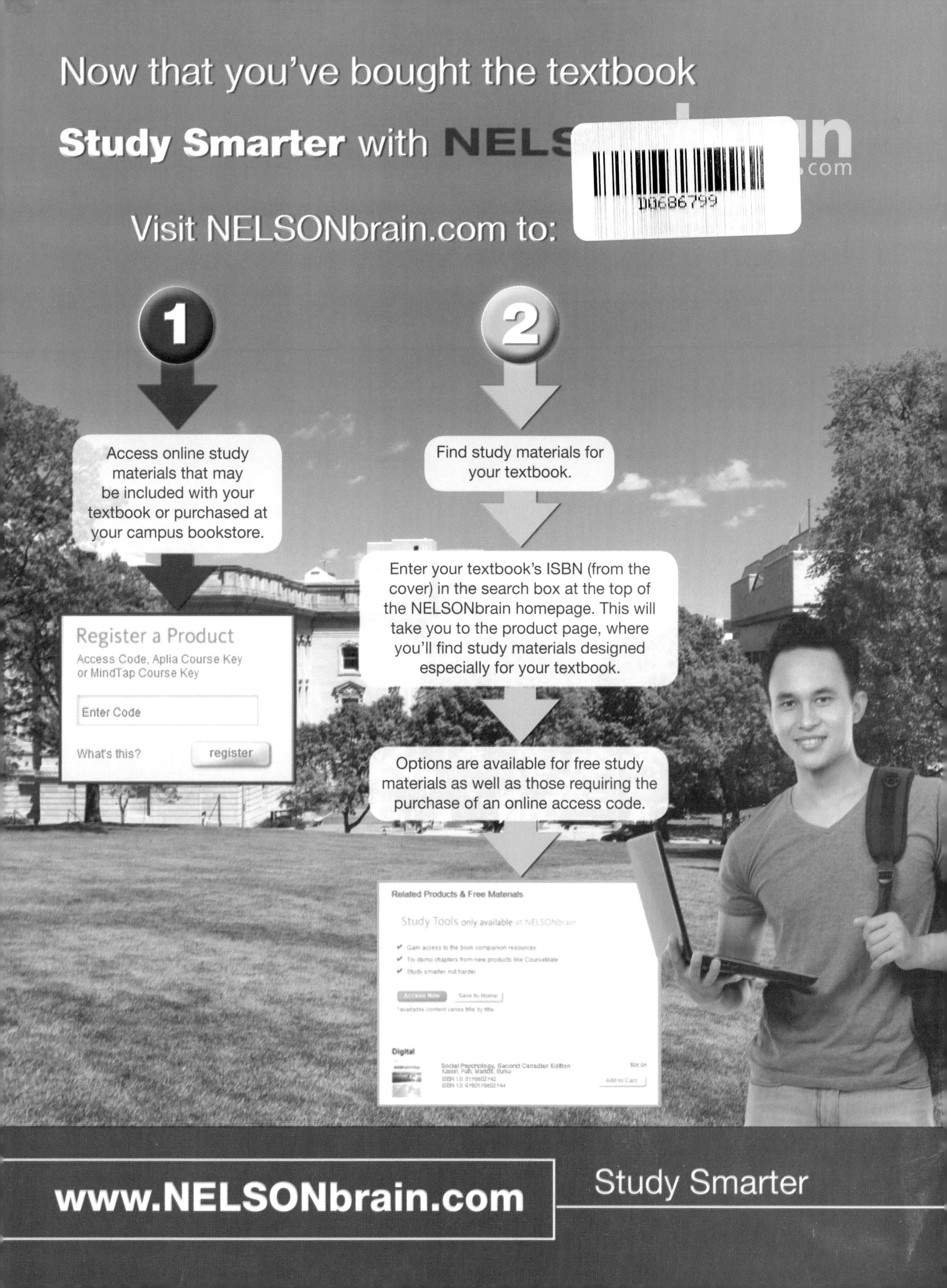
Now that you've bought the textbook
Study Smarter with NELSONbrain.com
Visit NELSONbrain.com to:
1
Access online study materials that may be included with your textbook or purchased at your campus bookstore.
Register a Product
Access Code, Aplia Course Key or MindTap Course Key
Enter Code
What's this?
register
2
Find study materials for your textbook.
Enter your textbook's ISBN (from the cover) in the search box at the top of the NELSONbrain homepage. This will take you to the product page, where you'll find study materials designed especially for your textbook.
Options are available for free study materials as well as those requiring the purchase of an online access code.
Related Products & Free Materials
Study Tools only available at NELSONbrain
Digital
Social Psychology, Second Canadian Edition
www.NELSONbrain.com
Study Smarter

SOCIAL PSYCHOLOGY

SECOND CANADIAN EDITION

SAUL KASSIN
John Jay College

STEVEN FEIN
Williams College

HAZEL ROSE MARKUS
Stanford University

TARA M. BURKE
Ryerson University

NELSON EDUCATION

NELSON EDUCATION

Social Psychology, **Second Canadian Edition**

by Saul Kassin, Steven Fein, Hazel Rose Markus, and Tara M. Burke

Vice President, Editorial Higher Education:
Anne Williams

Executive Editor:
Lenore Taylor-Atkins

Marketing Manager:
Ann Byford

Developmental Editor:
Brenda McLoughlin

Photo Researcher:
Daniela Glass

Permissions Coordinator:
Daniela Glass

Content Production Manager:
Claire Horsnell

Production Service:
Cenveo Publisher Services

Copy Editor:
Linda Szostak

Proofreader:
Manikandan

Indexer:
Christa Ramey

Senior Manufacturing Coordinator:
Joanne McNeil

Design Director:
Ken Phipps

Managing Designer:
Franca Amore

Interior Design:
Diane Beasley

Cover Design:
Liz Harasymczuk

Cover Image:
© Chris Joseph/All Canada Photos/ Corbis

Compositor:
Cenveo Publisher Services

Printer:
RR Donnelley

Printed and bound in the United States of America.
1 2 3 4 15 14 13 12

For more information contact Nelson Education Ltd., 1120 Birchmount Road, Toronto, Ontario, M1K 5G4. Or you can visit our Internet site at http://www.nelson.com

Library and Archives Canada Cataloguing in Publication

Social psychology / Saul Kassin ... [et al.]. — 2nd Canadian ed.

Includes bibliographical references and indexes.
ISBN-13: 978-0-17-650274-4

1. Social psychology—Textbooks. I. Kassin, Saul M.

HM1033.S623 2012
302 C2012-904066-5

ISBN-13: 978-0-17-650274-4
ISBN-10: 0-17-650274-2

We dedicate this book to our families,
friends, students, and colleagues.

Contents

PART III Social Influence

8 Group Processes 270

PART IV Social Relations

9 Attraction and Close Relationships 312

Preface

The world of the twenty-first century is both an exciting and a tumultuous place right now—more so, it seems, than at any other time in recent memory. On the one hand, it has never been easier to share information, opinions, pictures, music, and footage of live events as they occur with people from all corners of the world. On the other hand, we are surrounded by deep social and political divisions, ethnic conflict, economic turmoil, and an ever-present threat of terrorism and other acts of violence. As Charles Dickens (1859) said in *A Tale of Two Cities*, "It was the best of times, it was the worst of times."

Encircled by its place in science and by current world events, social psychology—its theories, research methods, and basic findings—has never been more relevant or more important. We used to think of social psychology as a discipline that is slow to change. As in other sciences, we thought, knowledge accumulates in small increments, one step at a time. Social psychology has no "critical" experiments, no single study can "prove" a theory, and no single theory can fully explain the complexities of human social behaviour. While all this remains true, the process of revising this textbook always shows us how complex, dynamic, and responsive our field can be. As the world around us rapidly changes—socially, politically, technologically, and in other respects—so too does social psychology.

As always, we had two main goals for this revision. Our first goal was to present the most important and exciting perspectives in the field as a whole, with a special focus on Canadian points of view. To communicate the depth of social psychology, we have expanded our coverage to include recent developments in areas such as social neuroscience and the role of cultural influences and perspectives. Second, we want this book to serve as a good teacher outside the classroom. While speaking the student's language, we always want to connect social psychology to current events in politics, sports, business, law, entertainment, uses of the Internet, and other life domains.

What's New in This Edition

For the second Canadian edition, we have tried to capture some subtle but important shifts within the field so that the Canadian reader can feel the pulse of social psychology *today* in each and every page of this textbook.

The Content

Comprehensive, Up-to-Date Scholarship The bedrock of teaching is knowledge. The second Canadian edition offers a broad, balanced, mainstream look at social psychology. Thus, there are detailed descriptions of classic studies from social psychology's historical warehouse, as well as the latest research findings—some hot off the presses—from hundreds of new references. Among the new additions are many Canadian studies that add a uniquely Canadian perspective to the book. In particular, we draw your attention to the following topics, which are either new to this edition or have received expanded coverage:

Chapter 1
- Contributions of women to early social psychology research
- Introduction to cultural perspectives in social psychology
- Introduction to social neuroscience and brain-imaging research

Chapter 2
- Uses of technology in social psychology research
- The distinction between qualitative and quantitative research
- The challenges of doing research across cultures
- Limits of self-report and its alternatives

Chapter 3
- Culture and self-esteem
- Vicarious self-perception
- Self-regulation and its aftereffects
- Ironic mental processes

Chapter 4
- Mind perception
- Recent research on human lie detection

Chapter 5
- The nature of racism
- Implicit racism and other forms of implicit prejudice
- Evolutionary perspectives on intergroup perception biases
- Cultural influences on social identity
- Self-regulation of prejudice
- Stereotype threat effects in nonacademic domains

Chapter 6
- Cross-cultural attitudes
- Links between implicit attitudes and behaviour
- Perceptual consequences of cognitive dissonance

Chapter 7
- Social influence and imitation in humans
- Obedience in the twenty-first century
- fMRI images of conformity and exclusion

Chapter 8
- Cultural influences on group cohesiveness
- The underuse of expertise in groups
- Group dynamics challenges posted by "virtual teams"
- Factors that influence cooperation in groups
- Negotiation strategies

Chapter 9
- The speed-dating phenomenon and research paradigm
- Cultural influences on romantic love
- Longitudinal effects of life stressors on marital satisfaction

Chapter 10
- Biological and evolutionary approaches to helping
- Culture and helping
- Empathy and helping among animals and human infants

- The bystander effect
- Moods and helping
- Intergroup biases in helping behaviour

Chapter 11
- Social neuroscience perspectives on aggression and its control
- Effects of social rejection and ostracism on aggression

Appendices
- The chapter on law from the first Canadian edition has been condensed into an appendix (Appendix A) to make room for new material about social psychology and health (Appendix B).

Overview of Changes

As the preceding list shows, this second Canadian edition contains a good deal of new material. In particular, you will see that we have zeroed in on developments within four important domains: social neuroscience, implicit processes, evolutionary theory, and cultural perspectives. Across chapters, as always, we have made it a point to illustrate the relevance of social psychology to current Canadian events, and to ask students to stop and reflect on their commonsense conceptions.

Social Neuroscience The first domain concerns social neuroscience and the fMRI brain-imaging studies that are poised to enlighten our understanding of the human social experience. Social neuroscience has not fully arrived, and researchers are still raising questions about how to interpret the newly observed links between brain activity and self-referential thoughts, social perceptions, motives, emotions, and behaviour. While we acknowledge the current limitations, we also want to provide students with a glimpse of this exciting new fusion of social psychology and neuroscience.

Implicit Processes We have expanded coverage and integrated the increasingly developed distinction between implicit and explicit processes. In matters relating to the unconscious, psychology owes a debt of gratitude to Freud. After some resistance, social psychologists have also come to realize the importance of the conscious-unconscious distinction when it comes to self-esteem, priming, stereotyping, prejudice, attitudes, ambivalence, social influence, and other core topics. Hence, we describe recent work involving the Implicit Association Test, or IAT, and the ongoing debate about what it measures, what it means, and what behaviours it predicts.

Evolutionary Theory We continue in this edition to represent various evolutionary perspectives on human nature, at the heart of which is the notion that we humans, like other species, have an ancestral past that predisposes us, albeit flexibly, to behave in ways that are adapted to promote survival and reproduction. Evolutionary psychologists today seek to explain a wide range of social phenomena—such as snap judgments in social perception, prejudice, helping, aggression, beauty, mate selection, and romantic jealousy. To some extent, this perspective is still controversial. To another extent, it has become part of the mainstream, with respected journals filled with studies and critiques of evolutionary psychology. This edition fully integrates the approach, its findings, and its limitations with the rest of social psychology.

Cultural Perspectives In this edition, we have continued both to cover and to fully integrate current research on cultural influences in social behaviour. Social psychologists have long been fascinated by similarity and difference—among cultural groups and between racial and ethnic groups within cultures. As the people of the world have come into closer contact, researchers have broadened their scope from the situational snapshot to a fuller account of people in their cultural milieu. Cultural phenomena, once marginalized, are now fully integrated into social psychology. As in our previous edition, every chapter now contains one, two, or three sections on the role of culture. These sections appear within the body of the text and are richly accompanied by photographs, rather than boxed or set apart.

As social psychology is now a truly international discipline, this book also includes many new citations to research conducted throughout Europe, Asia, Australia, and other parts of the world. We believe that the study of human diversity—from the perspectives of researchers who themselves are a diverse lot—can help students become better informed about social relations as well as about ethics and values.

Connections with Current Events To cover the world of social psychology is one thing. To use the principles of social psychology to explain events in the real world is quite another. The events of 9/11 changed the world. In different ways not yet fully discernible, so did the more recent severe economic recession. More than ever, we remain convinced that connecting theory to real life is the single best way to heighten student interest and involvement.

The second Canadian edition is committed to making social psychology *relevant.* Indeed, we invite you to flip open the book to any page and start reading. Soon, you'll come across a passage, a figure, a table, a photo, or a cartoon that refers to people, places, events, and issues that are prominent in contemporary Canadian culture. You'll read about Boston Bruins defenseman Zdeno Chara's hit on Montreal Canadiens player Max Pacioretty; how celebrities such as Don Cherry or Avril Lavigne can influence our behaviour; stories about Canadian Olympic athletes; events in Canadian politics; flash mobs; the death of Raymond Silverfox in RCMP custody; the Vancouver riot that broke out when the Boston Bruins beat the Vancouver Canucks in the Stanley Cup Finals; and the wrongful conviction of Thomas Sophonow.

You will also find—within the margins—various quotations, song lyrics, public opinion poll results, and "factoids". These high-interest items are designed to further illustrate the connectedness of social psychology to a world beyond the academic institution.

Social Psychology and Common Sense In an earlier edition, we introduced a feature that we remain excited about. Building on a discussion in Chapter 1 about the links (and lack thereof) between social psychology and common sense, each substantive chapter opens with "Putting Common Sense to the Test," a set of true/false questions designed to assess the student's intuitive beliefs about material later contained in that chapter. Some examples: "Sometimes, the harder you try to control a thought, feeling, or behaviour, the less likely you are to succeed," "People often come to like what they suffer for," "Opposites attract," and "Groups are less likely than individuals to invest more in a project that is failing." The answers to these questions are revealed in a marginal box after the topic is presented in the text. These answers are then explained at the end of each chapter. We think that students will find this exercise engaging. It will also enable them, as they read, to check their intuitive beliefs against the findings of social psychology and to notice the discrepancies that exist.

The Organization

Of all the challenges faced by course instructors and textbooks, perhaps the greatest one is to put information together in a way that is accurate and easy to understand. A strong organizational framework helps in meeting this challenge. There is nothing worse for a student than having to wade through a "laundry list" of endless studies whose connection with each other remains a profound mystery. A strong structure thus facilitates the development of conceptual understanding.

But the tail should not wag the dog. Since organizational structure is a means to an end, not an end in itself, we believe that it should be kept simple and unobtrusive. We present social psychology within five major parts, a heuristic structure that teachers and students have found sensible and easy to follow. The book opens with two *Introduction* chapters on the history, subject matter, and research methods of social psychology (Part I). As before, we then move to an intra-individual focus on *Social Perception* (Part II), and shift outward to *Social Influence* (Part III) and *Social Relations* (Part IV). We conclude with two appendices about the applications of social psychology (Part V) in the fields of law and health. We realize that some instructors prefer to reshuffle the deck to develop a chapter order that better fits their own approach. There is no problem in doing this. Each chapter stands on its own and does not require that others be read first.

The Presentation

Even when the content of a textbook is accurate and up to date, and even when its organization is sound, there is still the matter of presentation. As the teacher "outside the classroom," a good textbook should facilitate learning. Thus, every chapter contains the following pedagogical features:

- A narrative preview, chapter outline, and commonsense quiz called *Putting Common Sense to the Test* (beginning with Chapter 3).
- Key terms highlighted in the text, defined in the margin, listed at the end of the chapter, and reprinted in an alphabetized glossary at the end of the book. Both the list and the glossary provide page numbers for easy location of each term.
- Numerous bar graphs, line graphs, tables, sketches, photographs, flow charts, and cartoons that illustrate, extend, enhance, and enliven material in the text. Some of these depict classic images and studies from social psychology's history; others are contemporary, often "newsy."
- At the end of each chapter, a comprehensive bulleted review summarizing the major sections and points.

Ancillaries

For Instructors

Nelson Education Teaching Advantage (NETA) • The Nelson Education Teaching Advantage (NETA) program delivers research-based instructor resources that promote student engagement and higher-order thinking to enable the success of Canadian students and educators.

Instructors today face many challenges. Resources are limited, time is scarce, and a new kind of student has emerged: one who is juggling school with work, has gaps in his or her basic knowledge, and is immersed in technology in a way that has led to a completely new style of learning. In response, Nelson Education has gathered a group of dedicated instructors to advise us on the creation of richer and more flexible ancillaries that respond to the needs of today's teaching environments.

The members of our editorial advisory board have experience across a variety of disciplines and are recognized for their commitment to teaching. They include:

Norman Althouse, Haskayne School of Business, University of Calgary
Brenda Chant-Smith, Department of Psychology, Trent University
David DiBattista, Department of Psychology, Brock University
Roger Fisher, Ph.D.
Scott Follows, Manning School of Business Administration, Acadia University
Jon Houseman, Department of Biology, University of Ottawa
Glen Loppnow, Department of Chemistry, University of Alberta
Tanya Noel, Department of Biology, York University
Gary Poole, Director, Centre for Teaching and Academic Growth and School of Population and Public Health, University of British Columbia
Dan Pratt, Department of Educational Studies, University of British Columbia
Mercedes Rowinsky-Geurts, Department of Languages and Literatures, Wilfrid Laurier University

In consultation with the editorial advisory board, Nelson Education has completely rethought the structure, approaches, and formats of our key textbook ancillaries. We've also increased our investment in editorial support for our ancillary authors. The result is the Nelson Education Teaching Advantage and its key components: *NETA Engagement, NETA Assessment, NETA Presentation,* and *NETA Digital.* Each component includes one or more ancillaries prepared according to our best practices and may also be accompanied by documentation explaining the theory behind the practices.

NETA Engagement presents materials that help instructors deliver engaging content and activities to their classes. Instead of Instructor's Manuals that regurgitate chapter outlines and key terms from the text, NETA Enriched Instructor's Manuals (EIMs) provide genuine assistance to teachers. The EIMs answer questions such as *What should students learn? Why should students care?* and *What are some common student misconceptions and stumbling blocks?* EIMs not only identify the topics that cause students the most difficulty, but also describe techniques and resources to help students master these concepts. Dr. Roger Fisher's *Instructor's Guide to Classroom Engagement (IGCE)* accompanies every Enriched Instructor's Manual. (Information about the NETA Enriched Instructor's Manual prepared for *Social Psychology* is available on the instructors' website, www.socialpsych2Ce.nelson.com/instructor).

NETA Assessment relates to testing materials—not only Nelson's Test Banks and Computerized Test Banks, but also web quizzes available on the CourseMate site. Under *NETA Assessment,* Nelson's authors create multiple-choice questions that reflect research-based best practices for constructing effective questions, and for testing both recall and higher-order thinking. Our guidelines were developed by David DiBattista, a 3M National Teaching Fellow whose recent research as a professor of psychology at Brock University has focused on multiple-choice testing. All Test Bank authors receive training at workshops conducted by Professor DiBattista, as do the copy editors assigned to each Test Bank. A copy of *Multiple Choice Tests: Getting Beyond Remembering,* Professor DiBattista's guide to writing effective tests, is included with every Nelson Test Bank/Computerized Test Bank package. (Information about the NETA Test Bank prepared for *Social Psychology* is available on the instructors' website, www.socialpsych2Ce.nelson.com/instructor).

NETA Presentation has been developed to help instructors make the best use of PowerPoint in their classrooms. With a clean and uncluttered design developed by Maureen Stone of StoneSoup Consulting, NETA Presentation features slides with improved readability, more multimedia and graphic materials, activities to use in class, and tips for instructors on the Notes page. A copy of *NETA Guidelines for*

Classroom Presentations by Maureen Stone is included with each set of PowerPoint slides. (Information about the NETA PowerPoint prepared for *Social Psychology* is available on the instructors' website, www.socialpsych2Ce.nelson.com/instructor).

NETA Digital is a framework based on Arthur Chickering and Zelda Gamson's seminal work "Seven Principles of Good Practice In Undergraduate Education" (AAHE Bulletin, 1987) and the follow-up work by Chickering and Stephen C. Ehrmann, "Implementing the Seven Principles: Technology as Lever"(AAHE Bulletin, 1996). This aspect of the NETA program guides the writing and development of our digital products to ensure that they appropriately reflect the core goals of contact, collaboration, multimodal learning, time on task, prompt feedback, active learning, and high expectations. The resulting focus on pedagogical utility, rather than technological wizardry, ensures that all of our technology supports better outcomes for students.

Downloadable instructor ancillaries are provided on the Instructor's Resource website, www.socialpsych2Ce.nelson.com/instructor, giving instructors the ultimate tool for customizing lectures and presentations. The Instructors website includes:

- **NETA Engagement:** The Enriched Instructor's Manual was written by Anomi Bearden, Red Deer College. It is organized according to the textbook chapters and addresses eight key educational concerns, such as typical stumbling blocks student face and how to address them. Other features include Learning Objectives, Classroom Activities, and Other Resources.
- **NETA Assessment:** The Test Bank was written by Dawn Macaulay, Humber Institute of Technology and Advanced Learning. It includes over 1500 multiple-choice questions written according to NETA guidelines for effective construction and development of higher-order questions. Also included are 70 essay questions. Test Bank files are provided in Word format for easy editing and in PDF format for convenient printing whatever your system.

  The Computerized Test Bank by ExamView® includes all the questions from the Test Bank. The easy-to-use ExamView software is compatible with Microsoft Windows and Mac OS. Create tests by selecting questions from the question bank, modifying these questions as desired, and adding new questions you write yourself. You can administer quizzes online and export tests to WebCT, Blackboard, and other formats.
- **NETA Presentation:** Microsoft® PowerPoint® lecture slides for every chapter have been created by Corey Isaacs, University of Western Ontario. There is an average of 25 slides per chapter, many featuring key figures, tables, and photographs from *Social Psychology* 2ce. NETA principles of clear design and engaging content have been incorporated throughout.
- **Image Library:** This resource consists of digital copies of figures, short tables, and photographs used in the book. Instructors may use these jpegs to create their own PowerPoint presentations.
- **DayOne:** Day One—Prof InClass is a PowerPoint presentation that you can customize to orient your students to the class and their text at the beginning of the course.

For Students

CourseMate for *Social Psychology*, Second Canadian Edition • Nelson Education's CourseMate for *Social Psychology*, Second Canadian Edition, brings course concepts to life with interactive learning and exam-preparation tools that integrate with the printed textbook. Students activate their knowledge through quizzes, games, and flashcards, among many other tools.

CourseMate

CourseMate provides immediate feedback that enables students to connect results to the work they have just produced, increasing their learning efficiency. It encourages contact between students and faculty: Instructors can choose to monitor their students' level of engagement with CourseMate, correlating the students' efforts to their outcomes. Instructors can even use CourseMate's quizzes to practise "Just in Time" teaching by tracking results in the Engagement Tracker and customizing their lesson plans to address students' learning needs.

Watch student comprehension and engagement soar as your class engages with CourseMate. Instructors, ask your Nelson representative for a demonstration.

***Readings in Social Psychology: The Art and Science of Research Reader,* Eighth Edition (ISBN 9780840033000)** • This anthology contains 16 original articles, each with a brief introduction and questions to stimulate critical thinking about "doing" social psychology. These articles represent some of the most creative and accessible research in the field, both classic and contemporary, of topical interest to students.

CourseMate

The more you study, the better the results. Make the most of your study time by accessing everything you need to succeed in one place. Read your textbook, take notes, review flashcards, watch videos, and take practice quizzes—online with CourseMate.

Acknowledgments

Textbooks are the product of a team effort. Thanks to everyone at Nelson Education who worked to make this new edition a reality. I'd like to thank Lenore Taylor-Atkins for her foresight and dedication to the creation of a Canadian edition, as well as her colleagues who provided guidance on Canadian market needs and trends. Brenda McLoughlin and Sandy Matos attended to the development of this edition and I am grateful for their guidance and support throughout the project. Thanks also to Claire Horsnell, and Devanand Srinivasan and his team, who handled the production phase of the project, to Linda Szostak, the copy editor, and to Theresa Fitzgerald, who oversaw the development of the ancillaries. Finally, to Madison and Scott Pincombe, this is for you.

Several colleagues have guided us through their feedback on this and the previous Canadian edition. Each of these teachers and scholars has helped to make this a better book. I thank them for their invaluable insights, comments, and suggestions:

David Bourgeois, St. Mary's University
Rory Coughlan, Trent University
Ken Fowler, Memorial University
Christine Lomore, St. Francis Xavier University
Jennifer Steele, York University

Tara M. Burke
Ryerson University

About the Authors

Saul Kassin is a Distinguished Professor of Psychology at John Jay College of Criminal Justice in New York, and Massachusetts Professor of Psychology at Williams College, Williamstown, Massachusetts. Born and raised in New York City, he received his Ph.D. from the University of Connecticut, followed by a postdoctoral fellowship at the University of Kansas, a U.S. Supreme Court Judicial Fellowship, and a visiting professorship at Stanford University. In addition to authoring textbooks, he has co-authored and edited *Confessions in the Courtroom, The Psychology of Evidence and Trial Procedure, The American Jury on Trial,* and *Developmental Social Psychology.* Several years ago, Kassin pioneered the scientific study of false confession, an interest that continues to this day. He has also studied the impact of this and other evidence on the attributions, social perceptions, and verdicts of juries.

Steven Fein is Professor of Psychology at Williams College, Williamstown, Massachusetts. Born and raised in Bayonne, New Jersey, he received his A.B. from Princeton University and his Ph.D. in social psychology from the University of Michigan. He has been teaching at Williams College since 1991, with time spent teaching at Stanford University in 1999. His edited books include *Emotion: Interdisciplinary Perspectives, Readings in Social Psychology: The Art and Science of Research,* and *Motivated Social Perception: The Ontario Symposium.* His research interests concern stereotyping and prejudice, suspicion and attributional processes, social influence, and self-affirmation theory.

Hazel Rose Markus is the Davis-Brack Professor in the Behavioral Sciences at Stanford University. She also co-directs the Research Institute of the Stanford Center for Comparative Studies in Race and Ethnicity. Before moving to Stanford in 1994, she was a professor at the University of Michigan, where she received her Ph.D. Her work focuses on how the self-system, including current conceptions of self and possible selves, structures and lends meaning to experience. Born in England of English parents and raised in San Diego, California, she has been persistently fascinated by how nation of origin, region of the country, gender, ethnicity, race, religion, and social class shape self and identity. With her colleague Shinobu Kitayama at the University of Michigan, she has pioneered the experimental study of how culture and self influence one another. Some of her recent co-edited books include *Culture and Emotion: Empirical Studies of Mutual Influence, Engaging Cultural Differences: The Multicultural Challenge in Liberal Democracies, Just Schools: Pursuing Equal Education in Societies of Difference,* and *Doing Race: 21 Essays for the 21st Century.*

Tara M. Burke is an Associate Professor of Psychology at Ryerson University in Toronto, Ontario. Born and raised in Toronto, she received her B.A. from the University of Western Ontario and her M.A. and Ph.D. in social psychology from the University of Toronto. She has been at Ryerson University since 1999, where she was the recipient of a Teaching Excellence Award, honouring her for her work in teaching courses such as Social Psychology, Psychology and Law, and Introductory Psychology. Her research interests include social influence (applied to areas such as jury decision-making, pre-trial publicity, and the psychology of alibis), wrongful convictions, and research ethics.

1

Bob Mahoney/The Image Works

What Is Social Psychology?

This chapter introduces you to the study of social psychology. We begin by defining social psychology and identifying how it is distinct from but related to some other areas of study, both outside and within psychology. Next, we review the history of the field. We conclude by looking forward, with a discussion of the important themes and perspectives that are propelling social psychology into a new century.

A few years from now, you may receive a letter in the mail, inviting you to a high school or university reunion. You'll probably feel a bit nostalgic, and you'll begin to think about those old school days. What thoughts will come to mind first? Will you remember the terrific English teacher you had in Grade 11? Will you think about the excitement you felt when you completed your first chemistry lab? Will a tear form in your eye as you remember how inspiring your social psychology class was?

Perhaps. But what will probably dominate your thoughts are the people you knew in school and the interactions you had with them—the long and intense discussions about everything imaginable; the loves you had, lost, or wanted so desperately to experience; the time you made a fool of yourself at a party; the effort of trying to be accepted by a fraternity, sorority, or clique of popular people; the day you sat in the pouring rain with your friends while watching a football game.

ABC via Getty Images

Strangers quickly become celebrities as millions of people tune in to watch them relate to each other on "reality" shows. Pictured here is Canadian Jillian Harris, who appeared in a recent season of *The Bachelorette*. Viewers wondered which of the featured bachelors she would choose. The enormous popularity of shows like this illustrates part of the appeal of social psychology—people are fascinated with how we relate to one another.

We focus on these social situations because we are social beings. We forge our individual identities not alone but in the context of other people. We work, play, and live together. We hurt and help each other. We define happiness and success for each other. And we don't fall passively into social interactions; we actively seek them. We visit family, make friends, give parties, build networks, go on dates, pledge an enduring commitment, and decide to have children. We watch others, speculate about them, and predict who will wind up with whom, whether in real life or on "reality" TV shows like *The Bachelor* or *Jersey Shore*. Many of us text or tweet each other about everything we're doing, or we spend lots of time on social networking sites such as Facebook, interacting with countless peers from around the world, and adding hundreds or even thousands of "friends" to our social networks.

You've probably seen the movie *It's a Wonderful Life*. When the hero, George Bailey, was about to kill himself, the would-be angel Clarence didn't save him by showing him how much personal happiness he'd miss if he ended his life. Instead, he showed George how much his life had touched the lives of others and how many people would

Man is a social animal.
—Benedict Spinoza, *Ethics*

be hurt if he were not a part of their world. It was these social relationships that saved George's life, just as they define our own.

One of the exciting aspects of learning about social psychology is discovering how basic and profoundly important these social relationships are to the human animal. And research continues to find new evidence for and point to new implications of our social nature. Consider, for example, this recent set of research findings:

- Whether hurting from a physical pain, or from an emotional one, the same areas of the brain are activated. Therefore, social loss, such as a romantic breakup, may actually be experienced as physical pain (Kross, Berman, Mischel, Smith, & Wager, 2011).
- People who have experience with other cultures demonstrate more creative tendencies. This suggests that multicultural experiences help to keep us more open-minded and enable us to be more flexible thinkers (Maddux & Galinsky, 2009).
- Having close friends is associated with health benefits. Researchers have found that children and teens with fewer friends are more likely to experience depression, and be sick more often than their more popular peers (Bukowski, Laursen, & Hoza, 2010; Haas, Schaefer, & Kornienko, 2010).

Taken together, these studies demonstrate how basic and important is our connection to other people, and how much we benefit from social interaction and are hurt—not just metaphorically but even physically—from social isolation or rejection.

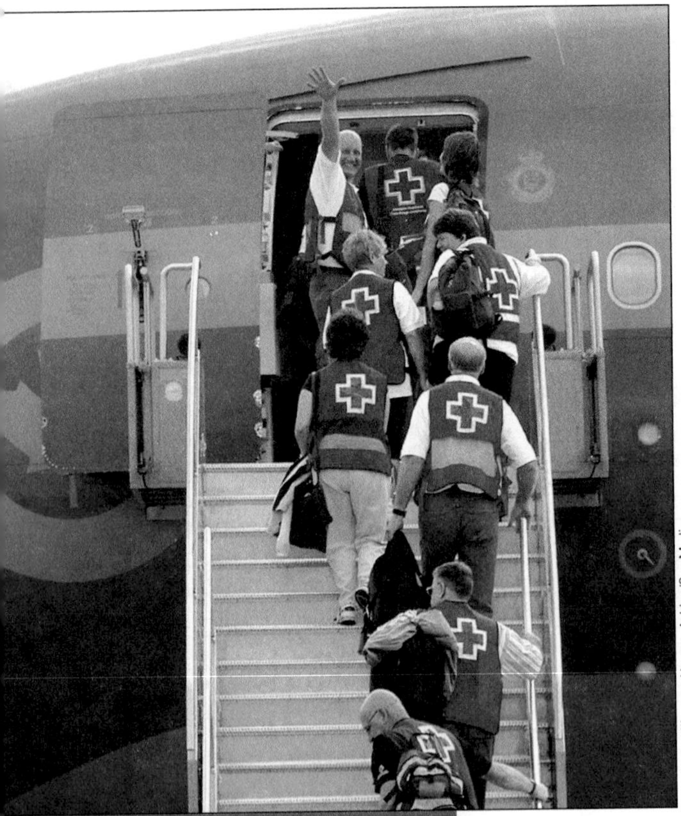
Belleville Intelligencer/Jeremy Ashley/Sun Media

Are some people, such as these members of the Canadian Red Cross, naturally altruistic, or can anyone display courage and heroism under the right conditions?

Precisely because we need and care so much about social interactions and relationships, the social contexts in which we find ourselves can influence us profoundly. You can find many examples of this kind of influence in your own life. Have you ever laughed at a joke you didn't get just because those around you were laughing? Do you present yourself in one way with one group of people and in quite a different way with another group? The power of the situation can also be much more subtle, and yet more powerful, than in these examples, as when another's unspoken expectations about you literally seem to cause you to become a different person.

The relevance of social psychology is evident in everyday life, of course, such as when two people become attracted to each other, or when a group tries to coordinate its efforts on a project. Dramatic events can heighten its significance all the more; we seek answers to the kinds of questions that social psychologists study—questions about hatred and violence, about intergroup conflict and suspicion, as well as about heroism, cooperation, and the capacity for understanding across cultural, ethnic, racial, religious, and geographic divides. We are reminded of the need for a better understanding of social psychological issues as we read the latest news about death and destruction, or sometimes, hope, from the Middle East, see footage of death and destruction in the wake of a tsunami, or are confronted with the reality of an all-too-violent world as nearby as our own neighbourhoods and campuses. We also appreciate the majesty and power of social connections as we recognize the courage of a firefighter, read about the charity of a donor, or see the glow in the eyes of a new parent. These are all—the bad and the good, the mundane and the extraordinary—part of the fascinating landscape of social psychology.

DreamPictures/Getty Images

Our social relationships and interactions are extremely important to us. Most people seek out and are profoundly affected by other people. This social nature of the human animal is what social psychology is all about.

Not only will you learn interesting and relevant research findings throughout this book, you will also learn *how* social psychologists have discovered this evidence. It is an exciting process, and one that we are enthusiastic about sharing with you. The purpose of this first chapter is to provide you with a broad overview of the field of social psychology. By the time you finish it, you should be ready and (we hope) eager for what lies ahead.

What Is Social Psychology?

We begin by previewing the new territory you're about to enter. Then we define social psychology and map out its relationship to sociology and some other disciplines within the field of psychology.

Defining Social Psychology

Social psychology is the scientific study of how individuals think, feel, and behave in a social context. Let's look at each part of this definition.

Scientific Study There are many approaches to understanding how people think, feel, and behave. We can learn about human behaviour from novels, films, history, and philosophy, to name just a few possibilities. What makes social psychology different from these artistic and humanistic endeavours is that social psychology is a science. It applies the *scientific method* of systematic observation, description, and measurement to the study of the human condition. How, and why, social psychologists do this is explained in Chapter 2.

How Individuals Think, Feel, and Behave Social psychology concerns an amazingly diverse set of topics. People's private, even nonconscious beliefs and attitudes, their most passionate emotions, their heroic, cowardly, or merely mundane public behaviours—these all fall within the broad scope of social psychology. In this way, social psychology differs from other social sciences such as economics and political

social psychology
The scientific study of how individuals think, feel, and behave in a social context.

CP/Montreal Gazette/Dave Sidaway

A celebrity like Don Cherry can influence the attitudes and behaviours of millions of people. When he recommended a hat honouring the Canadian Forces Personnel Support Agency during a "Coach's Corner" segment on *Hockey Night in Canada*, sales of the hats skyrocketed.

science. Research on attitudes (see Chapter 6) offers a good illustration. Whereas economists and political scientists may be interested in people's economic and political attitudes, respectively, social psychologists investigate a wide variety of attitudes and contexts, such as individuals' attitudes toward particular groups of people or how their attitudes are affected by their peers or their mood. In doing so, social psychologists strive to establish general principles of attitude formation and change that apply in a variety of situations, rather than exclusively to particular domains.

Note the word *individuals* in our definition of *social psychology*. This word points to another important way in which social psychology differs from some other social sciences. Sociology, for instance, typically classifies people in terms of their nationality, race, socioeconomic class, and other *group factors*. In contrast, social psychology typically focuses on the psychology of the *individual*. Even when social psychologists study groups of people, they usually emphasize the behaviour of the individual in the group context.

A Social Context Here is where the "social" in social psychology comes into play and how social psychology is distinguished from other branches of psychology. As a whole, the discipline of psychology is an immense, sprawling enterprise, the 800-pound gorilla of the social sciences, concerned with everything from the actions of neurotransmitters in the brain to the actions of music fans in a mosh pit. What makes social psychology unique is its emphasis on the social nature of individuals.

However, the "socialness" of social psychology varies. Attempting to establish general principles of human behaviour, social psychologists sometimes examine nonsocial factors that affect people's thoughts, emotions, motives, and actions. For example, they may study whether hot weather causes people to behave more aggressively (Anderson, 2001; Anderson & Huesmann, 2003). What is social about this is the behaviour: people hurting each other. In addition, social psychologists sometimes study people's thoughts or feelings about nonsocial things, such as people's attitudes toward Nike versus New Balance basketball shoes. How can attitudes toward basketball shoes be of interest to social psychologists? One way is if these attitudes are influenced by something social, such as whether having Steve Nash's endorsement of Nike makes people like Nike and perhaps even ultimately buy Nike shoes. Both examples, determining whether heat causes an increase in aggression or whether Steve Nash causes an increase in sales of Nike shoes, are *social* psychological pursuits because the thoughts, feelings, or behaviours either (a) concern other people or (b) are influenced by other people.

The "social context" referred to in the definition of *social psychology* does not have to be real or present. Even the implied or imagined presence of others can have important effects on individuals (Allport, 1985). For example, if people imagine receiving positive or negative reactions from others, their self-esteem can be affected significantly (Smart Richman & Leary, 2009). And if young people are asked to imagine living a day in the life of a professor, they are likely to perform better later on an analytic test; however, if they instead imagine being a cheerleader, they perform worse (Galinsky et al., 2008)!

Social Psychological Questions and Applications

For those of us fascinated by social behaviour, social psychology is a dream come true. Just look at ■ Table 1.1 and consider a small sample of the questions you'll explore in this textbook. As you can see, the social nature of the human animal is what social psychology is all about. Learning about social psychology is learning about ourselves and our social worlds. And because social psychology is scientific rather than anecdotal, systematic rather than haphazard, it provides insights that would be impossible to gain through intuition or experience alone.

The value of social psychology's perspective on human behaviour is widely recognized. Courses in social psychology are often required for undergraduate majors in business, education, and journalism as well as in psychology and sociology. Although many advanced graduates with a Ph.D. in social psychology hold faculty appointments in universities, others work in medical centres, law firms, government agencies, and a variety of business settings involving investment banking, marketing, advertising, human resources, negotiating, and social networking.

The number and importance of these applications continue to grow. Judges are drawing on social psychological research to render landmark decisions, and lawyers are depending on it to select juries and to support or refute evidence. Healthcare professionals are increasingly aware of the role of social psychological factors in the prevention and treatment of disease. Indeed, we can think of no other field of study that offers expertise that is more clearly relevant to so many different career paths.

TABLE 1.1

Examples of Social Psychological Questions

Social Perception: What Affects the Way We Perceive Ourselves and Others?

- Why do people sometimes sabotage their own performance, making it more likely that they will fail? (Ch. 3)
- How do people in East Asia often differ from North Americans in the way they explain people's behaviour? (Ch. 4)
- Where do stereotypes come from, and why are they so resistant to change? (Ch. 5)

Social Influence: How Do We Influence Each Other?

- Why do we often like what we suffer for? (Ch. 6)
- How do salespeople sometimes trick us into buying things we never really wanted? (Ch. 7)
- Why do people often perform worse in groups than they would have alone? (Ch. 8)

Social Interaction: What Causes Us to Like, Love, Help, and Hurt Others?

- How similar or different are the sexes in what they look for in an intimate relationship? (Ch. 9)
- When is a bystander more or less likely to help you in an emergency? (Ch. 10)
- Does exposure to TV violence, or to pornography, trigger aggressive behaviour? (Ch. 11)

Applying Social Psychology: How Does Social Psychology Help Us Understand Questions About Law and Health?

- Why do people sometimes confess to crimes they did not commit? (Appendix A)
- How does stress affect one's health, and what are the most effective ways of coping with stressful experiences? (Appendix B)

The Power of the Social Context: An Example of a Social Psychology Experiment

The social nature of people runs so deep that even that which seems so personal and unique to ourselves—our own senses of identity, of how we value ourselves—can be influenced subtly but significantly by merely being reminded about what is considered normative when it comes to judging our own appearance. This point is illustrated in research done by Erin Strahan and her colleagues (2008) at Wilfred Laurier University, where they explored the impact of media images on body satisfaction ratings by female undergraduate students (see ▶ Figure 1.1). They wanted to see if they could change whether a participant was feeling bad or good about her body by manipulating how aware she was of the cultural norms (i.e., 'thin is in') that we generally endorse in North America.

It is well known that many images portrayed in the media promote an unrealistic and unattainable goal for normal, healthy women. Previous research has found that those types of unrealistic images can lead some women to feel worse about their own bodies. However, understanding why that happens, or under what conditions, is

FIGURE 1.1

How Do I Look?

This graph shows the results of an experiment by Strahan and others (2008) in which female undergraduates exposed to either 'thin' commercials or neutral commercials were asked about their overall body satisfaction, and to what extent they were concerned with the opinions of others. The results depicted here show that if a woman had seen a thin model, she was more likely to have lower body satisfaction, lower feelings of self-worth, and report being more concerned with how other people might see her. If a woman had seen only neutral media images, however, her overall feelings of self-worth were not affected. These results suggest that when unrealistic cultural norms around body image are made salient, women become more concerned with how others might judge them. Because the norms are unattainable, and they can't live up to this image, they judge themselves more negatively.

(Based on Strahan et al., 2008.)

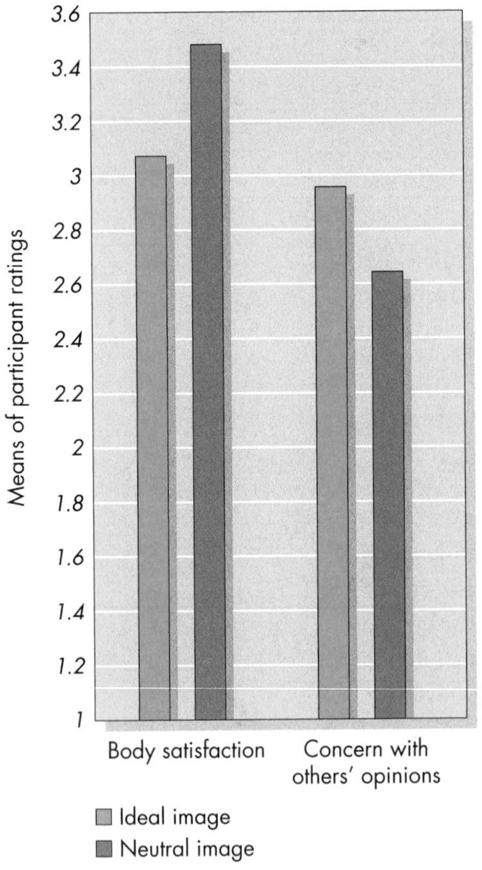

not always so clear-cut. Strahan and her colleagues (2008) proposed that, by viewing these images, women are reminded that other people are judging them based on their appearance, and so their own sense of self-worth suffers when they determine that they cannot live up to these expectations.

To test this idea, the researchers asked half of the women in their study to watch commercials with very thin, very attractive models (e.g., a Victoria's Secret ad), while others watched more neutral images (e.g., an ad for a cellphone). After a short break, they asked the women to rate themselves on a variety of measures, including self-worth and self-esteem scales. They also asked them to indicate how concerned they were with the opinions of other people. Consistent with previous research, those who viewed the thin images reported being less satisfied with their bodies. Interestingly, Strahan and her colleagues found that women exposed to the thin models described themselves as being more concerned with other people's opinions compared to women who had only viewed the neutral images. They concluded that by watching the commercials with the thin models, women were reminded of what was considered attractive, based on cultural norms. That, in turn, led to a greater awareness of how other people might judge them, and therefore greater dissatisfaction with their own appearance and decreased feelings of self-worth. It seems that simply being reminded of what is expected, or considered normal, within a particular social context can impact our feelings of self-worth when we worry that we do not live up to those ideals and that other people might evaluate us negatively. Remember that no one actually judged the women for their appearance in this study—they were simply reacting to how they imagined others would judge them, based on activation of those norms.

However, the news is not all bad; these same researchers created an intervention designed to challenge the cultural norms around ideal body size. Adolescent boys and girls participated in a series of information sessions and activities that provided them with a 'toolbox' of techniques for countering these unrealistic norms. They found that girls who had seen the thin models but who had also been exposed to the intervention were much less likely to base their self-worth on their appearance, and they reported being less concerned about the opinions of others. A bit of good news, then, as we will see as well throughout this book, is that making changes to the social context in a more positive way, such as promoting positive rather than negative expectancies about an individual or group, can have powerfully positive effects.

Social Psychology and Related Fields: Distinctions and Intersections

Social psychology is sometimes confused with certain other fields of study. Before we go on, it is important to clarify how social psychology is distinct from these other fields. At the same time, it is important to illustrate some of the ways in which interesting and significant questions can be addressed through interactions between social psychology and these other fields (see Table 1.2).

TABLE 1.2

Distinctions Between Social Psychology and Related Fields: The Case of Research on Prejudice

To see the differences between social psychology and related fields, consider an example of how researchers in each field might conduct a study of prejudice.

Field of Study	Example of How a Researcher in the Field Might Study Prejudice
Sociology	Measure how prejudice varies as a function of social or economic class.
Clinical psychology	Test various therapies for people with antisocial personalities who exhibit great degrees of prejudice.
Personality psychology	Develop a questionnaire to identify men who are very high or low in degree of prejudice toward women.
Cognitive psychology	Manipulate exposure to a member of some category of people and measure the thoughts and concepts that are automatically activated. (*A study of prejudice in this field would, by definition, be at the intersection of cognitive and social psychology.*)
Social psychology	Manipulate various kinds of contact between individuals of different groups, and examine the effect of these manipulations on the degree of prejudice exhibited.

Social Psychology and Sociology Sociologists and social psychologists share an interest in many issues, such as violence, prejudice, cultural differences, and marriage. As noted, however, sociology tends to focus on the group level, whereas social psychology tends to focus on the individual level. For example, sociologists might track the political attitudes of the middle class in Canada, whereas social psychologists might examine some of the specific factors that make individuals prefer one political candidate to another.

In addition, although there are many exceptions, social psychologists are more likely than sociologists to conduct experiments in which they manipulate some variable and determine the effects of this manipulation using precise, quantifiable measures.

Despite these differences, sociology and social psychology are clearly related. Indeed, many sociologists and social psychologists share the same training and publish in the same journals. When these two fields intersect, the result can be a more complete understanding of important issues. For example, interdisciplinary research on stereotyping and prejudice has examined the dynamic roles of both societal and immediate factors, such as how particular social systems or institutional norms and beliefs affect individuals' attitudes and behaviours (Eagly & Fischer, 2009; Jackson, 2011; van der Toorn, Tyler, & Jost, 2011).

Social Psychology and Clinical Psychology Tell people not very familiar with psychology that you are taking a social psychology class, and they are likely to say things like "Oh, great, now you're going to start psychoanalyzing me" or "Finally, maybe you can tell me why everyone in my family is so messed up." The assumption underlying these reactions, of course, is that you are studying clinical, or abnormal, psychology. Clinical psychologists seek to understand and treat people with psychological difficulties or disorders. Social psychologists do not focus on disorders; rather, they focus on the more typical ways in which individuals think, feel, behave, and influence each other.

There are, however, many fascinating ways in which clinical and social psychology intersect. Both, for example, may address how people cope with anxiety or pressure in social situations; how depressed and nondepressed individuals differ in the way they perceive or act toward other people; or how being bullied or stereotyped by others can affect individuals' health and feelings of self-worth (Amodio, 2009; Bosson, Pinel, & Thompson, 2008; Brodish & Devine, 2009; Conklin et al., 2009; Seeds, Harkness, & Quilty, 2010).

Social Psychology and Personality Psychology Both personality psychology and social psychology are concerned with individuals and their thoughts, feelings, and behaviours. However, personality psychology seeks to understand differences between

Skjold Photography/The Image Works

Are young children more likely to become aggressive after watching a television show depicting violence? Do violent video games make teenagers more aggressive? These are some of the questions that social psychology addresses.

individuals that remain relatively stable across a variety of situations, whereas social psychology seeks to understand how social factors affect most individuals, *regardless of* their different personalities.

In other words, personality psychologists are interested in cross-situational consistency. They may ask, "Is this person outgoing and friendly almost all the time, in just about any setting?" Social psychologists are interested in how different situations cause different behaviours. They may ask, "Are people in general more likely to seek out companionship when they are made anxious by a situation than when they are made to feel relaxed?"

These examples show the contrast between the fields; but in fact, personality psychology and social psychology are very closely linked. The Canadian Psychological Association has more than 25 different divisions, and yet personality psychologists and social psychologists share the same division. The reason for the high degree of connection between social psychology and personality psychology is that the two areas complement each other so well. For example, some social psychologists examine how receiving negative feedback (a situational factor) can have different effects on people as a function of whether their self-esteem is high or low (an individual-difference factor), or whether exposure to violent images on TV (a situational factor) is especially likely to trigger aggressiveness in particular types of children (an individual-difference factor) (Freedman, 2002; Bijvank et al., 2009; Park & Maner, 2009).

Social Psychology and Cognitive Psychology Cognitive psychologists study mental processes such as thinking, learning, remembering, and reasoning. Social psychologists are often interested in these same processes. More specifically, though, social psychologists are interested in how people think, learn, remember, and reason with respect to social information and in how these processes are relevant to social behaviour.

The last two decades have seen an explosion of interest in the intersection of cognitive and social psychology. The study of *social cognition* is discussed in more detail later in this chapter, and it is a focus throughout this text, especially in Part II on Social Perception.

Social Psychology and Common Sense

After reading about a theory or finding of social psychology, you may sometimes think, "Of course. I knew that all along. Anyone could have told me that." This "knew-it-all-along" phenomenon often causes people to question how social psychology is different from common sense, or traditional folk wisdom. After all, why would any of the following social psychological findings be surprising?

- Beauty and brains don't mix: Physically attractive people tend to be seen as less smart than physically unattractive people.

- People will like an activity more if you offer them a large reward for doing it, causing them to associate the activity with the positive reinforcement.
- People think that they're more distinctive than they really are: They tend to underestimate the extent to which others share the same opinions or interests.
- Playing contact sports or violent video games releases aggression and makes people less likely to vent their anger in violent ways.

We will have more to say about each of these statements later.

Common sense may seem to explain many social psychological findings after the fact. The problem is distinguishing common-sense fact from common-sense myth. After all, for most common-sense notions, there is an equally sensible-sounding notion that says the opposite. Is it "Birds of a feather flock together" or "Opposites attract"? Is it "Two heads are better than one" or "Too many cooks spoil the broth"? Which are correct? We have no reliable way to answer such questions through common sense or intuition alone.

Social psychology, unlike common sense, uses the scientific method to put its theories to the test. How it does so will be discussed in greater detail in the next chapter. But before we leave this section, one word of caution: Those four "findings" listed earlier? *They are all false.* Although there may be sensible reasons to believe each of the statements to be true, research indicates otherwise. Therein lies another problem with relying on common sense: Despite offering very compelling predictions and explanations, it is sometimes wildly inaccurate. And even when it is not completely wrong, common sense can be misleading in its simplicity. Often there is no simple answer to a question such as "Does absence make the heart grow fonder?" In reality, the answer is more complex than common sense would suggest, and social psychological research reveals how such an answer depends on a variety of factors.

To emphasize these points, and to encourage you to think critically about social psychological issues *before* as well as after learning about them, this textbook contains a feature called "Putting Common Sense to the Test." Beginning with Chapter 3, each chapter opens with a few statements about social psychological issues that will be covered in that chapter. Some of the statements are true, and some are false. As you read each statement, make a prediction about whether it is true or false, and think about *why* this is your prediction. Marginal notes throughout the chapter will tell you whether the statements are true or false. In reading the chapter, check not only whether your prediction was correct but also whether your reasons for the prediction were appropriate. If your intuition wasn't quite on the mark, think about what the right answer is and how the evidence supports that answer. There are few better ways of learning and remembering than through this kind of critical thinking.

From Past to Present: A Brief History of Social Psychology

People have probably been asking social psychological questions for as long as humans could think about each other. Certainly, early philosophers such as Plato offered keen insights into many social psychological issues. But no systematic and scientific study of social psychological issues developed until the end of the nineteenth century. The field of social psychology is therefore a very young one. Recent years have marked a tremendous interest in social psychology and an injection of many new scholars into the field. As social psychology begins its second century, it is instructive to look back to see how the field today has been shaped by the people and events of its first century.

"Psychology has a long past, but only a short history."
—Herman Ebbinghaus, *Summary of Psychology*

The Birth and Infancy of Social Psychology: 1880s–1920s

Like most such honours, the title "founder of social psychology" has many potential recipients, and not everyone agrees on who should prevail. There is ample evidence, for example, that, while not necessarily being explicitly referred to as social psychology, research and discourse on related topics was being discussed prior to the twentieth century (Lubek & Apfelbaum, 2000). Most historians would, however, point to the American psychologist Norman Triplett, who is credited with having published the first research article in social psychology at the end of the nineteenth century (1897–1898). Triplett's work was noteworthy because, after observing that bicyclists tended to race faster when racing in the presence of others than when simply racing against a clock, he designed an experiment to study this phenomenon in a carefully controlled, precise way. This scientific approach to studying the effects of the social context on individuals' behaviour can be seen as marking the birth of modern-day social psychology.

A case can also be made for the French agricultural engineer Max Ringelmann. Ringelmann's research was conducted in the 1880s but wasn't published until 1913. In an interesting coincidence, Ringelmann also studied the effects of the presence of others on the performance of individuals. In contrast to Triplett, however, Ringelmann noted that individuals often performed worse on simple tasks such as pulling rope when they performed the tasks with other people. The issues addressed by these two early researchers continue to be of vital interest, as will be seen later in Chapter 8 on Group Processes.

Photo by Bryn Lennon/Getty Images

Alberto Contador (centre, yellow jersey) races on the way to winning his third Tour de France in July 2010. Would Contador and his fellow cyclists have raced faster or slower if they were racing individually against the clock rather than racing simultaneously with their competitors? More generally, what effect does the presence of others have on an individual's performance? The two founders of social psychology, American psychologist Norman Triplett and French agricultural engineer Max Ringelmann, sought answers to questions such as these. Chapter 8 on Group Processes brings you up-to-date on the latest research in this area.

Despite their place in the history of social psychology, neither Triplett nor Ringelmann actually established social psychology as a distinct field of study. Credit for this creation goes to the writers of the first three textbooks in social psychology: the English psychologist William McDougall (1908) and two Americans, Edward Ross (1908) and Floyd Allport (1924). Allport's book in particular, with its focus on the interaction of individuals and their social context and its emphasis on the use of experimentation and the scientific method, helped establish social psychology as the discipline it is today. These authors announced the arrival of a new approach to the social aspects of human behaviour. Social psychology was born. Some of the initial influence of this new discipline was evident in Canada when McGill University, in Montreal, offered a course in Social Psychology as early as 1913 (Ferguson, 1992).

A Call to Action: 1930s–1950s

What one person would you guess has had the strongest influence on the field of social psychology? Various social psychologists, as well as psychologists of other areas, might be mentioned in response to this question. But someone who was not a psychologist at all may have had the most dramatic impact on the field: Adolf Hitler.

Hitler's rise to power and the ensuing turmoil caused people around the world to become desperate for answers to social psychological questions about what causes violence, prejudice and genocide, conformity and obedience, and a host of other social problems and behaviours. In addition, many social psychologists living in Europe in

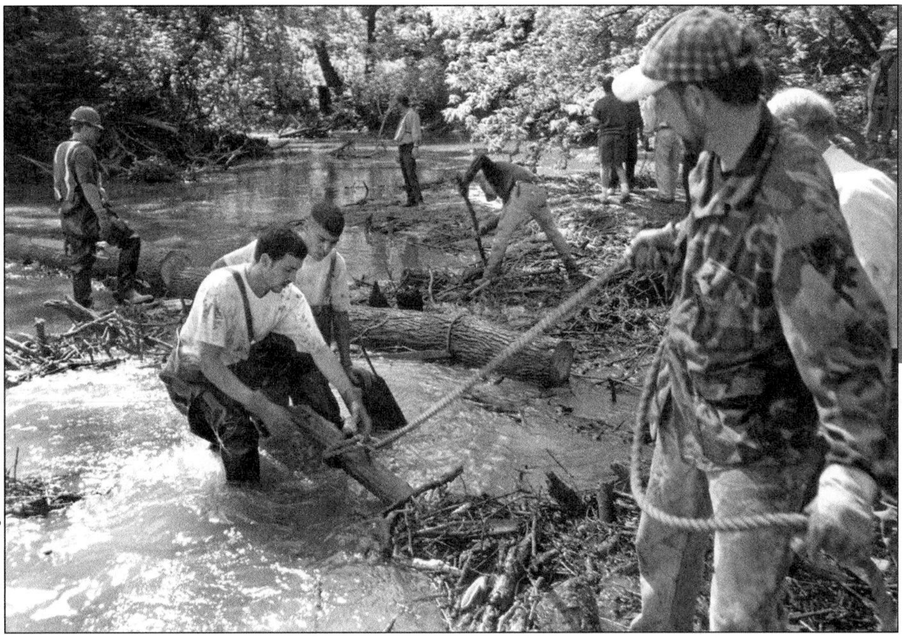

Jim West/The Image Works

What determines whether people are likely to act to conserve their environment, as these students did by volunteering their time to clean up a beach? Built on the legacy of Kurt Lewin, one of the leading figures in the development of the field, applied social psychology contributes to the solution of numerous social problems, such as environmental conservation.

the 1930s fled to Canada and the United States and helped establish a critical mass of social psychologists who would give shape to the rapidly maturing field. The years just before, during, and soon after World War II marked an explosion of interest in social psychology.

In 1936, Gordon Allport (younger brother of Floyd, author of the 1924 textbook) and a number of other social psychologists formed the Society for the Psychological Study of Social Issues (SPSSI). The name of the society illustrates these psychologists' concern for making important, practical contributions to society. Also in 1936, a social psychologist named Muzafer Sherif published groundbreaking experimental research on social influence. As a youth in Turkey, Sherif had witnessed groups of Greek soldiers brutally killing his friends. After immigrating to the United States, Sherif drew on this experience and began to conduct research on the powerful influences groups can exert on their individual members. Sherif's research was crucial for the development of social psychology because it demonstrated that it is possible to study complex social processes such as conformity and social influence in a rigorous, scientific manner. This innovation laid the foundation for what was to become one of the major topics in social psychology. Research and theory on social influence are discussed throughout this text, particularly in Part III on Social Influence.

Another great contributor to social psychology, Kurt Lewin, fled the Nazi onslaught in Germany and immigrated to the United States in the early 1930s. He was a bold and creative theorist whose concepts have had lasting effects on the field (e.g., Lewin, 1935, 1947). Among the fundamental principles of social psychology that Lewin helped establish were the following:

1. Behaviour is a function of the interaction between the person and the environment. This position, which later became known as the **interactionist perspective** (Blass, 1991), emphasized the dynamic interplay of internal and external factors, and marked a sharp contrast from other major psychological paradigms during his lifetime: psychoanalysis, with its emphasis on internal motives and fantasies; and behaviourism, with its focus on external rewards and punishments.

2. Social psychological theories should be applied to important, practical issues. Lewin researched a number of practical issues, such as how to persuade Americans

interactionist perspective
An emphasis on how both an individual's personality and environmental characteristics influence behaviour.

at home during the war to conserve materials to help the war effort; how to promote more economical and nutritious eating habits; and what kinds of leaders elicit the best work from group members. Through these studies, Lewin showed how social psychology could enlarge our understanding of social problems and contribute to their solution. Built on Lewin's legacy, applied social psychology flourishes today in areas such as advertising, business, education, environmental protection, health, law, politics, public policy, religion, and sports. Throughout this text, we draw on the findings of applied social psychology to illustrate the implications of social psychological principles for our daily lives. In Appendix A and Appendix B, two applications of social psychology are discussed in detail: law and health. One of Lewin's statements can be seen as a call to action for the entire field: "No research without action, no action without research."

During World War II, many social psychologists answered Lewin's call as they worked for the Canadian and U.S. governments to investigate how to protect soldiers from the propaganda of the enemy, how to persuade citizens to support the war effort, how to select officers for various positions, and other practical issues. During and after the war, social psychologists sought to understand the prejudice, aggression, and conformity the war had brought to light. The 1950s saw many major contributions to the field of social psychology. For example, Gordon Allport (1954) published *The Nature of Prejudice*, a book that continues to inspire research on stereotyping and prejudice more than a half century later. Solomon Asch's (1951) demonstration of how willing people are to conform to an obviously wrong majority amazes students even today. Leon Festinger (1954, 1957) introduced two important theories—one concerning how people try to learn about themselves by comparing themselves to other people, and one about how people's attitudes can be changed by their own behaviour—that remain among the most influential theories in the field. These are just a sample of a long list of landmark contributions made during the 1950s.

One thing appears to be missing from this list: there are no women scholars noted among these impressive ranks. This is not because women were not doing noteworthy research. Instead, it was the case that women—despite having the same professional training and credentials as their male counterparts—were more often excluded from academic appointments, and so their contributions were not always duly noted. Several of the earliest female members of the SPSSI were students of Kurt Lewin, but none of them were ever elected to leadership roles within that organization. Other early members, despite making substantive contributions to social psychology, were recognized only because of their more well-known spouses. For example, Caroline Wood Sherif collaborated extensively with her husband Muzafer, but it was not until much later in her career that this was acknowledged (Unger et al., 2010). Similarly, Marie Jahoda was one of the prominent social psychologists who emigrated from Europe but, despite her own academic credentials, it was her husband's position at Columbia University that first opened the door to an academic position for her in North America (Rutherford, Unger, & Cherry, 2011; Unger et al., 2010). She became the first woman to be elected president of the SPSSI in 1951. With the remarkable contributions and impact of researchers during this time, social psychology was clearly, and irrevocably, on the map.

Confidence and Crisis: 1960s–Mid-1970s

In spectacular fashion, Stanley Milgram's research in the early and middle 1960s linked the post-World War II era with the coming era of social revolution. Milgram's research was inspired by the destructive obedience demonstrated by Nazi officers and ordinary citizens in World War II, but it also looked ahead to the civil disobedience that was beginning to challenge institutions in many parts of the world. Milgram's experiments, which demonstrated individuals' vulnerability to the destructive commands of authority, became the most famous research in the history of social psychology. This research is discussed in detail in Chapter 7.

With its foundation firmly in place, social psychology entered a period of expansion and enthusiasm. In the 1970s the Canadian government expanded its funding programs, attracting many social psychologists from the United States (Adair, 2005). The sheer range of its investigations was staggering. Social psychologists considered how people thought and felt about themselves and others. They studied interactions in groups and social problems such as why people fail to help others in distress. They also examined aggression, physical attractiveness, and stress. For the field as a whole, it was a time of great productivity.

Ironically, it was also a time of crisis and heated debate. Many of the strong disagreements during this period can be understood as a reaction to the dominant research method of the day: the laboratory experiment. Critics of this method asserted that certain practices were unethical, that experimenters' expectations influenced their participants' behaviour, and that the theories being tested in the laboratory were historically and culturally limited (Gergen, 1973; Kelman, 1967; Rosenthal, 1976). Lubek and Apfelbaum (2000) describe the "cultural isolationism" and "methodolotry" that were present during this time, arguing that the definitions of what constituted "research" within the field became even narrower, based on the historical narratives that were written. They also made note of the fact that much of the feminist research, so important to shaping social psychology, was left out of this discussion. Those who favoured laboratory experimentation, on the other hand, contended that their procedures were ethical, their results valid, and their theoretical principles widely applicable (McGuire, 1967). For a while, social psychology seemed split in two.

An Era of Pluralism: Mid-1970s–1990s

Fortunately, both sides won. As we will see in the next chapter, more rigorous ethical standards for research were instituted, more stringent procedures to guard against bias were adopted, and more attention was paid to possible cross-cultural differences in behaviour. But the baby was not thrown out with the bathwater. Laboratory experiments continued. They did, however, get some company, as a single-minded attachment to one research method evolved into a broader acceptance of many methods. A pluralistic approach recognizes that because no one research method is perfect and because different topics require different kinds of investigations, a range of research techniques is needed. The various research methods used by today's social psychologists are described in the next chapter.

Pluralism in social psychology extends far beyond its methods. There are also important variations in what aspects of human behaviour are emphasized. Some social psychology research takes what we might call a "hot" perspective, focusing on *emotion* and *motivation* as determinants of our thoughts and actions. Other research in this field takes a "cold" perspective that emphasizes the role of *cognition*, examining the ways in which people's thoughts affect how they feel, what they want, and what they do. Of course, some social psychologists examine behaviour from both perspectives separately as well as interactively. Integrating such different perspectives is characteristic of the pluralism that the field has come to embrace in recent years.

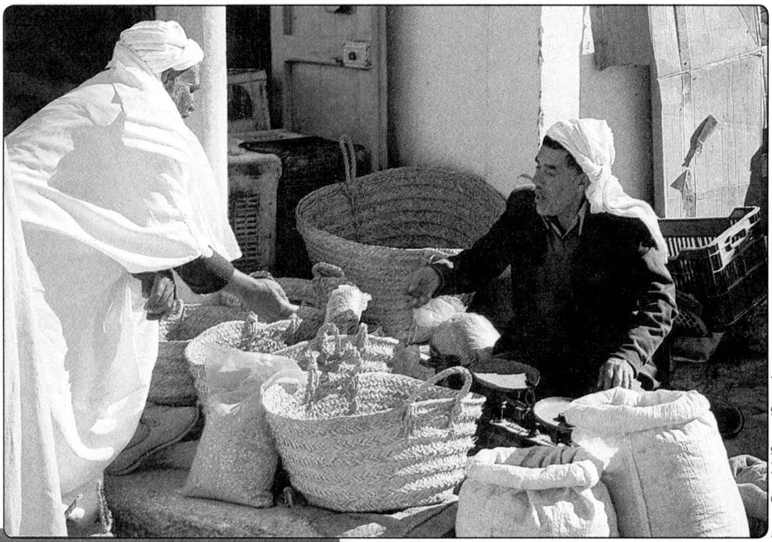

Social psychologists are becoming increasingly interested in cross-cultural research, which helps us break out of our culture-bound perspective. Many of our behaviours differ across cultures. In some cultures, for example, people are expected to negotiate about the price of the products they buy, as in this market in Tunisia. In other cultures, such bargaining would be highly unusual and cause confusion and distress.

Another source of pluralism in social psychology is its development of international and multicultural perspectives. Although, as we have seen, individuals from many countries helped establish the field, social psychology achieved its greatest professional recognition in Canada and the United States. At one point, it was estimated that 75 to 90 percent of social psychologists lived in North America (Smith & Bond, 1993; Triandis, 1994). Indeed, some called social psychology "culture-bound" (Berry et al., 1992) and "largely monocultural" (Moghaddam et al., 1993). However, this aspect of social psychology began to change rapidly in the 1990s, reflecting not only the different geographic and cultural backgrounds of its researchers and participants but also the recognition that many social psychological phenomena once assumed to be universal may actually vary dramatically as a function of culture You can find evidence of this new appreciation of the role of culture in every chapter of this textbook. While there is a great deal of similarity between the types of research conducted on both sides of the border, Canadian research has a strong focus on our cultural identity as well as uniquely Canadian issues, such as bilingualism and multiculturalism (Adair, 2005).

Social Psychology in a New Century

As we began the twenty-first century, social psychology began its second hundred years. The field today continues to grow in number and diversity of researchers and research topics, areas of the world in which research is conducted, and industries that hire social psychologists and apply their work.

Throughout this text, we emphasize the most current, cutting-edge research in the field, along with the classic findings of the past. In the remainder of the chapter, we focus on a few of the exciting themes and perspectives emerging from current research—research that is helping to shape the social psychology of the new century.

Integration of Emotion, Motivation, and Cognition

If any one perspective dominated the final quarter of social psychology's first century, it may have been **social cognition**, the study of how we perceive, remember, and interpret information about ourselves and others. Social psychologists demonstrated that these social-cognitive processes are critically important to virtually every area in the field. Social-cognitive explanations were so powerful that the roles of "hotter" influences, such as emotions and motivations, often took a back seat. Social cognition continues to flourish, but one of the more exciting developments in the field is the re-emergence of interest in how individuals' emotions and motivations influence

social cognition
The study of how people perceive, remember, and interpret information about themselves and others.

their thoughts and actions. Especially exciting is the fact that the social-cognitive approach is not necessarily seen as being at odds with approaches that emphasize motivations and emotions. Instead, there is a new push to integrate these perspectives, as in research investigating how people's motivations influence nonconscious cognitive processes, and vice versa (Bargh & Morsella, 2009; Forgas & Fitness, 2008; Moskowitz & Grant, 2009; Smith & Collins, 2009; Spencer et al., 2003).

One issue illustrating the integration of "hot" and "cold" variables concerns the conflict between wanting to be right and wanting to feel good about oneself. Most of us hold two very different motivations simultaneously: On the one hand, we want to be accurate in our judgments about ourselves and others. On the other hand, we *don't* want to be accurate if it means we will learn something bad about ourselves or those closest to us. These goals can pull our cognitive processes in very different directions. How we perform the required mental gymnastics is an ongoing concern for social psychologists.

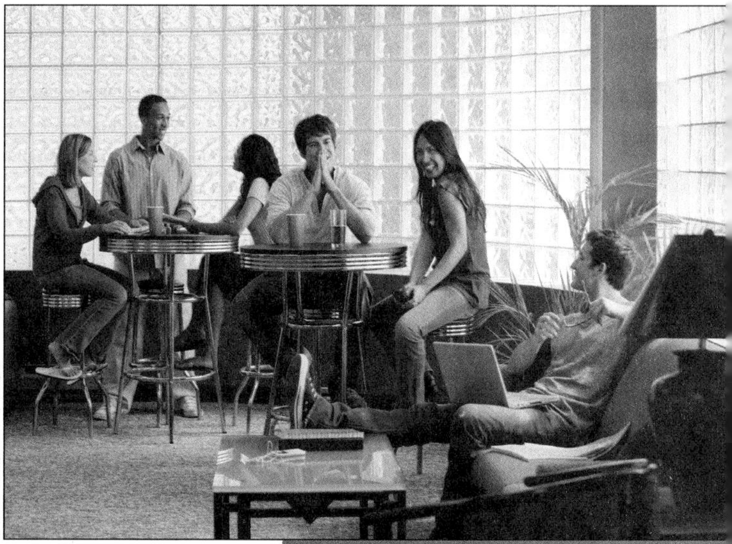

© JupiterImages/Getty Images

We are constantly making judgments about our own behaviour, as well as the behaviour of others. Such judgments may help us feel good about ourselves, although at times they may come at the expense of accuracy.

Another theme running through many chapters of this book is the growing interest in distinguishing between automatic and controllable processes and in understanding the dynamic relationship between them (Hassin, Bargh, & Zimerman, 2009; Moons, Mackie, & Garcia-Marques, 2009; Stewart & Payne, 2008). For example, there is a great deal of new evidence concerning whether and when stereotypes can be activated in one's mind automatically—that is, quickly and spontaneously, with no awareness, intention, or effort, and possibly even against one's will. Participants in many social psychology experiments are often surprised—to their great dismay—when they learn that their reactions during the study were biased by stereotypes (such as about the person's race or age) that they in fact did not believe in. On the other hand, there also is growing evidence that even such automatic reactions can be controlled under particular conditions. The automatic and controlled nature of a variety of processes and behaviours relevant to social psychology will no doubt continue to be an exciting area of research in the coming years.

Biological and Evolutionary Perspectives

As the technology available to researchers evolves, biological perspectives are increasingly being integrated into all branches of psychology, and this integration should continue to grow in social psychology. We are, of course, biological organisms, and it is clear that our brains and bodies influence, and are influenced by, our social experiences. This dynamic can be seen in a great deal of contemporary research, such as in studies demonstrating the cardiovascular effects of being the target of racism, or research illustrating that the manner in which people respond to stress can influence their athletic performance (Peters et al., 2011; Salomon & Jagusztyn, 2008; Sherman et al., 2009; Worthy, Markman, & Maddox, 2009).

Social psychologists have been concerned with physiological influences and responses for many years. Examples of this interest can be found throughout the textbook, especially in discussions of self-perception, attribution, attitude change, attraction, and aggression. A particularly exciting recent development is the emergence of the subfield of **social neuroscience**—the study of the relationship between neural and social processes. Social neuroscience is part of a flourishing set of research that explores how the social world affects the brain and biology, and vice versa.

Recent research has investigated such issues as how individuals' likelihood of acting aggressively may be influenced by their neurological responses to social rejection; gender differences in neuroendocrine reaction to stress; how our genes and our culture interact to help determine the attributions we make; and the relationship between activity in various brain structures, such as the amygdala, and how people respond to members of their own or a different racial group (Eisenberger et al., 2007; Kelly et al., 2008; Kim et al., 2010; Lieberman, 2010; Van Bavel, Packer, & Cunningham, 2008).

Recent advances in **behavioural genetics**—a subfield of psychology that examines the effects of genes on behaviour—has triggered new research to investigate such matters as the extent to which aggression is an inherited trait and the roles that genes play in individuals' sexual orientation or identity (Buckholtz & Meyer-Lindenberg, 2008; James, 2005).

Evolutionary psychology, which uses the principles of evolution to understand human behaviour, is another growing area that is sparking new research in social psychology. According to this perspective, to understand a social psychological issue such as jealousy, we should ask how the psychological mechanisms underlying jealousy today may have evolved from the natural-selection pressures our ancestors faced. Evolutionary psychological theories can then be used to explain and predict gender differences in jealousy, the situational factors most likely to trigger jealousy, and so on (Buss, 2007; Easton & Shackelford, 2009; Edlund & Sagarin, 2009). This perspective is discussed in many places in the textbook, especially in Part IV on Social Relations.

social neuroscience
The study of the relationship between neural and social processes.

behavioural genetics
A subfield of psychology that examines the role of genetic factors in behaviour.

evolutionary psychology
A subfield of psychology that uses the principles of evolution to understand human social behaviour.

culture
A system of enduring meanings, beliefs, values, assumptions, institutions, and practices shared by a large group of people and transmitted from one generation to the next.

cross-cultural research
Research designed to compare and contrast people of different cultures.

multicultural research
Research designed to examine racial and ethnic groups within cultures.

Cultural Perspectives

Because of the fantastic advancements in communication technologies in recent years and the globalization of the world's economies, it is faster, easier, and more necessary than ever before for people from vastly different cultures to interact with one another. Thus, our need and desire to understand how we are similar to and different from one another are greater than ever as well. Social psychology is currently experiencing tremendous growth in research designed to give us a better understanding and appreciation of the role of culture in all aspects of social psychology.

What is meant by "culture" is not easy to pin down, as many researchers think of culture in very different ways. At the start of the twentieth century, Wilhelm Wundt, a founding father of modern psychology, viewed the mind as a product of culture (*Völkerpsychologie*) and explored how language, for example, could tell us about this process (Danziger, 2001; Kroger & Scheibe, 1990). Broadly speaking, **culture** may be considered to be a system of enduring meanings, beliefs, values, assumptions, institutions, and practices shared by a large group of people and transmitted from one generation to the next. Whatever the specific definition, it is clear that how individuals perceive and derive meaning from their world are influenced profoundly by the beliefs, norms, and practices of the people and institutions around them.

Increasing numbers of social psychologists are evaluating the universal generality or cultural specificity of their theories and findings by conducting **cross-cultural research**, in which they examine similarities and differences across a variety of cultures. More and more social psychologists are also conducting **multicultural research**, in which they examine racial and ethnic groups within cultures.

These developments are already profoundly influencing our view of human behaviour. For example, a rapidly growing body of cross-cultural research has revealed important distinctions between the collectivist cultures typically found in Africa, Asia, and Latin America and the individualistic ones more commonly found in North America and Europe. The implications of these differences can be seen throughout the textbook. Consider, for instance, our earlier discussion of the integration of "hot" and "cold" variables in contemporary social psychology, in which we mentioned the conflict people have between wanting to be right and wanting to feel good about themselves. Cross-cultural research has shown that how people try to juggle these two goals can differ dramatically across cultures. Several researchers have found, for example, that people from individualistic cultures are more likely than people from collectivist cultures to seek out or focus on information that makes them feel good about themselves rather than information that points to the need for improvement (Heine, 2007). For example, Carl Falk and others (2009) asked Japanese or European-Canadian individuals to indicate which of a variety of desirable and undesirable traits characterized themselves. ▶ Figure 1.2 illustrates the results of the study, demonstrating that European-Canadian participants were far more likely to choose desirable than undesirable traits as characteristic of themselves, while Japanese participants were much more balanced between desirable and undesirable traits.

▶FIGURE 1.2

Self-Descriptions Across Cultures

Japanese or European-Canadian research participants were presented with a list of desirable (e.g., sincere, intelligent) and undesirable (e.g., cruel, indecisive) traits and asked which traits were characteristic of themselves. The European-Canadian participants (the two bars on the left) were much more likely to choose desirable than undesirable traits, but the Japanese participants (the two bars on the right) chose a much more balanced mix of traits.

(Based on Falk et al., 2009.)

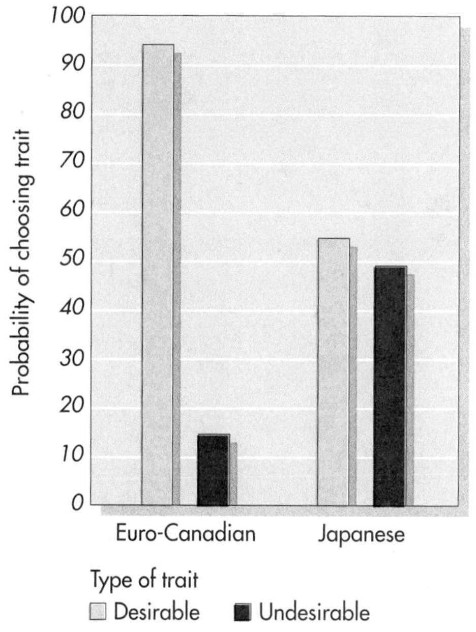

Within a particular society, people are often treated differently as a function of social categories such as gender, race, physical appearance, and so on. Boys and girls, for example, may be raised differently by their parents, confronted with different expectations by teachers, exposed to different types of advertising and marketing, and offered different kinds of jobs. In a sense, then, despite their frequent and intimate contact, women and men may develop and live in distinct subcultures. Social psychologists have studied the role of sociocultural factors in a variety of domains, such as conformity, leadership style, and aggression. Recent research is not only extending this tradition, it is sometimes turning it on its ear by illustrating that many previous research programs were flawed as a result of taking a male-dominated approach. New research on aggression, for example, illustrates that most of the older research focused almost exclusively on the forms of aggression typical of boys, thereby failing to recognize important issues relevant to aggression among girls.

These are but a few examples of the cultural research taking place today. In this text, we describe studies conducted in dozens of countries, representing every populated continent on Earth. As our knowledge expands, we should be able to see much more clearly both the behavioural differences among cultures and the similarities we all share.

Some social psychology textbooks devote a separate chapter to culture or to culture and gender. We chose not to do so. Because we believe that sociocultural influences are inherent in all aspects of social psychology, we chose instead to integrate discussions of the role of culture and gender throughout the textbook.

New Technologies

Advances in technologies that allow researchers to see images of the brain at work, through non-invasive procedures, have had a profound effect on several areas of psychology, including social psychology. A growing number of social psychologists are using techniques such as *positron emission tomography* (*PET*), *event-related potential* (*ERP*), *transcranial magnetic stimulation* (*TMS*), and *functional magnetic resonance imaging* (*fMRI*) to study the interplay of the brain and discrete thoughts, feelings, and behaviours. Social psychology research today benefits from other technological advances as well, such as new and better techniques to measure hormone levels, to code people's everyday dialogue into quantifiable units, and to present visual stimuli to research participants at fractions of a second and then record the number of milliseconds it takes the participants to respond to these stimuli. Researchers are just beginning to use virtual reality technology to examine a number of social psychological questions. James Blascovich and others have created The Research Center for Virtual Environments and Behavior at the University of California at Santa Barbara and have been conducting fascinating research on issues such as conformity, group dynamics, aggression and altruism, and eyewitness testimony (e.g., McCall et al., 2009). Because participants in these experiments are immersed in a virtual reality that the experimenters create for them, the researchers can test questions that would be impractical, impossible, or unethical without this technology.

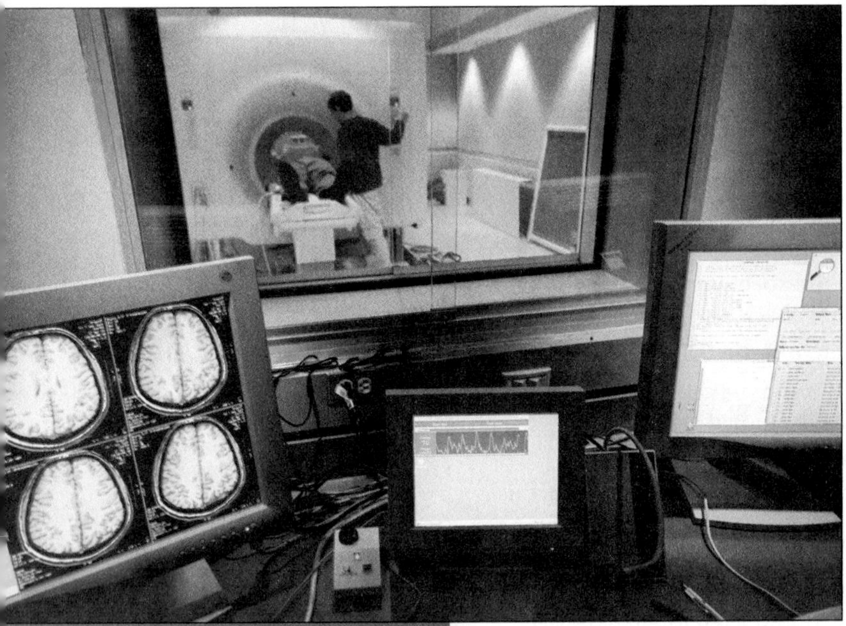
Jeff Miller/University of Wisconsin-Madison

Advances in technology enable social psychologists to extend their research in exciting new directions, such as by using functional magnetic resonance imaging (fMRI) to study activation in the brain in response to various thoughts or stimuli.

While the various ways that we access information and communicate with each other develop and change at a rapid pace, social psychology research grows along with it. Social psychologists around the world can now not only communicate and collaborate much more easily, but also gain access to research participants from populations that would otherwise never have been available. These developments have sparked the field's internationalization, perhaps its most exciting course in this new century. World War II triggered an explosion of social psychological research in North America; the Internet is extending this research to the rest of the world.

The Internet itself is also becoming a provocative topic of study. As more people interact with each other through email and social networking sites, there is growing interest in studying how attraction, prejudice, group dynamics, and a host of other social psychological phenomena unfold online versus offline (Toma et al., 2008; Weisbuch et al., 2009; Williams & Mendelsohn, 2008).

We would be presumptuous, and probably naive, to try to predict how new communication and computer technologies will influence the ways in which people interact in the coming years; but it probably is safe to predict that their influence will be great. As more and more people fall in love online, or fall into social isolation, or react with anxiety or violence to the loss of individual privacy, social psychology will explore these issues. We expect that some students reading this textbook today will be among those explorers in the years to come.

REVIEW

What Is Social Psychology?

Defining Social Psychology

- Social psychology is the scientific study of how individuals think, feel, and behave in a social context.
- Like other sciences, social psychology relies on the systematic approach of the scientific method.
- Distinctive characteristics of social psychology include a focus on the individual as well as a broad perspective on a variety of social contexts and behaviours.
- The "socialness" of social psychology varies, as social psychologists sometimes examine how nonsocial factors affect social thoughts, feelings, and behaviours and sometimes study how social factors influence nonsocial thoughts, feelings, and behaviours.

Social Psychological Questions and Applications

- Social psychologists study a large variety of fascinating questions about people and their social worlds. The scope and relevance of these questions to so many important aspects of our lives make social psychology applicable to many careers and interests.

The Power of the Social Context: An Example of a Social Psychology Experiment

- In one experiment that illustrates how thinking about others can influence our own self-perceptions, female undergraduates who were made aware of cultural norms regarding thinness experienced a decrease in their overall body satisfaction ratings and reported being more concerned with the opinions of others.

Social Psychology and Related Fields: Distinctions and Intersections

- Social psychology is related to a number of different areas of study, including sociology, clinical psychology, personality psychology, and cognitive psychology. Important work is being done at the intersection of social psychology and each of these fields.
- Social psychology tends to focus on individuals, whereas sociology tends to focus on groups. In addition, social psychology is less likely than sociology to study the relation between broad societal variables and people's behaviours and is more likely to use experimentation.
- In contrast to clinical psychology, social psychology focuses not on disorders but, rather, on the more typical ways in which individuals think, feel, behave, and interact.
- Personality psychology focuses on differences between individuals that remain relatively stable across a variety of situations; social psychology focuses on how social factors affect most individuals, regardless of their different personalities.
- Cognitive and social psychologists share an interest in mental processes such as thinking, learning, remembering, and reasoning; but social psychologists focus on the relevance of these processes to social behaviour.

Social Psychology and Common Sense

- Many social psychological theories and findings appear to be like common sense. One problem with common sense, however, is that it may offer conflicting explanations and provide no way to test which one is correct. Another problem is that common sense is often oversimplified and therefore misleading.

From Past to Present: A Brief History of Social Psychology

The Birth and Infancy of Social Psychology: 1880s–1920s

- Early research by Triplett and Ringelmann established an enduring topic in social psychology: how the presence of others affects an individual's performance.
- The first social psychology textbooks in 1908 and 1924 began to give the emerging field of social psychology its shape.

A Call to Action: 1930s–1950s

- Social psychology began to flourish because the world needed an explanation for the violence of war and solutions to it.
- Sherif's work laid the foundation for later studies of social influence, and the legacy of Kurt Lewin is still evident throughout much of social psychology.
- The 1940s and 1950s saw a burst of activity in social psychology that firmly established it as a major social science.

Confidence and Crisis: 1960s–Mid-1970s

- Stanley Milgram's experiments demonstrated individuals' vulnerability to the destructive commands of authority.
- While social psychology was expanding in many new directions, there was also intense debate about the ethics of research procedures, the validity of research results, and the generalizability of conclusions drawn from the research.

An Era of Pluralism: Mid-1970s–1990s

- During the 1970s, social psychology began to take a pluralistic approach that continues today in its research methods, views on human behaviour, and development of international and multicultural perspectives; this approach continues today.

Social Psychology in a New Century

- Several exciting themes and perspectives are helping to shape the beginning of social psychology's second century.

Integration of Emotion, Motivation, and Cognition

- Researchers are becoming more interested in how emotion, motivation, and cognition can operate together in influencing individuals' thoughts, feelings, and behaviours.
- A great deal of recent social psychological research has explored the automatic versus controllable nature of a number of processes, such as stereotyping.

Biological and Evolutionary Perspectives

- Biological perspectives, including perspectives based on neuroscience, genetics, and evolutionary principles, are being applied to the study of social psychological issues such as gender differences, relationships, and aggression.

Cultural Perspectives

- Increasing numbers of social psychologists are evaluating the universal generality or cultural specificity of their theories and findings by examining similarities and differences across cultures as well as between racial and ethnic groups within cultures.
- For example, in one experiment, Canadian participants chose more desirable than undesirable traits as characteristic of themselves, whereas Japanese participants chose a balance of desirable and undesirable traits.

New Technologies

- Advances in technology, such as improved brain imaging techniques, have given rise to groundbreaking research in social psychology.
- Virtual reality technology enables researchers to test questions that otherwise would be impractical, impossible, or unethical.
- The Internet has fostered communication and collaboration among researchers around the world, enabled researchers to study participants from diverse populations, and inspired researchers to investigate whether various social psychological phenomena are similar or different online versus offline.
- As rapidly advancing technologies change how individuals communicate and access information, the ways in which they interact are also likely to change. The social psychology of the next era will explore these issues.

Key Terms

behavioural genetics (18)
cross-cultural research (18)
culture (18)
evolutionary psychology (18)
interactionist perspective (13)
multicultural research (18)
social cognition (16)
social neuroscience (18)
social psychology (5)

2

Barry Rosenthal/Image Bank/Getty Images

Doing Social Psychology Research

This chapter examines how social psychologists do their research. We begin by asking, "Why should you learn about research methods?" We answer this question by discussing how learning about research methods can benefit you both in this course and beyond. Then we consider how researchers come up with and develop ideas and begin the research process. Next, we provide an overview of the research designs that social psychologists use to test their ideas. Finally, we turn to important questions about ethics and values in social psychology.

"The most exciting phrase to hear in science, the one that heralds new discoveries, is not 'Eureka!' (I found it!) but 'That's funny....'"

—Isaac Asimov

It's a familiar situation. You're starting a new term at school, and you're just beginning to settle into a new schedule and routine. You're looking forward to your new courses. In general, it's an exciting time. But there's one major catch: As you spend more and more time with your new classmates and new responsibilities, you're leaving someone behind. It could be a boyfriend or girlfriend, a spouse, or a close friend—someone who is not involved in what you are doing now. You may now live far apart from each other, or your new commitments in school may be keeping you apart from each other much more than you'd like. The romantic in you says, "Together forever." Or at least, "No problem." But the realist in you worries a bit. Will your love or friendship be the same? Can it survive the long distance, or the new demands on your time, or the new people in your respective environments? Your friends or family may have advice to offer in this situation. Some might smile and reassure you, "Don't worry. Remember what they say, 'Absence makes the heart grow fonder.' This will only strengthen your relationship." Others might call you aside and whisper, "Don't listen to them. Everybody knows, 'Out of sight, out of mind.' You'd better be careful."

Taking your mind off this problem, you begin to work on a class project. You have the option of working alone or as part of a group. Which should you do? You consult the wisdom of common sense. Maybe you should work in a group. After all, everyone knows that "two heads are better than one." As some members of your group begin to miss meetings and shirk responsibilities, though, you remember that "too many cooks spoil the broth." Will you regret having been so quick to decide to join this group? After all, haven't you been taught to "look before you leap?" Then again, if you had waited and missed the chance to join the group, you might have regretted your inaction, recalling that "he who hesitates is lost."

Questions about the course of relationships, the efficiency of working in groups, and the regret of action versus inaction are social psychological questions. And because we all are interested in predicting and explaining people's behaviours and their thoughts and feelings about each other, we all have our own opinions and intuitions about social psychological matters. If the discipline of social psychology were built on the personal experiences, observations, and intuitions of everyone who is interested in social psychological questions, it would be chock full of interesting theories and ideas; but it would also be a morass of contradictions, ambiguities, and relativism. Instead, social psychology is built on the scientific method.

Scientific? It's easy to see how chemistry is scientific. When you mix two specific compounds in the lab, you can predict exactly what will happen. The compounds will act the same way every time you mix them if the general conditions in the lab are the same. But what happens when you mix together two chemists, or any two people, in a social context? Sometimes you get great chemistry between them; other times you get apathy or even repulsion. How, then, can social behaviour, which seems so variable, be studied scientifically?

To many of us in the field, that's the great excitement and challenge of social psychology—the fact that it is so dynamic and diverse. Furthermore, in spite of these characteristics, social psychology can, and should, be studied according to scientific principles. Social psychologists develop specific, quantifiable hypotheses that can be tested empirically. If these hypotheses are not supported by the results of a study, we still learn something—and we can revise our methods and start again. In addition, social scientists report the details of how they conduct their tests so that others can try to replicate their findings. They integrate evidence from across time and place. And slowly but steadily, they build a consistent and ever more precise understanding of human nature. How social psychologists investigate social psychological questions scientifically is the focus of this chapter. Before we explain the methodology they use, we first explain a bit about why it's important and interesting for you to learn about these matters.

Why Should You Learn About Research Methods?

© Richard Nowitz/National Geographic Society/Corbis

We are bombarded with information in our everyday lives, such as in the countless advertisements designed to persuade us to buy particular products or adopt particular opinions or attitudes. Learning the methods used in social psychology research can help students become more sophisticated consumers of this information.

One very practical reason for learning about research methods is that it will help you better understand and learn the material in this book, which will in turn help you on exams and in subsequent courses. Let's look more closely at why this is so. Because social psychology is so relevant to our everyday lives, and because there are so many commonsense notions about social psychological questions, separating myths from truths can be difficult. Most of us don't have an intuition about particular questions concerning quantum mechanics, but we do have intuitions about, say, whether people work better alone or in groups. If you simply read a list of social psychological findings about issues such as this, without knowing and understanding the evidence that social psychologists have produced to support the findings, you may discover later that the task of remembering which were the actual findings and which were merely your own intuitions is difficult. This task is sometimes especially challenging in multiple-choice exams. The right answer might seem very plausible; but then again, so might some of the wrong answers, just as there are good reasons to believe both that "two heads are better than one" and that "too many cooks spoil the broth." Learning about the evidence on which the true research findings and theories are based should help you distinguish the correct from the plausible but incorrect answers.

But the benefits of learning about research methods go far beyond the academic. Training in research methods in psychology can improve your reasoning about real-life events (Lehman et al., 1988; Leshowitz et al., 2002; VanderStoep & Shaughnessy, 1997). It can make you a better, more sophisticated consumer of information in general. We are constantly bombarded with "facts" from the media, from sales pitches, and from other people. Much of this information turns out to be wrong or, at best, oversimplified and misleading. We are told about the health benefits of eating certain kinds of food, or the social status benefits of driving a certain kind of car or wearing a certain kind of shoe. To each of these pronouncements, we should say, "Prove it." What is the evidence? What alternative explanations might there be? For example, a commercial tells us that most doctors prefer a particular (and relatively expensive) brand of aspirin. So should we buy this brand? Think about what it was compared with. Perhaps the doctors didn't prefer that brand of aspirin over other (and cheaper) brands of aspirin but rather were asked to compare that brand of aspirin with several non-aspirin products for a particular problem. In that event, the doctors may have preferred *any* brand of aspirin over non-aspirin products for that need. Thinking like a scientist while reading this text will foster a healthy sense of doubt about claims like these. You will be in a better position to critically evaluate the information to which you're exposed and separate fact from fiction.

"Education is not the filling of a pail, but the lighting of a fire."

—William Butler Yeats

Developing Ideas: Beginning the Research Process

The research process involves coming up with ideas, refining them, testing them, and interpreting the meaning of the results obtained. This section describes the first stage of research, coming up with ideas. It also discusses the role of hypotheses and theories and of basic and applied research.

Asking Questions

Every social psychology study begins with a question. And the questions come from everywhere. As discussed in Chapter 1, the first social psychology experiment published was triggered by the question "Why do bicyclists race faster in the presence of other bicyclists?" (Triplett, 1897–1898). Inspiration can come from a variety of sources, from the distressing, such as a gruesome murder and the inaction of witnesses to that murder (Latané & Darley, 1970); to something perplexing, such as the under-representation of women in math and science (Ceci et al., 2011); to the amusing, such as the lyrics of a country song suggesting that to the men in a bar, the female patrons seem prettier as closing time approaches (Johnco et. al, 2010).

Questions also come from reading about research that has already been done. Solomon Asch (1946), for example, read about Muzafer Sherif's (1936) demonstration of how individuals in a group conform to others in the group when making judgments about a very ambiguous stimulus (mentioned in Chapter 1 and described in Chapter 7 on Conformity). Asch questioned whether people would conform to the opinions of others in a group even when it was quite clear that the group was wrong. He tested this question, and the results surprised him and the rest of the field: People often did conform even though it was clear that the group was wrong. Thus, one of the most famous experiments in the field inspired an even more famous experiment.

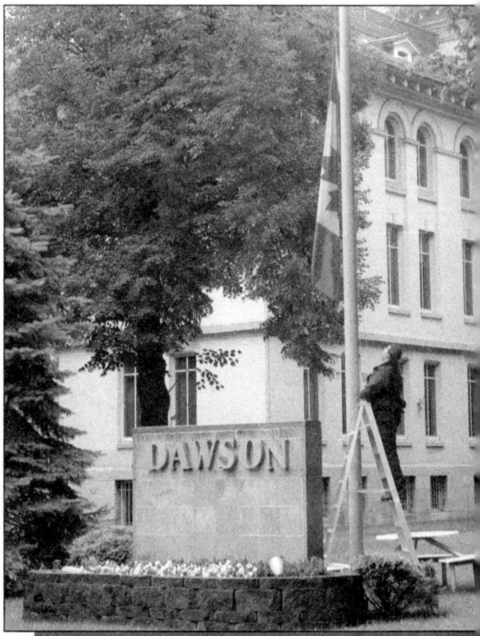

The Canadian Press/Paul Chiasson

On September 13, 2006, 25-year-old Kimveer Gill opened fire on students at Dawson College in Montréal, Québec. One student was killed and 19 others were injured. Gill committed suicide at the scene. He left a letter praising the actions of Eric Harris and Dylan Klebold, who killed 12 students and a teacher in a school shooting at Columbine High School in 1999. Over the years, tragic incidents like these have inspired social psychologists to conduct research on violence and a wide range of other important social problems.

Searching the Literature

Once the researcher has an idea, whether it came from personal observation, folk wisdom, a news story, or previous findings, it is important to see what research has already been done on this topic and related topics. While you may find information about all kinds of research on the Internet using a search engine such as Google, many

"Give people facts and you feed their minds for an hour. Awaken curiosity and they feed their own minds for a lifetime."

—Ian Russell

"The currency of science is not truth, but doubt."

—Dennis Overbye

of the sites you find—such as Wikipedia—may vary wildly in their relevance, accuracy, and quality. One of the best ways to search for published materials on topics of interest is by using an electronic database of published research. Some of these databases, such as PsycArticles and PsycINFO, are specific to the psychology literature; others are more general. When you use an electronic database, you can search hundreds of thousands of published articles and books in seconds. You can type in names of authors, key words or phrases, years, or the like, and instantly receive summaries of articles that fit your search criteria. Once you have found some relevant articles, there is a good chance that they will refer to other articles that are also relevant. Going from article to article, sometimes called *treeing*, can prove very valuable in tracking down information about the research question.

More often than not, the researcher's original question is changed in one way or another during the course of searching the literature. The question should become more precise, more specific to particular sets of conditions that are likely to have different effects, and more readily testable.

Hypotheses and Theories

An initial idea for research may be so vague that it amounts to little more than a hunch or an educated guess. Some ideas vanish with the break of day. But others can be shaped into a **hypothesis**—an explicit, testable prediction about the conditions under which an event will occur. Based on observation, existing theory, or previous research findings, one might test a hypothesis such as "Teenage boys are more likely to be aggressive toward others if they have just played a violent video game for an hour than if they played a nonviolent video game for an hour." This is a specific prediction, and it can be tested empirically. Formulating a hypothesis is a critical step toward planning and conducting research. It allows us to move from the realm of common sense to the rigours of the scientific method.

As hypotheses proliferate and data are collected to test the hypotheses, a more advanced step in the research process may take place: the proposal of a **theory**—an organized set of principles used to explain observed phenomena. Theories are usually evaluated in terms of three criteria: simplicity, comprehensiveness, and their ability to generate new hypotheses (known as generativity). All else being equal, the best theories are elegant and precise; encompass all of the relevant information; and lead to new hypotheses, further research, and better understanding.

In social psychology, there are many theories. Social psychologists do not attempt the all-encompassing grand theory, such as those of Freud or Piaget, which you may have studied in introductory psychology. Instead, they rely on more precise "mini-theories" that address limited and specific aspects of the way people behave, make explicit predictions about behaviour, and allow meaningful empirical investigation. Consider, for example, Daryl Bem's (1967, 1972) self-perception theory, which is discussed in Chapter 3 on the Social Self. Bem proposed that when people's internal states, such as a feeling or attitude, are difficult for them to interpret, they infer this feeling or attitude by observing their own behaviour and the situation in which it takes place. This theory did not apply to all situations; rather, it was specific to situations in which people made inferences about their own actions when their own internal states were somewhat ambiguous. Though more limited in scope than a grand theory of personality or development, self-perception theory did generate numerous specific, empirically testable hypotheses.

Good social psychological theories inspire subsequent research. Specifically, they stimulate systematic studies designed to test various aspects of the theories and

hypothesis
A testable prediction about the conditions under which an event will occur.

theory
An organized set of principles used to explain observed phenomena.

the specific hypotheses that are derived from them. A theory may be quite accurate and yet have little worth if it cannot be tested. Conversely, a theory may make an important contribution to the field even if it turns out to be wrong. The research it inspires may prove more valuable than the theory itself, as the results shed light on new truths that might not have been discovered without the directions suggested by the theory.

Indeed, when Bem introduced self-perception theory to the field, it generated a great deal of attention and controversy. Part of its value as a good theory was that it helped organize and make sense of evidence that had been found in previous studies. Furthermore, it generated testable new hypotheses. Many scholars doubted the validity of the theory, however, and conducted research designed to show that it was wrong. In short, both supporters and doubters of the theory launched a wave of studies, which ultimately led to a greater understanding of the processes described in Bem's theory.

Students new to social psychology are often surprised by the lack of consensus in the field. In part, such disagreement reflects the fact that social psychology is a relatively young science (Kruglanski, 2001). At this stage in its development, premature closure is a worse sin than contradiction or even confusion. But debate is an essential feature of even the most mature science. It is the fate of all scientific theories to be criticized and, eventually, surpassed.

"[Close cooperation between theoretical and applied psychology] can be accomplished ... if the theorist does not look toward applied problems with highbrow aversion or with a fear of social problems, and if the applied psychologist realizes that there is nothing so practical as a good theory."

—Kurt Lewin

Basic and Applied Research

Is testing a theory the purpose of research in social psychology? For some researchers, yes. **Basic research** seeks to increase our understanding of human behaviour and is often designed to test a specific hypothesis from a specific theory. **Applied research** has a different purpose: to make use of social psychology's theories or methods to enlarge our understanding of naturally occurring events and to contribute to the solution of social problems.

Despite their differences, basic research and applied research are closely connected in social psychology. Some researchers switch back and forth between the two—today basic, tomorrow applied. Some studies test a theory and examine a real-world phenomenon simultaneously. As a pioneer in both approaches, Kurt Lewin (1951) set the tone when he encouraged basic researchers to be concerned with complex social problems and urged applied researchers to recognize how important and practical good theories are.

Refining Ideas: Defining and Measuring Social Psychological Variables

To test their hypotheses, researchers always must decide how they will define and measure the variables in which they are interested. This is sometimes a straightforward process. For example, if you are interested in comparing how quickly people run a 100-metre dash when alone and when racing against another person, you can rely on well-established ways to define and measure the variables in question. Many other times, however, the process is less straightforward. If you are interested in studying the effects of alcohol intoxication on aggression, for example, you must first decide how you are going to define "alcohol intoxication" and "aggression." There may be countless ways to do this. Which ones should you pick?

basic research
Research designed to increase the understanding of human behaviour, often by testing hypotheses based on a theory.

applied research
Research designed to enlarge the understanding of naturally occurring events and to find solutions to practical problems.

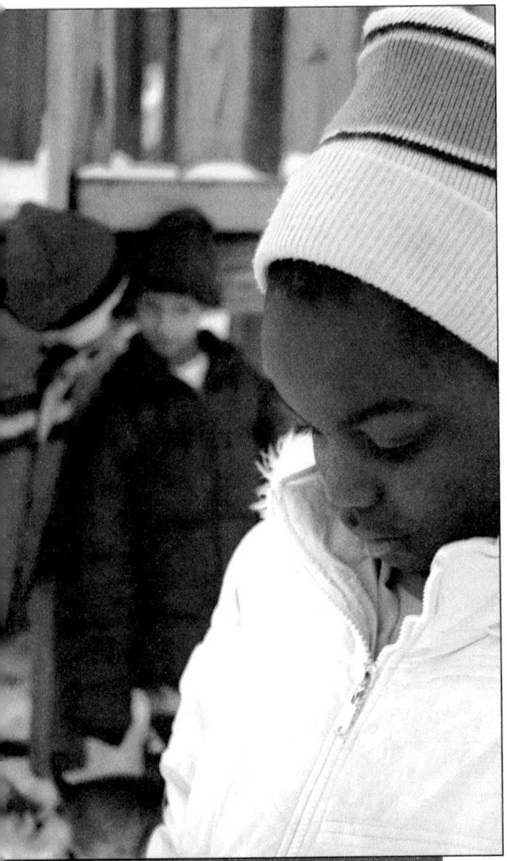

Thinkstock

From this picture, we can guess that the child standing alone on the playground is lonely, but how do researchers precisely define and measure conceptual variables like loneliness? Researchers may use any of a number of approaches, such as asking people how they feel or observing their behaviour.

Conceptual Variables and Operational Definitions: From the Abstract to the Specific

When a researcher first develops a hypothesis, the variables typically are in an abstract, general form. These are *conceptual variables.* Examples of conceptual variables include prejudice, conformity, attraction, love, violence, group pressure, and social anxiety. In order to test specific hypotheses, we must then transform these conceptual variables into variables that can be manipulated or measured in a study. The specific way in which a conceptual variable is manipulated or measured is called the **operational definition** of the variable. For example, a researcher might operationally define "conformity" in a particular study as the number of times a participant indicated agreement with the obviously wrong judgments made by a group of confederates. Part of the challenge and fun of designing research in social psychology is taking an abstract conceptual variable such as love or group pressure and deciding how to operationally define it so as to manipulate or measure it.

Using the example above, let's say you wanted to study the effects of alcohol intoxication on aggression. One of the conceptual variables might be whether or not participants are intoxicated. There are several ways of measuring this variable, most of which are relatively straightforward. For instance, one researcher might operationally define intoxication as when a participant has a blood alcohol level of .10 or more, while another might define it as when a participant says that he or she feels drunk. A second conceptual variable in this study would be aggression. Measuring aggression in experiments is particularly difficult because of ethical and practical issues—researchers cannot let participants in their studies attack each other. Researchers interested in measuring aggression are thus often forced to measure relatively unusual behaviours, such as administering shocks or blasts of noise to another person as part of a specific task.

Often, there is no single best way to transform a variable from the abstract (conceptual) to the specific (operational). A great deal of trial and error may be involved. However, sometimes there are systematic, statistical ways of checking how valid various manipulations and measures are, and researchers spend a great deal of time fine-tuning their operational definitions to best capture the conceptual variables they wish to study.

Researchers evaluate the manipulation and measurement of variables in terms of their **construct validity**. Construct validity refers to the extent to which (1) the manipulations in an experiment really manipulate the conceptual variables they were designed to manipulate and (2) the measures used in a study (experimental or otherwise) really measure the conceptual variables they were designed to measure.

operational definition
The specific procedures for manipulating or measuring a conceptual variable.

construct validity
The extent to which the measures used in a study measure the variables they were designed to measure and the manipulations in an experiment manipulate the variables they were designed to manipulate.

Measuring Variables: Using Self-Reports, Observations, and Technology

Social psychologists measure variables in many ways, but most can be placed into one of two categories: self-reports and observations. We discuss each of these methods in the next sections, along with how advances in technology are enabling social psychologists to measure variables in new ways.

Self-Reports: Going Straight to the Source Collecting *self-reports*—in which participants disclose their thoughts, feelings, desires, and actions—is a widely used measurement technique in social psychology. Self-reports can consist of individual questions or sets of questions that together measure a single conceptual variable. One popular self-report measure, the Rosenberg Self-Esteem Scale, consists of a set

The Canadian Press/Adrian Wyld

Self-reports can also be misleading when information is gathered from some groups and not from others. In June 2010, the Conservative government announced its plan to replace the long-form census with a voluntary survey. Member of Parliament Marc Garneau, the Liberal Industry, Science and Technology critic, spoke out against the plan. He argued that a census has to be mandatory in order to collect data from a wide variety of people. Without input from different groups, the government might not have the information it needs to develop effective policies.

of questions that measures individuals' overall self-esteem. For example, respondents are asked the extent to which they agree with statements such as "I feel that I have a number of good qualities," and "All in all, I am inclined to feel that I'm a failure." This scale is used in a wide variety of settings, and many researchers consider it to have good construct validity (Heatherton & Wyland, 2003; Franck et al., 2008; Supple & Plunkett, 2011).

Self-reports give the researcher access to an individual's beliefs and perceptions. But self-reports are not always accurate and can be misleading. For example, the desire to look good to ourselves and to others can influence how we respond. Research using a procedure called the "bogus pipeline" indicates that participants who are led to believe that their responses will be verified by an infallible lie-detector, report facts about themselves more accurately and endorse socially unacceptable opinions more frequently than those not told about such a device. The bogus pipeline is, in fact, bogus; no such infallible device exists. But belief in its powers discourages people from lying (Gannon, 2007; Imhoff & Banse, 2009; Roese & Jamieson, 1993).

Self-reports are also affected by the way that questions are asked, such as how they are worded or in what order or context they are asked (Schwarz & Oyserman, 2010). For example, 88 percent of participants in a study indicated that they thought condoms were effective in stopping AIDS when condoms were said to have a "95 percent success rate." (See Table 2.1.) However, when condoms were said to have a "5 percent failure rate," (which is merely another way of saying the same thing as a 95 percent success rate), only 42 percent indicated that they thought condoms were effective (Linville et al., 1992). Jonathon Schuldt and others (2011) found that conservative voters in the United States were more likely to agree that the planet is being affected by "climate change" (60.2 percent) than they were when asked about "global warming" (44 percent).

"Clemson here. How may I disappoint you?"

© Dean Vietor/The New Yorker Collection/ www.cartoonbank.com

This person would probably score low on Rosenberg's Self-Esteem Scale.

Even the exact same question can elicit very different responses depending on the context in which the question occurs. For example, all individuals contacted in

TABLE 2.1

How Self-Reports Can Be Affected by Context

Are condoms effective in preventing the spread of AIDS? Responses to this question can differ significantly depending on context. Participants told that condoms had a "95% success rate" were much more likely to say that condoms were effective than were participants told they had a "5% failure rate," even though these two rates are functionally the same thing.
(Linville et al., 1992.)

Statement Given to Participants	Percent Who Said Condoms Were Effective
"Condoms have a 95% success rate."	88
"Condoms have a 5% failure rate."	42

one telephone survey were asked how important the issue of skin cancer was in their lives, but this question was asked either before or after a series of questions about other health concerns. Even though the wording of the question was identical, respondents rated skin cancer as significantly more important if the question was asked first than if it came after the other health questions (Rimal & Real, 2005).

Another reason self-reports can be inaccurate is that they often ask participants to report on thoughts or behaviours from the past, and participants' memory for these thoughts or behaviours may be suspect. To minimize this problem, psychologists have developed ways to reduce the time that elapses between an actual experience and the person's report of it. For example, some use *interval-contingent* self-reports, in which respondents report their experiences at regular intervals, usually once a day. They may report events since the last report, or how they feel at the moment, or both. Researchers may also collect *signal-contingent* self-reports. Here, respondents report their experiences as soon as possible after being signalled to do so, usually by means of a beeper. Finally, some researchers collect *event-contingent* self-reports, in which respondents report on a designated set of events as soon as possible after such events have occurred. For example, the Rochester Interaction Record (RIR) is an event-contingent self-report questionnaire used by respondents to record every social interaction lasting ten minutes or more that occurs during the course of the study, usually a week or two (Downie et al., 2008; Nezlek et al., 2011).

Whatever their differences, most self-report methods require participants to provide specific answers to specific questions. In contrast, *narrative studies* collect lengthy responses on a general topic. Narrative materials can be generated by participants at the researcher's request or taken from other sources (such as diaries, speeches, books, or chat room discussions). These accounts are then analyzed in terms of a coding scheme developed by the researcher. For example, the researcher might code diaries for evidence of changes in behaviour toward other groups, or narrative statements to determine the impact of perspective taking on mental health (Page-Gould et al., 2008; Seih et al., 2011).

Observations Self-reports are not the only available window on human behaviour. Researchers can also observe people's actions. Sometimes these observations are very simple, as when a researcher notes which of two items a person selects. At other times, however, the observations are more elaborate and (like the coding of narrative accounts) require that interrater reliability be established. **Interrater reliability** refers to the level of agreement among multiple observers of the same behaviour. Only when different observers agree can the data be trusted.

The advantage of observational methods is that they avoid our sometimes faulty recollections and distorted interpretations of our own behaviour. Actions can speak louder than words. Of course, if individuals know they are being observed, their behaviours, like their self-reports, may be biased by the desire to present themselves in a favourable light. Therefore, researchers sometimes make observations much more subtly. For example, in an experiment concerning attitudes toward people with schizophrenia, researchers in London, Ontario, told participants they would be meeting a young woman with the disorder. One measure of the participant's attitude was how

interrater reliability
The degree to which different observers agree on their observations.

close he or she chose to sit to the chair where the young woman was expected to sit; seating distance was therefore used to demonstrate a bias that might not be revealed using more overt measures (Norman et al., 2010).

Jeff Greenberg/The Image Works, Inc.

Observational methods provide a useful alternative to self-reports. For example, studies of young children, whose verbal skills are limited, often rely on observations.

Technology Social psychologists of course use more than merely their eyes and ears to observe their participants. Advances in technology offer researchers exciting new tools that enable them to make extremely precise, subtle, and complex observations that were beyond the dreams of social psychologists just a generation or so ago. Various kinds of equipment are used to measure physiological responses, such as changes in heart rate, levels of particular hormones, and sexual arousal. Computers are used to record the speed with which participants respond to stimuli, such as how quickly they can identify the race of people in photographs, or the presence of a weapon in the hands of a white or black man (Bishara & Payne, 2009; Gonsalkorale et al., 2011). Eye-tracking technology is used to measure exactly where and for how long participants look at particular parts of a stimulus, such as an advertisement or a video (Crosby et al., 2008; DeWall et al., 2009; Pieters et al., 2010).

Most recently, social psychologists have begun to open a window into the live human brain—fortunately, without having to lift a scalpel. Brain-imaging technologies take and combine thousands of images of the brain in action. As mentioned in Chapter 1, many social psychology studies today use functional magnetic resonance imaging (fMRI) scans to provide researchers with visual images of activity in parts of the brain while the research participant is thinking, making decisions, responding to audio or visual stimuli, and so on. These images can show researchers what parts of the brain seem to "light up"—or show increased activity—in response to a particular stimulus or situation. For example, although participants in a study of racism may show no signs of any racial or sexist biases on their self-reports or through easily observable behaviour in the lab, these same participants may show increased activity in parts of their brain associated with feelings of threat or strong emotion when they see pictures of or think about people from a particular racial group or gender (Mitchell et al., 2009; Van Bavel et al., 2008).

Testing Ideas: Research Designs

Social psychologists use several different methods to test their research hypotheses and theories. While some social psychological issues can be studied using **qualitative research** approaches, including open-ended responses, observations, and interviews, the field generally emphasizes a **quantitative research** approach, where numerical data is collected in an objective, systematic, and quantifiable way. Social psychologists do not simply seek out evidence that supports their ideas; rather, they test their ideas in ways that could very clearly prove them wrong.

qualitative research
The collection of data through open-ended responses, observation, and interviews.

quantitative research
The collection of numerical data through objective testing and statistical analysis.

The most popular and preferred research method in social psychology is experimentation, in which researchers can test cause-and-effect relationships, such as whether exposure to a violent television program causes viewers to behave more aggressively. We emphasize the experimental approach in this book. In addition, we report the results of many studies that use another popular approach: correlational research, which looks for associations between two variables without establishing cause and effect. We also report the results of studies that use a relatively new technique called meta-analysis, which integrates the research findings of many different studies. Before describing these approaches, though, we turn to an approach with which we all are very familiar: descriptive research. This is the approach used in opinion polls, ratings of the popularity of TV shows, box scores in the sports section, and the like.

Descriptive Research: Discovering Trends and Tendencies

One obvious way of testing ideas about people is simply to record how frequently or how typically people think, feel, or behave in particular ways. The goal of *descriptive research* in social psychology is, as the term implies, to describe people and their thoughts, feelings, and behaviours. This method can test questions such as: What percentage of people who encounter a person lying on the sidewalk would offer to help that person? What do men and women say are the things most likely to make them jealous of their partner? Particular methods of doing descriptive research include observing people, studying records of past events and behaviours, and surveying people. We discuss each of these methods in this section.

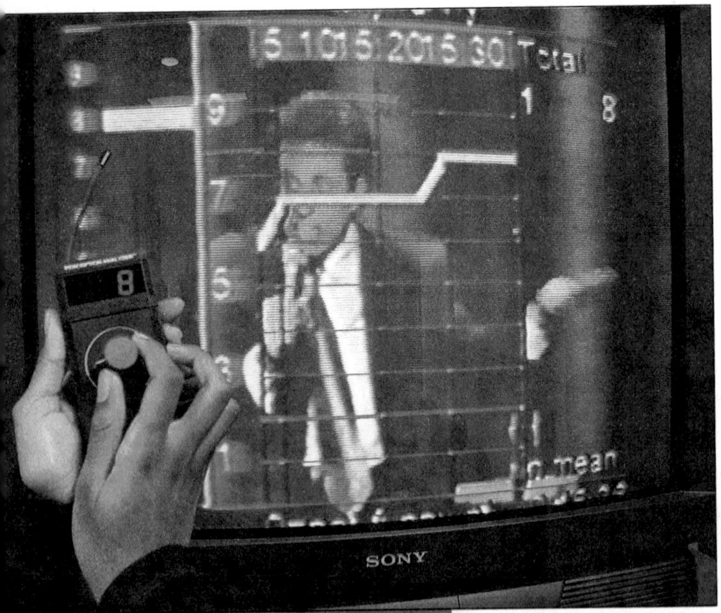

© Joanne Pasila/one2

Computerized video technology, such as this Perception Analyzer, allows researchers to track participants' moment-by-moment reactions to events on the screen (in this case, a comedian's performance). It can also simultaneously display the average ratings of groups of participants in a graph superimposed over the video. This technology can help researchers study the dynamics of social influence.

Observational Studies We can learn about other people by simply observing them, of course, and some social psychological questions can be addressed through observational studies. For example, researchers (Hawkins et al., 2001; Pepler & Craig, 1995) wanted to know how common bullying is among schoolchildren in Canada, and how often peers step in to help those who are being bullied. Is bullying an infrequent occurrence, revolving around a handful of bullies, or is it a widespread problem? Are there gender differences in bullying or in peer interventions? To investigate these questions, the researchers used hidden cameras and microphones to record the incidents of bullying and peer interventions in a number of schools in Canada (with the permission of the schools and parents). This peek into the schoolyard enabled the researchers to discover that the problem of bullying is much more pervasive than many people believe, and they were able to report the frequency with which particular forms of aggression, and helping, occurred. We might also want to learn more about *why* bullying occurs, rather than just how often. For example, Robert Thornberg and Sven Knutsen (2011), using both quantitative and qualitative research methods, surveyed Grade 9 students in Sweden regarding their explanations for bullying at their school. Interestingly, they found that most of those surveyed believed that bullying was attributable to either the victim or the bully, rather than to any societal or school-related pressures. Similarly, Jami-Leigh Sawyer and others (2011) conducted in-depth interviews with parents of children who were bullied at school. They identified key issues and themes that need to be considered when trying to understand the impact of bullying on children, such as how bullying is defined or when this type of behaviour is disclosed. As you can see, findings from both qualitative and quantitative research could be used to suggest strategies for reducing the prevalence and harmful impact of bullying among schoolchildren.

TV news magazine shows including *W5* and *the fifth estate* often use hidden cameras to record people's behaviours. The ethics of this can be troublesome; we return to the issue of ethics in research later in the chapter. In addition to ethical matters, though, questions of accuracy may arise in connection with these news programs. TV reporters and journalists often are more interested in telling a good story than in being scientifically sound, so we should be careful when drawing general conclusions from their presentations. A news program may show footage that is consistent with the point of view of their overall story—for example, footage demonstrating that certain kinds of people are treated worse by car salespeople or auto mechanics than others—but may not show footage that is inconsistent with this point of view. Social psychologists are trained to be systematic and unbiased in their observations and to report all of the data that are relevant to the research question, not just the data that support a particular hypothesis.

Archival Studies Archival research involves examining existing records of past events and behaviours, such as newspaper articles, medical records, diaries, sports statistics, personal ads, crime statistics, or hits on a Web page. A major advantage of archival measures is that, because the researchers are observing behaviour secondhand, they can be sure that they did not influence the behaviour by their presence. A limitation of this approach is that available records are not always complete or sufficiently detailed, and they may have been collected in a nonsystematic manner.

Archival measures are particularly valuable for examining cultural and historical trends. In Chapter 11 on Aggression, for example, we report a number of trends concerning the rate of violent crime in Canada and how it has changed in recent years, and we report differences in homicide rates in countries around the world. These data come from archival records, such as the records of police stations, or the Royal Canadian Mounted Police (RCMP). Other examples of archival research include a study by Deborah Connolly, Heather Price, and Don Read (2006) from Simon Fraser University that investigated the role of social science experts in cases that involve child sexual assault alleged to have been committed long before the case comes to trial, and a study that compared the academic performance of Quebec college students with or without disabilities (Jorgensen et al., 2005).

"Just as we suspected—they're beginning to form a boy band."

Observational research can reveal some fascinating—and sometimes disturbing!—insights into social behaviour.

Surveys It seems that nobody in politics these days sneezes without first conducting an opinion poll. Surveys have become increasingly popular in recent years, and they are conducted on everything from politics, to attitudes about social issues, to the percentages of women and men who squeeze rather than fold or roll their toothpaste tubes (OK, we'll tell you: 63 percent say they squeeze, according to a June 2009 poll on Vizu.com). Conducting surveys involves

Many social psychological questions are addressed using surveys, which can be conducted over the phone, by mail, via the Internet, or face-to-face in field settings such as this city street.

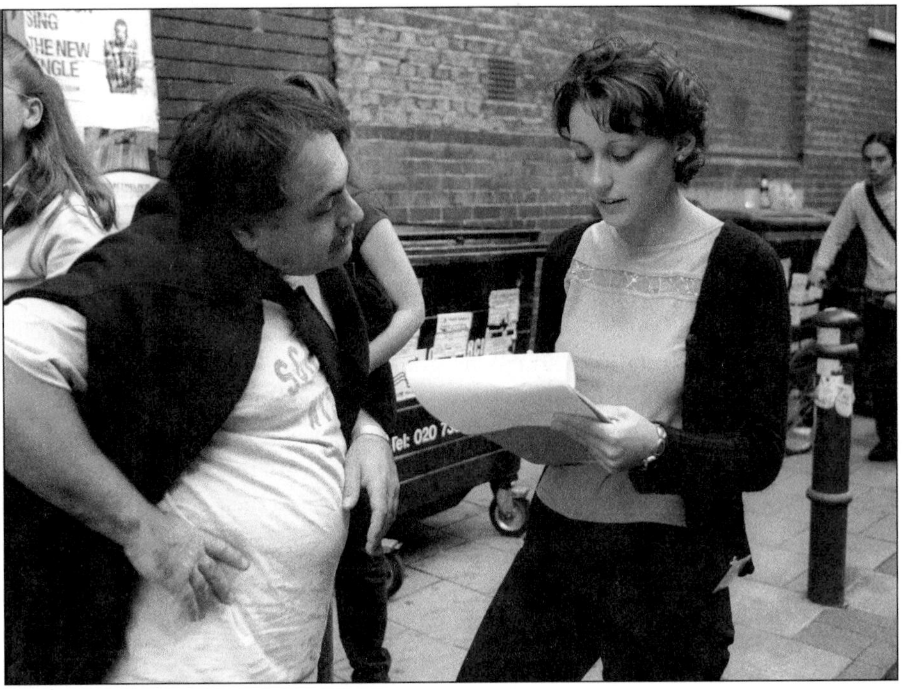

© Janine Wiedel Photolibrary/Alamy

asking people questions about their attitudes, beliefs, and behaviours. Surveys can be conducted in person, over the phone, by mail, or via the Internet. Many social psychological questions can be addressed only with surveys because they involve variables that are impossible or unethical to observe directly or manipulate, such as people's sexual behaviours or their optimism about the future.

Although anyone can conduct a survey (and sometimes it seems that everyone does), there is a science to designing, conducting, and interpreting the results of surveys. Like other self-report measures, surveys can be affected strongly by subtle aspects of the wording and context of questions, and survey researchers are trained to consider these issues and to test various kinds of wording and question ordering before conducting their surveys.

One of the most important issues that survey researchers face is how to select the people who will take part in the survey. The researchers first must identify the *population* in which they are interested. Is this survey supposed to tell us about the attitudes of Canadians in general, shoppers at Loblaws, or students in Introduction to Social Psychology at University X, for example? From this general population, the researchers select a subset, or *sample*, of individuals. For a survey to be accurate, the sample must be similar to, or representative of, the population on important characteristics such as age, sex, race, income, education, and cultural background. The best way to achieve this representativeness is to use **random sampling**, a method of selection in which everyone in a population has an equal chance of being selected for the sample. Survey researchers use randomizing procedures, such as tables of randomly distributed numbers generated by computers, to decide how to select individuals for their samples. To see the importance of proper random sampling, consider the results of the 2010 federal election in Canada. Ekos—a respected polling firm—failed to accurately predict the outcome of the election based in part on random sampling errors (Ekos Research Associates, 2011). They predicted a Conservative minority win, but were quite surprised when the Conservatives won by a large majority.

random sampling
A method of selecting participants for a study so that everyone in a population has an equal chance of being in the study.

Correlational Research: Looking for Associations

Although there is much to learn from descriptive research, social psychologists typically want to know more. Most research hypotheses in social psychology concern the relationship between variables. For example, is there a relationship between people's gender and their willingness to ask for help from others, or between how physically attractive people are and how much money they make?

One way to test such hypotheses is with correlational research. Like descriptive research, **correlational research** can be conducted using observational, archival, or survey methods. Unlike descriptive research, however, correlational approaches measure the *relationship* between different variables. The extent to which variables relate to each other, or correlate, can suggest how similar or distinct two different measures are (for example, how related people's self-esteem and popularity are) and how well one variable can be used to predict another (for example, how well we can predict university success from high school grades). It is important to note that researchers doing correlational research typically do not manipulate the variables they study; they simply measure them.

Correlation Coefficient When researchers examine the relationship between variables that vary in quantity (such as temperature or degree of self-esteem), they can measure the strength and direction of the relationship between the variables and calculate a statistic called a **correlation coefficient**. Correlation coefficients can range from − 1.0 to + 1.0. The absolute value of the number (the number itself, without the positive or negative sign) indicates how strongly the two variables are associated. The larger the absolute value of the number, the stronger the association between the two variables, and thus the better either of the variables is as a predictor of the other. Whether the coefficient is positive or negative indicates the direction of the relationship. A positive correlation coefficient indicates that as one variable increases, so does the other. For example, smoking and lung cancer are positively correlated; higher levels of smoking are associated with an increased likelihood of developing lung cancer and lower levels of smoking are associated with a decreased chance of developing lung cancer. This correlation is not perfect; some people who are heavy smokers will not develop lung cancer, and some people who never smoke, or smoke very little, will. Therefore, the correlation is less than +1.0; but it is greater than 0, because there is some association between the two. A negative coefficient indicates that the two variables go in opposite directions: As one goes up, the other tends to go down. For example, number of classes missed and GPA are likely to be negatively correlated. And a correlation close to 0 indicates that there is no consistent relationship at all. These three types of patterns are illustrated in ▶ Figure 2.1. Because few variables are perfectly related to each other, most correlation coefficients do not approach +1.0 or −1.0 but have more moderate values, such as − .39 or + .57.

Correlations obtained at a single point in time across a number of individuals are called *concurrent*. For example, you might be interested in testing the hypothesis that physically attractive people tend to make more money than less attractive people. You could measure the physical attractiveness of many different people somehow (such as by taking their pictures and asking a dozen other people to rate their physical appearance) and then ask them how much money they make. Correlations also can be obtained at different times from the same individuals. These correlations are called *prospective*. Prospective studies are especially useful in determining whether certain behaviours at a particular age are associated with other behaviours at a later age. For example, you might want to see whether people's degree of optimism at the age of 20 is correlated with how happy they feel at the age of 40. You would record the level of

Based on the results of a study of undergraduate students, Scott W. VanderStoep and John J. Shaughnessy (1997) concluded that studying research methods in psychology can give students "some general skills that they can use while watching the evening news, shopping for automobiles, voting, or deciding whether to adopt a new weight-loss technique they saw advertised."

correlational research Research designed to measure the association between variables that are not manipulated by the researcher.

correlation coefficient A statistical measure of the strength and direction of the association between two variables.

In the 2011 Canadian federal election, pollsters initially predicted that Jack Layton's New Democrats might win a few seats in Quebec in addition to the one they already held. In fact, the New Democrats gained strength throughout the election campaign and eventually won 59 out of 75 Quebec seats, becoming Canada's official Opposition party. As people begin to rely more on computers and smartphones for communication, polling companies are finding that they need to look beyond landline telephone surveys for new ways to collect data. However, there are concerns that moving data collection online will result in polls that do not fairly represent the entire population.

The Canadian Press/Peter McCabe

© Graham Oliver/Juice Images/Corbis

Similarity is correlated with attraction – the more similar two people are, the more attractive they are likely to find each other. But a correlation cannot identify the cause of this association. Chapter 9 on Attraction and Close Relationships discusses both correlational and experimental research on the role of similarity in the attraction process.

optimism of a number of 20-year-olds by using a questionnaire designed to measure optimism; and 20 years later, you'd ask these same individuals to complete a questionnaire designed to measure how happy they are.

Advantages and Disadvantages of Correlational Research Correlational research has many advantages. It can study the associations of naturally occurring variables that cannot be manipulated or induced—such as gender, race, ethnicity, and age. It can examine phenomena that would be difficult or unethical to create for research purposes, such as love, hate, and abuse. And it offers researchers a great deal of freedom in where variables are measured. Participants can be brought into a laboratory especially constructed for research purposes, or they can be approached in a real-world setting (often called "the field") such as a shopping mall or airport.

Despite these advantages, however, correlational research has one very serious disadvantage. And here it is in bold letters: **Correlation is not causation.**

In other words, a correlation cannot demonstrate a cause-and-effect relationship. Instead of revealing a specific causal pathway from one variable, A, to another variable, B, a correlation between variables A and B contains within it three possible causal effects: A could cause B; B could cause A; or a third variable, C, could cause both A and B. For example, imagine learning that the number of hours per night one sleeps is negatively correlated with the number of colds one gets. This means that as the amount of sleep increases, colds decrease in frequency; conversely, as sleep decreases, colds become more frequent. One reasonable explanation for this relationship is that lack of sleep (variable A) causes people to become more vulnerable to colds (variable B). Another reasonable explanation, however, is that people who have colds can't sleep well, and so colds (variable B) cause lack of sleep (variable A). A third reasonable explanation is that some other variable (C) causes both lack of sleep and greater frequency of colds. This third variable could be stress. Indeed, stress has many effects on people, as will be discussed in Appendix B (Health).

FIGURE 2.1

Correlations: Positive, Negative, and None

Correlations reveal a systematic association between two variables. Positive correlations indicate that variables are in sync: Increases in one variable are associated with increases in the other, decreases with decreases. Negative correlations indicate that variables go in opposite directions: Increases in one variable are associated with decreases in the other. When two variables are not systematically associated, there is no correlation.

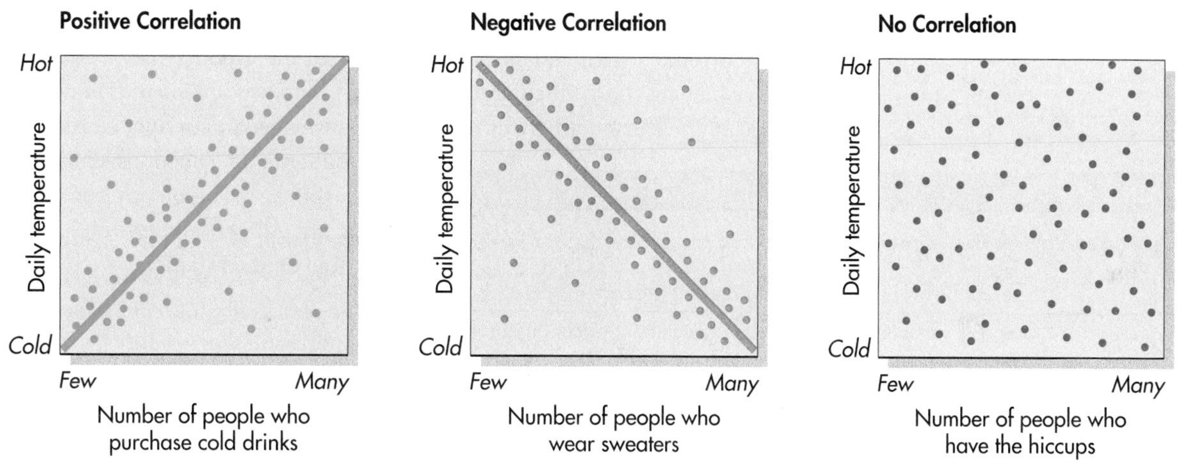

Figure 2.2 describes another correlation that can be explained in many ways—the correlation between playing violent video games and aggression.

As sure as death and taxes, there will be many, many times in your life when you'll encounter reports in the media that suggest cause-and-effect relationships based on correlational research. One of the great benefits of learning and gaining experience with the material in this chapter is that you can see the flaws in media reports like these and not be taken in by them. Correlation is not causation.

Do we learn nothing, then, from correlations? To say that would be to take caution too far. Correlations tell researchers about the strength and direction of relationships between variables, thus helping them understand these variables better and allowing them to use one variable to predict the other. Correlations can be extremely useful in developing new hypotheses to guide future research. And by gathering large

FIGURE 2.2

Explaining Correlations: Three Possibilities

The correlation between one variable (A) and another variable (B) could be explained in three ways. Variable A could cause changes in variable B, or variable B could cause changes in variable A, or a third variable (C) could cause similar changes in both A and B, even if A and B did not influence each other. For example, a correlation between how often children play violent video games and how aggressively they behave could be explained in the following ways:

(1) Playing violent video games causes aggressive behaviour.

(2) Children who behave aggressively like to play a lot of violent video games.

(3) Children who have family troubles, such as parents who are not very involved in the children's development, tend both to play a lot of violent video games and to behave aggressively.

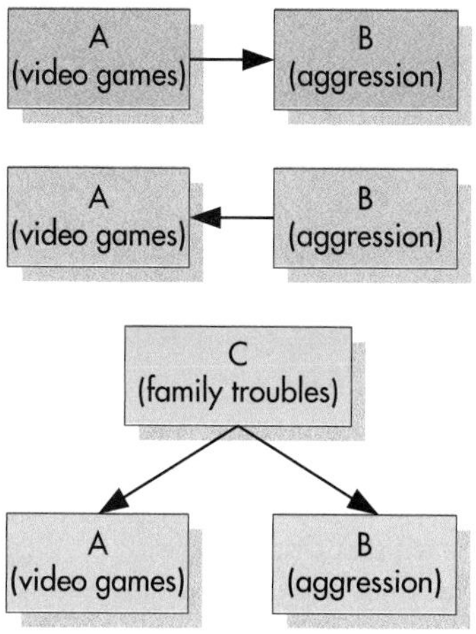

sets of correlations and using complicated statistical techniques to crunch the data, we can develop highly accurate predictions of future events. But still, correlation is not causation.

Experiments: Looking for Cause and Effect

Social psychologists often do want to examine cause-and-effect relationships. Although it is informative to know, for example, that playing a lot of violent video games is correlated with violent behaviour in real life, the inevitable next question is whether playing these video games *causes* an increase in violent behaviour. If we want to examine cause-and-effect relationships, we need to conduct an **experiment**. Experiments in social psychology range from the very simple to the incredibly elaborate. All of them, however, share two essential characteristics.

TABLE 2.2

Correlations Versus Experiments

	Correlational Research	Experimental Research
What does it involve?	Measuring variables and the degree of association between them	Random assignment to conditions and control over the events that occur; determining the effects of manipulations of the independent variable(s) on changes in the dependent variable(s)
What is the biggest advantage of using this method?	Enables researchers to study naturally occurring variables, including variables that would be too difficult or unethical to manipulate	Enables researchers to determine cause-and-effect relationships—that is, whether the independent variable can cause a change in the dependent variable

1. The researcher has *control* over the experimental procedures, manipulating the variables of interest while ensuring uniformity elsewhere. In other words, all participants in the research are treated in exactly the same manner—except for the specific differences the experimenter wants to create. By exercising control, the researcher attempts to ensure that differences obtained after the experimental manipulation are produced only by that manipulation and are not affected by other events in the experiment.
2. Participants in the study are *randomly* assigned to the different manipulations (called "conditions") included in the experiment. If there are two conditions, who goes where may be determined by simply flipping a coin. If there are many conditions, a computer program may be used. But however it's done, **random assignment** means that participants are not assigned to a condition on the basis of their personal or behavioural characteristics. Through random assignment, the experimenter attempts to ensure a level playing field: *On average, the participants randomly assigned to one condition are no different from those assigned to another condition.* Differences that appear between conditions after an experimental manipulation can therefore be attributed to the impact of that manipulation and not to any pre-existing differences between participants.

Because of experimenter control and random assignment of participants, an experiment is a powerful technique for examining cause and effect. Both characteristics serve the same goal: to eliminate the influence on participants' behaviour of any factors other than the experimental manipulation. By ruling out alternative explanations for research results, we become more confident that we understand just what has, in fact, caused a certain behaviour to occur. ■ Table 2.2 summarizes the distinctions between correlational and experimental research.

experiment
A form of research that can demonstrate causal relationships because the experimenter has control over the events that occur and participants are randomly assigned to conditions.

random assignment
A method of assigning participants to the various conditions of an experiment so that each participant in the experiment has an equal chance of being in any of the conditions.

Random Sampling Versus Random Assignment You may recall that we mentioned random sampling earlier, in connection with surveys. It's important to remember the differences between random *sampling* and random *assignment*. ■ Table 2.3 summarizes these differences. Random sampling concerns how individuals are selected to be in a study; it is important for generalizing the results obtained from a sample to a broader population, and it is therefore very important for survey research. Random assignment concerns not who is selected to be in the study but, rather, how participants in the study are assigned to different conditions, as explained previously. Random assignment is essential to experiments because it is necessary for determining cause-and-effect relationships; without it, there is always the possibility that any differences found between the conditions in a study were caused by pre-existing differences among participants. Random sampling, in contrast, is not necessary for establishing causality. For that reason, and because random sampling is difficult and expensive, very few experiments use random sampling. We consider the implications of this fact later in the chapter.

TABLE 2.3

Random Sampling Versus Random Assignment

	Random Sampling	Random Assignment
What does it involve?	Selecting participants to be in the study so that everyone from a population has an equal chance of being a participant in the study	Assigning participants (who are already in the study) to the various conditions of the experiment so that each participant has an equal chance of being in any of the conditions
What is the biggest advantage of using this procedure?	Enables researchers to collect data from samples that are representative of the broader population; important for being able to generalize the results to the broader population	Equalizes the conditions of the experiment so that it is very unlikely that the conditions differ in terms of pre-existing differences among the participants; essential to determine that the independent variable(s) caused an effect on the dependent variable(s)

Laboratory and Field Experiments Most experiments in social psychology are conducted in a *laboratory* setting, usually located in a university, so that the environment can be controlled and the participants carefully studied. Social psychology labs do not necessarily look like stereotypical laboratories with liquid bubbling in beakers or expensive equipment everywhere (although many social psychology labs are indeed very "high-tech"). They can resemble ordinary living rooms or even game rooms. The key point here is that the laboratory setting enables researchers to have control over the setting, measure participants' behaviours precisely, and keep conditions identical for participants.

Field research is conducted in real-world settings outside of the laboratory. Researchers interested in studying helping behaviour, for example, might conduct an experiment in a public park. The advantage of field experiments is that people are more likely to act naturally in a natural setting than in a laboratory in which they know they are being studied. The disadvantage of field settings is that the experimenter often has less control and cannot ensure that the participants in the various conditions of the experiment will be exposed to the same things.

To better understand how an experiment in social psychology works, let's consider the relationship between moods and culture. Imagine that someone shows you a handful of pens. Most of the pens are of one colour (e.g., black), and a minority of the pens are of a different colour (e.g., blue). You can choose to keep one of the pens. Do you choose a colour from the majority or the minority? Believe it or not, there is a consistent cultural difference in how people make this choice. People from Western cultures, such as Canada, tend to choose the uncommon pen colour, whereas people from East Asian cultures, such as Korea, tend to choose the majority pen colour.

This cultural difference was explored in an interesting way in a recent experiment by Claire Ashton-James and others (2009). The researchers hypothesized that being in a positive mood makes people more likely to explore novel thoughts and behaviours, which can result in their acting in ways that are inconsistent with how people in their culture typically behave. In one of their experiments, research participants were from either Western (European, Euro-Canadian)

Ariel Skelley/Corbis

In field research, people are observed in real-world settings. Field researchers may observe children in a schoolyard, for example, to study any of a variety of social psychological issues, such as friendship patterns, group dynamics, conformity, helping, aggression, and cultural differences.

FIGURE 2.3

Mood and Culture

Research participants from Western or East Asian backgrounds were put in a positive or negative mood and then were given a choice to keep one of several pens. Most of the pens were in one colour, but one or two were in a different colour. Western participants were more likely to choose the uncommon colour when in a negative mood rather than in a positive mood, whereas East Asian participants showed the opposite pattern. These results supported the hypothesis that positive moods can make individuals act in ways that are inconsistent with their cultural norms.

(Based on Ashton-James et al., 2009.)

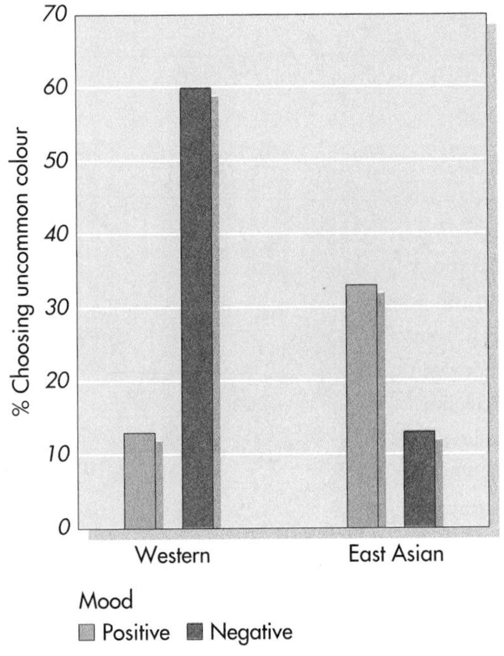

or East Asian backgrounds, and they were presented with the pen choice described above. Before looking at the pens, though, the participants were randomly assigned to be placed into a positive or negative mood. How was mood manipulated? The participants in the positive-mood condition listened to a very pleasant, upbeat piece of classical music (by Mozart), and those in the negative-mood condition listened to a much more serious, rather depressing piece (by Rachmaninov).

Figure 2.3 depicts the results of this study. The bars in the graph depict what percentage of participants in each condition chose the uncommon pen. Among the Western participants, as can be seen in the left half of the graph, those put in a positive mood were *less* likely to choose the uncommon pen compared to those in the negative-mood condition. The opposite was true for the East Asian participants: those put in a positive mood were *more* likely to choose the uncommon pen compared to those in the negative-mood condition. The results, therefore, supported the researchers' predictions: positive moods did make individuals more likely to act in ways that deviated from the norms of their cultures.

Independent and Dependent Variables Now that you have seen an example of an experiment, let's focus on some of the specific elements. In an experiment, researchers manipulate one or more **independent variables** and examine the effect of these manipulations on one or more **dependent variables.** In the experiment described above, some participants were randomly assigned to either the positive or negative mood condition. This was the independent variable. The dependent variable in that experiment was what colour pen the participant chose. It was the dependent variable because the researchers were interested in seeing if it would *depend* on (that is, be influenced by) the manipulation of the independent variable.

Subject Variables Some experiments include variables that are neither dependent nor truly independent. The gender or ethnicity of the participants may vary, for example, and researchers may be interested in examining some of these differences. The variables cannot be manipulated and randomly assigned, so they are not true independent variables, nor are they influenced by the independent variables, so they are not dependent variables. Variables such as these are called **subject variables,** because they characterize pre-existing differences among the subjects, or participants, in the experiment. If a study includes subject variables but no true, randomly assigned independent variable, it is not a true experiment. But experiments often include subject variables along with independent variables so that researchers can test whether the independent variables have the same or different effects on different kinds of participants. In our example of the impact of mood on pen choice, the participants' cultural background was a variable of interest—some were of Western background, some were of East Asian background. Thus, cultural background was a subject variable.

independent variable
In an experiment, a factor that experimenters manipulate to see if it affects the dependent variable.

dependent variable
In an experiment, a factor that experimenters measure to see if it is affected by the independent variable.

subject variable
A variable that characterizes pre-existing differences among the participants in a study.

Statistical Significance When you review the results of a study, such as our moods and culture example, how do you know whether these findings are meaningful? Could they simply be the result of chance? After all, if you flip a coin ten times, you might get six tails and four heads. Is the difference between six and four a meaningful difference? Surely it isn't—one could expect differences like this from random luck alone. Results obtained in an experiment are examined with statistical analyses that allow the researcher to determine how likely it is that the results could have occurred by chance. The standard convention is that if the results could have occurred by chance five or fewer times in 100 possible outcomes, then the result is *statistically significant* and should be taken seriously.

The fact that results are statistically significant does not mean, however, that they are absolutely certain. In essence, statistical significance is an attractive betting proposition. The odds are quite good (at least 95 out of 100) that the effects obtained in the study were due to the experimental manipulation of the independent variable. But there is still the possibility (as high as five out of 100) that the findings occurred by chance. This is one reason why it is important to try to *replicate* the results of an experiment—to repeat the experiment and see if similar results are found. If similar results are found, the probability that these results could have occurred by chance both times is less than one out of 400 (5 percent times 5 percent).

Statistical significance is relevant not only for the results of experiments but also for many other kinds of data as well, such as correlations. A correlation between two variables may be statistically significant or not, depending on the strength of the correlation and the number of participants or observations in the data.

When the results of some research are reported in the media or in an advertisement, it's not always clear from the reporting whether the results are statistically significant, so it is important to be very cautious when learning about them. You can be sure, however, that whenever we report in this textbook that there is a difference between conditions of an experiment or that two variables are correlated, these results are statistically significant.

Internal Validity: Did the Independent Variable Cause the Effect? When an experiment is properly conducted, its results are said to have **internal validity**. There is reasonable certainty that the independent variable did, in fact, cause the effects obtained on the dependent variable (Cook & Campbell, 1979). As noted earlier, both experimenter control and random assignment seek to rule out alternative explanations of the research results, thereby strengthening the internal validity of the research.

Experiments also include *control groups* for this purpose. Typically, a control group consists of participants who experience all of the experimental procedures except the experimental treatment. For example, if we included a 'neutral mood' condition in the moods and culture study by Ashton-James and others (2009), this could be considered a control group, which provided a baseline against which to compare the choices of those in the good mood, versus those in the bad mood, conditions.

Outside the laboratory, creating control groups in natural settings that examine real-life events raises many practical and ethical problems. For example, research on new medical treatments for deadly diseases, such as AIDS, can create a terrible dilemma. Individuals randomly assigned to the control group receive the standard treatment, but they are excluded for the duration of the study from what could turn out to be a life-saving new intervention. Yet without such a comparison, it is extremely difficult to determine which new treatments are effective and which are useless. Although many AIDS activists used to oppose including control groups in treatment research, they have become more supportive of this approach (Gorman, 1994).

internal validity
The degree to which there can be reasonable certainty that the independent variables in an experiment caused the effects obtained on the dependent variables.

In assessing internal validity, researchers need to consider their own role as well. Unwittingly, they can sometimes sabotage their own research. Here's how:

- Before they conduct a study, experimenters usually make an explicit prediction, or at least have a strong expectation, about the effect of an independent variable.
- If they know what conditions participants have been assigned to, they may, without realizing it, treat participants in different conditions differently.
- Because the experimenters' behaviour can affect the participants' behaviour, the results could then be produced by the experimenters' actions rather than by the independent variable.

The best way to protect an experiment from the influence of experimenters' expectations—called **experimenter expectancy effects** (Rosenthal, 1976)—is to keep experimenters uninformed about assignments to conditions. If they do not know the condition to which a participant has been assigned, they cannot treat participants differently as a function of their condition. Of course, there may be times when keeping experimenters uninformed is impossible or impractical. In such cases, the opportunity for experimenter expectancy effects to occur can at least be reduced—specifically, by minimizing the interaction between experimenters and participants. For example, rather than receiving instructions directly from an experimenter, participants can be asked to read the instructions on a computer screen.

External Validity: Do the Results Generalize? In addition to guarding internal validity, researchers are concerned about **external validity**, the extent to which the results obtained under one set of circumstances would also occur in a different set of circumstances (Berkowitz & Donnerstein, 1982). When an experiment has external validity, its findings can be assumed to generalize to other people and to other situations. Both the participants in the experiment and the setting in which it takes place affect external validity.

Because social psychologists often seek to establish universal principles of human behaviour, their ideal sample of participants should be representative of all human beings, all over the world. Such an all-inclusive representative sample has never been seen and probably never will be. Representative samples of more limited populations do exist and can be achieved by random sampling of a population, which was discussed earlier in the chapter. But, as also mentioned earlier, social psychologists rarely study representative samples. Usually, they rely on convenience samples drawn from populations that are readily available to them, which explains why so much social psychological research is conducted on university students. There are very practical reasons for the use of convenience samples. Representative samples are fine for surveys requiring short answers to a short list of questions. But what about complex, time-consuming experiments? The expense of bringing participants from diverse geographic areas into the lab would be staggering. Fortunately, researchers are using Internet-based data collection more and more frequently, which can allow for far more diverse sets of participants. There are numerous challenges associated with this approach as well, however, such as having less control over what participants are seeing or doing as they participate in the study from afar.

Advocates of convenience samples also contend that there is no contradiction between universal principles and particular participants. Indeed, the more basic the principle, the less it matters who participates in the research. For example, various people or cultures might differ in the *form* of aggression they typically exhibit when angry; but the situational factors that cause people to be more likely to exhibit

experimenter expectancy effects
The effects produced when an experimenter's expectations about the results of an experiment affect his or her behaviour toward a participant and thereby influence the participant's responses.

external validity
The degree to which there can be reasonable confidence that the results of a study would be obtained for other people and in other situations.

Fabian Cevallos/Sygma/Corbis

The settings in which children attend school can vary dramatically across cultures. Here students sit outside in a class in Imbabura, Ecuador. Recognizing cultural variation has become increasingly important in social psychology today, and social psychologists are conducting their research across a wider range of cultures and contexts than ever before.

aggressive behaviour, however that aggression is expressed, may be similar for most individuals no matter where they are from or what experiences they have had. Yet, in spite of these arguments, the drawbacks to convenience samples are clear—an important consideration given the need for social psychology to become more inclusive. The growing interest in cross-cultural research in the field is certainly one step in the right direction.

External validity is also affected by the setting in which the research is conducted. Because field research occurs in real-life natural settings rather than in the artificial arrangements of a laboratory, aren't its results more generalizable to actual behaviour? The answer depends on where you stand on the issue of mundane versus experimental realism (Aronson & Carlsmith, 1968).

Mundane realism refers to the extent to which the research setting resembles the real-world setting of interest. In order to study interpersonal attraction, Theodore Newcomb (1961) set up an entire college dormitory—a striking example of mundane realism. Advocates of mundane realism contend that if research procedures are more realistic, research findings are more likely to reveal what really goes on.

In contrast, **experimental realism** refers to the degree to which the experimental setting and procedures are real and involving to the participant, regardless of whether they resemble real life or not. According to those who favour experimental realism, if the experimental situation is compelling and real to the participants while they are participating in the study, their behaviour in the lab—even if the lab is in the basement of the psychology building—will be as natural and spontaneous as their behaviour in the real world. The majority of social psychologists who conduct experiments emphasize experimental realism.

Deception in Experiments Researchers who strive to create a highly involving experience for participants often rely on **deception**, providing participants with false information about experimental procedures. Toward this end, social psychologists sometimes employ **confederates**, who act as though they are participants in the experiment but are really working for the experimenter. For example, Pamela Regan and Delia Gutierrez (2005) had confederates, pretending to be ordinary shoppers, approach individuals in a supermarket to ask for $0.25 toward various items such

mundane realism
The degree to which the experimental situation resembles places and events in the real world.

experimental realism
The degree to which experimental procedures are involving to participants and lead them to behave naturally and spontaneously.

deception
In the context of research, a method that provides false information to participants.

confederate
Accomplice of an experimenter who, in dealing with the real participants in an experiment, acts as if he or she is also a participant.

as milk (considered a high-need item), cookie dough (a low-need item), or alcohol (low-need with negative connotations). The researchers wanted to see if the sex of the participant and the perceived need associated with the item would influence helping behaviour; in this case, need associated with the item played a greater role in helping than sex of the participant. Deception not only strengthens experimental realism but also confers other benefits: It allows the experimenter to manufacture situations in the laboratory that would be difficult to observe in a natural setting; to study potentially harmful behaviours, such as aggression, in a regulated, safe manner; and to assess people's spontaneous reactions rather than socially acceptable presentations. Studies have shown that participants are rarely bothered by deception and often particularly enjoy studies that use it (Smith & Richardson, 1983). Nevertheless, the use of deception creates some serious ethical concerns, which we examine later in this chapter.

Meta-Analysis: Combining Results Across Studies

We have seen that social psychologists conduct original descriptive, correlational, and experimental studies to test their hypotheses. Another way to test hypotheses in social psychology is to use a set of statistical procedures to examine, in a new way, relevant research that has already been conducted and reported. This technique is called **meta-analysis.** By "meta-analyzing" the results of a number of studies that have been conducted in different places and by different researchers, a social psychologist can measure precisely how strong and reliable particular effects are. For example, studies published concerning the effects of alcohol on aggression may sometimes contradict each other. Sometimes alcohol increases aggression; sometimes it doesn't. By combining the data from all the studies that are relevant to this hypothesis and conducting a meta-analysis, a researcher can determine what effect alcohol typically has, how strong that effect typically is, and perhaps under what specific conditions that effect is most likely to occur. This technique, which was developed relatively recently, is being used with increasing frequency in social psychology today, and we report the results of many meta-analyses in this textbook.

Culture and Research Methods

The study by Ashton-James and others (2009) on the effects of mood on Western and East Asian participants' pen choices is only one example of the growing interest in studying culture in social psychology. One of the advantages of this approach is that it provides better tests of the external validity of research that has been conducted in any one setting. By examining whether the results of an experiment generalize to a very different culture, social psychologists can begin to answer questions about the universality or cultural specificity of their research. It is important to keep in mind that when a finding in one culture does not generalize well to another culture, this should be seen not simply as a failure to replicate but also as an opportunity to learn about potentially interesting and important cultural differences, and about how and why these differences affect the issue being studied.

As important and exciting as these cultural investigations are, however, they offer special challenges to researchers. For one thing, there are important cultural differences in the assumptions individuals make and the information they tend to give as they respond to questions on a survey (Schwarz et al., 2010). Susanne

meta-analysis
A set of statistical procedures used to review a body of evidence by combining the results of individual studies to measure the overall reliability and strength of particular effects.

Haberstroh and others (2002), for example, found that individuals from a culture that promotes interdependent, collectivistic values and self-concepts (such as China) are more likely to take into account question context when completing a questionnaire than are respondents from cultures associated with a more independent, individualistic orientation (such as Germany). Another difference between cultures concerns how willing people are to answer personal questions as part of a research study. North Americans are used to answering personal questions, for example, but people in some cultures feel much more uncomfortable talking about themselves (Fiske, 2002).

Nairán Ramírez-Esparza and others (2009) recently demonstrated an interesting difference in data from self-report and observational measures as a function of culture. Ramírez-Esparza and her colleagues compared Mexican participants and native English-speaking American participants (none of whom were foreign or bicultural) in how sociable they rated themselves on a questionnaire and how sociable their actual behaviour was. The behaviour was assessed by means of voice-activated digital recorders that all participants wore during their daily activities for two days. As can be seen in Figure 2.4, although the Mexican participants rated themselves as no more sociable than did the American participants on a questionnaire, the Mexican participants' behaviour was observed to be significantly more sociable than Americans' behaviour (such as in time spent talking with other people).

When doing cross-cultural or multicultural studies, researchers must be careful also about issues as basic as language. Another study by Ramírez-Esparza and others (2008) illustrates this point. They found that bilingual Mexican-American participants rated themselves as less agreeable on a questionnaire if the questions were in Spanish rather than English, but their behaviour was observed to be higher in agreeableness during an interview if it was conducted in Spanish than if it was conducted in English.

FIGURE 2.4

Culture and Sociability: Self-Reports Versus Observations

Mexican and American participants completed questionnaires that assessed how sociable they were. This self-report measure showed no significant difference between the two groups. However, through the use of voice recorders worn by the participants for two days, the researchers could observe and measure how sociably the participants behaved, such as in how much they socialized or talked with other people. On this observational measure, Mexican participants were judged to be much more sociable than were the American participants.

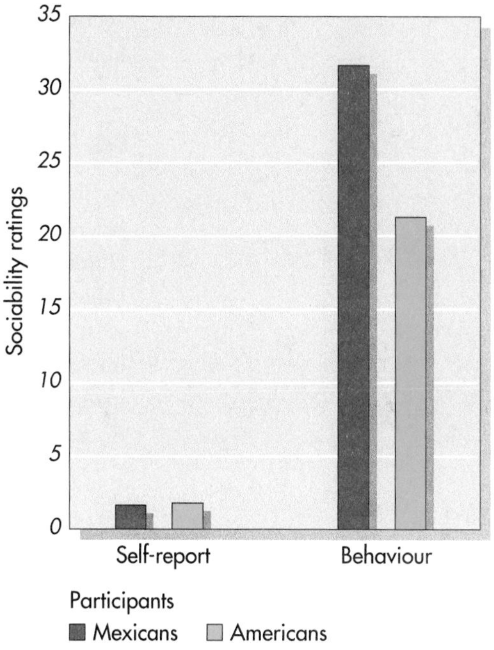

Ethics and Values in Social Psychology

Regardless of where research is conducted and what method is used, ethical issues must always be considered. Researchers in all fields have a moral and legal responsibility to abide by ethical principles. In social psychology, the use of deception has caused particular concern (Hertwig & Ortmann, 2008; Jamison et al., 2008; Kimmel et al., 2011), and several studies have provoked fierce debate about whether they went beyond the bounds of ethical acceptability. For example, Stanley Milgram (1963) designed a series of experiments to address the question "Would people obey orders to harm an innocent person?" To test this question, he put volunteers into a situation in which an experimenter commanded them to administer painful electric shocks to someone they thought was another volunteer participant (in fact, the other person was a confederate who was not actually receiving any shocks). The experiment had extremely high experimental realism—many of the participants experienced a great deal of anxiety and stress as they debated whether they should disobey the experimenter or continue to inflict pain on another person. The details and results of this experiment will be discussed in Chapter 7 on Conformity, but suffice it to say that the results of the study made people realize how prevalent and powerful obedience can be.

Milgram's research was inspired by the obedience displayed by Nazi officers in World War II. No one disputes the importance of his research question. What has been debated, however, is whether the significance of the research topic justified exposing participants to possibly harmful psychological consequences. Under today's provisions for the protection of human participants, Milgram's classic experiments probably could not be conducted in their original form, although as we discuss further in Chapter 7, some researchers have tried to replicate his findings using modified methods.

Milgram's research was by no means the only social psychological research to trigger debates about ethics. Several studies in the history of social psychology have sparked a great deal of controversy. And it is not only the controversial studies that receive scrutiny. Today, virtually every prospective social psychology study is evaluated for its ethics by other people before the study can be conducted. In the following sections, we describe current policies and procedures as well as continuing concerns about ethics and values in social psychological research.

Research Ethics Boards

In Canada, experts from the Canadian Institutes of Health Research (CIHR), the Natural Science and Engineering Research Council (NSERC), and the Social Science and Humanities Research Council (SSHRC) form the Interagency Advisory Panel on Research Ethics (PRE or the Panel). This panel provides guidance regarding ethical issues associated with human participant research. Their Tri-Council Policy Statement: Ethical Conduct for Research Involving Humans (TCPS2, 2010) includes the requirement that all research involving human subjects be reviewed and approved by an institutional Research Ethics Board (REB) to ensure that the welfare of participants is adequately protected.

Informed Consent

"[Objectivity in science] is the willingness (even the eagerness in truly honorable practitioners) to abandon a favored notion when testable evidence disconfirms key expectations."

—Stephen Jay Gould

Besides submitting their research to government-mandated REBs, researchers must also abide by their profession's code of ethics. The statement of ethics of the Canadian Psychological Association (CPA), called the *Canadian Code of Ethics for Psychologists* (2000), considers a wide range of ethical issues, including those related to research procedures and practices. The CPA *Code* stipulates that researchers are obligated to guard the rights and welfare of all those who participate in their studies.

One such obligation is to obtain **informed consent**. Individuals must be asked whether they wish to participate in the research project and must be given enough information to make an informed decision. Researchers should not proceed if "consent is given under any conditions of coercion, undue pressure, or undue reward." Participants must also know that they are free to withdraw from participation in the research at any point.

In principle, informed consent is absolutely essential for the protection of human participants. Only if you know what you will be getting into can you decide whether you want to participate in a study. In practice, however, it can be difficult to ensure that consent is, in fact, informed. Often, the information given to participants is vague because the researchers do not want to tell the participants so much that their responses during the study will be affected. Other times, the information can be so detailed and complex that many participants don't fully understand it. To make the practice of obtaining informed consent as effective as the principle says it should be, we need more research on how best to communicate this information.

informed consent
An individual's deliberate, voluntary decision to participate in research, based on the researcher's description of what will be required during such participation.

Debriefing: Telling All

Have you ever participated in psychological research? If so, what was your reaction to this experience? Have you ever been deceived about the hypothesis or procedures of a study in which you were a participant? If so, how did you feel about it? Most research on participants' reactions indicates that they have positive attitudes about their participation, even when they were deceived about some aspects of a study (Christensen, 1988; Epley & Huff, 1998). Indeed, deceived participants sometimes have expressed more favourable opinions than those who have not been deceived, presumably because studies involving deception are often interesting and creative (Smith & Richardson, 1983).

These findings are reassuring, but they do not remove the obligation of researchers to use deception only when nondeceptive alternatives are not feasible. In addition, whenever deception has been used, there is a special urgency to the requirement that, once the data have been collected, researchers fully inform their participants about the nature of the research in which they have participated. This process of disclosure is called **debriefing**. During a debriefing, the researcher goes over all procedures, explaining exactly what happened and why. Deceptions are revealed, the purpose of the research is discussed, and the researcher makes every effort to help the participant feel good about having participated. A skillful debriefing takes time and requires close attention to the individual participant.

Values and Science: Points of View

Ethical principles are based on moral values. These values set standards for and impose limits on the conduct of research, just as they influence individuals' personal behaviour. When the potential benefits of research for humankind are high and the potential costs are ethically acceptable, there is a moral imperative to try to carry out the research. But when the human costs are too high in terms of the suffering of participants, the moral imperative is to refrain. Ethical issues are an appropriate focus for moral values in science, but do values affect science in other ways as well? Consider this statement from the *Canadian Code of Ethics for Psychologists*: "Psychologists are not expected to be value-free or totally without self-interest in conducting their activities. However, they are expected to understand how their backgrounds, personal needs, and values interact with their activities, to be open and honest about the influence of such factors, and to be as objective and unbiased as possible under the circumstances" (2000, p. 27).

Infatuated by important topics, wrestling with beliefs about right and wrong, under the thumb of those who control funding for research—all this seems a long way from "objective and unbiased." It's such a long way that perhaps the search for objectivity is only a self-serving illusion. Perhaps the more forthright approach is to adopt a psychology of political advocacy: "championing causes that one believes good for the culture ... condemning movements or policies that seem inimical to human welfare" (Gergen, 1994, p. 415).

But there is another view. From this perspective, science can never be completely unbiased and objective because it is a human enterprise. Scientists choose what to study and how to study it; their choices are affected by personal values as well as by professional rewards. To acknowledge these influences, however, is not to embrace them. Quite the contrary. Such influences are precisely why the scientific method is so important.

As Stanley Parkinson (1994) puts it, "Scientists are not necessarily more objective than other people; rather, they use methods that have been developed to minimize self-deception" (p. 137). By scrutinizing their own behaviour and adopting the rigours

debriefing
A disclosure, made to participants after research procedures are completed, in which the researcher explains the purpose of the research, attempts to resolve any negative feelings, and emphasizes the scientific contribution made by the participants' involvement.

of the scientific method, scientists attempt to free themselves of their preconceptions and, thereby, to see reality more clearly, even if never perfectly.

You've read what others have said about values and science. But what do you think about all this? How do values influence science? How *should* values affect scientific inquiry? You might consider these questions as you read about the research reported throughout this book.

Your introduction to the field of social psychology is now complete. In these first two chapters, you have gone step-by-step through a definition of social psychology, a review of its history and discussion of its future, an overview of its research methods, and a consideration of ethics and values. As you study the material presented in the coming chapters, those of us who wrote this book invite you to share our enthusiasm. You can look forward to information that overturns common-sense assumptions, to lively debate and heated controversy, and to a better understanding of yourself and other people. Welcome to the world according to social psychology. We hope you enjoy it!

REVIEW

Why Should You Learn About Research Methods?

- Because common sense and intuitive ideas about social psychological issues can be misleading and contradictory, it is important to understand the scientific evidence on which social psychological theories and findings are based.
- Studying research methods in psychology improves people's reasoning about real-life events and information presented by the media and other sources.

Developing Ideas: Beginning the Research Process

Asking Questions

- Ideas for research in social psychology come from everywhere—personal experiences and observations, events in the news, and other research.

Searching the Literature

- Before pursuing a research idea, it is important to see what research has already been done on this and related topics.
- Electronic databases provide access to a wealth of information, both in the psychology literature and in more general sources.

Hypotheses and Theories

- Formulating a hypothesis is a critical step toward planning and conducting research.
- Theories in social psychology are specific rather than comprehensive and generate research that can support or disconfirm them. They should be revised and improved as a result of the research they inspire.

Basic and Applied Research

- The goal of basic research is to increase understanding of human behaviour.
- The goal of applied research is to increase understanding of real-world events and contribute to the solution of social problems.

Refining Ideas: Defining and Measuring Social Psychological Variables

Conceptual Variables and Operational Definitions: From the Abstract to the Specific

- Researchers often must transform abstract, conceptual variables into specific operational definitions that indicate exactly how the variables are to be manipulated or measured.
- Construct validity is the extent to which the operational definitions successfully manipulate or measure the conceptual variables to which they correspond.

Measuring Variables: Using Self-Reports, Observations and Technology

- In self-reports, participants indicate their thoughts, feelings, desires, and actions.
- Self-reports can be distorted by efforts to make a good impression, as well as by the effects of the wording and context of questions.
- To increase the accuracy of self-reports, some approaches emphasize the need to collect self-reports as soon as possible after participants experience the relevant thoughts, feelings, or behaviours.
- Narrative studies analyze the content of lengthy responses on a general topic.
- Observations are another way for social psychologists to measure variables.
- New and improved technologies enable researchers to measure physiological responses, reaction times, eye movements, and activity in regions of the brain.

Testing Ideas: Research Designs

- Most social psychologists test their ideas by using objective, systematic, and quantifiable methods.

Descriptive Research: Discovering Trends and Tendencies

- In descriptive research, social psychologists record how frequently or typically people think, feel, or behave in particular ways.
- One form of descriptive research is observational research, in which researchers observe individuals systematically, often in natural settings.
- In qualitative research, researchers go beyond the numbers to (in some cases) better understand why a particular behaviour occurs.
- In archival research, researchers examine existing records and documents such as newspaper articles, diaries, and published crime statistics.
- Surveys involve asking people questions about their attitudes, beliefs, and behaviours.
- Survey researchers identify the population to which they want the results of the survey to generalize, and they select a sample of people from that population to take the survey.
- To best ensure a sample that is representative of the broader population, researchers should randomly select people from the population to be in the survey.

Correlational Research: Looking for Associations

- Correlational research examines the association between variables.
- A correlation coefficient is a measure of the strength and direction of the association between two variables.
- Positive correlations indicate that as scores on one variable increase, scores on the other variable increase; and that as scores on one variable decrease, scores on the other decrease.
- Negative correlations indicate that as scores on one variable increase, scores on the other decrease.
- Correlation does not indicate causation; the fact that two variables are correlated does not necessarily mean that one causes the other.
- Correlations can be used for prediction and for generating hypotheses.

Experiments: Looking for Cause and Effect

- Experiments require (1) control by the experimenter over events in the study and (2) random assignment of participants to conditions.
- Random sampling concerns how people are selected to be in a study, whereas random assignment concerns how people who are in the study are assigned to the different conditions of the study.
- Experiments are often conducted in a laboratory so that the researchers can have control over the context and can measure variables precisely.
- Field experiments are conducted in real-world settings outside the laboratory.
- Experiments examine the effects of one or more independent variables on one or more dependent variables.
- Subject variables are variables that characterize preexisting differences among the participants.
- Results that are statistically significant could have occurred by chance five or fewer times in 100 possible outcomes.
- Experimental findings have internal validity to the extent that changes in the dependent variable can be attributed to the independent variables.
- Control groups strengthen internal validity; experimenter expectancy effects weaken it.
- Research results have external validity to the extent that they can be generalized to other people and other situations.
- A representative sample strengthens external validity; a convenience sample weakens it.
- Mundane realism is the extent to which the research setting seems similar to real-world situations.
- Experimental realism is the extent to which the participants experience the experimental setting and procedures as real and involving.
- Deception is sometimes used to increase experimental realism.
- Confederates act as though they are participants in an experiment but actually work for the experimenter.

Meta-Analysis: Combining Results Across Studies

- Meta-analysis uses statistical techniques to integrate the quantitative results of different studies.

Culture and Research Methods

- There is growing interest in studying the role of culture in social psychology.
- As important and exciting as these cultural investigations are, they offer special challenges to researchers.

Ethics and Values in Social Psychology

- Ethical issues are particularly important in social psychology because of the use of deception in some research.

Research Ethics Boards

- Established by the federal government, REBs are responsible for reviewing research proposals to ensure that the welfare of participants is adequately protected.

Informed Consent

- The Canadian Psychological Association's code of ethics requires psychologists to secure informed consent from research participants.

Debriefing: Telling All

- Most participants have positive attitudes about their participation in research, even if they were deceived about some aspects of the study.
- Whenever deception has been used in a study, a full debriefing is essential; the researchers must disclose the facts about the study and make sure that the participant does not experience any distress.

Values and Science: Points of View

- Moral values set standards for and impose limits on the conduct of research.
- There are various views on the relation between values and science. Few believe that there can be a completely value-free science, but some advocate trying to minimize the influence of values on science, whereas others argue that values should be recognized and encouraged as an important factor in science.

Key Terms

applied research (29)
basic research (29)
confederate (45)
construct validity (30)
correlation coefficient (37)
correlational research (37)
debriefing (49)
deception (45)
dependent variable (42)
experiment (40)
experimental realism (45)
experimenter expectancy effects (44)
external validity (44)
hypothesis (28)
independent variable (42)
informed consent (48)
internal validity (43)
interrater reliability (32)
meta-analysis (46)
mundane realism (45)
operational definition (30)
qualitative research (33)
quantitative research (33)
random assignment (40)
random sampling (36)
subject variable (42)
theory (28)

3

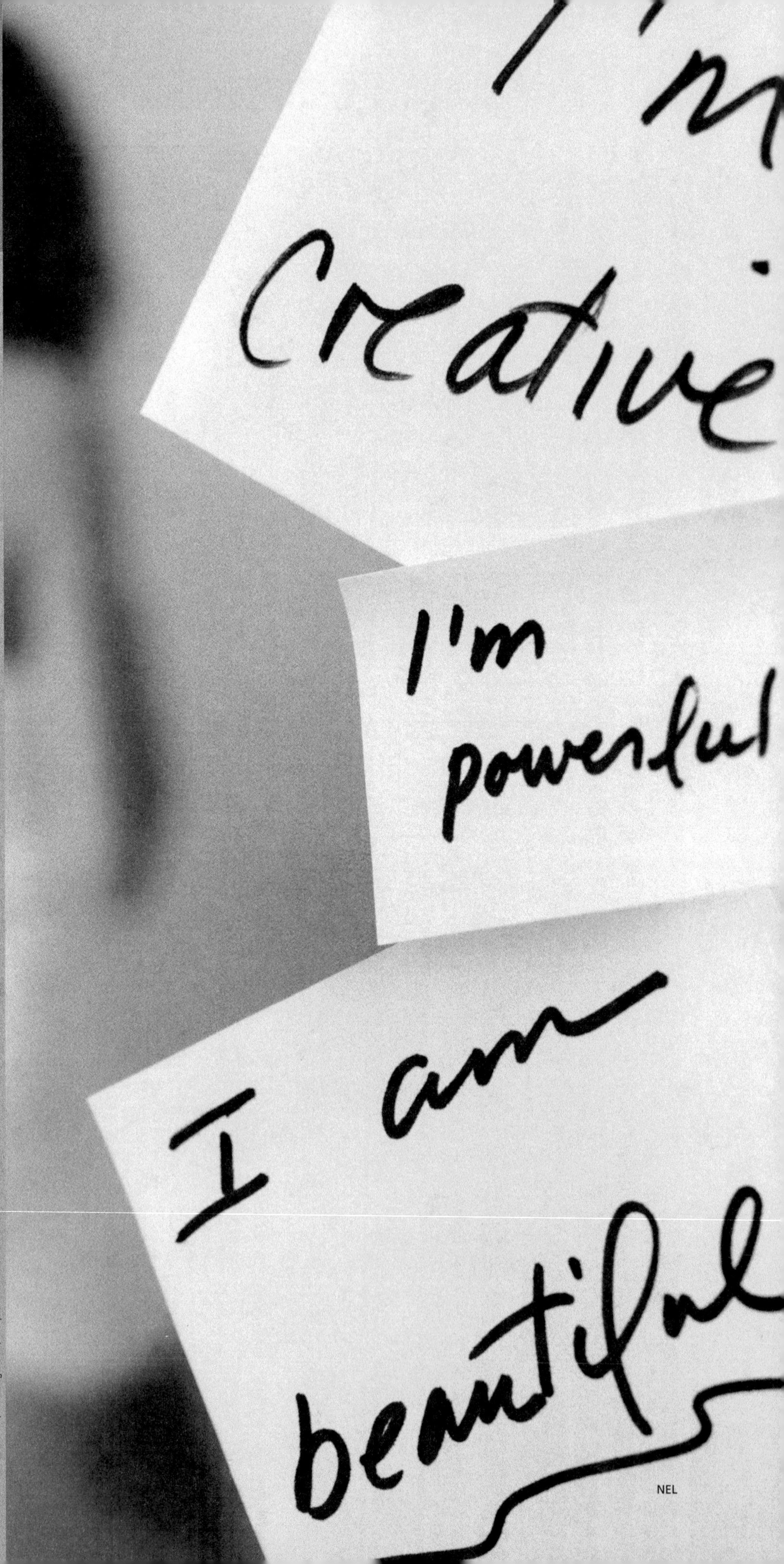

Lars Klove/The Image Bank/Getty

The Social Self

This chapter examines three interrelated aspects of the "social self." First, it considers the self-concept and the question of how people come to understand their own actions, emotions, and motivations. Second, it considers self-esteem, the affective component, and the question of how people evaluate themselves and defend against threats to their self-esteem. Third, it considers self-presentation, a behavioural manifestation of the self, and the question of how people present themselves to others. As we will see, the self is complex and multi-faceted.

Putting
COMMON SENSE
to the Test

Circle Your Answer

T F Humans are the only animals who recognize themselves in the mirror.

T F Smiling can make you feel happier.

T F Sometimes the harder you try to control a thought, feeling, or behaviour, the less likely you are to succeed.

T F People tend to be overly optimistic about their future.

T F People often sabotage their own performance in order to protect their self-esteem.

T F It's more adaptive to alter one's behaviour than to stay consistent from one social situation to the next.

Can you imagine living a meaningful or coherent life without a clear sense of who you are? In *The Man Who Mistook His Wife for a Hat,* neurologist Oliver Sacks (1985) described such a person—a patient named William Thompson. According to Sacks, Thompson suffered from an organic brain disorder that impairs a person's memory of recent events. Unable to recall anything for more than a few seconds, Thompson was always disoriented and lacked a sense of inner continuity. The effect on his behaviour was startling. Trying to grasp a constantly vanishing identity, Thompson would construct one tale after another to account for who he was, where he was, and what he was doing. From one moment to the next, he would improvise new identities—a grocery store clerk, minister, or medical patient, to name just a few. In social settings, Thompson's behaviour was especially intriguing. As Sacks (1985) observed,

> The presence of others, other people, excite and rattle him, force him into an endless, frenzied, social chatter, a veritable delirium of identity-making and -seeking; the presence of plants, a quiet garden, the nonhuman order, making no social demands upon him, allow this identity-delirium to relax, to subside (p. 110).

Thompson's plight is unusual, but it highlights two important points—one about the private "inner" self, the other about the "outer" self we show to others. First, the capacity for self-reflection is necessary for people to feel as if they understand their own motives and emotions and the causes of their behaviour. Unable to ponder his own actions, Thompson appeared vacant and without feeling—"desouled," as Sacks put it. Second, the self is heavily influenced by social factors. Thompson himself seemed compelled to put on a face for others and to improvise characters for the company he kept. We all do, to some extent. We may not create a kaleidoscope of multiple identities as Thompson did, but the way we manage ourselves is influenced by the people around us.

This chapter examines the ABCs of the self: A for *affect*, B for *behaviour*, and C for *cognition*. First, we ask a cognitive question: How do people come to know themselves, develop a self-concept, and maintain a stable sense of identity? Second, we explore an affective, or emotional, question: How do people evaluate themselves, enhance their self-images, and defend against threats to their self-esteem? Third, we confront a behavioural question: How do people regulate their own actions and present themselves to others according to interpersonal demands? As we'll see, the self is a topic that in recent years has attracted unprecedented interest among social psychologists (Leary & Tangney, 2003; Sedikides & Spencer, 2007; Swann & Bosson, 2010).

The Self-Concept

Have you ever been at a noisy gathering, struggling to have a conversation over music and the chatter of voices, and yet managed to hear someone at the other end of the room mention your name? If so, then you have experienced the "cocktail party effect"—the tendency of people to pick a personally relevant stimulus out of a complex environment (Moray, 1959; Wood & Cowan, 1995). To the cognitive psychologist, this phenomenon shows that people are selective in their attention. To the social psychologist, it also shows that the self is an important object of our own attention.

The term **self-concept** refers to the sum total of beliefs that people have about themselves. But what, specifically, does the self-concept consist of? According to Hazel Markus (1977), the self-concept is made up of cognitive molecules called **self-schemas**: beliefs about oneself that guide the processing of self-relevant information. Self-schemas are to an individual's total self-concept what hypotheses are to a theory, or what books are to a library. You can think of yourself as masculine or feminine, as independent or dependent, as liberal or conservative, as introverted or extroverted. Indeed, any specific attribute may have relevance to the self-concept for some people but not for others. The self-schema for body weight is a good example. People who regard themselves as extremely overweight or underweight, or for whom body image is a conspicuous aspect of the self-concept, are considered *schematic* with respect to weight. For body-weight schematics, a wide range of otherwise mundane events—a trip to the supermarket, new clothing, dinner at a restaurant, a day at the beach, or a friend's eating habits—may trigger thoughts about the self. In contrast, those who do not regard their own weight as extreme or as an important part of their lives are *aschematic* on that attribute (Markus et al., 1987).

Elements of the Self-Concept

Clearly, the self is a special object of our attention. Whether you are mentally focused on a memory, a conversation, a foul odour, the song in your head, your growling stomach, or this sentence, consciousness is like a "spotlight." It can shine on only one object at a point in time, but it can shift rapidly from one object to another and process information outside of awareness. In this spotlight, the self is front and centre. But is the self so special that it is uniquely represented in the neural circuitry of the brain? And is the self a uniquely human concept, or do other animals also distinguish the self from everything else?

self-concept
The sum total of an individual's beliefs about his or her own personal attributes.

self-schema
A belief people hold about themselves that guides the processing of self-relevant information.

Is the Self Specially Represented in the Brain? As illustrated by the story of William Thompson that opened this chapter, our sense of identity is biologically rooted. In *The Synaptic Self: How Our Brains Become Who We Are*, neuroscientist Joseph LeDoux (2002) argues that the synaptic connections within the brain provide the biological base for memory, which makes possible the sense of continuity that is needed for a normal identity. In *The Lost Self: Pathologies of the Brain and Identity*, Todd Feinberg and Julian Keenan (2005) describe how the self can be transformed and even completely destroyed by severe head injuries, brain tumours, diseases, and exposure to toxic substances that damage the brain and nervous system.

Social neuroscientists are starting to explore these possibilities. Using PET scans, fMRI, and other imaging techniques that can capture the brain in action, these researchers are finding that certain areas become more active when laboratory participants see a picture of themselves rather than a picture of others (Platek et al., 2008), when asked to judge whether they are 'above average' compared to their peers on various personality traits (Beer & Hughes, 2010), and when they take a first-person perspective while playing a video game as opposed to a third-person perspective (David et al., 2006). As we will see throughout this chapter, the self is a frame of reference that powerfully influences our thoughts, feelings, and behaviours. Not all aspects of the self are housed in a single structure of the brain. However, the bulk of research does seem to suggest that various self-based processes can be traced to activities occurring in certain areas of the brain (Northoff et al., 2011; Qin & Northoff, 2011).

Do Non-Human Animals Show Self-Recognition? When you stand in front of a mirror, what do you see? If you were a dog, a cat, or some other animal, you would not realize that the image you see is you, your own reflection. Except for human beings, only great apes—chimpanzees, gorillas, and orangutans—seem capable of self-recognition. How can we possibly know what non-humans think about mirrors? In a series of studies, Gordon Gallup (1977) placed different species of animals in a room with a large mirror. At first, they greeted their own images by vocalizing, gesturing, and making other social responses. After several days, the great apes—but not the other animals—began to use the mirror to pick food out of their teeth, groom themselves, blow bubbles, and make faces for their own entertainment. From all appearances, the apes recognized themselves.

In other studies, Gallup anaesthetized the animals, then painted an odourless red dye on their brows, and returned them to the mirror. Upon seeing the red spot, only the apes spontaneously reached for their own brows—proof that they perceived the image as their own (Povinelli et al., 1997; Keenan et al., 2003). Among apes, this form of self-recognition emerges in young adolescence and is stable across the lifespan, at least until old age (de Veer et al., 2003). By using a similar red dye test (but without anaesthetizing the infants), developmental psychologists have found that most human infants begin to recognize themselves in the mirror between the ages of 18 and 24 months (Lewis & Brooks-Gunn, 1979). Today, many researchers believe that self-recognition among great apes and human infants is the first clear expression of the concept "me" (Boysen & Himes, 1999).

Recent research suggests that certain intelligent non-primates can also recognize themselves. In one study, researchers at a New York aquarium found that two bottlenose dolphins marked with black ink often stopped to examine themselves in a mirror (Reiss & Marino, 2001). Similarly, Fabienne Delfour and Ken Marten (2001) found that killer whales and false killer whales spent more time in front of a mirror than whales only exposed to a window. Finally, researchers found that three Asian elephants placed in front of a jumbo-sized mirror used the mirror to inspect themselves—as when they moved their trunks to see the insides of their mouths, a part of the body they usually cannot see (Plotnik et al., 2006).

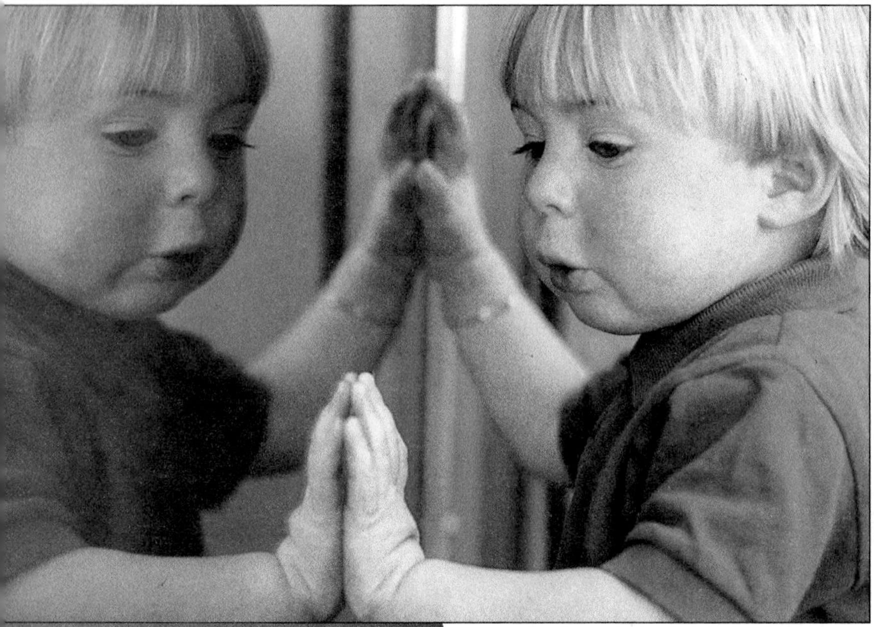

Ursula Markus/Photo Researchers

Infants begin to recognize themselves in the mirror at 18 to 24 months of age.

What Makes the Self a Social Concept? The ability to see yourself as a distinct entity is a necessary first step in the evolution and development of a self-concept. The second step involves social factors. Sociologist Charles Horton Cooley (1902) introduced the term *looking-glass self* to suggest that other people serve as a mirror in which we see ourselves. Expanding on this idea, George Herbert Mead (1934) added that we often come to know ourselves by imagining what significant others think of us and then incorporating these perceptions into our self-concepts. More recently, Susan Andersen and Serena Chen (2002) theorized that the self is "relational"—that we draw our sense of who we are from our past and current relationships with the significant others in our lives.

It is interesting that when Gallup tested his apes, those that had been raised in isolation—without exposure to peers—did not recognize themselves in the mirror. Only after such exposure did they begin to show signs of self-recognition. Among human beings, our self-concepts match our *perceptions* of what others think of us. But there's a hitch: What we think of ourselves often does not match what specific others *actually* think of us (Kenny & DePaulo, 1993; Shrauger & Schoeneman, 1979; Tice & Wallace, 2003; Vazire & Carlson, 2010).

Humans are the only animals who recognize themselves in the mirror. FALSE.

In recent years, social psychologists have broken new ground in the effort to understand the social self. People are not born thinking of themselves as reckless, likeable, shy, or outgoing. So where do their self-concepts come from? In the coming pages, five sources are considered: introspection, perceptions of our own behaviour, the influences of other people, autobiographical memories, and the cultures in which we live.

Introspection

Let's start at the beginning: How do people achieve insight into their own beliefs, attitudes, emotions, and motivations? Common sense makes this question seem ludicrous. After all, don't you know what you think because *you* think it? And don't you know how you feel because *you* feel it? Look through popular books on how to achieve self-insight, and you'll find the answers to these questions to be yes. Whether the prescribed technique is meditation, psychotherapy, religion, dream analysis, or hypnosis, the advice is basically the same: Self-knowledge is derived from introspection, a looking inward at one's own thoughts and feelings.

If these how-to books are correct, it stands to reason that no one can know you as well as you know yourself. Thus, people tend to assume that for others to know you at all, they would need information about your private thoughts, feelings, and other inner states—not just about your behaviour. But is this really the case? Most social psychologists are not sure that this faith in introspection is justified. Several years ago, Richard Nisbett and Timothy Wilson (1977) found that research participants often cannot accurately explain the causes or correlates of their own behaviour. This observation forced researchers to confront a thorny question: Does introspection improve the accuracy of self-knowledge?

"Look, babe. At this point, you've reinvented yourself so many times you're back to who you were at the start."

In some ways, our sense of self is malleable and subject to change.

In *Strangers to Ourselves,* Wilson (2002) says no, that introspection can sometimes impair self-knowledge. In a series of studies, he found that the attitudes people reported having about different objects corresponded closely to their behaviour toward those objects. The more participants said they enjoyed a task, the more time they spent on it; the more attractive they found a scenic landscape, the more pleasure they revealed in their facial expressions; the happier they said they were with a current dating partner, the longer the relationship ultimately lasted. Ironically, however, after participants were told to analyze the reasons for how they felt, the attitudes that they reported no longer corresponded to their behaviour. Human beings keep mentally busy processing information, which is why we often fail to understand our own thoughts, feelings, and behaviours. Apparently, it is possible to think too much and be too analytical, only to get confused.

People also have difficulty projecting forward and predicting how they would feel in response to future emotional events—a process known as **affective forecasting**. How happy would you be six months after winning a million-dollar lottery? Or, how unhappy would you be if injured in an automobile accident? In a series of studies, Timothy Wilson and Daniel Gilbert (2003, 2005) asked research participants to predict how they would feel after various positive and negative life events and compared their predictions to how others experiencing those events said they actually felt. Consistently, they found that people overestimate the strength and duration of their emotional reactions, a phenomenon they call the *impact bias.* In one study, junior professors predicted that receiving tenure would increase their happiness levels for several years, yet professors who actually received tenure were no happier at that later point than those not granted tenure. In a second study, voters predicted they would be happier a month after an election if their candidate won than if he or she lost. In actuality, supporters of the winning and losing candidates did not differ in their happiness levels one month after the election.

There are two possible reasons for the impact bias in affective forecasting. First, when it comes to negative life events—such as an injury, illness, or big financial loss—people do not fully appreciate the extent to which our psychological coping mechanisms help us to cushion the blow. In the face of adversity, human beings can be remarkably resilient—and not as devastated as we fear we will be (Gilbert et al., 1998). In fact, people are even more likely to overlook the coping mechanisms that *others* use. The result is a self–other difference by which we tend to predict that others will suffer even longer than we will (Igou, 2008).

A second reason for these overestimates is that when we introspect about the emotional impact on us of a future event—say, the breakup of a close relationship—we become so focused on that single event that we neglect to take into account the effects of other life experiences. For example, in a study conducted at the University of Waterloo, researchers found that the impact bias was less evident among East Asian participants than among Euro-Canadians. In one study that took place on a cool and rainy day, they asked participants how enjoyable the weather was at that time, as well

affective forecasting
The process of predicting how one would feel in response to future emotional events.

as how happy they anticipated they would be when the weather warmed up to at least 20 degrees Celsius. When the weather did warm up some weeks later, they once again measured happiness. They found that Euro-Canadians (who tend to focus more on individual events) predicted greater happiness in their future compared to East Asians (who tend to think more holistically), but actual measures of happiness did not differ between the two groups (Lam et al., 2005). To become more accurate in our predictions, then, we need to force ourselves to think more broadly about *all* the events that impact us.

Perceptions of Our Own Behaviour

Regardless of what we can learn from introspection, Daryl Bem (1972) believes that people can learn about themselves the same way outside observers do—by watching their own behaviour. Bem's **self-perception theory** is simple yet profound. To the extent that internal states are weak or difficult to interpret, people infer what they think or how they feel by observing their own behaviour and the situation in which that behaviour takes place. Think about it. Have you ever listened to yourself argue with someone, only to realize with amazement how angry you were? Have you ever devoured a sandwich in record time, only then to conclude that you must have been incredibly hungry? In each case, you made an inference about yourself by watching your own actions.

© Edward Frascino/The New Yorker Collection/www.cartoonbank.com.

"I don't sing because I am happy. I am happy because I sing."

As suggested by self-perception theory, we sometimes infer how we feel by observing our own behaviour.

There are limits to self-perception, of course. According to Bem, people do not infer their own internal states from behaviour that occurred in the presence of compelling situational pressures such as reward or punishment. If you argued vehemently or wolfed down a sandwich because you were paid to do so, you probably would not assume that you were angry or hungry. In other words, people learn about themselves through self-perception only when the situation alone seems insufficient to have caused their behaviour.

A good deal of research supports self-perception theory. When people are gently coaxed into doing something, and when they are not otherwise certain about how they feel, they come to view themselves in ways that are consistent with the behaviour (Chaiken & Baldwin, 1981; Kelly & Rodriguez, 2006; Schlenker & Trudeau, 1990). Thus, research participants induced to describe themselves in flattering terms scored higher on a later test of self-esteem than did those who were led to describe themselves more modestly (Jones et al., 1981; Rhodewalt & Agustsdottir, 1986). Similarly, those who were manoeuvred by leading questions into describing themselves as introverted or extroverted—whether or not they really were—came to define themselves as such later on, unless they were certain of this aspect of their personality (Fazio et al., 1981; Swann & Ely, 1984). British author E.M. Forster anticipated the theory well when he asked, "How can I tell what I think 'til I see what I say?"

Self-perception theory may have even more reach than Bem had anticipated. Bem argued that people sometimes learn about themselves by observing their *own* freely chosen behaviour. But might you also infer something about yourself by observing the behaviour of *someone else* with whom you completely identify? In a series of studies, Noah Goldstein and Robert Cialdini (2007) demonstrated this phenomenon, which they call vicarious self-perception. In one experiment, for example, they asked university students to listen to an interview with a fellow student who had agreed afterward to spend a few extra minutes helping out on a project on homelessness. Before listening to the interview, all the participants were fitted with an EEG recording device

self-perception theory
The theory that when internal cues are difficult to interpret, people gain self-insight by observing their own behaviour.

on their foreheads that allegedly measured brain activity as they viewed a series of images and words. By random assignment, some participants but not others were then told that their brainwave patterns closely resembled that of the person whose interview they would soon hear—a level of resemblance, they were told, that signalled genetic similarity and relationship closeness. Would participants in this similarity feedback condition draw inferences about themselves by observing the behaviour of a fellow student? Yes. In a post-interview questionnaire, these participants (compared to those in the no-feedback control group) rated themselves as more sensitive and as more self-sacrificing if the student whose helpfulness they observed was said to be similar, biologically. What's more, when the session was over, 93 percent of those in the similarity condition agreed to spend some extra time themselves helping the experimenter—compared to only 61 percent in the no-feedback control group.

Self-Perceptions of Emotion Draw the corners of your mouth back and up and tense your eye muscles. Okay, relax. Now raise your eyebrows, open your eyes wide, and let your mouth drop open slightly. Relax. Now pull your brows down and together and clench your teeth. Relax. If you followed these directions, you would have appeared to others to be feeling first happy, then fearful, and finally angry. The question is: How would you have appeared to yourself?

Social psychologists who study emotion have asked precisely that question. Viewed within the framework of self-perception theory, the **facial feedback hypothesis** states that changes in facial expression can trigger corresponding changes in the subjective experience of emotion. In the first test of this hypothesis, James Laird (1974) told participants that they were taking part in an experiment on activity of the facial muscles. After attaching electrodes to their faces, he showed them a series of cartoons. Before each one, the participants were instructed to contract certain facial muscles in ways that created either a smile or a frown. As Laird predicted, participants rated what they saw as funnier, and reported feeling happier, when they were smiling than when they were frowning. In follow-up research, people were similarly induced through posed expressions to experience fear, anger, sadness, and disgust (Duclos et al., 1989).

Facial feedback can evoke and magnify certain emotional states. It's important to note, however, that the face is not *necessary* to the experience of emotion. Neuropsychologists recently tested a 21-year-old woman who suffered from bilateral facial paralysis and found that despite her inability to outwardly *show* emotion, she reported *experiencing* various emotions in response to positive and negative visual images (Keillor et al., 2003).

How does facial feedback work? Laird argues that facial expressions affect emotion through a process of self-perception: "If I'm smiling, I must be happy." Consistent with this hypothesis, Chris Kleinke and others (1998) asked people to emulate either the happy or angry facial expressions that were depicted in a series of photographs. Half the participants saw themselves in a mirror during the task; the others did not. Did these manipulations affect mood states? Yes. Compared to participants in a no-expression control group, those who put on happy faces felt better, and those who put on angry faces felt worse. As predicted by self-perception theory, the differences were particularly pronounced among participants who saw themselves in a mirror.

Other expressive behaviours, such as body posture, can also provide us with sensory feedback and influence the way we feel. When people feel proud, they stand erect with their shoulders raised, chest expanded, and head held high *(expansion)*. When dejected, however, people slump over with their shoulders drooping and head bowed *(contraction)*. Clearly, your emotional state is revealed in the way you carry yourself. But is it also possible that the way you carry yourself affects your emotional state?

facial feedback hypothesis
The hypothesis that changes in facial expression can lead to corresponding changes in emotion.

Can people lift their spirits by expansion or lower their spirits by contraction? Yes. Sabine Stepper and Fritz Strack (1993) arranged for people to sit in either a slumped or an upright position by varying the height of the table they had to write on. Those forced to sit upright reported feeling more pride after succeeding at a task than did those who were placed in a slumped position. Similarly, Pablo Briñol and others (2009) instructed participants to write down either three positive or three negative personal traits that would relate to their future job performance; half of them completed this task while slumped over (doubtful posture) or while sitting up straight (confident posture). For those with a confident posture, listing positive thoughts led to the most favourable self-evaluations, but for those listing negative thoughts, the effect was the opposite—they had the worst self-evaluations. They were either confidently positive, or confidently negative!

Self-Perceptions of Motivation Without quite realizing it, Mark Twain was a self-perception theorist. In *The Adventures of Tom Sawyer,* written in the late 1800s, he quipped, "There are wealthy gentlemen in England who drive four-horse passenger coaches twenty or thirty miles on a daily line, in the summer, because the privilege costs them considerable money; but if they were offered wages for the service that would turn it into work then they would resign." Twain's hypothesis— that reward for an enjoyable activity can undermine interest in that activity—seems to contradict our intuition and a good deal of psychological research. After all, aren't we all motivated by reward, as B.F. Skinner and other behaviourists have declared? The answer depends on how *motivation* is defined.

Smiling can make you feel happier.
TRUE.

As a keen observer of human behaviour, Twain anticipated a key distinction between intrinsic and extrinsic motivation. *Intrinsic motivation* originates in factors within a person. People are said to be intrinsically motivated when they engage in an activity for the sake of their own interest, the challenge, or sheer enjoyment. Eating a fine meal, listening to music, spending time with friends, and engaging in a hobby are among the activities that you might find intrinsically motivating. In contrast, *extrinsic motivation* originates in factors outside the person. People are said to be extrinsically motivated when they engage in an activity as a means to an end, for tangible benefits. It might be for money, grades, or recognition; to fulfill obligations; or to avoid punishment. As the behaviourists have always said, people do strive for reward. The question is: What happens to the intrinsic motivation once that reward is no longer available?

From the standpoint of self-perception theory, Twain's hypothesis makes sense. When someone is rewarded for listening to music, playing a game, or eating a tasty food, his or her behaviour becomes *over*justified, or *over*rewarded, and can be attributed to extrinsic as well as intrinsic motives. This **overjustification effect** can be dangerous: Observing that their own efforts have paid off, people begin to wonder if the activity was ever worth pursuing in its own right.

Research shows that when people start getting "paid" for a task they already enjoy, they sometimes lose interest in it. In an early demonstration of this phenomenon, Mark Lepper and his colleagues (1973) gave preschool children an opportunity to play with colourful felt-tipped markers—an opportunity most could not resist. By observing how much time the children spent on the activity, the researchers were able to measure their intrinsic motivation. Two weeks later, the children were divided into three groups, all about equal in terms of initial levels of intrinsic motivation. In one, the children were simply asked to draw some pictures with the markers. In the second, they were told that if they used the markers, they would receive a "Good Player Award," a certificate with a gold star and a red ribbon. In a third group, the children were not offered a reward for drawing pictures, but—like those in the second group—they received a reward when they were done.

overjustification effect
The tendency for intrinsic motivation to diminish for activities that have become associated with reward or other extrinsic factors.

About a week later, the teachers placed the markers and paper on a table in the classroom while the experimenters observed through a one-way mirror. Since no rewards were offered on this occasion, the amount of free time the children spent playing with the markers reflected their intrinsic motivation. As predicted, those children who had expected and received a reward for their efforts were no longer as interested in the markers as they had been. Children who had not received a reward were not adversely affected, nor were those who had unexpectedly received the reward. Having played with the markers without the promise of reward, these children remained intrinsically motivated (see ▶ Figure 3.1).

▶ FIGURE 3.1

Paradoxical Effects of Reward on Intrinsic Motivation

In this study, an expected reward undermined children's intrinsic motivation to play with felt-tipped markers. Children who received an unexpected reward or no reward did not lose interest.

(Lepper et al., 1973.)

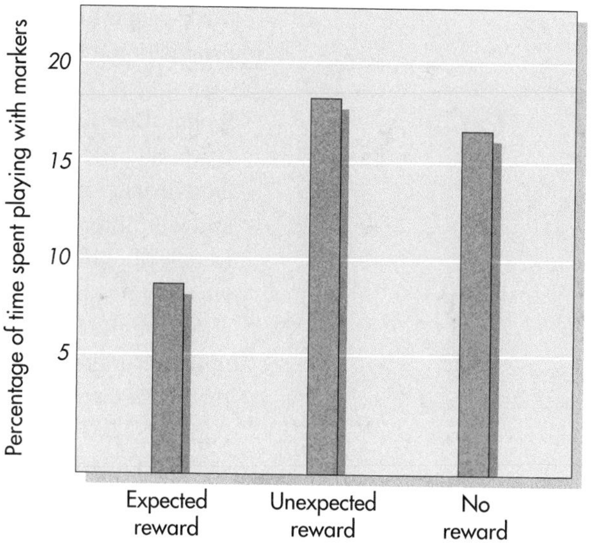

The paradox that reward can undermine rather than enhance intrinsic motivation has been observed in many settings and with both children and adults (Deci & Ryan, 1985; Enzle & Anderson, 1993; Pittman & Heller, 1987; Remedios et al., 2005; Tang & Hall, 1995). Accept money for a leisure activity, and before you know it, what used to be "play" comes to feel more like "work." In the long run, this can have negative effects on the quality of performance. In a series of studies, Teresa Amabile (1996) and others had participants write poems, draw or paint pictures, make paper collages, and generate creative solutions to business dilemmas. Consistently, they found that people are more creative when they feel interested and challenged by the work itself than when they feel pressured to make money, fulfill obligations, meet deadlines, win competitions, or impress others. In one study, Amabile had art experts rate the works of professional artists and found that the artists' commissioned work (art they were contracted for) was judged as lower in quality than their non-commissioned work. People are likely to be more creative when they are intrinsically motivated in relation to the task, not compelled by outside forces.

But wait. If extrinsic benefits serve to undermine intrinsic motivation, should teachers and parents *not* offer rewards to their children? And are the employee incentive programs so often used in business doomed to fail, as some (Kohn, 1993) have suggested? It all depends on how the reward is perceived—and by whom. If a reward is presented in the form of verbal praise that is perceived to be sincere, or as a special "bonus" for superior performance, then it can actually *enhance* intrinsic motivation by providing positive feedback about competence—as when people win competitions, scholarships, or a pat on the back from people they respect (Cameron & Pierce, 1994; Eisenberger & Cameron, 1996; Henderlong & Lepper, 2002).

The notion that intrinsic motivation is undermined by some types of reward but not others was observed by Nicola Lacetera and Mario Macis (2010) in their study of blood donors in Italy. They found that donors who were told they might receive a small amount of money for giving blood were more likely to indicate that they would subsequently stop donating their blood, compared to donors who were offered a voucher for the same amount. The authors suggested this was because an offer of money led to the donors feeling 'greedy'; one way to minimize that feeling would be to stop donating altogether.

Copyright © [1973] by the American Psychological Association. Reproduced with permission. From M.R. Lepper, D. Greene, and K.E. Nisbett (1973) "Undermining Children's Intrinsic Interest with Extrinsic Reward: A Test of the 'Overjustification' Hypothesis," *Journal of Personality and Social Psychology*, 28, 129-137. The use of APA information does not imply endorsement by APA.

Individual differences in motivational orientation toward work must also be considered. For intrinsically oriented people who say that "What matters most to me is enjoying what I do" and that "I seldom think about salary and promotions," reward may be unnecessary—and may even be detrimental (Amabile et al., 1994). Yet for people who are highly focused on the achievement of certain goals—whether at school, at work, or in sports—extrinsic inducements such as grades, scores, bonuses, trophies, and the thrill of competition—tend to boost their intrinsic motivation (Durik & Harackiewicz, 2007; Harackiewicz & Elliot, 1993).

Influences of Other People

As we noted earlier, Cooley's (1902) theory of the looking-glass self emphasized that other people help us define ourselves. In this section, we will see the importance of this proposition to our self-concepts.

Social Comparison Theory Suppose a stranger were to ask, "Who are you?" If you had only a minute or two to answer, would you mention your ethnic or religious background? What about your hometown? Would you describe your talents and your interests or your likes and dislikes? When asked this question, people tend to describe themselves in ways that set them apart from others in their immediate vicinity (McGuire & McGuire, 1988). For example, Rudolf Kalin and J.W. Berry (1995) report on the results of two national surveys conducted in 1974 and 1991 examining multicultural and ethnic attitudes. In the 1991 survey, most Canadians identified themselves as "Canadian" but in Quebec most identified themselves as "Provincial" (Quebecois), whereas in the 1974 survey, those in Quebec identified themselves as "French Canadian." Interestingly, the researchers found that despite this difference, all respondents maintained a strong attachment to Canada. They explain this by noting that in a country as diverse as Canada, multiple loyalties are possible; "Individuals can feel pride in, and allegiance to, smaller communities (e.g., ethnic groups) nested within the larger community of the nationstate (p. 1)." The implication is intriguing: Change someone's social surroundings, and you can change that person's spontaneous self-description.

This reliance on distinguishing features in self-description indicates that the self is "relative," a social construct, and that we define ourselves in part by using family members, friends, acquaintances, and others as a benchmark (Mussweiler & Rüter, 2003; Mussweiler & Strack, 2000). Indeed, that is what Leon Festinger (1954) proposed in his **social comparison theory**. Festinger argued that when people are uncertain of their abilities or opinions—that is, when objective information is not readily available—they evaluate themselves through comparisons with similar others. The theory seems reasonable, but is it valid? Over the years, social psychologists have put social comparison theory to the test, focusing on two key questions: (1) *When* do we turn to others for comparative information? (2) Of all the people who inhabit Earth, *with whom* do we choose to compare ourselves? (Chanal & Sarrazin, 2007; Suls & Wheeler, 2000).

As Festinger proposed, the answer to the "when" question appears to be that people engage in social comparison in states of uncertainty, when more objective means of self-evaluation are not available. In fact, recent studies suggest that Festinger may have understated the role of social comparison processes—that people may judge themselves in relation to others even when more objective standards are available. For example, William Klein (1997) asked university students to make a series of judgments of artwork. Giving false feedback, he then told the students that 60 percent or 40 percent of their answers were correct—and that this was 20 percent higher or lower than the average among students. When they later rated their own skill at the task, participants were influenced not by their absolute scores, but by where they stood in relation to their peers. For them, it was better to have had a 40 percent score that was above average than a 60 percent score that was below average. However, the tendency to

social comparison theory
The theory that people evaluate their own abilities and opinions by comparing themselves to others.

view ambiguous information in a self-enhancing way is more likely when participants receive information about their own and others' performance at the same time (Klein et al., 2006).

The "with whom" question has also been the subject of many studies. The answer seems to be that when we evaluate our own taste in music, value on the job market, or athletic ability, we look to others who are similar—or different—to us in relevant ways (Goethals & Darley, 1977; Wheeler et al., 1982)—a choice that we make automatically, without necessarily being aware of it (Gilbert et al., 1995). For example, Penelope Lockwood and others (2002) explored the extent to which a student's academic motivation could be affected by focusing on a role model who ostensibly had strategies similar to their own for achieving success. Participants at the University of Toronto were primed to think about strategies that either helped to "successfully promote this [positive] outcome" (p. 856) or to "successfully prevent this [negative] outcome" (p. 856). They then read a statement by a role model who appeared to have either a success promotion or failure avoidance strategy. The participant's own academic motivation was increased when the role model had a strategy congruent to his or her own; those who were primed to focus on promotion strategies were motivated by positive role models, while those who were primed to think about the avoidance of failure were motivated by negative role models. While we may generally compare ourselves to those who are similar to us, there are exceptions to this rule. Later in the chapter, we will see that people often cope with personal inadequacies by focusing on others who are *less* able or *less* fortunate than themselves.

Two-Factor Theory of Emotion People seek social comparison information to evaluate their abilities and opinions. Do they also turn to others to determine something as personal and subjective as their own emotions? In classic experiments on affiliation, Stanley Schachter (1959) found that when people were frightened into thinking they would receive painful electric shocks, most sought the company of others who were in the same predicament. Nervous and uncertain about how they should be feeling, participants wanted to affiliate with similar others, presumably for the purpose of comparison. Yet when they were not fearful, and expected only mild shocks, or when the "others" were not taking part in the same experiment, participants preferred to be alone. As Schachter put it, "Misery doesn't just love any kind of company; it loves only miserable company" (p. 24).

Intrigued by the possibilities, Schachter and his research team took the next step. Could it be, they wondered, that when people are uncertain about how they feel, their emotional state is actually determined by the reactions of others around them? In answer to this question, the researchers proposed that two factors are necessary to feel a specific emotion. First, the person must experience the symptoms of physiological arousal—such as a racing heart, perspiration, rapid breathing, and tightening of the stomach. Second, the person must make a *cognitive interpretation* that explains the source of the arousal. And that is where the people around us come in: Their reactions help us interpret our own arousal.

To test this provocative **two-factor theory of emotion**, Schachter and Jerome Singer (1962) injected male volunteers with epinephrine, a drug that heightens physiological arousal. Although one group was forewarned about the drug's effects, a second group was not. Members of a third group were injected with a harmless placebo. Before the drug (which was described as a vitamin supplement) actually took effect, participants were left alone with a male confederate introduced as another participant who had received the same injection. In some sessions, the confederate behaved in a euphoric manner. For 20 minutes, he happily bounced around, doodling on scratch paper, sinking jump shots into the wastebasket, flying paper airplanes across

two-factor theory of emotion The theory that the experience of emotion is based on two factors: physiological arousal and a cognitive interpretation of that arousal.

the room, and playing with a hula-hoop. In other sessions, the confederate displayed anger, ridiculing a questionnaire they were filling out and, in a fit of rage, ripping it up and hurling it into the wastebasket.

Think for a moment about these various combinations of situations. As the drug takes effect, participants in the *drug-informed* group will begin to feel their hearts pound, their hands shake, and their faces flush. Having been told to expect these symptoms, however, they need not search for an explanation. Participants in the *placebo* group will not become aroused in the first place, so they will have no symptoms to explain. But now consider the plight of those in the *drug-uninformed* group, who suddenly become aroused without knowing why. Trying to identify the sensations, these participants, according to the theory, should take their cues from someone else in the same predicament—namely, the confederate.

In general, the experimental results supported Schachter and Singer's line of reasoning. Drug-uninformed participants reported feeling relatively happy or angry depending on the confederate's performance. In many instances, they even exhibited similar kinds of behaviour. One participant, for example, "threw open the window and, laughing, hurled paper basketballs at passersby." In the drug-informed and placebo groups, however, participants were, as expected, less influenced by these social cues.

Schachter and Singer's two-factor theory of emotion has attracted a good deal of controversy, as some studies have corroborated their findings but others have not. Overall, it now appears that one limited but important conclusion can safely be drawn: When people are unclear about their own emotional states, they sometimes interpret how they feel by watching others (Reisenzein, 1983). The "sometimes" part of the conclusion is important. For others to influence your emotion, your level of physiological arousal cannot be too intense, or else it will be experienced as aversive—regardless of the situation (Maslach, 1979; Zimbardo et al., 1993). Also, research shows that other people must be present as a possible explanation for arousal *before* its onset. Once people are aroused, they turn for an explanation to events that preceded the change in their physiological state (Schachter & Singer, 1979; Sinclair et al., 1994).

In subsequent chapters, we will see that the two-factor theory of emotion has far-reaching implications for passionate love, anger and aggression, and other affective experiences.

Autobiographical Memories

Philosopher James Mill once said, "The phenomenon of the Self and that of Memory are merely two sides of the same fact." If the story of patient William Thompson at the start of this chapter is any indication, Mill was right. Without autobiographical memories—recollections of the sequences of events that have touched your life (Fivush et al., 2003; Rasmussen & Bernsten, 2009; Rubin, 1996; Thompson et al., 1998)—you would have no coherent self-concept. Think about it. Who would you be if you could not remember your parents or childhood playmates, your successes and failures, the places you lived, the schools you attended, the books you read, and the teams you played for? Clearly, memories shape the self-concept. In this section, we will see that the self-concept shapes our personal memories as well (Conway & Pleydell-Pearce, 2000).

"The nice thing about having memories is that you can choose."

—William Trevor

When people are prompted to recall their own experiences, they typically report more events from the recent than from the distant past. There are, however, two consistent exceptions to this recency rule. The first is that older adults retrieve a large number of personal memories from their adolescence and early adult years—a "reminiscence bump" found across many cultures that may occur because these years are busy and formative in one's life (Conway et al., 2005; Fitzgerald, 1988; Jansari & Parkin, 1996). A second exception is that people tend to remember transitional "firsts." Reflect for a moment on your university career. What events pop to mind—and when did they occur? Did you come up with the day you arrived on campus or the first time you met your closest friend? What about notable classes, parties, or sports events? It seems that, in particular, positive events, or those that are surprising and unexpected, are the most likely to be remembered (Dickson et al., 2011). Among students, events that occur during busy transitional periods, such as the first two months of their first year of university, are disproportionally recalled (Pillemer et al., 1996). Obviously, not all experiences leave the same impression.

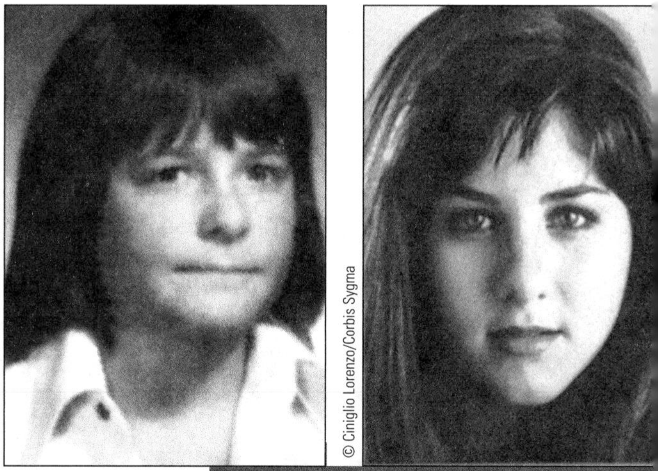

Pacific Coast News

© Ciniglio Lorenzo/Corbis Sygma

Although adults recall more events from the recent than distant past, people are filled with memories from late adolescence and early adulthood. These formative years are nicely captured by high-school yearbook photos—such as those of actors Michael J. Fox and Jennifer Aniston. (ClassMates.com, Yearbook Archives.)

Roger Brown and James Kulik (1977) coined the term *flashbulb memories* to describe these enduring, detailed, high-resolution recollections, and speculated that humans are biologically equipped for survival purposes to "print" these dramatic events in memory. These flashbulb memories are not necessarily accurate, or even consistent over time. When asked, for example, how he heard about the infamous September 11, 2001, terrorist attacks, then U.S. President George W. Bush gave different accounts on three occasions when asked what he was doing and who told him the news (Greenberg, 2004). Accurate or not, these recollections "feel" special and serve as prominent landmarks in the biographies that we tell about ourselves (Conway, 1995; Talarico & Rubin, 2007).

By linking the present to the past and providing us with a sense of inner continuity, autobiographical memory is a vital part of—and can be shaped by—our identity. Our current view of ourselves is often affected by our views of our past selves, as well as our views of our future selves (Wilson & Ross, 2003). In particular, people are often motivated to distort the past in ways that are self-inflated. According to Anthony Greenwald (1980), "The past is remembered as if it were a drama in which the self was the leading player" (p. 604).

For example, Michael Ross (1989) found that after people were persuaded by an expert who said that frequent tooth brushing was desirable, they reported, in the context of a subsequent experiment, having brushed more often in the previous two weeks. Illustrating that memory can be biased rather than objective, these participants "updated" the past in light of their new attitude. In a second study, Harry Bahrick and others (1996) asked undergraduates to recall all of their high school grades and then checked the accuracy of these reports against the actual transcripts. Overall, the majority of grades were recalled correctly. But most of the errors in memory were grade *inflations*—and most of these were made when the actual grades were *low* (see ▶ Figure 3.2).

Do these findings support sociologist George Herbert Mead's (1934) contention that our visions of the past are like pure "escape fancies ... in which we rebuild the world according to our hearts' desires" (pp. 348–349)? Not necessarily. In a series of studies, Ian Newby-Clark and Michael Ross (2003) asked students at the University of Waterloo to recall significant events from their own lives and to anticipate significant events likely to occur in their future. They found that although people are hopeful about the future, anticipating mostly positive events, their recollections from the past are more balanced. Most people feel as if they have been fortunate in their lives,

▶ FIGURE 3.2

Distortions in Memory of High School Grades

Undergraduate students were asked to recall their high school grades, which were then checked against their actual transcripts. These comparisons revealed that most errors in memory were grade inflations. Lower grades were recalled with the least accuracy (and the most inflation). It appears that people sometimes revise their own past to suit their current self-image.

(Bahrick et al., 1996.)

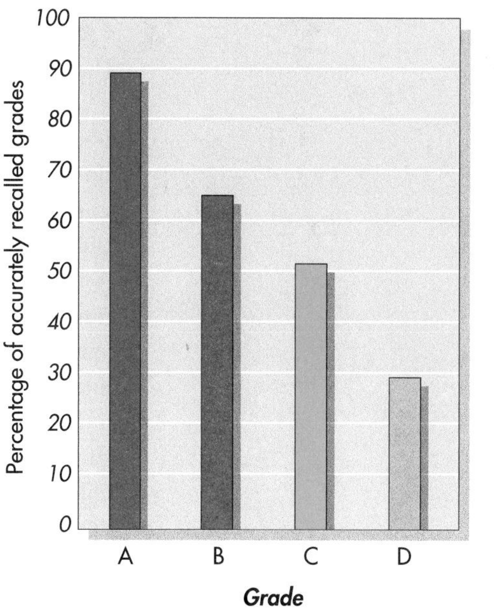

From Bahrick et al., Psychological Science, 1996, Vol 7, pp. 266-271. Copyright © 1996 Blackwell Publishing. Reprinted with permission.

J.P. Laffont/Corbis Sygma.

CP/Moose Jaw Times/Mark Taylor

Reflecting an interdependent view of the self, children in Japan are taught to fit into the community. Reflecting a more independent view of the self, children in Canada are encouraged to express their individuality.

but they are as quick to recall becoming ill or their parents divorcing, as they are to recall meeting a boyfriend or girlfriend, or graduating from high school.

Culture and the Self-Concept

The self-concept is also influenced by cultural factors. In North America, it is said that "the squeaky wheel gets the grease"; in Japan, it is said that "the nail that stands out gets pounded down." Thus Canadian parents try to raise their children to be independent, self-reliant, and assertive (a "cut above the rest"), whereas Japanese children are raised to fit into their groups and community.

The preceding example illustrates two contrasting cultural orientations. One values *individualism* and the virtues of independence, autonomy, and self-reliance. The other orientation values *collectivism* and the virtues of interdependence, cooperation, and social harmony. Under the banner of individualism, one's personal goals take priority over group allegiances. In collectivist cultures, by contrast, the person is, first and foremost, a loyal member of a family, team, company, church, and state motivated to be part of a group—not different, better, or worse (Triandis, 1994). In what countries are these orientations the most extreme? In a worldwide study of 117 000 employees of IBM, Geert Hofstede (2001) found that the most fiercely individualistic people were from the United States, Australia, the United Kingdom, Canada, and the Netherlands—in that order. The most collectivist people were from Guatemala, Ecuador, Panama, Venezuela, Indonesia, and Pakistan.

It's also important to realize that individualism and collectivism are not simple opposites on a continuum and that the similarities and differences between countries do not fit a simple pattern. Daphna Oyserman and others (2002) conducted a meta-analysis of many thousands of respondents in 83 studies. Within the United States, they found that African Americans were the most individualistic subgroup and that Asian and Latino Americans were the most collectivistic. Comparing nations, they found that Americans as a group are relatively individualistic. Collectivist orientations varied within Asia, however, as the Chinese were more collectivistic than Japanese and Korean respondents. Charissa Cheah and Larry Nelson (2004) found that within a Canadian Aboriginal population (a minority culture), not all group members identify with their heritage culture. While Aboriginal students were more likely to endorse collectivist ideals, such as interdependence and the maintenance of group balance and harmony, compared to European Canadian students, this was only found among Aboriginal students who held more traditional values.

Individualism and collectivism are so deeply ingrained in a culture that they mould our very self-conceptions and identities. According to Hazel Markus and Shinobu Kitayama (1991), most North Americans and Europeans have an *independent* view of the self. In this view, the self is an entity that is distinct, autonomous, self-contained, and endowed with unique dispositions. Yet in much of Asia, Africa, and Latin America, people hold an *interdependent* view of the self. Here, the self is part of a larger social network that includes one's family, co-workers, and others with whom one is socially connected. People with an independent view say that "the only person you can count on is yourself" and "I enjoy being unique and different from others." In contrast, those with an interdependent view are more likely to agree that "I'm partly to blame if one of my family members or co-workers fails" and "my happiness depends on the happiness of those around me" (Rhee et al., 1995; Singelis, 1994; Triandis et al., 1998). These contrasting orientations—one focused on the personal self, the other on a collective self—are depicted in ▶ Figure 3.3.

Research confirms that there is a close link between cultural orientation and conceptions of the self. David Trafimow and his colleagues (1991) had North American and Chinese college students complete 20 sentences beginning with "I am...." The Americans were more likely to fill in the blank with trait descriptions ("I am shy"), whereas the Chinese were more likely to identify themselves by group affiliations ("I am a college student"). It's no wonder that in China, one's family name comes *before* one's personal name. Similar differences are found between Australians and Malaysians (Bochner, 1994).

These cultural orientations can influence the way we perceive, evaluate, and present ourselves in relation to others. Markus and Kitayama (1991) identified two interesting differences between East and West. The first is that people in individualistic cultures strive for personal achievement, while those living in collectivist cultures derive more satisfaction from the status of a valued group. Thus, whereas North Americans tend to overestimate their own contributions to a team effort, take credit for success, and blame others for failure, people from collectivist cultures underestimate their own role and present themselves in more modest, self-effacing terms in relation to other members of the group (Akimoto & Sanbonmatsu, 1999; Heine et al., 2000). For example, Christopher Lo and others (2011) compared responses from participants in Canada, the United States, China, and Japan to a survey asking about the qualities that define who they are as a person. They were asked to write down five positive and five negative attributes that they felt they possessed. While the

▶ FIGURE 3.3

Cultural Conceptions of Self

As depicted here, different cultures foster different conceptions of the self. Many westerners have an *independent* view of the self as an entity that is distinct, autonomous, and self-contained. Yet many Asians, Africans, and Latin Americans hold an *interdependent* view of the self that encompasses others in a larger social network.

(Markus & Kitayama, 1991.)

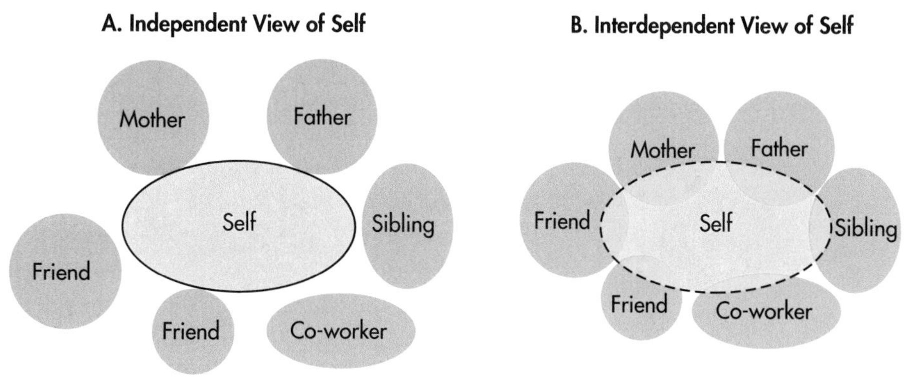

Copyright © [1999] by the American Psychological Association. Reproduced with permission. From H. Kim and H.R. Markus (1999) "Deviance or Uniqueness, Harmony or Conformity? A Cultural Analysis," *Journal of Personality and Social Psychology, 77*, 785-800. The use of APA information does not imply endorsement by APA.

researchers generally found similar results between the Eastern and Western participants, they did note that Easterners tended to be more self-critical and less self-enhancing than their Western counterparts.

A second consequence of these differing conceptions of the self is that university students in the West may see themselves as less similar to others than do students from the East. This difference reinforces the idea that individuals with independent conceptions of the self believe they are unique. In fact, our cultural orientations toward conformity or independence may lead us to favour similarity or uniqueness in all things. In a fascinating study, Heejung Kim and Hazel Markus (1999) showed abstract figures to subjects from the United States and Korea. Each figure contained nine parts. Most of the parts were identical in shape, position, and direction. One or more were different. Look at ▶ Figure 3.4. Which of the nine subfigures within each group do you like most? The American participants liked the subfigures that were unique or in the minority, while Korean subjects preferred those that "fit in" as part of the group. It seems that our culturally ingrained orientations to conformity and independence leave a mark on us, leading us to form preferences for things that "fit in" or "stand out."

▶ FIGURE 3.4

What's Your Preference: Similarity or Uniqueness?

Which subfigure within each set do you prefer? Kim and Markus (1999) found that Americans tend to like subfigures that "stand out" as unique or in the minority, while Koreans tend to like subfigures that "fit in" with the surrounding group.

(Kim & Markus, 1999.)

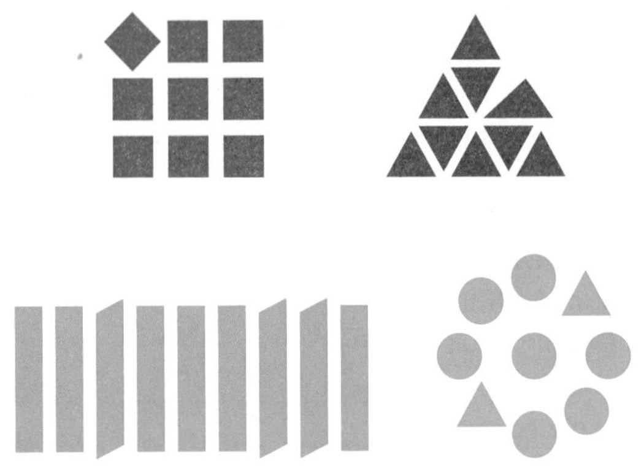

Are people from disparate cultures locked into thinking about the self in either personal or collective terms, or are both aspects of the self present in everyone, to be expressed according to the situation? A study by Michael Ross and others (2002) demonstrated that it is possible to activate different cultural mindsets that in turn affect bicultural individuals' self-perceptions. Chinese-born students living in Canada were asked to complete self-perception questionnaires in either Chinese or English. Compared to the Canadian-born participants of either Chinese or European descent, the Chinese-born participants responding in Chinese reported higher agreement with Chinese beliefs, were more likely to note their cultural background, and reported significantly lower self-esteem. It appears that each of us have both personal and collective aspects of the self to draw on—and that the part that comes to mind depends on the situation we are in.

The more closely social psychologists examine cultures and their impact on how people think, the more complex is the picture that emerges. Clearly, research documents the extent to which conceptions of the self are influenced by the individualist and collectivist impulses within a culture. But there are other core differences as well. Kaiping Peng and Richard Nisbett (1999) note that people in East Asian cultures think in dialectical terms about contradictory characteristics—accepting, for example, that apparent opposites (such as black and white, friend and enemy, strong and weak) can coexist within a single person either at the same time or as a result of changes over time. Grounded in Eastern traditions, **dialecticism** is a system of thought characterized by the acceptance of such contradictions through compromise, as implied by the Chinese proverb, "Beware of your friends, not your enemies." This thought style contrasts sharply with the North American and European perspective, grounded in Western logic, by which people differentiate seeming opposites on the assumption that if one is right, the other must be wrong. Interestingly, some research has shown that East Asians are more willing than Americans to see and accept contradictory aspects of themselves (Spencer-Rodgers et al., 2009), as seen in their willingness to accept both positive and negative aspects of themselves at the same time (Boucher et al., 2009).

dialecticism
An Eastern system of thought that accepts the existence of contradictory characteristics within a single person.

Self-Esteem

How do you feel about yourself? Are you generally satisfied with your appearance, personality, abilities, and friendships? Are you optimistic about your future? When it comes to the self, people are hardly cool, objective, dispassionate observers. Rather, we are judgmental, emotional, and highly protective of our **self-esteem**—an affectively charged component of the self.

The word *esteem* comes from the Latin *aestimare,* which means "to estimate or appraise." Self-esteem thus refers to our positive and negative evaluations of ourselves (Coopersmith, 1967). Some individuals have higher self-esteem than others do—an attribute that can have a profound impact on the way they think and feel about themselves. It's important to keep in mind, however, that although some of us have higher self-esteem than others, a feeling of self-worth is not a single trait etched permanently in stone. Rather, it is a state of mind that varies in response to success, failure, changes in fortune, social interactions, and other life experiences (Heatherton & Polivy, 1991). Also, because the self-concept is made up of many self-schemas, individuals typically view parts of the self differently: Some parts they judge more favourably, or see more clearly or as more important, than other parts (Pelham, 1995; Pelham & Swann, 1989). Indeed, just as individuals differ according to how high or low their self-esteem is, they also differ in the extent to which their self-esteem is stable or unstable. As a general rule, self-esteem is a trait that is stable from childhood through old age (Trzesniewski et al., 2003). Yet for some people in particular, self-esteem seems to fluctuate up and down in response to daily experiences—which makes them highly responsive to praise and overly sensitive to criticism (Baldwin & Sinclair, 1996; Kernis &Waschull, 1995; Schimel et al., 2001).

The Need for Self-Esteem

You and just about everyone else on the planet seem to have a need for self-esteem, as we all want to see ourselves in a positive light. This observation about human motivation is beyond dispute. But let's step back for a moment and ask, why? Why do we have this need for self-esteem?

At present, there are two social psychological answers to this question. One theory, proposed by Mark Leary and Roy Baumeister (2000), is that people are inherently social animals and that the desire for self-esteem is driven by this more primitive need to connect with others and gain their approval. In this way, our sense of self-esteem serves as a "sociometer," a rough indicator of how we're doing in the eyes of others. The threat of social rejection thus lowers self-esteem, which activates the need to regain approval and acceptance.

Alternatively, Jeff Greenberg, Sheldon Solomon, and Thomas Pyszczynski (1997) have proposed Terror Management Theory to help explain our need for self-esteem. According to this theory, we humans are biologically programmed for self-preservation. Yet we are conscious of—and terrified by—the inevitability of our own death. We cope with this deeply rooted fear by constructing and accepting cultural worldviews about how, why, and by whom Earth was created; explanations of the purpose of our existence; and a sense of history filled with heroes, villains, and momentous events. These worldviews provide meaning and purpose and a buffer against anxiety. In a series of

self-esteem
An affective component of the self, consisting of a person's positive and negative self-evaluations.

experiments, these investigators found that people react to graphic scenes of death, or to the thought of their own death, with intense defensiveness and anxiety. When given positive feedback on a test, however, which boosts their self-esteem, that reaction is muted.

In many ways, satisfying the need for self-esteem is critical to our entire outlook on life. People with positive self-images tend to be happy, healthy, productive, and successful. They are also confident, bringing to new challenges a winning and motivating attitude—which leads them to persist longer at difficult tasks, sleep better at night, maintain their independence in the face of peer pressure, and suffer fewer ulcers. In contrast, people with negative self-images tend to be more depressed, pessimistic about the future, and prone to failure. Lacking confidence, they bring to new tasks a losing attitude that traps them in a vicious, self-defeating cycle. Expecting to fail, and fearing the worst, they become anxious, exert less effort, and "tune out" on important challenges. People with low self-esteem don't trust their own positive self-appraisals (Josephs et al., 2003). And when they fail, they tend to blame themselves, which makes them feel even less competent (Brockner, 1983; Brown & Dutton, 1995). Low self-esteem may even be hazardous to your health. Some research suggests that becoming aware of one's own negative attributes adversely affects the activity of certain white blood cells in the immune system, thus compromising the body's capacity to ward off disease (Strauman et al., 1993; 2004).

Does high self-esteem ensure desirable life outcomes? This seemingly simple question is now the subject of debate. Jennifer Crocker and Lora Park (2004) argue that the process of pursuing self-esteem itself is costly. Specifically, they point to research showing that in trying hard to boost and maintain their self-esteem, people often become anxious, avoid activities that risk failure, neglect the needs of others, and suffer from stress-related health problems. Self-esteem has its benefits, they concede, but striving for it can also be costly. Ulrich Orth and others (2012), in an analysis of longitudinal data spanning four generations, conclude that self-esteem tends to peak at around age 50, and then declines as one ages, and, perhaps surprisingly, that self-esteem is more likely to be the cause of particular life outcomes, rather than the consequence. Challenging the conclusion that self-esteem is not worth striving for, William Swann and others (2007) note that although a person's overall, or *global*, sense of self-worth may not be predictive of positive life outcomes, people with specific domains of self-esteem benefit in more circumscribed ways. In other words, research suggests that individuals with high self-esteem specifically for public speaking, mathematics, or social situations will outperform those who have less self-confidence in the domains of public speaking, mathematics, and social situations, respectively.

Are There Gender and Race Differences?

Just as individuals differ in their self-esteem, so, too, do social and cultural groups. Think about it. If you were to administer a self-esteem test to thousands of people all over the world, would you find that some segments of the population score higher than others? Would you expect to see differences in the averages of men and women, blacks and whites, or inhabitants of different cultures? Believing that self-esteem promotes health, happiness, and success, and concerned that some groups are disadvantaged in this regard, researchers have indeed made these types of comparisons.

Are there gender differences in self-esteem? Over the years, a lot has been written in the popular press about the inflated but fragile "male ego," the low self-regard among adolescent girls and women, and the resulting gender-related "confidence gap" (Orenstein, 1994). Despite such claims, a study of 66 schoolchildren, ages 11 and 12 in Southwestern Ontario, found no difference in self-esteem levels between the boys and girls in its sample (Bosacki et al., 1997).

Researchers have also wondered if low self-esteem is a problem for members of stigmatized minority groups—historically, victims of prejudice and discrimination. Does membership in a minority group deflate one's sense of self-worth? Based on the combined results of studies involving more than half a million respondents, Bernadette Gray-Little and Adam Hafdahl (2000) reported that black children, adolescents, and adults consistently score higher—not lower—than their white counterparts on measures of self-esteem (see also Twenge & Crocker, 2002). Such counterintuitive findings have been dubbed the "puzzle of self-esteem" (Simmons, 1978). Some have suggested that perhaps Blacks—more than other minorities—are able to preserve their self-esteem in the face of adversity by attributing negative outcomes to the forces of discrimination and using this adversity to build a sense of group pride. In this regard, Twenge and Crocker (see ▶ Figure 3.5) found that self-esteem scores of black Americans, relative to those of white Americans, have risen over time—from the pre-civil rights days of the 1950s to the present. It also may be the case that one devalues any attribute upon which one's group does poorly, and instead focuses on those attributes upon which one's group excels; thus a stigmatized group protects its self-esteem (Verkuyten, 2005).

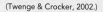

▶ **FIGURE 3.5**

Self-Esteem in U.S. Minorities

Through a meta-analysis, Twenge and Crocker (2002) found that African Americans score higher on self-esteem tests relative to whites, but that Hispanic American, Asian American, and Native American minorities score lower.

(Twenge & Crocker, 2002.)

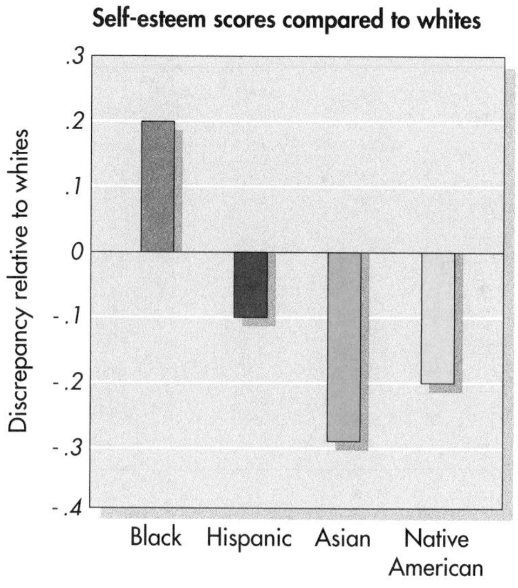

Culture and Self-Esteem

Variations in self-esteem have also been observed among people from different parts of the world. Earlier we saw that inhabitants of individualistic cultures tend to view themselves as distinct and autonomous, whereas those in collectivist cultures view the self as part of an interdependent social network. Do these different orientations have implications for self-esteem? Steven Heine and his colleagues (1999) believe that they do. Comparing the distribution of self-esteem scores in Canada and Japan, they found that whereas most Canadians' scores clustered in the high-end range, the majority of Japanese respondents scored in the centre of that same range.

Is the self-esteem of the Japanese truly less inflated than that of North Americans (a conclusion also suggested by their tendency to talk about themselves in critical, self-effacing terms)? Or do Japanese respondents, high in self-esteem, simply feel compelled to present themselves modestly to others (as a function of the collectivist need to "fit in" rather than "stand out")? To answer this question, Roman Tafarodi and others (2011) asked students at the University of Toronto and at two universities in Japan to complete measures of self-esteem. Instructions for completion of the measure included conditions whereby students were either warned against false modesty (assumed to be a Japanese trait) or warned against self-promotion (considered to be a Canadian trait). In contrast to participants who received standard instructions with the measure, Canadian students primed to avoid self-promotion were less likely to endorse statements measuring self-worth and efficacy, whereas Japanese students primed with anti-modesty instructions were more likely to agree with such statements. Thus, the researchers argue that differences in self-esteem scores generally found between the two groups could be directly related to an awareness of normative pressures to respond according to the dictates of the culture.

Given the possibility that awareness of social norms could influence scores on these types of measures, some researchers have tried to develop more indirect, subtle, "implicit" tests. In a timed word-association study, for example, Anthony Greenwald and Shelly Farnham (2000) found that despite their non-inflated scores on self-esteem tests, Asian Americans—just like their European American counterparts—were quicker to associate themselves with positive words such as *happy* and *sunshine* than with negative words such as *vomit* and *poison.* This suggests that people from individualist and collectivist cultures are similarly motivated to think highly of themselves—that the need for people to see themselves in a positive light is universal, or "pancultural" (Sedikides et al., 2003). The observed differences, they argue, stem from the fact that cultures influence *how* we seek to fulfill that need: Individualists present themselves as unique and self-confident, while collectivists present themselves as modest, equal members of a group. From this perspective, people are tactical in their self-enhancements, exhibiting self-praise or humility depending on what is desirable within their cultural surroundings (Lalwani et al., 2006; Sedikides et al., 2005).

Heine and his colleagues agree only in part with this interpretation of the research. They, too, argue that all people have a need for positive self-regard, wanting to become "good selves" within their own culture. They note, however, that in the effort to achieve this goal, Westerners and other individualists tend to use self-enhancement tactics to stand out, confirm, and express themselves, while East Asians and other collectivists tend to maintain face in order to fit in, improve the self, and adjust to the standards set by their groups. In short, the basic need for positive self-regard is universal but the specific drive toward self-enhancement is culturally ingrained (Heine, 2005; Heine & Hamamura, 2007).

Self-Discrepancy Theory

What determines how people feel about themselves? According to E. Tory Higgins (1989), our self-esteem is defined by the match or mismatch between how we see ourselves and how we want to see ourselves. To demonstrate, try the following exercise. On a blank sheet of paper, write down ten traits that describe the kind of person you think you *actually* are (smart? easygoing? sexy? excitable?). Next, list ten traits that describe the kind of person you think you *ought* to be, characteristics that would enable you to meet your sense of duty, obligation, and responsibility. Then make a list of traits that describe the kind of person you would like to be, an *ideal* that embodies your hopes, wishes, and dreams. If you follow these instructions, you should have three lists: your actual self, your ought self, and your ideal self.

Research has shown that these lists can be used to predict your self-esteem and your emotional well-being. The first list is your self-concept. The others represent your personal standards, or *self-guides.* To the extent that you fall short of these standards, you will have lowered self-esteem, negative emotion, and, in extreme cases, a serious affective disorder. The specific consequence depends on which self-guide you fail to achieve. If there's a discrepancy between your actual and ought selves, you will feel guilty, ashamed, and resentful. You might even suffer from excessive fears and anxiety-related disorders. If the mismatch is between your actual and ideal selves, you'll feel disappointed, frustrated, unfulfilled, and sad. In the worst-case scenario, you might even become depressed (Boldero & Francis, 2000; Higgins, 1999; Scott & O'Hara, 1993; Strauman, 1992). Our self-discrepancies may even set into motion a self-perpetuating process. Participating in a study of body images, women with high rather than low discrepancies between their actual and ideal selves were more likely to compare themselves with thin models in TV commercials, which further increased their body dissatisfaction and depression (Bessenoff, 2006).

It's clear that every one of us must cope with some degree of self-discrepancy. Nobody is perfect. Yet we do not all suffer from the emotional consequences. The reason, according to Higgins (1989), is that self-esteem depends on a number of factors. One is simply the amount of discrepancy. The more of it there is, the worse we feel. Another is the importance of the discrepancy to the self. The more important the domain in which we fall short, again, the worse we feel. A third factor is the extent to which we focus on our self-discrepancies. The more focused we are, the greater the harm. This last observation raises an important question: What causes us to be more or less focused on our personal shortcomings? For an answer, we turn to self-awareness theory.

"I have the true feeling of myself only when I am unbearably unhappy."

—Franz Kafka

The Self-Awareness "Trap"

If you carefully review your daily routine—classes, work, chores at home, leisure activities, social interactions, and meals—you will probably be surprised at how little time you actually spend thinking about yourself. In a study that illustrates this point, more than 100 people, ranging in age from 19 to 63, were equipped for a week with electronic beepers that sounded every two hours or so between 7:30 a.m. and 10:30 p.m. Each time the beepers went off, participants interrupted whatever they were doing, wrote down what they were thinking at that moment, and filled out a brief questionnaire. Out of 4700 recorded thoughts, only 8 percent were about the self. For the most part, attention was focused on work and other activities. In fact, when participants were thinking about themselves, they reported feeling relatively unhappy and wished they were doing something else (Csikszentmihalyi & Figurski, 1982).

Self-Focusing Situations The finding that people may be unhappy while they think about themselves is interesting, but what does it mean? Does self-reflection bring out our personal shortcomings the way staring into a mirror draws our gaze to every blemish on the face? Is self-awareness an unpleasant mental state from which we need to retreat?

Many years ago, Robert Wicklund and his colleagues theorized that the answer is yes (Duval & Wicklund, 1972; Wicklund, 1975; Silvia & Duval, 2001). According to their **self-awareness theory**, people are not usually self-focused, but certain situations predictably force us to turn inward and become the objects of our own attention. When we talk about ourselves, glance in a mirror, stand before an audience or camera, watch ourselves on videotape, or behave in a conspicuous manner, we enter into a state of heightened self-awareness that leads us naturally to compare our behaviour to some standard. This comparison often results in a negative discrepancy and a temporary reduction in self-esteem as we discover that we fall short. Thus, people often experience a negative mood state when placed in front of a mirror (Fejfar & Hoyle, 2000; Hass & Eisenstadt, 1990; Phillips & Silvia, 2005). Interestingly, Japanese people—already highly concerned about their public "face"—are unaffected by the added presence of a mirror (Heine et al., 2008).

In fact, the more self-focused people are in general, the more likely they are to find themselves in a bad mood (Flory et al., 2000) or depressed (Pyszczynski & Greenberg, 1987). People who are self-absorbed are also more likely to suffer from alcoholism, anxiety, and other clinical disorders (Ingram, 1990; Mor & Winquist, 2002).

Is there a solution? Self-awareness theory suggests two basic ways of coping with such discomfort: (1) "Shape up" by behaving in ways that reduce our self-discrepancies, or (2) "ship out" by withdrawing from self-awareness. According to Charles Carver and Michael Scheier (1981), the solution chosen depends on whether people think they can reduce their self-discrepancy and whether they're pleased with the progress they

self-awareness theory
The theory that self-focused attention leads people to notice self-discrepancies, thereby motivating either an escape from self-awareness or a change in behaviour.

make once they try (Duval et al., 1992). If so, they tend to match their behaviour to personal or societal standards; if not, they tune out, look for distractions, and turn attention away from the self. This process is depicted in ▶ Figure 3.6.

In general, research supports the prediction that when people are self-focused, they tend to behave in ways that are consistent either with their own personal values or with socially accepted ideals (Gibbons, 1990). Two interesting field studies illustrate this point. In one, Halloween trick-or-treaters—children wearing masks, costumes, and painted faces—were greeted at a researcher's door and left alone to help themselves from a bowl of candy. Although the children were asked to take only one piece, 34 percent violated the request. When a full-length mirror was placed behind the candy bowl, however, the number of violators dropped to 12 percent. Apparently, the mirror forced the children to become self-focused, leading them to behave in a way that was consistent with public standards of desirable conduct (Beaman et al., 1979). In a second study, conducted in England, customers at a lunch counter were trusted to pay for their coffee, tea, and milk by depositing money into an unsupervised "honesty box." Hanging on the wall behind the counter was a poster that featured a picture of flowers or a pair of eyes. By calculating the ratio of money deposited to drinks consumed, researchers observed that people paid nearly three times more money in the presence of the eyes (Bateson et al., 2006). Similar results were found for littering in a cafeteria; when the poster of the eyes was present, littering decreased by half as compared to when the flower poster was present (Ernest-Jones et al., 2011).

Self-awareness theory states that if a successful reduction of self-discrepancy seems unlikely, individuals will take a second route: escape from self-awareness. Roy Baumeister (1991) speculates that drug abuse, sexual masochism, spiritual ecstasy, binge eating, and even suicide all serve this escapist function. Even television may serve as a form of escape. In one study, Sophia Moskalenko and Steven Heine (2003) brought students into a laboratory and tested their actual-ideal self-discrepancies twice. Half watched a brief TV show on nature before filling out the second measure. In a second study, students were sent home with the questionnaire and instructed to fill it out either before or after watching TV. In both cases, those who watched TV had lower self-discrepancies on the second measure. In yet a third study, students who were told they had done poorly on an IQ test spent more time watching TV while waiting in the lab than those who were told they had succeeded. Perhaps TV and other forms of entertainment enable people to "watch their troubles away."

▶ FIGURE 3.6

The Causes and Effects of Self-Awareness

Self-awareness pressures people to reduce self-discrepancies either by matching their behaviour to personal or societal standards or by withdrawing from self-awareness.

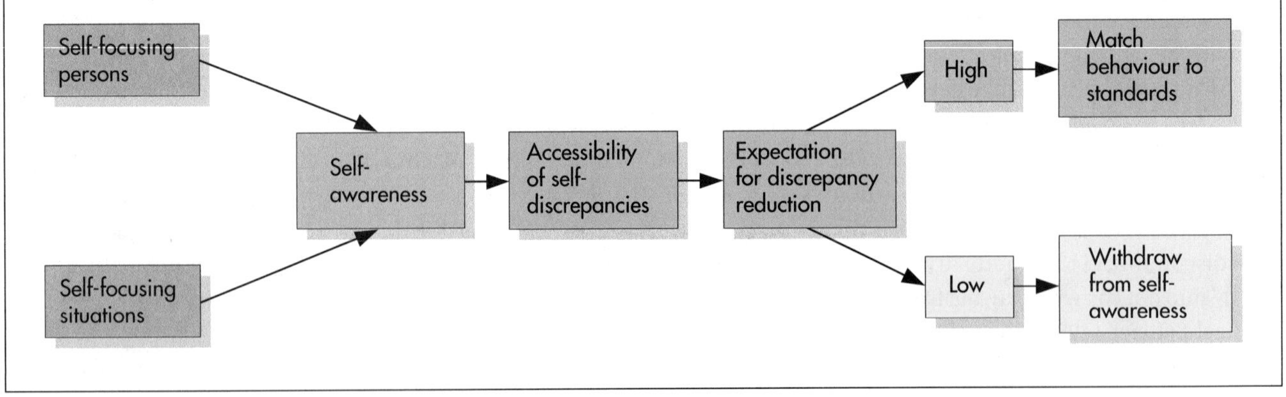

One particularly disturbing health implication concerns the use of alcohol. According to Jay Hull, people often drown their sorrows in a bottle as a way to escape the negative implications of self-awareness. To test this hypothesis, Hull and Richard Young (1983) administered what was supposed to be an IQ test to male participants and gave false feedback suggesting that they had either succeeded or failed. Supposedly as part of a separate study, those participants were then asked to taste and rate different wines. As they did so, experimenters kept track of how much they drank during a 15-minute tasting period. As predicted, participants who were prone to self-awareness drank more wine after failure than after success, presumably to dodge the blow to their self-esteem. Among participants not prone to self-awareness, there was no difference in alcohol consumption. These results come as no surprise. Indeed, many of us expect alcohol to grant this form of relief (Leigh & Stacy, 1993) and help us manage our emotional highs and lows (Cooper et al., 1995).

TABLE 3.1

How Self-Conscious Are You?

These sample items appear in the Self-Consciousness Scale. How would you describe yourself on the public and the private aspects of self-consciousness?

(Fenigstein et al., 1975.)

Items That Measure Private Self-Consciousness

- I'm always trying to figure myself out.
- I'm constantly examining my motives.
- I'm often the subject of my fantasies.
- I'm alert to changes in my mood.
- I'm aware of the way my mind works when I work on a problem.

Items That Measure Public Self-Consciousness

- I'm concerned about what other people think of me.
- I'm self-conscious about the way I look.
- I'm concerned about the way I present myself.
- I usually worry about making a good impression.
- One of the last things I do before leaving my house is look in the mirror.

Claude Steele and Robert Josephs (1990) believe that alcoholic intoxication provides more than just a means of tuning out on the self. By causing people to lose touch with reality and shed their inhibitions, it also evokes a state of "drunken self-inflation." In one study, for example, participants rated their actual and ideal selves on various traits—some important to self-esteem, others not important. After drinking either an 80-proof vodka cocktail or a harmless placebo, they re-rated themselves on the same traits. As measured by the perceived discrepancy between actual and ideal selves, participants who were drinking expressed inflated views of themselves on traits they considered important (Banaji & Steele, 1989).

Self-Focusing Persons Just as *situations* evoke a state of self-awareness, certain *individuals* are characteristically more self-focused than others. Research has revealed an important distinction between **private self-consciousness**—the tendency to introspect about our inner thoughts and feelings—and **public self-consciousness**—the tendency to focus on our outer public image (Buss, 1980; Fenigstein et al., 1975). ■ Table 3.1 presents a sample of items used to measure these traits.

Private and public self-consciousness are distinct traits. People who score high on a test of private self-consciousness tend to fill in incomplete sentences with first-person pronouns, are quick to make self-descriptive statements, and are acutely aware of changes in their internal bodily states (Mueller, 1982; Eichstaedt & Silvia, 2003). In contrast, those who score high on a measure of public self-consciousness are sensitive to the way they are viewed from an outsider's perspective. Thus, when people were asked to draw a capital letter E on their foreheads, 43 percent of those with high levels of public self-consciousness, compared with only 6 percent of those with low levels, oriented the E so that it was backward from their own standpoint but correct for an outside observer (Hass, 1984). People who are high in public self-consciousness are also particularly sensitive to the extent to which others share their opinions (Fenigstein & Abrams, 1993).

private self-consciousness
A personality characteristic of individuals who are introspective, often attending to their own inner states.

public self-consciousness
A personality characteristic of individuals who focus on themselves as social objects, as seen by others.

FIGURE 3.7

Revolving Images of Self

According to self-awareness theory, people try to meet either their own standards or standards held for them by others—depending, perhaps, on whether they are in a state of private or public self-consciousness. As Scheier and Carver (1983, p. 123) put it, there are "two sides of the self: one for you and one for me."

(Snyder et al., 1983.)

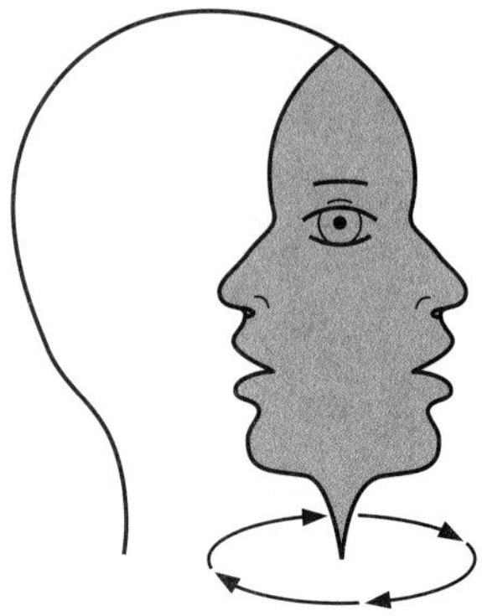

The distinction between private and public self-awareness has implications for the ways in which we reduce self-discrepancies. According to Higgins (1989), people are motivated to meet either their own standards or the standards held for them by significant others. If you're privately self-conscious, you listen to an inner voice and try to reduce discrepancies relative to your own standards; if you're publicly self-conscious, however, you try to match your behaviour to socially accepted norms. As illustrated in Figure 3.7, there may be "two sides of the self: one for you and one for me" (Scheier & Carver, 1983, p. 123).

Self-Regulation and Its Limits

To this point, we have seen that self-focused attention can motivate us to control our behaviour and strive toward personal or social ideals. To achieve these goals— which enables us to reduce the self-discrepancies that haunt us—we must engage in self-regulation, the processes by which we seek to control or alter our thoughts, feelings, behaviours, and urges (Carver & Scheier, 1998). From lifting ourselves out of bed in the morning to dieting, running the extra mile, smiling politely at people we really don't like, and working when we have more exciting things to do, the exercise of self-control is something we do all the time (Forgas et al., 2009).

Mark Muraven and Roy Baumeister (2000) have theorized that self-control is a limited inner resource that can temporarily be depleted by usage. There are two components to their theory. The first is that all self-control efforts draw from a single common reservoir. The second is that exercising self-control is like flexing a muscle: Once used, it becomes fatigued and loses strength, making it more difficult to re-exert self-control—at least for a while, until the resource is replenished. Deny yourself the ice cream sundae that tickles your sweet tooth and you'll find it more difficult to hold your temper when angered. Try to conceal your stage fright as you stand before an audience and you'll find it harder to resist the urge to watch TV when you should be studying.

Thus far, research supports this provocative hypothesis. In one study, Muraven and Baumeister (1998) had participants watch a brief clip from *Mondo Cane*, an upsetting film that shows scenes of sick and dying animals exposed to radioactive waste. Some of the participants were instructed to stifle their emotional responses to the clip, including their facial expressions; others were told to amplify or exaggerate their emotional responses; a third group received no special instructions. Both before and after the movie, self-control was measured by the length of time that participants were able to squeeze a handgrip exerciser without letting go. As predicted, those who had to inhibit or amplify their emotions during the film—but not those in the third group—lost their willpower in the handgrip task between the first time they tried it and the second (see Figure 3.8). Other studies have since confirmed the point: After people exert self-control in one task, their capacity for self-regulation is weakened (even if they were just changing their mindset)—causing them to talk too much, disclose too much, or brag too much in a later social situation (Hamilton et al., 2011; Vohs et al., 2005).

It appears that we can control ourselves just so much before self-regulation fatigue sets in, causing us to "lose it." What might this mean, then, for people who are constantly regulating their behaviour? To find out, Kathleen Vohs and Todd Heatherton (2000) showed a brief and dull documentary to individual female undergraduates, half of whom were chronic dieters. Placed in the viewing room—either within arm's reach (high temptation) or ten feet away (low temptation)—was a bowl filled with snacks that included candy, peanuts, and chips, that participants were free to sample. After watching the movie, they were taken to another room for an ice cream taste test and told they could eat as much as they wanted. The question is: How much ice cream did they consume? The researchers predicted that dieters seated within reach of the bowl would have to fight the hardest to avoid snacking—an act of self-control that would cost them later. The prediction was confirmed. As measured by the amount of ice cream consumed in the taste test, dieters in the high-temptation condition ate more ice cream than did all nondieters and dieters in the low-temptation situation. What's more, a second study showed that dieters who had to fight the urge in the high-temptation situation were later less persistent—and quicker to give up—on a set of impossible cognitive problems they were asked to solve.

New research suggests that self-regulation fatigue sets in because exerting self-control is physically taxing, as measured by the extent to which it consumes glucose, a vital source of bodily energy (e.g., Bauer & Baumeister, 2011). Across a range of experiments, Matthew Gailliot and others (2007) had participants engage in an act of self-control—such as suppressing a word, thought, or emotion—before and after which blood samples were taken. Consistently, they found that acts of self-control—relative to similar acts not requiring self-control—were followed by reduced blood glucose levels and a lessened capacity for additional self-control. What's more, these researchers were able to counteract these adverse effects merely by feeding participants sugared lemonade between tasks, which restored glucose to the bloodstream.

FIGURE 3.8

Self-Control as a Limited Inner Resource

Participants were shown an upsetting film and told to amplify or suppress their emotional responses to it (a third group received no self-control instruction). Before and afterward, self-control was measured by persistence at squeezing a handgrip exerciser. As shown, the two groups that had to control their emotions during the film—but not those in the third group—later lost their willpower on the handgrip.

(Muraven & Baumeister, 1998.)

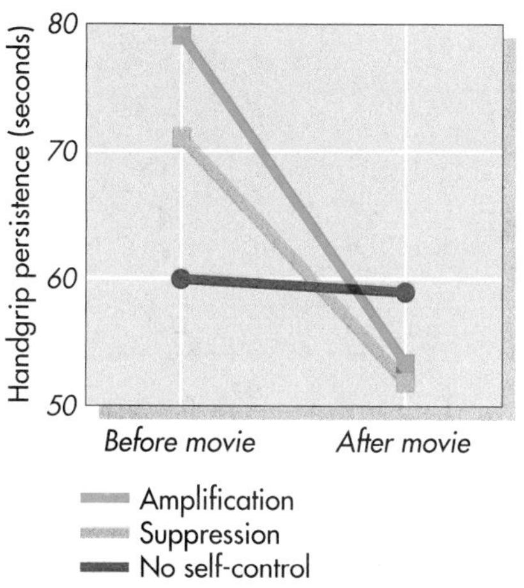

Is it possible to counteract self-regulation fatigue through psychological intervention alone, without the calories associated with glucose consumption? Brandon Schmeichel and Kathleen Vohs (2009) reasoned that people might be able to restore their capacity for self-control by stopping to mentally bolster or "affirm" their sense of who they are. To test this hypothesis, they asked participants to write a short story. To vary the exercise of self-control, some but not others were prohibited from using certain letters of the alphabet (try writing even a short paragraph without using the letters *a* or *n* and you will appreciate the discipline that is needed!). Afterward, all participants were administered a classic pain tolerance task that required them to soak one hand in a tub of circulating ice-cold water for as long as they could, until it was too painful to continue. Between the two tasks, "self-affirmation" participants were given a chance to express a core value by writing an essay about the one personal characteristic they find most important (such as family relations, friendships, creativity, or athletics). Others wrote about some less important characteristic. Can a small act of self-affirmation counteract the effects of self-regulation fatigue on cold tolerance? Yes. Among participants in the no-affirmation condition, the prior act of self-control sharply reduced their tolerance to cold pain from an average of 78 seconds to 27 seconds. Among those who were prompted to self-affirm, however, the adverse effect of the first self-control task on pain tolerance was erased.

Ironic Mental Processes

There's another possible downside to self-control that is often seen in sports when athletes become so self-focused under pressure that they stiffen up and "choke." While many athletes rise to the occasion, the pages of sports history are filled with stories of basketball players who lose their touch in the final minute of a championship game, or of tennis players who lose their serve, all when it matters most. "Choking" seems to be a paradoxical type of failure caused by thinking too much. When you learn a new motor activity, like how to throw a curve ball or land a jump, you must think through the

"The highest possible stage in moral culture is when we recognize that we ought to control our thoughts."

—Charles Darwin

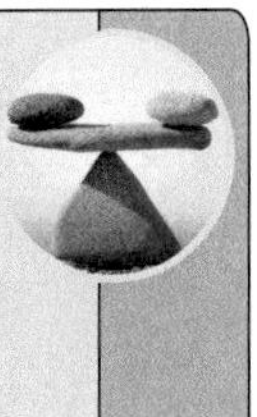

Sometimes the harder you try to control a thought, feeling, or behaviour, the less likely you are to succeed. TRUE.

mechanics in a slow and cautious manner. As you get better, however, your movements become automatic, so you do not have to think about timing, breathing, the position of your head and limbs, or the distribution of your weight. You relax and just do it. Unless trained to perform while self-focused, athletes under pressure often try their hardest not to fail, become self-conscious, and think too much—which disrupts the fluid and natural flow of their performance (Baumeister, 1984; Beilock & Carr, 2001; Lewis & Linder, 1997).

The paradoxical effects of attempted self-control are evident in other situations, too. Studying what he calls *ironic processes,* Daniel Wegner (1994) has found that, at times, the harder you try to inhibit a thought, feeling, or behaviour, the less likely you are to succeed. Try not to think about a white bear for the next 30 seconds, he finds, and that very image intrudes upon consciousness with remarkable frequency. Instruct the members of a jury to disregard inadmissible evidence, and the censored material is sure to pop to mind as they deliberate. Try not to worry about how long it's taking to fall asleep, and you'll stay awake. Try not to laugh in class, think about the chocolate cake in the fridge, or scratch the itch on your nose—well, you get the idea.

According to Wegner, every conscious effort at maintaining control is met by a concern about failing to do so. This concern automatically triggers an "ironic operating process" as the person, trying hard *not* to fail, searches his or her mind for the unwanted thought. The ironic process will not necessarily prevail, says Wegner. Sometimes we can put the imaginary white bear out of mind. But if the person is cognitively busy, distracted, tired, hurried, or under stress, then the ironic process, because it "just happens," will prevail over the intentional process, which requires conscious attention and effort. Thus, Wegner (1997) notes that "any attempt at mental control contains the seeds of its own undoing" (p. 148).

Ironic processes have now been observed in a wide range of behaviours. In an intriguing study of this effect on the control of motor behaviour, Wegner and his colleagues (1998) had participants hold a pendulum (a crystalline pendant suspended from a nylon fishing line) over the centre of two intersecting axes on a glass grid, which formed a +. Some participants were instructed simply to keep the pendulum steady, while others were more specifically told not to allow it to swing back and forth along the horizontal axis. Try this yourself, and you'll see that it's not easy to prevent all movement. In this experiment, however, the pendulum was more likely to swing horizontally when this direction was specifically forbidden. To further examine the role of mental distraction, the researchers instructed some participants to count backward from a thousand by sevens while controlling the pendulum. In this situation, the ironic effect was even greater. Among those who specifically tried to prevent horizontal movement but could not concentrate fully on the task, the pendulum swayed freely back and forth—in the forbidden direction (see ▶ Figure 3.9). It may seem both comic and tragic, but at times our efforts at self-control backfire, thwarting even the best of intentions.

▶ FIGURE 3.9

Ironic Effects of Mental Control

In this study, participants tried to hold a pendulum motionless over a grid. As illustrated in the tracings shown here, they were better at the task when simply instructed to keep the pendulum steady (*a*) than when specifically told to prevent horizontal movement (*c*). Among participants who were mentally distracted during the task, this ironic effect was even greater (*b* and *d*).

(Wegner et al., 1998.)

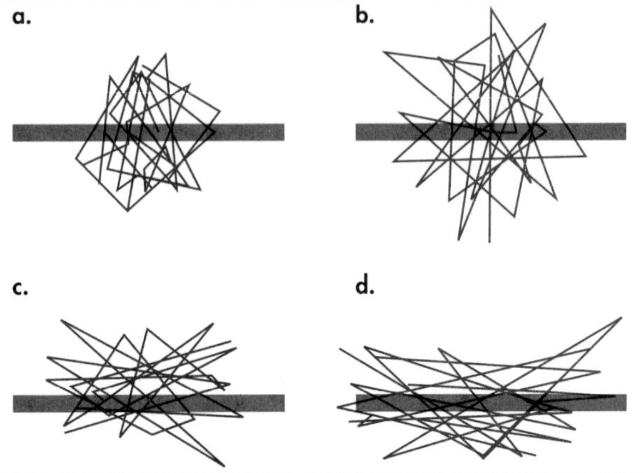

REUTERS/Leonhard Foeger (CANADA)

MCT via Getty Images

Why do some athletes choke under pressure and others rise to the occasion? While Manuel Osborne-Paradis was widely expected to win Canada's first gold medal in the men's downhill at the 2010 Winter Olympics, he instead finished a disappointing seventeenth. In contrast, Joanie Rochette overcame the heartbreaking death of her mother just two days before the start of the figure skating competition, and took home a bronze medal.

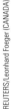

Mechanisms of Self-Enhancement

We have seen that self-awareness can create discomfort and lower self-esteem by focusing attention on discrepancies. We have seen that people often avoid focusing on themselves and turn away from unpleasant truths, but that such avoidance is not always possible. And we have seen that efforts at self-regulation often fail and sometimes even backfire. How, then, does the average person cope with his or her faults, inadequacies, and uncertain future?

In Western cultures, most people think highly of themselves most of the time. Consistently, research has shown that participants see positive traits as more self-descriptive than negative ones, rate themselves more highly than they rate others, rate themselves more highly than they are rated by others, exaggerate their control over life events, and predict that they have a bright future (Sedikides & Gregg, 2008; Taylor, 1989). Research shows that people overrate their effectiveness as speakers to an audience (Keysar & Henly, 2002), overestimate their contributions to a group and the extent to which they would be missed if absent (Savitsky et al., 2003), and selectively recall positive feedback about themselves while neglecting the negative (Green et al., 2008). People also overestimate their intellectual and social abilities across a wide range of domains. What's particularly interesting about this tendency is that those who are least competent are the most likely to overrate their performance. In a series of studies, Justin Kruger and David Dunning (1999) found that American college students with the lowest scores on tests of logic, grammar, and humour were the ones who most grossly overestimated their own abilities (on average, their scores were in the lowest 12 percent among peers, yet they estimated themselves to be in the 62nd percentile). These investigators also found that when the low-scorers were trained to be more competent in these areas, they became more realistic in their self-assessments. Ignorance, as they say, is bliss.

"We don't see things as they are, we see them as we are."
—Anaïs Nin

Other research, too, shows that people tend to exhibit **implicit egotism**, a nonconscious and subtle form of self-enhancement. This is well illustrated in the finding that people rate the letters in their name more favourably than other letters of the alphabet (Hoorens & Nuttin, 1993). In an article entitled "Why Susie Sells Seashells by the Seashore," Brett Pelham and his colleagues (2002) argue that we form positive associations to the sight and sound of our own name and thus are drawn to other people, places, and entities that share this most personal aspect of "self." In a thought-provoking series of studies, these researchers examined several important life choices

implicit egotism
A nonconscious form of self-enhancement.

that we make and found that people exhibit small but statistically detectable preferences for things that contain the letters of their own first or last name. For example, men and women are more likely than would be predicted by chance to live in places (Michelle in Manitoba, George in Guelph), attend schools (Wendy from the University of Western Ontario), and choose careers (Dennis and Denise as dentists) whose names resemble their own. Indeed, marriage records found on various genealogical websites reveal that people are disproportionately likely to marry others with first or last names that resemble their own (Jones et al., 2004). In a subtle but remarkable way, we unconsciously seek out reflections of the self in our surroundings.

This recent research on implicit egotism shows that we tend to hold ourselves in high regard. And it's not that we consciously or openly flatter ourselves. The response is more like a reflex. Indeed, when research participants are busy or distracted as they make self-ratings, their judgments are quicker and even more favourable (Hixon & Swann, 1993; Paulhus et al., 1989). We can't all be perfect, nor can we all be better than average. So what supports this common illusion? In this section, we examine four methods that people use to rationalize or otherwise enhance their self-esteem: self-serving cognitions, self-handicapping, basking in the glory of others, and downward social comparisons.

People tend to be overly optimistic about their future. TRUE.

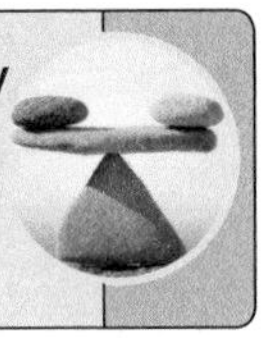

Self-Serving Cognitions When students receive exam grades, those who do well take credit for their success; those who do poorly complain about the instructor and the test questions. When researchers have articles accepted for publication, they credit the quality of their work; when articles are rejected, they blame the editor and reviewers. When gamblers win a bet, they see themselves as skillful; when they lose, they moan and groan about fluke events that transformed near victory into defeat. Whether people are high or low in self-esteem, explain their outcomes publicly or in private, and try to be honest or to make a good impression, there is bias. Across a range of cultures, people tend to take credit for success and to distance themselves from failure (Mezulis et al., 2004; Schlenker et al., 1990), while seeing themselves as objective, not biased (Pronin, 2007).

Lara Solt/Dallas Morning News/Corbis

In casinos, racetracks, and lotteries, gamblers lose billions of dollars a year. This self-defeating behaviour persists in part because people exaggerate their control over random events. For example, many slot-machine addicts mistakenly think that they can find "hot" machines that have not recently surrendered a jackpot.

Most of us are also unrealistically optimistic. University students who were asked to predict their own future compared with that of the average person believed that they would graduate higher in their class, get a better job, have a happier marriage, and bear a gifted child. They also believed they were less likely to get fired or divorced, have a car accident, become depressed, be victimized by crime, or suffer from a heart attack (Weinstein, 1980). In sports, politics, health, and social issues, people exhibit an optimistic bias about their own future, judging desirable events as more likely to occur than undesirable events (Lench, 2009; Massey et al., 2011).

Obviously, the future is not always bright, so what supports this unwavering optimism? People seem to harbour illusions of control, overestimating the extent to which they can influence personal outcomes that are not, in fact, within their power to control (Langer, 1975; Thompson, 1999). In a series of classic experiments on the illusion of control, Ellen Langer (1975) found that undergraduates bet more money in a chance game of high-card when their opponent seemed nervous rather than confident, and were more reluctant to sell a lottery ticket if they'd chosen the number themselves than if it was assigned.

Self-Handicapping "My dog ate my homework." "I had a flat tire." "My alarm didn't go off." "My computer crashed." "I had a bad headache." "The referee blew the call." On occasion, people make excuses for their past performance. Sometimes they even come up with excuses in anticipation of future performance. Particularly when people are afraid that they might fail in an important situation, they use illness, shyness, anxiety, pain, trauma, and other complaints as excuses (Kowalski, 1996; Snyder & Higgins, 1988). The reason people do this is simple: By admitting to a limited physical or mental weakness, they can shield themselves from what could be the most shattering implication of failure—a lack of ability.

One form of excuse-making that many of us can relate to is *procrastination*—a purposive delay in starting or completing a task that is due at a particular time (Ferrari et al., 1995). Some people procrastinate chronically, while others do so only in certain situations. There are many reasons why someone might put off what needs to get done—whether it's studying for a test, shopping for Christmas, or preparing for the April 30 tax deadline. According to Joseph Ferrari (1998), one "benefit" of procrastinating is that it helps to provide an excuse for possible failure.

Making verbal excuses is one way to cope with the threatening implications of failure. Under certain conditions, this strategy is taken one step further: Sometimes people actually sabotage their own performance. It seems like the ultimate paradox, but there are times when we purposely set *ourselves* up for failure in order to preserve our precious self-esteem. First described by Stephen Berglas and Edward Jones (1978), **self-handicapping** refers to actions people take to handicap their own performance in order to build an excuse for anticipated failure. To demonstrate, Berglas and Jones recruited students for an experiment supposedly concerning the effects of drugs on intellectual performance. All the participants worked on a 20-item test of analogies and were told that they had done well, after which they expected to work on a second, similar test. For one group, the problems in the first test were relatively easy, leading participants to expect more success in the second test; for a second group, the problems were insoluble, leaving participants confused about their initial success and worried about possible failure. Before seeing or taking the second test, participants were given a choice of two drugs: Actavil, which was supposed to improve performance, and Pandocrin, which was supposed to impair it.

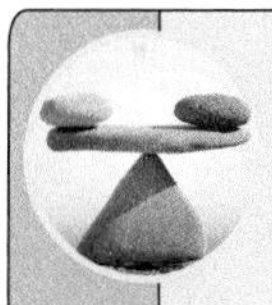

People often sabotage their own performance in order to protect their self-esteem. TRUE.

Although no drugs were actually administered, most participants who were confident about the upcoming test selected the Actavil. In contrast, males—but not females—who feared the outcome of the second test chose the Pandocrin. By handicapping themselves, these men set up a convenient excuse for failure—an excuse, we should add, that may have been intended more for the experimenter's benefit than for the benefit of the participants themselves. Indeed, a follow-up study showed that although self-handicapping occurs when the experimenter witnesses the participants' drug choice, it is reduced when the experimenter is not present while that choice is being made (Kolditz & Arkin, 1982).

Some people use self-handicapping as a defence more than others do (Rhodewalt, 1990), and there are different ways to use it. For example, men often handicap themselves by taking drugs (Higgins & Harris, 1988) or neglecting to practice (Hirt et al., 1991), while women tend to report stress and physical symptoms (Smith et al., 1983). Another tactic is to set one's goals too high, as perfectionists like to do, which sets up failure—but not for a lack of ability (Hewitt et al., 2003; Schultheiss & Brunstein, 2000). Still another paradoxical tactic used to reduce performance pressure is to play down our own ability, lower expectations, and predict for all to hear that we

self-handicapping
Behaviours designed to sabotage one's own performance in order to provide a subsequent excuse for failure.

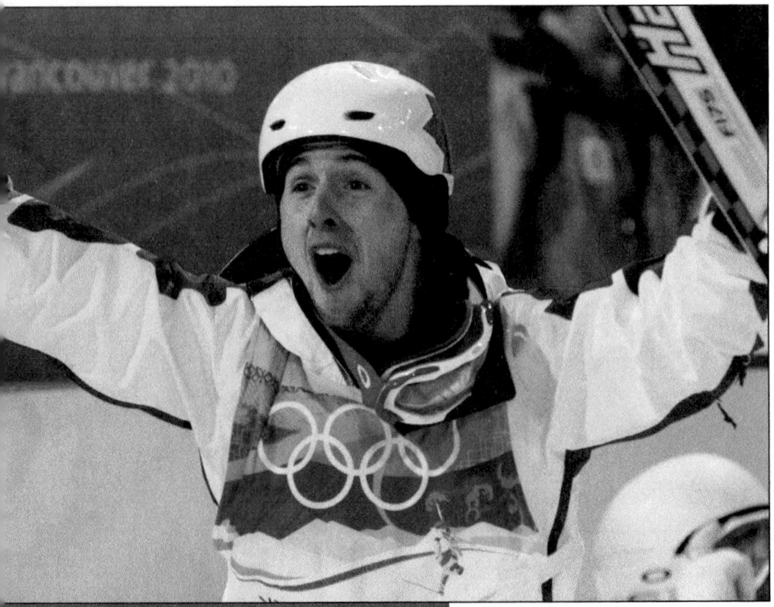

COC/Mike Ridewood

In 2010, freestyle skier Alexandre Bilodeau became the first Canadian athlete to win a gold medal at a Canadian Olympics. When Canadians won more gold medals than any other country, sports fans celebrated across the country. And why not? "We" won!

will fail—a self-presentation strategy known as "sandbagging" (Gibson & Sachau, 2000). People also differ in their reasons for self-handicapping. Dianne Tice (1991) found that people who are low in self-esteem use self-handicapping to set up a defensive, face-saving excuse in case they fail, while those who are high in self-esteem use it as an opportunity to claim extra credit if they succeed.

Whatever the tactics and whatever the goal, self-handicapping appears to be an ingenious strategy: With the odds seemingly stacked against us, the self is insulated from failure and enhanced by success. By easing the pressure to succeed, self-handicapping might even enable us to enjoy what we're doing without worrying so much about how well we do it (Deppe & Harackiewicz, 1996). Of course, this strategy is not without a cost. Sabotaging ourselves—by not practicing, or by drinking too much, using drugs, faking illness, or setting goals too high—objectively increases the risk of failure. What's worse, it does not exactly endear us to others. Frederick Rhodewalt and his colleagues (1995) found that participants did not like their partners in an experiment when they thought that these partners had self-handicapped by claiming they did not care, were anxious, or were medically impaired. Women are particularly suspicious and critical of people who self-handicap (Hirt et al., 2003).

Basking in the Glory of Others To some extent, your self-esteem is influenced by individuals and groups with whom you identify. According to Robert Cialdini and his colleagues (1976), people often **bask in reflected glory (BIRG)** by showing off their connections to successful others. Cialdini's team first observed BIRGing on the university campuses of Arizona State, Louisiana State, Notre Dame, Michigan, Pittsburgh, Ohio State, and Southern California. On the Monday mornings after football games, they counted the number of school sweatshirts worn on campus and found that more of them were worn if the team had won its game on the previous Saturday. In fact, the larger the margin of victory, the more school shirts were counted.

To evaluate the effects of self-esteem on BIRGing, Cialdini gave students a general-knowledge test and rigged the results so half would succeed and half would fail. The students were then asked to describe in their own words the outcome of a recent football game. In these descriptions, students who thought they had just failed a test were more likely than those who thought they had succeeded to share in their team's victory by exclaiming that "*we* won" and to distance themselves from defeat by lamenting how "*they* lost." In another study, participants coming off a recent failure were quick to point out that they had the same birth date as someone known to be successful—thus BIRGing by a merely coincidental association (Cialdini & De Nicholas, 1989).

If self-esteem is influenced by our links to others, how do we cope with friends, family members, teammates, and co-workers of low status? Again, consider sports fans, an interesting breed. As loudly as they cheer in victory, they often turn and jeer their teams in defeat. This behaviour seems fickle, but it is consistent with the notion that people derive part of their self-esteem from associations with others. In one study, participants took part in a problem-solving team that then succeeded, failed, or received no feedback about its performance. Participants were later offered a chance to take home a team badge. In the success and no-feedback groups, 68 and 50 percent, respectively, took badges; in the failure group, only 9 percent did (Snyder et al., 1986).

bask in reflected glory (BIRG) To increase self-esteem by associating with others who are successful.

It seems that the tendency to bask in reflected glory is matched by an equally powerful tendency to CORF—that is, to "cut off reflected failure."

Additional research confirms that the failures of others with whom we identify can influence our own sense of well-being. In one study, Edward Hirt and his colleagues (1992) found that avid sports fans temporarily lost faith in their own mental and social abilities after a favourite team suffered defeat. Reflected failure may even have physiological effects on the body. Paul Bernhardt and others (1998) took saliva samples from male students before and after they watched a basketball or soccer game between their favourite team and an archrival. By measuring changes in testosterone levels after the game, these investigators found that men who witnessed their teams in defeat had lowered levels of testosterone, the male sex hormone, compared to those who had watched their team win.

Downward Social Comparisons Earlier, we discussed Festinger's (1954) theory that people evaluate themselves by social comparison with similar others. But let's contemplate the *implications*. If the people around us achieve more than we do, what does that do to our self-esteem? Perhaps adults who shy away from class reunions in order to avoid having to compare themselves with former classmates are acting out an answer to that question.

Festinger fully realized that people don't always seek out objective information and that social comparisons are sometimes made in self-defence. When a person's self-esteem is at stake, he or she often benefits from making **downward social comparisons** with others who are less successful, less happy, or less fortunate (Hakmiller, 1966; Wills, 1981; Wood, 1989). Research shows that people who suffer some form of setback or failure adjust their social comparisons in a downward direction (Gibbons et al., 2002)—and these comparisons have an uplifting effect on their mood and on their outlook for the future (Aspinwall & Taylor, 1993; Gibbons & McCoy, 1991).

Although Festinger never addressed the issue, Anne Wilson and Michael Ross (2000) at the University of Waterloo note that in addition to making social comparisons between ourselves and similar others, we make *temporal* comparisons between our past and present selves. In one study, these investigators had students describe themselves; in another, they analyzed the autobiographical accounts of celebrities appearing in popular magazines. In both cases, they counted the number of times the self-descriptions contained references to past selves, to future selves, and to others. The result: People made more comparisons to their own past selves than to others, and most of these temporal comparisons were favourable. Other research has confirmed the basic point. Keenly aware of how "I'm better today than when I was younger," people use downward temporal comparisons the way they use downward social comparisons as a means of self-enhancement (Zell & Alicke, 2010).

Whether people make upward or downward social comparisons can have striking implications for health-related issues. When victimized by tragic life events (perhaps a crime, an accident, a disease, or the death of a loved one) people like to *affiliate* with others in the same predicament who are adjusting well, role models who offer hope and guidance. But they tend to *compare* themselves with others who are worse off, a form of downward social comparison (Taylor & Lobel, 1989). Clearly, it helps to know that life could be worse, which is why most cancer patients compare themselves with others in the same predicament but who are adjusting less well than they are. In a study of 312 women who had early-stage breast cancer and were in peer support groups, Laura Bogart and Vicki Helgeson (2000) had the patients report every week for seven weeks on instances in which they talked to, heard about, or thought about another patient. They found that 53 percent of all the social comparisons made

downward social comparison
The defensive tendency to compare ourselves with others who are worse off than we are.

were downward, to others who were worse off, while only 12 percent were upward, to others who were better off. (The remainder were "lateral" comparisons to similar or dissimilar others.) Bogart and Helgeson also found that the more often patients made these social comparisons, the better they felt.

Interviews of women with breast cancer tell the story. One woman who had only a lump removed wondered, "How awful it must be for women who have had a full mastectomy." An older woman who had a mastectomy said, "The people I really feel sorry for are these young gals. To lose a breast when you're so young must be awful." Yet a young mastectomy patient derived comfort from the fact that "if I hadn't been married, this thing would have really gotten to me" (Taylor, 1989, p. 171). As these quotes poignantly illustrate, there's always someone else with whom we can favourably compare—and this downward comparison makes us feel better (VanderZee et al., 1996).

Unfortunately, it's not always possible to defend the self via downward comparison. Think about it. When a sibling, spouse, or close friend has more success than you do, what happens to your self-esteem? Abraham Tesser (1988) predicted two possible reactions. On the one hand, you might feel proud of your association with this successful other, as in the process of basking in reflected glory. If you've ever bragged about the achievements of a loved one as if they were your own, you know how "reflection" can bolster self-esteem. On the other hand, you may feel overshadowed by the success of this other person and experience *social comparison jealousy*—a mixture of emotions that include resentment, envy, and a drop in self-esteem. According to Tesser, the key to whether one feels the pleasure of reflection or the pain of jealousy is whether the other person's success is self-relevant. When close friends surpass us in ways that are vital to our self-concepts, we become jealous and distance ourselves from them in order to keep up our own self-esteem. When intimate others surpass us in ways that are not important, however, we take pride in their triumphs through a process of reflection (Tesser & Collins, 1988; Tesser et al., 1989).

Personal and cultural factors may also influence the way people react to the success of others. For some people—as in those from collectivist cultures, whose concept of self is expanded to include friends, relatives, co-workers, classmates, and others with whom they identify—the success of another may bolster, not threaten, self-esteem. To test this hypothesis, Wendi Gardner and her colleagues (2002) brought pairs of friends into the laboratory together for a problem-solving task. They found that when they led the friends to think in collectivist terms, each derived pleasure, not jealousy and threat, from the other's greater success.

Are Positive Illusions Adaptive?

Psychologists used to maintain that an accurate perception of reality was vital to mental health. In recent years, however, this view has been challenged by research on the mechanisms of self-defence. Consistently, as we have seen, people preserve their self-esteem by deluding themselves and others with biased cognitions, self-handicapping, BIRGing, and downward comparisons. Are these strategies a sign of health and well-being, or are they symptoms of disorder?

When Shelley Taylor and Jonathon Brown (1988) reviewed the relevant research, they found that individuals who are depressed or low in self-esteem actually have more realistic views of themselves than do most others who are better adjusted. Their self-appraisals are more likely to match appraisals of them made by neutral observers; they make fewer self-serving attributions to account for success and failure; they are less likely to exaggerate their control over uncontrollable events; and they make more balanced predictions about their future. Based on these results, Taylor and Brown reached the provocative conclusion that positive illusions promote happiness, the desire to care for others, and the ability to engage in productive work—hallmark attributes of mental health: "These illusions help make each individual's world a warmer and more active and beneficent place in which to live" (p. 205). Research involving people under stress—such as men infected with HIV—shows that perceived control, optimism, and other positive illusions are "health-protective" psychological resources that help people cope with adversity (Taylor et al., 2000). As a result, people with high self-esteem appear better adjusted in personality tests and in interviews that are rated by friends, strangers, and mental health professionals (Taylor et al., 2003).

Not everyone agrees with the notion that it is adaptive in the long run to wear rose-coloured lenses. Roy Baumeister and Steven Scher (1988) warned that positive illusions can give rise to chronic patterns of self-defeating behaviour, as when people escape from self-awareness through alcohol and other drugs, self-handicap themselves into failure and underachievement, deny health-related problems until it's too late for treatment, and rely on the illusion of control to protect them from the tender mercies of the gambling casino. From an interpersonal standpoint, C. Randall Colvin and others (1995) found that people with inflated rather than realistic views of themselves were rated less favourably on certain dimensions by their own friends. In Baumeister and Scher's studies, self-enhancing men were seen as boastful, condescending, hostile, and less considerate of others; self-enhancing women were seen as more hostile, more defensive and sensitive to criticism, more likely to overreact to minor setbacks, and less well liked. People with inflated self-images may make a good first impression on others, but they are liked less and less as time wears on (Paulhus, 1998).

In a study that illustrates this possible dark side of high self-esteem, Todd Heatherton and Kathleen Vohs (2000) administered a standard self-esteem test to pairs of unacquainted university students and then brought them together for a brief conversation. Just before meeting, one student within each pair took a "Remote Associates Test," which involved finding one word that connects sets of three seemingly unrelated words (for example, *lick, sprinkle,* and *mines* were linked by the word *salt*). For half of these target students, the test was pitched as experimental and the problems given to them were easy to solve. Others were told that the test measured achievement potential and were given very difficult problems— leading them to perform, supposedly, worse than average. Did this ego-threatening feedback affect the students' behaviour—and the impressions they made on their interaction partners? Look at ▶ Figure 3.10 and you'll see that in the no-ego-threat group, the high and low self-esteem students were equally well liked. In the ego-threat situation, however, students with high self-esteem became less likeable; in fact, they were rated by their partners as rude, unfriendly, and arrogant.

Realism or illusion, which orientation is more adaptive? As social psychologists debate the short-term and long-term effects of positive illusions, it's clear that there is no simple answer (Kim & Chiu, 2011). For now, the picture that has emerged is this: People who harbour positive illusions of themselves are likely to enjoy the benefits and achievements of high self-esteem. But these same individuals may pay a price in other ways—as in their relations with others. So what are we to conclude? Do positive illusions motivate personal achievement but

▶ FIGURE 3.10

The Dark Side of High Self-Esteem

University students who were high or low in self-esteem were given ego-threatening or nonthreatening feedback about their intelligence before interacting with a fellow student. As shown, the high and low self-esteem students in the no-threat group were liked equally by their partners (left). In the ego-threat group, however, the high self-esteem students were liked less than those with lower self-esteem (right). It seems that high self-esteem people who feel threatened become boastful and abrasive.

(Heatherton & Vohs, 2000.)

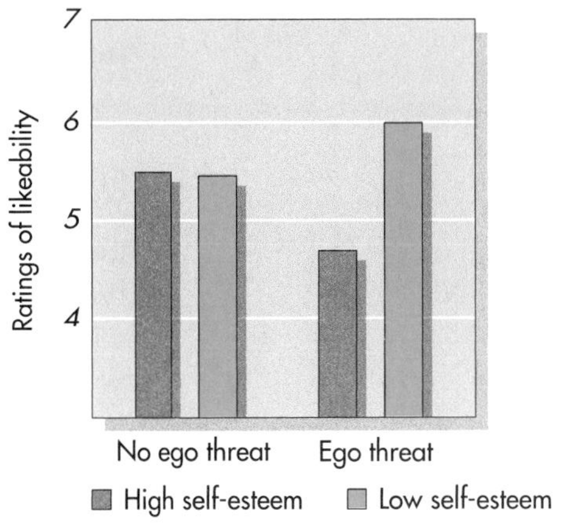

alienate us socially from others? Is it adaptive to see oneself in slightly inflated terms, but maladaptive to take a view that is too biased? It will be interesting to see how this thorny debate is resolved in the years to come.

Self-Presentation

The human quest for self-knowledge and self-esteem tells us about the inner self. The portrait is not complete, however, until we paint in the outermost layer, the behavioural expression of the social self. Most people are acutely concerned about the image they present to others. The fashion industry, diet centres, cosmetic surgeries designed to reshape everything from eyelids to breasts, and the endless search for miracle drugs that grow hair, remove hair, whiten teeth, freshen breath, and smooth out wrinkles, all exploit our preoccupation with physical appearance. Similarly, we are concerned about the impressions we convey through our public behaviour, not only in person, but on social networking sites such as Facebook. What, as they say, will the neighbours think?

Thomas Gilovich and others (2000) have found that people are so self-conscious in public settings that they are often subject to the *spotlight effect,* a tendency to believe that the social spotlight shines more brightly on them than it really does. In one set of studies, participants were asked to wear a T-shirt with a flattering or embarrassing image into a room full of strangers, after which they estimated how many of those strangers would be able to identify the image. Demonstrating that people self-consciously feel as if all eyes are upon them, the T-shirted participants overestimated by 23–40 percent the number of observers who had noticed and could recall what they were wearing. Not only do we overestimate the likelihood that other people will even notice a change in our appearance, when people commit a public social blunder, they later overestimate the negative impact of their behaviour on those who had observed them (Lawson, 2010; Savitsky et al., 2001).

In *As You Like It,* William Shakespeare wrote, "All the world's a stage, and all the men and women merely players." This insight was first put into social science terms by sociologist Erving Goffman (1959), who argued that life is like a theatre and that each of us acts out certain *lines,* as if from a script. Most important, said Goffman, is that each of us assumes a certain *face,* or social identity, that others politely help us to maintain. Inspired by Goffman's theory, social psychologists study **self-presentation**: the process by which we try to shape what others think of us and what we think of ourselves (Schlenker, 2003). An act of self-presentation may take many different forms. It may be conscious or unconscious, accurate or misleading, intended for an external audience or for ourselves. In this section, we look at the various goals of self-presentation and the ways in which people try to achieve these goals.

The Two Faces of Self-Presentation

There are basically two types of self-presentation, each serving a different motive. *Strategic self-presentation* consists of our efforts to shape others' impressions in specific ways in order to gain influence, power, sympathy, or approval. Prominent examples of strategic self-presentation are everywhere: in personal ads, on Internet message boards, in political campaign promises, in defendants' appeals to the jury. The specific goals include the desire to be seen as likeable, competent, moral, dangerous, or helpless. Whatever the goal may be, people find it less effortful to present themselves in ways that are accurate rather than contrived (Vohs et al., 2005).

self-presentation
Strategies people use to shape what others think of them.

To illustrate this point, Beth Pontari and Barry Schlenker (2000) instructed research participants who were introverted or extroverted to present themselves to a job interviewer in a way that was consistent or inconsistent with their true personality. Without distraction, all participants successfully presented themselves as introverted or extroverted, depending on the task they were given. But could they present themselves as needed if, during the interview, they also had to keep an eight-digit number in mind for a memorization test? In this situation, cognitively busy participants self-presented successfully when asked to convey their true personalities but not when asked to portray themselves in a way that was out of character.

The specific identities that people try to present vary from one person and situation to another. There are, however, two strategic self-presentation goals that are very common. The first is *ingratiation,* a term used to describe acts that are motivated by the desire to "get along" with others and be liked. The other is *self-promotion,* a term used to describe acts that are motivated by a desire to "get ahead" and gain respect for one's competence (Arkin, 1981; Jones & Pittman, 1982).

On the surface, it seems easy to achieve these goals. When people want to be liked, they put their best foot forward, smile a lot, nod their heads, express agreement, and, if necessary, use favours, compliments, and flattery. When people want to be admired for their competence, they try to impress others by talking about themselves and immodestly showing off their status, knowledge, and exploits. In both cases, there are tradeoffs. As the term *brown-nosing* all too graphically suggests, ingratiation tactics need to be subtle or else they will backfire (Jones, 1964). People also do not like those who relentlessly trumpet and brag about their own achievements (Godfrey et al., 1986) or who exhibit a "slimy" pattern of being friendly to their superiors but not to subordinates (Vonk, 1998).

Self-presentation may give rise to other problems as well. In a provocative article entitled "Self-Presentation Can Be Hazardous to Your Health," Mark Leary and his colleagues (1994) reviewed evidence suggesting that the need to project a favourable public image can lure us into unsafe patterns of behaviour. For example, self-presentation concerns can increase the risk of AIDS (when men are too embarrassed to buy condoms and talk openly with their sex partners), skin cancer (when people bake under the sun to get an attractive tan), eating disorders (when women over-diet or use amphetamines, laxatives, and forced vomiting to stay thin), drug abuse (when teenagers smoke, drink, and use drugs to impress their peers), and accidental injury (when young men drive recklessly to appear brave and fearless to others).

"Great-looking tie!"

Ingratiation is a strategy often used to curry favour.

The second self-presentation motive is *self-verification*: the desire to have others perceive us as we truly perceive ourselves. According to William Swann (1987), people are highly motivated to verify their existing self-concept in the eyes of others. Swann and his colleagues have gathered a great deal of evidence for this hypothesis—and have found, for example, that people selectively elicit, recall, and accept personality feedback that confirms their self-conceptions. In fact, people sometimes bend over backward to correct others whose impressions are positive but mistaken. In one study, participants interacted with a confederate who later said that they seemed dominant or submissive. When the comment was consistent with the participant's self-concept, it was accepted at face value. Yet when it was inconsistent, participants went out of their way to prove the confederate wrong: Those who perceived themselves as dominant but were labelled submissive later behaved more assertively than usual; those who viewed themselves as submissive but were labelled dominant subsequently became even more docile (Swann & Hill, 1982).

Self-verification seems desirable, but wait: Do people who have a negative self-concept want others to share that impression? Nobody is perfect, and everyone has some faults. But do we really want to verify these faults in the eyes of others? Do those of us who feel painfully shy, socially awkward, or insecure about an ability want others to see these weaknesses? Or would we prefer to present ourselves as bold, graceful, or competent? What happens when the desire for self-verification clashes with the need for self-enhancement?

Seeking to answer this question, Swann and his colleagues (1992) asked each participant to fill out a self-concept questionnaire and then choose an interaction partner from two other participants—one who supposedly had evaluated the participant favourably; the other, unfavourably. The result? Although participants with a positive self-concept chose partners who viewed them in a positive light, a majority of those with a negative self-concept preferred partners who confirmed their admitted shortcomings. In a later study, 64 percent of participants with low self-esteem, compared with only 25 percent of those with high self-esteem, sought clinical feedback about their weaknesses rather than their strengths when given a choice (Giesler et al., 1996).

If people seek self-verification from laboratory partners, it stands to reason that they would want the same from their close relationships. In a study of married couples, husbands and wives separately answered questions about their self-concepts, spouses, and commitment to the marriage. As predicted, people who had a positive self-concept expressed more commitment to partners who appraised them favourably, while those with a negative self-concept felt more committed to partners who appraised them *un*favourably (Swann et al., 1992).

Regarding important aspects of the self-concept, research shows that people would rather reflect on and learn more about their positive qualities than their negative ones (Sedikides, 1993). Still, it appears that the desire for self-verification is powerful—and can even, at times, overwhelm the need for self-enhancement. We all want to make a good impression, but we also want others in our lives to have an accurate impression, one that is compatible with our own self-concept (Swann, 1999).

Individual Differences in Self-Monitoring

Although self-presentation is a way of life for all of us, it differs considerably among individuals. Some people are generally more conscious of their public image than others. Also, some people are more likely to engage in strategic self-presentation, while others seem to prefer self-verification. According to Mark Snyder (1987), these differences are related to a personality trait he called **self-monitoring**: the tendency to regulate one's own behaviour to meet the demands of social situations.

Individuals who are high in self-monitoring appear to have a repertoire of selves from which to draw. Sensitive to strategic self-presentation concerns, they are poised, ready, and able to modify their behaviour as they move from one situation to another. As measured by the Self-Monitoring Scale (Snyder, 1974; Snyder & Gangestad, 1986), they are likely to agree with such statements as "I would probably make a good actor" and "In different situations and with different people, I often act like very different persons." In contrast, low self-monitors are self-verifiers by nature, appearing less concerned about the propriety of their behaviour. Like character actors always cast in the same role, they express themselves in a consistent manner from one situation

self-monitoring
The tendency to change behaviour in response to the self-presentation concerns of the situation.

to the next, exhibiting what they regard as their true and honest self. On the Self-Monitoring Scale, low self-monitors say that "I can only argue for ideas which I already believe" and "I have never been good at games like charades or improvisational acting" (see ■ Table 3.2).

TABLE 3.2

Self-Monitoring Scale

Are you a high or low self-monitor? For each statement, answer True or False. When you are done, give yourself one point if you answered T to items 4, 5, 6, 8, 10, 12, 17, and 18. Then give yourself one point if you answered F to items 1, 2, 3, 7, 9, 11, 13, 14, 15, and 16. Count your total number of points. This total represents your Self-Monitoring Score. Among North American college students, the average score is about 10 or 11.

(Snyder & Gangestad, 1986.)

1. I find it hard to imitate the behaviour of other people.
2. At parties and social gatherings, I do not attempt to do or say things that others will like.
3. I can only argue for ideas that I already believe.
4. I can make impromptu speeches even on topics about which I have almost no information.
5. I guess I put on a show to impress or entertain others.
6. I would probably make a good actor.
7. In a group of people I am rarely the centre of attention.
8. In different situations and with different people, I often act like very different persons.
9. I am not particularly good at making other people like me.
10. I'm not always the person I appear to be.
11. I would not change my opinions (or the way I do things) in order to please someone or win their favour.
12. I have considered being an entertainer.
13. I have never been good at games like charades or improvisational acting.
14. I have trouble changing my behaviour to suit different people and different situations.
15. At a party I let others keep the jokes and stories going.
16. I feel a bit awkward in company and do not show up quite as well as I should.
17. I can look anyone in the eye and tell a lie with a straight face (if for a right end).
18. I may deceive people by being friendly when I really dislike them.

Social psychologists disagree on whether the Self-Monitoring Scale measures one global trait or a combination of two or more specific traits. They also disagree about whether high and low self-monitors represent two discrete types of people or just points along a continuum. Either way, the test scores do appear to predict important social behaviours (Gangestad & Snyder, 2000). Concerned with public image, high self-monitors go out of their way to learn about others with whom they might interact and about the rules for appropriate conduct. Then, once they have the situation sized up, they modify their behaviour accordingly. If a situation calls for conformity, high self-monitors conform (Cheng & Chartrand, 2003). By contrast, low self-monitors maintain a relatively consistent posture across these situations (Snyder & Monson, 1975). As they are highly attuned to their own inner dispositions, low self-monitors may adjust their behaviour in response to feedback about their own characteristics (DeMarree et al., 2005). Consistent with the finding that high self-monitors are more concerned than lows about what other people think, research conducted in work settings shows that high self-monitors receive higher performance ratings and more promotions, and they are more likely to emerge as leaders (Day et al., 2002).

In the coming chapters, we will see that because so much of our behaviour is influenced by social norms, self-monitoring is relevant to many aspects of social psychology. There are also interesting developmental implications. A survey of 18- to 73-year-olds revealed that self-monitoring scores tend to drop with age— presumably because as people get older, they become more settled and secure about their personal identities (Reifman et al., 1989). For now, however, ponder this question: Is it better to be a high or low self-monitor? Is one orientation inherently more adaptive than the other?

The existing research does not enable us to make this kind of value judgment. Consider high self-monitors. Quite accurately, they regard themselves as pragmatic, flexible, and adaptive, and as able to cope with the diversity of life's roles. But they could also be described as fickle or phoney opportunists, more concerned with appearances than with reality and willing to change colours like a chameleon just to fit in. Now think about low self-monitors. They describe themselves as principled and forthright;

they are without pretence, always speaking their minds so others know where they stand. Of course, they could also be viewed as stubborn, insensitive to their surroundings, and unwilling to compromise in order to get along. Concerning the relative value of these two orientations, then, it is safe to conclude that neither high nor low self-monitoring is necessarily undesirable—unless carried to the extreme. Goffman (1955) made the same point many years ago:

> Too little perceptiveness, too little savoir faire, too little pride and considerateness, and the person ceases to be someone who can be trusted to take a hint about himself or give a hint that will save others embarrassment. Too much savoir faire or too much considerateness and he becomes someone who is too socialized, who leaves others with the feeling that they do not know how they really stand with him, nor what they should do to make an effective long-term adjustment. (p. 227)

It's more adaptive to alter one's behaviour than to stay consistent from one social situation to the next. FALSE.

Epilogue: The Multi-Faceted Self

Throughout human history, writers, poets, philosophers, and personality theorists have portrayed the self as an enduring aspect of personality, as an invisible "inner core" that is stable over time and slow to change. The struggle to "find yourself" and "be true to yourself" is based on this portrait. Indeed, when people over 85 years old were asked to reflect on their lives, almost all said that despite having changed in certain ways, they had remained essentially the same person (Troll & Skaff, 1997). In recent years, however, social psychologists have focused on change. In doing so, they have discovered that at least part of the self is malleable—moulded by life experiences and varying from one situation to the next. From this perspective, the self has many different faces.

When you look in the mirror, what do you see, one self or many? Do you see a person whose self-concept is enduring or one whose identity seems to change from time to time? Do you see a person whose strengths and weaknesses are evaluated with an objective eye or one who is insulated from unpleasant truths by mechanisms of self-defence? Do you see a person who has an inner, hidden self that is different from the face shown to others?

Based on the material presented in this chapter, the answer to such questions seems always to be the same: The self has all these characteristics. More than 100 years ago, William James (1890) said that the self is not simple but complex and multi-faceted. Based on current theories and research, we can now appreciate just how right James was. Sure, there's an aspect of the self-concept that we come to know only through introspection and that is stable over time. But there's also an aspect that changes with the company we keep and the information we get from others. When it comes to self-esteem, there are times when we are self-focused enough to become acutely aware of our shortcomings. Yet there are also times when we guard ourselves through self-serving cognitions, self-handicapping, BIRGing, and downward social comparisons. Then there is the matter of self-presentation. It's clear that each of us has a private self that consists of our inner thoughts, feelings, and memories. But it is equally clear that we also have an outer self, portrayed by the roles we play and the masks we wear in public. As you read through the pages of this text, you will see that the cognitive, affective, and behavioural components of the self are not separate and distinct but interrelated. They are also of great significance for the rest of social psychology.

REVIEW

The Self-Concept

- The self-concept is the sum total of a person's beliefs about his or her own attributes. It is the cognitive component of the self.

Elements of the Self-Concept

- Using brain scans, social neuroscientists find that certain areas become relatively more active when people process self-relevant information.
- Recognizing oneself as a distinct entity is the first step in the development of a self-concept.
- Human beings and apes are the only animals to recognize their mirror-image reflections as their own.
- Cooley's "looking-glass" self suggests that social factors are a necessary second step.

Introspection

- People believe that introspection is a key to knowing the true self.
- But research shows that introspection sometimes diminishes the accuracy of self-reports.
- People also tend to overestimate their emotional reactions to future positive and negative events.

Perceptions of Our Own Behaviour

- Bem's self-perception theory holds that when internal states are difficult to interpret, we infer our inner states by observing our own behaviour and the surrounding situation.
- Based on self-perception theory, the facial feedback hypothesis states that facial expressions can produce, not just reflect, an emotion state (smiling can cause us to feel happy).
- But it's unclear if the emotion occurs via self-perception or because facial expressions trigger physiological changes that produce the emotional response.
- Also derived from self-perception theory, studies of the overjustification effect show that people sometimes lose interest in activities for which they are rewarded.
- But if a reward is seen as a "bonus" for superior performance, then it can enhance intrinsic motivation by providing positive feedback.

Influences of Other People

- According to social comparison theory, people often evaluate their own opinions and abilities by comparing themselves to similar others.
- Schachter and Singer proposed that the experience of emotion is based on two factors: physiological arousal and a cognitive label for that arousal.
- Under certain conditions, people interpret their own arousal by watching others in the same situation.

Autobiographical Memories

- Memory of one's life events is critical to the self-concept.
- When people recall life experiences, they typically report more events from the recent past than from the distant past, though some types of memories are generally more vivid and lasting than others.
- Autobiographical memories are shaped by self-serving motives, as people overemphasize their own roles in past events.

Culture and the Self-Concept

- Cultures foster different conceptions of self.
- Many Europeans and North Americans hold an independent view of the self that emphasizes autonomy.
- People in certain Asian, African, and Latin American cultures hold an interdependent view of the self that encompasses social connections.
- These cultural differences influence the way we perceive, feel about, and present ourselves in relation to others.

Self-Esteem

- Self-esteem refers to a person's positive and negative evaluations of the self.

The Need for Self-Esteem

- People have a need for high self-esteem and want to see themselves in a positive light.
- People with low self-esteem often find themselves caught in a vicious cycle of self-defeating behaviour.

Are There Gender and Race Differences?

- Among adolescents and young adults, males have higher self-esteem than females do, although the difference is very small, particularly among older adults.
- Black Americans outscore white Americans on self-esteem tests, indicating, perhaps, that stigmatized minorities focus on their positive attributes.

Culture and Self-Esteem

- Cross-cultural comparisons suggest that people from collectivist cultures, compared to those in individualistic cultures, see or present themselves in a modest light relative to others.
- Researchers are seeking to determine whether collectivists have a less inflated self-esteem or simply feel compelled to present themselves modestly to others.
- Everyone has a need for positive self-regard; individualists and collectivists seek to fulfill that need in different ways.

Self-Discrepancy Theory

- Self-esteem can be defined by the match between how we see ourselves and how we want to see ourselves. Large self-discrepancies are associated with negative emotional states.

- Discrepancies between the actual and ideal selves are related to feelings of disappointment and depression.
- Discrepancies between the actual and the ought selves are related to shame, guilt, and anxiety.
- These emotional effects depend on the amount of discrepancy and whether we are consciously focused on it.

The Self-Awareness "Trap"

- In general, people spend little time actually thinking about themselves.
- But certain situations (mirrors, cameras, audiences) increase self-awareness, and certain people are generally more self-conscious than others.
- Self-awareness forces us to notice self-discrepancies and can produce a temporary reduction in self-esteem.
- To cope, we either adjust our behaviour to meet our standards or withdraw from the self-focusing situation. Heavy drinking can be viewed as a means of escaping from self-awareness.

Self-Regulation and Its Limits

- Self-control can temporarily be depleted by usage.
- This depletion effect can be reversed, enabling additional self-control, by the consumption of glucose and by self-affirmation.

Ironic Mental Processes

- Due to the operation of ironic processes, our efforts at self-control may also backfire, causing us to think, feel, and act in ways that are opposite to our intentions.
- Choking under pressure is an ironic phenomenon often seen in sports.

Mechanisms of Self-Enhancement

- Most people think highly of themselves and have unconscious positive associations with things related to the self.
- People protect their self-esteem in four major ways: through self-serving cognitions, such as taking credit for success and denying the blame for failure; self-handicapping, in order to excuse anticipated failure; basking in reflected glory, which boosts their self-esteem through associations with successful others; and downward social comparisons to others who are less well off.
- When others surpass us in ways that are important to us, we become jealous and distance ourselves from them. When surpassed in ways that are not self-relevant, we feel pride and seek closeness.

Are Positive Illusions Adaptive?

- Recent research suggests that certain positive illusions may foster high self-esteem and mental health.
- An alternative view is that such illusions promote self-defeating behaviour patterns and that people with inflated views of themselves are liked less by others.

Self-Presentation

- We care deeply about what others think of us and often believe that the social spotlight shines more brightly on us than it really does.
- Self-presentation is the process by which we try to shape what others think of us and even what we think of ourselves.

The Two Faces of Self-Presentation

- There are basically two types of self-presentation, each of which serves a different motive: strategic self-presentation (through which we try to shape others' impressions in order to be liked or seen as competent) and self-verification (through which we try to get others to perceive us as we perceive ourselves).

Individual Differences in Self-Monitoring

- Individuals differ in the tendency to regulate their behaviour to meet the demands of social situations.
- High self-monitors modify their behaviour, as appropriate, from one situation to the next.
- Low self-monitors express themselves in a more consistent manner, exhibiting at all times what they see as their true self.

Epilogue: The Multi-Faceted Self

- As this chapter has shown, the self is not simple but complex and multi-faceted.

Key Terms

affective forecasting (59)
bask in reflected glory (BIRG) (84)
dialecticism (70)
downward social comparison (85)
facial feedback hypothesis (61)
implicit egotism (81)
overjustification effect (62)
private self-consciousness (77)
public self-consciousness (77)
self-awareness theory (75)
self-concept (56)
self-esteem (71)
self-handicapping (83)
self-monitoring (90)
self-perception theory (60)
self-presentation (88)
self-schema (56)
social comparison theory (64)
two-factor theory of emotion (65)

Putting COMMON SENSE *to the Test*

Humans are the only animals who recognize themselves in the mirror.

False. *Studies have shown that the great apes (chimpanzees, gorillas, and orangutans) are also capable of self-recognition.*

Smiling can make you feel happier.

True. *Consistent with the facial feedback hypothesis, facial expressions can trigger or amplify the subjective experience of emotion.*

Sometimes the harder you try to control a thought, feeling, or behaviour, the less likely you are to succeed.

True. *Research on ironic processes in mental control has revealed that trying to inhibit a thought, feeling, or behaviour often backfires.*

People tend to be overly optimistic about their future.

True. *In general, people see themselves as more likely than average to have positive outcomes and less likely to have negative ones.*

People often sabotage their own performance in order to protect their self-esteem.

True. *Studies have shown that people often handicap their own performance in order to build an excuse for anticipated failure.*

It's more adaptive to alter one's behaviour than to stay consistent from one social situation to the next.

False. *High and low self-monitors differ in the extent to which they alter their behaviour to suit the situation they are in, but neither style is inherently more adaptive.*

4

Perceiving Persons

This chapter examines how people come to know, or think that they know, other persons. First, we introduce the elements of social perception—those aspects of persons, situations, and behaviour that guide initial observations. Next, we examine how people make explanations, or attributions, for the behaviour of others and how they form integrated impressions based on initial perceptions and attributions. We then consider confirmation biases, the subtle ways in which initial impressions lead people to distort later information, setting in motion a self-fulfilling prophecy.

Putting
COMMON SENSE
to the Test

Circle Your Answer

T F The impressions we form of others are influenced by superficial aspects of their appearance.

T F Adaptively, people are skilled at knowing when someone is lying rather than telling the truth.

T F Like social psychologists, people are sensitive to situational causes when explaining the behaviour of others.

T F People are slow to change their first impressions on the basis of new information.

T F The notion that we can create a "self-fulfilling prophecy" by getting others to behave in ways we expect is a myth.

T F People are more accurate at judging the personality of friends and acquaintances than of strangers.

In March 2011, Boston Bruins captain Zdeno Chara hit Montreal Canadiens forward Max Pacioretty into the boards, propelling his head into a stanchion—one of several large metal poles holding up the Plexiglas around the hockey rink. The result was a severe concussion and a broken vertebra for Pacioretty—he was out for the rest of the season. Was it Chara's intent to hurt Pacioretty, or was it simply an unfortunate accident? Some argued that the hit would have been fine if it happened anywhere else on the ice—but in this case it was the wrong hit at the wrong time. Chara stated in multiple news outlets, "That's not my style to (try to) hurt somebody. I always play hard. I play physical but I never try to hurt anybody so I'm hoping he's okay." Was his statement sincere? On the other hand, others believed that Chara knew full well that the post was there, and that he was aware of what he was doing. Pacioretty said on TSN Insider, "I believe he was trying to guide my head into the turnbuckle. We all know where the turnbuckle is. It wasn't a head shot like a lot of head shots we see but I do feel he targeted my head into the turnbuckle." Many were outraged when the NHL decided not to fine, nor suspend, Chara. Police in Quebec initially launched a criminal investigation, but ultimately declined to file charges.

Many years earlier, in October 1993, Saskatchewan farmer Robert Latimer killed his 12-year-old daughter Tracy. Tracy suffered from cerebral palsy, had endured several painful surgeries, and was both physically and mentally disabled. Latimer ran a hose from the exhaust on his truck into the cab where she sat, and then watched while she died. Was he a compassionate father, desperate to put his daughter out of her daily misery and relieve her suffering, or was he a callous father, trying to free himself of the exhausting daily rituals required to keep his daughter alive? Whatever the explanation, he was found guilty of second degree murder, began serving his life sentence in 2001, and was eventually granted full parole in November 2010.

Eric Bolte, QMI Agency

In March of 2011, Zdeno Chara's hit on Max Pacioretty caused Pacioretty to suffer a severe concussion and a broken vertebra. Was the hit intentional, or was Chara sincere when he said he never meant to hurt Pacioretty? Could it simply have been an unfortunate accident, a natural by-product of an aggressive game? As social perceivers, these are the types of questions we often ask ourselves in trying to understand people.

Whatever the topic—sports, politics, business, or personal events closer to home—we are all active and interested participants in **social perception**, the processes by which people come to understand one another. This chapter is divided into four sections. First, we look at the "raw data" of social perception: persons, situations, and behaviour. Second, we examine how people explain and analyze behaviour. Third, we consider how people integrate their observations into a coherent impression of other persons. Fourth, we discuss some of the subtle ways in which our impressions create a distorted picture of reality, often setting in motion a self-fulfilling prophecy. As you read this chapter, you will notice that the various processes are considered from a perceiver's vantage point. Keep in mind, however, that in the events of life, you are both a *perceiver* and a *target* of others' perceptions.

Observation: The Elements of Social Perception

As our opening examples suggest, understanding others may be difficult, but it's a vital part of everyday life. How do we do it? What kinds of evidence do we use? We cannot actually "see" someone's mental or emotional state, motives, or intentions, any more than a detective can see a crime that has already been committed. So, like a detective who tries to reconstruct events by turning up witnesses, fingerprints, blood samples, and other evidence, the social perceiver comes to know others by relying on indirect clues—the elements of social perception. These clues arise from three sources: persons, situations, and behaviour.

Persons: Judging a Book by Its Cover

Have you ever met someone for the first time and immediately formed an impression based only on a quick "snapshot" of information? As children, we were told not to judge a book by its cover, that things are not always what they seem, that appearances are deceptive, and that all that glitters is not gold. As adults, however, we can't seem to help ourselves.

To illustrate the rapid-fire nature of the process, Janine Willis and Alexander Todorov (2006) showed undergraduate students photographs of unfamiliar faces for one-tenth of a second, half a second, or a full second. Whether the students judged the faces for how attractive, likable, competent, trustworthy, or aggressive they were, their ratings—even at the briefest exposure—were quick and were highly correlated with judgments that other observers made without time-exposure limits (see Table 4.1). Flip quickly through the pages of an illustrated magazine, and you may see for yourself that it takes a mere fraction of a second to form an impression of a stranger from his or her face.

If first impressions are quick to form, on what are they based? In 500 BCE, the mathematician Pythagoras looked into the eyes of prospective students to determine if they were gifted. At about the same time, Hippocrates, the founder of modern medicine, used facial features to make diagnoses of life and death. In the nineteenth century, Viennese physician Franz Gall introduced a carnival-like science called phrenology and claimed that he could assess people's character by the shape of their skulls.

social perception
A general term for the processes by which people come to understand one another.

And in 1954, psychologist William Sheldon mistakenly concluded from flawed studies of adult men that there is a strong link between physique and personality.

People may not measure each other by bumps on the head, as phrenologists used to do, but first impressions are influenced in subtle ways by a person's height, weight, skin colour, hair colour, tattoos, eyeglasses, facial beauty, and other aspects of appearance (Alley, 1988; Herman et al., 1986; Rhodes & Zebrowitz, 2002). As social perceivers, we also form impressions of people that are often accurate based on a host of indirect telltale cues. In *Snoop: What Your Stuff Says About You*, Sam Gosling (2008) describes research he has conducted showing that people's personalities can be revealed in the knickknacks found in their offices and dormitory rooms, the identity claims they make on Facebook pages, the books that line their shelves, and the types of music that inhabit their iPods. Similarly, Donald Kluemper and others (2012) found that raters could reliably predict student grade point averages based on information posted on students' Facebook pages. We may even be influenced by a person's name. For example, Robert Young and others (1993) found that fictional characters with "old generation" names such as Harry, Walter, Dorothy, and Edith were judged to be less popular and intelligent than those with "young generation" names such as Kevin, Michael, Lisa, and Michelle.

TABLE 4.1

First Impressions in a Fraction of a Second

Participants rated unfamiliar faces based on pictures they saw for one-tenth of a second, half a second, or a full second. Would their impressions stay the same or change with unlimited time? As measured by the correlations of these ratings with those made by observers who had no exposure time limits, the results showed that ratings were highly correlated even at the briefest exposure times. Giving participants more time did not increase these correlations.

Traits being judged	.10 sec	.50 sec	1 sec
Trustworthy	.73	.66	.74
Competent	.52	.67	.59
Likable	.59	.57	.63
Aggressive	.52	.56	.59
Attractive	.69	.57	.66

(Willis & Todorov, 2006.)

Janine Willis, Alexander Todorov "First Impressions: Making Up Your Mind After a 100-Ms Exposure to a Face," from *Psychological Science Volume 17 Number 7*, copyright © 2006. Reprinted by Permission of SAGE Publications.

The impressions we form of others are influenced by superficial aspects of their appearance. TRUE.

The human face in particular attracts more than its share of attention. Since the time of ancient Greece, human beings have practised physiognomy—the art of reading character from faces. We may not realize it, but this tendency persists today. For example, Ran Hassin and Yaacov Trope (2000) found that people prejudge others in photographs as kind-hearted rather than mean-spirited based on such features as

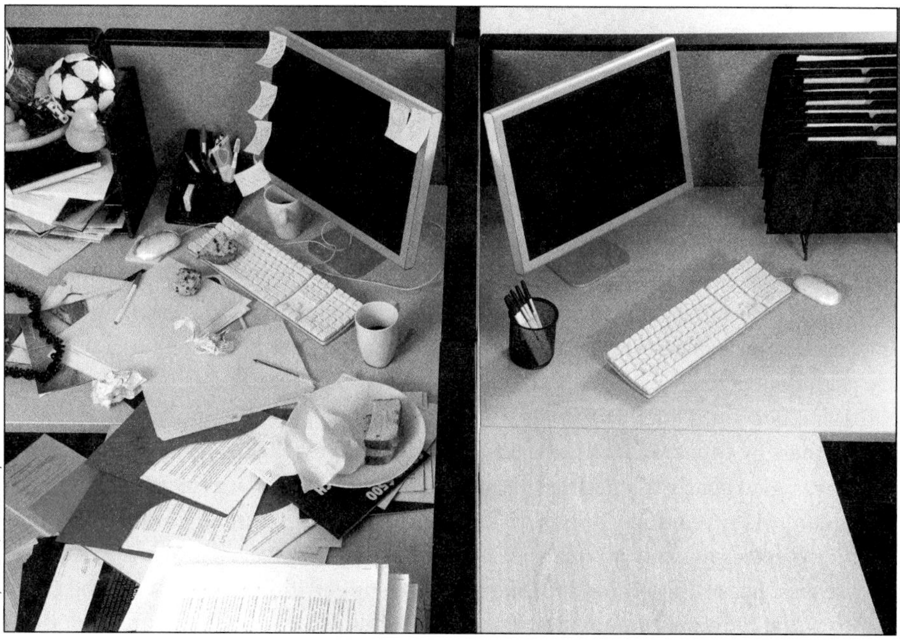

Look at these two office cubicles, side by side. Do these images lead you to form any impressions of their inhabitants? If so, do you suppose these impressions would be accurate or misleading?

Monalyn Gracia/PhotoLibrary

a full round face, curly hair, long eyelashes, large eyes, a short nose, full lips, and an upturned mouth. Interestingly, these researchers also found that just as people read traits *from* faces, at times they read traits *into* faces based on prior information. In one study, for example, participants who were told that a man was kind—compared to those who were told he was mean—later judged his face to be fuller, rounder, and more attractive.

In their studies of the human face, Diane Berry and Leslie Zebrowitz-McArthur (1986) found that adults who have baby-faced features—large, round eyes, high eyebrows, round cheeks, a large forehead, smooth skin, and a rounded chin—tend to be seen as warm, kind, naive, weak, honest, and submissive. In contrast, adults who have mature features—small eyes, low brows and a small forehead, wrinkled skin, and an angular chin—are seen as stronger, more dominant, and more competent. Thus, in small-claims court, judges are more likely to favour baby-faced defendants who are accused of intentional wrongdoing, but they tend to rule against baby-faced individuals accused of negligence (Zebrowitz & McDonald, 1991).

To explore the impact of facial features on person judgments, Nicholas Rule and Nalini Ambady (2011) asked undergraduate students at the University of Toronto to rate the faces of 92 of the managing partners of the top 100 law firms in the United States. Participants rated each face on a number of traits such as competence, maturity, dominance, and likeability. Blending competence, dominance, and facial maturity into one measure of 'Power,' the authors found that the Power ratings correlated significantly with the firms' profitability. That is, the firms with the greatest financial success also tended to have leaders who were rated highly on competence, dominance, and facial maturity—and those ratings were based only on a photograph!

As research by Malcolm Grant and others (2002) demonstrates, sometimes we even infer attitudes that we assume an individual holds, just on the basis of their face. Undergraduates at Memorial University viewed head-and-shoulders shots of individuals ranging from those in their late teens to their late seventies. Participants attributed conservative attitudes to the men in the photos for issues such as homosexuality and child rearing, while they judged the women in the photos to be more conservative when it came to religion. Attractive people were deemed to be the most liberal, and older adults the most conservative.

Of course the accuracy of such decisions isn't always clear. Christopher Olivola and Alexander Todorov (2010) explored this issue by using data from a website where users post photos of themselves, and then invite people to guess facts about them. On the basis of the photo, raters answer questions such as "Does this person do drugs?" or "Has this person ever been arrested?" They compared the online responses to a secondary survey sample that provided them with base-rate data as to how often people, in general, would fall into one of those categories (e.g., what percentage of people get arrested). They found that online raters—even when given feedback after each photo as to whether they were right or wrong—were far less accurate in their judgments than they would have been, had they ignored the target's appearance and simply guessed according to base-rate information. Thus, they far more often decided the person in the photo had 'been arrested' or 'did drugs' than would have been predicted based on the likelihood of these events occurring in the general population.

What accounts for these findings? And why, in general, are people so quick to judge others by appearances? To begin with, human beings are programmed by evolution to respond gently to infantile features so that real babies are treated with tender loving care. Many years ago, Nobel Prize–winning ethologist Konrad Lorenz noted that infantile features in many animal species seem to trigger a special nurturing response to cuteness. Recently, this old idea derived new support from a brain-imaging study showing that a frontal brain region associated with love and other positive emotions is activated when people are exposed, even fleetingly, to pictures of babies' faces but not to pictures of the faces of other adults (Kringelbach et al., 2008).

Our reflex-like response to babies is understandable. But do we really respond in the same way to baby-faced adults and, if so, why? Leslie Zebrowitz believes that we do—that we associate infantile features with helplessness traits and then overgeneralize this expectation to baby-faced adults. Consistent with this point, she and her colleagues found in a recent brain-imaging study that the region of the brain that was activated by pictures of babies' faces was also activated by pictures of baby-faced men (Zebrowitz et al., 2009).

Other researchers also believe that people as social perceivers have a tendency to overgeneralize in making snap judgments. Alexander Todorov and others (2008) find that people are quick to perceive unfamiliar faces as more or less trustworthy—an important judgment we must often make—and that we do so by focusing on features that resemble the expressions of happiness and anger (a trustworthy face has a U-shaped mouth and raised eyebrows; in an untrustworthy face, the mouth curls down and the eyebrows form a V). In other words, faces are seen as trustworthy if they look happy, an emotion that signals a person who is safe to approach, and untrustworthy if they look angry, an emotion that signals danger to be avoided.

Situations: The Scripts of Life

In addition to the beliefs we hold about persons, each of us has preset notions about certain types of situations—"scripts" that enable us to anticipate the goals, behaviours, and outcomes likely to occur in a particular setting (Abelson, 1981; Read, 1987). Based on past experience, people can easily imagine the sequences of events likely to unfold in a typical greeting or at the shopping mall or dinner table. The more experience you have in a given situation, the more detail your scripts will contain.

In *Do's and Taboos Around the World*, Roger Axtell (1993) describes many scripts that are culture specific. In Bolivia, dinner guests are expected to fully clean their plates to prove that they enjoyed the meal. Eat in an Indian home, however, and you'll see that many native guests will leave some food on the plate to show the host that they had enough to eat. Social scripts of this nature can influence perceptions and behaviour.

Behavioural scripts can be quite elaborate. Studying the "first date" script, John Pryor and Thomas Merluzzi (1985) asked undergraduate students to list the sequence of events that take place in this situation. From these lists, a picture of a typical North American first date emerged. Listed here are ten of the 16 steps that were identified: (1) male arrives; (2) female greets male at door; (3) female introduces date to parents or roommate; (4) male and female discuss plans and make small talk; (5) they go to a movie; (6) they get something to eat or drink; (7) male takes female home; (8) if interested, he remarks about a future date; (9) they kiss; (10) they say good night. Sound familiar? Pryor and Merluzzi then randomized their list of events and asked participants to arrange them into the appropriate order. They found that those with extensive dating experience were able to organize the statements more quickly than those who had less dating experience. For people who are familiar with a script, the events fall into place like the pieces of a puzzle. In fact, more than 20 years later, despite changes in gender and dating norms, research shows that this basic script has remained essentially the same (Morr Serewicz & Gale, 2008).

Knowledge of social settings provides an important context for understanding other people's verbal and nonverbal behaviour. For example, this knowledge leads us to expect someone to be polite during a job interview, playful at a picnic, and rowdy

"Our faces, together with our language, are social tools that help us navigate the social encounters that define our 'selves' and fashion our lives."
—Alan J. Fridlund

at a keg party. Scripts influence social perceptions in two ways. First, we sometimes see what we expect to see in a particular situation. In one study, participants looked at photographs of human faces that had ambiguous expressions. When told that the person in the photo was being threatened by a vicious dog, they saw the expression as fearful; when told that the individual had just won money, participants interpreted the *same* expression as a sign of happiness (Trope, 1986). Second, people use what they know about social situations to explain the causes of human behaviour. As described later in this chapter, an action seems to offer more information about a person when it departs from the norm than when it is common. In other words, you would learn more about someone who is rowdy during a job interview or polite at a keg party than if it were the other way around (Jones & Davis, 1965).

Behavioural Evidence

An essential first step in social perception is to recognize what someone is doing at a given moment. Identifying actions from movement is surprisingly easy. Even when actors dressed in black move about in a dark room with point lights attached only to the joints of their bodies, people easily recognize such complex acts as walking, running, jumping, exercising, and falling (Johansson et al., 1980). This ability is found in people of all cultures (Barrett et al., 2005) and enables them to recognize themselves and other specific individuals, such as friends, strictly on the basis of their movements (Loula et al., 2005).

More interesting, perhaps, is that people derive *meaning* from their observations by dividing the continuous stream of human behaviour into discrete units. By having participants observe someone on videotape and press a button whenever they detect a meaningful action, Darren Newtson and his colleagues (1987) have found that some perceivers break the behaviour stream into a large number of fine units, whereas others break it into a small number of gross units. While watching a baseball game, for example, you might press the button after each pitch, after each batter, after every inning, or only after runs are scored. The manner in which people divide a stream of behaviour can influence perceptions in important ways. Research participants who are told to break an event into fine units rather than gross units attend more closely, detect more meaningful actions, and remember more details about the actor's behaviour than do gross-unit participants (Lassiter et al., 1988).

In a new and developing area of research, social psychologists are interested in **mind perception**, the process by which people attribute humanlike mental states to various animate and inanimate objects, including other people. Studies show that people who identify someone's actions in high-level terms rather than low-level terms (for example, by describing the act of "painting a house" as "trying to make a house look new," not just "applying brush strokes") are also more likely to attribute humanizing thoughts, feelings, intentions, consciousness, and other states of mind to that actor (Kozak et al., 2006).

Although people do not tend to attribute mental states to inanimate objects, in general the more humanlike a target object is, the more likely we are to attribute to it qualities of "mind." In a series of studies, Carey Morewedge and others (2007) found that whether people are asked to rate different animals in nature (such as a sloth, turtle, housefly, deer, wolf, and hummingbird); cartoon robots or human beings whose motion was presented in slow, medium, and fast speeds; or a purple blob oozing down a city street at the same, slower, or faster pace than the people around it, the result is always the same: People see inner qualities of mind in target objects that superficially resemble humans in their speed of movement.

mind perception
The process by which people attribute humanlike mental states to various animate and inanimate objects, including other people.

Asking "What kinds of things have minds?", Heather Gray and her colleagues (2007) conducted an online survey in which they presented more than 2000 respondents with an array of human and nonhuman characters, such as a seven-week-old fetus, a five-month-old infant, an adult man, a man in a vegetative state, a dead woman, a frog, the family dog, a chimpanzee, God, and a sociable robot. They then asked respondents to rate the extent to which each character possessed various mental capacities such as pleasure, pain, fear, pride, embarrassment, memory, self-control, and morality. Once statistically combined, the results showed that people perceive minds along two dimensions: agency (a target's ability to plan and execute behaviour) and experience (the capacity to feel pleasure, pain, and other sensations). Overall, the more "mind" respondents attributed to a character, the more they liked it, valued it, wanted to make it happy, and wanted to rescue it from destruction. Interestingly, when participants are asked to focus on a target's physical characteristics, attributions regarding the target's agency *decrease*, but attributions of his or her experience *increase* (Gray et al., 2011). That is, they see the target as less capable, but more likely to experience pain or pleasure. As the authors of this study note, this is problematic if a woman applying for a job is judged primarily on her physical attributes, and therefore unfairly viewed as being 'too emotional.' On the other hand, a doctor seeing a patient as a 'body' may be more careful to avoid causing that patient pain.

The Silent Language of Nonverbal Behaviour Behavioural cues are used not only to identify someone's actions but also to determine his or her inner states. Knowing how another person is feeling can be tricky because people often try to hide their true emotions. Have you ever had to suppress your rage at someone, mask your disappointment after failure, feign surprise, make excuses, or pretend to like something just to be polite? Sometimes people come right out and tell us how they feel. At other times, however, they do not tell us, they are themselves not sure, or they actively try to conceal their true feelings. For these reasons, we often tune in to the silent language of **nonverbal behaviour**.

What kinds of nonverbal cues do people use in judging how someone else is feeling? In *The Expression of the Emotions in Man and Animals*, Charles Darwin (1872) proposed that the face expresses emotion in ways that are innate and understood by

nonverbal behaviour
Behaviour that reveals a person's feelings without words—through facial expressions, body language, and vocal cues.

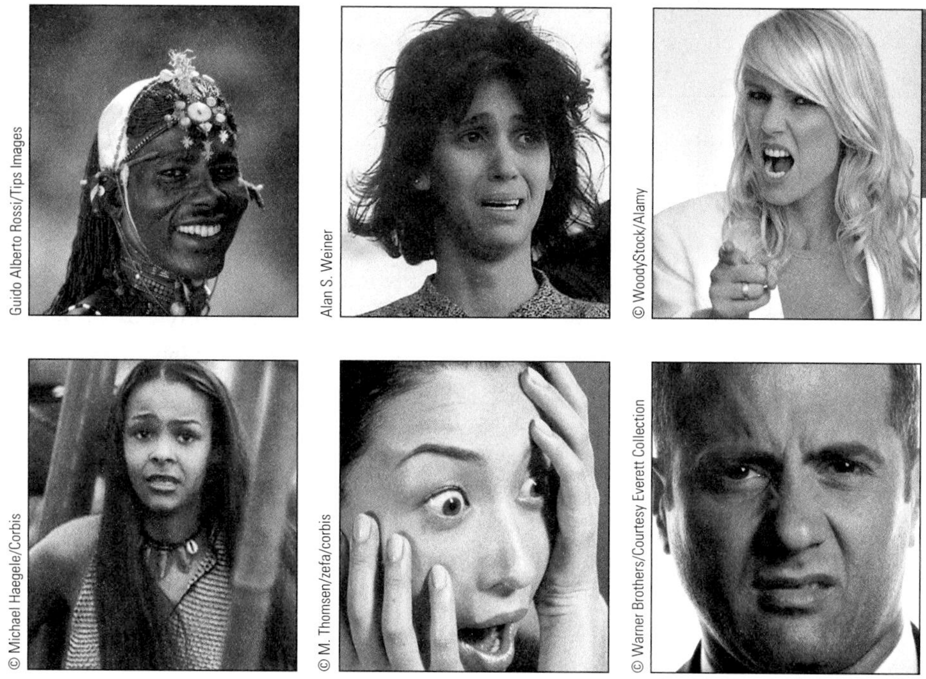

Can you tell how these individuals are feeling? If you are like most people, regardless of your culture, you will have little trouble recognizing the emotions portrayed.

people all over the world. Contemporary research supports this notion. Numerous studies have shown that when presented with photographs similar to those shown above, people can reliably identify at least six "primary" emotions: happiness, fear, sadness, anger, surprise, and disgust. In one study, participants from ten different countries—Estonia, Germany, Greece, Hong Kong, Italy, Japan, Scotland, Sumatra, Turkey, and the United States—exhibited high levels of agreement in their recognition of these emotions (Ekman et al., 1987). More recently, shame, embarrassment, contempt, and compassion have been discussed as possible contenders for 'basic emotion' status, but it is still not clear if they are as readily recognized. For example, in one study, participants were more likely to correctly label an expression as 'shame' when that emotion was included as an option in a forced-choice format accompanying the photograph, but not when they were asked to spontaneously interpret the face (Widen et al., 2011); in another, children regularly interpreted a 'disgust' face as 'anger' (Widen & Russell, 2010).

From one end of the world to the other, it is clear that a smile is a smile and a frown is a frown, and that just about everyone knows what they mean—even when these expressions are "put on" by actors and not genuinely felt (Gosselin et al., 1995). Still, the results do not fully support the claim that basic emotions are "universally" recognized from the face (Russell, 1994). To determine the extent to which emotions are universally recognized or culturally specific, Hillary Elfenbein and Nalini Ambady (2002) meta-analyzed 97 studies involving a total of 22 148 participants from 42 different countries. As shown in ▶ Figure 4.1, they found support for both points of view. On the one hand, people all over the world are able to recognize the primary emotions from photographs of facial expressions. On the other hand, people are 9 percent more accurate at judging faces from their own national, ethnic, or regional groups than from members of less familiar groups—indicating that we enjoy an "ingroup advantage" when it comes to knowing how those who are closest to us are feeling. Darwin believed that the ability to recognize emotion in others has survival value for all members of a species. This hypothesis suggests that it is more important to identify some emotions than others. For example, it may be more adaptive to be wary of someone who is angry, and hence prone to lash out in violence, than someone who is happy, a nonthreatening emotion. Indeed, studies have shown that angry faces arouse us and cause us to frown even when presented subliminally, without our awareness (Dimberg & Ohman, 1996; Dimberg et al., 2000). Illustrating what Christine and Ranald Hansen (1988) called the "anger superiority effect," researchers have found that people are quicker to spot—and slower to look away from—angry faces in a crowd than faces with neutral and less threatening emotions (Fox et al., 2002; Horstmann & Bauland, 2006). Of course, what people search for may be conditioned by a current motivational state. In a visual search task resembling "Where's Waldo?", research participants who were led to fear social rejection and loneliness were quicker to spot faces in diverse crowds that wore welcoming smiles than other expressions (DeWall et al., 2009).

▶ FIGURE 4.1

How Good Are People at Identifying Emotions in the Face?

A meta-analysis of emotion recognition studies involving 22 148 participants from 42 countries confirmed that people all over the world can recognize the six basic emotions from posed facial expressions.

(Elfenbein & Ambady, 2002.)

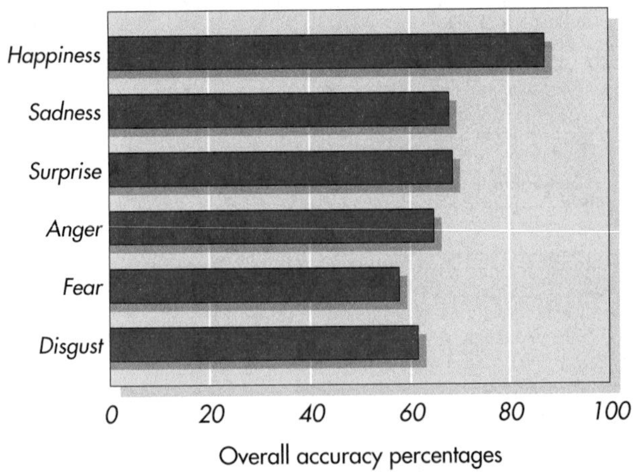

Disgust is another basic emotion that has adaptive significance. When confronted with an offensive stimulus such as a foul odour, spoiled food, feces, rotting flesh, or the sight of mutilation, people react with an aversion that shows in the way they wrinkle the nose, raise the upper lip, and gape. This visceral reaction is often accompanied by nausea and can facilitate the expulsion of bad food from the mouth (Rozin & Fallon, 1987; Rozin et al., 2000). In nature, food poisoning is a real threat, so it is adaptive for us to recognize disgust in the face of others. To illustrate, Bruno Wicker and others (2003) had 14 men watch video clips of people smelling pleasant, disgusting, or neutral odours. Afterward, these same men were exposed to the odours themselves. If you've ever inhaled the sweet, floury aroma of a bakery or inserted your nose into a carton of soured milk, you'll appreciate the different reactions that would appear on your face. Using functional magnetic resonance imaging, or fMRI, researchers monitored activity in the participants' brains throughout the experiment. They found that a structure in the brain known as the *insula* was activated not only when participants sniffed the disgusting odour but also when they watched *others* sniffing it. This result suggests that people more than recognize the face of disgust; they experience it at a neural level.

It's interesting to note that the social value of the face is evident to those who communicate online. When email first became popular, the written word was often misinterpreted—especially when the writer was trying to be funny—because it lacked the nonverbal cues that normally animate and clarify live interactions. To fill in this gap, emailers created smiley faces and other "emoticons" (emotion icons) from standard keyboard characters. Some routinely used emoticons, which are meant to be viewed with one's head tilted 90 degrees to the left, are shown in ▶ Figure 4.2 (Sanderson, 1993).

Other nonverbal cues can also influence social perception, enabling us to make quick and often accurate judgments of others based on "thin slices" of expressive behaviour (Ambady & Rosenthal, 1993). "Thin slicing is not an exotic gift," notes Malcolm Gladwell (2005), author of the best seller *Blink*. "It is a central part of what it means to be human" (p. 43). Social perceivers are often fluent readers of *body language*—the ways in which people stand, sit, walk, and express themselves with various gestures. For example, Elisha Babad (2005) asked high school students to watch 10-second clips of unfamiliar teachers' nonverbal behaviour and then predict whether the teacher would be helpful or not to either a high- or low-achieving student. She found that, compared to a non-student adult population, the high school students were far more accurate in their judgments, a finding she attributed to their implicit knowledge regarding 'typical' teacher behaviours that allowed them to more accurately interpret the nonverbal behaviour, even with only brief exposure. In another study, research participants were able to judge the intelligence of strangers accurately, as measured by standardized test scores, based only on hearing them read short sentences (Borkenau et al., 2004).

▶ FIGURE 4.2

Some Common Email "Emoticons"

In order to clarify the meaning of their written words, emailers often add smiles, winks, and other face-like symbols, or emoticons, to their electronic messages. One set of emoticons is shown here; you may be familiar with others.

(Sanderson, 1993.)

Wink	Smirk	Said smiling	Said frowning	Sardonic incredulity
'-)	:-,	:-)	:-(	;-)

Disgusted	Kiss, kiss	Clowning around	Said late at night	Said tongue-in-cheek
:-|	:-X	:*)	|-(	:-J

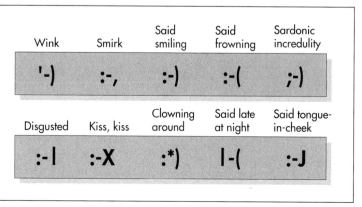

In communicating with others, people use conversational hand gestures such as the raised fist, the bye-bye wave, the thumbs up, and the extended middle finger, sometimes referred to as "flipping the bird" (Krauss et al., 1996). People also form impressions of others based on how they walk. Thus, men and women who have a youthful walking style—who sway their hips, bend their knees, lift their feet, and swing their arms—are seen as happier and more powerful than those who walk slowly, take shorter steps, and stiffly drag their feet (Montepare & McArthur, 1988). Some researchers have even suggested that male dance movements convey elements of their personality traits, as well as their levels of physical health, information that may be useful to a perceiver trying to determine if the dancer would make a good mate (Fink, et al., 2012).

Eye contact, or *gaze*, is another common form of nonverbal communication. People are highly attentive to eyes, often following the gaze of others. Look up, down, left, or right, and someone observing you will likely follow the direction of your eyes (Langton et al., 2000). Even one-year-old infants tend to follow gaze, looking toward or pointing at the object of an adult researcher's attention (Brooks & Meltzoff, 2002). Clearly, each of us is drawn like a magnet to another person's direct gaze. Controlled laboratory studies of this "eye contact effect" show that people who look us straight in the eye quickly draw and then hold our attention, increase arousal, and activate key "social" areas of the brain and that this sensitivity is present at birth (Senju & Johnson, 2009).

Eyes have been called the "windows of the soul." In many cultures, people tend to assume that someone who avoids eye contact is evasive, cold, fearful, shy, or indifferent; that frequent gazing signals intimacy, sincerity, self-confidence, and respect; and that the person who stares is tense, angry, and unfriendly. If you've ever conversed with someone who kept looking away, as if uninterested, then you would understand why people might form negative impressions from "gaze disengagement" (Mason et al., 2005). Sometimes eye contact is interpreted in light of a pre-existing relationship. If a relationship is friendly, frequent eye contact elicits a positive impression. If a relationship is not friendly, eye contact is seen in negative terms. It has been said that if two people lock eyes for more than a few seconds, they are going to either make love or kill each other (Kleinke, 1986; Patterson, 1983).

Another powerful, primitive form of nonverbal behaviour is *touch*—the congratulatory high-five, the sympathetic pat on the back, the joking elbow in the ribs, and the loving embrace being just a few familiar examples. Physical touching has long been regarded as an expression of friendship, nurturance, and sexual interest. But it may also serve other functions. Many years ago, Nancy Henley (1977) observed that men, older persons, and those of high socioeconomic status were more likely to touch women, younger persons, and individuals of lower status than the other way around. Henley's interpretation: that touching may be an expression not only of intimacy but of dominance and control. Is social touching reserved for those in power? It appears that the answer is no. After an exhaustive review of past research, Judith Hall and her colleagues (2005) found that although we tend to believe that people touch others more when they are dominant than when they are subordinate, there is no behavioural support for this hypothesis (though dominant people are more facially expressive, encroach more on others' personal space, speak louder, and are more likely to interrupt). Simple forms of touch, as when people greet each other, also provide us with thin slices of behavioural evidence. Think about the handshakes you've received in your life and whether the grips were firm or limp, strong or weak, dry or clammy, brief or lingering. Research suggests that the first impressions we form of others may be influenced by these qualities of a simple handshake (Bernieri & Petty, 2011; Chaplin et al., 2000).

As described by Axtell (1993), nonverbal communication norms vary from one culture to the next. So watch out! In Bulgaria, nodding your head means "no" and shaking your head sideways means "yes." In Germany and Brazil, the North American "okay" sign (forming a circle with your thumb and forefinger) is an obscene gesture. Personal-space habits also vary across cultures. Japanese people like to keep a comfortable distance while interacting. But in Puerto Rico and much of Latin America, people stand very close and backing off is considered an insult. Also beware of what you do with your eyes. In Latin America, locking eyes is a must; yet in Japan, too much eye contact shows a lack of respect. If you're in the habit of stroking your cheek, you should know that in Italy, Greece, and Spain it means that you find the person you're talking to attractive. And whatever you do, don't ever touch someone's head in Buddhist countries, especially Thailand. The head is sacred there.

John Stillwell/PA Photos/Landov

Touch is a powerful form of nonverbal behaviour and is often subject to strict cultural norms. In April 2009, First Lady Michelle Obama, meeting Queen Elizabeth II for the first time, put her arm around the Queen. Aghast, some commentators noted that this gesture breached protocol; others said it was appropriate because the Queen herself had embraced the First Lady.

Different cultures also have vastly different rules for greeting someone. In Finland, you should give a firm handshake; in France, you should loosen the grip; in Zambia, you should use your left hand to support the right; and in Bolivia, you should extend your arm if your hand is dirty. In Japan, people bow; in Thailand, they put both hands together in a praying position on the chest; and in Fiji, they smile and raise their eyebrows. In certain parts of Latin America, it is common for people to hug, embrace, and kiss upon meeting. And in most Arab countries, men greet one another by saying *salaam alaykum*, then shaking hands, saying *kaif halak*, and kissing each other on the cheek.

Distinguishing Truth from Deception Social perception is tricky because people often try to hide or stretch the truth about themselves. Poker players bluff to win money, witnesses lie to protect themselves, public officials make campaign promises they don't intend to keep, and acquaintances pass compliments to each other to be polite and supportive. On occasion, everyone tells something less than "the truth, the whole truth, and nothing but the truth." Can social perceivers tell the difference? Can *you* tell when someone is lying?

Sigmund Freud, the founder of psychoanalysis, once said that "no mortal can keep a secret. If his lips are silent, he chatters with his fingertips; betrayal oozes out of him at every pore" (1905, p. 94). Paul Ekman and Wallace Friesen (1974) revised Freud's observation by pointing out that some pores "ooze" more than others. Specifically, Ekman and Friesen proposed that some channels of communication are difficult for deceivers to control, while others are relatively easy. To test this hypothesis, they showed a series of films—some pleasant, others disgusting—to a group of female nurses. While watching, the nurses were instructed either to report their honest impressions of these films or to conceal their true feelings. Through the use of hidden cameras, these participants were videotaped. Others, acting as observers, then viewed the tapes and judged whether the participants had been truthful or deceptive. The results showed that judgment accuracy rates were influenced by which types of nonverbal cues the observers were exposed to. Observers who watched tapes that focused on the body were better at detecting deception than those who saw tapes focused on the face. The face can communicate emotion, but it is relatively easy for deceivers to control—unlike nervous movements of the hands and feet.

This study was the first of many. In these studies, one group of participants makes truthful or deceptive statements while another group reads the transcripts, listens to audiotapes or watches videotapes, and then tries to evaluate the statements. Consistently, in laboratories all over the world, results show that people are only about 54 percent accurate in judging truth and deception, too often accepting what others say at face value (Bond & DePaulo, 2006; Vrij, 2008). Although some social perceivers may be better than others at distinguishing truths and lies, individual differences are small (Bond & DePaulo, 2008). In fact, a good deal of research shows that professionals who are specially trained and who regularly make these kinds of judgments for a living—such as police detectives, judges, psychiatrists, customs inspectors, and those who administer lie-detector tests for government agencies including the military—are also highly prone to error (Ekman & O'Sullivan, 1991; Granhag & Strömwall, 2004; Meissner & Kassin, 2002; Vrij, 2008; see ■ Table 4.2).

What seems to be the problem? There are really two. The first is that there is a *mismatch* between the behavioural cues that actually signal deception and those used by perceivers to detect deception (Zuckerman et al., 1981; DePaulo et al., 2003). To be more specific, four channels of communication provide relevant information: words, the face, the body, and the voice. Yet when people have a reason to lie, the words they choose cannot be trusted, and they are generally able to control both their face and body (the voice is the most telling channel; when people lie, they tend to hesitate, then speed up and raise the pitch of their voice). In a survey of some 2500 adults in 63 countries, Charles Bond found that more than 70 percent believed that liars tend to avert their eyes—a cue that is not supported by any research. Similarly, most of Bond's survey respondents believed that people squirm, stutter, fidget, and touch themselves when they lie—also cues not supported by the research (Henig, 2006).

The second problem is that people tend to assume that the way to spot a liar is to watch for signs of stress in his or her behaviour. Yet in important real-life situations—for example, at a high-stakes poker table, the security screening area of an airport, or a police interrogation room—truth tellers are also likely to exhibit signs of stress. For this reason, researchers are seeking a different approach. For example, Aldert Vrij (2008; Vrij et al., 2011) theorizes that lying is harder to do and requires more thinking than telling the truth. Therefore, he argues, we should focus on behavioural cues that betray cognitive effort. This realization has led Vrij and others to create more challenging types of interviews that could expose deception. In one study, they asked truth tellers and liars to recount their stories in reverse chronological order. This task was a lot harder and more effortful for the deceivers to do, which made the interviewers better able to distinguish between truths and lies (Vrij et al., 2008).

TABLE 4.2

Can the "Experts" Distinguish Truth and Deception?

Lie-detection experts with experience at making judgments of truth and deception were shown brief videotapes of 10 women telling the truth or lying about their feelings. Considering that there was a 50–50 chance of guessing correctly, the accuracy rates were remarkably low. Only a sample of U.S. Secret Service agents posted a better-than-chance performance.

Observer Groups	Accuracy Rates (%)
College students	52.82
CIA, FBI, and military	55.67
Police investigators	55.79
Trial judges	56.73
Psychiatrists	57.61
U.S. Secret Service agents	64.12

(Ekman & O'Sullivan, 1991.)

In a second study, those interviewing suspects who had committed a mock crime withheld certain details of that crime while questioning some suspects but not others. Using this "strategic disclosure" technique, the interviewers made more accurate judgments of who was lying by catching those who had committed the mock crime in various inconsistencies—such as claiming that they were never present at the crime scene, unaware that they had left fingerprints—which the interviewers did not disclose until later (Hartwig et al., 2005). Similarly, recent evidence suggests that police officers are indeed better at detecting deception than laypersons when the statements they are asked to verify reflect "high stakes" lies (e.g., those that describe events that are personally relevant or have clear consequences for the liar) compared to when they are asked to analyze a "low stakes" (or more trivial) lie, as the former presumably require more cognitive resources to create than the latter (O'Sullivan et al., 2009).

In light of these findings, it appears that social perceivers tune in to the wrong channels of communication. Too easily seduced by the silver tongue, the smiling face, and the restless body, we often fail to notice the quivering voice. Too focused on how stressed a person seems while speaking—an emotional state that afflicts not only guilty liars but innocent truth tellers who stand falsely accused—we fail to notice the amount of effort it takes someone to recite their story or answer a question.

Adaptively, people are skilled at knowing when someone is lying rather than telling the truth. FALSE.

Attribution: From Elements to Dispositions

To interact effectively with others, we need to know how they feel and when they can be trusted. But to understand people well enough to predict their future behaviour, we must also identify their inner *dispositions*: stable characteristics such as personality traits, attitudes, and abilities. Since we cannot actually see dispositions, we infer them indirectly from what a person says and does. In this section, we look at the processes that lead us to make these inferences.

Attribution Theories

Do you ever think about the influence that you have on other people? What about the roles of heredity, childhood experiences, and social forces? Do you wonder why some people succeed while others fail? Individuals differ in the extent to which they feel a need to explain the uncertain events of human behaviour (Weary & Edwards, 1994). Among students, for example, those who major in psychology are more curious about people than are those who major in one of the natural sciences (Fletcher et al., 1986). Although there are vast differences among us, people in general tend to ask "why?" when they confront events that are important, negative, or unexpected (Hastie, 1984; Weiner, 1985) and when understanding these events has personal relevance (Malle & Knobe, 1997).

"It's not you, Frank, it's me—I don't like you."

People make personal and situational attributions all the time in an effort to make sense of their social world.

To make sense of our social world, we try to understand the causes of other people's behaviour. But what kinds of explanations do we make, and how do we go about making them? In a classic book entitled *The Psychology of Interpersonal Relations*, Fritz Heider (1958) took the first step toward answering these questions. To Heider, we are all scientists of a sort. Motivated to understand others well enough to manage our social lives, we observe, analyze, and explain their behaviour. The explanations we come up with are called *attributions*, and the theory that describes the process is called **attribution theory**. The questions posed at the beginning of the chapter regarding Zdeno Chara and Robert Latimer are questions of attribution.

Ask people to explain why their fellow human beings behave as they do—why they succeed or fail, laugh or cry, work or play, or help or hurt others—and you'll see that they come up with complex explanations often focused on whether the behaviour is intentional or unintentional (Malle et al., 2000). Interested in how people answer these *why* questions, Heider found it particularly useful to group the explanations people give into two categories: *personal* and *situational.* Consider the Chara case. What led him to hit Pacioretty the way he did? Did he intend to hurt him? He said no. But what caused the behaviour? Was it because he had a history of being an aggressive player and he liked taking on other players (a **personal attribution**), or because of an unfortunate accident that occurred in a naturally aggressive game (a **situational attribution**). Rudy Kafer and others (1993) explored the attributions surrounding the horrific massacre of 14 women by Marc Lepine at the École Polytechnique in Montreal in 1989. Lepine, blaming feminists for "ruining his life," walked through the school ordering the men to leave and shooting the women. Was his behaviour the result of a general acceptance in society of violence against women, or the result of his own rage and pathology? They found that to some extent women and men differed in their attributions; women were more likely to attribute the massacre to the killer (a personal attribution), whereas men were more likely to endorse the societal explanation (a situational attribution). The task for the attribution theorist is not to determine the true *causes* of such an event but, rather, to understand people's *perceptions* of causality. Heider's insights provided an initial spark for a number of formal models that together came to be known as attribution theory (Weiner, 2008). For now, we describe two of these theories.

Jones's Correspondent Inference Theory According to Edward Jones and Keith Davis (1965), each of us tries to understand other people by observing and analyzing their behaviour. Jones and Davis's *correspondent inference theory* predicts that people try to infer from an action whether the act itself corresponds to an enduring personal characteristic of the actor. Is the person who commits an act of aggression a beast? Is the person who donates money to charity an altruist? To answer these kinds of questions, people make inferences on the basis of three factors.

The first factor is a person's degree of *choice*. Behaviour that is freely chosen is more informative about a person than behaviour that is coerced. In one study, participants read a speech, presumably written by a student, that either favoured or opposed Fidel Castro, then the communist leader of Cuba. Some participants were told that the student had freely chosen this position, and others were told that the student had been assigned the position by a professor. When asked to determine the student's true attitude, participants were more likely to assume a correspondence between the essay (behaviour) and the student's attitude (disposition) when the student had had a choice than when he or she had been assigned to the role (Jones & Harris, 1967; see ▶ Figure 4.3). Keep this study in mind. It supports correspondent inference theory; but as we will see later, it also demonstrates one of the most tenacious biases of social perception.

The second factor that leads people to make dispositional inferences is the *expectedness* of behaviour. As previously noted, an action tells us more about a person when it departs from the norm than when it is typical, part of a social role, or otherwise expected under the circumstances (Jones et al., 1961). Thus, people think they know more about a student who wears three-piece suits to class or a citizen

attribution theory
A group of theories that describe how people explain the causes of behaviour.

personal attribution
Attribution to internal characteristics of an actor, such as ability, personality, mood, or effort.

situational attribution
Attribution to factors external to an actor, such as the task, other people, or luck.

who openly refuses to pay taxes than about a student who wears blue jeans to class or a citizen who files tax returns on April 30.

Third, people consider the intended *effects* or consequences of someone's behaviour. Acts that produce many desirable outcomes do not reveal a person's specific motives as clearly as acts that produce only a single desirable outcome (Newtson, 1974). For example, you are likely to be uncertain about exactly why a person stays on a job that is enjoyable, high paying, and in an attractive location—three desirable outcomes, each sufficient to explain the behaviour. In contrast, you may feel more certain about why a person stays on a job that is tedious and low paying but is in an attractive location—only one desirable outcome.

FIGURE 4.3

What Does This Speechwriter Really Believe?

As predicted by correspondent inference theory, participants who read a student's speech (behaviour) were more likely to assume that it reflected the student's true attitude (disposition) when the position taken was freely chosen (left) rather than assigned (right). But also note the evidence for the fundamental attribution error. Even participants who thought the student had been assigned a position inferred the student's attitude from the speech.

(Jones & Harris, 1967.)

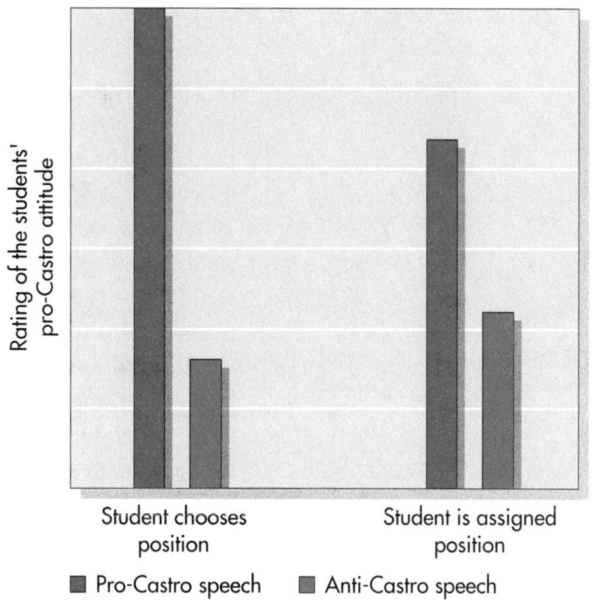

Reprinted from *Journal of Experimental Social Psychology, Vol. 3,* "The Attribution of Attitudes," by E.G. Jones and K.E. Harris, pp. 1-24. Copyright ©1967, with permission from Elsevier.

Kelley's Covariation Theory Correspondent inference theory seeks to describe how perceivers try to discern an individual's personal characteristics from a slice of behavioural evidence. However, behaviour can be attributed not only to personal factors but to situational factors as well. How is this distinction made? In the opening chapter, we noted that the causes of human behaviour can be derived only through *experiments.* That is, one has to make more than a single observation and compare behaviour in two or more settings in which everything stays the same except for the independent variables. Like Heider, Harold Kelley (1967) believes that people are much like scientists in this regard. They may not observe others in a laboratory, but they too make comparisons and think in terms of "experiments." According to Kelley, people make attributions by using the **covariation principle**: In order for something to be the cause of a behaviour, it must be present when the behaviour occurs and absent when it does not. Three kinds of covariation information are particularly useful: consensus, distinctiveness, and consistency.

To illustrate these concepts, imagine you are standing on a street corner one hot, steamy evening minding your own business, when all of a sudden a stranger comes out of an air-conditioned movie theatre and blurts out, "Great flick!" Looking up, you don't recognize the movie title, so you wonder what to make of this "recommendation." Was the behaviour (the rave review) caused by something about the person (the stranger), the stimulus (the film), or the circumstances (say, the air-conditioned theatre)? Possibly interested in spending a night at the movies, how would you proceed to explain what happened? What kinds of information would you want to obtain?

Thinking like a scientist, you might seek out *consensus information* to see how different persons react to the same stimulus. In other words, how do other moviegoers feel about this film? If others also rave about it, the stranger's behaviour is high in consensus and is attributed to the stimulus. If others are critical of the same film, the behaviour is low in consensus and is attributed to the person. Still thinking like a scientist, you might also want to have *distinctiveness information* to see how the same

covariation principle
A principle of attribution theory holding that people attribute behaviour to factors that are present when a behaviour occurs and absent when it does not.

person reacts to different stimuli. In other words, how does this moviegoer react to other films? If the stranger is generally critical of other films, then the target behaviour is high in distinctiveness and is attributed to the stimulus. If the stranger raves about everything, however, then the behaviour is low in distinctiveness and is attributed to the person. Finally, you might seek *consistency information* to see what happens to the behaviour at another time when the person and the stimulus both remain the same. How does this moviegoer feel about this film on other occasions? If the stranger raves about the film on video as well as in the theatre, the behaviour is high in consistency. If the stranger does not always enjoy the film, the behaviour is low in consistency. According to Kelley, behaviour that is consistent is attributed to the stimulus when consensus and distinctiveness are also high and to the person when they are low. In contrast, behaviour that is low in consistency is attributed to transient circumstances, such as the temperature of the movie theatre.

Kelley's theory and the predictions it makes are represented in ▶ Figure 4.4. Does this model describe the kinds of information you seek when you try to determine what causes people to behave as they do? Often it does. Research shows that research participants who are instructed to make attributions for various events do, in general, follow the logic of covariation (Cheng & Novick, 1990; Fosterling, 1992; McArthur, 1972). However, this research also shows that individuals have their own attributional styles, so people often disagree about what caused a particular behaviour (Robins et al., 2004). There are two ways in which social perceivers differ. First, individuals vary in the extent to which they believe that human behaviours are caused by personal characteristics that are fixed ("Everyone is a certain kind of person; there is not much that can be done to really change that") or malleable ("People can change even their most basic qualities") (Dweck et al., 1995). Second, some individuals are more likely than others to process information in ways that are coloured by self-serving motivations (von Hippel et al., 2005).

▶ FIGURE 4.4

Kelley's Covariation Theory

For behaviours that are high in consistency, people make personal attributions when there is low consensus and distinctiveness (top row) and stimulus attributions when there is high consensus and distinctiveness (bottom row). Behaviours that are low in consistency (not shown) are attributed to passing circumstances.

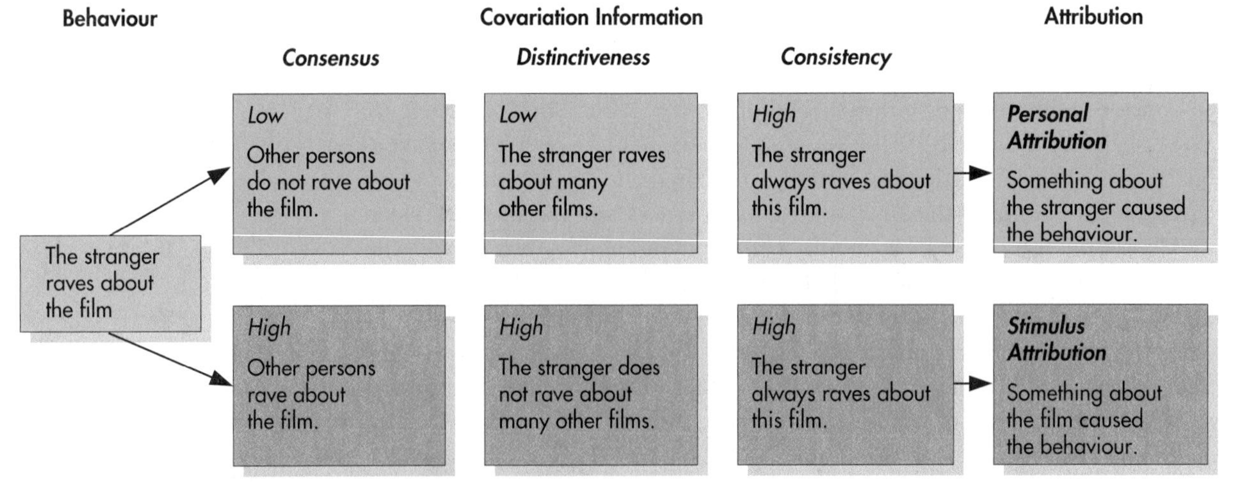

Attribution Biases

When the theories of attribution were first proposed, they were represented by such complicated flow charts, formulas, and diagrams that many social psychologists began to wonder: Do people really analyze behaviour in the way that one might expect of computers? Do people have the time, motivation, or cognitive capacity for such elaborate and mindful processes? The answer is sometimes yes, sometimes no. As social perceivers, we are limited in our ability to process all relevant information, or we may lack the kinds of training needed to employ fully the principles of attribution theory. More important, we often don't make an effort to think carefully about our attributions. With so much to explain and not enough time in a day, people take mental shortcuts, cross their fingers, hope for the best, and get on with life. The problem is that speed brings bias and perhaps even a loss of accuracy. In this section, we examine some of these shortcuts and their consequences.

Cognitive Heuristics According to Daniel Kahneman, Amos Tversky, and others, people often make attributions and other types of social judgments by using cognitive heuristics: information-processing rules of thumb that enable us to think in ways that are quick and easy but that frequently lead to error (Gilovich et al., 2002; Kahneman et al., 1982; Nisbett & Ross, 1980).

One rule of thumb that has particularly troublesome effects on attribution is the **availability heuristic**, a tendency to estimate the odds that an event will occur by how easily instances of it pop to mind. To demonstrate this phenomenon, Tversky and Kahneman (1973) asked research participants: Which is more common, words that start with the letter *r* or words that contain *r* as the third letter? In actuality, the English language has many more words with *r* as the third letter than as the first. Yet most people guessed that more words begin with *r*. The reason? It's easier to bring to mind words in which *r* appears first. Apparently, our estimates of likelihood are heavily influenced by events that are readily available in memory (MacLeod & Campbell, 1992).

The availability heuristic can lead us astray in two ways. First, it gives rise to the **false-consensus effect**, a tendency for people to overestimate the extent to which others share their opinions, attributes, and behaviours. This bias is pervasive. Regardless of whether people are asked to predict how others feel about same sex marriage, the privatization of healthcare, abortion, certain types of music, or norms for appropriate behaviour, they exaggerate the percentage of others who behave similarly or share their views (Krueger, 1998; Ross, Greene, & House, 1977).

To illustrate the effect, Joachim Krueger (2000) asked participants in a study to indicate whether or not they had certain personality traits. Then they were asked to estimate the percentage of people in general who have these same traits. Participants' beliefs about other people's personalities were biased by their own self-perceptions. In part, the false-consensus bias is a by-product of the availability heuristic. We tend to associate with others who are like us in important ways, so we are more likely to notice and recall instances of similar rather than dissimilar behaviour (Deutsch, 1989). Interestingly, people do *not* exhibit this bias when asked to predict the behaviour of people from groups other than their own (Mullen et al., 1992). People also do not exhibit this bias when predicting aspects of others for which they see themselves as distinct rather than typical (Karniol, 2003).

A second consequence of the availability heuristic is that social perceptions are influenced more by one vivid life story than by hard statistical facts. Have you ever wondered why so many people buy lottery tickets despite the astonishingly low odds

availability heuristic
The tendency to estimate the likelihood that an event will occur by how easily instances of it come to mind.

false-consensus effect
The tendency for people to overestimate the extent to which others share their opinions, attributes, and behaviours.

"A single death is a tragedy; a million is a statistic."
—Joseph Stalin

or why so many travellers are afraid to fly even though they are more likely to perish in a car accident? These behaviours are symptomatic of the **base-rate fallacy**—the fact that people are relatively insensitive to numerical base rates, or probabilities, and are influenced instead by graphic, dramatic events such as the sight of a multimillion-dollar lottery winner celebrating on TV or a photograph of bodies being pulled from the wreckage of a plane crash. The base-rate fallacy can thus lead to various misperceptions of risk. Indeed, people overestimate the number of those who die in shootings, fires, floods, and terrorist bombings, and underestimate the death toll caused by heart attacks, strokes, diabetes, and other mundane events (Slovic et al., 1982). Made relevant by recently acquired fears of terrorism, research shows that people's perceptions of risk are affected more by fear, anxiety, and other emotions than by cold probabilities (Loewenstein et al., 2001; Slovic, 2000). At times the result can be capricious and downright irrational. Consistent with the fact that people tend to fear things that sound unfamiliar, participants in one study rated fictional food additives as more hazardous to health when the names were difficult to pronounce, such as Hnegripitrom, than when they were easier to pronounce, such as Magnalroxate (Song & Schwarz, 2009). Interestingly, it appears that this effect can work both ways. Researchers at Brock University in Niagara found that participants were willing to pay more for a wine that was hard to pronounce; those that thought their wine came from the "Tselepou" winery felt it was worth $16 a bottle, compared to $14 for the slightly easier to pronounce "Titakis" wines (Mantonakis & Galiffi, 2011).

People can also be influenced by how easy it is to imagine events that did *not* occur. As thoughtful and curious beings, we often are not content to accept what happens to us or to others without wondering, at least in private, "What if...?" According to Daniel Kahneman and Dale Miller (1986), people's emotional reactions to events are often coloured by **counterfactual thinking**, the tendency to imagine alternative outcomes that might have occurred but did not. There are different types of counterfactual thoughts. If we imagine a result that is better than the actual result, then we're likely to experience disappointment, regret, and frustration. If the imagined result is worse, then we react with emotions that range from relief and satisfaction to elation. Thus, the psychological impact of positive and negative events depends on the way we think about "what might have been" (Roese, 1997; Roese & Olson, 1995). What domains of life trigger the most counterfactual thinking—and the regret that often follows? Summarizing past research, Neal Roese and Amy Summerville (2005) found that people's top three regrets centre, in order, on education ("I should have stayed in school"), career ("If only I had applied for that job"), and romance ("If only I had asked her out")—all domains that present us with opportunities that we may or may not realize.

Obviously, people don't immerse themselves in counterfactual thought after every experience. Research shows that we are more likely to think about what might have been—often with feelings of regret—after negative outcomes that result from actions we take rather than from those we don't take (Byrne & McEleney, 2000). Consider an experience that may sound all too familiar: You take a multiple-choice test and after reviewing an item you had struggled over, you want to change the answer. What do you do? Over the years, research has shown that most changes in test answers are from incorrect to correct. Yet most students harbor the "first instinct fallacy" that it is best to stick with one's original answer. Why? Justin Kruger and his colleagues (2005) found that this myth arises from counterfactual thinking: that students are more likely to react with regret and frustration ("If only I had ...") after changing a correct answer than after failing to change an incorrect answer.

According to Victoria Medvec and Kenneth Savitsky (1997), certain situations—such as being on the *verge* of a better or worse outcome, just above or below some

base-rate fallacy
The finding that people are relatively insensitive to consensus information presented in the form of numerical base rates.

counterfactual thinking
The tendency to imagine alternative events or outcomes that might have occurred but did not.

cut-off point—make it especially easy to conjure up images of what might have been. The implications are intriguing. Imagine, for example, that you are an Olympic athlete and have just won a silver medal—a remarkable feat. Now imagine that you have just won the bronze medal. Which situation would make you feel better? Rationally speaking, you should feel more pride and satisfaction with the silver medal. But what if your achievement had prompted you to engage in counterfactual thinking? What alternative would preoccupy your mind if you had finished in second place? Where would your focus be if you had placed third? Is it possible that the athlete who is better off objectively will feel worse?

During the 1996 Summer Olympics, Nike ran a counterfactual—and controversial—advertisement: "You don't win silver, you lose gold."

To examine this question, Medvec and her colleagues (1995) videotaped 41 athletes in the 1992 Summer Olympic Games at the moment they realized they had won a silver or a bronze medal and again, later, during the medal ceremony. Then they showed these tapes, without sound, to people who did not know the order of finish. These participants were asked to observe the medalists and rate their emotional states on a scale ranging from "agony" to "ecstasy." The intriguing result, as you might expect, was that the bronze medalists, on average, seemed happier than the silver medalists. Was there any more direct evidence of counterfactual thinking? In a second study, participants who watched interviews with many of these same athletes rated the silver medalists as more negatively focused on finishing second rather than first, and the bronze medalists as more positively focused on finishing third rather than fourth. For these world-class athletes, feelings of satisfaction were based more on their thoughts of what might have been than on the reality of what was.

The Fundamental Attribution Error By the time you finish reading this textbook, you will know the cardinal lesson of social psychology: People are profoundly influenced by the *situational* context of behaviour. This point is not as obvious as it may seem. For instance, parents are often surprised to hear that their mischievous child, the family monster, is a perfect angel in the classroom. And students are often surprised to observe that their favourite professor, so eloquent in the lecture hall, may stumble over words in less formal gatherings. These reactions are symptomatic of a well-documented aspect of social perception. When people explain the behaviour of others, they tend to overestimate the role of personal factors and overlook the impact of situations. Because this bias is so pervasive, and sometimes so misleading, it has been called the **fundamental attribution error** (Ross, 1977).

Evidence of the fundamental attribution error was first reported in the Jones and Harris (1967) study described earlier, in which participants read an essay presumably written by a student. In that study, participants were more likely to infer the student's true attitude when the position taken had been freely chosen than when they thought that the student had been assigned to it. But look again at Figure 4.3, and you'll notice that even when participants thought that the student had no choice but to assert a position, they still used the speech to infer his or her attitude. This finding has been repeated many times. Whether the essay topic is nuclear power, abortion, drug laws, or the death penalty, the results are essentially the same (Jones, 1990). As these types of inferences are based on incorrect assumptions regarding the correspondence between an actor's behaviour and his or her disposition, the fundamental attribution error is also referred to as the correspondence bias (Howell & Shepperd, 2011; Miller, 1984).

fundamental attribution error
The tendency to focus on the role of personal causes and underestimate the impact of situations on other people's behaviour. This error is sometimes called correspondence bias.

People fall prey to the fundamental attribution error even when they are fully aware of the situation's impact on behaviour. In one experiment, the participants themselves were assigned to take a position, whereupon they swapped essays and rated each other. Remarkably, they still jumped to conclusions about each other's attitudes (Miller et al., 1981). In another experiment, participants inferred attitudes from a speech even when they were the ones who had assigned the position to be taken (Gilbert & Jones, 1986).

A fascinating study by Lee Ross and his colleagues (1977) demonstrates the fundamental attribution error in a more familiar setting, the TV quiz show. By a flip of the coin, participants in this study were randomly assigned to play the role of either the questioner or the contestant in a quiz game while spectators looked on. In front of the contestant and spectators, the experimenter instructed the questioner to write ten challenging questions from his or her own store of general knowledge. If you are a trivia buff, you can imagine how esoteric such questions can be: Who was the founder of eBay? What team won the NHL Stanley Cup in 1968? It is no wonder that contestants correctly answered only about 40 percent of the questions asked. When the game was over, all participants rated the questioner's and the contestant's general knowledge on a scale of 0 to 100.

Picture the events that transpired. The questioners appeared more knowledgeable than the contestants. After all, they knew all the answers. But a moment's reflection should remind us that the situation put the questioner at a distinct advantage (there were no differences between the two groups on an objective test of general knowledge). Did participants take the questioners' advantage into account, or did they assume that the questioners actually had greater knowledge? The results were startling. Spectators rated the questioners as above average in their general knowledge and the contestants as below average. The contestants even rated themselves as inferior to their partners. Like the spectators, they too were fooled by the loaded situation (see Figure 4.5).

FIGURE 4.5

Fundamental Attribution Error and the TV Quiz Show

Even though the simulated quiz show situation placed questioners in an obvious position of advantage over contestants, observers rated the questioners as more knowledgeable (right). Questioners did not overrate their general knowledge (left); but contestants rated themselves as inferior (middle) and observers rated them as inferior as well. These results illustrate the fundamental attribution error.

(Ross, Amabile, and Steinmetz, 1977.)

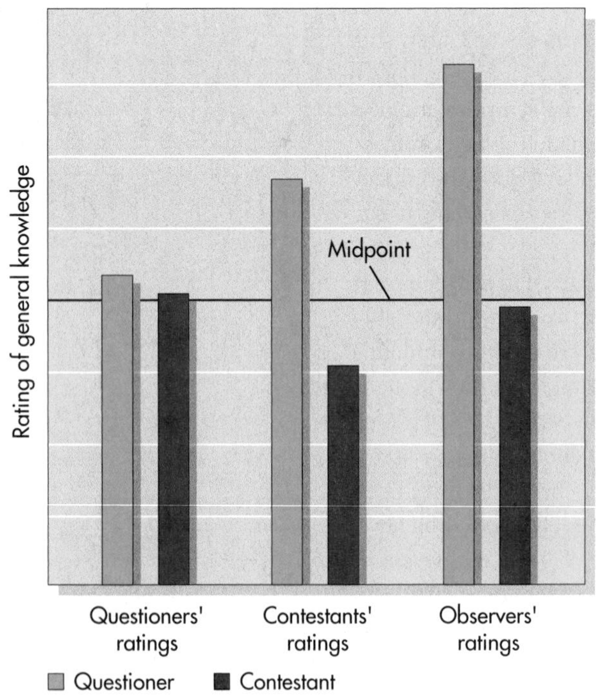

What's going on here? Why do social perceivers consistently make assumptions about persons and fail to appreciate the impact of situations? According to Daniel Gilbert and Patrick Malone (1995), the problem stems in part from *how* we make attributions. Attribution theorists used to assume that people survey all the evidence and then decide on either a personal or a situational attribution. Instead, it now appears that social perception is a two-step process: First we identify the behaviour and make a quick personal attribution; then we correct or adjust that inference to account for situational influences. At least for those raised in a Western culture, the first step is simple and automatic, like a reflex; the second requires attention, thought, and effort (see Figure 4.6). At present, social neuroscience researchers are beginning to use neuroimaging to probe the brain for evidence of this model (Lieberman et al., 2004).

Several research findings support this hypothesis. First, without realizing it, people often form quick impressions of others based on a brief glimpse at a face or sample of behaviour (Newman & Uleman, 1989; Todorov & Uleman, 2004). Second, perceivers are *more*

FIGURE 4.6

Two-Step Model of the Attribution Process

Traditional attribution theories assumed that we analyze behaviour by searching for a personal or situational cause. The two-step model suggests that people make personal attributions automatically and then must consciously adjust that inference in order to account for situational factors.

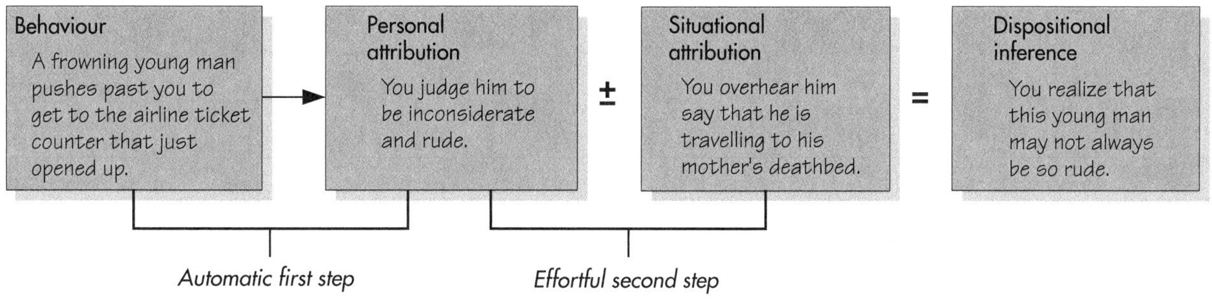
Behaviour
A frowning young man pushes past you to get to the airline ticket counter that just opened up.
Personal attribution
You judge him to be inconsiderate and rude.
±
Situational attribution
You overhear him say that he is travelling to his mother's deathbed.
=
Dispositional inference
You realize that this young man may not always be so rude.
Automatic first step
Effortful second step

likely to commit the fundamental attribution error when they are cognitively busy, or distracted, as they observe the target person than when they pay full attention (Gilbert et al., 1992; Trope & Alfieri, 1997). Since the two-step model predicts that personal attributions are automatic but that the later adjustment for situational factors requires conscious thought, it makes sense to suggest that when attention is divided, when the attribution is made hastily, or when perceivers lack motivation, the second step suffers more than the first. As Gilbert and his colleagues (1988) put it, "The first step is a snap, but the second one's a doozy" (p. 738).

Why is the first step such a snap, and why does it seem so natural for people to assume a link between acts and personal dispositions? One possible explanation is based on Heider's (1958) insight that people see dispositions in behaviour because of a perceptual bias, something like an optical illusion. When you listen to a speech or watch a quiz show, the actor is the conspicuous *figure* of your attention; the situation fades into the *background* ("out of sight, out of mind," as they say). And according to Heider, people attribute events to factors that are perceptually conspicuous, or *salient*. To test this hypothesis, Shelley Taylor and Susan Fiske (1975) varied the seating arrangements of observers who watched as two actors engaged in a carefully staged conversation. In each session, the participants were seated so that they faced actor A, actor B, or both actors. When later questioned about their observations, they rated the actor they faced as the more dominant member of the pair, the one who set the tone and direction.

© Roth Stock/Everett Collection

How knowledgeable is this man? Alex Trebek has hosted the TV quiz show, Jeopardy! since 1984. As host, Trebek reads questions to contestants, and then reveals the correct answers. In light of the quiz show study by Ross and others (1977), which illustrates the fundamental attribution error, viewers probably see Trebek as highly knowledgeable—despite knowing that the answers he recites are provided to him as part of his job.

People may commit the fundamental attribution error when they explain the behaviour of others, but do they exhibit the same bias in explaining their own behaviour? Think about it. Are you shy or outgoing, or does your behaviour depend on the situation? Are you calm or intense, quiet or talkative, lenient or firm? Or, again, does your behaviour in these respects depend primarily on the situation? Now think of a friend, and answer the same questions about his or her behaviour. Do you notice a difference? Chances are, you do. Research shows that people are more likely to say, "It depends on the situation" to describe themselves than to describe others (Goldberg, 1978).

Like social psychologists people are sensitive to situational causes when explaining the behaviour of others. FALSE.

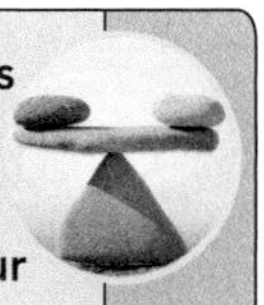

The tendency to make personal attributions for the behaviour of others and situational attributions for ourselves is called the **actor-observer effect** and has been widely demonstrated (Jones & Nisbett, 1972; Watson, 1982). In one study, 60 prison inmates and their counsellors were asked to explain why the inmates had committed their offences. The counsellors cited enduring personal characteristics; the prisoners referred to transient situational factors (Saulnier & Perlman, 1981).

Culture and Attribution

Attribution researchers used to assume that people all over the world explained human behaviour in the same ways. It is now clear, however, that the culture in which we live shapes in subtle but profound ways the kinds of attributions we make about people, their behaviour, and social situations (Nisbett, 2003). Consider the contrasting orientations between Western cultures (whose members tend to believe that persons are autonomous, motivated by internal forces, and responsible for their own actions) and non-Western "collectivist" cultures (whose members take a more holistic view that emphasizes the relationship between persons and their surroundings).

actor-observer effect
The tendency to attribute our own behaviour to situational causes and the behaviour of others to personal factors.

Do these contrasting cultural worldviews influence the attributions we make? Is it possible that the fundamental attribution error is a uniquely western phenomenon? To answer these questions, Joan Miller (1984) asked Americans and Asian Indians of varying ages to describe the causes of positive and negative behaviours they had observed in their lives. Among young children, there were no cultural differences. With increasing age, however, the American participants made more personal attributions, while the Indians made more situational attributions (see ▶ Figure 4.7).

▶ FIGURE 4.7

Fundamental Attribution Error: A Western Bias?

American and Asian Indian participants of varying ages described the causes of negative actions they had observed. Among young children, there were no cultural differences. With increasing age, however, Americans made more personal attributions, and Indian participants made more situational attributions. Explanations for positive behaviours followed a similar pattern. This finding suggests that the fundamental attribution error is a Western phenomenon.

(J. G. Miller, 1984.)

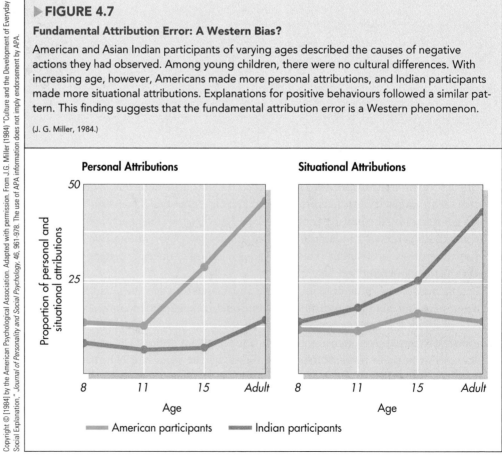

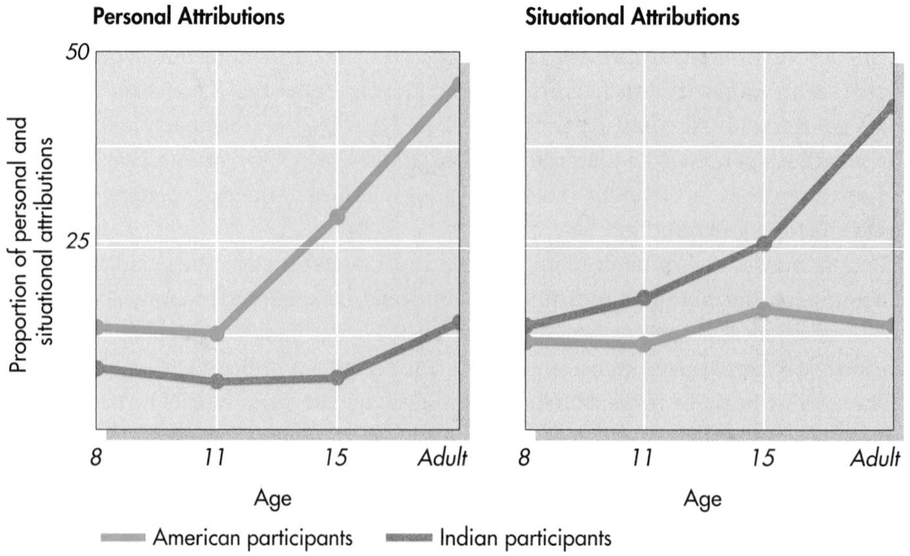

Testing this hypothesis in different ways, other studies as well have revealed that people form habits of thought, learning to make attributions according to culturally formed beliefs about the causes of human behaviour (Lieberman et al., 2005; Masuda & Kitayama, 2004; Miyamoto & Kitayama, 2002).

According to Ara Norenzayan and Richard Nisbett (2000), cultural differences in attribution are founded on varying folk theories about human causality. Western cultures, they note, emphasize the individual person and his or her attributes, whereas East Asian cultures focus on the background or field that surrounds that person. To test this hypothesis, they showed American and Japanese students underwater scenes featuring a cast of small fish, small animals, plants, rocks, and coral—and one or more large, fast-moving *focal* fish, the stars of the show. Moments later, when asked to recount what they had seen, both groups recalled details about the focal fish to a nearly equal extent, but the Japanese reported far more details about the supporting cast in the background. Other researchers, too, have observed cultural differences in the extent to which people notice, think about, and remember the details of situational contexts (Ishii et al., 2003; Kitayama et al., 2003; Masuda & Nisbett, 2001). Compared to the inhabitants of most western cultures, people from East Asia tend to see humans as more malleable and likelier to be influenced by social groups, situations, and other contextual factors (Choi et al., 1999). As such, they are less prone to commit the fundamental attribution error first identified by Jones and Harris (Miyamoto & Kitayama, 2002).

James T. Spencer/Photo Researchers

Look at this tropical underwater scene, then turn away and try to recount as much of it as you can. What did you notice? What did you forget? When researchers showed American and Japanese students underwater scenes, they found that while both groups recalled the focal fish (like the large blue one shown here), the Japanese recalled more about the elements of the background.

Clearly, the world is becoming a global village characterized by increasing racial and ethnic diversity within countries. Many people who migrate from one country to another become *bicultural* in their identity, retaining some of their ancestral heritage while adopting some of the lifestyles and values of their new homeland. How do these bicultural individuals make attributions for human behaviour? Is it possible that they view people through one cultural frame or the other, depending on which one is brought to mind? It's interesting that when shown a picture of one fish swimming ahead of a group, and asked why, Americans see the lone fish as *leading* the others (a personal attribution), while Chinese see the same fish as being *chased* by the others (a situational attribution). But what about bicultural social perceivers? In a study of China-born students attending university in California, researchers presented images symbolizing one of the two cultures (such as the U.S. and Chinese flags), administered the fish test, and found that compared to students exposed to the American images, those who saw the Chinese images made more situational attributions, seeing the lone fish as being chased rather than as leading (see ▶ Figure 4.8). Apparently, it is possible for us to hold differing cultural worldviews at the same time and to perceive others within either frame, depending on which culture is brought to mind (Hong et al., 2000; Oyserman & Lee, 2008).

FIGURE 4.8

Attributions Within Cultural Frames

When one fish swims ahead of others in a group, Americans see that fish as ***leading*** the others (a personal attribution), while Chinese see it as being ***chased*** by the others (a situational attribution). In a study of bicultural Chinese students attending college in California, Ying-yi Hong and others (2000) displayed visual images that symbolized the United States or China before administering this fish test. As you can see, compared to students who were not first shown any images (centre), the tendency to make situational attributions was more common among those exposed to Chinese images (right) and less common among those exposed to American images (left). For people familiar with both worldviews, it appears that social perceptions are fluid—and depend on which culture is brought to mind.

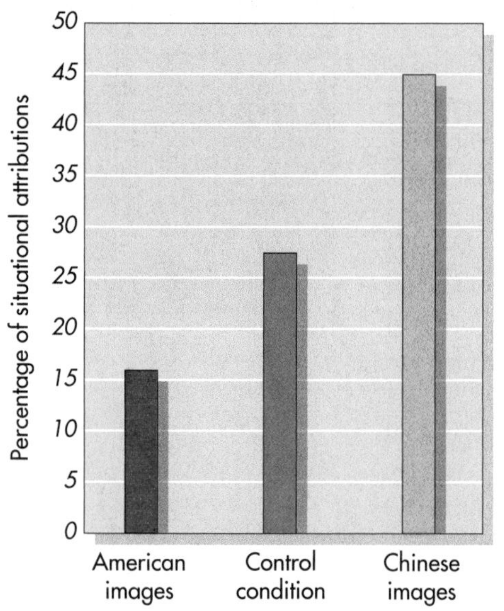

Motivational Biases

As objective as we try to be, our social perceptions are sometimes coloured by personal needs, wishes, and preferences. To illustrate, look at the object in Figure 4.9. What do you see? In a series of studies, Emily Balcetis and David Dunning (2006) showed stimuli like this one to students who thought they were participating in a taste-testing experiment. The students were told that they would be randomly assigned to taste either freshly squeezed orange juice or a vile, greenish, foul-smelling "organic" drink—depending on whether a letter or a number was flashed on a laptop computer. For those told that a letter would assign them to the orange juice condition, 72 percent saw the letter "B." For those told that a number would assign them to the orange juice, 61 percent saw the number "13." In some very basic ways, people have a tendency to see what they want to see.

People have a strong need for self-esteem, and this motive can lead us to make favourable, self-serving, and one-sided attributions for our own behaviour. In Chapter 3, we saw that research with students, teachers, parents, workers, athletes, and others shows that we take more credit for success than for failure. Similarly, people seek more information about their strengths than about their weaknesses, overestimate their contribution to group efforts, exaggerate their control, and predict a rosy future. The false-consensus effect described earlier also has a self-serving side to it. It seems that we overestimate the extent to which others think, feel, and behave as we do, in part to reassure ourselves that our own ways are correct, normal, and socially appropriate (Alicke & Largo, 1995). This positivity bias in attributions is ubiquitous. Through a meta-analysis of 266 studies involving thousands of participants, Amy Mezulis and others (2004) found that except in some Asian cultures, "the self-serving bias is pervasive in the general population" (p. 711).

According to David Dunning and his colleagues, the need for self-esteem can bias our social perceptions in other subtle ways, too—even when we don't realize that the self is implicated. For example, do you consider yourself to be a "people-person," or are you more of a "task-oriented" type? And which of the two styles do you think makes for great leadership? It turns out that students who describe themselves as people-oriented see social skills as necessary for good leadership, while those who are more task-focused see a task orientation as better for leadership. Hence, people tend to judge favourably others who are similar to themselves, rather than different, on key characteristics (McElwee et al., 2001).

At times, personal defensive motives lead us to blame others for their misfortunes. Consider the following classic experiment. Participants thought they were taking part in an emotion-perception study. One person, actually a confederate, was selected randomly to take a memory test while the others looked on. Each time the confederate made a mistake, she was jolted by a painful electric shock (actually, there was no shock; what participants saw was a staged videotape). Since participants knew that only the luck of the draw had kept them off the "hot seat," you might think they would react with sympathy and compassion. Not so. In fact, they belittled the hapless confederate (Lerner & Simmons, 1966).

Melvin Lerner (1980) argues that the tendency to be critical of victims stems from our deep-seated **belief in a just world**. According to Lerner, people need to view the world as a just place in which we "get what we deserve" and "deserve what we get"—a world where hard work and clean living always pay off and where laziness and a sinful lifestyle are punished. To believe otherwise is to concede that we, too, are vulnerable to the cruel twists and turns of fate. Research suggests that the belief in a just world can help victims cope and serves as a buffer against stress. But how might this belief system influence our perceptions of *others*? If people cannot help or compensate the victims of misfortune, they turn on them. Thus, it is often assumed that poor people are lazy, that crime victims are careless, that battered wives provoke their violent and abusive husbands, and that gay men and woman with AIDS are promiscuous. In addition, a tendency to believe in a just world may be related to one's long-term goals; that is, in order to achieve a long-term goal we need to believe that the world is a fair and just place. That if we work hard to achieve these goals, we will eventually realize them (Hafer et al., 2005). As you might expect, cross-national comparisons reveal that people in poorer countries are less likely than those in more affluent countries to believe in a just world (Furnham, 2003).

FIGURE 4.9

Motivated Visual Perception: How People See What They Want to See

Look at the image below. What do you see, the letter B or the number 13? The stimulus itself is ambiguous and can plausibly be seen either way. Research participants who thought they were in a taste-testing experiment were told that they'd be assigned to taste orange juice or a foul-smelling green drink depending on whether a letter or a number was flashed on a laptop computer. For those told that a ***letter*** would yield orange juice, 72 percent saw the image as "B." For those told that a ***number*** would yield orange juice, 61 percent saw a "13." This difference shows that sometimes people see what they ***want*** to see.

(Balcetis & Dunning, 2006.)

The tendency to disparage victims may seem like just another symptom of the fundamental attribution error: too much focus on the person and not enough on the situation. But the conditions that trigger this tendency suggest there is more to it. Studies have shown that accident victims are held more responsible for their fate when the consequences of the accident are severe rather than mild (Walster, 1966), when the victim's situation is similar to the perceiver's (Shaver, 1970), when the perceiver is generally anxious about threats to the self (Thornton, 1992), and when the perceiver identifies with the victim (Aguiar et al., 2008). The more threatened we feel by an apparent injustice, the greater is the need to protect ourselves from the dreadful implication that it could happen to us—an implication we defend by disparaging the victim. Ironically, some research shows that people may also satisfy their belief in a just world by *enhancing* members of disadvantaged groups—for example, by inferring that poor people are happy and that obese people are sociable, both attributes that restore justice by compensation (Kay & Jost, 2003; Kay et al., 2005).

In a laboratory experiment that reveals part of this process at work, participants at Brock University watched a TV news story about a boy who was robbed and beaten. Some were told that the boy's assailants were captured, tried, and sent to prison. Others were told that the assailants fled the country, never to be brought to trial—a story that strains one's belief in a just world. Afterward, participants were asked to name as quickly as they could the colours in which various words in a list were typed (for example, the word *chair* may have been written in blue, *floor* in yellow, and *wide* in red). When the words themselves were neutral, all participants—regardless of which story they had seen—were equally fast at naming the colours. But when the words pertained to justice (words such as *fair* and *unequal*), those who had seen the justice-threatened version of the story were more distracted by the words and, hence, slower to name the colours. In fact, the more distracted they were, the more they derogated the victim. With their cherished belief in a just world threatened, these participants became highly sensitive to the concept of "justice"—and quick to disparage the innocent victim (Hafer, 2000).

belief in a just world
The belief that individuals get what they deserve in life, an orientation that leads people to disparage victims.

Integration: From Dispositions to Impressions

When behaviour is attributed to situational factors, we do not generally make inferences about the actor. However, personal attributions often lead us to infer that a person has a certain disposition—that the leader of a failing business is incompetent, for example, or that the enemy who extends the olive branch seeks peace. Human beings are not one-dimensional, however, and one trait does not a person make. To have a complete picture of someone, social perceivers must assemble the various bits and pieces into a unified impression.

Information Integration: The Arithmetic

Once personal attributions are made, how are they combined into a single coherent picture of a person? How do we approach the process of **impression formation**? Do we simply add up all of a person's traits and calculate a mental average, or do we combine the information in more complicated ways? Anyone who has written or received letters of recommendation will surely appreciate the practical implications. Suppose that you're told an applicant is friendly and intelligent, two highly favourable qualities. Would you be more or less impressed if you then learned that this applicant was also prudent and even-tempered, two moderately favourable qualities? If you are more impressed, then you are intuitively following a *summation* model of impression formation: The more positive traits there are, the better. If you are less impressed, then you are using an *averaging* model: The higher the average value of all the various traits, the better.

impression formation
The process of integrating information about a person to form a coherent impression.

To quantify the formation of impressions, Norman Anderson (1968) had research participants rate the desirability of 555 traits on a 7-point scale. By calculating the average ratings, he obtained a *scale value* for each trait (*sincere* had the highest scale value; *liar* had the lowest). In an earlier study, Anderson (1965) used similar values and compared the summation and averaging models. Specifically, he asked a group of participants to rate how much they liked a person described by two traits with extremely high scale values *(H, H)*. A second group received a list of four traits, including two that were high and two that were moderately high in their scale values *(H, H, M1, M1)*. In a third group, participants received two extremely low, negative traits *(L, L)*. In a fourth group, they received four traits, including two that were low and two that were moderately low *(L, L, M2, M2)*. What effect did the moderate traits have on impressions? As predicted by an averaging model, the moderate traits diluted rather than added to the impact of the highly positive and negative traits. The practical implication for those who write letters of recommendation is clear. Applicants are better off if their letters include only the most glowing comments and omit favourable remarks that are somewhat more guarded in nature.

Getty Images

What sort of impression might people have of WikiLeaks founder Julian Assange? What sort of weighting would you give to any positive information you learned about him?

After extensive amounts of research, it appears that although people tend to combine traits by averaging, the process is somewhat more complicated. Consistent with Anderson's (1981) **information integration theory**, impressions formed of others are based on a combination, or integration, of (1) personal dispositions of the perceiver and (2) a *weighted* average, not a simple average, of the target person's characteristics (Kashima & Kerekes, 1994). Let's look more closely at these two sets of factors.

Deviations from the Arithmetic

Like other aspects of our social perceptions, impression formation does not follow the rules of cold logic. Weighted averaging may describe the way most people combine different traits, but the whole process begins with a warm-blooded human perceiver, not a computer. Thus, certain deviations from the "arithmetic" are inevitable.

Perceiver Characteristics To begin with, perceivers differ in the kinds of impressions they form of others. Some people seem to measure everyone with an intellectual yardstick; others look for physical beauty, a warm smile, a good sense of humour, or a firm handshake. Whatever the attribute, each of us is more likely to notice and recall certain traits than others (Bargh et al., 1988; Higgins et al., 1982). Thus, when people are asked to describe a group of target individuals, there's typically more overlap between the various descriptions provided *by* the same *perceiver* than there is between those provided *for* the same *target* (Dornbusch et al., 1965; Park, 1986). Part of the reason for the differences among perceivers is that we tend to use ourselves as a standard, or frame of reference, when evaluating others. Compared with the inert couch potato, for example, the serious jock is more likely to see others as less active and athletic (Dunning & Hayes, 1996). As we saw earlier, people also tend to see their own skills and traits as particularly desirable for others to have (McElwee et al., 2001).

A perceiver's current, temporary *mood* can also influence the impressions formed of others (Forgas, 2000). For example, Joseph Forgas and Gordon Bower (1987) told research participants that they had performed very well or poorly on a test of social adjustment. As expected, this feedback altered their moods; it also affected their outlook on others. When presented with behavioural information about various characters, participants spent more time attending to positive facts and formed more favourable impressions when they were happy than when they were sad. Follow-up research shows that people who are induced into a happy mood are also more optimistic, more lenient, and less critical in the attributions they make for others who succeed or fail (Forgas & Locke, 2005). They are also more likely to interpret another person's smile as genuine and heartfelt (Forgas & East, 2008).

Priming Effects Clearly, the combined effects of stable perceiver differences and fluctuating moods point to an important conclusion: that to some extent, impression formation is in the eye of the beholder. The characteristics we tend to notice in other people also change from time to time, depending on recent experiences. Have you ever noticed that once a seldom-used word slips into a conversation, it is often repeated over and over again? If so, you have observed **priming**, the tendency for frequently or recently used concepts to come to mind easily and influence the way we interpret new information.

The effect of priming on person impressions was first demonstrated by E. Tory Higgins and others (1977). Research participants were presented with a list of trait words, ostensibly as part of an experiment on memory. In fact, the task was designed as a priming device to plant certain ideas in their minds. Some participants read words that evoked a positive image: *brave, independent, adventurous.* Others read words that evoked a more negative image: *reckless, foolish, careless.* Later, in what they thought to

information integration theory
The theory that impressions are based on perceiver dispositions and a weighted average of a target person's traits.

priming
The tendency for recently used or perceived words or ideas to come to mind easily and influence the interpretation of new information.

be an unrelated experiment, participants read about a man who climbed mountains, drove in a demolition derby, and tried to cross the Atlantic Ocean in a sailboat. As predicted, their impressions were shaped by the trait words they had earlier memorized. Those exposed to positive words later formed more favourable impressions of the character than those exposed to negative words. All the participants read exactly the same description, yet they formed different impressions depending on what was already on their minds. In fact, priming seems to work best when the prime words are presented so rapidly that people are not even aware of the exposure (Bargh & Pietromonaco, 1982).

Recent research now shows that our motivations, and even our social behaviours, are also subject to the automatic effects of priming without awareness. In one provocative study, John Bargh and Tanya Chartrand (1999) gave participants a "word search" puzzle that contained either neutral words or words associated with achievement motivation (*strive, win, master, compete, succeed*). Afterward, the participants were left alone and given three minutes to write down as many words as they could from a set of Scrabble letter tiles. When the three-minute limit was up, they were signalled over an intercom to stop. Did these participants, driven to obtain a high score, stop on cue or continue to write? Through the use of hidden cameras, the experimenters observed that 57 percent of those primed with achievement-related words continued to write after the stop signal—compared to only 22 percent in the control group.

Looking at priming effects on social behaviour, Bargh, Chen, and Burrows (1996) gave people 30 sets of words presented in scrambled order ("he it hides finds instantly") and told them to use some of the words in each set to form grammatical sentences. After explaining the test, which would take about five minutes, the experimenter told participants to locate him down the hall when they were finished so he could administer a second task. So far, so good. But when participants found the experimenter, he was in the hallway immersed in a conversation—and he stayed in that conversation for ten full minutes without even acknowledging their presence. What's a person to do, wait patiently or interrupt? The participants didn't know it, but some had worked on a scrambled word test that contained many "politeness" words (*yield, respect, considerate, courteous*), while others had been exposed to words related to rudeness (*disturb, intrude, bold, bluntly*). Would these test words secretly prime participants, a few minutes later, to behave in one way or the other? Yes. Compared with those given the neutral words to unscramble, participants primed for rudeness were more likely—and those primed for politeness were less likely—to break in and interrupt the experimenter (see ▶ Figure 4.10).

What accounts for this effect of priming, not only on our social perceptions but also on our behaviour? The link between perception and behaviour is automatic; it happens like a mindless reflex. Present scrambled words that prime the "elderly" stereotype (*old, bingo*) and research participants walk out of the experiment more slowly as if mimicking an elderly person (Dijksterhuis & Bargh, 2001). But why? Joseph Cesario and others (2006) suggest that the automatic priming of behaviour is an adaptive social mechanism that helps us to prepare for upcoming encounters with a primed target—if we are so motivated. After measuring participants' attitudes toward the elderly, these researchers predicted and found that those who liked old people walked more slowly after priming (as if synchronizing with a slow friend), while those who disliked old people walked more quickly (as if fleeing from such an interaction).

Target Characteristics Just as not all social perceivers are created equal, neither are all traits created equal. In recent years, personality researchers have discovered, across cultures, that individuals can reliably be distinguished from one another along five broad traits, or factors: extroversion, emotional stability, openness to experience, agreeableness, and conscientiousness (De Raad, 2000; McCrae & Costa, 2003; Wiggins, 1996). Some of these factors are easier to judge than others. Based on their review of 32 studies, David Kenny and others (1994) found that social perceivers are most likely to agree in their judgments of a target's extroversion—that is, the extent to which he or she is sociable, friendly, fun-loving, outgoing, and adventurous. It seems that this characteristic is easy to spot—and different perceivers often agree on it even when rating a target person whom they are seeing for the first time.

The valence of a trait—whether it is considered socially desirable or undesirable— also affects its impact on our final impressions. Specifically, research shows that people exhibit a *trait negativity bias,* the tendency for negative information to weigh more heavily than positive information (Rozin & Royzman, 2001; Skowronski & Carlston, 1989). This means that we form more extreme impressions of a person who is said to be untrustworthy than of one who is said to be honest. We tend to view others favourably, so we are quick to take notice and pay careful attention when this expectation is violated (Pratto & John, 1991). One bad trait may be enough to destroy a person's reputation—regardless of other qualities.

When you think about it, it's probably adaptive for people to stay alert for—and pay particularly close attention to—negative information. Research suggests that people are quicker to sense their exposure to subliminally presented negative words such as *bomb, thief, shark,* and *cancer,* than to positive words such as *baby, sweet, friend,* and *beach* (Dijksterhuis & Aarts, 2003). This sensitivity to negative information is found in infants less than a year old (Vaish et al., 2008). It can even be "seen" in the brain (Smith et al., 2003). In one study, for example, Tiffany Ito and others (1998) exposed research participants to slides that depicted images that were positive (a red Ferrari, people enjoying a roller coaster), negative (a mutilated face, a handgun pointed at the camera), or neutral (a plate, a hair dryer). Using electrodes attached to participants' scalps, these researchers recorded electrical activity in different areas of the brain during the slide presentation. Sure enough, they observed that certain types of activity were more pronounced when participants saw negative images than when they saw stimuli that were positive or neutral. It appears that, as these researchers commented, "negative information weighs more heavily on the brain" (p. 887).

FIGURE 4.10

The Priming of Social Behaviour Without Awareness

Would waiting participants interrupt the busy experimenter? Compared with those who had previously been given neutral words to unscramble (centre), participants given politeness words were less likely to cut in (left), and those given rudeness words were more likely to cut in (right). These results show that priming can influence not only our social judgments but our behaviour as well.

(Bargh, Chen, and Burrows, 1996.)

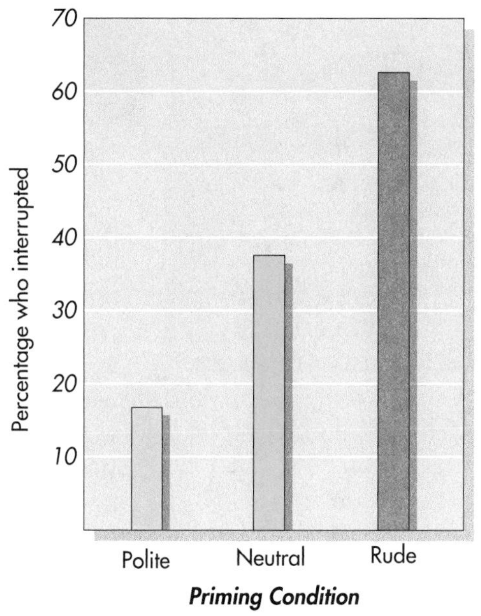

The impact of trait information on our impressions of others depends not only on characteristics of the perceiver and target but on context as well. Two contextual factors are particularly important in this regard: (1) implicit theories of personality and (2) the order in which we receive information about one trait relative to other traits.

Implicit Personality Theories In 2010, Russell Williams, a commander at the Canadian Forces Base in Trenton, Ontario, was arrested, and eventually convicted, on charges that included break and enter, forcible confinement, sexual assault, and murder. Williams was a decorated soldier who had, at one time, been a pilot for high-ranking dignitaries, including the Queen and the Prime Minister. His neighbours, with whom he and his wife had shared dinners and played cards, were stunned. It's

Bill Ross/Corbis Images

Thinkstock

Brain research shows that when people are exposed to negative emotional images—such as the car bomb on the right as opposed to the beach scene on the left—activity in certain parts of the brain is more pronounced.

easy to understand why people initially reacted to the charges with such disbelief. He just didn't seem like *the kind of person* who could commit such cold-blooded acts. That reaction was based on an **implicit personality theory**—a network of assumptions that we hold about relationships among various types of people, traits, and behaviours. Knowing that someone has one trait thus leads us to infer that he or she has other traits as well (Bruner & Tagiuri, 1954; Schneider, 1973; Sedikides & Anderson, 1994). For example, you might assume that a person who is unpredictable is also dangerous or that someone who speaks slowly is also slow-witted. You might also assume that certain traits are linked to certain behaviours (Reeder, 1993; Reeder & Brewer, 1979).

Solomon Asch (1946) was the first to discover that the presence of one trait often implies the presence of others. Asch told one group of research participants that an individual was "intelligent, skilful, industrious, warm, determined, practical and cautious." Another group read an identical list of traits, except that the word *warm* was replaced by *cold.* Only the one term was changed, but the two groups formed very different impressions. Participants inferred that the warm person was also happier and more generous, good-natured, and humorous than the cold person. When two other words were varied (*polite* and *blunt*), however, the differences were less pronounced. Why? Asch concluded that *warm* and *cold* are **central traits**, meaning that they imply the presence of certain other traits and exert a powerful influence on final impressions. Other researchers have observed similar effects (Stapel & Koomen, 2000). In fact, the impact of central traits is not limited to studies using trait lists. When undergraduate students in different classes were led to believe that a guest lecturer was a warm or a cold person, their impressions after the lecture were consistent with these beliefs—even though he gave the same lecture to everyone (Kelley, 1950; Widmeyer & Loy, 1988).

The Primacy Effect The order in which a trait is discovered can also influence its impact. It is often said that first impressions are critical, and social psychologists are quick to agree. Studies show that information often has greater impact when presented early in a sequence rather than late, a common phenomenon known as the **primacy effect**.

In another of Asch's (1946) classic experiments, one group of participants learned that a person was "intelligent, industrious, impulsive, critical, stubborn, and envious." A second group received exactly the same list but in reverse order. Rationally speaking, the two groups should have felt the same way about the person. But instead, participants who heard the first list in which the more positive traits came first formed more favourable impressions than did those who heard the second list. Similar findings were obtained among participants who watched a videotape of a woman taking an aptitude test. In all cases, she correctly answered 15 out of 30 multiple-choice questions. But participants who observed a pattern of initial success followed by failure perceived the woman as more intelligent than did those who observed the opposite pattern of failure followed by success (Jones et al., 1968). There are exceptions, but as a general rule, people tend to be more heavily influenced by the "early returns."

implicit personality theory
A network of assumptions people make about the relationships among traits and behaviours.

central traits
Traits that exert a powerful influence on overall impressions.

primacy effect
The tendency for information presented early in a sequence to have more impact on impressions than information presented later.

What accounts for this primacy effect? There are two basic explanations. The first is that once perceivers think they have formed an accurate impression of someone, they tend to pay less attention to subsequent information. Thus, when research participants read a series of statements about a person, the amount of time they spent reading the items declined steadily with each succeeding statement (Belmore, 1987).

Does this mean we are doomed to a life of primacy? Not at all. If unstimulated or tired, our attention may wane. But if perceivers are sufficiently motivated to avoid tuning out and are not pressured to form a quick first impression, then primacy effects are diminished (Anderson & Hubert, 1963; Kruglanski & Freund, 1983). Thus, in one study, students "leaped to conclusions" about a target person on the basis of preliminary information when they were mentally fatigued from having just taken a two-hour exam—but not when they were fresh, alert, and motivated to pay attention (Webster et al., 1996). In addition, Arie Kruglanski and Donna Webster (1996) have found that some people are more likely than others to "seize" upon and "freeze" their first impressions. Indeed, they find that individuals differ in their **need for closure**, the desire to reduce ambiguity. People who are low in this regard are open-minded, deliberate, and perhaps even reluctant to draw firm conclusions about others. In contrast, those who are high in the need for closure tend to be impulsive and impatient, and to form quick and lasting judgments of others.

More unsettling is the second reason for primacy, known as the *change-of-meaning hypothesis.* Once people have formed an impression, they start to interpret inconsistent information in light of that impression. Asch's research shows just how malleable the meaning of a trait can be. When people are told that a kind person is *calm,* they assume that he or she is gentle, peaceful, and serene. When a cruel person is said to be *calm,* however, the same word is interpreted to mean cool, shrewd, and calculating. There are many examples to illustrate the point. Based on your first impression, the word *proud* can mean self-respecting or conceited, *critical* can mean astute or picky, and *impulsive* can mean spontaneous or reckless.

It is remarkable just how creative we are in our efforts to transform a bundle of contradictions into a coherent, integrated impression. For example, the person who is said to be "good" but also "a thief" can be viewed as a Robin Hood type of character (Burnstein & Schul, 1982). Asch and Henri Zukier (1984) presented people with inconsistent trait pairs and found that they used different strategies to reconcile the conflicts. For example, a brilliant-foolish person may be seen as "very bright on abstract matters, but silly about day-to-day practical tasks"; a sociable-lonely person has "many superficial ties, but is unable to form deep relations"; and a cheerful-gloomy person may simply be someone who is "moody."

Confirmation Biases: From Impressions to Reality

> "Please your majesty," said the knave, "I didn't write it and they can't prove I did; there's no name signed at the end." "If you didn't sign it," said the King, "that only makes the matter worse. You must have meant some mischief, or else you'd have signed your name like an honest man."

This exchange, taken from Lewis Carroll's *Alice's Adventures in Wonderland,* illustrates the power of existing impressions. It is striking but often true: Once people make up their minds about something—even if they have incomplete information—they become more and more unlikely to change their minds when confronted with new evidence. Political leaders thus refuse to withdraw their support for government programs that don't work, and scientists stubbornly defend their theories in the face

need for closure
The desire to reduce cognitive uncertainty, which heightens the importance of first impressions.

"It is a capital mistake to theorize before you have all the evidence. It biases the judgment."

—Arthur Conan Doyle

of conflicting research data. These instances are easy to explain. Politicians and scientists are personally invested in their opinions, as pride, funding, and reputation may be at stake. But what about people who more innocently fail to revise their opinions, often to their own detriment? What about the baseball manager who clings to old strategies that are ineffective, or the trial lawyer who always selects juries according to false stereotypes? Why are they often so slow to face the facts? As we will see, people are subject to various **confirmation biases**—tendencies to interpret, seek, and create information in ways that verify existing beliefs.

Perseverance of Beliefs

Imagine you are looking at a slide that is completely out of focus. Gradually, it becomes focused enough so that the image is less blurry. At this point, the experimenter wants to know if you can recognize the picture. The response you're likely to make is interesting. Participants in experiments of this type have more trouble making an identification if they watch the gradual focusing procedure than if they simply view the final, blurry image. In the mechanics of the perceptual process, people apparently form early impressions that interfere with their subsequent ability to "see straight" once presented with improved evidence (Bruner & Potter, 1964). As we will see in this section, social perception is subject to the same kind of interference, which is another reason why first impressions often stick like glue even after we are forced to confront information that discredits them.

Consider what happens when you're led to expect something that does not materialize. In one study, John Darley and Paget Gross (1983) asked participants to evaluate the academic potential of a nine-year-old girl named Hannah. One group was led to believe that Hannah came from an affluent community in which both parents were well-educated professionals (high expectations). A second group thought she was from a run-down urban neighbourhood and that both parents were uneducated blue-collar workers (low expectations). As shown in ▶ Figure 4.11, participants in the first group were slightly more optimistic in their ratings of Hannah's potential than were those in the second group. In each of these groups, however, half the participants then watched a videotape of Hannah taking an achievement test. Her performance on the tape seemed average. She correctly answered some difficult questions but missed others that were relatively easy. Look again at Figure 4.11 and you'll see that even though all participants saw the same tape, Hannah now received much lower ratings of ability from those who thought she was poor, and higher ratings from those who thought she was affluent. Apparently, presenting an identical body of mixed evidence did not extinguish the biasing effects of beliefs—it *fuelled* these effects.

Events that are ambiguous enough to support contrasting interpretations are like inkblots: We see in them what we want or expect to see. Illustrating this point, researchers had people rate from photographs the extent to which pairs of adults and children resembled each other. Interestingly, the participants did not see more resemblance in parents and offspring than in random pairs of adults and children. Yet when told that certain pairs were related, they did "see" a resemblance, even when the relatedness information was false (Bressan & Dal Martello, 2002).

What about information that plainly disconfirms our beliefs? What then happens to our first impressions? Craig Anderson and his colleagues (1980) addressed this question by supplying participants with false information. After they had time to think about the information, they were told that it was untrue. In one experiment, half the participants read case studies suggesting that people who take risks make better firefighters than do those who are cautious. The others read cases suggesting

confirmation bias
The tendency to seek, interpret, and create information that verifies existing beliefs.

FIGURE 4.11

Mixed Evidence: Does it Extinguish or Fuel First Impressions?

Participants evaluated the potential of a schoolgirl. Without seeing her test performance, those with high expectations rated her slightly higher than did those with low expectations. Among participants who watched a tape of the girl taking a test, the expectations effect was even greater.

(Darley & Gross, 1983.)

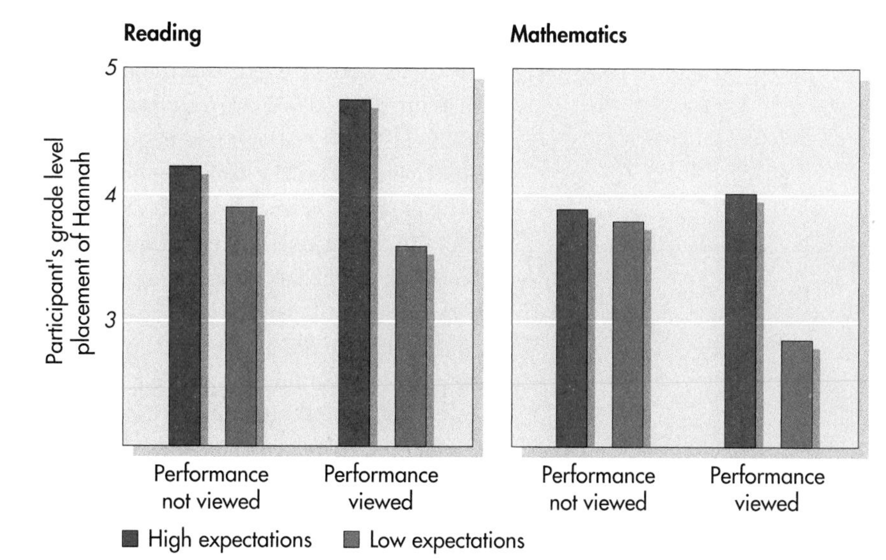

the opposite conclusion. Next, participants were asked to come up with a theory for the suggested correlation. The possibilities are easy to imagine: "He who hesitates is lost" supports risk-taking, whereas "You have to look before you leap" supports caution. Finally, participants were led to believe that the session was over and were told that the information they had received was false, manufactured for the sake of the experiment. Participants, however, did not abandon their firefighter theories. Instead they exhibited **belief perseverance**, sticking to initial beliefs even after these had been discredited. Apparently, it's easier to get people to build a theory than to convince them to tear it down.

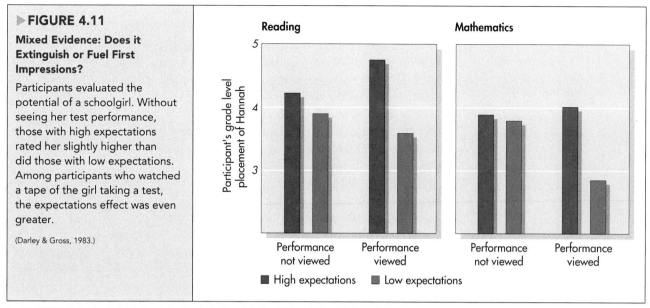

People are slow to change their first impressions on the basis of new information. TRUE.

Why do beliefs often outlive the evidence on which they are supposed to be based? The reason is that when people conjure up explanations that make sense, those explanations take on a life of their own. In fact, once people form an opinion, that opinion becomes strengthened when they merely *think* about the topic, even if they do not articulate the reasons for it (Tesser, 1978). And therein lies a possible solution. By asking people to consider why an *alternative* theory might be true, we can reduce or eliminate the belief perseverance effects to which they are vulnerable (Anderson & Sechler, 1986).

Confirmatory Hypothesis Testing

Social perceivers are not passive recipients of information. Like detectives, we ask questions and actively search for clues. But do we seek information objectively, or are we inclined to confirm the suspicions we already hold?

Mark Snyder and William Swann (1978) addressed this question by having pairs of participants who were strangers to one another take part in a getting-acquainted interview. In each pair, one participant was to interview the other. But first, that participant was falsely led to believe that his or her partner was either introverted or extroverted (actually, the participants were assigned on a random basis to these conditions) and was then told to select questions from a prepared list. Those who thought they were talking to an introvert chose mostly introvert-oriented questions ("Have you ever felt left out of some social group?"), while those who thought they were talking to an extrovert asked extrovert-oriented questions ("How do you liven up a party?"). Expecting a certain kind of person, participants unwittingly sought evidence that

belief perseverance
The tendency to maintain beliefs even after they have been discredited.

confirmed their expectations. By asking loaded questions, in fact, the interviewers actually gathered support for their beliefs. Thus, neutral observers who later listened to the tapes were also left with the mistaken impression that the interviewees really were as introverted or extroverted as the interviewers had assumed.

This last part of the study is powerful, but in hindsight not all that surprising. Imagine yourself on the receiving end of an interview. Asked about what you do to liven up parties, you would probably talk about organizing group games, playing dance music, and telling jokes. On the other hand, if you were asked about difficult social situations, you might talk about being nervous before oral presentations or about what it feels like to be the new kid on the block. In other words, simply by going along with the questions that are asked, you supply evidence confirming the interviewer's beliefs. Thus, perceivers set in motion a vicious cycle: Thinking someone has a certain trait, they engage in a one-sided search for information; and in doing so, they create a reality that ultimately supports their beliefs (Zuckerman et al., 1995).

Are people so blinded by their existing beliefs that they cannot manage an open and objective search for evidence? It depends. In the task devised by Snyder and Swann, people conduct a biased, confirmatory search for information. Even professional counsellors trained in psychotherapy select questions designed to confirm their own hypotheses (Haverkamp, 1993). Thankfully, different circumstances produce less biasing results. When people are not certain of their beliefs and are concerned about the accuracy of their impressions (Kruglanski & Mayseless, 1988), when they are allowed to prepare their own interviews (Trope et al., 1984), or when the available nonconfirmatory questions are better than the confirmatory questions (Skov & Sherman, 1986), they tend to pursue a more balanced search for information.

Let's stop for a moment and contemplate what this research means for the broader question of why we often seem to resist changing our negative but mistaken impressions of others, more than our positive but mistaken impressions. Jerker Denrell (2005) argues that even when we form a negative first impression on the basis of all available evidence, and even when we interpret that evidence accurately, our impression may be misleading. The reason: *biased experience sampling.* Meet someone who seems likable and you may interact with that person again. Then, if he or she turns out to be twisted, dishonest, or self-centred, you'll be in a position to observe these traits and revise your impression. But if you meet someone you don't like, you will try to avoid that person in the future, cutting yourself off from new information and limiting the opportunity to revise your opinion. Attraction breeds interaction, which is why our negative first impressions in particular tend to persist.

The Self-Fulfilling Prophecy

In 1948, sociologist Robert Merton told a story about Cartwright Millingville, president of the Last National Bank in the U.S during the Depression of the 1930s. Although the bank was solvent, a rumour began to spread that it was floundering. Within hours, hundreds of depositors were lined up to withdraw their savings before no money was left to withdraw. The rumour was false, but the bank eventually failed. Using stories such as this, Merton proposed what seemed like an outrageous hypothesis: that a perceiver's expectation can actually lead to its own fulfillment, a **self-fulfilling prophecy**.

self-fulfilling prophecy
The process by which one's expectations about a person eventually lead that person to behave in ways that confirm those expectations.

Merton's hypothesis lay dormant within psychology until Robert Rosenthal and Lenore Jacobson (1968) published the results of a study entitled *Pygmalion in the Classroom.* Noticing that teachers had higher expectations of better students, they wondered if teacher expectations *influenced* student performance rather than the other way around. To address the question, they told teachers in a San Francisco elementary school that certain pupils were on the verge of an intellectual growth spurt. The results of an IQ test were cited but, in fact, the pupils had been randomly selected. Then eight months later, when real tests were administered, the "late bloomers" exhibited an increase in their IQ scores compared with children assigned to a control group. They were also evaluated more favourably by their classroom teachers.

When the Pygmalion study was first published, it was greeted with chagrin. If positive teacher expectations can boost student performance, can negative expectations have the opposite effect? And what about the social implications? Could it be that affluent children are destined for success and disadvantaged children are doomed to failure because educators hold different expectations of them? Many researchers were critical of the study itself and skeptical about the generality of the results. Unfortunately, though, these findings cannot be swept under the proverbial rug. In a review of additional studies, Rosenthal (1985) found that teacher expectations significantly predicted student performance 36 percent of the time. Mercifully, the predictive value of teacher expectancies seems to wear off, not accumulate, as children graduate from one grade to the next (Smith et al., 1999).

How might teacher expectations be transformed into reality? There are two points of view. According to Rosenthal (2002), the process involves covert communication. The teacher forms an initial impression of students early in the school year—based, perhaps, on their background or reputation, physical appearance, initial classroom performance, and standardized-test scores. The teacher then alters his or her behaviour in ways that are consistent with that impression. If initial expectations are high rather than low, the teacher gives the student more praise, attention, challenging homework, and better feedback. In turn, the student adjusts his or her own behaviour. If the signals are positive, the student may become energized, work hard, and succeed. If negative, there may be a loss of interest and self-confidence. The cycle is thus complete and the expectations confirmed.

While recognizing that this effect can occur, Lee Jussim and others (1996; Jussim & Harber, 2005) question whether teachers in real life are so prone in the first place to form erroneous impressions of their students. It's true, in many naturalistic studies, that the expectations teachers have at the start of a school year are later confirmed by their students—a result that is consistent with the notion that the teachers had a hand in producing that outcome. But wait. That same result is also consistent with a more innocent possibility: that perhaps the expectations that teachers form of their students are *accurate*. There are times, Jussim admits, when teachers may stereotype a student and, without realizing it, behave in ways that create a self-fulfilling prophecy. But there are also times when teachers can predict how their students will perform without necessarily influencing that performance (Alvidrez & Weinstein, 1999).

It's clear that self-fulfilling prophecies are at work in many settings—not only schools but also a wide range of organizations, including the military (Kierein & Gold, 2000; McNatt, 2000). In a study of 1000 men assigned to 29 platoons in the Israeli Defense Forces, Dov Eden (1990) led some platoon leaders but not others to expect that the groups of trainees they were about to receive had great potential (in fact, these groups were of average ability). After ten weeks, the trainees assigned to the high-expectation platoons scored higher than the others on written exams and on the ability to operate a weapon. The process may also be found in the criminal justice system, where police interrogate suspects. In one study, Kassin and others (2003) had some students but not others commit a mock crime, stealing $100 from a laboratory. All suspects were then questioned by student interrogators who were led to believe that their suspect was probably guilty or innocent. Interrogators who presumed guilt asked more incriminating questions, conducted more coercive interrogations, and tried harder to get the suspect to confess. In turn, this more aggressive style made the suspects sound defensive and led observers who later listened to the tapes to judge them guilty, even when they were innocent. Follow-up research has confirmed this self-fulfilling prophecy in the police interrogation room (Hill et al., 2008). Still other studies have shown that judges unwittingly bias juries (Hart, 1995), and that negotiators settle for lesser outcomes if they believe their counterparts are highly competitive (Diekmann et al., 2003).

The self-fulfilling prophecy is a powerful phenomenon (Darley & Fazio, 1980; Harris & Rosenthal, 1985; Rosenthal, 2002). But how does it work? How do social perceivers transform their own expectations of others into reality? Research indicates that the phenomenon occurs as a three-step process. First, a perceiver forms an impression of a target person—an impression that may be based on interactions with the target or on other information. Second, the perceiver behaves in a manner that is consistent with that first impression. Third, the target person unwittingly adjusts his or her behaviour to the perceiver's actions. The net result: behavioural confirmation of the first impression (see ▶ Figure 4.12).

Now let's straighten out this picture. It would be a sad commentary on human nature if each of us were so easily moulded by others' perceptions into appearing brilliant or stupid, introverted or extroverted, competitive or cooperative, warm or cold. The effects are well established, but there are limits. By viewing the self-fulfilling prophecy as a three-step process, social psychologists can identify the links in the chain that can be broken to prevent the vicious cycle.

Consider the first step, the link between one's expectations and one's behaviour toward the target person. In the typical study, perceivers try to get to know the target on only a casual basis and are not necessarily driven to form an accurate impression. But when perceivers are highly motivated to seek the truth (as when they are considering the target as a possible teammate or opponent), they become more objective—and often do not confirm prior expectations (Harris & Perkins, 1995; Hilton & Darley, 1991).

The link between expectations and behaviour depends in other ways on a perceiver's goals and motivations in the interaction (Snyder & Stukas, 1999). In one study, John Copeland (1994) put either the perceiver or the target into a position of relative power. In all cases, the perceiver interacted with a target who was said to be introverted or extroverted. In half the pairs, the perceiver was given the power to accept or reject the target as a teammate for a money-winning game. In the other half, it was the target who was empowered to choose a teammate. The two participants interacted, the interaction was recorded, and neutral observers listened to the tapes and rated the target person. So, did perceivers cause the targets to behave as introverted or

▶ **FIGURE 4.12**

The Self-Fulfilling Prophecy as a Three-Step Process

How do people transform expectations into reality? (1) A perceiver has expectations of a target person; (2) the perceiver then behaves in a manner consistent with those expectations; (3) the target unwittingly adjusts his or her behaviour according to the perceiver's actions.

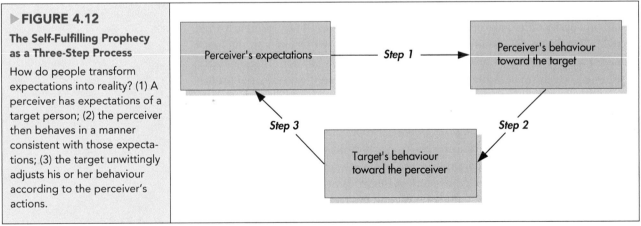

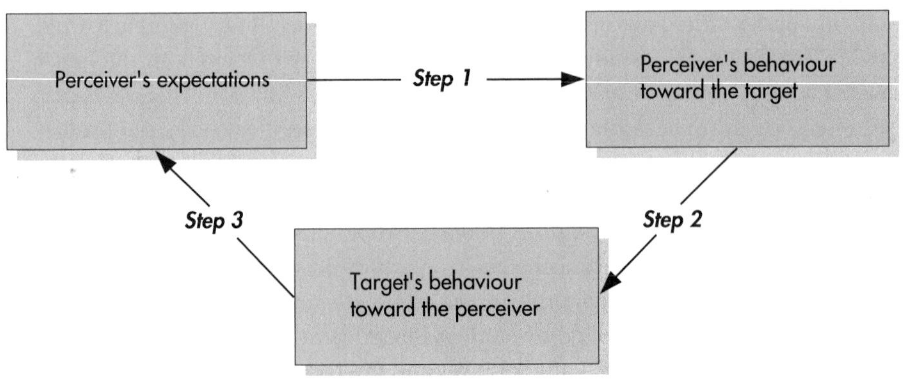

extroverted, depending on initial expectations? Yes and no. Illustrating what Copeland called "prophecies of power," the results showed that high-power perceivers triggered the self-fulfilling prophecy, as in past research, but that low-power perceivers did not. In the low-power situation, the perceivers spent less time getting to know the target person and more time trying to be liked.

Now consider the second step, the link between a perceiver's behaviour and the target's response. In much of the past research, as in much of life, target persons are not aware of the false impressions held by others. Thus, it is unlikely that Rosenthal and Jacobson's (1968) "late bloomers" knew of their teachers' high expectations or that Snyder and Swann's (1978) "introverts" and "extroverts" knew of their interviewers' misconceptions. But what if they had known? How would *you* react if you found yourself being cast in a particular light? When it happened to participants in one experiment, they managed to overcome the effect by behaving in ways that forced the perceivers to abandon their expectations (Hilton & Darley, 1985).

As you may recall from the discussion of self-verification in Chapter 3, this result is most likely to occur when perceiver expectations clash with a target person's self-concept. When targets who viewed themselves as extroverted were interviewed by perceivers who believed they were introverted (and vice versa), what changed as a result of the interaction were the perceivers' beliefs, not the targets' behaviour (Swann & Ely, 1984). Social perception is a two-way street—and the persons we judge have their own prophecies to fulfill.

The notion that we can create a "self-fulfilling prophecy" by getting others to behave in ways we expect is a myth. FALSE.

Social Perception: The Bottom Line

Trying to understand people—whether they are professional athletes, business leaders, trial lawyers, or loved ones closer to home—is no easy task. As you reflect on the material in this chapter, you will notice that there are two radically different views of social perception. One suggests that the process is quick and relatively automatic. Without much thought, effort, or awareness, people make rapid-fire snap judgments about others based on physical appearance, preconceptions, cognitive heuristics, or just a hint of behavioural evidence. According to a second view, however, the process is relatively mindful. People observe others carefully and reserve judgment until their analysis of the target person, behaviour, and situation is complete. As suggested by theories of attribution and information integration, the process is eminently logical. In light of recent research, it is now safe to conclude that both accounts of social perception are correct. Sometimes, our judgments are made instantly; at other times, they are based on a more painstaking analysis of behaviour. Either way, we often steer our interactions with others along a path that is narrowed by first impressions, a process that can set in motion a self-fulfilling prophecy. The various aspects of social perception, as described in this chapter, are summarized in ▶ Figure 4.13.

At this point, we must confront an important question: How *accurate* are people's impressions of each other? For years, this question has proved provocative but hard to answer (Cronbach, 1955; Kenny, 1994). Granted, people often depart from the ideals of logic and exhibit bias in their social perceptions. In this chapter alone, we have seen that perceivers typically focus on the wrong cues to determine if someone is lying; use cognitive heuristics without regard for numerical base rates; overlook the situational influences on behaviour; disparage victims whose misfortunes threaten their sense of justice; form premature first impressions; and interpret, seek, and create evidence in ways that support these impressions.

FIGURE 4.13

The Processes of Social Perception

Summarizing Chapter 4, this diagram depicts the processes of social perception. As shown, it begins with the observation of persons, situations, and behaviour. Sometimes, we make snap judgments from these cues. At other times, we form impressions only after making attributions and integrating these attributions. Either way, our impressions are subject to confirmation biases and the risk of a self-fulfilling prophecy.

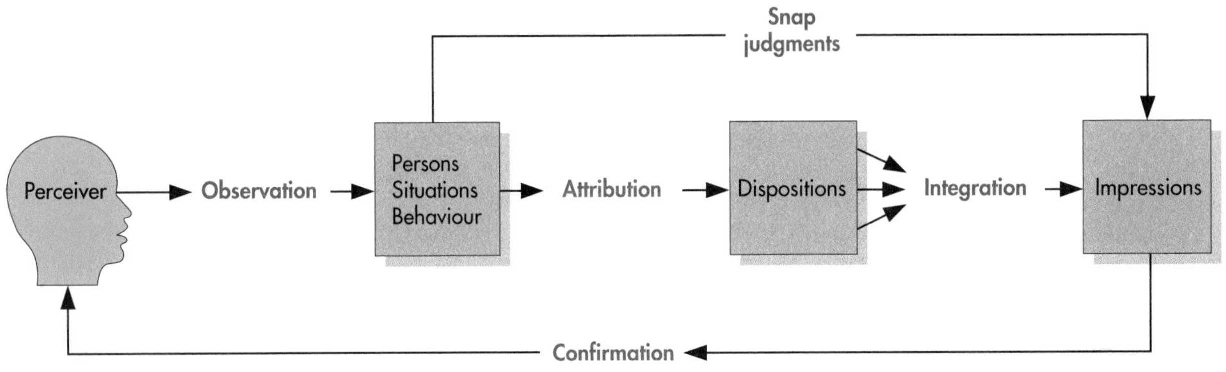

To make matters worse, we often have little awareness of our limitations, leading us to feel *overconfident* in our judgments. In a series of studies, David Dunning and his colleagues (1990) asked students to predict how a target person would react in various situations. Some made predictions about a fellow student whom they had just met and interviewed, and others made predictions about their roommates. In both cases, participants reported their confidence in each prediction, and accuracy was determined by the responses of the target persons themselves. The results were clear: Regardless of whether they judged a stranger or a roommate, the students consistently overestimated the accuracy of their predictions. In fact, Kruger and Dunning (1999) found that people who scored low rather than high on tests of spelling, logic, grammar, and humour appreciation were later the most likely to overestimate their own performance. Apparently, poor performers are doubly cursed and don't know what they don't know (Dunning et al., 2003), and they don't know they are biased (Ehrlinger et al., 2005).

Standing back from the material presented in this chapter, you may find the list of shortcomings, punctuated by the problem of overconfidence, to be long and depressing. So, how can this list be reconciled with the triumphs of civilization? Or to put it another way, "If we're so dumb, how come we made it to the moon?" (Nisbett & Ross, 1980, p. 249).

Many years ago, Herbert Simon (1956) coined the term *satisficing* (by combining *satisfying* and *sufficing*) to describe the way people make judgments that, while not logically perfect, are good enough. Today, many psychologists believe that people operate by a principle of "bounded rationality"—that we are rational *within bounds* depending on our abilities, motives, available time, and other factors. In a book entitled *Simple Heuristics That Make Us Smart,* Gerd Gigerenzer and others (1999) noted that people seldom compute intricate probabilities to make decisions; rather, they "reach into an adaptive toolbox filled with fast and frugal heuristics" (p. 5). They also note that these heuristics often serve us well enough.

It is true that people fall prey to the biases identified by social psychologists, and probably even to some that have not yet been noticed. It is also true that we often get fooled by con artists, misjudge our partners in marriage, and hire the wrong job applicants. As Thomas Gilovich (1991) pointed out, more North Americans believe in ESP than in evolution, and there are 20 times more astrologers in the world than astronomers. The problem is, these biases can have harmful consequences—giving rise, as we'll see in Chapter 5, to stereotypes, prejudice, and discrimination. Yet despite our imperfections, there are four reasons to be guardedly optimistic about our competence as social perceivers:

1. The more experience people have with each other, the more accurate they are. For example, although people have a limited ability to assess the personality of strangers they meet in the laboratory, they are generally better at judging their own friends and acquaintances (Kenny & Acitelli, 2001; Levesque, 1997; Malloy & Albright, 1990).
2. Although we are not good at making global judgments of others (that is, at knowing what people are like across a range of settings), we are able to make more circumscribed predictions of how others will behave in our own presence. You may well misjudge the personality of a roommate or co-worker, but to the extent that you can predict your roommate's actions at home or your co-worker's actions on the job, the mistakes may not matter (Swann, 1984).
3. Social perception skills can be enhanced in people who are taught the rules of probability and logic (Kosonen & Winne, 1995; Nisbett et al., 1987). For example, graduate students in psychology—because they take courses in statistics—tend to improve in their ability to reason about everyday social events (Lehman et al., 1988).
4. People can form more accurate impressions of others when motivated by a concern for accuracy and open-mindedness than when motivated by a need for immediacy, confirmation, and closure (Kruglanski & Webster, 1996). Many studies described in this chapter have shown that people exhibit less bias when there is an incentive for accuracy within the experiment (Kunda, 1990; Neuberg, 1989)—as when the perceiver judges a prospective teammate's ability to facilitate success in a future task (Fiske & Neuberg, 1990) or a future dating partner's *social* competence (Goodwin et al., 2002).

To summarize, research on the accuracy of social perceptions offers a valuable lesson: To the extent that we observe others with whom we have had time to interact, make judgments that are reasonably specific, have some knowledge of the rules of logic, and are sufficiently motivated to form an accurate impression, the problems that plague us can be minimized. Indeed, just being aware of the biases described in this chapter may well be a necessary first step toward a better understanding of others.

People are more accurate at judging the personality of friends and acquaintances than of strangers. TRUE.

REVIEW

Observation: The Elements of Social Perception

- To understand others, social perceivers rely on indirect clues—the elements of social perception.

Persons: Judging a Book by Its Cover

- People often make snap judgments of others based on physical appearances (for example, adults with baby-faced features are seen as having childlike qualities).

Situations: The Scripts of Life

- People have preconceptions, or "scripts," about certain types of situations. These scripts guide our interpretations of behaviour.

Behavioural Evidence

- People derive meaning from behaviour by dividing it into discrete, meaningful units.
- Nonverbal behaviours are often used to determine how others are feeling.
- From facial expressions, people all over the world can identify the emotions of happiness, fear, sadness, surprise, anger, and disgust.
- Body language, gaze, and touch are also important forms of nonverbal communication.
- People use nonverbal cues to detect deception but are often not accurate in making these judgments because they pay too much attention to the face and neglect cues that are more revealing.

Attribution: From Elements to Dispositions

- Attribution is the process by which we explain people's behaviour.

Attribution Theories

- People begin to understand others by making personal or situational attributions for their behaviour.
- Correspondent inference theory states that people learn about others from behaviour that is freely chosen, that is unexpected, and that results in a small number of desirable outcomes.
- From multiple behaviours, we base our attributions on three kinds of covariation information: consensus, distinctiveness, and consistency.

Attribution Biases

- People depart from the logic of attribution theory in two major ways.
- First, we use cognitive heuristics—rules of thumb that enable us to make judgments that are quick but often in error.
- Second, we tend to commit the fundamental attribution error, overestimating the role of personal factors and underestimating the impact of situations.

Culture and Attribution

- Cultures differ in their implicit theories about the causes of human behaviour.
- Studies show, for example, that East Asians are more likely than Americans to consider the impact of the social and situational contexts of which they are a part.

Motivational Biases

- Our attributions for the behaviour of others are often biased by our own self-esteem motives.
- Needing to believe in a just world, people often criticize victims and blame them for their fate.

Integration: From Dispositions to Impressions

Information Integration: The Arithmetic

- The impressions we form are usually based on an averaging of a person's traits, not on a summation.
- According to information integration theory, impressions are based on perceiver predispositions and a weighted average of individual traits.

Deviations from the Arithmetic

- Perceivers differ in their sensitivity to certain traits and in the impressions they form.
- Differences stem from stable perceiver characteristics, priming from recent experiences, implicit personality theories, and the primacy effect.

Confirmation Biases: From Impressions to Reality

- Once an impression is formed, people become less likely to change their minds when confronted with nonsupportive evidence.
- People tend to interpret, seek, and create information in ways that confirm existing beliefs.

Perseverance of Beliefs

- First impressions may survive in the face of inconsistent information.
- Ambiguous evidence is interpreted in ways that bolster first impressions.
- The effect of evidence that is later discredited perseveres because people formulate theories to support their initial beliefs.

Confirmatory Hypothesis Testing

- Once perceivers have beliefs about someone, they seek further information in ways that confirm those beliefs.

The Self-Fulfilling Prophecy

- As shown by the effects of teacher expectancies on student achievement, first impressions set in motion a self-fulfilling prophecy.
- This is the product of a three-step process: (1) A perceiver forms an expectation of a target person; (2) the perceiver behaves accordingly; and (3) the target adjusts to the perceiver's actions.
- This self-fulfilling prophecy effect is powerful but limited in important ways.

Social Perception: The Bottom Line

- Sometimes, people make snap judgments; at other times, they evaluate others by carefully analyzing their behaviour.
- Research suggests that our judgments are often biased and that we are overconfident.
- Still, there are conditions under which we are more competent as social perceivers.

Key Terms

Putting COMMON SENSE *to the Test*

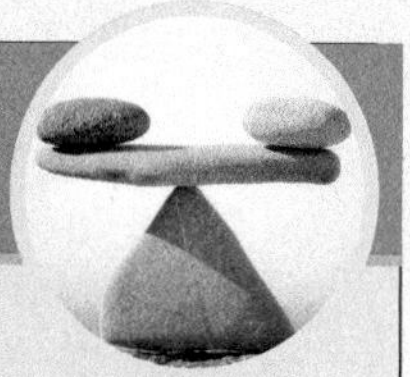

The impressions we form of others are influenced by superficial aspects of their appearance.

True. *Research shows that first impressions are influenced by height, weight, clothing, facial characteristics, and other aspects of appearance.*

Adaptively, people are skilled at knowing when someone is lying rather than telling the truth.

False. *People frequently make mistakes in their judgments of truth and deception, too often accepting what others say at face value.*

Like social psychologists, people are sensitive to situational causes when explaining the behaviour of others.

False. *In explaining the behaviour of others, people overestimate the importance of personal factors and overlook the impact of situations—a bias known as the "fundamental attribution error."*

People are slow to change their first impressions on the basis of new information.

True. *Studies have shown that once people form an impression of someone, they become resistant to change even when faced with contradictory new evidence.*

The notion that we can create a "self-fulfilling prophecy" by getting others to behave in ways we expect is a myth.

False. *In the laboratory and in the classroom, a perceiver's expectation can actually lead to its own fulfillment.*

People are more accurate at judging the personality of friends and acquaintances than of strangers.

True. *People often form erroneous impressions of strangers but tend to be more accurate in their judgments of friends and acquaintances.*

5

"Police receive training to make them more sensitive to weapons, but they don't get training to undo unconscious race stereotypes or biases."

—Anthony Greenwald

Stereotypes, Prejudice, and Discrimination

This chapter considers how people think, feel, and behave toward members of social groups. We begin by examining the nature of the problem—how aspects of stereotyping, prejudice, and discrimination have changed dramatically in recent years, as well as how persistent they can be. Next, we examine two sets of causes underlying these problems: The first set emphasizes intergroup and motivational factors, and the second set emphasizes cognitive and cultural factors. We then consider some of the effects of being the target of these biases, and we conclude with some ways to reduce stereotypes, prejudice, and discrimination today and in the future.

Putting
COMMON SENSE
to the Test

Circle Your Answer

T F Children do not tend to show biases based on race; it is only after they become adolescents that they learn to respond to people differently based on race.

T F Very brief exposure to a member of a stereotyped group does not lead to biased judgments or responses, but longer exposure typically does.

T F Even brief exposure to sexist television commercials can significantly influence the behaviours of men and women.

T F A black student is likely to perform worse on an athletic task if the task is described as one reflecting sports intelligence than if it is described as reflecting natural athletic ability.

T F Groups with a history of prejudice toward each other tend to become much less prejudiced after they are made to interact with each other in a desegregated setting.

In December 2008, Raymond Silverfox, a 43-year-old member of the Little Salmon Carmacks First Nation, died in police custody. He had been brought in earlier that evening due to public drunkenness. It was not the charges levied that were in dispute, but rather the treatment he received at the hands of the RCMP officers who oversaw his detention. It is alleged that over a 13-hour period, the officers watched, and laughed at, a live feed of Mr. Silverfox in his cell, while he vomited 26 times and lost control of his bowels. They did not clean up his cell, offer him a change of clothing (something they always had on hand) when he repeatedly soiled his own, nor seek medical attention despite his repeated vomiting. When one officer noticed that he no longer appeared to be breathing, he was removed from his cell, but by then it was too late; he died a short time later in hospital. As reported on the CBC website on May 4, 2010, according to interim grand chief Ruth Massie, Silverfox's death was the result of racism: "Without a doubt, these attitudes and stereotypes led to the death of Mr. Silverfox. Racist assumptions were made, and cultural stereotypes were employed as evidenced by the conduct and comments made by the RCMP members and guards involved." No criminal charges were ultimately filed against the officers in the case after a coroner inquest ruled that Silverfox died of natural causes. However, Silverfox's daughter launched a civil suit against the RCMP in the fall of 2010, believing that "racism and willful neglect" led to her father's death. A few months after the Silverfox inquest, another First Nations man, Robert Stone, also died in RCMP custody, under similar circumstances. Did racism play a role in the deaths of Silverfox and Stone? Did stereotypes associated with the First Nations population lead the officers to ignore the signs that Silverfox was in serious medical distress? Or was this simply a matter of an unfortunate series of events? Although we can never know for sure, there is ample research discussed in the present chapter that makes it clear

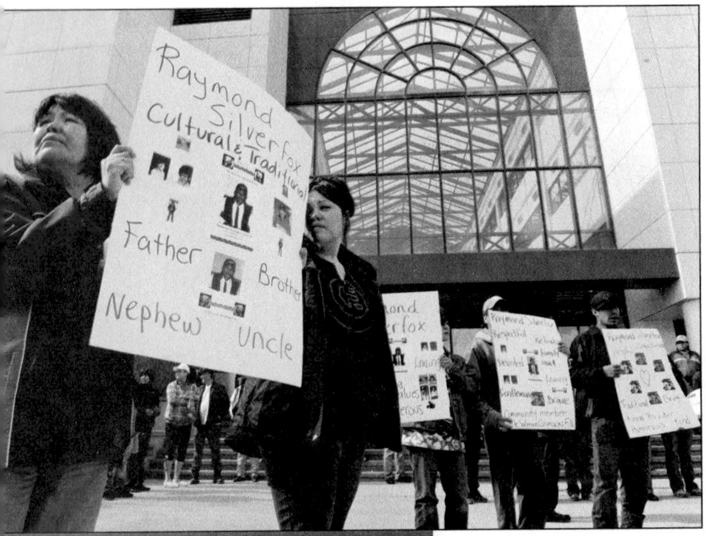

© Mike Thomas/Yukon News

The death of Raymond Silverfox while in the custody of the RCMP raises serious issues about racism and prejudice in Canada. Did negative stereotypes of First Nations peoples contribute to his death?

that our perception of others can be profoundly influenced by the act of perceiving them as a member of a group.

When Barack Obama was sworn in as the president of the United States in 2009, he took his presidential oath in the U.S. capital where only a few lifetimes before, African slaves did much of the work to build it. While being elected as the first black man to hold the highest office in the United States represents a remarkable evolution in race relations, there were numerous other signs that not everyone was happy with this development. After his election, white supremacist and other hate groups saw huge growths in number and activity, threats against the president's life jumped by about 400 percent compared to those made against his (white) predecessor, and sales of guns and ammunition skyrocketed. Such outcomes remind us that stereotypes, prejudice, and discrimination continue to play a profoundly important and destructive—though often more subtle—role in contemporary life. As we will see throughout this chapter, while there has certainly been progress, the journey is far from complete.

To address these issues, we begin by taking a close look at the nature of the problem of intergroup bias in contemporary life. Although there is a long list of groups that are the targets of stereotypes, prejudice, and discrimination, in this first section we focus primarily on racism and sexism, as they have been the focus of the large majority of research. Later in the chapter, we address some of the key causes and important consequences of intergroup biases, and we close by discussing some of the most promising directions in efforts to reduce these problems.

THE CANADIAN PRESS/Sean Kilpatrick

Barack Obama is the first member of a racial minority group to become president of the United States.

The Nature of the Problem: Persistence and Change

The election of a member of an historically oppressed minority group to the highest office in the United States, coupled with the prejudices that were revealed during and after the campaign, together reflect the dynamic nature of stereotypes, prejudice, and discrimination today. While examples of blatant, overt prejudice and discrimination remain all too prevalent, much progress has certainly been made. How much and how satisfactory that progress is, though, remains open for some debate. White Americans tend to perceive greater racial progress than other Americans, in part because the former see things more from the perspective of how far things have come, whereas the latter see things more from the perspective of how far the country still has to go (Brodish et al., 2008; Eibach & Ehrlinger, 2006). What is harder to debate is the fact that in general, stereotyping, prejudice, and discrimination are seen as less acceptable than ever before, although exceptions to this exist—such as the recent increase in prejudice against immigrants or people perceived to be "foreigners" in many countries around the world (Coenders et al., 2008; Zick et al., 2008) (see ▶ Figure 5.1).

In this section, we discuss some of the progress that has been made, along with the persistence of more subtle forms of bias. To provide a focus for reviewing the relevant research and to reflect the topics that have most dominated the research literature, we will concentrate in this section on racism and sexism in particular—even though many of the points hold true across a wide variety of targets of stereotypes, prejudice, and discrimination. Before turning to racism and sexism, however, we begin by defining these terms, along with several other relevant concepts.

FIGURE 5.1

Unfavourable Views Toward Jews and Muslims in Europe

This graph shows the median percentages of respondents from six countries (Britain, France, Germany, Poland, Russia, and Spain) with unfavourable opinions of Jews and Muslims in 2005 and 2008. Attitudes became more negative during this three-year period.

(Kohut & Wike, 2008.)

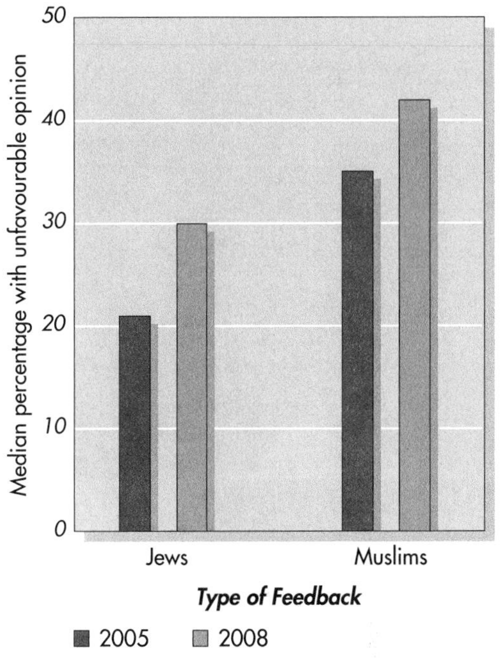

Kohut, A., & Wike, R. "Xenophobia on the Continent." *National Interest*, Oct. 30, 2008. www.nationalinterest.org. Reprinted by permission.

Defining Our Terms

Given the complexity of these issues, defining concepts such as prejudice or racism is no simple matter. Debates persist about how best to define the terms—how broad or specific they should be, whether they should focus on individual or institutional levels, and so on. For example, one way to define **racism** is as prejudice and discrimination based on a person's racial background. It is important to realize, however, that racism exists at several different levels. At the individual level, as this definition reflects, any of us can be racist toward anyone else. At the institutional and cultural levels, in contrast, some people are privileged while others are advantaged. For example, institutions that tend to accept or hire individuals connected to the people who already are in the institution (providing them with an advantage over others applying), or cultural values that favour the status quo (whereby some people are in a privileged position over others), may unwittingly perpetuate racism. Therefore, another way to define racism is as institutional and cultural practices that promote the domination of one racial group over another (Jones, 1997). Similarly, **sexism** may be defined as prejudice and discrimination based on a person's gender, or as institutional and cultural practices that promote the domination of one gender (typically men) over another (typically women).

For the purposes of this chapter, we define **stereotypes** as beliefs or associations that link whole groups of people with certain traits or characteristics. **Prejudice** consists of negative feelings about others because of their connection to a social group. While stereotypes concern associations or beliefs and prejudice concerns feelings, **discrimination** concerns behaviours—specifically negative behaviours directed against persons because of their membership in a particular group. Stereotypes, prejudice, and discrimination can operate somewhat independently, but they often influence and reinforce each other. Finally, a **group** is defined as two or more people perceived as having at least one of the following characteristics: (1) direct interactions with each other over a period of time; (2) joint membership in a social category based on sex, race, or other attributes; (3) a shared, common fate, identity, or set of goals. We see people in fundamentally different ways if we consider them to constitute a group rather than simply an aggregate of individuals. We also see people in fundamentally different ways if we consider them to be part of our ingroup or as part of an outgroup. Groups that we identify with—our country, religion, political party, even our hometown sports team—are called **ingroups**, whereas groups other than our own are called **outgroups**.

racism
Prejudice and discrimination based on a person's racial background, or institutional and cultural practices that promote the domination of one racial group over another.

sexism
Prejudice and discrimination based on a person's gender, or institutional and cultural practices that promote the domination of one gender over another.

stereotype
A belief or association that links a whole group of people with certain traits or characteristics.

prejudice
Negative feelings toward persons based on their membership in certain groups.

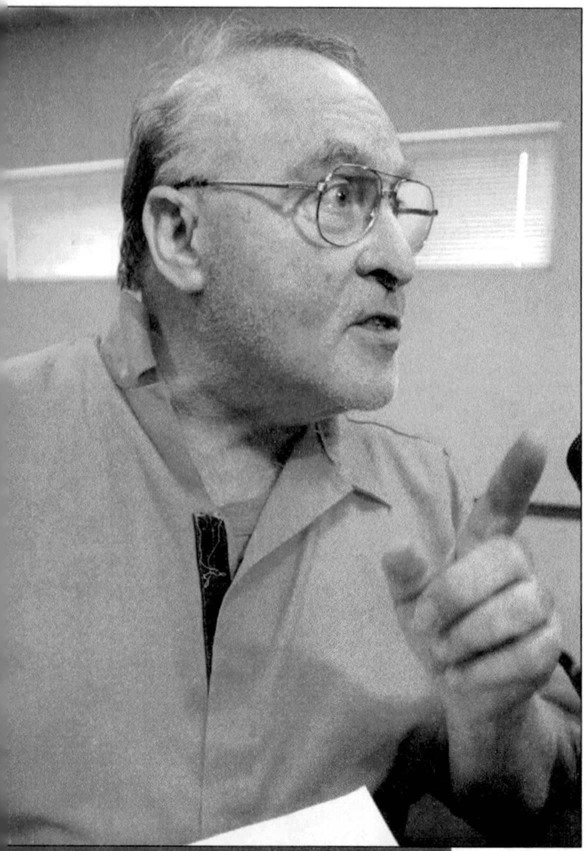

CP/Aaron Harris

There is nothing subtle about the racism exhibited by Holocaust denier Ernst Zundel. Before being deported from Canada, he distributed hate literature and maintained a website where he posted his racist views.

Racism: Current Forms and Challenges

In 1996, *National Geographic* magazine featured a story about Toronto, Ontario. While the article itself was quite complimentary toward the Canadian city, quotes were included from known Holocaust denier Ernst Zundel. Zundel blamed Blacks in Canada for rapes and drive-by shootings, and reportedly stated, "I'm objecting to allowing hordes of racially unabsorbable populations to invade the living space of a specific race." Zundel, who lived in Canada for 40 years, immigrated here when he was 19 to avoid being conscripted into the German army. In the late 1970s, Zundel began distributing pamphlets with titles such as "The Hitler We Loved and Why" and "Did Six Million Really Die?" He spent his years in Canada distributing hate literature (to a substantial mailing list) until his mailing privileges were suspended, and he also maintained a controversial website where he freely posted his racist views about whomever he pleased.

In 2003, Zundel was deemed a threat to Canadian society and human rights. He was deported back to Germany in March 2005. The outrage expressed by the Canadian people at Zundel's statements indicates that societal standards and values are changing, so that blatant racism is increasingly less acceptable. But racism can also be much more subtle, lurking beneath surfaces and behind corners. We may see its shadow and not be sure whether it is real or an apparition. Subtle, undercover forms of racism can be just as hurtful as more blatant forms, in part because their subtlety allows them to slip through people's defenses. In this section of the chapter, we consider some of the blatant and subtle forms and consequences of racism.

A close examination of legislation, opinion polls, sociological data, and social psychological research indicates that racial prejudice and discrimination have been lessening in North America over the last several decades (Dovidio & Gaertner, 1998; Dovidio et al., 2002)—although they may once again be on the rise in Western Europe. In a classic study of ethnic stereotypes published in 1933, Daniel Katz and Kenneth Braly found that white college students viewed the average white American as smart, industrious, and ambitious. Yet they saw the average black American as superstitious, ignorant, lazy, and happy-go-lucky. In multiple follow-up surveys with demographically similar samples of white students conducted from 1951 through 2001, these negative images of Blacks largely faded (Dovidio et al., 1996; Madon et al., 2001). For example, in 1987, only 48 percent of participants agreed with the statement "It's all right for Blacks and Whites to date each other," compared to 69 percent agreement in 1997 (Peterson, 1997).

The election of Barack Obama has been seen by many, both within and outside the United States, as a significant sign of racial progress. For example, University of Washington students, in a study by Cheryl Kaiser and others (2009), completed questionnaires about their perception of racial progress both just before and soon after the election. In only the span of a few weeks, the students' perception of racial progress in the United States increased significantly. The flip side of the coin, however, is that support for policies that address racial inequality and perceptions of how much farther the United States still needs to go to achieve racial equality decreased significantly. The authors of this research found these latter findings troubling because, as they report, "there are pervasive racial disparities in virtually all aspects of American society" (p. 558). Indeed, racial biases in employment, salaries, housing, bank credit, charges from car dealerships, and a whole host of other measures continue to exist (Pager & Shepherd, 2008). In sum, then, there are legitimate reasons to celebrate racial

discrimination
Negative behaviour directed against persons because of their membership in a particular group.

group
Two or more persons perceived as related because of their interactions with each other over time, membership in the same social category, or common fate.

ingroups
Groups with which an individual feels a sense of membership, belonging, and identity.

outgroups
Groups with which an individual does not feel a sense of membership, belonging, or identity.

progress. Racism, however, remains a fact of life and is by no means limited merely to the actions of some fringe individuals or groups. And as we will see in the following section, it exists in ways that escape the recognition of most people.

Modern Racism As noted earlier, researchers have pointed to the existence of subtle, covert forms of racism. One example is **modern racism**—a subtle form of prejudice that surfaces in direct ways whenever it is safe, socially acceptable, or easy to rationalize. Modern racism is far more subtle and most likely to be present under the cloud of ambiguity. According to theories of modern racism, many people are racially ambivalent. They want to see themselves as fair, but they still harbour feelings of anxiety and discomfort concerning other racial groups (Hass et al., 1992). There are several specific theories of modern racism, but they all emphasize contradictions and tensions that lead to subtle, often unconscious forms of prejudice and discrimination (Gawronski et al., 2008; Levy et al., 2006; Sears & Henry, 2005; Son Hing et al., 2008). For example, white British students in a study by Gordon Hodson and others (2005) read about either a white or a black defendant in a robbery case. When the evidence against the defendant was strong and unambiguous, the students were as likely to judge the white defendant guilty as the black defendant. However, when the situation was more ambiguous because some of the most incriminating information against the defendant was ruled inadmissible and therefore technically should be ignored (but often is used by jurors somewhat anyway), the students were significantly more likely to judge the black defendant guilty than the white defendant. This situation was ambiguous because although the students knew that they weren't supposed to use the inadmissible evidence, they also knew that the evidence suggested that the defendant was indeed guilty. So either a guilty or not-guilty verdict could be justified; it is in ambiguous situations such as this that racial biases are more likely to emerge.

Many Whites who feel that they are not prejudiced admit that on some occasions they do not react toward Blacks (or to other groups, such as gay men) as they should—an insight that causes them to feel embarrassed, guilty, and ashamed (Monteith et al., 2002). Indeed, when they have reason to suspect that racism could bias their judgments, low-prejudice Whites may show an *opposite* bias on explicit, consciously controlled tasks, responding more favourably to Blacks than to Whites (Dovidio et al., 1997; Fein et al., 1997; Norton et al., 2006; Wyer, 2004).

Just as with any other form of prejudice, individuals differ in the degree to which they exhibit underlying racist tendencies. But because of the covert nature of these tendencies, measuring the differences is difficult. Several questionnaires have been developed to ask individuals relatively subtle, indirect questions about their attitudes toward particular groups, including the Modern Racism Scale (McConahay, 1986), and scales designed to measure subtle forms of racism in Western Europe (Pettigrew & Meertens, 1995; Tougas et al., 1995). Although these scales have been used successfully in many studies (e.g., Wittenbrink et al., 1997), other research has demonstrated that people who are highly motivated to control their expressions of prejudice may score low on them, even if they do harbour prejudiced attitudes (Dunton & Fazio, 1997; Plant & Devine, 1998). Part of the limitation of these scales is that they *explicitly* ask respondents about their attitudes toward various groups, when research today is showing more and more how *implicit* these attitudes can be (Blair, 2001; Fazio & Olson, 2003).

Implicit Racism To contrast it from explicit racism, many scholars call racism that operates unconsciously and unintentionally **implicit racism**. Undetected by individuals who want to be fair and unbiased, implicit racism—along with other forms of implicit prejudice—can skew their judgments, feelings, and behaviours, without inducing the guilt that more obvious, explicit forms of racism would trigger.

modern racism
A form of prejudice that surfaces in subtle ways when it is safe, socially acceptable, and easy to rationalize.

implicit racism
Racism that operates unconsciously and unintentionally.

Implicit racism may be subtle, but its effects can be profound. For example, Jennifer Eberhardt and others (2006) studied predictors of whether a criminal defendant was likely to be sentenced to death. Examining more than 600 death-penalty-eligible cases tried in Philadelphia between 1979 and 1999, these researchers found that in cases involving a white victim, the more the defendant's physical appearance was stereotypically black, the more likely he would be sentenced to death. It is very unlikely that many of the judges or jurors were consciously aware of this bias, but the evidence reveals significant discrimination.

Again, the question of how to detect and measure implicit racism is a challenging one. Because of its implicit nature, covert measures that do not require individuals to answer questions about their attitudes typically are used. By far the most well-known measure of this kind is the **Implicit Association Test (IAT)**, first developed and tested by Anthony Greenwald and others (1998). The IAT, discussed in more detail in Chapter 6, measures the extent to which two concepts are associated. It measures implicit racism toward Blacks, for example, by comparing how quickly or slowly participants associate black cues (such as a black face) with negative and positive concepts, compared to how quickly or slowly they make the same kinds of associations with white cues. Other IATs focus on associations concerning older versus younger people, men versus women, and so on. It has sparked an explosion of research in the past decade about racism and other forms of prejudice and discrimination, with already more than 500 scientific publications (Smith & Nosek, 2010). To see how it works, try visiting the IAT website by typing "Implicit Association Test" in a search engine.

Implicit racial bias as measured by the IAT has been found between groups around the world and even among children as young as six years old. Such research demonstrates that whereas older children and adults begin to control or change their explicit prejudices and show less bias on explicit measures, the IAT continues to reveal implicit racism throughout development (Baron & Banaji, 2006; Dunham et al., 2008; Newheiser & Olson, 2012).

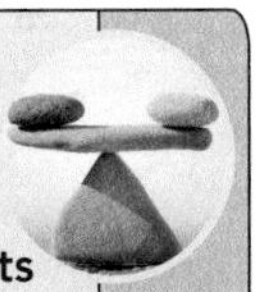

Children do not tend to show biases based on race; it is only after they become adolescents that they learn to respond to people differently based on race. FALSE.

Additional measures of implicit biases are being added to researchers' toolboxes (Bluemke & Friese, 2008; Olson & Fazio, 2004; Payne et al., 2005; Sekaquaptewa et al., 2003; Sriram & Greenwald, 2009; von Hippel et al., 2009). Regardless of the specific measure, social psychologists have found that individuals' degree of implicit racism sometimes predicts differences in their perceptions of and reactions to others as a function of race. This is particularly true regarding very subtle, often nonverbal behaviours, such as how far one chooses to sit from or how much eye contact one makes with a member of a different race (Amodio & Devine, 2006; Greenwald et al., 2009). This research is not without some controversy, however. On the one hand, some scholars have raised important questions about implicit measures, particularly the IAT, asking what they really measure, how useful they are for predicting behaviour, and how their results should be interpreted (Blanton et al., 2009; Karpinski & Hilton, 2001). On the other hand, a recent meta-analysis of a decade's worth of studies on the IAT found that in socially sensitive domains of interracial and other intergroup behaviour, when norms against explicit prejudice are likely to be strong, IAT measures of implicit prejudice predicted biased reactions and behaviour significantly better than did measures of explicit prejudice (Greenwald et al., 2009). It is to the sensitive domains of interracial perceptions and interactions that we turn in the following section.

Implicit Association Test (IAT) A covert measure of unconscious attitudes, it is derived from the speed at which people respond to pairings of concepts, such as black or white with good or bad.

Interracial Perceptions The divides between racial and ethnic groups tend to be more vast and may promote stronger feelings of hostility, fear, and distrust than the divides based on other social categories, such as those based on gender, appearance, age, and so on. One factor that can keep these negative feelings strong is the relative lack of contact between people of different racial and ethnic groups. In addition, in contemporary society, the stigma of being perceived as racist is especially troubling for most people (Crandall & Eshlemen, 2003). This combination of less contact, stronger negative emotions, and greater anxiety about appearing racist makes interracial perception and interaction particularly challenging and fraught with emotion and tension.

A number of studies have demonstrated that Whites may be quicker to perceive hostility or anger in black faces than white faces, and that this may be especially true for people relatively high in implicit racism. For example, Kurt Hugenberg and Galen Bodenhausen (2003, 2004) found that individuals' levels of implicit racism predicted how biased they were in perceiving hostility in black faces. White participants watched brief movies of facial expressions of white or black targets. In their first study, the facial expression began as displaying hostility and gradually became more neutral. In a second study, the expression began as neutral and gradually became more hostile. The participants' task was to indicate when the face no longer expressed the initial emotion—in other words, when did the emotion change from hostile to neutral in the first study, or from neutral to hostile in the second study? The researchers found that participants with relatively high levels of implicit bias, as measured by the IAT, saw the black faces as staying hostile longer in the first study, and becoming hostile more quickly in the second study, relative to the white faces. Participants who showed relatively low racism on the IAT did not show this bias. In a later study, these authors found that participants who showed a strong race bias on the IAT were more likely to categorize a racially ambiguous face as black if the face expressed hostility than if it expressed happiness.

More recently, Paul Hutchings and Geoffrey Haddock (2008) found similar effects with white British students. When students saw pictures of racially ambiguous faces, for example, those students high in implicit racism, as measured by the IAT, were more likely to categorize the faces as black if the faces were angry than if they were happy or neutral. Students low in implicit racism, in contrast, did not show this bias. (See ▶ Figure 5.2.)

▶FIGURE 5.2

Seeing Anger in Black Faces

White British students saw pictures of racially ambiguous faces such as these. Students high in implicit racism, as measured by the IAT, were more likely to categorize the faces as Black if the faces were angry than if they were happy or neutral. Students low in implicit racism did not show this bias.

(Hutchings & Haddock, 2008.)

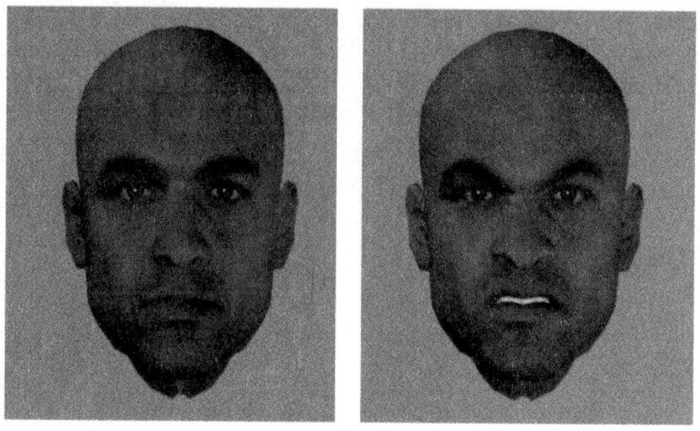

Reprinted from *Journal of Experimental Social Psychology, 44, 5,* M. Hutchings, P.B. & Haddock, G. (2008), Look black in anger: The role of implicit prejudice in the categorization and perceived emotional intensity of racially ambiguous faces, 1418-1420. Reprinted with permission from Elsevier.

Research using brain-imaging techniques has shown that just perceiving a member of a racial outgroup may trigger different, more emotional reactions than perceiving an ingroup member. This is a conclusion suggested in a study by Allen Hart and others (2000). They monitored the brain activity of white and black participants using a functional magnetic resonance imaging (fMRI) technique while they showed the participants pictures of individuals from their racial ingroup or outgroup. The fMRI revealed differential responses in the amygdala, a structure in the brain associated with emotion. Pictures of racial outgroup members tended to elicit stronger amygdala activation than did pictures of ingroup members. Elizabeth Phelps and others (2000) also found that white participants showed greater amygdala activation in response to black than white faces. In addition, this greater activation was associated with higher levels of implicit prejudice.

Since these initial studies, several other researchers have found further support for heightened amygdala activity in response to racial outgroup faces (e.g., Amodio, 2008; Ronquillo et al., 2007; Rule et al., 2010; Wheeler & Fiske, 2005). Interestingly, the effect of black faces on white participants' amygdala activity may depend on the direction of the eye gaze of the faces depicted. Jennifer Richeson, Sophie Trawalter, and their colleagues (Richeson et al., 2008; Trawalter et al., 2008) found that white participants showed greater amygdala activity and paid greater attention in response to black than white faces, but only if the faces displayed direct eye gaze (as if the person was looking at the participant). The effects were eliminated if the targets' eyes were closed or appeared to be looking elsewhere. Such results reflect the fact that direct eye contact from an outgroup member is much more likely to convey a threat (Boll et al., 2011).

Interracial Interactions If perceptions of a member of a racial outgroup are associated with various biases and emotional reactions, interracial interactions may be all the more complex and challenging. This is evident in a study by Wendy Mendes and others (2002), in which non-black participants interacted with either a black or a white confederate on a series of tasks. Participants were more likely to exhibit cardiovascular reactions (such as changes in the amount of blood pumped by the heart per minute) associated with feelings of threat if the confederate was black than if the confederate was white.

When engaging in interracial interactions, Whites may be concerned about a number of things, including not wanting to be, or appear to be, racist. They may therefore try to regulate their behaviours, become particularly vigilant for signs of distrust or dislike from their interaction partners, and so on. What should ideally be a smooth-flowing normal interaction can become awkward and even exhausting. This, in turn, can affect their partner's perceptions of them, possibly leading to the ironic outcome of their appearing to be racist because they were trying not to be. A number of researchers have been examining such phenomena (e.g., Amodio et al., 2007; Devine et al., 2005). According to Jacquie Vorauer (2003; Vorauer & Sasaki (2011), for example, individuals engaging in intergroup interactions often activate *metastereotypes*, or thoughts about the outgroup's stereotypes about them, and worry about being seen as consistent with these stereotypes.

Jennifer Richeson, Nicole Shelton, and their colleagues have found across a variety of recent experiments that for white participants, particularly if they score relatively high on a measure of implicit racism, interacting with a black individual can be cognitively and emotionally exhausting because they are so worried about appearing racist (Richeson & Shelton, 2010; Richeson & Trawalter, 2008; Shelton & Richeson, 2007; Shelton et al., 2009). For example, Trawalter and others (2011) found that white participants who were concerned with appearing prejudiced had increased stress responses during an interracial encounter, and also demonstrated more behavioural anxiety, compared to their less concerned counterparts. In addition, over the course of a year, these differences became more pronounced; those worried about appearing prejudiced displayed *more* physiological and behavioural distress after repeated interracial encounters, while those not concerned with how they appeared displayed *decreasing* levels of arousal.

It should not be surprising, then, that people sometimes try to avoid interracial interaction for fear of appearing racist or being treated in a racist way. This avoidant behaviour in turn can have the ironic effect of making things all the worse. This is illustrated in the work of Philip Goff, Claude Steele, and Paul Davies (2008). White male students were led to believe that they would engage in a conversation with either two white partners or two black partners. The students sat farther away from their partners if they thought the conversation was going to be about a racially sensitive topic (racial profiling) than they did if they thought they would be discussing a less racially relevant topic (relationships).

University of Manitoba researchers Jacquie Vorauer and Cory Turpie (2004) examined intimacy-building behaviours toward a same-sex white or First Nations individual with whom a white participant thought he or she would be subsequently partnered. After viewing a videotape of the target individual introducing himself or herself, participants were asked to record a message that would be viewed by their partner. When creating their own video, those high in prejudice were less likely to engage in intimacy-building behaviours, such as self-disclosure and maintaining eye contact, as long as they were not concerned with being evaluated, as evidenced by their lower public self-consciousness scores. However, when evaluation concerns were present, it was actually the low-prejudice individuals who engaged in fewer intimacy-building behaviours, which in turn led them to treat a First Nations individual less positively compared to those high in prejudice. Thus, for some individuals, trying to avoid appearing racist can take so much effort and self-focus that it ironically decreases one's awareness of the other person present.

As is evident from the example above, anxieties and challenges associated with intergroup interactions are not limited to those between Whites and Blacks, despite the fact that the majority of research has focused on this particular intergroup dynamic. For example, social psychologists are studying related issues involving other social categories, such as those concerning HIV-positive employees (Barron, Hebl, & Paludi, 2011), sexual orientation (Barron & Hebl, 2011), physical disabilities (Dovidio, Pagotto, & Hebl, 2011) and those who are facially stigmatized (Madera & Hebl, 2012).

Sexism: Ambivalence and Double Standards

As with racism, old-fashioned blatant displays of sexism are less socially accepted today than in in the past, although they continue to exist at a frequency and with an intensity that would surprise many. As with racism, researchers have been documenting and studying modern and implicit forms of sexism that tend to escape the notice of most people, but that can exert powerful discriminatory effects (Swim & Hyers, 2009).

There are some ways that sexism is different, however. Gender stereotypes are distinct from virtually all other stereotypes in that they are *prescriptive* rather than merely *descriptive.* That is, they indicate what many people in a given culture believe men and women *should* be. Few Canadians, for example, think that gay men should be artistic and sensitive or that old people should be forgetful and conservative; but many think that women should be nurturing and that men should be unemotional. Even though ambition and drive are valued in our society, women who exhibit such traits may be viewed in especially harsh terms, contributing to the double standards that are the hallmark of sexism (Cuddy et al., 2004; Prentice & Carranza, 2002; Rudman & Glick, 2001).

Another way that sexism is unique concerns the degree to which the ingroup and outgroup members interact. Men and women are intimately familiar with each other. They come from the same families, and typically (although certainly not always) grow up together, can be attracted to one another, live together, and produce and raise children together. Because of this, sexism involves more ambivalence between positive and negative feelings and beliefs than is typical of racism and other forms of prejudice and discrimination.

In this section, we will focus on this ambivalence and on some of the double standards that exist in sexism in degrees that are not as evident in most other forms of discrimination. Later in the chapter, we will explore the related issues of gender stereotypes and how they are perpetuated.

Ambivalent Sexism Overall, stereotypes of women tend to be more positive than stereotypes of men (Eagly et al., 1994); however, the positive traits associated with

FIGURE 5.3

Hostile Sexism Across Countries

Respondents from 19 countries completed measures of hostile and benevolent sexism. The average hostile sexism scores for male respondents from 11 of these countries are depicted here. The countries are listed from left to right in order of how unequal the sexes are in terms of political and economic power as defined by United Nations' criteria. It is clear both from this figure and from the data more generally that hostile sexism is positively correlated with gender inequality. Though not depicted in this graph, benevolent sexism is also positively correlated with gender inequality.

(Data from Glick, based on author correspondence.)

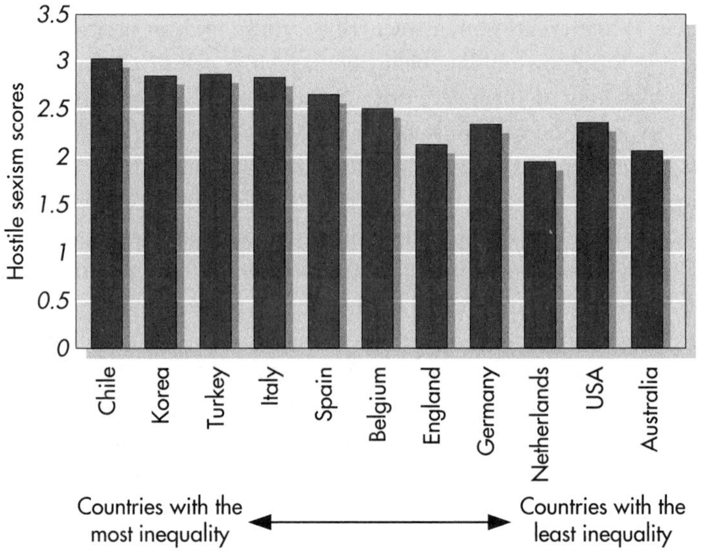

women are less valued in important domains such as business than the positive traits associated with men.

These contradictions are reflected in Peter Glick and Susan Fiske's (2001; 2011) concept of **ambivalent sexism**. Ambivalent sexism consists of two elements: *hostile sexism*, characterized by negative, resentful feelings about women's abilities, value, and ability to challenge men's power; and *benevolent sexism*, characterized by affectionate, chivalrous feelings founded on the potentially patronizing belief that women need and deserve protection. Although hostile sexism is clearly more negative and many women feel favourably toward men who exhibit benevolent sexism (Durán, Moya, & Megías, 2011; Kilianski & Rudman, 1998; Moya et al., 2007), the two forms of sexism are positively correlated. In a study of 15 000 men and women in 19 nations across six continents, Glick, Fiske, and others (2000) found strong support for the notion of prevalent ambivalent sexism around the world. Among their most intriguing findings is the fact that people from countries with the greatest degree of economic and political inequality between the sexes tend to exhibit the most hostile *and* benevolent sexism. Figure 5.3 depicts the average hostile sexism scores for each of several countries.

Benevolent sexism, on the surface, does not strike many women or men as terribly troubling, but it certainly fuels sexism and contributes to negative reactions, particularly to women who defy traditional gender roles and stereotypes. Indeed, studies from several countries around the world have found links between benevolent sexism and accepting myths about rape or evaluating women more negatively if they have been acquaintance-raped, particularly if the women are perceived to have acted inappropriately for a woman (such as being "unlady-like") (Chapleau et al., 2007; Viki et al., 2004; Yamawaki, 2007).

ambivalent sexism
A form of sexism characterized by attitudes about women that reflect both negative, resentful beliefs and feelings, and affectionate, chivalrous, but potentially patronizing beliefs and feelings.

Sex Discrimination: Double Standards and Pervasive Stereotypes Many years ago, Philip Goldberg (1968) asked female students to evaluate the content and writing style of some articles. When the material was supposedly written by John McKay rather than Joan McKay, it received higher ratings, a result that led Goldberg to wonder if even women were prejudiced against women. Certain other studies showed that people often devalue the performance of women who take on tasks usually reserved for men (Lott, 1985) and attribute their achievements to luck rather than ability (Deaux & Emswiller, 1974; Nieva & Gutek, 1981). These findings generated a lot of attention, but it now appears that this kind of devaluation of women is not commonly found in similar studies. More than a hundred studies modelled after Goldberg's indicate that people are not generally biased by gender in the evaluation of performance (Swim & Sanna, 1996; Top, 1991).

This does not mean, however, that sex discrimination no longer exists all these years after the Goldberg study. In many parts of the world, blatant sexism is still quite evident, of course. For example, in Iran, some people supported recent attempts at reforms to benefit women, but those in power reacted with hostile resistance. In Saudi Arabia, women are prohibited from driving. China is notorious for policies such as selective abortion to support a cultural preference for sons over daughters (Saleton, 2009). Other examples are less dramatic but still important. How many female airline pilots have you met lately? What about male secretaries? Look at ■ Table 5.1, and you'll notice some striking results regarding women's occupational choices. The question is, of course, what explains these differences? Decades of social science research point to sexist attitudes and discrimination as a key part of the equation. Sex discrimination during the early school years may pave the way for diverging career paths in adulthood. Then, when equally qualified men and women compete for a job, gender considerations enter in once again, as some research indicates that business professionals favour men for so-called masculine jobs (such as a manager for a machinery company) and women for so-called feminine jobs (such as a receptionist) (Eagly, 2004).

Even when women and men have comparable jobs, the odds are good that the women will be paid less than their male counterparts and will be confronted with a so-called glass ceiling that makes it harder or impossible for women to rise to the highest positions of power in a business or organization (Barreto et al., 2009; Gorman & Kmec, 2009; Leicht, 2008). Women are also frequently confronted with a hostile, unfair work environment. Canadian estimates of workplace sexual harassment toward women range from 42 percent to 80 percent (National Forum on Health, 2000). Women vying for jobs and career advancement are often confronted with a virtually impossible dilemma: They are seen as more competent if they present themselves with stereotypically masculine rather than feminine traits; yet they are also perceived as less socially skilled and attractive—a perception that may ultimately cost them the job or career advancement they were seeking (Eagly, 2004; Jackson et al., 2001; Phelan et al., 2008; Rudman & Glick, 2001).

TABLE 5.1

Women in Work Settings in Selected Countries Around the World (by percent)

These international labour statistics show some of the differences across nations in the distribution of women in the workforce, as well as the fairly consistent tendency for women to be especially likely to work in clerical occupations and as service and sales workers rather than in positions as legislators, senior officials, managers, or craft and trade workers. The numbers below indicate the percent of workers in each category who are women.

	Total Workforce	Clerks	Craft and Trade Workers	Legislators, Senior Officials, Managers	Sales and Service Workers
Australia	45%	67%	5%	37%	68%
Canada	47	77	8	37	63
Columbia	39	58	19	46	61
Costa Rica	37	57	14	27	54
Egypt	21	29	3	11	10
Iran	18	24	23	13	11
Israel	46	74	5	30	60
Italy	39	59	14	33	57
Republic of Korea	42	52	15	9	63
Mexico	37	61	24	31	54
Morocco	27	25	19	12	6
Netherlands	45	69	5	28	69
United Kingdom	46	78	8	34	76

(Data from International Labor Office, 2008.)

Causes of the Problem: Intergroup and Motivational Factors

No one is immune from stereotyping, prejudice, and discrimination. Therefore, although there are individual differences—clearly some people are more prejudiced than others, for example—social psychological explanations tend to address factors that make most of us either more or less vulnerable to these intergroup biases. In this section, we focus on perspectives that emphasize intergroup and motivational factors. In the section that follows, we examine perspectives that emphasize cultural and cognitive factors. It is important to point out here, though, that these different perspectives are not mutually exclusive. They often overlap and work together in accounting for the complexities and pervasiveness of stereotyping, prejudice, and discrimination.

Fundamental Motives Between Groups

A fundamental tenet of social psychology is the social nature of the human animal. Both in our evolutionary history and in contemporary life, humans live, play, work, and fight in groups. This was true in our evolutionary history and remains true today. A fundamental motive that evolved in our species and in other primates is the need to affiliate with relatively small groups of similar others. These affiliations serve the more basic motive of self-protection. One implication of this is the evolved tendency in people even today to divide the world into ingroups and outgroups—"us" versus "them"—and to favour the former over the latter in numerous ways. Negative stereotypes of outgroups can help justify the desire to exclude outgroups, and the stereotypes in turn can fuel even more prejudice and discrimination.

FIGURE 5.4

Fears in the Dark

Canadian participants evaluated Canadians (their ingroup) and Iraqis (an outgroup) on traits that were associated with high threat or low threat. They did this while in a bright or extremely dark room. The higher the bars on this graph, the more favourably they evaluated Canadians than Iraqis on these traits. Participants showed greater ingroup favouritism in ratings of high-threat traits when in a dark environment compared to a bright environment. Darkness did not affect ratings on low-threat traits.

(Schaller et al., 2003.)

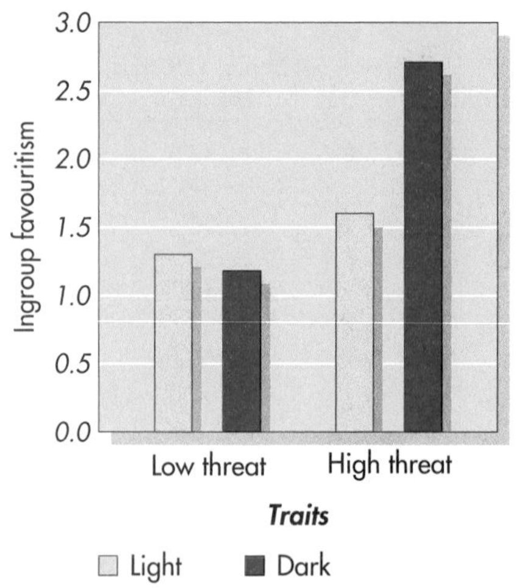

Mark Schaller and his colleagues (Crandall et al., 2011; Schaller et al., 2003; Kenrick et al., 2010; Neuberg et al., 2010) have conducted some fascinating studies that address these points. For example, one set of studies demonstrated that when people's motive to protect themselves is aroused (such as by watching frightening scenes from a movie in which a serial killer stalks a woman through a dark basement), they are more likely to misperceive the emotion of an outgroup member—but not an ingroup member—as anger (Maner et al., 2005). In one particularly creative set of experiments, Schaller and others (2003) hypothesized that being in a completely dark environment would trigger people's self-protective motive more than being in a bright environment, and that this would activate stereotypes about the threatening nature of outgroups. Consistent with this hypothesis, undergraduate students at the University of British Columbia showed greater outgroup bias against Iraqis (relative to ingroup Canadians) when evaluating groups on threat-relevant traits (hostile, untrustworthy) when they were in a dark room than when they were in a light room. Darkness did not affect ratings on low-threat traits (ignorant, closed-minded). (See Figure 5.4.)

The desire to form ingroups and exclude outsiders from them is reflected in a number of ways. According to *optimal distinctiveness theory*, for example, people try to balance the desire to belong and affiliate with others, on the one hand, and the desire to be distinct and differentiated from others, on the other hand (Abrams, 2009; Brewer, 2007). This may drive people to identify with relatively small ingroups and to distance themselves from outgroups and from individuals whose group status is ambiguous (Castano et al., 2002).

Robbers Cave: A Field Study in Intergroup Conflict

In the summer of 1954, a small group of 11-year-old boys—all white, healthy, middle-class youngsters, all strangers to one another—arrived at a 200-acre camp located in a densely wooded area of the Robbers Cave State Park, Oklahoma. The boys spent the first week or so hiking, swimming, boating, and camping out. After a while, they gave themselves a group name and printed it on their caps and T-shirts. At first, the boys thought they were the only ones at the camp. Soon, however, they discovered that there was a second group and that tournaments had been arranged between the two groups.

What these boys didn't know was that they were participants in an elaborate study conducted by Muzafer Sherif and his colleagues (1961). Parents had given permission for their sons to take part in an experiment for a study of competitiveness and cooperation. The two groups were brought in separately, and only after each had formed its own culture was the other's presence revealed. Now, the "Rattlers" and the "Eagles" were ready to meet. They did so under tense circumstances, competing against each other in football, a treasure hunt, a tug-of-war, and other events. For each event, the winning team was awarded points, and the tournament winner was promised a trophy, medals, and other prizes. Almost overnight, the groups turned into hostile antagonists; and their rivalry escalated into a full-scale war. Group flags were burned, cabins were ransacked, and a food fight that resembled a riot exploded in the mess hall. Keep in mind that the participants in this study were well-adjusted boys, not street-gang members. Yet, as Sherif (1966) noted, a naive observer would have thought the boys were "wicked, disturbed, and vicious" (p. 85).

Creating a monster through competition was easy. Restoring the peace, however, was not. First, the experimenters tried saying nice things to the Rattlers about the Eagles and vice versa, but the propaganda campaign did not work. Then the two groups were brought together under noncompetitive circumstances, but that didn't help either. What did eventually work was the introduction of **superordinate goals**, mutual goals that could be achieved only through cooperation between the groups. For example, the experimenters arranged for the camp truck to break down, and both groups were needed to pull it up a steep hill. This strategy worked like a charm. By the end of camp, the two groups were so friendly that they insisted on travelling home on the same bus. In just three weeks, the Rattlers and Eagles experienced the kinds of changes that often take generations to unfold: They formed close-knit groups, went to war, and made peace.

The events of Robbers Cave mimicked the kinds of conflict that plague people all over the world. The simplest explanation for this conflict is competition. Assign strangers to groups, throw the groups into contention, stir the pot, and soon there's conflict. Similarly, the intergroup benefits of reducing the focus on competition by activating superordinate goals are also evident around the world. Consider, for example, the remarkable aftermath of the natural disasters that befell Greece and Turkey in 1999. Fraught with conflict and mistrust for generations, Greek-Turkish relations improved dramatically in the wake of earthquakes that rocked both countries. Television images of Turkish rescue workers pulling a Greek child from under a

superordinate goal
A shared goal that can be achieved only through cooperation among individuals or groups.

pile of rubble in Athens generated an outpouring of goodwill. Uniting against a shared threat, as the boys in Robbers Cave did when the camp truck broke down, the two nations began to bridge a significant gulf (Kinzer, 1999).

Realistic Conflict Theory

The view that direct competition for valuable but limited resources breeds hostility between groups is called **realistic conflict theory** (Levine & Campbell, 1972). As a simple matter of economics, one group may fare better than another group in the struggle for land, jobs, or power. The loser becomes frustrated and resentful, the winner feels threatened and protective—and before long, conflict heats to a rapid boil. Chances are, a good deal of prejudice in the world is driven by the realities of competition (Coenders et al., 2008; Duckitt & Mphuthing, 1998; Stephan et al., 2005; Zárate et al., 2004).

But there is much more to prejudice than real competition. First, the "realistic" competition for resources may in fact be imagined—a perception in the mind of an individual who is not engaged in any real conflict. Second, people may become resentful of other groups, not because of their conviction that their own security or resources are threatened by these groups, but because of their sense of **relative deprivation**—the belief that they fare poorly compared with others (Pettigrew et al., 2008; Walker & Smith, 2002). What matters to the proverbial Smiths is not the size of their house per se, but whether it is larger than the Jones's house next door.

Social Identity Theory

Why are people so sensitive about the status and integrity of their ingroups, relative to rival outgroups, even when personal interests are not at stake? Could it be that personal interests really are at stake but that these interests are more subtle and psychological than a simple competition for valuable resources? If so, could that explain why people all over the world believe that their own nation, culture, language, and religion are better and more deserving than others?

These questions were first raised in a study of high school boys in Bristol, England, conducted by Henri Tajfel and his colleagues (1971). The boys were shown a series of dotted slides, and their task was to estimate the number of dots on each slide. The slides were presented in rapid-fire succession, so the dots could not be counted. Later, the experimenter told the participants that some people are chronic "overestimators" and others are "underestimators." As part of a second entirely separate task, participants were divided into two groups. They were told that for the sake of convenience, one group consisted of overestimators and the other of underestimators, and participants knew which group they were in. (In fact, they were divided randomly.) Participants were then told to allocate points to other participants that could be cashed in for money.

This procedure was designed to create *minimal groups*—persons categorized on the basis of trivial, minimally important similarities. Tajfel's overestimators and underestimators were not long-term rivals, did not have a history of antagonism, were not frustrated, did not compete for a limited resource, and were not even acquainted with each other. Still, participants consistently allocated more points to members of their own group than to members of the other group. This pattern of discrimination, called **ingroup favouritism**, has been found in studies performed in many countries and using a variety of measures (Capozza & Brown, 2000; Scheepers et al., 2006). The preference for ingroups is so powerful that its effects can be elicited simply by the

realistic conflict theory
The theory that hostility between groups is caused by direct competition for limited resources.

relative deprivation
Feelings of discontent aroused by the belief that one fares poorly compared to others.

ingroup favouritism
The tendency to discriminate in favour of ingroups over outgroups.

Ashley Fraser/Ottawa Citizen. Reprinted by permission.

On July 1 each year, Canadians enjoy a national holiday and celebrate their Canadian identity.

language we use. Charles Perdue and others (1990) found that subtly priming "ingroup" pronouns such as *we*, *us*, and *ours* triggered positive emotions in participants, while "outgroup" pronouns such as *they*, *them*, and *theirs* elicited negative emotions.

To explain ingroup favouritism, Tajfel (1982) and John Turner (1987) proposed **social identity theory**. According to this theory, each of us strives to enhance our self-esteem, which has two components: (1) a personal identity, and (2) various collective or social identities that are based on the groups to which we belong. In other words, people can boost their self-esteem through their own personal achievements or through affiliation with successful groups. What's nice about the need for social identity is that it leads us to derive pride from our connections with others, even if we don't receive any direct benefits from these others (Gagnon & Bourhis, 1996). What's sad, however, is that we often feel the need to belittle "them" in order to feel secure about "us." Religious fervour, racial and ethnic conceit, and aggressive nationalism may all fulfill this more negative side of our social identity. The theory is summarized in ▶ Figure 5.5.

social identity theory
The theory that people favour ingroups over outgroups in order to enhance their self-esteem.

Basic Predictions Two basic predictions arise from social identity theory: (1) Threats to one's self-esteem heighten the need for ingroup favouritism, and (2) expressions of ingroup favouritism enhance one's self-esteem. Research generally supports

▶ FIGURE 5.5

Social Identity Theory

According to Social Identity Theory, people strive to enhance self-esteem, which has two components: a personal identity and various social identities that derive from the groups to which we belong. Thus, people may boost their self-esteem by viewing their ingroups more favourably than outgroups.

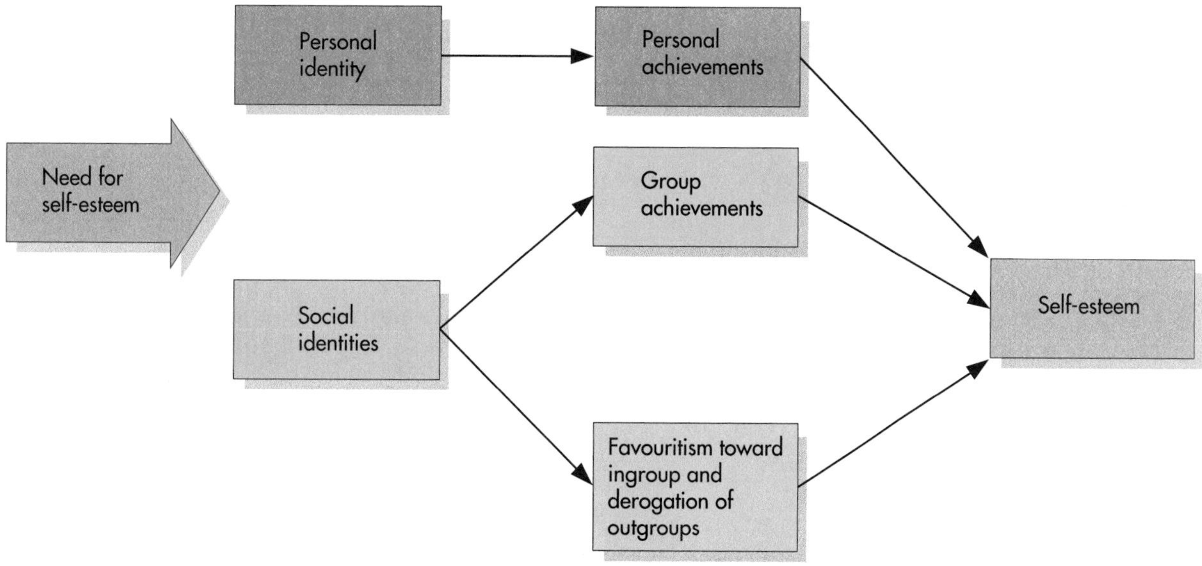

these predictions (Baray et al., 2009; Petersen & Blank, 2003; Scheepers, Ellemers, & Sintemaartensdijk, 2009).

Steven Fein and Steven Spencer (1997; 2008) proposed that threats to one's self-esteem can lead individuals to use available negative stereotypes to derogate members of stereotyped groups, and that by derogating others they can feel better about themselves. For example, in one study, they gave participants positive or negative feedback about their performance on a test of social and verbal skills—feedback that temporarily bolstered or threatened their self-esteem. These participants then took part in what was supposed to be a second experiment in which they evaluated a job applicant. All participants received a photograph of a young woman, her resumé, and a videotape of a job interview. Half the participants were given information suggesting that the woman (named Julie Goldberg) was Jewish. The other half was given information suggesting that the woman (named Maria D'Agostino) was not Jewish. On the campus where the study was held, there was a popular negative stereotype of the "Jewish American Princess" that often targeted upper-middle-class Jewish women from the New York area.

As predicted by social identity theory, there were two important results (see Figure 5.6). First, among participants whose self-esteem had been lowered by negative feedback, Julie Goldberg was rated more negatively than Maria D'Agostino—even though their pictures and their credentials were the same. Second, negative-feedback participants given a chance to belittle the Jewish woman later exhibited a post-experiment increase in self-esteem—the more negatively they evaluated the

FIGURE 5.6

Self-Esteem and Prejudice

Participants received positive or negative feedback and then evaluated a female job applicant believed to be Italian or Jewish. There were two key results: (1) participants whose self-esteem had been lowered by negative feedback evaluated the woman more negatively when she was Jewish than when she was Italian (left); and (2) negative-feedback participants given the opportunity to belittle the Jewish woman showed a post-experiment increase in self-esteem (right).

(Fein & Spencer, 1997.)

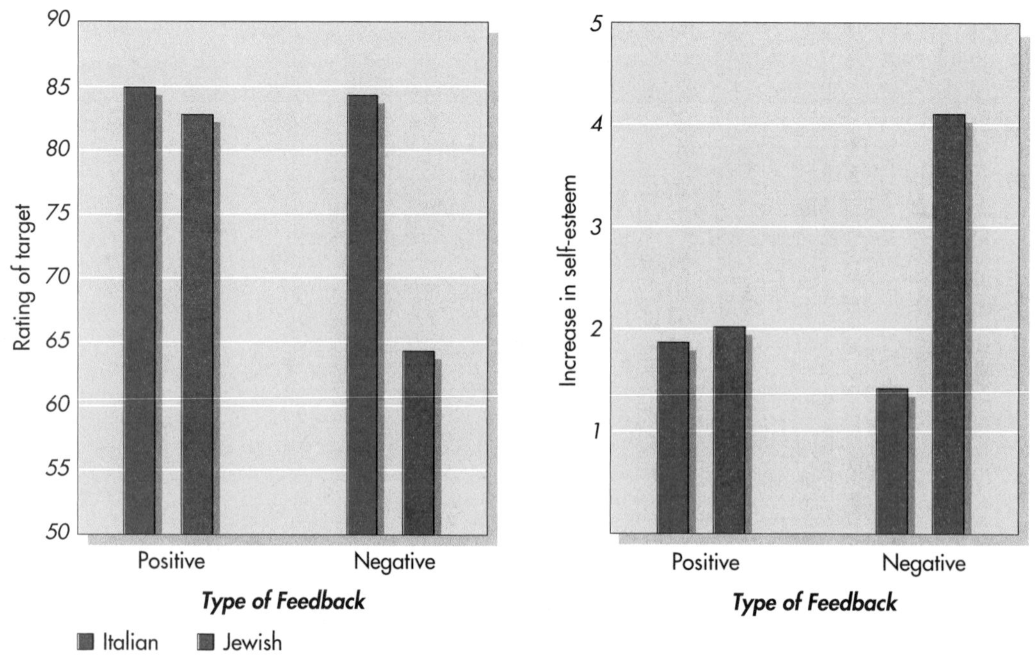

Jewish woman, the better these participants felt about themselves. In sum, a blow to one's self-image evokes prejudice and the expression of prejudice helps to restore self-image.

Interestingly, some research suggests that self-esteem is not always what it appears to be. Christian Jordan, Steven Spencer, and Mark Zanna (2005) describe how some people with high self-esteem are outwardly (or explicitly) quite secure in this view, whereas others who consciously consider themselves to have high self-esteem may be harbouring doubts and require more reinforcement of their positive self-view. Undergraduate participants at the University of Waterloo, all of whom were initially chosen for their high scores on an explicit measure of self-esteem, were given negative feedback about their performance on a bogus intelligence test. They then read about a case of student misconduct; some read that the student was a First Nations member, whereas others read that the student was white. They were then given the opportunity to suggest an appropriate punishment for the offender. What they found was that participants with lower implicit self-esteem (i.e., those who were less confident in their outward belief in their high self-esteem) recommended more severe punishments for the First Nations student than for the white student, while participants with high implicit self-esteem recommended similar punishments in both conditions.

Patrik Giardino/Corbis

Being part of a small, close-knit group can be an important, rewarding part of one's personal identity.

Situational and Individual Differences Recent work has extended social identity theory by making more specific distinctions among various types of esteem-relevant threats (such as whether the threat is to the group's status or to the individual's role within the group), types of groups (such as whether a group has high or low status in a culture), and types of ingroup members (such as whether the members are strongly or weakly identified with their group) (Platow et al., 2005; Scheepers & Ellemers, 2005; Schmitt et al., 2006; Wann & Grieve, 2005). Greater ingroup identification, for example, has been found across many studies to be associated with stronger social identity effects. Shana Levin and her colleagues (2003) reported that the Lebanese participants in their study who most strongly felt identified with the group "Arabs" were especially likely to report supporting terrorist organizations and feeling that the September 11, 2001 attacks on the United States were justified. And Manfred Schmitt and Juergen Maes (2002) found that the more East Germans identified with East Germany, the more they showed increased ingroup bias when making comparisons with West Germany during the German unification process—an effect heightened by increased feelings of relative deprivation during unification.

Culture and Social Identity

Cultural differences can also influence social identity processes. Collectivists are more likely than individualists to value their connectedness and interdependence with the people and groups around them, and their personal identities are tied closely with their social identities. However, according to a number of researchers, people from collectivist cultures are less likely than people from individualist cultures to show biases favouring their ingroups in order to boost their self-esteem (Heine, 2005; Lehman et al., 2004; Snibbe et al., 2003; Yuki, 2003). In one study, for example, Japanese students exhibited less ingroup-enhancing bias than Japanese-Canadian students, who, in turn, exhibited less bias than European-Canadian students (Heine et al., 2001). It isn't the case that collectivists do not favour their ingroup at all. Rather, collectivists are not as compelled to enhance their ingroup as a way of enhancing their own self-esteem. For example, Kenichiro Nakashima and others (2008) showed that when participants' self-esteem was threatened, individuals with independent self-construals showed more ingroup favouritism, whereas individuals with interdependent self-construals did not.

Although they tend not to be driven by self-esteem desires, collectivists do show some biases favouring their ingroups—indeed, being oriented strongly toward one's ingroup may be considered a highly desired and valued way of being (Capozza et al., 2000; Chen et al., 2002; Heine & Raineri, 2009). And although collectivists may be less likely to overtly exaggerate the strengths of their ingroups, some research indicates that they draw sharper distinctions between ingroup and outgroup members than individualists do (Gudykunst & Bond, 1997).

Motives Concerning Intergroup Dominance and Status

Although our membership in various social groups gives us an important part of our personal identity, not all of the groups to which we belong are equally likely to be important to our sense of self. According to Marilynn Brewer and Cynthia Pickett (1999; Brewer, 2003), one important consideration is the relative size and distinctiveness of one's ingroup. Noting that people want to belong to groups that are small enough for them to feel unique, Brewer and Pickett observed that ingroup loyalty and outgroup prejudice are more intense for groups that are in the minority than for members of large and inclusive majorities. People also vary in their ideologies about intergroup relations in society, such as concerning equality and access to power and social mobility. Individuals in groups that benefit from advantages that other groups do not have may be motivated to justify and protect those advantages. For example, a growing body of research has examined the **social dominance orientation**—a desire to see one's ingroups as dominant over other groups and a willingness to adopt cultural values that facilitate oppression over other groups. Such an orientation would be illustrated when individuals endorse sentiments such as "Some groups of people are simply inferior to other groups," and "If certain groups stayed in their place, we would have fewer problems." A person with a social dominance orientation would also likely disagree with statements such as "Group equality should be our ideal." Research in numerous countries throughout the world has found that ingroup identification and outgroup derogation can be especially strong among people with a social dominance orientation (Duckitt & Sibley, 2009; Levin et al., 2009; Sidanius et al., 2007).

Social dominance orientations promote self-interest. But some ideologies support a social structure that may actually oppose one's self-interest, depending on the status of one's groups. John Jost and his colleagues (2009) have focused on what they call *system justification*—processes that endorse and legitimize existing social arrangements. System-justifying beliefs protect the status quo. Groups with power, of course, may promote the status quo to preserve their own advantaged position. But although some disadvantaged groups might be able to improve their circumstances if they were willing to challenge an economic or political system, members of disadvantaged groups with a system-justifying orientation think that the system is fair and just; they may admire and even show *outgroup* favouritism—toward more powerful outgroups.

social dominance orientation A desire to see one's ingroups as dominant over other groups and a willingness to adopt cultural values that facilitate oppression over other groups.

Causes of the Problem: Cognitive and Cultural Factors

The previous section focused on causes of stereotyping, prejudice, and discrimination that on some level serve individuals' needs or motives, such as the motive to feel good about oneself and one's groups. In this section, we turn to perspectives that put greater emphasis on how stereotyping, prejudice, and discrimination result from the basic ways that people learn information available in their culture and process information about people. This is not to say that motivations and intergroup conflicts are not relevant to these cognitive processes. Indeed, we will see in this section a number of ways that people's goals or fears can influence how they process or apply information. The emphasis, however, is on causes that are rooted in cognitive and cultural factors.

Social Categorization

As perceivers, we routinely sort single objects into groups rather than think of each as unique. Biologists classify animals into species; archaeologists divide time into eras; geographers split Earth into regions. Likewise, people sort each other into groups on the basis of gender, race, and other common attributes in a process called **social categorization**. In some ways, social categorization is natural and adaptive. By grouping people the way we group foods, animals, and other objects, we form impressions quickly and use past experience to guide new interactions. With so many things to pay attention to in our social worlds, we can save time and effort by using peoples' group memberships to make inferences about them (Bodenhausen & Hugenberg, 2009; Fiske & Taylor, 2008; Gaertner et al., 2010). Children learn about social categories quite early and therefore become aware of and use stereotypes when they are very young (Levy & Hughes, 2009; Stangor, 2009).

There is, however, a serious drawback to the time and energy saved through social categorization. Like lumping apples and oranges together because both are fruit, categorizing people leads us to overestimate the differences between groups and to underestimate the differences within groups (Ford & Tonander, 1998; Krueger et al., 1989; Spears, 2002; Stangor & Lange, 1994; Wyer et al., 2002). According to Jeffrey Sherman and others (2009), people tend to learn features about majority groups earlier than features about minority groups. When they learn about minority groups, they tend to focus more on features that differentiate them from the majority, thereby magnifying the perceived differences between groups.

The distinctions between social categories may be seen as more rigid, even more biologically rooted, than they actually are. Many people assume, for example, that there is a clear genetic basis for classifying people by race. The fact is, however, that how societies make distinctions between races can change dramatically as a function of historical contexts. For instance, it was fairly common for Americans in the early part of the twentieth century to consider Irish Americans as distinct from Whites, but today such thinking is quite rare. Moreover, biologists, anthropologists, and psychologists have noted that there is more genetic variation within races than between them (Eberhardt & Goff, 2004; Marks, 1995; Markus, 2008; Ore, 2000). The categories we apply to others often say more about ourselves than they say about them. For example, Melissa Williams and Jennifer Eberhardt (2008) found that people who tend to think of race as a stable, biologically determined entity are less likely to interact with racial outgroup members and are more likely to accept racial inequalities than are people who see race as more socially determined.

social categorization
The classification of persons into groups on the basis of common attributes.

Each of us is a member of multiple social categories, but some categorizations—particularly race, gender, and age—are more likely to quickly dominate our perceptions than others (Ito & Urland, 2003; Yzerbyt & Demoulin, 2010). Other factors can influence how we categorize others. Cognitive factors, such as whether we have been primed to think about a particular category, as well as motivational factors, such as our immediate needs in a situation, can determine whether, for example, we will see a black male firefighter primarily by race, gender, or occupation (Bodenhausen & Macrae, 1998; Castelli et al., 2004).

Ingroups Versus Outgroups Although grouping humans is much like grouping objects, there is a key difference. When it comes to social categorization, perceivers themselves are members or non-members of the categories they use. As we have already discussed in this chapter, the strong tendency to carve the world into "us" (ingroups) and "them" (outgroups) has important consequences.

One cognitive consequence is that we exaggerate the differences between our ingroup and other outgroups. Ingroup members often care a great deal about preserving distinctions between their ingroup and outgroups (Castano et al., 2002). For example, many Quebecers (an example of an ingroup, when viewed as separate from the rest of Canada) have repeatedly argued for distinct society status including having French as their sole official language despite the fact that at the federal level, the rest of Canada (a potential outgroup) is officially both French and English. Because perceived similarities are minimized and perceived differences are maximized, stereotypes are formed and reinforced.

Another consequence is a phenomenon known as the **outgroup homogeneity effect**, whereby perceivers assume that there is a greater similarity among members of outgroups than among members of one's own group. In other words, there may be fine and subtle differences among "us," but "they" are all alike (Linville & Jones, 1980).

Research shows that outgroup homogeneity effects are common and evident around the world (Bartsch et al., 1997; Linville, 1998; Read & Urada, 2003). Indeed there are many real-life examples. People from China, Korea, Taiwan, and Vietnam see themselves as different from one another, of course, but to many Western eyes they are all Asian. Business majors like to talk about "engineering types"; engineers talk about "business types"; liberals lump together all conservatives; and teenagers lump together all "old people." To people outside the group, outgroup members can even seem to look alike—people are less accurate in distinguishing and recognizing faces of members of racial groups other than their own, especially to the extent that they are unfamiliar with these other groups (Chiroro et al., 2008; Pauker et al., 2009; Stahl et al., 2008; Young & Hugenberg, 2012).

There are several reasons for the tendency to perceive outgroups as homogeneous. First, we often do not notice subtle differences among outgroups because we have little personal contact with them. Think about your family or your favourite sports team, and specific individuals come to mind. Think about an unfamiliar outgroup, however, and you are likely to think in abstract terms about the group as a whole. Indeed, the more familiar people are with an outgroup, the less likely they are to perceive it as homogeneous.

A second problem is that people often do not encounter a representative sample of outgroup members. A student from one school who encounters students from a rival school only when they cruise into town for a football game, screaming at the top of their lungs, sees only the most avid rival fans—hardly a diverse lot (Linville et al., 1989; Quattrone, 1986). People sometimes perceive their own group to be homogeneous when they first join it, but over time, as they become more familiar with fellow

outgroup homogeneity effect The tendency to assume that there is greater similarity among members of outgroups than among members of ingroups.

group members, they see their group as more diverse relative to outgroups (Ryan & Bogart, 1997).

Lack of familiarity and lack of diversity of experiences with outgroup members are two reasons why "*they* all look alike," but there's more to the story than that. Research using brain imaging or cognitive methods has found that merely categorizing people as ingroup or outgroup members influences how perceivers process information about them, even if familiarity is held constant. For example, student participants in experiments by Kurt Hugenberg and Olivier Corneille (2009) were exposed to unfamiliar faces of people who were the same race as the participants. These faces were categorized as ingroup members (from the same university as the participants) or outgroup members (from a rival university). The students processed faces more holistically (that is, they integrated the features of the faces into a global representation of the overall face) when they had been categorized as being from their ingroup, than when they had been categorized as members of the outgroup.

Jay Van Bavel and others (2008) found related results when they exposed participants to unfamiliar white or black faces. The participants showed greater neural activity in particular areas of the brain, such as the orbitofrontal cortex, when the faces were labelled as being from an ingroup than when they were labelled as being from an outgroup (see ▶ Figure 5.7). In addition, this greater activity in the orbitofrontal cortex was correlated significantly with the degree to which the participants reported preferring the ingroup faces over the outgroup faces. It is interesting to note that the categorization of faces as ingroup or outgroup had a much stronger effect on orbitofrontal cortex activity and on preference for the faces than did the variable of whether the faces were white or black.

▶ FIGURE 5.7

Neural Activity and Ingroup Bias

Participants saw photographs of unfamiliar white and black faces. When the faces were said to be members of their ingroup, participants showed greater neural activity in particular areas of the brain, including the two areas highlighted here, the fusiform gyrus and the orbitofrontal cortex. Greater activation in the orbitofrontal cortex was also associated with stronger self-reported preference for ingroup faces.

(Van Bavel et al., 2008.)

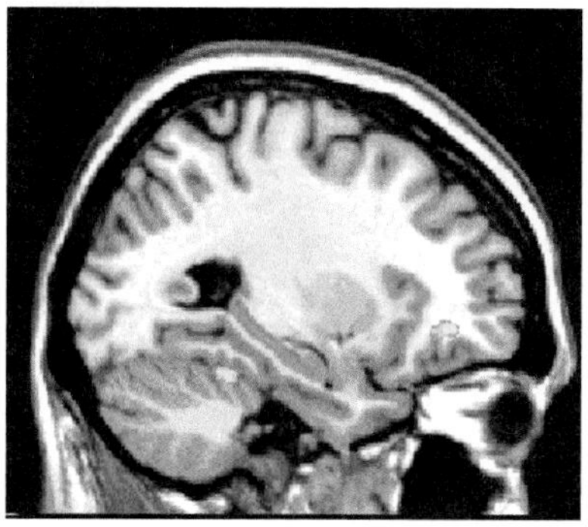

Van Bavel, J.J., Packer, D.J., & Cunningham, W.A.(2008). The neural substrates of in-group bias: A functional magnetic resonance imaging investigation. *Psychological Science 19, 1131-1139*, copyright © 2008 by Association of Psychological Science. Reprinted by Permission of SAGE Publications.

Dehumanizing Outgroups Perceivers may not only process outgroup members' faces more superficially—they also sometimes process them more like objects than like fellow human beings. This was a conclusion suggested by Lasana Harris and Susan Fiske (2006). When participants in their research saw pictures of people from a variety of groups, fMRI showed activation in their medial prefrontal cortex, which is thought to be necessary for social cognition. However, this activation was not evident in response to images of either nonhuman objects or people from particularly extreme outgroups, such as addicts or the homeless. In the latter case, regions of the brain associated with feelings such as disgust were more likely to be activated, leading to a dehumanizing view of the outgroup member. This in turn may allow individuals to be less concerned with treating outgroup members poorly (Harris & Fiske, 2011).

A rapidly growing number of social psychological investigations have illustrated both the subtle and not-so-subtle ways that people see or treat outgroup members as less than fully human (Demoulin et al., 2009; Haslam et al., 2008; Kwan & Fiske, 2008). Dehumanization has played a role in atrocities throughout history, such as in the Nazi propaganda that characterized the Jews in Germany as disease-spreading rats and Blacks as half-apes.

How Stereotypes Survive and Self-Perpetuate

Social categorization helps give rise to stereotypes, which offer us quick and convenient summaries of social groups. It is clear, however, that they often cause us to overlook the diversity within categories and to form mistaken impressions of specific individuals. Given their shortcomings, why do stereotypes endure? We turn now to some of the mechanisms that help perpetuate stereotypes.

Illusory Correlations One way in which stereotypes endure is through the **illusory correlation**, a tendency for people to overestimate the link between variables that are only slightly or not at all correlated (Meiser & Hewstone, 2006; Risen et al., 2007; Sherman et al., 2009; Stroessner & Plaks, 2001). Illusory correlations result from two different processes. First, people tend to overestimate the association between variables that are *distinctive*—variables that capture attention simply because they are novel or deviant. When two relatively unusual events happen together, that combination may stick in people's minds, and this can lead people to overestimate an association between the two events. For example, if people see a story on the news about a person who was recently released from a mental institution (a rarely encountered category of person) committing a brutal murder (an uncommon behaviour), they may remember the link between mental patient and murder better than if a more commonly encountered type of person committed the murder or than if a former mental patient did something more common.

The implications for stereotyping are important: Unless otherwise motivated, people overestimate the joint occurrence of distinctive variables such as minority groups and deviant acts. Even children in Grade 2 may perceive these false associations (Johnston & Jacobs, 2003).

Second, people tend to overestimate the association between variables that they already expect to go together. For example, in one study, participants were presented with lists of paired words, such as *lion-tiger*, *lion-eggs*, *bacon-tiger*, and *bacon-egg*. The participants tended to overestimate the frequency of pairings that had meaningful, expected associations (*lion-tiger*, *bacon-eggs*), even if such pairings actually occurred no more frequently than less expected pairings (*lion-eggs*, *bacon-tiger*) (Chapman, 1967). David Hamilton and Terrence Rose (1980) found that stereotypes can lead people to expect social groups and traits to fit together like bacon and eggs, and to overestimate the frequency with which they've actually observed these associations. The implications for stereotyping are important here as well: People overestimate the joint occurrence of variables they expect to be associated with each other, such as stereotyped groups and stereotypic behaviours.

Attributions People also maintain their stereotypes through how they explain the behaviours of others. Chapter 4 discusses how perceivers make attributions, or explanations, about the causes of other people's behaviours and how these attributions can sometimes be flawed. These flaws can help perpetuate stereotypes. For example, although we know from research that discrimination can impair the performance of stereotyped individuals, perceivers may fail to take this effect into account when explaining this underperformance and instead see it as evidence that supports the negative stereotype. In this way, perceivers may see confirmation of the stereotype instead of recognizing the consequences of discrimination. On the other hand, when people see others acting in ways that seem to contradict a stereotype, they may be more likely to think about situational factors in order to explain the surprising behaviour. Rather than accept a stereotype-disconfirming behaviour at face value, such as a woman defeating a man in an athletic contest, perceivers imagine the situational factors that might explain away this apparent exception to the rule, such as random luck, ulterior motives, or other special circumstances. In this way, perceivers can more easily maintain their stereotypes of these groups (Karpinski & von Hippel, 1996; Schnake & Ruscher, 1998; Sekaquaptewa et al., 2003; Sherman et al., 2005; Wigboldus et al., 2004).

illusory correlation
An overestimate of the association between variables that are only slightly or not at all correlated.

THE CANADIAN PRESS/Adrian Wyld

Women who play rough contact sports—such as these members of the Olympic gold medal-winning Canadian women's hockey team—defy gender stereotypes. But rather than change their gender stereotypes, many perceivers subtype these women and dismiss them as exceptions.

Subtyping Have you ever noticed that people often manage to hold negative views about a social group even when they like individual members of that group? One of the unnerving paradoxes of social perception is that stereotypes stubbornly survive one disconfirmation after the next. Gordon Allport (1954) recognized this phenomenon half a century ago. He wrote, "There is a common mental device that permits people to hold prejudgments even in the face of much contradictory evidence. It is the device of admitting exceptions.... By excluding a few favoured cases, the negative rubric is kept intact for all other cases" (p. 23). Confronted with a woman who does not seem particularly warm and nurturing, for example, people can either develop a more diversified image of females or toss the mismatch into a special subtype—say, "career women." To the extent that people create this subtype, their existing image of women in general will remain relatively intact (Carnaghi & Yzerbyt, 2007; Deutsch & Fazio, 2008; Hewstone & Lord, 1998; Wilder et al., 1996).

Confirmation Biases and Self-Fulfilling Prophecies Imagine learning that a mother yelled at a one-year-old girl, that a lawyer behaved aggressively, and that a Boy Scout grabbed the arm of an elderly woman crossing the street. Now imagine that a construction worker yelled at a one-year-old girl, that a homeless man behaved aggressively, and that an ex-con grabbed the arm of an elderly woman crossing the street. Do very different images of these actions come to mind? This is a fundamental effect of stereotyping: Stereotypes of groups influence people's perceptions and interpretations of the behaviours of group members. This is especially likely when a target of a stereotype behaves in an ambiguous way; perceivers reduce the ambiguity by interpreting the behaviour as consistent with the stereotype (Dunning & Sherman, 1997; Kunda et al., 1997). For example, in one study, black and white sixth-grade boys saw pictures and descriptions of ambiguously aggressive behaviours (such as one child bumping into another). Both the black and the white boys judged the behaviours as more mean and threatening if the behaviours were performed by black boys than by white boys (Sagar & Schofield, 1980).

The effect of stereotypes on individuals' perceptions is a type of confirmation bias, which, as we saw in Chapter 4, involves peoples' tendencies to interpret, seek, and create information that seems to confirm their expectations. In a clever demonstration of this bias (specifically in the context of interpreting information), Jeff Stone and

FIGURE 5.8

"White Men Can't Jump"?

Students listened to a basketball game and evaluated one particular player. Half of the students were led to believe that the player was black, the other half, that he was white. Consistent with their stereotypes, the students perceived the player as having more physical ability if they thought he was black and as having more "court smarts" if they thought he was white.

(Stone et al., 1997.)

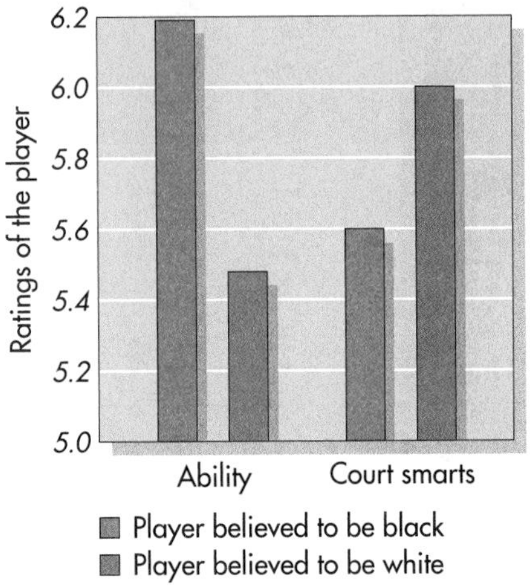

his colleagues (1997) had students listen to a college basketball game. Some were led to believe that a particular player was white; others thought he was black. After listening to the game, all of the students were asked to evaluate how the player had performed in the game. Consistent with racial stereotypes, those students who believed the player was black rated him as having played better and more athletically, whereas those who thought he was white rated him as having played with more intelligence and hustle (see Figure 5.8).

Stereotypes are held not just by individuals but typically by many people within a culture, and they are often perpetuated through repeated communications. In a classic demonstration, Gordon Allport and Leo Postman (1947) showed participants a picture of a subway train filled with passengers. In the picture were a black man dressed in a suit and a white man holding a razor (see Figure 5.9). One participant viewed the scene briefly and then described it to a second participant who had not seen it. The second participant communicated the description to a third participant and so on, through six rounds of communication. The result: In more than half the sessions, the final participant's report indicated that the black man, not the white man, held the razor. Some participants even reported that he had waved it in a threatening manner.

Confirmation biases are bad enough. But even more disturbing are situations in which stereotyped group members themselves are led to behave in stereotype-confirming ways. In other words, stereotypes can create self-fulfilling prophecies. As noted in Chapter 4, a self-fulfilling prophecy occurs when a perceiver's false expectations about a person cause the person to behave in ways that confirm those expectations. Stereotypes can trigger such behavioural confirmation (Rosenthal, 2002). Consider a classic experiment by Carl Word and others (1974) involving a situation of great importance in people's lives: the job interview. White participants, without realizing it, sat farther away, made more speech errors, and held shorter interviews when interviewing black applicants (who were actually experimental confederates) than white applicants. In a second study, white interviewers were asked to treat white job applicants as the black applicants had been treated in the

FIGURE 5.9

How Racial Stereotypes Distort Social Perceptions

After briefly viewing this picture, one participant described it to a second participant, who described it to a third, and so on. After six rounds of communication, the final report often placed the razor held by the white man into the black man's hand. This study illustrates how racial stereotypes can distort social perception.

(Adapted from Allport & Postman, 1947.)

first study (i.e., shorter interviews, farther social distance, and so on). Being exposed to this colder interpersonal style then led the white applicants to behave in a nervous and awkward manner; thus the applicants "confirmed" what the interviewers seemed to expect of them and this hurt their overall interview performance.

Are Stereotypes Ever Accurate? We have been discussing how stereotypes survive despite evidence that should disconfirm them, or how stereotypes distort perceptions and behaviours based on false expectations. But this can raise the question of whether stereotypes are ever accurate. Like people, stereotypes are not all alike. Some are more accurate than others. Although many stereotypes are based on completely illusory information or perceptions, some do stem from a kernel of truth, and still others may be fairly accurate. For example, researchers at the University of British Columbia asked attractive individuals—for whom beauty is stereotypically associated with goodness—to rate themselves on a number of personality traits. They then asked undergraduate participants to make personality judgments of these same individuals and found that, not only were the attractive targets rated more positively than less attractive people (following the stereotype), but perceiver's personality ratings of these individuals were also more accurate (Lorenzo, Biesanz, & Human, 2010)! Lee Jussim and others (2009; Madon et al., 1998) argue that stereotypes tend to be much more accurate than the majority of researchers who study stereotypes acknowledge.

But the question of accuracy is more complicated than it may appear. First, the meaning of "accurate" can be debated. "Accurate" could mean that stereotypes reflect universal, stable, possibly genetic differences; or it could mean that stereotypes reflect differences that exist under particular sets of societal and historic conditions (with the qualification that these differences may well change if conditions change). Most social psychologists focus on the latter meaning.

"Not everybody's life is what they make it. Some people's life is what other people make it."

—Alice Walker

Second, imagine that you believe that members of a particular social category tend to be rude. If you encounter a member of this group and anticipate that she is likely to be rude, you may react toward her in a cold, unfriendly way. This in turn may cause her to act rudely toward you in return. Was your expectation of that person accurate? In a sense, it was: She *was* rude to you, just as you expected. But clearly your own behaviour may have caused the rudeness. This self-fulfilling prophecy creates a reality that seems to render the stereotype accurate, even if it was false in the first place.

Reuters/Corbis

Satirist Rick Mercer plays up ingroup and outgroup differences when he asks unsuspecting Americans unusual questions about Canada. For example, he has gotten some Americans to agree that the capital building of Canada is an igloo and others to sign a petition asking the Canadian government to stop putting our elderly citizens on ice floes!

Culture and Socialization

When you stop to think about it, the list of well-known stereotypes seems endless. Consider some examples: Math majors are geeks, athletes are dumb, librarians are quiet, Italians are emotional, accountants are dull, Canadians are polite, Americans are loud, white men can't jump, and used-car salespeople can't be trusted as far as you can throw them. Dividing people into social categories, including ingroups and outgroups, certainly is a key factor in the formation of stereotypes and prejudices. But with so many stereotypes and prejudices, many of which are shared around the world, it is clear that at some level we are somehow taught these stereotypes from our culture. We turn now to examine those processes.

Socialization refers to the processes by which people learn the norms, rules, and information of a culture or group. It is often said that people must be taught to hate. People learn stereotypes and prejudice through role models, group norms, and the culture at large (Castelli et al., 2003; Devine, 1989; Guimond, 2000; Pettigrew, 1958). Like hairstyles and musical preferences, individuals' racial prejudices are affected dramatically by those of their peers, family, and other social contacts. Merely overhearing a racial slur by a stranger can increase people's expressions of prejudice (Greenberg & Pyszczynski, 1985). One author of this textbook recalls a time when he was about eight years old and his two best friends suddenly turned on him and derisively called him a "Jew ball." They had never thought of him as different from them or categorized him as Jewish before, and yet on this day, suddenly Jewishness was relevant—and negative to them. But why then, and how did they come up with "Jew ball"? Only much later did it become clear that they had misheard their father say "Jew boy." Trying to model their father's values, they used a version of this expression against their friend, and thereafter they saw him in a different way. The biased lens through which the father saw people was passed down to the next generation.

Although it certainly isn't always the case, the stereotypes and prejudices of a parent can influence the stereotypes and prejudices of a child, often in implicit ways (Castelli et al., 2009). More generally, and more pervasively, the stereotypes and prejudices exhibited by peers, the popular media, and one's culture are part of the air each of us breathes as we develop, and the influences can be obvious or subtle.

To narrow our discussion of these cultural and socialization processes, we will focus on gender stereotypes and sexism, but it is important to recognize that these processes are relevant to all kinds and targets of stereotypes, prejudice, and discrimination.

Gender Stereotypes: Blue for Boys, Pink for Girls When a baby is born, the first words uttered ring loud and clear: "It's a boy!" or "It's a girl!" In many hospitals, the newborn boy immediately is given a blue hat and the newborn girl a pink hat. The infant receives a gender-appropriate name and is showered with gender-appropriate gifts. Over the next few years, the typical boy is supplied with toy trucks, baseballs, pretend tools, guns, and chemistry sets; the typical girl is furnished with dolls, stuffed animals, pretend make-up kits, kitchen sets, and tea sets. As they enter school, many expect the boy to earn money by delivering newspapers and to enjoy math and video games, while they expect the girl to babysit and to enjoy crafts, music, and social activities. These distinctions persist in university, as more male students major in economics and the sciences, and more female students major in the arts, languages, and humanities. In the work force, more men become doctors, construction workers, auto mechanics, airplane pilots, investment bankers, and engineers. In contrast, more women become secretaries, schoolteachers, nurses, flight attendants, bank tellers, and stay-at-home moms.

The traditional pinks and blues are not as distinct today as they used to be. Many gender barriers of the past have broken down, and the colours have somewhat blended together. Nevertheless, the stereotypes—and, as we discussed earlier, sexism—persists.

What do people say when asked to describe the typical man and woman? Males are said to be more adventurous, assertive, aggressive, independent, and task-oriented; females are thought to be more sensitive, gentle, dependent, emotional, and people-oriented. These images are so universal that they were reported by 2800 university students from 30 different countries of North and South America, Europe, Africa, Asia, and Australia (Williams & Best, 1982). The images are also salient to young children, who distinguish men from women well before their first birthday; identify themselves and others as boys or girls by three years of age; form gender-stereotypic beliefs and preferences about stories, toys, and other objects soon after that; and then use their simplified stereotypes in judging others and favouring their own gender over the other in intergroup situations (Golombok & Hines, 2002; Knobloch et al., 2005).

Children also begin quite early to distinguish between stereotypically masculine and feminine behaviours. One study, for instance, found that by their second birthday, toddlers exhibited more surprise when adults performed behaviours inconsistent with gender roles (Serbin et al., 2002). In another study, preschool-age boys and girls liked a new toy less if they were told that it was a toy that opposite-sex children liked (Martin et al., 1995).

Although biological and evolutionary factors may play a role in some of these preferences, it is clear that children have ample opportunity to learn gender stereotypes and roles from their parents and other role models. A meta-analysis of more than 40 studies showed a significant correlation between parents' gender stereotypes and their children's gender-related thinking (Tenenbaum & Leaper, 2002).

Beliefs about males and females are so deeply ingrained that they influence the behaviour of adults literally the moment a baby is born. In a fascinating study, the first-time parents of 15 girls and 15 boys were interviewed within 24 hours of the babies' births. There were no differences between the male and female newborns in height, weight, or other aspects of physical appearance. Yet the parents of girls rated their babies as softer, smaller, and more finely featured. The fathers of boys saw their sons as stronger, larger, more alert, and better coordinated (Rubin et al., 1974). Could it be there really were differences that only the parents were able to discern? Doubtful. In another study, Emily Mondschein and others (2000) found that mothers of 11-month-old girls underestimated their infants' crawling ability, whereas mothers of 11-month-old boys overestimated it.

James Leynse/Corbis SABA

AP Photo/Andy Wong/CP Images

The Blues and the Pinks. Even a very quick look at a toy store illustrates dramatic differences in how boys and girls are socialized. For example, boys are encouraged to play active, loud, and violent games (top), while girls are encouraged to engage in quieter, nurturing role-play (bottom).

As they develop, boys and girls receive many divergent messages, in many different settings. For example, Alicia Chang and others (2011) found that mothers of 22-month-old infant boys spend almost twice as much time talking to them about numbers than do mothers of infant girls. They suggest that this may decrease girls' awareness of these concepts, leading them to have less interest in them later in life. Providing further evidence of the differences in how parents speak to boys compared to girls, Barbara Morrongiello and Tess Dawber (2000) showed mothers videotapes of children engaging in somewhat risky activities on a playground and asked them to stop the tape and indicate whatever they would ordinarily say to their own child in the situation shown. Mothers of daughters intervened more frequently and more quickly than did mothers of sons. As shown in ■ Table 5.2, mothers of daughters were more likely to caution the child about getting hurt, whereas mothers of sons were more likely to encourage the child's risky playing. Additional research by Morrongiello and others (2000) revealed that although boys typically experience more injuries from risky playing than girls, all children by the age of six tend to think that girls are at greater risk of injury than boys.

TABLE 5.2

What Mothers Would Say

Mothers of young children watched a videotape of another child playing on a playground and engaging in somewhat risky behaviours, such as standing on top of a structure and leaning far over to look underneath. The mothers were instructed to stop the videotape whenever they would say something to the child if the child were theirs, and to indicate what they would say. Mothers of daughters stopped the tape much more often than mothers of sons to express caution ("Be careful!"), worry about injury ("You could fall!"), and directives to stop ("Stop that this instant!"). In contrast, mothers of sons were more likely to indicate encouragement ("Good job! Let me see you go higher.").

(Adapted from Morrongiello & Dawber, 2000.)

	Frequency of Statement by:	
Context of Statement	Mothers of Girls	Mothers of Boys
Caution	3.9	0.7
Worry about injury	9.2	0.2
Directive to stop	9.3	0.6
Encouragement	0.5	3.0

Reprinted from *Journal of Experimental Child Psychology, 76, 89-103,* Morrongiello & Dawber, Mothers' Responses to Sons and Daughters Engaging in Injury-Risk Behaviors on a Playground: Implications for Sex Differences in Injury Rates, Copyright 2000, with permission from Elsevier.

Social Role Theory As children develop, they begin to look at the larger culture around them and see who occupies what roles in society, as well as how these roles are valued. According to Alice Eagly's (1987; Eagly et al., 2004) **social role theory**, although the perception of sex differences may be based on some real differences, it is magnified by the unequal social roles that men and women occupy.

The process involves three steps. First, through a combination of biological and social factors, a division of labour between the sexes has emerged over time—at home and in the work setting. Men are more likely to work in construction or business; women are more likely to care for children and to take lower-status jobs. Second, since people behave in ways that fit the roles they play, men are more likely than women to wield physical, social, and economic power. Third, these behavioural differences provide a continuing basis for social perception, leading us to perceive men as dominant and women as domestic "by nature," when in fact the differences reflect the roles they play. In short, sex stereotypes are shaped by—and often confused with—the unequal distribution of men and women into different social roles (see ▶ Figure 5.10). According to this theory, perceived differences between men and women are based on real behavioural differences that are mistakenly assumed to arise from gender rather than from social roles.

According to a Statistics Canada poll, men and women are much more likely to share household responsibilities than they were 20 years ago. Whereas only 54 percent of married men with children reported helping out around the house in 1986, that number rose to 71 percent by 2006 (Statistics Canada, 2006).

social role theory
The theory that small gender differences are magnified in perception by the contrasting social roles occupied by men and women.

Social role theory and socialization processes more generally can of course be extended beyond gender stereotypes and sexism. Seeing that some groups of people occupy particular roles in society more than other people do can fuel numerous stereotypes and prejudices. One extremely important factor in determining what kinds of people we see in what kinds of roles is the popular media. We examine some of the effects associated with media exposure next.

Media Effects More than ever, children, adolescents, and adults seem to be immersed in popular culture transmitted via the mass media. Watching TV shows

▶FIGURE 5.10

Eagly's Social Role Theory of Gender Stereotypes

According to social role theory, stereotypes of men as dominant and women as subordinate persist because men occupy higher-status positions in society. This division of labour, a product of many factors, leads men and women to behave in ways that fit their social roles. But rather than attribute the differences to these roles, people attribute the differences to gender.

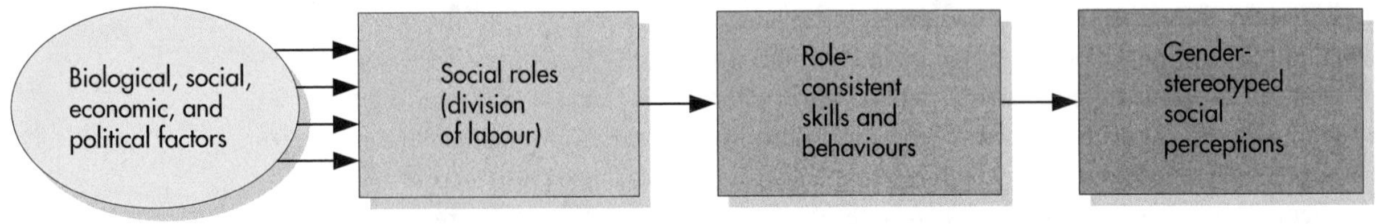

on our iPods or cellphones while on the stationary bike at the gym, checking out the latest viral video sweeping the Internet while taking a break at the office or coffee shop, seeing advertisements popping up on our computer screens like weeds, glancing at the tabloid cover shots of the latest starlet hounded by relentless paparazzi—there often seems no escape. Through the ever-present media, we are fed a steady diet of images of people. These images have the potential to perpetuate stereotypes and discrimination.

Fortunately, the days are gone when the media portrayed women and people of colour in almost exclusively stereotypical, powerless roles. Still, research indicates that some stereotyping persists—for example, in music videos and TV commercials, programs, and cartoons in countries around the world (Bartsch et al., 2000; Klein & Shiffman, 2009; Messineo, 2008; Nassif & Gunter, 2008; Ward et al., 2005).

David Reed/Corbis

Karl Prouse/Catwalking/Getty Images

Although looking at images of attractive people is a pleasant experience for many people, these popular images may also produce negative consequences—perpetuating stereotypes and promoting dangerous behaviours among those who try to achieve what are often impossible, unhealthy standards of masculinity and femininity.

More to the point is the fact that media depictions can influence viewers, often without the viewers realizing it (Ward & Friedman, 2006). Think about TV commercials for beer or men's cologne. There's a good chance that the commercials that come to mind include images of women as sex objects whose primary purpose in the ads is to serve as "the implied 'reward' for product consumption" (Rudman & Borgida, 1995, p. 495). Can these commercials affect not only men's attitudes toward women, but their immediate behaviour as well? Yes, according to research by Laurie Rudman and Eugene Borgida (1995). Male undergraduates in their study watched a videotape containing either sexist TV commercials or TV commercials for similar products that contained no sexual imagery. After watching the commercials, each participant went to a room to meet and interview a woman, who actually was a confederate of the experimenter. Each student's interaction with the woman was secretly videotaped. Later, female judges watched these videotaped interactions and evaluated the male students' behaviour toward the female confederate on several dimensions. The results revealed that the men who had seen sexist commercials were rated as behaving in a more sexualized, objectifying manner than the men who had seen the neutral ads. Having been primed with images of women as sex objects on TV, the men treated the woman in objectifying ways.

TV commercials also influence women's attitudes and behaviour. Studies have shown that female university students who had just watched a set of commercials in which the female characters were portrayed in stereotypic fashion tended to express lower self-confidence, less independence, and fewer career aspirations than did those who viewed stereotype-irrelevant or counter-stereotypical ads. They even performed more poorly on a difficult math test (Davies et al., 2002; Geis et al., 1984; Jennings et al., 1980).

Immersed in popular culture, people implicitly learn stereotypes about how men and women are supposed to look. Media images of impossibly thin or proportioned female models can have powerful effects on women's body images and esteem and are implicated in the near-epidemic incidence of eating disorders and debilitating anxiety over physical appearance, particularly among young European American women (Henderson-King et al., 2001; Moradi et al., 2005; Ward & Friedman, 2006). The media's impact may be especially negative among individuals who already have concerns about their appearance or are particularly concerned with other people's opinions. This idea found support in a recent meta-analysis conducted by Stephen Want (2009), a researcher at Ryerson University. Interestingly, he found that media effects on body dissatisfaction measures were *smallest* across the studies when women were specifically asked to focus on the appearance of the models in the images, as opposed to studies where participants were led to believe that the images were secondary to the real purpose of the study.

It appears that women may be most vulnerable to sexualized, objectifying images when they are not very mindful of them (Henderson-King et al., 2001). While standing in the checkout line, flipping through a magazine, or half-watching a TV commercial, women process these images but may not think much about them in terms of the potentially dangerous messages they convey. These messages can sneak in under the radar and have unnerving effects. However, when made more mindful of the exaggerated or sexist implications of these images, women may respond to these images very differently, such as by seeing them as exaggerations or unreal fantasies, and so they are better armed against their threatening implications.

Even brief exposure to sexist television commercials can significantly influence the behaviours of men and women. TRUE.

Men's body images may also be affected by the media. A meta-analysis of 25 studies—some correlational and some experimental—found a significant relationship between men's perceptions that the mass media was creating pressure about acceptable male bodies and feeling dissatisfied with their bodies (Barlett et al., 2008). Research points to a growing number of teenage boys and men who are hurting themselves through their obsession with their bodies as they try to gain muscle mass while remaining extremely lean. Here, too, the media appear to play a critical role. Indeed, graphic images of muscular and lean male models have become increasingly prevalent of late. More and more cases come to light every year of boys and young men copying star athletes by taking steroids and other drugs that can make them look more like their role models but that can seriously threaten their health (Gray & Ginsberg, 2007; Hanc, 2006; Hargreaves & Tiggemann, 2009; Hobza & Rochlen, 2009; Parent & Moradi, 2011; Taylor, 2006).

It is clear that the portrayals of different groups of people can vary dramatically from one culture to another. This is true also for body image—what is considered the norm or ideal in the mainstream media in Western culture is not the same as the norm or ideal in other cultures or even in subcultures within Western culture. What is considered beautiful in one culture may be considered too thin, too heavy, or too muscular in another culture, and these differences in ideals as represented in the most popular media of a culture lead to different effects on the body-related self-esteem and behaviours of individuals (Bailey, 2008; Jung & Lee, 2006; Schooler, 2008).

The media can also play a role in promoting *positive* norms. This was demonstrated recently in an unusual year-long field experiment in Rwanda, which has been the site of terrible war, genocide, and intergroup conflict, particularly between the Hutus and Tutsis. Elizabeth Levy Paluck (2009) had Rwandans listen to a radio soap opera (radio being the most important form of mass media there) over the course of a year. She randomly assigned half to listen to a soap opera about conflicts that paralleled real conflicts in the country but that were solved in ways that modelled intergroup cooperation and communication, nonviolence, and opposition to prejudice. The other half of the participants listened to a soap opera about health issues. At the end of the year, those Rwandans who listened to the soap opera promoting positive intergroup norms had significantly more positive feelings about intergroup cooperation, trust, and interactions.

Stereotype Content Model

The relative status and relations between groups in a culture influence the content of the culture's stereotypes about these groups. This is a central point in the **stereotype content model** (Cuddy et al., 2008; Fiske et al., 2009; 2012). According to this model, many group stereotypes vary along two dimensions: warmth and competence. Groups may be considered high on both dimensions, low on both, or high on one dimension but low on the other. For example, the elderly may be stereotyped as high on warmth but low on competence.

The stereotype content model proposes that stereotypes about the competence of a group are influenced by the relative *status* of that group in society—higher relative status is associated with higher competence. Stereotypes about the warmth of a group are influenced by perceived *competition* with the group—greater perceived competition is associated with lower warmth. For example, groups that are of low status but that remain compliant and do not try to upset the status quo are likely to be stereotyped as low in competence but high in warmth. A wave of immigrants who enter a country with low status but compete for jobs and resources, on the other hand, may be seen as low in both competence and warmth.

To put it into concrete terms, think about stereotypes about two categories of women. Housewives may be seen as having warm traits, such as being caring and nurturing, and having traits associated with lack of competence, such as being passive. Stereotypes of female executives in the corporate world, however, consist of much colder attributes, such as being demanding and cutthroat, along with competent attributes such as being strong. When stereotypes are high on one dimension but low on the other, group members can face a difficult challenge. A female business leader who comes off as very warm may be seen as less competent, for example. Similarly, if she comes off as very competent, she may be seen as less warm.

Researchers have found support for the stereotype content model both with experiments—in which perceived status and intergroup competition are manipulated—and from correlational studies conducted around the world (Caprariello et al., 2009; Cuddy et al., 2009).

Is Stereotyping Inevitable? Automatic Versus Intentional Processes

Part of the power of stereotypes is that they can bias our perceptions and responses even if we don't personally agree with them. In other words, we don't have to believe a stereotype for it to trigger illusory correlations and self-fulfilling prophecies, or to bias how we think, feel, and behave toward group members. Sometimes just being aware of stereotypes in one's culture is enough to cause these effects. Moreover, stereotypes can be activated without our awareness. These findings raise a provocative, and potentially depressing, question: Is stereotyping inevitable? When we encounter people from other groups, do our stereotypes of these groups always become activated in our minds? Can we do anything to prevent this from happening? Most people believe that they can resist stereotyping others, but recent research paints a far more complex picture.

Stereotypes as (Sometimes) Automatic Patricia Devine (1989) distinguishes between automatic and controlled processes in stereotyping. She argues that people have become highly aware of the contents of many stereotypes through cultural influences, such as lessons learned from parents and images in the media. Because of this high awareness, people automatically activate stereotypes whenever they are exposed to members of groups for which popular stereotypes exist. Thus, just as many of us are

stereotype content model
A model proposing that the relative status and competition between groups influence group stereotypes along the dimensions of competence and warmth.

automatically primed to think *eggs* after hearing *bacon and* ..., we are also primed to think of concepts relevant to a stereotype when we think of a stereotyped group. To be sure, we can try to prevent this activated stereotype from influencing our judgments or behaviours. As noted earlier, however, we are often unaware that a particular stereotype has been activated or how it can influence our perceptions and behaviours (Bargh, 1997). Thus, the stereotype can affect us in spite of our good intentions.

Very brief exposure to a member of a stereotyped group does not lead to biased judgments or responses, but longer exposure typically does. FALSE.

In her study, Devine exposed white participants to **subliminal presentations** on a computer monitor. For one group, these presentations consisted of words relevant to stereotypes about black people, such as "Africa," "ghetto," "welfare," and "basketball." Subliminally presented information is presented so quickly that perceivers do not even realize that they have been exposed to it. Thus, these students were not consciously aware that they had seen these words. Those who were subliminally primed with many of these words activated the black stereotype, which subsequently led them to interpret another person's behaviour in a more negative, hostile light. These effects occurred *even among participants who did not consciously endorse the stereotypes in question.*

subliminal presentation
A method of presenting stimuli so faintly or rapidly that people do not have any conscious awareness of having been exposed to them.

Devine's theory sparked an explosion of interest in these issues. Are we automatically biased by stereotypes, including those we disagree with? And are we inevitably prone to stereotyping after merely being exposed to stereotypes prevalent in our culture? Such questions are very complex, but within the past several years, social psychologists have made great strides in addressing them. It is now clear that stereotype activation can be triggered implicitly and automatically, influencing subsequent thoughts, feelings, and behaviours even among perceivers who are relatively low in prejudice. But it also is clear that several factors can make such activation more or less likely to happen.

Some stereotypes are more likely than others to come to mind quickly and easily for any given person. For example, people in Western Europe may be quicker to activate the "skinhead" stereotype than people in South America. How much exposure individuals have to a stereotype, and therefore how accessible the stereotype is in their mind, varies across time and cultures.

Another factor is how prejudiced the perceiver is. It is important to consider the kind and amount of information that perceivers encounter. If perceivers are exposed to only very minimal, emotionally neutral information, such as a category label (e.g., "black" or "gay") or a photo of a member of the group, automatic stereotype activation may depend on a perceiver's degree of prejudice. That is, people low in prejudice are less likely to automatically activate the stereotype based on this information than people higher in prejudice (Kawakami et al., 1998; Lepore & Brown, 1997, 2002; Wittenbrink et al., 1997).

In the following sections, we explore several other sets of factors that help determine when stereotyping is and isn't inevitable. See ■ Table 5.3 for a summary.

TABLE 5.3

Automatic Stereotype Activation: Important Factors

Based on the relevant research, we can propose the following as some of the factors that are important in determining when people are more or less likely to activate stereotypes automatically.

Factors That Make Automatic Activation More Likely	Factors That Make Automatic Activation Less Likely
Cognitive Factors	
■ Stereotype is accessible (e.g., recently activated or primed)	■ Exposure to counter-stereotypic group members
■ Depleted cognitive resources due to prior attempts to suppress stereotypic thinking, fatigue, age, intoxication	■ Knowledge of personal information about the individual.
Cultural Factors	
■ Popular stereotype in culture	■ Not common stereotype in culture
■ Norms and values that accept stereotyping	■ Norms and values that are opposed to stereotyping
Motivational Factors	
■ Motivated to make inferences about the person quickly	■ Motivated to avoid prejudice
■ Motivated to feel superior to other person	■ Motivated to be fair, egalitarian
Personal Factors	
■ Endorse stereotypes, high in prejudice	■ Disagree with stereotypes, low in prejudice

Flor Marcelino became the first woman of colour to be elected to the Legislative Assembly of Manitoba. Whether people are likely to immediately categorize her based on her race, her gender, or her occupation depends on a combination of cognitive, cultural, and motivational factors.

Motivation: Fuelling Activation There is a growing recognition of the role that motivational factors can play in stereotype activation (Blair, 2002; Bodenhausen et al., 2003; Gollwitzer & Schaal, 2001; Gonsalkorale et al., 2011; Kunda & Spencer, 2003; Spencer et al., 2003). Whether or not we realize it, we often have particular goals when we encounter others, such as wanting to learn about them, impress them, get to our next task and not be interrupted by them, and so on. Some sets of goals make us more likely to activate stereotypes, and others have the opposite effect.

One important goal is the desire to maintain, protect, and perhaps enhance one's self-image and self-esteem. These goals can lead even people low in prejudice to activate negative stereotypes. For example, when their self-esteem is threatened, people may become motivated to stereotype others so that they will feel better about themselves (Fein & Spencer, 1997). Motivated in this way, they may also become more likely to activate stereotypes automatically. To demonstrate these points, Steven Spencer and others (1998) conducted a series of experiments in which they threatened some participants' self-esteem by making them think that they had done poorly on an intelligence test. These participants became more likely to automatically activate negative stereotypes about Blacks or Asians when exposed briefly, even subliminally, to a drawing or videotape of a member of the stereotyped group.

Trying to protect one's self-image cannot only promote activation of some stereotypes, but it can also inhibit activation of others. For example, imagine interacting with a black doctor. Two different stereotypes could come to mind about this person—about doctors and about black people. Lisa Sinclair and Ziva Kunda found that when white Canadian students in their study received praise from a black doctor, not only did they activate positive stereotypes about doctors, but they also simultaneously *inhibited* activation of negative stereotypes about Blacks—a pattern presumably driven by the desire to see the person who praised them as especially smart and successful. If this is the effect that praise brings about, will criticism have the opposite effect? Sinclair and Kunda's (1999, 2000) research suggests that it can. They found that when a stereotyped group member criticizes or even simply disagrees with participants, the participants become more likely to activate negative stereotypes about the group (see ▶ Figure 5.11).

Motivation: Putting on the Brakes Although we may have nonconscious motives to stereotype others, clearly many people today often are motivated to not stereotype or discriminate against others. This motivation may be *externally* driven—not wanting to *appear* to others to be prejudiced. It may also or instead be *internally* driven—not wanting to *be* prejudiced, regardless of whether or not others would find out (Dunton & Fazio, 1997; Plant & Devine, 1998, 2009). Internally motivated individuals are likely to be more successful at controlling stereotyping and prejudice, even on implicit measures, but even they are vulnerable to the strong power of automatic stereotyping and implicit biases.

The question is: Can you actually prevent yourself from activating a negative stereotype? For instance, what if you try really hard to resist thinking about the stereotype? As noted in Chapter 3 in our discussion of ironic mental processes, sometimes

FIGURE 5.11

Motivated Stereotype Inhibition and Activation

Participants received either praise or criticism about their performance from either a black man or a white man who they were led to believe was a doctor. A computer task that measured how quickly the participants could respond to various stimuli was used to assess whether they activated stereotypes about Blacks. Compared to the reaction times of participants who received neither praise nor criticism ("no-feedback controls"), quicker reaction times indicate stereotype *activation*, whereas longer reaction times suggest stereotype *suppression*. Participants criticized by the black doctor strongly activated the black stereotypes, whereas participants praised by the black doctor inhibited black stereotypes.

(Sinclair & Kunda, 1999.)

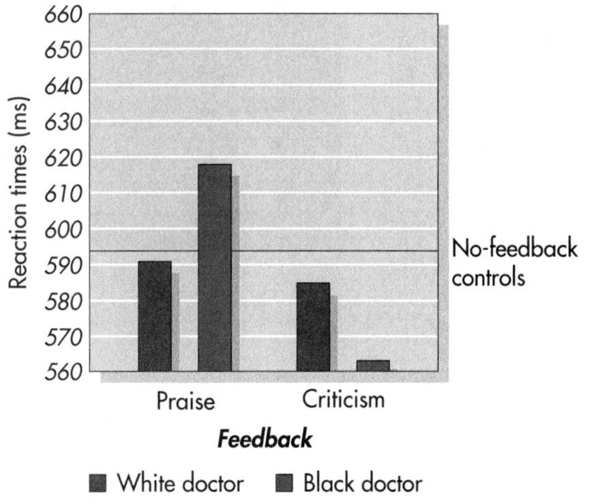

the harder you try to suppress an unwanted thought, the less likely you are to succeed.

Research on the effectiveness of trying to suppress stereotyping is mixed. On the one hand, it can sometimes cause a post-suppression rebound: After a person spends energy suppressing a stereotype, the stereotype pops up even more, like a volleyball that's been held under water (e.g., Macrae et al., 1994). Other research suggests that when people are intrinsically motivated to suppress a stereotype that they truly don't believe in, they may be successful at avoiding rebound effects. People who care deeply about not being prejudiced or who are often motivated by egalitarian goals can become much more efficient and successful in suppressing stereotypes (Gordijn et al., 2004; Monteith et al., 1998; Moskowitz et al., 2004; Wyer, 2007).

For example, according to the *self-regulation of prejudiced responses model* proposed by Margo Monteith and others (2002; Monteith & Mark, 2005, 2009), people who are truly motivated to be fair and unprejudiced are often confronted with the sad reality that they have failed to live up to that goal. These realizations lead to unpleasant emotions such as guilt. As individuals experience such feelings of guilt repeatedly, they begin to develop expertise at recognizing the situations and stimuli that tend to trigger these failures, and therefore they can exert more control over them. In so doing, they begin to interrupt what had been automatic stereotype activation.

Exerting Control: The Need for Cognitive Resources Trying to suppress stereotyping takes mental effort, and using this effort can drain individuals of cognitive resources for some period of time (Gordijn et al., 2004; Richeson & Trawalter, 2005). Some people are more likely than others to have the cognitive resources available to inhibit stereotyping. One factor is age. Older people have a harder time suppressing stereotypes than younger people, which may explain in part why older people often appear more prejudiced than younger people (Henry et al, 2009; von Hippel & Henry, 2011). Being intoxicated makes even younger people have a difficult time with suppressing thoughts or inhibiting impulses (e.g., consider the dreaded drunk dialing or texting). It may come as little surprise, therefore, that intoxication impairs people's ability to control stereotype activation and application (Bartholow et al., 2006; Schlauch et al., 2009).

Being physically tired or being affected by strong emotion or arousal can sap perceivers of the cognitive resources necessary to avoid stereoptyping (Bless et al., 1996; Gilbert & Hixon, 1991; Lambert et al., 2003). In an intriguing demonstration of this, Galen Bodenhausen (1990) classified participants by their circadian arousal patterns, or biological rhythms, into two types: "morning people" (who describe themselves as most alert early in the morning) and "night people" (who say they peak much later, in the evening). By random assignment, participants took part in an experiment in human judgment that was scheduled at either 9 a.m. or 8 p.m. The result? Morning people were more likely to use stereotypes when tested at night; night owls were more likely to do so early in the morning.

As discussed in Chapter 3, exercising self-control is like flexing a muscle, and muscles can become fatigued from use. This fatigue seems to be not just metaphorical—exerting self-control actually seems to consume glucose—a source of energy—in people's blood (Gailliot et al., 2007). In a particularly creative recent experiment, Matthew Gailliot and others (2009) had participants consume a drink sweetened either with sugar or an artificial sweetener (the sugar would raise their blood glucose level, but the artificial sweetener would not). After a brief delay to allow time for the drink manipulation to have its effect on blood glucose, participants were presented a picture of a young man said to be gay, and were asked to write for five minutes about a typical day in his life. The participants' prejudice toward homosexuals was assessed using a questionnaire.

As can be seen in ▶ Figure 5.12, participants who scored low in prejudice toward homosexuals on the questionnaire tended to avoid making derogatory statements about the gay man in their essays—regardless of which drink they consumed. However, among the participants who were relatively high in anti-gay prejudice, those who consumed the sugarless drink made significantly more derogatory statements than did those who consumed the high-sugar drink. In other words, the energy boost from the sugar drink seemed to give the high-prejudice participants the energy they needed to control their prejudice.

▶FIGURE 5.12

Needing Sugar to Stay Sweet?

Participants wrote a brief essay about a young man who they learned was gay. Participants whose scores on a measure of prejudice toward gays suggested that they were relatively low in prejudice tended to not make derogatory statements about the gay man in their essays, regardless of whether they drank a glucose-boosting high-sugar drink or a glucose-neutral sugarless drink. However, the participants who were relatively high in anti-gay prejudice were much more likely to make derogatory comments if they drank the sugarless drink. By raising their blood glucose, the high-sugar drink presumably gave these participants the energy needed to successfully inhibit expression of their prejudice.

(Gaertner et al., 2010.)

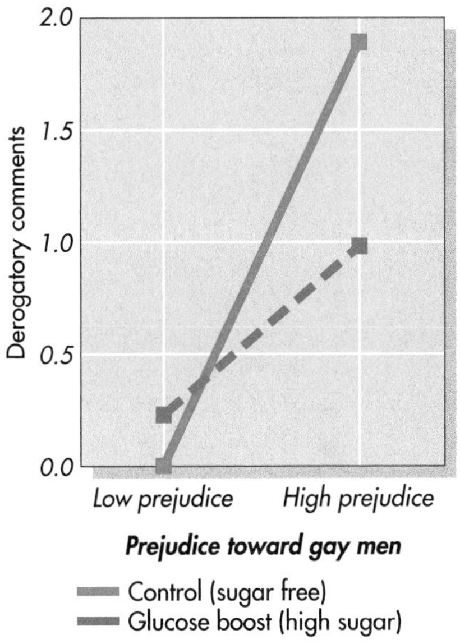

Gaertner, S.L., Dovidio, J.F., & Houlette, M.A., (2010). Social Categorization. In J.F. Dovidio, M. Hewstone, P. Glick, & V.M. Esses (Eds.), *Handbook of Prejudice, Stereotyping, and Discrimination*. London: Sage. Copyright © 2010. Reprinted by permission of Sage.

Exerting Control: Additional Factors Rather than to try not to think about it, one of the best strategies for avoiding the influence of stereotypes is to try instead to activate thoughts about the *individual* who happens to be a member of that group. In a provocative series of studies, Ziva Kunda and others (2002) exposed white Canadian participants to a videotape of an interview with a black person and found that these participants tended to activate stereotypes associated with this group within 15 seconds of exposure. However, if they continued to be exposed to the individual for 12 minutes and learned more information about him or her, they no longer exhibited any stereotype activation. Interestingly, if they were later provided with information indicating that this black person disagreed with them on a verdict in a court case, the stereotype was once again activated.

When we have specific personal information about an individual, stereotypes and other preconceptions can lose relevance and have less impact on how we respond to that person (Brewer & Feinstein, 1999; Fiske et al., 1999; Hilton & Fein, 1989; Kunda et al., 2003; Yzerbyt et al., 1998).

Researchers continue to explore ways to give people control over stereotyping. Techniques include receiving training and practice in resisting stereotype activation when confronted with information about a group; being primed with counter-stereotypic examples (such as female business leaders and scientists, or well-loved members of outgroups); and taking the perspective of a member of the stereotyped group (Dasgupta, 2009; Galinsky & Ku, 2004; Kawakami et al., 2000, 2007; Olson & Fazio, 2006; Stewart et al., 2010).

A Threat in the Air: Effects on the Targets of Stereotypes and Prejudice

We are all the targets of other people's stereotypes and prejudices. We are stereotyped and treated differently based on how we look, how we talk, and where we come from. None of us is immune from having our work evaluated in a biased way, our motives questioned, or our attempts at making new friends rejected because of stereotypes and prejudices.

But for the targets of some stereotypes and prejudices, these concerns are relentless and profound. For them, there seem to be few safe havens. Social psychologists often refer to these targets as *stigmatized*—"individuals who, by virtue of their membership in a particular social group, or by possession of particular characteristics, are targets of negative stereotypes, are vulnerable to being labelled as deviant, and are devalued in society" (Major & Crocker, 1993, p. 345). What are some of the effects of being stigmatized by stereotypes and prejudice? In this section, we first examine some of the effects that perceiving that one is being discriminated against can have on individuals. We then focus on the impact that a perceived threat of being stereotyped can have on individuals' performance, particularly regarding the academic achievement of women and minorities.

Perceiving Discrimination

In *Color-Blind*, writer Ellis Cose (1997), who is black, tells a story about how he was treated in a job interview 20 years ago. He was an award-winning newspaper reporter at the time and was hoping to land a job with a national magazine. The editor he met with was pleasant and gracious, but he said that the magazine didn't have many black readers. "All the editor saw was a young black guy, and since *Esquire* was not in need of a young black guy, they were not in need of me ... he had been so busy focusing on my race that he was incapable of seeing *me* or my work" (p. 150). Then a few years later, and in light of affirmative action, Cose was asked if he was interested in a position in a firm as corporate director of equal opportunity. "I was stunned, for the question made no sense. I was an expert neither on personnel nor on equal employment law; I was, however, black, which seemed to be the most important qualification" (p. 156).

The targets of stigmatizing stereotypes wonder frequently whether and to what extent others' impressions of them are distorted through the warped lens of social categorization. Over time, such suspicions can be deeply frustrating. In particular situations, however, they can have both positive and negative consequences. In a study by Jennifer Crocker and her colleagues (1991), black participants described themselves on a questionnaire, supposedly to be evaluated by an unknown white student who sat in an adjacent room. Participants were told that they were either liked or disliked by this student on the basis of the student's evaluation of the questionnaire; then they took a self-esteem test. If the participants thought that the white student could not see them and did not know their race, their self-esteem scores predictably rose after positive feedback and declined after negative feedback. But when participants thought the evaluating student had seen them through a one-way mirror, negative feedback did *not* lower their self-esteem. In this situation, participants blamed the unfavourable evaluations on prejudice. However, there was a drawback: Participants who received positive feedback and thought they had been observed through a one-way mirror showed a *decrease* in self-esteem. The reason? Instead of internalizing the credit for success, these participants attributed the praise to patronizing, reverse discrimination.

Attributing negative feedback to discrimination can sometimes protect one's self-esteem, but it can have costs as well. First, such an attribution can sometimes be inaccurate, and the recipient of the feedback might miss an opportunity to learn information relevant for self-improvement. Consider the dilemma faced by a white teacher who wants to give negative feedback to a black student regarding an essay the student has written. If the student dismisses this criticisms as biased, he or she may fail to learn from the teacher's advice. But if the teacher sugarcoats the feedback in an attempt to avoid the appearance of racism, the student may likewise fail to learn. Studying this dilemma in a pair of experiments, Geoffrey Cohen and others (1999) came up with a twofold prescription for solving it. What they found was that black students responded most positively to negative feedback when the teacher both (a) made it clear that he or she had high standards, and (b) assured students that they had the capacity to achieve those standards. Without such wise mentoring, the students' frequent experience of ambiguity about the sincerity or fairness of feedback can diminish their confidence in and accuracy about what they really do and do not know well (Aronson & Inzlicht, 2004). Second, although attributing negative feedback to discrimination can protect one's overall self-esteem, it can also make people feel as if they have less personal control over their lives. Individuals from low-status groups may be threatened by this vulnerability to discrimination and thus feel worse about themselves when they perceive that they were discriminated against—especially if they have reason to think that the discrimination against them could persist over time (Schmitt et al., 2002). Such concerns can have tremendous costs: Perceiving persistent discrimination over time is associated with a number of physical and mental health problems and with drug use (Gibbons et al., 2004, 2012; Pascoe & Smart Richman, 2009; Williams et al., 2003).

Whether a person is more or less likely to perceive discrimination based on his or her group membership, or to be affected negatively by such perceptions, depends in part on how and to what extent the target identifies with his or her stigmatized group. Several studies have shown, for example, that individuals are more likely to perceive discrimination against them based on their membership in a group if they are highly identified with the group or if they believe that others are often prejudiced against their group (Inzlicht et al., 2008; Major et al., 2003, 2007; Sellers & Shelton, 2003).

Stereotype Threat

Easily one of the most exciting developments in the field has been the tremendous wave of research triggered by a theory introduced by Claude Steele in the mid-1990s. Steele proposed that in situations in which a negative stereotype can apply to certain groups, members of these groups can fear being seen "through the lens of diminishing stereotypes and low expectations" (1999, p. 44). Steele (1997) calls this predicament **stereotype threat**, for it hangs like "a threat in the air" while the individual is in the stereotype-relevant situation. The predicament can be particularly threatening for individuals whose identity and self-esteem are invested in domains for which the stereotype is relevant. Steele argues that stereotype threat plays a crucial role in influencing the intellectual performance and identity of stereotyped group members. More recently, Steele and his colleagues (2002; Adams et al., 2006) have broadened the scope of their analysis to include *social identity threats* more generally, which are not necessarily tied to specific stereotypes but instead reflect a more general devaluing of a person's social group.

According to Steele's theory, stereotype threat can hamper achievement in academic domains in two ways. First, reactions to the "threat in the air" can directly interfere with performance—for example, by increasing anxiety and triggering distracting thoughts. Second, if this stereotype threat is chronic in the academic domain, it can cause individuals to *disidentify* from that domain—to dismiss the domain as no longer relevant to their self-esteem and identity. To illustrate, imagine a black student and a

stereotype threat
The experience of concern about being evaluated based on negative stereotypes about one's group.

FIGURE 5.13

Stereotype Threat and Academic Performance

Black and white students took a very difficult standardized verbal test. Before taking the test, some students were told that it was a test of their intellectual ability, but others were told that it was simply a research task unrelated to intellectual ability. All students' scores on this test were adjusted based on their scores from standardized college entrance verbal examinations. Despite this adjustment, black students did significantly worse than white students on the test if it had been introduced as a test of intellectual ability (left). In contrast, among the students who had been told that the test was unrelated to ability, black students and white students performed equally well (right).

(Steele & Aronson, 1995.)

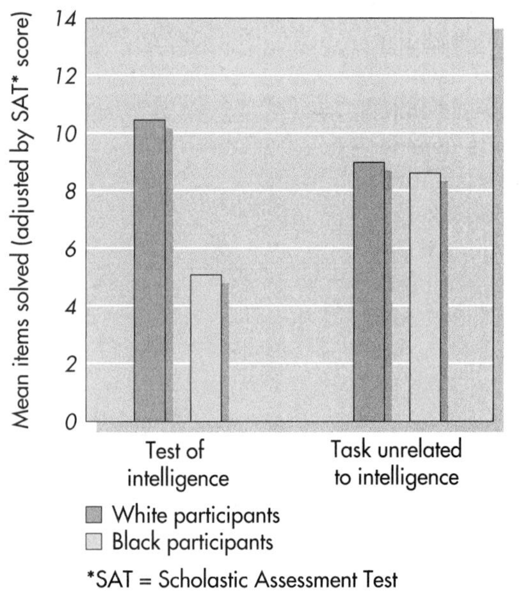

white student who enter high school equally qualified in academic performance. Imagine that while taking a particularly difficult test at the beginning of the school year, each student struggles on the first few problems. Both students may begin to worry about failing, but the black student may have a whole set of additional worries about appearing to confirm a negative stereotype of Blacks. Even if the black student doesn't believe the stereotype at all, the threat of being reduced to a stereotype in the eyes of those around her can trigger anxiety and distraction, impairing her performance. And if she experiences this threat in school frequently—perhaps because she stands out as one of only a few black students in the school or because she is treated by others in a particular way—the situation may become too threatening to her self-esteem. To buffer herself against the threat, she may disidentify with school; if so, her academic performance will become less relevant to her identity and self-esteem. In its place, some other domain of life, such as social success or a particular non-academic talent will become a more important source of identity and pride.

The Original Experiments Steele and others conducted a series of experiments in which they manipulated factors likely to increase or decrease stereotype threat as students took academic tests. For example, Steele and Joshua Aronson (1995) had black and white students from a highly selective university take a very difficult standardized verbal test. To some participants, it was introduced as a test of intellectual ability; to others, it was a laboratory problem-solving task unrelated to ability. Steele and Aronson reasoned that because of the difficulty of the test, *all* the students would struggle with it. If the test was said to be related to intellectual ability, however, the black students would also feel the threat of a negative stereotype. In contrast, if the test was simply a laboratory task and not a real test of intelligence, then negative stereotypes would be less applicable, and the stereotype threat would be reduced. In that case, black students would be less impaired while taking the test. As shown in Figure 5.13, the results supported these predictions.

Thus, a seemingly minor change in the setting—a few words about the meaning of a test—had a powerful effect on the black students' performance. In a second study, the researchers used an even more subtle manipulation of stereotype threat: whether students were asked to report their race just before taking the test (which was described as unrelated to ability). Making them think about race for a few seconds just before taking the test impaired the performance of black students but had no effect on white students.

Steele's theory predicts that because negative stereotypes concerning women's advanced math skills are prevalent, women may often experience stereotype threat in settings relevant to these skills. Reducing stereotype threat in these settings, therefore, should reduce the underperformance that women tend to exhibit in these areas. To test this idea, Steven Spencer and others (1999) recruited male and female students who were good at math and felt that math was important to their identities. The researchers gave these students a very difficult standardized math test, one on which all of them would perform poorly. Before taking the test, some students were told that the test generally showed no gender differences—thereby implying that the negative stereotype of women's ability in math was not relevant to this particular test. Other students were told that the test did generally show gender differences. As Steele's theory predicted, women performed worse than men when they were told that the test typically produced gender differences, but they performed as well as men when told that the test typically did not produce gender differences.

An interesting experiment by Barbara Fredrickson and others (1998) also examined how the math performance of women can be affected by the context in which they are tested. Male and female participants in their study were asked to evaluate some consumer products, including an item of clothing that they tried on and wore for some amount of time. For some participants, the clothing was a one-piece swimsuit; for others, it was a crewneck sweater. While wearing the clothing alone in a room in front of a mirror, each participant took a math test. Fredrickson and her colleagues proposed that because women in our society are made to feel more shame and anxiety about their bodies than are men, they should feel more anxious when taking the test while wearing the swimsuit, whereas men should be relatively unaffected by the manipulation of clothing. As can be seen in ▶ Figure 5.14, the results supported their predictions. After adjusting the participants' test scores based on their past performance on standardized math tests, these researchers found that women did significantly worse when wearing a swimsuit than a sweater, whereas men's performance was unaffected by the clothing manipulation.

▶ FIGURE 5.14

The Swimsuit Becomes You

While wearing either a sweater or swimsuit in front of a mirror, male and female students took a challenging standardized math test. All students' scores on this test were adjusted based on their scores from standardized college entrance math examinations. The men's scores were unaffected by what clothes they were wearing (left). The women's scores were affected (right): Women did significantly worse on the test if they were wearing a swimsuit than if they were wearing a sweater.

(Fredrickson et al., 1998.)

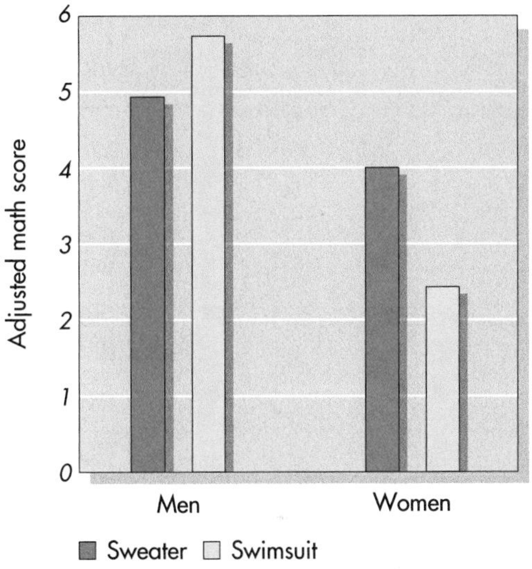

The Prevalence and Diversity of Threats Since these original studies, research inspired by the theory of stereotype threat grew at a stunningly fast pace. The evidence for underperformance due to stereotype threat is quite strong and broad. It has been found both in the laboratory and in real-world settings, including schools and businesses. Although much of the research has documented the power of the effects of stereotype threat on black people and women (Nguyen & Ryan, 2008), the scope of the research extends much farther. Stereotype threats can affect any group for which strong, well-known negative stereotypes are relevant in particular settings. Social identity threats can be more general than that, affecting groups that may be devalued even in the absence of specific negative stereotypes about a particular domain.

The examples of these threats run far and wide. For example, many white athletes feel stereotype threat whenever they step onto a court or playing field where they constitute the minority. Will the white athlete feel the added weight of this threat while struggling against other athletes in a game? To address this question, Jeff Stone and others (1999) had black and white students play miniature golf. When the experimenters characterized the game as diagnostic of "natural athletic ability," the white students did worse. But when they characterized it as diagnostic of "sports intelligence," the black students did worse.

Stereotype threat can undermine the performance of individuals from any group for which strong, well known, negative stereotypes are relevant. White male basketball players, for example, may experience stereotype threat in the presence of a black majority.

Here is a small sample of groups whose performance in various domains was hurt by stereotype threat, as demonstrated in experiments around the world (Aronson et al., 1999; Ben-Zeev et al., 2005; Chasteen et al., 2005; Croizet & Claire,

A black student is likely to perform worse on an athletic task if the task is described as one reflecting sports intelligence than if it is described as reflecting natural athletic ability. TRUE.

1998; Frantz et al., 2004; Gonzales et al., 2002; Kray et al., 2002; Maass et al., 2008; Picho & Stephens, 2012; Quinn et al., 2004; Seacat & Mickelson, 2009; Sekaquaptewa & Thompson, 2003; Spencer & Castano, 2007; Yeung & von Hippel, 2008; Yopyk & Prentice, 2005):

- Low-socioeconomic-status students in France and the United States on a verbal test when the test was said to be diagnostic of intellectual ability
- European American men on a math test when compared with Asians
- Ugandan girls on a math test in a co-ed rather than an all-female school
- Women playing chess on the computer when they were told that their opponent was male
- Women on an engineering test after interacting with sexist men
- White participants taking an IAT when they thought the test was diagnostic of racism
- Individuals with a history of mental illness on a test of reasoning ability when asked about their illness before taking the test
- Women on a negotiation task when success on the task was said to be associated with masculine traits
- Men on a negotiation task when success on the task was said to be associated with feminine traits
- Student athletes primed to think about their identity as athletes before taking a difficult math test
- Overweight individuals primed to think about weight-related stereotypes
- Older adults on a memory test when it was presented as a memory test rather than an impression formation task
- Women driving after being reminded of demeaning stereotypes about female drivers (causing women in a driving simulator to crash into jaywalkers!)

Because individuals are members of multiple groups, they can feel either threatened or emboldened by a stereotype—depending on which of their social identities has been activated. Consider, for example, a study by Margaret Shih and others (1999) in which Asian women were examined. In North America, there is a negative stereotype about women and math but a positive stereotype about Asians and math. The researchers found that these women performed worse on a math test when their gender identity was made salient (by means of questions they had to answer about their gender before taking the test), whereas they performed better on the test when their ethnic identity was made salient. In an interesting follow-up, though, Sapna Cheryan and Galen Bodenhausen (2000) reported that if the high expectations of Asian women's math abilities are made particularly salient to them as they are about to take a math test, the concern about living up to these expectations can itself be distracting, leading to a "choking" effect and worse performance.

In general, members of a group that has the relative advantage of being favourably compared to an outgroup that is targeted by a negative stereotype (for example, that men are better than women in math) may benefit from what Gregory Walton and Geoffrey Cohen (2004) call *stereotype lift*. In a meta-analysis of 43 relevant studies, members of non-stereotyped groups tended to perform better on tasks when the stereotype threat against the outgroup was relevant than when it was reduced. Reducing the threat, such as reassuring the targeted group that a particular test is not relevant to a negative stereotype, therefore not only improves the performance of the targeted group but also seems to remove some of the boost that the non-stereotyped group members get from being in the allegedly "superior" group.

Stereotype Threat Effects: Causes and Solutions How exactly does stereotype threat interfere with performance? And who within a target group is most vulnerable to these effects? These are among the questions currently being investigated. It is clear that one does not need to *believe in* a negative stereotype in order for it to have an effect. Just knowing about the stereotype seems to be enough—particularly if the individual identifies strongly with the group and cares about performing well.

Stereotype threat exerts its effects through multiple processes (Schmader et al., 2008). One of these is by triggering physiological arousal, which may interfere with people's ability to perform well on the task at hand (Ben-Zeev et al., 2005; Blascovich et al., 2001; O'Brien & Crandall, 2003). Another is by causing threatened individuals to try to suppress thoughts about the stereotype, which can have the ironic effect of draining cognitive resources away from the task they are working on (Logel et al., 2009, 2012). Stereotype threat also impairs threatened individuals' working memory, which of course impairs task performance (Schmader & Johns, 2003). It can also cause negative thoughts, worry, and feelings of dejection, and can cause individuals to focus more on trying to avoid failure than to achieve success. Each of these effects can undermine performance (Brodish & Devine, 2009; Croizet et al., 2004; Keller & Dauenheimer, 2003).

But although stereotype threat effects are widespread, the growing body of research on this subject also gives us reason to hope. Social psychologists have been uncovering ways that people can be better protected against these threats. These include being reminded of traits, qualities, or other things that make people feel good about themselves, even about things unrelated to the domain under threat; blurring boundaries between groups; coping with threat by using humour; attributing the arousal triggered by the threat to something nonthreatening; thinking of examples of other group members who have been successful in the domain under threat; and being reminded of other categories to which one belongs that are considered favourably in the domain (such as women taking a math test being reminded of positive stereotypes of "university students") (Ben-Zeev et al., 2005; Ford et al., 2004; McIntyre et al., 2003; Rosenthal & Crisp, 2006; Rydell et al., 2009).

Perhaps the finding most encouraging for readers of this section of the textbook is that simply learning about stereotype threat may help protect individuals from its effects. Women who were educated about stereotype threat in one study did not show the underperformance that women showed who had not learned about this research (Johns et al., 2005).

Part of the reason for the initial excitement when Claude Steele introduced this theory was that it spoke to a profound social problem but offered encouragement rather than pessimism. It illustrated that making even small changes in the situational factors that give rise to stereotype threat can reduce the tremendous weight of negative stereotypes, allowing the targets of stereotypes to perform to their potential. In fact, outside of the laboratory, Steele and his colleagues were quick to apply their theory by creating a model program in a real university setting. By creating what Steele calls a "wise" environment that fosters interracial contact and cooperation and reduces factors that contribute to stereotype threat, these researchers found that the black students in their program showed almost no underperformance in their grades and were much less likely than other black students to drop out of school (Steele, 1997).

Reducing Stereotypes, Prejudice, and Discrimination

The description of the Raymond Silverfox tragedy that opened this chapter and the exciting research of Claude Steele and others that closed the last section illustrate some of the problems and prospects concerning stereotypes, prejudice, and discrimination. In this final section, we focus on some of the approaches that have been suggested for combating stereotypes, prejudice, and discrimination more generally, and we point to directions we expect future research to follow on the road toward more progress.

Intergroup Contact

One of the classic books written on prejudice is Gordon Allport's (1954) *The Nature of Prejudice*. The book was unprecedented in its scope and gave important insights into the social psychology of prejudice. One of the many enduring ideas that Allport advanced was the **contact hypothesis**, which states that under certain conditions, direct contact between members of rival groups will reduce stereotyping, prejudice, and discrimination.

contact hypothesis
The theory that direct contact between hostile groups will reduce prejudice under certain conditions.

Around the time of the publication of this book, in the historic 1954 case of *Brown v. Board of Education of Topeka*, the U.S. Supreme Court ruled that racially separate schools were inherently unequal, in violation of the U.S. Constitution. In part, the decision was informed by empirical evidence supplied by 32 eminent social scientists on the harmful effects of segregation on the self-esteem and academic achievement of black students as well as on race relations (Allport et al., 1953). The Supreme Court's decision propelled the United States into a large-scale social experiment. What would be the effect?

The reality was that desegregation proceeded slowly. In Ontario, the law allowing segregation of black and white students wasn't repealed until 1964, when it was criticized by Leonard Braithwaite, Ontario's first Black MPP. The last segregated school in Ontario closed in 1965, and the last segregated school in Canada—found in Nova Scotia—didn't close until 1983. In the United States, there were stalling tactics, lawsuits, and vocal opposition to busing. Many schools remained untouched until the early 1970s. Then, as the dust began to settle, research brought the grave realization that little had changed—that contact between black and white schoolchildren was not having the

AP/Wide World Photos

AP Photo/John J. Lent/CP images

(Left) Students at Central High School in Little Rock, Arkansas, in September 1957, shout insults at Elizabeth Eckford, 16, as she walks toward the school entrance. National Guardsmen blocked the entrance and would not let her enter. (Right) Jackie Robinson became the first black player to cross "the colour line" and play Major League Baseball when he was promoted from the Montreal Royals to the Brooklyn Dodgers in 1947. This moment marked the beginning of the integration of major league sports.

intended effect. Walter Stephan (1986) reviewed studies conducted during and after desegregation and found that although 13 percent reported a decrease in prejudice among whites, 34 percent reported no change, and 53 percent reported an increase. These findings forced social psychologists to challenge the wisdom of their testimony to the Supreme Court and to re-examine the contact hypothesis that had guided that advice in the first place.

"See that man over there?"
"Yes."
"Well, I hate him."
"But you don't know him."
"That's why I hate him."
—Gordon Allport

Is the original contact hypothesis wrong? No. Although desegregation did not immediately produce the desired changes, it's important to realize that the conditions necessary for successful intergroup contact did not exist in the public schools. No one ever claimed that deeply rooted prejudices could be erased just by throwing groups together. According to the contact hypothesis, four conditions must exist for contact to succeed. These conditions are summarized in ■ Table 5.4.

A series of meta-analyses by Thomas Pettigrew and Linda Tropp (2000, 2006, 2008) involving more than 500 studies and a quarter of a million participants in 38 nations has found reliable support for the benefits of intergroup contact in reducing prejudice, particularly when the contact satisfies at least some of the conditions in Table 5.4. Pettigrew and Tropp (2008) propose that contact reduces prejudice by (1) enhancing knowledge about the outgroup, (2) reducing anxiety about intergroup contact, and (3) increasing empathy and perspective taking. Although many problems have plagued school and other desegregation efforts, such findings offer cause for optimism.

One of the most successful demonstrations of desegregation took place on the baseball diamond. In 1945, the Montreal Royals, a triple-A minor league affiliate of the Brooklyn Dodgers, signed a young black man, Jackie Robinson, to play on the team. Robinson's opportunity came through Dodgers owner Branch Rickey, who felt that integrating baseball was both moral and good for the game (Pratkanis & Turner, 1994). Rickey knew all about the contact hypothesis and was assured by a social scientist friend that a team could furnish the conditions needed for it to work: equal status among teammates, personal interactions, dedication to a common goal, and a positive climate from the owner, managers, and coaches. Montreal—a city that for the most part embraced Jackie—provided stark contrast to his initial days travelling with the team, when he faced many obstacles on the road, including death threats. When the Royals won the "Little World Series" in 1946, thanks in large part to Jackie, he was promoted to the Dodgers. On April 15, 1947, Jackie Robinson became the first black man to break the colour barrier in American sports. The rest is history. Although Robinson did face a great deal of racism, he endured, and baseball was integrated. At the end of his first year, Jackie Robinson was named rookie of the year; and in 1962, he was elected to the Baseball Hall of Fame. At his induction ceremony, Robinson asked three people to stand beside him: his mother, his wife, and his friend Branch Rickey.

Herb Carnegie may be a less familiar name to many students. As a gifted player in the semi-professional Quebec Provincial Hockey League, Carnegie was named most valuable player in three consecutive seasons. Despite his recognized skill on the ice, Carnegie never made it to the National Hockey League—a victim of a colour barrier in hockey that was not broken until 1958, when Willie O'Ree began playing for the Boston Bruins. While Carnegie never made it to the NHL, he was perhaps even better known for his work off the ice. After

TABLE 5.4

The Contact Hypothesis: Critical Conditions

Four conditions are deemed very important for intergroup contact to serve as a treatment for racism. However, many desegregated schools have failed to create a setting that meets these conditions.

1. *Equal status* The contact should occur in circumstances that give the two groups equal status.
2. *Personal interaction* The contact should involve one-on-one interactions among individual members of the two groups.
3. *Cooperative activities* Members of the two groups should join together in an effort to achieve superordinate goals.
4. *Social norms* The social norms, defined in part by relevant authorities, should favour intergroup contact.

Courtesy of the Carnegie Family

Rick Eglinton/GetStock.com

Herb Carnegie, an outstanding minor league hockey player, was never invited to play in the National Hockey League. Instead, Carnegie devoted his life to the development and support of young people with big dreams, just like his own. His experiences on and off the ice inspired others, and paved the way for many of them to realize their potential. Today there are more than 25 Black players in the NHL.

retiring from hockey, Carnegie went on to start the Future Aces Hockey School, the first registered hockey school in Canada, and the Herbert H. Carnegie Future Aces Foundation, which provides scholarships to youth who display qualities associated with being an exemplary citizen. Carnegie received numerous awards and accolades throughout his life, including eight medals for community service and inductions into ten Halls of Fame. In recognition of Carnegie's lifetime of working with young people, the Toronto District School Board voted to dedicate a week each September to honour his legacy. Carnegie continued his philanthropic and charitable endeavors until his death in 2012 at the age of 92. How Carnegie felt about his treatment as a black man coming up through the ranks in the early days of Canadian hockey is clear enough from the title of his autobiography: "*A Fly in a Pail of Milk: The Herb Carnegie Story*."

With more frequent and more meaningful contact across racial and ethnic divides, a variety of the kinds of barriers we've discussed in this chapter can be weakened. For example, a longitudinal study of dating in college by Shana Levin and others (2007) revealed that white, Asian American, and Latino students who dated outside their group more during university showed less ingroup bias and intergroup anxiety at the end of university than students who did not date outside their own racial group. Elizabeth Page-Gould and others (2008) actually created cross-group friendships between Latinos/as and whites in an experiment by having them meet for a few weeks and perform closeness-building tasks together. This experience had a number of positive intergroup effects, one of which was that participants who had initially been relatively high in implicit prejudice began to initiate more intergroup interactions.

The Jigsaw Classroom

Groups with a history of prejudice toward each other tend to become much less prejudiced soon after they are made to interact with each other in a desegregated setting. FALSE.

As the third condition in Table 5.4 indicates, cooperation and shared goals are necessary for intergroup contact to be successful. Yet the typical classroom is filled with competition, exactly the wrong ingredient. Picture the scene. The teacher stands in front of the class and asks a question. Many children wave their hands, each straining to catch the teacher's eye. Then, as soon as one student is called on, the others groan in frustration. In the competition for the teacher's approval, they are losers—hardly a scenario suited to positive intergroup contact. To combat this problem in the classroom, Elliot Aronson and his colleagues (1978) developed a cooperative learning method called the **jigsaw classroom**. In newly desegregated public schools, they assigned Grade 5 students to small racially and academically mixed groups. The material to be learned within each group was divided into subtopics, much the way a jigsaw puzzle is broken into pieces. Each student was responsible for learning one piece of the puzzle, after which all members took turns teaching their material to one another. In this system, everyone—regardless of race, ability, or self-confidence—needs everyone else if the group as a whole is to succeed.

jigsaw classroom
A cooperative learning method used to reduce racial prejudice through interaction in group efforts.

The method produced impressive results (Aronson, 2004). Compared with children in traditional classes, those in jigsaw classrooms grew to like each other more, liked school more, were less prejudiced, and had higher self-esteem. What's more, academic test scores improved for minority students and remained the same for white students. Much like an interracial sports team, the jigsaw classroom offers a promising way to create a truly integrated educational experience. It also provides a model of how to use interpersonal contact to promote greater tolerance of diversity.

Shared Identities

One important consequence of the jigsaw classroom technique is that individuals became more likely to classify outgroup members as part of their own ingroup. Instead of seeing racial or ethnic "others" within the classroom, the students now see fellow classmates, all in the same boat together. A growing body of research has emerged in support of the idea that intergroup contact emphasizing shared goals and fates, and that involves overlapping group memberships (such that an individual in one's outgroup in one context will be in his or her ingroup in another context), can be very successful at reducing prejudice and discrimination—specifically by changing how group members categorize each other (Bettencourt & Dorr, 1998; Brewer & Gaertner, 2004; Ray et al., 2008; Van Bavel & Cunningham, 2009).

According to the Common Ingroup Identity Model developed by John Dovidio and Samuel Gaertner (Dovidio et al., 2009; Gaertner & Dovidio, 2009; Gaertner et al., 2010), this change comes about through two separate processes: *de*categorization and *re*categorization. *Decategorization* leads people not only to pay less attention to categories and intergroup boundaries, but also to perceive outgroup members as individuals. *Recategorization*, in turn, leads people to change their conception of groups, allowing them to develop a more inclusive sense of the diversity characterizing their own ingroup. By recognizing members of an outgroup as ingroup members, just as the Rattlers and Eagles did when they converted from competitors to collaborators in Robbers Cave, "they" becomes "we," and a common ingroup identity can be forged.

Changing Cultures and Motivations

Earlier in the chapter, we reported some of the research showing the role that popular media can play in perpetuating stereotypes and prejudice. It is at the cultural level that much potential for positive change can be found as well. Exposure to images that reflect the diversity within social groups, for example, can help weaken stereotypes and combat their automatic activation. These images might also change people's tendency to see groups as relatively fixed entities and help them see groups as dynamic entities with less rigid borders.

Motivations, norms, and values can and often do change over time. Here again, popular culture is a key player. People—especially younger people—look to images in popular culture as well as to their peers and role models for information about what attitudes and behaviours are cool or out of date. We also look to our peers to get a sense of the local norms around us, including norms about stereotypes and prejudice (e.g., Crandall & Eshleman, 2003; Fein et al., 2003; Paluck, 2009; Stangor et al., 2001). In a particular high school, a student might feel comfortable calling a friend a "fag" and mean little by it and think nothing of it, and yet several months later in university this student might realize how wrong that would be to do in his or her new setting, and feel guilty for ever having done so. If this lesson is learned, it's more likely to have been learned by watching and interacting with one's peers than from having been lectured to about diversity and sensitivity by a campus speaker. Learning these norms can make us motivated to adopt them. Legislating against hate speech, unequal treatment, and hostile environments can also be an important weapon, of course. Although they can create resistance and backlashes, laws and policies requiring behavioural change can—if done right, with no suggestion of compromise, and with important leaders clearly behind them—cause hearts and minds to follow (Aronson, 1992).

Social psychologists today recognize that more and more people are motivated to not be prejudiced. The motivation may begin as a concern with not appearing to others to be prejudiced, but for many it becomes internalized—a much more effective antidote (Devine et al., 2005; Monteith et al., 2002).

Much of the hope, therefore, rests with what is at the very core of social psychology: the social nature of the human animal. Some of our baser instincts, such as intergroup competition that breeds intergroup biases, may always be present, but we also can learn from each other the thoughts, values, and goals that make us less vulnerable to perpetuating or being the targets of stereotypes, prejudice, and discrimination.

REVIEW

- The death of an aboriginal man in RCMP custody, and the election of a black man to the presidency of the United States illustrate both the persistent challenges and the progress regarding stereotyping, prejudice, and discrimination in contemporary life.

The Nature of the Problem: Persistence and Change

Defining Our Terms

- At the individual level, racism and sexism are forms of prejudice and discrimination based on a person's racial or gender background. At the institutional and cultural level, racism and sexism involve practices that promote the domination of one racial group or gender over another.
- Stereotypes are beliefs or associations that link groups of people with certain characteristics.
- Prejudice refers to negative feelings toward persons based on their membership in certain groups.
- Discrimination is negative behaviour directed against persons because of their membership in a particular group.
- Ingroups are groups we identify with; we contrast these with outgroups.

Racism: Current Forms and Challenges

- Over the years, various data show a decline in negative views of black people.
- However, modern racism is more subtle and surfaces in less direct ways, particularly in situations where people can rationalize racist behaviour.
- People's ambivalence concerning race can lead them to exhibit biases in favour of or against particular groups, depending on the context.
- Racism often works implicitly, as stereotypes and prejudice can fuel discrimination without conscious intent or awareness on the part of perceivers.
- Researchers use covert measures to detect and measure modern and implicit racism and other subtle forms of prejudice and discrimination. This includes the IAT.
- Individual differences in implicit racism can predict differences in perceptions of and reactions to others based on their race. For example, white perceivers who are relatively high in implicit racism are more likely to perceive hostility in the facial expressions of a black person than in the facial expressions of a white person.
- Seeing a member of a racial outgroup is associated with increased activation in the amygdala, a brain structure associated with emotion.
- Interracial interactions can feel threatening, can provoke anxiety, and can drain cognitive resources, particularly among people relatively high in implicit racism.
- Worried about appearing racist in these interactions, whites in particular may try to avoid interracial interactions, or they may go out of their way to avoid any mention of race even when it is relevant.

Sexism: Ambivalence and Double Standards

- Although similar in many other ways, sexism differs from other forms of prejudice and discrimination in part because gender stereotypes are more than just descriptive: They also indicate what the majority of people in a society believe men and women should be. Sexism is also unusual in that ingroup and outgroup members are so intimately familiar with each other.
- Ambivalent sexism reflects both hostile sexism, characterized by negative and resentful feelings toward women, and benevolent sexism, characterized by affectionate, chivalrous, but potentially patronizing feelings toward women.
- Individuals from countries with the greatest degree of economic and political inequality between men and women tend to exhibit high levels of both hostile and benevolent sexism.
- There are some striking sex differences in occupational choices and in the treatment that individuals experience in the workplace.
- Women often face a difficult dilemma: If they behave consistently with gender stereotypes, they may be liked more but respected less.

Causes of the Problem: Intergroup and Motivational Factors

Fundamental Motives Between Groups

- The tendency in people to divide the world into ingroups and outgroups—"us" versus "them"—and to favour the former over the latter in numerous ways is likely to be an evolved tendency due to the social nature of our species.
- When people's motives for self-protection are aroused, they show stronger biases against threatening outgroups.
- According to optimal distinctiveness theory, people try to balance the desire to belong with the desire to be distinct and differentiated from others.
- Being reminded about mortality triggers various ingroup biases, including negative stereotypes, and behaviour that demonstrates prejudice toward a variety of outgroups.

Robbers Cave: A Field Study in Intergroup Conflict

- In the Robbers Cave study, boys divided into rival groups quickly showed intergroup prejudice. This prejudice was reduced when the boys were brought together through tasks that required intergroup cooperation.

Realistic Conflict Theory

- Realistic conflict theory maintains that direct competition for resources gives rise to prejudice.

Social Identity Theory

- Participants categorized into arbitrary minimal groups discriminate in favour of the ingroup.
- Social identity theory proposes that self-esteem is influenced by the fate of social groups with which we identify.
- Research shows that threats to the self cause individuals to derogate outgroups, and that this behaviour in turn increases self-esteem.
- Ingroup favouritism is more intense among people whose identity is closely tied to their group.

Culture and Social Identity

- Cultural differences can influence social identity processes. Individualists are more likely than collectivists to try to boost their self-esteem through overt ingroup-enhancing biases.

Motives Concerning Intergroup Dominance and Status

- People with a social dominance orientation exhibit a desire to see their ingroups as dominant over other groups, and they tend to identify more strongly with their ingroup and to be more likely to disparage members of outgroups.
- People who tend to endorse and legitimize existing social arrangements can show signs of outgroup favouritism even when their group holds a relatively disadvantaged position in society.

Causes of the Problem: Cognitive and Cultural Factors

Social Categorization

- The tendency for people to group themselves and others into social categories is a key factor in stereotype formation and prejudice.
- Social categories can be energy-saving devices that allow perceivers to make quick inferences about group members, but these categories can lead to inaccurate judgments.
- People tend to exaggerate the differences between ingroups and outgroups.
- The outgroup homogeneity effect is the tendency to assume that there is more similarity among members of outgroups than there is among members of ingroups.
- Research using brain imaging and cognitive methods has found that merely categorizing people as outgroup members can lead perceivers to process information about outgroup members less deeply.
- Perceivers sometimes dehumanize outgroups in a variety of ways.How Stereotypes Survive and Self-Perpetuate
- People perceive illusory correlations between groups and traits when the traits are distinctive or when the correlations fit prior notions.
- People tend to make attributions about the causes of group members' behaviours in ways that help maintain their stereotypes.
- Group members who do not fit the mold are often subtyped, leaving the overall stereotype intact.
- The stereotypes that people hold about group members can lead them to behave in biased ways toward those members, sometimes causing the latter to behave consistently with the stereotypes. The stereotypes thus produce a self-fulfilling prophecy.
- Some stereotypes are more accurate than others, but judging the accuracy of stereotypes is challenging, in part because "accuracy" can have different meanings.

Culture and Socialization

- We often learn a tremendous amount of information relevant to stereotypes, prejudice, and discrimination without even realizing it by absorbing what we see around us in our culture, groups, and families.
- Boys and girls tend to show gender-stereotypical preferences for things like toys at very early ages.
- Gender stereotypes are so deeply ingrained that they bias perceptions of males and females from the moment they are born.
- Perceived differences between men and women are magnified by the contrasting social roles they occupy.
- The mass media foster stereotypes of various groups.
- Portrayals of men and women in advertising and other forms of media can influence the behaviour and attitudes of men and women.
- A recent field experiment in Rwanda demonstrated the positive effect the media can have in promoting anti-prejudice norms.

Stereotype Content Model

- Many group stereotypes vary along two dimensions: warmth and competence.
- The stereotype content model proposes that stereotypes about the competence of a group are influenced by the relative status of that group in society, and that stereotypes about the warmth of a group are influenced by perceived competition with the group.

Is Stereotyping Inevitable? Automatic Versus Intentional Processes

- Stereotypes are often activated without our awareness and operate at an unconscious, or implicit, level.
- Stereotype activation occurs automatically under some conditions. In these cases, stereotypes can influence individuals' perceptions and reactions concerning others even when they don't believe in the stereotypes.
- Stereotype activation can be influenced by a number of factors, including how accessible various stereotypes are in perceivers' minds and how prejudiced the perceivers are.
- Some motivations make stereotype activation more likely to occur and others make it less likely. For example, when perceivers are highly motivated to feel better about themselves, they may become more likely to activate some stereotypes and suppress others.
- Simply trying to suppress stereotypes from being activated can sometimes backfire, although it can work for people who are intrinsically motivated and do not believe the stereotype.
- Some individuals can become relatively expert at regulating prejudiced responses because they recognize the situational factors that have caused them to fail to live up to their egalitarian ideals in the past.
- Trying to suppress stereotyping can be cognitively tiring. When age, fatigue, intoxication, or other cognitive impairment reduces people's cognitive resources, they are less able to control their stereotypes.
- One experiment found that high-prejudice individuals were better able to inhibit their prejudice if their glucose levels were raised by a high-sugar drink.
- Recent research suggests that a variety of strategies—such as training, taking the perspective of others, and thinking of examples that counter stereotypes—can help suppress automatic activation of stereotypes.

A Threat in the Air: Effects on the Targets of Stereotypes and Prejudice

- Stigmatized groups are negatively stereotyped and devalued in society.

Perceiving Discrimination

- When members of stigmatized groups perceive others' reactions to them as discrimination, they experience both benefits and drawbacks to their self-esteem and feelings of control.

Stereotype Threat

- Situations that activate stereotype threat cause individuals to worry that others will see them in negative and stereotypical ways.
- Stereotype threat can impair the performance and affect the identity of members of stereotyped or devalued groups. Slight changes in a setting can reduce stereotype threat and its negative effects significantly.
- Stereotype threat can cause black and female students to fail to perform to their potential in academic settings.
- Research has documented a huge and growing list of groups whose members show underperformance and performance-impairing behaviours when a negative stereotype about their abilities is made relevant.
- Stereotype threat causes its effects through multiple processes. Stereotype threat can lead to increased arousal, trigger attempts to suppress negative stereotypes, impair working memory, and cause individuals to feel dejection-related emotions or to engage in negative thinking.
- Research points to ways that members of stereotyped groups can be protected against these negative effects.
- Learning about stereotype threat may protect members of targeted groups against its negative effects.

Reducing Stereotypes, Prejudice, and Discrimination

Intergroup Contact

- Although, according to the contact hypothesis, desegregation should reduce prejudice, it did not cure the problem in the absence of key conditions of intergroup contact: equal status, personal interactions, the need to achieve a common goal, and social norms. When these conditions are met, intergroup contact tends to be much more successful in reducing prejudice.

The Jigsaw Classroom

- Schools often fail to meet the conditions for reducing prejudice, in part because competition is too high. One program that is designed to foster intergroup cooperation and interdependence suggests that the right kinds of contact can improve attitudes and behaviours in a school setting.

Shared Identities

- Recent research has demonstrated that changing how group members categorize each other can reduce prejudice and discrimination; for example, by recognizing the ways group members share a common identity with members of other groups.

Changing Cultures and Motivations

- Changes in the kinds of information perpetuated in one's culture can alter how one perceives social groups.
- As the general culture and local norms change to promote values that are consistent with fairness and diversity and that are not consistent with prejudice and discrimination, individuals' motivations can change accordingly.

Key Terms

ambivalent sexism (148)
contact hypothesis (180)
discrimination (141)
group (141)
illusory correlation (160)
implicit racism (143)
Implicit Association Test (IAT) (144)
ingroup favouritism (153)
ingroups (141)
jigsaw classroom (182)
modern racism (143)
outgroup homogeneity effect (158)
outgroups (141)
prejudice (141)
racism (141)
realistic conflict theory (152)
relative deprivation (152)
sexism (141)
social categorization (157)
social dominance orientation (156)
social identity theory (153)
social role theory (166)
stereotype (141)
stereotype content model (169)
stereotype threat (175)
subliminal presentation (170)
superordinate goals (151)

Putting COMMON SENSE *to the Test*

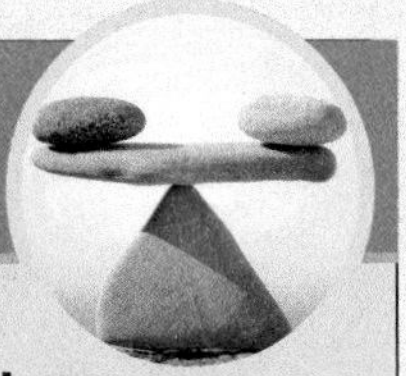

Children do not tend to show biases based on race; it is only after they become adolescents that they learn to respond to people differently based on race.

False. *Children learn about social categories quite early and use stereotypes when they are very young. Children show biases in favour of the racial ingroup on both explicit and implicit measures.*

Very brief exposure to a member of a stereotyped group does not lead to biased judgments or responses, but longer exposure typically does.

False. *Even very brief exposure to a member of a stereotyped group can activate the stereotype about the group, and this activation can bias subsequent judgments and reactions. Learning more information about the individual, however, sometimes reduces the effects of the stereotype.*

Even brief exposure to sexist television commercials can significantly influence the behaviours of men and women.

True. *Exposure to sexist commercials can make men behave in more sexist ways toward women and can make women engage in more stereotypical behaviours.*

A black student is likely to perform worse on an athletic task if the task is described as one reflecting sports intelligence than if it is described as reflecting natural athletic ability.

True. *Research on stereotype threat suggests that black students are likely to be concerned about being seen through the lens of negative stereotypes concerning their intelligence if the task is described as one that is diagnostic of their sports intelligence—a situation that could undermine their performance. White students tend to show the opposite effect: Their performance is worse if the task is described as reflecting natural athletic ability.*

Groups with a history of prejudice toward each other tend to become much less prejudiced soon after they are made to interact with each other in a desegregated setting.

False. *When the contact between groups involves unequal status between them, lacks personal interaction between individual group members, and does not involve cooperation to achieve shared goals, contact is not likely to reduce prejudice.*

6

Image Source/RF/Corbis

Attitudes

This chapter examines social influences on attitudes. We define attitudes and then discuss how they are measured and when they are related to behaviour. Then we consider two methods of changing attitudes. First, we look at source, message, and audience factors that win persuasion through the media of communication. Second, we consider theories and research showing that people often change their attitudes as a consequence of their own actions.

Putting **COMMON SENSE** *to the Test*

Circle Your Answer

- T F Researchers can tell if someone has a positive or negative attitude by measuring physiological arousal.
- T F In reacting to persuasive communications, people are influenced more by superficial images than by logical arguments.
- T F People are most easily persuaded by commercial messages that are presented without their awareness.
- T F The more money you pay people to tell a lie, the more they will come to believe it.
- T F People often come to like what they suffer for.

Abortion. Same sex marriages. Quebec separatism. Immigration. Tuition increases. Aboriginal autonomy. Stephen Harper. Israelis and Palestinians. Anyone who follows recent events knows how passionately people feel about the issues of the day. Attitudes and the mechanisms of attitude change, or persuasion, are a vital part of human social life. This chapter addresses three sets of questions: (1) What is an attitude, how can it be measured, and what is its link to behaviour? (2) What kinds of persuasive messages lead people to change their attitudes? (3) Why do we often change our attitudes as a result of our own actions?

The Study of Attitudes

Should smoking be prohibited in public places? Would you rather listen to rock or hip hop, drink Coke or Pepsi, work on a PC or a Mac? Should Quebec secede from the rest of Canada? As these questions suggest, each of us has positive and negative reactions to various persons, objects, and ideas. These reactions are called **attitudes**. Skim the chapters in this book, and you'll see just how pervasive attitudes are. You'll see, for example, that self-esteem is an attitude we hold about ourselves, that attraction is a positive attitude toward another person, and that prejudice is a negative attitude often directed against certain groups. Indeed, the study of attitudes—what they are, where they come from, how they can be measured, what causes them to change, and how they interact with behaviour—is central to the whole field of social psychology (Ajzen, 2001; Forgas, Cooper, & Crano, 2010; Petty & Chaiken, 2004;).

attitude
A positive, negative, or mixed reaction to a person, object, or idea.

▶ **FIGURE 6.1**

Four Possible Reactions to Attitude Objects

As shown, people evaluate objects along both positive and negative dimensions. As a result, our attitudes can be positive, negative, ambivalent, or indifferent.

(Cacioppo et al., 1997.)

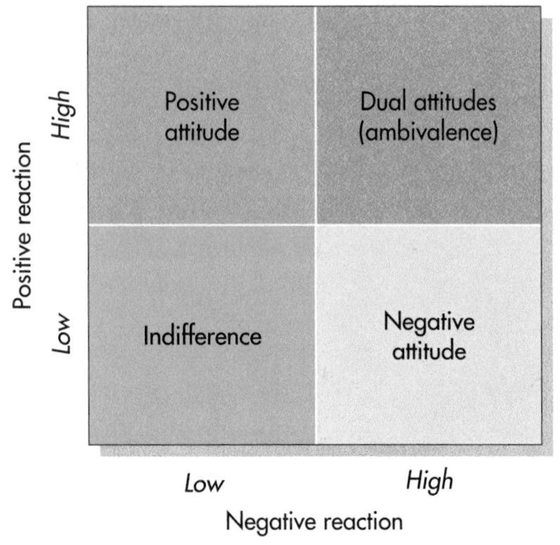

An attitude is a positive, negative, or mixed evaluation of an object, expressed at some level of intensity—nothing more, nothing less. *Like, love, dislike, hate, admire,* and *detest* are the kinds of words that people use to describe their attitudes. It's important to realize that attitudes cannot simply be represented along a single continuum ranging from wholly positive to wholly negative—as you might expect if attitudes were like the balance knob on a stereo that directs sound to the left or right speaker, or like the lever on a thermostat that raises or lowers temperature. Rather, as depicted in ▶ Figure 6.1, our attitudes can vary in strength along both positive and negative dimensions. In other words, we can react to something with positive affect, with negative affect, with ambivalence (strong but mixed emotions), or with apathy and indifference (Cacioppo et al., 1997). In fact, at times people can have both positive and negative reactions to the same attitude object without feeling conflict. Someone who is openly positive toward racial minorities but harbours unconscious prejudice is a case in point (Wilson et al., 2000).

Everyone routinely forms positive and/or negative evaluations of the people, places, objects, and ideas they encounter. This process is often instantaneous and automatic, like a reflex action (Bargh et al., 1996; Cunningham et al., 2003; Duckworth et al., 2002; Ferguson & Zayas, 2009). It now appears, however, that individuals differ in the extent to which they tend to react to stimuli in strong positive and negative terms. What about you—do you form opinions easily? Do you have strong likes and dislikes? Or do you tend to react in more objective, non-evaluative ways? People who describe themselves as high rather than low in the *need for evaluation* are more likely to view their daily experiences in judgmental terms. They are also more opinionated on a whole range of social, moral, and political issues (Bizer et al., 2006; Cronley et al., 2010; Jarvis & Petty, 1996).

Before we examine the elusive science of attitude measurement, let's stop for a moment and ponder this question: Why do we bother to have attitudes? Does forming positive and negative judgments of people, objects, and ideas serve any useful purpose? Over the years, researchers have found that attitudes serve important functions, such as enabling us to judge, quickly and without much thought, whether something we encounter is good or bad, helpful or hurtful, and to be sought or avoided (Maio & Olson, 2000). The problem is that having preexisting attitudes about persons, objects, and ideas can lead us to become closed-minded, bias the way we interpret new information, and make us more resistant to change. Russell Fazio and others (2000) found that people who were focused on their positive or negative attitudes toward computerized faces, compared to those who were not, were later slower to notice when the faces were "morphed" and no longer the same.

How Attitudes Are Measured

In 1928, Louis Thurstone published an article entitled *Attitudes Can Be Measured.* What Thurstone failed to anticipate, however, is that attitude measurement is a tricky business. One review of research uncovered more than 500 different methods of determining an individual's attitudes (Fishbein & Ajzen, 1972).

Self-Report Measures The easiest way to assess a person's attitude about something is to ask. All over the world, public opinion is assessed on a range of issues—in politics, the economy, healthcare, foreign affairs, science and technology, sports and entertainment, and lifestyles. Simply by asking, Ipsos-Reid polls have revealed that the majority of Canadians prefer a public (versus private) health-care system; think that the NHL should ban fighting; believe that gun violence is a result of gangs, drugs and lenient judges; and that Canadian children prefer grilled cheese to peanut butter and jelly sandwiches.

Donald Weber/Stringer/Getty Images

As seen in this pro-marijuana rally, people are often very passionate about their attitudes.

Self-report measures are direct and straightforward. But attitudes are sometimes too complex to be measured by a single question. As you may recall from Chapter 2, one problem recognized by public opinion pollsters is that responses to attitude questions can be influenced by their wording, the order and context in which they are asked, and other extraneous factors (Schwarz, 1999; Tourangeau et al., 2000). For example, Bärbel Knauper and Norbert Schwarz (2004) found that respondents over the age of 65 are more likely to agree to response alternatives presented to them last in a list—a recency effect—due to natural declines in processing speed and working memory capacity. That is, if the question requires a respondent to remember a range of alternatives, older adults may have more difficulty keeping all of these options in mind, and so agree with the last option they hear.

Recognizing the shortcomings of single-question measures, researchers who study people's social and political opinions often use multiple-item questionnaires known as **attitude scales** (Robinson, Shaver, & Wrightsman, 1991, 1998). Attitude scales come in different forms, perhaps the most popular being the *Likert Scale,* named after its inventor, Rensis Likert (1932). In this technique, respondents are presented with a list of statements about an attitude object and are asked to indicate on a multiple-point scale how strongly they agree or disagree with each statement. Each respondent's total attitude score is derived by summing his or her responses to all the items. However, regardless of whether attitudes are measured by one question or by a full-blown scale, the results should be taken with caution. All self-report measures assume that people express their true opinions. Sometimes this assumption is reasonable and correct, but often it is not. Wanting to make a good impression on others, people are generally reluctant to admit to their failures, vices, weaknesses, unpopular opinions, and prejudices.

One approach to this problem is to increase the accuracy of self-report measures. To get respondents to answer attitude questions more truthfully, researchers sometimes use the **bogus pipeline**, an elaborate mechanical device that supposedly records our true feelings like a lie-detector test. While the machine actually has no ability to detect anything, participants can be convinced that it does. Not wanting to get caught in a lie, respondents tend to answer attitude questions more honestly, and with less concern over looking good to the questioner, when they think that deception would be detected by the bogus pipeline (Jones & Sigall, 1971; Roese & Jamieson, 1993). For example, Roger Tourangeau and others (1997) found that people were more likely to admit to drinking too much, using cocaine, having frequent oral sex, and not exercising enough when the bogus pipeline was used than when it was not. In a recent test of the bogus pipeline technique, Kristin Grover and Carol Miller (2012) hooked up participants to a sensor that they were told measured either their physiological reaction to the study or the honesty of their responses to the questions put to them—like a lie detector might. Participants then read a story about a man named Dan, who has

attitude scale
A multiple-item questionnaire designed to measure a person's attitude toward some object.

bogus pipeline
A fake lie-detector device that is sometimes used to get respondents to give truthful answers to sensitive questions.

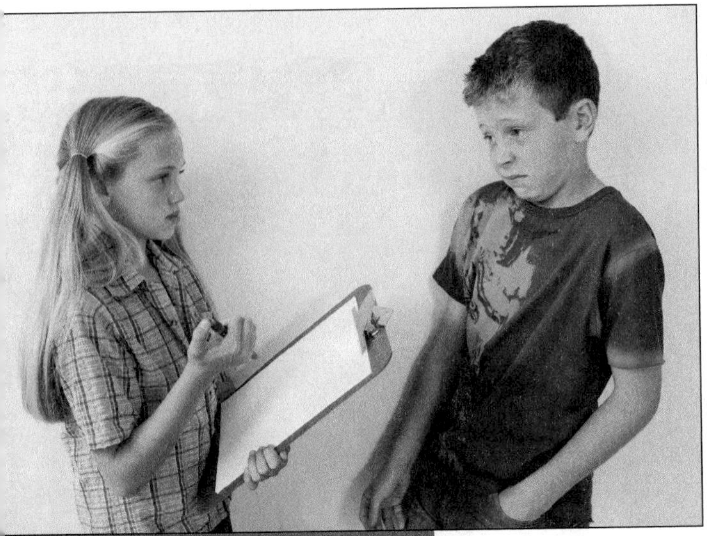
Radius Images/Corbis

Facial expressions and body language can reveal a lot about our attitudes.

AIDS, and were asked several questions assessing their overall acceptance of someone like him. They found that those in the lie detection (bogus pipeline) condition reported being less accepting of Dan compared to those who were not told that they could be caught in a lie. These results suggest that people are more concerned with *wanting* to appear accepting of, rather than actually accepting, a person with AIDS.

Covert Measures A second general approach to the self-report problem is to collect indirect, covert measures of attitudes that cannot be controlled. One possibility in this regard is to use observable behaviour such as facial expressions, tone of voice, and body language. In one study, Gary Wells and Richard Petty (1980) secretly videotaped students as they listened to a speech and noticed that when the speaker took a position that the students agreed with (that tuition costs should be lowered), most made vertical head movements. But when the speaker took a contrary position (that tuition costs should be raised), head movements were in a horizontal direction. Without realizing it, the students had signalled their attitudes by nodding and shaking their heads.

Although behaviour provides clues, it is far from perfect as a measure of attitudes. Sometimes, we nod our heads because we agree; at other times, we nod to be polite. The problem is that people monitor their overt behaviour just as they monitor self-reports. But what about internal, physiological reactions that are difficult, if not impossible, to control? Does the body betray how we feel? In the past, researchers tried to divine attitudes from involuntary physical reactions such as perspiration, heart rate, and pupil dilation. The result, however, was always the same: Measures of arousal reveal the intensity of one's attitude toward an object but not whether that attitude is positive or negative. On the physiological record, love and hate look very much the same (Petty & Cacioppo, 1983).

Although physiological arousal measures cannot distinguish between positive and negative attitudes, some exciting alternatives have been discovered. One is the **facial electromyograph (EMG)**. As shown in ▶ Figure 6.2, certain muscles in the face contract when we are happy, and different facial muscles contract when we are sad. Some of the muscular changes cannot be seen with the naked eye, however, so the facial EMG is used. To determine whether the EMG can be used to measure the affect associated with attitudes, John Cacioppo and Richard Petty (1981) recorded facial muscle activity of students as they listened to a message with which they agreed or disagreed. The agreeable message increased activity in the cheek muscles—the facial pattern characteristic of happiness. The disagreeable message sparked activity in the forehead and brow area—the facial patterns associated with sadness and distress. Outside observers who later watched the participants were unable to see these subtle changes. Apparently, the muscles in the human face reveal smiles, frowns, and other reactions to attitude objects that otherwise are hidden from view (Cacioppo et al., 1986; Roddy, Stewart, & Barnes-Holmes, 2011; Tassinary & Cacioppo, 1992).

facial electromyograph (EMG) An electronic instrument that records facial muscle activity associated with emotions and attitudes.

From a social neuroscience perspective, electrical activity in the brain may also assist in the measure of attitudes. In 1929, Hans Burger invented a machine that could detect, amplify, and record "waves" of electrical activity in the brain through electrodes pasted to the surface of the scalp. The instrument is called an *electroencephalograph*, or EEG, and the information it provides takes the form of line tracings called *brain waves*. Based on an earlier discovery, that certain patterns of electrical brain activity are triggered by exposure to stimuli that are novel or inconsistent, Cacioppo and his colleagues (1993) had participants list ten items they liked and ten items they did not like within various object categories (fruits, sports, movies, universities, etc.). Later, these participants were brought into the laboratory, wired to an EEG, and presented with a list of category words that depicted the objects they liked and disliked. The result: Brainwave patterns normally triggered by inconsistency increased more when a disliked stimulus appeared after a string of positive items, or when a liked stimulus was shown after a string of negative items, than when either stimulus evoked the same attitude as the items that preceded it.

Today, social psychologists are also starting to use new forms of brain imaging in the measurement of attitudes. For example, in one study, researchers used fMRI to record brain activity in participants as they read names of famous—and infamous—figures, such as Bill Cosby and Adolph Hitler. When the names were read, they observed greater activity in the amygdala, a structure in the brain associated with emotion—regardless of whether participants were asked to evaluate the famous figures (Cunningham et al., 2003). This suggests that people react automatically to positive and negative attitude objects. Although more research is needed, it appears that attitudes may be measurable by electrical activity in the brain.

FIGURE 6.2

The Facial EMG: A Covert Measure of Attitudes?

The facial EMG makes it possible to detect differences between positive and negative attitudes. Notice the major facial muscles and recording sites for electrodes. When people hear a message with which they agree rather than disagree, there is a relative increase in EMG activity in the depressor and zygomatic muscles, but a relative decrease in the corrugator and frontalis muscles. These changes cannot be seen with the naked eye.

(Cacioppo & Petty, 1981.)

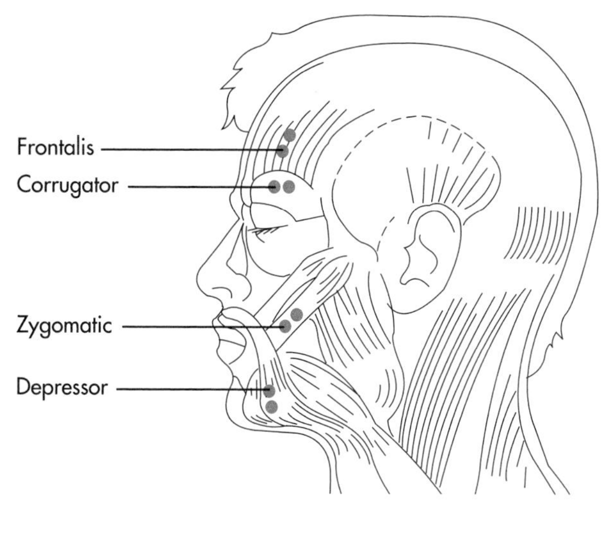

The Implicit Association Test (IAT) When it comes to covert measurement, one particularly interesting development is based on the notion that each of us has **implicit attitudes** that we cannot self-report in questionnaires because we are not aware of having them (Fazio & Olson, 2003). To measure these attitudes, Anthony Greenwald, Mahzarin Banaji, Brian Nosek, and others have developed the *Implicit Association Test*, or *IAT*. As we saw in Chapter 5, the IAT measures the speed with which people associate pairs of concepts (Greenwald et al., 1998).

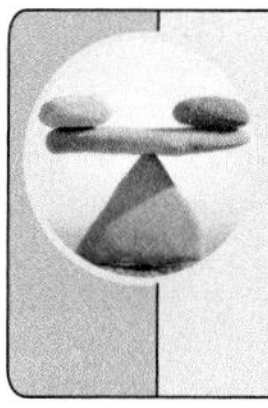

Researchers can tell if someone has a positive or negative attitude by measuring physiological arousal. FALSE.

You can complete tests that measure your implicit attitudes about race, age, gender, and many other constructs, and with many international sites, including a Canadian site, you can review tests and results that are most relevant to you. If you want to take a test that measures your implicit racial attitudes, you go through a series of stages. First, you are asked to categorize black or white faces as quickly as you can, for example, by pressing a left-hand key in response to a black face and a right-hand key for a white face. Next, you are asked to categorize a set of words, for example, by pressing a left-hand key for positive words (*love, laughter, friend*) and a right-hand key for negative words (*war, failure, evil*). Once you have become familiar with the categorization task, the test combines faces and words. You may be asked, for example, to press the left-hand key if you see a black face or positive word, and a right-hand key for a white face or negative word. Then, in the fourth stage, the opposite pairings are presented—black or negative, white or positive. Black and white faces are then interspersed in a quick sequence of trials, each time paired with a positive or negative word. In rapid-fire succession, you have to press one key or another in response to stimulus pairs such as *black-wonderful, black-failure, white-love, black-laughter, white-evil, white-awful, black-war*, and *white-joy*. As you work through the

Copyright © [1999] by the American Psychological Association, Reproduced with permission. From J.T. Cacioppo and R.E. Petty (1981) "Electromyograms as Measures of Extent and Affectivity of Information Processing," *American Psychologist, 36, 441-456.* The use of APA information does not imply endorsement by APA.

implicit attitude
An attitude—such as prejudice—that one is not aware of having.

▶ FIGURE 6.3

The Implicit Association Test (IAT)

Through a sequence of tasks, the IAT measures implicit racial attitudes toward, for example, Blacks by measuring how quickly people respond to *black-bad/white-good* word pairings relative to *black-good/white-bad* pairings. Responding faster to the first pairing indicates a negative association to Blacks.

(Greenwald et al., 2003.)

list, you may find that some pairings are harder and take longer to respond to than others. In general, people are quicker to respond when liked faces are paired with positive words and disliked faces are paired with negative words, than the other way around. Using the IAT, your implicit attitudes about Blacks can thus be detected by the speed it takes you to respond to *black-bad/white-good* pairings relative to *black-good/white-bad* pairings. The test takes only about ten minutes to complete. When you're done, you receive the results of your test and an explanation of what it means (see ▶ Figure 6.3).

From 1998 to the present, visitors to this site have completed millions of tests, at a rate of approximately 15 000 tests per week! In questionnaires, interviews, public opinion polls, and Internet surveys, people don't tend to reveal their stereotypes, prejudices, or other unpopular attitudes. Yet on the IAT, respondents have exhibited an average implicit preference for self over other, white over black, young over old, thin over obese, and the stereotype that links males with careers and females with family (Greenwald et al., 2003; Nosek et al., 2002; Nosek, Greenwald, & Banaji, 2005). Because more and more researchers are using these kinds of indirect measures, social psychologists who study attitudes find themselves in the midst of a debate over whether the IAT is methodologically sound, what IAT scores mean, how the implicit attitudes revealed in the IAT are formed and then changed, how these attitudes predict or influence behaviour, and how they differ from the more explicit attitudes that we consciously hold and report (Blanton et al., 2009; Buhrmester, Blanton, & Swann, Jr., 2011; Gawronski & Bodenhausen, 2006; Petty et al., 2009; Wittenbrink & Schwarz, 2007).

Do implicit attitudes matter? Do millisecond differences in response times on a computerized test really predict behaviour in real-world settings of consequence? And what does it mean when one's implicit and explicit attitudes clash? The importance of these questions cannot be overstated. If the IAT reveals unconscious prejudices that people do not self-report, should individuals be scrutinized in the laboratory for hidden motives underlying various potentially unlawful behaviours—as when a police officer shoots a black suspect, fearing that he or she is armed; as when an employer hires a male applicant over a female applicant, citing his credentials as opposed to discrimination; or as when a jury chooses to convict an Aboriginal defendant on the basis of ambiguous evidence?

Kristin Lane and others (2007) have speculated about the relevance of implicit attitudes in law. But is their speculation justified? Some researchers are critical of strong claims concerning the predictive validity of the IAT, citing the need for more behavioural evidence (Blanton et al., 2009). For example, while Canadian IAT scores may demonstrate negative attitudes toward Blacks, it is not clear that these negative attitudes would necessarily translate into differential treatment for these individuals in court. Then again, Jeffrey Rachlinski and others (2009) did find evidence that U.S. trial judges primed with words associated with African Americans were more likely to hand down harsher sentences—and this behaviour was predicted by the judges' IAT scores.

Based on a meta-analysis of 122 IAT studies involving 15 000 participants, Greenwald and others (2009) concede that people's implicit attitudes are generally less predictive of behaviour than their explicit attitudes. They also find, however, that IAT measures are better when it comes to socially sensitive topics such as race, where people often distort their self-reports.

Other researchers have suggested alternate methods to measure implicit attitudes. For example, Sarah Roddy and others (2011) found greater overlap between anti-fat attitudes detected by facial EMG and the **Implicit Relational Assessment Procedure (IRAP)**—a technique similar to the IAT that focuses on cognition and specific relations rather than general associations—than between the EMG and the IAT. Rather than choosing between only two categories (e.g., good/bad), respondents using the IRAP must also decide between two relational terms (e.g., similar/opposite). If you were taking this test to assess your racial attitudes, you might see a pairing of 'black/wonderful', but then you would have to decide whether you think the relationship between that pair of words is true or not. Proponents of the IRAP argue that it is a better measure of behavioural intentions than the IAT (Holmes et al., 2006; Roddy, Stewart, Barnes-Holmes, 2011).

How Attitudes Are Formed

How did you become liberal or conservative in your political values? Why do you favour or oppose same-sex marriage? What draws you toward or away from organized religion?

One hypothesis, first advanced by Abraham Tesser (1993), is that strong likes and dislikes are rooted in our genetic makeup. Research shows that on some issues, the attitudes of identical twins are more similar than those of fraternal twins, and that twins raised apart are as similar to each other as those who are raised in the same home. This pattern of evidence suggests that people may be predisposed to hold certain attitudes. Indeed, Tesser found that when asked about attitudes for which there seems to be a predisposition (such as attitudes toward sexual promiscuity, religion, and the death penalty), research participants were quicker to respond and less likely to alter their views toward social norms. Tesser speculated that individuals are disposed to hold certain strong attitudes as a result of inborn physical, sensory, and cognitive skills, temperament, and personality traits. Other twin studies, too (see ▶ Figure 6.4), have supported the notion that people differ in their attitudes toward a range of issues in part because of genetically rooted differences in their biological makeup (Olson et al., 2001).

Whatever dispositions nature provides us with, our most cherished attitudes often form as a result of our exposure to attitude objects; our history of rewards and punishments; the attitudes that our parents, friends, and enemies express; the social and cultural context in which we live; and other types of experiences. In a classic naturalistic study, Theodore Newcomb (1943) surveyed the political attitudes of students at Bennington College in Vermont. At the time, Bennington was a women's college that drew its students from conservative and mostly affluent families. Once there, however, the students encountered professors and older peers who held more liberal views. Newcomb found that as the women moved from their first year to graduation, they became progressively more liberal.

Implicit Relational Assessment Procedure (IRAP)
A way of measuring unconscious attitudes, similar to the IAT, that focuses on cognition and specific relations rather than general associations.

FIGURE 6.4

Genetic Influences on Attitudes

In this study, 672 twins individually rated their attitudes on a range of issues and activities. Indicating the role of genetic factors, there were higher correlations among pairs of identical twins than among pairs of fraternal twins.

(Olson et al., 2001.)

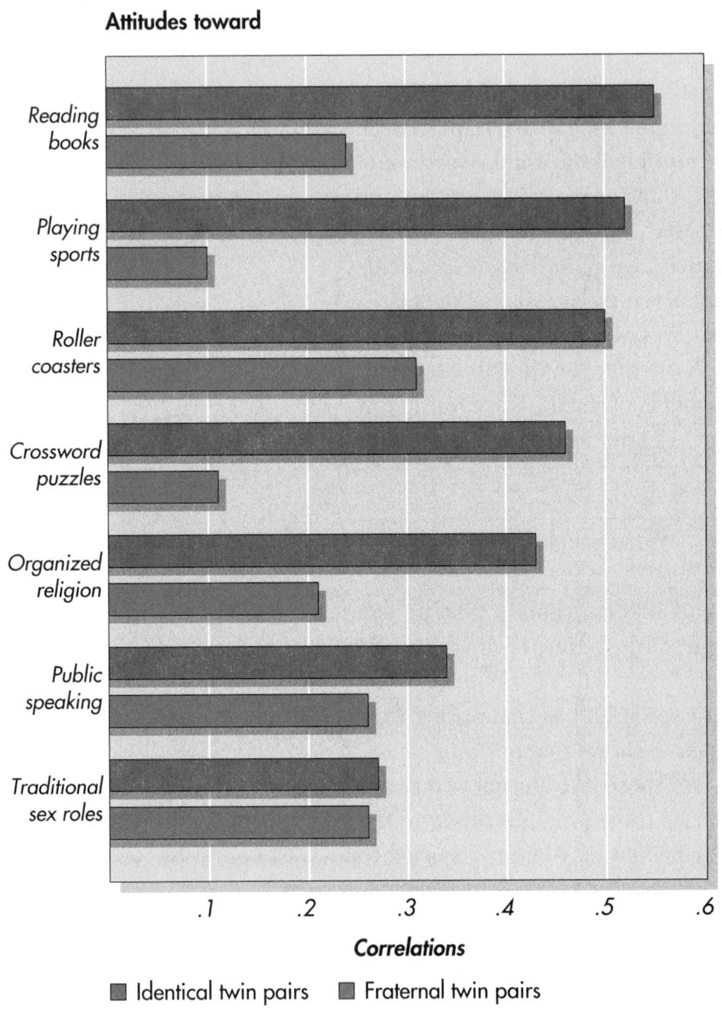

Clearly, attitudes are formed through basic processes of learning. For example, numerous studies have shown that people can form strong positive and negative attitudes toward neutral objects that somehow are linked to emotionally charged stimuli. In a classic study, university students were presented with a list of adjectives that indicate nationality (*German, Swedish, Dutch, Italian, French,* and *Greek*), each of which was repeatedly presented with words that had very pleasant (*happy, gift, sacred*) or unpleasant (*bitter, ugly, failure*) connotations. When the participants later evaluated the nationalities by name, they were more positive in their ratings of those that had been paired with pleasant words than with unpleasant words (Staats & Staats, 1958).

More recent studies of "evaluative conditioning" have further shown that implicit and explicit attitudes toward neutral objects can form by their association with positive and negative stimuli, even in people who are not conscious of this association (De Houwer et al., 2001; Olson & Fazio, 2001; Walther et al., 2005). That's why political leaders all over the world wrap themselves in national flags to derive the benefit of positive associations, while advertisers strategically pair their products with sexy models, uplifting music, beloved celebrities, nostalgic images, and other positive emotional symbols.

The Link Between Attitudes and Behaviour

People take for granted the notion that attitudes influence behaviour. We assume that voters' opinions of opposing candidates predict the decisions they make on election day, that consumers' attitudes toward competing products influence the purchases they make, and that feelings of prejudice trigger negative acts of discrimination. Yet as sensible as these assumptions seem, the link between attitudes and behaviour is far from perfect.

Sociologist Richard LaPiere (1934) was the first to notice that attitudes and behaviour don't always go hand in hand. In the 1930s, LaPiere took a young Chinese American couple on a three-month, 16 000 km automobile trip, visiting 250 restaurants, campgrounds, and hotels across the United States. Although prejudice against Asians was widespread at the time, the couple was refused service only once. Yet when LaPiere wrote back to the places they had visited and asked if they would accept Chinese patrons, more than 90 percent of those who returned an answer said they would not. Self-reported attitudes did not correspond with behaviour.

This study was provocative but seriously flawed. LaPiere measured attitudes several months after his trip, and during that time the attitudes may have changed. He also did not know whether those who responded to his letter were the same people who had greeted the couple in person. It was even possible that the Chinese couple were served wherever they went only because they were accompanied by LaPiere himself.

Despite these problems, LaPiere's study was the first of many to reveal a lack of correspondence between attitudes and behaviour. In 1969, Allan Wicker reviewed the applicable research and concluded that attitudes and behaviour are correlated only weakly, if at all. Sobered by this conclusion, researchers were puzzled: Could it be that the votes we cast do *not* follow from our political opinions, that consumers' purchases are *not* based on their attitudes toward a product, or that discrimination is *not* related to underlying prejudice? Is the study of attitudes useless to those interested in human social behaviour? No, not at all. It became apparent that researchers needed to understand when attitudes do predict behaviours, and when they don't. Determining the conditions necessary for attitude-behaviour consistency has been a key focus of social psychological researchers, not to mention marketing experts, since the early days of LaPiere. When Stephen Kraus (1995) analyzed all of this research, he concluded that "attitudes significantly and substantially predict future behaviour" (p. 58). In fact, Kraus calculated that there would have to be 60 983 new studies reporting a zero correlation before this conclusion would have to be revised. Based on their recent meta-analysis of 41 additional studies, Laura Glasman and Dolores Albarraín (2006) went on to identify some of the conditions under which attitudes most clearly predict future behaviour.

Attitudes in Context One important factor is the level of *correspondence,* or similarity, between attitude measures and behaviour. Perhaps the reason that LaPiere (1934) did not find a correlation between self-reported prejudice and discrimination was that he had asked proprietors about Asians in general but then observed their actions toward only one couple. To predict a single act of discrimination, he should have measured people's more specific attitudes toward a young, well-dressed, attractive Chinese couple accompanied by an American professor.

Analyzing more than a hundred studies, Icek Ajzen and Martin Fishbein (1977) found that attitudes correlate with behaviour only when attitude measures closely match the behaviour in question. Illustrating the point, Andrew Davidson and James Jaccard (1979) tried to use attitudes to predict whether women would use birth control pills within the next two years. Attitudes were measured in a series of questions ranging from very general ("How do you feel about birth control?") to very specific ("How do you feel about using birth control pills during the next two years?"). The more specific the initial attitude question was, the better it predicted the behaviour. Other researchers as well have replicated this finding (Kraus, 1995).

The link between our feelings and our actions should also be placed within a broader context. Attitudes are one determinant of social behaviour, but there are other determinants as well. This limitation formed the basis for Fishbein's (1980) theory of reasoned action, which Ajzen (1991) then expanded into his **theory of planned behaviour**. According to these theories, our attitudes influence our behaviour through a process of deliberate decision making—and their impact is limited in four respects (see ▶ Figure 6.5).

theory of planned behaviour The theory that attitudes toward a specific behaviour combine with subjective norms and perceived control to influence a person's actions.

First, as just described, behaviour is influenced less by general attitudes than by attitudes toward a specific behaviour. Second, behaviour is influenced not only by attitudes but also by *subjective norms*—our beliefs about what others think we should do. As we'll see in Chapter 7, social pressures to conform often lead us to behave in ways that are at odds with our inner convictions. Third, according to Ajzen, attitudes

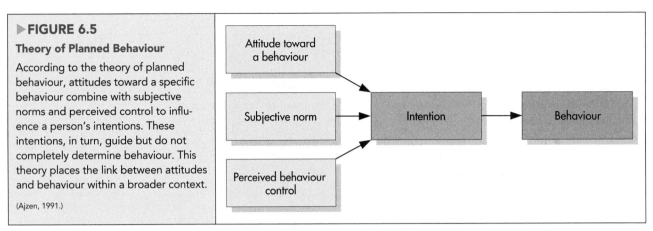

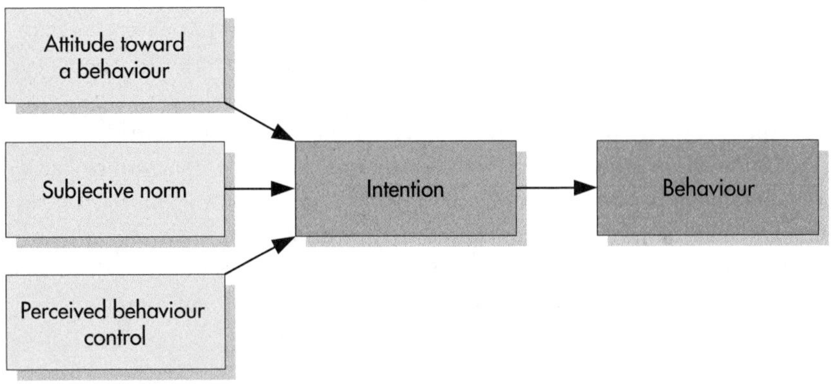

FIGURE 6.5
Theory of Planned Behaviour
According to the theory of planned behaviour, attitudes toward a specific behaviour combine with subjective norms and perceived control to influence a person's intentions. These intentions, in turn, guide but do not completely determine behaviour. This theory places the link between attitudes and behaviour within a broader context.

(Ajzen, 1991.)

give rise to behaviour only when we perceive the behaviour to be within our *control.* To the extent that people lack confidence in their ability to engage in some behaviour, they are unlikely to form an intention to do so. Fourth, although attitudes (along with subjective norms and perceived control) contribute to an *intention* to behave in a particular manner, people often do not or cannot follow through on their intentions.

A good deal of research supports the theories of reasoned action and planned behaviour (Ajzen & Fishbein, 2005; Madden et al., 1992). Indeed, this general approach, which places the link between attitudes and behaviours in a broader context, has successfully been used to predict a wide range of important and practical behaviours—such as using condoms, obeying speed limits, and eating healthy foods (Albarracin et al., 2001; Conner et al., 2002; Elliott et al., 2003; Poon et al., 2011).

Strength of the Attitude According to the theories of reasoned action and planned behaviour, specific attitudes combine with social factors to produce behaviour. Sometimes attitudes have more influence on behaviour than do other factors; sometimes they have less influence. In large part, it depends on the importance, or *strength,* of the attitude. Each of us has some views that are nearer and dearer to the heart than others. Computer jocks often become attached to PCs or Macs, while political activists have fiery passions for one political party over others. In each case, the attitude is held with great confidence and is difficult to change (Petty & Krosnick, 1995).

Why are some attitudes stronger than others? David Boninger and others (1995) have identified three psychological factors that consistently seem to distinguish between our strongest and weakest attitudes. They found that the attitudes people held most passionately were those that concerned issues that (1) directly affected their own outcomes and self-interests; (2) related to deeply held philosophical, political, and religious values; and (3) were of concern to their close friends, family, and social ingroups. This last, highly social, point is important. Research shows that when people are surrounded by others who are like-minded, the attitudes they hold are stronger and more resistant to change (Lun, Whitchurch, & Glenn, 2007; Visser & Mirabile, 2004).

Several factors indicate the strength of an attitude and its link to behaviour. One is that people tend to behave in ways that are consistent with their attitudes when they are well informed. For example, in one study, students were questioned about their views on various environmental issues and later were asked to take action—to sign petitions, participate in a recycling project, and so on. The more informed students were, the more consistent their environmental attitudes were with their behaviour (Kallgren & Wood, 1986).

Second, the strength of an attitude is indicated not only by the *amount* of information on which it is based but also by *how* that information was acquired. Research shows that attitudes are more stable and more predictive of behaviour when they are born of direct personal experience than when based on indirect, second-hand information. In a series of experiments, for example, Russell Fazio and Mark Zanna (1981) introduced two groups of participants to a set of puzzles. One group worked on sample puzzles; the other group merely watched someone else work on them. All participants were then asked to rate their interest in the puzzles (attitude) and were given an opportunity to spend time on them (behaviour). As it turned out, attitudes and behaviours were more consistent among participants who had previously sampled the puzzles.

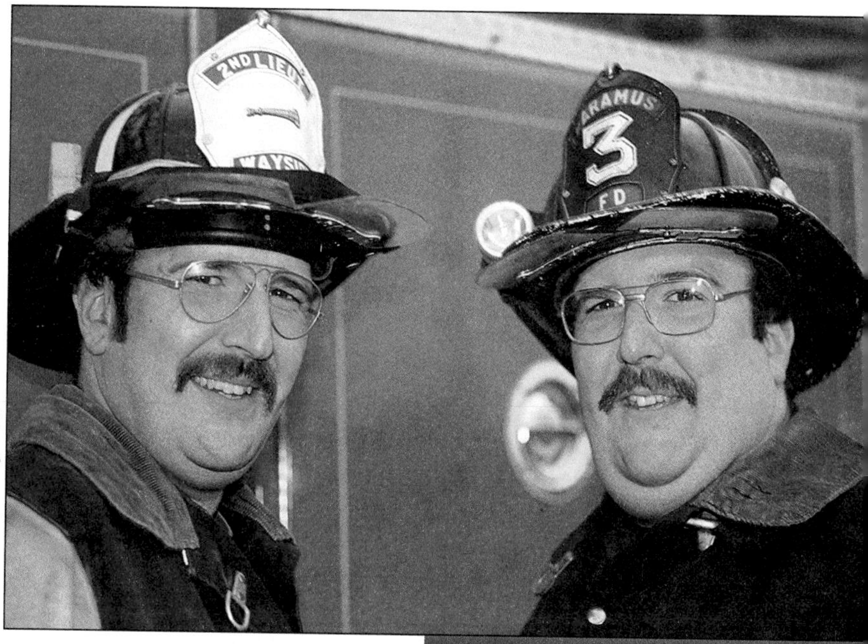

©Thomas Wanstall/The Image Works

Chances are, these identical twins have more in common than being firefighters. Research suggests that people may be genetically predisposed to hold certain attitudes.

Third, an attitude can be strengthened, ironically, by an attack against it from a persuasive message. According to Zakary Tormala and Richard Petty (2002), people hold attitudes with varying degrees of certainty, and they become more confident after they successfully resist changing that attitude in response to a persuasive communication. In one study, for example, researchers confronted university students with an unpopular proposal to add senior comprehensive exams as a graduation requirement. Each student read a pro-exam argument that was described as strong or weak, after which they were asked to write down counter-arguments and indicate their attitude toward the policy. The result: Students who continued to oppose the policy despite reading what they thought to be a strong argument became even more certain of their opinion.

Generally, when people resist a strong message and believe that they have done so in a compelling way, they become more certain of their attitude and more likely to form a behavioural intention that is consistent with it. When people resist a persuasive message "by the skin of their teeth," however, and see their own counter-arguments as weak, they become less certain of their initial attitude and more vulnerable to subsequent attack (Tormala et al., 2006). Even if a person's belief in his or her own thoughtful response is incorrect, it can influence the strength of the attitude in question (Barden & Petty, 2008). For example, Wonkyong Lee and others (2009), compared a population of self-described weekly adult smokers in Thailand to a similar population in Malaysia. While both countries have similar policies regarding the control of tobacco, Thailand has a longer history of enforcing such control, and is generally more strict when it comes to the production of tobacco than Malaysia. When comparing attitudes toward smoking amongst the populations, they found that Thai respondents indicated levels of regret regarding their smoking behaviour consistent with levels found in western countries, including Canada, at 92 percent compared to 79 percent in Malaysia. Interestingly, 49 percent of the Malaysian population rationalized their decision to keep smoking, whereas less than 10 percent of the Thai population did the same. Those in Thailand also reported intentions to quit at a higher rate than those in Malaysia. Thus, the researchers argue that in the presence of social norms to not smoke, these higher levels of regret, fewer rationalizations, and greater intentions to quit are much more likely to lead an individual to plan to and eventually quit smoking.

A fourth key factor is that strong attitudes are highly accessible to awareness, which means they are quickly and easily brought to mind (Fazio, 1990). To return to our earlier examples, computer jocks think often about their computer preferences, and political activists think often about their party allegiances. It turns out that many attitudes—not just those we feel strongly about—are easily brought to mind by the mere sight of, or even just the mention of, an attitude object (Bargh et al., 1992). When this happens, the attitude can trigger behaviour in a quick, spontaneous way or by leading us to think carefully about how we feel and how to respond (Fazio & Towles-Schwen, 1999). For example, researchers with the International Tobacco Control Policy Evaluation Project (ITC), headed by Geoff Fong at the University of Waterloo, have found that more prominent warnings about the dangers of smoking at places where cigarettes are sold leads to an increase in reported interest in quitting, as well as to an increase in quit-smoking attempts. When comparing Canada, the United States, the United Kingdom, and Australia, they determined that the larger, more prominent warnings found in Australia had a greater impact on intentions to quit than the less obtrusive, or weaker, warnings generally found in the other countries (Li et al., 2012). Perhaps seeing the warning regularly (and prominently) helps to keep the idea of quitting more accessible to smokers in countries where smoking is not considered to be normative behaviour.

To summarize, research on the link between attitudes and behaviour leads to an important conclusion. Our evaluations of an object do not always determine our actions because other factors must be taken into account. However, when attitudes are strong and specific to a behaviour, the effects are beyond dispute. Under these conditions, voting *is* influenced by political opinions, consumer purchasing *is* affected by product attitudes, and racial discrimination *is* rooted in feelings of prejudice. Attitudes are important determinants of behaviour. The question now is, how can attitudes be changed?

Persuasion by Communication

On a day-to-day basis, we are all involved in the process of changing attitudes. Advertisers flood consumers with ad campaigns designed to sell cars, soft drinks, running shoes, computers, and Internet services. Likewise, politicians make speeches, pass out bumper stickers, and kiss babies to win votes. Attitude change is sought whenever parents socialize their children, scientists advance theories, religious groups seek converts, financial analysts recommend stocks, or trial lawyers argue cases to a jury. Some appeals work; others do not. Some are soft and subtle; others are hard and blatant. Some serve the public interest, whereas others serve personal interests. The point is, there is nothing inherently evil or virtuous about changing attitudes, a process known as **persuasion**. We do it all the time.

Television provides a major outlet for commercial persuasion. The average Canadian watches just over 21 hours of TV per week—and views roughly 20 000 commercials per year (Statistics Canada, 2010).

If you wanted to change someone's attitude on an issue, you'd probably try by making a persuasive *communication.* Appeals made in person and through the mass media rely on the spoken word, the written word, and the image that is worth a thousand words. What determines whether an appeal succeeds or fails? To understand why certain approaches are effective while others are not, social psychologists have, for many years, sought to understand *how* and *why* persuasive communications work. For that, we need a road map of the persuasion process.

persuasion
The process by which attitudes are changed.

Two Routes to Persuasion

It's a familiar scene in politics: Every few years, various candidates launch extensive campaigns for office. In a way, if you've seen one election, you've seen them all. The names and dates may change; but over and over again, opposing candidates accuse each other of ducking the issues and turning the election into a flag-waving popularity contest. True or not, these accusations show that politicians are keenly aware that they can win votes through two different methods. They can stick to the issues, or they can base their appeals on other grounds. Interestingly, these "other grounds" can well determine who wins an election. In *The Political Brain*, Drew Westen (2007) presents a wealth of research evidence indicating that in the marketplace of politics, emotions trump reason. Based on a combination of laboratory experiments and public opinion polls, other political psychologists agree (Brader, 2006, 2011; Neuman et al., 2007).

To account for these two alternative approaches to persuasion, Richard Petty and John Cacioppo (1986) proposed a dual-process model of persuasion. This model assumes that we do not always process communications the same way. When people think critically about the contents of a message, they are said to take a **central route to persuasion** and are influenced by the strength and quality of the arguments. When people do not think critically about the contents of a message but focus instead on other cues, they take a **peripheral route to persuasion**. As we'll see, the route taken depends on whether one is willing and able to scrutinize the information contained in the message itself. Over the years, this model has provided an important framework for understanding the factors that elicit persuasion (Petty & Wegener, 1999).

The Central Route In the first systematic attempt to study persuasion, Carl Hovland and his colleagues (1949, 1953) started the Yale Communication and Attitude Change Program. They proposed that for a persuasive message to have influence, the recipients of that message must learn its contents and be motivated to accept it. According to this view, people can be persuaded only by an argument they attend to, comprehend, and retain in memory for later use. Regardless of whether the message takes the form of a personal appeal, a newspaper editorial, a Sunday sermon, a TV commercial, or a pop-up window on a website, these basic requirements remain the same.

A few years later, William McGuire (1969) reiterated the information-processing steps necessary for persuasion and, like the Yale group before him, distinguished between the learning, or *reception*, of a message, a necessary first step, and its later *acceptance*. In fact, McGuire (1968) used this distinction to explain the surprising finding that a recipient's self-esteem and intelligence are unrelated to persuasion. In McGuire's analysis, these characteristics have opposite effects on reception and acceptance. People who are smart or high in self-esteem are better able to learn a message but are less likely to accept its call for a change in attitude. People who are less smart or low in self-esteem are more willing to accept the message but may have trouble learning its contents. Overall, then, neither group is generally more vulnerable to persuasion than the other—a prediction that is supported by a good deal of research (Rhodes & Wood, 1992).

Anthony Greenwald (1968) and others then argued that persuasion requires a third, intermediate step: **elaboration**. To illustrate, imagine you are offered a job and your prospective employer tries to convince you over lunch to accept. You listen closely, learn the terms of the offer, and understand what it means. But if it's a really important interview, your head will spin with questions as you weigh the pros and cons and contemplate the implications: Would I have to move? Is there room for advancement? Am I better off staying where I am? When confronted with personally significant messages, we don't just listen for the sake of collecting information—we

central route to persuasion
The process by which a person thinks carefully about a communication and is influenced by the strength of its arguments.

peripheral route to persuasion
The process by which a person does not think carefully about a communication and is influenced instead by superficial cues.

elaboration
The process of thinking about and scrutinizing the arguments contained in a persuasive communication.

In elections, candidates try to win votes by addressing the issues, as in speeches (the central route), or through the use of celebrities, music, "spontaneous" photo-ops, and other theatrics (the peripheral route).

think about that information. The message is then effective to the extent that it leads us to focus on favourable rather than unfavourable thoughts.

These theories of attitude change all share the assumption that the recipients of persuasive appeals are attentive, active, critical, and thoughtful. This assumption is correct—some of the time. When it is, and when people consider a message carefully, their reaction to it depends on the strength of its contents. In these instances, messages have greater impact when they are easily learned rather than difficult, when they are memorable rather than forgettable, and when they stimulate favourable rather than unfavourable elaboration. Ultimately, strong arguments are persuasive, and weak arguments are not. On the central route to persuasion, the process is eminently thoughtful.

It's important to note, however, that thinking carefully about a persuasive message does not mean that the process is objective or that it necessarily promotes truth-seeking. At times, each of us prefers to hold a particular attitude—which leads us to become biased in our processing of information (Petty & Wegener, 1999). For example, students were less likely to be persuaded by a proposed tuition hike to fund campus improvements when the increase would take effect in one year, thus raising the personal stakes, than by a proposal to raise tuition in eight years (Darke & Chaiken, 2005). To further complicate matters, there are times when people want to hold the right attitudes, but believing they may be biased or overly influenced by nonrelevant factors, they try to correct for that bias—sometimes with an ironic result: overcorrection. In one study, for example, audience members who were forewarned that people are prone to agree with speakers they like later exhibited more attitude change in response to a speaker who was clearly *not* likeable (Petty et al., 1998).

The Peripheral Route "The receptive ability of the masses is very limited, their understanding small; on the other hand, they have a great power of forgetting." The author of this statement was Adolf Hitler (1933, p. 77). Believing that people are incompetent processors of information, Hitler relied heavily in his propaganda on the use of slogans, uniforms, marching bands, flags, and other symbols. For Hitler, "Meetings were not just occasions to make speeches, they were carefully planned theatrical productions in which settings, lighting, background music, and the timing of entrances were devised to maximize the emotional fervor of an audience" (Qualter, 1962, p. 112). Do these ploys work? Can the masses be so handily manipulated into persuasion? History shows that they can. Audiences are not always thoughtful. Sometimes people do not follow the central route to persuasion but instead take a shortcut through the peripheral route. Rather than try to learn the message and think through the issues, they respond with little effort on the basis of superficial, peripheral cues.

On the peripheral route to persuasion, people will often evaluate a communication by using simple-minded heuristics, or rules of thumb (Chaiken, 1987; Chen & Chaiken, 1999). If a communicator has a good reputation, speaks fluently, or writes well, we tend to assume that his or her message must be correct. And when a speaker has a reputation for being honest, people think less critically about the contents of his or her communication (Priester & Petty, 1995). Likewise, we assume that a message must be correct if it contains a long litany of arguments, or statistics, or an impressive list of supporting experts; if it's familiar; if it elicits cheers from an audience; or if the speaker seems to be arguing against his or her own interests. In some cases, simply knowing that an argument has majority support will get people to change their attitudes (Giner-Sorolla & Chaiken, 1997).

On the mindless peripheral route, people are also influenced by a host of attitude-irrelevant factors, such as cues from their own body movements. In one study, participants viewed and rated graphic symbols or word-like stimuli (*surtel, primet*) while using an exercise bar to either stretch their arms out (which mimics what we do to push something away) or flex their arms in (which we do to bring something closer). These stimuli were later judged to be more pleasant when associated with the flexing of the arm than with the stretching-out motion (Cacioppo et al., 1993; Priester et al., 1996).

Route Selection Thanks to Petty and Cacioppo's (1986) two-track distinction between the central and peripheral routes, we can better understand why the persuasion process seems so logical on some occasions yet so illogical on others—why voters may select candidates according to issues or images, why juries may base their verdicts on evidence or a defendant's appearance, and why consumers may base their purchases on marketing reports or product images. The process that is engaged depends on whether the recipients of a persuasive message have the *ability* and the *motivation* to take the central route or whether they rely on peripheral cues instead.

To understand the conditions that lead people to take one route or the other, it's helpful to view persuasive communication as the outcome of three factors: a *source* (who), a *message* (says what and in what context), and an *audience* (to whom). Each of these factors influences a recipient's approach to a persuasive communication. If a source speaks clearly, if the message is important, if there is a bright, captive, and involved audience that cares deeply about the issue and has time to absorb the information, then audience members will be willing and able to take the effortful central route. But if the source speaks at a rate too fast to comprehend, if the message is trivial or too complex to process, or if audience members are distracted, pressed for time, or uninterested, then the less strenuous peripheral route is taken.

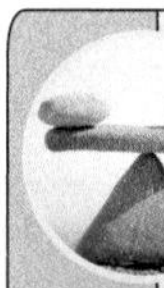

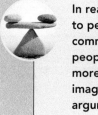

In reacting to persuasive communications, people are influenced more by superficial images than by logical arguments. FALSE.

▶ Figure 6.6 presents a road map representing the path to persuasive communication. In the next three sections, we will follow this map from the input factors (source, message, and audience), through the central or peripheral route processing strategies, to the final destination: persuasion.

▶ FIGURE 6.6

Two Routes to Persuasion

Based on characteristics of the source, message, and audience, recipients of a communication take either a central or a peripheral route to persuasion. On the central route, people are influenced by strong arguments and evidence. On the peripheral route, persuasion is based more on heuristics and other superficial cues. This two-process model helps explain how persuasion can seem logical on some occasions and illogical on others.

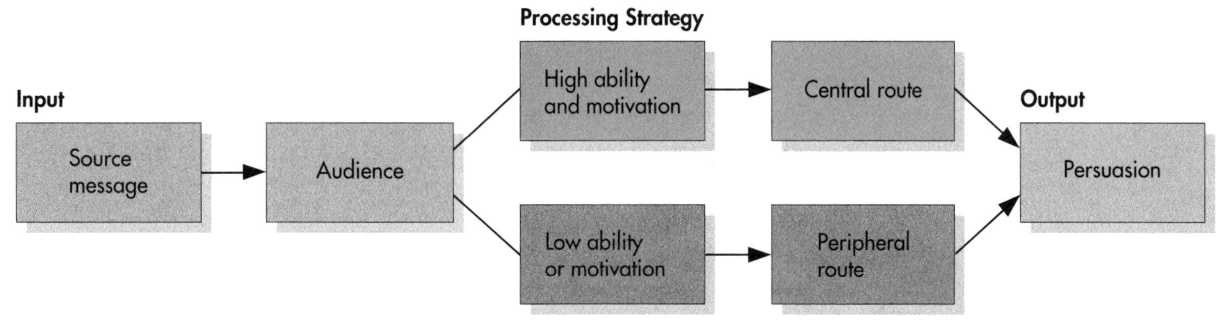

The Source

Hockey player Sydney Crosby has been paid millions of dollars per year to endorse the Tim Hortons brand, and other commercial products. Why is Crosby considered an effective spokes-person? What makes some communicators, in general, more effective than others? As we'll see, there are two key attributes: credibility and likeability.

Credibility Imagine you are waiting in line in a supermarket, and you catch a glimpse of an amazing headline: "Doctors Discover Cure for AIDS!" As your eye wanders across the front page, you discover that you are reading a tabloid magazine such as the sensationalistic *National Enquirer*. What would you think? Next, imagine that you are reading through scientific periodicals in a university library, and you come across a similar article—but this time it appears in the *New England Journal of Medicine*. Now what would you think?

Chances are, you'd react with more excitement to the medical journal than to the supermarket tabloid—even though both sources report the same news item. In a study conducted during the cold war era of the 1950s, participants read a speech advocating the development of nuclear submarines. The speech elicited more agreement when it was attributed to an eminent American physicist than when the source was said to be the Soviet government newspaper *Pravda* (Hovland & Weiss, 1951). Likewise, when participants read a speech favouring more lenient treatment of juvenile offenders, they changed their attitudes more when they thought the speaker was a judge rather than a convicted drug dealer (Kelman & Hovland, 1953). Now, after more than 50 years of research, it is clear that high-credibility sources are generally more persuasive than low-credibility sources (Pornpitakpan, 2004). Why are some sources more believable than others? Why were the medical journal, the physicist, and the judge more credible than the tabloid, *Pravda,* and the drug dealer? For communicators to be seen as credible, they must have two distinct characteristics: (1) competence, or expertise, and (2) trustworthiness. *Competence* refers to a speaker's ability. People who are knowledgeable, smart, or well spoken, or who have impressive credentials, are persuasive by virtue of their expertise (Hass, 1981). Experts can have a disarming effect on us. We assume they know what they're talking about. So when they speak, we listen. And when they take a position, even one that is extreme, we often yield. Unless an expert contradicts us on issues that are personally important, we tend to accept what he or she says without too much scrutiny (Maddux & Rogers, 1980)—even when the message itself is ambiguous (Chaiken & Maheswaran, 1994).

Still, we are confronted by plenty of experts in life whose opinions do not sway us. The reason is that expertise alone is not enough. To have credibility, communicators must also be *trustworthy*—that is, they must be seen as willing to report what they know truthfully and without compromise. What determines whether we trust a communicator? To some extent, we make these judgments on the basis of stereotypes. Recently, for example, a poll conducted by Ipsos-Reid (2012) asked about 1000 Canadians to rate the trustworthiness levels associated with various occupational categories. They found that pharmacists, doctors, soldiers, airline pilots, and teachers were rated the highest, while car salespeople and politicians were at the bottom.

In judging the credibility of a source, we are armed by common sense with a simple rule of caution: Beware of those who have something to gain from successful persuasion. If a speaker has been bought off, has an axe to grind, or is simply telling us what we want to hear, we suspect him or her of bias. This rule sheds light on a classic dilemma in advertising concerning the value of celebrity spokespersons: The more products a celebrity endorses, the less trustworthy he or she appears to consumers (Tripp et al., 1994). In the courtroom, the same rule of caution can be used to evaluate witnesses. In one study, research participants served as jurors in a mock trial in which a man claimed that his exposure to an industrial chemical at work had caused him to contract cancer. Testifying in support of this claim was a biochemist who was paid either $4800 or $75 for his expert testimony. You might think that jurors would be more impressed by the scientist when he commanded the higher fee. Yet, when highly paid, the expert was perceived to be a "hired gun"—and was, as a result, less believable and less persuasive (Cooper & Neuhaus, 2000).

AFP/Getty Images

Can celebrities help to sell products? Targeting the peripheral route to persuasion, the advertising industry seems to think so.

The self-interest rule has other interesting implications. One is that people are impressed by others who take unpopular stands or argue against their own interests. When research participants read a political speech accusing a large corporation of polluting a local river, those who thought that the speechmaker was a pro-environment candidate addressing a staunch environmentalist group perceived him to be biased, while those who thought he was a pro-business candidate talking to company supporters assumed he was sincere (Eagly et al., 1978). Trust is also established by speakers who are not purposely trying to change our views. Thus, people are influenced more when they think that they are accidentally overhearing a communication than when they receive a sales pitch clearly intended for their ears (Walster & Festinger, 1962). That's why advertisers sometimes use the "overheard communicator" trick, in which the source tells a buddy about a new product that really works. Feeling as if they are eavesdropping on a personal conversation, viewers assume that what one friend says to another can be trusted.

Likeability More than anything else, the celebrity power of Sydney Crosby is based on his athletic dominance, his popularity, and his youthful charm. But do these qualities enhance someone's impact as a communicator? Yes. As Dale Carnegie (1936) implied in the title of his classic bestseller, *How to Win Friends and Influence People,* being liked and being persuasive go hand in hand. The question is, what makes a communicator likeable? As we'll see in Chapter 9, two factors that spark attraction are *similarity* and *physical attractiveness.*

Just as source similarity can spark persuasion, dissimilarity can have the opposite inhibiting effect. In a study of people's taste in music, Clayton Hilmert and others (2006) introduced participants to a confederate who seemed to like the same or different kinds of music, such as rock, pop, country, or classical. Others did not meet a confederate. When later asked to rate a particular song, participants were positively influenced by the similar confederate's opinion and negatively influenced by the dissimilar confederate's opinion. In fact, although the effect is more potent when the points of similarity seem relevant to the attitude in question (Berscheid, 1966), the participants in this study were also more or less persuaded by a confederate whose similarities or differences were wholly unrelated to music—for example, when the confederate had similar or different interests in shopping, world politics, museums, trying new foods, or surfing the Internet. The effect of source similarity on persuasion has obvious implications for those who wish to exert influence. We're all similar to one another in some respects. We might agree in politics, share a common friend, have similar tastes in food, or enjoy spending summers on the same beach. Aware of the social benefits of similarity, the astute communicator can thus use common bonds to enhance his or her impact on an audience.

Advertisers are so convinced that beauty sells products that they pay millions of dollars for supermodels and celebrities to appear in their ads. Here Charlize Theron appears in an ad for Dior watches.

When it comes to physical attractiveness, advertising practices presuppose that beauty is also persuasive. After all, billboards, magazine ads, and TV commercials are filled with young and glamorous "supermodels" who are tall and slender (for women) or muscular (for men) and who have hard bodies, glowing complexions, and radiant smiles. Sure, these models can turn heads, you may think, but can they change attitudes and behaviours?

In a study that addressed this question, Shelly Chaiken (1979) had male and female U.S. college students approach others on campus. They introduced themselves as members of an organization that wanted the university to stop serving meat during breakfast and lunch. In each case, these student assistants gave reasons for the position and then asked respondents to sign a petition. The result: Attractive communicators were able to get 41 percent of respondents to sign the petition, whereas those who were less attractive succeeded only 32 percent of the time.

Additional research has shown that attractive male and female salespersons elicit more positive attitudes and purchasing intentions from customers then less attractive salespersons, even when they are up front about their desire to make a sale (Messner, Reinhard, & Sporer, 2008).

When What You Say Is More Important Than Who You Are To this point, it must seem as if the source of a persuasive message is more important than the message itself. Is this true? Advertisers have long debated the value of high-priced celebrity endorsements. David Ogilvy (1985), a leader in advertising, used to say that celebrities are not effective because viewers know they've been bought and paid for. Ogilvy was not alone in his skepticism. Still, many advertisers scramble furiously to sign high-priced models, entertainers, and athletes. The bigger the star, supposedly, the more valuable the endorsement.

Compared with the contents of a message, does the source really make the difference that advertisers pay for? Are we so impressed by the expert, and so drawn to the charming face, that we embrace whatever they have to say? And are we so scornful of non-experts and unattractive people that their presentations fall on deaf ears? In light of what is known about the central and peripheral routes to persuasion, the answer to these questions is "it depends."

First, a recipient's level of involvement plays an important role. When a message has personal relevance to your life, you pay attention to the source and think critically about the message, arguments, and implications. When a message does not have relevance, however, you may take the source at face value and spend little time scrutinizing the information. For example, Richard Petty and others (1981) had students listen to a speaker who proposed that seniors should be required to take comprehensive exams in order to graduate. Three aspects of the communication situation were varied. First, participants were led to believe that the speaker was either an education professor at Princeton University or a high school student. Second, participants heard either well-reasoned arguments and hard evidence or a weak message based only on anecdotes and personal opinion. And third, participants were told either that the proposed exams might be used the following year (Uh oh, that means me!) or that they would not take effect for another ten years (Who cares, I'll be long gone by then!).

As predicted, personal involvement determined the relative impact of source expertise and speech quality. Among participants who would not be affected by the proposed change, attitudes were based largely on the speaker's credibility: The professor was persuasive, the high school student was not. Among participants who thought that the proposed change would affect them directly, attitudes were based on the quality of the speaker's proposal: Strong arguments were persuasive, weak arguments were not.

As depicted in ▶ Figure 6.7, people followed the source rather than the message under low levels of involvement, illustrating the peripheral route to persuasion. But message factors outweighed the source under high levels of involvement, when participants cared enough to take the central route to persuasion. Likewise, research has shown that the tilt toward likeable and attractive communicators is reduced when recipients take the central route (Chaiken, 1980).

There is a second limit to source effects. It is often said that time heals all wounds. Well, it may also heal the effects of a bad reputation. Hovland and Weiss (1951) varied communicator credibility (for example, the physicist versus *Pravda*) and found that the change had a large and immediate effect on persuasion. But when they remeasured attitudes four weeks later, the effect had vanished. Over time, the attitude change produced by the credible source decreased, and the change caused by the noncredible source increased. This latter finding of a delayed persuasive impact of a low-credibility communicator is called the **sleeper effect**.

To explain this unforeseen result, the Hovland research group proposed the *discounting cue hypothesis.* According to this hypothesis, people immediately discount the arguments made by noncredible communicators; but over time, they dissociate what was said from who said it. In other words, we tend to remember the message but forget the source (Pratkanis et al., 1988). To examine the role of memory in this process, Kelman and Hovland (1953) reminded a group of participants of the source's identity before reassessing their attitudes. If the sleeper effect was due to forgetting, they reasoned, then it could be eliminated through reinstatement of the link between the source and the message. As shown in ▶ Figure 6.8, they were right. When participants' attitudes were measured after three weeks, those who were not reminded of the source showed the usual sleeper effect. Those who were reminded of the source did not. For the latter participants, the effects of high and low credibility endured. Recent studies by cognitive psychologists have confirmed that, over time, people "forget" the connection between a message and its source (Underwood & Pezdek, 1998).

▶ FIGURE 6.7

Source Versus Message: The Role of Audience Involvement

People who were high or low in their personal involvement heard a strong or weak message from an expert or nonexpert. For high-involvement participants (left), persuasion was based on the strength of arguments, not on source expertise. For low-involvement participants (right), persuasion was based more on the source than on the arguments. Source characteristics have more impact on those who don't care enough to take the central route to persuasion.

(Petty et al., 1981.)

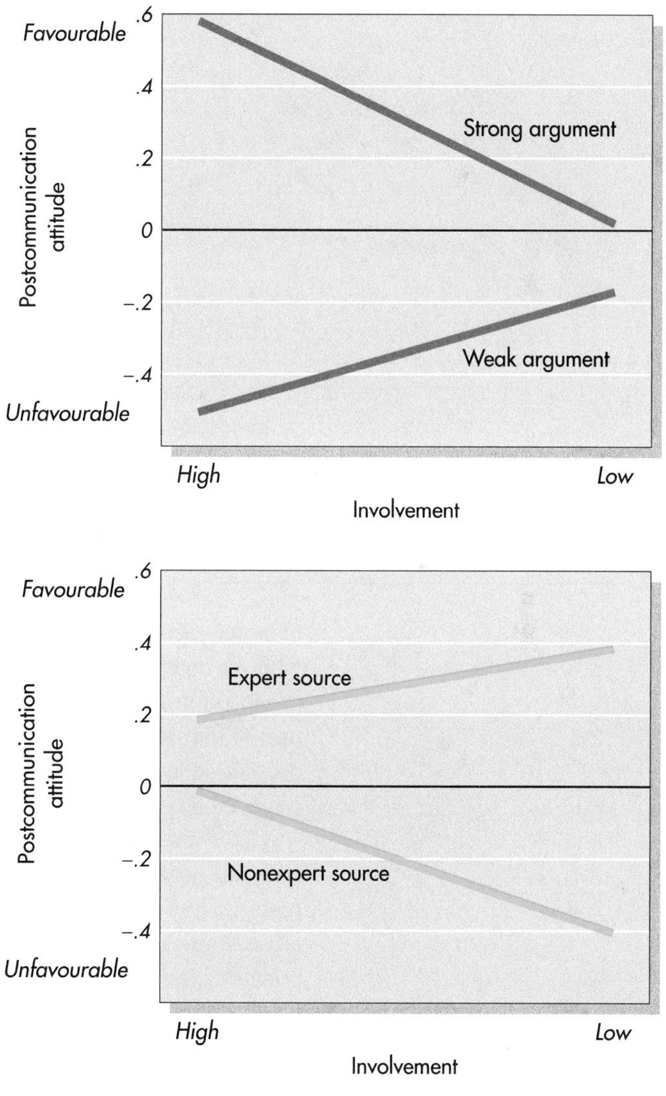

The sleeper effect generated a good deal of controversy. There was never a doubt that credible communicators lose some impact over time. But researchers had a harder time finding evidence for delayed persuasion by noncredible sources. Exasperated by their own failures to obtain this result, Paulette Gillig and Anthony Greenwald (1974) thus wondered, "Is it time to lay the sleeper effect to rest?" The answer, as it turned out, was no. More recent research showed that the sleeper effect is reliable—provided that participants do not learn who the source is until *after* they have received the original

sleeper effect
A delayed increase in the persuasive impact of a noncredible source.

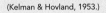

▶ **FIGURE 6.8**

The Sleeper Effect

In Experiment 1, participants changed their immediate attitudes more in response to a message from a high-credibility source than in response to a message from a low-credibility source. When attitudes were remeasured after three weeks, the high-credibility source lost impact, and the low-credibility source gained impact—the sleeper effect. In Experiment 2, the sleeper effect disappeared when participants were reminded of the source.

(Kelman & Hovland, 1953.)

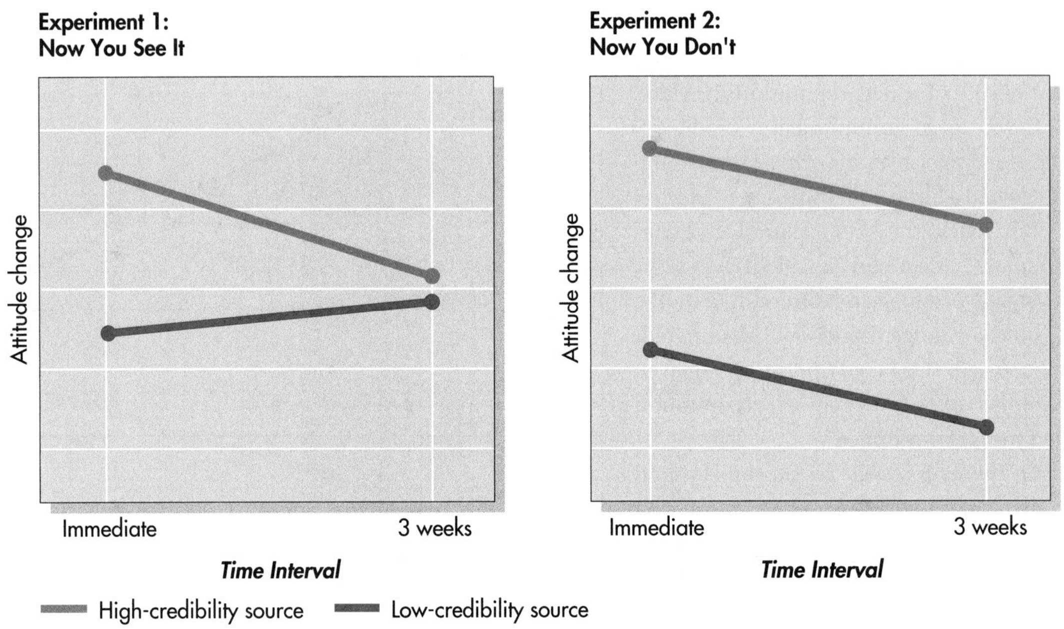

message (Greenwald et al., 1986; Gruder et al., 1978; Pratkanis et al., 1988). In addition, while we may be fully aware of whether or not a source is credible at the start of a persuasive communication, it appears we don't always choose to use that information as part of our decision-making processes. It may depend in part on whether conditions present encourage us to rely on it, or not (Klettke,Graesser, & Powell, 2010; Sparks & Rapp, 2011).

To appreciate the importance of timing, imagine that you're surfing the Internet and you come across what appears to be a review of a new CD. Before you begin reading, however, you notice in the fine print that this so-called review is really an advertisement. Aware that you can't always trust what you read, you skim the ad and reject it. Now imagine the same situation, except that you read the entire ad before realizing what it is. Again, you reject it. But notice the difference. This time, you have read the message with an open mind. You may then have rejected it; but after a few weeks, the information sinks in and influences your evaluation of the CD. This experience illustrates the sleeper effect.

The Message

Obviously, not all sources are created equal; some are more credible or likeable than others. On the peripheral route to persuasion, audiences are influenced heavily, maybe too heavily, by these and other source characteristics. But when people care about an issue, the strength of a message determines its impact. On the central route to persuasion, what matters most is whether a scientist's theory is supported by the data, whether a company has a sound product. Keep in mind, however, that the target of a persuasive appeal comes to know a message only through the medium of communication: *what* a person has to say and *how* that person says it.

Informational Strategies Communicators often struggle over how to present an argument to maximize its impact. Should a message be long and crammed with facts or short and to the point? Is it better to present a highly partisan, one-sided message or to take a more balanced, two-sided approach? And how should the various arguments be ordered—from strongest to weakest or the other way around? These are the kinds of questions often studied by persuasion researchers (Crano & Prislin, 2008; Petty et al., 1997).

Often, the most effective strategy to use depends on whether members of the audience process the message on the central or the peripheral route. Consider message length. When people process a message lazily, with their eyes and ears half-closed, they often fall back on a simple heuristic: The longer a message, the more valid it must be. In this case, word length gives the superficial appearance of factual support regardless of the quality of the arguments (Petty & Cacioppo, 1984; Wood et al., 1985). Thus, as David Ogilvy (1985) concluded from his years of advertising experience, "The more facts you tell, the more you sell" (p. 88).

When people process a communication carefully, however, length is a two-edged sword. If a message is long because it contains lots of supporting information, then longer does mean better. The more supportive arguments you can offer, or the more sources you can find to speak on your behalf, the more persuasive will be your appeal (Harkins & Petty, 1981). But if the added arguments are weak, or if the new sources are redundant, then an alert audience will not be fooled by length alone. When adding to the length of a message dilutes its quality, an appeal might well *lose* impact (Friedrich et al., 1996; Harkins & Petty, 1987).

"The truth is always the strongest argument."
—Sophocles

When opposing sides try to persuade an audience, presentation order becomes a relevant factor as well. Imagine you are a juror in a high-profile criminal case. The Crown has the chance to present their case first, and then it is the Defence's turn. Do you think this order provides an advantage to one side over the other? If you believe that information presented first has more impact, you'd predict a *primacy effect* (advantage to the Crown). If you believe that the information presented last has the edge, you'd predict a *recency effect* (advantage to the Defence).

There are good reasons for both predictions. On the one hand, first impressions are important. On the other hand, memory fades over time, and people often recall only the last argument they hear before making a decision. In light of these contrasting predictions, Norman Miller and Donald Campbell (1959) searched for the "missing link" that would determine the relative effects of primacy and recency. They discovered that the missing link is *time.* In a jury simulation study, they had people (1) read a summary of the plaintiff's case, (2) read a summary of the defendant's case, and (3) make a decision. The researchers varied how much time separated the two messages and then how much time elapsed between the second message and the decisions. When participants read the second message right after the first and then waited a whole week before reporting their opinion, a primacy effect prevailed, and the side that came first was favoured. Both messages faded equally from memory, so only the greater impact of first impressions was left. Yet when participants made a decision immediately after the second message but a full week after the first, there was a recency effect. The second argument was fresher in memory, thus favouring the side that went last. Using these results as a guideline, let's return to our original question: What is the impact on a jury in terms of the order of presentation? As you can see in the

TABLE 6.1

Effects of Presentation Order and Timing on Persuasion

A study by Miller and Campbell (1959) demonstrated the effect of presentation order and the timing of opposing arguments on persuasion.

	Conditions				Results
1. **Message 1**	**Message 2**	One week	Decision		**Primacy**
2. **Message 1**	One week	**Message 2**	Decision		**Recency**
3. **Message 1**	**Message 2**	Decision			None
4. **Message 1**	One week	**Message 2**	One week	Decision	None

third row of ■ Table 6.1, if the Defence proceeds immediately after the Crown finishes its case (no delay), there is no effect of presentation order.

Message Discrepancy Persuasion is a process of changing attitudes. But just how much change should be sought? Before addressing an audience, speakers confront what is perhaps the most critical strategic question: How extreme a position should they take? How *discrepant* should a message be from the audience's existing position in order to have the greatest impact? Common sense suggests two opposite answers. One approach is to take an extreme position in the hope that the more change you advocate, the more you get. Another approach is to exercise caution and not push for too much change so that the audience will not reject the message outright. Which approach seems more effective? Imagine trying to convert your politically conservative friends into liberals, or the other way around. Would you stake out a radical position in order to move them toward the centre, or would you preach moderation so as not to be cast aside?

Research shows that communicators should adopt the second, more cautious approach. To be sure, some discrepancy is needed to produce a change in attitude. But the relationship to persuasion can be pictured as an upside-down U, with the most change being produced at moderate amounts of discrepancy (Bochner & Insko, 1966). A study by Kari Edwards and Edward Smith (1996) helps to explain why taking a more extreme counter-attitudinal position is counterproductive. These investigators first measured people's attitudes on a number of hot social issues—for example, whether lesbian and gay couples should adopt children, or whether employers should give preference in hiring to minorities. Several weeks later, they asked these same people to read, think about, and rate arguments that were either consistent or inconsistent with their own prior attitudes. The result: When given arguments to read that preached attitudes that were discrepant from their own, the participants spent more time scrutinizing the material and judged the arguments to be weak. Apparently, people are quick to refute and reject persuasive messages they don't agree with. In fact, the more personally important an issue is to us, the more stubborn and resistant to change we become (Zuwerink & Devine, 1996).

CP/Ryan Remiorz

Before her death in 2005, Heather Crowe became a well-known face of the antismoking movement in Canada. Despite never having smoked a day in her life, she died of lung cancer. She believed this was the result of spending more than 40 years of her life as a waitress in a restaurant where she was surrounded by second-hand smoke.

Fear Appeals Many trial lawyers say that to win cases, they have to appeal to jurors through the heart rather than through the mind. The evidence is important, they admit; but what really matters is whether the jury reacts to their client with anger, disgust, sympathy, or sadness. Of course, very few messages are entirely based on rational argument or on emotion. And it's possible that the best approach to take depends on whether the attitude is rooted more in a person's beliefs or in his or her feelings about the object or issue in question (Edwards, 1990; Millar & Millar, 1990).

Fear is a particularly primitive and powerful emotion, serving as an early warning system that signals danger. Not surprisingly, the use of fear-based appeals to change attitudes has proven to be effective. Certain religious cults use scare tactics to indoctrinate new members. So do public health organizations that graphically portray the victims of cigarette smoking, drugs, overeating, drinking and driving, and unsafe sex. Political campaigns are notorious for negative advertising. The most hard-hitting and controversial negative ad ever was a TV commercial that aired just once, on September 7, 1964. In an ad to reelect then U.S. Democratic President Lyndon Johnson, running against Republican Barry Goldwater, a young girl pictured in a field counted to ten as she picked the petals off a daisy. As she reached nine, an adult voice broke in and counted down from ten to zero, followed by a nuclear explosion and this message: "Vote for President Johnson on November 3. The stakes are too high for you to stay home."

Is fear effective? If so, is it better to arouse a little nervousness or to trigger a full-blown anxiety attack? To answer these questions, social psychologists have compared the effects of communications that vary in the level of fear they arouse. In the first such study, Irving Janis and Seymour Feshbach (1953) found that high levels of fear arousal did not generate increased agreement with a communication. Since then, however, research has shown that high fear can be highly effective (de Hoog et al., 2007), particularly when information regarding an unfamiliar issue is being presented (De Pelsmacker, Cauberghe, & Dens, 2011).

Fear arousal increases the incentive to change for those who do not actively resist it, but its ultimate impact depends on the strength of the arguments and on whether the message also contains reassuring advice on how to avoid the threatened danger (Keller, 1999; Leventhal, 1970; Rogers, 1983). This last point is important. Without specific instructions on how to cope, people feel helpless, panic, and tune out the message. In one study, for example, participants with a chronic fear of cancer were less likely than others to detect the logical errors in a message that called for regular cancer checkups (Jepson & Chaiken, 1990). When clear instructions are included, however, high dosages of fear can be effective. Antismoking films that tell smokers how to quit thus elicit more negative attitudes about cigarettes when they show gory lung-cancer operations than charts filled with dry statistics (Leventhal et al., 1967). Driving-safety films are more effective when they show broken bones and bloody accident victims than controlled collisions involving plastic crash dummies (Rogers & Mewborn, 1976). In a recent meta-analysis of 105 studies, however, Natascha de Hoog and others (2007) found that communications that arouse fear need not be gruesome to be effective. Simply put, the more vulnerable people feel about a threatened outcome, the more attentive they are to the message and the more likely they are to follow the recommendations contained within it (Das et al., 2003; de Hoog et al., 2005).

Positive Emotions It's interesting that just as fear helps to induce a change in attitude, so do positive emotions. In one study, people were more likely to agree with a series of controversial arguments when they snacked on peanuts and soda than when they did not eat (Janis et al., 1965). In another study, participants liked a TV commercial more when it was embedded in a program that was upbeat rather than sad (Mathur & Chattopadhyay, 1991). Research shows that people are "soft touches" when they are in a good mood. Depending on the situation, food, drinks, a soft reclining chair, tender memories, a success experience, breathtaking scenery, and pleasant music can lull us into a positive emotional state ripe for persuasion (Schwarz et al., 1991).

According to Alice Isen (1984), people see the world through rose-coloured glasses when they are feeling good. Filled with high spirits, we become more sociable, more generous, and generally more positive in our outlook. We also make decisions more quickly and with relatively little thought. The result: positive feelings activate the peripheral route to persuasion, facilitating change and allowing superficial cues to take on added importance (Petty et al., 1993; Worth & Mackie, 1987).

What is it about feeling good that leads us to take shortcuts rather than the more effortful central route to persuasion? There are three possible explanations. One is that a positive emotional state is cognitively distracting, causing the mind to wander and impairing our ability to think critically about the persuasive arguments (Mackie & Worth, 1989; Mackie et al., 1992). A second explanation is that when people are in a good mood, they assume that all is well, let down their guard, and become somewhat lazy processors of information (Schwarz, 1990). A third explanation is that when people are happy, they become motivated to savour the moment and maintain their happy mood, not spoil it by thinking critically about new information (Wegener & Petty, 1994).

This last notion raises an interesting question: What if happy people were presented with a positive, uplifting persuasive message? Would they still appear cognitively distracted, or lazy, or would they pay close attention in order to prolong the rosy glow? To find out, Duane Wegener and his colleagues (1995) showed some U.S. college students a funny segment from the TV show *Late Night with David Letterman.* Others, less fortunate, watched a sombre scene from an HBO movie, *You Don't Have to Die.* All students were then asked to read and evaluate either an uplifting, pro-attitudinal article about a new plan to cut tuition, or a distressing, counter-attitudinal article about a new plan to raise tuition. In half the cases, the article they read contained strong arguments; in the others, the arguments were weak. Did the students read the material carefully enough to distinguish between the strong and weak arguments? Those in the sombre condition clearly did. Among those in the happy condition, however, the response depended on whether they expected the message to be one they wanted to hear. When the happy students read about a tuition increase, they tuned out and were equally persuaded by the strong and weak arguments. When they read about the proposal to cut tuition, however, they were persuaded more when the arguments were strong than when they were weak. Being in a good mood, and receiving a pro-attitudinal message that would not spoil it, these happy students took the effortful central route to persuasion.

Subliminal Messages In 1957, Vance Packard published *The Hidden Persuaders,* an exposé of techniques used by advertising agencies on New York's Madison Avenue. As the book climbed the bestseller list, it awakened in the public a fear of being manipulated by forces they could not see or hear. What had Packard uncovered? In the 1950s, amid growing fears of communism and the birth of rock 'n' roll, a number of advertisers were said to have used *subliminal advertising,* the presentation of commercial messages outside of conscious awareness. It all started in a drive-in movie theatre in New Jersey, where the words "Drink Coke" and "Eat popcorn" were secretly flashed on the screen during intermissions for a third of a millisecond. Although the audience never noticed the message, Coke sales were said to have increased 18 percent and popcorn sales 58 percent over a six-week period (Brean, 1958).

This incident was followed by many others. In 1958, the Canadian Broadcasting Corporation announced that they were going to present a subliminal message during a half-hour show, although the specific message ("telephone now") was not made public. While no increase in telephone usage was found, many viewers reported that they were suddenly hungry or thirsty. Apparently they erroneously attributed these feelings to what they expected the subliminal message to be, perhaps based on the reported results of the 'Eat Popcorn' study. Later, in books entitled *Subliminal Seduction* (1973) and *The Age of Manipulation* (1989), William Bryan Key charged that advertisers routinely sneak faint sexual images in visual ads to heighten the appeal of their products. Several years ago, concerns were also raised about subliminal messages in rock music. In one case, the families of two boys who committed suicide blamed the British rock group Judas Priest for subliminal lyrics ("Do it") that promoted Satanism and suicide (*National Law Journal,* 1990). Based in part on research presented by Canadian social psychologists John Vokey and J. Don Read (1985), the judge concluded that Judas Priest was not to blame as there was no evidence to support the idea of subliminal persuasion. Despite this, it's clear that many people believe in the power of hidden persuaders.

At the time of the New Jersey theatre scandal, research on the topic was so sketchy, and the public so outraged by the sinister implications, that the matter was quickly dropped. But today there is renewed interest in subliminal influences, as well as new research developments. In one recent field study, for example, researchers played traditional German or French music, on alternating days for two weeks, at a supermarket display of wines. Keeping track of sales, they found that of the total number of wines bought, 83 percent were German on German-music days and 65 percent were French on French-music days. Yet when asked the reasons for their choices, customers did not cite the music as a factor, suggesting that they were not aware of the effect it had on them (North et al., 1999).

In what has become a multimillion-dollar industry, companies today sell self-help videos, tapes, and CDs that play new age music or nature sounds and also contain fleeting messages that promise to help you relax, lose weight, stop smoking, make friends, raise self-esteem, and even improve your sex life. Can subliminal messages really trigger behaviour without our awareness? In 1982, Timothy Moore reviewed the existing research and concluded that "what you see is what you get"—nothing, "complete scams." Moore was right. The original Coke-and-popcorn incident was later exposed as a publicity stunt, a hoax (Pratkanis, 1992). In fact, controlled experiments on subliminal self-help CDs that promise to raise self-esteem, improve memory, or lose weight, show that they offer no therapeutic benefits (Greenwald et al., 1991; Merikle & Skanes, 1992).

If there is no solid evidence of subliminal influence, why, you may wonder, does research demonstrate perception without awareness in studies of priming, as we described in Chapter 4, but not in studies of subliminal persuasion? If you think about it, the two sets of claims are different. In the laboratory, subliminal exposures have a short-term effect on simple judgments and actions. But in claims of subliminal persuasion, the exposure is presumed to have long-term effects on eating and drinking, consumer purchases, voter sentiment, or even the most profound of violent acts, suicide. Psychologists agree that people can process information at an unconscious level, but they're also quick to note that this processing is "analytically limited" (Greenwald, 1992).

Erin Strahan and others (2002) suggest that although people *perceive* subliminal cues, those cues will not *persuade* them to take action unless they are already motivated to do so. To test this hypothesis, they brought thirsty University of Waterloo students into the lab for a marketing study and provided drinking water to some but not to others. Then, as part of a test administered by computer, they subliminally exposed these students to neutral words (*pirate, won*) or thirst-related words (*thirst, dry*). Did the subliminal "thirsty" message later lead the students, like automatons, to drink more in a taste test of the Kool-Aid beverages? Yes and no. ▶ Figure 6.9 shows that the subliminal thirst primes had little impact on students whose thirst had just been quenched, but they quite clearly increased consumption among those who were water-deprived and thirsty. For a subliminal message to influence behaviour, it has to strike "while the iron is hot."

Other researchers have since extended this interesting effect in important ways. In one study, participants who were subliminally presented with the name of a specific soft drink, Lipton Ice, were later more likely to report that they would select

Courtesy of American Association of Advertising Agencies

PEOPLE HAVE BEEN TRYING TO FIND THE BREASTS IN THESE ICE CUBES SINCE 1957.

The advertising industry is sometimes charged with sneaking seductive little pictures into ads.
 Supposedly, these pictures can get you to buy a product without your even seeing them.
 Consider the photograph above. According to some people, there's a pair of female breasts hidden in the patterns of light refracted by the ice cubes.
 Well, if you really searched you probably *could* see the breasts. For that matter, you could also see Millard Fillmore, a stuffed pork chop and a 1946 Dodge.
 The point is that so-called "subliminal advertising" simply doesn't exist. Overactive imaginations, however, most certainly do.
 So if anyone claims to see breasts in that drink up there, they aren't in the ice cubes.
 They're in the eye of the beholder.
ADVERTISING
ANOTHER WORD FOR FREEDOM OF CHOICE.
American Association of Advertising Agencies

For years, advertisers have defended against the charge that they embed suggestive and sexual images in print ads. This piece by the American Association of Advertising Agencies addresses the claim.

People are most easily persuaded by commercial messages that are presented without their awareness. **FALSE.**

▶**FIGURE 6.9**

Subliminal Influence

Thirsty and nonthirsty research participants were subliminally exposed to neutral or thirst-related words. Afterward they participated in a beverage taste test in which the amount they drank was measured. You can see that the subliminal thirst cues had little impact on nonthirsty participants, but they did increase consumption among those who were thirsty. Apparently, subliminal cues can influence our behaviour when we are otherwise predisposed.

(Strahan et al., 2002.)

Reprinted from *Journal of Experimental Social Psychology 38 (2002)*, Erin J. Strahan et al, Subliminal priming and persuasion: Striking while the iron is hot, 556-556, Copyright 2002, with permission from Elsevier.

need for cognition (NC)
A personality variable that distinguishes people on the basis of how much they enjoy effortful cognitive activities.

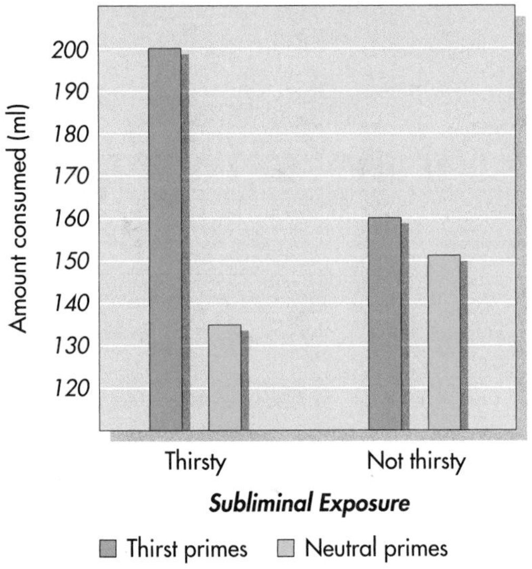

that particular brand over others—provided they were thirsty (Karremans, Stroebe, & Claus, 2006). In a second study, participants were subliminally presented with a logo for one brand of dextrose (a sugar pill) or another, after which they worked on a task that required intense concentration. The results showed that when given an opportunity to enhance their concentration, participants were more likely to select and consume the subliminally advertised brand than the other brand—provided they were mentally tired and in need of a boost (Bermeitinger et al., 2009).

The Audience

Although source and message factors are important, the astute communicator must also take his or her audience into account. Presentation strategies that succeed with some people fail with others. Audiences on the central route to persuasion, for example, bear little resemblance to those found strolling along the peripheral route. In this section, we'll see that the impact of a message is influenced by two additional factors: the recipient's personality and his or her expectations.

Right from the start, social psychologists tried to identify types of people who were more or less vulnerable to persuasion. But it turned out that very few individuals are *consistently* easy or difficult to persuade. Based on this insight, the search for individual and group differences is now guided by an interactionist perspective. Assuming that each of us can be persuaded more in some settings than in others, researchers look for an appropriate "match" between characteristics of the message and the audience. Thus we ask: What kinds of messages turn *you* on?

The Need For Cognition Earlier, we saw that people tend to process information more carefully when they are highly involved. Involvement can be determined by the importance and self-relevance of a message. According to Cacioppo and Petty (1982), however, there are also individual differences in the extent to which people become involved and take the central route to persuasion. Specifically, they have found that individuals differ in the extent to which they enjoy and participate in effortful cognitive activities, or, as they call it, the **need for cognition (NC)**. People who are high rather than low in their need for cognition like to work on hard problems, search for clues, make fine distinctions, and analyze situations. These differences can be identified by the items contained in the Need for Cognition Scale, some of which appear in ■ Table 6.2.

The need for cognition has interesting implications for changing attitudes. If people are prone to approach or avoid effortful cognitive activities, then the prepared communicator could design messages unique to a particular audience. In theory, the high-NC audience should receive information-oriented appeals, and the low-NC audience should be treated to appeals that rely on the use of peripheral cues. The theory is fine, but does it work? Can a message be customized to fit the information-processing style of its recipients? In one test of this hypothesis, participants read an editorial that consisted of either a strong or a weak set of arguments. As predicted, the higher their NC scores were, the more the participants thought about the material, the better they later recalled it, and the more persuaded they were by the strength of its arguments (Cacioppo et al., 1983).

In a recent example of this effect, Gale Sinatra and others (2012) measured students' attitudes toward climate change. Participants first completed a standard NC scale, as well as a "willingness to take action" scale created by the researchers. They then read a persuasive message discussing the negative impact of humans on climate change. They found that those participants who were high in NC were more persuaded by the message and subsequently expressed a greater willingness to take action on this issue, compared to those low in NC. While a strong argument can persuade people high in need for cognition, those who score lower on this measure are more likely to be persuaded by cues found along the peripheral route—such as a speaker's reputation and physical appearance, the reactions of others in the audience, and a positive mood state (Cacioppo et al., 1996). At times, they are mindlessly influenced by a reputable source even when his or her arguments are weak (Kaufman et al., 1999).

TABLE 6.2

Need for Cognition (NC) Scale: Sample Items

Are you high or low in the need for cognition? These statements are taken from the NC Scale. If you agree with items 1, 3, and 5 and disagree with items 2, 4, and 6, you would probably be regarded as high in NC.

(Cacioppo & Petty, 1982.)

1. I really enjoy a task that involves coming up with new solutions to problems.
2. Thinking is not my idea of fun.
3. The notion of thinking abstractly is appealing to me.
4. I like tasks that require little thought once I've learned them.
5. I usually end up deliberating about issues even when they do not affect me personally.
6. It's enough for me that something gets the job done; I don't care how or why it works.

Self-Monitoring Just as people high in the need for cognition crave information, other personality traits are associated with an attraction to other kinds of messages. Consider the trait of *self-monitoring.* As described in Chapter 3, high self-monitors regulate their behaviour from one situation to another out of concern for public self-presentation. Low self-monitors are less image conscious and behave instead according to their own beliefs and preferences. In the context of persuasion, high self-monitors may be particularly responsive to messages that promise desirable social images. Whether the product is beer, soda, blue jeans, or cars, this technique is common in advertising, where often the image is the message.

To test the self-monitoring hypothesis, Mark Snyder and Kenneth DeBono (1985) showed image- or information-oriented print ads to high and low self-monitors. In an ad for Irish Mocha Mint coffee, for example, a man and woman were depicted as relaxing in a candlelit room over a steamy cup of coffee. The image-oriented version promised to "Make a chilly night become a cozy evening," while the informational version offered "A delicious blend of three great flavours—coffee, chocolate, and mint." As predicted, high self-monitors were willing to pay more for products after reading imagery ads, while low self-monitors were influenced more by the information-oriented appeals (see Figure 6.10). Imagery can even influence the way high self-monitors evaluate a product, independent of its quality. DeBono and others (2003) presented people with one of two perfume samples packaged in more or

FIGURE 6.10

Informational and Image-Oriented Ads: The Role of Self-Monitoring

High and low self-monitors estimated how much they would pay for products presented in image-oriented or informational magazine ads. As shown, high image-oriented self-monitors preferred products depicted in image-oriented ads (left), while low self-monitors preferred those depicted in informational ads (right).

(Snyder & DeBono, 1985.)

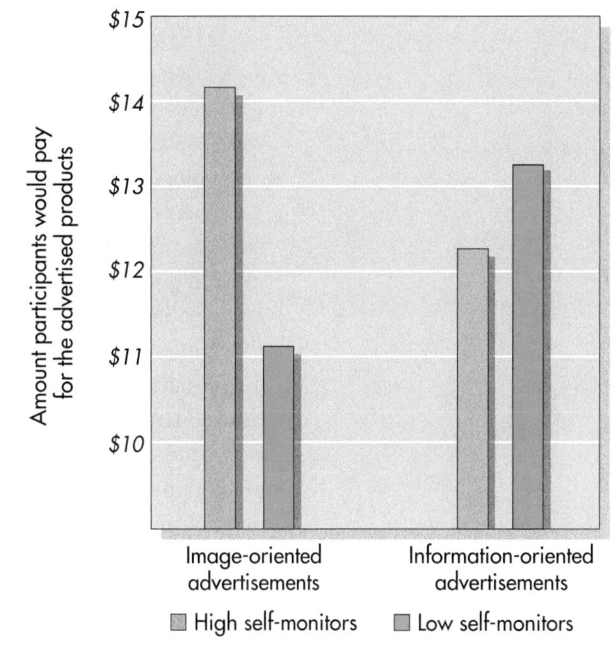

TABLE 6.3

Strategies for Resisting Persuasion

Strategy	Example
Attitude bolstering	"I reassure myself of facts that support the validity of my belief."
Counter-arguing	"I would talk to myself and play devil's advocate."
Social validation	"I also rely on others with the same opinion to be there for me."
Negative affect	"I tend to get angry when someone tries to change my beliefs."
Assertions of confidence	"I doubt anybody could change my viewpoint."
Selective exposure	"Most of the time I just ignore them."
Source derogation	"I look for faults in the person presenting the challenging belief."

(Jacks & Cameron, 2003.)

"Strategies for Resisting Persuasion" by Jacks and Cameron. *Basic and Applied Social Psychology, 25, 145-161.* Reprinted by permission of the publisher (Taylor & Francis Ltd, http://www.tandf.co.uk/journals.)

less attractive bottles. Whereas low self-monitors preferred the more pleasant-scented fragrance, high self-monitors preferred whatever scent came from the more attractive bottles.

Forewarning and Resistance When our attitudes or values come under attack, we can succumb to the challenge and change the attitude, or we can resist it and maintain the attitude. There are different means of resistance. In a series of studies, Julia Jacks and Kimberly Cameron (2003) asked people to describe and rate the ways in which they manage to resist persuasion in their attitudes on abortion or the death penalty. They identified seven strategies—the most common being attitude bolstering ("I think about all the reasons I believe the way I do"), and the least common being source derogation ("I look for faults in the person who challenges my belief"). These means of resistance are listed in ■ Table 6.3.

What leads people to invoke these mechanisms of resistance? Does it help to be forewarned that your attitude is about to come under attack? Perhaps the toughest audience to persuade is the one that knows you're coming. When people are aware that someone is trying to change their attitude, they become more likely to resist. All they need is some time to collect their thoughts and come up with a good defence. Jonathan Freedman and David Sears (1965) first discovered this when they told high school students to expect a speech on why teenagers should not be allowed to drive (an unpopular position, as you can imagine). The students were warned either 2 or 10 minutes before the talk began, or not at all. Those who were the victims of a sneak attack were the most likely to succumb to the speaker's position. Those who had a full 10 minutes' warning were the least likely to agree. To be forewarned is to be forearmed. But why?

At least two processes are at work here. To understand them, let's take a closer look at what forewarning does. Participants in the Freedman and Sears (1965) study were put on notice in two ways: (1) They were informed of the position the speaker would take, and (2) they were told that the speaker intended to change their attitudes. Psychologically, these two aspects of forewarning have different effects.

The first effect is purely cognitive. Knowing in advance what position a speaker will take enables us to come up with counter-arguments and, as a result, to become more resistant to change. To explain this effect, William McGuire (1964) drew an analogy: Protecting a person's attitudes from persuasion, he said, is like inoculating the human body against disease. In medicine, injecting a small dose of infection into a patient stimulates the body to build up a resistance to it. According to this **inoculation hypothesis**, an attitude can be immunized the same way. As with flu shots and other vaccines, our defences can be reinforced by exposure to weak doses of the opposing position before we actually encounter the full presentation. Studies of negative political ads show that inoculation can be used to combat the kinds of attack messages that sometimes win elections (Pfau et al., 1990).

inoculation hypothesis
The idea that exposure to weak versions of a persuasive argument increases later resistance to that argument.

Simply knowing that someone is trying to persuade us also elicits a motivational reaction as we brace ourselves to resist the attempt regardless of what position is taken. As a TV viewer, you have no doubt heard the phrase "And now, we pause for a message from our sponsor." What does this warning tell us? Not knowing yet who the sponsor is, even the grouchiest among us is in no position to object. Yet imagine how you would feel if an experimenter said to you, "In just a few minutes, you will hear a message prepared according to well-established principles of persuasion and designed to induce you to change your attitudes." If you are like the participants who actually heard this forewarning, you might be tempted to reply, "Oh yeah? Try me!" Indeed, subjects rejected that message without counter-argument and without much advance notice (Hass & Grady, 1975).

When people think that someone is trying to change their attitude or otherwise manipulate them, a red flag goes up. That red flag is called **psychological reactance**. According to Jack Brehm's theory of psychological reactance, all of us want the freedom to think, feel, and act as we (not others) choose. When we sense that a cherished freedom is being threatened, we become motivated to maintain it. And when we sense that a freedom is slipping away, we try to restore it (Brehm & Brehm, 1981). One possible result is that when a communicator comes on too strong, we may react with *negative attitude change,* by moving in the direction opposite to the one advocated—even, ironically, when the speaker's position agrees with our own (Heller et al., 1973). As Kyle Murray and Gerald Häubl, marketing professors at the University of Alberta warn, "Given the risks of triggering psychological reactance among current and potential users, market leaders should be careful about becoming too dominant and appearing too *successful.* Ironically, it may be good business to support and even cultivate competitors" (2012, p. 14). Sometimes, the motive to protect our freedom to think as we choose trumps our desire to hold a specific opinion. Reactance can trigger resistance to persuasion in two ways. Once aroused, the reactant target of attempted persuasion may simply shut down in a reflex-like response, or disagree in a more thoughtful manner by questioning the credibility of the source and counter-arguing the message (Silvia, 2006).

In a series of print ads with the slogan "Think different," Apple Computer paid tribute to Albert Einstein, Muhammad Ali, Pablo Picasso (shown here with Apple CEO Steve Jobs), and other creative geniuses. In a highly individualistic campaign, Apple saluted "The crazy ones. The misfits. The rebels. The troublemakers. The round pegs in the square holes. The ones who see things differently."

However, forewarning does not always increase resistance to persuasion, because the effects are not that simple. Based on a meta-analysis of 48 experiments, Wendy Wood and Jeffrey Quinn (2003) found that when people are forewarned about an impending persuasive appeal on a topic that is personally not that important, they start to agree before they even receive the message in order to keep from appearing vulnerable to influence. Yet when people are forewarned about a persuasive appeal on a topic that is of personal importance, they feel threatened and think up counter-arguments to bolster their attitude. This cognitive response strengthens their resistance to change once that appeal is delivered.

"To do just the opposite is also a form of imitation."
—Lichtenberg

Culture and Persuasion

A message is persuasive to the extent that it meets the psychological needs of its audience. In this regard, cultural factors also play a subtle but important role. In earlier chapters, we saw that cultures differ in the extent to which they are oriented toward individualism versus collectivism. In light of these differences, Sang-Pil Han and Sharon Shavitt (1994) compared the contents of magazine advertisements in the United States, an individualistic country, and Korea, a country with a collectivistic orientation. They found that while U.S. advertising slogans were focused more on personal benefits, individuality, competition, and self-improvement ("She's got a style all her own," "Make your way through the crowd"), Korean ads appealed more to the integrity, achievement, and well-being of one's family and other ingroups ("An exhilarating way to provide for

psychological reactance
The theory that people react against threats to their freedom by asserting themselves and perceiving the threatened freedom as more attractive.

your family," "Celebrating a half-century of partnership"). Clearly, there are different ways to appeal to the members of these two cultures as can be seen in the way celebrity endorsements are used in the two cultures. In the United States, celebrities tend to portray themselves using or talking directly about a product; in Korean commercials that appeal to belongingness, family, and traditional values, celebrities are more likely to play the role of someone else without being singled out (Choi et al., 2005). To be persuasive, a message should appeal to the culturally shared values of its audience.

Persuasion by Our Own Actions

Anyone who has ever acted on stage knows how easy it is to become so absorbed in a role that the experience seems real. Feigned laughter can make an actor feel happy, and crocodile tears can turn into sadness.

Role-Playing: All the World's a Stage

Most of us know how it feels to be coaxed into behaviour that is at odds with our inner convictions. People frequently engage in attitude-discrepant behaviour as part of a job, for example, or to please others. As commonplace as this seems, it raises a profound question. When we play along, saying and doing things that are privately discrepant from our own attitudes, do we begin to change those attitudes as a result? How we feel can determine the way we act. Is it also possible that the way we act can determine how we feel?

According to Irving Janis (1968), attitude change persists more when it is inspired by our own behaviour than when it stems from passive exposure to a persuasive communication. Janis conducted a study in which one group of participants listened to a speech that challenged their positions on a topic, and others were handed an outline and asked to give the speech themselves. As predicted, participants changed their attitudes more after giving the speech than after listening to it (Janis & King, 1954). According to Janis, role-playing works because it forces people to learn the message. That is why people remember arguments they come up with on their own better than they remember arguments provided by others (Slamecka & Graff, 1978). In fact, attitude change is more enduring even when people who read a persuasive message merely *expect* that they will later have to communicate it to others (Boninger et al., 1990).

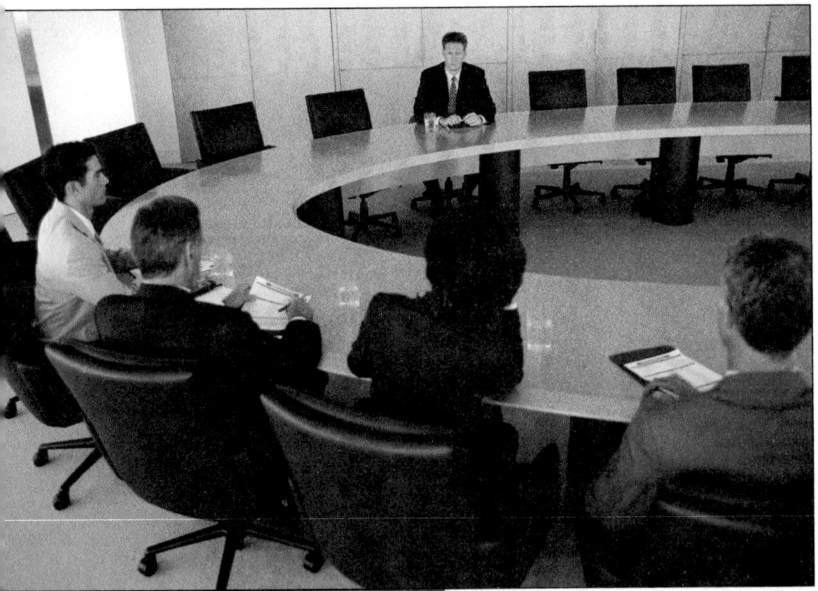

© Larry Hirshowitz/CORBIS

In a job interview, candidates typically try their best to show they are a good "fit" to the organization, even if this is a little bit of an act. But what happens after they get the job? Do their existing attitudes determine their actions, or does their new role ultimately reshape their attitudes?

But there's more to role-playing than improved memory. The effects of enacting a role can be staggering, in part because it is so easy to confuse what we do, or what we say, with how we really feel. Consider one of the most compelling examples of the power of role-playing to change behaviour, and also perhaps to influence attitudes.

The Stanford Prison Study It is no secret that many prisons are overcrowded and that the situation has worsened as a result of recently toughened sentencing guidelines. It is also no secret that prison life can be cruel, violent, and degrading. The setting is highly oppressive and regimented, many prison guards are abusive, and many inmates fall into a state of despair (Paulus, 1988). Thus, it is natural for social psychologists to wonder: Is there something in the situation, or in the individuals, that leads guards and prisoners to behave as they do? Would the rest of us react in the same way?

For ethical reasons, one obviously cannot place research participants inside a real prison. So, many years ago, a team of researchers from Stanford University did the next best thing. They constructed their own prison in the basement of the psychology department building (Haney et al., 1973; Haney & Zimbardo, 1998; Zimbardo et al., 1973). Complete with iron-barred cells, a solitary-confinement closet, and a recreation area for guards, the facility housed 21 participants—all healthy and stable men between the ages of 17 and 30 who had answered a newspaper ad promising $15 a day for a two-week study of prison life. By the flip of a coin, half the participants were designated as guards and the other half became prisoners. Neither group was told specifically how to fulfill its role.

On the first day, each of the participant prisoners was unexpectedly "arrested" at his home, booked, fingerprinted, and driven to the simulated prison by officers of the local police department. These prisoners were then stripped, searched, and dressed in loose-fitting smocks with an identification number, a nylon stocking to cover their hair, and rubber sandals. A chain was bolted to the ankle of each prisoner. The guards were dressed in khaki uniforms and supplied with nightsticks, handcuffs, reflector sunglasses, keys, and whistles. The rules specified that prisoners were to be called by number, routinely lined up to be counted, fed three bland meals, and permitted three supervised toilet visits per day. The stage was set. It remained to be seen just how seriously the participants would take their roles and react to one another in this novel setting.

The events of the next few days were startling. Filled with a sense of power and authority, a few guards became progressively more abusive. They harassed the inmates, forced them into crowded cells, woke them during the night, and subjected them to hard labour and solitary confinement. These guards were particularly cruel when they thought they were alone with a prisoner. The prisoners themselves were rebellious at first, but their efforts were met with retaliation. Soon they all became passive and demoralized. After 36 hours, the experimenters had to release their first prisoner, who was suffering from acute depression. On subsequent days, other prisoners had to be released. By the sixth day, those who remained were so shaken by the experience that the study was terminated. It is reassuring, if not remarkable, that after a series of debriefing sessions, participants seemed to show no signs of lasting distress.

This study has been criticized on methodological and ethical grounds (Banuazizi & Movahedi, 1975; Savin, 1973). Still, the results are fascinating. Within a brief period of time, under relatively mild conditions, and with a group of men not prone to violence, the Stanford study recreated some of the prisoner and guard behaviours actually found behind prison walls. Were they simply carrying out their assigned roles, or had the role also changed their attitudes, so that once well meaning individuals—now in the role of a guard—could justify their dehumanizing treatment of the mock-prisoners?

Wondering if these same findings would emerge today in the twenty-first century, social psychologists Steve Reicher and Alex Haslam (2006) worked in the spring of 2002 with the British Broadcasting Corporation (BBC) to create a survivor-like reality TV special called *The Experiment*, modelled after Zimbardo's study. Shown in four episodes, the television special brought together 15 men, all of whom were carefully screened, were warned that they would be exposed to hardships, and were randomly assigned to prisoner and guard roles. Determined to set limits, monitor events closely, and adhere to ethical guidelines for research with human subjects,

Haslam and Reicher did not fully recreate the conditions of the original study and did not observe the same kinds of brutality from the guards. In their view, these findings challenge the conclusion that normal people can be dehumanized by the mere assignment to institutional roles.

One other profound question has arisen concerning the Stanford prison study: Did the behaviour of guards reflect on the power of the situation they were in, or were the men who took part in the study uniquely prone to violence? Recently, Thomas Carnahan and Sam McFarland (2007) posted two newspaper ads—one, like Zimbardo's, for a study on prison life; the other, identical in every way except that it omitted the words "prison life." Those who volunteered for the prison study scored higher on tests that measure aggressiveness, authoritarianism, and narcissism, and lower on tests that measure empathy and altruism. Reflecting on the differences, these researchers suggested that, rather than the roles being to blame, perhaps the Stanford prison study had attracted individuals who were prone to antisocial behaviour. In response, Haney and Zimbardo (2009) note that volunteers in the original study were also tested and that no personality differences were found between them and the general population. More importantly, they note, no differences were found between those assigned to prisoner and guard roles within the experiment.

Reiterating his belief in the power of the situation, Zimbardo (2007) points to the striking parallels between the behaviours observed in his simulated prison and the sadistic abuses of real prisoners in 2004, more than 30 years later, by military guards at the Abu Ghraib Prison in Iraq. Indeed, the defense statements of several of the guards on trial for Abu Ghraib abuses included the claim that they were 'just following orders.' Noting that various social psychological factors create a "perfect storm" that leads good people to behave in evil ways, Zimbardo refers to this unfortunate transformation as the "Lucifer Effect," named after God's favourite angel, Lucifer, who fell from grace and ultimately became Satan.

On a much smaller scale than the prison example indicates, think about the times you've dished out compliments you didn't mean, or smiled at someone you didn't like, or nodded your head in response to a statement you disagreed with. We often shade what we say just to please a particular listener. What's fascinating is not that we make adjustments to suit others, but that this role-playing has such powerful effects on our own private attitudes. For example, participants in one study read about a man and then described him to someone else, who supposedly liked or disliked him. As you might expect, participants described the man in more positive terms when their listener was favourably disposed. In the process, however, they also convinced themselves. At least to some extent, "saying is believing" (Higgins & Rholes, 1978).

Consider the implications. We know that attitudes influence behaviour—as when people help those whom they like and hurt those whom they dislike. But research on role-playing emphasizes the flip side of the coin—that behaviour can determine attitudes. Perhaps we come to like people because we have helped them and blame people whom we have hurt. To change people's inner feelings, then, maybe we should begin by focusing on their behaviour. Why do people experience changes of attitude in response to changes in their own behaviour? One answer to this question is provided by the theory of cognitive dissonance.

Cognitive Dissonance Theory: The Classic Version

Many social psychologists believe that people are strongly motivated by a desire for cognitive consistency—a state of mind in which one's beliefs, attitudes, and behaviours are all compatible with each other (Abelson et al., 1968). Cognitive consistency theories seem to presuppose that people are generally logical. However, Leon Festinger (1957) turned this assumption on its head. Struck by the irrationalities of human behaviour, Festinger proposed **cognitive dissonance theory**, which states that a powerful motive to maintain cognitive consistency can give rise to irrational and sometimes maladaptive behaviour.

TABLE 6.4

Ways to Reduce Dissonance

"I need to be on a diet, yet I just dived headfirst into a tub of chocolate fudge brownie ice cream." If this were you, how would you reduce dissonance aroused by the discrepancy between your attitude and your behavior?

Techniques	Examples
Change your attitude.	"I don't really need to be on a diet."
Change your perception of the behaviour.	"I hardly ate any ice cream."
Add consonant cognitions.	"Chocolate ice cream is very nutritious."
Minimize the importance of the conflict.	"I don't care if I'm overweight—life is short!"
Reduce perceived choice.	"I had no choice; the ice cream was served for this special occasion."

According to Festinger, all of us hold many cognitions about ourselves and the world around us. These cognitions include everything we know about our own beliefs, attitudes, and behaviour. Although generally our cognitions coexist peacefully, at times they clash. Consider some examples. You say you're on a diet, yet you just dived headfirst into a chocolate mousse. Or you waited in line for hours to get into a rock concert, and then the band was disappointing. Or you baked for hours under the hot summer sun, even though you knew of the health risks. Each of these scenarios harbours inconsistency and conflict. You have already committed yourself to one course of action, yet you realize that what you did is inconsistent with your attitude.

Under certain specific conditions, discrepancies such as these can evoke an unpleasant state of tension known as cognitive dissonance. But discrepancy doesn't always produce dissonance. If you broke a diet for a Thanksgiving dinner with the family, your indiscretion would not lead you to experience dissonance. Or if you mistakenly thought the ice cream you ate was low in calories, only later to find out the truth, then, again, you would not experience much dissonance. As we'll see, what really hurts is knowing that you committed yourself to an attitude-discrepant behaviour freely and with some knowledge of the consequences. When that happens, dissonance is aroused, and you become motivated to reduce it. There are many possible ways to do so, as shown in ■ Table 6.4. These include rationalizing that everyone else is also a hypocrite (McKimmie et al., 2003), denying personal responsibility for the behaviour (Gosling et al., 2006), and trivializing the issue in question (Starzyk et al., 2009). Often, the easiest way is to change your attitude to bring it in line with your behaviour.

"Man is the only animal that learns by being hypocritical. He pretends to be polite and then, eventually, he becomes polite."

—Jean Kerr

Right from the start, cognitive dissonance theory captured the imagination. Festinger's basic proposition is simple, yet its implications are far-reaching. In this section, we examine three research areas that demonstrate the breadth of what dissonance theory has to say about attitude change.

Justifying Attitude-Discrepant Behaviour: When Doing Is Believing Imagine for a moment that you are a participant in a classic study by Leon Festinger and J. Merrill Carlsmith (1959). As soon as you arrive, you are greeted by an experimenter who says that he is interested in various measures of performance. Wondering what that means, you all too quickly find out. The experimenter hands you a wooden board containing 48 square pegs in square holes and asks you to turn each peg a quarter turn to the left, then a quarter turn back to the right, then back to the left, then back again to the right. The routine seems endless. After 30 minutes, the experimenter comes to your rescue. Or does he? Just when you think things are looking up, he hands you another board, another assignment. For the next half-hour, you are to take 12 spools of thread off the board, put them back, take them off, and put them back again. By now, you're just about ready to tear your hair out. As you think back over better times, even the first task begins to look good.

cognitive dissonance theory
The theory that holding inconsistent cognitions arouses psychological tension that people become motivated to reduce.

"It's a crazy idea, but it just might work."

One way to reduce dissonance is to minimize the importance of the conflict.

Finally, you're done. After one of the longest hours of your life, the experimenter lets you in on a secret: There's more to this experiment than meets the eye. You were in the control group. To test the effects of motivation on performance, other participants are being told that the experiment will be fun and exciting. You don't realize it, but you are now being set up for the critical part of the study. Would you be willing to tell the next participant that the experiment is enjoyable? As you hem and haw, the experimenter offers to pay for your services. Some participants are offered \$1; others are offered \$20. In either case, you agree to help out. Before you know it, you find yourself in the waiting room trying to dupe an unsuspecting fellow student (who is really a confederate).

By means of this elaborate, staged presentation, participants were goaded into an attitude-discrepant behaviour, an action that was inconsistent with their private attitudes. They knew how dull the experiment really was, yet they raved about it. Did this conflict arouse cognitive dissonance? It depends on how much the participants were paid. Suppose you were one of the lucky ones offered \$20 for your assistance. By today's standards, that payment would be worth \$80—surely a sufficient justification for telling a little white lie, right? Feeling well compensated, these participants experienced little if any dissonance. But wait. Suppose you were paid only \$1. Surely your integrity is worth more than that, don't you think? In this instance, you have **insufficient justification** for going along—so you need a way to cope. According to Festinger (1957), unless you can deny your actions (which is not usually possible), you'll feel pressured to change your attitude about the task. If you can convince yourself that the experiment wasn't that bad, then saying it was interesting is all right.

The results were just as Festinger and Carlsmith had predicted. When the experiment was presumably over, participants were asked how they felt about the pegboard tasks. Those in the control group who did not mislead a confederate openly admitted that the tasks were boring. So did those in the \$20 condition, who had ample justification for what they did. However, participants who were paid only \$1 rated the experiment as somewhat enjoyable. Having engaged in an attitude-discrepant act without sufficient justification, these participants reduced cognitive dissonance by changing their attitude. The results can be seen in ▶ Figure 6.11.

Two aspects of this classic study are noteworthy. First, it showed the phenomenon of self-persuasion: When people behave in ways that contradict their attitudes, they sometimes go on to change those attitudes—without exposure to a persuasive communication. Demonstrating the power of this phenomenon, Michael Leippe and Donna Eisenstadt (1994) found that white students who were coaxed into writing essays in favour of new scholarship funds only for black students later reported more favourable attitudes in general toward Blacks in general. The second major contribution of Festinger and Carlsmith's results is that they contradicted the time-honoured belief that big rewards produce greater change. In fact, the more money participants were offered for their inconsistent behaviour, the more justified they felt and the less likely they were to change their attitudes.

insufficient justification
A condition in which people freely perform an attitude-discrepant behaviour without receiving a large reward.

insufficient deterrence
A condition in which people refrain from engaging in a desirable activity, even when only mild punishment is threatened.

Just as a small reward provides insufficient justification for attitude-discrepant behaviour, mild punishment is **insufficient deterrence** for attitude-discrepant *non*-behaviour. Think about it. What happens when people refrain from doing something they really want to do? Do they devalue the activity and convince themselves that they never really wanted to do it in the first place? In one study, children were prohibited from playing with an attractive toy by being threatened with a mild or a severe punishment. All participants refrained. As cognitive dissonance theory predicts, however, only those faced with the mild punishment—an insufficient deterrent—later showed disdain for the forbidden toy. Those who confronted the threat of severe punishment did not (Aronson & Carlsmith, 1963). Once again, cognitive dissonance theory turned common sense on its head: the less severe the threatened punishment, the greater the attitude change produced.

▶ FIGURE 6.11

The Dissonance Classic

Participants in a boring experiment (attitude) were asked to say that it was enjoyable (behaviour) to a fellow student. Those in one group were paid $1 to lie; those in a second group were offered $20. Members of a third group, who did not have to lie, admitted that the task was boring. So did the participants paid $20—ample justification for what they did. Participants paid only $1, however, rated the task as more enjoyable. Behaving in an attitude-discrepant manner without justification, the $1 participants reduced dissonance by changing their attitude.

(Festinger & Carlsmith, 1959.)

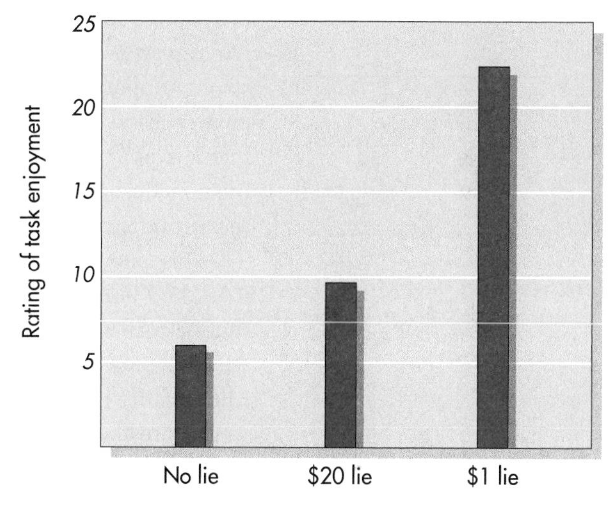

From "Cognitive Consequences of Forced Compliance," by L. Festinger and J.M. Carlsmith (1959), *Journal of Abnormal and Social Psychology, 58, 203-210.* Reprinted with permission.

Justifying Effort: Coming to Like What We Suffer For Have you ever spent tons of money or tried really hard to achieve something, only to discover later that it wasn't worth all the effort? This kind of inconsistency between effort and outcome can arouse cognitive dissonance and motivate a change of heart toward the unsatisfying outcome. The hypothesis is simple but profound: we alter our attitudes to justify our suffering.

In a classic test of this hypothesis, Elliot Aronson and Judson Mills (1959) invited female students to take part in a series of group discussions about sex. But there was a hitch. Because sex is a sensitive topic, participants were told that they would have to pass an "embarrassment test" before joining the group. The test consisted of reading sexual material aloud in front of a male experimenter. One group of participants experienced what amounted to a *severe* initiation in which they had to recite obscene words and lurid passages taken from paperback novels. A second group underwent a *mild* initiation in which they read a list of more ordinary words pertaining to sex. A third group was admitted to the discussions without an initiation test.

Moments later, all participants were given headphones and permitted to eavesdrop on the group they would soon be joining. Actually, what they heard was a tape-recorded discussion about "secondary sex behaviour in the lower animals." It was dreadfully boring. When it was over, participants were asked to rate how much they liked the group members and their discussion. Keep in mind what dissonance theory predicts: The more time or money or effort you choose to invest in something, the more anxious you will feel if the outcome proves disappointing. One way to cope with this inconsistency is to alter your attitudes. That's exactly what happened. Participants who had endured a severe initiation rated the discussion group more favourably than did those who had endured little or no initiation.

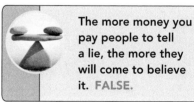

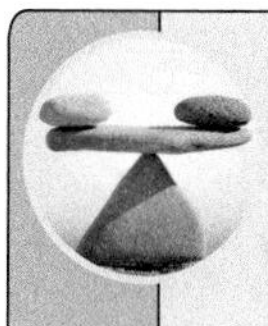

The more money you pay people to tell a lie, the more they will come to believe it. FALSE.

Social embarrassment is not the only kind of "effort" we feel the need to justify to ourselves. As a general rule, the more you pay for something—whether you pay in physical exertion, pain, time, or money—the more you will come to like it. This principle has provocative implications. For example, research suggests that the harder psychotherapy patients have to work at their own treatment, the more likely they are to feel better when that treatment is over (Axsom, 1989; Axsom & Cooper, 1985).

Justifying Difficult Decisions: When Good Choices Get Even Better Whenever we make difficult decisions—whether to marry, what school to attend, or what job to accept—we feel dissonance. By definition, a decision is difficult when the alternative courses of action are about equally desirable. Marriage offers comfort and stability; staying single enables us to seek out exciting new relationships. One job might pay more money; the other might involve more interesting work. Once people make tough decisions like these, they are at risk, as negative aspects of the chosen alternatives and positive aspects of the alternatives not chosen are at odds with their decisions. According to dissonance theory, people rationalize whatever they decide by exaggerating the positive features of the chosen alternative and the negative features of the unchosen alternative.

In an early test of this hypothesis, Jack Brehm (1956) asked female participants to evaluate various consumer products, presumably as part of a marketing research project. After rating a toaster, a coffee pot, a radio, a stopwatch, and other products, participants were told that they could take one home as a gift. In the high-dissonance condition, they were offered a difficult choice between two items they found equally attractive. In the low-dissonance group, they were offered an easier choice between a desirable and an undesirable item. After receiving the gift, participants read a few research reports and then reevaluated all the products. The results provided strong support for dissonance theory. In the low-dissonance group, the participants' post-decision ratings were about the same as their predecision ratings. But in the high-dissonance condition, ratings increased for the chosen item and decreased for the nonchosen item. Participants torn between two equivalent alternatives coped by reassuring themselves that they had made the right choice.

People often come to like what they suffer for. TRUE.

This phenomenon appears in a wide range of settings. For example, Robert Knox and James Inskter (1968) took dissonance theory to the racetrack and found that bettors who had already placed $2 bets on a horse were more optimistic about winning than were those still standing in line. Similarly, Dennis Regan and Martin Kilduff (1988) visited several polling stations on election day and found that voters were more likely to think that their candidates would win when interviewed after submitting their ballots than before. Since bets and votes cannot be taken back, people who had committed themselves to a decision were motivated to reduce post-decision dissonance. So they convinced themselves that the decision they made was right.

Cognitive Dissonance Theory: A New Look

Following in Festinger's bold footsteps, generations of social psychologists have studied and refined the basic theory (Cooper, 2007; Harmon-Jones & Mills, 1999). Nobody disputes the fact that when people are gently coaxed into performing an attitude-discrepant behaviour, they often go on to change their attitudes. In fact, people will feel discomfort and change their attitudes when they disagree with others in a group (Matz & Wood, 2005) or even when they observe inconsistent behaviour from others with whom they identify—a process of vicarious dissonance (Cooper & Hogg, 2007). Researchers have also examined possible perceptual consequences of cognitive dissonance. In one study, Emily Balcetis and David Dunning (2007) took students to the crowded centre of campus and asked them to put on—and walk around in—a costume consisting of a grass skirt, a coconut bra, a flower lei around the neck, and a plastic fruit basket on the head. Embarrassing as it was to appear this way in public, all the participants walked across campus in this costume. In a high-choice condition, they were led to believe that they could decline in favour of a different task (insufficient justification). In a low-choice condition, they were told that no alternative tasks were available (sufficient justification). How bad was it? Afterward, all the students were asked to estimate the distance they had walked from one point to the other. Needing to justify their embarrassing antics, those in the high-choice condition underestimated how far they had walked relative to those in the low-choice condition. Apparently, the motivation to reduce dissonance can alter our visual representations of the natural environment.

Through systematic research, however, it became evident early on that Festinger's (1957) original theory was not to be the last word. People do change their attitudes to justify attitude-discrepant behaviour, effort, and difficult decisions. But for dissonance to be aroused, certain conditions must be present. As first summarized by Joel Cooper and Russell Fazio's (1984) "new look" at dissonance theory, we now have a pretty good idea of what those conditions are.

Getty Images

Suggesting that people need to justify difficult irrevocable decisions to quell the dissonance they arouse, researchers found that gamblers who had already bet on a horse rated themselves as more certain of winning than those who were still waiting to place a bet.

According to Cooper and Fazio, four steps are necessary for the arousal and reduction of dissonance. First, the attitude-discrepant behaviour must produce unwanted *negative consequences.* Recall the initial Festinger and Carlsmith (1959) study. Not only did participants say something they knew to be false, they also deceived a fellow student into taking part in a painfully boring experiment. Had these participants lied without causing hardship, they would *not* have changed their attitudes to justify the action (Cooper et al., 1974). To borrow an expression from schoolyard basketball, "no harm, no foul." In fact, it appears that negative consequences arouse dissonance even when people's actions are consistent with their attitudes—as when college students who wrote against fee hikes were led to believe that their essays had backfired, prompting a university committee to favour an increase (Scher & Cooper, 1989).

The second necessary step in the process is a feeling of *personal responsibility* for the unpleasant outcomes of behaviour. Personal responsibility consists of two factors. The first is the freedom of *choice.* When people believe they had no choice but to act as they did, there is no dissonance and no attitude change (Linder et al., 1967). Had Festinger and Carlsmith coerced participants into raving about the boring experiment, the participants would not have felt the need to further justify what they did by changing their attitudes. But the experimental situation led participants to think that their actions were voluntary and that the choice was theirs. Pressured without realizing it, participants believed that they did not have to comply with the experimenter's request.

For people to feel personally responsible, they must also believe that the potential negative consequences of their actions were *foreseeable* at the time (Goethals et al., 1979). When the outcome could not realistically have been anticipated, then there's no dissonance and no attitude change. Had Festinger and Carlsmith's participants lied in private, only later to find out that their statements had been tape-recorded for subsequent use, then, again, they would not have felt the need to further justify their behaviour.

The third necessary step in the process is physiological *arousal.* Right from the start, Festinger viewed cognitive dissonance as a state of discomfort and tension that people seek to reduce—much like hunger, thirst, and other basic drives. Research has shown that this emphasis was well placed. In a study by Robert Croyle and Joel Cooper (1983), participants wrote essays that supported or contradicted their own attitudes. Some were ordered to do so, but others were led to believe that the choice was theirs. During the session, electrodes were attached to each participant's fingertips to record physiological arousal. As predicted by cognitive dissonance theory, those who freely wrote attitude-discrepant essays were the most aroused—an observation made by other researchers as well (Elkin & Leippe, 1986). In fact, participants who write attitude-discrepant essays in a "free-choice" situation report feeling high levels of discomfort—which subside once they change their attitudes (Elliot & Devine, 1994).

The fourth step in the dissonance process is closely related to the third. It isn't enough to feel generally aroused. The person must also make an *attribution* for that arousal to his or her own behaviour. Suppose you just lied to a friend, or studied for an exam that was cancelled, or made a tough decision that you might soon regret. Suppose further that although you are upset, you believe that your discomfort is caused by some external factor, not by your dissonance-producing behaviour. Under these circumstances, will you exhibit attitude change as a symptom of cognitive dissonance? Probably not. When participants were led to attribute their dissonance-related arousal to a drug they had supposedly taken (Zanna & Cooper, 1974), to the anticipation of painful electric shocks (Pittman, 1975), or to a pair of prism goggles that they had to wear (Losch & Cacioppo, 1990), attitude change did not occur. ▶ Figure 6.12 summarizes these steps in the production and reduction of dissonance.

In addition, there are cross-cultural findings demonstrating that dissonance reduction is not universal. Steven Heine and Darrin Lehman (1997) compared Japanese participants (who come from a culture based on an interdependent view of oneself) to a Canadian sample (where one is likely to view oneself as independent) in a free-choice paradigm. Canadian participants were much more likely to provide rationalizations for their choices in the task, whereas the Japanese participants did not; there was no dissonance reduction in this group.

To this day, social psychologists continue to debate the "classic" and "new look" theories of cognitive dissonance. On the one hand, research has shown that attitude-discrepant actions do not always produce dissonance, in part because not everyone cares about being cognitively consistent (Cialdini et al., 1995), and in part because a change in attitude often seems to require the production of negative consequences (Johnson et al., 1995). On the other hand, some researchers have found that inconsistency alone can trigger cognitive dissonance, even without the negative consequences. For example, Eddie Harmon-Jones and others (1996) had people drink a Kool-Aid beverage that was mixed with sugar or vinegar. The researchers either told participants (no choice) or asked them (high choice) to state in writing that they liked the beverage and then toss these notes, which were not really needed, into the wastebasket. Afterward, they rated how much they really liked the drink. You may have noticed that this experiment parallels the Festinger and Carlsmith study, with one key exception: For participants in the high-choice situation who consumed vinegar and said they liked it, the lie—although it contradicted their true

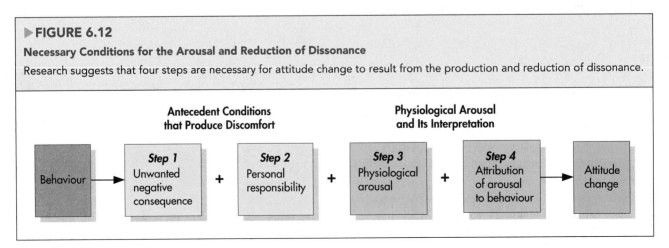

▶ FIGURE 6.12

Necessary Conditions for the Arousal and Reduction of Dissonance

Research suggests that four steps are necessary for attitude change to result from the production and reduction of dissonance.

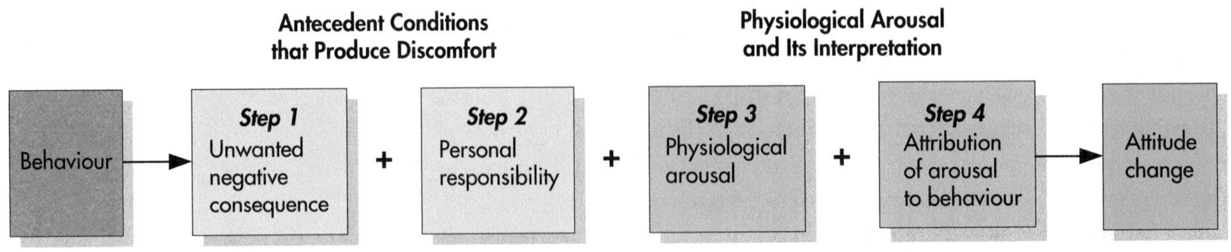

attitudes—did not cause harm to anyone. Did they experience dissonance that they would have to reduce by overrating the vinegar Kool-Aid? Yes. Compared with participants who lied about the vinegar in the no-choice situation, those in the high-choice situation rated its taste as more pleasant. The lie was harmless, but the feeling of inconsistency still forced a change in attitude.

Alternative Routes to Self-Persuasion

It is important to distinguish between the empirical facts as uncovered by dissonance researchers and the theory that is used to explain them. The facts themselves are clear: Under certain conditions, people who behave in attitude-discrepant ways go on to change their attitudes. Whether this phenomenon reflects a human need to reduce dissonance, however, is a matter of some controversy. Over the years, three other explanations have been proposed.

Self-Perception Theory Daryl Bem's (1965) *self-perception theory,* as described in Chapter 3, posed the first serious challenge to dissonance theory. Noting that people don't always have first-hand knowledge of their own attitudes, Bem proposed that we infer how we feel by observing ourselves and the circumstances of our own behaviour. This sort of self-persuasion is not fuelled by the need to reduce tension or justify our actions. Instead, it is a cool, calm, and rational process in which people interpret ambiguous feelings by observing their own behaviour. But can Bem's theory replace dissonance theory as an explanation of self-persuasion?

Bem confronted this question head-on. What if neutral observers who are not motivated by the need to reduce dissonance were to read a step-by-step description of a dissonance study and predict the results? This approach to the problem was ingenious. Bem reasoned that observers can have the same behavioural information as the participants themselves but not experience the same personal conflict. If observers generate the same results as real participants, it shows that dissonance arousal is not necessary for the resulting changes in attitudes.

To test his hypothesis, Bem (1967) described the Festinger and Carlsmith study to observers and had them guess participants' attitudes. Some were told about the $1 condition, some were told about the $20 condition, and others read about the control group procedure. The results closely paralleled the original study. As observers saw it, participants who said the task was interesting for $20 didn't mean it—they just went along for the money. But those who made the claim for only $1 must have been sincere. Why else would they have gone along? As far as Bem was concerned, participants themselves reason the same way. No conflict, no arousal—just inference by observation.

So should we conclude that self-perception, not dissonance, is what's necessary to bring about attitude change? That's a tough question. It's not easy to come up with a critical experiment to distinguish between these theories. Both predict the same results, but for different reasons. And both offer unique support for their own points of view. On the one hand, Bem's observer studies show that dissonance-like results *can* be obtained without arousal. On the other hand, the subjects of dissonance manipulations *do* experience arousal, which seems necessary for attitude change to take place. Can we say that one theory is right and the other wrong?

Fazio and others (1977) concluded that both theories are right but in different situations. When people behave in ways that are strikingly at odds with their attitudes, they feel the unnerving effects of dissonance and change their attitudes to rationalize their actions. When people behave in ways that are not terribly discrepant from how they feel, however, they experience relatively little tension and form their attitudes as a matter of inference. In short, highly discrepant behaviour produces attitude change through dissonance, whereas slightly discrepant behaviour produces change through self-perception.

Impression-Management Theory Another alternative to a dissonance view of self-persuasion is based on *impression-management theory,* which says that what matters is not a motive to *be* consistent but a motive to *appear* consistent. Nobody wants to be called fickle or be seen by others as a hypocrite. So we calibrate our attitudes and behaviours only publicly just to present ourselves to others in a particular light (Baumeister, 1982; Tedeschi et al., 1971). Or perhaps we are motivated not by a desire to appear consistent but by a desire to avoid being held responsible for the unpleasant consequences of our actions (Schlenker, 1982). Either way, this theory places the emphasis on our concern for self-presentation. According to this view, participants in the Festinger and Carlsmith study simply did not want the experimenter to think they had sold out for a paltry sum of money.

If the impression-management approach is correct, then cognitive dissonance does not produce attitude change at all—only reported change. In other words, if research participants were to state their attitudes anonymously, or if they were to think that the experimenter could determine their true feelings through covert measures, then dissonance-like effects should vanish. Sometimes, the effects do vanish; but other times, they do not. In general, studies have shown that although self-persuasion can be motivated by impression management, it can also occur in situations that do not clearly arouse self-presentation concerns (Baumeister & Tice, 1984).

Self-Esteem Theories A third competing explanation relates self-persuasion to the self. According to Elliot Aronson, acts that arouse dissonance do so because they threaten the self-concept, making the person feel guilty, dishonest, or hypocritical, and motivating a change in attitude or future behaviour (Aronson, 1999; Stone et al., 1997). This being the case, perhaps Festinger and Carlsmith's participants needed to change their attitudes toward the boring task in order to repair damage to the self, not to resolve cognitive inconsistency.

If cognitive dissonance is aroused only by behaviour that lowers self-esteem, then people with already low expectations of themselves should not be affected: "If a person conceives of himself as a 'schnook,' he will expect to behave like a schnook" (Aronson, 1969, p. 24). In fact, Jeff Stone (2003) found that when students were coaxed into writing an essay in favour of a tuition increase (a position that contradicted their attitude) and into thinking about their own standards of behaviour, those who had high self-esteem changed their attitude to meet their behaviour, as dissonance theory would predict, more than those who had low self-esteem. Claude Steele (1988) takes the notion two steps further. First, he suggests that a dissonance-producing situation—engaging in attitude-discrepant behaviour, exerting wasted effort, or making a difficult decision—sets in motion a process of *self-affirmation* that serves to revalidate the integrity of the self-concept. Second, this revalidation can be achieved in many ways, not just by resolving dissonance. Self-affirmation theory makes a unique prediction: If the active ingredient in dissonance situations is a threat to the self, then people who have an opportunity to affirm the self in other ways will not suffer from the effects of dissonance. Give Festinger and Carlsmith's $1 participants a chance to donate money, help a victim in distress, or solve a problem, and their self-concepts should bounce back without further need to justify their actions.

Research provides support for this hypothesis. For example, Steele and his colleagues (1993) gave people positive or negative feedback about a personality test they had taken. Next, they asked them to rate ten popular music CDs and then offered them a choice of keeping either their fifth- or sixth-ranked CD. Soon after making the decision, participants were asked to rate the CDs again. As predicted by dissonance theory, most inflated their ratings of the chosen CD relative to the album that was not chosen. The key word, however, is *most.* Among positive-feedback participants, ratings did not change. Why not? According to Steele, these participants had just enjoyed a self-affirming experience—enough to overcome the need to reduce dissonance.

When we compare the major theories of self-persuasion, we see that each alternative challenges a different aspect of dissonance theory. Self-perception theory assumes that attitude change is a matter of inference, not motivation. Impression-management theory maintains that the change is more apparent than real, reported for the sake of public self-presentation. Self-affirmation theory contends that the motivating force is a concern for the self and that attitude change will not occur when the self-concept is affirmed in other ways.

Steele's research suggests that there are many possible ways to repair the dissonance damaged self. But if these efforts at indirect self-affirmation fail, would cognitive dissonance return and pressure a change in attitude? Yes. In one study, students were asked (high-choice) or told (low-choice) to deliver an attitude-discrepant speech advocating that a popular campus tradition (running nude on the evening of the first snowfall) be banned. For those in the high-choice condition, cognitive dissonance was aroused, pressuring a change in attitude favouring the ban. Students in a third group who were subsequently given an opportunity to self-affirm by expressing some cherished values felt less discomfort and exhibited less attitude change. For them, self-affirmation provided the necessary relief. However, among students in a fourth group—who self-affirmed but then received negative feedback about the values they expressed—cognitive dissonance returned, pressuring a change in attitude toward the ban. In essence, cognitive dissonance and its impact on attitudes re-emerged from the failed attempt at self-affirmation (Galinsky et al., 2000; see ▶ Figure 6.13).

To summarize, dissonance theory maintains that people change their attitudes to justify their attitude-discrepant behaviours, efforts, and decisions. Self-perception theory argues that the change occurs because people infer how they feel by observing their own behaviour. Impression-management theory claims that the attitude change is spurred by self-presentation concerns. And self-affirmation theory says that the change is motivated by threats to the self (see ▶ Figure 6.14).

▶ FIGURE 6.13

When Self-Affirmation Fails

Students gave a dissonant speech advocating a ban on a popular campus tradition. Compared to those in a low-choice situation, students in a high-choice group changed their attitude more to favour the ban. As self-affirmation theory predicts, those given a chance to express their values afterward did not then favour the ban—unless their values were poorly received. Self-affirmation can repair the dissonance-damaged self. When it fails, however, cognitive dissonance returns to pressure the change in attitude.

(Galinsky et al., 2000.)

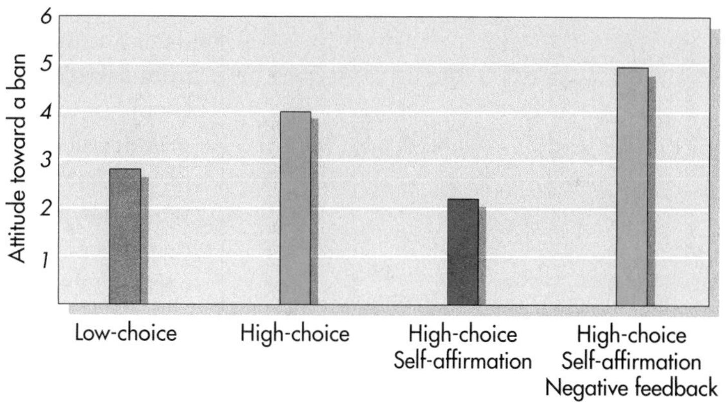

FIGURE 6.14

Theories of Self-Persuasion: Critical Comparisons

Here we compare the major theories of self-persuasion. Each alternative challenges a different aspect of dissonance theory. Self-perception theory assumes that attitude change is a matter of inference, not motivation. Impression-management theory maintains that the change is more apparent than real, reported for the sake of public self-presentation. Self-affirmation theory contends that the motivating force is a concern for the self and that attitude change will not occur when the self-concept is affirmed in other ways.

	Theories			
	Cognitive Dissonance	*Self-Perception*	*Impression Management*	*Self-Affirmation*
Is the attitude change motivated by a desire to reduce discomfort?	Yes	No	Yes	Yes
Does a person's private attitude really change?	Yes	Yes	No	Yes
Must the change be directly related to the attitude-discrepant behaviour?	Yes	Yes	Yes	No

FIGURE 6.15

Cognitive Dissonance as Both Universal and Culturally Dependent

Researchers compared Canadian and Japanese research participants in a post-decision dissonance study in which they ranked ordered items on a menu, chose their top dishes, and then ranked the list again. Half made the choices for themselves; the others were asked to imagine a close friend. When deciding for themselves, only the Canadians exhibited a significant justification effect; when deciding for a friend, however, Japanese participants exhibited the stronger effect.

(Hoshino-Browne et al., 2005.)

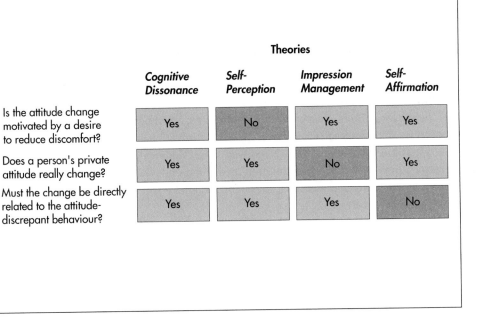

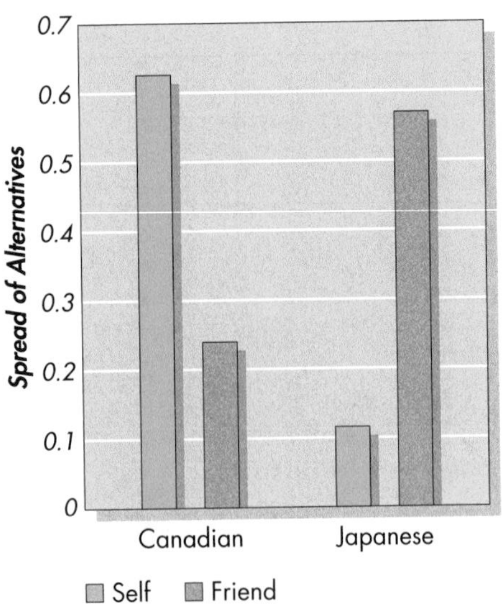

Cultural Influences on Cognitive Dissonance

Over the years, social psychologists have presumed that the cognitive dissonance effects uncovered in 50 years of research and described in this chapter are universal and characteristic of human nature. More and more, however, it appears that cultural context may influence both the arousal and reduction of cognitive dissonance.

In Western cultures, individuals are expected to make decisions that are consistent with their personal attitudes and to make those decisions free from outside influences. In East Asian cultures, however, individuals are also expected to make decisions that benefit their ingroup members and to take the well-being of others into account in making those decisions. In light of these differences, Etsuko Hoshino-Browne and colleagues (2005) compared the reactions of European-Canadian and Japanese research participants in a post-decision dissonance experiment in which they rank-ordered items on a menu by choosing their top 10 dishes. Then they ranked the list again. Half made the choices for themselves, and the others were asked to imagine a close friend whose tastes they knew and choose on behalf of that friend. Did participants show the classic post-decision justification effect, becoming more positive in their ratings of the chosen items relative to nonchosen items? Yes and no. When they made decisions for themselves, only the Canadian participants exhibited a significant justification effect. When Japanese participants made decisions for a friend, however, they exhibited the stronger effect (see Figure 6.15).

To sum up, cognitive dissonance is both universal and dependent on culture. At times everyone feels and tries to reduce dissonance, but cultures influence the conditions under which these processes occur.

Changing Attitudes

Attitudes and attitude change are an important part of social life. In this chapter, we have seen that persuasion can be achieved in different ways. The most common approach is through communication from *others.* Faced with newspaper editorials, junk mail, books, TV commercials, Internet ads, and other messages, we take one of two routes to persuasion. On the central route, attitude change is based on the merits of the source and his or her communication. On the peripheral route, it is based on superficial cues. Either way, the change in attitude often precipitates a change in behaviour.

A second, less obvious means of persuasion originates within *ourselves.* When people behave in ways that run afoul of their true convictions, they often go on to change their attitudes. Once again, there is not one route to change, but many. In this regard, cognitive dissonance, self-perception, impression management, and self-esteem concerns are among the possible avenues. From attitudes to behaviour and back again, the processes of persuasion are complex and interwoven.

REVIEW

The Study of Attitudes

- An attitude is an affective, evaluative reaction toward a person, place, issue, or object.

How Attitudes Are Measured

- The most common way to measure attitudes is through self-reports, such as attitude scales.
- To get respondents to answer questions honestly, the bogus pipeline may be used.
- Covert measures may also be used. Such measures include nonverbal behaviour, the facial electromyograph (EMG), brain-wave patterns, the Implicit Association Test (IAT), and the Implicit Relational Assessment Procedure.

How Attitudes Are Formed

- Twin studies suggest that people may be genetically predisposed to hold certain attitudes.
- However, research shows that attitudes are formed by experience and learning, as when people develop strong attitudes toward neutral objects because of their association with positive and negative stimuli.

The Link Between Attitudes and Behaviour

- Attitudes do not necessarily correlate with behaviour; but under certain conditions, there is a high correlation.
- Attitudes predict behaviour best when they're specific rather than general, and strong rather than weak.
- Attitudes compete with other influences on behaviour.

Persuasion by Communication

- The most common approach to changing attitudes is through a persuasive communication.

Two Routes to Persuasion

- When people think critically about a message, they take the central route to persuasion and are influenced by the strength of the arguments.
- When people do not think carefully about a message, they take the peripheral route to persuasion and are influenced by peripheral cues.
- The route taken depends on whether people have the ability and the motivation to fully process the communication.

The Source

- Attitude change is greater for messages delivered by a source that is credible (competent and trustworthy).
- Attitude change is also greater when the source is likeable (similar and attractive).
- When an audience has a high level of personal involvement, source factors are less important than message quality.
- The sleeper effect shows that people often forget the source but not the message, so the effects of source credibility dissipate over time.

The Message

- On the peripheral route, lengthy messages are persuasive. On the central route, length works only if the added information does not dilute the message.
- Whether it is best to present an argument first or second depends on how much time elapses—both between the two arguments and between the second argument and the final decision.
- Messages that are moderately discrepant from an audience's attitudes will inspire change, but highly discrepant messages will be scrutinized and rejected.
- High-fear messages motivate attitude change when they contain strong arguments and instructions on how to avoid the threatened danger.
- Positive emotion also facilitates attitude change because people are easier to persuade when they're in a good mood.
- Research shows that subliminal messages do not produce meaningful or lasting changes in attitudes.

The Audience

- People are not consistently difficult or easy to persuade.
- Rather, different kinds of messages influence different kinds of people.
- People who are high in the need for cognition are persuaded more by the strength of the arguments.
- People who are high in self-monitoring are influenced more by appeals to social images.
- To be persuasive, a message should also appeal to the cultural values of its audience.
- Forewarning increases resistance to persuasive influence. It inoculates the audience by providing the opportunity to generate counter-arguments, and it arouses psychological reactance.

Culture and Persuasion

- Communications are successful to the extent that they appeal to the cultural values of an audience.
- Research shows that North Americans are persuaded more by individualistic ads, whereas East Asians prefer collectivistic ads.

Persuasion by Our Own Actions

Role-Playing: All the World's a Stage

- The way people act can influence how they feel, as behaviour can determine attitudes.
- This was demonstrated by the Stanford Prison Study.

Cognitive Dissonance Theory: The Classic Version

- Under certain conditions, inconsistency between attitudes and behaviour produces an unpleasant psychological state called cognitive dissonance.
- Motivated to reduce the tension, people often change their attitudes to justify (1) attitude-discrepant behaviour, (2) wasted effort, and (3) difficult decisions.

Cognitive Dissonance Theory: A New Look

- According to the "new look" version of cognitive dissonance theory, four conditions must be met for dissonance to be aroused: (1) an act with unwanted consequences, (2) a feeling of personal responsibility, (3) arousal or discomfort, and (4) attribution of the arousal to the attitude-discrepant act.
- Social psychologists continue to debate whether dissonance can be aroused by cognitive inconsistency when no unwanted consequences are produced.

Alternative Routes to Self-Persuasion

- Alternative explanations of dissonance-related attitude change have been proposed.
- Self-perception theory states that people logically infer their attitudes by observing their own behaviour.
- Impression-management theory says that people are motivated only to appear consistent to others.
- Self-esteem theories state that dissonance is triggered by threats to the self-concept and can be reduced indirectly, without a change in attitude, through self-affirming experiences.

Cultural Influences on Cognitive Dissonance

- Recently, social psychologists have wondered whether cognitive dissonance effects are universal or specific to Western cultures.
- Research suggests that people all over the world will try to reduce dissonance when it arises, but that the conditions that arouse it are influenced by cultural context.

Changing Attitudes

- Through persuasive communications and the mechanisms of self-persuasion, the processes of changing attitudes and behaviour are complex and interwoven.

Key Terms

attitude (189)
attitude scale (191)
bogus pipeline (191)
central route to persuasion (201)
cognitive dissonance theory (221)
elaboration (201)
facial electromyograph (EMG) (192)
implicit attitude (193)
Implicit Relational Assessment Procedure (IRAP) (195)
inoculation hypothesis (216)
insufficient deterrence (222)
insufficient justification (222)
need for cognition (NC) (214)
peripheral route to persuasion (201)
persuasion (200)
psychological reactance (217)
sleeper effect (207)
theory of planned behaviour (197)

Putting COMMON SENSE *to the Test*

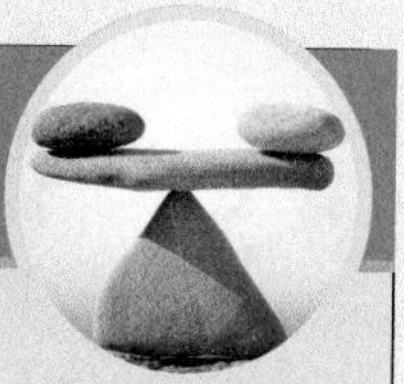

Researchers can tell if someone has a positive or negative attitude by measuring physiological arousal.

False. *Measures of arousal can reveal how intensely someone feels, but not whether the person's attitude is positive or negative.*

In reacting to persuasive communications, people are influenced more by superficial images than by logical arguments.

False. *As indicated by the dual-process model of persuasion, people can be influenced by images or arguments—depending on their ability and motivation to think critically about the information.*

People are most easily persuaded by commercial messages that are presented without their awareness.

False. *There is no research evidence to support the presumed effects of subliminal ads.*

The more money you pay people to tell a lie, the more they will come to believe it.

False. *Cognitive dissonance studies show that people believe the lies they are underpaid to tell as a way to justify their own actions.*

People often come to like what they suffer for.

True. *Studies show that the more people work or suffer for something, the more they come to like it as a way to justify their effort.*

7

Kevin Miller/Stone/Getty Images

Conformity

This chapter examines ways in which social influences are "automatic." We then look at three processes. First, we consider the reasons why people exhibit conformity to group norms. Second, we describe the strategies used to elicit compliance with direct requests. Third, we analyze the causes and effects of obedience to the commands of authority. The chapter concludes with a discussion of the continuum of social influence.

Putting
COMMON SENSE
to the Test

Circle Your Answer

T F When all members of a group give an incorrect response to an easy question, most people most of the time conform to that response.

T F An effective way to get someone to do you a favour is to make a first request that is so large the person is sure to reject it.

T F In experiments on obedience, most participants who were ordered to administer severe shocks to an innocent person refused to do so.

T F As the number of people in a group increases, so does their impact on an individual.

T F Conformity rates vary across different cultures and from one generation to the next.

Picture yourself sitting in a mall food court, enjoying your lunch, perhaps taking a break from some holiday shopping, when a strange thing happens. A young women sitting alone at a table close by suddenly stands up and starts belting out the Hallelujah Chorus from Handel's Messiah. Before you can even react, more than 100 other people from around the food court who moments ago were apparently simply fellow diners join in, perfectly on cue. On November 13th, 2010, this was the experience of lunchtime diners in a London, Ontario mall. Similarly, in June 2009, in York, England, feathers flew outside of the well-known Yorkshire Museum and Gardens when 500 good-natured Facebook users appeared, pillows in hand, for a mass pillow fight that lasted five minutes. In Rome, 300 people entered a book and music store and asked the staff for titles that did not exist. In Paris, people congregated under the pyramid of the Louvre and fell lifelessly to the ground. Illustrating the viral power of the Internet to serve as a vehicle for social influence, each of these crowds was a "flash mob"—a group of people who received instructions over the Internet, gathered voluntarily at a set time and place, performed some silly but harmless action, and dispersed. Other examples of flash mobs can be found in New York, Amsterdam, Berlin, Oslo, Melbourne, Budapest, and other cities around the world.

Sometimes, the social influences that move us are not entertaining and funny but potentially hazardous to our health. Consider the unusual events that occurred on a Vancouver bus in 2004 when several people, including the bus driver and the paramedics called to treat him, became violently ill and had to be hospitalized. It was initially believed that a "suspicious" passenger had poisoned them, after the driver reported an "unusual odour." All quickly recovered and no medical explanation for their illness was ever found. An epidemiologist at the University of British Columbia labelled it a case of "mass psychogenic illness"—a profound form of social influence previously documented by Jones et al. (2000).

"We are discreet sheep; we wait to see how the drove is going and then go with the drove."

—Mark Twain

Flash mobs reveal the awesome power of social influence. The effects that people have on each other can also be seen in the most mundane of human events. Thus, sports fans spread the "wave" around a stadium or chant "de-fence" in a spectacular show of unison. TV producers insert canned laughter into sitcoms to increase viewer

Michael Stuparyk/Getstock.com

This flash mob, following instructions they received over the Internet, gathered at the Toronto Eaton Centre in February 2010 to dance together and create an online video. The event was organized in honour of Erika Heller, who died from colon cancer.

responsiveness. Political candidates trumpet the inflated results of their own favourable public opinion polls to attract new voters to their side. And bartenders, waiters, and waitresses stuff dollar bills into their tip jars as a way to get customers to follow suit. As they say, "Monkey see, monkey do."

You don't need to be a social psychologist to know that we have an impact on each other's behaviour. The question is, how, and with what effect? The term *social influence* refers to the ways in which people are affected by the real and imagined pressures of others (Nolan, Schultz, Cialdini, Goldstein & Griskevicius, 2008; Kiesler & Kiesler, 1969). The kinds of influences brought to bear on an individual come in different shapes and sizes. In this chapter, we look at social influences that are mindless and automatic; then we consider three forms of influence that vary in the degree of pressure exerted on an individual—*conformity, compliance,* and *obedience.* As depicted in ▶ Figure 7.1, conformity, compliance, and obedience are not distinct, qualitatively different "types" of influence. In all three cases, the influence may emanate from a person, a group, or an institution. And in all instances, the behaviour in question may be constructive (helping oneself or others), destructive (hurting oneself or others), or neutral. It is useful to note, once again, that social influence varies, as points along a continuum, according to the degree of pressure exerted on the individual. It is also useful to note that we do not always succumb under pressure. People may conform or maintain their independence from others; they may comply with direct requests or react with assertiveness; they may obey the commands of authority or oppose powerful others in an act of defiance. In this chapter, we examine the factors that lead human beings to yield to or resist social influence.

Social Influence as "Automatic"

Before we consider the explicit forms of social influence depicted in Figure 7.1, whereby individuals choose whether to "go along," it's important to note that, as social animals, humans are vulnerable to a host of subtle, almost reflex-like influences. Without realizing it, we often yawn when we see others yawning and laugh when we hear others laughing. In an early study, Stanley Milgram and others (1969) had research confederates stop on a busy street in New York City, look up, and gawk

▶ FIGURE 7.1

Continuum of Social Influence

Social influences vary in the degree of pressure they bring to bear on an individual. People may (1) *conform* to group norms or maintain their independence, (2) *comply* with requests or be assertive, and (3) *obey* or defy the commands of authority.

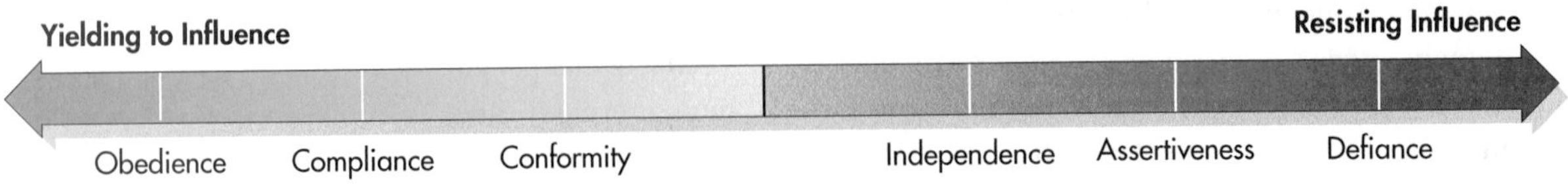

at the sixth-floor window of a nearby building. Films shot from behind the window indicated that about 80 percent of passersby stopped and gazed up when they saw the confederates.

Do we really imitate one another automatically, without thought and without conflict? It appears that we do. In recent years, controlled studies of human infants have shown that sometimes shortly after birth, babies not only look at faces but—to the delight of parents all over the world—often mimic gestures such as moving the head, pursing the lips, and sticking out the tongue (Bremner, 2002; Gopnik et al., 1999).

You may not realize it, but human adults unwittingly mimic each other all the time. To demonstrate, Tanya Chartrand and John Bargh (1999) set up participants to work on a task with a partner, a confederate who exhibited the habit of rubbing his face or shaking his foot. Hidden cameras recording the interaction revealed that, without realizing it, participants mimicked these motor behaviours, rubbing their face or shaking a foot to match their partner's behaviour. Chartrand and Bargh dubbed this phenomenon the "chameleon effect," after the lizard that changes colours according to its physical environment (see ▶ Figure 7.2). The reason for this nonconscious form of imitation, they speculated, is that people interact more smoothly when they are behaviourally "in sync" with one another. Accordingly, Chartrand and Bargh turned the tables in a second study, instructing their confederate to match in subtle ways the mannerisms of some participants but not others. Sure enough, participants who had been mimicked liked the confederate more than those who had not.

Further demonstrating the social function of mimicry, people mimic others more when they are motivated to affiliate than when they are not (Hove & Risen, 2009; Lakin & Chartrand, 2003). In one experiment, Mariëlle Stel and others (2010) demonstrated that expectations regarding whether we will like or dislike someone can affect the extent to which we will mimic them. They asked participants to view a one-minute videotape of a woman being interviewed. While the content of the video itself was emotionally neutral, prior to watching it, participants were given background information indicating the woman was either helpful, unhelpful, or that she would simply be discussing helping behaviour in general (the control condition). When participants were told that the woman in the video was helpful (i.e., more likeable), they were significantly more likely to mimic her behaviours, compared to those who were assigned to the unhelpful (i.e., unlikeable) or control condition.

The human impulse to mimic others may have adaptive social value, but these types of effects can also be found in nonsocial situations. In one study, Roland Neumann and Fritz Strack (2000) had people listen to an abstract philosophical speech that was recited on tape in a happy, sad, or neutral voice. Afterward, participants rated their own mood as more positive when they heard the happy voice and as more negative when they heard the sad voice. Apparently, even though the participants and speakers never interacted, the speaker's emotional state was socially contagious—an automatic effect that can be described as a form of "mood contagion."

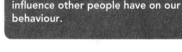

"I don't know why. I just suddenly felt like calling."

Often we are not aware of the influence other people have on our behaviour.

▶FIGURE 7.2

The Chameleon Effect

This graph shows the number of times per minute that participants rubbed their face or shook their foot when with a confederate who was rubbing his face or shaking his foot.

(Chartrand & Bargh, 1999.)

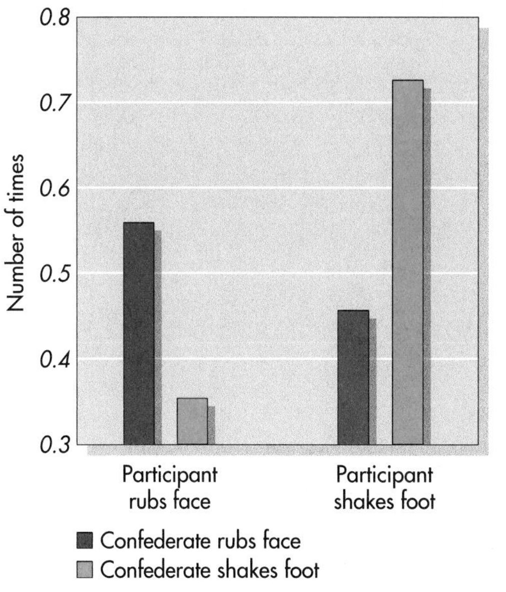

It is also important to realize that mimicry is a dynamic process, as when two people who are walking together or dancing become more and more coordinated over time. To demonstrate, Michael Richardson and others (2005) sat pairs of students side by side to work on visual problems while swinging a handheld pendulum as "a distraction task." The students did not need to be synchronized in their swinging tempo in order to get along or solve the problems. Yet when each could see the other's pendulum (and even without speaking), their tempos gradually converged over time—like two hearts beating as one.

Conformity

It is hard to find behaviours that are *not* in some way affected by exposure to the actions of others. When social psychologists talk of **conformity**, they specifically refer to the tendency of people to change their perceptions, opinions, and behaviour in ways that are consistent with group norms. With this definition in mind, would you call yourself a conformist or a nonconformist? For instance, do you ever feel inclined to follow what others are saying or doing? At first, you may deny the tendency to conform and, instead, declare your individuality. But think about it. When was the last time you appeared at a formal wedding dressed in blue jeans or remained seated during the national anthem at a sports event? People find it difficult to breach social norms. In an interesting demonstration of this point, social psychology research assistants were supposed to ask subway passengers to give up their seats—a conspicuous violation of the norm of acceptable conduct. Many of the assistants could not carry out their assignment. In fact, some of those who tried it became so anxious that they pretended to be ill just to make their request appear justified (Milgram & Sabini, 1978).

With conformity being so widespread, it is interesting and ironic that research participants (at least in North America) who are coaxed into conforming to a group norm will often not admit it, or perhaps even be aware of it. Sometimes, our willingness to admit that we conform depends on who we are explaining this to. In a clever series of studies that included both social psychologists and undergraduate psychology students as participants, Jetten and others (2006) found that those who viewed their status in a group as being more junior relative to their audience were also more willing to agree that they were sometimes conformist, while their more senior colleagues viewed themselves as nonconformist. Almost all of their participants, however, viewed themselves as being less conformist than the average person. While part of the explanation for this may lie in the self-protective nature of seeing oneself as being better than average, it also may be the case that whereas people judge others by their overt behaviour and the degree to which it matches what others are doing, they tend to judge themselves by focusing inward and introspecting about their thought processes, which blinds them to their own conformity (Pronin et al., 2007).

People understandably have mixed feelings about conformity. After all, some degree of conformity is essential if individuals are to coexist peacefully, as when people assume their rightful place in a waiting line. Yet at other times, conformity can have harmful consequences, as when people drink too heavily at parties or tell offensive ethnic jokes because others are doing the same. For the social psychologist, the goal is to understand the conditions that promote conformity and the reasons for that behaviour.

conformity
The tendency to change our perceptions, opinions, or behaviour in ways that are consistent with group norms.

The Early Classics

In 1936, Muzafer Sherif published a classic laboratory study of how norms develop in small groups. His method was ingenious. Male students, who believed they were participating in a visual perception experiment, sat in a totally darkened room. Approximately 4.5 metres in front of them, a small dot of light appeared for two seconds, after which participants were asked to estimate how far it had moved. This procedure was repeated several times. Although participants didn't realize it, the dot of light always remained motionless. The movement they thought they saw was merely an optical illusion known as the *autokinetic effect:* in darkness, a stationary point of light appears to move, sometimes erratically, in various directions.

At first, participants sat alone and reported their judgments to the experimenter. After several trials, Sherif found that they settled in on their own stable perceptions of movement, with most estimates ranging from two to 25 centimetres. During the next three days, people returned to participate in three-person groups.

As before, lights were flashed, and participants, one by one, announced their estimates. As shown in ▶ Figure 7.3, initial estimates varied considerably, but participants later converged on a common perception. Eventually, each group established its own set of norms.

▶ FIGURE 7.3

A Classic Case of Suggestibility

This graph, taken from Sherif's study, shows how three participants' estimates of the apparent movement of light gradually converged. Before they came together, their perceptions varied considerably. Once in groups, however, participants conformed to the norm that had developed.

(Sherif, 1936.)

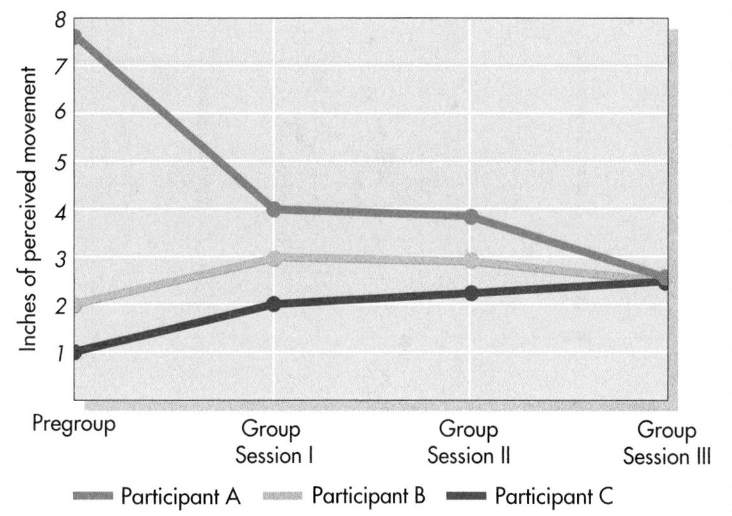

The Psychology of Social Norms, by Muzafa Sherif, 1936 and 1966 Harper and Row. Reproduced by permission.

Some 15 years after Sherif's demonstration, Solomon Asch (1951) constructed a very different task for testing how people's beliefs affect the beliefs of others. To appreciate what Asch did, imagine yourself in the following situation. You sign up for a psychology experiment and when you arrive, you find six other students waiting around a table. Soon after you take an empty seat, the experimenter explains that he is interested in the ability to make visual discriminations. As an example, he asks you and the others to indicate which of three comparison lines is identical in length to a standard line.

That seems easy enough. The experimenter then says that after each set of lines is shown, you and the others should take turns announcing your judgments out loud in the order of your seating position. Beginning on his left, the experimenter asks the first person for his judgment. Seeing that you are in the next-to-last position, you patiently await your turn. The opening moments pass uneventfully. The discriminations are clear, and everyone agrees on the answers. On the third set of lines, however, the first participant selects what is quite clearly the wrong line. Huh? What happened? Did he suddenly lose his mind, his eyesight, or both? Before you have the chance to figure this one out, the next four participants choose the same wrong line. Now what? Feeling as if you have entered the Twilight Zone, you wonder

Asch, S. E. (1955). Opinions and social pressure. *Scientific American, 193*, 31-35. Reproduced with permission. Copyright © 1955 Scientific American, Inc. All rights reserved

After two uneventful rounds in Asch's study, the participant (seated second from the right) faces a dilemma. The answer he wants to give in the third test of visual discrimination differs from that of the first five confederates, who are all in agreement. Should he give his own answer, or conform to theirs?

FIGURE 7.4

Line Judgment Task Used in Asch's Conformity Studies

Which comparison line—A, B, or C—is the same in length as the standard line? What would you say if you found yourself in the presence of a unanimous majority that answered A or C? The participants in Asch's experiments conformed to the majority about a third of the time.

(Asch, 1955.)

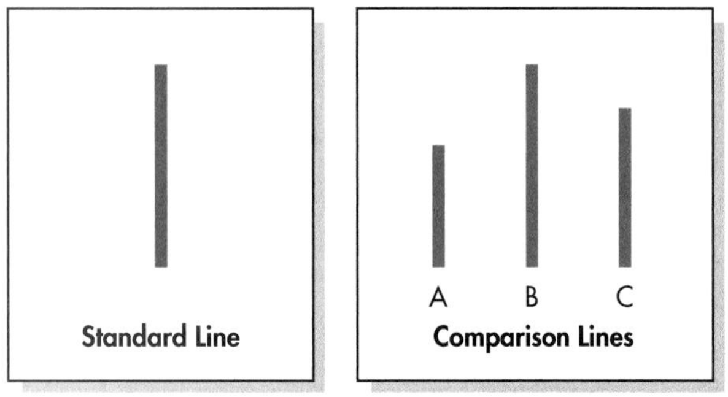

if you misunderstood the task. And you wonder what the others will think if you have the nerve to disagree. It's your turn now. You rub your eyes and take another look. What do you see? More to the point, what do you do?

Figure 7.4 gives an idea of the bind in which Asch's participants found themselves—caught between the need to be right and the desire to be liked (Insko et al., 1982; Ross et al., 1976). As you may suspect by now, the other "participants" were actually confederates—and had been trained to make incorrect judgments on 12 out of 18 presentations. There seems little doubt that the real participants knew the correct answers. In a control group, where they made judgments in isolation, they made almost no errors. Yet Asch's participants went along with the incorrect majority about 37 percent of the time—far more often than most of us would ever predict. Not everyone conformed, of course. About 25 percent refused to agree on any of the incorrect judgments. Yet 50 percent went along on at least half of the critical presentations, with the remaining participants conforming on an occasional basis. Similarly high levels of conformity were observed when Asch's study was repeated 30 years later and in recent studies involving other cognitive tasks (Larsen, 1990; Schneider & Watkins, 1996).

Let's compare Sherif's and Asch's classic studies of social influence. Obviously, both studies demonstrate that our visual perceptions can be heavily influenced by others. But how similar are they, really? Did Sherif's and Asch's participants exhibit the same kind of conformity, and for the same reasons, or was the resemblance in their behaviour more apparent than real?

From the start, it was clear that these studies differed in some important ways. In Sherif's research, participants were quite literally "in the dark," so they naturally turned to others for guidance. When physical reality is ambiguous and we are uncertain of our own judgments, as in the autokinetic situation, others can serve as a valuable source of information (Festinger, 1954). Asch's participants found themselves in a much more awkward position. Their task was relatively simple, and they could see with their own eyes what answers were correct. Still, they often followed the incorrect majority. In interviews, many of Asch's participants reported afterward that they went along with the group even though they were not convinced. Many of those who did not conform said they felt "conspicuous" and "crazy," like a "misfit" (Asch, 1956, p. 31).

Worldwide, more than 2 billion people, accounting for more than 30 percent of the planet's population, have access to the Internet (Internet World Stats, 2011). In Canada alone, almost 78 percent of us have access. This being the case, you may wonder: Do the social forces that influence people in the face-to-face encounters studied by Sherif and Asch also operate in virtual groups, where members are somewhat anonymous? The answer is yes. McKenna and Bargh (1998) observed behaviour in a number of Internet newsgroups, or blogs, in which people with common interests posted and responded to messages on a range of topics, from obesity and sexual orientation to money and the stock market. The social medium in this situation was "remote." Still, these researchers found that in newsgroups that brought together people with "hidden identities" (such as gay men and lesbians who had concealed their sexuality from others), members were highly responsive to social feedback. Those who posted messages that were met with approval rather than

When all members of a group give an incorrect response to an easy question, most people most of the time conform to that response. **FALSE.**

disapproval later became more active participants of the newsgroup. When it comes to social support and rejection, even virtual groups have the power to shape our behaviour (Bargh & McKenna, 2004; Williams et al., 2000).

David Turnley/Corbis

Nonconformists often pay a price for dissent. Nelson Mandela spent 27 years in prison for speaking out against apartheid in South Africa.

Why Do People Conform?

The Sherif and Asch studies demonstrate that people conform for two very different reasons: one informational, the other normative (Crutchfield, 1955; Deutsch & Gerard, 1955). Through **informational influence**, people conform because they want to be correct in their judgments and they assume that when others agree on something, they must be right. In Sherif's autokinetic task, as in other difficult or ambiguous tasks, it's natural to assume that four eyes are better than two. Hence, research shows that eyewitnesses trying to recall a crime or some other event will alter their recollections—and even create false memories—in response to what they hear other witnesses report (Gabbert et al., 2003; Garry et al., 2008). **Normative influence**, however, leads people to conform because they fear the consequences of appearing deviant. It's easy to see why. Research shows that individuals who stray from a group norm are often disliked, rejected, ridiculed, and laughed at (Levine, 1989; Schachter, 1951). These negative social reactions can be hard to take. In a series of controlled studies, people who were socially *ostracized*—by being neglected, ignored, and excluded in a live or Internet chat room conversation—reacted by feeling hurt, angry, and alone (Williams et al., 2002). In fact, in a brain-imaging study, young people who were left out by other players in a three-person Internet game called "Cyberball" exhibited elevated activity in a part of the brain normally associated with physical pain (Eisenberger, 2012; Eisenberger et al., 2003, 2007). In *Ostracism: The Power of Silence,* Kipling Williams (2001) notes that some people get so distressed when they are rejected that they become passive, numb, and lethargic—"as though they had been hit with a stun gun" (p. 159).

Usually, informational and normative influences operate jointly. Even though some of Asch's participants said they had conformed just to avoid being different, others said that they came to agree with their group's erroneous judgments. Is that possible? At the time, Asch had to rely on what his participants reported in interviews. Thanks to recent developments in social neuroscience, however, researchers can now peer into the socially active brain. In an ingenious medical school study that illustrates the point, Gregory Berns and others (2005) put 32 adults into a visual–spatial perception experiment in which they were asked to "mentally rotate" two geometric objects to determine if they were the same or different. As in the original Asch study, the participants were accompanied by four confederates who unanimously made incorrect judgments on certain trials. Unlike in the original study, however, participants were placed in an fMRI scanner while engaged in the task. There were two noteworthy results. First, participants conformed to 41 percent of the group's incorrect judgments. Second, these conforming judgments were accompanied by heightened activity in a part of the brain that controls spatial awareness—not in areas associated with conscious decision making. These results suggest that the group altered perceptions, not just behaviour.

Still, the distinction between informational and normative influence is important, not just for understanding why people conform, but because the two types

informational influence
Influence that produces conformity when a person believes others are correct in their judgments.

normative influence
Influence that produces conformity when a person fears the negative social consequences of appearing deviant.

FIGURE 7.5

Distinguishing Types of Conformity

People made judgments under conditions in which they had a high or a low level of motivation. Regardless of whether the judgment task was difficult or easy, there were moderate levels of conformity when participants had low motivation (left). But when they were highly motivated (right), participants conformed more when the task was difficult.

(Baron et al., 1996.)

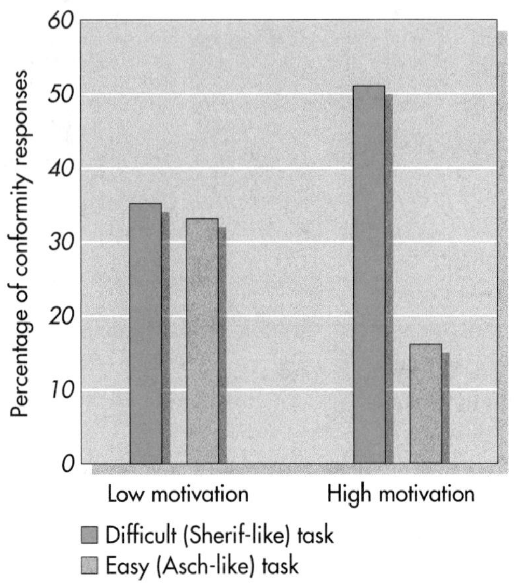

of influence produce different types of conformity: private and public (Allen, 1965; Kelman, 1961). Like beauty, conformity may be skin deep, or it may penetrate beneath the surface. **Private conformity**, also called true acceptance or conversion, describes instances in which others cause us to change not only our overt behaviour, but our minds as well. To conform at this level is to be truly persuaded that others are correct. In contrast, **public conformity** (sometimes called compliance, a term that is used later in this chapter to describe a different form of influence) refers to a superficial change in behaviour. People often respond to normative pressures by pretending to agree even when privately they do not. This often happens when we want to curry favour with others. The politician who tells constituents whatever they want to hear is a case in point.

How, you might be wondering, can social psychologists ever tell the difference between the private and public conformist? After all, both exhibit the same change in their observable behaviour. The difference is that compared with someone who merely acquiesces in public, the individual who is truly persuaded maintains that change long after the others are out of the picture. When this distinction is applied to Sherif's and Asch's research, the results come out as expected. At the end of his study, Sherif (1936) retested participants alone and found that their estimates continued to reflect the norm previously established in their group—even among those who were retested a full year after the experiment (Rohrer et al., 1954). In contrast, when Asch (1956) had participants write their answers privately, their level of conformity dropped sharply (Deutsch & Gerard, 1955; Mouton et al., 1956).

In a study that demonstrates both processes, Robert S. Baron and others (1996) had people, in groups of three (one participant and two confederates), act as eyewitnesses. First they would see a picture of a person, then they would try to pick that person out of a lineup. In some groups, the task was difficult, like Sherif's, since participants saw each picture only once, for half a second. For other groups, the task was easier, like Asch's, in that they saw each picture twice for a total of ten seconds. How often did participants conform when the confederates made the wrong identification? It depended on how motivated they were. When the experimenter downplayed the task as only a "pilot study," the conformity rates were 35 percent when the task was difficult and 33 percent when it was easy. But when participants were offered a financial incentive to do well, conformity went up to 51 percent when the task was difficult—and down to 16 percent when it was easy (see Figure 7.5). With pride and money on the line, the Sherif-like participants conformed more, and the Asch-like participants conformed less.

Table 7.1 summarizes the comparison of Sherif's and Asch's studies and the depths of social influence that they demonstrate. Looking at this table, you can see that the difficulty of the task is crucial. When reality cannot easily be validated by physical evidence, as in the autokinetic situation, people turn to others for information and conform because they are truly persuaded by that information. When reality is clear, however, the cost of dissent becomes the major issue. As Asch found, it can be difficult to depart too much from others even when you know that they—not you—are wrong. So you play along. Privately, you don't change your mind. But you nod your head in agreement anyway.

private conformity
The change of beliefs that occurs when a person privately accepts the position taken by others.

public conformity
A superficial change in overt behaviour, without a corresponding change of opinion, produced by real or imagined group pressure.

Majority Influence

Realizing that people often succumb to peer pressure is only the first step in understanding the process of social influence. The next step is to identify the situational and personal factors that make us more or less likely to conform. We know that people tend to conform when the social pressure is intense and they are insecure about how to behave. But what creates these feelings of pressure and insecurity? Here, we look at five factors: the size of the group, a focus on norms, the presence of an ally, gender differences, and culture.

TABLE 7.1

Two Types of Conformity

A comparison of Sherif's and Asch's studies suggests different kinds of conformity for different reasons. Sherif used an ambiguous task, so others provided a source of information and influenced the participants' true opinions. Asch used a task that required simple judgments of a clear stimulus, so most participants exhibited occasional public conformity in response to normative pressure but privately did not accept the group's judgments.

Experimental Task	Primary Effect of Group	Depth of Conformity Produced
Sherif's ambiguous autokinetic effect	Informational influence	Private acceptance
Asch's simple line judgments	Normative influence	Public conformity

Group Size: The Power in Numbers Common sense would suggest that as the number of people in a majority increases, so should their impact. Actually, it is not that simple. Asch (1956) varied the size of groups, using 1, 2, 3, 4, 8, or 15 confederates, and he found that conformity increased with group size—but only up to a point. Once there were three or four confederates, the amount of *additional* influence exerted by the rest was negligible. Other researchers have obtained similar results (Gerard et al., 1968).

Beyond the presence of three or four others, additions to a group are subject to the law of "diminishing returns" (Knowles, 1983; Mullen, 1983). As we will see later, Bibb Latané (1981) likens the influence of people on an individual to the way light bulbs illuminate a surface. When a second bulb is added to a room, the effect is dramatic. When the tenth bulb is added, however, its impact is barely felt, if at all. Economists say the same about the perception of money. An additional dollar seems greater to the person who has only $3 than to the person who has $300.

Another possible explanation is that as more and more people express the same opinion, an individual is likely to suspect that they are acting either in "collusion" or as "spineless sheep." According to David Wilder (1977), what matters is not the actual number of others but one's perception of how many distinct others, thinking independently, there are. Indeed, Wilder found that people were more influenced by two groups of two than by one four-person group and by two groups of three than by one six-person group. Conformity increased even further when people were exposed to three two-person groups. When faced with a majority opinion, we do more than just count the number of warm bodies—we try to assess the number of independent minds.

A Focus on Norms The size of a majority may influence the amount of pressure that is felt, but social norms give rise to conformity only when we know and focus on those norms. This may sound like an obvious point, yet we often misperceive what is normative—particularly when others are too afraid or embarrassed to publicly present their true thoughts, feelings, and behaviours.

One common example of this "pluralistic ignorance" concerns perceptions of alcohol usage. In a survey of university students, Clayton Neighbors and others, 2006 found that most students overestimated both the frequency and the amount of alcohol consumed by their peers. Unfortunately, those students who believed their peers drank more, and more often, were more likely to be consuming greater quantities of alcohol a year later.

David Frazier/Photo Researchers, Inc.

Courtesy of Vicki Gould

Whether in sports stadiums or at a favourite restaurant, social norms influence us when they are brought to awareness by the current or past behaviour of others.

Knowing how others are behaving in a situation is necessary for conformity, but these norms are likely to influence us only when they are brought to our awareness, or "activated." Robert Cialdini and his colleagues have demonstrated this point in studies on littering. In one study, researchers had confederates pass out handbills to amusement park visitors and varied the amount of litter that appeared in one section of the park (an indication of how others behave in that setting). The result: The more litter there was, the more likely visitors were to toss their handbills to the ground (Cialdini et al., 1990). A second study showed that passersby were most influenced by the prior behaviour of others when their attention was drawn to the existing norm. In this instance, people were observed in a parking garage that was either clean or cluttered with cigarette butts, candy wrappers, paper cups, and trash. In half of the cases, the norm that was already in place—clean or cluttered—was brought to participants' attention by a confederate who threw paper to the ground as he walked by. In the other half, the confederate passed by without incident. As participants reached their cars, they found a "Please Drive Safely" handbill tucked under the windshield wiper. Did they toss the paper to the ground or take it with them? The results showed that people were most likely to conform (by littering more when the garage was cluttered than when it was clean) when the confederate had littered—an act that drew attention to the norm (Cialdini et al., 1991).

An Ally in Dissent: Getting By with a Little Help In Asch's initial experiment, participants found themselves pitted against unanimous majorities. But what if they had an ally, a partner in dissent? Asch investigated this issue and found that the presence of a single confederate who agreed with the participant reduced conformity by almost 80 percent. This finding, however, does not tell us why the presence of an ally was so effective. Was it because he or she *agreed* with the participant or because he or she *disagreed* with the majority? In other words, were the views of the participants strengthened because a dissenting confederate offered validating information or because dissent per se reduced *normative* pressures?

A series of experiments explored these two possibilities. In one, Vernon Allen and John Levine (1969) led participants to believe they were working together with four confederates. Three of these others consistently agreed on the wrong judgment. The fourth one then either followed the majority, agreed with the participant, or made a third judgment, which was also incorrect. This last variation was the most interesting: Even when the confederate did not validate his or her own judgment, participants conformed less often to the majority. In another study, Allen and Levine (1971) varied the competence of the ally. Some participants received support from an average person. In contrast, others found themselves supported by someone who wore very thick glasses and complained that he could not see the visual displays. Not a very reassuring ally, right? Wrong. Even though participants derived less comfort from this supporter than from one who seemed more competent at the task, his presence still reduced their level of conformity.

Two important conclusions follow from this research. First, it is substantially more difficult for people to stand alone for their convictions than to be part of even a tiny minority. Second, *any* dissent—whether it validates an individual's opinion or not—can break the spell cast by a unanimous majority and reduce the normative pressures to conform.

Gender Differences Are there gender differences in conformity? Based on Asch's initial studies, social psychologists used to think that women, once considered the "weaker" sex, conform more than men. In light of more recent research, however, it appears that two additional factors have to be considered. First, sex differences depend on how comfortable people are with the experimental task. Frank Sistrunk and John McDavid (1971) had male and female participants answer questions on stereotypically masculine, feminine, and gender-neutral topics. Along with each question, participants were told the percentage of others who agreed or disagreed. Although females conformed to the contrived majority more on the masculine items, males conformed more on the feminine items (there were no sex differences on the neutral questions). This finding suggests that one's familiarity with the issue at hand, not gender, is what affects conformity. Ask about football or video war games, and most women acquiesce more than most men. Ask about family planning and fashion design, and the pattern is reversed (Eagly & Carli, 1981).

A second factor is the type of social pressure people face. As a general rule, sex differences are weak and unreliable. But there is an important exception: In face-to-face encounters, where people must openly disagree with each other, small differences do emerge. In fact, when participants think they are being observed, women conform more and men conform less than they do in a more private situation (Eagly & Chravala, 1986; Eagly et al., 1981). Why does being "in public" create such a divergence in behaviour? Alice Eagly (1987) argues that in front of others, people worry about how they come across and feel pressured to behave in ways that are viewed as acceptable within traditional gender-role constraints. At least in public, men make it a point to behave with fierce independence and autonomy, while women play a gentler, more docile role. In a replication of Asch's study, Susan Alizadeh Fard (2010) found that conformity rates among the women increased only when their status was manipulated to make them feel inferior to others in the room. Conformity levels were the same for men and women in the 'superior group.' Therefore, gender may not be enough of an explanation for differing levels of conformity—status and group identity should be considered, too.

Cultural Influences Linked together by space, language, religion, and a common history, each cultural group has its own ideologies, music, fashions, foods, laws, customs, and manners of expression. As many tourists and exchange students have come to learn, sometimes the hard way, the social norms that influence human conduct can vary in significant ways from one part of the world to another.

In *Do's and Taboos Around the World*, R. E. Axtell (1993) warns world travellers about some of these differences. Dine in an Indian home, he notes, and you should leave food on the plate to show the host that the portions were generous and that you had enough to eat. Yet as a dinner guest in Bolivia, you would show your appreciation by cleaning your plate. Shop in an outdoor market in Iraq, and you should expect to negotiate the price of everything you buy. Plan an appointment in Brazil, and the person

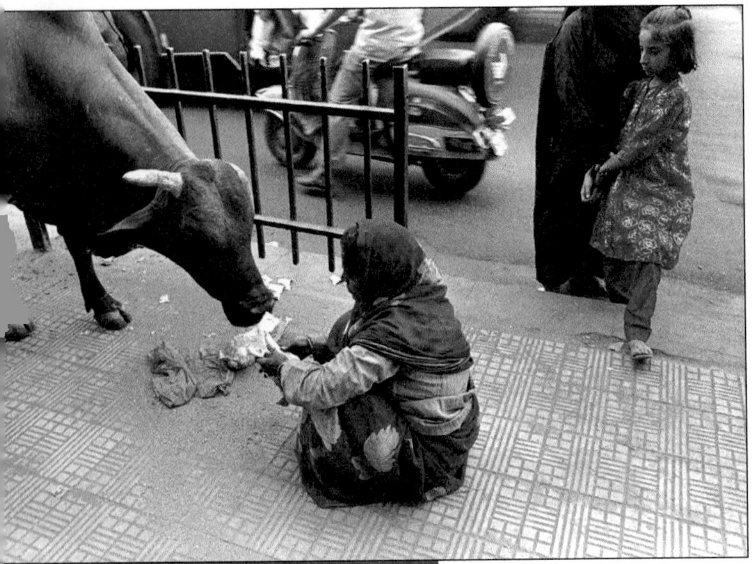

©John Moore/The Image Works

In Canada, where cows are considered mainly a food source, we would likely be surprised to see one on the sidewalk. In India, however, cows are considered sacred and are welcome to roam freely on the streets.

you're scheduled to meet is likely to be late. Nothing personal. Even the way we space ourselves from each other is culturally determined. Americans, Canadians, British, and Northern Europeans keep a polite distance between themselves and others—and feel "crowded" by the touchier, nose-to-nose style of the French, Greeks, Arabs, Mexicans, and people of South America.

In addition to social norms, there are also hundreds of *religions* that people identify with—the most common being Christianity (33 percent), Islam (21 percent), Hinduism (14 percent), and Buddhism (6 percent), with Judaism (0.22 percent) and others claiming fewer adherents. Roughly 16 percent of the world's population is not affiliated with a religion (Adherents.com 2005). Patty Van Cappellen and others (2011) explored the relationship between religion and conformity. They first primed their participants with religious concepts by showing them words such as "wedding" and "salvation," or neutral words such as "sandal" and "handkerchief." Participants then completed a task requiring them to estimate how many letter 'a's appeared on a computer screen. They were told that estimates from three previous participants were visible on the bottom of the screen, although they were free to disregard those if they wished. Higher levels of conformity were found for those in the religious prime condition, but it wasn't overall religiosity levels that explained this result. Rather, it appears that for more submissive people, religious primes activated their tendency to conform. According to the researchers, this may be because the religious words are associated with submissive tendencies in general, or because these words simply activated feelings of cooperation and trust in these individuals.

Just as cultures differ in their social and religious norms, so, too, they differ in the extent to which people adhere to those norms. As we saw in Chapter 3, there are two different cultural orientations toward persons and their relationships to groups. Some cultures value **individualism** and the virtues of independence, autonomy, and self-reliance, while others value **collectivism** and the virtues of interdependence, cooperation, and social harmony. Under the banner of individualism, personal goals take priority over group allegiances. Yet in collectivistic cultures, the person is, first and foremost, a loyal member of a family, team, company, church, and state.

Early research across nations showed that autonomy and independence are most highly valued in the United States, Australia, Great Britain, Canada, and the Netherlands, in that order. In contrast, other cultures value social harmony and "fitting in" for the sake of community, the most collectivist people being from Venezuela, Colombia, Pakistan, Peru, Taiwan, and China (Hofstede, 1980). Although it now appears that cultures differ in other more complicated ways and that individuals differ even within cultures (Oyserman et al., 2002), it is clear that nations on average vary in their orientations on the dimension of individualism (Schimmack et al., 2005). Generally, however, conformity rates are higher in cultures that are collectivistic rather than individualistic in their orientation (Bond & Smith, 1996).

individualism
A cultural orientation in which independence, autonomy, and self-reliance take priority over group allegiances.

collectivism
A cultural orientation in which interdependence, cooperation, and social harmony take priority over personal goals.

Minority Influence

It's not easy for individuals to express unpopular views or enlist support from others. Philosopher Bertrand Russell once said, "Conventional people are roused to frenzy by departure from convention, largely because they regard such departure as criticism of themselves." He may have been right. Although people who stand up for their beliefs against the majority are generally seen as competent and honest, they are also disliked and often rejected (Bassili & Provencal, 1988; Levine, 1989). It's no wonder that people think twice before expressing positions that are unpopular. In a series of survey studies that revealed what he called the "minority slowness effect," John Bassili (2003) asked people about their attitudes on social policy issues like affirmative action or about their likes and dislikes for various celebrities, sports, foods, places, and activities. Consistently, and regardless of topic, respondents who held minority opinions were slower to answer the questions than those in the majority.

Resisting the pressure to conform and maintaining one's independence may be socially difficult, but not impossible. History's famous heroes, villains, and creative minds are living proof: Joan of Arc, Muhammad, Charles Darwin, and Gandhi, to name just a few, were dissenters of their time who continue to capture the imagination. Then there's human behaviour in the laboratory. Social psychologists were so intrigued by Asch's initial finding that participants conformed 37 percent of the time that textbooks such as this one routinely refer to "Asch's conformity study." Yet the overlooked flip side of the coin is that Asch's participants refused to acquiesce 63 percent of the time—thus also indicating the power of independence (Friend et al., 1990).

Thanks to Serge Moscovici, Edwin Hollander, and others, we now know quite a bit about **minority influence** and about the strategies that effective nonconformists use to act as agents of social change (De Dreu & De Vries, 2001; Hollander, 1985; Maass & Clark, 1984; Moscovici et al., 1985; Mugny & Perez, 1991).

The Power of Style According to Moscovici, majorities are powerful by virtue of their sheer *numbers*, while nonconformists derive power from the *style* of their behaviour. It is not just what they say that matters, but how they say it. To exert influence, says Moscovici, those in the minority must be forceful, persistent, and unwavering in support of their position. Yet at the same time, they must appear flexible and open-minded. Confronted with a consistent but even-handed dissenter, members of the majority will sit up, take notice, and rethink their own positions.

Why should a consistent behavioural style prove effective? One possible reason is that unwavering repetition draws attention from those in the mainstream, which is a necessary first step to social influence. Another possibility is that consistency signals that the dissenter is unlikely to yield, which leads those in the majority to feel pressured to seek compromise. A third possible reason is that when confronted with someone who has the self-confidence and dedication to take an unpopular stand without backing down, people assume that he or she must have a point. Unless a dissenter is perceived in negative terms—as biased, obstinate, or just plain crazy—this situation stimulates others to reexamine their own views (Moskowitz, 1996). Of course, it helps to be seen as part of "us" rather than "them." Research shows that dissenters have more influence when people identify with them and perceive them to be similar in ways that are positive and relevant (Turner, 1991; Wood et al., 1996).

Based on a meta-analysis of 97 experiments investigating minority influence, Wendy Wood and her colleagues (1994) concluded that there is strong support for the consistency hypothesis. In one classic study, for example, Moscovici and others (1969) turned Asch's procedure on its head by confronting people with a *minority* of confederates who made incorrect judgments. In groups of six, participants took part in what was supposed to be a study of colour perception. They viewed a series of slides—all blue, but varying in intensity. For each slide, the participants took turns naming the colour. The task was simple, but two confederates announced

minority influence
The process by which dissenters produce change within a group.

that the slides were green. When the confederates were *consistent*—that is, when both made incorrect green judgments for all slides—they had a surprising degree of influence. About a third of all participants incorrectly reported seeing at least one green slide, and eight percent of all responses were incorrect. Subsequent research confirmed that the perception of consistency increases minority influence (Clark, 2001; Crano, 2000).

A Chip Off the Old Block? Regardless of which strategy is used, minority influence is a force to be reckoned with. But does it work just like the process of conformity, or is there something different about the way that minorities and majorities effect change? Some theorists believe that a *single process* accounts for both directions of social influence—that minority influence is just like a "chip off the old block" (Latané & Wolf, 1981; Tanford & Penrod, 1984). Others have taken a *dual-process* approach (Moscovici, 1980; Nemeth, 1986). In this second view, majorities and minorities exert influence in very different ways. Majorities, because they have power and control, elicit public conformity by bringing stressful normative pressures to bear on the individual. But minorities, because they are seen as seriously committed to their views, produce a deeper and more lasting form of private conformity, or *conversion,* by leading others to rethink their original positions.

To evaluate these single- and dual-process theories, researchers have compared the effects of majority and minority viewpoints on participants who are otherwise neutral on an issue in dispute. On the basis of this research, two conclusions can be drawn. First, the relative impact of majorities and minorities depends on whether the judgment that is being made is objective or subjective, a matter of fact or opinion. In a study conducted in Italy, Ann Maass and others (1996) found that majorities have greater influence on factual questions, for which only one answer is correct ("What percentage of its raw oil does Italy import from Venezuela?"), but that minorities exert equal impact on opinion questions, for which there is a range of acceptable responses ("What percentage of its raw oil *should* Italy import from Venezuela?"). People feel freer to stray from the mainstream on matters of opinion—when there is no right or wrong answer.

The second conclusion is that the relative effects of majority and minority viewpoints depend on how conformity is measured. To be sure, majorities have a decisive upper hand on direct or public measures of conformity. After all, people are reluctant to stray conspicuously from the group norm. But on more indirect or private measures of conformity—when participants can respond without a fear of appearing deviant—minorities exert a strong impact (Clark & Maass, 1990; Moscovici & Personnaz, 1991; Wood et al., 1996). As Moscovici so cogently argued, each of us is changed in a meaningful but subtle way by minority opinion. Because of social pressures, we may be too intimidated to admit it; but the change is unmistakable (Wood et al., 1994).

According to Charlan Nemeth (1986), dissenters serve a valuable purpose regardless of whether their views are correct. Simply by their willingness to stay independent, minorities can force other group members to think more carefully, more openly, and more creatively about a problem, thus enhancing the quality of a group's decision making. In one study, participants exposed to a minority viewpoint on how to solve anagram problems later found more novel solutions themselves (Nemeth & Kwan, 1987). In a second study, those exposed to a consistent minority view on how to recall information later recalled more words from a list they were trying to memorize (Nemeth et al., 1990). And in a third study, interacting groups that contained one dissenting confederate produced more original analyses of complex business problems (Van Dyne & Saavedra, 1996).

Compliance

In conformity situations, people follow implicit group norms. But another common form of social influence occurs when others make direct *explicit* requests of us in the hope that we will comply. Situations calling for **compliance** take many forms. These include a friend's request for help, sheepishly prefaced by the question, "Can you do me a favour?" They also include the pop-up ad on the Internet designed to lure you into clicking onto a commercial site and the salesperson's pitch for business prefaced by the dangerous words, "Have I got a deal for you!" Sometimes, the request itself is upfront and direct; what you see is what you get. At other times, it is part of a subtle and more elaborate manipulation.

How do people get others to comply with self-serving requests? How do police interrogators get crime suspects to confess? How do TV evangelists draw millions of dollars in contributions for their ministries? How do *you* exert influence over others? Do you use threats, promises, politeness, deceit, or reason? Do you hint, coax, sulk, negotiate, throw tantrums, or pull rank whenever you can? To a large extent, the compliance strategies we use depend on how well we know a person, our status within a relationship, our personality, culture, and the nature of the request.

By observing the masters of influence—advertisers, fundraisers, politicians, and business leaders—social psychologists have learned a great deal about the subtle but effective strategies that are commonly used. What we see is that people often get others to comply with their requests by setting traps. Once caught in one of these traps, the unwary victim often finds it difficult to escape.

The Language of Request

How a request is phrased can affect our levels of compliance. Consider, for example, requests that sound reasonable but offer no real reason for compliance. Ellen Langer and her colleagues (1978) have found that words alone can sometimes trick us into submission. In their research, an experimenter approached people who were using a library photocopier and asked to cut in. Three different versions of the request were used. In one, participants were simply asked, "Excuse me. I have five pages. May I use the Xerox machine?" In a second version, the request was justified by the added phrase "because I'm in a rush." As you would expect, more participants stepped aside when the request was justified (94 percent) than when it was not (60 percent). A third version of the request, however, suggests that the reason offered had little to do with the increase in compliance. In this case, participants heard the following: "Excuse me. I have five pages. May I use the Xerox machine because I have to make some copies?" If you read this request closely, you'll see that it really offered no reason at all. Yet 93 percent in this condition complied! It was as if the appearance of a reason, triggered by the word *because,* was all that was necessary. Indeed, Langer (1989) finds that the mind is often on "automatic pilot," as we respond *mindlessly* to words without fully processing the information they are supposed to convey. At least for requests that are small, "sweet little nothings" may be enough to win compliance.

It is interesting that although the state of mindlessness can make us vulnerable to compliance, it can also have the opposite effect. For example, many city dwellers automatically walk past panhandlers on the street looking for a handout. Perhaps the way to increase compliance in such situations is to disrupt this mindless refusal response by making a request that is so unusual that it piques the target person's interest. In one study, a confederate approached people on the street and made a request that was either typical ("Can you spare a quarter?") or atypical ("Can you spare 17¢?").

compliance
Changes in behaviour that are elicited by direct requests.

Con artists prosper from the tendency for people to respond mindlessly to requests that sound reasonable but offer no real basis for compliance.

The result: Atypical pleas elicited more comments and questions from those who were targeted—and produced a 60 percent increase in the number of people who gave money (Santos et al., 1994). In another study, researchers went door-to-door selling holiday cards and gained more compliance when they disrupted the mindless process and reframed the sales pitch. They sold more cards when they said the price was "300 pennies—that's $3, it's a bargain" than when they simply asked for $3 (Davis & Knowles, 1999).

The Norm of Reciprocity

A simple, unstated, but powerful rule of social behaviour known as the *norm of reciprocity* dictates that we treat others as they have treated us (Gouldner, 1960). On the negative side, this norm can be used to sanction retaliation against those who cause us harm: "An eye for an eye." On the positive side, it leads us to feel obligated to repay others for acts of kindness. Thus, when we receive gifts, invitations, and free samples, we usually go out of our way to return the favour.

The norm of reciprocity contributes to the predictability and fairness of social interaction. However, it can also be used to exploit us. Dennis Regan (1971) examined this possibility in the following study. Individuals were brought together with a confederate—who was trained to act in a likeable or unlikeable manner—for an experiment on "aesthetics." In one condition, the confederate did the participant an unsolicited favour. He left during a break and returned with two bottles of Coca-Cola, one for himself and the other for the participant. In a second condition, he returned from the break empty-handed. In a third condition, participants were treated to a Coke—but by the experimenter, not the confederate. The confederate then told participants in all conditions that he was selling raffle tickets at 25¢ apiece and asked if they would be willing to buy any. On the average, participants bought more raffle tickets when the confederate had earlier brought them a soft drink than when he had not. The norm of reciprocity was so strong that they returned the favour even when the confederate was not otherwise a likeable character. In fact, participants in this condition spent an average of 43¢ on raffle tickets. At a time when soft drinks cost less than a quarter, the confederate made a handsome quick profit on his investment!

It's clear that the norm of reciprocity can be used to trap us into compliance. Research conducted in restaurants shows that waiters and waitresses can increase their tip percentages by writing "Thank you" on the back of the customer's check, by drawing a happy face on it, or by placing candy on the check tray (Rind & Strohmetz, 2001; Strohmetz et al., 2002). But does receiving a favour make us feel indebted forever, or is there a time limit to this social rule of thumb? In an experiment designed to answer this question, Jerry Burger and others (1997) used Regan's soft drink favour and had the confederate try to "cash in" with a request either immediately or one week later. The result: Compliance levels increased in the immediate condition but not after a full week had passed. People may feel compelled to reciprocate, but that feeling—at least for small acts of kindness—is relatively short-lived.

Some people are more likely than others to exploit the reciprocity norm. According to Martin Greenberg and David Westcott (1983), individuals who use reciprocity to elicit compliance are called "creditors" because they always try to keep others in their debt so they can cash in when necessary. On a questionnaire that measures *reciprocation ideology,* people are identified as creditors if they agree with such statements as "If someone does you a favour, it's good to repay that person with a greater favour."

On the receiving end, some people more than others try not to accept favours that might later set them up to be exploited. On a scale that measures *reciprocation wariness,* people are said to be wary if they express the suspicion, for example, that "asking for another's help gives them power over your life" (Eisenberger et al., 1987).

Setting Traps: Sequential Request Strategies

People who raise money or sell for a living know that it often takes more than a single plea to win over a potential donor or customer. Social psychologists share this knowledge and have studied several compliance techniques that are based on making two or more related requests. *Click!* The first request sets the trap. *Snap!* The second captures the prey. In a fascinating book entitled *Influence: Science and Practice,* Robert Cialdini (2001) describes a number of sequential request tactics in vivid detail. These methods are presented in the following pages.

The Foot in the Door Folk wisdom has it that one way to get a person to comply with a sizable request is to start small. First devised by travelling salespeople peddling vacuum cleaners, hairbrushes, cosmetics, magazine subscriptions, and encyclopedias, the trick is to somehow get your "foot in the door." The expression need not be taken literally, of course. The point of the **foot-in-the-door technique** is to break the ice with a small initial request that the customer can't easily refuse. Once that first commitment is elicited, the chances are increased that another, larger request will succeed.

Jonathan Freedman and Scott Fraser (1966) tested the impact of this technique in a series of field experiments. In one, an experimenter pretending to be employed by a consumer organization telephoned a group of female homemakers in Palo Alto, California, and asked if they would be willing to answer some questions about household products. Those who consented were then asked a few innocuous questions and thanked for their assistance. Three days later, the experimenter called back and made a considerable, almost outrageous, request. He asked the women if they would allow a handful of men into their homes for two hours to rummage through their drawers and cupboards so they could take an inventory of household products.

The foot-in-the-door technique proved to be very effective. When participants were confronted with only the very intrusive request, 22 percent consented. Yet among those surveyed earlier, the rate of agreement more than doubled, to 53 percent. This basic result has now been repeated over and over again. People are more likely to donate time, money, blood, the use of their home, and other resources once they have been induced to go along with a small initial request. Although the effect is seldom as dramatic as that obtained by Freedman and Fraser, it does appear in a wide variety of circumstances—and increases compliance rates, on average, by about 13 percent (Burger, 1999).

The practical implications of the foot-in-the-door technique are obvious. But why does it work? Several explanations have been suggested. One that seems plausible is based on self-perception theory—that people infer their attitudes by observing their own behaviour. This explanation suggests that a two-step process is at work. First, by observing your own behaviour in the initial situation, you come to see yourself as the kind of person who is generally cooperative when approached with a request. Second, when confronted with the more burdensome request, you seek to respond in ways that maintain this new self-image. By this logic, the foot-in-the-door technique should succeed only when you attribute an initial act of compliance to your own personal characteristics.

foot-in-the-door technique
A two-step compliance technique in which an influencer sets the stage for the real request by first getting a person to comply with a much smaller request.

Based on a review of dozens of studies, Jerry Burger (1999) concludes that the research generally supports the self-perception account. Thus, if the first request is too trivial or if participants are paid for the first act of compliance, they won't later come to view themselves as inherently cooperative. Under these conditions, the technique does *not* work. Likewise, the effect occurs only when people are motivated to be consistent with their self-images. If participants are unhappy with what the initial behaviour implies about them, if they are too young to appreciate the implications, or if they don't care about behaving in ways that are personally consistent, then again the technique does not work. Other processes may be at work, but it appears that the foot opens the door by altering *self*-perceptions, leading people who agree to the small initial request—without any compensation—to see themselves as helpful (Burger & Caldwell, 2003). In fact, this process can occur even when a person tries to comply with the initial small request but fails. In a series of studies, Dariusz Dolinski (2000) found that when people were asked if they could find directions to a nonexistent street address or decipher an unreadable message—small favours they could not satisfy—they, too, become more compliant with the next request.

Knowing that a foot in the door increases compliance is both exciting and troubling—exciting for the owner of the foot, troubling for the owner of the door. As Cialdini (2001) put it, "You can use small commitments to manipulate a person's self-image; you can use them to turn citizens into 'public servants,' prospects into 'customers,' prisoners into 'collaborators.' And once you've got a person's self-image where you want it, he or she should comply *naturally* with a whole range of requests that are consistent with this new self-view" (p. 67).

Spencer Platt/Getty Images

Low-balling is a common technique used in selling cars.

Low-Balling Another two-step trap, perhaps the most unscrupulous of all compliance techniques, is also based on the "start small" idea. Imagine yourself in the following situation. You're at a local automobile dealership. After some negotiation, the salesperson offers a great price on the car of your choice. You cast aside other considerations and shake hands on the deal; and as the salesperson goes off to "write it up," you begin to feel the thrill of owning the car of your dreams. Absorbed in fantasy, you are interrupted by the sudden return of the salesperson. "I'm sorry," he says. "The manager would not approve the sale. We have to raise the price by another $450. I'm afraid that's the best we can do." As the victim of an all-too-common trick known as **low-balling**, you are now faced with a tough decision. On the one hand, you're wild about the car. You've already enjoyed the pleasure of thinking it's yours; and the more you think about it, the better it looks. On the other hand, you don't want to pay more than you bargained for, and you have an uneasy feeling in the pit of your stomach that you're being duped. What do you do?

low-balling
A two-step compliance technique in which the influencer secures agreement with a request but then increases the size of that request by revealing hidden costs.

Salespeople who use this tactic are betting that you'll go ahead with the purchase despite the added cost. If the way research participants behave is any indication, they are often right. In one study, experimenters phoned introductory psychology students and asked if they would be willing to participate in a study for extra credit. Some were told up front that the session would begin at the uncivilized hour of 7 a.m. Knowing that, only 31 percent volunteered. But other participants were low-balled. Only *after* they agreed to participate did the experimenter inform them of the 7 a.m. starting time. Would that be okay? Whether it was okay or not, the procedure achieved its objective—the sign-up rate rose to 56 percent (Cialdini et al., 1978).

Low-balling is an interesting technique. Surely, once the low ball has been thrown, many recipients suspect that they were misled. Yet they go along. Why? The reason appears to be based on the psychology of commitment (Kiesler, 1971). Once people make a particular decision, they justify it to themselves by thinking of all its positive aspects. As they get increasingly committed to a course of action, they grow more resistant to changing their mind, even if the initial reasons for the action have been changed or withdrawn entirely. In the automobile dealership scenario, you might very well have decided to purchase the car because of the price. But then you would have thought about its sleek appearance, the leather interior, and the cool sunroof. By the time you learned that the price would be more than you'd bargained for, it would be too late—you would already have been hooked.

Low-balling also produces another form of commitment. When people do not suspect duplicity, they feel a nagging sense of unfulfilled obligation to the person with whom they negotiated. Thus, even though the salesperson was unable to complete the original deal, you might feel obligated to buy anyway, having already agreed to make the purchase. This commitment to the other person may account for why low-balling works better when the second request is made by the same person who made the initial request than when it is made by someone else (Burger & Petty, 1981). It may also explain why people are most vulnerable to the low-ball when they make their commitment in public rather than in private (Burger & Cornelius, 2003).

The Door in the Face Although shifting from an initial small request to a larger one can be effective, as in the foot-in-the-door and low-ball techniques, oddly enough the opposite is also true. Cialdini (2007) describes the time he was approached by a Boy Scout and asked to buy two $5 tickets to an upcoming circus. Having better things to do with his time and money, he declined. Then the boy asked if he would be interested in buying chocolate bars at a dollar apiece. Even though he doesn't like chocolate, Cialdini—an expert on social influence—bought two of them! After a moment's reflection, he realized what had happened. Whether the Boy Scout planned it that way or not, Cialdini had fallen for what is known as the **door-in-the-face technique**.

The technique is as simple as it sounds. An individual makes an initial request that is so large it is sure to be rejected, and then comes back with a second, more reasonable request. Will the second request fare better after the first one has been declined? Plagued by the sight of uneaten chocolate bars, Cialdini and others (1975) tested the effectiveness of the door-in-the-face technique. They stopped students on campus and asked if they would volunteer to work without pay at a counselling centre for juvenile delinquents. The time commitment would be forbidding: roughly two hours a week for the next two years! Not surprisingly, everyone who was approached politely slammed the proverbial door in the experimenter's face. But then the experimenter followed up with a more modest proposal, asking the students if they would be willing to take a group of delinquents on a two-hour trip to the zoo. The strategy worked like a charm. Only 17 percent of the students confronted with only the second request agreed. But of those who initially declined the first request, 50 percent said yes to the zoo trip. You should note that the door-in-the-face technique does not elicit only empty promises. Most research participants who comply subsequently do what they've agreed to do (Cialdini & Ascani, 1976).

Why is the door-in-the-face technique such an effective trap? One possibility involves the principle of *perceptual contrast:* To the person exposed to a very large initial request, the second request "seems smaller." In this case, $2 worth of candy bars is not bad compared with $10 for circus tickets. Likewise, taking a group of kids to the zoo seems trivial compared with two years of volunteer work. As intuitively sensible as this explanation seems, Cialdini and others (1975) concluded that perceptual contrast is only partly responsible for the effect. When participants heard the large request

door-in-the-face technique
A two-step compliance technique in which an influencer prefaces the real request with one that is so large that it is rejected.

without actually having to reject it, their rate of compliance with the second request (25 percent) was only slightly larger than the 17 percent rate of compliance exhibited by those who heard only the small request.

A second, more compelling explanation for the effect involves the notion of *reciprocal concessions.* A close cousin of the reciprocity norm, this refers to the pressure to respond to changes in a bargaining position. When an individual backs down from a large request to a smaller one, we view that move as a concession that we should match by our own compliance. Thus, the door-in-the-face technique does not work if the second request is made by a different person (Cialdini et al., 1975). Nor does it work if the first request is so extreme that it comes across as an insincere "first offer" (Schwarzwald et al., 1979). On an emotional level, refusing to help on one request may trigger feelings of guilt—which we can reduce by complying with the second, smaller request (O'Keefe & Figge, 1997; Millar, 2002).

An effective way to get someone to do you a favour is to make a first request that is so large the person is sure to reject it. **TRUE.**

That's Not All, Folks! If the notion of reciprocal concessions is correct, then a person shouldn't actually have to refuse the initial offer for the shift to a smaller request to work. Indeed, another familiar sales strategy manages to use concession without first eliciting refusal. In this strategy, a product is offered at a particular price; but then, before the buyer has a chance to respond, the seller adds, "And that's not all!" At that point, either the original price is reduced, or a bonus is offered to sweeten the pot. The seller, of course, intends all along to make the so-called concession.

This ploy, called the **that's-not-all technique**, seems awfully transparent, right? Surely, no one falls for it, right? Jerry Burger (1986) was not so sure. He predicted that people are more likely to make a purchase when a deal seems to have improved than when the same deal is offered right from the start. To test this hypothesis, Burger set up a booth at a campus fair and sold cupcakes. Some customers who approached the table were told that the cupcakes cost 75¢ each. Others were told that they cost a dollar; but then, before they could respond, the price was reduced to 75¢. Rationally speaking, Burger's manipulation did not affect the ultimate price, so it should not have affected sales. But it did. When customers were led to believe that the final price represented a reduction, sales increased from 44 to 73 percent.

that's-not-all technique
A two-step compliance technique in which the influencer begins with an inflated request, and then decreases its apparent size by offering a discount or bonus.

At this point, let's step back and look at the various compliance techniques described in this section. All of them are based on a two-step process that involves a shift from a request of one size to another. What differs is whether the small or large request comes first and how the transition between steps is made (see ■ Table 7.2). Moreover, all these strategies work in subtle ways by manipulating the target person's self-image, commitment to the product, feelings of obligation to the seller, or perceptions of the real request. It is even possible to increase compliance by prefacing the request with "How are you feeling?"—a question that tends to elicit a favourable first response from strangers (Howard, 1990). When you consider these various traps, you have to wonder whether it's ever possible to escape.

TABLE 7.2

Sequential Request Strategies

Various compliance techniques are based on a sequence of two related requests. *Click!* The first request sets the trap. *Snap!* The second captures the prey. Research has shown that the four sequential request strategies summarized in this table are all effective.

Request Shifts	Technique	Description
From small to large	Foot in the door	Begin with a very small request; secure agreement; then make a separate, larger request.
	Low-balling	Secure agreement with a request, and then increase the size of that request by revealing hidden costs.
From large to small	Door in the face	Begin with a very large request that will be rejected; then follow up with a more modest request.
	That's not all	Begin with a somewhat inflated request; then immediately decrease the apparent size of that request by offering a discount or bonus.

Assertiveness: When People Say No

Cialdini (2007) opens his book with a confession: "I can admit it freely now. All my life I've been a patsy." As a past victim of compliance traps, he is not alone. Many people find it difficult to be assertive in interpersonal situations. Faced with an unreasonable request from a friend, spouse, or stranger, they become anxious at the mere thought of putting a foot down and refusing to comply. Indeed, there are times when it is uncomfortable for anyone to say no. However, just as we can maintain our autonomy in the face of conformity pressures, we can also refuse direct requests—even clever ones. The trap may be set, but you don't have to get caught.

"Your Honour, has anyone ever told you what a wry, sensuous mouth you have?"

Compliance techniques are likely to backfire when seen as transparent attempts at influence.

According to Cialdini, being able to resist the pressure of compliance rests, first and foremost, on being vigilant. If a stranger hands you a gift and then launches into a sales pitch, you should recognize the tactic for what it is and not feel indebted by the norm of reciprocity. And if you strike a deal with a salesperson who later reneges on the terms, you should be aware that you're being thrown a low ball. Indeed, that is exactly what happened to one of the authors of this book. After a full Saturday afternoon of careful negotiation at a local car dealer, he and his wife finally came to terms on a price. Minutes later, however, the salesperson returned with the news that the manager would not approve the deal. The cost of an air conditioner, which was originally to be included, would have to be added on to the price. Familiar with the research, the author turned to his wife and exclaimed, "It's a trick; they're low-balling us!" Realizing what was happening, she became furious, went straight to the manager, and made such a scene in front of other customers that he backed down and honoured the original deal.

What happened in this instance? Why did recognizing the attempted manipulation produce such anger and resistance? As this story illustrates, compliance techniques work smoothly only if they are hidden from view. The problem is not only that they are attempts to influence us, but that they are deceptive. Flattery, gifts, and other ploys often elicit compliance—but not if they are perceived as insincere (Jones, 1964), and not if the target has a high level of reciprocity wariness (Eisenberger et al., 1987). Likewise, the sequential request traps are powerful to the extent that they are subtle and cannot be seen for what they are (Schwarzwald et al., 1979). People don't like to be hustled. In fact, feeling manipulated typically leads us to react with anger, psychological reactance, and stubborn noncompliance ... unless the request is a command and the requester is a figure of authority.

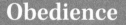

"Knowledge is power, and if you know when a clever technique is being used on you, then it becomes easier to ignore it."

—Burke Leon

Obedience

From the day we are born, we are taught that it's important to respect legitimate forms of leadership. Most people think twice before defying parents, teachers, employers, coaches, and government officials. The problem is, mere symbols of authority—titles, uniforms, badges, or the trappings of success, even without the necessary credentials—can sometimes turn ordinary people into docile servants. Leonard Bickman (1974) demonstrated this phenomenon in a series of studies in which a male research assistant

© Topham/The Image Works

Taken to the extreme, blind obedience can have devastating results. In World War II, Nazi officials killed millions, many said, "because I was just following orders."

stopped passersby on the street and ordered them to do something unusual. Sometimes, he pointed to a paper bag on the ground and said, "Pick up this bag for me!" At other times, he pointed to an individual standing beside a parked car and said, "This fellow is over-parked at the meter but doesn't have any change. Give him a dime!" Would anyone really take this guy seriously? When he was dressed in street clothes, only a third of the people stopped and followed his orders. But when he wore a security guard's uniform, nearly 9 out of every 10 people obeyed! Even when the uniformed assistant turned the corner and walked away after issuing his command, the vast majority of passersby followed his orders. Clearly, uniforms signify the power of authority (Bushman, 1988).

Blind **obedience** may seem funny; but if people are willing to take orders from a total stranger, how far will they go when it really matters? As the pages of history attest, the implications are sobering. In World War II, Nazi officials participated in the deaths of millions of Jews, as well as Poles, Russians, Gypsies, and homosexuals. Yet when tried for these crimes, their defence was always the same: "I was following orders."

Surely, you may be thinking, the Holocaust was a historical anomaly that says more about the Nazis as prejudiced, frustrated, and sick individuals than about the situations that lead people in general to commit acts of destructive obedience. In *Hitler's Willing Executioners,* historian Daniel Goldhagen (1996) argues on the basis of past records that many Germans were willing anti-Semitic participants in the Holocaust—not ordinary people forced to follow orders. But two lines of evidence suggest that attaching responsibility to the German people is far too simple an explanation of what happened. First, interviews with Nazi war criminals and doctors who worked in concentration camps have suggested the provocative and disturbing conclusion that these people were "utterly ordinary" (Arendt, 1963; Lifton, 1986; Von Lang & Sibyll, 1983). Second, the monstrous events of World War II do not stand alone in modern history. Even today, crimes of obedience, including both suicide bombings and torture, are being committed throughout the world (Kelman & Hamilton, 1989; Haritos-Fatouros, 2002). On extraordinary occasions, obedience is carried to its limit. In 1978, 900 members of the People's Temple cult obeyed an order from the Reverend Jim Jones to kill themselves. In 1997, in a small Quebec town, five disciples of the Order of the Solar Temple took sedatives and then blew up their cottage; according to the doctrines of the cult, this allowed them to ascend to the stars. Fanatic cult members have committed mass suicide before, and they will likely do so again (Galanter, 1999).

Milgram's Research: Forces of Destructive Obedience

obedience
Behaviour change produced by the commands of authority.

During the time that Adolf Eichmann was being tried for his Nazi war crimes, Stanley Milgram (1963) began a dramatic series of experiments that culminated in his 1974 book *Obedience to Authority.* For many years, the ethics of this research has been the focus of much debate. Those who say it was not ethical point to the potential

From the film *Obedience,* copyright 1968 by Stanley Milgram, copyright renewed 1993 by Alexandra Milgram and distributed by Penn State Media Sales.

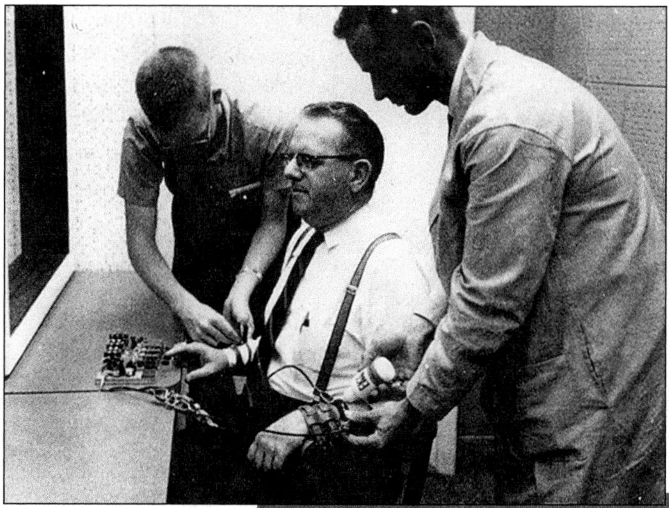

By using Milgram's shock generator (left), participants in Milgram's studies believed they were shocking Mr. Wallace, the man being strapped into his chair (right).

psychological harm to which the participants were exposed. In contrast, those who believe that Milgram's research met appropriate ethical standards emphasize the contribution it makes to our understanding of an important social problem. They conclude that, on balance, the extreme danger that destructive obedience poses for all humankind justified Milgram's unorthodox methods. Consider both sides of the debate, which were summarized in Chapter 2, and make your own judgment. Now, however, take a more personal look. Imagine yourself as one of the approximately 1000 participants who found themselves in the following situation.

The experience begins when you arrive at a Yale University laboratory and meet two men. One is the experimenter, a stern young man dressed in a grey lab coat and carrying a clipboard. The other is a middle-aged gentleman named Mr. Wallace, an accountant who is slightly overweight and average in appearance. You exchange introductions, and then the experimenter explains that you and your co-participant will take part in a study on the effects of punishment on learning. After lots have been drawn, it is determined that you will serve as the teacher and that Mr. Wallace will be the learner. So far, so good.

Soon, however, the situation takes on a more ominous tone. You find out that your job is to test the learner's memory and administer electric shocks of increasing intensity whenever he makes a mistake. You are then escorted into another room, where the experimenter straps Mr. Wallace into a chair, rolls up his sleeves, attaches electrodes to his arms, and applies "electrode paste" to prevent blisters and burns. As if that isn't bad enough, you may overhear Mr. Wallace telling the experimenter that he has a heart problem. The experimenter responds by conceding that the shocks will be painful but reassures Mr. Wallace that they will not cause "permanent tissue damage." In the meantime, you can personally vouch for how painful the shocks are because the experimenter stings you with one that is supposed to be mild. From there, the experimenter takes you back to the main room, where you are seated in front of a "shock generator," a machine with 30 switches that range from 15 volts, labelled "slight shock," to 450 volts, labelled "XXX."

"Far more, and far more hideous, crimes have been committed in the name of obedience than have ever been committed in the name of rebellion."

—C. P. Snow

Your role in this experiment is straightforward. First you read a list of word pairs to Mr. Wallace through a microphone. Then you test his memory with a series of multiple-choice questions. The learner answers each question by pressing one of four switches that light up signals on the shock generator. If his answer is correct, you move on to the next question. If it is incorrect, you announce the correct answer and shock him. When you press the appropriate shock switch, a red light flashes above it, relay switches click inside the machine, and you hear a loud buzzing sound go off in the learner's room. After each wrong answer, you're told, the intensity of the shock should be increased by 15 volts.

You aren't aware, of course, that the experiment is rigged and that Mr. Wallace—who is actually a confederate—is never really shocked. As far as you know, he gets zapped each time you press one of the switches. As the session proceeds, the learner makes more and more errors, leading you to work your way up the shock scale. As you reach 75, 90, and 105 volts, you hear the learner grunt in pain. At 120 volts, he begins to shout. If you're still in it at 150 volts, you hear the learner cry out, "Experimenter! That's all. Get me out of here. My heart's starting to bother me now. I refuse to go on!" Screams of agony and protest continue. At 300 volts, he says he absolutely refuses to continue. By the time you surpass 330 volts, the learner falls silent and fails to respond—not to be heard from again. ■ Table 7.3 lists his responses in grim detail.

TABLE 7.3

The Learner's Protests in the Milgram Experiment

As participants administered progressively more intense shocks, they heard the learner moan, groan, protest, and complain. All participants heard the same programmed set of responses. Eventually, the learner fell silent and ceased to respond.

(Milgram, 1974.)

75 volts	Ugh!
90 volts	Ugh!
105 volts	Ugh! (louder)
120 volts	Ugh! Hey this really hurts.
135 volts	Ugh!!
150 volts	Ugh!!! Experimenter! That's all. Get me out of here. I told you I had heart trouble. My heart's starting to bother me now. Get me out of here, please. My heart's starting to bother me. I refuse to go on. Let me out.
165 volts	Ugh! Let me out! (shouting)
180 volts	Ugh! I can't stand the pain. Let me out of here! (shouting)
195 volts	Ugh! Let me out of here. Let me out of here. My heart's bothering me. Let me out of here! You have no right to keep me here! Let me out! Let me out of here! Let me out! Let me out of here! My heart's bothering me. Let me out! Let me out!
210 volts	Ugh!! Experimenter! Get me out of here. I've had enough. I won't be in the experiment any more.
225 volts	Ugh!
240 volts	Ugh!
255 volts	Ugh! Get me out of here.
270 volts	(Agonized scream.) Let me out of here. Let me out of here. Let me out of here. Let me out. Do you hear? Let me out of here.
285 volts	(Agonized scream.)
300 volts	(Agonized scream.) I absolutely refuse to answer any more. Get me out of here. You can't hold me here. Get me out. Get me out of here.
315 volts	(Intensely agonized scream.) I told you I refuse to answer. I'm no longer part of this experiment.
330 volts	(Intense and prolonged agonized scream.) Let me out of here. Let me out of here. My heart's bothering me. Let me out, I tell you. (Hysterically) Let me out of here. Let me out of here. You have no right to hold me here. Let me out! Let me out! Let me out! Let me out of here! Let me out! Let me out!

Somewhere along the line, you turn to the experimenter for guidance. "What should I do? Don't you think I should stop? Shouldn't we at least check on him?" You might even confront the experimenter head-on and refuse to continue. Yet in answer to your inquiries, the experimenter—firm in his tone and seemingly unaffected by the learner's distress—prods you along as follows:

- Please continue (or please go on).
- The experiment requires that you continue.
- It is absolutely essential that you continue.
- You have no other choice; you must go on.

What do you do? In a situation that begins to feel more and more like a bad dream, do you follow your own conscience or obey the experimenter?

Milgram described this procedure to psychiatrists, students, and middle-class adults, and he asked them to predict how they would behave. On average, these groups estimated that they would call it quits at the 135-volt level. Not a single person thought he or she would go all the way to 450 volts. When asked to predict the percentage of *other* people who would deliver the maximum shock, those interviewed gave similar estimates. The psychiatrists estimated that only one out of 1000 people would exhibit that kind of extreme obedience. They were wrong. In Milgram's initial study, involving 40 men, participants exhibited an alarming degree of obedience, administering an average of 27 out of 30 possible shocks. In fact, 26 of the 40 participants—*65 percent*—delivered the ultimate punishment of 450 volts.

The Obedient Participant At first glance, you may see these results as a lesson in the psychology of cruelty and conclude that Milgram's participants were seriously disturbed. But research does not support such a simple explanation. To begin with, those in a control group who were not prodded along by an experimenter refused to continue early in the shock sequence. Moreover, Milgram found that virtually all participants, including those who administered severe shocks, were tormented by the experience. Many of them pleaded with the experimenter to let them stop. When he refused, they went on. But, in the process, they trembled, stuttered, groaned, perspired, bit their lips, and dug their fingernails into their flesh. Some burst into fits of nervous laughter. On one occasion, said Milgram, "we observed a [participant's] seizure so violently convulsive that it was necessary to call a halt to the experiment" (1963, p. 375).

Was Milgram's 65 percent baseline level of obedience attributable to his unique sample of male participants? Not at all. Forty women who participated in a later study exhibited precisely the same level of obedience: 65 percent threw the 450-volt switch. Before you jump to the conclusion that something was amiss in the community surrounding Yale University, consider the fact that Milgram's basic finding has been obtained in several different countries and with children as well as students and older adults (Shanab & Yahya, 1977, 1978). Obedience in the Milgram situation is so universal that it led one author to ask, "Are we all Nazis?" (Askenasy, 1978).

The answer, of course, is no. An individual's character can make a difference; and some people, depending on the situation, are far more obedient than others. In the aftermath of World War II, a group of social scientists, searching for the root causes of prejudice, sought to identify individuals with an *authoritarian personality* and developed a questionnaire known as the F-Scale to measure it (Adorno et al., 1950; Stone et al., 1993). What they found is that people who get high scores on the F-Scale (F stands for "Fascist") are rigid, dogmatic, sexually repressed, ethnocentric, intolerant of dissent, and punitive. They are submissive toward figures of authority but aggressive toward subordinates. Indeed, people with high F scores are also more willing than low scorers to administer high-intensity shocks in Milgram's obedience situation (Elms & Milgram, 1966). Examining the scores of more than 4000 Canadian university students and more than 2500 of their parents, Robert Altemeyer (2004) has concluded that those who score the highest on authoritarian scales are also among the most prejudiced in society.

Although personality characteristics may make someone vulnerable or resistant to destructive obedience, what seems to matter most is the situation in which people find themselves. By carefully altering particular aspects of his basic scenario, in more than 20 variations of the basic experiment, Milgram was able to identify factors that increase and decrease the 65 percent baseline rate of obedience (see ▶ Figure 7.6). Three factors in particular are important: the authority figure, the proximity of the victim, and the experimental procedure (Blass, 1992; Miller, 1986).

The Authority What is most remarkable about Milgram's findings is that a lab-coated experimenter is *not* a powerful figure of authority. Unlike a military superior, employer, or teacher, the psychology experimenter in Milgram's research could not ultimately enforce his commands. Still, his physical presence and his apparent

▶ FIGURE 7.6

Factors That Influence Obedience

Milgram varied many factors in his research program. Without commands from an experimenter, fewer than 3 percent of the participants exhibited full obedience. Yet in the standard baseline condition, 65 percent of participants followed the orders. To identify factors that might reduce this level, Milgram varied the location of the experiment, the status of the authority, the participant's proximity to the victim, and the presence of confederates who rebel. The effects of these variations are illustrated here.

(Milgram, 1974.)

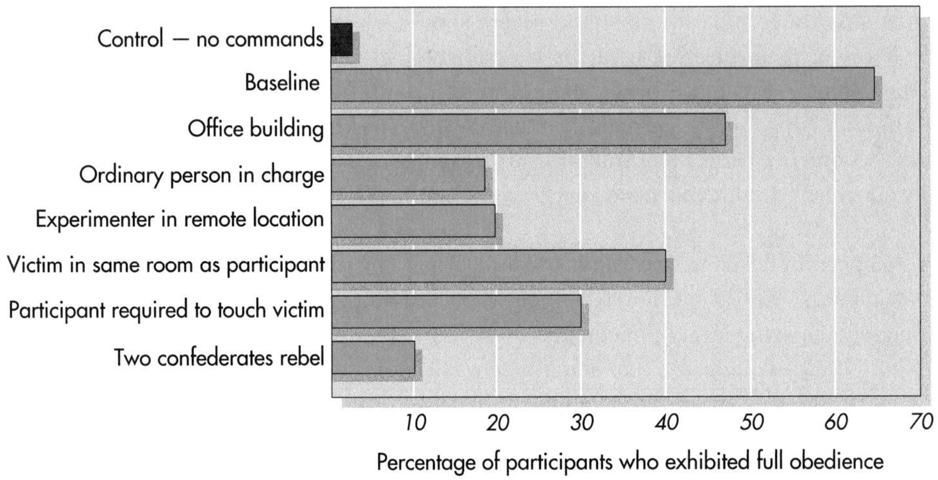

legitimacy played major roles in drawing obedience. When Milgram diminished the experimenter's status by moving his lab from the distinguished surroundings of Yale University to a rundown urban office building in nearby Bridgeport, Connecticut, the rate of total obedience dropped to 48 percent. When the experimenter was replaced by an ordinary person—supposedly another participant—there was a sharp reduction to 20 percent. Similarly, Milgram found that when the experimenter was in charge but issued his commands by telephone, only 21 percent fully obeyed. (In fact, when the experimenter was not watching, many participants in this condition feigned obedience by pressing the 15-volt switch.) One conclusion, then, is clear. At least in the Milgram setting, destructive obedience requires the physical presence of a prestigious authority figure.

If an experimenter can exert such control over research participants, imagine the control wielded by truly powerful authority figures—present or not. An intriguing field study examined the extent to which hospital nurses would obey unreasonable orders from a doctor they did not know. Using a fictitious name, a male physician called several female nurses on the phone and told them to administer a drug to a specific patient. His order violated hospital regulations. The drug was uncommon, the dosage was too large, and the effects could have been harmful. Yet out of the 22 nurses who were contacted, 21 had to be stopped as they prepared to obey the doctor's orders (Hofling et al., 1966).

The Victim Situational characteristics of the victim are also important in destructive obedience. Milgram noted that Nazi war criminal Adolf Eichmann felt sick when he toured concentration camps but only had to shuffle papers from behind a desk to play his part in the Holocaust. Similarly, the B-29 pilot who dropped the atom bomb on Hiroshima in World War II said of his mission, "I had no thoughts, except what I'm supposed to do" (Miller, 1986, p. 228). These events suggest that because Milgram's participants were physically separated from the learner, they were able to distance themselves emotionally from the consequences of their actions.

To test the impact of a victim's proximity on destructive obedience, Milgram seated the learner in one of his studies in the same room as the participant. Under these conditions, only 40 percent fully obeyed. When participants were required to physically grasp the victim's hand and force it onto a metal shock plate, full obedience dropped to 30 percent. These findings represent significant reductions from the 65 percent baseline. Still, three out of ten participants were willing to use brute force in the name of obedience.

The Procedure Finally, there is the situation created by Milgram. A close look at the dilemma his participants faced reveals two important aspects of the experimental procedure. First, participants were led to feel relieved of any personal sense of *responsibility* for the victim's welfare. The experimenter said up front that he was accountable. When participants were led to believe that *they* were responsible, their levels of obedience dropped considerably (Tilker, 1970). The ramifications of this finding are immense. In the military and other organizations, individuals often occupy positions in a hierarchical chain of command. Eichmann was a middle-level bureaucrat who received orders from Hitler and transmitted them to others for implementation. Caught between individuals who make policy and those who carry it out, how personally responsible do those in the middle feel? Wesley Kilham and Leon Mann (1974) examined this issue in an obedience study that cast participants in one of two roles: the *transmitter* (who took orders from the experimenter and passed them on), and the *executant* (who actually pressed the shock levers). As they predicted, transmitters were more obedient (54 percent) than executants (28 percent).

The second feature of Milgram's scenario that promoted obedience is gradual escalation. Participants began the session by delivering mild shocks and then, only gradually, escalated to voltage levels of high intensity. After all, what's another 15 volts compared with the current level? By the time participants realized the frightening implications of what they were doing, it had become more difficult for them to escape (Gilbert, 1981). This sequence is much like the foot-in-the-door technique. In Milgram's words, people become "integrated into a situation that carries its own momentum. The subject's problem ... is how to become disengaged from a situation which is moving in an altogether ugly direction" (1974, p. 73). We should point out that obedience by momentum is not unique to Milgram's research paradigm. As reported by Amnesty International, many countries today torture political prisoners—and those who are recruited for the dirty work are trained, in part, through an escalating series of commitments (Haritos-Fatouros, 2002).

Milgram in the Twenty-First Century

When Stanley Milgram published the results of his first experiment in 1963, at the age of 28, a *New York Times* headline read: "Sixty-Five Percent in Test Blindly Obey Order to Inflict Pain." Milgram had pierced the public consciousness and was poised to become one of the most important and controversial figures in psychology—and beyond. In a fascinating biography, *The Man Who Shocked the World*, Thomas Blass (2004) tells of how Milgram became interested in obedience and the impact his studies have had on social scientists, legal scholars, the military, and popular culture around the world

In experiments on obedience, most participants who were ordered to administer severe shocks to an innocent person refused to do so. FALSE.

(Milgram's obedience book has been translated into 11 languages). Now, in an age filled with threats of global conflict, extremism, terrorism, economic desperation, and new forms of lethal weaponry, obedience to authority is an issue of such importance that social psychologists all over the world continue to ponder its ramifications (Benjamin & Simpson, 2009; Blass, 2009).

Would the same results as Milgram's be repeated today, in a different but analogous situation? To answer this question, Dutch researchers Wim Meeus and Quinten Raaijmakers (1995) constructed a moral dilemma like Milgram's. Rather than command participants to inflict physical pain, however, they arranged for them to cause psychological harm. When participants arrived at a university laboratory, they met a confederate supposedly there to take a test as part of a job interview. If the confederate passed the test, he'd get the job; if he failed, he would not. As part of a study of performance under stress, the experimenter told participants to distract the test-taking applicant by making an escalating series of harassing remarks. On cue, the applicant pleaded with participants to stop, became angry, faltered, and eventually fell into a state of despair and failed. As in Milgram's research, the question was straightforward: How many participants would obey orders through the entire set of 15 stress remarks, despite the apparent harm caused to a real-life job applicant? In a control group that lacked a prodding experimenter, no one persisted. But when the experimenter ordered them to go on, 92 percent exhibited complete obedience despite seeing the task as unfair and distasteful. It appears that obedience is a powerful aspect of human nature brought about by the docile manner in which people relate to figures of authority—even today.

In a more recent—and even more direct—attempt to revisit Milgram, Jerry Burger (2009) conducted a "partial replication" for which he paid $50 to 70 men and women, a diverse group that ranged from 20 to 81 years old, and used the same procedure. In the original experiment, the learner first protested and asked to stop at 150 volts, at which point nearly all participants paused and indicated a reluctance to continue. Some outright refused at this point. Of those participants who did continue, however, most went all the way (Packer, 2008). On the basis of this finding, Burger followed the Milgram protocol up to 150 volts in order to estimate the number of participants who would have pulled the switch at 450 volts. He also added a condition in which a defiant confederate posing as another participant refused to continue (see ▶ Figure 7.7).

In light of post-Milgram changes in standards for research ethics, Burger took additional precautions; he excluded from the study individuals he feared would experience too much stress, and then he informed and reminded participants three times that they could withdraw from the study at any time without penalty.

Despite all that has changed in 45 years, the obedience rate was not appreciably lower.

▶ FIGURE 7.7

Obedience in the Twenty-First Century

In the version of the experiment that Burger modelled, 83 percent of Milgram's original participants continued past 150 volts. Forty-five years later, Burger saw a slight drop to 70 percent. Note, too, that the obedience rate dropped only slightly, to 63 percent, among participants who saw a defiant confederate refuse to continue. These results show that obedience to authority may have declined a bit over the years, but it has by no means extinguished.

(Burger, 2009.)

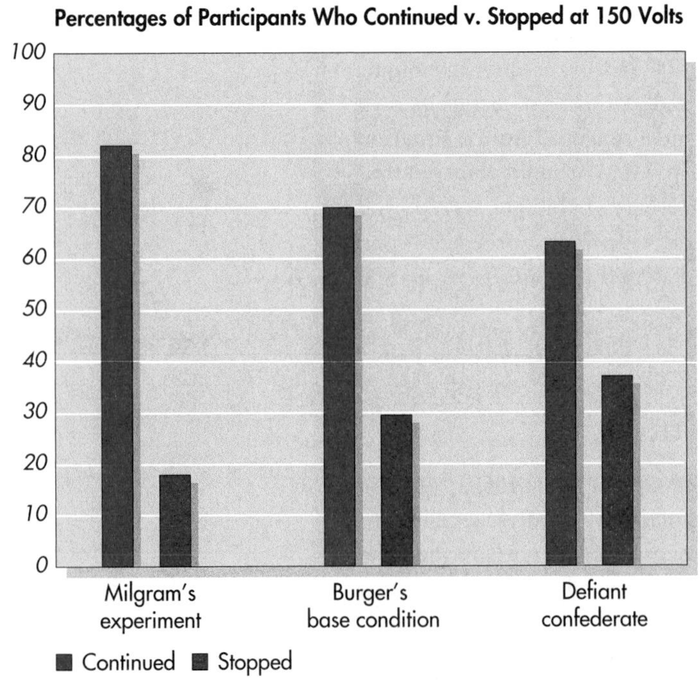

In the experiment that Burger modelled, 83 percent of Milgram's participants had continued past 150 volts. In Burger's more recent study, 70 percent did the same (it can be estimated, therefore, that 55 percent would have exhibited full 450-volt obedience in the original experiment). Two additional results proved interesting: (1) Just as Milgram had found, there were no differences between men and women; and (2) the obedience rate declined only slightly, to 63 percent, among participants who saw a defiant confederate refuse to continue.

Already this new replication has drawn a good deal of interest and commentary. Alan Elms (2009), a graduate student and collaborator of Milgram's in the 1960s, is cautious about comparing Burger's "obedience lite" procedure to Milgram's but eager to see it revitalize the research program Milgram had initiated. Arthur Miller (2009), author of *The Obedience Experiments*, voices the same cautious excitement. Thomas Blass (2009), author of the Milgram biography, *The Man Who Shocked the World*, sees Burger's experiment as an important milestone and demonstrates the stability and resilience of obedience in human social behaviour. In contrast, Jean Twenge (2009) notes that relative to an obedience rate of 83 percent among Milgram's male participants, only 67 percent of Burger's men exhibited 150-volt obedience, an encouraging decline. While impressed with the power of Milgram's situation, Twenge is hopeful that destructive obedience is less prevalent today, in the twenty-first century, than in the past.

Before leaving the Milgram studies, consider an awkward but important moral question: By providing a situational explanation for the evils of Nazi Germany or of modern-day terrorism, are social psychologists unwittingly excusing the perpetrators? Does blaming what they did on the situation let them off the responsibility hook? In a series of studies, Arthur Miller and others (1999) found that after people were asked to come up with explanations for acts of wrongdoing, they tended to be more forgiving of the individuals who committed those acts—and were seen as more forgiving by others. This appearance of forgiveness was certainly not Milgram's intent, nor is it the intent of other researchers today who seek to understand cruelty, even while continuing to condemn it. Miller and his colleagues are thus quick to caution, "To explain is not to forgive" (p. 265).

Defiance: When People Rebel

It is easy to despair in light of the impressive array of forces that compel people toward blind obedience. But there's also good news. Just as social influence processes can breed subservience to authority, they can also breed rebellion and defiance. Few people realize it, but this phenomenon, too, was seen during World War II. In *Resistance of the Heart*, historian Nathan Stoltzfus (1996) describes a civil protest in Berlin in which the non-Jewish wives of 2000 newly captured Jews congregated outside the prison. The women were there, initially, seeking information about their husbands. Soon they were filling the streets chanting and refusing to leave. After eight straight days of protest, the defiant women prevailed. Fearing the negative impact on public opinion, the Nazis backed down and released the men.

Are the actions of a group harder to control than the behaviour of a single individual? Consider the following study. Pretending to be part of a marketing research firm, William Gamson and others (1982) recruited people to participate in a supposed discussion of "community standards." Scheduled in groups of nine, participants were told that their discussions would be videotaped for a large oil company that was suing the manager of a local service station who had spoken out against higher gas prices. After receiving a summary of the case, most participants sided with

AP/Nasser Nasser/CP images

Political protests allow the public to express their displeasure at the decisions made by their political leaders. Research shows that it is easier for people to behave defiantly in groups than alone.

the station manager. But there was a hitch. The oil company wanted evidence to win its case, said the experimenter—posing as the discussion coordinator. He told each of the group members to get in front of the camera and express the company's viewpoint. Then he told them to sign an affidavit giving the company permission to edit the tapes for use in court.

You can see how the obedience script was supposed to unfold. Actually, only one of 33 groups even came close to following the script. In all others, people became incensed by the coordinator's behaviour and refused to continue. Some groups were so outraged that they planned to take action. One group even threatened to blow the whistle on the firm by calling the local newspapers. Faced with one emotionally charged mutiny after another, the researchers had to discontinue the experiment.

Why did this study produce such active, often passionate revolt when Milgram's revealed such utterly passive obedience? Could it reflect a change in values from the 1960s, when Milgram's studies were run? Results from studies such as Burger's (2009) contradict the suggestion that people would conform less today than in the past, and an analysis of obedience studies has revealed that there is no correlation between the year a study was conducted and the level of obedience that it produced (Blass, 1999). So what accounts for the contrasting results? One key difference is that people in Milgram's studies took part alone, and those in Gamson's were in groups. As Michael Walzer noted, "Disobedience, when it is not criminally but morally, religiously, or politically motivated, is always a *collective* act" (cited in R. Brown, 1986, p. 17).

"A little rebellion now and then is a good thing."
—Thomas Jefferson

Our earlier discussion of conformity indicated that the mere presence of one ally in an otherwise unanimous majority gives individuals the courage to dissent. Perhaps the same holds true for obedience. Notably, Milgram never had more than one participant present in the same session. But in one experiment, he did use two confederates who posed as co-teachers along with the real participant. In these sessions, one confederate refused to continue at 150 volts, and the second refused at 210 volts. These models of disobedience had a profound influence on participants' willingness to defy the experimenter: In their presence, only 10 percent delivered the maximum level of shock (see Figure 7.7).

We should add that the presence of a group is not a perfect safeguard against destructive obedience. Groups can trigger aggression, as we'll see in Chapter 11. For example, the followers of Jim Jones were together when they collectively followed his command to die. And lynch mobs are just that—groups, not individuals. Clearly, there is power in sheer numbers. That power can be destructive, or it can be used for constructive purposes. Indeed, the presence and support of others often provide the extra ounce of courage that people need to resist orders they find offensive.

The Continuum of Social Influence

As we have seen, social influence on behaviour ranges from the implicit pressure of group norms, to the traps set by direct requests, to the powerful commands of authority. In each case, people choose whether to react with conformity or independence, compliance or assertiveness, obedience or defiance. At this point, let's step back and ask two important questions. First, although different kinds of pressure influence us for different reasons, is it possible to predict all effects with a single, overarching principle? Second, what does the theory and research on social influence say about human nature?

Social Impact Theory

In 1981, Bibb Latané proposed that a common bond among the different processes involved in social influence leads people toward or away from such influence. Specifically, Latané proposed **social impact theory**, which states that social influence of any kind—the total impact of others on a target person—is a function of the others' strength, immediacy, and number. According to Latané, social forces act on individuals in the same way that physical forces act on objects. Consider, for example, how overhead lights illuminate a surface. The total amount of light cast on a surface depends on the strength of the bulbs, their distance from the surface, and their number. As illustrated in the left portion of Figure 7.8, the same factors apply to social impact.

The *strength* of a source is determined by his or her status, ability, or relationship to a target. The stronger the source, the greater the influence. When people view the other members of a group as competent, they are more likely to conform in their judgments. When it comes to compliance, sources enhance their strength by making targets feel obligated to reciprocate a small favour. And to elicit obedience, authority figures gain strength by wearing uniforms or flaunting their prestigious affiliations.

Immediacy refers to a source's proximity in time and space to the target. The closer the source, the greater its impact. Milgram's research offers the best example. Obedience rates were higher when the experimenter issued commands in person rather than from a remote location; and when the victim suffered in close proximity to the participant, he acted as a contrary source of influence and obedience levels dropped. Consistent with this hypothesis, Latané and others (1995) asked individuals to name up to seven people in their lives and to indicate how far away those people lived and how many memorable interactions they'd had with them. In three studies, the correlation was the same: the closer others are, geographically, the more impact they have on us.

Jennie Woodcock/Reflections Library/Corbis

According to social impact theory, this "intervention" should prove persuasive.

Finally, the theory predicts that as the *number* of sources increases, so does their influence—at least up to a point. You may recall that when Asch (1956) increased the number of live confederates in his line-judgment studies from one to four, conformity levels rose; yet further increases had only a negligible additional effect.

Social impact theory also predicts that people sometimes resist social pressure. According to Latané, this resistance is most likely to occur when social impact is *divided* among many strong and distant *targets*, as seen in the right part of Figure 7.8. There should be less impact on a target who is strong and far from the source than on one who is weak and close to the source; and there should be less impact on a target who is accompanied by other target persons than on one who stands alone. Thus, we have seen that conformity is reduced by the presence of an ally and that obedience rates drop when people are in the company of rebellious peers.

social impact theory
The theory that social influence depends on the strength, immediacy, and number of source persons relative to target persons.

FIGURE 7.8

Social Impact: Source Factors and Target Factors

According to social impact theory, the total influence of other people on a target individual depends on three factors related to the source persons: their strength (size of source circles), immediacy (distance to the target), and number (number of source circles). Similarly, the total influence is diffused, or reduced, by the strength (size of target circles), immediacy (distance from source circle), and number of target persons.

(Latané, 1981.)

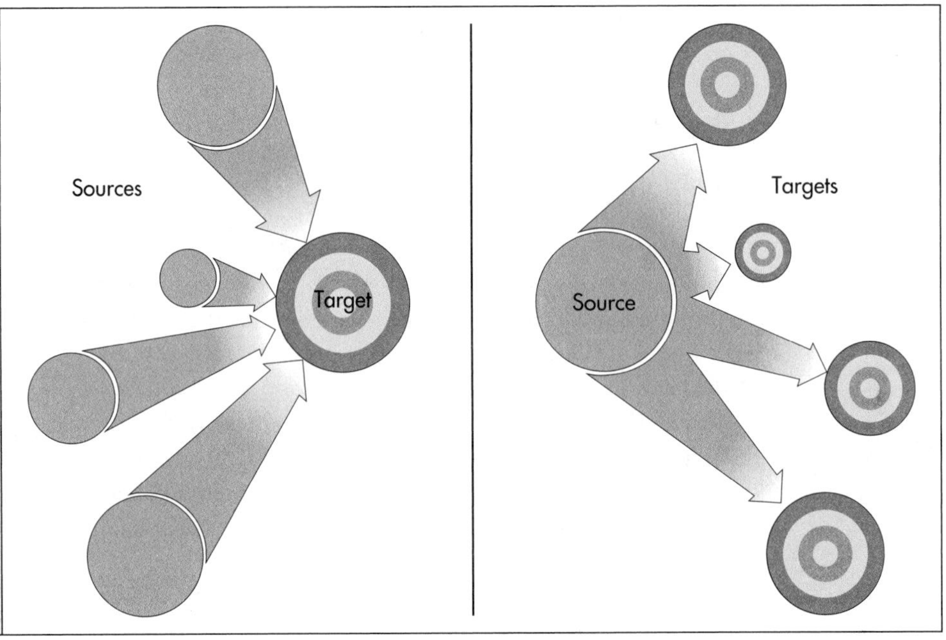

Over the years, social impact theory has been challenged, defended, and refined on various grounds (Jackson, 1986; Mullen, 1985; Sedikides & Jackson, 1990). On the one hand, critics say that it does not enable us to *explain* the processes that give rise to social influence or answer *why* questions. On the other hand, the theory enables us to *predict* the emergence of social influence and determine *when* it will occur. Whether the topic is conformity, compliance, or obedience, this theory has set the stage for interesting new research in the years to come.

As the number of people in a group increases, so does their impact on an individual. FALSE.

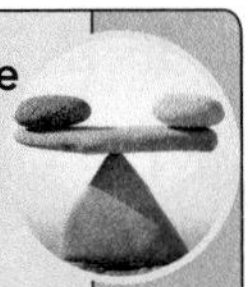

A number of social psychologists have recently argued that social impact is a fluid, dynamic, ever-changing process (Vallacher et al., 2002). Latané and Todd L'Herrou (1996) thus refined the theory in that vein. By having large groups of participants interact through email, for example, and by controlling their lines of communication, they found that the individuals within the network formed "clusters." Over time, neighbours (participants who were in direct contact) became more similar to each other than did those who were more distant (not in direct contact) within the network. Referring to the geometry of social space, Latané and L'Herrou note that in the real world, immediacy cannot be defined strictly in terms of physical distance. "Walls between houses, rivers through towns, open spaces between cities, these and other spatial discontinuities all tend to prevent the equal flow of influence among all members of a population" (p. 1229). Speculating on the role of computer technology, they also note that social impact theory has to account for the fact that, more and more, people interact in cyberspace—perhaps making physical proximity a less relevant factor.

Perspectives on Human Nature

From the material presented in this chapter, what general conclusions might you draw about human nature? Granted, social influence is more likely to occur in some situations than in others. But are people generally malleable or unyielding? Is there a tilt toward accepting influence or toward putting up resistance?

Conformity rates vary across different cultures and from one generation to the next. TRUE.

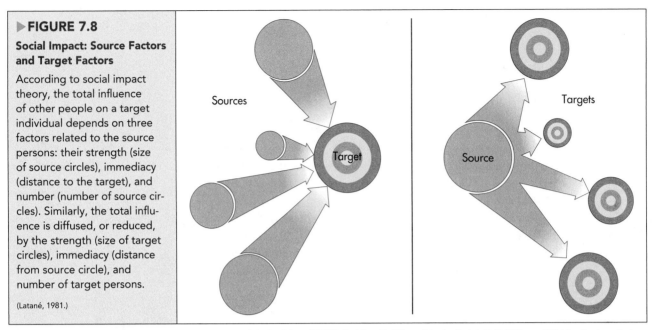

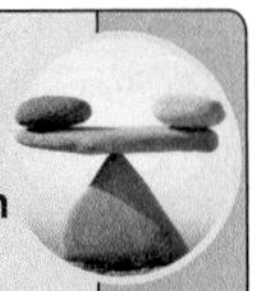

There is no single, universal answer to these questions. As we saw earlier, some cultures value autonomy and independence, while others place more emphasis on conformity to one's group. Even within a given culture, values may change over time. To demonstrate the point, ask yourself: If you were a parent, what traits would you like your child to have? When this question was put to American mothers in 1924, they chose "obedience" and "loyalty," key characteristics of conformity. Yet when mothers were asked the same question in 1978, they cited "independence" and "tolerance of others," key characteristics of autonomy. Similar trends were found in surveys conducted in West Germany, Italy, England, and Japan (Remley, 1988)—and in laboratory experiments, where conformity rates are somewhat lower today than in the past (Bond & Smith, 1996).

Is it possible that today's children—tomorrow's adults—will exhibit greater resistance to the various forms of social influence? If so, what effects will this trend have on society as a whole? Cast in a positive light, conformity, compliance, and obedience are good and necessary human responses. They promote group solidarity and agreement—qualities that keep groups from being torn apart by dissension. Cast in a negative light, a lack of independence, assertiveness, and defiance are undesirable behaviours that lend themselves to narrow-mindedness, cowardice, and destructive obedience—often with terrible costs. For each of us, and for society as a whole, the trick is to strike a balance.

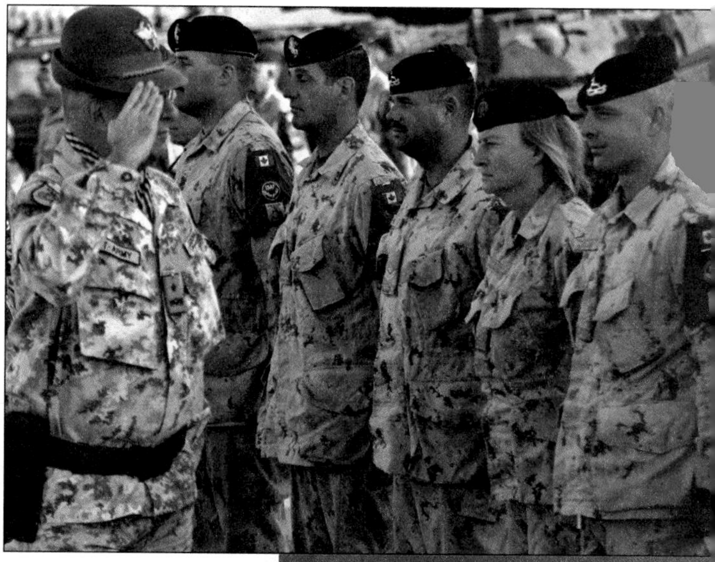

Omar Sobhani/Reuters/Corbis

According to social impact theory, an officer will exert influence to the extent that he or she is strong (in a position of power), immediate (physically close), and numerous (backed by others in the institution) relative to his or her trainees.

REVIEW

- Conformity, compliance, and obedience are three kinds of social influence, varying in the degree of pressure brought to bear on an individual.

Social Influence as "Automatic"

- Sometimes we are influenced by other people without our awareness.
- Studies show that people mimic each other's behaviours and moods, perhaps as a way of smoothing social interactions.

Conformity

- Conformity is the tendency for people to change their behaviour to be consistent with group norms.

The Early Classics

- Two classic experiments illustrate contrasting types of conformity.
- Sherif presented groups of participants with an ambiguous task and found that their judgments gradually converged.
- Using a simpler line-judgment task, Asch had confederates make incorrect responses and found that participants went along about a third of the time.

Why Do People Conform?

- Sherif found that people exhibit private conformity, using others for information in an ambiguous situation.
- Asch's studies indicated that people conform in their public behaviour to avoid appearing deviant.

Majority Influence

- As the size of an incorrect unanimous majority increases, so does conformity—up to a point.
- People conform to perceived social norms when these norms are brought to mind.

- The presence of one dissenter reduces conformity, even when he or she disagrees with the participant and lacks competence at the task.
- Women conform more than men on "masculine" tasks and in face-to-face settings, but not on "feminine" or gender-neutral tasks or in private settings.
- Conformity rates are higher in cultures that value collectivism than in those that value individualism.

Minority Influence

- Sometimes minorities resist pressures to conform and are able to influence majorities.
- In general, minority influence is greater when the source is an ingroup member.
- According to Moscovici, minorities can exert influence by taking a consistent and unwavering position.
- Majority influence is greater on direct and public measures of conformity, but minorities show their impact in indirect or private measures of conformity.
- By forcing other group members to think more openly about a problem, minorities enhance the quality of a group's decision making.
- People gain courage to resist conformity pressures after watching others do the same.

Compliance

- A common form of social influence occurs when we respond to direct requests.

The Language of Request

- People are more likely to comply when they are taken by surprise and when the request *sounds* reasonable.

The Norm of Reciprocity

- We often comply when we feel indebted to a requester who has done us a favour.
- People differ in the extent to which they use reciprocity for personal gain and are wary of falling prey to this strategy.

Setting Traps: Sequential Request Strategies

- Four compliance techniques are based on a two-step request: The first step sets a trap, and the second elicits compliance.
- Using the foot-in-the-door technique, a person sets the stage for the "real" request by first getting someone to comply with a smaller request.
- In low-balling, one person gets another to agree to a request but then increases the size of it by revealing hidden costs. Despite the increase, people often follow through on their agreement.
- With the door-in-the-face technique, the real request is preceded by a large one that is rejected. People then comply with the second request because they see it as a concession to be reciprocated.
- The that's-not-all technique begins with a large request. Then the apparent size of the request is reduced by the offer of a discount or bonus.

Assertiveness: When People Say No

- Many people find it hard to be assertive. Doing so requires that we be vigilant and recognize the traps.

Obedience

- When the request is a command, and the requester is a figure of authority, the resulting influence is called obedience.

Milgram's Research: Forces of Destructive Obedience

- In a series of experiments, participants were ordered by an experimenter to administer increasingly painful shocks to a confederate.
- Sixty-five percent obeyed completely but felt tormented by the experience.
- Obedience levels are influenced by various situational factors, including a participant's physical proximity to both the authority figure and the victim.
- Two other aspects of Milgram's procedure also contributed to the high levels of obedience: (1) participants did not feel personally responsible, and (2) the orders escalated gradually.
- In more recent studies, people exhibited high rates of obedience when told to inflict psychological harm on another person.

Milgram in the Twenty-First Century

- Milgram's studies have remained relevant and controversial into the twenty-first century.
- Researchers note that a situational explanation for acts of destructive obedience does not forgive them.
- A recent "partial replication" of Milgram's shock study suggests that most people are still fully obedient today.

Defiance: When People Rebel

- Just as processes of social influence breed obedience, they can also support acts of defiance, since groups are more difficult to control than individuals.
- Provision of a situational explanation for cruel behaviour does not excuse that behaviour.

The Continuum of Social Influence

Social Impact Theory

- Social impact theory predicts that social influence depends on the strength, immediacy, and number of sources who exert pressure relative to target persons who absorb that pressure.

Perspectives on Human Nature

- There is no single answer to the question of whether people are conformists or nonconformists.
- There are cross-cultural differences in social influence, and values change over time even within specific cultures.

Key Terms

collectivism (246)
compliance (249)
conformity (238)
door-in-the-face technique (253)
foot-in-the-door technique (251)
individualism (246)
informational influence (241)
low-balling (252)
minority influence (247)
normative influence (241)
obedience (256)
private conformity (242)
public conformity (242)
social impact theory (265)
that's-not-all technique (254)

Putting COMMON SENSE *to the Test*

When all members of a group give an incorrect response to an easy question, most people most of the time conform to that response.

False. *In Asch's classic conformity experiments, respondents conformed only about a third of the time.*

An effective way to get someone to do you a favour is to make a first request that is so large the person is sure to reject it.

True. *This approach, known as the door-in-the-face technique, increases compliance by making the person feel bound to make a concession.*

In experiments on obedience, most participants who were ordered to administer severe shocks to an innocent person refused to do so.

False. *In Milgram's classic research, 65 percent of all participants obeyed the experimenter and administered the maximum possible shock.*

As the number of people in a group increases, so does their impact on an individual.

False. *Increasing group size boosts the impact on an individual only up to a point, beyond which further increases have very little added effect.*

Conformity rates vary across different cultures and from one generation to the next.

True. *Research shows that conformity rates are higher in cultures that are collectivistic rather than individualistic in orientation, and values change over time even within cultures.*

8

Reuters

Group Processes

This chapter examines social influence in a group context. First, we focus on the fundamentals of groups, in which we discuss issues such as why people are drawn to groups and how groups develop. We then turn to how the behaviour of individuals is affected by the presence of others. Then we focus on group performance and discuss why the whole (the group decision or performance) is different from the sum of its parts (the attitudes and abilities of the group members). In the final section, we examine how groups intensify or reconcile their differences.

Putting
COMMON SENSE
to the Test

Circle Your Answer

- T F People will cheer louder when they cheer as part of a group than when they cheer alone.
- T F People brainstorming as a group come up with a greater number of better ideas than the same number of people working individually.
- T F Group members' attitudes about a course of action usually become more moderate after group discussion.
- T F Groups are less likely than individuals to invest more and more resources in a project that is failing.
- T F Large groups are more likely than small groups to exploit a scarce resource that the members collectively depend on.

In June 2011, many Canadians were glued to their television sets watching game 7 of the Stanley Cup final between the Vancouver Canucks and the Boston Bruins. Shortly after the Canucks' 4-0 loss to the Bruins, downtown Vancouver erupted in violence. As angry and unruly crowds roamed the streets, stores were looted, police cars were overturned, fires were started, and countless fights broke out. This was an unfortunate, and surprising, black eye for a city that a year previous had been praised for its successful handling of massive crowds while hosting the 2010 Olympic Winter Games. As attribution theory (discussed in detail in Chapter 4) might predict, some in the media spoke of 'hooligans' and 'criminals,' while others commented that this was simply the result of 'crowd behaviour.' While media images depicting the riots made their way around the globe that night, one conclusion might be that people from Vancouver are violent and aggressive as a group. But this of course would not be fair, nor would it be accurate. Indeed, there is another much more uplifting side to this story; by noon of the next day, more than 15 000 people had signed up on Facebook to help clean up the mess left by the rioters. Thus, while groups can sometimes make bad decisions, at other times individuals will come together as a group and do great things.

All this reveals a fascinating fact: *Groups can be quite different from the sum of their parts.* When you think about that statement, it suggests something almost mystical or magical about groups, like quantum physics. How can a group be better—or worse—than its individual members? The math may not seem to add up, but the theory and research discussed in this chapter will help answer this question.

People are often at their best—and their worst—in groups. It is through groups that individuals form communities, pool resources, and share successes. But it is also through groups that stereotypes turn into oppression, frustrations turn into mob violence, and conflicts turn into wars. In this chapter, we first introduce the fundamentals of what groups are and how they develop. Then we examine groups on several

It has become fairly commonplace in recent years for the anger and frustration felt by fans after their team's loss to escalate to mayhem and destruction.

THE CANADIAN PRESS/Ryan Remiorz

levels. At the individual level, we explore how individuals are influenced by groups; at the group level, we explore how groups perform; and at the intergroup level, we explore how groups interact with each other in cooperation and competition.

Fundamentals of Groups

We begin our exploration of groups by asking the basic questions: What is a group? Why do people join groups? We then examine how individuals are socialized into, or out of, groups, and how groups develop over time. We then focus on three important aspects of groups: roles, norms, and cohesiveness.

What Is a Group? Why Join a Group?

What Is a Group? The question might seem simple, but if you step back and think about it, the answer is less obvious. For example, many students are members of a variety of groups on Facebook. Are these really groups? You may be part of a large social psychology class. Is this a group identity that is meaningful to you?

In Chapter 5, we focused on how individuals perceive groups and group members. In that context, we characterized a group as a set of individuals with at least one of the following characteristics: (1) direct interactions with each other over a period of time; (2) joint membership in a social category based on sex, race, or other attributes; (3) a shared fate, identity, or set of goals. The current chapter focuses on groups themselves rather than on others' perceptions of groups and group members. In this context, we emphasize the first and third criteria: direct interactions among group members over a period of time, and a shared fate, identity, or set of goals.

"You think because you understand 'one,' you must understand 'two,' because one and one make two. But you must also understand 'and.'"
—Ancient Sufi saying

Groups vary in the extent to which they are seen as distinct entities, such as whether they have rigid boundaries that make them distinct from other groups. In other words, some groups seem more "groupy" than others (Crawford & Salaman, 2012; Kurebayashi et al., 2012; Rutchick et al., 2008). On the very low end of the dimensions of entity or social integration would be people attending a concert or working out near each other in a gym. Rather than being considered a real group, such assemblages are sometimes called **collectives**—people engaging in a common activity but having little direct interaction with each other (Milgram & Toch, 1969). Much more integrated groups include tight-knit clubs, sports teams, or work teams—groups that engage in very purposeful activities with a lot of interaction over time and clear boundaries of who is in and not in the group.

Groups come in all shapes and sizes: large and small, highly organized and quite informal, short term and long lasting. Sometimes group membership is involuntary. You didn't choose your family, for example, or your social class. But membership in many groups is voluntary. You decide to join an existing group or get together with others to create a brand new one. Why do people join groups? We address this question next.

People join a group for any of several reasons, such as to affiliate with others, obtain social status, and interact with individual group members. These musicians from the Canadian Youth Orchestra toured Canada together in the summer of 2010.

Why Join a Group? The complexity and ambitions of human life require that we work in groups, at least some of the time. Neither symphonies nor football games can be played by one person alone, and many types of work require team effort.

At a fundamental level, people may have an innate need to belong to groups, stemming from evolutionary pressures that increased people's chances of survival and reproduction when they lived in groups rather than in isolation. Indeed, according to the *social brain hypothesis*, the unusually large size of primates' brains evolved because of their unusually complex social worlds (Dunbar, 2008, 2012; Shultz & Dunbar, 2010). The results of neuroimaging research demonstrate that brain regions such as the amygdala, intricately involved in social information processing, can actually increase in size as our social networks get bigger, to help us cope with the greater demand on our cognitive resources (Bickart et al., 2011; Sallet et al., 2011). As Mark Van Vugt and Mark Schaller (2008) state in their review of research on contemporary human group dynamics from an evolutionary perspective: "Humans may well have evolved a range of psychological mechanisms that promote an attraction to and capacity for living in groups" (p. 1).

For humans, attraction to group life serves not only to protect against threat and uncertainty in a physical sense, but also to gain a greater sense of personal and social identity. According to social identity theory, which was discussed in Chapter 5, an important part of people's feelings of self-worth comes from their identification with particular groups. This is also at the root of why being rejected by a group is one of life's most painful experiences (Jones, Carter-Sowell, & Kelly, 2011; Williams, 2009). As social beings, we come to understand ourselves and our place in the world with reference to the groups that constitute our identities (Bizumic et al., 2009; Haslam et al., 2009; Swann & Bosson, 2010). Certainly the appeal of joining a variety of virtual groups and building a large group of friends on social network sites is fueled by the feelings of social identity and connectedness that they foster.

Socialization and Group Development

Once an individual has joined a group, a process of adjustment takes place. The individual assimilates into the group, making whatever changes are necessary to fit in. At the same time, the group accommodates the newcomer, making whatever changes are necessary

collective
People engaged in common activities but having minimal direct interaction.

TABLE 8.1

Stages of Group Development

- Forming: Members try to orient themselves to the group. They often act in polite, exploratory ways with each other.
- Storming: Members try to influence the group so that it best fits their own needs. They become more assertive about the group's direction and what roles they would like to play in the group. A great deal of conflict and hostility may arise, along with feelings of excitement about what might be achieved.
- Norming: Members try to reconcile the conflicts that emerged during storming and develop a common sense of purpose and perspective. They establish norms and roles and begin to feel more commitment to the group.
- Performing: Members try to perform their tasks and maximize the group's performance. They operate within their roles in the group and try to solve problems to allow them to achieve their shared goals.
- Adjourning: Members disengage from the group, distancing themselves from the other members and reducing their activities within the group. This may occur if members believe that the benefits of staying in the group no longer outweigh the costs.

(Based on Tuckman, 1965; Tuckman & Jensen, 1977.)

to include that individual. Socialization of a new member into a group often relies heavily on the relationship between newcomers and established members (Pinto et al., 2010). Newcomers model their behaviour on what the old-timers do; old-timers may hold explicit training sessions for newcomers, serve as mentors, or develop close personal relationships with them to help them be successful in the group. Effectively socializing new members can produce short-term and long-term benefits for the group as a whole. Conversely, poor socialization can lead to many bad outcomes, including suppressing the potential contributions of newcomers or creating a lot of turnover and instability in the group (Levine & Choi, 2010; Moreland & Levine, 2002).

Just as an individual's relationship with the group changes over time, the dynamics in the group as a whole change across time as well. Group development may proceed through several stages. Bruce Tuckman (1965; Tuckman & Jensen, 1977) proposed a particularly memorable set of stages through which groups often develop: forming, storming, norming, performing, and adjourning. These stages are described in ■ Table 8.1. According to this model, groups gradually progress from a period of initial orientation through stages of conflict, compromise, and action, followed by a period of withdrawal if the group no longer satisfies members' needs.

Although many groups seem to pass through these stages, not all groups do. Contemporary theory on group development offers more complex models of group development, including the recognition that groups often develop in ways that are not linear, and that different groups may develop in different ways (e.g., Chang et al., 2006; Sauer, 2011). For example, Connie Gersick (1988, 1994) observed that groups often do not proceed gradually through a uniform series of stages but instead operate in starts and stops, going through periods of relative inactivity until triggered by awareness of time and deadlines. According to Gersick, many groups adopt a problem-solving strategy very quickly—much quicker than Tuckman's theory suggests—but then they procrastinate until they have wasted about half the time they have allotted for the task, after which point they spring into action. Think about the work groups that *you've* been a part of. Do the stages described in Table 8.1 seem to apply, or do the groups described by Gersick seem more familiar to you?

Roles, Norms, and Cohesiveness

Despite their variation in specific characteristics, important features in most groups are an expected set of tasks for members (roles), rules of conduct for members (norms), and forces that push members together (cohesiveness). We consider each of these features in the following sections.

Roles People's roles in a group, their set of expected behaviours, can be formal or informal. Formal roles are designated by titles: teacher or student in a class, vice president or account executive in a corporation. Informal roles are less obvious but still powerful. For example, Robert Bales (1958) proposed that regardless of people's titles, enduring groups give rise to two fundamental types of roles: an instrumental role to help the group achieve its tasks, and an expressive role to provide emotional support and maintain morale. The same person can fill both roles, but often the roles are assumed by different individuals, and which of these roles is emphasized in groups may fluctuate over time depending on the needs of the group.

Having a set of clear roles can be beneficial to a group. A meta-analysis of studies involving more than 11 000 individuals found a significant negative correlation between role ambiguity and job performance—the more role ambiguity, the worse one's job performance (Tubre & Collins, 2000). Teams often strive to organize themselves and to distribute task roles based on group members' particular skills and preferences. The better a team does in assigning roles that match the individual's characteristics, the better the individual will function in the group. However, when a person's role in the group is ambiguous, conflicts with other roles the person has (as when a group member needs to be demanding but also is the person who typically provides emotional support to others), or changes over time, stress and loss of productivity are likely to result (Chen et al., 2009; Lu et al., 2008).

Norms In addition to roles for its members, groups also establish *norms,* rules of conduct for members. Like roles, norms may be either formal or informal. Fraternities and sororities, for example, usually have written rules for the behaviour expected from their members. Informal norms are more subtle. What do I wear? How hard can I push for what I want? Who pays for this or that? Figuring out the unwritten rules of the group can be a time-consuming and, sometimes, anxiety-provoking endeavour.

Researchers have investigated the development and consequences of a huge array of group norms, involving everything from binge drinking, drug use, smoking, risky sexual behaviour, and prejudice to the use of language and symbols in Internet groups and gaming (Hittner & Kennington, 2008; Karasek et al., 2012; Latkin et al., 2009; Martey & Stromer-Galley, 2007; Zitek & Hebl, 2007). Brendan McAuliffe and others (2003) found that even a group norm of individualism can be established, resulting in members conforming to the norm of not conforming!

Blowing the Whistle: Resisting Norms to Reveal Serious Problems Sometimes, breaking a group norm can be very difficult and even traumatic for a group member. Co-workers are especially reluctant to report the unethical behaviour of others on their work teams, fearing the social consequences of reporting on a member of the group (Yeargain & Kessler, 2010). Indeed, Benoit Monin and others (2008) demonstrated in a series of experiments how individuals who refused to go along with the norm were strongly disliked by their fellow participants, even when it was clear that the norm was rather immoral. Consultants involved in employee relations frequently observe the dilemma that workers in cohesive teams face when they witness unethical conduct. As one consultant noted, "[Team workers] have a fear they'll be seen as divisive. We're social animals, and we so very much want to belong" (Armour, 1998, p. 6B).

Aaron Lynett/Ottawa Citizen. Reprinted by permission.

Joanna Gualtieri broke group norms when she came forward with evidence that office staff at the Department of Foreign Affairs were spending lavish amounts of money on travel at taxpayers' expense.

Breaking the "business as usual" norms by coming forward with information about unethical behaviour takes great courage, as the pressure to keep silent can be enormous. Joanna Gualtieri, a lawyer who worked for the Department of Foreign Affairs, uncovered evidence of lavish spending on travel by office staff, all at the expense of Canadian taxpayers. When Gualtieri came forward with her allegations, she claims her bosses tried to censor her and gave her a dead-end job to keep her quiet. Gualtieri eventually launched a $20 million harassment lawsuit, one that dragged through the courts for almost 12 years. Finally, in 2010, an agreement with the Federal Government was reached, although the terms of the settlement are confidential. Today, Gualtieri is Director of FAIR (Federal Accountability Initiative for Reform), an organization that supports legislation designed to protect whistle-blowers and promote free speech in the workplace.

Cohesiveness Breaking group norms is especially difficulty in groups that are cohesive. **Group cohesiveness** refers to the forces exerted on a group that push its members closer together (Cartwright & Zander, 1960; Festinger, 1950). Various factors contribute to cohesiveness including commitment to the group task, attraction to group members, group pride, and number and intensity of interactions (Dion, 2000; Klassen & Krawchuk, 2009).

An interesting question is whether cohesiveness makes groups perform better. It may seem obvious that it should, but in fact the relationship is not a simple one. The causal relationship works both ways. On the one hand, when a group is cohesive, group performance often improves; on the other hand, when a group performs well, it often becomes more cohesive. Many team athletes recognize that winning creates team chemistry even more than team chemistry creates winning. In their meta-analysis of the research on cohesiveness and group performance, Brian Mullen and Carolyn Copper (1994) found stronger evidence that performance affects cohesiveness than that cohesiveness affects performance. They also found that the positive relationship between cohesiveness and group performance may depend on the size of the group: The relationship tended to be stronger in small groups than in large ones. In a study comparing young Canadian athletes, ages 12 to 17, researchers found that those who were considered "starters" on a team (meaning they were on the field first, and tended to get more playing time) perceived their teams to be more cohesive than the "non-starters" (Jeffery-Tosoni et al., 2011).

Subsequent meta-analyses and longitudinal studies have provided more evidence showing that group cohesion can lead to better performance, but other variables tend to be important in predicting when and to what extent this effect may emerge (Beal et al., 2003; Gully et al., 1995, Tekleab et al., 2009). For example, a meta-analysis of 46 studies of cohesiveness in sports teams found not only a generally positive correlation between cohesiveness and team performance, but also that the relationship was particularly strong for female sports teams—possibly because women tend to be more interdependent than men (Carron et al., 2002).

Culture and Cohesiveness

More than ever before, people work in groups that are culturally diverse. Work teams in the business world may consist of individuals from around the globe. It is becoming all the more important, then, to understand how group dynamics may differ across cultures. For example, Norman Wright and Glyn Drewery (2006) hypothesized that the factors that affect a group's cohesiveness will vary as a function of whether the group members are from collectivistic or individualistic cultures. Consistent with this idea, they found that if some group members did not carry their share of the workload or came late to meetings, group cohesiveness was more likely to suffer among Japanese and Pacific Islanders than among Anglos.

Group cohesiveness
The extent to which forces exerted on a group push its members closer together.

How concerned group members are about hurting group cohesiveness by engaging in heated debates—and the effects of such debates on group performance—may also vary across culture. Roger Nibler and Karen Harris (2003) studied five-person groups of strangers and friends in China and the United States. The groups' task was to rank 15 items to be taken aboard a lifeboat from a ship that was about to sink. This task tends to trigger a fair amount of initial disagreement among group members until a consensus can be reached. With the Chinese groups and the groups of American strangers, these kinds of disagreements tended to be perceived as troubling and interfered with group performance. To the groups of American friends, in contrast, these disagreements were more likely to be seen as simply part of a freewheeling debate, and the sense of freedom to exchange opinions and disagree with one another tended to improve performance on this task.

Individuals in Groups: The Presence of Others

When we engage in activities in groups, we are in the presence (either physically or virtually) of others. It's an obvious point, but some of its consequences are profound and surprising. In this section, we focus on three important effects that the presence of others can have on individuals: social facilitation, social loafing, and deindividuation.

Social Facilitation: When Others Arouse Us

Social psychologists have long been fascinated by how the presence of others affects behaviour. In Chapter 1, we reported that one of the founders of social psychology was Norman Triplett, whose article *The Dynamogenic Factors in Pace-making and Competition* (1897–1898) is often cited as one of the earliest publications in the field. This is likely due, in part, to his use of experimental procedures more akin to modern day social psychological paradigms (Stroebe, 2012). Triplett began his research by studying the official bicycle records from the Racing Board of the League of American Wheelmen for the 1897 season. He noticed that cyclists who competed against others performed better than those who cycled alone against the clock. After dismissing various theories of the day (our favourite is "brain worry"), he proposed his own hypothesis: The presence of another rider releases the competitive instinct, which increases nervous energy and enhances performance. To test this proposition, Triplett had 40 children wind up fishing reels, which caused a small flag to move along a 4-metre course. The children alternated between performing alone and working in parallel, working in one of two pre-determined sequences that Triplett created to help rule out practice or fatigue effects. On average, winding time was faster when the children worked side by side than when they worked alone, although Michael Strube (2005), using modern statistical techniques to reanalyze Triplett's original data, argues the results are not nearly as straightforward as Triplett's report suggested.

Later research following Triplett's studies proved disappointing. Sometimes the presence of others (side by side or with an audience out front) enhanced performance; at other times, performance declined. It seemed that Triplett's promising lead had turned into a blind alley, and social psychologists had largely abandoned this research by World War II. But years later, Robert Zajonc (1965, 1980) saw a way to reconcile the contradictory results by integrating research from experimental psychology with social psychological research. Zajonc offered an elegant solution: The presence of others increases arousal, which can affect performance in different ways, depending on the task at hand. Let's see how this works.

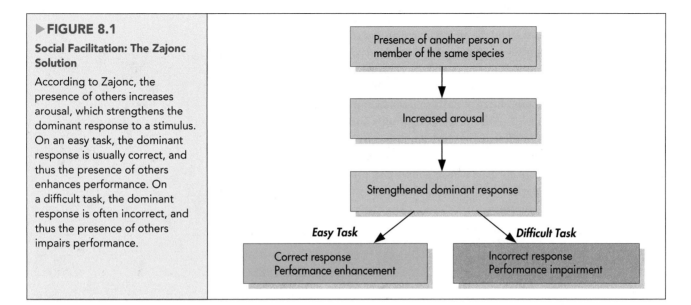

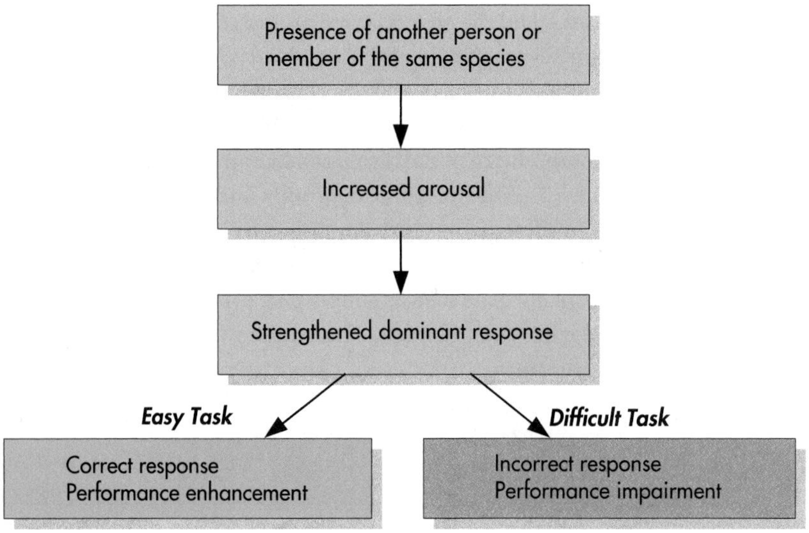

FIGURE 8.1

Social Facilitation: The Zajonc Solution

According to Zajonc, the presence of others increases arousal, which strengthens the dominant response to a stimulus. On an easy task, the dominant response is usually correct, and thus the presence of others enhances performance. On a difficult task, the dominant response is often incorrect, and thus the presence of others impairs performance.

The Zajonc Solution According to Zajonc, the road from presence to performance requires three steps.

1. The presence of others creates general physiological *arousal*, which energizes behaviour. Based on experimental psychology research and principles of evolution, Zajonc argued that all animals, including humans, tend to become aroused when in the presence of *conspecifics*—that is, members of their own species.
2. Increased arousal enhances an individual's tendency to perform the *dominant response*. The dominant response is the reaction elicited most quickly and easily by a given stimulus. Here again, Zajonc drew from experimental psychology research, particularly research concerning learning.
3. The quality of an individual's performance varies according to the type of *task*. On an easy task (one that is simple or well learned), the dominant response is usually correct or successful. But on a difficult task (one that is complex or unfamiliar), the dominant response is often incorrect or unsuccessful.

Putting these three steps together (see Figure 8.1) yields the following scenarios. Suppose you are playing the violin. If you're an excellent player and are performing a well-learned, familiar arrangement, having other people around should enhance your performance—the presence of others will increase your arousal, which will enhance your dominant response. Because this arrangement is so well learned, your dominant response will be to perform it well. However, if you are just learning to play the violin and you are unfamiliar with this arrangement, the presence of others is the last thing you'll want. The increase in arousal should enhance the dominant response, which in this case would be *unsuccessful* violin playing.

When you think about it, this makes intuitive sense. If you are just learning how to perform some complicated task, such as playing the violin or riding a bike, it helps if you are not aroused. In contrast, if you are already good at the task, you may need the extra "juice" that comes from performing in front of others to help you rise to new heights and perform even better than you would if performing alone. Sports fans may be able to think of many instances in which the best athletes seem to rise to the occasion when the pressure is on, while lesser athletes "choke" under the same kind of pressure. And physical performances are not the only ones influenced; the effects also hold for social judgment or cognitive tasks, such as forming impressions of others, dealing with the effects of cognitive dissonance, or solving math problems (Lambert et al., 2003; Martinie et al., 2010; Park & Catrambone, 2007).

Taken as a package, these two effects of the presence of others—helping performance on easy tasks but hurting performance on difficult tasks—are known as **social facilitation**. Unfortunately, this term has been a prime source of confusion for countless students. The trick is to remember that the presence of others facilitates the *dominant* response, not necessarily the task itself. This facilitation of the dominant response does, in effect, facilitate easy tasks, but it makes difficult tasks even more difficult.

Zajonc says that social facilitation is universal—occurring not only in human activities but also among other animals, even insects. Have you ever wondered, for instance, how well a cockroach performs in front of other cockroaches? Neither did we—that is, we wouldn't have if not for the ever-creative Bob Zajonc. Zajonc and his colleagues (1969) had cockroaches placed in a brightly lit start box connected to a darkened goal box. When the track was a simple one, with a straight runway between the start box and the goal box, cockroaches running in pairs ran more quickly toward the goal box than did those running alone. But in a more complex maze, with a right turn required to reach the goal box, solitary cockroaches outraced pairs.

FP/Getty Images

Through social facilitation, professional athletes like up-and-coming Canadian tennis sensation Milos Raonic benefit from the presence of an audience when performing well-learned actions. On the other hand, when first learning to play, a novice would be advised not to try it at centre court, Wimbledon, in front of an arousing crowd!

In a particularly creative follow-up experiment, Zajonc and his colleagues found that cockroaches completed the easy maze faster, and the difficult maze slower, if they raced in front of a crowd of spectator cockroaches than if they raced with no audience. You may wonder, how did the researchers get cockroaches to participate as spectators? The researchers placed cockroaches in Plexiglas "audience boxes" along either side of the maze, and this "audience" produced social facilitation.

Social Facilitation Research Today Zajonc's formulation revived interest in the issues raised by Triplett's early research, and suddenly the inconsistent findings that had been reported began to make sense. The results of a meta-analysis of 241 studies were consistent with much of Zajonc's account (Bond & Titus, 1983). And despite its long history, research today continues to explore ways that social facilitation can influence human behaviour. Researchers are also beginning to find neurological and physiological evidence consistent with predictions based on the theory, such as evidence concerning patterns of brain activation and cardiovascular responses (Blascovich et al., 1999; Wagstaff et al., 2008).

Social facilitation effects have been demonstrated in a variety of settings. For example, Tova Rosenbloom and others (2007) found that individuals taking their driving test alone were more likely to pass than those paired with another testee in the car. Matthew Rockloff and Nancy Greer (2011) asked gamblers playing on an Electronic Gaming Machine (EGM) to place bets while alone, or in front of a 5-person or 25-person audience; they found that participants' bets decreased as the size of the audience increased. Interestingly, in this case the audience was not even physically present; while participants assumed they were watching a live video feed of the audience, it was in fact previously recorded. Thus it appears the social facilitation effects can be found even in the presence of a virtual other as with a real other person.

Even non-human characters may be human-like enough to cause arousal and social facilitation effects. Students in Sung Park and Richard Catrambone's (2007) experiment completed tasks either alone, in the company of another person, or next to a computer that showed a "virtual" person—a computer-generated three-dimensional display that seemed to breathe, blink, and display subtle facial movements—that

social facilitation
A process whereby the presence of others enhances performance on easy tasks but impairs performance on difficult tasks.

▶ FIGURE 8.2

Virtual Human and Social Facilitation

This is an image of what the virtual person looked like in the study by Sung Park and Richard Catrambone (2007). The presence of this virtual human watching participants triggered social facilitation effects.

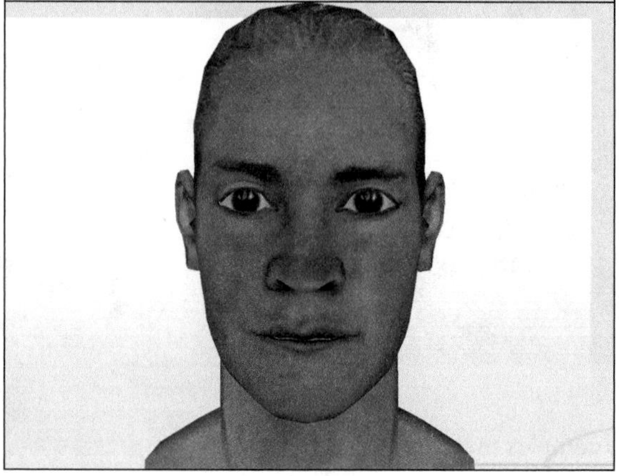

Park & Catrambone , Human Factors: The Journal of the Human Factors and Ergonomics Society, vol. 49 no. 6 1054-1060, 2007. Reprinted by permission of SAGE Publications.

appeared to watch them (see ▶ Figure 8.2). Social facilitation effects were just as strong in the presence of a virtual other as with a real other person.

Alternative Explanations for Social Facilitation Social facilitation effects have been replicated across many domains, but not all of Zajonc's theory has received universal support. Zajonc proposed that the **mere presence** of others is sufficient to produce social facilitation. Some have argued, however, that the presence of others will produce social facilitation only under certain conditions. These issues have produced various alternative explanations of social facilitation.

The first and most thoroughly researched alternative, **evaluation apprehension theory**, proposes that performance will be enhanced or impaired only in the presence of others who are in a position to evaluate that performance (Geen, 1991; Henchy & Glass, 1968). In other words, it's not simply because others are around that I'm so aroused and therefore inept as I try to learn to snowboard on a crowded mountain. Rather, it's because I worry that the others are watching and probably laughing at me, possibly uploading a video of my performance to YouTube. These concerns increase my dominant response, which, unfortunately, is falling.

Another approach to social facilitation, **distraction-conflict theory**, points out that being distracted while we're working on a task creates attentional conflict (Baron, 1986; Sanders, 1981). We're torn between focusing on the task and inspecting the distracting stimulus. Conflicted about where to pay attention, our arousal increases. Trying to isolate these different causes in an experiment can be challenging. For example, one study tried to manipulate evaluation apprehension while keeping mere presence constant by having confederates in one condition be present but blindfolded (supposedly in preparation for a perception study) while participants worked on a task. The presence of confederates who were not blindfolded led to increased dominant responses for participants; however, blindfolded confederates did not trigger this effect, presumably because participants would not be concerned about being evaluated by these others (Cottrell et al., 1968).

So is one of these theories right and the others wrong? Probably not. It seems likely that all three of the basic elements described by these theories (mere presence, evaluation, and attention) can contribute to the impact others have on our own performance (Uziel, 2007, 2010). For example, the mere presence account can explain social facilitation among cockroaches better than the evaluation apprehension account can, but evaluation apprehension is better than mere presence at explaining why blindfolded others have less impact than others who are not blindfolded. An integration of these different explanations may offer the best account of all. As we are about to see in the next section, there is even more to the story of how individuals are affected by the presence of others.

mere presence theory
A theory holding that the mere presence of others is sufficient to produce social facilitation effects.

evaluation apprehension theory
A theory holding that the presence of others will produce social facilitation effects only when those others are seen as potential evaluators.

distraction-conflict theory
A theory holding that the presence of others will produce social facilitation effects only when those others distract from the task and create attentional conflict.

Social Loafing: When Others Relax Us

The tasks employed in research on social facilitation produce individually identifiable results. That is, individual behaviour can be identified and evaluated. But on some tasks, efforts are pooled so that the specific performance of any one individual cannot be determined. That other founder of social psychology, French agricultural engineer Max Ringelmann, investigated group performance on these kinds of collective endeavours. In research conducted during the 1880s, Ringelmann discovered that, compared with what people produced when they worked on their own, individual output declined when they worked together on simple tasks like pulling a rope or pushing a cart (Kravitz & Martin, 1986; Ringelmann, 1913).

Why did individual output decline? One explanation is that the individuals exerted less effort when they acted collectively, but another explanation is that the individuals simply demonstrated poor coordination when working together—some pulled while others relaxed, and vice versa. How can you distinguish lack of effort from poor coordination in a task like this? Nearly 100 years after Ringelmann's research, Alan Ingham and his colleagues (1974) answered this question by using a rope-pulling machine and blindfolding participants. In one condition, participants were led to *think* that they were pulling with a bunch of other participants; and in another condition, the participants were informed that they were pulling alone (which, in fact, they were). The researchers told the participants to pull as hard as they could. Ingham and colleagues were able to measure exactly how hard each individual participant pulled; they observed that the participants pulled almost 20 percent harder when they thought they were pulling alone than when they thought they were pulling with others. Naoki Kugihara (1999) recently found a similar decline in rope-pulling among Japanese men (but not women) in a collective setting.

"We just haven't been flapping them hard enough."

Individuals often don't try as hard in groups as they do alone. If they can be convinced that their efforts will pay off, however, their output can soar.

Bibb Latané and his colleagues (1979) found that group-produced reductions in individual output, which they called **social loafing**, are common in other types of tasks as well. For example, imagine being asked as part of a psychology experiment to cheer or clap as loudly as you can. Common sense might lead you to think that you would cheer and clap louder when doing this together with others in a group than when performing alone because you would be less embarrassed and inhibited if others were doing the same thing as you. But Latané and his colleagues found that when performing collectively, individual students loafed—they exerted less effort. The noise generated by each individual decreased as the size of the group increased (see ▶ Figure 8.3, on page 282). This social loafing occurred even among cheerleaders, who are supposed to be experts at cheering and clapping with others!

Social loafing is not restricted to simple motor tasks. Sharing responsibility with others reduces the amount of effort that people put into more complex motor tasks, such as swimming in a relay race; cognitive tasks, such as completing memory, math, or verbal tests; and important, enduring real-world behaviours, such as working collaboratively on collective farms or team projects (Liden et al., 2004; Miles & Greenberg, 1993; Plaks & Higgins, 2000; Weldon et al., 2000). When others are there to pick up the slack, people slack off.

But social loafing is not inevitable; a number of factors can reduce it. Social loafing is less likely to occur when one of the following conditions is present:

- People believe that their own performance can be identified and thus evaluated, by themselves or others.
- The task is important or meaningful to those performing it.
- People believe that their own efforts are necessary for a successful outcome.
- The group expects to be punished for poor performance.

social loafing
A group-produced reduction in individual output on easy tasks where contributions are pooled.

FIGURE 8.3

Social Loafing: When Many Produce Less

Social loafing is a group-produced reduction in individual output on simple tasks. In this study, college students were told to cheer or clap as loudly as they could. The noise produced by each of them decreased as the size of the group increased.

(Latané et al., 1979.)

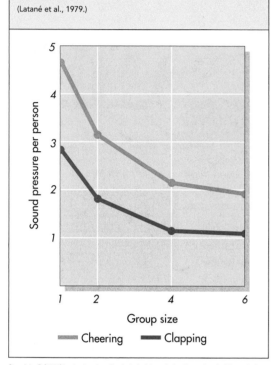

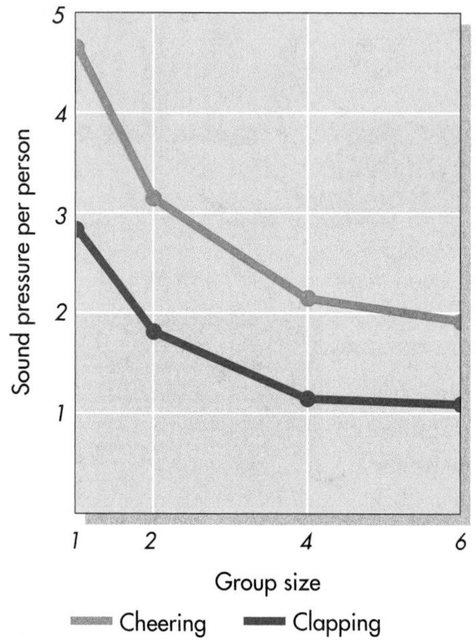

- The group is small.
- The group is cohesive—that is, membership in the group is valuable and important to the members, and the individuals like each other.

Businesses have taken note of social loafing and have applied these research findings in an effort to reduce it in the workplace. For example, when employees "*cyberloaf*" by spending work time surfing the Internet, checking Facebook, and answering personal emails, their productivity can suffer (Henle et al., 2009; Liberman, 2011). One result is that workers' actions on the job are coming under increasing surveillance as the number of computer keystrokes they make per hour or the content of their calls, emails, or Internet browsing can be recorded electronically.

Although everyone is vulnerable to social loafing, some people may be more or less prone to it than others. Hwee Tan and Min-Li Tan (2008), for example, found that people high in conscientiousness were less likely to engage in social loafing. Other factors associated with reduced social loafing include being very task oriented, having "a winning orientation," and being relatively high in achievement motivation (Hart et al., 2004; Høigaard & Ommundsen, 2007; Stark et al., 2007).

Collective Effort Model Several researchers have constructed theoretical accounts to explain the findings about when social loafing is more or less likely to occur (e.g., Guerin, 2003; Shepperd & Taylor, 1999). One influential analysis is by Karau and Williams (2001), who proposed the **collective effort model**. This model asserts that individuals try hard on a collective task when they think their efforts will help them achieve outcomes that they personally value. If the outcome is important to individual members of the group, and if they believe that they can help achieve the desired outcome, then these individuals are likely to engage in *social compensation*—specifically, by increasing their efforts on collective tasks to try to compensate for the anticipated social loafing or poor performance of other group members. Conversely, if the outcome is not personally important to individual members, if they believe that their contribution won't affect the outcome very much, or if they feel they are unable to compensate for the anticipated social loafing of other members, then they are likely to exert less effort. This is sometimes called the *sucker effect:* Nobody wants to be the "sucker" who does all the work while everyone else goofs off, so everyone withholds effort, and the result is very poor group performance (Houldsworth & Mathews, 2000; Hütter & Diehl, 2011; Kerr, 1983; Shepperd, 1993). The next time you work on a group project, such as a paper that you and several other students are supposed to write together, consider the factors that increase and decrease social loafing. You might want to try to change aspects of the situation so that all group members are motivated to do their share of the work.

People will cheer louder when they cheer as part of a group than when they cheer alone. FALSE.

collective effort model
The theory that individuals will exert effort on a collective task to the degree that they think their individual efforts will be important, relevant, and meaningful for achieving outcomes that they value.

Culture and Social Loafing

Steven Karau and Kipling Williams (1993) conducted a meta-analysis of 78 studies and found social loafing to be a reliable phenomenon, displayed across numerous tasks and in countries around the world. Recent research has even demonstrated social loafing among children as young as five years old (Arterberry et al., 2007). Despite its prevalence around the world, some group and cultural differences in tendencies to socially loaf have been found.

Karau and Williams's meta-analysis found that social loafing was less prevalent among women than men, and less prevalent among people from East Asian, collectivist cultures (such as China, Japan, and Taiwan) than among people from Western, individualist cultures (such as those in Canada and the United States).

In an interesting twist, Ying-yi Hong and others (2008) hypothesized that there are times when people from collectivistic cultures may be especially likely to socially loaf. Because people from these cultures tend to be concerned with behaving consistently with group norms, they may be tempted to socially loaf if they are working in a group that has established a norm of low productivity and effort. The researchers found support for this idea in a set of studies with Chinese students. When these students engaged in a task with co-workers who were not being productive, the participants reduced their own efforts if they thought their effort would be evident to their co-workers. Not wanting to publicly deviate from the group norm, these students conformed to the norm of working less hard.

Bruce Miller/Alamy

Here, Chinese farmers cooperate on a task in which individual contributions cannot be identified. Social loafing on such tasks occurs less often in Eastern cultures than in Western ones.

Facilitation and Loafing: Unifying the Paradigms

Social facilitation and social loafing represent two separate research traditions, but the connection between them—the fact that both arise in the presence of others—has prompted some investigators to attempt a unified approach that highlights the arousal associated with possible performance evaluation (Jackson & Williams, 1985; Sanna, 1992). The typical pattern of results is diagrammed in ▶ Figure 8.4. A unified view of social facilitation and social loafing has important practical implications for maximizing performance when individuals are working together. In team sports, for

▶ FIGURE 8.4

Unifying the Paradigms: Presence and Evaluation

The relationship between the presence of others and the potential for evaluation is the key to a unified paradigm of social facilitation and social loafing. When individual performance can be evaluated, the presence of others enhances performance on easy tasks but impairs performance on difficult endeavours. When contributions are pooled across individuals, the pattern reverses, as performance declines on easy tasks but improves on difficult ones.

(Adapted from Jackson & Williams, 1985; Sanna, 1992.)

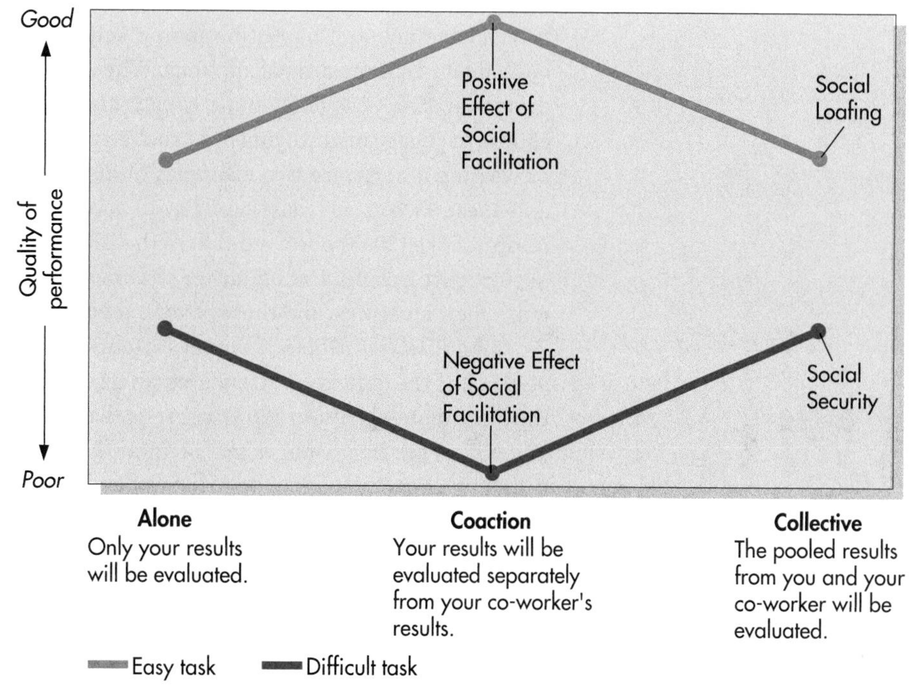

example, coaches would be well advised to evaluate each player's performance against a weak opponent, but to stress team spirit and overall group effort during a tough game. Unification is also historically satisfying: two of the founders of social psychology, Triplett and Ringelmann, together at last.

Deindividuation

Although we spend much of our lives in the presence of others, there are times when behaviour in collectives can be quite extraordinary. Nineteenth-century French scholars, Gabriel Tarde (1890) and Gustave Le Bon (1895) maintained that, under the sway of the crowd, people turn into copycat automatons or, worse still, uncontrollable mobs. More than a century later, their warnings of what are often known as "the group mind" or "mob behaviour" still resonate when the latest example of a group gone wild with rioting or looting makes the news, as happened in Vancouver after the Canucks loss.

There is no doubt that the destructive capacity of collectives has left a bloody trail through human history. What turns an unruly crowd into a violent mob? It is clear that many of the factors described in Chapter 11 on Aggression contribute to violence by groups as well as by individuals. Possible factors include imitation of aggressive models, intense frustration, high temperatures, alcohol consumption, and the presence of weapons that trigger aggressive thoughts and actions. But there's also **deindividuation**, the loss of a person's sense of individuality and the reduction of normal constraints against deviant behaviour. Most investigators believe that deindividuation is a collective phenomenon that occurs only in the presence of others (Diener et al., 1976; Festinger et al., 1952). Philip Zimbardo (1969) observed that arousal, anonymity, and reduced feelings of individual responsibility together contribute to deindividuation. In the case of the Vancouver riots, described at the start of the chapter, all three elements that Zimbardo specified were present: The fans were very *aroused* by their team's loss, the thousands of fans pouring out of the arena provided the individuals with relative *anonymity*, and these factors, quite possibly along with alcohol consumed during the game, contributed to reduced feelings of individual *responsibility*.

According to Steven Prentice-Dunn and Ronald Rogers (1982, 1983), two types of environmental cues—accountability cues and attentional cues—make deviant behaviours such as this rioting more likely to occur. *Accountability cues* affect the individual's cost-reward calculations. When accountability is low, those who commit deviant acts are less likely to be caught and punished, and people may deliberately choose to engage in gratifying but usually inhibited behaviours. Being in a large crowd or wearing a mask are two examples of instances when accountability may be low, and these factors are associated with more extreme and destructive behaviours. Andrew Silke (2003) observed that of the 500 violent interpersonal attacks he studied in Northern Ireland, the offenders in almost half of the incidents wore disguises to mask their identities, and those attacks tended to be the most violent.

Attentional cues focus a person's attention away from the self. In this "deindividuated state," the individual attends less to internal standards of conduct, reacts more to the immediate situation, and is less sensitive to long-term consequences of behaviour (Diener, 1980). Behaviour slips out from the bonds of cognitive control, and people act on impulse. When you are at a party with very loud music and flashing lights, you may be swept up with the pulsating crowd and feel your individual identity slipping away. In laboratory research, groups of participants placed in a highly stimulating environment (loud music, colourful video games) were more uninhibited, extreme, and aggressive in their actions (Diener, 1979; Spivey & Prentice-Dunn, 1990).

One context where many people spend a lot of time and where both accountability and attentional cues are likely to be low is online. If you've ever been part of an online

deindividuation
The loss of a person's sense of individuality and the reduction of normal constraints against deviant behaviour.

community where people can post comments anonymously, there is a good chance that you've witnessed some of the nasty effects of deindividuation. Many well-intentioned sites or discussions, or even the comments sections linked to online newspaper stories, videos, or celebrity gossip blogs, soon devolve into a torrent of crude, hostile, and prejudiced venting and taunting that would never happen without the cloak of anonymity. In a survey of nearly 4000 middle-school students, for example, Robin Kowalski and Susan Limber (2007) found that nearly 11 percent of the students had been cyber bullied (i.e., through email, instant messaging, and chat rooms), and that 48 percent of the time, the victim didn't know the identity of their attacker. As Michael Moore and others (2012) note, in the face of an anonymous attack, the victim will be less able to defend himself or herself, while there is little chance the attacker will face any consequences.

One particularly creative set of field experiments by Edward Diener and Arthur Beaman and their colleagues (Beaman et al., 1979; Diener et al., 1976) demonstrated how accountability cues and attentional cues can affect behaviour on a night when many otherwise well-behaved individuals act in antisocial ways: Halloween. When you think about it, Halloween can be a perfect time to study deindividuation; children often wear costumes with masks, travel in large groups at night, and are highly aroused. In one study, the researchers unobtrusively observed more than 1300 children who came trick-or-treating to 27 homes spread around Seattle, Washington. At each of these homes, a researcher met and greeted the children, who were either alone or in groups. In one condition, the researcher asked the children their names and where they lived; in another condition, the researcher did not ask them any questions about their identities. When asked to identify themselves, the children should have become more self-aware and more accountable for their actions. Children who were not asked to reveal their identities should have felt relatively deindividuated, safe, and anonymous in their costumes.

The children were then invited to take *one* item from a bowl full of candy and were left alone with the bowl. Hidden observers watched to see how many pieces of candy each child took. What did the observers see? The children who were in a group were more likely to break the rule and take extra candy than were children who were alone. Add anonymity to the presence of a group, and children became even more likely to do so. In other words, the children were most likely to take extra candy when they were the most deindividuated—when they were in a group and had not been asked to identify themselves. Being in a large crowd can decrease both accountability and self-awareness. Perhaps because of this double impact, larger groups are associated with greater violence (Mullen, 1986). For example, in 2010, a 16-year-old Vancouver teenager was an apparent victim of a gang rape while attending a rave. She was drugged, then allegedly attacked by up to seven youths, while others videotaped the assault. Photos and videos of the assault were then uploaded and distributed widely through various social media sites. None of those alleged to have been involved have so far been brought to justice; despite the number of people attending the party, and the presence of the videotaped evidence, it has been difficult identifying the individual attackers.

Moving from Personal to Social Identity Despite the association between crowds and violence, the loss of personal identity does not always produce antisocial behaviour. In a study conducted by Robert Johnson and Leslie Downing (1979), female undergraduates donned garments resembling either robes worn by Ku Klux Klan members or nurses' uniforms. Half of the participants were individually identified throughout the study; the others were not. All of the participants were then given the opportunity to increase or decrease the intensity of electric shocks delivered to a supposed other participant (actually, an experimental confederate) who had previously behaved in an obnoxious manner. Participants wearing Ku Klux Klan costumes increased shock levels in both the identified and anonymous conditions. However, among those in

FIGURE 8.5

Deindividuation and Social Identity

Group members who saw each other as individuals were more likely to be persuaded by strong arguments, whereas deindividuated members of the group were less likely to notice the quality of the argument presented and instead conform only to the extent that they identified with the group itself.

(Based on Lee, 2008.)

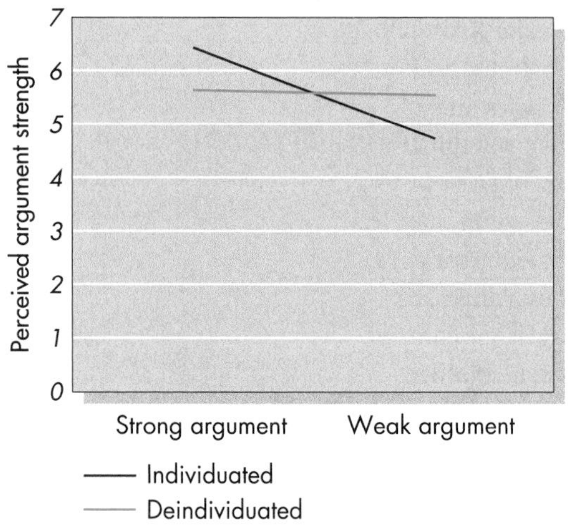

nurse's apparel, anonymous participants *decreased* shock intensity four times more frequently than did identified participants!

These findings make a telling point: Sometimes becoming less accountable, or less self-aware, allows us to be more responsive to the needs of others. According to the **social identity model of deindividuation effects (SIDE)**, whether deindividuation affects people for better or for worse seems to reflect the characteristics and norms of the group immediately surrounding the individual, as well as the group's power to act according to these norms (Cronin & Reicher, 2009; Kim & Park, 2011; Lee, 2008). In order to test this theory, Eun-Ju Lee (2008) told undergraduate participants that they would be interacting with three other people, via computer, while they considered various options in response to a choice dilemma. Though the participants didn't know it, the 'three others' were actually just identities constructed by the experimenter. Those in the 'individuation' condition first had a chance to introduce themselves to the other members of the group and to provide some personal information about themselves, such as their favourite colour or television show. Those in the 'deindividuation' condition skipped this step, and moved on to the choice tasks. After the participant decided between two courses of action for each dilemma, they were then able to see what the other group members ostensibly chose; in every case, their responses were programmed to be the opposite of whatever choice the participant made. In addition to the choice made, the rationale for the decisions of the group members was presented; half of the participants saw strong arguments for why their partners chose the opposite solution, while half saw weak arguments. Each participant was then given a chance to indicate how valid and persuasive they found the arguments presented by the other group members. As can be seen in Figure 8.5, those who were in the deindividuation condition didn't differentiate between strong or weak arguments—they processed everything the same. On the other hand, those who were given a chance to talk about themselves—to be seen as individuals within the group—were significantly more likely to notice whether the other group members' arguments were strong or weak. In addition, the individuated group conformed to the group opinion only when they were presented with a good rationale for doing so.

As personal identity and internal controls are submerged, social identity emerges and conformity to the group increases. If a group defines itself ("us") in terms of prejudice and hatred against another group ("them"), deindividuation can ignite an explosion of violence. But if a group defines itself in terms of concern for the welfare of others, deindividuation can spark an expansion of goodness. The consequences of losing your personal identity depend on what you lose it to.

Group Performance: Problems and Solutions

social identity model of deindividuation effects (SIDE) A model of group behaviour that explains deindividuation effects as the result of a shift from personal identity to social identity.

Social facilitation, social loafing, and deindividuation all can affect individuals whether they are working in real groups or are merely part of a collective or crowd. In this section, we examine processes that are specific to groups, where interaction among members is more direct and meaningful. We focus on how well groups perform, and in doing so, we address a fundamental question: Aren't two or more heads generally better than one? Although eight people typically can out-produce a lone individual, do eight people working together in a group typically outperform the sum of eight people working individually? Although this often is true, you may be surprised to learn how often and in what ways groups perform worse than their potential would suggest. We also discuss when and how groups are more likely to perform well.

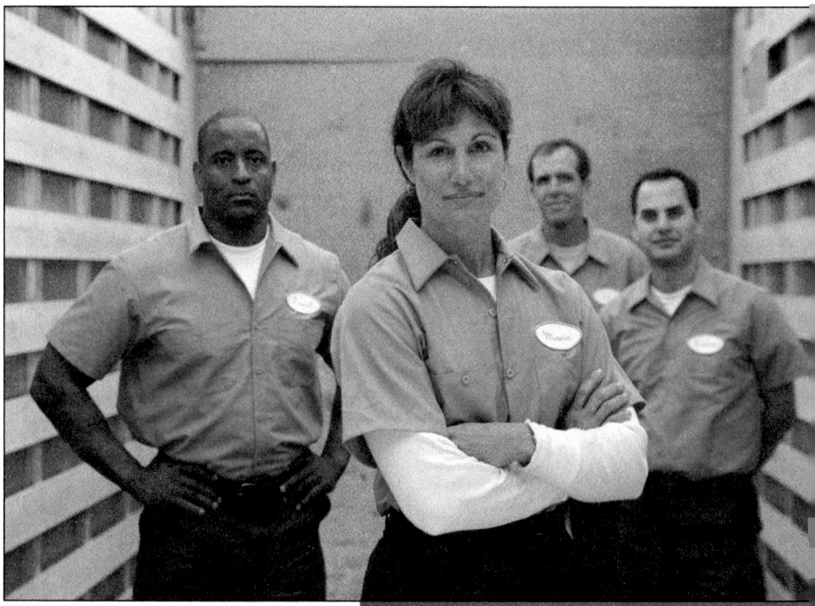

Walter Hodges/Corbis

Group members are often the same, but different. That is, while they may appear similar, they can still maintain unique attributes.

Process Loss and Types of Group Tasks

According to Ivan Steiner (1972), when a group performs worse than its potential, it experiences **process loss**. Process loss refers to the reduction of group productivity due to problems in the dynamics of a group. According to Steiner, some types of group tasks are more vulnerable to process loss than others.

For instance, on an *additive* task, the group product is the *sum* of all the members' contributions. Donating to a charity is an additive task, and so is making noise at a pep rally. As we have seen, people often indulge in social loafing during additive tasks, which creates process loss. Of course, groups usually outperform a single individual. However, each member's contribution may be less than it would be if that person worked alone.

On a *conjunctive* task, the group product is determined by the individual with the *poorest* performance. Mountain-climbing teams are engaged in such a task; the "weakest link" will determine their success or failure. Because of this vulnerability to the poor performance of a single group member, group performance on conjunctive tasks tends to be worse than the performance of a single, average individual.

On a *disjunctive* task, the group product is (or can be) determined by the performance of the individual with the *best* performance. Trying to solve a problem or develop a strategy may be a disjunctive task: What the group needs is a single successful idea, regardless of the number of failures. In principle, groups have an edge on individuals in the performance of disjunctive tasks: The more people involved, the more likely it is that someone will make a breakthrough. In practice, however, group processes can interfere with coming up with ideas and getting them accepted—resulting in process loss.

For example, groups may not realize which group members have the best ideas or are most expert, or may feel that there is less support for the group to achieve its goals as the size of the group increases and so exert less effort overall (Mueller, 2012; Soll & Larrick, 2009). Have you ever had the experience of *knowing* you had the right idea but were unable to convince others in your group until it was too late? If so, then you have experienced first-hand the problem of process loss on a disjunctive task. Fortunately, as groups gain experience with each other, they can become better at recognizing and utilizing the expertise of their members (Bonner & Baumann, 2008, 2012). We will discuss strategies that can help groups recognize and utilize expertise a bit later.

On some kinds of tasks, groups can even show *process gain,* in which they outperform even the best members. Patrick Laughlin and his colleagues (2008; Carey & Laughlin, 2012) propose that groups can perform better than the best individuals on tasks in which the correct answer is clearly evident to everyone in the group once it is presented, and in which the work can be divided up so that various subgroups work on different aspects of the task.

process loss
The reduction in group performance due to obstacles created by group processes, such as problems of coordination and motivation.

The Image Bank/Getty Images

Just as the strength of a chain depends on its weakest link, the group product of a conjunctive task is determined by the individual with the poorest performance. In mountain climbing, for example, if one person slips or falls, the whole team is endangered.

Brainstorming

During the 1950s, advertising executive Alex Osborn developed a technique called **brainstorming**, designed to enhance the creativity and productivity of problem-solving groups. The ground rules for brainstorming call for a freewheeling, creative approach:

- Express *all* ideas that come to mind, even if they sound crazy.
- The more ideas, the better.
- Don't worry whether the ideas are good or bad, and don't criticize anyone's ideas; they can be evaluated later.
- All ideas belong to the group, so members should feel free to build on each other's work.

Osborn (1953) claimed that by using these procedures, groups could generate more and better ideas than could individuals working alone. The gimmick caught on. Brainstorming was soon a popular exercise in business, government, and education; and it remains so today. But when the research caught up with the hype, it turned out that Osborn's faith in the group process was unfounded. In fact, "nominal groups" (several individuals working alone) produce a greater number of better ideas than do real groups in which members interact with each other (Boddy, 2012). Brainstorming can indeed be effective, but people brainstorming individually produce more and higher-quality ideas than the same number of people brainstorming together. One meta-analysis concluded that brainstorming groups are only about half as productive as an equal number of individuals working alone (Mullen et al., 1991). Rather than being inspired by each other and building on each other's ideas, people brainstorming in a group underperform (Nijstad & Stroebe, 2006; Paulus & Brown, 2007).

The top half of Table 8.2 presents several possible explanations that have been proposed for why brainstorming is ineffective. It's particularly ironic, then, that people who engage in group brainstorming typically think that it works wonderfully. Despite the research evidence, brainstorming is still a popular device in many organizations. People who participate in interactive brainstorming groups evaluate their own performance more favourably than do individuals in nominal groups. They also enjoy themselves more. And those who have not participated in an interactive brainstorming group believe that such groups are highly productive. Both the experienced and the inexperienced cling to the illusion that group brainstorming is much better than individual brainstorming (Nijstad & Stroebe, 2006).

There are strategies to improve productivity while also promoting the enjoyment that group brainstorming can produce. For example, training people in effective brainstorming, alternating types of brainstorming sessions (such as by having members brainstorm alone and then together), or carefully pacing the amount and timing of information that any one group member must attend to are each strategies that have been shown to improve group performance (Ferreira et al., 2011; Paulus et al., 2006; Paulus & Brown, 2007).

Computers offer a new and promising way to improve group brainstorming. Electronic brainstorming combines the freedom of working alone at a computer with the stimulation of receiving the ideas of others on a screen. The bottom of Table 8.2 presents some of the factors that make this type of brainstorming effective.

brainstorming
A technique that attempts to increase the production of creative ideas by encouraging group members to speak freely without criticizing their own or others' contributions.

TABLE 8.2

Brainstorming in Groups: Problems and Solutions

Factors That Reduce the Effectiveness of Group Brainstorming

- Production blocking: When people have to wait their turn to speak, they may forget their ideas, may be too busy trying to remember their ideas to listen to others or to generate new ones, or may simply lose interest.
- Free riding: As others contribute ideas, individuals may feel less motivated to work hard themselves. They see their own contributions as less necessary or less likely to have much impact.
- Evaluation apprehension: In the presence of others, people may be hesitant to suggest wild, off-the-wall ideas for fear of looking foolish and being criticized. Even if they are willing to suggest such ideas, they may spend time preparing to justify them—time they otherwise could have spent coming up with more ideas.
- Performance matching: Group members work only as hard as they see others work. Once the other three factors have reduced the performance of a brainstorming group, performance matching can help maintain this relatively inferior performance.

Why Electronic Brainstorming Is Effective

- Production blocking is reduced because members can key in ideas whenever they come to mind.
- Free riding can be reduced by having the computer keep track of each member's input.
- Evaluation apprehension is reduced because group members contribute their ideas anonymously.
- Performance matching is reduced because group members spend less time focusing on the performance of others as they key in their own ideas. In addition, performance matching is less of a problem because the initial performance of groups brainstorming electronically is likely to be high.
- Group members can benefit by seeing the ideas of others, which can inspire new ideas they might not otherwise have considered.

The results of a meta-analysis on the existing research on electronic brainstorming is encouraging (DeRosa et al., 2007). Groups using electric brainstorming tend to perform much better than other brainstorming groups and almost as well as nominal groups. When the group is relatively large (more than eight people), electronic brainstorming groups may even perform better than nominal groups. Brainstorming may have found its true home in a technology that Osborn could only have dreamed of all of those years ago.

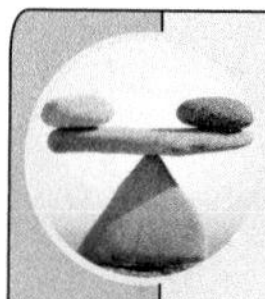

People brainstorming as a group come up with a greater number of better ideas than the same number of people working individually. FALSE.

Group Polarization

People typically are attracted to groups that share their attitudes, and those who disagree with the group usually leave by their own choice or are ejected by the others. But similar does not mean identical. Although the range of opinion is relatively restricted, there are still differences. What do you think should be the result of a group discussion of these differing points of view? For example, imagine that a group is discussing whether someone should behave in a risky or a cautious manner, such as whether an entrepreneur should risk trying to expand his or her business or whether an employee in a stable but boring job should quit and take a more creative job in a new but unproven Internet company. Are groups more likely to advocate risky or cautious decisions about issues like these?

"A committee should consist of three men, two of whom are absent."
—Herbert Beerbohm Tree

Common sense suggests two alternative predictions. Perhaps the most reasonable prediction is that after the group members discuss their differing points of view, the group decision will represent an overall compromise as everyone moves toward the group average. But common sense also suggests another prediction. Many people familiar with committees agree that forming a committee is a good way *not* to get something done. The idea is that individuals are willing to take risks and implement new ideas, whereas groups tend to be cautious and slow moving. Wary of leading the group toward a risky decision, people often become more cautious in their views as they discuss them with the other group members.

"A committee is a cul-de-sac down which ideas are lured and then quietly strangled."
—Barnett Cock

So, which prediction is the correct one—movement toward the average attitude or movement toward caution? James Stoner (1961) tested this question by comparing decisions made by individuals with decisions made by groups, and he found that *neither* prediction was correct: Group decisions tended to be *riskier* than individuals' decisions. Was this a fluke? Several subsequent studies found similar results, and the tendency for groups to become riskier than the average of the individuals became known as the *risky shift* (Cartwright, 1971).

But the story doesn't end there. Later studies seemed to contradict the idea of the risky shift, finding that for some choices, groups tended to become more *cautious* (Knox & Safford, 1976). How can we make sense of these contradictory findings?

Researchers concluded that group discussion tends to enhance or exaggerate the initial leanings of the group. Thus, if most group members initially lean toward a risky position on a particular issue, the group's position becomes even riskier after the discussion; but if group members in general initially lean toward a cautious position, the group discussion leads to greater caution. This effect is called **group polarization**—the exaggeration through group discussion of initial tendencies in the thinking of group members (Moscovici & Zavalloni, 1969; Myers & Lamm, 1976).

Group polarization is not restricted to decisions involving risk versus caution. Any group decision can be influenced by group polarization, although it is more likely to occur when important, rather than unimportant, issues are being discussed. Consider, for example, racial prejudice. In one study, high school students responded to an initial questionnaire and were classified as high, medium, or low on racial prejudice. Groups of like-minded students then met for a discussion of racial issues, with their individual attitudes on these issues assessed before and after their interaction. Group polarization was dramatic. Students low in prejudice to begin with were even less prejudiced after the group discussion; students moderate or high in prejudice became even more prejudiced (Myers & Bishop, 1970).

What creates group polarization? Three processes are usually emphasized:

1. According to *persuasive arguments theory*, the greater the number and persuasiveness of the arguments to which group members are exposed, the more extreme their attitudes become. If most group members favour a cautious decision, for example, most of the arguments discussed will favour caution, giving the members more and more reason to think caution is the correct approach (Pavitt, 1994; Vinokur & Burnstein, 1974).

2. According to *social comparison theory*, in a group discussion, people may discover more support for their own opinion than they had originally anticipated. This discovery then sets up a new, more extreme norm and motivates group members to go beyond that norm. If believing X is good, then believing twice X is even better. By adopting a more extreme attitudinal position, people can distinguish themselves in the group in a manner approved by the group (Lamm & Myers, 1978).

3. In addition, group polarization is influenced by a concept you may recall from Chapter 5: *social categorization*, the tendency for people to categorize themselves and others in terms of social groups. The social categorization approach compares how individuals react to information from ingroups (to which they belong or want to belong) and outgroups (to which they don't belong and don't want to belong). Ingroup members may want to distinguish their group from other groups, and so they overestimate the extremity of their group's position and distance themselves from the position of an outgroup (Hogg et al., 1990; McGarty et al., 1992).

group polarization
The exaggeration through group discussion of initial tendencies in the thinking of group members.

Now that you know about group polarization, you should be able to see evidence of it often as you observe the groups around you. At a broad level, it seems that political groups today have become more and more polarized, moving to extremes rather than toward moderation and compromise. On a smaller level, observe how the culture of a team may evolve over the course of a season, or follow the attitudes of a group as it prepares for a debate and you're likely to see group polarization develop through the processes just described.

Group members' attitudes about a course of action usually become more moderate after group discussion. FALSE.

Groupthink

The processes involved in group polarization may set the stage for an even greater, and perhaps more dangerous, bias in group decision making. There are numerous examples of high-level groups making decisions that in hindsight seem remarkably ill-conceived.

For example, in May 2000, a criminal investigation began in Walkerton, Ontario, after 7 people died and more than 2000 residents became ill after drinking local water. It turned out that the town's water supply contained the deadly *E. coli* bacteria after a storm caused cow manure to wash into a town well. The investigation revealed that many people who worked for the city were aware that the water was contaminated, but rather than warning the public and cleaning it up, they covered it up. The chlorination system, which may have helped to avert the tragedy, was not working at the time the storm occurred, and in fact had not been working properly for some time. Rather than fixing this, those in charge instead falsified the logs for any required water tests.

Or consider one of the greatest fiascos in U.S. history: the decision to invade Cuba in 1961. When John Kennedy became president of the United States in 1961, he assembled one of the most impressive groups of advisers in the history of American government. These individuals—highly intelligent, educated at the best universities, led by a new president brimming with ambition, charisma, and optimism—were called "the best and the brightest" (Halberstam, 1972). But the Kennedy administration had inherited a plan from the previous administration to invade Cuba at the Bay of Pigs in order to spark a people's revolt that would overthrow Fidel Castro's government. After much deliberation, Kennedy and his advisers eventually approved an invasion plan that in hindsight was hopelessly flawed. For example, once the invaders landed at the Bay of Pigs, they were to be supported by anti-Castro guerrillas camped in the mountains nearby. But had Kennedy and his advisers consulted a map, they might have noticed that the invaders were actually set to land 80 miles away from these mountains and were separated from them by a huge swamp. Ultimately, the invasion failed miserably. The invaders were quickly killed or captured, the world was outraged at the United States, and Cuba allied itself more closely with the Soviet Union—exactly the opposite of what Kennedy had intended. The United States was humiliated. After the fiasco, Kennedy himself wondered, "How could we have been so stupid?" (Janis, 1982).

"'It is always best on these occasions to do what the mob do. 'But suppose there are two mobs?' suggested Mr. Snodgrass. 'Shout with the largest,' replied Mr. Pickwick."

—Charles Dickens

According to Irving Janis (1982), the answer to this question, and similar questions that could be posed of any of the other fiascos we've described, lies in a particular kind of flawed group dynamic that he called **groupthink**, an excessive tendency to seek concurrence among group members. Groupthink emerges when the need for agreement takes priority over the motivation to obtain accurate information and make appropriate decisions. ▶ Figure 8.6, on page 292, outlines the factors that contribute to groupthink, along with its symptoms and consequences.

groupthink
A group decision-making style characterized by an excessive tendency among group members to seek concurrence.

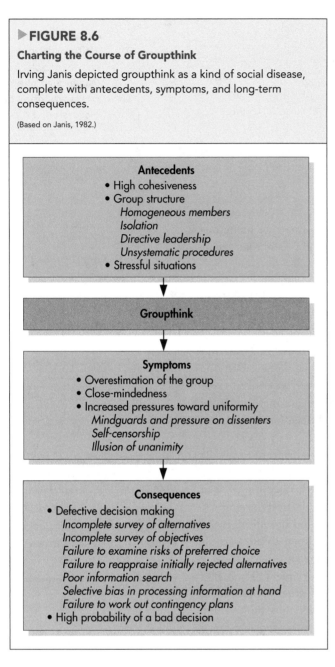

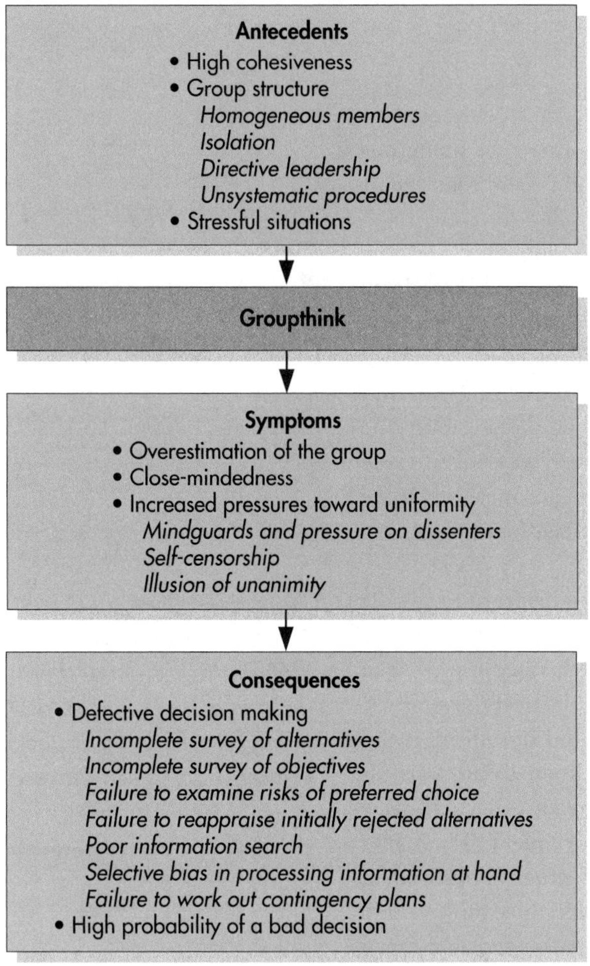

Antecedents
• High cohesiveness
• Group structure
Homogeneous members
Isolation
Directive leadership
Unsystematic procedures
• Stressful situations
Groupthink
Symptoms
• Overestimation of the group
• Close-mindedness
• Increased pressures toward uniformity
Mindguards and pressure on dissenters
Self-censorship
Illusion of unanimity
Consequences
• Defective decision making
Incomplete survey of alternatives
Incomplete survey of objectives
Failure to examine risks of preferred choice
Failure to reappraise initially rejected alternatives
Poor information search
Selective bias in processing information at hand
Failure to work out contingency plans
• High probability of a bad decision

FIGURE 8.6

Charting the Course of Groupthink

Irving Janis depicted groupthink as a kind of social disease, complete with antecedents, symptoms, and long-term consequences.

(Based on Janis, 1982.)

Janis believed that three characteristics contribute to the development of groupthink:

1. Since *highly cohesive groups* are more likely to reject members with deviant opinions, Janis thought they would be more susceptible to groupthink.
2. *Group structure* is also important. Groups that are composed of people from similar backgrounds, isolated from other people, directed by a strong leader, and lacking in systematic procedures for making and reviewing decisions should be particularly likely to fall prey to groupthink.
3. Finally, Janis emphasized that *stressful situations* can provoke groupthink. Under stress, urgency can overrule accuracy, and the reassuring support of other group members becomes highly desirable.

In Janis's formulation, groupthink is a kind of social disease, and infected groups display the behavioural symptoms indicated in the middle of Figure 8.6. For example, Kennedy and his advisers exhibited *overestimation of the group,* assuming that as "the best and the brightest," they could pull off a little invasion, even if some of the details were worrisome. And the refusal of those in charge of the Walkerton water supply to ask for outside help once they realized there was a problem clearly illustrated the symptom of *closed-mindedness.* Another symptom, *pressures toward uniformity,* was evident in both these examples. In groupthink, group members may censor their own thoughts or act as "mindguards" to discourage deviant thoughts by other group members. During the planning of the Bay of Pigs invasion, the president's brother, Robert Kennedy, served as a mindguard and warned dissenting members to keep quiet, helping to foster an *illusion of unanimity.*

When alternatives are not considered, the behavioural symptoms of groupthink can result in the defective decision making outlined in Figure 8.6. In turn, a defective decision-making process increases the likelihood that a group will make bad decisions.

Research on Groupthink Groupthink is a rather distinctive theory in social psychology. On the one hand, its impact has been unusually broad. It is discussed in a variety of disciplines outside of psychology, including business, political science, and communication, and it has spawned numerous workshops as well as a best-selling management training video. Yet, on the other hand, there is not a great deal of empirical support for the model, certainly not in proportion to its fame. This may be partly due to the difficulty of experimentally testing such a broad set of variables in high-pressure group settings. In addition, many researchers disagree with Janis about the specific conditions that make groups vulnerable to groupthink (Baron, 2005; Choi & Kim, 1999; Henningsen et al., 2006; Kramer, 1998; 't Hart et al., 1995; Tetlock, 1998; Whyte, 1998). But when multiple antecedents of groupthink are evident simultaneously, such as high cohesiveness, a strong and controlling leader, and a great deal of stress, groups are particularly vulnerable to the kinds of faulty decision making that Janis described (Esser, 1998; Mullen et al., 1994).

Preventing Groupthink To guard against groupthink, Janis urged groups to make an active effort to process information more carefully and accurately. He recommended that decision-making groups use the following strategies:

- To avoid isolation, groups should consult widely with outsiders.
- To reduce conformity pressures, leaders should explicitly encourage criticism and not take a strong stand early in the group discussion.
- To establish a strong norm of critical review, subgroups should separately discuss the same issue, a member should be assigned to play devil's advocate and question all decisions and ideas, and a "second chance" meeting should be held to reconsider the group decision before taking action.

"On second thought, don't correct me if I'm wrong."

A controlling leader who discourages disagreement can promote groupthink, leading to bad decisions.

Research has shown empirical support for the effectiveness of some strategies in curtailing groupthink tendencies. These include inserting someone in the group to play the role of a "reminder" who is responsible for informing the group about the dangers of biased decision making; making individual group members believe that they will be held personally responsible for the outcome of their group's decisions; increasing the diversity of group members; and creating a group norm encouraging critical thinking and discouraging the search for concurrence (Kroon et al., 1991; Postmes et al., 2001; Schultz et al., 1995; t'Hart, 1998). And as we will see a bit later in the chapter, computer-based technology can be used during meetings to help avoid groupthink.

Escalation Effects

A specific kind of trap that can be very costly to organizations and businesses is known as the **escalation effect** (sometimes referred to as *entrapment*). Escalation effects occur when commitment to a failing course of action is increased to justify investments already made (Haslam et al., 2006; Keil et al., 2007; Staw, 1997). Laboratory experiments show that groups are more likely to escalate commitment to a failing project, and are likely to do so in more extreme ways, than are individuals (Dietz-Uhler, 1996; Whyte, 1993).

In numerous instances, groups, businesses, and governments have incurred huge costs because they kept throwing more money, time, and other resources into a project that should have been terminated long before (Ross & Staw, 1986). For example, in 2009, the Auditor General for Ontario completed his report documenting the spending fiasco that became known as the eHealth scandal. In 2000, the Federal government set aside $500 million to start the process of creating electronic health records for all Canadians. In Ontario, the goal was to have switched over to this new system by 2015. However, by 2008, with millions already spent, little progress had been made. The Auditor General ultimately concluded that over $1 billion of taxpayers' money was wasted on this process, with outrageous, and in many cases unaccounted for, spending on consultants, salaried staff, no-bid contracts, and even on office decoration.

escalation effect
The condition in which commitments to a failing course of action are increased to justify investments already made.

Toronto Star/Vince Talatta

Sarah Kramer, the former head of eHealth Ontario, was fired from her job in the wake of the eHealth spending scandal.

Communicating Information and Utilizing Expertise

One of the biggest flaws in how groups perform is that they often fail to use all the information or skills that group members have (Hackman & Katz, 2010). In this section, we will explore some of the dynamics that cause this problem, as well as some factors that can help groups better communicate and use important information.

Biased Sampling Imagine that you are part of a group that is discussing which of several candidates should be supported in an election. You have read some potentially damaging personal information about one of the candidates, and you assume that the others are also aware of it. If you observe during group discussion that nobody else mentions this information, you may further assume that the others don't think the information is relevant or credible; so you may not mention it yourself. Other group members may also have unique bits of information known only to them. For similar reasons, these pieces of information fail to enter the discussion. In the end, the discussion is dominated by information everyone in the group already knew, while the unshared information never makes it to the table. This illustrates what Garold Stasser (1992; Stasser & Titus, 2003) termed **biased sampling**. Because of biased sampling, a group may fail to consider important information that is not common knowledge in the group. Inadequately informed, the group may make a bad decision. A recent meta-analysis by Jessica Mesmer-Magnus and Leslie DeChurch (2009) of 72 studies involving almost 5000 groups found that biased sampling is a frequent and significant problem in groups. Groups that do a better job of sharing information tend to perform much better and are more cohesive.

"Nor is the people's judgment always true: The most may err as grossly as the few."
—John Dryden

Research has discovered several conditions in which biased sampling is less likely to occur. When group members are aware that not everyone has access to the same information, they are more likely to share their information with the group (Schittekatte & van Hiel, 1996; Stasser & Birchmeier, 2003). Leaders who encourage a lot of group participation are more likely to elicit unshared (as well as shared) information during group discussions than are more directive leaders (Larson et al., 1998). In addition, as groups gain more experience, they often become better at sharing information (Greitemeyer et al., 2006).

Groups are less likely than individuals to invest more and more resources in a project that is failing. FALSE.

Other kinds of mindsets can also promote more thorough information sharing in groups. For instance, Adam Galinsky and Laura Kray (2004) found that priming some groups to think counterfactually—that is, to imagine alternative outcomes that easily could have happened but did not—prompted these groups to discuss unshared information, and to make the correct decision, significantly more often than the groups that were not primed.

biased sampling
The tendency for groups to spend more time discussing shared information (information already known by all or most group members) than unshared information (information known by only one or a few group members).

Information Processing and Transactive Memory Even if a group has all the available information, group members must process that information and use it to make judgments or perform tasks. How well do groups process information, compared with individuals? In general, groups are susceptible to the same information-processing biases as individuals—only more so. In reviewing the research on group information processing, Verlin Hinsz and others (1997) concluded, "If some bias, error, or tendency predisposes individuals to process information in a particular way, then groups exaggerate this tendency. However, if this bias, error, or tendency is unlikely among individuals processing the information (e.g., less than half the sample), then groups are even less likely to process information in this fashion" (pp. 49–50).

Groups can divide a large body of information into smaller portions and delegate different members to remember these more manageable portions, ideally by matching information to individuals based on their expertise and interest. This shared process is known as **transactive memory** and helps groups remember more information more efficiently than individuals (Peltokorpi, 2012; Wegner et al., 1991). But process loss can occur in this domain as well. Social loafing may occur, for example, when group members don't do their share of the work while expecting others to pick up the slack. A particularly important problem is that groups may not distribute the tasks and roles among group members in a rational or efficient manner, for example, by matching individuals to tasks based on their skills, expertise, and preferences. Groups that develop good transactive memory systems are able to do this well, for example, by recognizing who knows what in the group, and this improves group performance significantly (Littlepage et al., 2008; Palazzolo et al., 2006).

Strategies for Improvement

Groups of researchers have found a variety of factors that promote better group dynamics, such as through better sharing of information and utilization of expertise. We turn to some of these next.

Norms and Goals As with so many aspects of group dynamics, group norms play an important role. Tom Postmes and others (2001) conducted an experiment in which groups were induced to develop a norm emphasizing either group consensus or independent critical analysis. Groups with the critical-thinking norm were much more likely to discuss unshared information (thereby avoiding biased sampling), and come to significantly more accurate decisions after group discussion than were groups with the consensus norm.

Groups, like individuals, tend to perform better on a task when they have specific, challenging, and reachable goals, particularly if the group members are committed to the goals and believe they have the ability to achieve them. Such goals are generally more effective than "do your best" goals or no goals at all (Latham & Locke, 2007; Wegge et al., 2007). You've probably worked in many groups for which the goal was simply to "do your best." Despite the popularity of such goals, the research clearly shows that they are not as effective as specific goals. As Edwin Locke and Gary Latham (2002) concluded from their review of 35 years' worth of studies, "When people are asked to do their best, they do not do so" (p. 706). People are indeed capable of better than their vaguely defined "best." In addition to having challenging and specific goals, groups are most likely to benefit when there are incentives in place for achieving these goals.

Training and Interventions Researchers have discovered several other strategies and factors that can enhance group processes. ■ Table 8.3, on page 296, presents a set of the conditions that Ruth Wageman and her colleagues (2009, 2012) suggest are best for team effectiveness. These suggestions are consistent with the principles that we have addressed throughout this chapter, and they help illustrate the tremendous value that understanding the social psychology of groups can have in the business world or wherever group performance is essential.

transactive memory A shared system for remembering information that enables multiple people to remember information together more efficiently than they could alone.

TABLE 8.3

Conditions for Team Effectiveness

Ruth Wageman and her colleagues (2009) reviewed the research on what makes teams most effective. Below is a list of some of the conditions they emphasize.

- Teams should be interdependent for some common purpose and have some stability of membership.
- The team's overall purpose should be challenging, clear, and consequential.
- Teams should be as small as possible and have clear norms that specify what behaviours are valued or are unacceptable.
- A reward system should provide positive consequences for excellent team performance.
- Technical assistance and training should be available to the team.

TABLE 8.4

How Computerized Group Support Systems Help Groups Avoid Groupthink

1. Allow group members to raise their concerns anonymously through the computer interface, enabling them to risk challenging group consensus without fear of direct attacks.
2. Reduce the directive role of the leader.
3. Enable group members to provide input simultaneously, so they don't have to wait for a chance to raise their ideas.
4. Allow the least assertive group members to state their ideas as easily as the most dominating.
5. Provide a systematic agenda of information gathering and decision making.
6. Keep the focus in the group meetings on the ideas themselves rather than on the people and relationships within the group.

(Based on Miranda, 1994.)

Another approach that research has shown to be effective is adopting interventions that stop the natural flow of behaviours in groups and compel the group members to explicitly think about how they should proceed (Woolley et al., 2008). For example, Andrea Gurtner and others (2007) found that group performance was improved significantly after an intervention was performed that induced the group to reflect on its performance and make explicit plans to implement strategies for improvement.

Computer Technology and Group Support Systems Some of the obstacles that get in the way of good group discussion and decision making can be reduced through the use of interactive computer programs. Recently there has been an explosion of research on the use of such programs. Often referred to as *group support systems (GSSs)* or *group decision support systems (GDSSs)*, these programs help remove communication barriers and provide structure and incentives for group discussions and decisions. Compared to groups employing more conventional face-to-face modes of discussion, groups that use these systems often do a better job of sampling information, communicating, and arriving at good decisions (Lim & Guo, 2008; Rains, 2005; Vathanophas & Liang, 2007). ■ Table 8.4 lists some of the ways that computerized group support systems can help groups avoid groupthink.

▌▌ Virtual Teams

Teams consisting of people who may be dispersed widely across the globe are a relatively recent (and rapidly growing) part of the business world. Recent estimates indicate that a majority of professional workers today spend time working in virtual teams (Cordery & Soo, 2008; Mathieu et al., 2008). Virtual teams, sometimes also called dispersed teams, are "groups of people who work interdependently with shared purpose across space, time, and organization boundaries using technology to communicate and collaborate" (Kirkman et al., 2002, p. 67). Due to globalization and a variety of related factors, virtual teams will be increasingly important in businesses and organizations.

Most of the factors that contribute to process loss in groups apply as well to virtual groups, but virtual groups may be especially vulnerable to some of these (Robert et al., 2009). Given the physical distances between members and how little interaction they may have with each other, virtual groups may have a harder time building cohesiveness, keeping membership stable, socializing new members, keeping roles clear, sharing information, and developing transactive memory systems that enable the members to recognize or recall who has what knowledge or expertise in the group. Special attention must be paid to virtual groups, therefore, to offset these problems. For example, according to Vishal Midha and Ankur Nandedkar (2012), using an online avatar as a representation of oneself to the group makes identity more salient and therefore decreases social loafing. In addition, frequent teleconferencing sessions and occasional short visits to allow dispersed group members to spend some time together can also help (Cordery & Soo, 2008; Hackman & Katz, 2010; Oshri et al., 2008).

Jon Feingersh/Getty Images

As new technology allows more and more diverse groups to communicate and work together, it is more important than ever that groups learn how to utilize the great benefits and minimize the costs of diversity in group processes.

Diversity

In the twenty-first century, groups around the world, whether in schools, organizations, businesses, sports, arts, or governments, are becoming increasingly diverse, most obviously in terms of sex, race, ethnicity, and cultural background. How does diversity affect group performance? How can a group best use diversity to its advantage? The answers to such questions—and even the meaning of *diversity*—are likely to change as society changes in terms of its demographics and attitudes. In addition, diversity is not restricted to demographic differences among group members, but can also mean differences in attitudes, personalities, skill levels, and so on. Thus, the issues surrounding diversity are particularly complex.

The evidence from empirical research concerning the effects of diversity on group performance is decidedly mixed (Cheng et al., 2012; Hackman & Katz, 2010; van Knippenberg & Schippers, 2007). On the one hand, diversity often is associated with negative group dynamics (Levine & Moreland, 1998; Maznevski, 1994; Rico et al., 2012). Miscommunications and misunderstandings are more likely to arise among heterogeneous group members, causing frustration and resentment, and damaging group performance by weakening coordination, morale, and commitment to the group. Cliques often form in diverse groups, causing some group members to feel alienated (Jackson et al., 1995; Maznevski, 1994). And even if diversity doesn't appear to hurt a group in any objective way, group members may *think* that it does. For example, S. Gayle Baugh and George Graen (1997) compared how diverse and homogeneous project teams rated their own effectiveness. Project teams that were diverse in terms of gender and race rated themselves as less effective—even though external evaluators judged the diverse teams to be no less effective than the homogeneous teams.

On the other hand, research has also demonstrated positive effects of diversity, such as on patterns of socialization, classroom dynamics, and complexity of group discussion (Antonio et al., 2004; Juvonen et al., 2006). As more and more organizations try to attract customers and investors from diverse cultures, diversity in personnel should offer more and more advantages. Cedric Herring (2009) analyzed data from over 1000 work establishments in the United States from 1996 to 1997 and found that racial diversity was associated with greater profits and market share. Given trends in populations, business, and attitudes, we can predict that the relationship between diversity and group success is likely to become more positive and consistent in the future. It remains for future research to investigate this hypothesis.

Conflict: Cooperation and Competition Within and Between Groups

Many of the most crucial issues confronting our world today involve conflicts between individuals and their groups or between groups. The desire of some individuals to consume valuable resources conflicts with the need of others to protect the environment for the greater good. A nation's claim to important territory or the right to nuclear arms conflicts with another nation's national security. In this section, we describe some of the dilemmas groups often must confront, and what factors influence whether individuals and groups act cooperatively or competitively in dealing with them. We also look at some of the factors that cause conflicts between groups to escalate or to be reduced, and we focus on an important mechanism for resolving group conflicts: negotiation.

Mixed Motives and Social Dilemmas

Imagine that you have to choose between cooperating with others in your group and pursuing your own self-interests, which can hurt the others. Examples of these mixed-motive situations are everywhere. An actor in a play may be motivated to try to "steal" a scene, a basketball player may be inclined to hog the ball, an executive may want to keep more of the company's profits, a family member may want to eat more than her fair share of the leftover birthday cake, and a citizen of Earth may want to use more than his fair share of finite, valuable resources. In each case, the individual can gain something by pursuing his or her self-interests; but if everyone in the group pursues self-interests, all of the group members will ultimately be worse off than if they had cooperated with each other. Each option, therefore, has possible benefits along with potential costs. When you are in a situation like this, you may feel torn between wanting to cooperate and wanting to compete, and these mixed motives create a difficult dilemma. What do you do?

Large groups are more likely than small groups to exploit a scarce resource that the members collectively depend on. TRUE.

The notion that the pursuit of self-interest can sometimes be self-destructive forms the basis for what is called a **social dilemma.** In a social dilemma, what is good for one is bad for all. If everyone makes the most self-rewarding choice, everyone suffers the greatest loss. This section examines how people resolve the tension between their cooperative and competitive inclinations in social dilemmas.

social dilemma
A situation in which a self-interested choice by everyone creates the worst outcome for everyone.

prisoner's dilemma
A type of dilemma in which one party must make either cooperative or competitive moves in relation to another party; typically designed in such a way that competitive moves are more beneficial to either side, but if both sides make competitive moves, they are both worse off than if they both cooperated.

The Prisoner's Dilemma We begin with a detective story. Two partners in crime are picked up by the police for questioning. Although the police believe they have committed a major offence, there is only enough evidence to convict them on a minor charge. In order to sustain a conviction for the more serious crime, the police will have to convince one of them to testify against the other. Separated during questioning, the criminals weigh their alternatives (see ▶ Figure 8.7). If neither confesses, they will both get light sentences on the minor charge. If both confess and plead guilty, they will both receive moderate sentences. But if one confesses and the other stays silent, the confessing criminal will secure immunity from prosecution while the silent criminal will pay the maximum penalty.

This story forms the basis for the research paradigm known as the **prisoner's dilemma.** In the two-person prisoner's dilemma, participants are given a series of

FIGURE 8.7

The Prisoner's Dilemma

In the original prisoner's dilemma, from which the game took its name, each of two criminals is offered immunity from prosecution in exchange for a confession. If both stay silent, both get off with a light sentence on a minor charge (upper left). If both confess, both receive a moderate sentence (lower right). But if one confesses while the other stays mum, the confessing criminal goes free and the silent one spends a long time in jail.

Prisoner B \ Prisoner A	No Confession (Cooperates with Prisoner B)	Confession (Competes with Prisoner B)
No Confession (Cooperates with Prisoner A)	A gets 1 year B gets 1 year	A gets 0 years B gets 10 years
Confession (Competes with Prisoner A)	A gets 10 years B gets 0 years	A gets 5 years B gets 5 years

choices in which they have the option of cooperating or competing with each other, but either option has potential costs. Consider an example: Imagine that you're Prisoner A in Figure 8.7. It appears that no matter what Prisoner B does, you're better off if you compete with B and confess. If B doesn't confess to the police (in other words, if he cooperates with you), you get a lighter sentence if you do confess (you would get no jail time) than if you don't confess (you would get one year in jail). If B does confess, you still get a lighter sentence if you confess than if you don't—five versus ten years. So, clearly, you should confess, right? But here's the dilemma: If you *both* confess, each of you gets five years. If *neither* of you confesses, each of you gets only one year. It's really a perplexing situation. What do you think you would do?

This kind of social dilemma is not limited to situations involving only two individuals at a time. Imagine, for example, being in a burning building or a sinking ship. Everyone might want to race for the exit or the lifeboats as quickly as possible and push others out of the way; but if everyone does that, more people will die in the panic. More lives will be saved if people leave in an orderly fashion. Soldiers engaged in combat may be better off individually if they take no chances and duck for cover, but if their comrades do the same thing, they will all be slaughtered by the enemy. Nations face such dilemmas as well. Two countries locked in an arms race would be better off if they stopped spending money and resources on weapons of mass destruction, but neither country wants to risk falling behind the other (Dawes, 1980).

Resource Dilemmas The prisoner's dilemma sets up a trap for those who play it: Attempts to gain an advantage will backfire if the other party also makes the competitive choice. This conflict of motives also forms the basis for another category of social dilemmas: **resource dilemmas**, which concern how two or more people share a limited resource. Resource dilemmas come in two basic types: (1) commons dilemmas, and (2) public goods dilemmas.

The commons dilemma is a situation in which, if people take as much as they want of a limited resource that does not replenish itself, nothing will be left for anyone. Robyn Dawes (1980) called this situation the take-some dilemma, one popular version of which is known as the "tragedy of the commons" (Hardin, 1968). In earlier times, people would let their animals graze on the town's lush, grassy commons. But if all the animals grazed to their hearts' content, and to their owners' benefit, the commons would be stripped, the animals' food supply diminished, and the owners' welfare threatened. Today, the tragedy of the commons is a clear and present danger on a global scale. Deforestation, air pollution, ocean dumping, massive irrigation,

resource dilemmas
Social dilemmas concerning how two or more people share a limited resource.

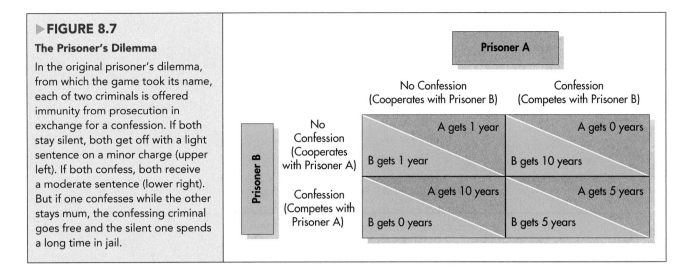

overfishing, commercial development of wilderness areas, a rapidly increasing population in some developing countries, and an over-consuming population in the richest nations—all pit individual self-interest against the common good. Selfish responses to commons dilemmas are social sins of commission; people take too much.

In public goods dilemmas, all of the individuals are supposed to contribute resources to a common pool. Examples of these public goods include the blood supply, public broadcasting, schools, libraries, roads, and parks. If no one gives, the service can't continue. If club members don't pay their dues or contribute their time, the club will fail. Again, private gain conflicts with the public good.

Solving Social Dilemmas: Groups and Individuals When does individual desire prevail in social dilemmas? When, in contrast, do people see beyond their own immediate potential for gain and consider the long-term benefits of cooperation? Social dilemmas pose a serious threat to the quality of life and even to life itself. How do people try to solve them? What factors make people more or less cooperative when faced with these dilemmas?

Fear and greed are two critically important factors in determining reactions to these dilemmas—the fear of being exploited by others and the greedy desire to maximize one's own outcomes. Trust, therefore, is essential in promoting cooperation because it reduces the fear of being exploited. Similarly, a sense of belongingness and identity with the greater group also promotes cooperation, because this perspective can reduce fear and greed (De Cremer et al., 2008; Ishii & Kurzban, 2008; Klapwijk & Van Lange, 2009). Another important factor is threat of punishment (Mulder, 2008). Groups that punish members who exploit the rest of the group are more likely to thrive. Indeed, according to evolutionary psychologists, punishing those who do not cooperate with the group is an evolved psychological mechanism because cooperation was crucial for survival (O'Gormon et al., 2008). A recent meta-analysis by Daniel Balliet, Laetitia Mulder, and Paul Van Lange (2011) confirmed that fear of punishment or the possibility of reward are both important factors affecting the level of cooperation exhibited by group members. When incentives are perceived as costly, as when there is evidence of a self-sacrificing component to benefit the greater good, overall levels of cooperation increase. Interestingly, punishments were also more effective when the group members were going to be working with the same group members again on subsequent tasks. In a related finding, Van Lange and others (2011) demonstrated that simply anticipating a future interaction with a group was enough to increase cooperation.

These are just a few of the variables that help determine competition or cooperation in social dilemmas. ■ Table 8.5 summarizes some of the factors that extensive research has identified as facilitating the best solutions to social dilemmas.

Groups tend to be more competitive in mixed-motive situations than individuals, in part due to the challenges inherent in establishing trust between groups than between individuals (McGlynn et al., 2009; Naquin & Kurtzberg, 2009). Because we are prone to perceive groups in less personalized or humanized ways than we perceive individuals, we are more likely to fear groups and to feel less inhibited about behaving in a greedy way toward them. We feel less shame or guilt in hurting an abstract *Other* than we do in hurting a specific person. In addition, group members feel less identifiable by members of the other group. The greater anonymity that a group offers frees individual group members to act in a self-interested, aggressive manner. This is one reason why large groups are more likely to exploit scarce resources than are small ones (Pruitt, 1998; Seijts & Latham, 2000; Wildschut et al., 2003).

The fact remains that social dilemmas also involve very large groups—a city, a province, a nation, the whole world. In these circumstances, the structural factors we have listed in Table 8.5 may be most appropriate. The importance of resolving social dilemmas well is crucial for maintaining the quality of our lives, both immediately but even more so for the future. Understanding the psychological and structural factors that affect groups' behaviours when confronted with these dilemmas is therefore one of the most vital contributions that social psychological research can make.

TABLE 8.5

Solving Social Dilemmas

Behaviour in a social dilemma is influenced by both psychological factors and structural arrangements. The characteristics listed here contribute to the successful solution of social dilemmas.

Psychological Factors

- Individual and cultural differences
  - Having a prosocial, cooperative orientation
  - Trusting others
  - Being a member of a collectivistic culture
- Situational factors
  - Being in a good mood
  - Having had successful experience managing resources and working cooperatively
  - Seeing unselfish models
  - Having reason to expect others to cooperate
- Group dynamics
  - Acting as an individual rather than in a group
  - Being in a small group rather than in a large group
  - Sharing a social identity or superordinate goals

Structural Arrangements

- Creating a payoff structure that rewards cooperative behaviour and/or punishes selfish behaviour
- Removing resources from the public domain and handing them over to private ownership
- Establishing an authority to control the resources

Individual and Gender Differences Although all of us struggle with social dilemmas, people differ in their own tendencies toward cooperation and competition. One individual difference concerns people's social value orientations. People with a *prosocial, cooperative* orientation seek to maximize joint gains; those with an *individualist* orientation seek to maximize their own gain; and those with a *competitive* orientation seek to maximize their own gain relative to that of others. People with a cooperative orientation are less likely to behave in a competitive, resource-consuming fashion than are people with individualistic or competitive orientations (Bogaert et al., 2008; De Cremer et al., 2008; van Dijk et al., 2009).

Although women often are stereotypically thought to be more cooperative and less individualistic than men, the evidence does not support this assumption. In a recent meta-analysis exploring sex differences in cooperation levels, Daniel Balliet and others (2011) found no evidence for sex differences in overall levels of cooperation. However, they did find that men tend to be *more* cooperative when interacting with other men, whereas women cooperate *less* when working with other women. Women were instead most likely to cooperate when working with men. The authors suggest several explanations for these findings, including the possibility that evolutionary pressures may be behind these results. That is, it may be adaptive for men to work together to gain resources, whereas women—competing for those resources—avoid helping other women who they may view as their competition. On the other hand, by cooperating with a man, a woman may help to increase his chances of success, which in turn increases his resources, thus making him a more attractive mate.

Culture and Social Dilemmas

Just as with gender differences, the expectation that there should be reliable cultural differences in responses to social dilemmas is stronger than the evidence found in the research thus far. Some studies have suggested that people and groups from collectivist cultures are more likely to cooperate in social dilemmas than people and groups from individualist cultures, while other studies have found similarities across cultures

(Ishii & Kurzban, 2008; Kopelman, 2009; Takemura & Yuki, 2007; Yamagishi et al., 2005). More specifically, however, it may be that collectivists tend to cooperate more when dealing with friends or ingroup members but compete more aggressively when dealing with strangers or outgroup members; this difference tends not to be as strong among individualists (De Dreu et al., 2007; Oyserman et al., 2002).

Conflict Escalation and Reduction

Social dilemmas can create important conflicts between groups, and how groups resolve these dilemmas can make the difference between war and peace. There are, of course, many other sources of conflict between groups. The very fact that groups differ from each other on any of a number of dimensions—religious, ethnic, racial, cultural, political—can spark conflict. Again and again, throughout human history, differences between groups explode in hatred and bloodshed. What fans the flames of an escalating conflict? And what can extinguish these flames? We address these questions in the remaining sections of the chapter.

Conflicts between groups are caused by many factors, including competition for scarce resources, stereotypes and prejudice, and competing ideologies. But once a conflict is in place, it can feed on itself. Indeed, *conflict spirals* are frequent, as one party annoys the other party, who retaliates, prompting a more extreme reaction from the first party, and so on (Brett et al., 1998; Rubin et al., 1994). ■ Table 8.6 lists several factors that contribute to conflict escalation. The first three factors concern group processes discussed earlier in the chapter. The fourth factor, concerning the capacity to use threat, may seem more surprising. We discuss this and a fifth factor (perceptions of the other) in the next sections.

Group conflict is tragically hard to stop. After an earthquake devastated much of Port-Au-Prince, Haiti, food and other resources were scare. When the man in the photo was caught by police while looting a downtown store, an angry mob grabbed him from the back of the police truck and proceeded to beat him, set him on fire, then leave him to die. While many in Haiti were similarly forced to scavenge for food and water, this man was singled out for being 'a thief.' Mob justice prevailed.

Threat Capacity It seems obvious that the ability to punish someone who engages in a prohibited behaviour can act as a deterrent to conflict escalation. You're less likely to mess with someone who can mess right back with you. If both parties hold their fire, a balance of terror can work. But having the capacity to attack can present an irresistible temptation to do so.

A classic study conducted by Morton Deutsch and Robert Krauss (1960) makes the point. These investigators had pairs of female participants engage in a simulated work environment in which each was in charge of a trucking company carrying merchandise over a road to a specific destination. Because they had to share parts of the road, they had to coordinate their efforts. However, in one condition of the study, one of the women in each pair had the capacity to take control of the road and block the other's progress, which would increase her own profit and reduce the other participant's profit. In another condition, both participants in each pair had this capacity. What was the result?

In general, when a participant had the ability to block the other, she did—and both participants suffered. Overall, participants earned more money if neither could block the other than if one of them could, and when *both* members of the pair could block the other, the participants earned least of all. These results suggest that once coercive means are available, people tend to use them, even when doing so damages their own outcomes.

TABLE 8.6

Factors That Promote and Sustain the Escalation of Between-Group Conflict

- The group polarization process, which increases the extremity of group members' attitudes and opinions
- Pressures for conformity such as group cohesiveness and groupthink, which make it difficult for individuals to oppose the group's increasingly aggressive position
- Escalation of commitment, which seeks to justify past investments through the commitment of additional resources
- Premature use of threat capacity, which triggers aggressive retaliation
- Negative perceptions of "the other," which promote acceptance of aggressive behaviour and enhance cohesiveness of the ingroup "us" against the outgroup "them"

Perceptions of the Other The fifth factor listed in Table 8.6 calls to mind our earlier discussion of stereotypes and prejudice, including the favouring of ingroups over outgroups (see Chapter 5). During conflict, the opposing group and its members are often perceived as "the other"—strange, foreign, alien. They are characterized in simplistic, exaggerated ways. Held at a psychological distance, the other becomes a screen on which it is possible to project one's worst fears. Indeed, groups often see each other as *mirror images:* They see in their enemies what their enemies see in them. As Urie Bronfenbrenner (1961) discovered when he visited the former Soviet Union during the Cold War, the Soviets saw Americans as aggressive, exploitative, and untrustworthy—just as the Americans saw them. The same is true of Israelis and Palestinians today.

Taken to extremes, negative views of the other can result in *dehumanization,* the perception that people lack human qualities or are "subhuman," and this can play a powerful role in escalating conflict and promoting prejudice or violence (Demoulin et al., 2009; Maoz & McCauley, 2008). For example, Victoria Esses and others (2008) demonstrated that Canadian refugees are often viewed in dehumanizing terms, and that the media may be partly to blame for these negative attitudes by printing editorials decrying refugees as 'liars and cheats' trying to take advantage of the system. Such contempt for those seeking assistance can then lead to a lack of support surrounding refugee policies in general. As the Nazis began the Holocaust, they released propaganda that characterized Jews as less than human—as rats that spread disease and needed to be exterminated. Dehumanization is the ultimate version of "us" versus "them," removing all religious and ethical constraints against the taking of human life. As George Orwell (1942) discovered during the Spanish Civil War, the cure for dehumanization is to restore the human connection. Sighting an enemy soldier holding up his trousers with both hands while running beside a nearby trench, Orwell was unable to take the easy shot: "I had come here to shoot at 'Fascists'; but a man who is holding up his trousers isn't a 'Fascist,' he is visibly a fellow creature, similar to yourself, and you don't feel like shooting at him" (p. 254).

Reducing Conflict Through GRIT A peacemaking strategy developed by Charles Osgood (1962) offers some hope for breaking a conflict between groups. In this strategy, called **graduated and reciprocated initiatives in tension-reduction (GRIT)**, one group takes the first move toward cooperation by making an initial concession. It then waits for the response from the other side and reciprocates that move: It responds to aggressiveness with aggressiveness and to cooperativeness with even more cooperativeness. Research on GRIT is encouraging; even people with a competitive orientation tend to respond cooperatively to this strategy, and the positive effects of GRIT can be enduring (Lindskold & Han, 1988; Yamagishi et al., 2005).

graduated and reciprocated initiatives in tension-reduction (GRIT)
A strategy for unilateral, persistent efforts to establish trust and cooperation between opposing parties.

Canadian Press/Adrian Wyld

In January 2011, Stephen Harper attended a meeting of the World Health Organization in Geneva to discuss ways to improve the health of mothers and children in the developing world. Such negotiations are both important and complex, involving nations with different resources, needs, relationships, and cultures. This highlights the usefulness of social psychological research, which has specified a number of factors that can make negotiations more or less likely to succeed.

Negotiation

Unilateral concessions are useful for beginning the peace process, but extended negotiations are usually required to reach a final agreement. Negotiations on complex issues such as nuclear arms control and international environmental protection, as well as efforts to make peace in volatile regions such as the Middle East, often go on for years or even decades.

But negotiations are not restricted to the international scene. Unions and management engage in collective bargaining to establish employee contracts. Divorcing couples negotiate the terms of their divorce, by themselves or through their lawyers. Dating couples negotiate about which movie to attend. Families negotiate about who does which annoying household chores. Indeed, negotiations occur whenever there is a conflict that the parties wish to resolve without getting into an open fight or relying on an imposed legal settlement. There is an immense amount of research on negotiation and bargaining (Harinck et al., 2011; Wagner & Druckman, 2012). Here, we focus on those findings most relevant to conflict reduction.

Keys to Successful Negotiating Conflicts can be reduced through successful negotiation. But what constitutes success in this context? Perhaps the most common successful outcome is a 50-50 compromise. Here, the negotiators start at extreme positions and gradually work toward a mutually acceptable midpoint. Some negotiators, however, achieve an even higher level of success. Most negotiations are not simply fixed-sum situations in which each side must give up something until a middle point is reached. Instead, there often exist ways in which both sides can benefit (Bazerman & Neale, 1992). When an **integrative agreement** is reached, both parties obtain outcomes that are superior to a 50-50 split.

Take, for instance, the tale of the orange and the two sisters (Follett, 1942). One sister wanted the juice to drink; the other wanted the peel for a cake. So they sliced the orange in half and each one took her portion. These sisters suffered from an advanced case of the *"fixed-pie" syndrome.* They assumed that whatever one of them won, the other lost. In fact, however, each of them could have had the whole thing: all of the juice for one, all of the peel for the other. An integrative agreement was well within their grasp, but they failed to see it. Unfortunately, research indicates that this happens all too often. Leigh Thompson and Dennis Hrebec (1996) conducted a meta-analysis of 32 experiments and found that in over 20 percent of negotiations that could have resulted in integrative agreements, the participants agreed to settlements that were worse for both sides. The ability to achieve integrative agreements is an acquired skill: experienced negotiators obtain them more often than do inexperienced ones (Thompson, 1990).

integrative agreement
A negotiated resolution to a conflict in which all parties obtain outcomes that are superior to what they would have obtained from an equal division of the contested resources.

It is always difficult for participants in a dispute to listen carefully to each other and to reach some reasonable understanding of each other's perspective. But communication in which both sides disclose their goals and needs is critically important in allowing each side to see opportunities for joint benefits (De Dreu et al., 2006). This may seem obvious, and yet people in negotiations very often fail to communicate their goals and needs. For one thing, negotiators tend to think that their goals and objectives are clearer to the other party than they actually are (Vorauer & Claude, 1998). Furthermore, in conflict negotiations each party is likely to distrust and fear the other. Neither wants to reveal too much for fear of losing power at the bargaining table. Again, this is part of the fixed-pie syndrome. But if one party does disclose information, the disclosure can have dramatic effects. If one side discloses, the other party becomes much more likely to do so, enhancing the likelihood of integrative agreement (Thompson, 1991).

In addition to disclosure of information, several other factors can improve negotiations and increase the chances that both sides will benefit. These factors include training negotiators in conflict-resolution techniques and using computerized negotiation support systems (Carbonneau et al., 2011; Taylor et al., 2008).

During particularly difficult or significant negotiations, outside assistance may be sought. Some negotiations rely on an *arbitrator,* who has the power to impose a settlement. But it is more common for conflicting parties to request the participation of a *mediator,* who works with them to try to reach a voluntary agreement. Traditionally, mediators have been employed in labour-management negotiations and international conflicts. But increasingly, mediators help resolve a wide range of other disputes, such as those involving tenants and landlords, divorcing couples, and feuding neighbours. Trained in negotiation and conflict management, mediators can often increase the likelihood of reaching a cooperative solution (Alexander, 2008; Carnevale, 2002).

Gender Differences As with gender differences concerning social dilemmas, the evidence for gender differences in negotiation is not as clear as many expect them to be. For example, Roderick Swaab and Dick Swaab (2009) recently found in a meta-analysis and in their own laboratory experiment that men achieved higher-quality agreements when negotiating under conditions in which there was no visual contact between the parties (such as via the phone or email). If there was visual contact, the men did better when there was no eye contact. Women showed the opposite pattern: Visual contact and eye contact were associated with higher-quality agreements. The authors speculate that the results may reflect differences in what makes men and women most comfortable. Whatever the exact cause, the results support the idea that gender differences in negotiation likely depend on a host of other variables.

Culture and Negotiation

As the world becomes smaller because of advances in technology, the globalization of business and the economy, and global threats concerning the environment and terrorism, the ability to negotiate effectively across cultures becomes increasingly important. Understanding cultural differences relevant to negotiation is therefore vital. Table 8.7 lists some common assumptions made by negotiators from Western, individualistic cultures that are not always shared by representatives from other cultures.

Consider, for example, our statement that good communication is a key ingredient in successful negotiation. Communication across cultures can present special challenges. Whereas an individualistic perspective emphasizes direct communication and confrontation, a collectivistic perspective emphasizes information sharing that is more indirect and a desire to avoid direct conflict. Individualistic negotiators may emphasize rationality, whereas a greater tolerance of contradiction and emotionality is characteristic of a collectivistic style—although collectivists prefer emotionality that is not confrontational. Negotiators from individualistic cultures are more likely to respond with a direct "no" to a proposal; negotiators from collectivistic cultures are more likely to refer to social roles and relationships. However, as Wendi Adair, a researcher at the University

TABLE 8.7

Cultural Assumptions About Negotiating

People from different cultures make different assumptions about the negotiation process. This table summarizes some assumptions commonly made by Western negotiators. It also presents some alternative assumptions that may be held by negotiators from other cultures. As you can see, such different assumptions could make it very difficult to reach a successful agreement. (Based on Brett & Gelfand, 2006, De Dreu et al., 2007, Gelfand et al., 2007, Giebels & Taylor, 2009, and Kimmel, 1994, 2000)

Assumptions Made by Negotiators from Western Countries	Alternatives
Negotiation is a business, not a social activity.	The first step in negotiating is to develop a trusting relationship between the individual negotiators.
Points should be made with rational, analytical arguments without contradiction	Arguments may be more holistic, and emotionality and contradiction may be tolerated.
Communication is direct and verbal.	Some of the most important communications are nonverbal or indirect.
Written contracts are binding; oral commitments are not.	Written contracts are less meaningful than oral communications because the nonverbal context clarifies intentions.
Current information and ideas are more valid than historical or traditional opinions and information.	History and tradition are more valid than current information and ideas. Information must be understood in its greater context.
Time is very important; punctuality is expected; deadlines should be set and adhered to.	Building a relationship takes time and is more important than punctuality; setting deadlines is an effort to humiliate the other party.

of Waterloo, points out, sometimes each side tries so hard to anticipate, and compensate for, differences, they may end up adjusting their cultural assumptions about negotiating too far—and this too can lead to an apparent mismatch in styles (Adair et al., 2009).

Reuters/Corbis-Bettman

Germans demonstrate against neo-Nazi groups and anti-Semitism. The sign "I am a foreigner worldwide" proclaims that since we are all foreigners somewhere, there is no "them," only a superordinate human identity as "us."

Finding Common Ground

Every conflict is unique, as is every attempt at conflict resolution. Still, all efforts to find a constructive solution to conflict require some common ground to build upon. Recognition of a *superordinate identity* is one way to establish common ground between groups in conflict. When group members perceive that they have a shared identity—a sense of belonging to something larger than and encompassing their own groups—the attractiveness of outgroup members increases, and interactions between the groups often become more peaceful.

Superordinate goals have another valuable characteristic: They can produce a superordinate identity. The experience of intergroup cooperation increases the sense of belonging to a single superordinate group. Even the mere expectation of a cooperative interaction increases empathy, which, in turn, enhances helpfulness and reduces aggression. Indeed, empathic connections between various members of each group can lay the foundation for an inclusive, rather than exclusive, social identity (Dovidio & Gaertner, 2010).

On the road to peace, both kinds of common ground are needed. Cooperation to meet shared goals makes similarities more visible, and a sense of a shared identity makes cooperation more likely. Those who would make peace, not war, realize that it is in their own self-interest to do so and understand that the cloak of humanity is large enough to cover a multitude of lesser differences.

REVIEW

Fundamentals of Groups

What Is a Group? Why Join a Group?

- Groups involve direct interactions among group members over a period of time and a shared common fate, identity, or set of goals.
- Groups vary in the extent to which they are seen as distinct entities.
- People join a group for a variety of reasons, including to perform tasks that can't be accomplished alone and to enhance self-esteem and social identity.
- Evolutionary scholars propose that attraction to groups is an evolved psychological mechanism.

Socialization and Group Development

- The socialization of newcomers into a group relies on the relationships they form with old-timers, who act as models, trainers, and mentors.
- Groups often proceed through several stages of development, from initial orientation through periods of conflict, compromise, and action.
- Some groups pass through periods of inactivity followed by sudden action in response to time pressures.

Roles, Norms, and Cohesiveness

- Establishing clear roles can help a group; but when members' roles are assigned poorly, are ambiguous, come in conflict with other roles, or undergo change, stress and poor performance can result.
- Teams in one experiment where group roles were matched to individuals' areas of expertise on the basis of tests of each individual's brain functioning performed especially well.
- Groups often develop norms that group members are expected to conform to. Group members who go against the norm may be disliked, threatened, or rejected.
- The relationship between cohesiveness and group performance is complex and depends on factors such as the size of the group, the kind of task the group is performing, and the kinds of norms that have been established.

Culture and Cohesiveness

- What behaviours affect group cohesiveness can vary significantly across cultures.
- When working in a group, people from collectivistic cultures may distinguish more between working with friends and strangers than do people from individualistic cultures.

Individuals in Groups: The Presence of Others

Social Facilitation: When Others Arouse Us

- In an early experiment, Triplett found that children performed faster when they worked side-by-side rather than alone.
- Social facilitation refers to two effects that occur when individual contributions are identifiable: The presence of others enhances performance on easy tasks but impairs performance on difficult tasks.
- Social facilitation effects have been found in a variety of domains. Even the "presence" of computerized images of people can trigger these effects.
- The theories of mere presence, evaluation apprehension, and distraction-conflict give different explanations of the cause of social facilitation; all three explanations probably account for some of the social facilitation effects.

Social Loafing: When Others Relax Us

- In early research on easy tasks involving pooled contributions, Ringelmann found that individual output declined when people worked with others. This social loafing effect has been replicated in numerous studies over the years.
- But social loafing is reduced or eliminated when people think their individual efforts will be important, relevant, and meaningful. In such cases, individuals may engage in social compensation in an effort to offset the anticipated social loafing of others.

Culture and Social Loafing

- Groups in collectivistic cultures may be more likely to have group norms that promote productive teamwork and discourage social loafing.

- People from collectivistic cultures may be likely to socially loaf if they are working in a group that has established a norm of low productivity and effort.

Facilitation and Loafing: Unifying the Paradigms

- A unified paradigm integrates social facilitation and social loafing.

Deindividuation

- Deindividuation diminishes a person's sense of individuality and reduces constraints against deviant behaviour.
- Two types of environmental cues can increase deviant behaviour: (1) Accountability cues, such as anonymity, signal that individuals will not be held responsible for their actions; and (2) attentional cues, such as intense environmental stimulation, produce a deindividuated state in which the individual acts impulsively.
- Large crowds can both increase anonymity and decrease self-awareness, which together can increase violent or other deviant behaviour.
- The effects of deindividuation depend on the characteristics of the immediate group. In the context of an antagonistic social identity, antisocial behaviour increases; in the context of a benevolent social identity, prosocial behaviour increases.

Group Performance: Problems and Solutions

Process Loss and Types of Group Tasks

- Because of process loss, a group may perform worse than it would if every individual performed up to his or her potential.
- Group performance is influenced by the type of task at hand (additive, conjunctive, or disjunctive).
- Among the factors that create process loss are social loafing, poor coordination, and failure to recognize the expertise of particular group members.
- Groups can do better than even the best members of the group on tasks that can be divided among subgroups and in which the correct answer is clearly demonstrable to the rest of the group members.

Brainstorming

- Contrary to illusions about the effectiveness of interactive brainstorming, groups in which members interact face-to-face produce fewer creative ideas than the same number of people working alone.
- Computer-based technology can improve group brainstorming.

Group Polarization

- When individuals who have similar, though not identical, opinions participate in a group discussion, their opinions become more extreme.
- Explanations for group polarization emphasize the number and persuasiveness of arguments heard, and social comparison with other group members.

Groupthink

- Groupthink refers to an excessive tendency to seek concurrence among group members.
- The symptoms of groupthink produce defective decision making, which can lead to a bad decision.
- Research to test the theory of groupthink has not produced as much evidence to support the theory as its fame might suggest.
- Groups may be more likely to experience groupthink if multiple contributing factors are present simultaneously, such as high cohesiveness, a strong and controlling leader, and a great deal of stress.
- Strategies that have been successful in helping groups avoid groupthink include consulting with outsiders, having the leader play a less controlling role, encouraging criticism and thorough information search, and having a group member play devil's advocate to challenge the consensus.

Escalation Effects

- Groups are susceptible to an escalation effect, which occurs when commitment to a failing course of action is increased to justify investments that have already been made. Instead of cutting its losses, groups essentially throw good money and time after bad.

Communicating Information and Utilizing Expertise

- Biased sampling refers to the tendency for groups to pay more attention to information that is already known by all or most group members than to important information that is known by only one or a few group members.
- Information may not be communicated adequately in a group because of problems in the group's communication network, such as suppression of relevant information at some point in the decision-making chain.
- Groups can remember more information than individuals through transactive memory, a shared process in which the information can be divided among the group members.

Strategies for Improvement

- Group norms fostering critical thinking can prevent biased sampling.
- Setting specific ambitious goals can improve group performance.
- Training groups in better group dynamics, such as how best to develop transactive memory, can be effective.
- Interventions that compel groups to stop and explicitly think about the best way to proceed can also improve group performance.

- Having experts in a group is not good enough to improve group performance; the presence of experts helps only if their presence is coupled with an intervention that requires the group to engage in collaborative planning.
- Computer technology can be used to guide group discussions and decision-making processes, which can help groups avoid problems such as groupthink.

Virtual Teams

- There is a growing trend in the business world toward teams that are dispersed across space and work interactively via technology, but such teams may be especially vulnerable to some of the factors that cause process loss. Therefore, special attention needs to be paid to virtual teams to offset these problems.

Diversity

- Research on the effects of diversity on group performance is rather mixed; both positive and negative effects have been found thus far.

Conflict: Cooperation and Competition Within and Between Groups

Mixed Motives and Social Dilemmas

- In mixed-motive situations, such as the prisoner's dilemma, there are incentives for both competition and cooperation.
- In a social dilemma, personal benefit conflicts with the overall good.
- Resource dilemmas involve sharing limited resources. In the commons dilemma, a group of people can take resources from a common pool, whereas in the public goods dilemma, the maintenance of a common resource requires the contributions of a group of people.
- Behaviour in a social dilemma is influenced by a number of psychological factors, including situational factors, group dynamics, and structural arrangements.
- Groups tend to be more competitive than individuals in mixed-motive situations.
- Individuals with a prosocial, cooperative orientation are less likely to behave in a competitive, resource-consuming fashion than are people with individualistic or competitive orientations.

Culture and Social Dilemmas

- Some studies have suggested that collectivists are more likely to cooperate in social dilemmas than are individualists, but the evidence is somewhat mixed.
- Collectivists may cooperate more when dealing with friends or ingroup members but compete more aggressively when dealing with strangers or outgroup members.

Conflict Escalation and Reduction

- Conflicts can escalate for many reasons, including conflict spirals and escalation of commitment.
- The premature use of the capacity to punish can elicit retaliation and escalate conflict.
- Perceptions of the other that contribute to conflict escalation include unfavourable mirror images and dehumanization.
- GRIT—an explicit strategy for the unilateral, persistent pursuit of trust and cooperation between opposing parties—is a useful strategy for beginning the peace process.

Negotiation

- Many negotiations have the potential to result in integrative agreements, in which outcomes exceed a 50-50 split; however, negotiators often fail to achieve such outcomes.
- Communication and an understanding of the other party's perspective are key ingredients of successful negotiation.
- Mediators can often be helpful in achieving success in negotiations.
- Differences between men and women in negotiation most likely emerge only in combination with other variables. For example, one line of research suggests that for women, negotiations go better when there is eye contact between the negotiators; for men, negotiations are more productive when there is no visual contact.

Culture and Negotiation

- People from different cultures may have very different assumptions and styles concerning negotiations, such as whether direct or indirect communication is preferred, how important is context and relationship building, and whether direct conflict should be avoided.
- Groups may go too far trying to accommodate another group's negotiation style, leading to further difficulties.

Finding Common Ground

- Superordinate goals and a superordinate identity increase the likelihood of a peaceful resolution of differences.

Key Terms

biased sampling (294)
brainstorming (288)
collective (273)
collective effort model (282)
deindividuation (284)
distraction-conflict theory (280)
escalation effect (293)
evaluation apprehension theory (280)
graduated and reciprocated initiatives in tension-reduction (GRIT) (303)
group cohesiveness (276)
group polarization (290)
groupthink (291)
integrative agreement (304)
mere presence theory (280)
prisoner's dilemma (298)
process loss (287)
resource dilemmas (299)
social dilemma (298)
social facilitation (279)
social identity model of deindividuation effects (SIDE) (286)
social loafing (281)
transactive memory (295)

Putting COMMON SENSE *to the Test*

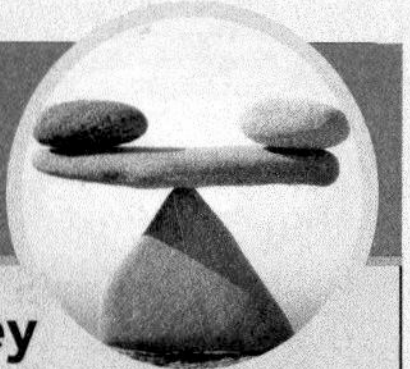

People will cheer louder when they cheer as part of a group than when they cheer alone.

False. *People tend to put less effort into collective tasks, such as group cheering, than into tasks when their individual performance can be identified and evaluated.*

People brainstorming as a group come up with a greater number of better ideas than the same number of people working individually.

False. *Groups in which members interact face-to-face produce fewer creative ideas when brainstorming than the same number of people brainstorming alone.*

Group members' attitudes about a course of action usually become more moderate after group discussion.

False. *Group discussion often causes attitudes to become more extreme as the initial tendencies of the group are exaggerated.*

Groups are less likely than individuals to invest more and more resources in a project that is failing.

False. *Although individuals often feel entrapped by previous commitments and make things worse by throwing good money (and other resources) after bad, groups are even more prone to having this problem.*

Large groups are more likely than small groups to exploit a scarce resource that the members collectively depend on.

True. *Large groups are more likely to behave selfishly when faced with resource dilemmas, in part because people in large groups feel less identifiable and more anonymous*

9

Fuse/Getty

Attraction and Close Relationships

Putting
COMMON SENSE
to the Test

Circle Your Answer

T F People seek out the company of others, even strangers, in times of stress.

T F Infants do not discriminate between faces considered attractive and unattractive in their culture.

T F People who are physically attractive are happier and have higher self-esteem than those who are unattractive.

T F When it comes to romantic relationships, opposites attract.

T F Men are more likely than women to interpret friendly gestures by the opposite sex in sexual terms.

T F After the honeymoon period, there is an overall decline in levels of marital satisfaction.

This chapter examines how people form relationships with each other. First, we describe the fundamental human need for being with others, why people affiliate, and the problem of loneliness. Then we consider various personal and situational factors that influence our initial attraction to specific others. Third, we examine different types of close relationships—what makes them rewarding, how they differ, the types of love they arouse, and the factors that keep them together or break them apart.

No topic fascinates the people of this planet more than interpersonal attraction. Needing to belong, we humans are obsessed about friendships, romantic relationships, dating, love, sex, reproduction, sexual orientation, marriage, and divorce. Playwrights, poets, and musicians write with eloquence and emotion about loves desired, won, and lost. North American television is filled with relationship-centred reality TV shows like *The Bachelor, The Bachelorette, Hooked up,* or *Fairy Tale,* the first Canadian reality show for gay men, lesbians, bisexual, and transgendered individuals. More and more, people are meeting romantic partners online, in Internet chat rooms, and on dating service websites, such as Match.com or eHarmony. Both in our hearts and in our minds, the relationships we seek and enjoy with other people are more important than anything else.

At one time or another, all of us have been startled by our reaction to someone we've met. Why, in general, are human beings drawn to each other? Why are we attracted to some people and yet indifferent to, or even repelled by, others? What determines how our intimate relationships evolve? What does it mean to love someone, and what problems are likely to arise along the way? As these questions reveal, attraction among people—from the first spark through the flames of an intimate connection—often seems like a kind of wild card in the deck of human behaviour. This chapter unravels some of the mysteries.

Being with Others: A Fundamental Human Motive

Although born helpless, human infants are equipped with reflexes that orient them toward people. They are uniquely responsive to human faces, they turn their head toward voices, and they are able to mimic certain facial gestures on cue. Then, a few weeks later, there is the baby's first smile, surely the warmest sign of all. Much to the delight of parents all over the world, the newborn seems an inherently social animal.

But wait. If you reflect on the amount of time you spend talking to, being with, flirting with, pining for, confiding in, or worrying about other people, you'll realize that we are all social animals. It seems that people need people.

According to Roy Baumeister and Mark Leary (1995), the need to belong is a basic human motive, "a pervasive drive to form and maintain at least a minimum quantity of lasting, positive, and significant interpersonal relationships" (p. 497). This general proposition is supported by everyday observation and a great deal of research. All over the world, people feel joy when they form new social attachments and react with anxiety and grief when these bonds are broken—as when separated from a loved one by distance, divorce, or death. The need to belong runs deep, which is why people are distressed when they are neglected by others, rejected, excluded, stigmatized, or ostracized—all forms of "social death" (Leary, 2001; Williams, 2007).

We care deeply about what others think of us, which is why we spend so much time and money to make ourselves presentable and attractive. In fact, some people are so worried about how they come across to others that they suffer from *social anxiety,* intense feelings of discomfort in situations that invite public scrutiny (Leary & Kowalski, 1995). One very familiar example is public speaking anxiety, or "stage fright"—a performer's worst nightmare. If you've ever had to make a presentation, only to feel weak in the knees and hear your voice quiver, you have endured a hint of this disorder. When sufferers are asked what there is to fear, the most common responses are: shaking and showing other signs of anxiety, going blank, saying something foolish, and being unable to continue (Stein et al., 1996). For people with high levels of social anxiety, the problem is also evoked by other social situations, such as eating at a public lunch counter, signing a cheque in front of a store clerk, and, for males, urinating in a crowded men's room. In extreme cases, the reaction can become so debilitating that the person just stays at home (Beidel & Turner, 1998; Crozier & Alden, 2005).

Our need to belong is a fundamental human motive. People who have a network of close social ties—in the form of lovers, friends, family members, and co-workers—tend to report being happier with their lives, and have higher levels of self-esteem, than those who live more isolated lives (Denissen et al., 2008; Diener et al., 1999; Leary, 2012; Leary & Baumeister, 2000). For example, researchers found that people with more Facebook friends, and therefore an ever-present audience to their personal updates, scored higher on measures of overall life satisfaction (Manago et al., 2012). In fact, as we will see in Appendix B in the section on health, people who are socially connected are also physically healthier and less likely to die a premature death (Hawkley & Cacioppo, 2010; Holwerda et al., 2012; House et al., 1988; Uchino et al., 1996).

The Thrill of Affiliation

As social beings, humans are drawn to each other. We work together, play together, live together, and often make lifetime commitments to grow old together. This social motivation begins with the **need for affiliation**, defined as a desire to establish social contact with others (McAdams, 1989). Individuals differ in the strength of their need for affiliation, but it seems that people are motivated to establish and maintain an *optimum* balance of social contact—sometimes craving the company of others, sometimes wanting to be alone—the way the body maintains a certain level of caloric intake. In an interesting study, Bibb Latané and Carol Werner (1978) found that laboratory rats were more likely to approach others of their species after a period of isolation and were less likely to approach others after prolonged contact. These researchers suggested that rats, like many other animals, have a built-in "sociostat" (social thermostat) to regulate their affiliative tendencies.

need for affiliation
The desire to establish and maintain many rewarding interpersonal relationships.

Is there evidence of a similar mechanism in humans? Shawn O'Connor and Lorne Rosenblood (1996) recruited students to carry portable beepers for four days. Whenever the beepers went off (on average, every hour), the students wrote down whether, at the time, they were *actually* alone or in the company of other people and whether, at the time, they *wanted* to be alone or with others. The results showed that the students were in the state they desired two-thirds of the time—and that the situation they wished to be in on one occasion predicted their actual situation the next time they were signalled. Whether it was solitude or social contact that the students sought, they successfully managed to regulate their own personal needs for affiliation.

People are motivated to establish and maintain an optimum level of social contact.

People may well differ in the strength of their affiliative needs, but there are times when we all want to be with other people. It is common to find the streets of major cities across North America filled with fans whenever the home team wins the final championship game. From one city to the next, jubilant fans stay long after the game ends, milling about and exchanging high-fives, slaps on the back, hugs, and kisses. It is clear that people want to celebrate together rather than alone.

Affiliating can satisfy us for other reasons as well. From others, we get energy, attention, stimulation, information, and emotional support (Hill, 1987). One condition that strongly arouses our need for affiliation is stress. Have you ever noticed the way neighbours who never stop to say hello come together in snowstorms, power failures, and other crises? Many years ago, Stanley Schachter (1959) theorized that external threat triggers fear and motivates us to affiliate—particularly with others who face a similar threat. In a laboratory experiment that demonstrated the point, Schachter found that people who were expecting to receive painful electric shocks chose to wait with other nervous participants rather than alone. So far, so good. But when Irving Sarnoff and Philip Zimbardo (1961) led participants to expect that they would be engaging in an embarrassing behaviour—sucking on large nipples and pacifiers—their desire to be with others fell off. It seemed puzzling. Why do people in fearful misery love company, while those in embarrassed misery seek solitude?

Yacov Rofé (1984) proposed a simple answer: utility. Rofé argued that stress increases the desire to affiliate only when being with others is seen as useful in reducing the negative impact of the stressful situation. Schachter's participants had good reason to believe that affiliation would be useful. They would have the opportunity to compare their emotional reactions with those of others to determine whether they really needed to be fearful. For those in the Sarnoff and Zimbardo study, however, affiliation had little to offer. Facing embarrassment, being with others is more likely to increase the stress than reduce it.

Returning to Schachter's initial study, what specific benefit do people get from being in the presence of others in times of stress? Research suggests that people facing an imminent threat seek each other out in order to gain *cognitive clarity* about the danger they are in. In one study, James Kulik and Heike Mahler (1989) found that hospital patients waiting for open-heart surgery preferred to have as roommates other patients who were post-operative rather than pre-operative, presumably because they were in a position to provide information about the experience. Patients in a second study who had been assigned post-operative rather than pre-operative roommates became less anxious about the experience and were later quicker to recover from the surgery (Kulik et al., 1996).

People seek out the company of others, even strangers, in times of stress. TRUE.

"Loneliness and the feeling of being unwanted is the most terrible poverty."
—Mother Teresa

Even in a laboratory setting, Kulik and others (1994) found that people anticipating the painful task of soaking a hand in ice-cold water (compared with those told that the task would not be painful) preferred to wait with someone who had already completed the task than with someone who had not. They also asked more questions of these experienced peers. Under stress, we adaptively become motivated to affiliate with others who can help us cope with an impending threat. Summarizing his own work, Schachter (1959) had noted that misery loves miserable company. Based on their more recent studies, Gump and Kulik (1997) further amended this assertion: "Misery loves the company of those in the same miserable situation" (p. 317).

The Agony of Loneliness

People need other people—to celebrate, share news with, commiserate with, talk to, and learn from. But some people are painfully shy, socially awkward, inhibited, and reluctant to approach others (Bruch et al., 1989). Shyness is a pervasive problem. Roughly 49 percent of all Americans describe themselves as shy, as do 31 percent in Israel, 40 percent in Germany, 55 percent in Taiwan, and 57 percent in Japan (Henderson & Zimbardo, 1998). In fact, it is estimated that 3 percent of the Canadian population suffers from social anxiety disorder—an extreme form of shyness, and less than half of those individuals seek help (*Canadian Community Health Survey (CCHS): Mental Health and Well-being,* 2002). People who are shy find it difficult to approach strangers, make small talk, telephone someone for a date, participate in small groups, or mingle at parties. What's worse, they often reject others, perhaps because they fear being rejected themselves. The sad result is a pattern of risk avoidance that sets them up for unpleasant and unrewarding interactions (Crozier, 2001).

Shyness can arise from different sources. In some cases, it may be an inborn personality trait. Jerome Kagan (1994) and others have found that some infants are highly sensitive to stimulation, inhibited, and cautious shortly after birth. In other cases, shyness develops as a learned reaction to failed interactions with others. Thus, interpersonal problems of the past can ignite social anxieties about the future (Leary & Kowalski, 1995). Not all shy infants grow up to become inhibited adults. But longitudinal research indicates that there is some continuity—that this aspect of our personalities may be predictable from our temperament and behaviour as young children. Thus, toddlers observed to be inhibited, shy, and fearful at age 3 were more likely than toddlers who were more outgoing to be socially isolated and depressed at age 21 (Caspi, 2000). Such differences can be seen in the adult brain. Elliott Beaton and others (2010) asked undergraduate participants at McMaster University to make gender discrimination decisions for faces displaying positive, negative, or neutral emotions. The task itself was simply to ensure the participants paid attention to the faces. Using fMRI, they were able to observe greater neural activation among shy participants who were viewing emotional faces, compared to the non-shy group. These findings suggest that shy individuals are overly sensitive to social cues, and therefore more reactive to any emotional expression; their fear of making an error then leads them to avoid social interaction altogether.

Whatever the source, shyness is a real problem—and it has painful consequences. Studies show that shy people evaluate themselves negatively, expect to fail in their social encounters, and blame themselves when they do. As a result, many shy people go into self-imposed isolation, which makes them feel lonely (Cheek & Melchior, 1990; Jackson et al., 2002). In part, the problem stems from a paralyzing fear of rejection, which inhibits people from making friendly or romantic overtures to those they are interested in. As demonstrated by a recent meta-analysis of 88 studies, people who experience rejection develop feelings of worthlessness, which leads to a decrease in their self-esteem (Gerber & Wheeler, 2009). If you ever wanted to approach someone you liked, only to stop yourself, you know that this situation often triggers an approach-avoidance conflict, pulling you between the desire for contact and a fear of being rejected. What's worse, research shows that people who fear rejection think that their friendly or romantic interest is transparent to others, which leads them to back off (Vorauer et al., 2003).

Loneliness is a sad and heart-wrenching emotion. To be lonely is to feel deprived about the nature of one's existing social relations (Hawley & Cacioppo, 2010). Some researchers have maintained that loneliness is triggered by a discrepancy between the level of social contact that a person has and the level he or she wants (Peplau & Perlman, 1982). Others find, more simply, that the less social contact people have, the lonelier they feel (Archibald et al., 1995). Who is lonely, and when? Loneliness is most likely to occur during times of transition or disruption—as in the first year at university, after a romantic breakup, or when a loved one moves far away. Surveys show that people who are unattached are lonelier than those who have romantic partners—but that those who are widowed, divorced, and separated are lonelier than people who have never been married. Contrary to the stereotypic image of the lonely old man passing time on a park bench, the loneliest groups in North American society are adolescents and young adults 18- to 30-years-old. In fact, loneliness seems to decline over the course of adulthood—at least until health problems in old age limit social activities (Peplau & Perlman, 1982).

How do people cope with this distressing state? When students were asked about the behavioural strategies they use to combat loneliness, 96 percent said they sometimes or often tried harder to be friendly to other people; 94 percent took their mind off the problem by reading or watching TV; and 93 percent tried extra hard to succeed at another aspect of life. Others said that they distracted themselves by running, shopping, washing the car, or staying busy at other activities. Still others sought new ways to meet people, tried to improve their physical appearance, or talked to a friend, relative, or therapist about the problem. Though fewer in number, some are so desperate that they use alcohol or drugs to wash away feelings of loneliness (Rook & Peplau, 1982).

The Initial Attraction

Affiliation is a necessary first step in the formation of a social relationship. But each of us is drawn to some people more than to others. If you've ever had a crush on someone, felt the tingly excitement of a first encounter, or enjoyed the first few moments of a new friendship, then you know the meaning of the term *attraction.* When you meet someone for the first time, what do *you* look for? Does familiarity breed fondness or contempt? Do birds of a feather flock together, or do opposites attract? Is beauty the object of your desire, or do you believe that outward appearances are deceiving? And what is it about a situation, or the circumstances of an initial meeting, that draws you in for more?

According to one perspective, people are attracted to others with whom a rewarding relationship seems possible (Byrne & Clore, 1970; Lott & Lott, 1974). The rewards may be direct—as when people provide us with attention, support, money, status, information, and other valuable commodities. Or the rewards may be indirect—as when it feels good to be with someone who is beautiful, smart, or funny, or who happens to be in our presence when times are good. A second perspective on attraction has also emerged in recent years—that of evolutionary psychology, the subdiscipline

loneliness
A feeling of deprivation about existing social relations.

© sven hagolani/Corbis

Dating services, such as Internet dating or speed dating, enable strangers to meet. Interested in first encounters of this nature, attraction researchers try to determine what factors draw people to each other.

that uses principles of evolution to understand human social behaviour. According to this view, human beings all over the world exhibit patterns of attraction and mate selection that favour the conception, birth, and survival of their offspring. This approach has a great deal to say about differences in this regard between men and women (Buss, 2004; Neuberg et al., 2010; Simpson & Kenrick, 1997).

Recognizing the role of rewards and the call of our evolutionary past provides broad perspectives for understanding human attraction. But there's more to the story. Much more. Over the years, social psychologists have identified many determinants of attraction and the development of intimate relationships (Berscheid & Regan, 2004; Miller & Perlman, 2009). It's important to note that most of the research has focused on heterosexuals, so we often do not know how well specific findings apply to the homosexual population. In Ontario, where same sex marriages have been legal since 2003, more than 4000 same-sex couples married within the first year of the new law. Canada, in fact, was the fourth country to legalize same-sex marriages (Rose, 2012). Therefore, it is important to realize that many of the basic processes described in this chapter affect the development of all close relationships—regardless of whether the individuals involved are gay, lesbian, or straight (Fingerhut et al., 2011; Kurdek, 2008).

Familiarity: Being There

It seems so obvious that people tend to overlook it. We are most likely to become attracted to someone whom we have seen and become familiar with. So let's begin with two basic and necessary factors in the attraction process: proximity and exposure.

The Proximity Effect It hardly sounds romantic, but the single best predictor of whether two people will get together is physical proximity, or nearness. Sure, we interact at remote distances with the help of telephones, email, Twitter, blogs, and message boards. These days it's common for people to find friends, lovers, and sexual partners on the Internet. Still, our most impactful social interactions occur among people who are in the same place at the same time (Latané et al., 1995).

To begin with, where we live influences the friends we make. Many years ago, Leon Festinger and his colleagues (1950) studied friendship patterns in married-student housing and found that people were more likely to become friends with residents of nearby apartments than with those who lived farther away. More recent research has also shown that students—who live in off-campus apartments, dormitories, or fraternity and sorority houses—tend to date those who live either nearby (Hays, 1985) or in the same type of housing as they do (Whitbeck & Hoyt, 1994).

The Mere Exposure Effect Proximity does not necessarily spark attraction, but to the extent that it increases frequency of contact, it's a good first step. Folk wisdom often suggests a dim view of familiarity, which is said to "breed contempt." Not so. In a series of experiments, Robert Zajonc (1968) found that the more often people saw a novel stimulus—whether it was a foreign word, a geometric form, or a human face—the more they came to like it. This phenomenon, which Zajonc called the **mere exposure effect**, has since been observed in more than 200 experiments (Bornstein, 1989).

People do not even have to be aware of their prior exposures for this effect to occur. In a typical study, participants are shown pictures of several stimuli, each for one to five milliseconds, which is too quick to register in awareness and too quick for anyone to realize that some stimuli are presented more often than others. After the presentation, participants are shown each of the stimuli and asked two questions: Do you like it, and have you ever seen it before? Perhaps you can predict the result. The more frequently the stimulus is presented, the more people like it. Yet when asked if they've ever seen the liked stimulus before, they say no. These results demonstrate that the mere exposure effect can influence us without our awareness (Kuntz-Wilson & Zajonc, 1980; Moreland & Beach, 1992). In fact, the effect is stronger under these conditions (Bornstein & D'Agostino, 1992; Zajonc, 2001). For example, Gül Günaydin and others (2012) showed participants 24 photos; 12 contained novel faces and 12 appeared to be novel but in fact contained morphed images of their significant other's face, blended with photos of strangers. After a brief exposure to each image, participants were asked to make trait judgments of the face, such as how trustworthy or attractive it was, and to report whether the photo resembled anyone they knew. They found that, even after removing from the analyses anyone who noted a resemblance to their partner, women were more likely to positively evaluate the faces that contained elements of their significant other.

Familiarity can even influence our self-evaluations. Imagine that you had a portrait photograph of yourself developed into two pictures—one that depicted your actual appearance and the other a mirror-image copy. Which image would you prefer? Which would a friend prefer? Theodore Mita and his colleagues (1977) tried this interesting experiment with female students and found that most preferred their own mirror images, while their friends liked the actual photos. In both cases, the preference was for the view of the face that was most familiar.

"Beauty is a greater recommendation than any letter of introduction."
—Aristotle

Physical Attractiveness: Getting Drawn In

What do you look for in a friend or romantic partner? Intelligence? Kindness? A sense of humour? How important, really, is a person's looks? As children, we were told that "beauty is only skin deep" and that we should not "judge a book by its cover." Yet as adults, we react more favourably to others who are physically attractive than to those who are not. Over the years, studies have shown that in the affairs of our social world, beauty is a force to be reckoned with (Eastwick et al., 2011; Langlois et al., 2000; Swami & Furnham, 2008).

The bias for beauty is pervasive. In one study, fifth-grade teachers were given background information about a boy or girl, accompanied by a photograph. All teachers received identical information, yet those who saw an attractive child saw that child as being smarter and more likely to do well in school (Clifford & Walster, 1973). In a second study, male and female experimenters approached students on a university campus and tried to get them to sign a petition. The more attractive the experimenters were, the more signatures they were able to get (Chaiken, 1979). In a third study, Texas judges set lower bail and imposed smaller fines on suspects who were rated as attractive rather than unattractive on the basis of photographs (Downs & Lyons, 1991). Finally, in a series of studies conducted in Canada and the United States, economists discovered that across occupational groups, physically attractive men and women earn more money than others who are comparable except for being less attractive (Hamermesh & Biddle, 1994; Judge et al., 2009). Across a range of job situations, people fare better if they are attractive than if they are not (Hosoda et al., 2003).

mere exposure effect
The phenomenon whereby the more often people are exposed to a stimulus, the more positively they evaluate that stimulus.

Perceptions of facial beauty are largely consistent across cultures. Those regarded as good-looking in one culture also tend to be judged as attractive by people from other cultures. The individuals pictured here are from Venezuela, Kenya, Japan, and the United States.

It all seems so shallow, so superficial. But before we go on to accept the notion that people prefer others who are physically attractive, let's stop for a moment and consider a fundamental question: What constitutes physical beauty? Is it an objective and measurable human characteristic like height, weight, or hair colour? Or is beauty a subjective quality, existing in the eye of the beholder? There are advocates on both sides.

What Is Beauty? Some researchers believe that certain faces are inherently more attractive than others. There are three sources of evidence for this proposition.

First, when people are asked to rate faces on a ten-point scale, there is typically a high level of agreement among children and adults, men and women, and people from the same or different cultures (Langlois et al., 2000). For example, Michael Cunningham and others (1995) asked Asian and Latino students, along with black and white American students, to rate the appearance of women from all these groups. Overall, some faces were rated more attractive than others, leading these investigators to argue that people everywhere share an image of what is beautiful.

People also tend to agree about what constitutes an attractive body. For example, men tend to be drawn to the "hourglass" figure seen in women of average weight whose waists are a third narrower than their hips, a shape thought to be associated with reproductive fertility. In general, women with a 0.7 WHR (a waist-to-hip ratio where the waist circumference is 70 percent of the hip circumference) are rated as more attractive by men from European cultures. In fact, when shown photographs of women before and after they had microfat grafting surgery (where fat tissue is taken from the waist and implanted on the buttocks, which lowers the WHR), people rated the post-operative photographs as more attractive—independent of any changes in body weight (Singh & Randall, 2007). In contrast, women like men with a waist-to-hip ratio that forms a tapering V-shaped physique, signalling more muscle than fat (Singh, 1993, 1995). If marriage statistics are any indication, women also seem to have a preference for height. Comparisons made in Europe indicate that married men are a full inch taller, on average, than unmarried men (Pawlowski et al., 2000).

Second, some researchers have identified physical features of the human face that are reliably associated with judgments of attractiveness, such as smooth skin, a pleasant expression, youthfulness, and a direct gaze (Ewing et al., 2010; Rhodes, 2006). Particularly intriguing are studies showing that people like faces in which the eyes, nose, lips, and other features are not too different from the average. Judith Langlois and Lori Roggman (1990) showed students both actual yearbook photos and computerized facial composites that "averaged" features from 4, 8, 16, or 32 of the photos. Time and again, they found that students preferred the averaged composites to the individual faces—and that the more faces used to form the composite, the more highly it was rated. Other studies have since confirmed this result (Jones et al., 2007; Langlois et al., 1994; Rhodes et al., 1999).

It seems odd that "averaged" faces are judged attractive when, after all, the faces we find the most beautiful are anything but average. What accounts for these findings? Langlois and others (1994) believe that people like averaged faces because they are more prototypically face-like and, as such, seem more familiar to us. Consistent with this notion, research shows that just as people are more attracted to averaged faces than to individual faces, they also prefer averaged dogs, birds, fish, cars, and wristwatches (Halberstadt & Rhodes, 2000, 2003).

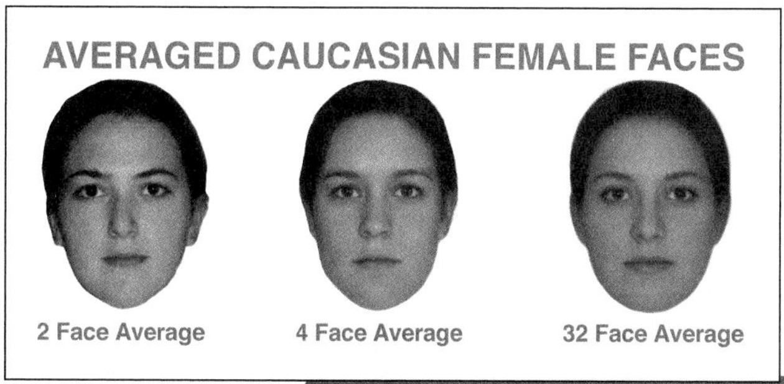

Courtesy of Dr. Judith Langlois; University of Texas, Austin

Computer-generated images that "average" the features of different faces are seen as more attractive than the individual faces on which they were based. Shown here is a set of female composites that combines 2, 4, and 32 faces. Which do you prefer?

(Langlois & Roggman, 1990.)

Other studies indicate that computerized averaging produces faces that are also symmetrical—and that symmetry is what we find attractive (Grammer & Thornhill, 1994; Mealey et al., 1999). Why do people prefer symmetrical faces in which the paired features on the right and left sides mirror each other? Although the research support is mixed, some evolutionary psychologists have speculated that symmetry is naturally associated with health, fitness, and fertility—qualities that are highly desirable in a mate (Rhodes et al., 2001; Shackelford & Larsen, 1999; Thornhill & Gangestad, 1993). Indeed, preference for symmetrical faces seems to depend in part on the availability of potential mates. When there are many options to choose from in a given population, the salience of facial cues (i.e., symmetry) increases to help distinguish between high versus low quality mates. However, when competition is scarce, symmetry becomes less important in judging overall attractiveness (Watkins et al., 2012).

A third source of evidence for the view that beauty is an objective quality is that babies who are far too young to have learned the culture's standards of beauty exhibit a nonverbal preference for faces considered attractive by adults. Picture the scene in an infant laboratory: A baby, lying on her back in a crib, is shown a series of faces previously rated by students. The first face appears and a clock starts ticking as the baby stares at it. As soon as the baby looks away, the clock stops and the next face is presented. The result: young infants spend more time tracking and looking at attractive faces than at unattractive ones—regardless of whether the faces are young or old, male or female, or black or white (Game et al., 2003; Langlois et al., 1991).

In contrast to this objective perspective, other researchers argue that physical attractiveness is subjective, and they point for evidence to the influences of culture, time, and the circumstances of our perception. One source of support for this view is that people from different cultures enhance their beauty in very different ways through face painting, makeup, plastic surgery, scarring, tattoos, hairstyling, the moulding of bones, the filing of teeth, braces, and the piercing of ears and other body parts—all contributing to the "enigma of beauty" (Newman, 2000). For example, Viren Swami and others (2012) compared acceptance of plastic surgery in a British sample of Caucasians, South Asians, and African Caribbeans, and found that Caucasians showed higher acceptance of plastic surgery, and were more likely to consider having it done themselves, than the other two groups. Plastic surgery tends to be marketed toward the creation of a Caucasian ideal and therefore may not appeal to those of other races or ethnicities. What people find attractive in one part of the world is often seen as repulsive in another part of the world (Landau, 1989).

"There is no known culture in which people do not paint, pierce, tattoo, reshape or simply adorn their bodies."

—Enid Schildkrout, anthropologist

Ideals also vary when it comes to bodies. Looking at preferences for female body size in 54 cultures, Judith Anderson and others (1992) found that heavy women are judged more attractive than slender women in places where food is frequently in short supply. In one study, for example, Douglas Yu and Glenn Shepard (1998) found that Matsigenka men living in the Andes mountains of southeastern Peru see female forms with "tubular" shapes—as opposed to hourglass shapes—as healthier, more attractive, and more desirable in a mate.

Infants do not discriminate between faces considered attractive and unattractive in their culture. FALSE.

Standards of beauty also change over time, from one generation to the next. Brett Silverstein and others (1986) examined the measurements of female models appearing in women's magazines from 1901 to 1981, and they found that "curvaceousness" (as measured by the bust-to-waist ratio) varied over time, with a boyish, slender look becoming particularly desirable in recent years. More recently, researchers took body measurements from all *Playboy* centrefolds, beginning with the first issue, in 1953, which featured Marilyn Monroe, through the last issue of 2001 and found that over time, models became thinner and had lower bust-to-waist ratios—away from the ample "hourglass" to a more slender, athletic, sticklike shape (Voracek & Fisher, 2002). Swami and others (2009) also found cultural differences relating to the waist-to-hips ratio (WHR) mentioned previously. South African men preferred a black woman with a high WHR and large breasts OR a white women, also with a high WHR, but with small breasts. In contrast, British Caucasians found most attractive the high WHR black women with small breasts or the high WHR white woman with large breasts.

Still other evidence for the subjective nature of beauty comes from many research laboratories. Time and again, social psychologists have found that our perceptions of someone's beauty can be inflated or deflated by various circumstances. Research shows, for example, that people often see others as more physically attractive if they have non-physical qualities (e.g., respectful) that make them likeable (Kniffin & Wilson, 2004). In addition, the more in love people are with their partners, the less attracted they are to others of the opposite sex (Johnson & Rusbult, 1989; Simpson et al., 1990).

Demonstrating further the importance of circumstance, Uriah Anderson and others (2010) found that 'high fertility' women (classified as such on the basis of their ovulation cycle in reference to the day they completed the study) paid more attention to attractive faces than did 'low fertility' women, though both groups showed equal recall for the faces later on. When it comes to men's attraction to women, another context factor concerns colour. The colour red is routinely associated with sex. In many species of primates, females display red swelling on their genitals, chest, or face as they near ovulation. In human rituals that date back thousands of years, girls painted red ochre on their face and body at the emergence of puberty and fertility. Today, women use red lipstick and rouge to enhance their appeal, red hearts symbolize Valentine's Day, red lingerie is worn to entice, and red-light districts signal the availability of sex through prostitution. Are men so conditioned by the colour red that its presence boosts their perceptions of attractiveness? In a study of the "red-sex link," Andrew Elliot and Daniela Niesta (2008) had male and female research participants rate female photos that were set against a solid red or white background. Everyone saw the same photos, yet the attractiveness ratings were highest among the men in the red background condition (see Figure 9.1).

FIGURE 9.1

Romantic Red: The Colour of Attraction?

In this experiment, students rated pictures of women that were set against a solid red or white background. Perhaps illustrating a learned association between the colour red and romance, male students—but not their female counterparts—rated the pictured women as more attractive in the red background condition.

(Elliot & Niesta, 2008.)

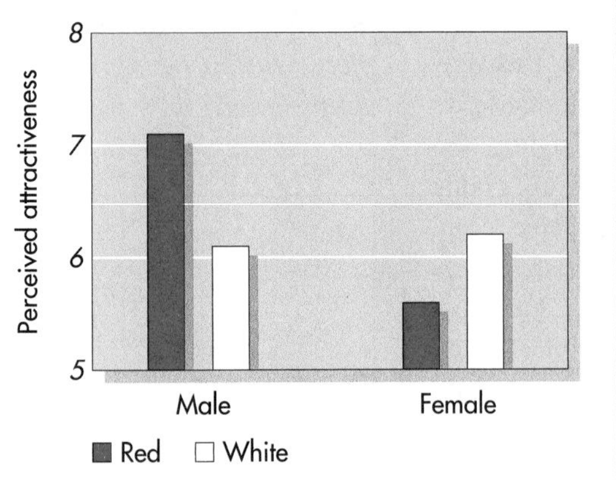

Why Are We Blinded by Beauty? Regardless of how beauty is defined, it's clear that people seen as physically attractive are at a social advantage. Perhaps that's why billions of dollars a year are spent on makeup, hair products, and cosmetic surgery to plump up sunken skin, peel and scrape wrinkles from the face, vacuum out fat deposits, lift faces, reshape noses, tuck in tummies, and enlarge or reduce breasts.

What creates the bias for beauty, and why are we drawn like magnets to people who are physically attractive? One possibility is that it is inherently rewarding to be in the company of people who are aesthetically appealing—that we derive pleasure from beautiful men and women the same way that we enjoy a breathtaking landscape or a magnificent work of art. Or perhaps the rewards are more extrinsic. Perhaps, for example, we expect the glitter of another's beauty to rub off on us. When average-looking men and women are seen alongside someone else of the same sex, they are rated as more attractive when the other person is good-looking, and as less attractive when he or she is plain-looking (Geiselman et al., 1984).

A second possible reason for the bias for beauty is that people tend to associate physical attractiveness with other desirable qualities—an assumption known as the **what-is-beautiful-is-good stereotype** (Dion et al., 1972). Think about children's fairy tales, where Snow White and Cinderella are portrayed as beautiful *and* kind, while the witch and stepsisters are said to be both ugly *and* cruel. This link between beauty and goodness can even be seen in Hollywood movies. Stephen Smith and others (1999) asked people to watch and rate the main characters who appeared in the 100 top-grossing movies between 1940 and 1990. They found that the more attractive the characters were, the more frequently they were portrayed as virtuous, romantically active, and successful. In a second study, these investigators showed students a film that depicted either a strong or a weak link between the beauty and goodness of the characters. Then, in a supposedly unrelated experiment, these students were asked to evaluate two graduate school applicants whose credentials were equivalent but whose photographs differed in terms of physical attractiveness. The result was both interesting and disturbing: Students who had watched a film depicting the beautiful-is-good stereotype were more likely than those who had watched a nonstereotypic film to favour the physically attractive applicant in their evaluations (see Figure 9.2). It appears that the entertainment industry unwittingly helps to foster and perpetuate our tendency to judge people by their physical appearance.

FIGURE 9.2

Media Influences on the Bias for Beauty

In this study, participants evaluated graduate school applicants who differed in their physical attractiveness. Indicating the power of the media to influence us, those who had first watched a stereotypic film in which beauty was associated with goodness were more likely to favour the attractive applicant than those who had first seen a nonstereotypic film.

(Smith et al., 1999.)

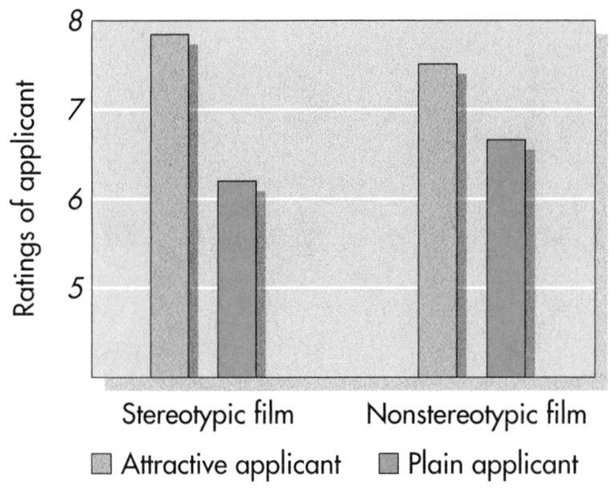

"Cyberdating works because the courting process is reversed; people get to know each other from the inside out."

—Trish McDermott, Match.com

Studies have shown that good-looking people are judged to be smart, successful, happy, well-adjusted, socially skilled, confident, and assertive—though also vain (Eagly et al., 1991). So, is this physical attractiveness stereotype accurate? Only to a limited extent. Research shows that good-looking people do have more friends, better social skills, and a more active sex life. But beauty is *not* related to objective measures of intelligence, personality, adjustment, or self-esteem. In these domains, popular perceptions appear to exaggerate the reality (Feingold, 1992b). It also seems that the specific nature of the stereotype depends on cultural conceptions of what is "good." When Ladd Wheeler and Youngmee Kim (1997) asked people in Korea to rate photos of various men and women, they found that people seen as physically attractive were also assumed to have "integrity" and "a concern for others"—traits that are highly valued in this collectivist culture. In contrast to what is considered desirable in more individualistic cultures, attractive people in Korea were not assumed to be dominant or assertive. What is beautiful is good; but what is good is, in part, culturally defined.

what-is-beautiful-is-good stereotype
The belief that physically attractive individuals also possess desirable personality characteristics.

Christie's Image/Corbis

This painting depicts a Greek myth in which Pygmalion, the King of Cyprus, sculpted his ideal woman in an ivory statue he called Galatea. Illustrating the power of a self-fulfilling prophecy, Pygmalion fell in love with his creation, caressed it, adorned it with jewellery, and eventually brought it to life.

If the physical attractiveness stereotype is true only in part, why does it endure? One possibility is that each of us creates support for the bias via the *self-fulfilling prophecy* model described in Chapter 4. In a classic study of interpersonal attraction, Mark Snyder and others (1977) brought together unacquainted pairs of male and female students. All the students were given biographical sketches of their partners. Each man also received a photograph of a physically attractive or unattractive woman, supposedly his partner. At that point, the students rated each other on several dimensions and had a phone-like conversation over headphones. The results were provocative. Men who thought they were interacting with a woman who was attractive (1) formed more positive impressions of her personality and (2) were friendlier in their conversational behaviour. And now for the clincher: (3) The female students whose partners had seen the attractive picture were later rated by listeners to the conversation as warmer, more confident, and more animated. Fulfilling the prophecies of their own expectations, men who expected an attractive partner actually created one. These findings call to mind the Greek myth of Pygmalion, who fell in love with a statue he had carved—and brought it to life.

The Benefits and Costs of Beauty No doubt about it, good-looking people have a significant edge. As a result, they are more popular, more sexually experienced, and more socially skilled. In light of these advantages, it's interesting that physical attractiveness is not a sure ticket to health, happiness, or high self-esteem (Diener et al., 1995; Feingold, 1992b; Langlois et al., 2000).

One problem is that highly attractive people can't always tell if the attention and praise they receive from others are due to their talent or just their good looks. A study by Brenda Major and others (1984) illustrates the point. Male and female participants who saw themselves as attractive or unattractive wrote essays that were later positively evaluated by an unknown member of the opposite sex. Half the participants were told that their evaluator would be watching them through a one-way mirror as they wrote the essay; the other half were led to believe that they could not be seen. In actuality, there was no evaluator, and all participants received identical, very positive evaluations of their work. Participants were then asked why their essay had been so favourably reviewed. The result: Those who saw themselves as unattractive felt better about the quality of their work after getting a glowing evaluation from someone who had seen them. Yet those who saw themselves as attractive and thought they had been seen attributed the glowing feedback to their looks—not to the quality of their work. For people who are highly attractive, positive feedback is sometimes hard to interpret (see ▶ Figure 9.3). This distrust may be well founded. In one study, many men and women openly admitted that they would lie in order to present themselves well to prospective dates—when those dates are highly attractive (Rowatt et al., 1999).

Another cost of having physical attractiveness as a social asset is the pressure to maintain one's appearance. In contemporary North American society, such pressure is particularly strong when it comes to the body. This focus on the human form can produce a healthy emphasis on nutrition and exercise. But it can also have distinctly unhealthy consequences as seen in a strange dichotomy whereby men pop steroids to build muscles while women over-diet in order to lose weight. In a startling finding, Timothy Judge and Daniel Cable (2011) demonstrated what they termed a weight double standard. As women gain weight, their salaries decrease, while for men the opposite is true; at least up until the point of obesity, gaining weight is associated with salary increases. Perhaps most remarkable, very thin women who subsequently gained a few pounds suffered the most in terms of salary disparities. In a weight-obsessed culture, having achieved, but then lost, that unrealistic ideal leads to the greatest consequences.

Particularly among young women, an obsession with thinness can give rise to serious eating disorders such as *bulimia* (food binges followed by purging) and *anorexia nervosa* (self-imposed starvation, which can be fatal). Although estimates vary, recent studies indicate that fewer than 1 percent of women suffer from anorexia, that 2 to 3 percent have bulimia, and that these rates are higher among female students than among non-students (Fairburn & Brownell, 2002; Smolak & Thompson, 2009; Striegel-Moore & Smolak , 2001).

Women are more likely than men to suffer from what Janet Polivy and others (1986) at the University of Toronto call the "modern mania for slenderness." This slender ideal is projected in the mass media. Studies have shown that young women who see magazine ads or TV commercials that feature ultra-thin models become more dissatisfied with their own bodies than those who view neutral materials (Posavac et al., 1998). Trying to measure up to the multi-million-dollar supermodels can only prove frustrating to most. What's worse, the cultural ideal for thinness may be set early in childhood. Several years ago, Kevin Norton and his colleagues (1996) projected the life-size dimensions of the original Ken and Barbie dolls that are popular all over the world. They found that both were unnaturally thin compared with the average young adult. In fact, the estimated odds that any young woman will have Barbie's shape are approximately 1 in 100 000.

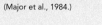

FIGURE 9.3

When Being Seen Leads to Disbelief

People who believed they were physically unattractive were more likely to cite the quality of their work as the reason for receiving a positive evaluation when they thought they were seen by the evaluator. However, people who believed they were attractive were less likely to credit the quality of their work when they thought they were seen.

(Major et al., 1984.)

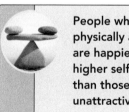

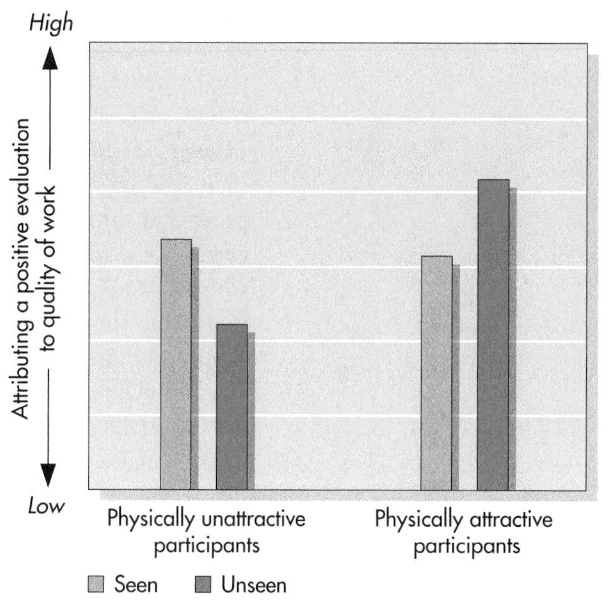

In sum, being beautiful may be a mixed blessing. There are some real benefits that cannot be denied, but there may be some costs as well. This trade-off makes you wonder about the long-term effects. Some years ago, Ellen Berscheid and others (1972) compared the physical attractiveness levels of students (based on yearbook pictures) to their adjustment when they reached middle age. There was little relationship between their appearance in youth and their later happiness. Those who were especially good-looking in university were more likely to be married, but they were not more satisfied with marriage or more content with life. Beauty may confer advantage, but it is not destiny.

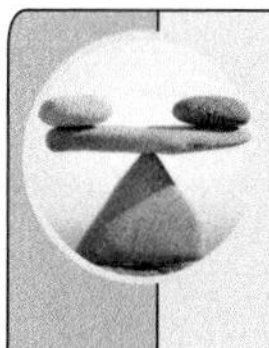

People who are physically attractive are happier and have higher self-esteem than those who are unattractive. FALSE.

First Encounters: Getting Acquainted

Proximity increases the odds that we will meet someone, familiarity puts us at ease, and beauty draws us in like magnets to a first encounter. But what determines whether sparks will fly in the early getting-acquainted stages of a relationship? In this section, we consider three characteristics of others that can influence our attraction: similarity, reciprocity, and being hard to get.

Liking Others Who Are Similar The problem with proverbial wisdom is that it very often contradicts itself. Common sense tells us that "birds of a feather flock together." Yet we also hear that "opposites attract." So which is it? Before answering this question, imagine sitting at a computer, meeting someone in an online chat room, and striking up a conversation about politics, sports, restaurants, where you live, or your favourite band—and you realize that the two of you have a lot in common. Now imagine the opposite experience of chatting with someone who is very different from you in his or her background, interests, values, and outlook on life. Which of the two strangers would you want to meet, the one who is similar or the one who is different?

Over the years, research has consistently shown that people tend to associate with others who are similar to themselves (Montoya et al., 2008). Four types of similarity are most relevant. The first is demographic. In a series of studies conducted at Dalhousie University, Sean Mackinnon and his colleagues (2011) demonstrated that, when given a choice, people tend to sit beside those who look like them based on any number of physical similarities, including hair length, race, or even whether the other person wears glasses! On a whole range of demographic variables—including age, education, race, religion, height, level of intelligence, and socioeconomic status—people who go together as friends, dates, or partners in marriage resemble each other more than randomly paired couples (Warren, 1966). These correlations cannot be used to prove that similarity causes attraction. A more compelling case could be made, however, by first measuring people's demographic characteristics and then determining whether these people, when they met others, liked those who were similar to them more than those who were dissimilar. This is what Theodore Newcomb (1961) did. In an elaborate study, Newcomb set up an experimental dormitory and found that students who were similar in their backgrounds grew to like each other more than did those who were dissimilar. Is demographic similarity still a factor even today, with all the choices we have in our diverse and multicultural society? Yes. Commenting on the persistently magnetic appeal of similarity, sociologist John Macionis (2003) notes that "Cupid's arrow is aimed by society more than we like to think." One unfortunate result, as we saw in Chapter 5, is that by associating only with similar others, people form social niches that are homogeneous—and divided along the lines of race, ethnic background, age, religion, level of education, and occupation (McPherson et al., 2001).

People can also be similar in other ways, as when they share the same opinions, interests, and values. The vast array of online dating sites illustrates the point. In addition to generic services such as Match.ca or eHarmony, all sorts of specialty services are specifically designed to bring together people of like minds—hence Jdate.com or DateMyPet.com. In one study, Paul Eastwick and others (2011) asked students to select three essential and three non-essential traits in a romantic partner. The students later read an online description of an opposite sex individual (a confederate) whose profile appeared to match either two of their essential, or two of their least essential, traits. Romantic interest in the person depicted in the profile was highest when the student thought this person embodied their essential traits. However, once given a chance to meet and interact with the person in the profile, differences between the essential and non-essential trait groups disappeared, in large part because students who met someone they didn't expect to be interested in ended up liking them more. Therefore, knowing that someone shares our ideals may have its greatest effect before an interaction, and increase the likelihood of initiating an interaction in the first place, rather than it really determining whether we eventually come to like (or love) someone.

What about the role of *attitude* similarity in attraction? Here, the time course is slower, because people have to get to know each other first. In Newcomb's study, the link between actual similarity and liking increased gradually during the school year. Laboratory experiments have confirmed the point. For example, Donn Byrne (1971) had people give their opinions on a whole range of issues and then presented them with an attitude survey supposedly filled out by another person (the responses were actually rigged). In study after study, he found that participants liked this other person better when they perceived his or her attitudes as being more similar to theirs (Byrne, 1997).

The link between attitudes and attraction can also be seen in dating and married couples, as research shows that the more similar two people are in the roles they like to play and the ways they like to spend leisure time, the more compatible they are (Lucier-Greer & Adler-Baeder, (2011). Apparently, birds of a feather that flock together also stay together. But wait. Does this necessarily mean that similarity breeds attraction, or might attraction also breed similarity? In all likelihood, both mechanisms are at work. Studies of dating couples show that when partners who are close discover that they disagree on important moral issues, they bring their views on these issues into alignment and become more similar from that point on (Davis & Rusbult, 2001).

According to Milton Rosenbaum (1986), attraction researchers have over-played the role of attitudinal similarity. Similarity does not spark attraction, he says; rather, *dis*similarity triggers repulsion—the desire to avoid someone. Rosenbaum maintains that people expect most others to be similar, which is why others who are different grab our attention. Taking this hypothesis one step further, David Lykken and Auke Tellegen (1993) argue that in mate selection, *all* forms of interpersonal similarity are irrelevant. After a person discards the 50 percent of the population who are least similar, they claim, a random selection process takes over.

So which is it: Are we turned on by others who are similar in their attitudes, or are we turned off by those who are different? As depicted in ▶ Figure 9.4, Donn Byrne and his colleagues proposed a two-step model that takes both reactions into account. First, they claim, we avoid associating with others who are dissimilar; then, among those who remain, we are drawn to those who are most similar (Byrne et al., 1986; Smeaton et al., 1989). Our reactions may also be influenced by expectations. People expect similarity from ingroup members—like fellow Liberals or Conservatives, or fellow straights or gays. In a series of studies, Fang Chen and Douglas Kenrick (2002) thus found that research participants were particularly attracted to outgroup members who expressed similar attitudes, and they were most repulsed by ingroup members who expressed dissimilar attitudes.

In addition to demographics and attitudes, a third source of similarity and difference is also at work, at least in romantic relationships. Have you ever noticed the way people react to couples in which one partner is gorgeous and the other plain? Typically, we are startled by "mismatches" of this sort, as if expecting people to pair off with others who are similarly attractive—not more, not less. This reaction has a basis in reality. Early on, laboratory studies showed that both men and women yearn for

▶ FIGURE 9.4

A Two-Stage Model of the Attraction Process

Proposed by Byrne and his colleagues (1986), the two-stage model of attraction holds that we first avoid dissimilar others and then approach similar others.

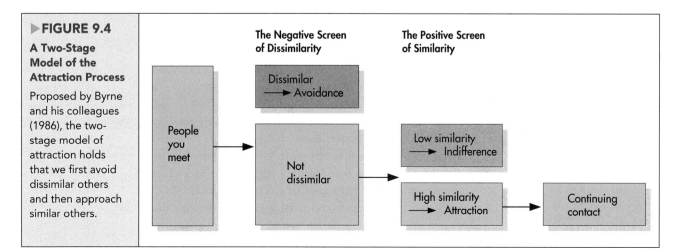

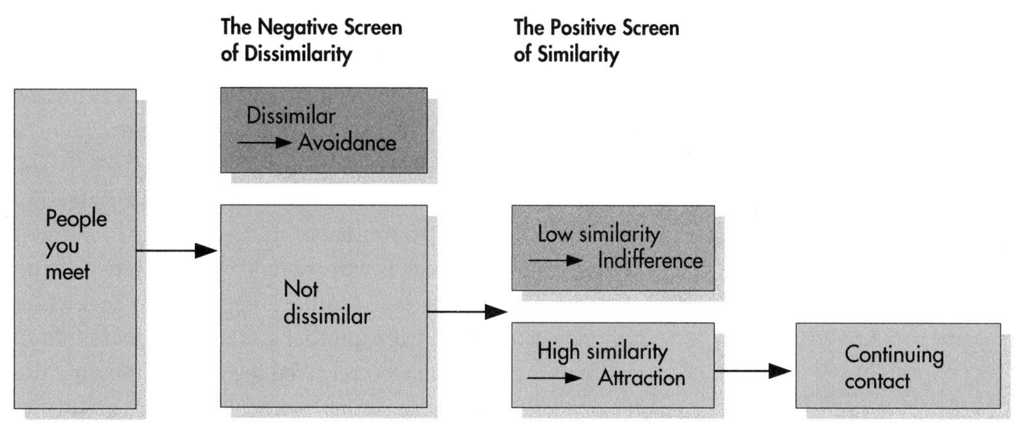

The pairing of Brad Pitt and Angelina Jolie nicely fits the expectations we tend to hold about the matching hypothesis.

partners who are highly attractive. Thus, when incoming first-year students at the University of Minnesota were randomly coupled for a dance, their desire for a second date was influenced more by their partner's physical attractiveness than by any other variable (Walster et al., 1966). In real-life situations, however, where one can be accepted or rejected by a prospective partner, people shy away from romantic encounters with others who are "out of their league" (Berscheid et al., 1971). Correlational studies of couples who are dating, engaged, living together, or married thus support a **matching hypothesis**—the idea that people tend to become involved romantically with others who are equivalent in their physical attractiveness (Feingold, 1988).

A fourth type of similarity can trigger attraction among strangers: a similarity in subjective experience. Imagine that a professor says something in class that strikes you as funny. You glance at the student next to you, who glances back, and the two of you burst out laughing, as if bonded by a private joke. Whenever two people who are at a common event laugh, cry, jump to their feet, cheer, shake their heads, or roll their eyes at the same time, they feel as if they have shared a subjective experience. Elizabeth Pinel and Anson Long (2012) called this experience "I-sharing" and theorized that people who I-share, even if they are otherwise dissimilar, feel a profound sense of connection to one another—like "kindred spirits."

Before concluding that similarity is the key to attraction, though, what about the common-sense notion that opposites attract? Many years ago, sociologists proposed the *complementarity* hypothesis, which holds that people seek others whose needs "oppose" their own—that people who need to dominate, for example, are drawn to those who are submissive (Winch et al., 1954). Is there any support for this view? Surprisingly, the answer is no. Sure, most human beings are romantically attracted to others of the opposite sex. But when it comes to fitting mutual needs and personality traits the way keys fit locks, research shows that complementarity does not influence attraction (Gonzaga et al., 2007; O'Leary & Smith, 1991).

When it comes to romantic relationships, opposites attract.
FALSE.

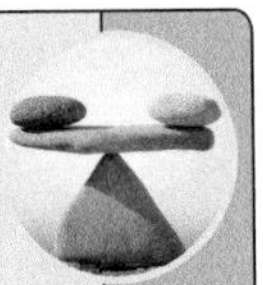

Liking Others Who Like Us Many years ago, Fritz Heider (1958) theorized that people prefer relationships that are psychologically "balanced" and that a state of imbalance causes distress. In groups of three or more individuals, a balanced social constellation exists when we like someone whose relationships with others parallel our own. Thus, we want to like the friends of our friends and the enemies of our enemies (Aronson & Cope, 1968). If you've ever had a good friend who dated someone you detested, then you know just how awkward and unpleasant an *un*balanced relationship can be. The fact is, we don't expect our friends and enemies to get along (Chapdelaine et al., 1994).

Between two people, a state of balance exists when the relationship is characterized by **reciprocity**—a mutual exchange between what we give and what we receive. Liking is mutual, which is why we tend to like others who indicate that they like us. In one experiment, Matthew Montoya and Chester Insko (2008) provided participants with bogus feedback from another student they were told they might have the opportunity to meet. Those who received feedback indicating the other person liked them reported liking them in return, believing that the other person had more benevolent intentions toward them (i.e., would look out for their interests), and had a greater

matching hypothesis
The proposition that people are attracted to others who are similar in physical attractiveness.

reciprocity
A mutual exchange between what we give and receive—for example, liking those who like us.

interest in meeting them. Feeling liked is important. When groups of men and women were asked to reflect on how they fell in love or developed friendships with specific people, many spontaneously said they had been turned on initially by the realization that they were liked (Aron et al., 1989).

But does reciprocity mean, simply, that the more people like us, the more we will like them back? Elliot Aronson and Darwyn Linder (1965) conducted an interesting study in which female students met in pairs several times to discuss various topics. In each pair, one student was a research participant, and her partner was a confederate. After each meeting, the participant overheard a follow-up conversation between the experimenter and the confederate in which she was discussed and evaluated. Over time, the confederate's evaluation of the participant either was consistently positive or negative or underwent a change— either from negative to positive (gain) or from positive to negative (loss). Put yourself in the participant's shoes. All else being equal, in which condition would you like your partner most? In this study, participants liked the partner more when her evaluation changed from negative to positive than when it was positive all along. As long as the "conversion" is gradual and believable, people like others more when their affection takes time to earn than when it comes easily.

Exploring whether expecting to like someone leads to liking, researchers have turned to speed dating, a fascinating new platform for men and women who are looking for a romantic relationship. In speed-dating events, individuals pay to have between ten and twenty-five very brief "dates" lasting no more than four minutes. After rotating like clockwork from one partner to another, participants—who wear nametags—let the event hosts know which partners, if any, they'd be interested in seeing again. If two participants double-match, the host provides each with the other's contact information so they can schedule a real date (Finkel & Eastwick, 2008). Mitja Back and others (2011) found that when speed dating, women who were not choosy (i.e., they selected many men) displayed flirtatious behaviours that led to them being chosen by many men; however, this didn't translate into more double-matches for them—they just appeared to be more popular overall. In contrast, men who were not choosy (i.e., they chose lots of women) were selected by fewer women. The flirtatious behaviours exhibited by both men and women were reciprocated, but only women were rewarded for it. Regardless, in neither case did it lead to more matches. Our own liking is therefore a poor indicator for determining who likes us.

Pursuing Those Who Are Hard to Get The study by Back and his colleagues (2011) suggests that to some extent we like others who are socially selective. This seems to support an old popular notion that you can spark romantic interest by playing hard to get. For example, some years ago, Ellen Fein and Sherri Schneider (1996) wrote a paperback book for women seductively titled *The Rules: Time-Tested Secrets for Capturing the Heart of Mr. Right.* What were the rules? Here's one: "Don't call him and rarely return his calls." Here's another: "Let him take the lead." In all cases, the theme was that men are charmed by women who are hard to get. It's an interesting hypothesis. Yet researchers have found that the **hard-to-get effect** is harder to get than they had originally anticipated (Walster et al., 1973). One problem is that we are turned *off* by those who reject us because they are committed to someone else or have no interest in us (Wright & Contrada, 1986). Another problem is that we prefer people who are moderately selective compared with those who are nonselective (they have no taste, or no standards) or too selective (they are arrogant) (Eastwick & Finkel, 2008).

hard-to-get effect
The tendency to prefer people who are highly selective in their social choices over those who are more readily available.

But now suppose that someone you are interested in is hard to get for external reasons. What if a desired relationship is opposed or forbidden by parents, as in the

Imageshop/Jupiter Images

Consistent with reactance theory, studies conducted in bars like this one have shown that men and women who are not in committed relationships see each other as more attractive as the night wears on.

story of Romeo and Juliet? What about a relationship threatened by catastrophe, as in the love story portrayed in the movie *Titanic*? What about distance, a lack of time, or renewed interest from a partner's old flame? As you may recall from Chapter 6, the theory of psychological reactance states that people are motivated to protect their freedom to choose and behave as they please. When a valued freedom is threatened, people reassert themselves, often by over-wanting the endangered behaviour—like the proverbial forbidden fruit (Brehm & Brehm, 1981).

Consider what happens when you think that your chance to get a date for the evening is slipping away. Is it true, to quote country-and-western musician Mickey Gilley, that "the girls all get prettier at closing time"? To find out, researchers entered some bars in Texas and asked patrons three times during the night to rate the physical attractiveness of other patrons of the same and opposite sex. As Gilley's lyrics suggested, people of the opposite sex were seen as more attractive as the night wore on (Pennebaker et al., 1979). The study is cute, but the correlation between time and attraction can be interpreted in other ways (perhaps attractiveness ratings rise with blood-alcohol levels!). In a follow-up study, Scott Madey and his colleagues (1996) also had patrons in a bar make attractiveness ratings throughout the night. They found that these ratings increased as the night wore on only among patrons who were not committed to a relationship. As reactance theory would predict, closing time posed a threat—which sparked desire—only to those on the lookout for a late-night date.

Another possible instance of passion fuelled by reactance can be seen in "the allure of secret relationships." In a fascinating experiment, Daniel Wegner and others (1994) paired up male and female students to play bridge. Within each foursome, one couple was instructed in writing to play footsie under the table—either secretly or in the open. Got the picture? After a few minutes, the game was stopped, and the players were asked to indicate privately how attracted they were to their own partner and to the opposite-sex member of the other team. The result: Students who played footsie in secret were more attracted to each other than those who played in the open or not at all. This finding is certainly consistent with reactance theory. But there may be more to it. First, as we'll see later, the thrill of engaging in a forbidden act, or the sheer excitement of having to keep a secret, may help fan the flames of attraction. Second, it is important to realize that keeping a secret romance from others can be so much of a burden that the relationship itself will suffer (Foster et al., 2010).

"Love ceases to be a pleasure when it ceases to be a secret."
—Aphra Behn

Finally, it's important to realize that there are situations in which reactance reduces interpersonal attraction. Have you ever tried to play the matchmaker by insisting that two of your unattached single friends get together? Be forewarned: Setting people up can backfire. Determined to preserve the freedom to make their own romantic choices, your friends may become *less* attracted to each other than they would have been without your encouragement (Wright et al., 1992).

Mate Selection: The Evolution of Desire

Before moving on to the topic of close relationships, let's stop and ponder this question: When it comes to the search for a short-term or long-term mate, are men and women similarly motivated? If not, what are the differences? Later in this chapter, we'll see that most men appear more sex-driven than most women—desiring more frequent and more casual sex, more partners, and more variety, all of which leads researchers in the area to conclude that "men desire sex more than women" (Baumeister et al., 2001, p. 270).

According to the evolutionary perspective, men and women differ in their mating strategies. Women are limited in the number of children they can bear, so they seek out men with the financial resources to support them and their offspring. Men, on the other hand, try to attract young and attractive (fertile) women who can bear them many children and help them carry on their genetic line.

The Evolutionary Perspective Why do these differences exist, and what do they mean? In *The Evolution of Desire,* David Buss (2003) argues that the answer can be derived from evolutionary psychology. According to this perspective, human beings all over the world exhibit mate-selection patterns that favour the conception, birth, and survival of their offspring—and women and men, by necessity, employ different strategies to achieve that common goal (Buss & Schmitt, 1993; Gangestad & Simpson, 2000; Trivers, 1972).

According to Buss, women must be highly selective because they are biologically limited in the number of children they can bear and raise in a lifetime. A woman must, therefore, protect those she has and so searches for a mate who possesses (or has the potential to possess) economic resources and is willing to commit those resources to support her offspring. The result is that women should be attracted to men who are older and financially secure or who have ambition, intelligence, stability, and other traits predictive of future success.

In contrast, men can father an unlimited number of children and ensure their reproductive success by inseminating many women. Men are restricted, however, by their ability to attract fertile partners and by their lack of certainty as to whether the babies born are actually their own. With these motives springing from their evolutionary past, men seek out women who are young and physically attractive (having smooth skin, full lips, lustrous hair, good muscle tone, and other youthful features)—attributes that signal health and reproductive fertility. To minimize their paternal uncertainty, men should also favour chastity, pursuing women they think will be sexually faithful rather than promiscuous.

To test this theory, Buss (1989) and a team of researchers surveyed 10 047 men and women in 37 cultures in North and South America, Asia, Africa, Eastern and Western Europe, and the Pacific. All respondents were asked to rank-order and rate the importance of various attributes in choosing a mate. The results were consistent with predictions. Both men and women gave equally high ratings to certain attributes, such as "having a pleasant disposition." But in the vast majority of countries, "good looks" and "no previous experience in sexual intercourse" were valued more by men, whereas "good financial prospect" and "ambitious and industrious" were more important to women. Analyses of personal ads appearing in magazines and newspapers have also revealed that in the dating marketplace, the "deal" is that women offer beauty, while men offer wealth (Feingold, 1992a; Rajecki et al., 1991; Sprecher et al., 1994). In the words of one investigator, the search for a heterosexual mate seems to feature "men as success objects and women as sex objects" (Davis, 1990). This may explain, in part, why Joseph Nedelec and Kevin Beaver (2011) found differences in how male and female interviewers in their study rated the attractiveness of the respondents. Women were significantly more likely than men to rate a male respondent as 'very attractive' or 'very unattractive.' They suggest that, from an evolutionary perspective, men may be more attuned to notice beauty cues in women but not in men, and this is reflected in their ratings.

Some researchers have suggested that these gendered preferences are not mere luxuries, but necessities in the mating marketplace. In Buss's (1989) study, men were more likely to prefer good looks, and women were more likely to prefer good financial prospects, but both sexes saw other characteristics—such as funny, dependable, and kind—as more important. But what happens in real life, where mate seekers who can't have it all must prioritize their desires? Studying "the necessities and luxuries in mate preferences," Norman Li and others (2011) asked research participants in the United States and Singapore to design their ideal long-term or short-term mate by purchasing different characteristics using "mate dollars." For long-term mates, men in both countries spent more play money on physical attractiveness, while women in both countries spent more on social status, although men and women also prioritized kindness. In the short-term partner condition, both men and women spent more on physical attractiveness. When mate seekers can't have it all and must therefore focus on what's most important, they prioritize their choices in the ways predicted by evolutionary theory (see ▶ Figure 9.5).

"Men seek to propagate widely, whereas women seek to propagate wisely."
—Robert Hinde

Also consistent with the evolutionary perspective is a universal tendency for men to seek younger women (who are most likely to be fertile), and for women to desire older men (who are most likely to have financial resources). These mate preferences appear to persist throughout the lifespan (Alterovitz & Mendelsohn, 2009). Buss (1989) found this age-preference discrepancy in all the cultures he studied, with men on average wanting to marry women who were 2.7 years younger and women wanting men who were 3.4 years older. Based on their analysis of personal ads, Douglas Kenrick and Richard Keefe (1992) found that men in their twenties are equally interested in younger women and slightly older women still of fertile age. But men in their thirties seek out women who are five years younger, while men in their fifties prefer women 10 to 20 years younger. In contrast, girls and women of all ages are attracted to men who are older than they are. These patterns can also be seen in marriage statistics taken from different cultures and generations. There is one interesting exception: teenage boys say they are most attracted to women who are slightly *older* than they are, women in their fertile twenties (Kenrick et al., 1996).

Also supportive of evolutionary theory is research on *jealousy*, "the dangerous passion"—a negative emotional state that arises from a perceived threat to one's relationship. Although jealousy is a common and normal human reaction, men and women may well be aroused by different triggering events. According to the theory, a man should be most upset by *sexual* infidelity because a wife's extramarital

▶ FIGURE 9.5
Sex Differences in Mate Preference: Evolutionary Necessities?
In this study, participants built an ideal long- or short-term mate by purchasing characteristics. For a long-term mate, men in both Singapore and the United States spent a higher percentage of money on physical attractiveness, compared to women who also valued social status somewhat more than men. For a short-term mate, both men and women focused on physical attractiveness. Data for the U.S. sample is displayed.

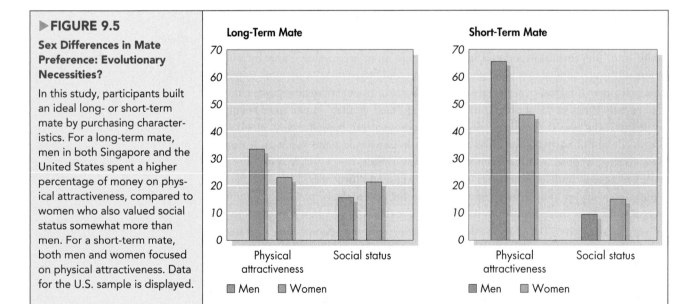

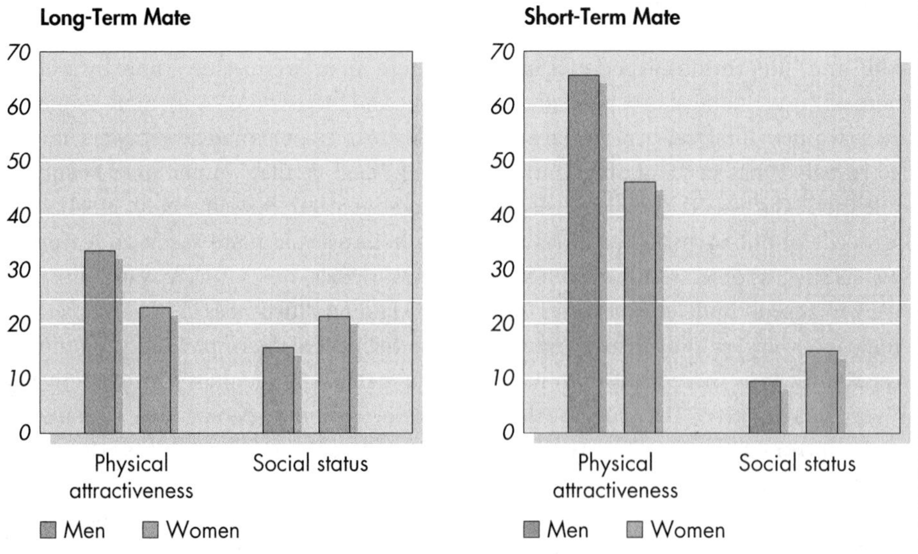

affair increases the risk that the children he supports are not his own. In contrast, a woman should feel threatened more by *emotional* infidelity because a husband who falls in love with another woman might leave and withdraw his financial support (Buss, 2000).

A number of studies support this hypothesis. In one, male and female students were asked whether they would be more upset if their romantic partner were to form a deep emotional attachment or have sexual intercourse with another person. Think for a moment about this choice. Which situation would *you* find more distressing? The results revealed a striking sex difference: 60 percent of the men said they would be more upset by a partner's sexual infidelity, but 83 percent of the women felt that emotional infidelity was worse (Buss et al., 1992).

In a second study, newly married husbands and wives were interviewed about how they would react if they suspected their partner of cheating. Interestingly, the men said they would use more "mate-retention" tactics (concealing or threatening the wife, or taking action against the male rival) when their wives were young and attractive. In contrast, women said they would use more mate-retention tactics (being watchful or enhancing their appearance) when married to men who strived for status and made more money (Buss & Shackelford, 1997). In a related study, men who had been away from their female partner for a significant period of time and who also believed there was a possibility she would cheat reported being more likely to sexually coerce her (e.g., by telling her he might have sex with another woman, or by using physical force) to gain compliance (McKibbin et al., 2011).

In a fourth study, male and female students in Argentina and Spain were asked to imagine their girlfriend or boyfriend flirting at a party with a person of the opposite sex—someone depicted as attractive or unattractive, and as socially dominant or submissive. The result: Men said they would be most jealous when their imagined male rival was dominant, while women were most jealous when their female rival was physically attractive (Buunk et al., 2011).

Sociocultural Perspectives Although the gender differences are intriguing, critics of the evolutionary approach are quick to argue that some of the results can be interpreted in terms that are "psychological" rather than "evolutionary." One common argument is that women trade youth and beauty for money not for reproductive purposes but, rather, because they often lack *direct* access to economic power. With this hypothesis in mind, Steven Gangestad (1993) examined women's access to wealth in each of the countries in Buss's cross-cultural study. He found that the more economic power women had, the more important male physical attractiveness was to them. This result suggests that it may be the generally low social and economic status of women relative to men that leads them to care less about the physical attributes of a potential mate.

Another argument concerns the finding that men are more fearful of a mate's sexual infidelity (which threatens paternal certainty), while women worry more about emotional infidelity (which threatens future support). First, in contrast to the explanation provided by evolutionary theory, some researchers have found that men become more upset over sexual infidelity not because of uncertain paternity, but because they reasonably assume that a married woman who has a sexual affair is also likely to have intimate feelings for her extramarital partner. In other words, the man's concern, like the woman's, may be over the threat to the relationship—not fatherhood issues (DeSteno & Salovey, 1996; Harris & Christenfeld, 1996). Second, although men and women react differently when asked to imagine a partner's sexual or emotional infidelity, they are equally more upset by emotional infidelity when asked to recall actual experiences from a past relationship (Harris, 2002).

Abbas/Magnum Photos

The Bari tribeswomen of Venezuela are sexually promiscuous. The Bari believe that a baby can have multiple fathers, so being promiscuous enables a woman to secure child support from many men. This exception to the evolutionary norm illustrates that human behaviour is flexible and that people can develop mating strategies to suit their cultural environment.

A third argument is that the differences typically found between the sexes are small compared to the similarities. This is an important point. A recent meta-analysis (Carpenter, 2012) of 172 studies found that, other than in the case of U.S. heterosexual American men, most men and women in other countries find emotional infidelity most distressing. For those whose partner is a man (i.e., heterosexual women or gay men), knowing their partner has developed an emotional attachment implies they have likely also engaged in sexual infidelity. For those who have female partners (i.e., heterosexual men or lesbians), evidence of a sexual infidelity implies that an emotional attachment is also present. In Buss's cross-cultural study, both men and women gave their highest ratings to such attributes as kindness, dependability, a good sense of humour, and a pleasant disposition (physical attractiveness and financial prospects did not top the lists). In fact, research shows that women desire physical attractiveness as much as men do when asked about what they want in a short-term casual sex partner (Li & Kenrick, 2006; Regan & Berscheid, 1997).

Finally, the sex differences often observed are neither predictable nor universal. Human societies are remarkably flexible in terms of the ways people adapt to their environments—and there are revealing exceptions to the rules that are supposed to govern human play on the evolutionary field. For example, David Geary (2000) points out that while human fathers spend less time at child care than mothers do, they are unique among mammals—including baboons and chimpanzees, our evolutionary cousins—in the amount of care they give to their offspring. Geary speculates that human men care for their children in part because they enjoy more paternal certainty than do other male primates.

Consider, too, the puzzling observation that most women of the Bari tribe in Venezuela are highly promiscuous. From an evolutionary standpoint, this behaviour does not seem adaptive since women who "sleep around" may scare off potential mates fearful of wasting their resources on children who are not their own. So why is female promiscuity the norm in this culture? In *Cultures of Multiple Fathers,* anthropologists Stephen Beckerman, Paul Valentine, and others note that the Bari—and some other aboriginal people in lowland South America—believe that a baby can have multiple fathers and that all men who have sex with a pregnant woman make a biological contribution to the unborn child (some groups assume that more than one father, or at least more than one insemination, are *required* to form a fetus). Thus, by taking many lovers, a woman increases the number of men who provide for her child. It appears that this strategy works. A multi-fathered Bari child is 16 percent more likely than a single-fathered child to survive to the age of 15 (Beckerman & Valentine, 2002).

Summing Up The evolutionary perspective offers social psychologists a fascinating but controversial perspective on relationships. The approach continues to draw criticism that the results are weak, limited, or explainable by nonevolutionary means (Harris, 2003; Hazan & Diamond, 2000; Pedersen et al., 2002). However, it also continues to generate new and interesting ideas. At present, scientists in this area are studying a range of issues—such as the possible links between facial appearance and health and fertility (Weeden & Sabini 2005; Young et al., 2011); the flexibility or "plasticity" of sexual orientation in men and women (Baumeister, 2000; LeVay, 2011; Lippa, 2006); the potentially deadly link between sexual jealousy and violence (Buss, 2000); women's ability to detect and prefer men who are intelligent (Prokosch et al., 2009); and the various sexual motives that can pull our attention toward physically attractive members of the opposite or same sex (Kunstman & Maner, 2011).

Close Relationships

Being attracted to people can be exhilarating or frustrating depending on how the initial encounters develop. How important is a good relationship to you? Researchers asked 300 students to weigh the importance of having a satisfying romantic relationship against the importance of other life goals (such as getting a good education, having a successful career, contributing to a better society) and found that 73 percent said they would sacrifice most other goals before giving up a good relationship (Hammersla & Frease-McMahan, 1990).

Intimate relationships often involve three basic components: (1) feelings of attachment, affection, and love; (2) the fulfillment of psychological needs; and (3) interdependence between partners, each of whom has a meaningful influence on the other. People have many significant relationships in their lives that contain one or more of these components, but social psychologists have concentrated their research on friends, dating partners, lovers, and married couples (Berscheid & Regan, 2005; Brehm et al., 2001; Hendrick & Hendrick, 2000; Sprecher & Fehr, 2011).

Not all intimate relationships contain all these ingredients. A summer romance is emotionally intense; but in the fall, both partners resume their separate lives. An "empty shell" marriage revolves around coordinated daily activities; but emotional attachment is weak, and psychological needs go unmet. Clearly, relationships come in different shapes and sizes. Some are sexual; others are not. Some involve partners of the same sex; others involve partners of the opposite sex. Some partners commit to a future together; others drop by for a brief stay. Feelings run the gamut from joyful to painful and from loving to hateful, with emotional intensity ranging all the way from mild to megawatt.

How do we advance from our first encounters to the intimate relationships that warm our lives? Do we proceed in stages, step by step, or by leaps and bounds? According to one perspective, relationships progress in order through a series of stages. For example, Bernard Murstein's (1986) *stimulus-value-role (SVR) theory* says there are three: (1) the stimulus stage, in which attraction is sparked by external attributes such as physical appearance; (2) the value stage, in which attachment is based on similarity of values and beliefs; and (3) the role stage, in which commitment is based on the performance of such roles as husband and wife. All three factors are important throughout a relationship, but each one is said to be first and foremost during only one stage.

In evaluating any stage theory, the critical issue is *sequence.* Does the value stage always precede the role stage, or might a couple work out roles before exploring whether their values are compatible? Most researchers do not believe that intimate relationships progress through a fixed sequence of stages. What then accounts for how they change? Every relationship has a developmental history with ups, downs, stalls, and accelerations. What pushes a relationship up, pulls it down, or keeps it steady? One common answer is *rewards.* Love, like attraction, depends on the experience of positive emotions in the presence of a partner. Step by step, as the rewards pile up, love develops. Or, as rewards diminish, love erodes. In reward theories of love, quantity counts. But some would disagree. Think about your own relationships. Are your feelings toward someone you love simply a more intense version of your feelings toward someone you like? Is the love of a close friend the same as the love of a romantic partner? If not, then you can appreciate that there are qualitative differences among relationships. Both views have something to offer. Progress on the road from attraction to love depends on the quantity of fuel in the tank *and* on the kind of engine providing the power. The next section examines the reward-based approach to building a relationship. Then we consider differences among the various types of relationships.

intimate relationship
A close relationship between two adults involving emotional attachment, fulfillment of psychological needs, or interdependence.

The Intimate Marketplace: Tracking the Gains and Losses

Earlier, we saw that people are initially attracted to others who provide them with direct or indirect rewards. But is "What's in it for me?" still important in a relationship that has blossomed and grown? Can an economic approach be used to predict the future of a close relationship?

Social Exchange Theory **Social exchange theory** is an economic model of human behaviour according to which people are motivated by a desire to maximize profit and minimize loss in their social relationships, just as they are in business (Homans, 1961; Thibaut & Kelley, 1959). The basic premise is simple: Relationships that provide more rewards and fewer costs will be more satisfying and endure longer. Between intimates, the rewards include love, companionship, consolation in times of distress, and sexual gratification if the relationship is of this nature. The costs include the work it takes to maintain a relationship, conflict, compromise, and the sacrifice of opportunities elsewhere.

The development of an intimate relationship is very clearly associated with the overall level of rewards and costs. Research has shown that dating couples who experience greater increases in rewards as their relationship progresses are more likely to stay together than are those who experience small increases or declines (Berg & McQuinn, 1986). People do not worry about costs during the honeymoon phase of a relationship (Hays, 1985). After a few months, however, both rewards and costs contribute to levels of satisfaction whether in heterosexual, gay, or lesbian couples (Kurdek, 1991a; Margolin & Wampold, 1981).

Rewards and costs do not arise in a psychological vacuum. People bring to their relationships certain expectations about the balance sheet to which they are entitled. John Thibaut and Harold Kelley (1959) coined the term *comparison level (CL)* to refer to this average expected outcome in relationships. A person with a high CL expects his or her relationships to be rewarding; someone with a low CL does not. Situations that meet or exceed a person's expectations are more satisfying than those that fall short. Even a bad relationship can look pretty good to someone who has a low CL.

According to Thibaut and Kelley, a second kind of expectation is also important. They coined the term *comparison level for alternatives (CLalt)* to refer to people's expectations about what they would receive in an alternative situation. If the rewards available elsewhere are believed to be high, a person will be less committed to staying in the present relationship (Drigotas & Rusbult, 1992). If people perceive few acceptable alternatives (a low CLalt), they will tend to remain, even in an unsatisfying relationship that fails to meet expectations (CL).

Of course, just as these alternatives can influence our commitment, a sense of commitment can influence our perceptions of the alternatives. To further explore this concept, Lisa Linardatos and John Lydon (2011) surveyed relationship satisfaction levels of students at McGill University in Montreal over a three-year period. Those who had incorporated their sense of self into their relationship and reported being committed and satisfied were categorized as having high (as opposed to low) relationship-specific identification. Students then completed a laboratory study they believed was exploring various ways people get to know each other through the use of technology. They first used a webcam to introduce themselves to another person (actually a confederate), and then watched the other person's video introduction. All subsequent interaction then took place using Instant Messaging (IM). Students in the control condition interacted with a same-sex confederate, while those in the

social exchange theory
A perspective that views people as motivated to maximize benefits and minimize costs in their relationships with others.

experimental (threat) condition interacted with an attractive member of the opposite sex. During the IM chat, the confederate posed a series of questions that were ordered in such a way that it would be difficult for students to avoid mentioning their partner. The result: In the control condition, students were equally likely to mention their partner (about 75 percent of the time) regardless of whether they were high or low in relationship-specific identification. However, for those in the threat condition (interacting with an attractive and apparently single member of their preferred sex), the results were quite different; 90 percent of high identifiers compared to 42 percent of low identifiers mentioned their partner! Those in committed relationships are therefore more likely to engage in behaviours that help to deflect or diminish threats from temptation or outside forces.

If you have ever been in love, you probably were not cold, calculating, and altogether objective in your perceptions of the alternatives. In close and intimate relationships, we act like lovers, not scientists, and harbour positive illusions. Research shows that people who are in love see other prospective partners as less appealing (Johnson & Rusbult, 1989; Simpson et al., 1990). They also tend to see their own partners and relationships through rose-coloured glasses (Gagne & Lydon, 2001; Sanderson & Evans, 2001; Swami & Allum, 2012). Those who have positive illusions about their romantic partners tend to report more satisfaction, love, and trust in their relationships (Murray et al., 1996; Murray & Holmes, 1999). Interestingly, the extent to which we are able to maintain these positive illusions may depend on our own levels of self-esteem. Sandra Murray and others (2009) found that people high in self-esteem use a '*commitment insurance*' system, allowing them to focus their attention on the value of their partner rather than on any perceived 'cost' of their relationship (i.e., a loss in autonomy). In contrast, people with low self-esteem may attempt to protect themselves psychologically by focusing on the costs of being with their partner in order to avoid becoming too attached to them; such a focus then undermines their relationship. It seems that seeing one's partner through those rose-coloured glasses is conducive to happy, stable relationships.

A third element in the social exchange is investment. An *investment* is something a person puts into a relationship that he or she cannot recover if the relationship ends. If you don't like the way an intimate relationship is working out, you can pack your clothes, grab your laptop, and drive away. But what about the time you put into trying to make it last? What about all the romantic and career opportunities you sacrificed along the way? As you might expect, investments increase commitment. Because of those things that we can't take with us, we're more likely to stay (Rusbult & Buunk, 1993).

Over the years, research has shown that the building blocks of the social exchange framework—as depicted in ▶ Figure 9.6, on page 338, and as incorporated into Caryl Rusbult and others' (1998) Investment Model—can be used to determine the level of commitment that partners bring to a relationship (Le & Agnew, 2003). This model is important because commitment levels predict how long relationships will last. In studies of dating and married couples, research shows that the best-adjusted ones are those in which each partner is committed and sees the other as mutually committed (Drigotas et al., 1999). Particularly important for the durability of a relationship, people who are committed are more likely to forgive and forget when their partners betray a spoken or unspoken relationship norm by flirting, lying, forgetting an anniversary, revealing an embarrassing story in public, or having an affair (Finkel et al., 2002).

equity theory
The theory that people are most satisfied with a relationship when the ratio between benefits and contributions is similar for both partners.

Equity Theory **Equity theory** is a specific version of how social exchange operates in interpersonal interactions (Adams, 1965; Messick & Cook, 1983; Walster et al.,

FIGURE 9.6

Relational Building Blocks

The building blocks of social exchange are rewards, costs, comparison level, comparison level for alternatives, and investments. These factors are strongly associated with the satisfaction and commitment partners experience in their relationship.

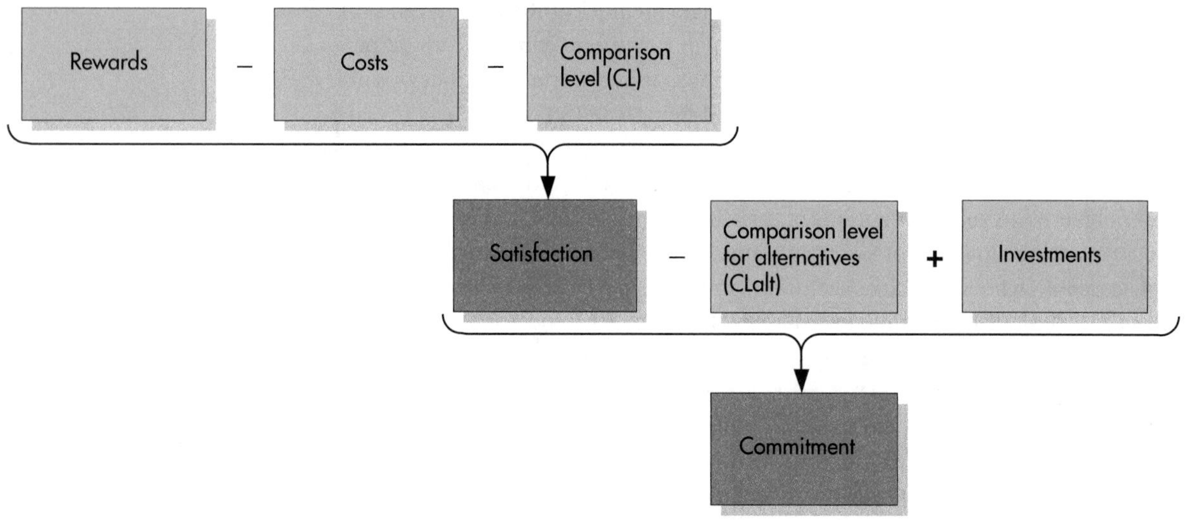

1978). According to this theory, people are most content with a relationship when the ratio between what they get out of it (benefits) and what they put into it (contributions) is similar for both partners. Thus, the basic equity formula is

$$\frac{\text{Your Benefits}}{\text{Your Contribution}} = \frac{\text{Your Partner's Benefit}}{\text{Your Partner's Contribution}}$$

Equity is different from equality. According to equity theory, the balance is what counts. So, if one partner benefits more from a relationship but also makes a greater contribution, then the situation is equitable. In an *in*equitable relationship, the balance is disturbed. One partner (called the *overbenefited*) receives more benefits than he or she deserves on the basis of contributions made, while the other partner (aptly called the *underbenefited*) receives fewer benefits than deserved.

Both overbenefit and underbenefit are unstable and often unhappy states. Underbenefited partners feel angry and resentful because they are giving more than their partner for the benefits they receive. At the same time, overbenefited partners feel guilty because they are profiting unfairly. Both kinds of inequity are associated with negative emotions in dating couples (Walster et al., 1978), married couples (Schafer & Keith, 1980), and the friendships of elderly widows (Rook, 1987). When it comes to satisfaction with a relationship, however, it is more unpleasant to feel underbenefited than overbenefited. People prefer to receive too much in life rather than too little—even if they feel bad about it (Grote & Clark, 2001; Hatfied et al., 1982; Sprecher, 2001).

If equity is so important, then any partner in a close relationship may at times feel a need to restore the balance sheet when he or she is feeling inferior, as if he or she is falling short, or insecure. According to Sandra Murray and John Holmes (2008), people in relationships naturally and unconsciously maintain something of a "trust-insurance system" by which they keep a tally of costs and benefits in order to detect and then repair possible imbalances.

Types of Relationships

Social exchange models focus on quantity: The more (rewards, equity), the better (satisfaction, endurance). But is reward always necessary? And what about the qualitative differences in our relationships? Does more reward turn casual acquaintances into friends, and friends into lovers, or are these types of relationships different from each other in other ways?

Exchange and Communal Relationships According to Margaret Clark and her colleagues, people operate by a reward-based model when they are in **exchange relationships**, which are characterized by an immediate tit-for-tat repayment of benefits. In these situations, people want costs to be quickly offset by compensation, leaving the balance at zero. But not all relationships fit this mould. Clark maintains that in **communal relationships**, partners respond to each other's needs and well-being over time, without regard for whether they have given or received a benefit (Clark, 1984; Clark & Mills, 1979).

Exchange relationships most often exist between strangers and casual acquaintances and in certain long-term arrangements such as business partnerships. In contrast, strong communal relationships are usually limited to close friends, romantic partners, and family members (Clark & Mills, 1993). Based on fieldwork in West Africa, Alan Fiske (1992) is convinced that this distinction applies to human interactions all over the world. But the cynics among us wonder: Are communal relationships truly free of social exchange considerations? Can people really give without any desire to receive, or do partners in a communal relationship follow a more subtle version of social exchange, assuming that the benefits will balance out in the long run? Clark and Judson Mills (1993) believe that true communal relationships do exist—that once a communal norm has been adopted in a relationship, regardless of how it started, the motivation to respond to the other's needs becomes automatic.

Secure and Insecure Attachment Styles Another interesting approach to understanding relationships is provided by Phillip Shaver, Cindy Hazan, and their colleagues, who have theorized that just as infants display different kinds of attachment toward their parents, so do adults exhibit specific **attachment styles** in their romantic relationships (Cassidy & Shaver, 1999; Mikulincer et al., 2011; Shaver & Mikulincer, 2012; Sprecher & Fehr, 2011).

For many years, child development psychologists had noticed that infants form intense, exclusive bonds with their primary caretakers. This first relationship is highly charged with emotion, and it emerges with regularity from one culture to the next. By observing the way babies react to both separations from and reunions with the primary caretaker, usually the mother, researchers also noticed that babies have different attachment styles. Those with *secure* attachments cry in distress when the mother leaves and then beam with sheer delight when she returns. Those with insecure attachments show one of two patterns. Some, described as *anxious,* cling and cry when the mother leaves but then greet her with anger or apathy upon her return. Others are generally more detached and *avoidant,* not reacting much on either occasion (Ainsworth et al., 1978).

How important is this first attachment? Does a secure and trusting bond in the first year of life lay a foundation for close relationships later in life? John Bowlby (1988), a psychiatrist and influential theorist, argues that there is a link—that infants form "internal working models" of attachment figures, and that these models guide their relationships later in life. Research shows that infants classified as securely attached are later more

exchange relationship
A relationship in which the participants expect and desire strict reciprocity in their interactions.

communal relationship
A relationship in which the participants expect and desire mutual responsiveness to each other's needs.

attachment style
The way a person typically interacts with significant others.

TABLE 9.1

Attachment Style

(Hazan & Shaver, 1987.)

Question: Which of the following best describes your feelings?

Answers and Percentages	Newspaper Sample	University Sample
Secure		
I find it relatively easy to get close to others and am comfortable depending on them and having them depend on me. I don't often worry about being abandoned or about someone getting too close to me.	56%	56%
Avoidant		
I am somewhat uncomfortable being close to others; I find it difficult to trust them completely, difficult to allow myself to depend on them. I am nervous when anyone gets too close, and often, love partners want me to be more intimate than I feel comfortable being.	25%	23%
Anxious		
I find that others are reluctant to get as close as I would like. I often worry that my partner doesn't really love me or won't want to stay with me. I want to merge completely with another person, and this desire sometimes scares people away.	19%	21%

positive in their outlook toward others (Cassidy et al., 1996). Looking back, adults with a secure attachment style described having positive family relationships, while avoidant and anxious adults recalled having problems with one or both parents (Feeney & Noller, 1990; Hazan & Shaver, 1987).

Whether or not adult attachment styles are rooted in the first year of life, the distinction among adults has proved to be a useful one. Read the descriptions of three attachment types in ■ Table 9.1. Which fits you best? Hazan and Shaver (1987) presented this task initially in a "love quiz" that appeared in a Denver, Colorado newspaper and then in a study of university students. As shown in Table 9.1, the distribution of responses was similar in the two samples, and it proved similar again in a later U.S.-wide sample of 8000 adults (Mickelson et al., 1997). In addition, the researchers found that people who have a secure attachment style report having satisfying relationships that are happy, friendly, based on mutual trust, and enduring. Cognitively, they see people as good-hearted, and they believe in romantic love. In contrast, avoidant lovers fear intimacy and believe that romantic love is doomed to fade; and anxious lovers report a love life full of emotional highs and lows, obsessive preoccupation, a greater willingness than others to make long-term commitments, and extreme sexual attraction and jealousy.

"I have studied love because it is my life's most difficult problem. Although I have made much progress, the 'impossible dream' of a truly fulfilling mutual love remains a goal I have yet to achieve."

—John Alan Lee

To some extent, our attachment styles can be seen in our everyday behaviour. For example, Lorne Campbell and others (2005) asked dating partners at the University of Western Ontario to keep a 14-day diary, and then videotaped the couples discussing a problem. They found that anxiously attached individuals were more likely to feel that there was greater conflict in the relationship and that the problems were escalating; independent raters noted that these individuals were more likely to be responsible for the escalation of conflict. There is also reason to believe that people's attachment styles influence their physiological reactions to relationship conflict. In one study, Sally Powers and her colleagues (2006) brought 124 university-age dating couples into the laboratory to discuss a heated conflict they'd been having. Before and after this "conflict negotiation task," the researchers took saliva samples from all participants to measure levels of cortisol, a stress hormone. The results showed that boyfriends and girlfriends who were insecurely attached exhibited more physiological stress in response to the conflict task than did those who were securely attached.

What about the future? Does the attachment style you endorse today foretell relational outcomes tomorrow? On this question, the evidence is mixed. People who are secure do tend to have more lasting relationships. But the prognosis for those classified as insecure is harder to predict, with the results less consistent. What's important to realize is that although styles of attachment are somewhat stable over time—perhaps as holdovers from infancy and childhood—they are not fixed or completely set in stone. For instance, Lee Kirkpatrick and Cindy Hazan (1994) tracked down participants from an earlier study and found, four years later, that 30 percent had different attachment styles. In keeping with the central theme of social psychology—that people are profoundly shaped by the situations they are in—research suggests that people may continuously revise their attachment styles in response to their own relationship experiences (Baldwin & Fehr, 1995; Keelan et al., 1994; Scharfe & Bartholomew, 1994).

How Do I Love Thee? Counting the Ways

The poet Elizabeth Barrett Browning asked, "How do I love thee?" and then went on to "count the ways"—of which there are many. When students were asked to list all the kinds of love that came to mind, they produced 216 items—such as friendship, parental, brotherly, sisterly, romantic, sexual, spiritual, obsessive, possessive, and puppy love (Fehr & Russell, 1991).

While concepts of love have been around for hundreds of years, it wasn't until the 1940s that researchers began to try to measure this thing called love in any sort of systematic way (Hatfield et al., 2012). Over the years, various schemes for classifying different types of love have been proposed (Sternberg & Barnes, 1998; Berscheid, 2010). On the basis of ancient writings, sociologist John Alan Lee (1988) identified three primary love styles—*eros* (erotic love), *ludus* (game-playing, uncommitted love), and *storge* (friendship love). As with primary colours, Lee theorized, these three styles can be blended together to form new secondary types of love, such as *mania* (demanding and possessive love), *pragma* (pragmatic love), and *agape* (other-oriented, altruistic love). On a scale designed to measure these "colours of love," men tend to score higher than women on *ludus,* while women score higher on *storge, mania,* and *pragma* (Hendrick & Hendrick, 1995).

Another popular taxonomy is derived from Robert Sternberg's (1986) **triangular theory of love**. According to Sternberg, there are eight basic subtypes of love (seven different forms of love and an eighth combination that results in non-love)—and all can be derived from the presence or absence of three components. The combination can thus be viewed as the vertices of a triangle (see ▶ Figure 9.7). These three components—and sample items used to measure each one—are described below:

Intimacy: The emotional component, which involves liking and feelings of closeness. ("I have a comfortable relationship with ___.")

Passion: The motivational component, which contains drives that trigger attraction, romance, and sexual desire. ("Just seeing ___ is exciting for me.")

Commitment: The cognitive component, which reflects the decision to make a long-term commitment to a loved partner. ("I will always feel a strong responsibility for ___.")

Research provides good support for this tri-component model of love (Sternberg, 1999). In one study, Arthur Aron and Lori Westbay (1996) asked people to rate 68 prototypical features of love and found that all the various features fell into three categories: passion *(gazing at the other, euphoria, butterflies in the stomach),* intimacy *(feeling free to talk about anything, supportive, understanding),* and commitment *(devotion, putting the other first, long-lasting).* In a second study, José Bauermeister and others (2011) found support for Sternberg's theory among self-identified sexual minority young men. When asked to describe their ideal romantic male partner, they endorsed items consistent with intimacy, passion, and commitment.

triangular theory of love
A theory proposing that love has three basic components—intimacy, passion, and commitment—which can be combined to produce eight subtypes.

In light of infant attachments, colours, triangles, and other love classification schemes that have been proposed over the years, one wonders: How many types

FIGURE 9.7

Sternberg's Triangular Theory of Love

According to Sternberg, various combinations of passion, intimacy, and commitment give rise to seven different types of love (although not shown, the absence of all three components produces an eighth result, non-love).

(Sternberg, 1986.)

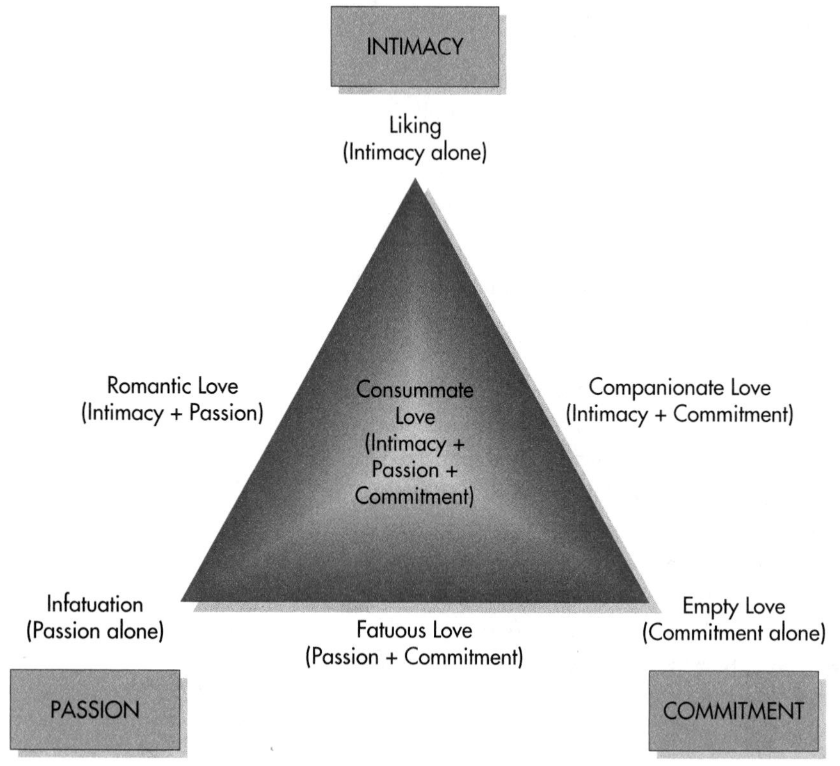

From R. Sternberg and M.L. Barnes (eds.) *The Psychology of Love*, Yale University Press, 1986. Reprinted with permission of Yale University Press.

of love are there, really? It's hard to tell. But there are two basic types that are built into all models: *liking*, the type of feeling you would have for a platonic friend, and *loving*, the kind of feeling you would have for a romantic partner. According to Zick Rubin (1973), liking and loving are two distinct reactions to an intimate relationship. There is some question, however, about how sharp the difference is. Kenneth and Karen Dion (1976) questioned casual daters, exclusive daters, engaged couples, and married couples. Although casual daters reported more liking than loving, liking and loving did not differ among those in the more committed dating relationships. More pointed is the two-pronged distinction made by Elaine Hatfield (1988) and others between passionate love and companionate love. According to Hatfield, **passionate love** is an emotionally intense *and often erotic* state of absorption in another person, whereas **companionate love** is a secure, trusting, and stable partnership, similar to what Rubin called liking.

Passionate Love: The Thrill of It Passionate love is an intense emotional state of absorption in another person. From ecstatic highs to agonizing lows, it is the bittersweet stuff of romance paperbacks, popular music, poems, and soap operas. What is passionate love, and where does it come from? According to Ellen Berscheid and Elaine Walster (later Hatfield) (1974), the key to understanding passionate love is to recognize that it is an emotion—and can be analyzed like any other emotion. Drawing on Schachter's (1964) two-factor theory of emotion (see Chapter 3), they theorized that passionate love requires two key ingredients: (1) a heightened state of physiological *arousal*, and (2) the *belief* that this arousal was triggered by the beloved person.

passionate love
Romantic love characterized by high arousal, intense attraction, and fear of rejection.

companionate love
A secure, trusting, stable partnership.

excitation transfer
The process whereby arousal caused by one stimulus is added to arousal from a second stimulus, and the combined arousal is attributed to the second stimulus.

Sometimes, the arousal-love connection is obvious—as when a person feels a surge of sexual desire at the sight of a romantic partner. At other times, however, the symptoms of arousal—such as a pounding heart, sweaty palms, and weak knees—can be hard to interpret. In the company of an attractive person, these symptoms may be attributed or "misattributed" to passionate love. Dolf Zillmann (1984) calls the process **excitation transfer**. According to Zillmann, arousal triggered by one stimulus can be transferred or added to the arousal from a second stimulus. The combined arousal is then perceived as having been caused only by the second stimulus.

Donald Dutton and Arthur Aron (1974) first tested this provocative hypothesis in a field study that took place on two bridges above the Capilano River in Vancouver. One was a narrow, wobbly suspension bridge (137 metres long and 1.5 metres wide, with a low handrail) that sways 70 metres above rocky rapids—a nightmare for anyone the least bit afraid of heights. The other bridge was wide, sturdy, and only 3 metres from the ground. Whenever an unaccompanied young man walked across one of these bridges, he was met by an attractive young woman who introduced herself as a research assistant, asked him to fill out a brief questionnaire, and gave her phone number in case he wanted more information about the project. As predicted, men who crossed the scary bridge were later more likely to call her than those who crossed the stable bridge. In an amusement park study of "love at first fright," Cindy Meston and Penny Frohlich (2003) similarly found that men and women who were not with a romantic partner rated a pictured person of the opposite sex as more attractive just after they rode on a roller coaster than before they began the ride. Perhaps terror can fan the hot flames of romance.

Shutterstock

According to excitation transfer theory, bodily arousal triggered by one stimulus can be misattributed to another stimulus. This theory suggests that the energy that springs from dancing may intensify a person's feelings for their partner, fanning the flames of passion.

Or maybe not. Maybe it's just a relief to be with someone when we're in distress. To rule out the possibility that it's relief rather than arousal that fuels attraction, Gregory White and his colleagues (1981) had to create arousal without distress. How? A little exercise can do it. Male participants ran in place for either two minutes or 15 seconds and then saw a videotape of a woman they expected to meet. The woman had been made up to look physically attractive or unattractive. After watching the video, participants rated her appearance. The result: Those who exercised for two minutes as opposed to only 15 seconds saw the physically attractive woman as even more attractive and the unattractive woman as less attractive. This study, and others like it (Allen et al., 1989), showed that arousal—even without distress—intensifies emotional reactions, positive or negative.

The implication of this research—that our passions are at the mercy of bridges, roller coasters, exercise, and anything else that causes the heart to race—is intriguing. It is certainly consistent with the common observation that people are vulnerable to falling in love when their lives are turbulent. But does the effect occur, as theorized, because people *mis*attribute their arousal to a person they have just met? Yes and no. Based on their review of 33 experiments, Craig Foster and others (1998) confirmed that the arousal-attraction effect does exist. They also found, however, that the effect occurs even when people know the actual source of their arousal—in other words, even without misattribution. According to these investigators, just being aroused, even if we know why, facilitates whatever is the most natural response. If the person we meet is good-looking and of the right sex, we become more attracted. If the person is not good-looking or is of the wrong sex, we become less attracted. No thought is required. The response is automatic.

In a book entitled *Lust: What We Know About Human Sexual Desire,* Pamela Regan and Ellen Berscheid (1999) present compelling evidence for the proposition that intense sexual desire and excitement are a vital part of passionate love. In this regard, they are quick to note that "loving" is different from "being in love." To illustrate, Berscheid and Meyers (1996) asked men and women to make three lists: people they loved, people they were in love with, and people they were sexually attracted to. As it turned out, only 2 percent of those in the "love" category also appeared in the sex list. Yet among those in the "in love" category, the overlap with sex was 85 percent.

And when Regan and her colleagues (1998) asked people to list the characteristics of romantic love, two-thirds cited sexual desire—more than the number who put happiness, loyalty, communication, sharing, or commitment on the list.

Romantic ideals notwithstanding, it is also clear that people have doubts about the staying power of passionate love. Does the fire within a relationship burn hot and bright over time, or is it just a passing fancy? Comparisons of couples at different stages of their relationships and longitudinal studies that measure changes in the same couples over time suggest that passionate love does diminish somewhat over time (Acker & Davis, 1992). Yet this decline may not be clearly defined or inevitable. In a recent study, Bianca Acevedo and Arthur Aron (2009) meta-analyzed past survey research and asked couples who had been together for varying lengths of time questions about passionate love. They found that although the initial "obsessional" aspect of passionate love clearly does diminish in long-term relationships ("I sometimes find it difficult to concentrate on work because thoughts of my partner occupy my mind"), there is a "romantic" aspect that often endures ("I would rather be with my partner than anyone else," "I want my partner—physically, emotionally, mentally"). In fact, in a sample of Americans who had been married at least 10 years, 40 percent reported still being "intensely" in love (O'Leary et al., 2012).

"True love never grows old."
—proverb

Companionate Love: The Self-Disclosure in It In contrast to the intense, emotional, and erotic nature of passionate love, companionate love is a form of affection found between close friends as well as lovers. Companionate relationships rest more on a foundation of mutual trust, caring, respect, friendship, and long-term commitment—characteristics that John Harvey and Julie Omarzu (2000) see as necessary for "minding the close relationship."

Compared with the passionate form of love, companionate love is less intense but in some respects deeper and more enduring. Susan Sprecher and Pamela Regan (1998) administered passionate and companionate love scales to heterosexual couples who had been together for varying amounts of time and found that passionate love scores of both men and women initially rose over time but then peaked and declined somewhat during marriage. Companionate love scores, however, did not similarly decline. Like the sturdy, steady tortoise in Aesop's fable, companionate love may seem outpaced by the flashier start of passionate love, but it can still cross the finish line well ahead.

Companionate love is characterized by high levels of **self-disclosure**, a willingness to open up and share intimate facts and feelings. In a way, self-disclosure is to companionate love what arousal is to passionate love. Think for a moment about your most embarrassing moment, your most cherished ambitions, or your sex life. Would you bare your soul on these private matters to a complete stranger? What about an acquaintance, date, friend, or lover? Whether or not to self-disclose—what, when, how much, and to whom—is a decision that each of us makes based on a consideration of what we stand to gain and lose in a relationship (Omarzu, 2000).

Still, it is the willingness to disclose intimate facts and feelings that lies at the heart of our closest and most intimate relationships (Derlega et al., 1993). Research shows that the more emotionally involved people are in a close relationship, the more they self-disclose to each other. Nancy Collins and Lynn Miller (1994) note three possible reasons for this correlation: (1) We disclose to people we like, (2) we like people who disclose to us, and (3) we like people to whom we have disclosed. Thus, among pairs of students brought together in a laboratory for brief getting-acquainted conversations, the more they self-disclosed, the better they felt about each other afterward (Vittengl & Holt, 2000). Results of a survey of Canadian couples revealed that, when it comes to sex, too, partners who self-disclose their likes and dislikes to each other are more satisfied sexually than those who are less open (MacNeil & Byers, 2009).

self-disclosure
Revelations about the self that a person makes to others.

Over the years, researchers have made three major observations about self-disclosure patterns in relationships. One is that partners reveal more to each other as their relationship grows over time. According to Irving Altman and Dalmas Taylor (1973), self-disclosure is a basic form of social exchange that unfolds as relationships develop. Their *social penetration theory* holds that relationships progress from superficial exchanges to more intimate ones. At first, people give relatively little of themselves to each other and receive little in return. If the initial encounters prove rewarding, however, the exchanges become both *broader* (covering more areas of their lives) and *deeper* (involving more sensitive areas). As shown in ▶ Figure 9.8, social interaction grows from a narrow, shallow sliver to a wider, more penetrating wedge.

A second observation is that patterns of self-disclosure change according to the state of a relationship. During a first encounter, and in the budding stages of a new relationship, people tend to reciprocate another's self-disclosure with their own—at a comparable level of intimacy. If a new acquaintance opens up, it is polite to match that self-disclosure by revealing more of ourselves. Once a relationship is well established, however, strict reciprocity occurs less frequently (Altman, 1973; Derlega et al., 1976). Among couples in distress, two different self-disclosure patterns have been observed. For some, both breadth and depth decrease as partners withdraw from each other and cease to communicate (Baxter, 1987). For others, the breadth of self-disclosure declines, but depth increases as the partners hurl cruel and angry statements at each other (Tolstedt & Stokes, 1984). In this case, the social *de*penetration process resembles neither the sliver of a superficial affiliation nor the wedge of a close relationship—but, rather, a long, thin dagger of discontent.

A third common observation is that individuals differ in the tendency to share private, intimate thoughts with others. For example, Kathryn Dindia and Mike Allen (1992) conducted a meta-analysis of 205 studies involving 23 702 white North

▶ FIGURE 9.8

From a Sliver to a Wedge

According to the theory of social penetration, as a relationship becomes closer, partners increase both the breadth (covering a wider range of topics) and depth (revealing more intimate information) of their exchanges.

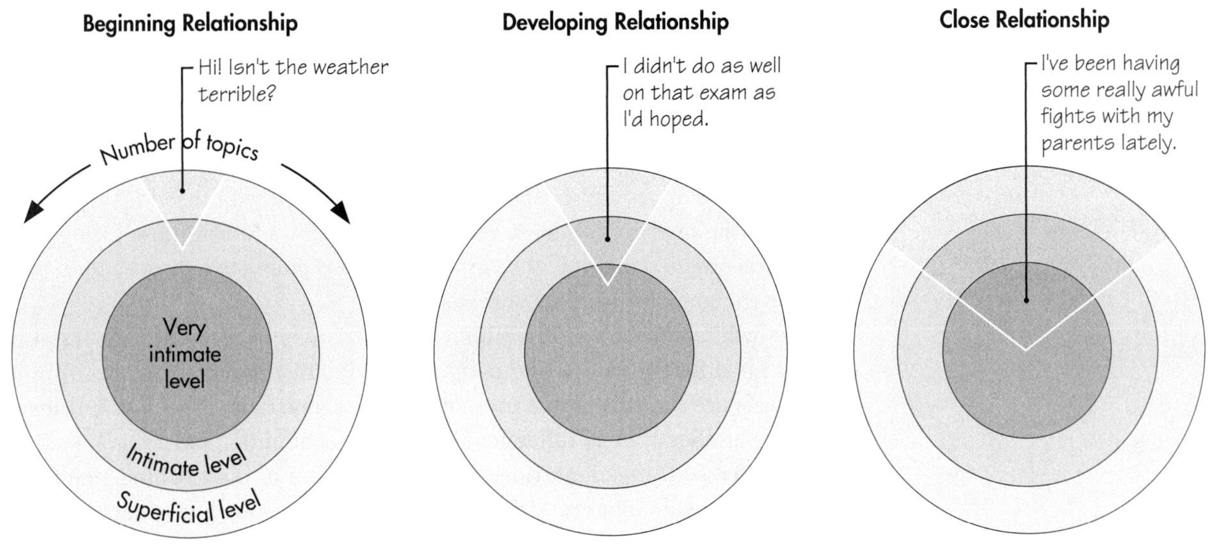

Americans and found, on average, that women are more open than men—and that people in general are more self-disclosing to women than to men. This being the case, it comes as no surprise that women rate their same-sex friendships more highly than men rate theirs. At least in North America, male friends seem to bond more by taking part in common activities, while female friends engage more in a sharing of feelings (Duck & Wright, 1993). As Paul Wright (1982) put it, women tend to interact "face-to-face;" men go "side-by-side." In a second study, Amanda Forest and Joanne Wood (2011) asked high or low self-esteem undergraduates at the University of Waterloo to disclose a sad personal event to another student, in an email. Half of the participants received a 'response' (actually written by the experimenter) containing caring and understanding phrases (e.g., "you must have felt bad"), while half received responses that were less expressive (e.g., "I know these kinds of things happen"). Students were then asked to send another email to the same person describing a second sad event. They found that students with low self-esteem, who believed they had a caring responsive partner, were far more likely to 'open up' in subsequent emails and be more expressive and self-disclosing than students with high self-esteem.

Culture, Attraction, and Relationships

In looking at attraction, desire, relationships, and love, one wonders: Are people all over the world similar or different? To what extent are these processes universal or different from one culture to another? In recent years, several social psychologists have raised these kinds of questions (Hatfield et al., 2007).

In his original cross-cultural study of mate selection, for example, Buss (1989) found that physical attractiveness is more important to men all over the world and that financial resources are more important to women—gender differences that appeared to be universal. Yet even Buss was struck by the powerful impact that culture had on mate preferences. In China, India, Indonesia, Iran, Taiwan, and the Palestinian territories of Israel, for example, people valued chastity in a mate. Yet in Finland, France, Norway, Sweden, the Netherlands, and West Germany, chastity was either unimportant or negatively valued.

When it comes to close relationships, research has shown that passionate love is a widespread and universal emotion. In surveys conducted throughout the world, William Jankowiak and Edward Fischer (1992) detected indications of passionate love in 147 out of 166 cultures as varied as Indonesia, China, Turkey, Nigeria, Trinidad, Morocco, Australia, and Micronesia. Drawing on this universality, some researchers have begun to explore the underlying neuroscience. For example, anthropologist Helen Fisher (2004) believes that romantic love is hard-wired in the neurochemistry of the brain. In particular, Fisher argues that the neurotransmitter dopamine, which drives animals to seek rewards such as food and sex, is essential to the pleasure that is felt when these drives are satisfied. Hence, she argues, dopamine levels are associated with both the highs of romantic passion and the lows of rejection. Citing evidence from studies of humans and other animals, she also points to neurochemical parallels between romantic love and substance addiction.

The willingness to marry without love is also subject to cultural variation. In light of the different values that pervade individualist and collectivist cultures, the differences are not surprising. In many cultures, marriage is seen as a transaction between families that is influenced by social, economic, and religious considerations. Indeed, arranged marriages are still common in India, China, many Muslim countries, and sub-Saharan Africa. So, when Robert Levine and others (1995) asked students from eleven countries about marrying without love, they found that the percentage who said they would do so ranged from 4 percent in the United States,

5 percent in Australia, and 8 percent in England, up to 49 percent in India and 51 percent in Pakistan.

In China, where a cultural premium is placed on devotion, respect, and obedience of children to parents and other family elders, there is far less emphasis on the Western "fairytale ideals" of love and romance (Higgins et al., 2002; Jackson et al., 2006). In recent surveys, young adults in China, more than in the United States, said they would be influenced in their mate selection decisions by parents and close friends—for example, that they would try to persuade their parents to accept a dating partner and stop dating that partner if their parents did not approve (Zhang & Kline, 2009).

Culture's influence on love is interesting. On the one hand, it could be argued that the rugged individualism found in Western cultures would inhibit the tendency to become intimate and interdependent with others. On the other hand, this same individualistic orientation leads people to give priority in making marital decisions to their own feelings—rather than to family concerns, social obligations, religious constraints, income, and the like (Dion & Dion, 1996).

DPA/The Image Works, Inc.

In a wedding ceremony that took place in Mumbai, Tushar Agarwal and his bride Richa are married. Fulfilling a tradition that seems strange to most North Americans, for whom being in love is essential, this Indian marriage was arranged.

Relationship Issues: The Male-Female "Connection"

Browse the shelves of any bookstore, and you'll see one paperback title after another on the general topic of gender. There are books for men and books for women, books that preach the masculine ideal and books that tell us how to be more feminine, books that portray men and women as similar and books that focus on differences, the so-called gender gap. Is it true, to borrow John Gray's (1997) provocative book title, that *Men Are from Mars, Women Are from Venus?* And if so, what are the implications when it comes to male-female relationships?

Men are more likely than women to interpret friendly gestures by the opposite sex in sexual terms. TRUE.

Sexuality One hundred years ago, Sigmund Freud shocked the scientific community by proposing psychoanalytic theory, which placed great emphasis on sex as a driving force in human behaviour. At the time, Freud's closest associates rejected this focus on sexual motivation. But was he wrong? Sexual images and themes pop up, quite literally, in our dreams, in the jokes we tell, in the TV shows we watch, in the novels we read, in the music we hear, and in the sex scandals that swirl around public figures in the news. It's no wonder that advertisers use sex to sell everything from blue jeans to perfumes, soft drinks, and cars.

Sex, a most private aspect of human relations, is difficult to study systematically. During the 1940s, biologist Alfred Kinsey and his colleagues (1948, 1953) conducted the first large-scale survey of sexual practices in the United States. Based on confidential interviews of more than 17 000 men and women, these researchers sought for the first time to describe what nobody would openly talk about: sexual activity. Many of his results were shocking, with reported sexual activity more frequent and more varied than anyone had expected. His books were instant bestsellers. Certain aspects of his methodology were flawed, however. For example, participants were mostly young, white, urban, and middle class—hardly a representative sample. He also asked leading questions to enable respondents to report on sexual activities—or make up stories (Jones, 1997). Kinsey died in 1954, but his Institute for Sex Research at Indiana University remains to this day a major centre for the study of human sexuality.

Since Kinsey's groundbreaking study, many sex surveys have been conducted, and they form part of the research history that has been chronicled, both seriously and with humour, in books with such titles as *Kiss and Tell: Surveying Sex in the Twentieth Century* (Ericksen & Steffen, 1999), and *Bonk: The Curious Coupling of Science and Sex* (Roach, 2008). The limits of self-reports—regardless of whether they are taken in face-to-face interviews, telephone surveys, or the Internet—is that we can never know for sure how accurate the results are. Part of the problem is that respondents may not be honest in their disclosures. But also problematic is that people differ in their interpretations of survey questions.

Consider this deceptively simple question: What does it mean to say you had sex? In an article published in *Sexual Health,* Stephanie Sanders and others (2010) asked a group of telephone survey respondents, "Would you say you *had sex* with someone if the most intimate behaviour you engaged in was ...?" The results showed that most respondents agreed that penile-vaginal intercourse constitutes having sex—while manual contact with genitals does not. Yet there was less consensus about penile-anal intercourse and oral-genital contact. This finding suggests that there is some ambiguity about what "having sex" actually means (see Table 9.2).

Researchers have used an array of methods to measure sexual attitudes and behaviour. Studies of everyday interactions reveal that men view the world in more "sexualized" terms. In 1982, Antonia Abbey arranged for pairs of male and female students to talk for five minutes, while other students observed the sessions. When she later questioned the actors and observers, Abbey found that the males were more sexually attracted to the females than vice versa. The males also rated the female actors as being more seductive and more flirtatious than the women had rated themselves as being. Among men more than women, eye contact, a compliment, a friendly remark, a brush against the arm, and an innocent smile are often interpreted as sexual come-ons (Kowalski, 1993). Despite all that has changed in recent years, these gender differences in perceptions of sexual interest still exist (Levesque et al., 2006).

Gender differences are particularly common in self-report surveys, where men report being more promiscuous, more likely to think about sex, more permissive, more likely to enjoy casual sex without emotional commitment, and more likely to fantasize about sex with multiple partners (Oliver & Hyde, 1993). When asked to select ten private wishes from a list, for example, most men and women similarly wanted love, health, peace on Earth, unlimited ability, and wealth. But more men than women also wanted "to have sex with anyone I choose" (Ehrlichman & Eichenstein, 1992). In a large-scale study of 16 000 respondents from 52 countries all over the world, David Schmitt (2003) found

TABLE 9.2

What Constitutes "Having Sex"?

In this study, men and women were asked, "Would you say you 'had sex' with someone if the most intimate behaviour you engaged in was ...?" As you can see, there was consensus for some behaviours, but disagreement for others.

(Sanders et al., 2010)

Contact	% Who Said Yes
You touched, fondled, or manually stimulated a partner's genitals.	44.9%
A partner touched, fondled, or manually stimulated your genitals.	48.1%
You had oral contact with a partner's genitals.	71.0%
A partner had oral contact with your genitals.	72.9%
Penile-anal intercourse	80.8%
Penile-vaginal intercourse	94.8%

From Sanders et al., 2010, "Misclassification bias: diversity in conceptualisations about having 'had sex'", *Sexual Health 7(1) 31–34* http://www.publish.csiro.au/nid/164/paper/SH09068.htm. Copyright © CSIRO PUBLISHING.

that men desire more sex partners and more sexual variety than women do—regardless of their relationship status or sexual orientation.

Sexual Orientation No discussion of human sexuality is complete without consideration of individual differences in **sexual orientation**—defined as one's sexual preference for members of the same sex (homosexuality), opposite sex (heterosexuality), or both sexes (bisexuality). How common is homosexuality, and where does it come from? Throughout history, and in all cultures, a vast majority of people have been heterosexual in their orientation. But how vast a majority is a subject of some debate. In a survey of Canadian men and women, 1.1 percent of Canadians identified themselves as gay or lesbian, and 0.9% identified themselves as bisexual (Canadian Community Health Survey, 2009). Together, large-scale surveys in the United States, Europe, Asia, and the Pacific suggest that the exclusively homosexual population in the world is 3 or 4 percent among men and about half that number among women (Diamond, 1993).

CP/Aaron Harris

Although researchers can only estimate the population prevalence of homosexuality, many men and women are openly gay. It isn't always easy, of course. In 2002, Marc Hall became the centre of a media storm when officials with the Durham Catholic District School Board in Oshawa, Ontario, refused to allow him to bring his boyfriend to the high school prom. He fought the ruling, and won.

Although an exclusive homosexual orientation is rare among humans and other animals, homosexual *behaviours* are more common. In *Biological Exuberance,* Bruce Bagemihl (1999) reports that sexual encounters among male-male and female-female pairs have been observed in more than 450 species— including giraffes, goats, birds, chimpanzees, and lizards.

Among humans, the incidence of homosexual behaviour varies from one generation and culture to the next, depending on prevailing attitudes. In *Same Sex, Different Cultures,* Gilbert Herdt (1998) notes that in part of the world, stretching from Sumatra to Melanesia, it's common for adolescent males to engage in homosexual activities before being of age for marriage—even though homosexuality as a permanent trait is rare. It's important, then, to realize that sexual orientation cannot be viewed in black-or-white terms but along a continuum. In the centre of that continuum, 1 percent of people describe themselves as actively *bi*sexual.

To explain the roots of homosexuality, various theories have been proposed. The Greek philosopher Aristotle believed that it was inborn but strengthened by habit; psychoanalysts argue that it stems from family dynamics, specifically a child's overattachment to a parent of the same or opposite sex; social learning theorists point to rewarding sexual experiences with same-sex peers in childhood. Yet there is little evidence to support these claims. In a particularly comprehensive study, Alan Bell and others (1981) interviewed 1500 homosexual and heterosexual adults about their lives. There were no differences in past family backgrounds, absence of a male or female parent, relationship with parents, sex abuse, age of onset of puberty, or high school dating patterns. Except for the fact that homosexual adults described themselves as less conforming as children, the two groups could not be distinguished by past experiences. Both groups strongly felt that their sexual orientation was set long before it was "official."

Increasingly, there is scientific evidence of a biological disposition. In a highly publicized study, neurobiologist Simon LeVay (1991) autopsied the brains of 19 homosexual men who had died of AIDS, 16 heterosexual men (some of whom had died of AIDS), and six heterosexual women. LeVay examined a tiny nucleus in the hypothalamus known to be involved in regulating sexual behaviour and known to be larger in heterosexual men than in women. The specimens were numerically coded, so LeVay did not know whether the donor he was examining was male or female,

sexual orientation
One's sexual preference for members of the same sex, opposite sex, or both sexes.

straight or gay. The result: In the male homosexual brains he studied, the nucleus was half the size as in male heterosexual brains—and comparable to those found in female heterosexual brains. This research is fully described in LeVay's (1993) book *The Sexual Brain.*

It's important to recognize that this study revealed only a correlation between sexual orientation and the brain, and cannot be used to draw conclusions about cause and effect. More convincing support for the biological roots of sexual orientation comes from twin studies suggesting that there is a genetic predisposition. Michael Bailey and Richard Pillard (1991) surveyed 167 gay men and their twins and adopted brothers. Overall, 52 percent of the identical twins were gay, compared to only 22 percent of fraternal twins and 11 percent of adoptive brothers. Two years later, Bailey and others (1993) conducted a companion study of lesbians with similar results.

The origins of sexual orientation are complex for two reasons. First, it's not clear that sexual orientation for men and women are similarly rooted. In Australia, Bailey and others (2000) had hundreds of pairs of twins rate their own sexuality on a seven-point continuum that ranged from "exclusively heterosexual" to "exclusively homosexual." Overall, 92 percent of both men and women saw themselves as exclusively heterosexual. Among the others, however, more women said that they had bisexual tendencies and more men said they were exclusively homosexual. In another study, a longitudinal investigation of 18- to 25-year-old women, Lisa Diamond (2003) found that more than a quarter of those who had initially identified themselves as lesbian or bisexual changed their orientation over the next five years—far more than is ever reported among men. These findings, and others (e.g., Lippa, 2006), compel the conclusion that women are sexually more flexible than men, having more *erotic plasticity.* Simply put, women are more likely to change sexual preferences over the course of a lifetime (Baumeister, 2000; Diamond, 2008; Peplau, 2003).

A second complicating factor is that although there is evidence for a biological disposition, this does not mean that there's a "gay gene" (Hamer et al., 1999). Daryl Bem (1996, 2000) sees the development of sexual orientation as a *psycho*biological process. According to Bem, genes determine a person's temperament at birth, leading some infants and young children to be naturally more active, energetic, and aggressive than others. These differences in temperament draw some children toward male playmates and "masculine" activities and others toward female playmates and "feminine" activities. Activity preferences in childhood may be biologically rooted, but what happens next is the psychological part. According to Bem, gender-conforming children come to see members of the opposite sex as different, unfamiliar, and arousing, even "exotic." Gender-nonconforming children, in contrast, come to see same-sex peers as different, unfamiliar, arousing, and exotic. Later, at puberty, as children become physically and sexually mature, they find that they are attracted to members of the same or opposite sex—depending on which is the more exotic. Bem describes his proposed chain of events as the "exotic becomes erotic" theory of sexual orientation.

At present, there is only sketchy support for this theory. It is true that genetic makeup can influence temperament and predispose a child to favour certain kinds of activities over others (Kagan, 1994). It is also true that gay men are more likely to have been viewed as "sissies" and that lesbians are more likely to have been seen as "tomboys" as children (Bailey & Zucker, 1995). It may even be true that people are genetically hard-wired to become sissies and tomboys as children (Bailey et al., 2000). But do peer preferences in childhood alter adult sexual orientation, as Bem suggests, because exotic becomes erotic? Or, is there a "gay gene" that fosters gender nonconformity in childhood as well as homosexuality in adolescence and adulthood? And can a single theory explain homosexuality in both men and women, or are separate theories needed, as some have suggested (Peplau et al., 1998)? At present, more research is needed to answer these questions and tease apart the biological and psychological influences. Either way, one point looms large: People do not seem to willfully choose their sexual orientation, nor can they easily change it.

Is there any reason to believe that the attraction process and the formation of intimate relationships are any different for same-sex couples? Not really. Recent research shows that gay men and lesbians meet people in the same ways as straights, by seeking out others who are attractive and similar in their attitudes; that their satisfaction and commitment levels are affected by social exchange and equity concerns just as they are in heterosexual relationships; and that they report levels of liking and loving in their intimate relationships that are comparable to those in heterosexual couples. Same-sex couples differ from straight couples in two ways: They are more likely to retain friendships with former sex partners after breaking up, and they tend to divide chores more equally within a household (Kurdek, 2005; Peplau & Fingerhut, 2007).

The Marital Trajectory Because we are social beings, having close relationships is important to us all—for our happiness and emotional well-being and even for our physical health and longevity. Yet sadly, for students living in Canada or the United States, roughly 40 to 50 percent of first marriages are likely to end in divorce. With just one previously divorced partner, the odds of divorce are even greater. This discrepancy—between the endurance most people want and the disruption they may have to confront—is dramatic. Couples break up, separate, and divorce. How do marriages evolve over time, and why do some last while others dissolve?

Ellen Berscheid and Harry Reis (1998) say that for social psychologists who study intimate relationships, this is the most frequently asked and vexing question. Is there a typical developmental pattern? No and yes. No, it's clear that all marriages are different and cannot be squeezed into a single mould. But yes, certain patterns do emerge when survey results are combined from large numbers of married couples that are studied over long periods of time. Lawrence Kurdek (1999) reported on a longitudinal study of married couples in which he measured each spouse's satisfaction every year for ten years (out of 522 couples he started with, 93 completed the study). Look at ▶ Figure 9.9, and you'll see that there is an overall decline in ratings of marital quality and that the ratings given by husbands and wives were very similar. Look more closely and you'll also see that there are two particularly sharp periods of decline.

▶ FIGURE 9.9

Marital Satisfaction over Time

In a longitudinal study that spanned ten years, married couples rated the quality of their marriages. On average, these ratings were high, but they declined among both husbands and wives. As you can see, there were two steep drops, occurring during the first and eighth years of marriage.

(Kurdek, 1999.)

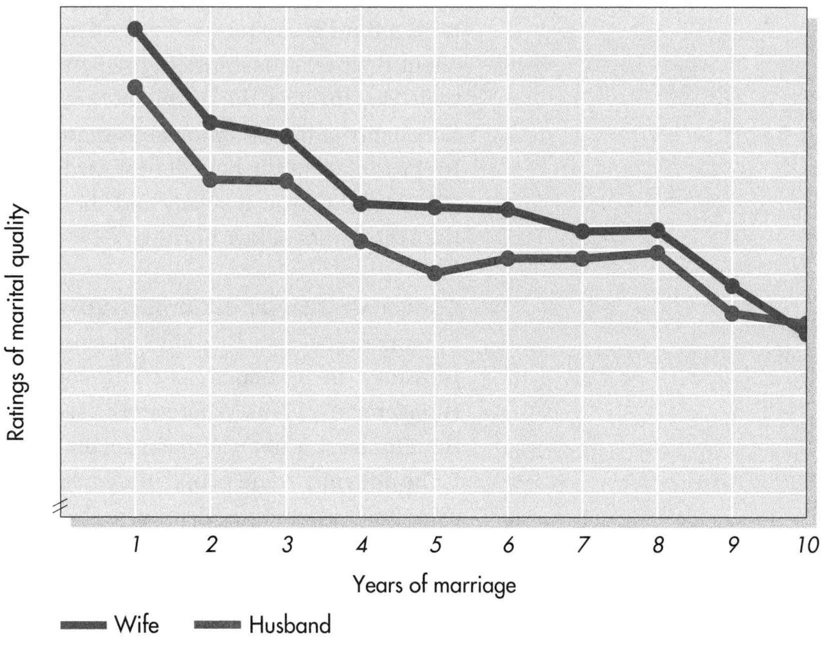

The first occurs during the first year of marriage. Apparently, while newlyweds tend to idealize each other and to enjoy an initial state of marital bliss (Murray et al., 1996), this "honeymoon" is soon followed by a decline in satisfaction (Bradbury, 1998). After some stabilization, a second decline is then observed at about the eighth year of marriage—a finding that is consistent with the popular belief in a "seven-year itch" (Kovacs, 1983). Then again, Nancy Frye and Benjamin Karney (2004) found that marital satisfaction ratings for spouses taken at 6-month intervals from 3 months to 2.5 years after their wedding reflected a global awareness of the state of their relationship (one with ups and downs), yet from a more day-to-day perspective, they viewed their recent past more positively, which in turn helps to keep the relationship moving forward.

Are there specific factors that predict future outcomes? In heterosexual couples that have a first child, the transition to parenthood hastens the sense of decline in both partners (Lawrence et al., 2008); cohabitating gay and lesbian couples do not self-report the lowered satisfaction often seen in heterosexual couples (Kurdek, 2008); and despite the initial dip, marital satisfaction increases again in middle age for parents whose children grow up, leave home, and empty the nest (Gorchoff et al., 2008). Boredom is also predictive of a loss in satisfaction. In a longitudinal study of 123 married couples, husbands and wives who felt like they were in a rut at one point in time were significantly less satisfied nine years later (Tsapelas et al., 2009).

After the honeymoon period, there is an overall decline in levels of marital satisfaction. TRUE.

Is there anything a couple can do to keep the honeymoon alive? Perhaps there is. Arthur Aron and his colleagues (2000) have theorized that after the exhilaration of a new relationship wears off, partners can combat boredom by engaging together in new and arousing activities. By means of questionnaires and a door-to-door survey, these researchers found that the more new experiences spouses said they had together, the more satisfied they were with their marriages. To test this hypothesis in a controlled experiment, they brought randomly selected couples into the laboratory, spread gymnasium mats across the floor, tied the partners together at a wrist and ankle, and had them crawl on their hands and knees, over a barrier, from one end of the room to the other—all while carrying a pillow between their bodies. Other couples were given the more mundane task of rolling a ball across the mat, one partner at a time. A third group received no assignment. Afterward, all participants were surveyed about their relationships. As predicted, the couples that had struggled and laughed their way through the novel and arousing activity reported more satisfaction with the quality of their relationships than did those in the mundane and no-task groups. It's possible that the benefit of shared participation in this study was short-lived. But maybe, just maybe, a steady and changing diet of exciting new experiences can help keep the flames of love burning.

Communication and Conflict Disagreements about sex, children, in-laws, and other matters can stir conflict in close relationships. Research shows that economic pressures, in particular, put an enormous amount of strain on marital relations (Conger et al., 1999). Whatever the cause, all couples experience some degree of friction. The issue is not whether it occurs but how we respond to it. One source of conflict is the difficulty some people have talking about their disagreements. When relationships break up, communication problems are indeed among the most common causes cited by straight and gay couples alike (Kurdek, 1991b; Sprecher, 1994). But what constitutes "bad communication"? Comparisons between happy and distressed couples have revealed a number of communication patterns that often occur in troubled relationships (Fincham, 2003).

One common pattern is called *negative affect reciprocity*—a tit-for-tat exchange of expressions of negative feelings. Generally speaking, expressions of negative affect within a couple trigger more in-kind responses than do expressions of positive affect. But negative affect reciprocity, especially in nonverbal behaviour, is greater in couples that are unhappy, distressed, and locked into a duel. For couples in distress, smiles pass by unnoticed, but every glare, every disgusted look, provokes a sharp reflex-like response. The result, as observed in unhappy couples around the world, is an inability to break the vicious cycle and terminate unpleasant interactions (Gottman, 1998).

Men and women react differently to conflict. Women usually report more intense emotions and are more expressive (Grossman & Wood, 1993). She tells him to "warm up," while he urges her to "calm down." Thus, unhappy marriages also tend to be characterized by a *demand/withdraw interaction pattern,* in which the wife demands to discuss the relationship problems, only to become frustrated when her husband withdraws from such discussions (Christensen & Heavey, 1993). This configuration is not unique to married couples. When dating partners were asked about how they typically deal with problems, the same female-demand/male-withdraw pattern was found (Vogel et al., 1999). Married or not, then, it's clear that couples caught in this bind often find themselves echoing the title of Deborah Tannen's (1990) popular book on gender differences in communication, *You Just Don't Understand.* According to John Gottman (1994), there is nothing wrong with either approach to dealing with conflict. The problem, he says, lies in the discrepancy—that healthy relationships are most likely when both partners have similar styles of dealing with conflict.

Whatever one's style, there are two basic approaches to reducing the negative effects of conflict. The first is so obvious that it is often overlooked: Increase rewarding behaviour in other aspects of the relationship. According to Gottman and Levenson (1992), marital stability rests on a "fairly high balance of positive to negative behaviours" (p. 230). If there is conflict over one issue, partners can and should search for other ways to reward each other. As the balance of positives to negatives improves, so should overall satisfaction, which can reduce conflict (Huston & Vangelisti, 1991). The second approach is to try to understand the other's point of view. Being sensitive to what the partner thinks and how he or she feels enhances the quality of the relationship (Honeycutt et al., 1993; Long & Andrews, 1990). What motivates individuals in the heat of battle to make that effort to understand? For starters, it helps if they agree that there is, in fact, a communication problem.

The attributions that partners make for each other's behaviours and the willingness to forgive are correlated with the quality of their relationship (Bradbury & Fincham, 1992; Fincham et al., 2007; Harvey & Manusov, 2001). As you might expect, happy couples make *relationship-enhancing attributions:* They see the partner's undesirable behaviours as caused by factors that are situational ("a bad day"), temporary ("It'll pass"), and limited in scope ("That's just a sore spot"). Yet they see desirable behaviours as caused by factors that are inherent in the partner, permanent, and generalizable to other aspects of the relationship. In contrast, unhappy couples flip the attributional coin on its tail by making the opposite attributions, called *distress-maintaining attributions.* Thus, while happy couples minimize the bad and maximize the good, distressed couples don't give an inch. In light of these differing attributional patterns, it would seem, over time, that happy couples would get happier and miserable couples more miserable. Do they? Yes. By tracking married couples in multi-year longitudinal studies, researchers have found that husbands and wives who made distress-maintaining causal attributions early in their marriage reported less satisfaction at a later point in time (Fincham et al., 2000; Karney & Bradbury, 2000). The link between causal attributions and marital bliss or distress may be reciprocal, with each influencing the other.

FIGURE 9.10

How Close Is Your Relationship?

The Inclusion of Other in the Self (IOS) Scale is a one-item, pictorial measure of relationship closeness. Choosing a picture with less overlap between the circles indicates less closeness; choosing one with more overlap indicates more closeness.

(Aron et al., 1992.)

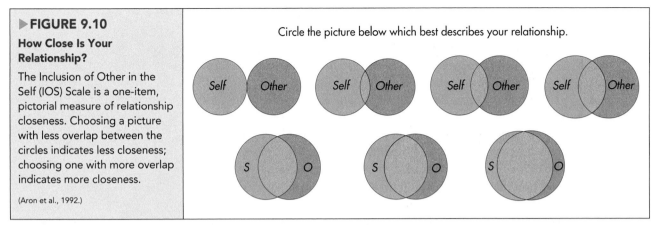

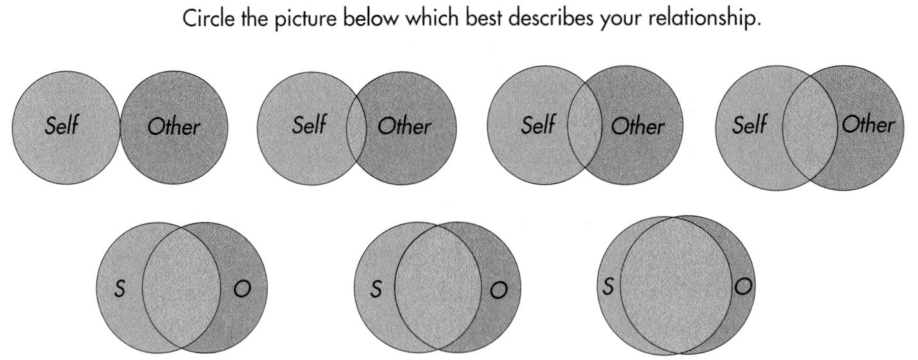

Copyright © [1992] by the American Psychological Association, Reproduced with permission. From A. Aron, E. Aron, and D. Smollan (1992) "Inclusion of the Other in the Self Scale and the Structure of Interpersonal Closeness," *Journal of Personality and Social Psychology, 63, 596-612.* The use of APA information does not imply endorsement by APA.

Breaking Up When an intimate relationship ends, the effect can be traumatic (Fine & Harvey, 2006). How do people cope? The answer is, it depends on the nature of the loss. One vital factor is the closeness of a relationship, or the extent to which the line between self and other becomes so blurred that mine and yours are one and the same. Indeed, Aron and others (1992) found that the longevity of a romantic relationship can be predicted by which diagram in ▶ Figure 9.10 people choose to describe their relationship. The more one incorporates a partner into the self, the more lasting the relationship is likely to be—but the more distress one anticipates if there is a breakup.

Another important factor in this regard is interdependence—the social glue that bonds us together. Research shows that the more interdependent couples are (as measured by the amount of time spent together, the variety of shared activities, and the degree of influence each partner has on the other), and the more invested they are in the relationship, the longer it is likely to last (Berscheid et al., 1989; Rusbult & Buunk, 1993)—and the more devastated they become when it ends (Fine & Sacher, 1997; Simpson, 1987). In trying to explain how people regulate the risks of forming close romantic relationships, Sandra Murray and others (2006) note that an ironic theme runs through much of the research: "The relationships that have the most potential to satisfy adult needs for interpersonal connection are the very relationships that activate the most anxiety about rejection" (p. 661). Those factors that contribute to the endurance of a relationship (closeness and interdependence) turn out to be the same factors that intensify distress and make coping more difficult after a relationship ends. So, how do you balance making the psychological investment necessary for a lasting relationship against holding back enough for self-protection?

In Canada and other western countries, various demographic markers indicate how problematic traditional forms of commitment have become: a high divorce rate, more single-parent families, more unmarried couples living together, and more never-married individuals. Yet the desire for long-term intimate relationships has never wavered or disappeared. To the contrary, people spend millions of dollars on online dating sites, gay men and lesbians seek legal recognition of same-sex marriages, the vast majority of divorced individuals remarry, and stepfamilies forge a new sense of what it means to be a "family." It seems that we are in the midst of a great and compelling search, as millions of men and women try to find ways to affiliate with, attract, get closer to, love, and commit themselves with permanence to others.

REVIEW

Being with Others: A Fundamental Human Motive

- The need to belong is a basic human motive, a pervasive drive to form and maintain lasting relationships.
- Stressful situations in particular motivate us to affiliate with others who face a similar threat.

The Thrill of Affiliation

- This social motivation begins with the need for affiliation, a desire to establish social contact with others.
- People differ in the strength of their affiliative needs.

The Agony of Loneliness

- Shyness is a pervasive problem that sets people up to have unrewarding interactions with others.
- People who are painfully shy are at risk for loneliness, a feeling of isolation, and social deprivation.

The Initial Attraction

- According to one perspective, people are attracted to others with whom the relationship is rewarding; rewards can be direct or indirect.
- Evolutionary psychologists argue that human beings exhibit patterns of attraction and mate selection that favour the passing on of their own genes.

Familiarity: Being There

- Proximity sets the stage for social interaction, which is why friendships are most likely to form between people who live near each other.
- Supporting the mere exposure effect, studies show that the more often people see a stimulus, the more they come to like it.
- We do not have to be aware of our prior exposures for the increase in liking to occur.

Physical Attractiveness: Getting Drawn In

- In a wide range of social settings, people respond more favourably to men and women who are physically attractive.
- Some researchers believe that certain faces (averaged and symmetrical) are inherently attractive—across cultures and to infants as well as adults.
- Others argue that beauty is in the eye of the beholder and point to the influences of culture, time, and context.
- One reason for the bias toward beauty is that it's rewarding to be in the company of others who are attractive.
- A second reason is that people associate beauty with other positive qualities, a belief known as the what-is-beautiful-is-good stereotype.
- People seen as physically attractive are more popular, more sexually experienced, and more socially skilled; however, they are not happier or higher in self-esteem.
- One reason physically attractive people are not happier is that they often discount the praise they get for non-social endeavours.
- Another problem with having beauty as a social asset is that people, notably women, feel pressured to keep up their appearance and are often dissatisfied with how they look.

First Encounters: Getting Acquainted

- People tend to associate with, befriend, and marry others who are similar in their demographic backgrounds, attitudes, and interests.
- People first avoid others who are dissimilar and then are drawn to those in the remaining group who are most similar to themselves.
- Supporting the matching hypothesis, people tend to become romantically involved with others who are equivalent in physical attractiveness.
- Contrary to popular belief, complementarity in needs or personality does not spark attraction.
- Illustrating the effects of reciprocity, we tend to like others who indicate that they like us.
- But people who are indiscriminate about who they like can be taken for granted and not liked as much by others.
- Research on the hard-to-get-effect shows that people like others best who are moderately selective in their social choices.

Mate Selection: The Evolution of Desire

- Evolutionary psychologists say that women seek men with financial security or traits predictive of future success in order to ensure the survival of their offspring.
- In contrast, men seek women who are young and attractive (physical attributes that signal health and fertility)—and not promiscuous (an attribute that diminishes certainty of paternity).
- Cross-cultural studies tend to support these predicted sex differences, but critics note that many results are not that strong and can be viewed in terms that are more psychological than evolutionary.

Close Relationships

- Intimate relationships include at least one of three components: feelings of attachment, fulfillment of psychological needs, and interdependence.
- Stage theories propose that close relationships go through specific stages, but evidence for a fixed sequence is weak.
- Two other views emphasize either a gradual accumulation of rewards or a sharp distinction between types of relationships.

The Intimate Marketplace: Tracking the Gains and Losses

- According to social exchange theory, people seek to maximize gains and minimize costs in their relationships.
- Higher rewards, lower costs, and an outcome that meets or exceeds a partner's comparison level (CL) predict high levels of satisfaction.
- Lower expectations about alternatives (CLalt) and more investment in the relationship are associated with higher levels of commitment.
- Equity theory holds that satisfaction is greatest when the ratio between benefits and contributions is similar for both partners.
- Both overbenefit and underbenefit elicit negative emotions, but the underbenefited are usually less satisfied.

Types of Relationships

- In exchange relationships, people are oriented toward reward and immediate reciprocity; in communal relationships, partners are responsive to each other's needs.
- People with secure attachment styles have more satisfying romantic relationships than do those with insecure (anxious or avoidant) styles.

How Do I Love Thee? Counting the Ways

- According to the triangular theory of love, there are eight subtypes of love produced by the combinations of intimacy, passion, and commitment.
- Inherent in all classifications of love are two types: passionate and companionate.
- Passionate love is an intense, emotional, often erotic state of positive absorption in another person.
- In one theory, passionate love is sparked by physiological arousal and the belief that the arousal was caused by the loved person.
- Consistent with excitation transfer, arousal can increase or decrease attraction, depending on the initial attractiveness of the person whom one is with.
- Compared with passionate love, companionate love is less intense but in some respects deeper and more enduring.
- Companionate love rests on mutual trust, caring, friendship, commitment, and willingness to share intimate facts and feelings.
- Self-disclosure between partners often becomes broader and deeper over time, though self-disclosure varies with the state of the relationship.

Culture, Attraction, and Relationships

- Although Buss identified universal gender differences in mate preference, he also found some striking cultural differences, for example, in differing preferences for chastity.
- The universality of passionate love has led some researchers to explore the neuroscientific bases for this experience.
- Cultures differ in the extent to which romantic love is seen as necessary for marriage.

Relationship Issues: The Male-Female "Connection"

- People vary in how they define what it means to "have sex."
- On average, men report being more sexually active than women and see opposite-sex interactions in more sexualized terms.
- An estimated 3 or 4 percent of men and 2 percent of women are exclusively homosexual in orientation.
- Both biological and environmental theories are used to explain the origins of homosexuality.
- When relationships break up, communication problems are among the most common causes.
- Unhappy couples engage often in negative affect reciprocity and exhibit a demand/withdraw interaction pattern.
- During conflict, women are more likely to be demanding; men are more likely to withdraw.
- Partners can reduce conflict by behaving in rewarding ways in other areas and by trying to understand each other's point of view.
- Happy couples make relationship-enhancing attributions, while unhappy couples make distress-maintaining attributions.
- On average, marital satisfaction starts high, declines during the first year, stabilizes, and then declines again at about the eighth year.
- Partners who are close and interdependent and for whom relationships are important to the self-concept (characteristics that normally promote stability) suffer more after breaking up.

Key Terms

attachment style (339)
communal relationship (339)
companionate love (342)
equity theory (337)
exchange relationship (339)
excitation transfer (342)
hard-to-get effect (329)
intimate relationship (335)
loneliness (317)
matching hypothesis (328)
mere exposure effect (319)
need for affiliation (314)
passionate love (342)
reciprocity (328)
self-disclosure (344)
sexual orientation (349)
social exchange theory (336)
triangular theory of love (341)
what-is-beautiful-is-good stereotype (323)

Putting COMMON SENSE *to the Test*

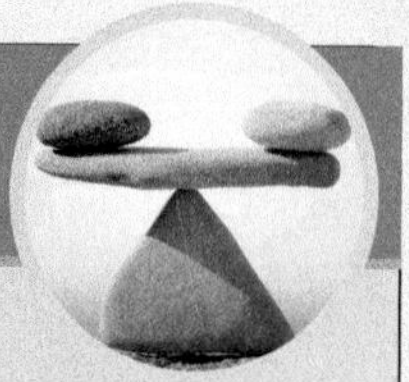

People seek out the company of others, even strangers, in times of stress.

True. *Research has shown that external threat causes stress and leads people to affiliate with others who are facing or have faced a similar threat.*

Infants do not discriminate between faces considered attractive and unattractive in their culture.

False. *Two-month-old infants spend more time gazing at attractive than unattractive faces, indicating that they do make the distinction.*

People who are physically attractive are happier and have higher self-esteem than those who are unattractive.

False. *Attractive people are at an advantage in their social lives, but they are not happier, better adjusted, or higher in self-esteem.*

When it comes to romantic relationships, opposites attract.

False. *Consistently, people are attracted to others who are similar—not opposite or complementary—on a whole range of dimensions.*

Men are more likely than women to interpret friendly gestures by the opposite sex in sexual terms.

True. *Experiments have shown that men are more likely than women to interpret friendly opposite-sex interactions as sexual come-ons.*

After the honeymoon period, there is an overall decline in levels of marital satisfaction.

True. *High marital satisfaction levels among newlyweds are often followed by a measurable decline during the first year and then, after a period of stabilization, by another decline at about the eighth year—a pattern found among parents and non-parents alike.*

10

Kevin Dodge/Corbis

Helping Others

Putting
COMMON SENSE
to the Test

Circle Your Answer

T F People are more likely to help someone in an emergency if the potential rewards seem high and the potential costs seem low.

T F In an emergency, a person who needs help has a much better chance of getting it if three other people are present than if only one other person is present.

T F People are much more likely to help someone when they're in a good mood.

T F People are much less likely to help someone when they're in a bad mood.

T F Attractive people have a better chance than unattractive people of getting help when they need it.

T F In any situation, people are more likely to help a friend succeed than a stranger.

T F Women seek help more often than men do.

This chapter describes the social psychology of giving and receiving help. First, we examine the evolutionary, motivational, situational, personal, and interpersonal factors that predict whether a potential helper will provide assistance to a person in need. Then, we consider people's reactions to receiving help. In the concluding section, we discuss the helping connection, the role of social ties in promoting helpfulness to others.

It was their bravery that compelled them to risk their lives, but it was their compassion that ultimately saved them. Six firefighters from New York City's Ladder Company Six were among the numerous firefighters, police officers, and other rescue workers who courageously climbed up the stairs of the World Trade Center on September 11, 2001. The jets that had flown into each of the Twin Towers of the skyscraper were hemorrhaging fuel, causing an inferno of unprecedented proportion. A massive stream of people trying to flee raced down the narrow stairs, passing the firefighters who were going up. Awed by their courage and resolve, people yelled encouragement and blessings to the firefighters as they passed them. Under the burden of more than 100 pounds of equipment, the men of Company Six reached the twenty-seventh floor of the North Tower when they heard the horrifying sound of the South Tower collapsing. Their captain ordered them to turn back, realizing that if the other tower could collapse, so could theirs.

On their way down, around the fourteenth or fifteenth floor, they encountered a frail woman named Josephine Harris. She had walked down almost 60 flights already, and she was exhausted. The firefighters helped her walk, but she was slowing them down dangerously. Their captain, John Jonas, was growing more anxious: "I could hear the clock ticking in the back of my head. I'm thinking, 'C'mon, c'mon. We've got to keep moving.'" But none of the six men considered leaving her—or any of the rest of the group—behind, so they slowly walked down together. Josephine didn't think she could go on, but one of the firefighters asked her about her family and told her that her children and grandchildren wanted to see her again. She continued, but finally collapsed as they got near the fourth floor. On the fourth floor, they tried to find a chair to carry her in. And then, the 110-story skyscraper collapsed.

Other rescue workers who had passed this slow-moving group on the stairs were killed on the floors below them. Virtually everyone who was still above them was killed. And yet somehow this group survived, trapped in an inexplicable pocket of safety amidst the unimaginable wreckage, along with two other firefighters, a Fire Department chief, and a Port Authority police officer. After a harrowing search for a

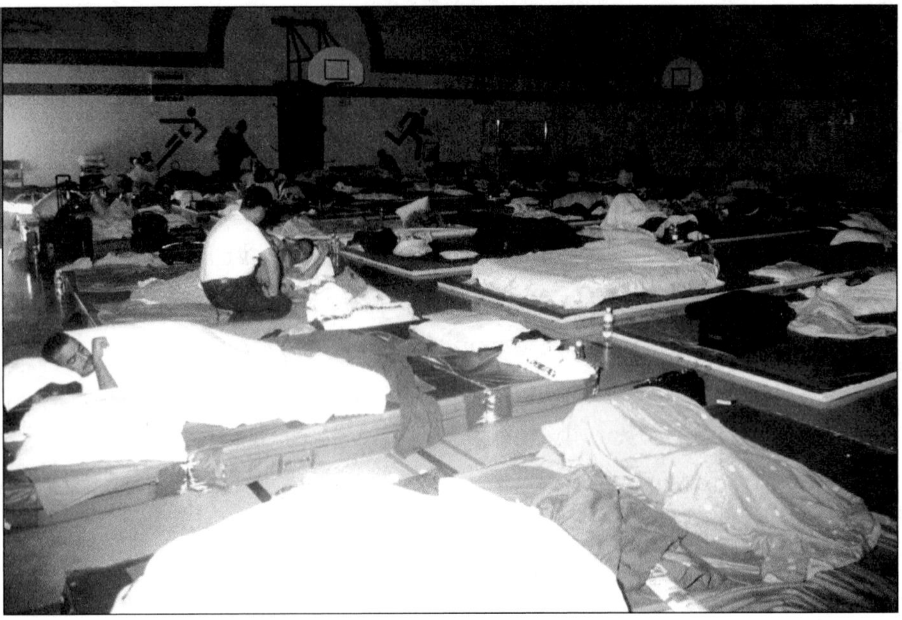

CP/Scott Cook

When all North American aircraft were grounded in the aftermath of the terrorist attacks in New York on September 11, 2001, Gander, Newfoundland, opened their schools, churches, and hearts to those that were stranded.

way out, eventually they found a small ray of light—a literal ray of hope—and followed it to safety.

The firefighters later called Josephine Harris their guardian angel and thanked *her* for saving *their* lives. They realized that had they not encountered her, they would have gone down the stairs faster, and had she not kept walking despite exhaustion, they would have been a few floors above—either way, they would have been killed. But Josephine Harris knew that she owed her life to these brave men, who risked seeing their own children again so that she could see hers.

There were many other heroes that day, including ordinary citizens whose acts of self-sacrifice to help others were not part of their job descriptions. Much of the help was behind the scenes, as in the cases of people volunteering endless hours doing the gruelling work of cleaning up the disaster area, helping the injured and the grieving, and donating money, clothes, and other resources. When American airspace was closed in response to the terrorist attacks, 240 flights were rerouted to Canada. Thirty-eight of those planes landed in Gander, Newfoundland, which has a population of approximately 10 000 people. According to passenger reports, the people of Gander could not have been more helpful. Consider this letter written to the *Cleveland Plain Dealer* thanking the people of Gander for their assistance:

> Everyone was extraordinarily thoughtful of each other. One woman must have put her life on hold and was constantly checking on us. She even came to the airport when we finally left to make sure we all were fine. I never saw her without a smile. The lady who ran the cafeteria along with many neighbours made hot meals and brought in casseroles each day. Students helped us to use e-mail, and we were able to use the phone to call our family. No organization with financial backing was behind this—this was a call to neighbours and friends to come and help those of us in need. We will never be able to think of Gander, Newfoundland, without remembering all the goodness and kindness that was showered upon us by our neighbours and friends from Canada. (Sweet, 2001, p. B6)*

When people read stories such as these, it is natural for them to wonder what they would have done. What makes some people, at some times, act to help others? The wonderful acts of helping during the chaos of 9/11 are inspiring, to be sure. But there were also many stories that day of people who turned their backs on others, even on people who had just helped them.

* Sweet, P. R. (October 1, 2001). "Surely Canada Is Our Best Friend, Closest Ally." *The Cleveland Plain Dealer*, p. B6

Every day there are numerous unheralded acts of helping others and of failing to help others. A volunteer works tirelessly in an AIDS clinic, a university student tutors a child, a congregation raises money for a religious cause, an older sister lets her little brother win at checkers. And yet every day someone ignores the screams outside his or her window, drives past motorists stranded on the side of a road, or tries to avoid making eye contact with a homeless person on the street.

Every few months we see a story like the one about Deborah Chiborak and Gerard Beernaerts from Manitoba. In April 2007 they found an elderly woman trapped on the railway tracks beneath her motorized scooter. They managed to lift it off her and pull her to safety seconds before the train came. While the victim escaped unscathed, Ms. Chiborak suffered back injuries. And all too often we also learn of a story like that of the unidentified 66-year-old woman who froze to death in Toronto in January 2011. She suffered from dementia and wandered away from her home in the middle of a bitterly cold night. She was found early the next morning in a driveway near her house by a newspaper delivery person, but by then it was too late. As reported in the *Toronto Star* on Monday, January 17, 2011, at least two neighbours heard her cries for help, and another saw her in distress. No one came to her assistance, or called 911.

There is no simple answer to the question of why some help and others don't, or why some situations lead to quick assistance and others to shocking displays of inaction. The determinants of helping behaviour are complex and multi-faceted. But social psychologists have learned a great deal about these determinants—and therefore about human nature. As you will see in the pages to come, some of their findings are quite surprising.

In this chapter, we examine several questions about helping: *Why* do people help? *When* do they help? *Who* is likely to help? *Whom* do they help? The concluding section concentrates on a major, recurring theme—social connection—that underlies much of the theory and research on helping.

Evolutionary and Motivational Factors: Why Do People Help?

Although few individuals reach the heights of heroic helping, virtually everyone helps somebody sometime. People give their friends a ride to the airport; donate money, food, and clothing for disaster relief; babysit for a relative; work as a volunteer for a charitable organization; pick up the mail for a neighbour who's out of town. The list of **prosocial behaviours**—actions intended to benefit others—is endless. But *why* do people help? Several factors have an impact.

In a survey conducted by Statistics Canada in 2010 asking about charitable activities in the previous 12 months, 47.6 percent of the population over the age of 15 indicated they had volunteered their time with their contributions totalling almost 2.1 billion hours, and 84 percent had made a charitable donation.

(Canada Survey of Giving, Volunteering and Participating, 2010).

Evolutionary Factors in Helping

We begin with evolution. Evolutionary scientists use principles of evolution to understand human social behaviour. Can evolutionary principles help explain why people help? At first glance, some may think it unlikely. From an evolutionary perspective, what possible function can there be in helping others, especially at the risk of one's own life? Doesn't risking one's life for others fly in the face of evolutionary principles like "survival of the fittest"?

The "Selfish Gene" In fact, evolutionary perspectives emphasize not the survival of the fittest individuals but the survival of the individuals' genes (Dawkins, 1989; Hamilton, 1964). From the perspective of evolution, human social behaviour should

prosocial behaviours
Actions intended to benefit others.

© Kennan Ward/CORBIS

Ellen Senisi/The Image Works, Inc.

Many animals groom each other, whether they are chimpanzees in Tanzania or schoolgirls in North America. According to evolutionary psychologists, such behaviour often reflects reciprocal altruism.

be analyzed in terms of its contribution to reproductive success in ancestral environments: the conception, birth, and survival of offspring over the course of many generations. If a specific social behaviour enhances reproductive success, the genetic underpinnings of that behaviour are more likely to be passed on to subsequent generations. In this way, the behaviour can eventually become part of the common inheritance of the species.

Of course, in order to reproduce, the individual must survive long enough to do so. Being helped *by* others should increase the chances of survival. But what about being helpful *to* others? Since helping others can be costly in terms of time and effort, and is sometimes dangerous to the helper, being helpful would seem to decrease one's chances of survival. Shouldn't any genetically based propensities for helping have dropped out of the gene pool long ago?

Not necessarily. There is another way to ensure that your genes survive, such as by promoting the survival of those who share your genetic makeup, even if you perish in the effort to help them. By means of this indirect route to genetic survival, the tendency to help genetic relatives, called **kin selection**, could become an innate characteristic—that is, a characteristic that is not dependent on learning for its development, although it can be influenced by learning, culture, and other factors. Kin selection is evident in the behaviour of many organisms. Just as humans often risk their lives to save close relatives, ground squirrels, capuchin monkeys, and many other mammals and birds emit an alarm to warn nearby relatives of a predator. The alarm helps their relatives but makes the individual who sounds the alarm more vulnerable to attack (Kokolakis et al., 2010; Schel et al., 2009; Silk & House, 2011; Wheeler, 2008). Similarly, lemurs sometimes rush to the aid of a fellow lemur held by a snake, putting themselves at risk as they mob the snake to save the lemur (Eberle & Kappeler, 2008).

kin selection
Preferential helping of genetic relatives, so that genes held in common will survive.

Because kinship selection serves the function of genetic survival, preferential helping of genetic relatives should be strongest when the biological stakes are particularly high. This appears to be the case. Steve Stewart-Williams (2007) asked undergraduate psychology students at McMaster University to first think about a cousin, acquaintance, close friend, or sibling in their social network. Research participants were then asked to think of a time in the previous two months when they had offered this person emotional support (low-cost condition), had provided a more involved level of help (e.g., helping during an illness: medium cost condition), or, in the high-cost condition, whether they would, hypothetically, be willing to donate a kidney or risk their own death or injury to help this person. As expected, they found that more helping occurred among those more closely related. (See ▶ Figure 10.1) There was one exception to this: friends received as much help as did more closely related kin. However, when they factored in the cost of the helping, a clearer pattern emerged. If the cost of helping was low, friends received the most help, whereas if the cost of helping was high, siblings were much more likely to be the beneficiaries.

Participants in a series of studies by Elaine Madsen and others (2007) did more than speculate about what they thought they would do in different hypothetical scenarios—these participants actually suffered in order to help others. The research participants were asked to hold a difficult position with their legs (from an isometric ski-training exercise). The longer they could hold the position, the more money would be earned for another person. However, the position became more and more painful to hold over time. Consistent with predictions based on kin selection, participants withstood the pain and held the position longer if they were doing so for a genetically close relative than for a more distant relative, a friend, or a charity. This effect was found among British students as well as among participants from Zulu populations in South Africa.

▶ FIGURE 10.1

Helping Kin When Risks Are High

Participants indicated how willing they would be to offer different types of help to a cousin, acquaintance, close friend, or sibling. The help was either low risk, medium risk, or high risk. For the lowest-risk help, friends received the most help. For higher-risk helping, in contrast, participants were more willing to help a sibling than a friend.

(Based on Stewart-Williams, 2007.)

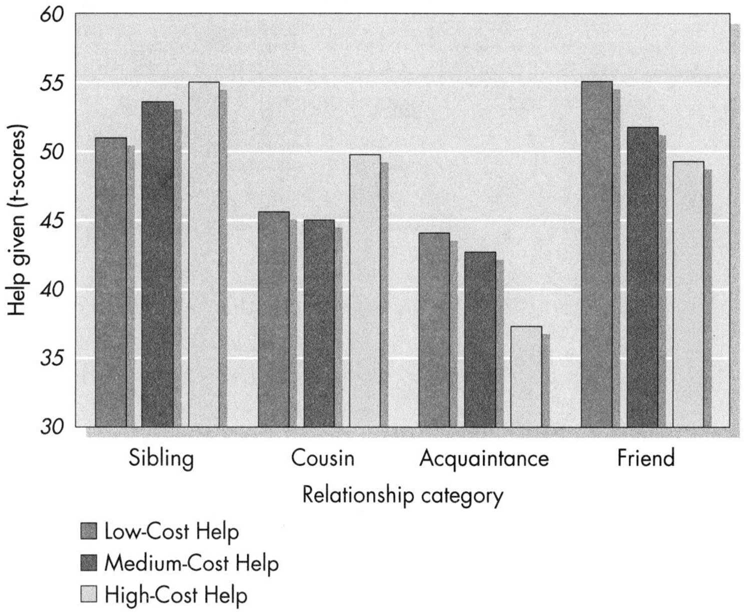

Reciprocal Altruism Kin selection provides only a partial explanation for helping. Relatives are not always helpful to each other. And even though relatives may get preferential treatment, most people help out non-kin as well. What's the reproductive advantage of helping someone who isn't related to you? The most common answer is reciprocity. Through *reciprocal altruism,* helping someone else can be in your best interests because it increases the likelihood that you will be helped in return (Krebs, 1987; Trivers, 1985). If Chris helps Sandy and Sandy helps Chris, both Chris and Sandy increase their chances of survival and reproductive success. Over the course of evolution, therefore, individuals who engage in reciprocal altruism should survive and reproduce more than individuals who do not, thus enabling this kind of altruism to flourish.

"Scratch my back and I'll scratch yours."

—Proverb

Robert Trivers (1971) cites several examples of reciprocal altruism in animals. Many animals groom each other; for instance, monkeys groom other monkeys and cats groom other cats. Large fish (such as groupers) allow small fish (such as wrasses) to swim in their mouths without eating them; the small fish get food for themselves and at the same time remove parasites from the larger fish. And chimps who share with other chimps at one feeding are repaid by the other chimps at another feeding; those who are selfish are rebuffed, sometimes violently, at a later feeding (de Waal, 1996, 2006). An additional illustration is provided by Robert Seyfarth and Dorothy Cheney (1984). In a creative field experiment, these researchers audiotaped female vervet monkeys calling out for help and then played the recorded vocalizations near other female

Jeff Irwin/Photo Researchers

Among the Amish, cooperation within the group is an essential feature of their way of life. Some evolutionary theorists believe that helping other members of one's social group is an innate tendency among all human beings.

monkeys. Half of these other monkeys heard a female who had recently groomed them; the other half heard a female who had not recently done so. Consistent with the idea of reciprocal altruism, they were significantly more likely to respond attentively to the request for help if the solicitor had just groomed them than if she had not. Interestingly, if the solicitor was genetically related to the monkeys who heard the tape, the monkeys' response was equally strong whether or not she had groomed them.

Learning to cooperate, therefore, can be rewarding for both parties. This is illustrated in a clever study by Frans de Waal and Michelle Berger (2000) where they observed same-sex pairs of capuchin monkeys working cooperatively in a test chamber to obtain a tray of food. The two monkeys were separated from each other by a mesh partition. One monkey by itself could not pull the tray, but the two monkeys could accomplish the task cooperatively. When successful, the monkey that wound up with the food consistently shared it with its helper. When rewarded in this way, the monkeys became even more likely to help each other on subsequent occasions.

In some human environments, reciprocal altruism is essential for survival even today. Consider, for example, the Northern Ache, who are indigenous peoples of northeastern Paraguay. Wesley Allen-Arave and others (2008) studied a group of Northern Ache who lived in households on a reservation and shared virtually all their food across households. The researchers found that households shared more food with other households that reciprocated in kind. Even among kin, sharing food was contingent on it being reciprocated. In other words, households shared more food with kin who were most likely to share with them.

Reciprocal altruism is not restricted to basic needs such as food acquisition. The passengers of one of those flights diverted to Gander after the 9/11 attacks were so grateful for the kindness and assistance they received that they created a scholarship for Gander students; it is now worth more than $1.5 million and has helped put more than 130 students through school. Consider another more common example—swapping music and videos online through file-sharing services. This may also be considered a form of reciprocal altruism, since an individual makes his or her own files available to others so that he or she can have access to theirs. (Of course, the record labels and movie studios have other terms for these activities, such as *criminal* and *unethical*.) Strong norms often develop in these peer-to-peer networks. An individual who downloads songs or videos from others' computers but doesn't make his or her own files available is likely to be chastised quickly and emphatically. Indeed, the development of norms and the punishment of individuals who deviate from the norm are key factors in maintaining reciprocal altruism, especially in groups of non-kin. Individuals may actively punish violators of the norm of reciprocity, despite the potential cost to themselves in doing so (Nelissen, 2008; Rilling et al., 2008; Singer et al., 2006).

The Altruistic Group Kin selection and reciprocal altruism emphasize helping specific others based on genetic relatedness or the probability of being helped in return. But much helping goes beyond these limits. For example, injured or sick animals are often aided by others in their group, even if they are unrelated and there is little chance that the recipients will return the favour (de Waal, 1996, 2008). Can altruism operate at a broader level than specific genes or specific reciprocal relationships between individuals?

According to Elliott Sober and David Wilson (1998; Wilson & Sober, 1994), group selection may play a role in accounting for the evolution of human psychology: groups with altruistic members may be more likely to thrive and avoid extinction than groups with only selfish individuals (O'Gorman et al., 2008; Wilson et al., 2008). Thus, cooperation and helpfulness for the good of the group (especially when the group faces an external threat) could be an innate, universal tendency (Wilson & Wilson, 2010). Franz de Waal (1996) reports remarkable instances of within-group helping among animals—for example, a Japanese monkey born without hands and feet who was fully accepted and helped by the other monkeys in its group. Some evolutionary scientists are skeptical of the concept of group selection, however, and it remains to be seen how this idea itself will evolve in the years to come (Brewer & Caporael, 2006; Price, 2008).

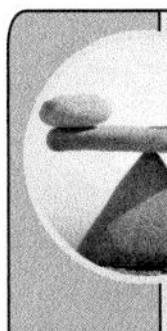

People are more likely to help someone in an emergency if the potential rewards seem high and the potential costs seem low. TRUE.

Rewards of Helping: Helping Others to Help Oneself

Whether or not it can be traced to evolutionary factors, one important reason why people help others is because it often is rewarding, even if the rewards are psychological rather than material. We all like the idea of being the hero, lifted onto the shoulders of our peers for coming to the rescue of someone in distress. Helping helps the helper.

The empirical evidence on this point is clear: People are much more likely to help when the potential rewards of helping seem high relative to the potential costs (Dovidio, 1984; Fritzsche et al., 2000; Piliavin et al., 1975; Shotland & Stebbins, 1983). This effect does not appear to be limited to the very individualistic cultures of Canada, the United States, and Western Europe; evidence has also been found in Sudan and in Japan, for example (Hedge & Yousif, 1992; Imai, 1991). Potential helpers around the world often seem to conduct a cost-benefit analysis not only when making deliberate decisions to behave prosocially, as when donating blood, but also in more impulsive, sudden decisions to intervene in an emergency.

Indeed, the **arousal: cost-reward model** of helping stipulates that both emotional and cognitive factors determine whether bystanders to an emergency will intervene (Dovidio et al., 2006). Emotionally, bystanders experience the shock and alarm of personal distress; this unpleasant state of arousal motivates them to do something to reduce it. What they do, however, depends on the "bystander calculus," their computation of the costs and rewards associated with helping. When potential rewards (to self and victim) outweigh potential costs (to self and victim), bystanders will help. But raise those costs and lower those rewards, and victims stand a good chance of having to do without (Fritzsche et al., 2000; Piliavin et al., 1981).

Feeling Good Helping often simply feels good. A growing body of research reveals a strong relationship between giving help and feeling better, including on measures of mental *and* physical health (Glomb et al., 2011; Omoto et al., 2009; Piliavin, 2003; Post, 2005). For example, a longitudinal study by Jane Piliavin and Erica Siegl (2007) found that doing volunteer work was associated with improvements in psychological well-being, and that volunteering for multiple organizations was associated with greater improvement. In a large-scale study of teenagers, Carolyn Schwartz and others (2009) found higher levels of well-being in teenage boys who regularly helped others in their family (e.g., by doing yardwork, or assisting with child care), and teenage girls who engaged in

arousal: cost-reward model The proposition that people react to emergency situations by acting in the most cost-effective way to reduce the arousal of shock and alarm.

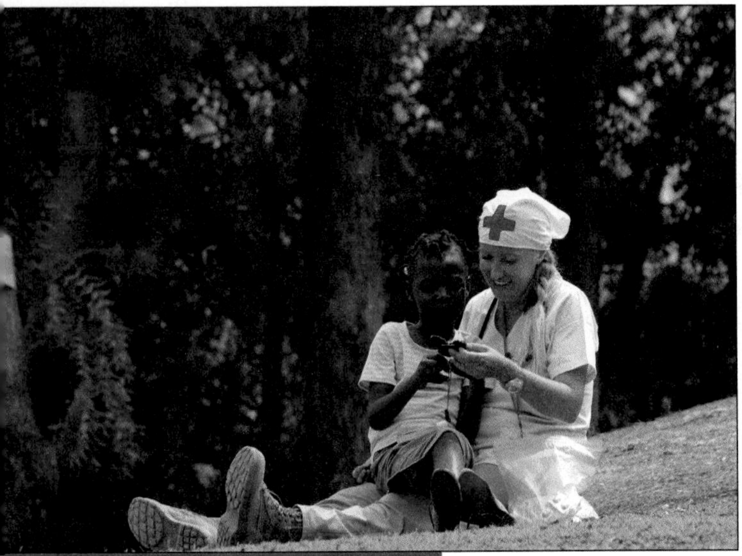

AP Photo/Andres Leighton

Volunteering one's time, energy, and skills to help others can make one feel good about oneself. Even if not financial, the rewards can be tremendous. Here, a volunteer doctor gives a gift to a Haitian girl at a camp for earthquake survivors in Port-au-Prince.

more generally helpful behaviours (e.g., giving directions to a stranger, helping a classmate with homework).

In a provocative set of studies using brain-imaging techniques, James Rilling and others (2002) examined the brain activity of women playing a Prisoner's Dilemma game, which, as was discussed in Chapter 8, is a game in which individuals compete or cooperate with each other for individual and joint payoffs. The researchers found that when the women were engaged in mutual cooperation during the game, activation was observed in areas of the brain that are linked to processing rewards. Despite the fact that these individuals could earn more money by competing with their partner after their partner had cooperated, their brain activity suggested that cooperation was intrinsically rewarding, and this feeling could reinforce altruism and inhibit selfishness. In a more recent study, researchers found that cooperation between men in the same Prisoner's Dilemma game could be increased by administering a dose of oxytocin—a hormone associated with, among other things, positive social interaction. The oxytocin helped the male participants learn to cooperate by understanding that the other person could be trusted to reciprocate (Rilling et al., 2012).

Even when helping doesn't feel good immediately, it can pay off in the long run. When parents reluctantly sacrifice relaxing with a good book or DVD at the end of a hard day to help their child finish some homework, they might not feel immediate joy from giving help; but in the long run, they will reap the benefits of their behaviour (Salovey et al., 1991). Children learn that helping others can be rewarding (Grusec, 1991). Younger children focus on the rewards they get from parents and others; but as they develop into adolescence, they begin to reward themselves for helping, taking pride in their actions. Their helpful behaviour can then be internally motivated, leading them to help even without the promise of immediate material or social rewards (Cialdini et al., 1981; Piliavin & Callero, 1991).

The process of helping others in order to feel good about oneself is often not conscious, but it can be. For example, participants in one study rated the relative importance of a number of considerations in deciding whether to help someone else. Two of the three considerations that the participants rated as most important concerned the rewards ("It would make me feel good about myself") and costs ("I might get hurt") of helping. The other consideration was "It's the right thing to do" (Smitherman, 1992). People's awareness that helping feels good is evident in the words offered by no less an authority than the venerable "Dear Abby," the world's most famous syndicated advice columnist. She offered this advice to her readers: "The surest way to forget your own troubles is to do something nice for those less fortunate. The adrenaline rush you'll get is more powerful than speed, and the 'high' is perfectly legal" ("Dear Abby," 2003).

In their **negative state relief model**, Robert Cialdini and his colleagues (1987) propose that because of this positive effect of helping, people who are feeling bad may be inclined to help others in order to improve their mood. Indeed, after experiencing a traumatic event, some individuals seek out opportunities to help others in order to feel better about themselves instead of becoming bitter and antisocial (Staub & Vollhardt, 2008; Vollhardt, 2009). Helping others may help one heal oneself.

negative state relief model The proposition that people help others in order to counteract their own feelings of sadness.

Being Good In addition to wanting to *feel* good, many of us are also motivated to *be* good. We want to help because we recognize that "It's the right thing to do."

Some situations are especially likely to call to mind norms that compel helpful behaviours. These may be everyday situations, as when encountering an elderly person in a parking lot who needs help getting grocery bags in her car. Sometimes norms can compel much more dramatic and risky action, particularly for individuals whose roles in a group or society give them responsibility in a situation. When the firefighters in Ladder Company six (described in the introduction of this chapter) risked their lives to stay with Josephine Harris, their actions were consistent with the idea of not leaving anyone behind who could be saved. Acts of helping like these may be triggered by norms and moral principles, but of course they can also serve to make the helpers feel good about themselves. Being good can feel good, and the heroic helper may be rewarded in multiple ways.

The Costs of Helping, or of Not Helping Clearly, helping has its rewards; but it has its costs as well. The firefighters in Ladder Company Six who risked their lives to help Josephine Harris were among the lucky ones. Not everyone is so lucky; in April 2011, 28-year-old Kearn Nedd was shot and killed when he tried to intervene during an armed robbery attempt at a charity poker game in Brampton, Ontario.

Other helpers have done more sustained and deliberate helping, such as the people who helped guide runaway slaves in the nineteenth-century American South through the underground railroad to places such as Canada or Mexico where they could live as free citizens, or the people who helped hide Jews during the Holocaust. Sharon Shepela and others (1999) call this type of thoughtful helping in the face of potentially enormous costs *courageous resistance.* And although giving help is often associated with positive affect and health, when the help involves constant and exhausting demands, which is often the case when taking long-term care of a very ill person, the effects on the helper's physical and mental health can be quite negative (Chow et al., 2011; Fujino & Okamura, 2009).

To lower some of the costs of helping, several provinces have created "Good Samaritan" laws that encourage people to provide or summon aid in an emergency—so long as they do not endanger themselves in the process. A component of such a law is that the would-be helper cannot be sued for coming to the aid of a victim should something not go according to plan. Other kinds of Good Samaritan laws increase the costs of failing to help. For example, Quebec has a "duty to rescue" law, which requires people to provide or summon aid in an emergency, as long as they do not endanger themselves in the process.

Altruism or Egoism: The Great Debate

At the end of 1996, *People* magazine honoured Binti Jua as one of the 25 "most intriguing people" of the year; and *Newsweek* named her "hero of the year." On August 16, while caring for her own 17-month-old daughter, Binti came across a three-year-old boy who had fallen about 6 metres onto a cement floor and been knocked unconscious. She picked up the boy and gently held him, rocking him softly, and then turned him over to paramedics. The "intriguing" thing about Binti is that she is a gorilla.

When the boy climbed over a fence and fell into the primate exhibit at the Brookfield Zoo, near Chicago, witnesses feared the worst. One paramedic said, "I didn't know if she was going to treat him like a doll or a toy." With her own daughter clinging to her back the entire time, Binti "protected the toddler as if he were her own," keeping other gorillas at bay and eventually placing him gently at the entrance where zookeepers and paramedics could get to him. "I could not believe how gentle she was," observed a zoo director (O'Neill et al., 1996, p. 72).

Associated Press

Binti Jua, a gorilla in the Brookfield Zoo, near Chicago, gently rocks a three-year-old boy who had fallen 6 metres into the primate exhibit. The gorilla was acclaimed a hero for her role in saving the boy. Did Binti Jua act out of kindness and empathy? Or did she simply do what she was taught to do—care for an infant? This episode brings the altruism debate to life—even in the animal world.

It was, of course, a terrific story; and it soon sparked a debate; was Binti's act a heartwarming example of altruism, motivated by kindness and compassion, or was it that Binti had received training in infant care before the birth of her own baby and had simply acted as she had been trained to act—with no kindness or compassion involved?

The same debate exists about human behaviour. Are humans ever truly **altruistic**—motivated by the desire to increase another's welfare? Or are our helpful behaviours always **egoistic**—motivated by selfish concerns or simple conformity to socialized norms? Many psychological theories assume an egoistic, self-interested bottom line. It is not difficult to imagine egoistic interpretations for almost any acts of helping, even the most seemingly altruistic ones. Tutoring the disadvantaged? It will look good on your resumé. Anonymously helping the homeless? It reduces your guilt. Risking your life for a stranger? Such heroism may benefit your reputation and status. So is all helping at some level egoistic?

Daniel Batson (2009; 2012) thinks not. As we will see in the following section, he believes that the motivation behind some helpful actions is at least in part truly altruistic.

The Empathy-Altruism Hypothesis Batson's model of altruism is based on his view of the consequences of **empathy**, which has long been viewed as a basic factor in promoting positive behaviour toward others. Although the definition of empathy has been much debated, most researchers regard empathy as a complex phenomenon with both cognitive and emotional components (Davis et al., 2004; de Waal, 2009; Eisenberg, 2010). The major cognitive component of empathy is *perspective taking:* using the power of imagination to try to see the world through someone else's eyes. A key emotional component of empathy is *empathic concern,* which involves other-oriented feelings, such as sympathy, compassion, and tenderness. In contrast to empathic concern is *personal distress,* which involves self-oriented reactions to a person in need, such as feeling alarmed, troubled, or upset.

According to Batson (2009; Batson et al., 2011) perspective taking is the first step toward altruism. If you perceive someone in need and imagine how *that person* feels, you are likely to experience other-oriented feelings of empathic concern, which in turn produce the altruistic motive to reduce the other person's distress. However, if you perceive someone in need and focus on your *own* feelings or on how *you* would feel in that person's situation, you are not adopting the perspective of the needy person; rather, you will experience self-oriented feelings of personal distress, which elicit the egoistic motive to reduce your distress. It's when your focus is on the other person that true altruism is possible. The basic features of Batson's **empathy-altruism hypothesis** are outlined in ▶ Figure 10.2.

A fascinating study suggests that human infants are capable of at least a rudimentary degree of perspective taking leading to helping behaviour. Felix Warneken and Michael Tomasello (2006) placed 18-month-old human infants with an adult experimenter. At various points in time, the experimenter appeared to have trouble reaching a goal. For example, he accidentally dropped a marker on the floor and tried unsuccessfully to reach it, or he couldn't put some magazines into a cabinet because the doors were closed. Twenty-two of the twenty-four infants tested in the study helped the experimenter in at least one of the tasks, and many infants helped on several tasks. In doing so, the infants apparently understood that the experimenter needed help—that is, that he was having trouble completing a task by himself.

altruistic
Motivated by the desire to improve another's welfare.

egoistic
Motivated by the desire to improve one's own welfare.

empathy
Understanding or vicariously experiencing another individual's perspective and feeling sympathy and compassion for that individual.

empathy-altruism hypothesis
The proposition that empathic concern for a person in need produces an altruistic motive for helping.

FIGURE 10.2

The Empathy-Altruism Hypothesis

According to the empathy-altruism hypothesis, taking the perspective of a person in need creates feelings of empathic concern, which produce the altruistic motive to reduce the other person's distress. When people do *not* take the other's perspective, they experience feelings of personal distress, which produce the egoistic motive to reduce their own discomfort.

(Based on Batson, 1991.)

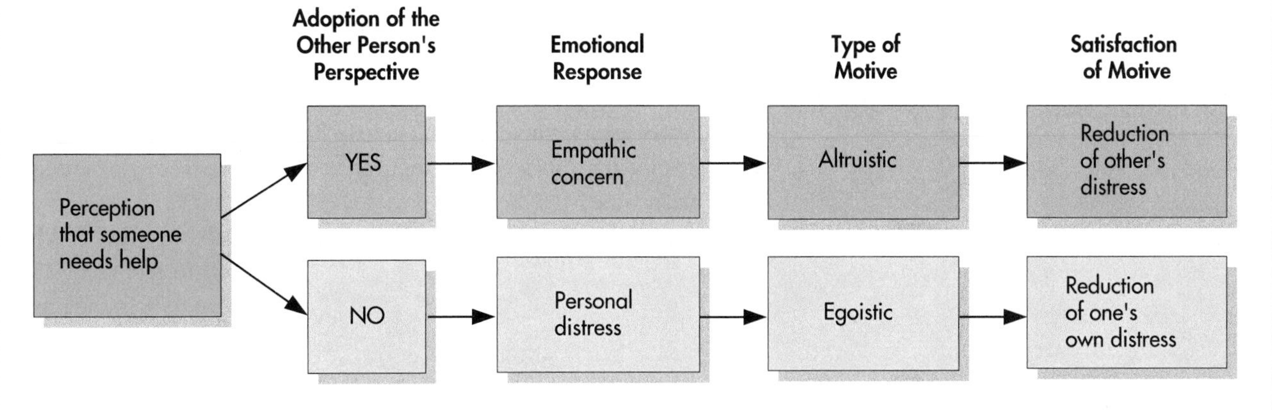

Two additional details are worth noting about the study. First, the experimenter never requested help from the infants, nor did he praise or reward the infants when they did help. Second, for every task he needed help with, the experimenter created a similar situation in which he did not seem to have a problem. For example, rather than accidentally drop the marker on the floor and try to reach it, the experimenter sometimes intentionally threw the marker on the floor and did not try to retrieve it. In these situations, the infants were not likely to take action such as picking up the marker. This suggested that when they did help the experimenter, the infants did so because they understood he was trying to achieve some goal. Other research that seems to demonstrate examples of empathy in primates such as chimpanzees and bonobos has led Frans de Waal (2008) to conclude, "There is now increasing evidence that the brain is hardwired for social connection, and that the same empathy mechanism proposed to underlie human altruism may underlie the directed altruism of other animals" (p. 292). To this point, recent studies involving fMRI scans and brain stimulation have highlighted areas of the brain that appear to be associated with empathy in humans (Hétu et al., 2012; Masten et al., 2011).

Now comes the hard part. How can we tell the difference between egoistic and altruistic motives? In both cases, people help someone else, but the helpers' reasons are different. Confronted with this puzzle, Batson came up with an elegant solution. It depends, he says, on whether one can obtain the relevant self-benefits without relieving the other's need. For example, when a person's motive is egoistic, helping should decline if it's easy for the individual to escape from the situation. When a person's motive is altruistic, however, help will be given regardless of the ease of escape.

Batson and others have conducted more than 30 experiments that have found support for the empathy-altruism hypothesis. For example, Batson and his colleagues (2007) demonstrated the role of both perspective taking and having warm emotional reactions to the other person in predicting helping. Students in this study read about a fictitious student named Bryan Banks who was hit by a car while running late to class and was seriously injured. The researchers manipulated perspective taking by varying the instructions given to the students. Those in the objective condition were asked to "try to take an objective perspective toward what is described. Try not to get caught up

FIGURE 10.3

Perspective Taking and Positive Emotions Underlying Helping

Students read about a fictitious student named Bryan who was injured. They were instructed either to take an objective perspective or to imagine Bryan's perspective. They also read information designed to make them feel either positive or negative emotions toward him. The bars in this graph reflect the percentage of students in each condition who agreed to help get class notes copied for Bryan. The combination of imagining Bryan's perspective and feeling positive emotions toward him led to the most helping.

(Based on Batson et al., 2007.)

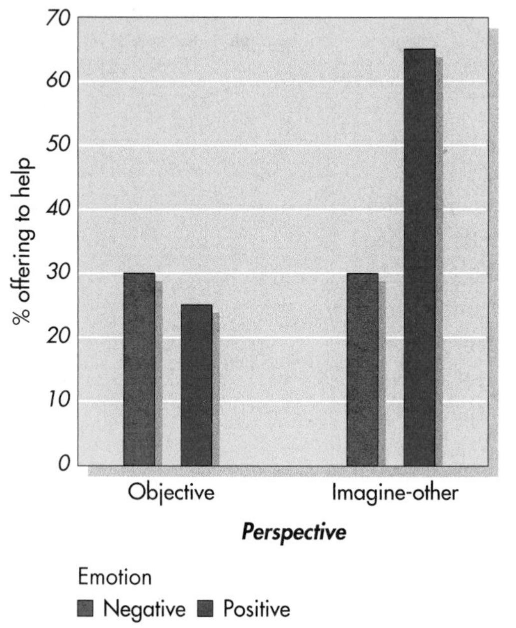

in how the student facing this difficulty feels; just remain objective and detached." The students in the imagine-perspective condition were asked to "try to imagine how the student facing this difficulty feels and how it is affecting his or her life."

The researchers also manipulated emotional reactions to Bryan. Students read that Bryan had been running late to class because he was stopped by an old woman who was lost and needed help finding her house. The students in one condition read that Bryan was very nice to the woman, whereas students in the other condition read that Bryan was rather nasty to her. Later, after they were led to think the study was completed, the students read a letter asking for volunteers to help Bryan by helping get class notes copied for him, a commitment that would take a couple of hours of their time.

As can be seen in Figure 10.3, participants who had been induced both to take Bryan's perspective and to feel emotionally positive toward him were more likely to sign up to help the injured student than were participants in any of the other conditions. In addition, and consistent with the empathy-altruism hypothesis, the more these students felt empathic concern for Bryan (as measured on a questionnaire), the more likely they were to step up and actually offer to help him.

Despite the evidence for the empathy-altruism hypothesis, it has its limits. For example, Batson has never claimed that *all* helping is altruistically motivated. There are multiple motives for helping, and many helpful acts are best explained in terms of the processes we consider elsewhere in this chapter. And any single helpful action can be the result of a mixture of egoistic and altruistic motives. Mark Snyder (1993) suggests, for example, that the most effective way to increase helping is to encourage people to recognize and feel comfortable with the convergence of self-oriented and other-oriented concerns.

Another limit is created by the fact that motives do not guarantee behaviour. Empathy leads to altruistic motivations, but not necessarily to helpful behaviours. For example, someone with empathic concern for another might not help this person if he or she fears that the potential cost of offering the help is too high under the circumstances (Abbate & Ruggieri, 2011; Batson et al., 1983). It is also the case that some individuals may tend to be more or less altruistic than others. For example, in a set of studies, Brent Simpson and Robb Willer (2008) found that individuals they classified as egoists tended to act prosocially when their reputations were at stake, but individuals they classified as altruists tended to act prosocially regardless of whether their reputations could be affected.

Altruism Versus Egoism: Convergence of Motivations On the surface, the debate between altruistic and egoistic accounts of helping may seem to be irrelevant quibbling about semantics or philosophy. After all, if someone pulls you out of a burning car, you don't care if your rescuer did it to increase the chances that your similar genes will be passed down to future generations, to be lauded as a hero as the action news team approaches with its cameras, or simply because he or she was concerned for your safety. You are just thankful that the person helped, no matter what the motivation.

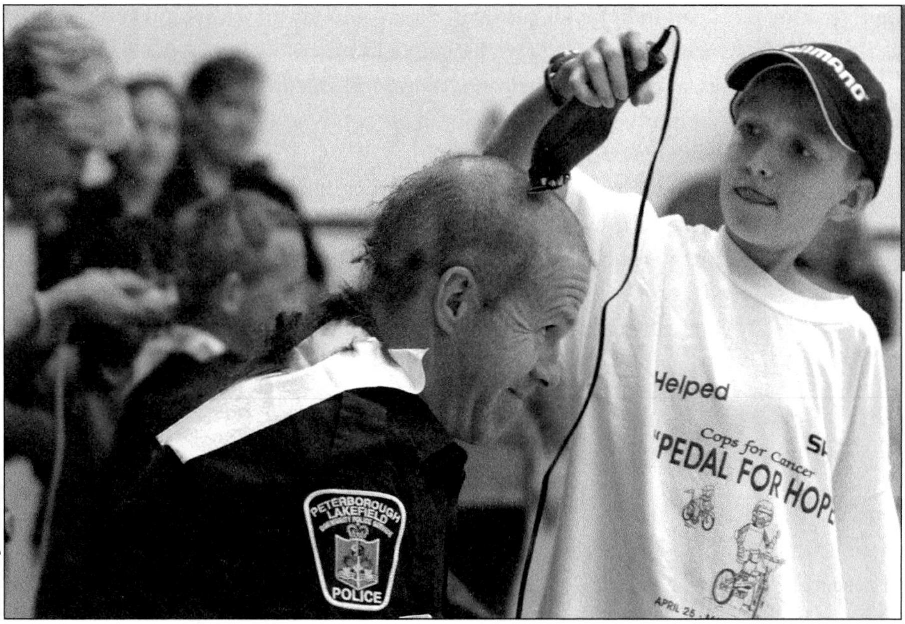

Peterborough Examiner/Clifford Skarstedt

The Canadian Cancer Society sponsors "Cops for Cancer"—fundraising events where police officers publicly shave their heads to raise money for the charity. According to the empathy-altruism hypothesis, taking the perspective of someone in need is the first step toward altruism.

The debate may also become less relevant when considering more long-term helping behaviour, such as volunteerism. People tend to volunteer not because of one specific motive, but due to multiple motives. Some of these are associated with empathy, such as perspective taking and empathic concern, whereas other motives are more egoistic, such as wanting to enhance one's résumé, relieve negative emotions, or conform to prosocial norms (Akintola, 2011; Anik et al., 2011; Hur, 2006; Mannino et al., 2011; Penner et al., 2005; Piferi et al., 2006). Allen Omoto and others (2009) have found that both other-focused motivation and self-focused motivation can impact volunteerism.

■ Table 10.1 lists five categories of motives that Allen Omoto and Mark Snyder (1995) determined were behind volunteers' decisions to help people with AIDS. One interesting finding was that volunteers who had initially endorsed self-oriented motives, such as gaining understanding and developing personal skills, remained active volunteers longer than did those who had initially emphasized other-oriented motives, such as humanitarian values and community concern. Why were the more egoistic goals associated with longer service? Snyder and Omoto (2008) have observed that purely altruistic

TABLE 10.1

Motivations to Volunteer to Help People with AIDS

Allen Omoto and Mark Snyder identified five categories of motivations underlying people's initial decisions to volunteer to help people with AIDS. Within each category, three examples of specific statements representative of the general motive are presented.

(Omoto & Snyder, 1995.)

Values
Because of my humanitarian obligation to help others
Because I enjoy helping other people
Because I consider myself a loving and caring person
Understanding
To learn more about how to prevent AIDS
To learn how to help people with AIDS
To deal with my personal fears and anxiety about AIDS
Personal Development
To get to know people who are similar to myself
To meet new people and make new friends
To gain experience dealing with emotionally difficult topics
Community Concern
Because of my sense of obligation to the gay community
Because I consider myself an advocate for gay-related issues
Because of my concern and worry about the gay community
Esteem Enhancement
To feel better about myself
To escape other pressures and stress in my life
To feel less lonely

motives may not keep individuals motivated long enough to withstand the personal costs associated with some kinds of prolonged helping.

Self-interest as a motive for helping, therefore, is not necessarily a bad thing. Indeed, the fact that many people find helping others to be so personally rewarding is a positive aspect of human nature. One's feelings of empathic concern for others are usually limited to a few other people at a time and perhaps to relatively brief periods. Those people who derive a great deal of personal satisfaction from helping others, however, may be motivated much more frequently and consistently to engage in helping behaviours. Indeed, commitment to prosocial actions can become an important part of one's identity (Piliavin et al., 2002; Snyder& Omoto, 2008).

Situational Influences: When Do People Help?

Thus far, we have focused on *why* people help others. We now turn to the question of *when* people help. We begin by discussing a remarkably creative and provocative set of research findings that make a surprising point: If you need help in an emergency, you may be better off if there is only one witness to your plight than if there are several. We then focus on a wide range of other situational factors on helping, including where we live, whether we are experiencing time pressure, what kind of mood we're in, and whether we've been exposed to particular role models or social norms.

The Unhelpful Crowd

On October 13, 2011, two-year-old Wang Yue wandered away from her home in Guangdong, a southeast province in China. After stepping into a small street in a nearby market, she was hit by a van. As can be seen in video footage that captured the incident, the driver of the van initially slowed down, but then sped away from the scene running over her body in the process. During the next 7 minutes, at least 18 people passed by her while she laid crying and bleeding in the street. A second vehicle then drove over her. Finally, a woman picking through garbage dragged her to the side of the road and helped get her to a hospital. Wang Yue died 8 days later.

The sad truth is that this kind of story of bystanders failing to act, while chilling, is not as uncommon as most people imagine. The most famous of these stories occurred more than four decades ago. It has remained famous in large part because of the fascinating social psychology research it inspired.

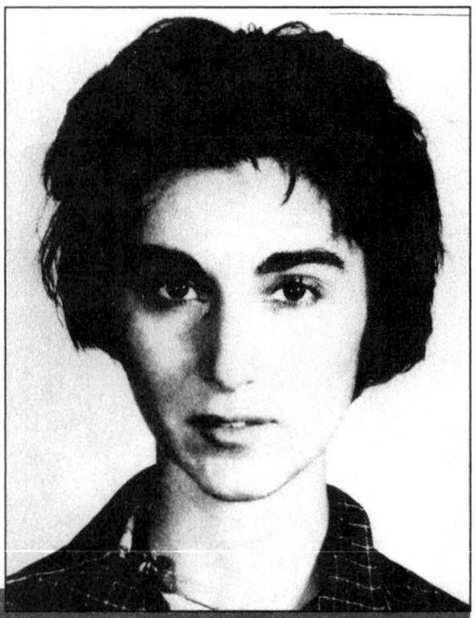
NY Times Pictures

How could 38 witnesses stand by and do nothing while Kitty Genovese was being murdered? Research conducted in the aftermath of the tragedy suggests that if there had been only one witness rather than almost 40, she might have had a better chance of receiving help, and she might be alive today.

The story begins at about 3:20 on the morning of March 13, 1964, in the New York City borough of Queens. Twenty-eight-year-old Kitty Genovese was returning home from her job as a bar manager. Suddenly, a man attacked her with a knife. She was stalked, stabbed, and sexually assaulted just 35 yards from her own apartment building. Lights went on and windows went up as she screamed, "Oh my God! He stabbed me! Please help me!" She broke free from her attacker twice, but only briefly. Thirty-eight of her neighbours witnessed her ordeal, but not one intervened. Finally, after nearly 45 minutes of terror, one man called the police. But before they got her to the hospital, Genovese was dead.

The murder of Kitty Genovese was shocking. Were her neighbours to blame? It seemed unlikely that all 38 of them could have been moral monsters. Most of the media attention focused on the decline of morals and values in contemporary society, and on the anonymity and apathy seen in large American cities such as New York. A few days after the incident, Bibb Latané and John Darley discussed over dinner the events and the explanations being offered for it. They were not convinced that these explanations were sufficient to account for why Kitty Genovese didn't get the help she needed; and they wondered if other, social psychological processes might have been at work. They speculated that because each witness to the attack could see that many other witnesses had turned on their lights and were looking out their windows, each witness might have assumed that others would, or should, take responsibility and call the police. To test their ideas, Latané and Darley (1970) set out to see if they could produce unresponsive bystanders under laboratory conditions. Let's take a look at one of their studies.

When a participant arrived, he or she was taken to one of a series of small rooms located along a corridor. Speaking over an intercom, the experimenter explained that he wanted participants to discuss personal problems often faced by students. Participants were told that, to protect confidentiality, the group discussion would take place over the intercom system, and the experimenter would not be listening. They were required to speak one at a time, taking turns. Some participants were assigned to talk with one other person; others joined larger groups of three or six people.

Although one participant did mention in passing that he suffered from a seizure disorder that was sometimes triggered by study pressures, the opening moments of the conversation were uneventful. But soon, an unexpected problem developed. When the time came for this person to speak again, he stuttered badly, had a hard time speaking clearly, and sounded as if he were in very serious trouble:

> *I could really-er-use some help so if somebody would-er-give me a little h-help-uhererer-er c-could somebody-er-er-help-er-uh-uh-uh [choking sounds].... I'm gonna die-er-er-I'm ... gonna die-er-help-er-er-seizure-er [chokes, then quiet].*

Confronted with this situation, what would *you* do? Would you interrupt the experiment, dash out of your cubicle, and try to find the experimenter? Or would you sit there—concerned, but unsure how to react?

As it turns out, participants' responses to this emergency were strongly influenced by the size of their group. Actually, all participants were participating alone, but tape-recorded material led them to believe that others were present. All the participants who thought that only they knew about the emergency left the room quickly to try to get help. In the larger groups, however, participants were less likely and slower to intervene. Indeed, 38 percent of the participants in the six-person groups never left the room at all! This research led Latané and Darley to a chilling conclusion: The more bystanders, the *less* likely the victim will be helped. This is the **bystander effect**, whereby the presence of others inhibits helping.

Before the pioneering work of Latané and Darley, most people would have assumed just the opposite. Isn't there safety in numbers? Don't we feel more secure rushing in to help when others are around to lend their support? Latané and Darley overturned this common-sense assumption and provided a careful, step-by-step analysis of the decision-making process involved in emergency interventions. In the following sections, we examine each of five steps in this process: noticing something unusual, interpreting it as an emergency, taking responsibility for getting help, deciding how to help, and providing assistance. We also consider the reasons why people sometimes fail to take one of these steps and, therefore, do not help. These steps, and the obstacles along the way, are summarized in ▶ Figure 10.4, on page 374.

In an emergency, a person who needs help has a much better chance of getting it if three other people are present than if only one other person is present. FALSE.

Noticing The first step toward being a helpful bystander is to notice that someone needs help or, at least, that something out of the ordinary is happening. Participants in the seizure study could not help but notice the emergency. In many situations, however, the problem isn't necessarily perceived as such. The presence of others can be distracting and can divert attention away from indications of a victim's plight. In addition, people may fail to notice that someone needs help because they are caught

bystander effect
The effect whereby the presence of others inhibits helping.

FIGURE 10.4

The Five Steps to Helping in an Emergency

On the basis of their analysis of the decision-making process in emergency interventions, Latané and Darley (1970) outlined five steps that lead to providing assistance. But there are obstacles that can interfere; and if a step is missed, the victim won't be helped.

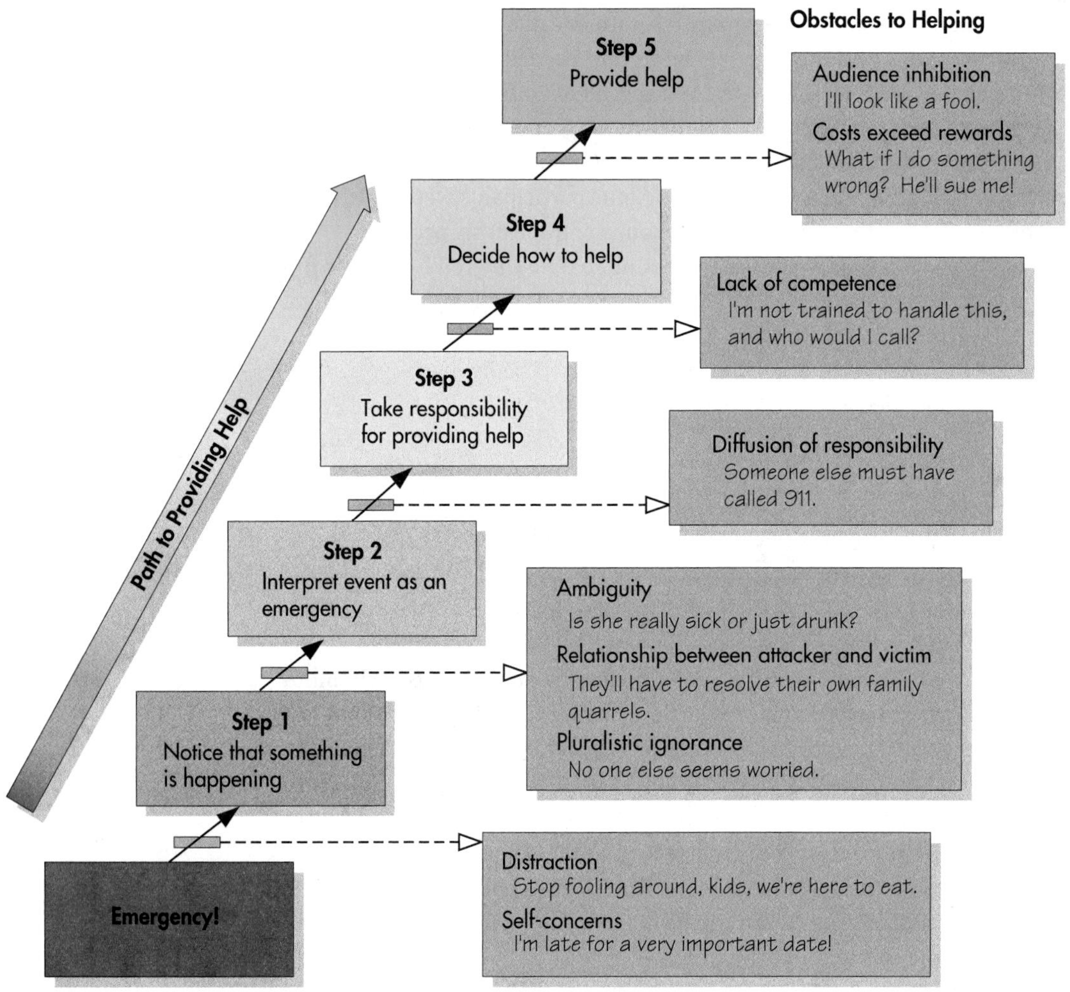

up in their own self-concerns. People who live in big cities and noisy environments may become so used to seeing people lying on sidewalks or hearing screams that they begin to tune them out, becoming susceptible to what Stanley Milgram (1970) called *stimulus overload.*

Interpreting Noticing the victim is a necessary first step toward helping, but it is not enough. People must interpret the meaning of what they notice. Cries of pain can be mistaken for shrieks of laughter; heart-attack victims can appear to be drunk. Evidence of this reasoning process was demonstrated by Ivy Chiu Loke and others (2011) at the University of Toronto who found differing levels of neural activation, measured using Event Related Potentials (ERP), depending on the expectedness of a behaviour described in a helping scnenario. The greatest activation occurred in situations where help wasn't given but was clearly needed, and when help wasn't needed, but was given anyway. So observers wonder: Does that person really need help?

In general, the more ambiguous the situation, the less likely it is that bystanders will intervene (Cismaru et al., 2010; Clark & Word, 1972).

Interpretations of the relationship between a victim and an attacker also affect whether help will be provided. Consider, for example, how people react when they see a woman attacked by a man. Research by Lance Shotland and Margaret Straw (1976) indicates that many observers of such an incident believe that the attacker and the victim have a close relationship as dates, lovers, or spouses—even when no information about the relationship is actually available. This inference can have very serious implications, since—as Shotland and Straw documented—intervening in domestic violence is perceived to be more dangerous to the helper and less desired by the victim than is intervening in an attack by a stranger. Given such beliefs, the response to a scene staged by Shotland and Straw was predictable: In the scene, a woman was supposedly being assaulted either by a stranger or by her husband. When being physically attacked, she either yelled, "Get away from me. I don't know you" (stranger condition) or "Get away from me. I don't know why I ever married you" (husband condition). More than three times as many observers tried to stop the assault by the stranger.

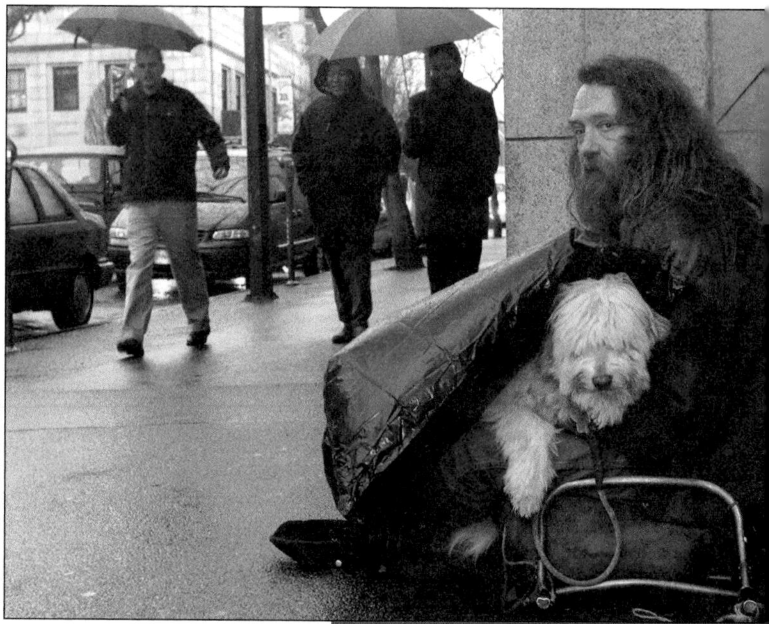

CP/Victoria Times Colonist/Debra Brash

The first step toward providing help is to notice that someone needs assistance. These people become "invisible" to potential helpers who pass them each day as they make their way to school or work, distracted by their own concerns or by the overwhelming stimuli of a big, bustling city.

It's not only women who are in danger if they are perceived as having a close relationship with their attacker: Children also suffer. The 1993 murder of two-year-old James Bulger by two ten-year-old boys was the British equivalent of the Kitty Genovese slaying. James was dragged, kicking and screaming, for two and a half miles from a shopping mall to a railroad track, where he was battered to death. Sixty-one people admitted that they had seen the boys. Most did nothing. One asked a few questions but didn't intervene. The reason? As one witness put it, he thought the boys were "older brothers taking a little one home." When people think "family," they think, "It's OK, it's safe." But sometimes it isn't.

Perhaps the most powerful information available during an emergency is the behaviour of other people. Startled by a sudden, unexpected, possibly dangerous event, each person looks quickly to see what others are doing. As everyone looks at everyone else for clues about how to behave, the entire group is paralyzed by indecision. When this happens, the person needing help is a victim of **pluralistic ignorance**. In this state of ignorance, each individual believes that his or her own thoughts and feelings are different from those of other people, even though everyone's behaviour is the same. Each bystander thinks that other people aren't acting because somehow they know there isn't an emergency. Actually, everyone is confused and hesitant, but taking cues from each other's inaction, each observer concludes that help is not required.

Latané and Darley (1968) put this phenomenon to the test in an experiment in which participants completed a questionnaire in a room in which they were either (a) alone; (b) with two confederates who remained passive and took no action; or (c) with two other naive participants, just like them. A few minutes after participants had started to fill out the questionnaire, smoke began to seep into the room through a vent. Was this an emergency? How do you think you would respond? Within four minutes, half of the participants who were working alone took some action, such as leaving the room to report the smoke to someone. Within six minutes—the

pluralistic ignorance
The state in which people mistakenly believe that their own thoughts and feelings are different from those of others, even when everyone's behaviour is the same.

maximum time allotted before the researchers terminated the experiment—three-quarters of these participants took action. Clearly, they interpreted the smoke as a potential emergency.

But what about the participants working in groups of three? Common sense suggests that the chances that *somebody* will take action should be greater when more people are present. But only one of the 24 participants in this condition took action within four minutes, and only three did so before the end of the study—even though, at that point, the smoke was so thick they had to fan it away from their faces to see the questionnaire. If these participants had interpreted the smoke as a potential emergency, they would have acted, because their own lives would have been at stake. But instead, they quickly, coolly looked at the reactions of the others in the room, saw that nobody else seemed too concerned, and so became convinced that nothing could be wrong.

Pluralistic ignorance is not restricted to emergency situations (Grant et al., 2009; Halbesleben, 2009; Reiber & Garcia, 2010; Zhu & Westphal, 2011). Have you ever sat through a class feeling totally lost? You want to ask a question, but you're too embarrassed. No one else is saying anything, so you assume they all find the material a snap. Finally, you dare to ask a question. And suddenly, hands shoot up in the air all over the classroom. No one understood the material, yet everyone assumed that everyone else was breezing along. Pluralistic ignorance in the classroom interferes with learning. In an emergency situation, it can lead to disaster—unless someone breaks out of the pack and dares to help. Then others are likely to follow.

Taking Responsibility Noticing a victim and recognizing an emergency are crucial steps; but by themselves, they don't ensure that a bystander will come to the rescue. The issue of responsibility remains. When help is needed, who is responsible for providing it? If a person knows that others are around, it's all too easy to place the responsibility on *them.* People often fail to help because of the **diffusion of responsibility**—the belief that others will or should intervene. Presumably, each of those 38 people who watched and listened to Kitty Genovese's murder thought someone else would do something to stop the attack. But remember those helpful participants in the seizure study who thought that they alone heard the other person's cry for help? Diffusion of responsibility cannot occur if an individual believes that only he or she is aware of the victim's need.

An interesting set of experiments by Stephen Garcia and others (2002) found that the presence of others can promote diffusion of responsibility even when they are present only in one's mind! Garcia and his colleagues (including John Darley) had participants simply *imagine* being in a crowd or being alone, and soon after, these participants were given an opportunity to help someone. The results indicated that participants who had just thought of being with many other people were less likely to help than were the participants who had imagined themselves alone.

Diffusion of responsibility usually takes place under conditions of anonymity. Bystanders who do not know the victim personally are more likely to see others as responsible for providing help. Accordingly, if the psychological distance between a bystander and the victim is reduced, there will be less diffusion of responsibility and more help. Reducing the psychological distance among bystanders can also counteract the diffusion of responsibility. Established groups in which the members know each other are usually more helpful than groups of strangers (Rutkowski et al., 1983). For example, in recent experiments, Mark Levine and Simon Crowther (2008) replicated the inhibiting effect of bystanders on helping when the bystanders were strangers, but they found that the effect did not occur when the bystanders were all friends.

diffusion of responsibility
The belief that others will or should take the responsibility for providing assistance to a person in need.

In addition, the diffusion of responsibility can be defeated by a person's role. A group leader, even if only recently assigned to that position, is more likely than other group members to act in an emergency (Baumeister et al., 1988). And some occupational roles increase the likelihood of intervention. Registered nurses, for example, do not diffuse responsibility when confronted by a possible physical injury (Cramer et al., 1988).

Deciding How to Help Having assumed the responsibility to help, the person must now decide how to help. Bystanders are more likely to offer direct help when they feel competent to perform the actions required. For instance, individuals who have received Red Cross training in first-aid techniques are more likely to provide direct assistance to a bleeding victim than are those without training (Shotland & Heinold, 1985).

But people who do not possess the skills that would make them feel competent to intervene directly often do have an option available. They can decide to help indirectly by calling for assistance from others. In many situations, indirect helping is by far the wiser course of action. Physical injuries are best treated by medical personnel; dangerous situations such as domestic violence are best handled by police officers; and that friendly looking individual standing by the side of a stalled car on a lonely road is best picked up by the highway patrol. Even people trained in CPR are now advised to call 911 before starting CPR on an adult victim. Calling others in to help is safe, simple, and effective. A prompt phone call can be a lifeline. Such a call might have saved Kitty Genovese's life.

Providing Help The final step in the intervention process is to take action. Here, too, the presence of others can have an impact. Latané and Darley point out that people sometimes feel too socially awkward and embarrassed to act helpfully in a public setting. When observers do not act in an emergency because they fear making a bad impression on other observers, they are under the influence of **audience inhibition**. Worrying about how others will view us does not, however, always reduce helping. When people think others will scorn them for failing to help, the presence of an audience *increases* their helpful actions (Garcia et al., 2009; Levine & Cassidy, 2010; Schwartz & Gottlieb, 1980).

The Bystander Effect Online One new application of the research on the bystander effect is in the world of electronic-based communication. Daniel Stalder (2008) reviewed recent studies on individuals' responses to email or Internet-based requests for help. Even here, the bystander effect emerged, indicating that the virtual presence of others reduced the likelihood that any one individual would intervene.

A sad example of the bystander effect in cyberspace occurred in February 2003. Twenty-one-year-old Brandon Vedas overdosed on drugs and lay dying in front of a room crowded with people, many of whom egged him on to take even more drugs. The modern-day twist was that this room was virtual—it was a chat room, and the bystanders watched via the webcam as Vedas, who used the name "Ripper" online, poisoned himself to death in his Phoenix, Arizona, bedroom. "That's not much," said a teenager from rural Oklahoma whose alias was "Smoke2K." "Eat more. I wanna see if you survive or if you just black out." Another wrote in, "Ripper—you should try to pass out in front of the cam." Not everyone was so callous. Some wrote in, warning Ripper to be careful; one wrote, "Don't OD on us, Ripper." One person did begin to call the police, but, astonishingly, others talked her out of it. Vedas posted his cell number with the instructions, "Call if I look dead." The last coherent words Vedas wrote were, "I told u I was hardcore" (Kennedy, 2003, p. 5).

audience inhibition
Reluctance to help for fear of making a bad impression on observers.

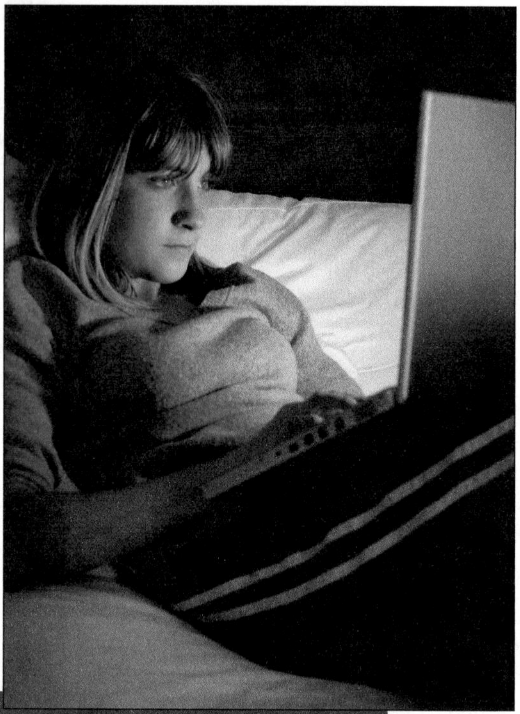

Although not physically in the same room, the virtual presence of others in an Internet chat room is enough to create the right conditions for the bystander effect to occur.

This incident was different from the Kitty Genovese one in several ways, including the fact that it was not clear if the onlookers could have done anything about this. Without knowing Ripper's real name or address, the police probably would not have been able to find him in time even had someone called promptly. But several processes central to Darley and Latané's research clearly were evident. Several witnesses suggested that "somebody" call poison control or the police but did not do so themselves. Some questioned whether Ripper was really dying or had just passed out. One person told another *not* to call the police because that could get Ripper arrested. Together, these Internet bystanders were struggling on the decision tree, spreading doubt and diffusion of responsibility.

The Legacy of the Bystander Effect Research As you can see in Figure 10.4, providing help in an emergency is a challenging process. At each step along the way, barriers and diversions can prevent a potential helper from becoming an actual one. In 2011, Peter Fischer and others conducted a meta-analysis of 53 studies on the bystander effect and concluded that the evidence continues to support the finding that the presence of others inhibits individual bystanders from helping. They did note, however, that the effect was readily reduced when the situation was clearly a dangerous one, and therefore helping was more obviously required.

When stories such as the hit and run of Wang Yue, or the woman with dementia who froze to death (both discussed earlier in the chapter) are covered in the news, the name "Kitty Genovese" invariably comes up. Given its enduring legacy, it is interesting to note that some of the original details reported about the witnesses to the Kitty Genovese murder—accounts that have been repeated countless times over the years since then—may, in fact, be inaccurate. Rachel Manning and others (2008) recently published an article suggesting that some of the witnesses may have called the police well before the police finally arrived. These were in the days before "911" calls, and it is impossible to know whether these calls were made or what may have been said in them. Manning and her colleagues also question whether 38 was the correct number of witnesses and suggest that far fewer were likely to have actually seen the incident, although possibly even more than 38 heard it.

To us, these questions are interesting but beside the main point. Whether fully accurate or not, these original reports were what inspired John Darley and Bibb Latané to pursue the line of research we have reported in this section, and that research has yielded valuable insight concerning the social psychology of bystander intervention. In addition, we have cited several other more recent stories from the news of tragic inaction of bystanders, and for every one we cite, there are dozens more. Latané and Darley's theorizing continues to help people understand how these incidents can occur.

Many of us who teach social psychology have stories of former students who witnessed an emergency and jumped in to help while consciously thinking of the lessons they'd learned about the bystander effect in their social psychology classes. Indeed, one of the authors of this book remembers being at a colloquium in a room filled with social psychologists when a loud crash suddenly emanated from an adjacent room. After a few seconds of delay, dozens of social psychologists burst out of their chairs, almost trampling each other as they rushed to see if there was an emergency. And the only ones of us who were not explicitly thinking "Darley & Latané" while doing so were the ones thinking "Latané & Darley."

Getting Help in a Crowd: What Should You Do? But what do all these stories and experiments teach you about what to do if you need help in the presence of many people? Is there anything you can do to enhance the chances that someone will come to your aid? Try to counteract the ambiguity of the situation by making it very clear that you do need help, and try to reduce diffusion of responsibility by singling out particular individuals for help, such as with eye contact, pointing, or direct requests (Moriarty, 1975; Shotland & Stebbins, 1980).

A study by P. M. Markey (2000) involving people in Internet chat rooms found results consistent with this advice. As the number of people present in each chat room group grew larger, individuals took increasingly more time to respond to someone's plea for help; however, this effect was eliminated when the person asking for help specified a particular individual's name (see ▶ Figure 10.5). In light of Brandon Vedas's overdose a few years later, this study of diffusion of responsibility in Internet chat rooms was chillingly prophetic.

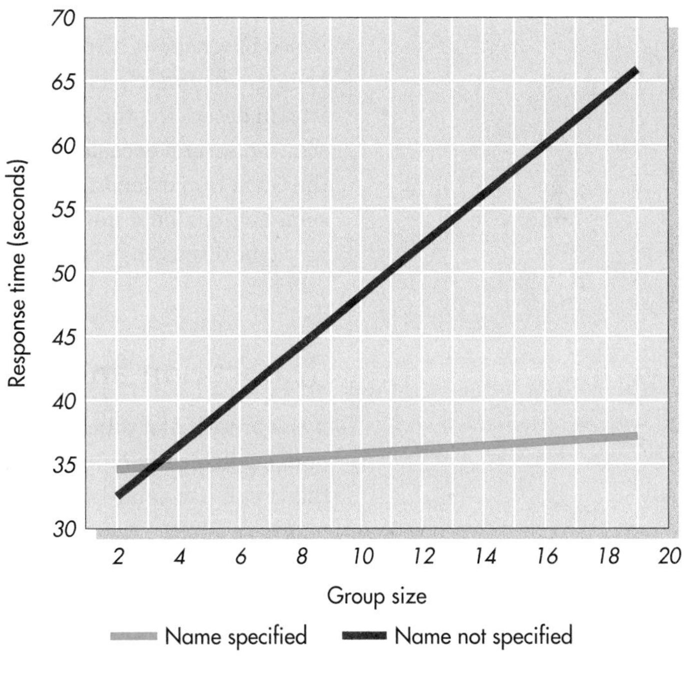

▦ Time Pressure

The presence of others can create obstacles at each step on the way toward helping in an emergency. Other factors, too, can affect multiple steps in this process. Our good intentions to help those in need can sometimes conflict with other motivations. One such source of conflict is time pressure. When we are in a hurry or have a lot on our minds, we may be so preoccupied that we fail to notice others who need help, we may become less likely to accept responsibility for helping someone, or we may decide that the costs of helping are too high because of the precious time that will be lost. When we have other demands on us that seem very important, getting involved in someone else's problems may seem like a luxury we can't afford (Batson et al., 1978). John Darley and Daniel Batson (1973) examined the role of time pressure in an experiment that produced what may be the most ironic finding in the history of social psychology.

Their study was based on the parable of the Good Samaritan, from the Bible. This parable tells the story of three different people—a priest, a Levite, and a Samaritan—each travelling on the road from Jerusalem to Jericho. Each encounters a man lying half-dead by the roadside. The priest and the Levite—both considered busy, important, and relatively holy people—pass by the man without stopping. The only one who helps is the Samaritan, a social and religious outcast of that time. A moral of the tale is that people with low status are sometimes more virtuous and display more sensitivity to others than those enjoying high status and prestige (Piff et al., 2010). Why? Perhaps in part because high-status individuals tend to be busy people, preoccupied with their

▶ **FIGURE 10.5**

Cyberhelping

In a study that extends Latané and Darley's research on the bystander effect by bringing it into cyberspace, individuals participating in an online chat room saw a plea for help from another person in the chat room. Consistent with Latané and Darley's findings, individuals responded more slowly if they thought many other people were in the chat room than if they thought there were few others present. However, if an individual's name was specified in the request for help, then that person responded quickly regardless of how many other people were in the chat room.

(Source: Markey, 2000.)

Group size

— Name specified ▬ Name not specified

Reprinted from *Computers in Human Behavior Vol. 16*, P.M. Markey, pp. 183-188. Copyright ©2000, with permission from Elsevier.

own concerns and rushing around to various engagements. Such characteristics may prevent them from noticing or deciding to help a victim in need of assistance.

Darley and Batson brought this ancient story to life. They asked seminary students to think about what they wanted to say in an upcoming talk. Half of them were told that the talk was to be based on the parable of the Good Samaritan; the other half expected to discuss the jobs that seminary students like best. All participants were then instructed to walk over to a nearby building where the speech would be recorded. At this point, participants were told that they were running ahead of schedule, that they were right on time, or that they were already a few minutes behind schedule. On the way to the other building, all participants passed a research confederate slumped in a doorway, coughing and groaning. Which of these future ministers stopped to lend a helping hand?

Perhaps surprisingly, the topic of the upcoming speech had little effect on helping. The pressure of time, however, made a real difference. Of those who thought they were ahead of schedule, 63 percent offered help—compared with 45 percent of those who believed they were on time and only 10 percent of those who had been told they were late. In describing the events that took place in their study, Darley and Batson noted that "on several occasions a seminary student going to give his talk on the parable of the Good Samaritan literally stepped over the victim as he hurried on his way!" These seminary students unwittingly demonstrated the very point that the parable they would be discussing warns against.

Location and Helping

If the presence of others often inhibits helping, do individuals have a worse chance of being helped in an emergency in a big city than in a small town? In the midst of the hectic pace and large crowds of a big city, are pleas for help more likely to go unanswered?

Although place of residence does not seem to affect how much those in close relationships help each other (Franck, 1980; Korte, 1980), a large city does have a number of characteristics that might reduce help to strangers. For example, as we discussed earlier in the context of "noticing" an emergency, Stanley Milgram (1970) proposed that cities produce stimulus overload among their inhabitants. Bombarded by sights and sounds, city residents may wear a coat of unresponsive armour to protect themselves from being overwhelmed by stimulation (Korte et al., 1975). Claude Fischer (1976) noted that the residents of large urban areas are a heterogeneous group composed of diverse nationalities, races, and ethnic backgrounds. Such diversity could diminish the sense of similarity with others, reduce empathic concern, and result in less helping. Also, residents of large cities may feel more anonymous and less accountable for their actions than residents of smaller communities, where people are more likely to know their neighbours.

Whatever the exact causes, people are less likely to help in urban areas than in rural ones. This relationship has been found in several countries, including Canada, Israel, Great Britain, and the Sudan (Hedge & Yousif, 1992; Steblay, 1987). For example, when Paul Amato (1983) studied 55 Australian communities, he found that spontaneous, informal help to strangers was greater where the population was smaller. Interestingly, a *Reader's Digest* poll rated the world's most "polite" cities and ranked Toronto third, behind New York and Zurich. One of the testers for *Reader's Digest* noted that, "Courtesy is the social lubricant that allows us—in these densely packed urban areas—to get along with each other. And without it, we'd be at each other's throats" (*Reader's Digest,* 2006).

In a similar vein, Robert Levine and his colleagues (2008) examined three kinds of spontaneous help offered to strangers in 24 U.S. cities. These measures of helping—all assessed in a downtown area during normal business hours on clear summer days—included picking up a pen that a stranger had apparently dropped accidentally; helping a stranger with a noticeable limp pick up a pile of magazines that the stranger had dropped; and responding to a stranger's request for change for a quarter by at least checking to see if they had change. They found that greater population size and population density (population per square mile) were associated with less helping. Levine and his colleagues also found that greater economic well-being of a city was associated with more helping.

Culture and Helping

Around the world as well, some cities seem to have more helpful citizens than others. Robert Levine and others (2001) conducted similar field experiments in a major city in each of 23 large countries around the world. ▌ Table 10.2 reports how the cities ranked in their propensity to help, with pedestrians in Rio de Janeiro, Brazil, exhibiting the highest rates of helping and pedestrians in Kuala Lampur, Malaysia, the lowest rates. Levine and his colleagues examined a number of measures of each city to try to determine what factors predicted these differences in helping, such as how hectic the pace of life seemed to be (as determined by pedestrians' walking speed), or how individualistic or collectivistic the culture was. Only two measures correlated with helping rates. One was a measure of economic well-being—cities from countries with the greatest levels of economic well-being tended to exhibit the least helping, although this relationship was not very strong (and is inconsistent with the findings from the research of Levine and his colleagues in the United States).

The other variable that predicted helping concerned the notion of what is called *simpatía* in Spanish or *simpático* in Portuguese. Some researchers report that this is an important element of Spanish and Latin American cultures and involves a concern with the social well-being of others (Markus & Lin, 1999; Sanchez-Burks et al., 2000). The five *simpatía* cultures in Levine and others' study did tend to show higher rates of helping than the non- *simpatía* cultures.

You may find it surprising that collectivism was not a predictor of helping, but the research on the relationship between individualism-collectivism and prosocial behaviour is quite mixed at this time. This inconsistency may stem in part from differences in the kinds of helping studied. Relative to individualists, collectivists may be more likely to help ingroup members, but they are less likely to help outgroup members (Conway et al., 2001; Kemmelmeier et al., 2006; Schwartz, 1990).

TABLE 10.2

Helping Around the World

Three types of spontaneous helping of a stranger were examined in field experiments in a major city in each of 23 different countries around the world. The top six and bottom six cities are listed below, along with their respective ranks on a measure of economic prosperity. Cities with asterisks are considered to have *simpatía* cultural values, which are characterized by a concern with the social well-being of others.

(Based on Levine et al., 2001.)

Top Six Cities for Helping

City	Helping Rank	Economic Rank
*Rio de Janeiro, Brazil	1	16
*San Jose, Costa Rica	2	15
Lilongwe, Malawi	3	22
Calcutta, India	4	21
Vienna, Austria	5	4
*Madrid, Spain	6	9

Bottom Six Cities for Helping

City	Helping Rank	Economic Rank
Taipei, Taiwan	18	[data unavailable]
Sofia, Bulgaria	19	17
Amsterdam, Netherlands	20	6
Singapore, Singapore	21	2
New York, United States	22	1
Kuala Lampur, Malaysia	23	10

Based on R.V. Levine, A. Norenzayan and K. Philbrock, "Cross-Cultural Differences in Helping Strangers," *Journal of Cross-Cultural Psychology*, *Vol. 32, pp. 543-560*. Copyright © 2001 by Sage Publications, Inc. Reprinted by permission of Sage Publications, Inc.

People are much more likely to help someone when they're in a good mood. **TRUE.**

Moods and Helping

Helping someone can put people in a better mood, but can being in a good mood increase people's likelihood of helping someone? Are we less likely to help if we're in a bad mood? What's your prediction?

Good Moods and Doing Good Over the course of a year, pedestrians in a U.S. city were stopped and asked to participate in a survey of social opinions. When Michael Cunningham (1979) tabulated their responses according to the weather conditions, he discovered that people answered more questions on sunny days than on cloudy ones. Moving his investigation indoors, Cunningham found that sunshine is truly golden: The more the sun was shining, the more generous were the tips left by restaurant customers. Sunshine and helping seem to go together, but what's the connection? Probably it's the mood we're in, as a sunny day cheers us up and a cloudy day damps us down.

When the sun is not shining, many people head for the mall. One of the more powerful sensations you can count on experiencing while strolling through the mall comes when you pass a bakery or coffee shop, the pleasant aroma of freshly baked chocolate chip cookies or freshly brewed French roast stopping you in your tracks. Robert Baron (1997) believed that these pleasant scents put people in a good mood, and he wondered if this good mood would make them more likely to help someone in need. He tested this with passersby in a large shopping mall. Each selected passerby was approached by a member of the research team and asked for change for a dollar. This interaction took place in a location containing either strong, pleasant odours (such as near a bakery or a coffee-roasting cafe) or no discernible odour (such as near a clothing store). As can be seen in ▶ Figure 10.6, people approached in a pleasant-smelling location were much more likely to help than people approached in a neutral-smelling location. Baron also found that people were in a better mood when they were in the pleasant-smelling environments. This effect on their mood appears to have caused their greater tendency to help.

Shoppers are not the only people at the mall affected by mood—the sales staff is affected, too. Joseph Forgas and others (2008) conducted a field experiment at four department stores in Sydney, Australia. The moods of salespersons were manipulated by having a confederate approach them and say either very complimentary things

▶ FIGURE 10.6

Scents and Sensibilities

People walking in a mall were approached by someone who asked them for change. This encounter took place in areas of the mall with either pleasant ambient odours or no clear odours. The stranger also gave the individuals a questionnaire that measured their moods on a five-point scale, ranging from 1 (very bad) to 5 (very good). As shown on the left, the people approached in a pleasant-smelling area were in a better mood than those approached in neutral-smelling locations. In addition (right), people were more likely to help the stranger by giving him change if they were in a pleasant-smelling area than if they were in a neutral-smelling area.

(Data from Baron, 1997.)

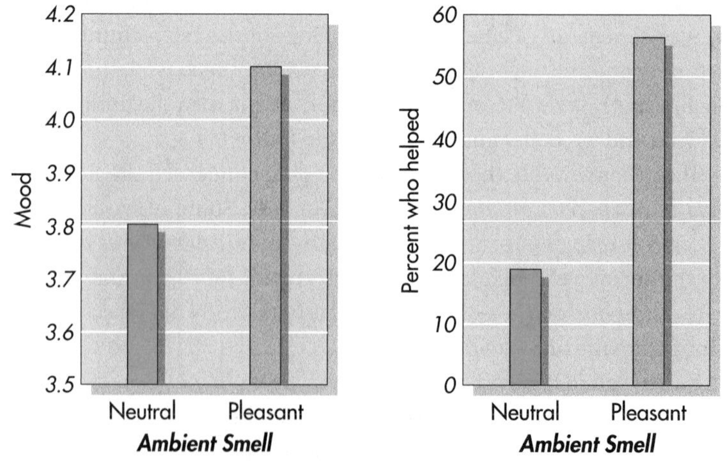

(e.g., "I am so impressed with the service at this store"), or negative things (e.g., "I am so disappointed with the service at this store"), or neutral things. A few seconds later, a second confederate approached the salesperson and asked for help finding an item that did not really exist. How much did the salesperson attempt to help this confederate?

The researchers predicted that the mood manipulation would not have much effect on the most experienced salespersons, as they would have a well-rehearsed set of responses to customer questions and would therefore respond accordingly. For the less experienced staff, however, Forgas and his colleagues expected that they would exert greater effort to help the customer if they had been put in a good mood. This is exactly what the results indicated.

Of course, sunshine and sweet scents are not the only enhancers of mood and helping. In fact, helping is increased by all kinds of pleasant, mood-lifting experiences, such as being successful at a task, reading pleasant positive statements, being offered a cookie, imagining a Hawaiian vacation, and listening to uplifting music (Aderman, 1972; Isen & Levin, 1972; North et al., 2004). On the job, being in a good mood seems to be the major determinant of a wide range of behaviours (such as helping co-workers, making constructive suggestions, and spreading good will) that improve workplace quality and increase organizational effectiveness (Isen, 2008; Tsai et al., 2007). When we're happy, we're helpful—a state of affairs known as the **good mood effect**.

TABLE 10.3

Good Moods Lead to Helping: Reasons and Limitations

Research shows that people in positive moods are more likely to help someone in need than are people in neutral moods. There are several explanations for this effect, as well as some limiting conditions that can weaken or reverse the help-promoting effects of good moods.

Why Feeling Good Leads to Doing Good

- *Desire to maintain one's good mood.* When we are in a good mood, we are motivated to maintain that mood. Helping others makes us feel good, and so it can help maintain a positive mood.
- *Positive expectations about helping.* If we have more positive expectations about the rewards of helping, we are more likely to help.
- *Positive thoughts.* Positive moods trigger positive thoughts, and if we have positive thoughts about others, we should like them more, which makes us more likely to help them.
- *Positive thoughts and expectations about social activities.* Positive moods trigger positive thoughts and expectations about interacting with others and engaging in social activities. These positive thoughts and expectations can promote interacting with others in prosocial ways, including helping them.

When Feeling Good Might Not Lead to Doing Good

- *Costs of helping are high.* If the anticipated costs of helping in a particular situation seem high, helping would put our good mood at risk. In this case, if we can avoid getting involved and thus maintain our good mood (for example, if we can justify our failure to help), we are less likely to help.
- *Positive thoughts about other social activities that conflict with helping.* If our good mood makes us want to go out and party with our friends, our motivation to engage in this social activity may prevent us from taking the time to notice or take responsibility for helping someone in need.

Why do good moods increase helping? There seem to be several factors at work. ■ Table 10.3 summarizes some of the reasons why feeling good often leads to doing good, and it also describes some of the forks in this road that can lead away from helping. Whatever its exact cause, the good mood effect kicks in quite early in life. It occurs among people of all ages, and even young children help more when they feel happy and cheerful (Moore et al., 1973).

Bad Moods and Doing Good Since a good mood increases helping, does a bad mood decrease it? Not necessarily. Under many circumstances, negative feelings can elicit positive behaviour toward others (Carlson & Miller, 1987; Estrada-Hollenbeck & Heatherton, 1998; Vollhardt, 2009). Imagine yourself in the following situation. A stranger approaches you on the street and asks you to use his camera to take his picture for a school project. You get ready, aim, and ... nothing. The camera doesn't work. Looking concerned, the stranger says the camera is rather delicate, asks if you touched any of the dials, and informs you that it will have to be fixed. You continue on your way down the street. As you pass a young woman, she drops a file folder containing some papers. Now, here's the question: Are you more likely

good mood effect
The effect whereby a good mood increases helping behaviour.

TABLE 10.4

Bad Moods and Helping: When Does Feeling Bad Lead to Doing Good, and When Doesn't It?

Research shows that people in negative moods are often more likely to help someone in need than are people in neutral moods. However, there are several limitations to this effect. This table summarizes some of the factors that make it more or less likely for people to do good when they feel bad.

When Negative Moods Make Us More Likely to Help Others

- If we take responsibility for what caused our bad mood ("I feel guilty for what I did.")
- If we focus on other people ("Wow, those people have suffered so much.")
- If we are made to think about our personal values that promote helping ("I really shouldn't act like such a jerk next time; I have to be nicer.")

When Negative Moods Make Us Less Likely to Help Others

- If we blame others for our bad mood ("I feel so angry at that jerk who put me in this situation.")
- If we become very self-focused ("I am so depressed.")
- If we are made to think about our personal values that do not promote helping ("I have to wise up and start thinking about my own needs more.")

to help the woman pick up her papers because you think you broke the other person's camera?

Probably. In an experiment that used this setup, 80 percent of participants who had been led to believe that they had broken the man's camera helped the woman pick up her papers; only 40 percent of participants who had had no broken-camera experience stopped to help (Cunningham et al., 1980). Thus, participants who unintentionally harmed one individual were more helpful to the next person. According to Roy Baumeister and others (1994), such spillover effects provide an especially vivid demonstration of the interpersonal nature of guilt and its function of enhancing, maintaining, and repairing relationships. Feeling guilty, they contend, motivates us to strengthen whatever social relations are at hand.

More generally, negative moods often promote helping. Why might this be? As noted earlier, people know that helping makes them feel good. This point underlies the negative state relief model, which we described earlier as proposing that people who are feeling bad are motivated to repair their mood and they realize that one way to do it is by helping others.

Although negative moods can boost helping, it is not always as strong and consistent a relationship as that between good moods and helping. As ■ Table 10.4 indicates, there are several limits to this effect. One important variable is whether people accept responsibility for their bad feelings (Rogers et al., 1982). Negative moods are less likely to promote helping if we blame others for them (such as when we're angry at another person) than if we take personal responsibility (such as when we regret a poor decision we just made). In addition, negative moods are less likely to increase helping if they cause us to become very self-focused (such as when we experience intense grief or depression or when we dwell on our own problems and concerns) than if they direct our focus outward (such as when we feel sad after watching a public service advertisement about child abuse) (Bagozzi & Moore, 1994; Fisher et al., 2008; Tangney et al., 1996).

People are much less likely to help someone when they're in a bad mood. FALSE.

Role Models and Social Norms: A Helpful Standard

We mentioned earlier that children become more aware as they get older of the potential benefits of helping. How, in general, do children learn about helping? One important way is through role models. Seeing important people in their lives behave prosocially, or antisocially, encourages children to follow suit. Role models can be real people in children's lives or characters they see on television (Moriarty & McCabe, 1977; Rushton, 1981a; Sprafkin et al., 1975). Indeed, although politicians, educators, researchers, and parents pay a great deal of attention to the negative effects of TV on children (discussed in Chapter 11 on Aggression), TV can also have positive effects on children through the modelling of prosocial behaviour. After reviewing extensive research literature, Susan Hearold (1986) concluded that the effect of prosocial TV on prosocial behaviour was about twice as large as the effect of TV violence on aggressive behaviour. She argued that rather than advocating primarily to "eliminate the negative" by removing shows with sex and violence, the public should focus more on "accentuating the positive" by encouraging the creation of more shows with prosocial themes and positive role models (p. 116). More recently, a meta-analysis of 34 studies involving more than 5000 children found a reliable positive effect of prosocial television on children's prosocial behavior, especially when specific acts of altruism were modelled on TV (Mares & Woodard, 2005).

Helpful models are important not only for children but for all of us. Observing helpful models increases helping in a variety of situations (Bryan & Test, 1967; Sarason et al., 1991; Siu et al., 2006). Even song lyrics can increase helping. Céline Jacob and others (2010) found that restaurant patrons in France gave larger tips to their waitress when they were exposed to background music containing prosocial, compared to neutral, lyrics.

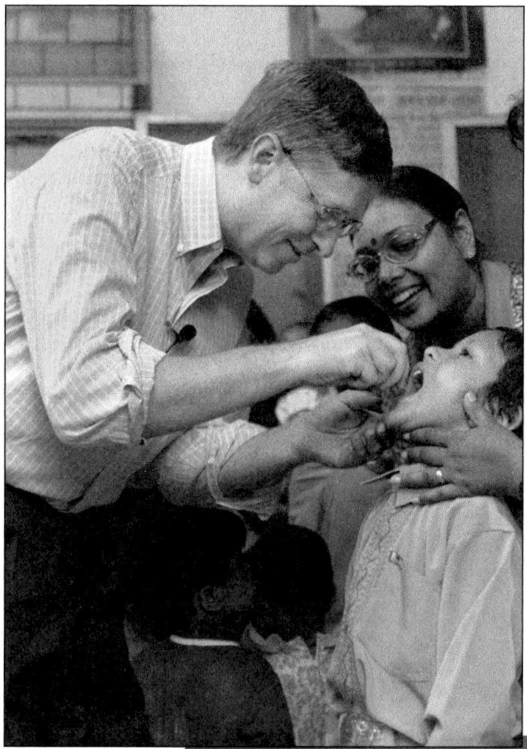

Jeff Christensen/Getty Images

Microsoft chairman Bill Gates has donated billions of dollars through the Bill and Melinda Gates Foundation to help reduce poverty and disease around the world. Here he administers an oral polio vaccine to Nikunj Kumar, 5, of New Delhi, India.

Why do people who exemplify helping inspire us to help? Three reasons stand out. First, they provide an example of behaviour for us to imitate directly. Second, when they are rewarded for their helpful behaviour, they teach us that helping is valued and rewarding, which strengthens our own inclination to be helpful. Third, the behaviour of these models makes us think about and become more aware of the standards of conduct in our society.

General rules of conduct established by society are called **social norms**. These norms embody standards of socially approved and disapproved behaviour. Two sets of social norms bear directly on when people are likely to help. The first consists of norms based on fairness. As we mentioned in Chapter 7, the *norm of reciprocity* establishes quid-pro-quo transactions as a socially approved standard: People who give to you should be paid back. We discussed reciprocal altruism earlier in this chapter; many animals, including humans, help those who have helped them. Equity is the basis of another norm calling for fairness in our treatment of others. The *norm of equity* prescribes that when people are in a situation in which they feel overbenefited (receiving more benefits than earned), they should help those who are underbenefited (receiving fewer benefits than earned). Such help restores an equitable balance (Walster et al., 1978).

Other social norms related to help go beyond an immediate sense of fairness to a larger sense of what is right. The **norm of social responsibility** dictates that people should help those who need assistance. This norm creates a sense of duty and obligation, to which people respond by giving more help to those in greater need of it (Berkowitz, 1972; Bornstein, 1994). When people are more motivated by concerns about *justice* or *fairness*, however, their intentions to help someone will be driven more by their belief that this person *deserves* their assistance than by their belief that he or she simply needs it (Lerner, 1998).

Concerns with reciprocity, equity, social responsibility, and justice can have powerful effects. Yet sometimes they fail to produce the helpful behaviour they prescribe. Why? One problem with social norms is their generality. They are so general, so abstract, that it is not clear when they apply. When you encounter two people fighting, should you follow the norm prescribing "Help those in need" or the one instructing you to "Mind your own business"? (Darley & Latané, 1970).

social norm
A general rule of conduct reflecting standards of social approval and disapproval.

norm of social responsibility
A moral standard emphasizing that people should help those who need assistance.

Personal Influences: Who Is Likely to Help?

As we have just seen, social psychological research addressing the question "When do people help?" has been quite productive. What about the question "Who is likely to help?" In this section, we consider some of the individual differences between people that address this question.

Are Some People More Helpful than Others?

What led to 12-year-old Craig Kielburger creating the "Free the Children" organization? One day Craig read a Toronto newspaper that detailed the plight of another boy his age a world away in Pakistan; Iqbal worked in a carpet factory 12 hours a day, six days a week. Craig and his friends began to discuss the case of Iqbal, and others like him, and his crusade for children's rights began. Free the Children, now a worldwide organization, has been nominated for a Nobel Peace Prize three times. Although situational factors clearly can overwhelm individual differences in influencing helping behaviours in many contexts (Latané & Darley, 1970), researchers have found some evidence that people who are more helpful than others in one situation are likely to be more helpful in other situations as well (Hampson, 1984; Hay & Cook, 2007; Rushton, 1981b). In addition, longitudinal research suggests that this individual difference may be relatively stable over time (Dovidio et al., 2006). For example, Nancy Eisenberg and others (2002) found that the degree to which preschool children exhibited spontaneous helping behaviour predicted how helpful they would be in later childhood and early adulthood.

"The purpose of human life is to serve and to show compassion and the will to help others."

—Albert Schweitzer

This individual difference in helpfulness appears to be partly based on genetics. Genetically identical (monozygotic) twins are more similar to each other in their helpful behavioural tendencies and their helping-related emotions and reactions, such as empathy, than are fraternal (dizygotic) twins, who share only a portion of their genetic makeup (Gregory et al., 2009; Knafo & Plomin, 2006; Knafo et al., 2008).

What Is the Altruistic Personality?

Even if we identify some people who help others a lot and other people who don't, we have not addressed the question of what distinguishes people who help from those who do not—other than their helpfulness, of course. What are the various components of the altruistic personality? Can we predict who is likely to be altruistic by looking at people's overall personalities?

Consider some examples of people who have acted very altruistically. Do they seem to have very similar personality traits and characteristics? Take, for example, Oskar Schindler, the wealthy German businessman during the Nazi regime who became the hero of the book and movie *Schindler's List*. Schindler was a shady operator, cheating in business and marriage, partying with sadistic German military officers. From his overall personality, could anyone have predicted his altruistic actions of risking his own life to save over 4000 Jews during the Holocaust? It is doubtful. What about more contemporary models of altruism? Consider Bill Gates, a computer geek who cofounded Microsoft and became the richest man in the world. He and his wife Melinda have pledged billions of dollars to charity, much of it to target health issues around the world. Or how about Bono, the Irish rock star, who has worked tirelessly to raise money and awareness about the plight of poor African nations. Or Mother Teresa, a Roman Catholic nun from Macedonia, who devoted her life to the poor in India.

The quest to discover the altruistic personality has not been an easy one. Much of the research conducted over the years has failed to find consistent, reliable personality characteristics that predict helping behaviour across situations. Some researchers have changed the nature of the quest, however, focusing on personality variables that predict helping in some specific situations rather than across all situations; and their studies have been more successful in identifying traits that predict such behaviour (Carlo et al., 2005; Finkelstein, 2009; Penner, 2004).

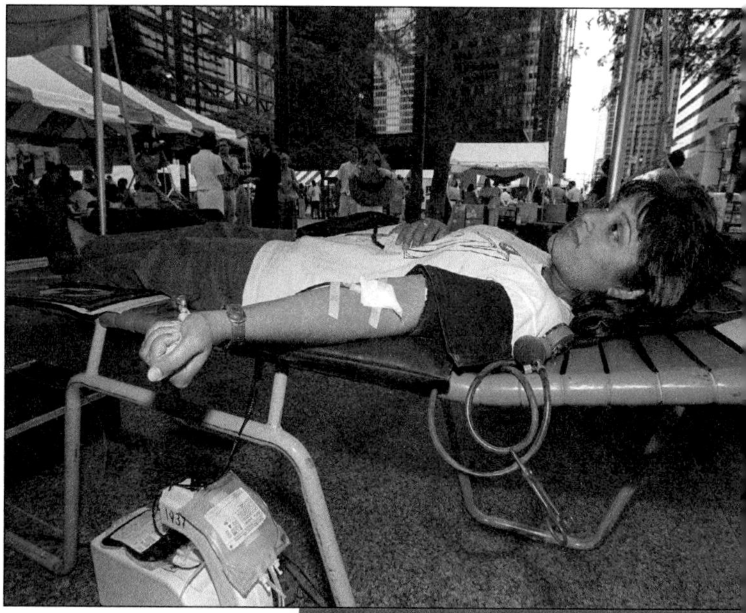

CP PICTURE ARCHIVE/Frank Gunn

According to Canadian Blood Services, every 60 seconds someone in Canada needs blood or a blood product. They rely on volunteers to replenish the supply. If people stopped giving blood, they estimate they would run out in four to six days.

Two qualities that the research thus far suggests are most essential for an altruistic personality are empathy and advanced moral reasoning (e.g., Eisenberg & Eggum, 2008; Eggum et al., 2011; Hoffman, 2000). We have already discussed empathy in this chapter, such as in the context of Batson's empathy-altruism hypothesis. Being able to take the perspective of others and experience empathy are associated positively with helping and other prosocial behaviours in children and adults (Albiero et al., 2009; Batson, 2009; Nakao & Itakura, 2009; Vaish et al., 2009).

The second characteristic associated with helping is moral reasoning. Children and adults who exhibit internalized and advanced levels of moral reasoning behave more altruistically than others. Such moral reasoning involves adhering to moral standards independent of external social controls, and taking into account the needs of others when making decisions about courses of action. In contrast, people whose reasoning is focused on their own needs or on the concrete personal consequences that their actions are likely to have tend not to engage in many helping behaviours (Carlo et al., 2011; Krebs & Rosenwald, 1994; Malti et al., 2009; Midlarsky et al., 1999; Schonert-Reichl, 1999).

The combination of empathy and advanced moral reasoning may be an especially strong predictor of helping tendencies. Paul Miller and his colleagues (1996) propose that "cold" cognitive moral principles may not be enough to trigger self-sacrificing prosocial action; however, helping is much more likely when these principles are activated together with the experience of "hot" empathic or sympathetic emotional responses to another's suffering.

Elizabeth Midlarsky, Stephanie Fagin-Jones, and their colleagues (Fagin-Jones & Midlarsky, 2007; Midlarsky et al., 2005) have conducted one fascinating line of research that suggests the importance of both empathy and moral reasoning. They contrasted the personalities of "non-Jewish heroes of the Holocaust"—people who risked their lives to help Jews despite having no expectation of any extrinsic rewards—with bystanders who did not help during the Holocaust. The researchers found that rescuers did indeed tend to differ from bystanders on a combination of several variables associated with prosocial behaviour, particularly empathic concern and moral reasoning. Both of these qualities are reflected in the quote of one woman who sheltered 30 Jews in her home in Poland: "Helping to give shelter was the natural thing to do, the human thing. When I looked into those eyes, how could I not care? Of course I was afraid—always afraid—but there was no choice but to do the only decent thing" (Midlarsky et al., 2005, p. 908).

"True kindness presupposes the faculty of imagining as one's own the suffering and joy of others."

—André Gide

Interpersonal Influences: Whom Do People Help?

However influential they might be, personal factors alone do not a helper make. The characteristics of the person in need are important as well. Are some people more likely than others to receive help? Are some helpers particularly responsive to certain kinds of individuals who need assistance? Here, we explore some of the interpersonal aspects of helping.

Attractive people have a better chance than unattractive people of getting help when they need it. TRUE.

Perceived Characteristics of the Person in Need

Although many characteristics of a person in need might affect whether that individual is helped, researchers have paid special attention to two characteristics: the personal attractiveness of the person in need and whether the person seems responsible for being in the position of needing assistance.

Attractiveness In Chapter 9, we described the social advantages enjoyed by physically attractive individuals. The bias for beauty also affects helping. Attractive people are more likely to be offered help and cooperation across a number of different settings, whether it be asking for directions on campus, playing a game that could be either competitive or cooperative, or requesting money in a health emergency (Farrelly et al., 2007; West & Brown, 1975; Wilson, 1978). One demonstration of this was a study by Peter Benson and his colleagues (1976) in a large metropolitan airport. Darting into a phone booth to make a call, each of 604 travellers discovered some materials supposedly left behind accidentally by the previous caller (but actually planted by the experimenters): a completed graduate school application form, a photograph of the applicant, and a stamped, addressed envelope. In some packets, the photo depicted a physically attractive individual; in others, the person was relatively unattractive. What was a busy traveller to do? When the researchers checked their mail, they found that people were more likely to send in the materials of the good-looking applicants than those of the less attractive applicants.

Attributions of Responsibility At some time or another, most students have had the experience of being asked to lend their class notes to a classmate. Has this ever happened to you? If so, you can compare your reactions with those of the students in a study conducted by Richard Barnes and his colleagues (1979). In this research, students received a call from an experimental confederate posing as another student, who asked to borrow their class notes to prepare for an upcoming exam. The reason for this request varied. To some students, the caller said, "I just don't seem to have the ability to take good notes. I really try to take good notes, but sometimes I just can't do it." Other students were told, "I just don't seem to have the motivation to take good notes. I really can take good notes, but sometimes I just don't try." You probably won't be surprised to learn that the caller received much more help from those who were informed he had tried yet failed than from those who were told he hadn't tried at all.

Bluntly stating that you didn't even try to help yourself may seem like an obvious way to ensure that others won't help you out. But even when the circumstances are more complex and the causes more subtle, people's beliefs about the needy individual's responsibility influence helping. For example, participants in an experiment by Pamela Dooley (1995) read scenarios about someone who had just been diagnosed with AIDS. If the participants read that the person had contracted the disease through a blood transfusion rather than through sexual activity or drug use, they considered the situation less controllable, and they felt more pity for the person. In addition, those who felt pity indicated a greater desire to engage in helping behaviours. Similarly, Michelle Lobchuk and others (2008) found that caregivers of people with lung cancer had more negative emotions and gave less supportive help if they believed the patient was largely responsible for their disease.

The Fit Between Giver and Receiver

Some potential helpers are particularly responsive to some kinds of potential recipients. In this section, we look at a variety of ways in which helping depends on the fit between a giver and a receiver.

Similarity: Helping Those Just Like Us We are more likely to help others who are similar to us. All kinds of similarity—from dress to attitudes to nationality—increase our willingness to help, and signs of dissimilarity decrease it (Dovidio, 1984).

There are probably several reasons underlying this effect. For one thing, as seen in Chapter 9, we are more likely to be attracted to and develop relationships with people who are similar to ourselves. In addition, people tend to empathize more with similar others or with people in their ingroups (Xu et al., 2009). The influence of similarity could even be a form of kin selection, as people may use similarity in appearance as a signal of potential kinship. People are much more likely to help fellow ingroup members than they are to help members of an outgroup (Bernhard et al., 2006; Kogut & Ritov, 2007; Stürmer et al., 2006). For example, in a study by Mark Levine and others (2005) a jogger (actually a confederate) who fell and seemed to be in pain with an injured ankle was more likely to be helped when he was wearing the shirt of the participant's favourite team than if he was wearing the shirt of a rival team, or a shirt with no logo.

The effects of similarity and ingroup status on helping suggest that members of the same race should help each other more than members of different races. However, in a meta-analysis of more than 30 studies, Donald Saucier and others (2005) found no consistent overall relationship between racial similarity and helping. What accounts for these inconsistencies? First, although helping can be a compassionate response to another, it can also be seen as a sign of superiority over the person who needs help, and this can greatly complicate the decision about helping someone (Ames et al., 2004; Vorauer & Sasaki, 2009). Second, public displays of racial prejudice risk social disapproval, and prejudiced individuals may bend over backward (in public, at least) to avoid revealing their attitudes. As discussed in Chapter 5, however, modern racism relies on more subtle forms of discrimination. For example, using a measure of implicit racial bias, Irena Stepanikova and others (2011) showed that helping decreased when a research participant, who was also high in prejudice, thought that his partner on a task was black. Consistent with predictions from theories of modern racism, Saucier and others' (2005) meta-analysis found that when the situation provides people with excuses or justifications for not helping, racial discrimination in helping is more likely.

Intergroup biases in helping can be reduced significantly, however, if the members of the different groups can perceive themselves as members of a common group. Through fostering perceptions of shared identities and highlighting similarities between individuals across groups, an ingroup and an outgroup can begin to see each other as more similar than different, thereby promoting helping and other positive behaviours (Dovidio et al., 2009; Gaertner & Dovidio, 2000).

Closeness: A Little Help for Our Friends As we would expect, people are usually more helpful toward those they know and care about than toward strangers or superficial acquaintances (Bell et al., 1995; Clark & Mills, 1993; Stewart-Williams, 2008). People in a *communal* relationship, such as close friends or romantic partners, feel mutual responsibility for each other's needs. People in an *exchange* relationship, such as acquaintances or business associates, give help with the expectation of receiving comparable benefits in return—"If I help you move your furniture, you'd better give me a ride to the airport." When people are, or desire to be, in a communal relationship with each other, they attend more to each other's needs, are more likely to help, and are less likely to be concerned with keeping track of rewards and costs. People in a communal relationship also feel better about having helped the other, and they feel worse if they were unable to help (Williamson et al., 1996). For example, Lara Aknin and others (2011) at the University of British Columbia asked participants to recall the last time they spent $20 on someone they considered to be a strong social tie (i.e., family member or good friend) or on someone with whom they have a weak tie (i.e., acquaintance), and then measured their level of happiness. They found the highest rates of happiness in those who recalled a time they spent the money on the person close to them.

So, common sense seems correct here: People help their friends more than strangers or acquaintances. But there may be an exception to this general rule, and it has to do with the helper's ego. If we can help a friend succeed in a task that is not very important to our identity or relevant to our ego, we are likely to do so and to delight in their success. But what if they succeed in doing something that we wish we could do at least as well? Would we help a friend shine in this case? According to the *self-evaluation maintenance model* (Erber & Tesser, 1994), people sometimes offer more help to a stranger than to a friend if the help is for something that can be threatening to the helper's ego. We may prefer that a stranger steal the spotlight than a friend whose success we'll be reminded of all too often.

In any situation, people are more likely to help a friend succeed than a stranger. FALSE.

Gender and Helping

Here's a quick, one-question quiz: Who helps more, men or women? Before you answer, consider the following situations:

A. Two strangers pass on the street. Suddenly, one of them needs help that might be dangerous to give. Other people are watching. The person in need is female.

B. Two individuals have a close relationship. Every so often, one of them needs assistance that takes time and energy to provide but is not physically dangerous. No one else is around to notice whether help is given. The person who needs help is either male or female.

Is your answer the same for both situations? It shouldn't be. Situation A is a classic male-helper scenario. Here, the helper is a "knight in shining armour"—physically brave and chivalrous, rescuing a lady in distress. Because social psychologists have tended to focus on these kinds of emergency situations, their research has found that, on the average, men are more helpful than women, and women receive more help than do men (Eagly & Crowley, 1986).

Situation B is the classic female-helper scenario. Every day, millions of women—mothers, sisters, wives, and female friends—provide support for their friends and loved ones, and they are more likely to provide this kind of help than are men (George et al., 1998; McGuire, 1994). Though it lacks the high drama of an emergency intervention, this type of helping, called "social support," plays a crucial role in the quality of our lives.

For types of helping that do not easily fit into either of these categories, the evidence for gender differences is not strong. In a field experiment conducted in six cities that examined whether people help a man or woman who dropped a pen, for example, there were no gender differences in who tended to help or in who was helped (Reysen & Ganz, 2006).

Gender is related not only to differences in helping behaviour but also to differences in the willingness to *seek* help. Have you ever had the experience of getting lost while driving with a member of the opposite sex? Who wanted to stop early on and ask for directions? Who kept insisting that help wasn't necessary? In this case, the male stereotype is true: For relatively minor problems, at least, men ask for help less frequently than do women—a difference replicated in several countries around the world (Chang, 2007; Mackenzie et al., 2006; Murray et al., 2008; Sherer, 2007). Seeking help is less socially acceptable for men and is more threatening to their self-esteem (Wills & DePaulo, 1991).

Flynn Larson/Phototonica/Getty Images

Men are less likely to seek help than women, possibly because it is more threatening to their self-esteem.

Women seek help more often than men do. TRUE.

Reactions to Receiving Help

The last time someone helped you, how did you feel? Grateful, relieved, comforted—anything else? Embarrassed, obligated, inferior? Receiving help is often a positive experience, but sometimes it has drawbacks for the recipient. There are costs in providing help, and there can be costs in receiving it.

Jeffrey Fisher and Arie Nadler have extensively examined people's reactions to receiving help (Fisher et al., 1982; Nadler & Fisher, 1986). According to their **threat-to-self-esteem model**, receiving help is experienced as *self-supportive* when the recipient feels appreciated and cared for, but as *self-threatening* when the recipient feels inferior and overly dependent.

People who are stigmatized by being the targets of negative stereotypes and feeling devalued in the larger society often face a difficult attributional dilemma when they receive help from members of nonstigmatized groups: Is the helping sincere and unassuming, is it well intentioned but patronizing, or is it controlling and designed to keep the recipient dependent? These are questions that members of nonstigmatized groups aren't as likely to consider when they receive help from another. Members of stigmatized groups may feel worse about themselves after receiving help from an outgroup member, particularly if the help was unsolicited (Blaine et al., 1995; Nadler et al., 2009; Schneider et al., 1996).

Culture and Who Receives Help

As we said earlier in the chapter, compared to individualists, collectivists may be more likely to help ingroup members but less likely to help outgroup members (Conway et al., 2001; Schwartz, 1990). Even within a culture, the extent to which individuals are individualistic or collectivistic can matter.

We also discussed earlier that people are less likely to help if they think the person is responsible for his or her plight. Elizabeth Mullen and Linda Skitka (2009) recently proposed that this may be a stronger influence on helping in an individualist culture—where individuals may be expected to have more control over their own fates—than in a collectivist one. On the other hand, perceptions of how much the person in need contributes to society might affect the helping decisions of collectivists—who have stronger norms of interdependence—more than of individualists.

To test these ideas, Mullen and Skitka had participants from the United States and the Ukraine (a more collectivistic society) read about 16 individuals who needed an organ transplant. Information about each individual suggested that some were

threat-to-self-esteem model
The theory that reactions to receiving assistance depend on whether help is perceived as supportive or threatening.

FIGURE 10.7

Who Should Receive Help? A Cross-Cultural Difference

Americans and Ukrainians were asked to decide which six of up to 16 individuals should receive an organ transplant. Participants were given information about the individuals that varied in terms of how personally responsible they seemed to be for their illnesses and how much they seemed to contribute to their society. Although participants in both countries preferred helping individuals who were not responsible for their illness and who made contributions to society, Americans' decisions were affected more by how responsible the person seemed, whereas Ukrainians' decisions were affected more by whether the person made contributions to society.

(Based on Mullen & Skitka, 2009.)

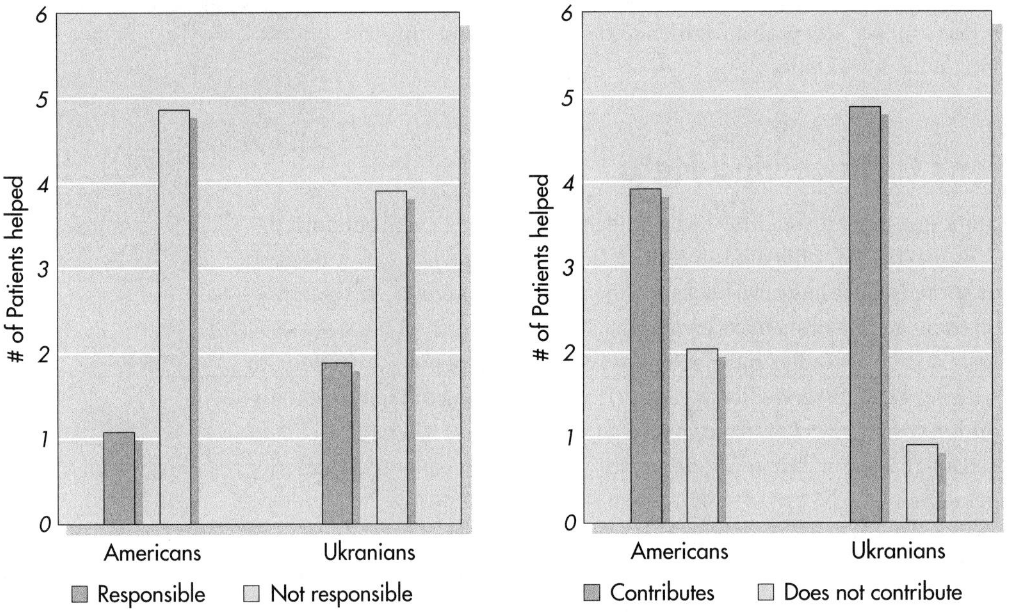

more responsible for their illness than others (e.g., a person continued to eat unhealthy foods and resist exercise despite warnings versus a person who had a genetically defective organ). The researchers also varied information about how much contribution the individuals seemed to make to society (e.g., a person who volunteers for multiple organizations versus a person who does not volunteer). After reading about all 16 people, participants were asked to indicate which of up to six of them should receive a transplant.

In both cultures, people were less likely to help patients who were more responsible for their organ failure or who made less contribution to society. However, as can be seen in Figure 10.7, the issue of personal responsibility played a bigger role in the decisions made by the Americans, whereas the issue of contribution to society played a bigger role in the decisions made by the Ukrainians.

The Helping Connection

Although whether or not people help others can be quite variable, there is a consistent theme that appears repeatedly in this chapter: a sense of connection. Throughout the chapter, this connection has taken various forms—genetic relatedness, empathic concern, sense of responsibility for someone, perceived similarity, shared group membership, and so on.

The importance of a sense of connection is vividly demonstrated by a cross-cultural comparison. First, consider one of the great social tragedies of our time: homelessness. In Canada, one of the richest countries on Earth, thousands of men, women, and children are without a home. Many sleep on the street, carry their belongings in grocery carts, and rummage through piles of garbage to find food. Now, compare Canada's homelessness with an anthropologist's account of life among the Moose (pronounced "MOH-say") in West Africa:

> Moose welcome anyone who wishes to join the community and move into the village. New arrivals have only to say where they wish to build their homes, and the user of the land in question gives it up for the newcomer's residence.... Each of the two years that I lived there, the well ran dry and villagers had to walk miles to get water for themselves and their stock from other villages, carrying it home on their heads. Each of these other villages shared their water until their wells were nearly dry, without expecting any reciprocation for the water. Even in these circumstances, any stranger who comes into the village may ask for a drink, and any visitor is offered water. (Fiske, 1991, pp. 190–191)

Among some of the poorest people on Earth, no one goes without shelter or remains thirsty as long as anyone has water to drink.

How can we account for the extraordinary difference between Canadian homelessness and Moose hospitality? Homelessness is, of course, a complex phenomenon affected by many specific economic and political factors. But it may also be a symptom of a profound loss of social connection in North American society (Wuthnow, 1991). Among the Moose, no such loss has occurred. Their sense of being intimately connected to others binds them to those who live in their village and to strangers who arrive in their midst.

The relationship between helping and interpersonal connection runs like a bright red thread through much of the research on helping. For example:

© DNAinfo/Ben Fractenberg

Connections forged between people who help each other can sometimes last a lifetime. In 2011, Ladder Company Six firefighters acted as pallbearers at the funeral of Josephine Harris, the woman they risked their lives to save nearly ten years earlier in the World Trade Center on September 11, 2001. Their selfless act of helping her may in turn have saved their own lives as the 110-story skyscraper collapsed around them.

- Evolutionary perspectives emphasize the genetic connection of reciprocal, kin, and within-group helping.
- Two kinds of connections lie at the heart of the empathy-altruism hypothesis: the cognitive connection of perspective taking and the emotional connection of empathic concern.
- In an emergency, bystanders who know the victim or know each other are more likely to intervene.
- People who respond empathically to another's suffering and consider the plight of others in their own moral reasoning are more likely to help than are others.
- Perceived similarity increases helping.
- In a close relationship, it's easier to give and more comfortable to receive.

Taken as a whole, these theories and research findings suggest that helping requires the recognition of individual human beings with whom we can have a meaningful connection. Which brings us back to Ladder Company Six, and the many others who risked, and even lost, their lives on September 11, 2001. Most of the people didn't know the others they were helping. But unexpectedly, horribly, fate had thrown them together, and suddenly their lives deeply mattered to each other. They felt responsible for each other. Many of those who helped in the face of grave danger may never have read the words that English poet John Donne wrote almost 400 years ago. But they would have understood them:

> No man is an island, entire of itself. Every man is a piece of the continent, a part of the main. If a clod be washed away by the sea, Europe is the less, as well as if a promontory were, as well as if a manor of thy friends or of thine own were. Any man's death diminishes me, because I am involved in mankind. And therefore never send to know for whom the bell tolls; it tolls for thee.

REVIEW

Evolutionary and Motivational Factors: Why Do People Help?

Evolutionary Factors in Helping

- Evolutionary perspectives emphasize two ways in which helping could become an innate, universal behavioural tendency: kin selection, in which individuals protect their own genes by helping close relatives; and reciprocal altruism, in which those who give also receive.
- Other evolutionary approaches include the idea of group selection, in which members of a social group help each other survive.

Rewards of Helping: Helping Others to Help Oneself

- People are much more likely to help when the potential rewards of helping seem high relative to the potential costs.
- Helping others often makes the helper feel good, it can relieve negative feelings such as guilt, and it is associated with better health.
- People who are feeling bad may be inclined to help others in order to feel relief from their negative mood.

Altruism or Egoism: The Great Debate

- According to the empathy-altruism hypothesis, taking the perspective of a person perceived to be in need creates the other-oriented emotion of empathic concern, which in turn produces the altruistic motive to reduce the other's distress.
- The self-oriented emotion of personal distress produces the egoistic motive to reduce one's own distress.
- When people are altruistically motivated, they will help even when escaping from the helping situation is easy.
- Alternatives to the empathy-altruism hypothesis include empathy-specific punishments for not helping and empathy-specific rewards for helping, such as negative state relief and empathic joy.
- Longer-term acts of helping, such as volunteerism, reflect both altruistic and egoistic motivations. Self-interested goals in this context can be a good thing because they promote a commitment to helping behavior to the extent that such goals are met.

Situational Influences: When Do People Help?

The Unhelpful Crowd

- Research on the bystander effect, in which the presence of others inhibits helping in an emergency, indicates why the five steps necessary for helping—noticing, interpreting, taking responsibility, deciding how to help, and providing help—may not be taken.
- The distractions of others and our own self-concerns may impair our ability to notice that someone needs help.
- Under ambiguous circumstances, some interpretations—such as the belief that an attacker and a victim have a close relationship or the mistaken inferences drawn from pluralistic ignorance—reduce bystander intervention.
- People may fail to take responsibility because they assume that others will—a phenomenon called diffusion of responsibility.
- Bystanders are less likely to offer direct aid when they do not feel competent to do so. They can, however, call for assistance from others.
- Even if people want to help, they may not do so if they fear that behaving in a helpful fashion will make them look foolish.
- Some recent research has demonstrated the bystander effect even in online contexts, when the bystanders are not physically present.
- The legacy of the bystander effect research and of the Kitty Genovese tragedy that inspired it endures, even as revisions are suggested to some of the research conclusions or to some of the details of the Genovese case.

Time Pressure

- When people are in a hurry, they are less likely to notice or choose to help others in need.

Location and Helping

- Residents of densely populated areas are less likely to provide spontaneous, informal help to strangers than are residents of smaller or less densely populated communities.

Culture and Helping

- Cross-cultural research has found variation in the helping rates of people in cities around the world. According to one study, people in cities with relatively low levels of economic well-being were somewhat more likely to help strangers, and people from *simpatía* cultures were more likely to help strangers than people from non-*simpatía* cultures.
- Research concerning the relationship between individualism-collectivism and helping has yielded rather mixed results. According to one analysis, collectivists may be more responsive than individualists to the immediate needs of a particular person, but less helpful in more abstract situations.

Moods and Helping

- A good mood increases helpfulness.
- People in a good mood may help in order to maintain their positive mood or because they have more positive thoughts and expectations about helpful behaviour, the person in need, or social activities in general.
- A bad mood can often increase helpfulness, such as when people feel guilty about something.
- People in a bad mood may be motivated to help others in order to improve their mood.
- A bad mood is less likely to increase helpfulness if the bad mood is attributed to the fault of others, or if it causes the person to become very self-focused.

Role Models and Social Norms: A Helpful Standard

- Observing a helpful model increases helping.
- Social norms that promote helping are based on a sense of fairness or on standards about what is right.
- Cultural differences exist in how people interpret and apply social norms.

Personal Influences: Who Is Likely to Help?

Are Some People More Helpful than Others?

- There is some evidence of relatively stable individual differences in helping tendencies.
- Recent findings suggest that there may be a genetic, heritable component to helpfulness.

What Is the Altruistic Personality?

- Some personality traits are associated with helpful behavioural tendencies, but no one set of traits appears to define the altruistic personality.
- Two qualities that do predict helping behaviours are empathy and advanced moral reasoning.

Interpersonal Influences: Whom Do People Help?

Perceived Characteristics of the Person in Need

- Attractive individuals are more likely to receive help than are those who are less attractive.
- People are more willing to help when they attribute a person's need for assistance to uncontrollable causes rather than to events under the person's control.

The Fit Between Giver and Receiver

- In general, perceived similarity to a person in need increases willingness to help.
- People are more likely to help members of their ingroups.
- Research on racial similarity has yielded inconsistent results.
- People usually help significant others more than strangers, except when helping threatens their own egos.

Gender and Helping

- Men help female strangers in potentially dangerous situations more than women do; women help friends and relations in everyday situations more than men do.
- Compared to women, men are more hesitant to seek help, especially for relatively minor problems.

Reactions to Receiving Help

- The threat-to-self-esteem model distinguishes between help perceived as supportive, which produces positive reactions, and help perceived as threatening, which creates negative reactions. Members of stigmatized groups sometimes feel worse after receiving unsolicited help from members of nonstigmatized groups.

Culture and Who Receives Help

- Some research has shown that people with a collectivistic orientation may be less likely to help outgroup members or strangers than are those with an individualistic orientation.

The Helping Connection

- Theory and research seem to indicate that helping requires the recognition of meaningful connections among individuals.

Key Terms

altruistic (368)
arousal: cost-reward model (365)
audience inhibition (377)
bystander effect (373)
diffusion of responsibility (376)
egoistic (368)
empathy (368)
empathy-altruism hypothesis (368)
good mood effect (383)
kin selection (362)
negative state relief model (366)
norm of social responsibility (385)
pluralistic ignorance (375)
prosocial behaviours (361)
social norm (385)
threat-to-self-esteem model (391)

Putting COMMON SENSE *to the Test*

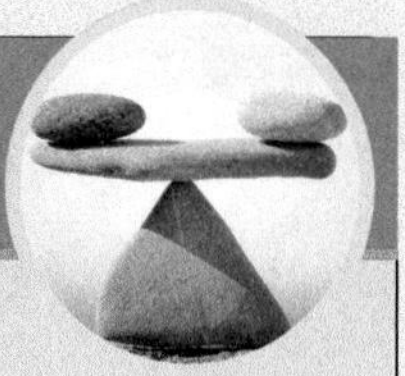

People are more likely to help someone in an emergency if the potential rewards seem high and the potential costs seem low.

True. *For both emergency situations and more long-term, well-planned helping, people's helping behaviours are determined in part by a cost-benefit analysis.*

In an emergency, a person who needs help has a much better chance of getting it if three other people are present than if only one other person is present.

False. *In several ways, the presence of others inhibits helping.*

People are much more likely to help someone when they're in a good mood.

True. *Compared to neutral moods, good moods tend to elicit more helping and other prosocial behaviours.*

People are much less likely to help someone when they're in a bad mood.

False. *Compared to neutral moods, negative moods often elicit more helping and prosocial behaviours. This effect depends on a number of factors, including whether people take responsibility for their bad mood or blame it on others; but in many circumstances, feeling bad leads to doing good.*

Attractive people have a better chance than unattractive people of getting help when they need it.

True. *People are more likely to help those who are attractive. This attractiveness can be based on physical appearance or friendliness.*

In any situation, people are more likely to help a friend succeed than a stranger.

False. *Although we tend to help those closest to us more than we help others, this tendency is often eliminated or even reversed if the task is very important to our own self-esteem and if our friend's success is threatening to our ego.*

Women seek help more often than men do.

True. *At least for relatively minor problems, men ask for help less frequently than women do.*

11

Roger Lemoyne/Getty Images

Aggression

In this chapter, we examine a disturbing aspect of human behaviour: aggression. First, we ask, "What is aggression?" and consider its definition. After describing how aggression may vary based on cultural, gender, and individual differences, we examine various theories concerning the origins of aggression. We then explore a variety of situational factors that influence when people are likely to behave aggressively. Next, we focus on two critically important issues in our society: media effects on aggression, including the consequences of exposure to media violence and pornography, and the intimate violence that can occur in close relationships. We conclude by discussing ways of reducing violence.

On June 2, 2012, 23-year-old Christopher Husbands walked into the food court of a busy downtown Toronto shopping mall and began shooting. Late-day shoppers grabbing a quick bite of dinner unwittingly found themselves in the middle of a dispute among gang members. While two individuals were specifically targeted by Husbands, six other people were injured. One of them, a 13-year-old boy visiting the mall with his family, was shot in the head. It was difficult for people to understand how individuals simply going about their daily lives could end up as victims of such random violence in Canada.

On July 22, 2011, Anders Breivik bombed government buildings in Norway, killing eight people. He then hunted down participants at a camp for the Youth Workers League, killing 69 others, mostly teenagers. He claimed his actions were in self-defense and that he was protecting his country from Muslims and other immigrants. Despite his cold-blooded killing of 77 innocent people, Breivik told his lawyer that he regretted that the final death toll wasn't higher.

The tragedy in Norway occurred 13 years after what has come to serve as a chilling icon of this sickening kind of aggression: the massacre at Columbine High School. On April 20, 1999, teenagers Dylan Klebold and Eric Harris, armed with a semi-automatic rifle, a semi-automatic handgun, two sawed-off shotguns, and more than 30 homemade bombs, terrorized the school. These boys first shot and killed two students in the school parking lot. Then they entered the cafeteria, where they threw pipe bombs and opened fire, filling the room with bullets.

Putting
COMMON SENSE
to the Test

Circle Your Answer

T F In virtually every culture, males are more violent than females.

T F For virtually any category of aggression, males are more aggressive than females.

T F Children who are spanked or otherwise physically disciplined (but not abused) for behaving aggressively tend to become less aggressive.

T F Blowing off steam by engaging in safe but aggressive activities (such as sports) makes people less likely to aggress later.

T F Exposure to TV violence in childhood is related to aggression later in life.

T F Men are much more likely than women to aggress against their spouses or partners.

T F Adults who as children were abused by their parents are less likely to inflict abuse on their own children than are other adults.

Reuters New Media Inc./Corbis

Eric Harris and Dylan Klebold are seen walking through Columbine High School on the day of their murderous rampage in April 1999.

From there, the boys went upstairs, shot a school police officer, and then shot and killed a teacher, ten other students, and themselves.

Profound questions are raised by these tragedies about the causes of aggression and violence. Each of these incidents reflects some of the factors associated with aggression that will be discussed in the pages that follow. This chapter examines the origins and immediate triggers of aggression. It focuses primarily on aggression by individuals; aggression by groups, such as rampaging mobs and warring nations, was discussed in Chapter 8. This chapter also discusses factors that reduce aggression.

What Is Aggression?

Although there are numerous ways one can define aggression, the definition that best represents the research today is that **aggression** is behaviour intended to harm another individual. "Harm" is an important word as it indicates that the aggressor is intending to leave the victim worse off than they were before. Aggressive behaviours come in many forms. Words as well as deeds can be aggressive. Quarrelling couples who intend their spiteful remarks to hurt are behaving aggressively. Spreading a vicious rumour about someone is another form of aggression. Even failure to act can be aggressive, if that failure is intended to hurt someone, such as by not helping someone avoid what you know will be a humiliating outcome.

AP Photo/Jack Smith, File

During their heavyweight boxing championship fight in June 1997, former champion Mike Tyson viciously bites champion Evander Holyfield's ear. After chewing off pieces of both of Holyfield's ears, Tyson was disqualified, and a near-riot ensued in the ring. Was Tyson's attack an instance of instrumental aggression, in which he bit Holyfield's ears in order to stop a fight he felt he could not win, or was it an example of emotional aggression, in which he lost his composure and snapped due to the frustration and pain he was experiencing?

To distinguish them from less harmful behaviours, extreme acts of aggression are called *violence.* Some other terms in the language of aggression refer to emotions and attitudes. *Anger* consists of strong feelings of displeasure in response to a perceived injury; the exact nature of these feelings (for example, outrage, hate, or irritation) depends on the specific situation. *Hostility* is a negative, antagonistic attitude toward another person or group. Anger and hostility are often closely connected to aggression, but not always. People can be angry with others and regard them with great hostility without ever trying to harm them. And aggression can occur without a trace of anger or hostility, as when a contract killer murders a perfect stranger in order to "make a killing" financially.

The aggression of a hired gun is an example of **instrumental aggression**, in which harm is inflicted as a means to a desired end. Aggression aimed at harming someone for personal gain, attention, or even self-defence fits this definition. If the aggressor believes that there is an easier way to obtain the goal, aggression would not occur. Some researchers call this type of aggression *proactive aggression.* In **emotional aggression**, the means and the end coincide. Harm is inflicted for its own sake. Some researchers call this type of aggression *reactive aggression.* Emotional aggression is often impulsive, carried out in the heat of the moment. The jealous lover strikes out in rage; fans of rival soccer teams go at each other with fists and clubs. Emotional aggression, however, can also be calm, cool, and calculating. Revenge, so the saying goes, is a dish best served cold.

Of course, sometimes it is hard to distinguish between instrumental and emotional aggression. Why did Mike Tyson viciously bite Evander Holyfield's ear during their 1997 championship boxing match? Was it a deliberate attempt to escape the embarrassment of being beaten by his opponent for the second time, or did he simply lose control and lash out against him in frustration? Perhaps no one, not even Tyson himself, can answer this question—in part because it is difficult to know where to draw the line between the two types of aggression and motives. Indeed, some scholars believe that all aggression is fundamentally instrumental, serving some need, and still others suggest that instrumental and emotional aggression are not distinct categories but endpoints on a continuum (Anderson & Huesmann, 2007; Tedeschi & Bond, 2001).

Culture, Gender, and Individual Differences

Just as not all types of aggression are alike, not all groups of people are alike in their attitudes and propensities toward aggression. Before we discuss the causes of aggression and what can be done about it, we need to consider how aggression is similar and how it differs across cultures, gender, and individuals.

Culture and Aggression

Based on information collected by the World Health Organization (2002), violence is the cause of death for more than 1.6 million people worldwide each year (see ▪ Table 11.1). In 2010, there were just over 22 000 sexual assaults reported to police in Canada, and 554 murders, the lowest homicide level since the 1960s. Do these numbers seem high or low to you? As a basis of comparison, the United States reported 14 748 murders and 84 767 forcible rapes in 2010, according to Federal Bureau of Investigation statistics. Though both of these statistics represent a dramatic decrease from the previous few years, the rates of murder, rape, and assault among 11 countries in the Americas (including Argentina, the Bahamas, Chile, Costa Rica, and the United States) are about double the world averages (Barber, 2006). ▶ Figure 11.1, on page 402, illustrates some of the variation in homicide rates around the world. Keep in mind, of course, that the United States has a much larger population than Canada. Despite this, Canada has for many years enjoyed a positive comparison in terms of crime statistics—rates of crimes in major Canadian cities are much lower than those found in similarly sized American cities.

TABLE 11.1	
The Violent Crime Clock	
The World Health Organization (2002) reported the following worldwide statistics:	
▪ One MURDER	every 60 seconds
▪ One DEATH DUE TO ARMED CONFLICT	every 100 seconds
▪ One AGGRAVATED ASSAULT	every 35 seconds
▪ One SUICIDE	every 40 seconds
(World Health Organization, 2002.)	

As discussed throughout the book, individualistic cultures place more emphasis on the values of independence, autonomy, and self-reliance, whereas collectivistic cultures place greater emphasis on the values of interdependence, cooperation, and social harmony. Gordon Forbes and others (2009) hypothesized that individualistic cultures, which are less concerned with social harmony and the avoidance of open conflict, are most likely to have a relatively high rate of aggression. To examine this idea, they asked students in China (a highly collectivistic culture), the United States (a highly individualistic culture), and Poland (a culture with intermediate levels of collectivism and individualism) to complete questionnaires about different types of aggression. The researchers found that aggression levels were highest in

aggression
Behaviour intended to harm another individual.

instrumental aggression
Inflicting harm in order to obtain something of value

emotional aggression
Inflicting harm for its own sake

FIGURE 11.1

Violence Around the World

These figures indicate the number of murders in one year per 100 000 people in each of several countries, according to United Nations statistics published in 2002. As can be seen, the frequency of murders varies widely around the world.

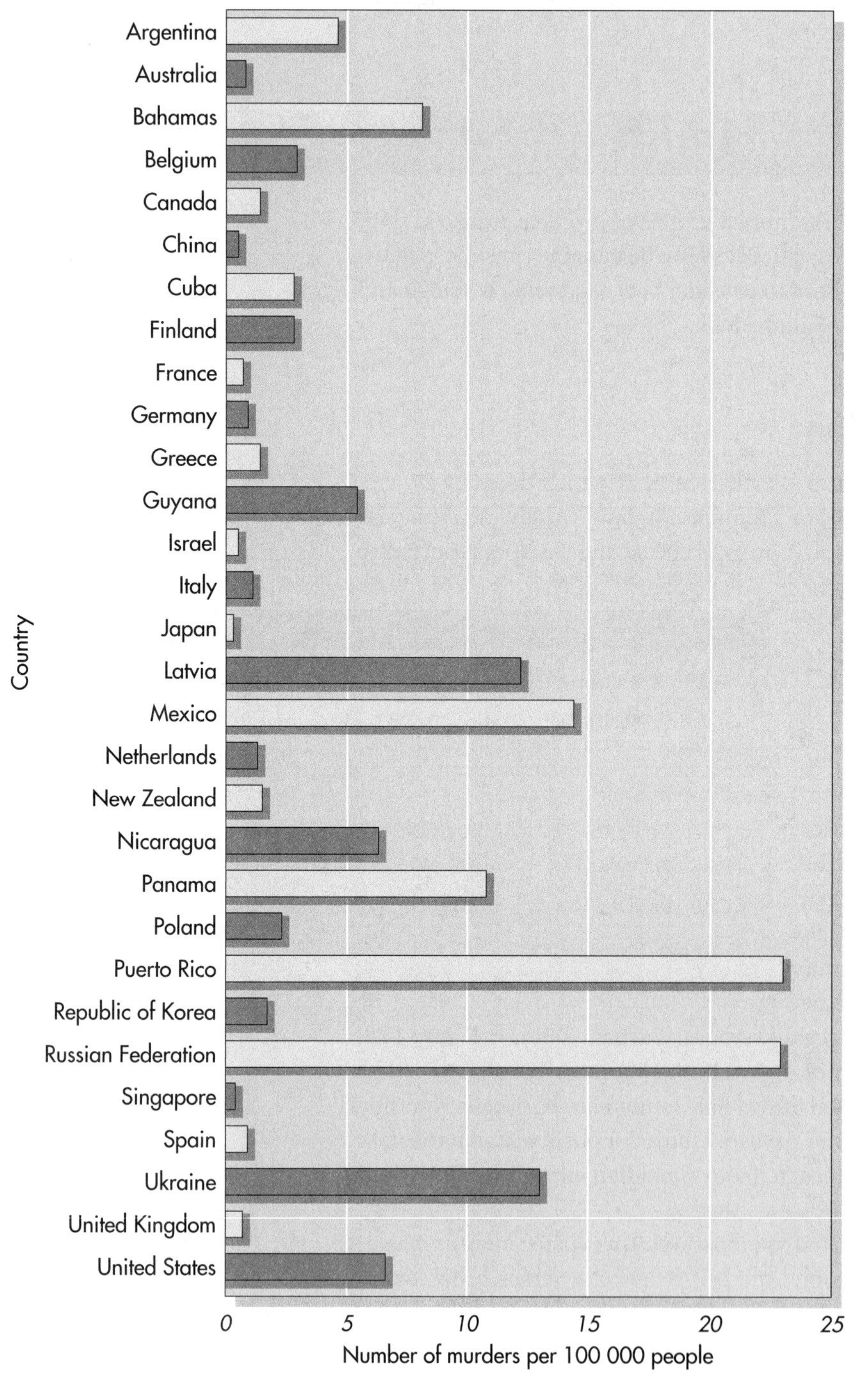

the United States and lowest in China, with Poland falling in the middle. Although there may be multiple reasons for these differences, Forbes and his colleagues believe that the results support their hypothesis that individualism is associated with aggression.

The forms violence typically takes, and people's attitudes toward various kinds of aggression, also differ internationally. Relative to most of the world, the United States has a tremendous amount of gun-related violence. The prevalence of handguns in the United States is exceptionally high, and even when compared to countries with which it shares much culturally, such as Canada, England, and Australia, attitudes about guns tend to be much more permissive and positive in the United States, especially among males (Cooke, 2004). Researchers believe that the higher murder rate in the United States is due to the prevalence of guns. Almost 67 percent of the murders in the United States in 2010 were committed with guns.

Cultures also differ in their attitudes about aggression. In a study involving students at 36 universities in 19 different countries around the world, there was considerable variation in how acceptable the students found different actions, such as a husband slapping a wife or vice versa (Douglas & Straus, 2006). In general, respondents from Europe were more approving of a husband slapping a wife than were respondents from Australia and New Zealand, who in turn tended to be somewhat more approving than respondents from North America. In contrast, these trends were reversed for the question of whether respondents had ever injured a dating partner—on this issue, North American rates tended to be highest.

What is considered to be aggression and unacceptable in relation to children also can differ across cultures. For example, in Japan, it is not uncommon for Japanese adult businessmen to grope schoolgirls on public transportation—a practice that would be considered aggressive and unacceptable in many other cultures. A 2004 survey conducted in Tokyo found that 64 percent of women in their 20s and 30s said that they had been groped in subways or subway stations (Ronzone, 2009).

Another example concerns female genital mutilation—any of several procedures in which, according to some estimates, the genitals of approximately 6000 girls a day are cut in several countries around the world, particularly in parts of Africa and Asia. The cultures that practice this consider it an important, sacred ritual; but the cultures that condemn it consider it an inhumane act of violence and have vigorously called for a worldwide ban (Leye et al., 2006; Rosenthal, 2006).

Bullying Around the World Children around the world are physically, sexually, or emotionally bullied by other students (Hong, & Espelage, 2012; Kanetsuna et al., 2006; Nesdale & Naito, 2005). The reported prevalence of bullying varies widely across research studies, with estimates on the low end suggesting that 5 or 10 percent of schoolchildren are involved in bullying, and estimates on the high end suggesting numbers as high as 70 to 90 percent (Borntrager et al., 2009; Due & Holstein, 2008; Olweus, 2004; Santalahti et al., 2008). Bullying behaviour appears to peak in the middle school years, from Grade 6 through Grade 8, is more likely to be perpetuated by boys than girls, and is increasingly seen in the form of cyberbullying (Hoertel et al., 2012; Law et al., 2012; Wang et al., 2012). When Wendy Craig and her colleagues (2000) set up hidden video cameras and microphones to get an unfiltered peek into aggression in schoolyards in Canada, they saw bullying in mid-sized schools at a rate of 4.5 episodes per hour. This team of researchers found in a later study that almost half of boys in Grade 8 and half the girls in Grade 9 reported having recently bullied others (Pepler et al., 2006).

These seemingly ordinary rites of childhood can lead to extraordinary suffering, including feelings of panic, nervousness, and distraction in school; recurring memories of abuse; depression and anxiety that can endure through adulthood; and even suicide (Birkett et al., 2009; Cassidy, 2009; Gladstone et al., 2006; Lund et al., 2009; Meltzer et al., 2011). It is worth noting that in most of the instances of school shootings during the past several years, the shooters had reportedly felt bullied or picked on by peers.

Non-Violent Cultures Although violence seems to be just about everywhere, a handful of societies stand out as non-violent exceptions. Bruce Bonta (1997) describes 25 societies around the world that are almost completely without violence. For example, the Chewong, who live in the mountains of the Malay Peninsula, do not even have words in their language for quarrelling, fighting, aggression, or warfare. The Amish, the Hutterites, and the Mennonites are all societies that reside in Canada and the relatively violent United States but remain remarkably non-violent. ■ Table 11.2 lists some of the other societies that Bonta identified as non-violent. What makes all of these societies so peaceful? According to Bonta, all but two of these 25 societies strongly oppose competition and endorse cooperation in all aspects of their lives. This raises the possibility that cooperation and lack of competition may promote non-violence.

Subcultures Within a Country There are important variations in aggression within particular societies as a function of age, class, race, and region. For example, teenagers and young adults have a much greater rate of involvement in violent crime—as both offenders and victims—than any other age group. The fact that the North American population has been aging in recent years is one of the reasons cited for the drop in violent crime rates. (Other factors that are noted frequently include longer jail

TABLE 11.2

Non-Violent Societies

In addition to those discussed in the text, this table lists a few of the other societies that Bruce Bonta (1997) identified as non-violent.

Society	Comments
Balinese (Indonesian island of Bali)	A researcher who was there for four years never witnessed one boy another beating boy.
G/wi (Central Kalahari Desert of southern Africa)	They abhor violence and take pleasure from fortunate events only if they are in the company of group members.
Inuit (Arctic regions, including those in Siberia, Alaska, Canada, and Greenland)	They use strategies to control anger and prevent violence; they have a strong fear of aggression.
Ladakhis (Tibetan Buddhist society in northern India)	Villagers indicate that they have no memory of any fighting in the village.
Zapotec (Native American society in southern Mexico)	"Several researchers have been fascinated that one community is particularly peaceful, with very strong values that oppose violence, in contrast to other communities nearby where fighting and machismo are comparable with the rest of Mexico" (p. 320).

sentences for criminals, more visible and community-oriented policing, a decline in the market for crack cocaine, tougher gun-control laws, and a strong economy.)

What about race? The National Parole Board of Canada's *Performance Monitoring Report* for 2010/11 indicated that Aboriginal offenders represented 21.5 percent of the federal offender population (compared to their overall representation in the population of 3.8 percent), and Blacks 9.1 percent (who comprise 2.5 percent of the Canadian population). Among incidents involving one victim and one offender in the United States in 2007, 92 percent of black murder victims were killed by black offenders, and 83 percent of white murder victims were slain by white offenders. Nevertheless, black Americans live in a much more violent America than do white Americans. For example, although African Americans represented about 13 percent of the U.S. population in 2005, they were victims of 49 percent of all murders, and 93 percent of those killed were killed by other black people (U.S. Department of Justice, 2007).

"The most persistent sound which reverberates through men's history is the beating of war drums."

—Arthur Koestler

Regional differences are also striking. In the United States, the murder rate is consistently highest in the South, followed by the West. Some scholars have attributed the greater violence in the South and West to a *culture of honour* that is prevalent among white males in these regions. The culture of honour encourages violent responses to perceived threats against one's status as an honourable, powerful man (Cohen et al., 1998; Vandello & Cohen, 2005). We will focus more on the culture of honour later in the chapter.

Gender and Aggression

In virtually every culture, males are more violent than females. TRUE.

Despite all the variation across cultures, one thing is universal: Men are more violent than women. This has been found in virtually all cultures studied around the world. According to Canadian statistics, women represent only 4 percent of the offender population in Canada. World Health Organization data indicate that, compared to women, men are almost four times more likely to be murdered in the United States, two times more likely in Finland, four times more likely in the Russian Federation, and nine times more likely in Mexico (Bulatao & VandenBos, 1996). Despite the significant variation in total violence from one country to another, the gender difference remains remarkably stable over time and place: Men commit the very large majority of homicides, and men comprise the very large majority of murder victims (Buss, 2004; Daly & Wilson, 1989).

What about aggression in general, as opposed to violence? In a meta-analysis involving hundreds of samples from numerous countries, John Archer (2006) found that males are consistently more physically aggressive than females. Females were as likely to feel anger as males, but they were much less likely to act on their anger in aggressive ways. Even among children between three and six years old, boys show higher rates of physical aggression than girls.

Men are more physically aggressive than women in most societies, but women, too, commit acts of physical violence. Here, a young woman is being brutally initiated into a gang by other female gang members.

So, does all this mean that the stereotype of males as more aggressive than females is correct? Not necessarily. Most of the research has focused on the aggression typical of males: physical aggression. But think back to our definition of aggression: It concerns intent to harm. There are many ways to harm someone other than through physical means. Recent research has recognized this, and the results challenge the notion that males are more aggressive than females. The findings emerging can be summarized by a child's remark noted by Britt Galen and Marion Underwood (1997) in their research on aggression among adolescent girls and boys: "Boys may use their fists to fight, but at least it's over with quickly; girls use their tongues, and it goes on forever" (p. 589).

This research reveals that although boys tend to be more *overtly* aggressive than girls, girls often are more *indirectly,* or *relationally,* aggressive than boys. Indirect forms of aggression include acts such as telling lies to get someone in trouble or shutting them out of desired activities. Relational aggression is one kind of indirect aggression, particularly targeting a person's relationships and social status, such as by threatening to end a friendship, engaging in gossip and backbiting, and trying to get others to dislike the target. Why are girls more likely to use relational aggression than boys? Nikki Crick and colleagues (Crick & Rose, 2000; Crick et al., 1999; Morales et al., 2005) believe it is because females typically care more about relationships and intimacy than males do and so may see injuring someone socially as particularly effective.

Numerous studies conducted in a variety of countries around the world have found that females tend to engage in indirect aggression more often than males (Archer, 2006; French et al., 2002; Galen & Underwood, 1997; Huesmann et al., 2003; Owens et al., 2000). The results of meta-analyses (Archer, 2004; Card et al., 2008) that have reviewed the very large amount of research literature on the topic have found a very small but statistically significant gender difference, with girls exhibiting somewhat more indirect aggression than boys (see ▶ Figure 11.2).

▶ FIGURE 11.2

Gender and Types of Aggression

A meta-analysis was conducted of 148 studies of direct and indirect aggression involving children and adolescents across several countries. The results indicate that the magnitude and direction of gender differences in aggression depend on the type of aggression. The heights of the bars in this graph indicate the degree to which boys show more aggression than girls; the higher the bar, the greater the difference in the amount of aggression exhibited by boys compared to girls. Across these various studies, the boys tend to be much more physically aggressive than girls. Boys also exhibit more direct verbal aggression than girls, but this difference is smaller. Regarding indirect aggression, however, girls tend to be more aggressive than boys. This difference is very small but is statistically reliable across the set of studies.

(Based on Card et al., 2008.)

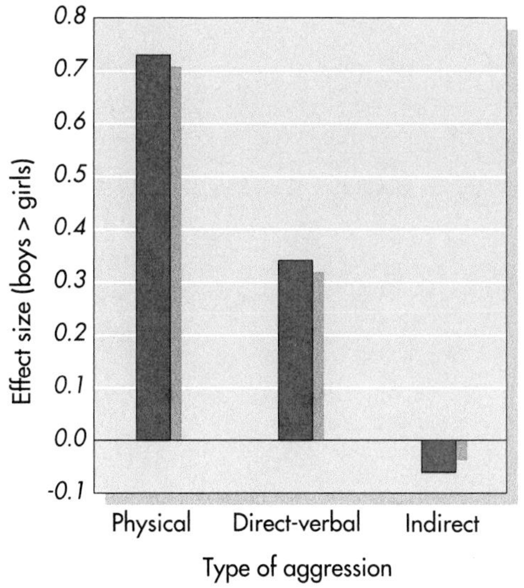

Individual Differences

Although it is clear that aggression can vary across cultures and gender, a different question is whether there is consistency in aggression within specific individuals. In other words, do some people simply tend to be more aggressive than others, across ages and situations? The evidence on this point is fairly clear: Although situational variables (as we will see later in this chapter) certainly do influence whether and how someone will aggress, there are some stable individual differences in aggressiveness. Aggression in childhood does predict aggression in adolescence and adulthood, along with adult criminality, alcohol abuse, and other antisocial behaviours. Similarly, low aggression in childhood predicts low aggression well into adulthood (Huesmann et al., 2009; Kokko et al., 2009; Vierikko et al., 2006).

Recent research by Annie Renouf and others (2010) at the Université du Québec à Montréal examined indirect aggression in French-Canadian children at 60 months, and then one year later, when the children had entered the school system. The children completed a series of cognitive tasks at 60 months, and then the following year their Kindergarten teachers were asked to complete a 10-item questionnaire assessing direct (e.g. "got into fights") and indirect (e.g. "said bad things behind someone's back") aggression. The result: children who are better able to understand the perspective of others (or who can understand that others have a perspective different from their own) were more likely to use indirect aggression. Children with the ability to take another's perspective were therefore more likely to also have the requisite skills to manipulate others, and to spread rumours, without getting caught.

Researchers have also explored whether there are specific personality types that are more likely to be associated with aggression (Lee & Ashton, 2012). Christopher Barlett and Craig Anderson (2012) found a link between the presence of traits such as disagreeableness and extraversion and the likelihood of noticing and reacting to aggression. Ann Bettencourt and others (2006) conducted a meta-analysis of 63 studies and found that people who tend to hold hostile cognitions, express anger, and exhibit irritability tend to behave more aggressively.

For virtually any category of aggression, males are more aggressive than females. FALSE.

Origins of Aggression

Regardless of these various cultural and gender differences, aggression has been a prevalent part of human interaction throughout human history and around the world. It is not surprising that many have speculated about the origins of aggression. Where does it come from? Are we *born* aggressive, or are we *taught* to be aggressive? Many have argued for one side or the other of the "nature-nurture" debate—the "nature" side holding that aggression is an innate characteristic of human beings and the "nurture" side holding that aggression is learned through experience. In this section, we look at the theory and research most relevant to tracing the origins of human aggression. In reviewing each perspective, we examine how well it can account for the overall prevalence of aggression, as well as for the cultural and gender differences that we have discussed.

Is Aggression Innate?

Innate characteristics are not contingent on learning for their development, although they can be influenced by learning, culture, and other factors. Here, we examine two approaches to the issue of whether aggression is innate: (1) evolutionary psychology accounts; and (2) biological factors, including genes, hormones, neurotransmitters, and brain and executive functioning.

Evolutionary Psychology Evolutionary psychological accounts of aggression use principles of evolution to understand both the roots and the contemporary patterns of human aggression. For example, in his provocative book, *The Most Dangerous Animal: Human Nature and the Origins of War*, David Livingstone Smith (2007) takes an evolutionary psychological perspective in his analysis of the origins of human warfare. This account emphasizes that human warfare originated not only to obtain valuable resources, but also to attract mates and forge intragroup bonds. While it might seem that in our evolutionary history it would have been the pacifists who would have been more likely to survive than the warriors, Smith argues that it was the warriors who would have been more likely to attract mates and be accepted as part of a group. Therefore, the individuals who could and would fight had greater chances for reproductive success, and they would pass down these tendencies to their offspring, and so on. The greater reproductive success of warriors over pacifists would result in the tendencies toward aggression and war to evolve to become part of human nature.

Evolutionary social psychology is geared not only to describe the origins of human social behaviour, but also to generate testable, falsifiable predictions. For example, evolutionary theories emphasize genetic survival rather than the survival of the individual. Because at least some of a person's genes can be transmitted through the reproductive success of genetic relatives, evolution should have favoured the inhibition of aggression against those who are genetically related to us. Consistent with that hypothesis, Martin Daly and Margo Wilson (1988, 1996, 2005) report that birth parents are much less likely to abuse or murder their own offspring than step-parents are to harm stepchildren. In two samples studied, preschool children living with a step-parent or foster parent were 70 to 100 times more likely to be fatally abused than were children living with both biological parents.

What can account for the gender differences in aggression? From a strictly evolutionary perspective, males are competitive with each other because females select high-status males for mating, and aggression is a means by which males traditionally have been able to achieve and maintain status. In addition, because human men, unlike women, cannot be sure that they are the true genetic parents of their children, men are predisposed to sexual jealousy. Behaviours triggered by sexual jealousy, including aggression and the threat of aggression, may be designed to enhance the male's confidence in his paternity of offspring. Consistent with evolutionary reasoning, crime statistics indicate that male-to-male violence is most likely to occur when one is perceived as challenging the other's status or social power, such as by attempting to humiliate him or to challenge his sexual relationships. Male-to-female violence is predominantly triggered by sexual jealousy (Duntley & Buss, 2008; Wilson & Daly, 1996).

In an interesting study by Michael Stirrat and others (2012), men with narrower faces were more likely to die a violent death than those with wider faces, a finding they attributed to a lack of physical dominance one would instead find in men with wider faces. Thus, a narrow face leads to poorer outcomes in intrasexual competition. Men with wider faces look scarier and are better at fighting! Wide-faced men are more likely to get in a fight, but according to this, they will be more successful, too. Thus, they may be more aggressive because they face less risk.

Of course, as noted earlier, women also aggress. From an evolutionary perspective, reproductive success is dependent on the survival of one's offspring, and because women are much more limited than men in terms of the number of children they can have, evolution presumably favoured those women who were committed to protecting their children. Indeed, much research on aggression by females has focused on maternal aggression, whereby females aggress to defend their offspring against threats by others. For example, females in a variety of species have been observed to attack male strangers who come too close to their offspring (Ferreira et al., 2000; Gammie et al., 2000). In a similar vein, Anne Campbell (1999) proposes that females tend to place a higher value on protecting their own lives—again, so as to protect their offspring. This hypothesis may explain not only why human males engage more often in risky, potentially self-destructive behaviours, but also why human females, when they do aggress, are more likely to use less obvious, and thus less dangerous, means—such as indirect or relational aggression rather than overt, physical aggression.

Behaviour Genetics Evolutionary psychology involves tying together evolution, genetic transmission, and behaviour. Behaviour genetics focuses on the latter two. As we said earlier, aggressiveness is a relatively stable personality characteristic; children relatively high in aggressiveness are more likely to be aggressive later in life. Can this aggressive personality type be due to genes? To answer this question, two types of studies are typically employed in research on humans. In twin studies, monozygotic twins (who are identical in their genetic makeup) are compared with dizygotic twins (who share only part of their genes). On any heritable trait, monozygotic twins will be more similar than dizygotic twins. Adoptee studies are also used in behaviour genetics research. On any inherited trait, adopted children will resemble their biological parents more than they resemble their adoptive parents.

Although twin and adoptee studies have produced some evidence supporting the heritability of human aggressive behaviour, the results overall have been somewhat mixed (Hines & Saudino, 2002; Miles & Carey, 1997; Rowe et al., 2008). One interesting finding from a study of twins in the Montreal area was that there was much stronger evidence for the role of genes in physical aggression than in indirect, relational aggression (Brendgen et al., 2005). In another study of young twins, Mara Brendgen and her colleagues (2011) found that when environmental stressors are present, there is a greater likelihood that a genetic predisposition for aggression is activated. On the other hand, when a child with this maladaptive predisposition encounters a more prosocial environment, such as when he or she enjoys a positive relationship with a teacher, aggressive behaviour is reduced and positive peer-to-peer interactions increase.

The Role of Testosterone In addition to the question of heritability, researchers have long been interested in determining what specific biological factors influence aggression (Renfrew, 1997). Because of the persistent sex differences in physical aggression found among humans and other animals, many researchers have wondered if testosterone plays a role. Although men and women both have this "male sex hormone," men usually have higher levels than do women. Research conducted on a variety of animals has found a strong correlation between testosterone levels and aggression. The relationship is far weaker among humans, however. Even so, a number of studies have documented an association between testosterone and aggression. Using diverse samples of people, such as young boys, prison inmates, university students, and elderly men, these studies tend to show a strong positive correlation between testosterone levels and physical aggression or violence (Book et al., 2001; Dabbs & Dabbs, 2005; Kuepper et al., 2010; Montoya et al., 2012; van Bokhoven et al., 2006). For example, one study found that fraternities whose members tended to have higher testosterone levels were more rambunctious and exhibited more crude behaviour than other fraternities; fraternities with lower testosterone levels tended to be more academically successful and socially responsible, and their members smiled more (Dabbs et al., 1996). The relationship between testosterone and aggression is not limited to males. Studies have also shown a positive relationship between testosterone and aggression and related behaviours (such as competitiveness) in women (Cashdan, 2003; Dabbs & Dabbs, 2005; von der Pahlen et al., 2002).

Look at your index and ring fingers. Which is longer? Believe it or not, your answer may be a clue to how aggressive you are likely to be! Well, that may be overstating it a bit, but research has shown some intriguing correlations among finger-length ratio, testosterone, and aggression. Men tend to have relatively longer ring fingers than index fingers; larger ratios (especially on the right hand) are considered more "masculine." Larger ratios are thought to be associated with exposure to higher prenatal testosterone levels. For example, Allison Bailey and Peter Hurd (2005) at the University of Alberta found that men with more masculine finger-length ratios had higher scores for the trait of physical aggression. This correlation did not emerge among women.

Intriguing as they are, such correlational findings cannot prove that testosterone causes aggression. There are alternative explanations. For example, aggression itself can cause temporary increases in testosterone—if the aggression is successful (Gladue et al., 1989; Mazur et al., 1992). Stress may also be involved: Higher levels of stress are associated with higher levels of testosterone (Thompson et al., 1990). Stress may simultaneously elevate both testosterone and aggression, resulting in a correlation that may reflect the effects of stress rather than the effects of testosterone.

For ethical reasons, researchers do not manipulate people's levels of testosterone to measure its effects on aggression and other behaviours. But Stephanie Van Goozen and others (1995; Cohen-Ketteinis & Van Goozen, 1997) have studied individuals who were voluntarily manipulating their sex hormones—transsexuals undergoing sex reassignment treatments. The researchers administered tests of aggression to 35 female-to-male transsexuals and 15 male-to-female transsexuals shortly before and three months after the start of cross-sex hormone treatment in a Dutch hospital. With their increase in male hormones, the female-to-male transsexuals exhibited increased aggression-proneness. In contrast, the deprivation of these hormones in the male-to-female group was associated with a decrease in aggression-proneness. It is important to note, however, that these changes in aggressiveness may have been caused not by the hormone treatment per se but, rather, by indirect factors such as the transsexuals' expectations or other people's reactions to them.

The Role of Serotonin Testosterone is not the only biological factor linked to human aggression. There has been an explosion of interest in the past decade concerning the role of the neurotransmitter serotonin (Beitchman et al., 2006; Carrillo et al., 2009; Crockett et al., 2008; Kuepper et al., 2010; Montoya et al., 2012). Neurotransmitters such as serotonin act as chemical messengers in the nervous system, transmitting information. Serotonin appears to work like a braking mechanism to restrain impulsive acts of aggression. Low levels of serotonin in the nervous systems of humans and many animals are associated with high levels of aggression. Drugs that boost serotonin's activity can dampen aggressiveness, along with a range of other impulsive and socially deviant behaviours.

Brain and Executive Functioning In addition to hormones and neurotransmitters, the frontal lobe of the brain is another hot topic in research on the biological underpinnings of human aggression. Researchers using a variety of techniques have found evidence linking abnormalities in frontal lobe structures with tendencies toward aggressive and violent behaviour (Hortensius et al., 2012; Miura, 2009; Potegal, 2011). The prefrontal cortex in particular has been implicated. Impaired prefrontal processing can disrupt what is called *executive functioning*, the cognitive abilities and processes that allow humans to plan or inhibit their actions. Executive functioning enables people to respond to situations in a reasoned, flexible manner, as opposed to being driven purely by external stimuli (Hoaken et al., 2007). A growing body of research finds a link between poor executive functioning and high aggression (Ellis et al., 2009; Raaijmakers et al., 2008; Seguin & Zelazo, 2005; Siever, 2008).

One noteworthy recent finding is that very aggressive teenagers showed different patterns of brain activity in response to witnessing someone else in pain than did less aggressive youth (Decety et al., 2009). In particular, when watching situations in which someone intentionally inflicted pain on another person, healthy teenagers showed brain activity associated with empathy. The highly aggressive teens, however, exhibited a pattern of brain activity associated with experiencing rewards, suggesting that they enjoyed watching others experience pain that someone intentionally inflicted on them. In addition, the aggressive teenagers showed less activation in areas associated with self-regulation and moral reasoning when seeing someone inflict pain on another than did the non-aggressive teenagers.

Is Aggression Learned?

Regardless of the precise contribution of genetic and biological factors, the importance of experience is clear: Aggressive behaviour is strongly affected by learning (Bandura, 1973). Rewards obtained by aggression today increase its use tomorrow. Such rewards come in two flavours: *positive reinforcement,* when aggression produces desired outcomes, and *negative reinforcement,* when aggression prevents or stops undesirable outcomes. The child who gets a toy by hitting the toy's owner is likely to hit again. So, too, the child who can stop other children from teasing by shoving them away has learned the fateful lesson that aggression pays. Children who see aggression producing more good outcomes, and fewer bad ones, are more aggressive than other children (Boldizar et al., 1989).

Rewards are one part of the learning equation, but what about punishment? Punishment is often promoted as a way to reduce aggressive behaviour. Can people learn not to act aggressively through punishment? Research suggests that punishment is most likely to decrease aggression when it (1) immediately follows the aggressive behaviour, (2) is strong enough to deter the aggressor, and (3) is consistently applied and perceived as fair and legitimate by the aggressor. However, such stringent conditions are seldom met, and when they are not met, punishment can backfire. When courts are overburdened and prisons are overcrowded, the relationship between crime and punishment can seem more like a lottery than a rational system in which the punishment fits the crime. In short, the *certainty* of punishment is more important than its *severity* (Berkowitz, 1998).

There are some other problems with punishment as well. Punishment perceived as unfair or arbitrary can provoke retaliation, creating an escalating cycle of aggression. Perhaps most troubling is that punishment, especially when delivered in an angry or hostile manner, offers a model to imitate. Murray Straus and his colleagues (Gámez-Guadix et al., 2010; Straus, 2000; Straus & Douglas, 2008; Winstok & Straus, 2011) have been outspoken critics of the use of *corporal punishment*—physical force (such as spanking, hitting, and pinching) intended to cause a child pain, but not injury, for the purpose of controlling or correcting the child's behaviour. A survey by Marie-Hélène Gagné and others (2007) at the University of Laval revealed that just over 66 percent of Quebec adults recalled being spanked as children. Those that had been spanked were themselves more in favour of this technique as a form of discipline. Numerous studies, however, report a *positive* relationship between corporal punishment and the likelihood of aggression: more corporal punishment is associated with more aggression. Elizabeth Gershoff (2002) investigated this issue with a meta-analysis of 88 studies conducted over six decades and involving more than 36 000 participants. Her analysis revealed strong evidence for a positive correlation between corporal punishment and several antisocial behaviours, such as aggression as a child, aggression as an adult, and adult criminal behaviour. As can be seen in ▶ Figure 11.3, both European American and African American mothers use a variety of techniques to discipline their children. While spanking was ranked last by each group, the mothers differed in the frequency with which they employed the techniques. For example, the European-American mothers were much more likely to try to reason with their child, or yell at them, compared to the African-American mothers (Lansford et al., 2012).

Children who are spanked or otherwise physically disciplined (but not abused) for behaving aggressively tend to become less aggressive. FALSE.

The relationship between parental corporal punishment and children's subsequent aggression is influenced by a number of factors, including the overall family environment, the emotions displayed by the parents during the punishment, and cultural and ethnic differences (Benjet & Kazdin, 2003; Pagani et al., 2009; Pinderhughes et al., 2000). For example, corporal punishment is less likely to increase aggressiveness when it is administered in the context of an overall warm and supportive parent-child relationship (Baumrind, 1997; Deater-Deckard et al., 1998).

▶ FIGURE 11.3

While both European-American and African-American mothers reported similar rankings for four different disciplinary techniques, the frequency of use for each technique was different. European-American mothers were more likely to use reason, or to yell at their child, compared to African-American mothers.

(Based on Lansford et al., 2012.)

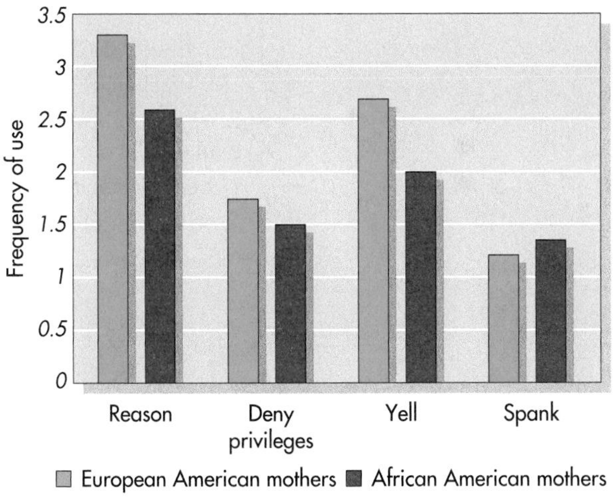

Social Learning Theory One of the authors of this book remembers many a late, cold afternoon during his middle school and high school years playing informal but competitive games of football and hockey with friends. Both games were played without protective equipment and were quite rough, but the way he and his friends played them, football was the more physically brutal of the two. Yet despite the fact that virtually every play culminated in a pile of boys jumping on the flattened body of an opponent, it was very rare that an actual fight would break out. When this same group of friends played hockey, on the other hand, virtually every single game they played featured at least one fight. Why? Although he was years away from his first social psychology class, this future social psychologist was quite sure that he and his friends were basing their behaviour on role models. Rarely had they seen professional football players stop and fight on the field. But rarely had they seen a professional hockey game in which that *didn't* happen.

The power of models to modify behaviour is a crucial tenet of Albert Bandura's (1977) **social learning theory**. Social learning theory emphasizes that we learn from the example of others as well as from direct experience with rewards and punishments. Models influence the prosocial, helpful behaviour described in Chapter 10. They also affect antisocial, aggressive behaviour. In a classic study, Bandura and his associates (1961) observed the behaviour of mildly frustrated children. Those who had previously watched an adult throw around, punch, and kick an inflatable doll were more likely to mimic that behaviour when they later played with the doll than were those who had watched a quiet, subdued adult. While not everyone would agree this was 'aggression'—it isn't necessarily the case that the children intended to harm the doll—it is certainly true that this behaviour could harm a person if exhibited in other circumstances.

social learning theory
The proposition that behaviour is learned through the observation of others as well as through the direct experience of rewards and punishments.

Mario Tama/Getty Images

Iraqi boys in Baghdad play with toy guns in January 2004, imitating the adult behaviour they have observed in their war-torn country.

People can learn more than specific aggressive behaviours from aggressive models. They also develop more positive attitudes and beliefs about aggression in general as they process and incorporate the social information from their environment. When repeatedly seeing aggression modelling by their parents, for example, children construct aggressive "scripts" that serve as guides for how to behave and solve social problems. These scripts can be activated automatically in various situations, leading to quick, often unthinking aggressive responses that follow the scripts we have been taught (Chen et al., 2012; Doh et al., 2012; Underwood et al., 2008).

Fortunately, changing the model can change the consequences: Non-aggressive models decrease aggressive behaviour. Observing a non-aggressive response to a provoking situation teaches a peaceful alternative and strengthens existing restraints against aggression. In addition, observing someone who is calm and reasonable may help an angry person settle down rather than lash out. Aggression can spread like wildfire. But nonviolence and prosocial behaviour, too, can be contagious (Donnerstein & Donnerstein, 1976; Gibbons & Ebbeck, 1997).

Bandura's social learning theory has been one of the most important social psychological approaches to the study of human aggression since his classic early experiments in the early 1960s. Its simplicity should not obscure the fact that it can help explain a great amount of human behaviour. Daniel Batson and Adam Powell (2003) wrote that social learning theory "has probably come closer to [the goal of accounting for the most facts with the fewest principles] than has any other theory in the history of social psychology" (p. 466).

Gender Differences and Socialization: "Boys Will Be Boys"

To account for gender differences in aggression, social learning approaches emphasize that males and females are taught different lessons about aggression—they are rewarded and punished differently for aggression and are presented with different models. Whether or not gender differences in aggressive behaviour originated from innate biological factors, today they are maintained and perpetuated through lessons that are passed on from one generation to the next about the acceptability of various kinds and degrees of aggression.

Most researchers agree that social roles have a strong influence on gender differences in physical aggression. As described in Chapter 5, males and females are socialized to fill different roles in society. Overt aggression tends to be more socially acceptable in stereotypically male roles than in female roles. Indeed, highly aggressive boys are often among the most popular and socially connected children in elementary school (Garandeau et al., 2011; Rodkin & Roisman, 2010). Boys who use their fists to deal with conflict are much more likely to be rewarded with increased social status than are girls, who might suffer scorn and ridicule for fighting. On the other hand, a girl who successfully uses relational aggression, such as through social manipulation, can reap social benefits more easily than a boy (Crick & Rose, 2000).

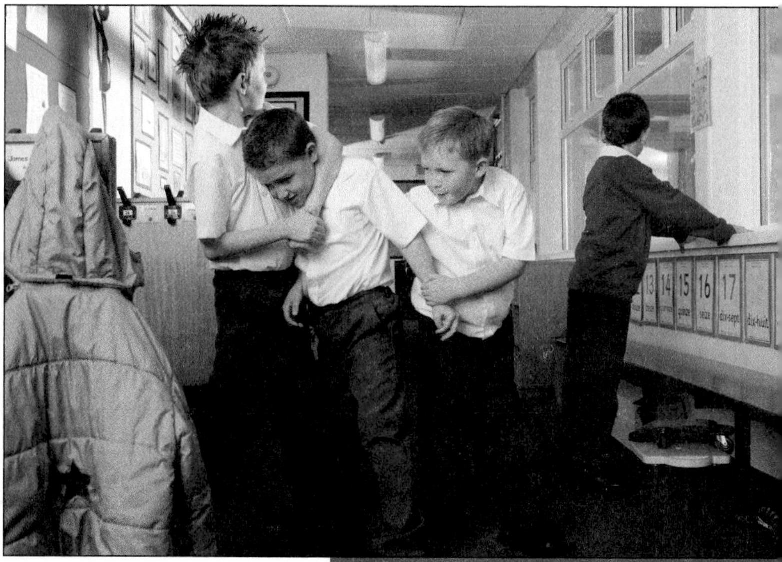
Echo/Getty

Roughhousing at school is often considered to be appropriate behaviour for boys, and a sign of their masculinity, whereas girls are expected to act more 'ladylike.'

Culture and Socialization: Cultures of Honour

Socialization of aggression also varies from culture to culture. In support of this statement is a study by Giovanna Tomada and Barry Schneider (1997) who report that adolescent boys in traditional villages in Italy are encouraged to aggress as an indication of their sexual prowess and preparation for their dominant role in the household. These authors believe that this is why schoolyard bullying among elementary schoolboys is significantly higher in Central and Southern Italy than it is in Norway, England, Spain, or Japan. Similarly, some researchers believe that *machismo*—which in its most stereotyped characterization prescribes that challenges, abuse, and even differences of opinion "must be met with fists or other weapons" (Ingoldsby, 1991, p. 57)—contributes to the fact that rates of violence are higher among Latin American men than European American men (Harris, 1995).

Machismo may represent one form of what anthropologists call a *culture of honour,* which emphasizes honour and social status, particularly for males, and the role of aggression in protecting that honour. Even minor conflicts or disputes are often seen as challenges to social status and reputation, and can therefore trigger aggressive responses. Several such subcultures exist around the world. In an extensive series of studies, Dov Cohen, Richard Nisbett, Joseph Vandello, and their colleagues have examined various cultures of honour. Their original focus was on white men in the American South (Nisbett & Cohen, 1996). Rates of violence are consistently higher in the South than in all other regions. Southerners are more likely than northerners to agree that "a man has the right to kill" in order to defend his family and house; and they are more accepting of using violence to protect one's honour than are people from other parts of the country. In fact, in a recent study, Ryan Brown and his colleagues (2009) found that high school students in States associated with a culture of honour were more likely to bring a weapon to school compared to students in northern States. There are two important notes, however: (1) the majority of students—more than 90 percent of them—do *not* bring weapons to school, and (2) Southerners are *not* more likely than other Americans to accept violence unrelated to the protection of honour.

In one series of experiments (Cohen et al., 1996), researchers investigated how white male students who had grown up either in the North or in the South responded to insults. The experiments, conducted on a large midwestern campus, involved an encounter that took place as the participant and a confederate were passing each other in a narrow hallway. The confederate did not give way to the participant, bumped into him, and hurled an insult. Compared with Northerners, Southerners were more likely to think that their masculine reputations had been threatened; exhibited greater physiological signs of being upset; appeared more physiologically primed for aggression (their testosterone levels rose); and engaged in more aggressive and dominant subsequent behaviour (gave firmer handshakes) and were more unwilling to yield to a subsequent confederate as they walked toward each other in a very narrow hallway. Interestingly, it appears that for some individuals who endorse this culture of honour, if they feel they have not succeeded in defending their reputation, they are also more likely to resort to violence against themselves, as evidenced by higher suicide rates in southern and western, compared to northern, States (Osterman & Brown, 2011).

Institutions support norms about the acceptability of honour-based violence. Cohen and Nisbett (1997) sent letters to employers all over the United States from a fictitious job applicant who admitted having been convicted of a felony. To half the employers, the applicant reported that he had impulsively killed a man who had been having an affair with his fiancée and had taunted him about it in a crowded bar. To the other half, the applicant reported that he had stolen a car because he needed the money to pay off debts. Employers from the South and the West (which has a culture of honour similar to the South's) were more likely than their northern counterparts to respond in an understanding and cooperative way to the letter from the convicted killer—but not from the auto thief.

Joseph Vandello, Dov Cohen, and their colleagues (2009) had participants from Chile (a culture that emphasizes honour) or Canada (a culture that is neutral concerning honour) listen to a tape of a man describing how he behaved violently toward his wife during a conflict. In one condition, the conflict was triggered when the husband thought she was flirting with another man at a party. In a different condition, the conflict was triggered by something having nothing to do with jealousy or threats to the man's honour. The Chilean participants rated the violence as more acceptable and rated the husband more positively across several dimensions than the Canadian participants did when the conflict was related to jealousy, but there was no cultural difference when the conflict was not related to jealousy or honour (see ▶ Figure 11.4).

A key to the aggression associated with cultures of honour is the fact that individuals in these cultures perceive aggressive responses to honour-based threats as the norm among their peers. That is, cultures of honour persist because the individuals believe that most people in their peer group have positive attitudes toward aggression (and negative attitudes toward not acting aggressively) in response to threats to one's honour (Vandello et al., 2008).

▶ FIGURE 11.4

Culture of Honour and Attitudes About Domestic Violence

Participants from Chile (a culture that emphasizes honour) or Canada (a neutral culture regarding honour) listened to a tape of a man describing his violent behaviour toward his wife during a conflict. When the conflict was not triggered by an honour-related issue, Chileans and Canadians did not differ in how acceptable they thought the violence was. When the conflict was triggered by the husband perceiving his wife flirting with another man at a party, however, the Chileans were significantly more accepting of the violence than were the Canadians.

(Based on Vandello et al., 2009.)

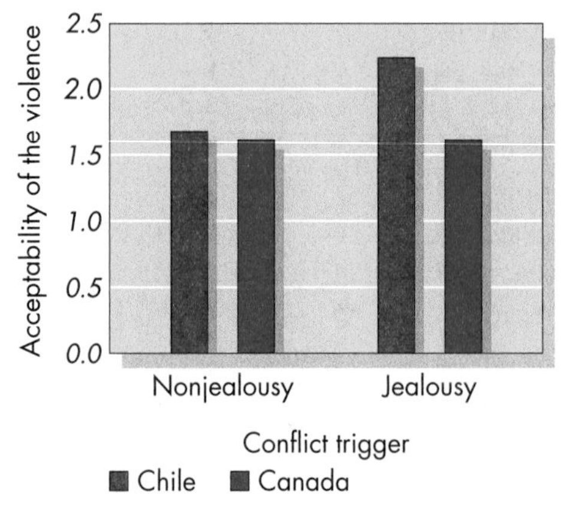

Nature Versus Nurture: A False Debate?

The origins of aggression are a source not only of scientific disagreement but also of political controversy. Heated debates about funding research and treatment programs frequently occur among politicians who disagree strongly on whether aggression is, to any significant extent, attributable to genetic inheritance or stable biological characteristics present at birth. However important it may be, this contentious issue should not obscure the considerable agreement that exists on other points. The effects of learning are not disputed; aggression is, at least to some extent, "made" by experience. Nor is there any doubt that in aggression, as in all human behaviour, biology and environment interact. The debate between nature and nurture may rage among politicians, but to scientists it is clear that the origins of human aggression represent a profound interaction of innate predispositions and environmental and social factors.

Situational Influences on Aggression

Whatever the ultimate causes of aggression, it is clear that specific, immediate situational factors can promote or inhibit aggressive thoughts and actions. In this section, we take a close look at several of these factors: frustration, negative affect, arousal, and factors that influence people's thoughts and information processing.

Frustration: Aggression as a Drive

In 1939, the year that World War II began, John Dollard and his colleagues published *Frustration and Aggression,* one of the most influential books on aggression ever written. This book sets forth two major propositions, which taken together are called the **frustration-aggression hypothesis**: (1) Frustration produced by interrupting a person's progress toward an expected goal will always elicit the motive to aggress, and (2) all aggression is caused by frustration.

Dollard and his colleagues claimed that the motive to aggress is a psychological drive that resembles physiological drives like hunger. According to this theory, just as food deprivation elicits a hunger drive, so frustration elicits an aggressive drive. Just as the hunger drive prompts the search for food, so the aggressive drive prompts the attempt to inflict injury. But what if we're unable to aggress against the source of our frustration? After all, we can't hit the boss; nor can we strike out against abstractions such as health problems or financial setbacks. Dollard and his colleagues believed that in such instances the aggressive drive can seep out in the form of **displacement**. Here, the inclination to aggress is deflected from the real target to a substitute. After a bad day at work or at school, do you sometimes come home and yell at the first available target—be it friend, family member, lover, or pet? If so, what is the effect on you? Does yelling at an innocent bystander reduce your inclination to take revenge on the person who gave you a hard time?

Drawing from the ancient idea of **catharsis**, Dollard and his colleagues believed that displacing aggression in these safer ways can be effective. Just as hunger can be satisfied by fast food as well as by an expensive steak, so any aggressive act should reduce the motive to engage in any other aggressive behaviour. Since the Dollard group defined aggression quite broadly—to include making hostile jokes, telling violent stories, cursing, and observing the aggression of others, real or fictional—they held out the hope that engaging in some relatively harmless pursuit could drain away energy from more violent tendencies.

The Frustration-Aggression Hypothesis: Does the Evidence Support It? Obviously, there is a connection between frustration and aggression. Break into a line of shoppers at the supermarket or interrupt a student cramming for an exam, and you can see it for yourself. On a more extreme level, it was clear that Dylan Klebold and Eric Harris of the Columbine massacre had been feeling extremely frustrated by their exclusion from popular cliques. Indeed, in 13 of the 15 school shootings between 1995 and 2001 that Mark Leary and others (2003) examined, the shooters had apparently been frustrated by social rejection.

frustration-aggression hypothesis
The idea that frustration always elicits the motive to aggress, and that all aggression is caused by frustration.

displacement
Aggressing against a substitute target because aggressive acts against the source of the frustration are inhibited by fear or lack of access.

catharsis
A reduction of the motive to aggress that is said to result from any imagined, observed, or actual act of aggression.

Aggressive behaviour on the road—what has been labelled "road rage"—is now a major problem in Canada as well as in many parts of the world. In a poll conducted by the Canadian Automobile Association (CAA, 2011), 86 percent of drivers indicated that 'road rage' was the most annoying bad habit they encountered. A large majority of these acts of aggression stem from frustration—such as frustration about being stuck in traffic or cut off by another driver.

Soon after the frustration-aggression theory was proposed, however, critics pointed out that the Dollard group had overstated their case. Early on, Neal Miller (1941), one of the originators of the hypothesis, acknowledged that frustration does not always produce aggressive inclinations. The other absolute, that all aggression is caused by frustration, was soon overturned as well. In the following pages, we will consider many other causes of aggression.

The concept of displacement was also subjected to close scrutiny. Some evidence suggested that societal frustrations arising from economic and social difficulties may fuel genocide and other forms of violence (such as lynchings) against outgroups (Hovland & Sears, 1940; Staub, 1996, 2004)—a reaction sometimes called *scapegoating*, which involves blaming a particular minority group or groups for the problems the overall society is facing. However, acceptance of the role of displacement in channelling aggressive behaviour soon diminished within the field after scholars pointed to theoretical weaknesses and inconclusive empirical evidence (Green et al., 1998; Marcus-Newhall et al., 2000; Zillmann, 1979). The tide may be turning yet again, though, as the concept of displacement seems to be making a comeback in recent years, sparked in part by a meta-analysis of 49 published articles that found reliable evidence for displaced aggression in response to provocation (Marcus-Newhall et al., 2000). More recently, David Barash and Judith Lipton (2011) have referred to this displacement as 'redirected' aggression and, given examples of it in many other non-human species, argue that to some extent it is a natural or hard-wired response.

The concept of catharsis also received a great deal of attention, perhaps because it seemed to offer a way to control aggression. Dollard and his colleagues described catharsis as a two-step sequence. First, aggression reduces the level of physiological arousal. Second, because arousal is reduced, people are less angry and less likely to aggress further. It sounds logical, and many people believe it. For example, Gordon Russell and his colleagues (1995) reported that more than two-thirds of Canadian respondents in their research agreed with statements reflecting a belief in the effectiveness of catharsis (such as the statement that participating in aggressive sports is a good way to get rid of aggressive urges). Catharsis has also been used by school administrators and others to justify violent sports (Bennett, 1991).

But, put to the test, catharsis has not lived up to its advertisement. Most researchers have concluded that the catharsis idea is a myth. It is more counterproductive than effective in reducing subsequent aggression (Bushman, 2002; Geen & Quanty, 1977). Here's why:

- Imagined aggression or the observation of aggressive models is more likely to increase arousal and aggression than to reduce them. Indeed, this is a central point of social learning theory.
- Actual aggression can lower arousal levels. However, if aggressive intent remains, "cold-blooded" aggression can still occur. Furthermore, if aggression-produced reduction of arousal feels good to the aggressor, this reward makes it more likely that aggression will occur again—another important point from social learning theory.

- Blowing off steam by hitting a punching bag or screaming may feel good to people who intuitively believe in catharsis. Yet their feelings of hostility and anger may persist—and possibly even increase.
- Even relatively low levels of aggression can chip away at restraints against more violent behaviour.

Aggressive behaviour may sometimes reduce the likelihood of further immediate aggression—but so can just letting the frustration simply dissipate over time. For that matter, a response incompatible with aggression, such as distracting oneself with laughter, can be more effective. In the long run, however, successful aggression sets the stage for more aggression later. In sum, relying on catharsis is dangerous medicine—more likely to inflame aggression than to put it out.

Frustration-Aggression Theory Revised After bearing so much criticism, the frustration-aggression hypothesis seemed torn and tattered. But Leonard Berkowitz's (1989) reformulation put the hypothesis in a new perspective. According to Berkowitz, frustration is but one of many unpleasant experiences that can lead to aggression by creating negative, uncomfortable feelings. It is these negative feelings, not the frustration itself that can trigger aggression. And as we'll see, negative feelings play a major role in influencing aggression.

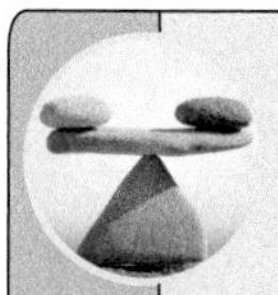

Blowing off steam by engaging in safe but aggressive activities (such as sports) makes people less likely to aggress later. FALSE.

Negative Affect

In addition to frustrating experiences, a wide variety of noxious stimuli and bad feelings can increase aggression: noise, crowding, physical pain, threatened self-esteem, social rejection, violent song lyrics, bad odours, and having your home team lose a professional football playoff game (Baumeister et al., 2000; Berkowitz, 1998; Brummert Lennings & Warburton, 2011; Leary et al., 2006; Panee & Ballard, 2002; Verona et al., 2002; Warburton et al., 2006). Most aggressive incidents can be directly linked to some type of provocation, and the negative affect caused by the provocation plays a critically important role in triggering aggression. Reactions to a very common unpleasant condition, hot weather, are especially intriguing. Many people assume that temperature and tempers rise together, while others think it's just a myth. Who is right?

Heat and Aggression: Losing Your Cool Craig Anderson and others have conducted extensive research on the question of whether heat leads to aggression; and data across time, cultures, and methodologies strongly support the notion that people lose their cool in hot temperatures and behave more aggressively (Anderson et al., 2000; Bushman et al., 2005). More violent crimes occur in the summer than in the winter, during hot years than in cooler years, and in hot cities than in cooler cities at any given time of year. The numbers of political uprisings, riots, homicides, assaults, rapes, and reports of violence all peak in the summer months (see ▶ Figure 11.5). Indirect acts of aggression also increase in excessive heat. As temperatures rise to uncomfortable levels, laboratory participants become more likely to interpret ambiguous events in hostile terms (Rule et al., 1987), and drivers in cars without air-conditioning become more likely to honk their horns at motorists whose cars are stalled in front of them (Kenrick & MacFarlane, 1986). Alan Reifman and others (1991) found that as the temperature rises, Major League Baseball pitchers are more likely to hit batters with a pitch; the pitchers aren't wilder in general (such as in their number of walks or wild pitches)—just more likely to hit batters (see ▶ Figure 11.6). Nathan DeWall and Brad Bushman (2009) recently

FIGURE 11.5

The Link Between Heat and Violence

Worldwide weather records and crime statistics reveal that more violent crimes are committed during the summer than in the other seasons.

(Anderson, 1989.)

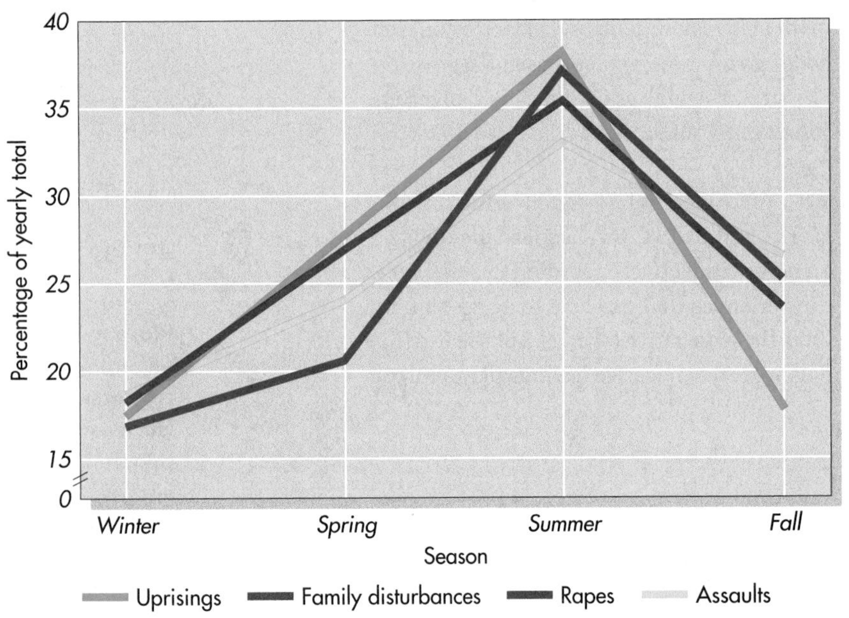

reported an intriguing result: participants who were exposed to words associated with hot temperatures (e.g., "boils," "roasted") were more likely to complete word fragments with aggressive words (e.g,. completing "ki__" with "kill" rather than with "kiss") compared to participants who saw neutral words, or words associated with cool temperatures.

Given the earlier discussion of the culture of honour and the high incidence of violence in the American South, you may wonder whether it is culture or heat that contributes to the violence. At this point, evidence points to both influences as important. Each probably has independent effects on aggression. In addition, they may interact with each other—for example, the relatively high temperatures of the region may support aggressive norms (Anderson et al., 2000; Nisbett & Cohen, 1996).

Social Rejection One of the most unpleasant feelings that people experience is being rejected or ostracized by others. A number of experiments have manipulated social rejection to examine its causal effect on a number of outcomes including aggression. For example, a participant in an experiment might find himself or herself suddenly ignored by the two other participants in the study, who engage in pleasant interactions only with each other. These studies have shown that social rejection increases

FIGURE 11.6

Temper and Temperature in Baseball

This figure shows the average number of players hit by pitches (HBPs) per game during the 1986 through 1988 Major League Baseball seasons. As the temperature increased, so did the likelihood that pitchers would hit batters (with balls often thrown around 90 miles per hour and often thrown at a batter's head). Players' general wildness or fatigue, as measured by walks, wild pitches, passed balls, and errors, did not increase with temperature, suggesting that the heat-HBP correlation may be due to hotter temperatures—and hotter tempers.

(Reifman et al., 1991.)

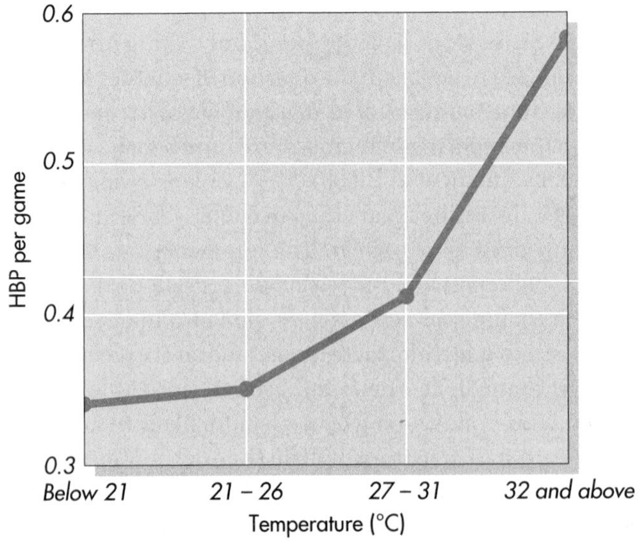

the likelihood of aggressive responses (Crescioni & Baumeister, 2009; Williams, 2007)—especially if the socially rejected individual is particularly sensitive to rejection (Ayduk et al., 2008).

Positive Affect If negative affect increases the likelihood of aggressing, can positive emotional reactions reduce it? Some evidence suggests that they can. For example, participants in one study were first angered by an experimental confederate. They were then shown funny cartoons or neutral pictures. Presented with an opportunity to retaliate by delivering electric shocks as part of a supposed learning experiment, those who had seen the cartoons delivered fewer shocks (Baron & Ball, 1974). Similarly, when participants were given a chance to aggress against another individual by requiring them to eat a spicy sauce, those participants who first experienced acceptance—in the form of assistance—by other players in an online game reduced their overall level of aggression compared to those who did not receive acceptance (DeWall et al., 2010). Feeling good appears to be incompatible with anger and aggression.

Arousal: "Wired" for Action

Research on affect clearly indicates that the type of emotion (positive or negative) influences aggression. The intensity of arousal is important as well. In Chapter 9, we described the process of *excitation transfer,* in which the arousal created by one stimulus can intensify an individual's emotional response to another stimulus. For example, men who engaged in vigorous exercise were later more attracted to an attractive female than were those who had barely moved (White et al., 1981). Physical exercise is a highly arousing but emotionally neutral experience. Can it increase aggression as well as attraction? The research of Dolf Zillmann (1983, 2003) suggests that it can. The scope of excitation transfer is not limited to physical exercise. Noise, violent motion pictures, arousing music—all have been shown to increase aggression. Heat has an interesting effect on arousal: Although people believe that heat lowers arousal, it actually increases it. This misperception makes heat a prime candidate for excitation transfer, as people are likely to misattribute arousal caused by heat to something else, such as anger, which can then lead to aggression (Anderson et al., 1996). Later in this chapter, we describe the effects of another arousing stimulus—pornography—on the inclination to aggress.

Thought: Automatic and Deliberate

Step by step, we have been making our way toward a comprehensive theory of social and situational influences on aggression, particularly emotional aggression. We've examined several kinds of unpleasant experiences (frustration, noxious stimuli, and provocation) that create negative affect. We've considered how arousal can contribute to aggression. The next step is to add cognition. People don't just feel; they also think. These thoughts may be as primitive as automatic, unconscious associations, or they may be higher-order, conscious deliberations. Both automatic and deliberate thoughts play a critically important role in aggressive behaviour.

Automatic Cognition: Situational Cues No other stable, industrialized country in the world comes even close to the United States in terms of the prevalence of guns used in violent crime. Guns, of course, are only an instrument—it's the people who are pulling the trigger. But social psychologist Leonard Berkowitz wondered whether guns were in fact entirely neutral. He hypothesized that the presence of a weapon can act as a situational cue that automatically triggers aggressive thoughts and feelings, thereby increasing the likelihood of aggression. In a classic study designed to test this idea, he and Anthony LePage (1967) had a confederate provoke male participants who could later respond by giving the confederate electric shocks (although in reality the confederate was not shocked). On a table near the shock apparatus just happened to be some objects scattered about, allegedly left there from a previous experiment. For half of the participants, these objects were a revolver and rifle, and for the other half, they were badminton racquets and shuttlecocks. Berkowitz and LePage found that participants delivered more shocks to the confederate when a revolver and rifle, rather than badminton racquets and shuttlecocks, were present. In other words, although they didn't use these weapons, their mere presence seemed to make the participants more aggressive. This tendency for the presence of guns to increase aggression is called the **weapons effect**. As Berkowitz put it: "The finger pulls the trigger, but the trigger may also be pulling the finger" (1968, p. 22).

Jennifer Klinesmith and others (2006) found that weapons had an effect on men's testosterone levels as well as on their aggression. Male students in this experiment handled either a handgun or a children's game for 15 minutes. Relative to the students who interacted with the game, students who interacted with the gun showed increased testosterone levels and exhibited greater aggression against another person.

In general, any object or external characteristic that is associated with (1) successful aggression or (2) the negative affect of pain or unpleasantness can serve as an aggression-enhancing situational cue (Berkowitz, 1993, 1998, 2012). Such cues can have very strong effects, increasing people's hostility and likelihood of aggressing. In addition, stimuli that would not serve as aggression-enhancing cues for some people can be aggression-enhancing cues for others. People who tend to be aggressive associate significantly more cues with aggression and hostility than do people who are not as chronically aggressive; thus, they are particularly prone to automatically activating aggression-related thoughts (Bushman, 1996, 1998).

Higher-Order Cognition: Cognitive Control Situational cues can trigger automatic associations. More complex information about one's situation, however, influences the deliberate, thoughtful consideration that we call higher-order cognitive processing. For example, an angry person might refrain from acting aggressively if the potential costs of fighting seem too high. In this case, the person might choose to flee rather than fight. In addition, people who believe that aggression is inappropriate in a particular situation or whose moral values and principles mandate non-violent behaviour, may realize that better alternatives to aggression exist (Huesmann & Guerra, 1997). The behaviour of other people in the immediate situation can also influence an individual's considerations. If one or more others in a group are reacting aggressively to the situation, aggression can be contagious (Levy & Nail, 1993).

Mitigating information indicating that an individual should not be held responsible for aggressive acts should also diminish perceived intent to harm. This was demonstrated in one study by Christopher Barlett and Craig Anderson (2011) when they asked participants to write a brief essay, and then provided them with feedback on their writing allegedly written by another student participant. In reality, all feedback was standardized and written by the experimenters. After receiving positive, negative, or neutral feedback, the participant was given the opportunity to select some puzzles—ranging from very easy to very difficult—for the other student to complete. When participants received negative feedback about their essay (i.e., 'this is the worst thing I have ever read'), they chose more difficult puzzles for the other student. But if

weapons effect
The tendency of weapons to increase the likelihood of aggression by their mere presence.

mitigating information
Information about a person's situation indicating that he or she should not be held fully responsible for aggressive actions.

they were subsequently informed that the other participant wrote what they did because they had broken up with their romantic partner the night before, aggressive behaviour decreased and easier puzzles were chosen.

People's thoughts about the intentions of other people can determine whether they are likely to respond aggressively. Some individuals exhibit a **hostile attribution bias** in that they tend to perceive hostile intent in others. For example, Christine Wickens and others (2011) at York University asked participants to keep a diary and write down their driving experiences every two days. They found that the majority of participants recorded negative driving experiences, with the most common annoyance being cut off or almost hit by another vehicle (sideswiped). Interestingly, participants rarely attributed any errors in driving to their own behaviour, or if they did, they had an excuse for why they did what they did. But they were quick to blame others for their driving mistakes!

Other researchers have found that socially maladjusted children who are chronically aggressive and have been rejected by their peers see hostile intent where others don't (Crick & Dodge, 1994). Such perceptions then increase their aggression, and their peers respond by rejecting them further, locking these children into an ever-escalating vicious cycle. Chronically aggressive adults, too, tend to expect and perceive hostility in others' motives and behaviours (Dill et al., 1997). Research has found hostile attribution bias to be associated with both physical and relational aggression (Bailey & Ostrov, 2008). A meta-analysis of more than 40 studies found strong support for the relationship between aggressive behaviour and hostile attributions of the intentions of peers (Orobio de Castro et al., 2002).

FIGURE 11.7

A Model of Situational Influences on Emotional Aggression

Unpleasant experiences and situational cues can trigger negative affect, high arousal, and aggression-related thoughts. Due to individual differences, some people are more likely than others to experience these feelings and thoughts. Higher-order thinking then shapes these feelings and thoughts into more well-defined emotions and behavioural intentions. Depending on the outcome of this thinking (which can occur beneath the individual's conscious awareness and can be affected by factors such as alcohol or stress), the individual may choose to aggress.

(Based on Anderson et al., 1996.)

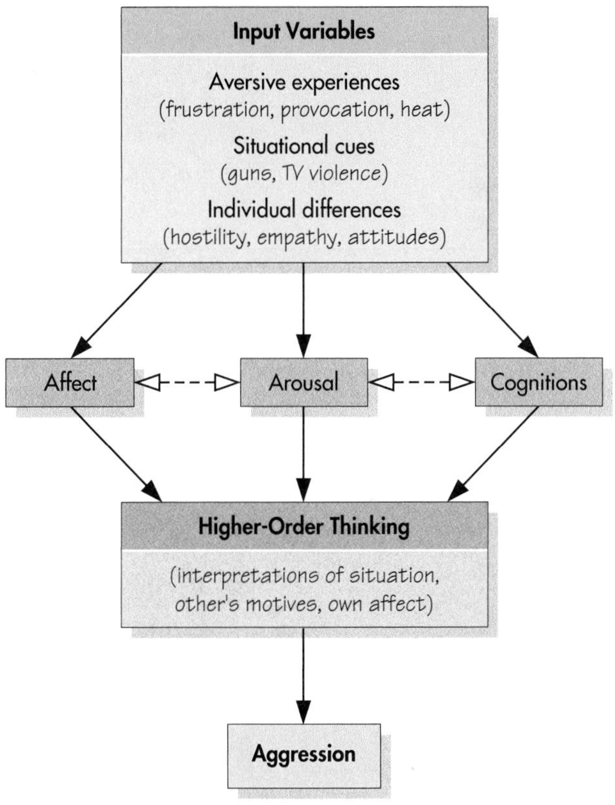

Alcohol Some conditions make it more difficult to engage in the higher-order processing that can inhibit aggressive impulses. High arousal, for example, impairs the cognitive control of aggression (Zillmann et al., 1975). So does alcohol. Alcohol is implicated in the majority of violent crimes, suicides, and automobile fatalities. The evidence is quite clear about this point: Alcohol consumption often increases aggressive behaviour (Bushman et al., 2012; Bushman & Cooper, 1990; Exum, 2006; Leonard et al., 2003). Even among individuals who are usually not aggressive, those who drink more aggress more (Bailey & Taylor, 1991; Pihl et al., 1997).

But *how* does alcohol increase aggression? A meta-analysis of 49 studies indicates that alcohol reduces anxiety, which in turn lowers people's inhibitions against aggressing (Ito et al., 1996). In addition, drinking disrupts the way we process information (Leonard, 1989). For example, Claude Steele and Robert Josephs (1990) propose that intoxication causes *alcohol myopia*; that is, alcohol narrows people's focus of attention. Intoxicated people respond to initial, salient information about the situation, but often miss later, more subtle indicators. In addition to its pharmacological

hostile attribution bias
The tendency to perceive hostile intent in others.

effects, alcohol can also affect aggressiveness because of people's *expectations* about alcohol's effects. The more people expect alcohol to affect them and make them more aggressive, the more likely it is that it will have that effect (Bègue et al., 2009; Quigley & Leonard, 2006).

Situational Influences: Putting It All Together

We have seen that negative affect, arousal, and aggression-related thoughts can lead to aggression. And a number of factors influence whether one is likely to experience negative affect, arousal, and aggressive thoughts, such as aversive experiences (frustration, crowding, heat, provocation), situational cues (guns, violent movies), and individual and cultural differences (chronic hostility, cultures of honour). ▶ Figure 11.7 diagrams how these various factors interact to lead to emotional aggression. Whether the affect, arousal, and thoughts translate into aggressive behaviour, however, may depend in part on the outcome of higher-order thinking, which can either inhibit aggression (such as by recognizing the danger of the situation or recognizing that what seemed like a provocation was really just an accident), or facilitate it (such as by perceiving that a provocation was intentional).

Media Effects

Having looked at origins and specific factors that contribute to aggression, we now focus on a special topic that has been a major concern of politicians, families, and social scientists alike for many years: violence in television, film, and other media. We explore two types of mass media presentations—non-sexual violence and pornography—in which the display of aggression may elicit more of it.

Violence in TV, Movies, Music Lyrics, and Video Games

On September 13, 2006, Kimveer Gill, a 25-year-old man, drove up to Dawson College in Montreal, pulled three guns from his car, and started shooting students. In total, Gill shot 20 people. Gill had no apparent connection or dispute with Dawson College or its students. Rather, it seemed, he had a tremendous amount of hostility toward the world in general. He had written numerous postings on the Internet about his loathing for humanity and about his fascination with guns, death, and violent video games. On a website popular with Goth culture, he had posted entries about his fantasies of killing people, many of which foreshadowed the events of September 13. "Life is a video game. You've got to die sometime," he wrote in one blog (Struck, 2006, p. A12). But do video games—or the violence depicted in other popular media—cause real-world aggression and violence?

Violence depicted in the media has been a target of attack and counterattack for decades. But the amount, intensity, and graphic nature of the violence have continued to escalate. Guy Paquette (2004) at Laval University analyzed the amount of violence on Canadian television on six different networks during one week in March over seven years. He recorded over 10 000 acts of physical and psychological violence and noted that violent acts had increased 50 percent between 1995 and 1998. Private networks in particular were three times more likely to show violent shows than were public networks. Interestingly, it is estimated that 80 percent of the violent programming in Canada originates in the United States.

The most violent TV shows ironically enough are targeted to children directly—namely, cartoons and other children's programming (*National Television Violence Study,* 1998). At the same time, children and adolescents are heavily exposed to depictions of violence in movies and video games. Particularly popular among young males is "professional" wrestling and mixed martial arts, which in recent years have become increasingly violent and graphic. Young men and women are also heavy consumers of music that includes violent imagery in its lyrics and accompanying videos. If consumers didn't enjoy violence in TV, film, music, videos, and video games, these media would not be featuring it. So can it really be harmful? We explore this question in the sections that follow.

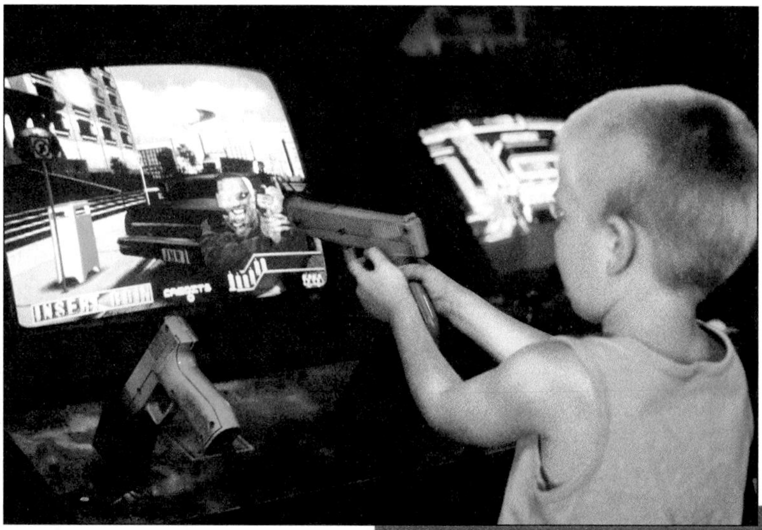

© D. Hurst/Alamy

Can playing violent video games cause children and young adults to become more aggressive and violent? A growing body of research suggests that it can.

Linking Media Violence to Real-World Violence Does life imitate art? Sometimes it seems that way. Brad Bushman, whose work is cited in several places in this chapter, first became interested in research on media violence when a store owner he knew was the victim of a heinous crime: Two armed men came into the store and forced the owner and customers into the basement, forced them to drink Drano (a highly corrosive, toxic fluid used to clean plumbing pipes), and put duct tape over their mouths. The day prior to the attack, these men had allegedly watched (three times) the Clint Eastwood movie *Magnum Force,* which features a scene depicting this very act of brutality (Leland, 1995). In January 2006, two Toronto teenagers were in court facing charges that their street racing led to the death of a cab driver. A copy of the video game "Need for Speed"—a game about drag racing and evading police—was found in one of the cars. People who have lost family members to violence that seemed to be copied directly from violent video games such as *Manhunt* and *Grand Theft Auto* have sued the makers and distributors of these violent games. According to one analysis, there were 400 copycat incidents in the United States and Canada in the month after the Columbine shooting, most of which were not fatal (Tobin, 2006). Yet no one can ever prove that a specific fictional depiction was the primary cause of a specific act of violence. There are always other possibilities.

If you ask people whether exposure to media violence causes real aggression, some would say they doubt that it does, or that there has never been clear evidence one way or another on this question. This view is echoed by some social scientists, including Jonathan Freedman at the University of Toronto, who argue that the relevant scientific evidence is weak and mixed, at best (Bushman et al., 2007; Freedman, 2002, 2007).

Other social psychological researchers argue the opposite; while media violence is neither a necessary nor a sufficient cause of real-world aggression and violence (that is, exposure to media violence does not necessarily cause one to aggress, nor is it ever the only cause of an act of aggression or violence), media violence can contribute to real aggression and violence.

Studying the effects of media violence on real-world aggression is particularly challenging because while correlational studies cannot determine causality, experiments are limited due to practical and ethical constraints. For instance, ethical considerations would not allow researchers to conduct experiments to study the kinds of real-world aggression that we want to understand. The best way to investigate the issue of media violence, therefore, is to use multiple methods, each of which has different sets of strengths and weaknesses. This is exactly what researchers in this area have done. Longitudinal research, which examines individuals' exposure to violent media early in life and then examines their real-world aggression years later, has found, for example, that the extent to which 8-year-olds watched violent TV predicts their aggressiveness and criminality as adults, even when statistically controlling for other factors such as socioeconomic status and parenting practices (Huesmann et al., 2003). (See ▶ Figure 11.8.) More recently, Paul Boxer and others found that childhood and adolescent preferences for violent media significantly predicted later violence and aggression (Boxer et al., 2009).

In experimental research, individuals are randomly assigned to watch or play with violent or non-violent media, and their aggressive thoughts, feelings, and behaviours are measured immediately after the exposure. In one experiment, for example, adolescent Dutch boys were randomly assigned to play either a violent or a non-violent video game for 20 minutes. Compared to the boys who played the non-violent video game, the boys who played the violent game behaved more aggressively after the game by delivering very loud, aversive blasts of noise against an opponent in a reaction-time task. This aggressive effect was especially strong among the boys who reported identifying most strongly with the main character in the video game. Some of these boys chose to blast their opponent with noise so loud that it could—according to the experimenter's instructions—cause permanent hearing loss to the other boy (although, in fact, no one actually received these noise blasts) (Konijn et al., 2007).

Violent video games have not been around as long as violent television, but there has been enough research on these games within the past decade that researchers have found reliable effects. For example, a recent meta-analysis by Craig Anderson and his colleagues (2010) of more than 130 research reports concluded that as the amount of time playing violent video games increases, so do aggressive behaviours, aggressive cognitions, and aggressive affect. In addition, more exposure to violent video games was associated with a lack of empathy and prosocial behaviour. They attribute such effects in part to players becoming both psychologically and emotionally invested with the game, a risk that may be greater among boys with lower educational abilities (Bijvank et al., 2012).

▶ FIGURE 11.8

Violent TV Viewing and Aggression 15 Years Later

A longitudinal study tracked individuals over a 15-year period. Based on how much TV violence they viewed as 8-year-olds, individuals were categorized as having viewed low (lower 20 percent), medium (middle 60 percent), or high (upper 20 percent) levels of TV violence. Their aggressiveness as adults was measured 15 years later. For both females and males, those who tended to watch the greatest amount of violent TV as children tended to be the most aggressive as adults.

(Based on Huesmann et al., 2003.)

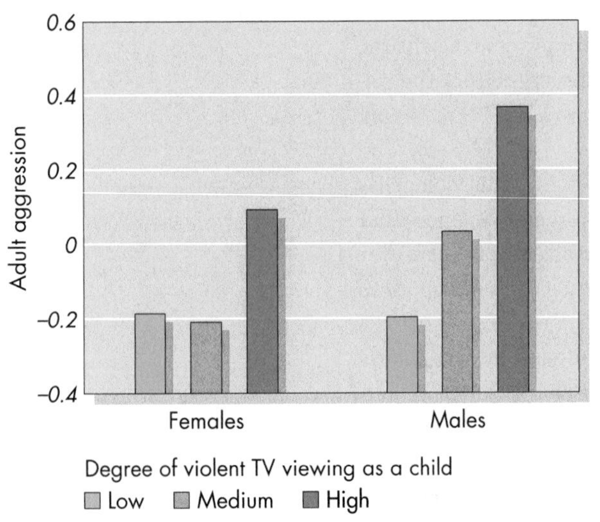

Of course, the media do not operate in a vacuum. People are influenced by their families, peers, social values, and opportunities for education and employment. Nor are all individuals the same; differences in personality can heat up or tone down the impact of exposure to aggressive displays. Media effects tend to be especially strong among people who are high in trait aggressiveness, irritability, or hostility as well as among those who lack empathy (Anderson & Bushman, 2002; Arriaga et al., 2006; Bushman & Huesmann, 2001).

How Does Media Violence Cause These Effects? The evidence from hundreds of studies makes it clear that media violence—whether from TV, movies, music lyrics or videos, video games, and so on—can have both immediate and long-term effects. Another question, though, is *how* it can have these effects. Social psychologists have found several paths through which media violence produces real-world aggression. Media violence can trigger aggressive and hostile thoughts, which in turn can lead individuals to interpret others' actions in hostile ways and promote aggression.

In one series of experiments, Peter Fischer and Tobias Greitemeyer (2006) found that male participants who had just listened to misogynous song lyrics recalled more negative attributes about women, reported more feelings of vengeance, and behaved more aggressively toward a female confederate than did male participants who had listened to neutral music. Listening to men-hating lyrics had a similar effect on female participants' aggressive-related responses toward men. Because of the sexual and sexist overtones of many video games, they may also promote sexist attitudes and behaviours (Dietz, 1998). Steven Fein and Emily Eustis (2001) found that male students with higher-than-average levels of hostility expressed more sexist attitudes after they participated in a video game that featured sexist behaviour. Other research has demonstrated that playing a violent video game for 20 minutes is enough to influence participants' responses regarding the likelihood of a character in a story behaving in an aggressive manner to solve an interpersonal dispute. These same participants were then more likely to behave in an aggressive manner, by blasting loud noise through a set of headphones, toward a confederate in a subsequent task. They concluded that the violent video game led to hostile intent, which then led to hostile behaviour (Hasan et al., 2012).

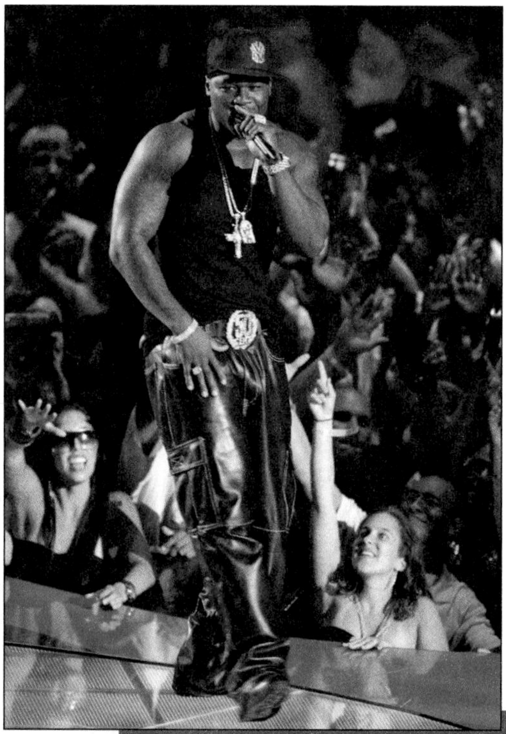
Kevin Winter/Getty Images

Rap star 50 Cent has achieved a great deal of popularity and acclaim over the past several years, while at the same time sparking controversy because of the violent nature of many of his songs. In December 2005, he was granted a temporary resident visa so that he could perform in Canada, after a Canadian MP tried to keep him out of Canada based on his criminal record and violent lyrics.

Another effect of media violence is that it desensitizes individuals to violence. **Desensitization** to violence refers to a reduction in emotion-related physiological reactivity to real violence. Desensitization is one form of *habituation.* A novel stimulus gets our attention and, if it's sufficiently interesting or exciting, elicits physiological arousal. But when we get used to something, our reactions diminish. Familiarity with violence reduces physiological arousal to new incidents of violence (Geen, 1981). Desensitized to violence, we may become more accepting of it.

For example, Kostas Fanti and his colleagues (2009) exposed participants to a series of 18 video clips, alternating between comedy scenes (e.g., from the television show *Friends*), and violent scenes (e.g., from the movie *A Clockwork Orange* or *Fight Club*). Although participants initially found the violent video clips aversive, after repeated exposure their enjoyment of the clips increased and their sympathy for the victims portrayed in the scenes decreased. In another experiment, male and female students who were randomly assigned to play a violent video game for 20 minutes subsequently took more than 450 percent longer to help an injured stranger than did participants who played a non-violent video game. (See ▶ Figure 11.9, on page 427.) Those who played the violent game also perceived the fight to be less serious than did those who played the non-violent game (Bushman & Anderson, 2009).

Another way that depictions of violence can affect people is through what George Gerbner and his colleagues (1986) call **cultivation**. Cultivation refers to the capacity of the mass media to construct a social reality that people perceive as true, even if it isn't. The media tend to depict the world as much more violent than it actually is. This can make people become more fearful, more distrustful, more likely to arm themselves, and more likely to behave aggressively in what they perceive to be a threatening situation (Nabi & Sullivan, 2001).

"I see television's violent content as therapeutic for the population."

—Jib Fowles, author of *The Case for Television Violence*

"The pervasiveness of false beliefs about catharsis makes them potentially harmful."

—Social psychologists Brad Bushman and Roy Baumeister

desensitization
Reduction in emotion-related physiological reactivity in response to a stimulus.

cultivation
The process by which the mass media (particularly television) construct a version of social reality for the public.

Can Media Cause Positive, Prosocial Effects? The vast amount of attention and research has focused on the negative effects of media, but can positive media

Exposure to TV violence in childhood is related to aggression later in life. TRUE.

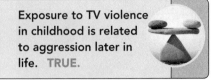

images and messages produce prosocial rather than antisocial effects? Although there is not a great deal of research on this yet, there are some encouraging results. Tobias Greitemeyer (2011) found that listening to music lyrics that promoted socially positive messages caused participants to behave more helpfully. In a separate study, the same author and his colleagues (2012) also found that exposure to prosocial video games (e.g., "Lemmings") made less accessible the aggressive cognitions and affect that, as discussed earlier, often lead to both direct and indirect aggressive behaviour.

Pornography

Just as citizens, scientists, and politicians have been concerned about the consequences of mass media presentations of violence, they have also been troubled by mass media displays of sexual material. Such displays are highly visible and widely available. Magazines, videos, and Internet sites cater to a wide range of sexual interests. Heavy metal, hip-hop, and rap groups often rely on obscenities to get their fans' attention. Pornographic websites and phone services rake in millions of dollars. Opposition to pornography is equally prominent. Parents, religious leaders, consumer groups, and feminist activists lobby legislators and go to court to obtain greater restraints on the availability of sexually explicit materials.

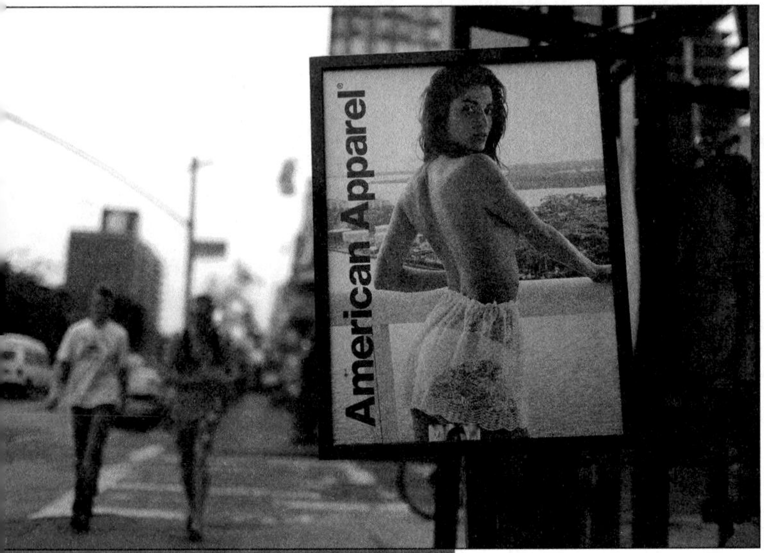

Getty Images

The question of whether exposure to erotic or pornographic images can influence aggression toward women has triggered a good deal of social psychological research over the years. The importance of understanding the impact of such material is underscored by the prevalence of such images in our society, such as this advertisement for American Apparel.

In a meta-analysis of 46 published studies, Elizabeth Oddone-Paolucci and others (2000) found that men were significantly more likely to report sexually aggressive behaviours and attitudes if they also reported exposure to pornography. Of course, this correlational evidence does not prove that pornography caused these behaviours and attitudes. Indeed, such evidence must be supported by experimental research, which we review below. But it is important to recognize the challenges of conducting research on such a controversial and sensitive issue. Even defining the variables is rarely straightforward. Past attempts to ban specific works, such as James Joyce's novel *Ulysses* and Robert Mapplethorpe's photos, indicate that the definitions of such terms as *obscenity, erotica,* and *pornography* are often a matter of personal opinion. One person's smut is another person's masterpiece. Because of the subjectivity in such definitions, the term **pornography** is used here to refer to explicit sexual material, regardless of its moral or aesthetic qualities. It is crucial, however, to distinguish between non-violent and violent pornography in discussing the relationship between pornographic displays and aggression.

Non-Violent Pornography Earlier in this chapter, we described how both arousal and affect can influence aggression. The results of research on non-violent pornography confirm the importance of these factors (Donnerstein et al., 1987). For many people, viewing attractive nudes elicits a pleasant emotional response and low levels of sexual arousal. This combination of positive affect and only moderate arousal is unlikely to trigger much aggression. Indeed, the research by Michael Seto and his colleagues (2001) at the Centre for Addiction and Mental Health in Toronto shows there is little support for a direct causal link between pornography use and sexual aggression. These researchers do note, however, that men who are already predisposed to sexually

pornography
Explicit sexual material.

offend are the most likely to be affected by pornography exposure. This latter point is also consistent with a conclusion reached by other researchers (Kingston et al., 2009; Vega & Malamuth, 2007). They propose that relatively aggressive men may interpret and react to the same images differently than less aggressive men, making them more likely to be affected by them in negative ways.

Violent Pornography Adding violence to pornography greatly increases the possibility of harmful effects. Violent pornography is a triple threat: It brings together high arousal; negative emotional reactions such as shock, alarm, and disgust; and aggressive thoughts. Numerous Internet sites—including many that are free and can be viewed easily by minors—focus specifically on images of sexual violence against women and use depictions of women's pain as a selling point (Gossett & Byrne, 2002).

According to a meta-analysis of 217 studies on the relationship between TV violence and aggression, violent pornography had a stronger effect than any other type of program (Paik & Comstock, 1994). Similar results were found with a more modest meta-analysis carried out on nine non-experimental studies (Hald et al., 2010). And there is substantial evidence that this effect is gender-specific. Male-to-male aggression is no greater after exposure to violent pornography than after exposure to highly arousing but non-violent pornography. Male-to-female aggression, however, is markedly increased (Donnerstein & Malamuth, 1997; Linz et al., 1987; Malamuth & Donnerstein, 1982). Furthermore, violent pornography is one of the few situational factors (along with guns and alcohol) that has been shown to increase aggression even in the absence of provocation. The prime ingredient in such materials is the portrayal of women as willing participants who "enjoy" their own victimization (Donnerstein & Berkowitz, 1981).

Not everyone is affected by violent pornography in the same way. Neil Malamuth has developed what he calls the "rapist's profile." Men fit the profile if they have relatively high levels of sexual arousal in response to violent pornography and also express attitudes and opinions indicating acceptance of violence toward women (see ■ Table 11.3, on page 428). These individuals report more sexually coercive behaviour in the past and more sexually aggressive intentions for the future. Among male students given an opportunity to retaliate against a female confederate who had angered them, those who fit the rapist's profile were more aggressive (Malamuth, 1983, 1986). In another study illustrating the volatile mix of negative attitudes and violent pornography, Dano Demaré and his colleagues (1993) found that male students' negative attitudes toward women and their frequent consumption of violent pornography each predicted the students' self-reported sexually aggressive intentions; the best prediction, however, was obtained when both pornography *and* attitudes were included in the equation.

The potential dangers of mixing violence and sexual arousal are not limited to the pornography industry. Many popular movies, video games, and music videos also mix the two frequently and strategically. This has been true in the movie industry since the time of silent movies, in which the hero saves the damsel in distress, who is perhaps tied to the train tracks; and it continues a century later as action movies try to top each other with increasingly arousing, graphic scenes of fighting and sex.

▶ FIGURE 11.9

Desensitizing Effects of Violent Media

Students were randomly assigned to play either a violent or a non-violent video game for 20 minutes. A few minutes after playing the game, while filling out a questionnaire, they heard what sounded like a fight outside the lab room. They could hear one person get injured and be left alone while clearly needing help. The students were led to believe that the experimenter was not around at this time. Consistent with the idea that violent media can desensitize people, the students who had played the violent game took more than 450 percent longer to come to the aid of this injured stranger than did the students who had played the non-violent game.

(Bushman & Anderson, 2009.)

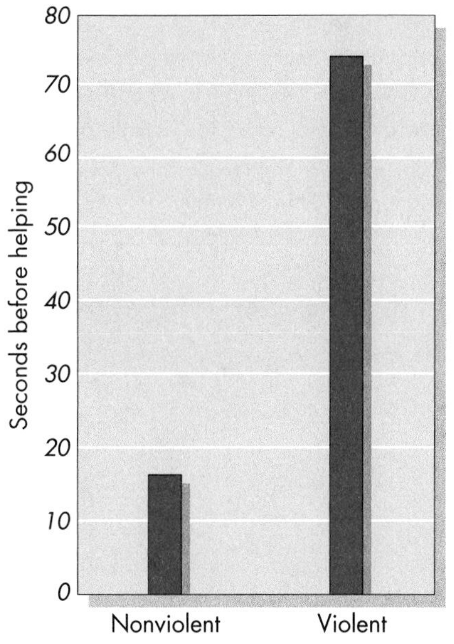

TABLE 11.3

Attitudes About Sex and Aggression

Widely used in research on pornography, these two scales assess attitudes about violence toward women and beliefs about the nature of rape. A few items from each scale are shown here.

(Based on Burt, 1980.)

Acceptance of Interpersonal Violence (Toward Women): AIV Scale

1. Being roughed up is sexually stimulating to many women.
2. Many times a woman will pretend she doesn't want to have intercourse because she doesn't want to seem loose, but she's really hoping the man will force her.
3. A man is never justified in hitting his wife.

Scoring: Persons scoring high in acceptance of violence toward women agree with items 1 and 2, but disagree with item 3.

Rape Myth Acceptance: RMA Scale

1. If a woman engages in necking or petting and she lets things get out of hand, it is her own fault if her partner forces sex on her.
2. Any female can get raped.
3. Many women have an unconscious wish to be raped, and may then unconsciously set up a situation in which they are likely to be attacked.
4. In the majority of rapes, the victim is promiscuous or has a bad reputation.

Scoring: Persons scoring high in acceptance of rape myths agree with items 1, 3, and 4, but disagree with item 2.

Numerous violent video games mix intense violence with gratuitously erotic images of women. These games offer what seems to be an especially dangerous combination of ingredients: a tremendous amount of violence; rewards for degrading women and treating them violently; and very arousing action and music. In at least one popular video game, players not only get to have their character kill numerous people and animals in numerous inventive ways, but they also can urinate on a woman before killing her. Meanwhile, professional wrestling organizations have become notorious for their frequent use of violence and sexual imagery targeted to young males. Defenders claim that viewing such material is harmless and offers a cathartic release for viewers, thereby reducing real-world violence. Opponents cite evidence pointing strongly against catharsis (Bushman, 2002; Forbes et al., 2006).

Intimate Violence: Trust Betrayed

All violence is shocking, but aggression between intimates is especially disturbing. We want to feel safe with those we know and love; and yet far too often, that sense of security is destroyed by violence. A recent international study examining rates of intimate partner violence found similar levels of violence between men and women in countries with more gender equality (e.g., the United States), whereas in countries with greater gender inequality (e.g.,Uganda), higher rates of female victimization were reported (Esquivel-Santoveña & Dixon, 2012). In Statistics Canada's 2009 *General Social Survey on Victimization,* it was found that girls and women are twice as likely as boys and men to be a victim of family violence. For example, women are four times more likely to report being sexually assaulted by their partner, and more than twice as likely to report being beaten. The victims of intimate violence are children as well as adults, and the assault that takes place is often sexual as well as physical. In this section, we examine two major types of intimate violence: sexual aggression among students, and physical aggression between partners.

Sexual Aggression Among University Students

Acquaintance rape (often called "date rape") is a serious problem among university students. In Canada, more than 20 percent of women on university campuses said they had had unwanted sexual intercourse because they were overwhelmed by their male partner (Canadian Federation of Students, 1999), and in a separate survey the same proportion of male students agreed that it was okay to sexually assault a women if they had spent money on her or had been dating her for a long time (Johnson, 1996). When all types of unwanted sexual interactions are included, a majority of women students and about a third of men say they have experienced coercive sexual contact (Cate & Lloyd, 1992; De Keseredy et al., 1993); Struckman-Johnson & Struckman-Johnson, 1994).

A number of factors are associated with sexual aggression among university students. Two of the most important are gender and alcohol. First, both men and women report that men are more likely to engage in coercive behaviour—psychological as well as physical—in order to obtain sex (Poppen & Segal, 1988). Second, alcohol consumption is involved in a majority of sexually aggressive incidents between university students (Cate & Lloyd, 1992; Lawyer et al., 2010). Not only does actual consumption increase aggressive behaviour, but the mere *belief* that one has consumed alcohol (even if one hasn't) heightens sexual arousal and sexual interest (Baron & Richardson, 1994). The cognitive effects of intoxication, in which salient cues are noticed but subtle ones are missed, may disrupt interpersonal communication (Farris et al., 2010). In addition, the anxiety-reducing effects of intoxication may weaken inhibitions against aggressive behaviour (Farris et al., 2008). These conclusions are consistent with the results of an experiment by Brian Marx and others (1999) in which male students listened to an audiotape of a simulated date rape. As illustrated in ▶ Figure 11.10, those participants who had consumed alcohol took significantly longer to determine that the man should refrain from attempting further sexual contact with the woman.

Women's perceptions and behaviours are also affected by alcohol. Several studies have found evidence suggesting that alcohol use (especially binge drinking) can make women more likely not only to take greater risks but also to fail to recognize danger and to feel less able to resist an assault effectively (Howard et al., 2008; Mouilso et al., 2012; Pumphrey-Gordon & Gross, 2007; Testa & Hoffman, 2012).

A recent particularly disturbing development has been the growing use of so-called date-rape drugs, such as Rohypnol (sometimes called "Roofies") or Gamma Hydroxy Butyrate (GHB, sometimes called "Liquid Ecstasy"), to render a person, often a date, helpless. Numerous stories around the world have documented their use in acquaintance rape by methods such as secretly putting the drug in a target's drink at a club or party.

▶ FIGURE 11.10

Alcohol and Perception of Sexual Aggression

Male students listened to an audiotape of what was designed to sound like a date rape. Before listening to the tape, some of the men consumed alcohol and others did not. The experimenter recorded how long it took each participant to determine that the man on the tape should stop attempting further sexual contact with the woman. Students who consumed alcohol took significantly longer to determine that the man should refrain from attempting further sexual contact.

(Marx et al.1999.)

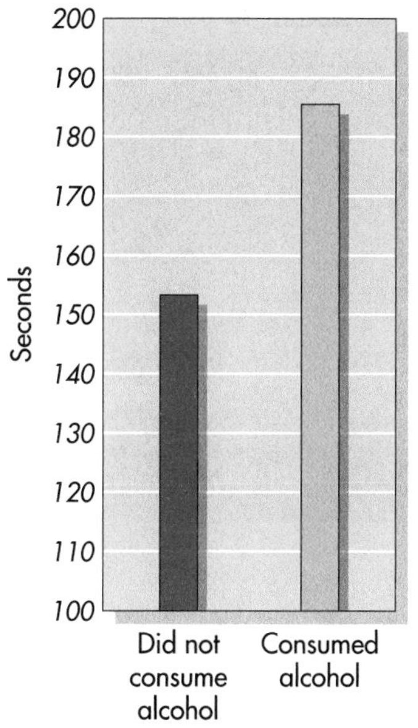

A third important factor concerns attitudes toward rape and toward women. As we indicated earlier, men who fit Malamuth's (1996) concept of the rapist's profile—relatively high sexual arousal in response to violent pornography and attitudes indicating acceptance of violence toward women (see Table 11.3)—report using more sexually coercive behaviour. In light of these findings, it is encouraging that rape-awareness workshops appear to reduce acceptance of rape myths and increase sympathy for female rape victims (Hong, 2000; Proto-Campise et al., 1998). Education has a crucial role to play in reducing sexual aggression.

Men are much more likely than women to aggress against their spouses or partners. FALSE.

Domestic Violence: Partner and Child Abuse

Partner Abuse In 2010, 89 Canadians were killed by their intimate partner, according to a Statistics Canada report. This was an overall decrease of 32 percent from 1980 statistics. A recent study found that 7 percent of Canadians over the age of 60 are victims of some type of intimate partner violence (Poole & Rietschlin, 2012). Of course, partner abuse is not limited to Canada; it is a worldwide phenomenon.

Scott Gries/Getty Images

AFP/Getty Images

Singers Rihanna and Chris Brown are seen here performing together in a concert in December 2008. Less than two months later, the image of this happy couple shattered when Brown was charged with assault for brutally beating Rihanna. In August 2009, Brown was sentenced to probation and community service. Violence targeting dating partners, spouses, and children occurs at alarming rates, and researchers point to several factors as contributing to this tragic problem.

A large-scale study of aggression between dating partners in high school was carried out in Canada and Italy. Similar rates of physical aggression were found in both countries with 33 percent of Canadian students and 34 percent of Italian students reporting at least one violent act (e.g., choking, punching, or beating) in a current or former relationship (Connolly and others, 2010).

Partner abuse is also not a new development; it has occurred throughout history. Indeed, evolutionary psychologists point to a number of factors that predict such behaviour, including males' concerns about paternity (in particular, uncertainty over whether they are the biological fathers of their children). These concerns are known to fuel intense sexual jealousy and distrust, both of which have been implicated in a large percentage of spousal homicides and acts of physical aggression (Buss & Duntley, 2005; Shackelford, 2001; Shackelford & Goetz, 2005).

One of the most surprising results of national surveys in 1975 and 1985 was the high level of wife-to-husband violence, which in terms of severe violence (such as kicking, hitting, beating, threatening with a weapon, and using a weapon) was consistently higher than the level of husband-to-wife abuse. Research on aggression during the early years of marriage has also found higher rates of wife-to-husband abuse (Frye & Karney, 2006; O'Leary et al., 1989). These statistics were initially met with doubt, but they have since received support from the results of research by Murray Straus and his colleagues (Douglas & Straus, 2006; Straus, 1999; Straus & Ramirez, 2005) and from a series of meta-analyses conducted by John Archer (2000, 2006), involving more than 80 published articles, books, and other sources of data concerning aggression between heterosexual partners in Canada, the United States, the United Kingdom, and three other countries.

These statistics tell only part of the story. Although women may aggress against men in intimate relationships as much as or somewhat more than men do against women, the consequences of aggression between partners tend to be much more damaging to women, who are more often killed, seriously injured, or sexually assaulted during domestic disputes than are men (Archer, 2000, 2006; Straus & Ramirez, 2005). As Barbara Morse (1995) put it, "Women were more often the victims of severe partner assault and injury not because men strike more often, but because men strike harder" (p. 251).

Like most aggressive actions, violence between partners is caused by multiple factors. Among the factors associated with increased partner aggression are personal characteristics (such as age, attitudes toward violence, drug and alcohol abuse, and personality), socioeconomic status (which includes income and education), interpersonal conflict, stress, social isolation, and the experience of growing up in a violent family (Herzberger, 1996, 2005; Tjaden & Thoennes, 2000). Several of these factors may help to explain why, according to Alysha Jones (2012) at the University of Manitoba, rates of violence among military couples is higher than in the civilian population.

Child Abuse Children who grow up in a violent family not only witness aggression; they often bear the brunt of it. Tragically, child abuse is not a rare occurrence. While it is difficult to get accurate estimates of child abuse, due to the hidden nature of the crime, a 1998 study estimated that more than 135 000 Canadian children had been abused. In 2006, there were 60 murders of children across Canada; 36 children were killed by a family member (Statistics Canada, 2008).

Like partner aggression, child abuse stems from multiple factors. Among the factors associated with increased child abuse are personal characteristics of the abusing parent (such as personality and substance abuse) and of the child (younger children are more often abused by family members); the family's socioeconomic status; stressful experiences; social isolation; marital conflict; and the abusing parent's having been abused as a child (Belsky, 1993; Davies & Cummings, 1994; Herzberger, 1996, 2005).

The Cycle of Family Violence At this point, you should begin to see a pattern emerging: the connection between violence in childhood and violence as an adult. This connection is called the **cycle of family violence**. Children who witness parental violence or who are themselves abused are more likely as adults to inflict abuse on intimate partners or their children, or, perhaps, to be victims of intimate violence (Fagan, 2005; Frey et al., 2009; Holt & Gillespie, 2008; Ireland & Smith, 2009). This intergenerational transmission of domestic violence is by no means inevitable, however. Most people who witness or experience abuse in their families of origin are not abusive or abused in their families of procreation. The cycle of family violence refers to a greater tendency, not an absolute certainty.

Adults who as children were abused by their parents are less likely to inflict abuse on their own children than are other adults. FALSE.

Reducing Violence

Multiple Causes, Multiple Cures

A variety of factors can contribute to aggression—and, as we have seen, the impact of any one factor often involves other factors simultaneously. Hot temperatures, for instance, influence arousal and aggressive thoughts as well as affect. The effects of watching violence in the media may depend on the chronic level of hostility that a viewer has. Thus, we cannot hope for a single, simple cure. The most effective strategies for reducing aggression recognize this complexity and work on multiple levels. Indeed, one of the most successful treatment programs for violent juvenile delinquents is called *multisystemic therapy*. This approach addresses individuals' problems at several different levels, including the needs of the adolescents and the many contexts in which they are embedded, such as family, peer group, school, and neighbourhood (Borduin et al., 2009; Curtis et al., 2009; Henggeler et al., 2009; Letourneau et al., 2009).

Situational and Sociocultural Factors What about steps to reduce aggression more generally? Given that negative affect and thinking contribute to aggression, reducing stressors such as frustration, discomfort, and provocation should reduce aggression. Toward this end, an improved economy, healthier living conditions, and social support are extremely important. The prevalence of weapons has also been associated with aggressive thoughts and emotions. Reducing the number of guns may

cycle of family violence The transmission of domestic violence across generations.

reduce not only access to the weapons but also the incidence of such thoughts and emotions. At the same time, teaching and modelling non-violent responses to frustrations and social problems—and encouraging thoughtful responses incompatible with anger, such as humour and relaxation—are among the most effective things we can do for our society's children, and for each other.

Having observed the relative non-violence of cultures that emphasize cooperation over competitiveness, social psychologists have concluded that cooperation and shared goals across groups are effective methods for reducing intergroup hostilities and aggression. In addition, because communities beset by broken windows and petty crime reveal a loss of control and support—thus possibly signalling to those who live there that aggression and antisocial behaviour are left unpunished—police departments in numerous cities have begun to crack down on relatively minor acts of vandalism and aggression in the hope that doing so will prevent more serious acts of violence (Taylor, 2000). Finally, changing the cost-reward payoffs associated with aggression can have profound effects on the aggressive tendencies exhibited within a culture. Socialization practices that reward prosocial rather than antisocial behaviour therefore have the potential to greatly reduce the tendency among boys, in particular, to engage in bullying, fighting, and other aggressive behaviours. Conversely, when violence is legitimized, we are all at risk.

Media Effects The media, of course, play an important role in legitimizing—even glorifying—violence. What, then, can we do about it? Government censorship is one answer; but it is not a very popular one, for a number of reasons. Another alternative is to use public pressure to increase media self-censorship. Of course, the most powerful kind of public pressure would be a commercial boycott. If violence did not sell, the media would not produce it. Unfortunately, however, violence continues to be a moneymaker.

Research on the effects of prosocial song lyrics, television, and video games are quite encouraging in this regard. If parents can help children select shows and games that provide compelling, vivid prosocial models for their children, the effects may be strong. Parents have also been advised to watch television with their children and to teach them how TV differs from real life, how imitating TV characters can produce undesirable outcomes, and how children might be harmed by watching TV. This kind of ongoing parental tutorial takes significant time and effort. But given the extent of media depictions of violence in our society, strengthening children's critical viewing skills is a wise investment.

At this point, education may well be the most effective approach. In addition to the role of parents in educating and supporting their children concerning consumption of media, school-based interventions may also help curb children's undesirable reactions to TV. Sahara Byrne (2009) recently conducted an experiment that demonstrated that exposing children to a media literacy intervention can reduce their willingness to use aggression after exposure to violent media.

Daniel Linz and others (1992) similarly advise educational efforts to increase viewers' critical skills in evaluating media depictions that link violence and sex. A model for such efforts can be found in the debriefing provided to research participants exposed to violent pornography in experiments (Donnerstein et al., 1987). This debriefing emphasizes that rape myths are inaccurate and that violent pornography is unrealistic. Among individuals presented with this information, there are long-term reductions in acceptance of rape myths.

Intimate Violence In addition to rape-awareness programs that debunk various rape myths and increase sensitivity, sex-education programs that emphasize the desirability of being respectful and considerate toward one's sexual partner are important tools in the effort to reduce sexual aggression. Many university campuses experience persistent problems with alcohol abuse, which can be a key factor in many rapes and other forms of sexual aggression. Preventing and treating alcohol abuse, therefore, can make for healthier, safer campuses.

Family violence, too, is a matter of grave societal concern; and, since it is caused by multiple factors, it must be addressed by a variety of approaches. Laws and programs that protect victims of abuse and reduce the likelihood of continued violence by abusers are vitally important. But family violence takes place in a larger context. As Peter Sidebotham and Jon Heron (2006) have observed, "The association between poverty and child maltreatment is one of the most consistent observations in the published research" (p. 499). Thus, protecting families from violence also requires providing family members with educational and employment opportunities. Furthermore, because abuse of alcohol and other drugs so often leads to family violence, better education about the effects of such substances, as well as support for individuals who need help dealing with them, would be a worthy investment not only for these individuals but also for the people around them.

Ultimately, effective communication is the key to reducing intimate violence. Jealousy and distrust contribute to much of the violence that occurs between intimate partners. Insensitivities to others' needs and fears, as well as acceptance of myths about rape, play important roles in sexual aggression. And children who grow up in abusive homes may learn aggressive scripts that teach them that the best way to respond to social problems is through aggression. Better communication can help address all of these problems.

"Since war begins in the minds of men, it is in the minds of men that the defenses of peace must be constructed."

—Constitution of UNESCO

Conclusions

We began this chapter with several stories of violence. A review of this chapter will reveal social psychological research in each section that is relevant to various aspects of the lives of the perpetrators involved in the events described. Some of the people behind these acts of violence grew up in a "culture of honour" that may have glorified violence in response to perceived threats to their status and manhood. Many experienced great frustrations in their lives, felt isolated and lonely, had easy access to weapons and hate-filled propaganda, and were consumers of brutal violence in TV shows, movies, and video games. Some were exposed to abuse within their families.

There exists no single profile of the kind of student who is most likely to lash out violently. Rather, the best way to predict those most likely to aggress is to listen to what the students themselves have to say, as many of them reveal, in one way or another, their aggressive thoughts and hostile attitudes. This conclusion parallels the crucial point we have already stated: Communication and social support are critically important factors in reducing violence.

Table 11.4 lists some of the possible steps suggested by the research we have reviewed. Personally, you may not agree that all of these actions are desirable, and

TABLE 11.4

Some Steps to Reduce Aggression and Violence

Although there may be reasons to endorse or reject these ideas, social psychological research on aggression suggests that each has the potential to reduce aggression.

- Enlarge opportunities to achieve the goals valued by society (such as social approval, status, financial success) through non-violent means.
- Reward non-aggressive behaviour.
- Provide attractive models of peaceful behaviour.
- Reduce all forms of aggression in our society, including physical punishment of children, capital punishment of criminals, and war.
- Reduce frustration by improving the quality of life in housing, healthcare, employment, and child care.
- Provide fans and air-conditioned shelters when it's hot.
- Reduce access to and display of weapons.
- Apologize when you've angered someone, and regard apologies as a sign of strength—not weakness. Encourage others to do likewise.
- Stop and think when you feel your temper rising. Control it instead of letting it control you.
- Discourage excessive drinking of alcohol and support efforts to provide treatment for alcohol abuse.
- Develop good communication skills in families and relationships, thereby helping to avoid misperceptions, jealousy, and distrust.
- Pay attention and respond to warning signs of trouble in adolescents, including social isolation, talk of violence, and consumption of violence-filled literature and other media.

you may prefer others that are not mentioned. What is important is to realize that each of us can do something to reduce aggression. There are many paths to take toward this common goal. And because aggression is caused by multiple factors, it is only through multiple paths that we can reach this goal.

REVIEW

What Is Aggression?

- Aggression is behaviour intended to harm another individual.
- Anger is an emotional response to perceived injury; hostility is an antagonistic attitude.
- Instrumental aggression is a means to obtain a desired outcome.
- In emotional aggression, harm is inflicted for its own sake.

Culture, Gender, and Individual Differences

Culture and Aggression

- The rates of violence and the forms violence takes vary dramatically from one society to another.
- Some research suggests that individualistic cultures tend to have higher rates of aggression than collectivistic cultures.
- The forms that aggression may take and attitudes about whether various practices should be considered aggression vary across cultures.
- Bullying is a persistent and widespread problem that affects a large number of young people in the world.
- Within a society, different subcultures exhibit different norms concerning aggression.
- Teenagers and young adults, and people in the Southern United States (compared to northern States) are the groups most prone to violence.

Gender and Aggression

- Men are more violent than women in virtually every culture and time period that has been studied.
- Males tend to be more overtly physically aggressive than females.
- Females are often more indirectly, or relationally, aggressive than males.

Individual Differences

- There is some stability in aggression: Aggression in childhood predicts aggression in adulthood.
- People who tend to hold hostile cognitions, express anger, and exhibit irritability tend to behave more aggressively.

Origins of Aggression

Is Aggression Innate?

- Evolutionary psychology views aggression as a universal, innate characteristic that has evolved from natural and sexual selection pressures.
- Evolutionary accounts propose that gender differences in aggression can be traced to competition for status (and the most desirable mates) and sexual jealousy.
- Some research suggests that individual differences in aggression are produced by genetic inheritance, but the overall evidence is somewhat mixed.
- The sex hormone testosterone and the neurotransmitter serotonin appear to play roles in human aggression.
- Impairments in several areas of the brain, especially to executive functioning, are associated with aggressiveness.
- Biological factors interact with social factors in producing or regulating aggression.

Is Aggression Learned?

- Aggression is increased by rewards.
- Aggression is decreased by punishment only under specific conditions that are often not met in the real world.
- Physical punishment of children is associated with increases in their subsequent aggressive behaviour.
- Social learning theory emphasizes the influence of models on the behaviour of observers.
- Models who obtain desired goals through the use of aggression and are not punished for their behaviour are the most likely to be imitated. But even punished models may encourage aggression by observers.
- Aggressive models teach not only specific behaviours but also more general attitudes and ideas about aggression and aggressive "scripts" that guide behaviour.
- Growing up in a household or community with a lot of aggression and violence increases the likelihood that one will become an aggressive person.
- Peaceful models can decrease aggressive responses by observers.

Gender Differences and Socialization: "Boys Will Be Boys"

- Gender and cultural differences in human aggression may be due in part to differences in socialization practices—lessons taught, reinforcements and punishments given, models offered, and roles and norms emphasized.

Culture and Socialization: Cultures of Honour

- A culture of honour promotes status-protecting aggression among white males in the American South and West, as well as among men in other parts of the world, such as in Brazil.

Nature Versus Nurture: A False Debate?

- Human aggression clearly is affected by learning and experience.
- In aggression, as in all human behaviour, biological and environmental influences interact.

Situational Influences on Aggression

Frustration: Aggression as a Drive

- The frustration-aggression hypothesis proposes that frustration produces the motive to aggress and that aggression is caused by frustration.
- But, in fact, frustration produces many motives, and aggression is caused by many factors.
- According to the frustration-aggression hypothesis, displacement occurs if aggression against the source of frustration is inhibited.
- The frustration-aggression hypothesis holds that engaging in any aggressive action reduces the motive to engage in further aggression, a process called catharsis.
- In the long run, however, aggression now is likely to increase aggression later.
- Frustration is only one of a number of unpleasant experiences that produce negative affect and increase aggression.
- Some studies support the idea of displacement of aggression; however, most research does not support the idea of catharsis as an effective means to reduce aggression.

Negative Affect

- A wide variety of noxious stimuli can create negative feelings and increase aggression.
- Hot temperatures are associated with increased aggression and violence.
- Experiencing social rejection is particularly aversive and can increase aggressive responses.
- Positive emotional responses are incompatible with negative affect and reduce retaliatory aggression.

Arousal: "Wired" for Action

- Highly arousing stimuli increase retaliatory aggression.

Thought: Automatic and Deliberate

- Situational cues associated with aggression, such as the presence of a gun, can automatically activate aggression-related thoughts and increase aggressive behaviour.
- Deliberate thoughts that affect aggression include the perception of the cost or appropriateness of aggression.
- The extent to which individuals perceive hostile intent in others is an important factor in predicting aggression.
- High arousal impairs the cognitive control of aggression, as does alcohol.

Situational Influences: Putting It All Together

- Aggression is influenced by separate and interactive influences of affect, arousal, and cognitions.

Media Effects

Violence in TV, Movies, Music Lyrics, and Video Games

- There is a tremendous amount of violence depicted in the media, and much of it is targeted to children and adolescents.
- A large number of studies, using a variety of different methods, have shown a significant positive relationship between exposure to media violence and real-world aggressive cognitions and behaviours.
- Exposure to TV violence in childhood is related to aggression later in life.
- In laboratory and field experiments, exposure to aggressive models increases aggressive behaviour among adults and children.
- Observing violence in the media can trigger aggressive cognitions and hostility.
- Because we habituate to familiar stimuli, repeated observations of violence desensitizes people to violence, reducing physiological arousal to new incidents. This desensitization can increase aggressive behaviour and decrease helping behaviour.
- Habitual viewing of media violence can suggest that aggression is rewarded, encourage imitation, and promote aggressive scripts, which can guide subsequent behaviour.
- Through cultivation of a social reality, the mass media can intensify fear of aggression and encourage aggressive behaviour.
- Prosocial song lyrics, TV programs, and video games can increase prosocial behavior.

Pornography

- In general, the evidence pointing to a causal link between viewing non-violent pornography and aggressive behaviour is weak, but the effect is stronger among individuals who are already predisposed to sexual aggression.
- Violent pornography increases aggression, particularly male-to-female aggression.
- When a female is portrayed as enjoying violent sex, even unprovoked men become more aggressive and more accepting of violence against women.
- The combination of interest in violent pornography and negative attitudes toward women is a strong predictor of self-reported sexual aggression in the past and sexually aggressive intentions for the future.

Intimate Violence: Trust Betrayed

Sexual Aggression Among University Students

- Men are more likely than women to engage in sexually coercive behaviour.
- Alcohol consumption is involved in a majority of sexually aggressive incidents.
- The combination of positive attitudes toward rape and negative attitudes toward women is associated with coercive sexual behaviour.

Domestic Violence: Partner and Child Abuse

- Sexual jealousy and distrust fuel a great deal of violence between intimate partners.
- National surveys reveal that women engage in more aggressive behaviour against a partner than do men; but women are more likely to be killed, seriously injured, or sexually abused by a partner.
- A shockingly high number of children are victimized—often by parents and caretakers.
- Children who witness parental violence or are themselves abused are more likely as adults to abuse their partners and their own children. But most people escape from this cycle of family violence.

Reducing Violence

Multiple Causes, Multiple Cures

- Recognizing that aggression has multiple levels of causes, multisystemic therapy has been effective in reducing aggressive behaviours among violent adolescents.
- Situational and sociocultural factors that can help reduce violence include avoidance of negative affect, aggressive thinking, the presence of weapons, competitiveness, minor acts of aggression and vandalism, and social rewards for aggressive behaviour.
- Models of non-violent responses to social problems are also useful in reducing violent behaviour.
- Educational efforts emphasizing the unrealistic nature of violent pornography have proved effective in reducing acceptance of rape myths.
- Sex-education and rape-awareness programs can be effective in helping prevent sexual aggression.
- Because of the role of alcohol in rape and other forms of sexual aggression, it is all the more important for university campuses to develop more effective prevention and treatments of alcohol abuse.
- Protecting the victims of family violence and preventing its recurrence require a wide range of interventions.

Conclusions

- Communication and social support are critically important factors in reducing violence.

Key Terms

aggression (400)
catharsis (415)
cultivation (425)
cycle of family violence (431)
desensitization (425)
displacement (415)
emotional aggression (400)
frustration-aggression hypothesis (415)
hostile attribution bias (421)
instrumental aggression (400)
mitigating information (420)
pornography (426)
social learning theory (411)
weapons effect (420)

Putting COMMON SENSE *to the Test*

In virtually every culture, males are more violent than females.

True. *In almost every culture and time period that have been studied, men commit the large majority of violent crimes.*

For virtually any category of aggression, males are more aggressive than females.

False. *Girls are often more indirectly, or relationally, aggressive than boys; and women often exhibit levels of aggression similar to men's when they have been provoked or when they feel relatively anonymous and deindividuated.*

Children who are spanked or otherwise physically disciplined (but not abused) for behaving aggressively tend to become less aggressive.

False. *Evidence indicates that the use of even a little physical punishment to discipline children is associated with increases in subsequent aggressive and antisocial behaviour by the children, even years later, although this relationship may depend on a variety of other factors.*

Blowing off steam by engaging in safe but aggressive activities (such as sports) makes people less likely to aggress later.

False. *Although people may be less likely to aggress immediately after such activities, initial aggression makes future aggression more, not less, likely.*

Exposure to TV violence in childhood is related to aggression later in life.

True. *Laboratory experiments, field experiments, and correlational research all suggest a link between exposure to violence on TV and subsequent aggressive behaviour.*

Men are much more likely than women to aggress against their spouses or partners.

False. *Some evidence suggests that women engage in more acts of serious aggression against their partners than men do; but men are much more likely to injure, sexually abuse, or kill their partners.*

Adults who as children were abused by their parents are less likely to inflict abuse on their own children than are other adults.

False. *Although most people who have experienced such abuse do break the cycle of family violence, on average they are more likely to abuse their own children than are people who have never experienced parental abuse.*

APPENDIX A

Law

This appendix examines applications of social psychology to the law. First, we consider three stages in the life of a jury trial: jury selection, an often controversial process; the courtroom drama, in which confessions, eyewitness identifications, and other types of evidence are presented; and jury deliberation, where the jury reaches a group decision. Next, we consider post-trial factors such as sentencing, the possible result of a guilty verdict. Finally, we discuss perceptions of justice both inside and outside the courtroom.

It seems there is always a high-profile trial in the news that spotlights a crime of sex, violence, money, passion, or celebrity, and captures our interest. The twenty-first century is still young, and yet we have already witnessed some very public, and in some cases sensational, legal cases including: the pending trial of Luka Magnotta, recently arrested and charged with the horrific torture, murder, and dismemberment of Jun Lin, a Chinese International student at Concordia University; the conviction of former Air Force Colonel Russell Williams for two murders and 82 fetish break-and-enters and thefts; the trial and subsequent conviction of Robert Pickton, the British Columbia pig farmer who murdered at least six women from downtown Vancouver between 1995 and 2002 and who has another 20 murder charges still pending. We even saw a world leader brought to trial—former Liberian president Charles Taylor was convicted in 2012 by an International Court for war crimes and crimes against humanity for his support of actions in Sierra Leone. He was sentenced to 50 years in prison.

Regardless of how you feel about these cases, they illustrate the profound importance of social psychology at work in the legal system, raising many questions: What kinds of people do lawyers think make good jurors, and why? Can partisans set aside their biases in decision making? How reliable are confessions, eyewitnesses, and other types of evidence presented in court? Are decision makers contaminated by pretrial publicity and other information not in evidence? How do juries reach their decisions after days, weeks, or months of presentations, often followed by exhausting deliberation? In this appendix, we take social psychology into the courtroom to answer these questions. But first, let's place the trial process in a broader context.

In the North American criminal justice system, trials are just the tip of an iceberg. Once a crime takes place, it must be detected and reported if it is to receive further attention. Through investigation, the police must then find a suspect and decide whether to make an arrest. If they do, the suspect is jailed or bail is set, and then the courts decide if there is sufficient evidence for a formal accusation. If there is sufficient evidence, then the Crown counsel and defence lawyers begin a lengthy process known as "discovery," during which they gather evidence. At this point, many defendants plead guilty as part of a deal negotiated by the lawyers. In cases that do go to trial, the ordeal does not then end with a verdict. After conviction, the judge imposes a sentence, and the defendant decides whether to appeal to a higher court. For those in prison, decisions concerning their release are made by parole boards.

The criminal justice apparatus is complex, and the actors behind the scenes are numerous. Yet through it all, the trial—a relatively infrequent event—is the heart and soul of the system. The threat of trial motivates parties to gather evidence and, later, to negotiate a deal. And when it's over, the trial by judge or jury forms the basis for sentencing and appeals decisions. Social psychologists have a lot to say about trials and other aspects of the legal system as well (Greene & Heilbrun, 2011; Pozzulo et al., 2011).

The issues that social psychologists are now studying are broad and varied. At present, for example, researchers in Canada are looking at how jurors view alibi evidence provided by a witness or a defendant (Burke et al., 2006; Burke & Marion, 2012), whether Muslim women should be allowed to testify in court wearing a veil (Maeder et al., 2012), how jurors deal with inconsistent evidence presented by multiple eyewitnesses (O'Neill & Pozzulo, 2012), whether girls are treated differently than boys when it comes to treatment-based bail conditions (Sprott & Doob, 2010), and how biased impressions of a victim can change the way evidence is perceived by jurors in a trial (Connolly & Gordon, 2011), to list just a few. Importantly, much of what social psychologists have discovered in the legal arena is not known to judges, lawyers, and lay people as a matter of common sense (Borgida & Fiske, 2007). In the coming pages, we divide the trial event into three basic stages: jury selection, the presentation of evidence, and the jury's deliberations.

Putting
COMMON SENSE
to the Test

Circle Your Answer

T F Contrary to popular opinion, women are harsher as criminal trial jurors than men are.

T F Without being beaten or threatened, innocent people sometimes confess to crimes they did not commit.

T F A person can fool a lie-detector test by suppressing arousal when questions about the crime are asked.

T F Eyewitnesses find it relatively difficult to recognize members of a race other than their own.

T F The more confident an eyewitness is about an identification, the more accurate it is likely to be.

T F One can usually predict a jury's final verdict by knowing where the individual jurors stand the first time they vote.

Jury Selection

If you're ever accused of a crime in Canada, or involved in a lawsuit, the *Canadian Charter of Rights and Freedoms* guarantees you many rights, including being presumed innocent until proven guilty; being tried within a reasonable time; and the right to a jury trial if the maximum punishment for the offense is imprisonment for five years or more. Such rights are considered essential to doing justice within a democracy. Yet, it often seems that whenever a controversial verdict is reached in a high-profile case, people, right or wrong, blame the 12 individuals who constituted the jury. That's why it is important to know how juries are selected.

© HO/Reuters/Corbis

CP Images

Reuters

North Americans are fascinated by trials, particularly when they involve sensational details, and horrific crimes. In recent years, high-profile trials involved former Air Force Colonel Russell Williams (left), who was found guilty of murder, as well as sexual assault and theft; Luka Magnotta (middle), charged with killing and dismembering a student and mailing the body parts to federal political parties in Ottawa and Vancouver schools; and Robert Pickton, the farmer from British Columbia convicted of the murders of six women; he has another 20 murder charges still pending (right).

Voir Dire

Jury selection is a three-stage process. First, the Sheriff's office is in charge of contacting the eligible jurors, based on voter registration lists and other sources to compile a master list of eligible citizens who live in the community. Second, so that a representative sample can be obtained, a certain number of people from the list are randomly drawn and summoned for duty. Before people who appear in court are placed on a jury, the court ensures that they don't know any of the people involved in the trial, including victims, the accused, and even the police officers overseeing the case. This screening process is formally known as the **voir dire**, but its use is very limited in Canada, compared to what you might find in the United States. For example, if you have ever read a John Grisham novel, you will have read about lawyers investigating prospective jurors, learning everything they can about them before they ever come to the trial. While this makes for thrilling reading, the process is typically far less dramatic. For example, if you are called for jury duty in Canada, it is likely that all that will be known about you is your name, address, and occupation. In most cases, based on this very limited information, the lawyers can either accept the juror (and they become part of the jury in this case), or they can "challenge" (reject) them. Each side (Crown and Defence) is given a limited number of what are called **peremptory challenges**; they don't need a reason to reject a juror, but they can excuse them nonetheless. What guides the decision to accept some jurors and reject others? These questions make the process of voir dire particularly interesting to social psychologists (Vidmar & Hans, 2007).

There are also unlimited **challenges for "cause"**; if one side feels that a juror may be unsuitable (based on reasons specified by law) or biased for a particular reason, such as the ethnicity or sexual orientation of the defendant, they may ask the judge to grant them the opportunity to challenge (ask further questions of) the jurors on these issues. If the judge agrees, then jurors can be questioned further. If there appears to be bias, then he or she is excused. In fact, if it can be demonstrated that an entire community is biased, perhaps because of pretrial publicity, then the trial might be postponed or moved to another location.

voir dire
The pretrial examination of prospective jurors by the judge or opposing lawyers to uncover signs of bias.

peremptory challenge
A means by which lawyers can exclude a limited number of prospective jurors without the judge's approval.

challenge for cause
A means by which lawyers can exclude an unlimited number of prospective jurors due to perceived bias, or unsuitableness for jury duty under the law.

Trial Lawyers as Intuitive Psychologists

Trial lawyers have been known to have some unusual ideas about who—or what—makes for a good juror. Under pressure to make choices quickly and without much information, lawyers may rely on implicit personality theories and stereotypes. As described in Chapter 4, an implicit personality theory is a set of assumptions that people make about how certain attributes are related to each other and to behaviour. When people believe that all members of a group share the same attributes, these implicit theories are called stereotypes.

As far as trial practice is concerned, how-to books claim that the astute lawyer can predict a juror's verdict by his or her gender, race, occupation, ethnic heritage, and other simple demographics. Still others offer selection advice based on faces, facial expressions, body language, and clothing. Perhaps the most interesting rule of thumb is also the simplest: "If you don't like a juror's face, chances are he doesn't like yours either!" (Wishman, 1986, pp. 72–73).

CP/Chuck Stoody

More than 600 people were summoned as potential jurors in the trial of serial killer Robert Pickton. Though the field for selection was large, the selection process lasted just two days.

The intuitive approach to jury selection by which lawyers use peremptory challenges may provide for colourful stories from inside the courtroom, but the consequences of this kind of stereotyping for justice can be troubling. For example, what if a Crown prosecutor used peremptory challenges to exclude from the jury all Whites or all Blacks, or all men or all women, possibly stripping the jury of the defendant's peers? Citing social psychological research on stereotyping and prejudice, Samuel Sommers and Michael Norton (2008) point to two problems: (1) The influence of conscious and unconscious racial stereotypes on social perceptions is prevalent and likely to influence lawyers in the courtroom; and (2) these racial biases are difficult to identify in specific instances because lawyers, like everyone else, typically do not acknowledge having been influenced by their stereotypes.

Contrary to popular opinion, women are harsher as criminal trial jurors than men are. **FALSE.**

If assumptions based on surface appearances were correct, it would be easy to predict how jurors would vote. But, although some experienced trial attorneys take pride in their jury-selection skills, researchers have found that most lawyers cannot effectively predict how jurors will vote, either on the basis of their intuitive rules of thumb (Olczak et al., 1991) or by relying on how prospective jurors answer questions during the voir dire (Kerr et al., 1991; Zeisel & Diamond, 1978).

The Courtroom Drama

Once a jury is selected, the trial officially begins, and much of the evidence previously gathered comes to life. The evidence produced in the courtroom can range far and wide, from confessions to autopsy results, medical tests, bloodstains, hair samples, handwriting samples, diaries, fingerprints, photographs, and business documents. The trial itself is a well-orchestrated event. Lawyers for both sides make opening statements. Witnesses then answer questions under oath. Lawyers make closing arguments. The judge instructs the jury. Yet there are many problems in this all-too-human enterprise: The evidence may not be accurate or reliable, jurors may be biased by extraneous factors, and judges' instructions may fall on deaf ears. In this section, we identify some of the problems and possible solutions.

Confession Evidence

Every now and then, an extraordinary event comes along that shakes the way you think. The Central Park jogger case was one of these events. In 1989, five boys, 14 to 16 years old, were found guilty of a monstrous assault and rape of a female jogger in New York's Central Park after they confessed, four of them on videotape, in vivid detail. Thirteen years later, a serial rapist named Matias Reyes stepped forward from prison to say that he alone, not the boys, had committed the crime. As part of an investigation of Reyes's claim, the district attorney DNA-tested the semen from the crime scene and found that it was a match: Reyes was the rapist. The five boys, now men, were innocent. Their confessions were false and the convictions were vacated (Kassin, 2002; Saulny, 2002).

Police Interrogations: Social Influence Under Pressure As these events unfolded, questions mounted: Why would five boys, or anyone else for that matter, confess to a crime they did not commit? Why, for example, would Romeo Phillion, already in prison on a robbery charge, confess to the murder of Ottawa firefighter Leopold Roy in 1967? He immediately recanted that confession, claiming it was only meant as a "bad joke"; however that confession, joke or not, ultimately led to his spending the next 32 years in prison.

While once it was not uncommon for police detectives to use bright lights, brute force, the rubber hose, and physical intimidation to get confessions, today the *Charter of Rights and Freedoms* requires the police to inform suspects of their rights to silence and to legal counsel—and the "third degree" tactics they use are more psychological in nature. In *Criminal Interrogation and Confessions,* the most popular how-to manual written for police, Fred Inbau and others (2001) have advised interrogators to put suspects into a small, bare, soundproof room—a physical environment designed to arouse feelings of social isolation, helplessness, and discomfort. Next, they present a vivid nine-step procedure designed to get suspects to confess (see ■ Table A.1). These steps are part of what is commonly referred to as the "Reid Technique."

In general, there are two approaches contained within this method of interrogation. One approach is to pressure the suspect into submission by expressing certainty of his or her guilt and even, at times, claiming to have damaging evidence such as fingerprints or an eyewitness. In this way, the accused is led to believe that it is futile to mount a defence. A second approach is to befriend the suspect, offer sympathy and friendly advice, and "minimize" the offence by offering face-saving excuses or blaming the victim. Lulled into a false sense of security, and led to expect leniency, the suspect caves in. These police tactics may sound as if they come from a television script, but in real life they are frequently used (Davis & Leo, 2012; Gudjonsson, 2003; Kassin et al., 2010; Leo & Davis, 2010).

Interestingly, there is nothing under Canadian law that guarantees a suspect

TABLE A.1

The Nine Steps of Interrogation

(Inbau et al., 2001.)

1. Confront the suspect with assertions of his or her guilt.
2. Develop "themes" that appear to justify or excuse the crime.
3. Interrupt all statements of innocence and denial.
4. Overcome all of the suspect's objections to the charges.
5. Keep the increasingly passive suspect from tuning out.
6. Show sympathy and understanding, and urge the suspect to tell all.
7. Offer the suspect a face-saving explanation for his or her guilty action.
8. Get the suspect to recount the details of the crime.
9. Convert that statement into a full written confession.

that their solicitor will be present while they are being interrogated, *unless they specifically request it,* in which case the police must immediately comply.

THE CANADIAN PRESS/Allison Jones

Tammy Marquardt was wrongly convicted and imprisoned for the murder of her two-and-a-half-year-old son. Her conviction was due in large part to the testimony of disgraced pathologist Charles Smith, who made misleading claims and inferences that went beyond the evidence and his expertise. After spending nearly 15 years in prison for a crime she didn't commit, Marquardt's conviction was finally overturned.

The Risk of False Confessions It could be argued that the use of trickery and deception does not pose a serious problem because innocent people never confess to crimes they did not commit. This assumption, however, is not always correct. As hard as it is to believe, there are a number of chilling cases on record. In fact, among prisoners convicted and later proved innocent by DNA evidence, 20 to 25 percent had given false confessions (Garrett, 2008; Scheck et al., 2000).

Sometimes innocent suspects confess as an act of *compliance,* merely to escape a bad situation. Douglas Firemoon and Joel Labadie were both charged (along with another youth) in the murder of 14-year-old Regina native Darrelle Exner, after admitting they had started to walk her home the night she was killed. All three suspects were subjected to the Reid technique; after hours and hours of interrogation, they each provided details of how they committed the crime—the problem was, they were innocent. Very long periods of time bring fatigue, despair, and a deprivation of sleep and other need states. Sometimes, suspects cooperate, thinking they will be allowed to go home once they confess. There are other instances in which interrogation causes innocent suspects to believe that they might be guilty of the crime, illustrating an even stronger form of social influence known as *internalization.*

Is it really possible to convince people that they are guilty of an act they did not commit? Based on an analysis of actual cases, Saul Kassin and Katherine Kiechel (1996) have found that two factors can increase this risk: (1) a suspect who lacks a clear memory of the event in question, and so is vulnerable to suggestion, and (2) the presentation of false evidence, a technique that the police sometimes use.

Confessions and the Jury: An Attributional Dilemma How does the legal system treat confessions brought out by various methods of interrogation? The procedure is straightforward. Whenever a suspect confesses but then withdraws the statement and goes to trial, the judge must determine whether the statement was voluntary or coerced. If the confession was clearly coerced—as when a suspect is isolated for a long period of time, deprived of food or sleep, threatened, or abused—it is excluded. If the confession is not coerced, it is admitted into evidence for the jury to evaluate.

In these cases, juries are thus confronted with a classic attributional dilemma: A suspect's statement may indicate guilt (personal attribution), or it may simply be a way to avoid the aversive consequences of silence (situational attribution). According to attribution theory, jurors should reject all confessions made in response to external pressure. But wait. Remember the fundamental attribution error? In Chapter 4, we saw that people tend to overattribute behaviour to persons and overlook the influence of situational forces. Is it similarly possible that jurors view suspects who confess as guilty, even if they were highly pressured to confess during interrogation?

"Before we begin, may I ask which of you is the good cop, and which is the bad?"

To examine this question, Kassin and Holly Sukel (1997) had mock jurors read one of three versions of a murder trial. In a control version that did not contain a confession, only 19 percent voted guilty. In a low-pressure version in which the defendant was said to have confessed immediately upon questioning, the conviction rate rose considerably, to 62 percent. But there was a third, high-pressure condition in which participants were told that the defendant had confessed out of fear and with his hands cuffed painfully behind his back. How did participants in this situation react? Reasonably, they judged the confession to be coerced, and they said it did not influence their verdicts. Yet the conviction rate in this situation significantly increased, this time to 50 percent. Apparently, people are powerfully influenced by evidence of a confession— even, sometimes, when they concede that this confession was coerced.

Without being beaten or threatened, innocent people sometimes confess to crimes they did not commit. TRUE.

The jury's reaction to confession evidence may also depend on how that evidence is presented. In a series of experiments, Daniel Lassiter and his colleagues (2001) taped mock confessions from three different camera angles so that either the suspect or the interrogator or both were visible. All participants heard the same exchanges of words, but those who watched the suspects saw the situations as less coercive than did those who focused on the interrogators. Follow-up research has shown that even the perceptions of experienced trial judges are influenced by these variations in camera perspective (Lassiter et al., 2007). Today, many police departments videotape confessions for presentation in court (Lassiter, 2010). The practical implications are striking. When the camera directs all eyes at the accused, jurors are likely to underestimate the amount of pressure exerted by the "hidden" interrogator.

The Lie-Detector Test

Often, people confess after being told that they have failed the **polygraph**, or lie-detector test. A polygraph is an electronic instrument that simultaneously records multiple channels of physiological arousal. The signals are picked up by sensors attached to different parts of the body. For example, rubber tubes are strapped around a suspect's torso to measure breathing; blood pressure cuffs are wrapped around the upper arm to measure pulse rate; and electrodes are placed on the fingertips to record sweat-gland activity, or perspiration. These signals are then boosted by amplifiers and converted into a visual display.

The polygraph is used to detect deception on the assumption that when people lie, they become anxious and aroused in ways that can be measured. Here's how the test is conducted. After convincing a suspect that the polygraph works and establishing his or her baseline level of arousal, the examiner asks a series of yes-no questions and compares how the suspect reacts to emotionally arousing *crime-relevant questions* ("Did you steal the money?") and *control questions* that are arousing but not relevant to the crime ("Did you take anything that did not belong to you when you were young?") In theory, suspects who are innocent—whose denials are truthful—should be more aroused by the control questions, while guilty suspects—whose denials are false— should be more aroused by the crime-relevant questions.

polygraph
A mechanical instrument that records physiological arousal from multiple channels; it is often used as a lie-detector test.

Does the lie-detector test really work? Many people think it is foolproof, but scientific opinion is split (Iacono & Lykken, 1997). Some researchers report accuracy rates of up to 80 to 90 percent (Honts, 1996; Raskin, 1986). Others believe that such claims are exaggerated and misleading (Lykken, 1998). One well-documented problem is that truthful persons too often fail the test. A second problem is that people who understand the test can fake the results. Studies show that you can beat the polygraph by tensing your muscles, squeezing your toes, or using other countermeasures while answering the *control* questions. By artificially inflating the responses to "innocent" questions, one can mask the stress that is aroused by lying on the crime-relevant questions (Honts et al., 1994).

What, then, are we to conclude? Careful reviews of the research suggest that there is no simple answer (Honts et al., 2002; Meijer & Verschuere, 2010; National Research Council, 2003). Under certain conditions—for example, when the suspect is naive and the examiner is competent—it is possible for the polygraph to detect truth and deception at fairly high levels of accuracy. Still, the problems are hard to overcome, which is why the Supreme Court of Canada ruled, in 1987, that polygraph test results are not admissible in courts of law. As an alternative, researchers are now trying to develop tests that distinguish between truth and deception through the measurement of involuntary electrical activity in the brain (Bashore & Rapp, 1993), pupil dilation when the person being tested is asked to lie, which requires more cognitive effort than telling the truth (Dionisio et al., 2001), and the use of fMRI to measure blood oxygen levels in areas of the brain associated with deception (Bhatt et al., 2009; McCabe et al., 2011).

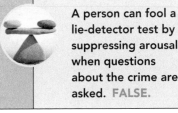

A person can fool a lie-detector test by suppressing arousal when questions about the crime are asked. FALSE.

Eyewitness Testimony

"I'll never forget that face!" When these words are uttered, police officers, judges, and juries all take notice. Often, however, eyewitnesses make mistakes. Consider the story of Thomas Sophonow, charged with murdering Barbara Stoppel while visiting his sister in Winnipeg, Manitoba, in 1981. Several eyewitnesses picked Sophonow out of a lineup. It seemed that the police had their killer. Sophonow spent four years in prison for this crime, although he maintained his innocence throughout. While he was eventually freed, four years later, it took another 15 years before he was officially found innocent. We will discuss the factors that helped to wrongfully convict him, below.

According to Rod Lindsay of Queen's University, as few as 40 and as many as 300 people are wrongfully convicted each year in Canada, primarily on the basis of mistaken eyewitness identification. Figures from the United States suggest that 77 000 people a year are charged with crimes solely on the basis of eyewitness evidence (Goldstein et al., 1989). Many of these eyewitness accounts are accurate, but many are not. Studies of wrongful convictions—cases in which an individual is convicted, but later exonerated by DNA evidence—have demonstrated that the number one reason people are wrongfully convicted is mistaken eyewitness identification (Connors et al., 1996; Wells, Memon, & Penrod, 2007).

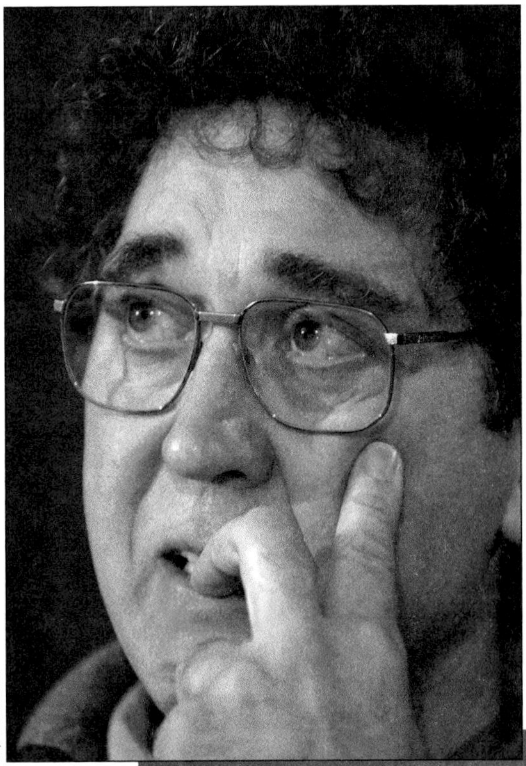
CP/Aaron Harris

Thomas Sophonow, despite an alibi and no physical evidence linking him to the crime, was wrongfully convicted for the murder of a 16-year-old waitress and spent four years in jail.

In 1999, the U.S. Department of Justice took a bold step in response to this problem, assembling a group of police, prosecutors, defence attorneys, and research psychologists—including two from Canada—to devise a set of "how-to" guidelines. Led by Gary Wells, this technical working group went on to publish *Eyewitness Evidence: A Guide for Law Enforcement* (U.S. Department of Justice, 1999; Wells et al., 2000).

As eyewitnesses, people can be called upon to remember just about anything—perhaps a face, an accident, or a conversation. To date, hundreds of tightly controlled studies of eyewitness testimony have been conducted. Based on this research, three conclusions can be drawn: (1) Eyewitnesses are imperfect, (2) certain personal and situational factors systematically influence their performance, and (3) judges, juries, and lawyers are not well informed about these factors (Cutler & Penrod, 1995; Lindsay et al., 2007; Wells & Quinliven, 2009).

People tend to think that human memory is like a digital video camera: If you turn on the power and focus the lens, all events will be recorded for subsequent playback. Unfortunately, it's not that simple. Over the years, researchers have found it useful to view memory as a three-stage process involving the *acquisition*, *storage*, and *retrieval* of information. The first of these stages, acquisition, refers to a witness's perceptions at the time of the event in question. Second, the witness rehearses and stores that information in memory to avoid forgetting. Third, the witness retrieves the information from storage when needed. This model suggests that errors can occur at three different points.

Acquisition Some kinds of persons and events are more difficult to perceive than others. Common sense tells us that brief exposure time, poor lighting, distance, physical disguise, and distraction can all limit a witness's perceptions. Research has uncovered other, less obvious factors as well.

Consider the effects of a witness's emotional state. Often people are asked to recall a bloody shooting, or a car wreck, or an assault—emotional events that trigger high levels of stress. Arousal has a complex effect on memory. Realizing the importance of what they are seeing, highly aroused witnesses zoom in on the central features of an event—perhaps the culprit, the victim, or a weapon. As a direct result of this narrowed field of attention, however, arousal impairs a witness's memory for other less central details (Brown, 2003; Christianson, 1992). Alcohol, a drug often involved in crime, also causes problems. When participants in one study witnessed a live staged crime, those who had earlier consumed fruit juice were more accurate in their recollections than were those who had been served an alcoholic beverage (Yuille & Tollestrup, 1990). Under the influence of alcohol, people can recognize the perpetrator in a lineup—but they too often make false identifications when the actual perpetrator is absent (Dysart et al., 2002).

There is still another important consideration. By varying the racial makeup of participants and target persons in laboratory and real-life interactions, researchers discovered that people find it relatively difficult to recognize members of a race other than their own—an effect known as the **cross-race identification bias** (Malpass & Kravitz, 1969). The finding that "they all look alike" (referring to members of other groups) is found reliably and in many different racial and ethnic groups. Indeed, Christian Meissner and John Brigham (2001) statistically combined the results of 39 studies involving a total of 5000 mock witnesses. As it turns out, these witnesses were consistently less accurate and more prone to making false identifications when they tried to recognize target persons from racial and ethnic groups other than their own.

Storage Can remembrances of the remote past be trusted? As you might expect, memory for faces and events tends to decline with the passage of time. Longer intervals between an event and its retrieval are generally associated with increased forgetting (Shapiro & Penrod, 1986). But not all recollections fade, and time alone does not cause memory slippage. Consider the plight of bystanders who witness firsthand such incidents as terrorist bombings, shootings, plane crashes, or fatal car accidents. Afterward, they may talk about what they saw, read about it, hear what other bystanders have to say, and answer questions from investigators and reporters. By the

cross-race identification bias
The tendency for people to have difficulty identifying members of a race other than their own.

▶ **FIGURE A.1**

Biasing Eyewitness Reports with Loaded Questions

Participants viewed a film of a traffic accident and then answered this question: "About how fast were these cars going when they (hit, smashed, or contacted) each other?" As shown, the wording of the question influenced speed estimates (top). One week later, it also caused participants to reconstruct their memory of other aspects of the accident (bottom).

(Loftus & Palmer, 1974.)

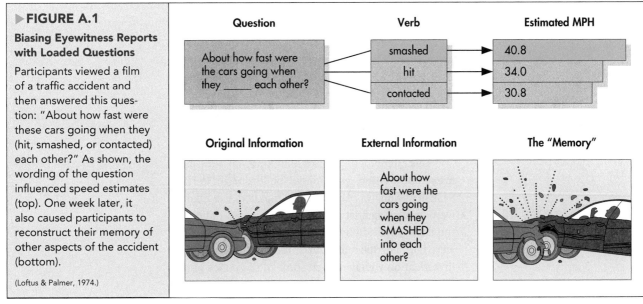

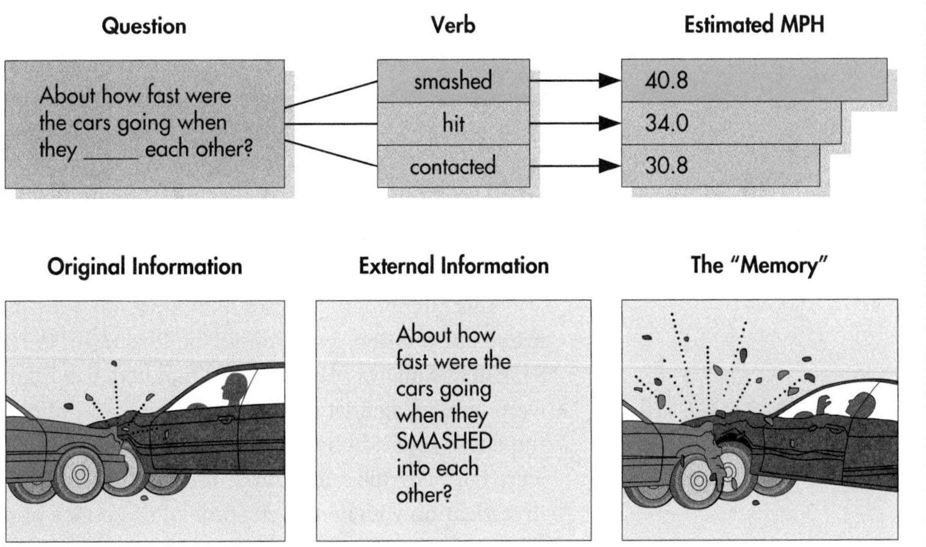

Adapted from *Journal of Verbal Learning and Verbal Behavior, Vol. 13, 1974*,.F. Loftus and J.C. Palmer, "Reconstruction of Automobile Destruction: An Example of the Interaction Between Language and Memory", pp. 585-589, Copyright 1974, with permission from Elsevier

time witnesses to these events are officially questioned, they are likely to have been exposed to so much post-event information that one wonders if their original memory is still "pure."

According to Elizabeth Loftus (1996), it probably is not. Many years ago, based on her studies of eyewitness testimony, Loftus proposed a theory of reconstructive memory. After people observe an event, she said, later information about that event—whether it's true or not—becomes integrated into the fabric of their memory. A classic experiment by Loftus and John Palmer (1974) illustrates the point. Participants viewed a film of a traffic accident and then answered questions, including: "About how fast were the cars going when they hit each other?" Other participants answered the same question, except that the verb *hit* was replaced by *smashed, collided, bumped,* or *contacted.* All participants saw the same accident, yet the wording of the question affected their reports. ▶ Figure A.1 shows that participants given the "smashed" question estimated the highest average speed, and those responding to the "contacted" question estimated the lowest. But there's more. One week later, participants were called back for more probing. Had the wording of the questions caused them to reconstruct their memories of the accident? Yes. When asked whether they had seen broken glass at the accident (none was actually present), 32 percent of the "smashed" participants said they had. As Loftus had predicted, what these participants remembered of the accident was based on two sources: the event itself and post-event information.

Eyewitnesses find it relatively difficult to recognize members of a race other than their own. TRUE.

This **misinformation effect** has aroused much controversy. It's clear that eyewitnesses can be compromised when they get misleading post-event information (Hasel & Kassin, 2009; Porter et al., 2010; Tiwari, 2012). But does post-event information actually alter a witness's real memory, so that it can never be retrieved again? Or do participants merely follow the experimenter's suggestion, leaving their true memory intact for retrieval under other conditions? Either way, whether memory is truly altered or not, it is clear that eyewitness *reports* are hopelessly biased by post-event information and that this effect can be hard to erase (Johnson & Seifert, 1998). These effects can also be dramatic. In one laboratory study, people were led through a process of imagination to create false memories of having performed some bizarre behaviours two weeks earlier—like balancing a spoon on the nose, sitting on dice, and rubbing lotion on a chair (Thomas & Loftus, 2002). As another example, Steve

misinformation effect
The tendency for false post-event information to become integrated into people's memory of an event.

Lindsay and others (2004) asked undergraduates at the University of Victoria to recall details of three childhood events, based on information provided by the parents of the students. Only two of the events were true; the third event, created by the researchers, was about the student playing a prank on their teacher. As a memory cue, half of the participants were also provided with their school class photos for the years during which the events were to have taken place. They found that rates of false memories soared in the class photo condition. Participants provided with class photos reported details of an event that never happened to them twice as often as those in the no-photo group.

This phenomenon raises an additional question. If adults can be misled by post-event information, what about children? In 1991, the small town of Martensville, Saskatchewan, was plunged into the media spotlight after allegations of sexual abuse were levelled against a family operating an unlicensed daycare centre. The extent of the abuse reported by the children was massive, and the particular events described were both horrific and bizarre, including stories of satanic rituals and torture. As the investigation widened, even some of the police officers who initially investigated the case were themselves charged!

Were the children's stories accurate? On the one hand, there were striking consistencies in the testimonies of the child witnesses. On the other hand, the therapists and investigators who conducted the interviews often prompted the children with suggestive leading questions, pressuring them to describe acts they had initially denied. Eventually, only one person was ever found guilty, and more than a decade later, the owners of the daycare successfully sued the Saskatchewan government for close to $1 million in compensation for their ordeal. Despite all charges being dropped against him, Ron Sterling, one of the owners, noted that the stigma of being charged as a child molester will follow him always. As Sterling stated on CBC's *the fifth estate* on February 12, 2003, "You're not anonymous anywhere. It doesn't matter where we go. There's always somebody who will stop and stare, point a finger."

Can suggestive interview procedures cause young children to confuse appearance and reality? At first, simple laboratory experiments conducted to test this idea showed that preschoolers were more likely than older children and adults to incorporate misleading "trick" questions into their memories for simple stories (Ceci et al., 1987). Other studies showed that interviewers could get young children to change their memories, or at least their answers, simply by repeating a question over and over—a situation that implies that the answer given is not good enough (Poole & White, 1991).

It is now apparent that repetition, misinformation, and leading questions can bias a child's memory report—and that preschoolers are particularly vulnerable in this regard. In dozens of studies, these procedures have led children to falsely report that they were touched, hit, kissed, and hugged; that a thief came into their classroom; that something "yukky" was put into their mouth; and even that a doctor had cut a bone from their nose to stop it from bleeding. Somehow, the courts must distinguish between true and false claims—and do so on a case-by-case basis. To assist in this endeavour, researchers have proposed that interviewing guidelines be set so that future child witnesses are questioned in an objective, nonbiasing manner (La Rooy et al., 2010).

"Do you swear to tell your version of the truth as you perceive it, clouded perhaps by the passage of time and preconceived notions?"

Retrieval For eyewitnesses, testifying is only the last in a series of efforts to retrieve what they saw from memory. Before witnesses reach the courtroom, they are questioned by police and lawyers, view a lineup or mug shots, and even assist in the construction of a facial composite or an artist's sketch of the perpetrator. Yet each of these experiences increases the risk of error and distortion.

Nothing an eyewitness does has greater impact than an identification from a lineup. When the police make an arrest, they often call on witnesses to view a photographic lineup that includes the suspect and five to seven other individuals. This procedure may take place within days of a crime or months later. Either way, the lineup often results in tragic cases of mistaken identity. Through the application of eyewitness research findings, this risk can be reduced (Wells et al., 1998; Wells et al., 2007).

Basically, four factors affect identification performance. The first is the lineup *construction.* To be fair, a lineup should contain four to eight innocent persons, or "foils," who match the witness's general description of the culprit or resemble the suspect in general appearance. Anything that makes a suspect distinctive, compared with the others, increases his or her chance of being selected (Buckhout, 1974). This is what happened to Thomas Sophonow; his picture stood out like a sore thumb. The culprit had been described as being quite tall, but Sophonow was the tallest person shown to the witnesses. His photo was the only one taken outdoors (wearing a cowboy hat), whereas the rest were taken indoors. Further, he was the only person from the photo lineup to then be asked to appear in a live lineup; it is no wonder that some of the witnesses found him to be "familiar" (Loftus, 2003)!

Second, lineup *instructions* to the witness are important. In a study by Roy Malpass and Patricia Devine (1981), students saw a staged act of vandalism, after which they attended a lineup. Half of the students received "biased" instructions: They were led to believe that the culprit was in the lineup. The others were told that he might or might not be present. Lineups were then presented either with or without the culprit. When the students received biased instructions, they felt compelled to identify *someone*—and often picked an innocent person (see ▪ Table A.2). When the criminal is present in the lineup, biased instructions are not problematic. When the criminal is not in the lineup, however—which occurs whenever the police suspect is innocent—biased instructions substantially increase the rate of mistaken identifications (Clark, 2005; Steblay, 1997).

Third, the *format* of a lineup also influences whether a witness feels compelled to make a selection. When witnesses are presented with a spread of photographs, they tend to make relative, multiple-choice-like judgments by comparing the different alternatives and picking the one who looks most like the criminal. This strategy increases the risk of making a false identification. The solution: When the same photos are shown sequentially, one at a time, witnesses tend to make absolute judgments by comparing each target person with their memory of the criminal. This situation diminishes the risk of a forced and often false identification, a finding confirmed in a recent meta-analysis of 72 studies comparing simultaneous to sequential lineups (Steblay et al., 2011).

The fourth factor is perhaps the most subtle, as it pertains to *familiarity-induced biases.* Research shows that people often remember a face but not the circumstances in which they saw that face. In one study, for example, participants witnessed a staged crime and then looked through mug shots. A few days later, they were asked to view a

TABLE A.2

Effects of Lineup and Instructions on False Identifications

After witnessing a crime, participants were told either that the culprit was in the lineup (biased instruction) or that he might or might not be present (unbiased instruction). Participants then viewed a lineup in which the real culprit was present or absent. Notice the percentage of participants in each group who identified an innocent person. Those who received the biased instruction were more likely to make a false identification, picking an innocent person rather than no one at all—especially when the real culprit was not in the lineup.

(Malpass & Devine, 1981.)

	Percentage of False Identifications	
	Unbiased Instructions	Biased Instructions
Culprit present	0	25
Culprit absent	33	78

lineup. The result was startling: Participants were just as likely to identify an innocent person whose photograph was in the mug shots as they were to pick the actual criminal (Brown et al., 1977). Many different studies have shown that witnesses will often identify from a lineup someone they had seen in another context, including innocent bystanders who also happened to be at the crime scene (Deffenbacher et al., 2006).

Courtroom Testimony Eyewitnesses can be inaccurate, but that's only part of the problem. The other part is that their testimony in court is persuasive and not easy to evaluate. To examine how juries view eyewitness testimony, Gary Wells, Rod Lindsay, and others conducted a series of experiments in which they staged the theft of a calculator in front of unsuspecting research participants, who were later cross-examined after trying to pick the culprit from a photo spread. Other participants, who served as mock jurors, observed the questioning and judged the witnesses. The results were sobering: Jurors overestimated how accurate the eyewitnesses were and could not distinguish between witnesses whose identifications were correct and those whose identifications were incorrect (Lindsay et al., 1981; Wells et al., 1979).

There appear to be two problems. First, the subject of human memory is not something people know about through common sense. Brian Cutler and others (1988) found that mock jurors were not sensitive enough to the effects of lineup instructions, the cross-race bias, and other aspects of an eyewitnessing situation in evaluating the testimony of an eyewitness (Abshire & Bernstein, 2003). Survey research shows that relative to experts, judges, prosecutors, defence attorneys, and, according to one study, even licensed psychologists also lack awareness of many of the factors described above that influence eyewitness memory (Benton et al., 2007; Magnussen & Melinder, 2012; Magnussen et al., 2008; Wise et al., 2011).

The more confident an eyewitness is about an identification, the more accurate it is likely to be. FALSE.

The second problem is that people tend to base their judgments of an eyewitness largely on how *confident* the witness is, a factor that is only modestly predictive of accuracy. This statement may seem surprising, but studies have shown that the witness who declares "I am absolutely certain" is often not more likely to be right than the one who appears unsure (Penrod & Cutler, 1995; Sporer et al., 1995; Wells & Murray, 1984). Why are eyewitness confidence and accuracy not highly related? The reason is that confidence levels can be raised and lowered by factors that do not have an impact on identification accuracy (Lüüs & Wells, 1994; Shaw, 1996).

For example, Gary Wells and Amy Bradfield (1998) found that eyewitnesses who were given positive feedback about their false identifications also went on to reconstruct other aspects of their eyewitnessing experience. In a series of studies, they showed participants a security camera videotape of a man who shoots a guard followed by a set of photographs that did not contain the actual gunman (in other words, all identifications made were false). The experimenter then said to some witnesses, but not to others, "Oh good. You identified the actual murder suspect." When witnesses were later asked about the whole experience, those given the confirming feedback recalled that they had paid more attention to the event, had a better view of the culprit, and found it easier to make the identification (see ▶ Figure A.2). Apparently, an eyewitness's confidence about the entire experience can be raised or lowered by social feedback—and this makes confidence even less predictive of accuracy (Bradfield et al., 2002; Rodriguez & Berry, 2010).

Nonevidentiary Influences

A trial is a well-orchestrated event that follows strict rules of evidence and procedure. The goal is to ensure that juries base their verdicts solely on the evidence and

FIGURE A.2

Biasing Effects of Post-Identification Feedback

Participants saw a gunman on videotape and then tried to make an identification from a set of photographs in which he was absent. Afterward, the experimenter gave some witnesses but not others confirming feedback about their selection. As shown, those given the confirming feedback later recalled that they had paid more *attention* to the event, had a better *view* of it, could make out *details* of the culprit's face, and found it *easier* to make the identification. They were also more willing to testify in court.

(Wells & Bradfield, 1998.)

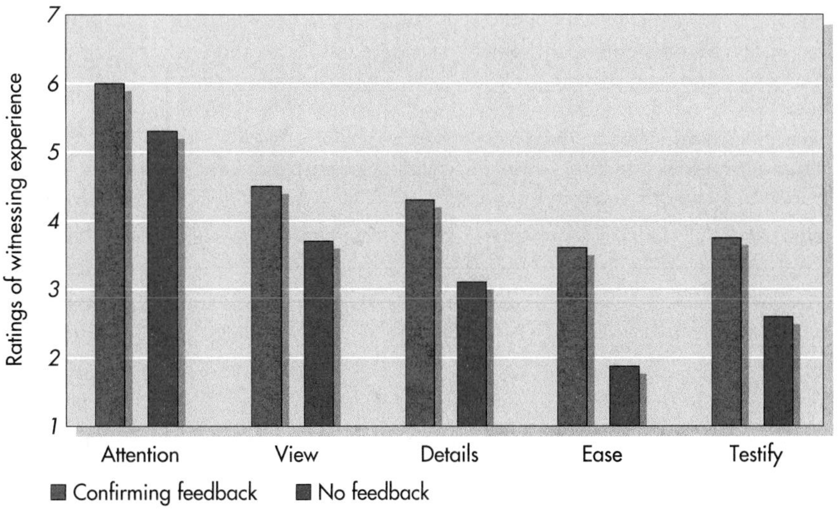

testimony presented in court—not on rumours, newspaper stories, a defendant's attire, and other information. The question is: To what extent is this goal achieved, and to what extent are jury verdicts tainted by nonevidentiary influences?

"It is a capital mistake to theorize before you have all the evidence. It biases the judgment."

—Sir Arthur Conan Doyle

Pretrial Publicity Many high-profile cases find their way into newspapers and other mass media long before they appear in court. In these instances, the legal system struggles with this dilemma: Does exposure to pretrial news stories corrupt prospective jurors? Public opinion surveys consistently show that the more people know about a case, the more likely they are to presume the defendant guilty, even when they claim to be impartial (Kovera, 2002; Moran & Cutler, 1991). There is nothing particularly mysterious about this result. The information in news reports usually comes from the police or Crown prosecutor's office, so it often reveals facts unfavourable to the defence. The real question is whether these reports have an impact on juries that go on to receive hard evidence in court and deliberate to a verdict.

To examine the effects of pretrial publicity, Geoffrey Kramer and his colleagues (1990) played a videotaped re-enactment of an armed robbery trial to hundreds of people participating in 108 mock juries. Before watching the tape, participants were exposed to news clippings about the case. Some read material that was neutral. Others read information that was incriminating—revealing, for example, that the defendant had a prior record or implicating him in a hit-and-run accident in which a small child was killed. Even though participants were instructed to base their decisions solely on the evidence, pretrial publicity had a marked effect. Among those exposed to neutral material, 33 percent voted guilty after deliberating in a jury. Among those exposed to the prejudicial material, that figure increased to 48 percent. What's worse, judges and defence lawyers could not identify in a simulated voir dire which jurors were biased by the publicity. As shown in Figure A.3, 48 percent of those who were questioned and not challenged—jurors who said they were unaffected—went on to vote guilty (Kerr et al., 1991). The impact of pretrial publicity is even more powerful when the news is seen on television rather than in print (Ogloff & Vidmar, 1994).

In Canada, a judge may issue a publication ban on evidence surrounding a case as a way to increase the chances of a defendant getting a fair trial, or to otherwise protect

FIGURE A.3

Contaminating Effects of Pretrial Publicity

In this study, participants were exposed to prejudicial or neutral news reports about a defendant, watched a videotaped trial, and voted before and after participating in a mock jury deliberation. As shown, pretrial publicity increased the conviction rate slightly before deliberations (left). After deliberations, however, it more clearly increased the conviction rate—even among participants perceived as impartial by judges and lawyers (right).

(Kerr et al., 1991.)

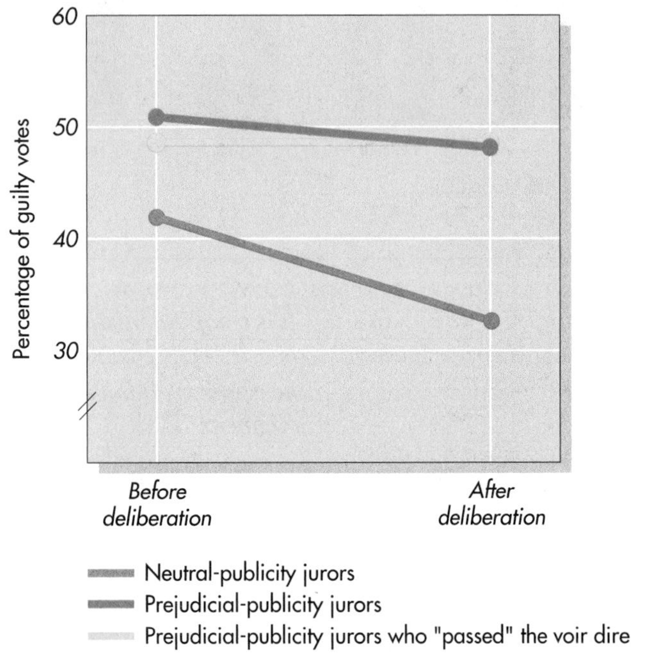

those involved in the case. For example, when Paul Bernardo and Karla Homolka were charged with the murders of two young schoolgirls, a ban was issued prohibiting the Canadian media from reporting on any of the evidence until after the trial. Despite this ban, however, the Internet was full of gruesome details of their crimes (many of the details were false, but that didn't stop the flow of information). In addition, some of the U.S. media did not honour the ban, allowing those that lived close to the U.S. border access to the lurid details presented in court. In this case at least, the publication ban did little to limit the amount of information available to potential jurors.

Pretrial publicity is potentially dangerous in two respects. First, it often divulges information that is not later allowed into the trial record. Jonathan Freedman and Tara Burke (1996) suggested that pretrial publicity is more likely to have an effect in such circumstances, as any potentially damaging information never officially becomes evidence and so can never be refuted in court. Second is the matter of timing. Because many news stories precede the actual trial, jurors learn certain facts even before they enter the courtroom. From what is known about the power of first impressions, the implications are clear. If jurors receive prejudicial news information about a defendant *before* trial, the concern is that this information will distort the way they interpret the facts of the case (Hope et al., 2004; Ruva et al., 2011).

Given that the results of many studies indicate that the biasing effects persist despite the practices of jury selection, the presentation of hard evidence, cautionary words from the judge, and jury deliberations, justice may demand that highly publicized cases be postponed or moved to other, less informed communities (Steblay et al., 1999; Studebaker & Penrod, 1997). For example, the trial for Paul Bernardo was moved from St. Catharines, Ontario, where the murders occurred, to Toronto, Ontario, where it was assumed a jury would be less likely to have been influenced by the sensational details of the crimes.

Inadmissible Testimony Just as jurors may be biased by news stories, so they occasionally receive extralegal information within the trial itself. Imagine that you are a juror in a case, and immediately after hearing a very powerful piece of evidence, one of the lawyers jumps up and says, "I object. Move to strike." The learned judge leans over and tells the jury to disregard the information that was just presented. Could you do it? Can people really strike information from their minds the way court reporters can strike it from the record? Can people on a jury resist the forbidden fruit of inadmissible testimony? Although common sense suggests they cannot, the research is mixed. In one study, a group of mock jurors read about a murder case based on evidence so weak that not a single juror voted guilty. A second group read the same case, except that the prosecution introduced an illegally obtained tape recording of a phone call made by the defendant: "I finally got the money to pay you off.... When you read the papers tomorrow, you'll know what I mean." The defence argued that the illegal tape should not be admissible, but the judge disagreed. At this point, the conviction rate increased to 26 percent. In a third group, as in the second, the tape was brought in and the defence objected. Yet this time, the judge sustained the objection and told jurors to disregard the tape. The result: 35 percent voted for conviction (Sue et al., 1973). A meta-analysis by Nancy Steblay and others (2006) concluded that instructions to disregard evidence do not deter jurors.

Why do people not follow a judge's order to disregard inadmissible evidence? There are a number of possible explanations (Lieberman & Arndt, 2000). Imagine yourself in the jury box, and three reasons will become apparent. First, the added instruction draws attention to the information in controversy. It's like being told *not* to think about white bears. As we saw in Chapter 3, trying to suppress a specific thought increases its tendency to intrude upon our consciousness (Wegner, 1994). A second reason is that a judge's instruction to disregard, much like censorship, restricts a juror's decision-making freedom. Accordingly, it can backfire by arousing reactance. Thus, when a judge emphasizes the ruling by *forbidding* jurors from considering the information ("You have no choice but to disregard it"), they become even *more* likely to use it (Wolf & Montgomery, 1977). The third reason is the easiest to understand: Jurors want to reach the right decision. If they stumble onto relevant information, they want to use it—whether it satisfies the law's technical rules or not. In other words, jurors find it hard to ignore information that seems relevant to a case (Wissler & Saks, 1985).

The Judge's Instructions

One of the most important rituals in any trial is the judge's instructions to the jury. It is through these instructions that juries are educated about relevant legal concepts, informed of the verdict options, admonished to disregard extralegal factors, and advised on how to conduct their deliberations. To make verdicts adhere to the law, juries are supposed to comply with these instructions. The task seems simple enough, but there are problems.

To begin with, the jury's intellectual competence has been called into question. For years, the courts have doubted whether jurors understood their instructions. One skeptical judge put it bluntly when he said, "these words may as well be spoken in a foreign language" (Frank, 1949, p. 181). To some extent, he was right. When actual instructions are tested with mock jurors, the results reveal high levels of misunderstanding—a serious problem in light of the fact that jurors seem to have many preconceptions about crimes and the requirements of the law.

Gordon Rose and James Ogloff (2001) compared the ability of undergraduate students, volunteers from jury panels, and first year law students from British Columbia to understand the judge's instructions in a drug conspiracy case. They found that comprehension levels were highest among the law-school students (approximately 70 percent), while students did about as well as jurors (in the 60- to 70-percent range). They described these overall levels of comprehension as "abysmally low" (p. 429). There is, however, reason for hope. Research has shown that when conventional instructions (which are poorly structured, esoteric, and filled with complex legal terms) are rewritten in plain English, comprehension rates increase markedly (Elwork et al., 1982; English & Sales, 1997).

A lack of comprehension is one reason that a judge's instructions may have little impact. But there is a second reason: Sometimes juries disagree with the law, thus raising the controversial issue of **jury nullification**. You may not realize it, but juries, because they deliberate in private, can choose to disregard, or "nullify," the judge's instructions. The pages of history are filled with poignant examples. Consider the case

jury nullification
The jury's power to disregard, or "nullify," the law when it conflicts with personal conceptions of justice.

of someone tried for euthanasia, or "mercy killing." By law, it is murder. But to the defendant, it might be a noble act on behalf of a loved one. Faced with this kind of conflict—an explosive moral issue on which public opinion is sharply divided—juries often evaluate the issue in human terms, use their own notions of common-sense justice, and vote despite the law for acquittal (Finkel, 1995; Horowitz & Willging, 1991; Niedermeier et al., 1999).

Jury Deliberation

Anyone who has seen the original movie *Twelve Angry Men* can appreciate how colourful and passionate a jury's deliberation can be. This film classic opens with a jury eager to convict a young man of murder—no ifs, ands, or buts. The group selects a foreperson and takes a show-of-hands vote. The result is an 11-to-1 majority, with actor Henry Fonda the lone dissenter. After many tense moments, Fonda manages to convert his peers, and the jury votes unanimously for acquittal.

It is often said that the unique power of the jury stems from the fact that individuals come together privately as one *group.* Is this assumption justified? *Twelve Angry Men* is a work of fiction, but does it realistically portray what transpires in the jury room? And in what ways does the legal system influence the group dynamics? By interviewing jurors after trials, and by recruiting people to participate on mock juries and then recording their deliberations, researchers have learned a great deal about the ways in which juries make their decisions.

The Everett Collection

In the classic movie Twelve Angry Men, Henry Fonda plays a lone juror who single-handedly converts his 11 guilty-voting peers to vote for acquittal. Sometimes life imitates art; in this case, it does not. Research shows that majorities on the first jury vote usually prevail in the final verdict.

Leadership in the Jury Room

In theory, all jurors are created equal. In practice, however, it is common for dominance hierarchies to develop. As in other decision-making groups, a handful of individuals lead the discussion, while others join in at a lower rate or watch from the sidelines, speaking only to cast their votes (Hastie et al., 1983). It's almost as if there is a jury within the jury. The question is, what kinds of people emerge as leaders?

It is often assumed that the foreperson is the leader. The foreperson, after all, calls for votes, acts as a liaison between the judge and jury, and announces the verdict in court. It seems like a position of importance, yet the selection process is very quick and casual. It's interesting that foreperson selection outcomes do follow a predictable pattern (Stasser et al., 1982). People of higher occupational status or with prior experience on a jury are frequently chosen. Sex differences are also common. Norbert Kerr and others (1982) examined the records of 179 trials held in San Diego and found that 50 percent of the jurors were female but 90 percent of the forepersons were male. Other patterns, too, are evident. The first person who speaks is often chosen as foreperson (Strodtbeck et al., 1957).

And when jurors deliberate around a rectangular table, those who sit at the heads of the table are more likely to be chosen than are those seated in the middle (Bray et al., 1978; Strodtbeck & Hook, 1961).

If you find such inequalities bothersome, fear not: Forepersons may act as nominal leaders, but they do *not* exert more than their fair share of influence over the group. In fact, although they spend more time than other jurors talking about procedural matters, they spend less time expressing opinions on the verdict (Hastie et al., 1983). Thus, it may be most accurate to think of the foreperson not as the jury's leader but as its moderator. In *Twelve Angry Men,* actor Martin Balsam—not Henry Fonda—was the foreperson. He was also among the least influential members of the jury.

The Dynamics of Deliberation

If the walls of the jury room could talk, they would tell us that the decision-making process typically passes through three stages (Hastie et al., 1983; Stasser et al., 1982). Like other problem-solving groups, juries begin in a relaxed *orientation* period during which they set an agenda, talk in open-ended terms, raise questions, and explore the facts. Then, once differences of opinion are revealed—usually after the first vote is taken—factions develop, and the group shifts abruptly into a period of *open conflict.* With the battle lines sharply drawn, discussion takes on a more focused, argumentative tone. Together, jurors scrutinize the evidence, construct stories to account for that evidence, and discuss the judge's instructions (Pennington & Hastie, 1992). If all jurors agree, they return a verdict. If not, the majority tries to achieve a consensus by converting the holdouts through information and social pressure. If unanimity is achieved, the group enters a period of *reconciliation,* during which it smoothes over the conflicts and affirms its satisfaction with the outcome. If the holdouts continue to disagree, the jury declares itself hung.

When it comes to decision-making *outcomes,* deliberations follow a predictable course first discovered by Harry Kalven and Hans Zeisel (1966). By interviewing the members of 225 juries, they were able to reconstruct how these juries split on their very first vote. Out of 215 juries that opened with an initial majority, 209 reached a final verdict consistent with that first vote. This finding—later bolstered by the results of mock jury studies (Kerr, 1981; Stasser & Davis, 1981; see ■ Table A.3)—led Kalven and Zeisel to conclude that "the deliberation process might well be likened to what the developer does for an exposed film; it brings out the picture, but the outcome is predetermined" (1966, p. 489). Henry Fonda's *Twelve Angry Men* heroics notwithstanding, one can usually predict the final verdict by knowing where the individual jurors stand the first time they vote. Indeed, juries are not generally more or less subject to bias than the individuals who comprise the groups. There is one reliable exception to this majority-wins rule. Juries that are equally divided in their initial vote are ultimately likely to return not-guilty verdicts, demonstrating what is known as a **leniency bias** favouring the defendant.

leniency bias
The tendency for jury deliberation to produce a tilt toward acquittal.

TABLE A.3

The Road to Agreement: From Individual Votes to a Group Verdict

Research has shown how verdicts are reached by mock juries that begin with different combinations of initial votes. You can see that the results support the majority-wins rule. But also note the evidence for a leniency bias: When the initial vote is split, juries gravitate toward acquittal.

(Kerr, 1981, as cited in Stasser et al., 1982.)

	Final Jury Verdicts (percent)		
Initial Votes (Guilty–Not Guilty)	Conviction	Acquittal	Hung
6–0	100	0	0
5–1	78	7	16
4–2	44	26	30
3–3	9	51	40
2–4	4	79	17
1–5	0	93	7
0–6	0	100	0

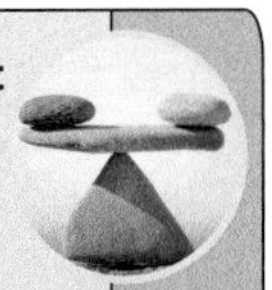

One can usually predict a jury's final verdict by knowing where the individual jurors stand the first time they vote. TRUE.

Knowing that the majority tends to prevail doesn't tell us how juries manage to resolve disagreements en route to a verdict. From the conformity studies discussed in Chapter 7, we know that there are two possibilities. Sometimes, people conform because, through a process of *informational influence,* they are genuinely persuaded by what others say. At other times, people yield to the pressures of *normative influence* by changing their overt behaviour in the majority's direction even though they disagree in private. Justice demands that juries reach a consensus through a vigorous exchange of views and information, not by heavy-handed social pressure. But is that how it works? Research shows that juries achieve unanimity not by one process or the other but by a combination of both (Kaplan & Schersching, 1981). Research also shows that certain factors can upset the delicate balance between informational and normative influence. Social pressure is increased, for example, in juries that vote by a public roll call or show of hands (Davis et al., 1989) and in deadlocked juries that are called into the courtroom and urged by the judge to resolve their differences (Smith & Kassin, 1993).

Of course, how members of a jury proceed in any given case can only be inferred from the results of studies using mock-jurors, archival research, or post-trial interviews with jurors in the United States, as jurors in Canada are strictly forbidden from discussing anything about the trial or their deliberations.

Jury Size

How many people does it take to form a jury? In keeping with the British tradition, 12 has long been the magic number and is still the norm in Canada for criminal trials. The American courts are today permitted to cut trial costs by using six-person juries in cases that do not involve the death penalty.

What is the impact of a six-person jury? The U.S. Supreme Court approached this question as a social psychologist would. It sought to determine whether the change would affect the decision-making process. Unfortunately, the Court misinterpreted the available research so badly that Michael Saks concluded it "would not win a passing grade in a high school psychology class" (1974, p. 18). Consider whether a reduction in size affects the ability of those in the voting minority to resist normative pressures. The Court did not think it would. Citing Asch's (1956) conformity studies, the Court argued that an individual juror's resistance depends on the *proportional* size of the majority. But is that true? Is the lone dissenter caught in a 5-to-1 bind as well insulated from the group norm as the minority in a 10-to-2 split? The Court argued that these 83-to-17 percent divisions are psychologically identical. But wait. Asch's research showed exactly the opposite— that the mere presence of a single ally enables dissenters to keep their independence better than anything else. Research has shown that the size of a jury has other effects, too. Michael Saks and Molli Marti (1997) conducted a meta-analysis of studies involving 15 000 mock jurors who deliberated in over 2000 6-person or 12-person juries. Overall, they found that the smaller juries were less likely to represent minority segments of the population. They were also more likely to reach a unanimous verdict and to do so despite deliberating for shorter periods of time.

Post-Trial: Sentencing

For defendants convicted of crimes, the jury's verdict is followed by a sentence. Sentencing decisions are usually made by judges, not juries, and they are often controversial. One reason for the controversy is that many people see judges as being too lenient (Stalans & Diamond, 1990). Another reason is that people disagree on the goals served by imprisonment. For many judges, the goal of a prison sentence is a practical one: to incapacitate offenders and deter them from committing future crimes. For many citizens, however, there is a more powerful motive at work: to exact retribution, or revenge, against the offender for his or her misdeeds. Research shows that people are driven by this "just deserts" motive, recommending sentences of increasing harshness for crimes of increasing severity—regardless of whether the offender is seen as likely to strike again (Carlsmith et al., 2002; Carlsmith, 2006; Darley et al., 2000).

Judges also disagree about sentencing-related issues. Thus, a common public complaint is that there is too much **sentencing disparity**—that punishments are inconsistent from one judge to the next. To document the problem, Anthony Partridge and William Eldridge (1974) compiled identical sets of files from 20 actual cases, sent them to 50 federal judges, and found major disparities in the sentences they said they would impose. In one case, for example, judges had read about a man who was convicted of extortion and tax evasion. One judge recommended a three-year prison sentence, while another recommended 20 years in prison and a fine of $65 000. It's hard to believe these two judges read the same case. But other studies have uncovered similar differences.

"It only makes a man worse to go to prison and be corrupted."

—E. M. Forster

Perceptions of Justice

People tend to measure the success of a legal system by its ability to produce fair and accurate results. But is that all there is to justice?

Justice as a Matter of Procedure

In a book entitled *Procedural Justice* (1975), John Thibaut and Laurens Walker proposed that our satisfaction with the way disputes are resolved—legal or otherwise—depends not only on outcomes but also on the procedures used to achieve those outcomes. People report being more satisfied with the outcome of a court proceeding when they believe that they have a voice in the proceedings, are treated with respect, and are judged by an impartial decision maker (Lind et al., 1990).

How people view their "day in court" may also depend on the model of justice practised in the courtroom where they find themselves. In the **adversarial model** as practised in North America, Great Britain, and a handful of other countries—the Crown (prosecution) and defence oppose each other, each presenting one side of the story in an effort to win a favourable verdict. In contrast, most other countries use an **inquisitorial model**, in which a neutral investigator gathers the evidence from both sides and presents the findings in court.

Researchers have found that regardless of whether they had won or lost the verdict, participants who took part in an adversarial trial were more satisfied than those involved in an inquisitorial trial. Even impartial observers preferred the adversarial proceedings (Walker et al., 1974; Lind, 1978). However, it seems that any method that offers participants a voice in the proceedings, including methods that are non-adversarial, is seen as most fair and just—not only in law, but also in business, politics, school settings, and intimate relationships (Folger & Greenberg, 1985; Sheppard, 1985).

sentencing disparity
Inconsistency of sentences for the same offence from one judge to another.

adversarial model
A dispute-resolution system in which the Crown (prosecution) and defence present opposing sides of the story.

inquisitorial model
A dispute-resolution system in which a neutral investigator gathers evidence from both sides and presents the findings in court.

Culture, Law, and Justice

When it comes to the basics of human behaviour, much of the research in this appendix can be universally applied, whether we are discussing police interrogations, eyewitness testimony, or decision making in the courtroom. Although the similarities are clear, they should not mask important cross-cultural differences. Because cultures have different norms, customs, and values, they also create different laws to regulate their citizens' behaviour.

Just as nations differ in the crime laws that are set, the study of *comparative law* shows that they also differ in the processes used to enforce these laws. In Great Britain, Canada, the United States, and Australia, the accused has a right to be tried by a jury composed of fellow citizens. In France, Russia, and Brazil, that right is reserved for only the most serious crimes. In India and throughout Asia, all defendants are tried by professional judges, not juries. Yet China recently introduced mixed panels consisting of one judge and two lay jurors. Beginning in 2009, Japan also started to use a quasi-jury system, called *saiban-in*, in which three law-trained judges and six lay citizens chosen by lottery come together to render verdicts and sentencing decisions by a majority vote.

Closing Statement

This appendix focuses on the trial process, the events that precede it, and the events that follow from it. Yet we've only scratched the surface. In recent years, more and more judges, lawyers, and policy makers have come to recognize that social psychology can make important contributions to the legal system. Thus, with increasing frequency, social psychologists are called on for expert advice in and out of court and are cited in the opinions written by judges. Clearly, the gathering, presentation, and evaluation of evidence are imperfect human enterprises and subject to bias. Through an understanding of social psychology, however, we can now identify some of the problems—and perhaps even the solutions.

REVIEW

- Embedded in a large criminal justice system, relatively few cases come to trial.
- Yet the trial is the heart and soul of the system.

Jury Selection

Voir Dire

- Once called for service, prospective jurors are questioned by the judge or lawyers in a process known as voir dire.
- Those who exhibit a clear bias are excluded. Lawyers may also strike a limited number through the use of peremptory challenges.

Trial Lawyers as Intuitive Psychologists

- Pressured to make juror selections quickly, lawyers rely on implicit personality theories and stereotypes.
- But general demographic factors do not reliably predict how jurors will vote.

The Courtroom Drama

- Once the jury is selected, evidence previously gathered is presented in court.

Confession Evidence

- The police employ various methods of interrogation.
- One method is to befriend the suspect and "minimize" the offence; a second is to scare the suspect into believing that it is futile to deny the charges.
- Under pressure, people sometimes confess to crimes they did not commit.
- Although juries are supposed to reject coerced confessions, their verdicts are still influenced by such evidence.

The Lie-Detector Test

- By recording physiological arousal, the polygraph can be used as a lie detector.
- Polygraphers report high rates of accuracy; but truthful persons are too often judged guilty, and the test can be fooled.

Eyewitness Testimony

- Eyewitness memory is a three-stage process involving acquisition, storage, and retrieval.
- During acquisition, witnesses who are highly aroused zoom in on the central features of an event but lose memory for peripheral details.
- Witnesses have trouble recognizing members of a race other than their own.
- During storage, misleading post-event information biases eyewitness memory.
- Young children are particularly suggestible in this regard.
- Lineups are biased when a suspect is distinctive, when the police imply that the criminal is in the lineup, when witnesses make relative judgments, and when the suspect is familiar for other reasons.
- In court, jurors overestimate eyewitnesses' accuracy and cannot distinguish between accurate and inaccurate witnesses.
- People are too readily persuaded by a witness's confidence—a factor that does not reliably predict identification accuracy.

Nonevidentiary Influences

- The more pretrial knowledge people have about a case, the more likely they are to presume the defendant guilty.
- Research shows that pretrial publicity can bias jury verdicts.
- Once inadmissible testimony leaks out in court, the jury is contaminated by it.
- A judge's cautionary instruction may worsen the situation by drawing attention to the forbidden testimony, arousing reactance, or leading jurors to see the information as relevant.

The Judge's Instructions

- The judge's instructions often have little impact, in part because they are often incomprehensible.
- The instructions are usually delivered after the evidence—after many jurors have formed an opinion.
- Jurors may not follow instructions that conflict with their own conceptions of justice, a phenomenon known as jury nullification.

Jury Deliberation

Leadership in the Jury Room

- Dominance hierarchies develop in the jury room.
- Certain people are more likely than others to be elected foreperson, but the foreperson tends to play the role of moderator rather than group leader.

The Dynamics of Deliberation

- Jury deliberations pass through three stages: orientation, open conflict, and reconciliation.
- The period of open conflict is filled with informational and normative pressures.
- When it comes to outcomes, the initial majority typically wins.

Jury Size

- While the U.S. Supreme Court has ruled that the use of 6-person juries is acceptable in criminal trials, the norm in Canada is still 12.
- Smaller juries do not deliberate for as long as 12-person juries and contain less minority representation.

Post-Trial: Sentencing

- Many people believe that judges are too lenient and that punishments for the same offence are often inconsistent from one case to another.
- Part of the problem is that people have different views of the goals of sentencing and punishment.

Perceptions of Justice

Justice as a Matter of Procedure

- Satisfaction with justice depends not only on winning and losing, but also on the procedures used to achieve the outcome.
- People of all cultures prefer models of justice that offer participants a voice in the proceedings and the opportunity to be judged by an impartial decision maker.

Culture, Law, and Justice

- Reflecting cultural and religious values, countries set different laws in an effort to regulate behaviour.

Closing Statement

- Increasingly, social psychologists have become involved in studying the legal system—identifying the problems and seeking solutions.

Key Terms

adversarial model (457)
challenge for cause (440)
cross-race identification bias (446)
inquisitorial model (457)
jury nullification (453)
leniency bias (455)
misinformation effect (447)
peremptory challenge (440)
polygraph (444)
sentencing disparity (457)
voir dire (440)

Putting COMMON SENSE *to the Test*

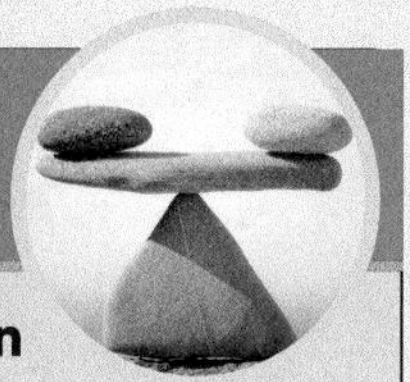

Contrary to popular opinion, women are harsher as criminal trial jurors than men are.

False. *Demographic factors such as gender do not consistently predict juror verdicts; men may be harsher in some cases, women in others.*

Without being beaten or threatened, innocent people sometimes confess to crimes they did not commit.

True. *Innocent suspects sometimes confess—either to escape an unpleasant situation or because they are led to believe they committed a crime they cannot recall.*

A person can fool a lie-detector test by suppressing arousal when questions about the crime are asked.

False. *It is possible to beat a lie-detector test—but by elevating arousal when "innocent" questions are asked, not by trying to suppress arousal in response to "guilty" questions.*

Eyewitnesses find it relatively difficult to recognize members of a race other than their own.

True. *Researchers have observed this cross-race identification bias in both laboratory and field settings.*

The more confident an eyewitness is about an identification, the more accurate it is likely to be.

False. *Studies have shown that eyewitness confidence does not reliably predict accuracy, in part because confidence is influenced by post-identification factors.*

One can usually predict a jury's final verdict by knowing where the individual jurors stand the first time they vote.

True. *As a result of both informational and normative group influences, the preference of the initial voting majority usually prevails.*

APPENDIX

B

Health

This appendix explores the social psychology of physical and mental health. We focus first on the links between stress and health. Four questions are asked in this regard: What causes stress? How does it affect the body? How do we appraise potentially stressful situations? What are some ways of coping with stress? Next, we discuss some of the social influences on treatment and prevention. We then conclude on a positive note, looking at the roots of happiness.

When Laurence Sterne, an eighteenth-century English novelist, weighed the value of good health, he concluded that it was "above all gold and treasure." The reasons that social psychologists study *mental health* and such disorders as anxiety and depression are obvious. We humans are inherently social creatures, and our psychological well-being can be both damaged and repaired by our relationships with other people. But social psychologists are also interested in *physical health*, a domain normally associated with medicine. Working in universities, medical schools, hospitals, and government agencies, many social psychologists are deeply involved in the emerging area of **health psychology**—the application of psychology to the promotion of physical health and the prevention and treatment of illness (Friedman, 2011; Gurung, 2010; Leventhal et al., 2008; Taylor, 2009).

You may wonder: What does social psychology have to do with catching a cold, having a heart attack, or being afflicted by cancer? If you could turn the clock back a few years and ask your family doctor, his or her reply would be "nothing." In the past, physical illness was considered a purely biological event. But this strict medical perspective has given way to a broader model, which holds that health is a joint product of biological, psychological, and social factors.

Part of the reason for this expanded view is that illness patterns over the years have changed in significant ways. According to Statistics Canada, between 1921 and 1925, the principal causes of death in Canada were contagious diseases such as tuberculosis, influenza, bronchitis and pneumonia. Today, none of these infectious illnesses are leading killers. Instead, Canadians are most likely to die (in order of risk) from cancer, heart disease, lower respiratory diseases, accidents, and diabetes. These diseases are sometimes preventable through changes in lifestyle, outlook, and behaviour. In light of research that has been conducted in recent years, this appendix focuses first on stress: what causes it, what it does to the body, and how we appraise stressful situations in order to cope with them. Next, we look at some social influences on the treatment and prevention of illness. Finally, we briefly consider the pursuit of happiness and life satisfaction.

Putting COMMON SENSE to the Test

Circle Your Answer

T F The accumulation of daily hassles does more to make people sick than catastrophes or major life changes.

T F Stress can weaken the heart, but it cannot affect the immune system.

T F When it comes to physical health, research does not support popular beliefs about the power of positive thinking.

T F People who have lots of friends are healthier and live longer than those who live more isolated lives.

T F As role models, celebrities have great influence over public health care decisions.

Stress and Health

Stress is an unpleasant state of arousal that arises when we perceive that the demands of a situation threaten our ability to cope effectively. Nobody knows the precise extent of the problem, but stress is a potent killer. Regardless of who you are, when you were born, or where you live, you have no doubt experienced stress. Sitting in rush-hour traffic, packing your belongings to move, losing your job and looking for work, getting married or divorced, getting into an argument with a close friend, worrying about an unwanted pregnancy or the health of your child, living in a high-crime neighbourhood, struggling to make financial ends meet, and caring for a loved one who is sick are examples of stresses and strains we all must live with. Whether the stress is short term or long term, serious or mild, no one is immune and there is no escape. But there are ways to cope.

According to Richard Lazarus and Susan Folkman (1984), the stress-and-coping process is an ongoing transaction between a person and his or her environment. Faced with an event that may prove threatening, our subjective **appraisal** of the situation determines how we will experience the stress and what **coping** strategies we will use—in other words, what thoughts, feelings, and behaviours we will employ to try to reduce the stress.

In the next two sections, we examine two questions that are relevant to health and well-being: (1) What causes stress? (2) How does stress "get into" the body? Then we look at appraisal and coping, processes that account for why an event that flattens one person can prove harmless to another. As all the pieces come together, we'll see that the answers to these questions provide a broad and useful model of the stress-and-coping process.

What Causes Stress?

There are many different sources of stress, or **stressors**, and these can be defined and measured in different ways (Cohen et al., 1995). What events do *you* find stressful? Try jotting down some of the stressors in your own life, and you'll probably find that the items on your list can be sorted into three major categories: catastrophes, major life events, and daily hassles.

Crises and Catastrophes

On March 11, 2011 one of the most powerful earthquakes ever recorded struck off the coast of Japan. While the devastation from the earthquake was extensive, it also triggered massive tsunami waves more than 40 metres high that wiped out coastal villages, towns, and cities, and killed more than 15 000 people. Seven years before, on December 26, 2004, a similar situation occurred when a massive earthquake struck deep under the Indian Ocean, triggering tsunamis that killed approximately 320 000

health psychology
The study of physical health and illness by psychologists from various areas of specialization.

stress
An unpleasant state of arousal in which people perceive the demands of an event as taxing or exceeding their ability to satisfy or alter those demands.

appraisal
The process by which people make judgments about the demands of potentially stressful events and their ability to meet those demands.

© MPAK/Alamy

Natural disasters, such as the March 2011 tsunami in Japan, can devastate entire populations.

According to the World Health Organization, the average life expectancy ranges from a low of 33 years in Swaziland to a high of 83 in Andorra. (The average life expectancy is 80 in Canada and 78 in the United States.)

people in a dozen countries. As a result of both disasters, thousands of survivors were injured and traumatized in the process.

The intense stress imposed on a population by such a natural catastrophe can also be caused by human beings. The September 11, 2001 terrorist attack in the United States was a different kind of tragedy that no one who was old enough to witness it will ever forget. In a survey of 560 American adults conducted later that week, 90 percent said they were experiencing some symptoms of stress and 44 percent reported "substantial" symptoms such as recurring thoughts, dreams, and memories; difficulty falling or staying asleep; difficulty concentrating on work; and unprovoked outbursts of anger (Schuster et al., 2001). Other events that can have similarly traumatic effects include war, motor vehicle accidents, plane crashes, violent crimes, physical or sexual abuse, the death of a loved one, and natural disasters such as fires, tornadoes, earthquakes, and floods (Kubany et al., 2000).

The scarring effects of large-scale disasters are without dispute. Based on their review of 52 studies, Anthony Rubonis and Leonard Bickman (1991) found that high rates of psychological disorders—such as anxiety, phobias, depression, alcohol abuse, and somatic complaints—are common among residents of areas that have been hit by these catastrophic events.

Major Life Events

Some people are lucky enough to avoid major catastrophes. But nobody can completely avoid stress. Indeed, change itself may cause stress by forcing us to adapt to new circumstances. This hypothesis was first proposed by Thomas Holmes and Richard Rahe (1967), who interviewed hospital patients and found that their illnesses had often been preceded by major changes in some aspect of their lives. Some of the changes were negative (getting hurt, divorced, or fired), but others were positive (getting married or promoted or having a baby). To measure life stress, Holmes and Rahe then devised the Social Readjustment Rating Scale (SRRS)—a checklist of 43 major life events each assigned a numerical value based on the amount of readjustment it requires. Among the events sampled (and the numerical values they were assigned) were the death of a spouse (100), divorce (73), imprisonment (63), marriage (50), job loss (47), pregnancy (40), school transfer (20), and even vacations (13).

The idea that change is inherently stressful has an intuitive ring about it, but there are two problems with this notion. First, although there is a statistical link between negative events and illness, research does not similarly support the claim that positive "stressors" such as taking a vacation, graduating, or winning a lottery are similarly harmful (Stewart et al., 1986). Happiness is not the absence of distress, nor is distress the absence of happiness. A person can simultaneously experience both emotions (Carver & Scheier, 1990), and the health consequences are different (Taylor, 1991). The second complicating factor is that the impact of any change depends on who the person is and how the change is interpreted. Moving to a new country, for example, is less stressful to immigrants who can speak the new language (Berry et al., 1992).

coping
Efforts to reduce stress.

stressor
Anything that causes stress.

Microstressors: The Hassles of Everyday Life

Think again about the sources of stress in your life, and catastrophes and other exceptional events will spring to mind. Yet the most common source of stress arises from the hassles that irritate us every day. Environmental factors such as population density, loud noise, extreme heat or cold, and cigarette smoke are all sources of stress. Car problems, long commutes, gas prices, waiting in lines, losing keys, bad work days, money troubles, and other "microstressors" also place a constant strain on us. Unfortunately, there is nothing "micro" about the impact of these stressors on health and well-being. Research by Paul Kohn and others (1991) at York University suggests that the accumulation of daily hassles contributes more to illness than do major life events. Interpersonal conflicts are the most upsetting of our daily stressors and have a longer-lasting impact than most others (Bolger et al., 1989).

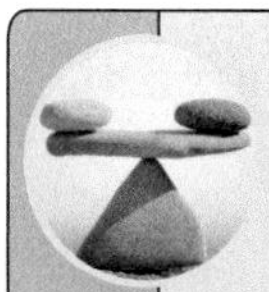

The accumulation of daily hassles does more to make people sick than catastrophes or major life changes. TRUE.

How Does Stress Affect the Body?

The term *stress* was first popularized by endocrinologist Hans Selye (1936). As a young medical student, Selye noticed that patients who were hospitalized for many different illnesses often had similar symptoms, such as muscle weakness, a loss of weight and appetite, and a lack of ambition. Maybe these symptoms were part of a generalized response to an attack on the body, he thought. In the 1930s, Selye tested this hypothesis by exposing laboratory rats to various stressors, including heat, cold, heavy exercise, toxic substances, food deprivation, and electric shock. As anticipated, the different stressors all produced a similar physiological response: enlarged adrenal glands, shrunken lymph nodes, and bleeding stomach ulcers. Borrowing a term from engineering, Selye called the reaction *stress*—a word that quickly became part of everyday language.

The General Adaptation Syndrome

According to Selye, the body naturally responds to stress in a three-stage process that he called the **general adaptation syndrome** (see ▶ Figure B.1, on page 466). Sparked by the recognition of a threat—such as a predator, an enemy soldier, a speeding car, or a virus—the body has an initial *alarm* reaction. To meet the challenge, adrenaline and other hormones are poured into the bloodstream, creating physiological arousal. Heart rate, blood pressure, and breathing rates increase, while slower, long-term functions such as growth, digestion, and the operation of the immune system are inhibited. At this stage, the body mobilizes all of its resources to ward off the threat. Next comes a *resistance* stage, during which the body remains aroused and on the alert. There is continued release of stress hormones, and local defenses are activated. But if the stress persists for a prolonged period of time, the body will fall into an *exhaustion* stage. According to Selye, our anti-stress resources are limited. In fact, however, research has shown that exhaustion occurs not because our stress-fighting resources are limited, but because their overuse causes other systems in the body to break down, which puts us at risk for illness and even death. Selye's basic model thus makes an important point: Stress may be an adaptive short-term reaction to threat, but over time it compromises our health and well-being.

The reason stress causes ulcers and other illnesses, then, is that the response is designed for acute physical emergencies, yet we turn it on often and for prolonged periods of time as we worry about taxes, mortgages, oral presentations, the job market, marital problems, and the inevitability of death.

general adaptation syndrome
A three-stage process (alarm, resistance, and exhaustion) by which the body responds to stress.

FIGURE B.1

The General Adaptation Syndrome

According to Selye (1936), the human body responds to threat in three phases: alarm, resistance, and exhaustion.

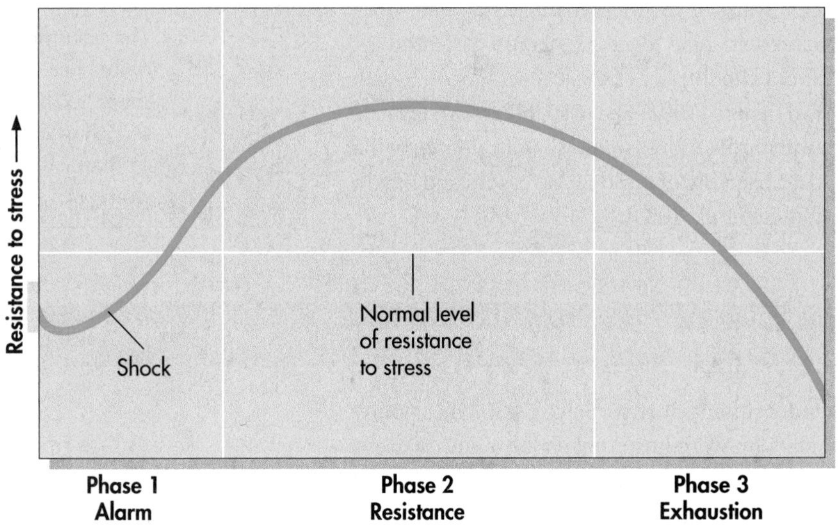

What Stress Does to the Heart

Heart disease and stroke are two of the three leading causes of death for Canadians. According to the Heart and Stroke Foundation, every year approximately 70 000 Canadians have heart attacks. One-quarter do not survive.

Several factors are known to increase the risk of these types of cardiovascular diseases, including smoking, alcohol, lack of physical exercise, obesity, high blood pressure. and high cholesterol. What's missing from the equation is another important risk factor: psychological stress—from work, from marital troubles, and from the negative life events that plague people who lack resources because of low socioeconomic status (Gallo & Matthews, 2003; Hogh et al., 2012; Matthews, 2005). Twenty-three percent of Canadians report a high level of life stress.

In 1956, cardiologists Meyer Friedman and Ray Rosenman were studying the relationship between cholesterol and coronary heart disease. After noticing that husbands were more likely than their wives to have cardiovascular disease, they speculated that work-related stress might be the reason (at the time, most women did not work outside the home). To test this hypothesis, Friedman and Rosenman interviewed 3000 healthy middle-aged men. Those who seemed the most hard driving, competitive, impatient, time conscious, and quick to anger were classified as having a **Type A personality** (also called coronary-prone behaviour pattern—a more optimistic label since it is easier to change a behaviour pattern than a personality). Roughly an equal number of men who were easygoing, relaxed, and laid back were classified as having a Type B personality. Interestingly, out of 258 men who went on to have heart attacks over the following nine years, 69 percent had been classified as Type A and only 31 percent as Type B (Rosenman et al., 1975).

By the early 1980s, the influence of the Type A behaviour pattern on heart disease was widely accepted. But science, like time, moves on. Later studies of Type A and heart disease obtained weaker results that varied depending on how Type A was measured and the kind of population that was studied (Matthews, 1988). Certainty about the bad effects of "hurry sickness" and "workaholism" began to crumble.

One issue that arose concerned measurement. Specifically, it turns out that the strength of the link between Type A behaviour and heart disease depends on how people are diagnosed. Apparently, the Type A pattern is more evident from a person's interview *behaviour* (whether he or she constantly checks the time, speaks quickly, interrupts the interviewer, and makes restless fidgety movements) than from *self-reports*. When interviews are used to make the diagnosis, 70 percent of men who have heart disease also have a Type A behaviour pattern—compared with only 46 percent of those who are healthy (Miller et al., 1991).

Type A personality
A pattern of behaviour characterized by extremes of competitive striving for achievement, a sense of time urgency, hostility, and aggression.

The Type A behaviour pattern was also refined conceptually, and a new line of inquiry sprang up. This research showed the primary toxic ingredient in coronary artery disease is *hostility*—as seen in people who are constantly angry, resentful, cynical, suspicious, and mistrustful of others (see ■ Table B.1). Apparently, people who are always in a negative emotional state and are quick to explode are besieged by stress. In the long run, chronic hostility and anger can be lethal (Miller et al., 1996; Myrtek, 2007; Siegman & Smith, 1994).

TABLE B.1

How "Hostile" Is Your Pattern of Behaviour?

- When in the express checkout line at the supermarket, do you often count the items in the baskets of the people ahead of you to be sure they aren't over the limit?
- When an elevator doesn't come as quickly as it should, do your thoughts quickly focus on the inconsiderate behaviour of the person on another floor who's holding it up?
- When someone criticizes you, do you quickly begin to feel annoyed?
- Do you frequently find yourself muttering at the television during a news broadcast?
- When you are held up in a slow line of traffic, do you quickly sense your heart pounding and your breath quickening?

(Williams, 1993.)

What Stress Does to the Immune System

Increasingly, it has become clear that psychological stress produces a wide range of effects on the body, including increases in the risk of chronic back pain, diabetes, appendicitis, upper respiratory infections, arthritis, herpes, gum disease, common colds, and some forms of cancer. How can stress have so broad a range of disabling effects? Answer: By compromising the body's immune system, the first line of defence against illness (Ader, 2007).

immune system
A biological surveillance system that detects and destroys "nonself" substances that invade the body.

The **immune system** is a complex surveillance system that fights bacteria, viruses, parasites, fungi, and other "nonself" substances that invade the body. The system contains more than a trillion specialized white blood cells called *lymphocytes* that circulate throughout the bloodstream and secrete chemical antibodies. These shark-like search-and-destroy cells protect us 24 hours a day by patrolling the body and attacking trespassers. The immune system is also equipped with large scavenger cells that zero in on viruses and cancerous tumours. Serving as a "sixth sense" for foreign invaders, the immune system continually renews itself. For example, during the few seconds it took to read this sentence, your body produced 10 million new lymphocytes.

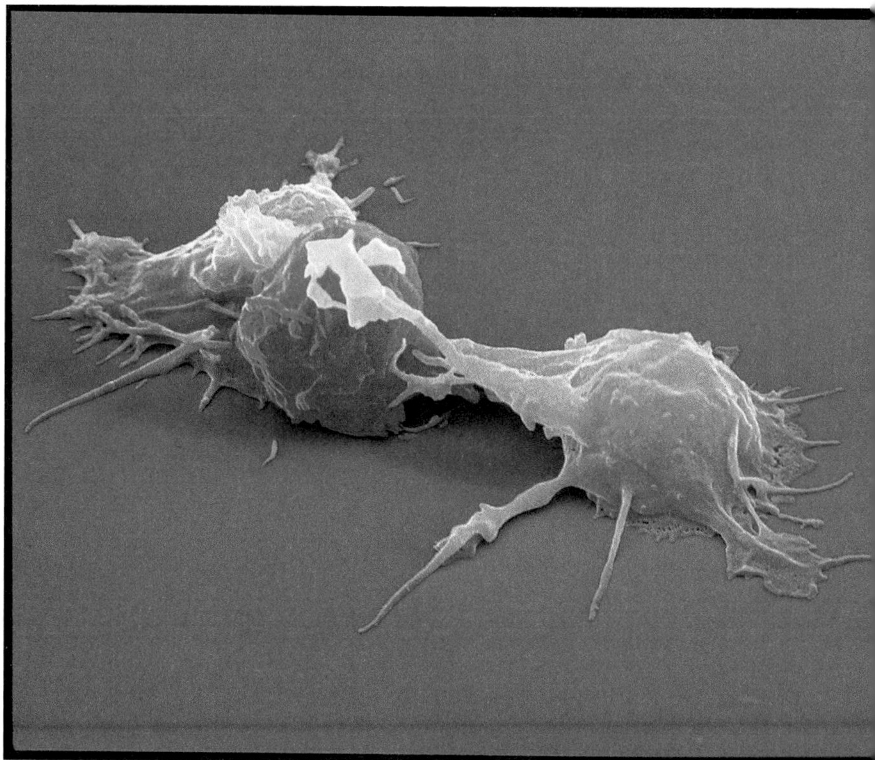
Meckes/Ottowa/Photo Researchers

This colour-enhanced microscopic image shows two "natural killer" immune cells (in yellow) engulfing and destroying a leukemia cell (in red). The human immune system contains more than a trillion specialized white blood cells.

It is now clear that stress can affect the immune system, at least temporarily. For example, intrigued by the fact that people often become sick and die shortly after they are widowed, R. W. Barthrop and others (1977) took blood samples from 26 men and women whose spouses had recently died. Compared with non-widowed controls, these grief-stricken spouses exhibited a weakened immune response. This demonstration was the first of its kind.

Additional studies soon revealed weakened immune responses in people deprived of sleep for a prolonged period of time, in students in the midst of final exams, in men and women recently divorced or separated, in people caring for a family member with Alzheimer's disease, in snake-phobic people who are exposed to a live snake, and in workers who have just lost their jobs. Even in the laboratory, people who are given complex arithmetic problems to solve or painful stimuli to tolerate exhibit changes in immune cell activity that last for one or more hours after the stress has subsided (Cohen & Herbert, 1996). Clearly, psychological states can "get into" the immune system. Hundreds of studies now show that the effects of stress on the immune system are complex. Brief stressors (such as a shark attack, a difficult exam, or an injury) can enhance the immune response in ways that are adaptive in the short term, but chronic life stressors (such as a high-pressure job, a distressed marriage, or a family death) can suppress the immune response over time, putting the organism at risk (Khanfer et al., 2011; Segerstrom & Miller, 2004).

The Links Between Stress and Illness

If chronic stress can weaken the immune system, are people who are stressed in life more likely to become sick? To test this hypothesis, Cohen and others (1998) interviewed 276 volunteers about recent life stressors, infected them with a cold virus, and then measured whether they developed a cold. They found that some types of stress were more toxic than others. Specifically, people who had endured *chronic* stressors that lasted for more than a month (like ongoing marital problems or unemployment) were more likely to catch a cold than those who had experienced *acute* short-term stress (such as a fight with a spouse or a reprimand at work). ▶ Figure B.2 shows that the longer a stressor had lasted, the more likely a person was to catch a cold. Over time, stress breaks down the body's immune system.

The effects of stress are clear. But it appears that certain personal characteristics can buffer people against the adverse health effects. In a follow-up study, Cohen and his colleagues (2006) found that the more sociable people were in life, the more resistant they were to developing the lab-induced cold. They also found that the more positively people *see themselves* on the socioeconomic status (SES) ladder relative to others in the population—regardless of their *actual* levels of education, occupation, and income—the less likely they were to catch the lab-induced cold (Cohen et al., 2008).

These common-cold studies are important because they demonstrate not only that stress can weaken the immune system, but also that it can leave us vulnerable to illness as a result. Does stress have similar effects on more serious illnesses? Can it, for example, hasten the spread of cancer? In an early test of this hypothesis, Madeline Visintainer and others (1982) implanted tumorous cancer cells into laboratory rats, some of which were then exposed repeatedly to shocks they could not escape. After one month, 50 percent of the animals not shocked died of cancer. Yet relative to that baseline, the death rate climbed to 73 percent among those subjected to the inescapable shock. This study was among the first to show that psychological states such as a feeling of helplessness can influence the spread of cancer.

The growth of tumours in helpless white laboratory rats is interesting, but does the same principle apply to people? For obvious ethical reasons, researchers cannot fill humans with despair or inject lethal tumours into their bodies to test the cause-and-effect chain directly. But they can examine the medical records of people whose lives have been struck by tragedy. Investigations of this sort have revealed that cancer appears more often than normal in people who are prone to being in a negative emotional state (Sklar & Anisman, 1981).

▶ FIGURE B.2

Stress Duration and Illness

A total of 276 volunteers were interviewed about recent life stress, and then were infected with a cold virus. As shown above, the more months a stressor had lasted, the more likely a person was to catch the cold. Over time, stress breaks down the body's immune system.

(Cohen et al., 1998.)

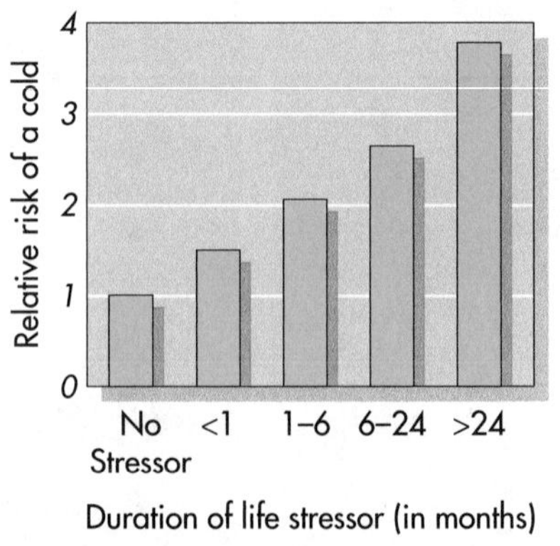

Cohen et al.

Let's be clear about what these results mean. Nobody disputes that cancer is caused by exposure to toxic substances and other biological factors. But individuals who are clinically depressed or under great stress have weakened immune systems and a heightened susceptibility to infectious agents, which, in some cases, may result in a higher death rate from cancer and other diseases as well (Gouin et al., 2012; Kiecolt-Glaser, 2009; Miller et al., 2009).

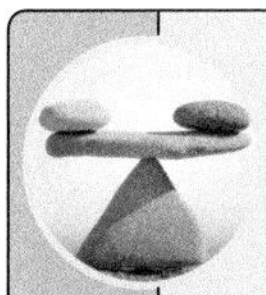

Stress can weaken the heart, but it cannot affect the immune system. FALSE.

Processes of Appraisal

The process of appraisal involves considering possible explanations for one's circumstances, and forming expectations about one's ability to cope with them. As will be discussed in the next section, how people come to view their life events and experiences can play a significant role in their overall health and well-being.

Attribution Styles

Depression is a mood disorder characterized by feelings of sadness, pessimism, and apathy and slowed thought processes. Other symptoms include disturbances in sleeping and eating patterns and a reduced interest in sex. Sometimes called the "common cold" of psychological disorders, depression is universal and widespread (Gotlib & Hammen, 2009). About twice as many women as men seek treatment for being depressed. According to the Public Health Agency of Canada, during the course of a lifetime, an estimated 8 percent of Canadian adults will suffer from a major depression. While depression has many causes, some researchers have focused on the attributions people make for the positive and negative events of their lives.

In 1975, Martin Seligman argued that depression results from **learned helplessness**, the acquired expectation that one cannot control important outcomes. In a classic series of experiments, Seligman had found that dogs strapped into a harness and exposed to painful electric shocks soon became passive and gave up trying to escape, even in new situations where escape was possible. In contrast, dogs that had not received uncontrollable shocks quickly learned the escape routine. As applied to humans, this finding suggested that prolonged exposure to uncontrollable events might similarly cause apathy, inactivity, a loss of motivation, and pessimism. Among human research participants, those exposed to inescapable bursts of noise thus failed to protect themselves in a later situation where the noise could be easily avoided. Seligman was quick to note that people who are exposed to uncontrollable events become, in many ways, like depressed individuals: discouraged, pessimistic about the future, and lacking in initiative. Thus, he saw depression as a form of learned helplessness.

The Human Capacity for Resilience

Stress affects people differently, an observation that led Suzanne Kobasa and her colleagues (1982) to wonder why some of us are more resilient than others in the face of stress. Kobasa studied some 200 business executives who were under stress. Many said they were frequently sick, affirming the link between stress and illness, while others had managed to stay healthy. The two groups were similar in terms of age, education, job status, income, and ethnic and religious background. But it

learned helplessness
A phenomenon in which experience with an uncontrollable event creates passive behaviour toward a subsequent threat to well-being.

was clear from various tests that they differed in their attitudes toward themselves, their jobs, and the people in their lives. Based on these differences, Kobasa identified a personality style that she called *hardiness*. She concluded that hardy people have three characteristics: (1) commitment—a sense of purpose with regard to one's work, family, and other domains; (2) challenge—an openness to new experiences and a desire to embrace change; and (3) control—the belief that one has the power to influence important future outcomes.

Research supports the general point that resilience, or hardiness, serves as a buffer against stress (Funk, 1992). As you might expect, most people are exposed to at least one highly traumatic event during the course of a lifetime, yet many of them are able to maintain their equilibrium and mental health. In fact, Vicki Helgeson and her colleagues (2006) note that many people who confront heart attacks, cancer, divorce, war, family illness, and other traumas will often find ways to accept, benefit, and grow from the experience.

Self-Efficacy When Kobasa and others (1982) first identified hardiness as an adaptive trait, they—and other researchers—were quick to notice that the perception of control is an important ingredient (Florian et al., 1995). Early on, research showed that the harmful effects of crowding, noise, heat, and other stressors are reduced when people think they can exert control over these aspects of their environment (Glass & Singer, 1972). The perception of control is especially meaningful for people whose lives are regulated to a large extent by others. For example, elderly residents of nursing homes who were given more control over daily routines became happier and more active (Langer & Rodin, 1976; Schulz, 1976).

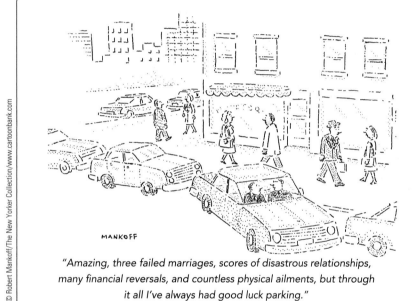

"Amazing, three failed marriages, scores of disastrous relationships, many financial reversals, and countless physical ailments, but through it all I've always had good luck parking."

People often have feelings of self-efficacy in some life domains but not others.

The perception of control refers to the expectation that our behaviours can produce satisfying outcomes. But people also differ in the extent to which they believe they can perform these behaviours in the first place. These concepts seem related, but in fact they refer to different beliefs, both of which are necessary for us to feel that we control important outcomes in our lives (Skinner, 1996). According to Albert Bandura (1997), these latter expectations are based on feelings of competence, or **self-efficacy**. Some individuals may be generally more confident than others, says Bandura, but self-efficacy is a state of mind that varies from one specific task and situation to another. In other words, you may have high self-efficacy about meeting new people, but not about raising your grades. Or you may have high self-efficacy about solving a math problem, but not about writing a paper.

self-efficacy
A person's belief that he or she is capable of the specific behaviour required to produce a desired outcome in a given situation.

Research on self-efficacy has shown that the more of it you have at a particular task, the more likely you are to take on that task, try hard, persist in the face of failure, and succeed. The implications for mental and physical health are particularly striking. For example, individuals with high self-efficacy on health-related matters are more likely, if they want, to stay physically fit, abstain from alcohol, and tolerate the pain of arthritis, childbirth, and migraine headaches (Maddux, 1995)—and even to stop smoking (Baldwin et al., 2006) or lose weight (Linde et al., 2006).

Dispositional Optimism The reason it is important to understand our attributions for past outcomes and our perceptions of control in present situations is that both have implications for our outlook on the future. In *Learned Optimism*, Seligman (1991) argues that optimists tend to blame failure on factors that are external, temporary, and specific, and to credit success to factors that are internal, permanent, and global. Thankfully, in light of the advantages that optimism brings, Suzanne Segerstrom (2006a), like Seligman, notes that even pessimists can retrain themselves to think in optimistic ways.

Consider your own view of the future. Are you the eternal optimist who looks on the bright side and generally expects good things to happen, or do you tend to believe in Murphy's Law, that if something can go wrong it will? By asking questions such as these, Michael Scheier and Charles Carver (1985) categorized students along this dimension and found that dispositional optimists reported fewer illness symptoms during the semester than did pessimists. Correlations between optimism and health are common. Studies have shown that optimists are more likely to take an active problem-focused approach in coping with stress (Carver et al., 2010; Nes & Segerstrom, 2006). As a result, they are more likely to complete a rehabilitation program for alcoholics; make a quicker, fuller recovery from coronary artery bypass surgery; and, among gay men concerned about AIDS, take a more active approach to the threat (Scheier & Carver, 1992).

The optimist proclaims we live in the best of all possible worlds; and the pessimist fears this is true.

—James Cabell

In the course of a lifetime, everyone has setbacks. But an optimistic disposition may help us better weather the storms. Let's be clear about what the research means. The mind is a powerful tool that can be used to hurt, heal, and protect the body (Ray, 2004). Still, no credible scientist believes that our attributions, perceptions of control, optimism, or other sources of resilience are the sole determinants of a long life. A positive outlook cannot guarantee future good health. So, although we should appreciate the powers of the mind to influence the body, it would be a cruel mistake to blame victims of illness for having a bad outlook on life. As Howard Friedman (1991) put it in *The Self-Healing Personality*, "We must walk a fine line between blaming patients on the one hand and absolving them of any role in their health on the other" (p. 96).

When it comes to physical health, research does not support popular beliefs about the power of positive thinking. FALSE.

It is also important to recognize that there may be drawbacks to positive thinking, especially if it leads us to see ourselves and the events around us in ways that are grossly unrealistic. As we saw in Chapter 3, people with overly positive views of themselves are sometimes disliked by their friends and seen as boastful, inconsiderate, and oversensitive to criticism (Colvin et al., 1995; Heatherton & Vohs, 2000). It may also be detrimental for people to believe that they have control over events when they do not. In a study of patients suffering from a loss of kidney function, those who felt that they had control over their health became more depressed, not less, after having a transplant that failed (Christensen et al., 1991). In a study of first-year law students, optimists exhibited a stronger immune response than did pessimists when their transition to law school was easy, but a weaker immune response when the transition was difficult (Segerstrom, 2006b). Faced with some setbacks, a sense of control can help us bounce back. But setting control expectations too high can do more harm than good in the wake of negative outcomes.

Ways of Coping with Stress

Leaving home. Studying for final exams. Breaking up with a boyfriend or girlfriend. Working long nights—or not at all. Waiting in long security lines at the airport. Feeling squeezed in a tight job market. Having children. Raising children. Struggling to meet the deadline to complete a textbook. Stress is inevitable. No one can prevent it. The best we can do is to minimize its harmful effects on our health. Depending on the person and stressor, people can cope by trying to solve the problem, talking to friends, inviting distractions, sleeping or drinking too much to escape, praying, brooding, venting, lashing out, laughing it off, getting outside help, pretending that all is well—or freaking out. Combining all psychological theories and research, it appears that there are about 400 specific ways to cope with stress (Skinner et al., 2003).

While noting that people can use different coping strategies, Richard Lazarus and Susan Folkman (1984) distinguished two general types. The first is **problem-focused coping**, cognitive and behavioural efforts to reduce stress by overcoming the source of the problem. Difficulties in school? Study harder, hire a tutor, or reduce your workload. Marriage on the rocks? Talk it out or see a counsellor. Problems at work? Consult with your boss or look for another job. The goal is to attack the source of stress. A second approach is **emotion-focused coping**, which consists of efforts to manage our emotional reactions to stressors rather than trying to change the stressors themselves. If you struggle at school, at work, or in a romantic relationship, you can keep a stiff upper lip, accept what is happening, tune out, or vent your emotions. According to Lazarus and Folkman, we tend to take an active, problem-focused approach when we think we can overcome a stressor, but fall back on an emotion-focused approach when we perceive the problem to be out of our control. Lisa Aspinwall and Shelley Taylor (1997) note that there is a third alternative: **proactive coping**, which consists of up-front efforts to ward off or modify the onset of a stressful event. As we'll see, coping is an ongoing process by which we try to prevent—not just react to—life's bumps and bruises.

Problem-Focused Coping

Problem-focused coping seems like the prime candidate for a starring role in the war against stress. Surely our most active and assertive efforts are associated with better health (Aspinwall & Taylor, 1992). And clearly, we often benefit from confronting a stressor head-on rather than avoiding it. Consider something we all are guilty of on occasion: procrastination, a purposive delay in beginning or completing a task, often accompanied by feelings of discomfort (Ferrari et al., 1995). In a longitudinal study of undergraduates enrolled in a health psychology class, Dianne Tice and Roy Baumeister (1997) administered a questionnaire at the start of the semester that assesses the extent to which people tend to procrastinate. True to their word, those students who were classified from their test scores as procrastinators turned in their term papers later than did their classmates and received lower grades. More interesting was the relationship to daily reports of stress and physical health. Early on, while procrastinators were in the "putting it off" stage of their projects, they were relatively stress-free compared with others. Later in the semester, however, as the deadline neared and passed, procrastinators were under greater stress and reported having more symptoms of illness. In the end, the short-term benefits of avoidance were outweighed by the long-term costs. In dealing with essential tasks, it is better to confront and control than to avoid.

When we use the word *control*, we usually have in mind active efforts to manage something: win an argument, work out a marital problem, or solve a problem at work. But control comes in many guises. Knowledge, for instance, is a form of control. Knowing why something happens increases your chance of making sure it goes your way—if not now, then the next time. Sometimes we can cope effectively with tragedies such as technological disasters, terrorist acts, and spousal abuse by blaming the

problem-focused coping
Cognitive and behavioural efforts to alter a stressful situation.

emotion-focused coping
Cognitive and behavioural efforts to reduce the distress produced by a stressful situation.

proactive coping
Up-front efforts to ward off or modify the onset of a stressful event.

perpetrators for their actions. In these situations, holding others responsible can force a helpful response, such as financial compensation or police protection.

But what about self-blame? Is it ever adaptive to cope with a bad situation by blaming oneself? According to Ronnie Janoff-Bulman (1979), it depends on whether you blame your behaviour or yourself as a person. People can change their own behaviour, she notes, so behavioural self-blame paves the way for control in an effort to reduce current stresses or avoid future ones. But it is not similarly adaptive, she warns, to blame your own enduring personal characteristics, which are harder to change.

Patricia Frazier (2003) offers a somewhat more complex perspective on blame, control, and coping. Clearly, she notes, it can be adaptive for the victims of rape and other traumas to own a sense of future control (Carver et al., 2000; Frazier et al., 2004). But noting that behavioural self-blame for a past trauma does not guarantee the prevention of future trauma, she distinguishes past, present, and future control—and what each implies about the dreaded possibility of a future recurrence. In a longitudinal study of female rape victims appearing in an emergency room, she assessed attributions of blame and responsibility, perceptions of control, and feelings of distress periodically from two weeks up to a year later. Overall, women blamed the rapist more than they blamed themselves, a tendency that strengthened over time. As in other studies, however, those who assigned more blame either to the rapist or to themselves were more distressed. Apparently, the problem with behavioural self-blame, once thought to be adaptive, is that it did not engender feelings of future safety. In this regard, the most useful sense of control was over the *present*: women who believed that they could help themselves get better and facilitate their own recovery were more optimistic about the future and the least distressed.

Emotion-Focused Coping

Stress is by definition an unpleasant and arousing experience that fills people with negative and unhealthy emotions. Do some coping mechanisms focus on this emotional aspect of adversity?

Positive Emotions: Building Blocks of Emotion-Focused Coping People who cope well and are resilient tend to experience positive emotions in the face of stress—a common capacity that Ann Masten (2001) termed "ordinary magic." How is it that positive emotions work like magic? On the basis of numerous studies, Barbara Fredrickson (2009) notes that positive emotions help people to *broaden* their outlook in times of stress so they can cope with adversity—in part by providing a welcome distraction from the anger, fear, and other negative states that increase blood pressure and arousal and narrow the focusing of attention. By coping with positive emotions in one specific situation after another, Fredrickson suggests, people over time *build* personal resources—learning, for example, how to stay calm, focused, in control, and capable of giving and receiving emotional support.

Shutting Down: Suppressing Unwanted Thoughts. Often we react to stress by shutting down and trying to deny or suppress the unpleasant thoughts and feelings. One specific form of avoidance coping is distraction. Research suggests that in situations where individuals have little actual control over events, distraction and other emotion-focused techniques are more effective in reducing distress than are problem-focused efforts to exert control (Auerbach et al., 1994; Strentz & Auerbach, 1988).

Although potentially effective, suppression of unwanted thoughts from awareness can also have a peculiar, paradoxical effect. As described in Chapter 3, Daniel

Wegner (1994, 1997) conducted a series of studies in which he told people not to think of a white bear and found that they could not then keep the image from popping to mind. What's more, he found that among participants who were permitted later to think about the bear, those who had earlier tried to suppress the image were unusually preoccupied with it, providing evidence of a rebound effect. Sometimes, the harder you try not to think about something, the less likely you are to succeed (Wegner et al., 1998). The solution: focused distraction. When participants were told to imagine a tiny red Volkswagen every time the forbidden bear intruded into consciousness, the rebound effect vanished (Wenzlaff & Wegner, 2000).

What do white bears and red cars have to do with coping? A lot. When people try to block stressful thoughts from awareness, the problem may worsen. That's where focused distraction comes in. In a study of pain tolerance, Delia Cioffi and James Holloway (1993) had people put a hand into a bucket of ice-cold water and keep it there until they could no longer bear the pain. One group was instructed to avoid thinking about the sensation. A second group was told to form a mental picture of their home. Afterward, those who had coped through suppression were slower to recover from the pain than were those who had used focused self-distraction. To manage stress—whether it's caused by physical pain, a strained romance, final exams, or problems at work—distraction ("think about lying on the beach") is a better coping strategy than mere suppression ("don't think about the pain").

Opening Up: Confronting One's Demons The research just described suggests that just as shutting down can sometimes have benefits, so too can the opposite form of coping: opening up. There are two aspects to this emotional means of coping with stress. The first is acknowledging and understanding our emotional reactions to important events; the second is expressing these inner feelings to ourselves and others (Stanton et al., 2000).

According to James Pennebaker (1997), psychotherapy, self-help groups, and various religious rituals have something in common: All offer a chance for people to confide in someone, spill their guts, confess, and talk freely about their troubles—maybe for the first time. To test for the healing power of opening up, Pennebaker conducted a series of controlled studies in which he brought students into a laboratory and asked them to talk into a tape recorder or write for 20 minutes either about past traumas or about trivial daily events. While speaking or writing, the students were upset and physiologically aroused. Many tearfully recounted accidents, failures, instances of physical or sexual abuse, loneliness, the death or divorce of their parents, shattered relationships, and their fears about the future. Soon these students felt better than ever. Pennebaker found that when they opened up, their systolic blood pressure levels rose during the disclosures, but then later dipped below their pre-experiment levels. The students even exhibited a decline in the number of times they visited the campus health centre over the next six months. Other studies, too, have shown that keeping personal secrets can be stressful and that "letting it out" and "getting it off your chest" can have true therapeutic effects on mental and physical health. These effects are especially strong when participants are comfortable with disclosure, when the disclosures are made across multiple sessions, and when the events being described are recent and traumatic (Frattaroli, 2006; Lepore & Smyth, 2002).

One explanation for the benefits of opening up is that talking about a problem can help you to sort out your thoughts, understand the problem better, and gain *insight*, in cognitive terms. Whatever the reason, it is clear that opening up, perhaps to someone else, can be therapeutic—provided that the listener can be trusted. This last point is critical: Despite the potential for gain, opening up can also cause great distress when

© Ann Johansson/Corbis

© Chuck Savage/CORBIS

Healthy distractions such as exercise are a good way to break out of the trap of self-focused depression. Unhealthy distractions, such as an alcohol binge, reduce self-focus at a self-destructive cost.

the people we confide in react with rejection or unwanted advice or, worse, betray what was said to others (Kelly & McKillop, 1996).

Self-Focus: Getting Trapped Versus Getting Out In Chapter 3, we saw that people spend little time actually thinking about the self—and when they do, they wish they were doing something else (Csikszentmihalyi & Figurski, 1982). According to self-awareness theory, self-focus brings out our personal shortcomings the way staring in a mirror draws our attention to every blemish on the face. It comes as no surprise, then, that self-focus seems to intensify some of the most undesirable consequences of emotion-focused coping. Here's the script.

The state of self-awareness can be induced in us by external stimuli such as mirrors, cameras, and audiences. Mood, too, plays a role. Peter Salovey (1992) found that, compared with a neutral mood state, both positive and negative moods increase awareness of the self. Thus, when a stressful event occurs, the negative feelings that arise magnify self-focus. What happens next depends on a person's self-esteem, as people with a negative self-concept experience more negative moods when self-focused than do those with a positive self-concept (Sedikides, 1992). As researchers at the Centre for Addiction and Mental Health and the Universities of Waterloo and Toronto recently confirmed, some students may turn to alcohol as a means of focusing awareness away from themselves (Aramakis et al., 2012). The end result is a self-perpetuating feedback loop: Being in a bad mood triggers self-focus, which in people with low self-esteem further worsens the mood. This vicious circle forms the basis for a self-focusing model of depression, according to which coping with stress by attending to your own feelings only makes things worse (Mor & Winquist, 2002; Pyszczynski & Greenberg, 1992).

Thankfully, there are healthier alternatives. To redirect attention away from the self, it helps to become absorbed in an activity such as aerobic exercise, gardening, writing, or reading a book. Whatever the activity, it should be difficult, demanding, and fully engaging. Ralph Erber and Abraham Tesser (1992) found that people who were in a bad mood felt better after performing a difficult task than a simple task or none at all. Difficult tasks, it appears, can "absorb" a bad mood.

Proactive Coping

According to Lisa Aspinwall and Shelley Taylor (1997), people often benefit from *proactive coping*, which consists of up-front efforts to ward off or modify the onset of a stressful event. Coping can be seen as an ongoing process by which we try to prevent as well as react to the bumps and bruises of daily life. Also as shown, the first line of defence involves the accumulation of resources—personal, financial, social, and otherwise—that can later, if needed, serve as a buffer against stress. In this section, we look at one possible resources: **social support**.

Social Support If the world is crashing down around you, what do you do? Do you try to stop it? Do you try to manage your emotions? Or do you try to get help from others? Throughout this book, we have seen that no man or woman is an island, that human beings are social animals, that people need people, and that to get by you need a little help from friends. But do our social nature and our connections to others have anything to do with health? The answer is yes. The evidence is now overwhelming that social support has therapeutic effects on our physical and psychological well-being (Cohen, 2004; Uchino, 2009).

David Spiegel of Stanford University's School of Medicine came to appreciate the value of social connections many years ago when he organized support groups for women with advanced breast cancer. The groups met weekly in 90-minute sessions to laugh, cry, share stories, and discuss ways of coping. Spiegel had fully expected the women to benefit emotionally from the experience. But he found something else he did not expect: These women lived an average of 18 months longer than did similar others who did not attend the groups. According to Spiegel (1993), "The added survival time was longer than any medication or other known medical treatment could be expected to provide for women with breast cancer so far advanced" (pp. 331–332).

Research findings like these are common. For example, married people are more likely than those who are single, divorced, or widowed to survive cancer for five years (Taylor, 1990), gay men infected with HIV are less likely to contemplate suicide if they have close ties than if they do not (Schneider et al., 1991), people who have a heart attack are less likely to have a second one if they live with someone than if they live alone (Case et al., 1992), and people, once married, who are then separated or divorced for long periods of time, are at an increased risk of early death (Sbarra & Nietert, 2009). Based on this type of research, Bert Uchino and his colleagues (1996) concluded that in times of stress, having social support lowers blood pressure, lessens the secretion of stress hormones, and strengthens immune responses.

Precisely because researchers agree that social support is vital to health, they have struggled mightily to come up with ways to measure it (Cohen et al., 2000). In some studies, social support is defined by the sheer *number of social contacts* that a person has. This measure can be useful, but a simple social contact model has some limitations. One is that it glosses over the fact that people who are trapped in bad relationships are sometimes more distressed, not less (Rook, 1984). Another problem is that having too many contacts can actually reduce levels of support. Consider the plight of the urban poor in India who are packed into overcrowded residences of up to 11 people per room. They are more stressed than people in less crowded conditions and have *less* social support, in part because they tend to withdraw (Evans & Lepore, 1993).

A second model of social support focuses on the *diversity* of a person's social network, one that consists, for example, of a spouse, close family members, friends, co-workers, and neighbours. Over the years, research has shown that people who are socially "integrated," who have connections to different types of people in different types of relationships, are healthier and live longer (Cohen & Janicki-Deverts, 2009).

A third model focuses on the quality of a person's relationships rather than their quantity. This *intimacy model* predicts that the key is to have a close relationship with a significant other who is emotionally on call for late-night conversations. Having one special relationship may be all a person needs. Thus, while many women with breast cancer benefit physically and emotionally from peer discussion groups, these groups

social support
The helpful coping resources provided by friends and other people.

are not needed by—and do not help—women who have supportive partners at home (Helgeson et al., 2000).

A fourth approach defines social support by *its perceived availability* (Sarason et al., 1983). Compared with people who are uncertain of what social resources they have, those who believe that ample support is available when needed cope more effectively. In almost any demanding situation you can imagine, perceived support is associated with better adjustment—even when these perceptions are not entirely accurate (Lakey & Cassady, 1990).

People who have lots of friends are healthier and live longer than those who live more isolated lives. TRUE.

Culture and Coping

Everyone in the world feels stress during the course of a lifetime. Whether the result of a natural disaster, the death of a loved one, the breakup of a relationship, war, serious illness, an accident, or the chronic microstressors of studying, working, and trying to make ends meet, stress is universal to the human experience. But do people in all cultures solve problems and cope in the same ways?

Most of the research on coping is conducted with people from Western cultures, in which individualism and independence are highly valued. Do people from collectivist cultures that value interdependence use the same coping mechanisms? The answer may not be as obvious as it seems. In view of the differences between Eastern and Western cultures, for example, one might predict that Asians are more likely than European Americans to cope with stress by turning to others for support. Yet Shelley Taylor and her colleagues (2004) found that when they asked students to describe what they do to relieve stress, only 39 percent of South Koreans (compared to 57 percent of Americans) said they sought social support. Additional research has confirmed this surprising cultural difference. Regardless of whether the source of stress is social, academic, financial, or health related; across age groups; and in diverse Asian samples that included Chinese, Japanese, Korean, and Vietnamese participants, the result is always the same: People from Asian cultures are less likely to seek out social support in times of stress.

Additional probing has shed light on this difference. In individualistic cultures, people often use others to service their personal goals. Yet in collectivist cultures, where social groups take precedence over the self, people are reluctant to strain their relationships by calling on others for support. This being the case, Heejung Kim and her colleagues (2008) distinguished between *explicit social support* (disclosing one's distress to others and seeking their advice, aid, or comfort) and *implicit social support* (merely thinking about or being with close others without openly asking for help). In a study that asked participants to imagine themselves in one of these two situations, Asian Americans reacted with more stress to the explicit social support situation, while European Americans found the more contained implicit situation more stressful (Taylor et al., 2007).

Treatment and Prevention

Understanding what social support is and how it operates is important in the study of health because so many of life's problems and prospects occur in a social context and so many of our efforts to cope with stress involve other people. Indeed, as we will see in this section, health psychologists are actively trying to find ways in which social influences can be used to improve the development of treatment and prevention programs.

Treatment: The "Social" Ingredients

Often, what ails us can be treated through medical intervention. The treatments vary widely—from a simple change in diet to vitamin supplements, aspirin, antibiotics, surgery, and the like. There is no doubt about it: Medicine is vital to health. In addition, however, treatment has a social component, what the family doctor used to call "bedside manner." What are the active social ingredients?

To begin to answer this question, let's consider research on the benefits of psychotherapy. Over the years, studies have shown that although there are vastly different schools of thought and techniques for doing psychotherapy, all approaches are somewhat effective and, surprisingly, all are generally equivalent (Smith et al., 1980; Wampold et al., 1997). Apparently, despite the surface differences, all psychotherapies have a great deal in common at a deeper level, and these common factors—more than the specific techniques used—provide the active ingredients necessary for change. What are some of these factors?

First, all healers—regardless of whether they are medical doctors, psychologists, or others—provide *social support*, a close human relationship characterized by warmth, expressions of concern, a shoulder to cry on, and someone to talk to. Earlier, we discussed the benefits to health and longevity of having social contacts. In psychological therapy, studies have shown that the better the "working alliance" between a therapist and client, the more favourable the outcome is likely to be (Horvath & Luborsky, 1993).

Second, all therapies offer a ray of *hope* to people who are sick, demoralized, unhappy, or in pain. In all aspects of life, people are motivated by upbeat, positive expectations. Although some of us are more optimistic than others, optimism is a specific expectation that can be increased or decreased in certain situations (Armor & Taylor, 1998). Indeed, a common aspect of all treatments is that they communicate and instill positive expectations. It has been suggested that high expectations can spark change even when they are not justified (Prioleau et al., 1983). This suggestion is consistent with the well-known placebo effect in medicine, whereby patients improve after being given an inactive drug or treatment. Believing can help make it so, which is how faith healers, shamans, and witch doctors all over the world have managed to perform "miracle cures" with elaborate rituals. Even modern medicine exploits the power of hope. As Walter Brown (1998) puts it, "The symbols and rituals of healing—the doctor's office, the stethoscope, the physical examination—offer reassurance" (p. 91).

A third important ingredient is *choice*. Allowing patients to make meaningful choices, such as deciding on a type of treatment, increases the effectiveness of treatments for alcoholism (Miller, 1985) and obesity (Mendonca & Brehm, 1983). Choosing to undergo an effortful or costly treatment is particularly beneficial in this regard. The person who voluntarily pays in time, money, or discomfort needs to self-justify that investment—a predicament sure to arouse cognitive dissonance (see Chapter 6). One way to reduce dissonance is to become ultra-motivated to succeed: "Why have I chosen to do this? Because I really want to get better." Perhaps because highly motivated individuals are more careful and conscientious about carrying out the prescribed treatment, they tend to improve more.

Prevention: Getting the Message Across

We live in what could aptly be described as the era of prevention in that many serious health threats are preventable. Just watch TV, leaf through a magazine, or surf the Internet: There are campaigns to persuade smokers to break the habit, sunscreens that protect the skin from harmful rays, and laws that mandate the use of seat belts. To a large extent, we know what to do and what not to do to promote good health and avoid disease and injury. But just how do we convince ourselves and others to translate that knowledge into action? Across a range of perspectives, several basic steps emerge (see ▶ Figure B.3).

The first step toward good health depends on the relative pleasure to be derived from healthy versus unhealthy behaviours. If a healthy behaviour is more enjoyable than an unhealthy one, then presumably all we need to do is try it out and we'll be convinced. Usually, however, it's not this easy. Many unhealthy habits are sinfully enjoyable, and many healthy behaviours require self-control. If they are to be convinced to switch, people have to recognize that their health is at risk. As described in Chapter 6, graphic fear appeals are a popular method of persuasion in commercial and public service advertisements: the gruesome lung-cancer operation to scare smokers into quitting, the bloody accident victim to get people to use seat belts. Fear appeals can be incredibly effective at changing attitudes and behaviour (de Hoog et al., 2007).

The next two steps toward good health involve other people. When those around us behave in healthful ways, they serve as role models that help set healthy norms. Direct modelling can be especially useful. Celebrities in particular have a great deal of influence over public health issues (Nattinger et al., 1998). Unfortunately, the sword of influence cuts both ways, which is why it is so troubling to see role models of *un*healthy behaviour among high-profile athletes, entertainers, and other celebrities who occupy centre stage.

Besides eliciting direct imitation, spokespersons contribute to the development of subjective norms, beliefs we hold about how people expect us to behave. According to the theories of reasoned action (Fishbein, 1980) and planned behaviour (Ajzen, 1991) presented in Chapter 6, both attitudes and subjective norms affect our intentions to take action.

Intervention strategies that make use of social pressure can be very effective. Unfortunately, subjective norms often sustain unhealthy behaviours. There are two reasons why this occurs. First, people who smoke or drink excessively overestimate the prevalence of such practices among their peers. Second, these inflated estimates serve to support and increase unhealthy practices at a later time. For example, Deborah Prentice and Dale Miller (1996) found that students who overestimate the

As role models, celebrities have great influence over public health care decisions. TRUE.

FIGURE B.3

Aiming for Good Health

Several major factors help convince people to engage in healthy practices. Recognition that a threat to health exists is a necessary first step. Positive models and healthy subjective norms encourage people to adopt health-protective behaviours. A sense of self-efficacy about being able to carry out healthy behaviours and the belief that such behaviours will be effective increase the likelihood of active efforts.

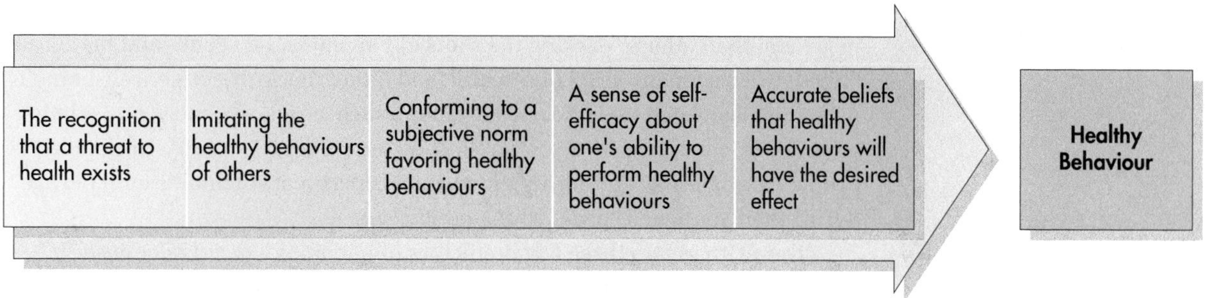

level of alcohol use on campus at the start of a school year are eventually more likely to conform to this misperception in their own attitudes and behaviour. For those trapped within this closed circle, the best way to cut through it is to provide accurate information about *who* does *what.* Prentice and Miller found that students who took part in a program designed to correct their misperceptions of campus norms actually consumed less alcohol six months later.

The fourth step to health emphasizes a person's confidence in his or her ability to succeed. Self-efficacy—the belief that we can do what needs to be done—enhances the adoption of various healthy behaviours, including safe-sex practices, not smoking, and abstinence from alcohol (Bandura, 1999; Maddux, 1995). If people don't know how to perform the necessary corrective behaviours, then they should be taught. For example, smoking-prevention programs often teach children techniques for resisting peer pressures and refusing the offer of a cigarette (Baum, 1984; Evans et al., 1984).

Finally, people need reliable and accurate information about the effectiveness of the healthy behaviours they are urged to adopt (Weinstein, 1989). If people believe that something works, they will be more likely to try it out.

The Pursuit of Happiness

Long before the emergence of social psychology, philosophers regarded happiness as the ultimate state of being. But what is happiness, and how is it achieved? Aristotle said it was the reward of an active life. Freud linked it with both work and love. Others have variously suggested that happiness requires money and power, health and fitness, religion, beauty, the satisfaction of basic needs, and an ability to derive pleasure from the events of everyday life. In recent years, social psychologists have applied their theories and methods to the study of this most basic human motive: the pursuit of happiness (Carr, 2011; Diener & Biswas-Diener, 2008; Franklin, 2010; Gilbert, 2006).

To study happiness—or subjective well-being, as social psychologists like to call it—one must be able to measure it. How do researchers know whether someone is happy? Simple: They ask. Better yet, they use questionnaires such as the Satisfaction with Life Scale, in which people respond to statements such as "If I could live my life over, I would change almost nothing" (Diener et al., 1984; Pavot & Diener, 1993). As Marcus Aurelius said, "No man is happy who does not think himself so."

In general, people who are happy also have cheerful moods, high self-esteem, physical health, a sense of personal control, more memories of positive as opposed to negative events, and optimism about the future (Myers & Diener, 1995). Predictably, the events of everyday life trigger fluctuations in mood. For example, people are most happy on Fridays and Saturdays and least happy on Mondays and Tuesdays (Larsen & Kasimatis, 1990).

But what determines our long-term satisfaction, and why are some of us happier in general than others? Seeking the roots of happiness, Ed Diener and his colleagues (1999) reviewed many years of research and found that **subjective well-being** is not meaningfully related to demographic factors such as age, sex, racial and ethnic background, IQ, education level, or physical attractiveness. Contrary to popular belief, people are not less happy during the so-called crisis years of midlife or in old age than during their youth and "peak" young-adult years.

subjective well-being
One's happiness, or life satisfaction, as measured by self-report.

Overall, there are three key predictors of happiness: *social relationships* (people with an active social life, close friends, and a happy marriage are more satisfied than those who lack these intimate connections), *employment status* (regardless of income, employed people are happier than those who are out of work), and *physical and mental health* (people who are healthy are happier than those who are not). Reflecting the impact of these factors, worldwide surveys of more than 100 000 respondents in 55 countries have shown that happiness levels vary from one culture to the next (Diener & Suh, 2000). Although rankings fluctuate a bit from survey to survey, national happiness ratings are consistently high in Denmark, Sweden, Switzerland, and Australia. Canada ranks fifth in the world, and the United States ranks seventh (Veenhoven, 1993). Perhaps the most interesting statistical relationship is between income and subjective well-being. We all know the saying that "money can't buy happiness"—although some people (particularly those who are financially strapped) do not believe it. But is wealth truly a key to happiness? To some extent, yes, but the evidence is complex.

Cross-national studies reveal a strong positive association between a nation's wealth and the subjective well-being of its people. There are some exceptions. But as a general rule, the more money a country has, the happier its citizens are, at least up to a point. Within any given country, however, the differences between wealthy and middle-income people are modest. And when comparisons within a single culture are made over time, there is no relationship between affluence and happiness. People in North America are, on average, two to three times richer now than 50 years ago—before we had computers, flat-screen TVs, BlackBerrys, iPhones, and digital cameras that fit into the palm of your hand—yet not necessarily any happier. According to the Global Barometer of Happiness, in 2011 only 60 percent of Canadians rated themselves as 'happy.' Interestingly, our overall happiness score was tied with Japan, despite the fact that during this same year, they experienced the devastating earthquake, tsunami, and nuclear crisis!

So what are we to conclude? At this point, it appears that having shelter, food, safety, and security is essential for subjective well-being. But once these basic needs are met, particularly in an already prosperous society, additional increases in wealth do not appreciably raise levels of happiness. Why doesn't money contribute more to subjective well-being? One reason is that our perceptions of wealth are not absolute but, instead, are relative to certain personally set standards (Parducci, 1995). These standards are derived from two sources: other people and our own past.

According to *social comparison theory*, as described in Chapter 3, people tend to naturally compare themselves to others and feel contented or deprived depending on how they fare in this comparison. That is why the middle-class worker whose neighbours cannot pay their bills feels fortunate, but the upper-class social climber who rubs elbows with the rich and famous feels deprived. This relativity may also help explain why there are only modest relationships between happiness and actual income, and perceptions of financial status (Johnson & Krueger, 2006).

It is also natural for people to use their own recent past as a basis of comparison. According to *adaptation-level theory*, our satisfaction with the present depends on the level of success to which we are accustomed. Get married, buy a new house, or make a killing in the stock market and you will surely enjoy a wave of euphoria. Before long, however, the glitter will wear off, and you will adapt to your better situation and raise your standard of comparison. Indeed, when Philip Brickman and others (1978) interviewed 22 people who had won between $50 000 and $1 million in a lottery, they found that these people did not rate themselves as happier than in the past. Compared to others from similar backgrounds, the winners said that they now derived less pleasure from routine activities such as shopping, reading, and talking to a friend.

There is one other possible and intriguing explanation for why money, per se, is not more predictive of happiness. Perhaps each of us, as a result of both biological and environmental factors, has a set baseline level of happiness, a "set point" toward which we gravitate. Evidence to support this notion includes the finding that ratings of happiness are higher among pairs of identical twins than among fraternal twins—leading David Lykken (2000) to suggest that there may be a genetic basis for having a certain set level of contentment, and that happiness levels, like personality traits, are relatively stable over time and place. This leads to the conclusion that some people are, in general, happier than others (DeNeve & Cooper, 1998).

The pursuit of happiness is a powerful human motive that is not fully understood. Although it appears that people are predisposed toward a particular set point, it is clear that happiness is not completely set in stone. In a study of national surveys that spanned from 1981 to 2007, other researchers found that average happiness ratings increased in 45 out of 52 countries in which multiple surveys were administered over time—an increase that was linked to increasing democratization in these countries (Inglehart et al., 2008). Realizing that happiness is malleable, both for individuals and for large populations, researchers are now seeking ways to produce sustainable increases in subjective well-being (Lyubomirsky et al., 2005).

REVIEW

Stress and Health

- Stress is an unpleasant state that arises when we perceive that the demands of an event strain our ability to cope effectively.
- A person's appraisal of a situation determines how stress is experienced and how he or she copes.
- Coping responses consist of the thoughts, feelings, and behaviours by which people attempt to reduce stress.

What Causes Stress?

- There are many different causes of stress, or stressors.

Crises and Catastrophes

- Natural disasters and other catastrophic events can have harmful and long-term effects on mental and physical health.

Major Life Events

- Early research suggested that all change is stressful.
- However, more recent studies suggest that only negative events are harmful.

Microstressors: The Hassles of Everyday Life

- The most common sources of stress are minor everyday hassles.
- Constant noise, job pressures, and living in shared space are all stressful in this regard.

How Does Stress Affect the Body?

- Selye coined the term *stress* upon observing that different stressors produce similar physiological effects on the body.

The General Adaptation Syndrome

- The body responds to stress in three stages: alarm, resistance, and exhaustion.
- The stress response is designed for acute emergencies, not for the constant long-term stress that humans often experience.

What Stress Does to the Heart

- Stress is a major risk factor in cardiovascular heart disease.
- Early research suggested that the hard-driving Type A personality, also called coronary behaviour pattern, is associated with heart disease.
- This link was found when the Type A pattern was assessed in structured interviews, but not when it was measured by questionnaire.
- Hostility is now known to be the "toxic" element in the Type A behaviour pattern.

What Stress Does to the Immune System

- The immune system contains specialized white blood cells called lymphocytes that detect and destroy foreign substances in the body.
- Laboratory and field research shows that stress affects the activity of these cells, sometimes resulting in a weakened immune response.
- Stress can "get into" the immune system by causing people to behave in unhealthy ways or by triggering the release of stress hormones that suppress immune cell activity.

The Links Between Stress and Illness

- Stress weakens the immune system, so people under stress are more likely to catch a cold when exposed to a virus.
- There may also be a link between negative emotional states and serious diseases such as cancer, but the evidence is less strong.

Processes of Appraisal

Attribution Styles

- According to the learned helplessness model of depression, exposure to an uncontrollable event sparks passive, apathetic, depression-like symptoms.
- Research shows that the attributions people make for their lack of control are of central importance.

The Human Capacity for Resilience

- Some individuals are more resilient than others in the face of stress, a trait called hardiness.
- The key ingredient of hardiness is the belief that one has the power to control future outcomes through one's own behaviour.
- Depending on the situation, people may have a high or low self-efficacy—the belief that they can perform the behaviours needed to produce positive outcomes.
- Some individuals are characteristically more optimistic than others, and optimism at one point in time is predictive of later positive health outcomes.

Ways of Coping with Stress

Problem-Focused Coping

- In problem-focused coping, people try to reduce stress by overcoming the source of the problem.
- Problem-focused coping is often effective, but at times there are drawbacks.
- For example, exerting control is physiologically taxing and can increase stress rather than reduce it.
- Also, both behavioural and characterological self-blame are associated with increased distress.

Emotion-Focused Coping

- In emotion-focused coping, people try to manage the emotional turmoil produced by a stressful situation.
- The best starting point is the experience of positive emotions.
- In situations that one cannot control, mental distraction and avoidance can reduce stress.
- But the suppression from awareness of unwanted thoughts and feelings can backfire, causing us to become preoccupied with them.
- Research shows that opening up and confronting one's feelings about upsetting events improves mental and physical health.
- Among people with low self-esteem, self-focus worsens their mood and heightens their distress.
- In contrast, it is helpful to become absorbed in demanding external activities such as reading, exercise, and gardening.

Proactive Coping

- As a first line of defense, people can ward off stress through proactive coping efforts such as the accumulation of resources.
- Friendships and other sources of social support have strong beneficial effects on physical health and psychological well-being.
- All researchers agree that social support is healthy, but they measure it in different ways, focusing on such factors as the number of social contacts a person has, the presence of special close relationships, or perceptions that social support is available.

Culture and Coping

- Stress is universal, but people from collectivist cultures appear to rely less often on social support as a means of coping than do people from individualist cultures.
- Recent research has identified that acceptance, avoidance, family support, religion, and private emotional outlets are the coping styles members of collectivist cultures use.

Treatment and Prevention

Treatment: The "Social" Ingredients

- Medical treatment includes an important social component.
- Doctors, therapists, and other health care workers provide patients with social support and a ray of hope.
- Choice of treatment is also an important factor, particularly when patients choose an effortful treatment, which increases commitment.

Prevention: Getting the Message Across

- Many causes of death are preventable through changes in lifestyle and behaviour, which is where social psychology comes in.
- First, people have to recognize that a threat to their health exists.
- Others serve as important role models and spokespersons for healthy or unhealthy behaviour.
- Subjective norms can also encourage healthy or unhealthy behaviours.
- A sense of self-efficacy enhances a person's adoption and maintenance of healthy behaviours.
- Accurate information is needed to sustain people's commitment to healthy behaviours.

The Pursuit of Happiness

- Most people report being relatively happy, but there are individual differences.
- Three important factors are social relationships, employment, and health.
- Evidence that money can buy happiness is mixed. More affluent nations tend to have happier citizens than less affluent nations, but correlations with groups of citizens within nations are modest.
- One reason for the limited association between wealth and happiness is that our perceptions of wealth are relative, not only to what others have, but also to what we have become accustomed to.
- Research suggests that each of us has a baseline level of happiness toward which we gravitate over time.
- Still, research shows that happiness levels are somewhat malleable in individuals and in nations.

Key Terms

appraisal (463)
coping (463)
emotion-focused coping (472)
general adaptation syndrome (465)
health psychology (462)
immune system (467)
learned helplessness (469)
proactive coping (472)
problem-focused coping (472)
self-efficacy (470)
social support (476)
stress (463)
stressor (463)
subjective well-being (480)
Type A personality (466)

Putting COMMON SENSE *to the Test*

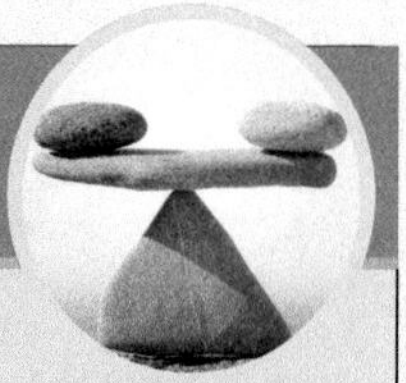

The accumulation of daily hassles does more to make people sick than catastrophes or major life changes.

True. *Car problems, arguments with friends, and other "microstressors" contribute more to our levels of stress than larger but less frequent stressors.*

Stress can weaken the heart, but it cannot affect the immune system.

False. *Recent research has shown that stress and other psychological states can alter the activity of white blood cells in the immune system and affect our resistance to illness.*

When it comes to physical health, research does not support popular beliefs about the power of positive thinking.

False. *Consistently, people who are optimistic—and situations that promote optimism—are associated with better health outcomes.*

People who have lots of friends are healthier and live longer than those who live more isolated lives.

True. *Across a range of studies, researchers have found that social support is strongly associated with positive health outcomes.*

As role models, celebrities have great influence over public health care decisions.

True. *As a result of all the media attention given to celebrities, the health care decisions they make exert a great deal of influence on others.*

actor-observer effect The tendency to attribute our own behaviour to situational causes and the behaviour of others to personal factors. *(p. 118)*

adversarial model A dispute-resolution system in which the Crown (prosecution) and defence present opposing sides of the story. *(p. 457)*

affective forecasting The process of predicting how one would feel in response to future emotional events. *(p. 59)*

aggression Behaviour intended to harm another individual. *(p. 400)*

altruistic Motivated by the desire to improve another's welfare. *(p. 368)*

ambivalent sexism A form of sexism characterized by attitudes about women that reflect both negative, resentful beliefs and feelings and affectionate, chivalrous, but potentially patronizing beliefs and feelings. *(p. 148)*

applied research Research designed to enlarge the understanding of naturally occurring events and to find solutions to practical problems. *(p. 29)*

appraisal The process by which people make judgments about the demands of potentially stressful events and their ability to meet those demands. *(p. 463)*

arousal: cost-reward model The proposition that people react to emergency situations by acting in the most cost-effective way to reduce the arousal of shock and alarm. *(p. 365)*

attachment style The way a person typically interacts with significant others. *(p. 339)*

attitude A positive, negative, or mixed reaction to a person, object, or idea. *(p. 189)*

attitude scale A multiple-item questionnaire designed to measure a person's attitude toward some object. *(p. 191)*

attribution theory A group of theories that describe how people explain the causes of behaviour. *(p. 110)*

audience inhibition Reluctance to help for fear of making a bad impression on observers. *(p. 377)*

availability heuristic The tendency to estimate the likelihood that an event will occur by how easily instances of it come to mind. *(p. 113)*

base-rate fallacy The finding that people are relatively insensitive to consensus information presented in the form of numerical base rates. *(p. 114)*

basic research Research designed to increase the understanding of human behaviour, often by testing hypotheses based on a theory. *(p. 29)*

bask in reflected glory (BIRG) To increase self-esteem by associating with others who are successful. *(p. 84)*

behavioural genetics A subfield of psychology that examines the role of genetic factors in behaviour. *(p. 18)*

belief in a just world The belief that individuals get what they deserve in life, an orientation that leads people to disparage victims. *(p. 121)*

belief perseverance The tendency to maintain beliefs even after they have been discredited. *(p. 129)*

biased sampling The tendency for groups to spend more time discussing shared information (information already known by all or most group members) than unshared information (information known by only one or a few group members). *(p. 294)*

bogus pipeline A fake lie-detector device that is sometimes used to get respondents to give truthful answers to sensitive questions. *(p. 191)*

brainstorming A technique that attempts to increase the production of creative ideas by encouraging group members to speak freely without criticizing their own or others' contributions. *(p. 288)*

bystander effect The effect whereby the presence of others inhibits helping. *(p. 373)*

catharsis A reduction of the motive to aggress that is said to result from any imagined, observed, or actual act of aggression. *(p. 415)*

central route to persuasion The process by which a person thinks carefully about a communication and is influenced by the strength of its arguments. *(p. 201)*

central traits Traits that exert a powerful influence on overall impressions. *(p. 126)*

challenge for cause A means by which lawyers can exclude an unlimited number of prospective jurors due to perceived bias, or unsuitableness for jury duty under the law. *(p. 440)*

cognitive dissonance theory The theory that holding inconsistent cognitions arouses psychological tension that people become motivated to reduce. *(p. 221)*

collective People engaged in common activities but having minimal direct interaction. *(p. 273)*

collective effort model The theory that individuals will exert effort on a collective task to the degree that they think their individual efforts will be important, relevant, and meaningful for achieving outcomes that they value. *(p. 282)*

collectivism A cultural orientation in which interdependence, cooperation, and social harmony take priority over personal goals. *(p. 246)*

communal relationship A relationship in which the participants expect and desire mutual responsiveness to each other's needs. *(p. 339)*

companionate love A secure, trusting, stable partnership. *(p. 342)*

compliance Changes in behaviour that are elicited by direct requests. *(p. 249)*

confederate Accomplice of an experimenter who, in dealing with the real participants in an experiment, acts as if he or she is also a participant. *(p. 45)*

confirmation bias The tendency to seek, interpret, and create information that verifies existing beliefs. *(p. 128)*

conformity The tendency to change our perceptions, opinions, or behaviour in ways that are consistent with group norms. *(p. 238)*

construct validity The extent to which the measures used in a study measure the variables they were designed to measure and the manipulations in an experiment manipulate the variables they were designed to manipulate. *(p. 30)*

contact hypothesis The theory that direct contact between hostile groups will reduce prejudice under certain conditions. *(p. 180)*

coping Efforts to reduce stress. *(p. 463)*

correlation coefficient A statistical measure of the strength and direction of the association between two variables. *(p. 37)*

correlational research Research designed to measure the association between variables that are not manipulated by the researcher. *(p. 37)*

counterfactual thinking The tendency to imagine alternative events or outcomes that might have occurred but did not. *(p. 114)*

covariation principle A principle of attribution theory holding that people attribute behaviour to factors that are present when a behaviour occurs and absent when it does not. *(p. 111)*

cross-cultural research Research designed to compare and contrast people of different cultures. *(p. 18)*

cross-race identification bias The tendency for people to have difficulty identifying members of a race other than their own. *(p. 446)*

cultivation The process by which the mass media (particularly television) construct a version of social reality for the public. *(p. 425)*

culture A system of enduring meanings, beliefs, values, assumptions, institutions, and practices shared by a large group of people and transmitted from one generation to the next. *(p. 18)*

cycle of family violence The transmission of domestic violence across generations. *(p. 431)*

debriefing A disclosure, made to participants after research procedures are completed, in which the researcher explains the purpose of the research, attempts to resolve any negative feelings, and emphasizes the scientific contribution made by the participants' involvement. *(p. 49)*

deception In the context of research, a method that provides false information to participants. *(p. 45)*

deindividuation The loss of a person's sense of individuality and the reduction of normal constraints against deviant behaviour. *(p. 284)*

dependent variable In an experiment, a factor that experimenters measure to see if it is affected by the independent variable. *(p. 42)*

desensitization Reduction in emotion-related physiological reactivity in response to a stimulus. *(p. 425)*

dialecticism An Eastern system of thought that accepts the existence of contradictory characteristics within a single person. *(p. 70)*

diffusion of responsibility The belief that others will or should take the responsibility for providing assistance to a person in need. *(p. 376)*

discrimination Negative behaviour directed against persons because of their membership in a particular group. *(p. 141)*

displacement Aggressing against a substitute target because aggressive acts against the source of the frustration are inhibited by fear or lack of access. *(p. 415)*

distraction-conflict theory A theory holding that the presence of others will produce social facilitation effects only when those others distract from the task and create attentional conflict. *(p. 280)*

door-in-the-face technique A two-step compliance technique in which an influencer prefaces the real request with one that is so large that it is rejected. *(p. 253)*

downward social comparison The defensive tendency to compare ourselves with others who are worse off than we are. *(p. 85)*

egoistic Motivated by the desire to improve one's own welfare. *(p. 368)*

elaboration The process of thinking about and scrutinizing the arguments contained in a persuasive communication. *(p. 201)*

emotion-focused coping Cognitive and behavioural efforts to reduce the distress produced by a stressful situation. *(p. 472)*

emotional aggression Inflicting harm for its own sake. *(p. 400)*

empathy Understanding or vicariously experiencing another individual's perspective and feeling sympathy or compassion for that individual. *(p. 368)*

empathy-altruism hypothesis The proposition that empathic concern for a person in need produces an altruistic motive for helping. *(p. 368)*

equity theory The theory that people are most satisfied with a relationship when the ratio between benefits and contributions is similar for both partners. *(p. 337)*

escalation effect The condition in which commitments to a failing course of action are increased to justify investments already made. *(p. 293)*

evaluation apprehension theory A theory holding that the presence of others will produce social facilitation effects only when those others are seen as potential evaluators. *(p. 280)*

evolutionary psychology A subfield of psychology that uses the principles of evolution to understand human social behaviour. *(p. 18)*

exchange relationship A relationship in which the participants expect and desire strict reciprocity in their interactions. *(p. 339)*

excitation transfer The process whereby arousal caused by one stimulus is added to arousal from a second stimulus and the combined arousal is attributed to the second stimulus. *(p. 342)*

experiment A form of research that can demonstrate causal relationships because the experimenter has control over the events that occur and participants are randomly assigned to conditions. *(p. 40)*

experimental realism The degree to which experimental procedures are involving to participants and lead them to behave naturally and spontaneously. *(p. 45)*

experimenter expectancy effects The effects produced when an experimenter's expectations about the results of an experiment affect his or her behaviour toward a participant and thereby influence the participant's responses. *(p. 44)*

external validity The degree to which there can be reasonable confidence that the results of a study would be obtained for other people and in other situations. *(p. 44)*

facial electromyograph (EMG) An electronic instrument that records facial muscle activity associated with emotions and attitudes. *(p. 192)*

facial feedback hypothesis The hypothesis that changes in facial expression can lead to corresponding changes in emotion. *(p. 61)*

false-consensus effect The tendency for people to overestimate the extent to which others share their opinions, attributes, and behaviours. *(p. 113)*

foot-in-the-door technique A two-step compliance technique in which an influencer sets the stage for the real request by first getting a person to comply with a much smaller request. *(p. 251)*

frustration-aggression hypothesis The idea that frustration always elicits the motive to aggress, and that all aggression is caused by frustration. *(p. 415)*

fundamental attribution error The tendency to focus on the role of personal causes and underestimate the impact of situations on other people's behaviour. This error is sometimes called correspondence bias. *(p. 115)*

general adaptation syndrome A three-stage process (alarm, resistance, and exhaustion) by which the body responds to stress. *(p. 465)*

good mood effect The effect whereby a good mood increases helping behaviour. *(p. 383)*

graduated and reciprocated initiatives in tension-reduction (GRIT) A strategy for unilateral, persistent efforts to establish trust and cooperation between opposing parties. *(p. 303)*

group Two or more persons perceived as related because of their interactions with each other over time, membership in the same social category, or common fate. *(p. 141)*

group cohesiveness The extent to which forces exerted on a group push its members closer together. *(p. 276)*

group polarization The exaggeration through group discussion of initial tendencies in the thinking of group members. *(p. 290)*

groupthink A group decision-making style characterized by an excessive tendency among group members to seek concurrence. *(p. 291)*

hard-to-get effect The tendency to prefer people who are highly selective in their social choices over those who are more readily available. *(p. 329)*

health psychology The study of physical health and illness by psychologists from various areas of specialization. *(p. 462)*

hostile attribution bias The tendency to perceive hostile intent in others. *(p. 421)*

hypothesis A testable prediction about the conditions under which an event will occur. *(p. 28)*

illusory correlation An overestimate of the association between variables that are only slightly or not at all correlated. *(p. 160)*

immune system A biological surveillance system that detects and destroys "nonself" substances that invade the body. *(p. 467)*

Implicit Association Test (IAT) A covert measure of unconscious attitudes, it is derived from the speed at which people respond to pairings of concepts, such as black or white with good or bad. *(p. 144)*

implicit attitude An attitude—such as prejudice—that one is not aware of having. *(p. 193)*

implicit egotism A nonconscious form of self-enhancement. *(p. 81)*

implicit personality theory A network of assumptions people make about the relationships among traits and behaviours. *(p. 126)*

implicit racism Racism that operates unconsciously and unintentionally. *(p. 143)*

Implicit Relational Assessment Procedure (IRAP) A way of measuring unconscious attitudes, similar to the IAT, that focuses on cognition and specific relations rather than general associations. *(p. 195)*

impression formation The process of integrating information about a person to form a coherent impression. *(p. 122)*

independent variable In an experiment, a factor that experimenters manipulate to see if it affects the dependent variable. *(p. 42)*

individualism A cultural orientation in which independence, autonomy, and self-reliance take priority over group allegiances. *(p. 246)*

information integration theory The theory that impressions are based on perceiver dispositions and a weighted average of a target person's traits. *(p. 123)*

informational influence Influence that produces conformity when a person believes others are correct in their judgments. *(p. 241)*

informed consent An individual's deliberate, voluntary decision to participate in research, based on the researcher's description of what will be required during such participation. *(p. 48)*

ingroup favouritism The tendency to discriminate in favour of ingroups over outgroups. *(p. 153)*

ingroups Groups with which an individual feels a sense of membership, belonging, and identity. *(p. 141)*

inoculation hypothesis The idea that exposure to weak versions of a persuasive argument increases later resistance to that argument. *(p. 216)*

inquisitorial model A dispute-resolution system in which a neutral investigator gathers evidence from both sides and presents the findings in court. *(p. 457)*

instrumental aggression Inflicting harm in order to obtain something of value. *(p. 400)*

insufficient deterrence A condition in which people refrain from engaging in a desirable activity, even when only mild punishment is threatened. *(p. 222)*

insufficient justification A condition in which people freely perform an attitude-discrepant behaviour without receiving a large reward. *(p. 222)*

integrative agreement A negotiated resolution to a conflict in which all parties obtain outcomes that are superior to what they would have obtained from an equal division of the contested resources. *(p. 304)*

interactionist perspective An emphasis on how both an individual's personality and environmental characteristics influence behaviour. *(p. 13)*

internal validity The degree to which there can be reasonable certainty that the independent variables in an experiment caused the effects obtained on the dependent variables. *(p. 43)*

interrater reliability The degree to which different observers agree on their observations. *(p. 32)*

intimate relationship A close relationship between two adults involving emotional attachment, fulfillment of psychological needs, or interdependence. *(p. 335)*

jigsaw classroom A cooperative learning method used to reduce racial prejudice through interaction in group efforts. *(p. 182)*

jury nullification The jury's power to disregard, or "nullify," the law when it conflicts with personal conceptions of justice. *(p. 453)*

kin selection Preferential helping of genetic relatives, so that genes held in common will survive. *(p. 362)*

learned helplessness A phenomenon in which experience with an uncontrollable event creates passive behaviour toward a subsequent threat to well-being. *(p. 469)*

leniency bias The tendency for jury deliberation to produce a tilt toward acquittal. *(p. 455)*

loneliness A feeling of deprivation about existing social relations. *(p. 317)*

low-balling A two-step compliance technique in which the influencer secures agreement with a request but then increases the size of that request by revealing hidden costs. *(p. 252)*

matching hypothesis The proposition that people are attracted to others who are similar in physical attractiveness. *(p. 328)*

mere exposure effect The phenomenon whereby the more often people are exposed to a stimulus, the more positively they evaluate that stimulus. *(p. 319)*

mere presence theory A theory holding that the mere presence of others is sufficient to produce social facilitation effects. *(p. 280)*

meta-analysis A set of statistical procedures used to review a body of evidence by combining the results of individual studies to measure the overall reliability and strength of particular effects. *(p. 46)*

mind perception The process by which people attribute human-like mental states to various animate and inanimate objects, including other people. *(p. 102)*

minority influence The process by which dissenters produce change within a group. *(p. 247)*

misinformation effect The tendency for false post-event misinformation to become integrated into people's memory of an event. *(p. 447)*

mitigating information Information about a person's situation indicating that he or she should not be held fully responsible for aggressive actions. *(p. 420)*

modern racism A form of prejudice that surfaces in subtle ways when it is safe, socially acceptable, and easy to rationalize. *(p. 143)*

multicultural research Research designed to examine racial and ethnic groups within cultures. *(p. 18)*

mundane realism The degree to which the experimental situation resembles places and events in the real world. *(p. 45)*

need for affiliation The desire to establish and maintain many rewarding interpersonal relationships. *(p. 314)*

need for closure The desire to reduce cognitive uncertainty, which heightens the importance of first impressions. *(p. 127)*

need for cognition (NC) A personality variable that distinguishes people on the basis of how much they enjoy effortful cognitive activities. *(p. 214)*

negative state relief model The proposition that people help others in order to counteract their own feelings of sadness. *(p. 366)*

nonverbal behaviour Behaviour that reveals a person's feelings without words—through facial expressions, body language, and vocal cues. *(p. 103)*

norm of social responsibility A moral standard emphasizing that people should help those who need assistance. *(p. 385)*

normative influence Influence that produces conformity when a person fears the negative social consequences of appearing deviant. *(p. 241)*

obedience Behaviour change produced by the commands of authority. *(p. 256)*

operational definition The specific procedures for manipulating or measuring a conceptual variable. *(p. 30)*

outgroup homogeneity effect The tendency to assume that there is greater similarity among members of outgroups than among members of ingroups. *(p. 158)*

outgroups Groups with which an individual does not feel a sense of membership, belonging, or identity. *(p. 141)*

overjustification effect The tendency for intrinsic motivation to diminish for activities that have become associated with reward or other extrinsic factors. *(p. 62)*

passionate love Romantic love characterized by high arousal, intense attraction, and fear of rejection. *(p. 342)*

peremptory challenge A means by which lawyers can exclude a limited number of prospective jurors without the judge's approval. *(p. 440)*

peripheral route to persuasion The process by which a person does not think carefully about a communication and is influenced instead by superficial cues. *(p. 201)*

personal attribution Attribution to internal characteristics of an actor, such as ability, personality, mood, or effort. *(p. 110)*

persuasion The process by which attitudes are changed. *(p. 200)*

pluralistic ignorance The state in which people mistakenly believe that their own thoughts and feelings are different from those of others, even when everyone's behaviour is the same. *(p. 375)*

polygraph A mechanical instrument that records physiological arousal from multiple channels; it is often used as a lie-detector test. *(p. 444)*

pornography Explicit sexual material. *(p. 426)*

prejudice Negative feelings toward persons based on their membership in certain groups. *(p. 141)*

primacy effect The tendency for information presented early in a sequence to have more impact on impressions than information presented later. *(p. 126)*

priming The tendency for recently used or perceived words or ideas to come to mind easily and influence the interpretation of new information. *(p. 123)*

prisoner's dilemma A type of dilemma in which one party must make either cooperative or competitive moves in relation to another party; typically designed in such a way that competitive moves are more beneficial to either side, but if both sides make competitive moves, they are both worse off than if they both cooperated. *(p. 298)*

private conformity The change of beliefs that occurs when a person privately accepts the position taken by others. *(p. 242)*

private self-consciousness A personality characteristic of individuals who are introspective, often attending to their own inner states. *(p. 77)*

proactive coping Up-front efforts to ward off or modify the onset of a stressful event. *(p. 472)*
problem-focused coping Cognitive and behavioral efforts to alter a stressful situation. *(p. 472)*
process loss The reduction in group performance due to obstacles created by group processes, such as problems of coordination and motivation. *(p. 287)*
prosocial behaviours Actions intended to benefit others. *(p. 361)*
psychological reactance The theory that people react against threats to their freedom by asserting themselves and perceiving the threatened freedom as more attractive. *(p. 217)*
public conformity A superficial change in overt behaviour, without a corresponding change of opinion, produced by real or imagined group pressure. *(p. 242)*
public self-consciousness A personality characteristic of individuals who focus on themselves as social objects, as seen by others. *(p. 77)*
qualitative research The collection of data through open-ended responses, observation, and interviews. *(p. 33)*
quantitative research The collection of numerical data through objective testing and statistical analysis. *(p. 33)*
racism Prejudice and discrimination based on a person's racial background, or institutional and cultural practices that promote the domination of one racial group over another. *(p. 141)*
random assignment A method of assigning participants to the various conditions of an experiment so that each participant in the experiment has an equal chance of being in any of the conditions. *(p. 40)*
random sampling A method of selecting participants for a study so that everyone in a population has an equal chance of being in the study. *(p. 36)*
realistic conflict theory The theory that hostility between groups is caused by direct competition for limited resources. *(p. 152)*
reciprocity A mutual exchange between what we give and receive—for example, liking those who like us. *(p. 328)*
relative deprivation Feelings of discontent aroused by the belief that one fares poorly compared to others. *(p. 152)*
resource dilemmas Social dilemmas concerning how two or more people share a limited resource. *(p. 299)*
self-awareness theory The theory that self-focused attention leads people to notice self-discrepancies, thereby motivating either an escape from self-awareness or a change in behaviour. *(p. 75)*
self-concept The sum total of an individual's beliefs about his or her own personal attributes. *(p. 56)*
self-disclosure Revelations about the self that a person makes to others. *(p. 344)*
self-efficacy A person's belief that he or she is capable of the specific behaviour required to produce a desired outcome in a given situation. *(p. 470)*
self-esteem An affective component of the self, consisting of a person's positive and negative self-evaluations. *(p. 71)*
self-fulfilling prophecy The process by which one's expectations about a person eventually lead that person to behave in ways that confirm those expectations. *(p. 130)*
self-handicapping Behaviours designed to sabotage one's own performance in order to provide a subsequent excuse for failure. *(p. 83)*
self-monitoring The tendency to change behaviour in response to the self-presentation concerns of the situation. *(p. 90)*
self-perception theory The theory that when internal cues are difficult to interpret, people gain self-insight by observing their own behaviour. *(p. 60)*
self-presentation Strategies people use to shape what others think of them. *(p. 88)*
self-schema A belief people hold about themselves that guides the processing of self-relevant information. *(p. 56)*
sentencing disparity Inconsistency of sentences for the same offence from one judge to another. *(p. 457)*
sexism Prejudice and discrimination based on a person's gender, or insitutional and cultural practices that promote the domination of one gender over another. *(p. 141)*
sexual orientation One's sexual preference for members of the same sex, the opposite sex, or both sexes. *(p. 349)*
situational attribution Attribution to factors external to an actor, such as the task, other people, or luck. *(p. 110)*
sleeper effect A delayed increase in the persuasive impact of a noncredible source. *(p. 207)*
social categorization The classification of persons into groups on the basis of common attributes. *(p. 157)*
social cognition The study of how people perceive, remember, and interpret information about themselves and others. *(p. 16)*
social comparison theory The theory that people evaluate their own abilities and opinions by comparing themselves to others. *(p. 64)*
social dilemma A situation in which a self-interested choice by everyone creates the worst outcome for everyone. *(p. 298)*
social dominance orientation A desire to see one's ingroups as dominant over other groups and a willingness to adopt cultural values that facilitate oppression over other groups. *(p. 156)*
social exchange theory A perspective that views people as motivated to maximize benefits and minimize costs in their relationships with others. *(p. 336)*
social facilitation A process whereby the presence of others enhances performance on easy tasks but impairs performance on difficult tasks. *(p. 279)*
social identity model of deindividuation effects (SIDE) A model of group behaviour that explains deindividuation effects as the result of a shift from personal identity to social identity. *(p. 286)*
social identity theory The theory that people favour ingroups over outgroups in order to enhance their self-esteem. *(p. 153)*
social impact theory The theory that social influence depends on the strength, immediacy, and number of source persons relative to target persons. *(p. 265)*
social learning theory The theory that behaviour is learned through the observation of others as well as through the direct experience of rewards and punishments. *(p. 411)*
social loafing A group-produced reduction in individual output on easy tasks where contributions are pooled. *(p. 281)*
social neuroscience The study of the relationship between neural and social processes. *(p. 18)*
social norm A general rule of conduct reflecting standards of social approval and disapproval. *(p. 385)*

social perception A general term for the processes by which people come to understand one another. *(p. 98)*

social psychology The scientific study of how individuals think, feel, and behave in a social context. *(p. 5)*

social role theory The theory that small gender differences are magnified in perception by the contrasting social roles occupied by men and women. *(p. 166)*

social support The helpful coping resources provided by friends and other people. *(p. 476)*

stereotype A belief or association that links a whole group of people with certain traits or characteristics. *(p. 141)*

stereotype content model A model proposing that the relative status and competition between groups influence group stereotypes along the dimensions of competence and warmth. *(p. 169)*

stereotype threat The experience of concern about being evaluated based on negative stereotypes about one's group. *(p. 175)*

stress An unpleasant state of arousal in which people perceive the demands of an event as taxing or exceeding their ability to satisfy or alter those demands. *(p. 463)*

stressor Anything that causes stress. *(p. 463)*

subject variable A variable that characterizes pre-existing differences among the participants in a study. *(p. 42)*

subjective well-being One's happiness, or life satisfaction, as measured by self-report. *(p. 480)*

subliminal presentation A method of presenting stimuli so faintly or rapidly that people do not have any conscious awareness of having been exposed to them. *(p. 170)*

superordinate goal A shared goal that can be achieved only through cooperation among individuals or groups. *(p. 151)*

that's-not-all technique A two-step compliance technique in which the influencer begins with an inflated request, and then decreases its apparent size by offering a discount or bonus. *(p. 254)*

theory An organized set of principles used to explain observed phenomena. *(p. 28)*

theory of planned behaviour The theory that attitudes toward a specific behaviour combine with subjective norms and perceived control to influence a person's actions. *(p. 197)*

threat-to-self-esteem model The theory that reactions to receiving assistance depend on whether help is perceived as supportive or threatening. *(p. 391)*

transactive memory A shared system for remembering information that enables multiple people to remember information together more efficiently than they could alone. *(p. 295)*

triangular theory of love A theory proposing that love has three basic components—intimacy, passion, and commitment—which can be combined to produce eight subtypes. *(p. 341)*

two-factor theory of emotion The theory that the experience of emotion is based on two factors: physiological arousal and a cognitive interpretation of that arousal. *(p. 65)*

Type A personality A pattern of behavior characterized by extremes of competitive striving for achievement, a sense of time urgency, hostility, and aggression. *(p. 466)*

voir dire The pretrial examination of prospective jurors by the judge or opposing lawyers to uncover signs of bias. *(p. 440)*

weapons effect The tendency of weapons to increase the likelihood of aggression by their mere presence. *(p. 420)*

what-is-beautiful-is-good stereotype The belief that physically attractive individuals also possess desirable personality characteristics. *(p. 323)*

References

Abbate, C. S., & Ruggieri, S. (2011). The fairness principle, reward, and altruistic behavior. *Journal of Applied Social Psychology, 41*, 1110–1120.

Abbey, A. (1982). Sex differences in attributions for friendly behavior: Do males misperceive females' friendliness? *Journal of Personality and Social Psychology, 42,* 830–838.

Abelson, R. P. (1981). Psychological status of the script concept. *American Psychologist, 36,* 715–729.

Abelson, R. P., Aronson, E., McGuire, W. J., Newcomb, T. M., Rosenberg, M. J., & Tannenbaum, P. H. (1968). *Theories of cognitive consistency: A sourcebook.* Chicago: Rand McNally.

Abrams, D. (2009). Social identity on a national scale: Optimal distinctiveness and young people's self-expression through musical preference. *Group Processes & Intergroup Relations, 12,* 303–317.

Abshire, J., & Bernstein, B. H. (2003). Juror sensitivity to the cross-race effect. *Law and Human Behavior, 27,* 471–480.

Acevedo, B. P., & Aron, A. (2009). Does a long-term relationship kill romantic love? *Review of General Psychology, 13,* 59–65.

Acker, M., & Davis, M. H. (1992). Intimacy, passion, and commitment in adult romantic relationships: A test of the triangular theory of love. *Journal of Social and Personal Relationships, 9,* 21–50.

Adair, J. G. (2005). The origins and development of social psychology in Canada. *International Journal of Psychology, 40,* 277–288.

Adair, W. L., Taylor, M. S., & Tinsley, C. H. (2009). Starting out on the right foot: Negotiation schemas when cultures collide. *Negotiation and Conflict Management Research, 2,* 138–163.

Adams, G., Garcia, D. M., Purdie-Vaughns, V., & Steele, C. M. (2006). The detrimental effects of a suggestion of sexism in an instruction situation. *Journal of Experimental Social Psychology, 42,* 602–615.

Adams, J. S. (1965). Equity in social exchange. *Advances in Experimental Social Psychology, 2,* 267–299.

Ader, R. (Ed.). (2007). *Psychoneuroimmunology* (4th ed.). Burlington, MA: Elsevier.

Aderman, D. (1972). Elation, depression, and helping behavior. *Journal of Personality and Social Psychology, 24,* 91–101.

Adherents.com. (2005). *Major religions of the world ranked by number of adherents.* Retrieved February 2, 2010, from http://www.adherents.com/Religions_By_Adherents.html.

Adorno, T., Frenkel-Brunswik, E., Levinson, D., & Sanford, R. N. (1950). *The authoritarian personality.* New York: Harper.

Aguiar, P., Vala, J., Correia, I., & Pereira, C. (2008). Justice in our world and in that of others: Belief in a just world and reactions to victims. *Social Justice Research, 21,* 50–68.

Ainsworth, M., Blehar, M. C., Waters, E., & Wall, S. (1978). *Patterns of attachment: A psychological study of the strange situation.* Hillsdale, NJ: Erlbaum.

Ajzen, I. (1991). The theory of planned behavior. *Organizational Behavior and Human Decision Processes, 50,* 179–211.

Ajzen, I. (2001). Nature and operation of attitudes. *Annual Review of Psychology, 52,* 27–58.

Ajzen, I., & Fishbein, M. (1977). Attitude-behavior relations: A theoretical analysis and review of empirical research. *Psychological Bulletin, 84,* 888–918.

Ajzen, I., & Fishbein, M. (2005). The influence of attitudes on behavior. In D. Albarracín, B. T. Johnson, & M. P. Zanna (Eds.), *The handbook of attitudes* (pp. 173–221). Hillsdale, NJ: Erlbaum.

Akimoto, S. A., & Sanbonmatsu, D. M. (1999). Differences in self-effacing behavior between European and Japanese Americans: Effect on competence evaluations. *Journal of Cross-Cultural Psychology, 30,* 159–177.

Akintola, O. (2011). What motivates people to volunteer? the case of volunteer AIDS caregivers in faith-based organizations in KwaZulu-natal, south Africa. *Health Policy and Planning, 26,* 53–62.

Aknin, L. B., Sandstrom, G. M., Dunn, E. W., & Norton, M. I. (2011). It's the recipient that counts: Spending money on strong social ties leads to greater happiness than spending on weak social ties. *PLoS ONE, 6*(2).

Albarracin, D., Johnson, B. T., Fishbein, M., & Muellerleile, P. A. (2001). Theories of reasoned action and planned behavior as models of condom use: A meta-analysis. *Psychological Bulletin, 127,* 142–161.

Albiero, P., Matricardi, G., Speltri, D., & Toso, D. (2009). The assessment of empathy in adolescence: A contribution to the italian validation of the basic empathy scale. *Journal of Adolescence, 32,* 393–408.

Alexander, N. (2008). The mediation metamodel: Understanding practice. *Conflict Resolution Quarterly, 26,* 97–122.

Alicke, M. D., & Largo, E. (1995). The role of the self in the false consensus effect. *Journal of Experimental Social Psychology, 31,* 28–47.

Allen, J. B., Kenrick, D. T., Linder, D. E., & McCall, M. A. (1989). Arousal and attribution: A response-facilitation alternative to misattribution and negative-reinforcement models. *Journal of Personality and Social Psychology, 57,* 261–270.

Allen, V. L. (1965). Situational factors in conformity. In L.Berkowitz (Ed.), *Advances in Experimental Social Psychology, 2,* 133–175.

Allen, V. L., & Levine, J. M. (1969). Consensus and conformity. *Journal of Experimental Social Psychology, 5,* 389–399.

Allen, V. L., & Levine, J. M. (1971). Social support and conformity: The role of independent assessment of reality. *Journal of Experimental Social Psychology, 7,* 48–58.

Allen-Arave, W., Gurven, M., & Hill, K. (2008). Reciprocal altruism, rather than kin selection, maintains nepotistic food transfers on an Ache reservation. *Evolution and Human Behavior, 29,* 305–318.

Alley, T. R. (1988). Social and applied aspects of perceiving faces. Hillsdale, NJ: Erlbaum.

Allport, F. H. (1924). *Social psychology.* Boston: Houghton Mifflin.

Allport, F. H., et al. (1953). The effects of segregation and the consequences of desegregation: A social science statement. *Minneapolis Law Review, 37,* 429–440.

Allport, G. W. (1954). *The nature of prejudice.* Reading, MA: Addison-Wesley.

Allport, G. W. (1985). The historical background of social psychology. In G. Lindzey & E. Aronson (Eds.), *Handbook of social psychology* (3rd ed., Vol. I, pp. 1–46). New York: Random House.

Allport, G. W., & Postman, L. J. (1947). *The psychology of rumor.* New York: Holt.

Altemeyer, R. (2004) Highly dominating, highly authoritarian personalities. *Journal of Social Psychology, 144,* 421–447.

Alterovitz, S. S.-R., & Mendelsohn, G. A. (2009). Partner preferences across the life span: Online dating by older adults. *Psychology and Aging, 24,* 513–517.

Altman, I. (1973). Reciprocity of interpersonal exchange. *Journal for Theory of Social Behavior, 3,* 249–261.

Altman, I., & Taylor, D. A. (1973). *Social penetration: The development of interpersonal relationships.* New York: Holt, Rinehart and Winston.

Alvidrez, A., & Weinstein, R. S. (1999). Early teacher perceptions and later student academic achievement. *Journal of Educational Psychology, 91,* 731–746.

Amabile, T. M. (1996). *Creativity in context.* New York: Westview.

Amabile, T. M., Hill, K. G., Hennessey, B. A., & Tighe, E. M. (1994). The work preference inventory: Assessing intrinsic and extrinsic motivation orientations. *Journal of Personality and Social Psychology, 66,* 950–967.

Amato, P. R. (1983). Helping behavior in urban and rural environments: Field studies based on a taxonomic organization of helping episodes. *Journal of Personality and Social Psychology, 45,* 571–586.

Ambady, N., & Rosenthal, R. (1993). Half a minute: Predicting teacher evaluations from thin slices of nonverbal behavior and physical attractiveness. *Journal of Personality and Social Psychology, 64,* 431–441.

Ames, D. R., Flynn, F. J., & Weber, E. U. (2004). It's the thought that counts: On perceiving how helpers decide to lend a hand. *Personality and Social Psychology Bulletin, 30,* 461–474.

Amodio, D. (2008). The social neuroscience of intergroup relations. *European Review of Social Psychology, 19,* 1–54.

Amodio, D. (2009). Intergroup anxiety effects on the control of racial stereotypes: A psychoneuroendocrine analysis. *Journal of Experimental Social Psychology, 45,* 60–67.

Amodio, D. M., & Devine, P. G. (2006). Stereotyping and evaluation in implicit race bias: Evidence for independent constructs and unique effects on behavior. *Journal of Personality and Social Psychology, 91,* 652–661.

Amodio, D. M., Kubota, J. T., Harmon-Jones, E., & Devine, P. G. (2007). Alternative mechanisms for regulating racial responses according to internal vs. external cues. *Social Cognitive and Affective Neuroscience, 1,* 1–26.

Andersen, S. M., & Chen, S. (2002). The relational self: An interpersonal social-cognitive theory. *Psychological Review, 109,* 619–645.

Anderson, C. A. (1989). Temperature and aggression: Ubiquitous effects of heat on occurrence of human violence. *Psychological Bulletin, 106,* 74–96.

Anderson, C. A. (2001). Heat and violence. *Current Directions in Psychological Science, 10,* 33–38.

Anderson, C. A., Anderson, K. B., & Deuser, W. E. (1996). Examining an affective framework: Weapon and temperature effects on aggressive thoughts, affect, and attitudes. *Personality and Social Psychology Bulletin, 22,* 366–376.

Anderson, C. A., Anderson, K. B., Dorr, N., DeNeve, K. M., & Flanagan, M. (2000). Temperature and aggression. In M. P. Zanna (Ed.), *Advances in experimental social psychology* (Vol. 32, pp. 63–133). San Diego, CA: Academic Press.

Anderson, C. A., & Bushman, B. J. (2002). The general aggression model: An integrated social-cognitive model of human aggression. *Annual Review of Psychology, 53,* 27–51.

Anderson, C. A., & Huesmann, L. R. (2007). Human aggression: A social-cognitive review. In M. A. Hogg & J. Cooper (Eds.), *The Sage handbook of social psychology* (pp. 259–287). London: Sage.

Anderson, C. A., Lepper, M. R., & Ross, L. (1980). Perseverance of social theories: The role of explanation in the persistence of discredited information. *Journal of Personality and Social Psychology, 39,* 1037–1049.

Anderson, C. A., & Sechler, E. S. (1986). Effects of explanation and counterexplanation on the development and use of social theories. *Journal of Personality and Social Psychology, 50,* 24–34.

Anderson, C. A., Shibuya, A., Ihori, N., Swing, E. L., Bushman, B. J., Sakamoto, A., Rothstein, H.R., & Saleem, M. (2010). Violent video game effects on aggression, empathy, and prosocial behavior in eastern and western countries: A meta-analytic review. *Psychological Bulletin, 136,* 151–173.

Anderson, J. L., Crawford, C. B., Nadeau, J., & Lindberg, T. (1992). Was the Duchess of Windsor right? A cross-cultural review of the socioecology of ideals of female body shape. *Ethology and Sociobiology, 13,* 197–227.

Anderson, N. H. (1965). Averaging versus adding as a stimulus combination rule in impression formation. *Journal of Experimental Social Psychology, 70,* 394–400.

Anderson, N. H. (1968). Likableness ratings of 555 personality-trait words. *Journal of Personality and Social Psychology, 9,* 272–279.

Anderson, N. H. (1981). *Foundations of information integration theory.* New York: Academic Press.

Anderson, N. H., & Hubert, S. (1963). Effects of concomitant verbal recall on order effects in personality impression formation. *Journal of Verbal Learning and Verbal Behavior, 2,* 379–391.

Anderson, U. S., Perea, E. F., Becker, D. V., Ackerman, J. M., Shapiro, J. R., Neuberg, S. L., & Kenrick, D. T. (2010). I only have eyes for you: Ovulation redirects attention (but not memory) to attractive men. *Journal of Experimental Social Psychology, 46,* 804–808.

Anik, L., Aknin, L. B., Norton, M. I., & Dunn, E. W. (2011). *Feeling good about giving: The benefits (and costs) of self-interested charitable behavior.* New York: Psychology Press.

Antonio, A. L., Chang, M. J., Hakuta, K., Kenny, D. A., Levin, S., & Milem, J. F. (2004). Effects of racial diversity on complex thinking in college students. *Psychological Science, 15,* 507–510.

Aramakis, V. B., Khamba, B. K., MacLeod, C. M., Poulos, C. X., & Zack, M. (2012). Alcohol selectively impairs negative self-relevant associations in young drinkers. *Journal of Psychopharmacology, 26,* 221–231.

Archer, J. (2000). Sex differences in aggression between heterosexual partners: A meta-analytic review. *Psychological Bulletin, 126,* 651–680.

Archer, J. (2004). Sex differences in aggression in real-world settings: A meta-analytic review. *Review of General Psychology, 8,* 291–322

Archer, J. (2005). Are women or men the more aggressive sex? In S. Fein, G. R. Goethals, & M. J. Sandstrom (Eds.), *Gender and aggression: Interdisciplinary perspectives.* Mahwah, NJ: Erlbaum.

Archer, J, (2006). Cross-cultural differences in physical aggression between partners: A social-role analysis. *Personality and Social Psychology Review, 10,* 133–153.

Archibald, F. S., Bartholomew, K., & Marx, R. (1995). Loneliness in early adolescence: A test of the cognitive discrepancy model of loneliness. *Personality and Social Psychology Bulletin, 21,* 296–301.

Arendt, H. (1963). *Eichmann in Jerusalem: A report on the banality of evil.* New York: Viking.

Arkin, R. M. (1981). Self-presentation styles. In J. T. Tedeschi (Ed.), *Impression management theory and social psychological research* (pp. 311–333). New York: Academic Press.

Armor, D. A., & Taylor, S. E. (1998). Situated optimism: Specific outcome expectancies and self-regulation. *Advances in Experimental Social Psychology, 30,* 309–379.

Armour, S. (1998, February 17). Office ethics: Teams make it hard to tattle. *USA Today,* p. 6B.

Aron, A., Aron, E. N., & Smollan, D. (1992). Inclusion of Other in the Self Scale and the structure of interpersonal closeness. *Journal of Personality and Social Psychology, 63,* 596–612.

Aron, A., Dutton, D. G., Aron, E. N., & Iverson, A. (1989).Experiences of falling in love. *Journal of Social and Personal Relationships, 6,* 243–257.

Aron, A., Norman, C. C., Aron, E. N., McKenna, C., & Heyman, R. E. (2000). Couples' shared participation in novel and arousing activities and experienced relationship quality. *Journal of Personality and Social Psychology, 78,* 273–284.

Aron, A., & Westbay, L. (1996). Dimensions of the prototype of love. *Journal of Personality and Social Psychology, 70,* 535–551.

Aronson, E. (1969). The theory of cognitive dissonance: A current perspective. *Advances in Experimental Social Psychology,* 4, 1-34.

Aronson, E. (1992). Stateways can change folkways. In R. M. Baird & S. E. Rosenbaum (Eds.), *Bigotry, prejudice, and hatred: Definitions, causes, and solutions* (pp. 185–201). Buffalo, NY: Prometheus.

Aronson, E. (1999). Dissonance, hypocrisy, and the self-concept. In E. Harmon-Jones & J. Mills (Eds.), *Cognitive dissonance: Progress on a pivotal theory in social psychology* (pp. 103–126). Washington, DC: American Psychological Association.

Aronson, E. (2004). Reducing hostility and building compassion: Lessons from the jigsaw classroom. In A. G. Miller (Ed.), *The social psychology of good and evil* (pp. 469–488). New York: Guilford.

Aronson, E., Blaney, N., Stephan, C., Sikes, J., & Snapp, M. (1978). *The jigsaw classroom.* Beverly Hills, CA: Sage.

Aronson, E., & Carlsmith, J. M. (1963). Effect of severity of threat on the devaluation of forbidden behavior. *Journal of Abnormal and Social Psychology, 66,* 584–588.

Aronson, E., & Carlsmith, J. M. (1968). Experimentation in social psychology. In G. Lindzey & E. Aronson (Eds.), *Handbook of social psychology* (Vol. 2, 2nd ed., pp. 1–79). Reading, MA: Addison-Wesley.

Aronson, E., & Cope, V. (1968). My enemy's enemy is my friend. *Journal of Personality and Social Psychology, 8,* 8–12.

Aronson, E., & Linder, D. (1965). Gain and loss of esteem as determinants of interpersonal attractiveness. *Journal of Experimental Social Psychology, 1,* 156–172.

Aronson, E., & Mills, J. (1959). The effect of severity of initiation on liking for a group. *Journal of Abnormal and Social Psychology, 59,* 177–181.

Aronson, J., & Inzlicht, M. (2004). The ups and downs of attributional ambiguity: Stereotype vulnerability and the academic self-knowledge of African American college students. *Psychological Science, 15,* 829–836.

Aronson, J., Lustina, M. J., Good, C., Keough, K., Steele, C. M., & Brown, J. (1999). When white men can't do math: Necessary and sufficient factors in stereotype threat. *Journal of Experimental Social Psychology, 35,* 29–46.

Arriaga, P., Esteves, F., Carneiro, P., & Monteiro, M. B. (2006). Violent computer games and their effects on state hostility and physiological arousal. *Aggressive Behavior, 32,* 358–371.

Arterberry, M. E., Cain, K. M., & Chopko, S. A. (2007). Collaborative problem solving in five-year-old children: Evidence of social facilitation and social loafing. *Educational Psychology, 27,* 577–596.

Asch, S. E. (1946). Forming impressions of personality. *Journal of Abnormal and Social Psychology, 41,* 258–290.

Asch, S. E. (1951). Effects of group pressure upon the modification and distortion of judgments. In H. Guetzkow (Ed.), *Groups, leadership, and men.* Pittsburgh, PA: Carnegie Press.

Asch, S. E. (1955, November). Opinions and social pressure. *Scientific American,* pp. 31–35.

Asch, S. E. (1956). Studies of independence and conformity: A minority of one against a unanimous majority. *Psychological Monographs, 70,* 416.

Asch, S. E., & Zukier, H. (1984). Thinking about persons. *Journal of Personality and Social Psychology, 46,* 1230–1240.

Ashton-James, C. E., Maddux, W. W., Galinsky, A. D., & Chartrand, T. L. (2009). Who I am depends on how I feel: The role of affect in the expression of culture. *Psychological Science, 20,* 340–346.

Askenasy, H. (1978). *Are we all Nazis?* Secaucus, NJ: Lyle Stuart.

Aspinwall, L. G., & Taylor, S. E. (1993). The effects of social comparison direction, threat, and self-esteem on affect, self-evaluation, and expected success. *Journal of Personality and Social Psychology, 64,* 708–722.

Aspinwall, L. G., & Taylor, S. E. (1992). Modeling cognitive adaptation: A longitudinal investigation of the impact of individual differences and coping on college adjustment and performance. *Journal of Personality and Social Psychology, 63,* 989–1003.

Aspinwall, L. G., & Taylor, S. E. (1997). A stitch in time: Self-regulation and proactive coping. *Psychological Bulletin, 121,* 417–436.

Auerbach, S. M., Kiesler, D. J., Strentz, T., Schmidt, J. A., & Serio, C. D. (1994). Interpersonal impacts and adjunctment to the stress of simulated captivity: An empirical test of the Stockholm Syndrome. *Journal of Social and Clinical Psychology, 13,* 207–221.

Axsom, D. (1989). Cognitive dissonance and behavior change in psychotherapy. *Journal of Experimental Social Psychology, 25,* 234–252.

Axsom, D., & Cooper, J. (1985). Cognitive dissonance and psychotherapy: The role of effort justification in inducing weight loss. *Journal of Experimental Social Psychology, 21,* 149–160.

Axtell, R. E. (1993). *Do's and taboos around the world* (3rd ed.). New York: John Wiley.

Ayduk, Ö., Gyurak, A., & Luerssen, A. (2008). Individual differences in the rejection-aggression link in the hot sauce paradigm: The case of rejection sensitivity. *Journal of Experimental Social Psychology, 44,* 775–782.

Babad, E. (2005). Guessing teachers differential treatment of high- and low-achievers from thin slices of their public lecturing behavior. *Journal of Nonverbal Behavior, 29,* 125–134.

Back, M. D., Penke, L., Schmukle, S. C., Sachse, K., Borkenau, P., & Asendorpf, J. B. (2011). Why mate choices are not as reciprocal as we assume: The role of personality, flirting and physical attractiveness. *European Journal of Personality, 25,* 120–132.

Bagemihl, B. (1999). *Biological exuberance: Animal homosexuality and natural diversity.* New York: St. Martin's Press.

Bagozzi, R. P., & Moore, D. J. (1994). Public service advertisements: Emotions and empathy guide prosocial behavior. *Journal of Marketing, 58,* 56–70.

Bahrick, H. P., Hall, L. K., & Berger, S. A. (1996). Accuracy and distortion in memory for high school grades. *Psychological Science, 7,* 265–271.

Bailey, A. A., & Hurd, P. L. (2005). Finger length ratio (2D:4D) correlates with physical aggression in men but not in women. *Biological Psychology, 68,* 215–222.

Bailey, C. A., & Ostrov, J. M. (2008). Differentiating forms and functions of aggression in emerging adults: Associations with hostile attribution biases and normative beliefs. *Journal of Youth and Adolescence, 37,* 713–722.

Bailey, D. S., & Taylor, S. P. (1991). Effects of alcohol and aggressive disposition on human physical aggression. *Journal of Research in Personality, 25,* 334–342.

Bailey, E. J. (2008). *Black America, body beautiful: How the African American image is changing fashion, fitness, and other industries.* Westport, CT: Praeger.

Bailey, J. M., Dunne, M. P., & Martin, N. G. (2000). Genetic and environmental influences on sexual orientation and its correlates in an Australian twin sample. *Journal of Personality and Social Psychology 78,* 524–536.

Bailey, J. M., & Pillard, R. C. (1991). A genetic study of male sexual orientation. *Archives of General Psychiatry, 48,* 1089–1096.

Bailey, J. M., Pillard, R. C., Neale, M. C., & Agyei, Y. (1993). Heritable factors influence sexual orientation in women. *Archives of General Psychiatry, 50,* 217–223.

Bailey, J. M., & Zucker, K. J. (1995). Childhood sex-typed behavior and sexual orientation: A conceptual analysis and quantitative review. *Development Psychology, 31,* 43–55.

Balcetis, E., & Dunning, D. (2006). See what you want to see: Motivational influences on visual perception. *Journal of Personality and Social Psychology, 91,* 612–625.

Balcetis, E., & Dunning, D. (2007). Cognitive dissonance and the perception of natural environments. *Psychological Science, 18,* 917–921.

Baldwin, A. S., Rothman, A. J., Hertel, A. W., Linde, J. A., Jeffery, R. W., Finch, E. A., & Lando, H. A. (2006). Specifying the determinants of the initiation and maintenance of behavior change: An examination of self-efficacy, satisfaction, and smoking cessation. *Health Psychology, 25,* 626–634.

Baldwin, M., & Fehr, B. (1995). On the instability of attachment style ratings. *Personal Relationships, 2,* 247–261.

Baldwin, M. W., & Sinclair, L. (1996). Self-esteem and "if . . . then" contingencies of interpersonal acceptance. *Journal of Personality and Social Psychology, 71,* 1130–1141.

Bales, R. F. (1958). Task roles and social roles in problem-solving groups. In E. E. Maccoby, T. M. Newcomb, & E. L. Hartley (Eds.), *Readings in social psychology* (3rd ed., pp. 437–447). New York: Holt.

Balliet, D., Mulder, L. B., & Van Lange, Paul A. M. (2011). Reward, punishment, and cooperation: A meta-analysis. *Psychological Bulletin, 137,* 594–615.

Balliet, D., Li, N.P., McFarlan, S.J., & Van Vugt, M. (2011). Sex differences in cooperation: A meta-analytic review of social dilemmas. Psychological Bulletin, 137, 881909

Banaji, M. R., & Steele, C. M. (1989). Alcohol and self-evaluation: Is a social cognition approach beneficial? *Social Cognition, 7,* 137–151.

Bandura, A. (1973). *Aggression: A social learning analysis.* Englewood Cliffs, NJ: Prentice-Hall.

Bandura, A. (1977). *Social learning theory.* Englewood Cliffs, NJ: Prentice-Hall.

Bandura, A. (1997). *Self-efficacy: The exercise of control.* New York: W. H. Freeman.

Bandura, A. (1999). A sociocognitive analysis of substance abuse: An agentic perspective. *Psychological Science, 10,* 214–218.

Bandura, A., Ross, R., & Ross, S. (1961). Transmission of aggression through imitation of aggressive models. *Journal of Abnormal and Social Psychology, 63,* 575–582.

Banuazizi, A., & Movahedi, S. (1975). Interpersonal dynamics in a simulated prison: A methodological analysis. *American Psychologist, 30,* 152–160.

Barash, D. P., & Lipton, J. E. (2011). *Payback: Why we retaliate, redirect aggression, and take revenge.* New York: Oxford University Press.

Baray, G., Postmes, T., & Jetten, J. (2009). When "I" equals "We": Exploring the relation between social and personal identity of extreme right-wing political party members. *British Journal of Social Psychology, 48,* 625–647.

Barber, N. (2006). Why is violent crime so common in the Americas? *Aggressive Behavior, 32,* 442–450.

Barden, J., & Petty, R. E. (2008). The mere perception of elaboration creates attitude certainty: Exploring the thoughtfulness heuristic. *Journal of Personality and Social Psychology, 95,* 489–509.

Bargh, J. A. (1997). The automaticity of everyday life. In R. S. Wyer (Ed.), *The automaticity of everyday life: Advances in social cognition* (Vol. 10, pp. 1–61). Mahwah, NJ: Erlbaum.

Bargh, J. A., Chaiken, S., Govender, R., & Pratto, F. (1992). The generality of the automatic attitude activation effect. *Journal of Personality and Social Psychology, 62,* 893–912.

Bargh, J. A., Chaiken, S., Raymond, P., & Hymes, C. (1996). The automatic evaluation effect: Unconditional automatic attitude activation with a pronunciation task. *Journal of Experimental Social Psychology, 31,* 104–128.

Bargh, J. A., & Chartrand, T. L. (1999). The unbearable automaticity of being. *American Psychologist, 54,* 462–479.

Bargh, J. A., Chen, M., & Burrows, L. (1996). Automaticity of social behavior: Direct effects of trait construct and stereotype activation on action. *Journal of Personality and Social Psychology, 71,* 230–244.

Bargh, J. A., Lombardi, W. J., & Higgins, E. T. (1988). Automaticity of chronically accessible constructs in person situation effects on person perception: It's just a matter of time. *Journal of Personality and Social Psychology, 55,* 599–605.

Bargh, J.A., & McKenna, K. Y. A. (2004). The internet and social life. *Annual Review of Psychology, 55,* 20.1–20.18.

Bargh, J. A., & Morsella, E. (2009). Unconscious behavioral guidance systems. In C. Agnew, D. Carlston, W. Graziano, & J. Kelly (Eds.), *Then a miracle occurs: Focusing on behavior in social psychological theory and research.* New York: Oxford University Press.

Bargh, J. A., & Pietromonaco, P. (1982). Automatic information processing and social perception: The influence of trait information presented outside of conscious awareness on impression formation. *Journal of Personality and Social Psychology, 43,* 437–449.

Barlett, C. P., & Anderson, C. A. (2011). Reappraising the situation and its impact on aggressive behavior. *Personality and Social Psychology Bulletin, 37,* 1564–1573.

Barlett, C. P., & Anderson, C. A. (2012). Direct and indirect relations between the big 5 personality traits and aggressive and violent behavior. *Personality and Individual Differences, 52,* 870-875.

Barlett, C. P., Vowels, C. L., & Saucier, D. A. (2008). Meta-analyses of the effects of media images on men's body-image concerns. *Journal of Social and Clinical Psychology, 27,* 279–310.

Barnes, R. D., Ickes, W., & Kidd, R. F. (1979). Effects of the perceived intentionality and stability of another's dependency on helping behavior. *Personality and Social Psychology Bulletin, 5,* 367–372.

Baron, A. S., & Banaji, M. R. (2006). The development of implicit attitudes: Evidence of race evaluations from ages 6 and 10 and adulthood. *Psychological Science, 17,* 53–58.

Baron, R. A. (1997). The sweet smell of ...helping: Effects of pleasant ambient fragrance on prosocial behavior in shopping malls. *Personality and Social Psychology Bulletin, 23,* 498–503.

Baron, R. A., & Ball, R. L. (1974). The aggression-inhibiting influence of nonhostile behavior. *Journal of Experimental Social Psychology, 10,* 23–33.

Baron, R. A., & Richardson, D. R. (1994). *Human aggression* (2nd ed.). New York: Plenum.

Baron, R. S. (1986). Distraction-conflict theory: Progress and problems. In L. Berkowitz (Ed.), *Advances in experimental social psychology* (Vol. 19, pp. 1–40). Orlando, FL: Academic Press.

Baron, R. S. (2005). So right it's wrong: Groupthink and the ubiquitous nature of polarized group decision making. In M. P. Zanna (Ed.), *Advances in experimental social psychology* (pp. 219–253). San Diego: Elsevier Academic Press.

Baron, R. S., Hoppe, S. I., Kao, C. F., Brunsman, B., Linneweh, B., & Rogers, D. (1996). Social corroboration and opinion extremity. *Journal of Experimental Social Psychology, 32,* 537–560.

Barreto, M., Ryan, M. K., & Schmitt, M. T. (2009). *The glass ceiling in the 21st century: Understanding barriers to gender equality.* Washington, DC: American Psychological Association.

Barrett, H. C., Todd, P. M., Miller, G. F., & Blythe, P. W. (2005). Accurate judgments of intention from motion cues alone: A cross-cultural study. *Evolution and Human Behavior, 26,* 313–331.

Barron, L. G., & Hebl, M. (2011). In M. A. Paludi, C. A. Paludi, and E. R. DeSouza (Eds.), *Sexual orientation: A protected and unprotected class.* Santa Barbara, CA: Praeger/ABC-CLIO.

Barron, L. G., Hebl, M., & Paludi, M. A. (2011). In M. A. Paludi, C. A. Paludi, and E. R. DeSouza (Eds.), *Reducing stigma about employees with HIV/AIDS: Workplace responses.* Santa Barbara, CA: Praeger/ABC-CLIO.

Bartholow, B. D., Dickter, C. L., & Sestir, M. A. (2006). Stereotype activation and control of race bias: Cognitive control of inhibition and its impairment by alcohol. *Journal of Personality and Social Psychology, 90,* 272–287.

Barthrop, R. W., Lazarus, L., Luckhurst, E., Kiloh, L. G., & Penny, R. (1977). Depressed lymphocyte function after bereavement. *Lancet, 1,* 834–839.

Bartsch, R. A., Burnett, T., Diller, T. R., & Rankin-Williams, E. E. (2000). Gender representation in television commercials: Updating an update. *Sex Roles, 43,* 735–743.

Bartsch, R. A., Judd, C. M., Louw, D. A., Park, B., & Ryan, C. S. (1997). Cross-national outgroup homogeneity: United States and South African stereotypes. *South African Journal of Psychology, 27,* 166–170.

Bashore, T. R., & Rapp, P. E. (1993). Are there alternatives to traditional polygraph procedures? *Psychological Bulletin, 113,* 3–22.

Bassili, J. N. (2003). The minority slowness effect: Subtle inhibitions in the expression of views not shared by others. *Journal of Personality and Social Psychology, 84,* 261–276.

Bassili, J. N., & Provencal, A. (1988). Perceiving minorities: A factor-analytic approach. *Personality and Social Psychology Bulletin, 14,* 5–15.

Bateson, M., Nettle, D., & Roberts, G. (2006). Cues of being watched enhance cooperation in a real-world setting. *Biology Letters*, 2, 412–414.

Batson, C. D. (1991). *The altruism question.* Hillsdale, NJ: Erlbaum.

Batson, C. D. (2009). In K. D. Markman, W. M. P. Klein, and J. A. Suhr (Eds.), *Two forms of perspective taking: Imagining how another feels and imagining how you would feel.* New York: Psychology Press.

Batson, C. D. (2012). In A. W. Kruglanski, and W. Stroebe (Eds.), *A history of prosocial behavior research.* New York: Psychology Press.

Batson, C. D., Ahmad, N., & Stocks, E. L. (2011). In D. Dunning (Ed.), *Four forms of prosocial motivation: Egoism, altruism, collectivism, and principlism.* New York: Psychology Press.

Batson, C. D., Cochran, P. J., Biederman, M. F., Blosser, J. L., Ryan, M. J., & Vogt, B. (1978). Failure to help when in a hurry: Callousness or conflict? *Personality and Social Psychology Bulletin, 4,* 97–101.

Batson, C. D., Eklund, J. H., Chermok, V. L., Hoyt, J. L., & Ortiz, B. G. (2007). An additional antecedent of empathic concern: Valuing the welfare of the person in need. *Journal of Personality and Social Psychology, 93,* 65–74.

Batson, C. D., O'Quin, K., Fultz, J., Vanderplas, M., & Isen, A. M. (1983). Influence of self-reported distress and empathy on egoistic versus altruistic motivation to help. *Journal of Personality and Social Psychology, 45,* 706–718.

Batson, C. D., & Powell, A. A. (2003). Altruism and prosocial behavior. In T. Millon & M. J. Lerner (Eds.), *Handbook of psychology: Personality and social psychology* (Vol. 5, pp. 463–484). New York: Wiley.

Bauer, I. M., & Baumeister, R. F. (2011). In K. D. Vohs, and R. F. Baumeister (Eds.), *Self-regulatory strength.* New York: Guilford Press.

Bauermeister, J. A., Johns, M. M., Pingel, E., Eisenberg, A., Santana, M. L., & Zimmerman, M. (2011). Measuring love: Sexual minority male youths ideal romantic characteristics. *Journal of LGBT Issues in Counseling, 5,* 102–121.

Baugh, S. G., & Graen, G. B. (1997). Effects of team gender and racial composition on perceptions of team performance in cross-functional teams. *Group and Organization Management, 22,* 366–383.

Baum, A. (Ed.). (1984). Social psychology and cigarette smoking [Special issue]. *Journal of Applied Social Psychology, 14*(3).

Baumeister, R. F. (1982). A self-presentational view of social phenomena. *Psychological Bulletin, 91,* 3–26.

Baumeister, R. F. (1984). Choking under pressure: Self-consciousness and paradoxical effects of incentives on skillful performance. *Journal of Personality and Social Psychology, 46,* 610–620.

Baumeister, R. F. (1991). *Escaping the self.* New York: Basic Books.

Baumeister, R. F. (2000). Gender differences in erotic plasticity: The female sex drive as socially flexible and responsive. *Psychological Bulletin, 126,* 347–374.

Baumeister, R. F., Catanese, K. R., & Vohs, K. D. (2001). Is there a gender difference in the strength of sex drive? Theoretical views, conceptual distinctions, and a review of relevant evidence. *Personality and Social Psychology Review, 5,* 242–273.

Baumeister, R. F., Chesner, S. P., Sanders, P. S., & Tice, D. M. (1988). Who's in charge here? Group leaders do lend help in emergencies. *Personality and Social Psychology Bulletin, 14,* 17–22.

Baumeister, R. F., & Leary, M. R. (1995). The need to belong: Desire for interpersonal attachments as a fundamental human motivation. *Psychological Bulletin, 117,* 497–529.

Baumeister, R. F., & Scher, S. J. (1988). Self-defeating behavior patterns among normal individuals: Review and analysis of common self-destructive tendencies. *Psychological Bulletin, 104,* 3–22.

Baumeister, R., Stillwell, A. M., & Hetherington, T. F. (1994). Guilt: An interpersonal approach. *Psychological Bulletin, 115,* 243–267.

Baumeister, R. F., & Tice, D. M. (1984). Role of self-presentation and choice in cognitive dissonance under forced compliance: Necessary or sufficient causes? *Journal of Personality and Social Psychology, 46,* 5–13.

Baumrind, D. (1997). Necessary distinctions. *Psychological Inquiry, 8,* 176–229.

Baxter, L. A. (1987). Self-disclosure and disengagement. In V. J. Derleg & J. H. Berg (Eds.), *Self-disclosure: Theory, research, and therapy* (pp. 155–174). New York: Plenum.

Bazerman, M. H., & Neale, M. A. (1992). *Negotiating rationally.* New York: Free Press.

Beal, D. J., Cohen, R. R., Burke, M. J., & McLendon, C. L. (2003, December). Cohesion and performance in groups: A meta-analytic clarification of construct relations. *Journal of Applied Psychology, 88,* 989–1004.

Beaman, A. L., Klentz, B., Diener, E., & Svanum, S. (1979). Objective self-awareness and transgression in children: A field study. *Journal of Personality and Social Psychology, 37,* 1835–1846.

Beaton, E. A., Schmidt, L. A., Schulkin, J., & Hall, G. B. (2010). Neural correlates of implicit processing of facial emotions in shy adults. *Personality and Individual Differences, 49,* 755–761.

Beckerman, S., & Valentine, P. (Eds.) (2002). Cultures of multiple fathers: The theory and practice of partible paternity in lowland South America. Gainesville, FL: University Press of Florida.

Beer, J. S., & Hughes, B. L. (2010). Neural systems of social comparison and the "above-average" effect. *NeuroImage, 49,* 2671–2679.

Bègue, L., Subra, B., Arvers, P., Muller, D., Bricout, V., & Zorman, M. (2009). A message in a bottle: Extrapharmacological effects of alcohol on aggression. *Journal of Experimental Social Psychology, 45,* 137–142.

Beidel, D. C., & Turner, S. M. (1998). Shy children, phobic adults: Nature and treatment of social phobia. Washington, DC: American Psychological Association.

Beilock, S. L., & Carr, T. H. (2001). On the fragility of skilled performance: What governs choking under pressure? *Journal of Experimental Psychology: General, 130,* 701–725.

Beitchman, J. H., Baldassarra, L., Mik, H., De Luca, V., King, N., Bender, D., Kennedy, J. L. (2006). Serotonin transporter polymorphisms and persistent, pervasive childhood aggression. *The American Journal of Psychiatry, 163,* 1103–1105.

Bell, J., Grekul, J., Lamba, N., Minas, C., & Harrell, W. A. (1995). The impact of cost on student helping behavior. *Journal of Social Psychology, 135,* 49–56.

Belmore, S. M. (1987). Determinants of attention during impression formation. *Journal of Experimental Psychology: Learning, Memory, and Cognition, 13,* 480–489.

Belsky, J. (1993). Etiology of child maltreatment: A developmental-ecological analysis. *Psychological Bulletin, 114,* 413–434.

Bem, D. J. (1965). An experimental analysis of self-persuasion. *Journal of Experimental Social Psychology, 1,* 199–218.

Bem, D. J. (1967). Self-perception: An alternative interpretation of cognitive dissonance phenomena. *Psychological Review, 74,* 183–200.

Bem, D. J. (1972). Self-perception theory. In L. Berkowitz (Ed.), *Advances in experimental social psychology* (Vol. 6, pp. 1–62). New York: Academic Press.

Bem, D. J. (1996). Exotic becomes erotic: A developmental theory of sexual orientation. *Psychological Review, 103,* 320–335.

Bem, D. J. (2000). Exotic becomes erotic: Interpreting the biological correlates of sexual orientation. *Archives of Sexual Behavior, 29,* 531–548.

Benjamin, L. T., & Simpson, J. A. (2009). The power of the situation: The impact of Milgram's obedience studies on personality and social psychology. *American Psychologist, 64,* 12–19.

Benjet, C., & Kazdin, A. E. (2003). Spanking children: The controversies, findings and new directions. *Clinical Psychology Review, 23,* 197–224.

Bennett, J. C. (1991). The irrationality of the catharsis theory of aggression as justification for educators' support of interscholastic football. *Perceptual and Motor Skills, 72,* 415–418.

Benson, P. L., Karabenick, S. A., & Lerner, R. M. (1976). Pretty pleases: The effects of physical attractiveness, race, and sex on receiving help. *Journal of Experimental Social Psychology, 12,* 409–415.

Benton, T. R., McDonnell, S., Ross, D. F., Thomas, W. N., & Bradshaw, E. (2007). In R. C. L. Lindsay, D. F. Ross, J. D. Read, and M. P. Toglia (Eds.), *Has eyewitness research penetrated the american legal system? A synthesis of case history, juror knowledge, and expert testimony.* Mahwah, NJ: Lawrence Erlbaum Associates Publishers.

Ben-Zeev, T., Fein, S., & Inzlicht, M. (2005). Arousal and stereotype threat. *Journal of Experimental Social Psychology, 41,* 174–181.

Berg, J. H., & McQuinn, R. D. (1986). Attraction and exchange in continuing and noncontinuing dating relationships. *Journal of Personality and Social Psychology, 50,* 942–952.

Berglas, S., & Jones, E. E. (1978). Drug choice as a self-handicapping strategy in response to noncontingent success. *Journal of Personality and Social Psychology, 36,* 405–417.

Berkowitz, L. (1968). Impulse, aggression, and the gun. *Psychology Today, 2*(4), pp. 18–22.

Berkowitz, L. (1972). Social norms, feelings, and other factors affecting helping and altruism. In L. Berkowitz (Ed.), *Advances in experimental social psychology.* (Vol. 6, pp. 63–108). New York: Academic Press.

Berkowitz, L. (1989). Frustration-aggression hypothesis: Examination and reformulation. *Psychological Bulletin, 106,* 59–73.

Berkowitz, L. (1993). *Aggression: Its causes, consequences, and control.* New York: McGraw-Hill.

Berkowitz, L. (1998). Affective aggression: The role of stress, pain, and negative affect. In R. G. Geen & E. Donnerstein (Eds.), *Human aggression: Theories, research, and implications for social policy* (pp. 49–72). San Diego: Academic Press.

Berkowitz, L. (2012). In Van Lange P. A. M., Kruglanski A. W. and Higgins E. T. (Eds.), *A cognitive-neoassociation theory of aggression.* Thousand Oaks, CA: Sage Publications Ltd.

Berkowitz, L., & Donnerstein, E. (1982). External validity is more than skin deep: Some answers to criticisms of laboratory experiments. *American Psychologist, 37,* 245–257.

Berkowitz, L., & LePage, A. (1967). Weapons as aggression-eliciting stimuli. *Journal of Personality and Social Psychology, 7,* 202–207.

Bermeitinger, C., Goelz, R., Johr, N., Neumann, M., Ecker, U., & Doerr, R. (2009). The hidden persuaders break into the tired brain. *Journal of Experimental Social Psychology, 45,* 320–326.

Bernhard, H., Fischbacher, U., & Fehr, E. (2006). Parochial altruism in humans. *Nature, 442,* 912–915.

Bernhardt, P. C., Dabbs, J. M., Fielden, J. A., & Lutter, C. D. (1998). Testosterone changes during vicarious experiences of winning and losing among fans at sporting events. *Physiology and Behavior, 65,* 59–62.

Bernieri, F. J., & Petty, K. N. (2011). The influence of handshakes on first impression accuracy. *Social Influence, 6,* 78-87.

Berns, G. S., Chappelow, J., Zink, C. F., Pagnoni, G., Martin-Skurski, M., & Richards, J. (2005). Neurobiological correlates of social conformity and independence during mental rotation. *Biological Psychiatry, 58,* 245–253.

Berry, D. S., & Zebrowitz-McArthur, L. (1986). Perceiving character in faces: The impact of age-related craniofacial changes in social perception. *Psychological Bulletin, 100,* 3–18.

Berry, J. W., Poortinga, Y. H., Segall, M. H., & Dasen, P. R. (1992). *Cross-cultural psychology: Research and application.* Cambridge, UK: Cambridge University Press.

Berscheid, E. (1966). Opinion change and communicator-communicatee similarity and dissimilarity. *Journal of Personality and Social Psychology, 4,* 670–680.

Berscheid, E. (2010). Love in the fourth dimension. *Annual Review of Psychology, 61,* 1–25.

Berscheid, E., Dion, K., Walster, E., & Walster, G. W. (1971). Physical attractiveness and dating choice: A test of the matching hypothesis. *Journal of Experimental Social Psychology, 7,* 173–189.

Berscheid, E., & Meyers, S. A. (1996). A social categorical approach to a question about love. *Personal Relationships, 3,* 19–43.

Berscheid, E., & Regan, P. (2004). *The psychology of interpersonal relationships.* Upper Saddle River, NJ: Prentice-Hall.

Berscheid, E., & Regan, P. C. (2005). *The psychology of interpersonal relationships.* Upper Saddle River, NJ: Prentice Hall.

Berscheid, E., & Reis, H. T. (1998). Attraction and close relationships. In D. Gilbert, S. Fiske, & G. Lindzey (Eds.), *Handbook of social psychology* (4th ed.). New York: McGraw-Hill.

Berscheid, E., Snyder, M., & Omoto, A. M. (1989). The relationship closeness inventory: Assessing the closeness of interpersonal relationships. *Journal of Personality and Social Psychology, 57,* 792–807.

Berscheid, E., & Walster, E. (1974). A little bit about love. In T. Huston (Ed.), *Foundations of interpersonal attraction* (pp. 355–381). New York: Academic Press.

Berscheid, E., Walster, E., & Campbell, R. (1972). *Grow old along with me.* Unpublished manuscript, Department of Psychology, University of Minnesota.

Bessenoff, & Gayle R. (2006). Can the media affect us? Social comparison, self-discrepancy, and the thin ideal. *Psychology of Women Quarterly, 30,* 239–251.

Bettencourt, B. A., & Dorr, N. (1998). Cooperative interaction and intergroup bias: Effects of numerical representation and cross-cut role assignment. *Personality and Social Psychology Bulletin, 24,* 1276–1293.

Bettencourt, B. A., Talley, A., Benjamin, A. J., & Valentine, J. (2006). Personality and aggressive behavior under provoking and neutral conditions: A meta-analytic review. *Psychological Bulletin, 132,* 751–777.

Bhatt, S., Mbwana, J., Adeyemo, A., Sawyer, A., Hailu, A., & VanMeter, J. (2009). Lying about facial recognition: An fMRI study. *Brain and Cognition, 69,* 382–390.

Bickart, K. C., Wright, C. I., Dautoff, R. J., Dickerson, B. C., & Barrett, L. F. (2011). Amygdala volume and social network size in humans. *Nature Neuroscience, 14,* 163–164.

Bickman, L. (1974). The social power of a uniform. *Journal of Applied Social Psychology, 4,* 47–61.

Bijvank, M. N., Konijn, E. A., & Bushman, B. J. (2012). "We don't need no education": Video game preferences, video game motivations, and aggressiveness among adolescent boys of different educational ability levels. *Journal of Adolescence, 35,* 153–162.

Bijvank, M. N., Konijn, E. A., Bushman, B. J., & Roelofsma, P. H. M. P. (2009). Age and violent-content labels make video games forbidden fruits for youth. *Pediatrics, 123,* 870–876.

Birkett, M., Espelage, D. L., & Koenig, B. (2009). LGB and questioning students in schools: The moderating effects of homophobic bullying and school climate on negative outcomes. *Journal of Youth and Adolescence, 38,* 989–1000.

Bishara, A. J., & Payne, B. K. (2009). Multinomial process tree models of control and automaticity in weapon misidentification. *Journal of Experimental Social Psychology, 45,* 524–534.

Bizer, G. Y., Tormala, Z. L., Rucker, D. D., & Petty, R. E. (2006). Memory-based versus on-line processing: Implications for attitude strength. *Journal of Experimental Social Psychology, 42,* 646–653.

Bizumic, B., Reynolds, K. J., Turner, J. C., Bromhead, D., & Subasic, E. (2009). The role of the group in individual functioning: School identification and the psychological well-being of staff and students. *Applied Psychology: An International Review, 58,* 171–192.

Blaine, B., Crocker, J., & Major, B. (1995). The unintended negative consequences of sympathy for the stigmatized. *Journal of Applied Social Psychology, 25,* 889–905.

Blair, I. V. (2001). Implicit stereotypes and prejudice. In G. B. Moskowitz (Ed.), *Cognitive social psychology: On the future of social cognition* (pp. 359–374). Mahwah, NJ: Erlbaum.

Blair, I. V. (2002). The malleability of automatic stereotypes and prejudice. *Personality and Social Psychology Review, 6,* 242–261.

Blanton, H., Jaccard, J., Klick, J., Mellers, B., Mitchell, G., & Tetlock, P. E. (2009). Strong claims and weak evidence: Reassessing the predictive validity of the IAT. *Journal of Applied Psychology, 94,* 567–582.

Blascovich, J., Mendes, W. B., Hunter, S. B., & Salomon, K. (1999). Social "facilitation" as challenge and threat. *Journal of Personality and Social Psychology, 77,* 68–77.

Blascovich, J., Spencer, S. J., Quinn, D., & Steele, C. (2001). African Americans and high blood pressure: The role of stereotype threat. *Psychological Science, 12,* 225–229.

Blass, T. (1991). Understanding behavior in the Milgram obedience experiment: The role of personality, situations, and their interactions. *Journal of Personality and Social Psychology, 60,* 398–413.

Blass, T. (1992). The social psychology of Stanley Milgram. *Advances in Experimental Social Psychology, 25,* 227–329.

Blass, T. (1999). The Milgram paradigm after 35 years: Some things we now know about obedience to authority. *Journal of Applied Social Psychology, 25,* 955–978.

Blass, T. (Ed.) (2000). *Obedience to authority: Current perspectives on the Milgram paradigm.* Mahwah, NJ: Erlbaum.

Blass, T. (2004). *The man who shocked the world.* New York: Basic Books.

Blass, T. (2009). From New Haven to Santa Clara: A historical perspective on the Milgram obedience experiments. *American Psychologist, 64,* 37–45.

Bless, H., Schwarz, N., & Wieland, R. (1996). Mood and the impact of category membership and individuating information. *European Journal of Social Psychology, 26,* 935–959.

Bluemke, M., & Friese, M. (2008). Reliability and validity of the Single-Target IAT (ST-IAT): Assessing automatic affect towards multiple attitude objects. *European Journal of Social Psychology, 38,* 977–997.

Bochner, S. (1994). Cross-cultural differences in the self-concept: A test of Hofstede's individualism/collectivism distinction. *Journal of Cross Cultural Psychology, 25,* 273–283.

Bochner, S., & Insko, C. A. (1966). Communicator discrepancy, source credibility, and opinion change. *Journal of Personality and Social Psychology, 4,* 614–621.

Boddy, C. (2012). The nominal group technique: An aid to brainstorming ideas in research. *Qualitative Market Research: An International Journal, 15,* 6–18.

Bodenhausen, G. V. (1990). Stereotypes as judgmental heuristics: Evidence of circadian variations in discrimination. *Psychological Science, 1,* 319–322.

Bodenhausen, G. V., & Hugenberg, K. (2009). Attention, perception, and social cognition. In F. Strack & J. Förster (Eds.), *Social cognition: The basis of human interaction* (pp. 1–22). Philadelphia: Psychology Press.

Bodenhausen, G. V., & Macrae, C. N. (1998). Stereotype activation and inhibition. In R. S. Wyer, Jr. (Ed.), *Stereotype activation and inhibition: Advances in Social Cognition* (Vol. 11, pp. 1–52). Mahwah, NJ: Erlbaum.

Bodenhausen, G. V., Macrae, C. N., & Hugenberg, K. (2003).Social cognition. In T. Millon & M. J. Lerner (Eds.), *Handbook of psychology: Personality and social psychology* (Vol. 5., pp. 257–282). New York: Wiley.

Bogaert, S., Boone, C., & Declerck, C. (2008). Social value orientation and cooperation in social dilemmas: A review and conceptual model. *British Journal of Social Psychology, 47,* 453–480.

Bogart, L. M., & Helgeson, V. S. (2000). Social comparisons among women with breast cancer: A longitudinal investigation. *Journal of Applied Social Psychology, 30,* 547–575.

Boldero, J., & Francis, J. (2000). The relation between self-discrepancies and emotion: The moderating roles of self-guide importance, location relevance, and social self-domain centrality. *Journal of Personality and Social Psychology, 78,* 38–52.

Boldizar, J. P., Perry, D. G., & Perry, L. (1989). Outcome values and aggression. *Child Development, 60,* 571–579.

Bolger, N., DeLongis, A., Kessler, R. C., & Schilling, E. A. (1989). Effects of daily stress and negative mood. *Journal of Personality and Social Psychology, 57,* 808–818.

Boll, S., Gamer, M., Kalisch, R., & Büchel, C. (2011). Processing of facial expressions and their significance for the observer in subregions of the human amygdala. *NeuroImage, 56,* 299–306.

Bond, C. F., Jr., & DePaulo, B. M. (2006). Accuracy of deception judgments. *Personality and Social Psychology Review, 10,* 214–234.

Bond, C. F., Jr., & DePaulo, B. M. (2008). Individual differences in judging deception: Accuracy and bias. *Psychological Bulletin, 134,* 477–492.

Bond, C. F., Jr., & Titus, L. J. (1983). Social facilitation: A meta-analysis of 241 studies. *Psychological Bulletin, 94,* 265–292.

Bond, R., & Smith, P. B. (1996). Culture and conformity: A meta-analysis of studies using Asch's (1952b, 1956) line judgment task. *Psychological Bulletin, 119,* 111–137.

Boninger, D. S., Brock, T. C., Cook, T. D., Gruder, C. L., & Romer, D. (1990). Discovery of reliable attitude change persistence resulting from a transmitter tuning set. *Psychological Science, 1,* 268–271.

Boninger, D. S., Krosnick, J. A., & Berent, M. K. (1995). Origins of attitude importance: Self-interest, social identification, and value relevance. *Journal of Personality and Social Psychology, 68,* 61–80.

Bonner, B. L., & Baumann, M. R. (2012). Leveraging member expertise to improve knowledge transfer and demonstrability in groups. *Journal of Personality and Social Psychology, 102,* 337–350.

Bonner, B. L., & Baumann, M. R. (2008). Informational intra-group influence: The effects of time pressure and group size. *European Journal of Social Psychology, 38,* 46–66.

Bonta, B. D. (1997). Cooperation and competition in peaceful societies. *Psychological Bulletin, 121,* 299–320.

Book, A. S., Starzyk, K. B., & Quinsey, V. L. (2001). The relationship between testosterone and aggression: A meta-analysis. *Aggression and Violent Behavior, 6,* 579–599.

Borduin, C. M., Schaeffer, C. M., & Heiblum, N. (2009). A randomized clinical trial of multisystemic therapy with juvenile sexual offenders: Effects on youth social ecology and criminal activity. *Journal of Consulting and Clinical Psychology, 77,* 26–37.

Borgida, E., & Campbell, B. (1982). Belief relevance and attitude-behavior consistency: The moderating role of personal experience. *Journal of Personality and Social Psychology, 42,* 239–247.

Borgida, E., & Fiske, S. T. (Eds.). (2007). Beyond common sense: Psychological science in the courtroom. New York: Wiley-Blackwell.

Borkenau, P., Mauer, N., Riemann, R., Spinath, F. M., & Angleitner, A. (2004). Thin slices of behavior as cues of personality and intelligence. *Journal of Personality and Social Psychology, 86,* 599–614.

Bornstein, R. F. (1989). Exposure and affect: Overview and meta-analysis of research, 1968–1987. *Psychological Bulletin, 106,* 265–289.

Bornstein, R. F. (1994). Dependency as a social cue: A meta-analytic review of research on the dependency-helping relationship. *Journal of Research in Personality, 28,* 182–213.

Bornstein, R. F., & D'Agostino, P. R. (1992). Stimulus recognition and the mere exposure effect. *Journal of Personality and Social Psychology, 63,* 545–552.

Borntrager, C., Davis, J. L., Bernstein, A., & Gorman, H. (2009). A cross-national perspective on bullying. *Child and Youth Care Forum, 38,* 121–134.

Bosacki, S., Innerd, W., & Towson, S. (1997). Field independence–dependence and self-esteem in preadolescents: does gender make a difference? *Journal of Youth and Adolescence, 26,* 1573–6601.

Bosson, J. K., Pinel, E. C., & Thompson, J. K. (2008). The affective consequences of minimizing women's body image concerns. *Psychology of Women Quarterly, 32,* 257–266.

Boucher, H. C., Peng, K., Shi, J., & Wang, L. (2009). Culture and implicit self-esteem: Chinese are 'good' and 'bad' at the same time. *Journal of Cross-Cultural Psychology, 40,* 24–45.

Bowlby, J. (1988). *A secure base.* New York: Basic Books.

Boxer, P., Huesmann, L. R., Bushman, B. J., O'Brien, M., & Moceri, D. (2009). The role of violent media preference in cumulative developmental risk for violence and general aggression. *Journal of Youth and Adolescence, 38,* 417–428.

Boysen, S. T., & Himes, G. T. (1999). Current issues and emerging theories in animal cognition. *Annual Review of Psychology 50,* 683–705.

Bradbury, T. N. (Ed.) (1998). *The developmental course of marital dysfunction.* New York: Cambridge University Press.

Bradbury, T. N., & Fincham, F. D. (1992). Attributions and behavior in marital interaction. *Journal of Personality and Social Psychology, 63,* 613–628.

Brader, T. (2006). Affective intelligence and beyond: Next steps in research on emotion in politics. *Political Communication Report, 16*(3), 1–6.

Brader, T. (2011). The political relevance of emotions: "Reassessing" revisited. *Political Psychology, 32,* 337–346.

Bradfield, A. L., Wells, G. L., & Olson, E. A. (2002). The damaging effect of confirming feedback on the relation between eyewitness certainty and identification accuracy. *Journal of Applied Psychology, 87,* 112–120.

Bray, R. M., Struckman-Johnson, C., Osborne, M., McFarlane, J., & Scott, J. (1978). The effects of defendant status on decisions of student and community juries. *Social Psychology, 41,* 256–260.

Brean, H. (1958, March 31). What hidden sell is all about. *Life,* pp. 104–114.

Brendgen, M., Dionne, G., Girard, A., Boivin, M., Vitaro, F., & Pérusse, D. (2005). Examining genetic and environmental effects on social aggression: A study of 6-year-old twins. *Child Development, 76,* 930–946.

Brendgen, M., Boivin, M., Dionne, G., Barker, E. D., Vitaro, F., Girard, A., Trembley, R., & Pérusse, D. (2011). Gene–environment processes linking aggression, peer victimization, and the teacher–child relationship. *Child Development, 82,* 2021–2036.

Brehm, J. W. (1956). Post-decision changes in desirability of alternatives. *Journal of Abnormal and Social Psychology, 52,* 384–389.

Brehm, S. S., & Brehm, J. W. (1981). *Psychological reactance: A theory of freedom and control.* New York: Academic Press.

Brehm, S. S., Miller R., Perlman, D., & Campbell, S. M. (2001). *Intimate relationships* (3rd ed.). New York: McGraw-Hill.

Bremner, J. G. (2002). The nature of imitation by infants. *Infant Behavior & Development, 25,* 65–67.

Bressan, P., & Dal Martello, M. F. (2002). *Talis Pater, Talis Filius:* Perceived resemblance and the belief in genetic relatedness. *Psychological Science, 13,* 213–218.

Brett, J. M., Shapiro, D. L., & Lytle, A. L. (1998). Breaking the bonds of reciprocity in negotiations. *Academy of Management Journal, 41,* 410–424.

Brewer, M. B. (2003). Optimal distinctiveness, social identity, and the self. In M. R. Leary & J. P. Tangney (Eds.), *Handbook of self and identity* (pp. 480–491). New York: Guilford.

Brewer, M. B. (2007). The importance of being we: Human nature and intergroup relations. *American Psychologist, 62,* 728–738.

Brewer, M. B., & Caporael, L. R. (2006). An evolutionary perspective on social identity: Revisiting groups. In M. Schaller (Ed.), *Evolution and social psychology* (pp. 143–161). Madison, CT: Psychosocial Press.

Brewer, M. B., & Feinstein, A. S. H. (1999). Dual processes in the cognitive representation of persons and social categories. In S. Chaiken & Y. Trope (Eds.), *Dual-process theories in social psychology* (pp. 255–270). New York: Guilford.

Brewer, M. B., & Gaertner, S. L. (2004). Toward reduction of prejudice: Intergroup contact and social categorization. In M. B. Brewer & M. Hewstone (Eds.), *Self and social identity* (pp. 298–318). Malden, MA: Blackwell.

Brewer, M. B., & Pickett, C. L. (1999). Distinctiveness motives as a source of the social self. In T. R. Tyler & R. M. Kramer (Eds.), *The psychology of the social self: Applied social research* (pp. 71–87). Mahwah, NJ: Erlbaum.

Brickman, P., Coates, D., & Janoff-Bulman, R. J. (1978). Lottery winners and accident victims: Is happiness relative? *Journal of Personality and Social Psychology, 36,* 917–927.

Briñol, P., Petty, R. E., & Wagner, B. (2009). Body posture effects on self-evaluation: A self-validation approach. *European Journal of Social Psychology, 39,* 1053–1064.

Brockner, J. (1983). Low self-esteem and behavioral plasticity: Some implications. In L. Wheeler & P. Shaver (Eds.), *Review of personality and social psychology* (Vol. 4, pp. 237–271). Beverly Hills, CA: Sage.

Brodish, A. B., Brazy, P. C., & Devine, P. G. (2008). More eyes on the prize: Variability in White Americans' perceptions of progress toward racial equality. *Personality and Social Psychology Bulletin, 34,* 513–527.

Brodish, A. B., & Devine, P. G. (2009). The role of performance-avoidance goals and worry in mediating the relationship between stereotype threat and performance. *Journal of Experimental Social Psychology, 45,* 180–185.

Bronfenbrenner, U. (1961). The mirror-image in Soviet-American relations. *Journal of Social Issues, 17,* 45–56.

Brooks, R., & Meltzoff, A. N. (2002). The importance of eyes: How infants interpret adult looking behavior. *Developmental Psychology, 38,* 958–966.

Brown, E., Deffenbacher, K., & Sturgill, W. (1977). Memory for faces and the circumstances of encounter. *Journal of Applied Psychology, 62,* 311–318.

Brown, J. D., & Dutton, K. A. (1995). The thrill of victory, the complexity of defeat: Self-esteem and people's emotional reactions to success and failure. *Journal of Personality and Social Psychology, 68,* 712–722.

Brown, J. M. (2003). Eyewitness memory for arousing events: Putting things into context. *Applied Cognitive Psychology, 17,* 93–106.

Brown, R. (1986). *Social psychology* (2nd ed.). New York: Free Press.

Brown, R., & Kulik, J. (1977). Flashbulb memories. *Cognition, 5,* 73–99.

Brown, R. P., Osterman, L. L., & Barnes, C. D. (2009). School violence and the culture of honor. *Psychological Science, 20,* 1400–1405.

Brown, W. A. (1998, January). The placebo effect. *Scientific American,* pp. 90–95.

Bruch, M. A., Gorsky, J. M., Collins, T. M., & Berger, P. A. (1989). Shyness and sociability examined: A multicomponent analysis. *Journal of Personality and Social Psychology, 57,* 904–915.

Brummert Lennings, H. I., & Warburton, W. A. (2011). The effect of auditory versus visual violent media exposure on aggressive behaviour: The role of song lyrics, video clips and musical tone. *Journal of Experimental Social Psychology, 47,* 794–799.

Bruner, J. S., & Potter, M. C. (1964). Interference in visual recognition. *Science, 144,* 424–425.

Bruner, J. S., & Tagiuri, R. (1954). Person perception. In G. Lindzey (Ed.), *Handbook of social psychology* (Vol. 2, pp. 634–654). Reading, MA: Addison-Wesley.

Bryan, J. H., & Test, M. A. (1967). Models and helping: Naturalistic studies in aiding behavior. *Journal of Personality and Social Psychology, 6,* 400–407.

Buckholtz, J. W., Meyer-Lindenberg, A. (2008). MAOA and the neurogenetic architecture of human aggression. *Trends in Neurosciences, 31,* 120–129.

Buckhout, R. (1974, December). Eyewitness testimony. *Scientific American,* pp. 23–31.

Buhrmester, M. D., Blanton, H., & Swann, W. B. (2011). Implicit self-esteem: Nature, measurement, and a new way forward. *Journal of Personality and Social Psychology, 100,* 365–385.

Bukowski, W. M., Laursen, B., & Hoza, B. (2010). The snowball effect: Friendship moderates escalations in depressed affect among avoidant and excluded children. *Development and Psychopathology, 22,* 749–757.

Bulatao, E. Q., & VandenBos, G. R. (1996). Workplace violence: Its scope and the issues. In G. R. VandenBos & E. Q. Bulatao (Eds.), *Violence on the job: Identifying risks and developing solutions* (pp. 1–23). Washington, DC: American Psychological Association.

Burger, J. M. (1986). Increasing compliance by improving the deal: The that's-not-all technique. *Journal of Personality and Social Psychology, 51,* 277–283.

Burger, J. M. (1999). The foot-in-the-door compliance procedure: A multiple-process analysis and review. *Personality and Social Psychology Review, 3,* 303–325.

Burger, J. M. (2009). Replicating Milgram: Would people still obey today? *American Psychologist, 64,* 1–11.

Burger, J. M., & Caldwell, D. F. (2003). The effects of monetary incentives and labeling on the foot-in-the-door effect: Evidence for a self-perception process. *Basic and Applied Social Psychology, 25,* 235–241.

Burger, J. M., & Cornelius, T. (2003). Raising the price of agreement: Public commitment and the low-ball compliance procedure. *Journal of Applied Social Psychology, 33,* 923–934.

Burger, J. M., Horita, M., Kinoshita, L., Roberts, K., & Vera, C. (1997). Effects of time on the norm of reciprocity. *Basic and Applied Social Psychology, 19,* 91–100.

Burger, J. M., & Petty, R. E. (1981). The low-ball compliance technique: Task or person commitment? *Journal of Personality and Social Psychology, 40,* 492–500.

Burke, T. M., & Marion, S. B. (2012). Alibi witnesses. In B. L. Cutler (Ed.), *Conviction of the innocent: Lessons from psychological research.* Washington, DC: American Psychological Association, 239256.

Burke, T. M., Turtle, J. W., & Olson, E. (2006). A psychological approach to the study of alibis. In M. Toglia, J. D. Read, D. Ross, & R. C. L. Lindsay (Eds.), *The Handbook of Eyewitness Psychology.* Mahwah, NJ: Erlbaum.

Burnstein, E., & Schul, Y. (1982). The informational basis of social judgments: The operations in forming an impression of another person. *Journal of Experimental Social Psychology, 18,* 217–234.

Burt, M. C. (1980). Cultural myths and supports for rape. *Journal of Personality and Social Psychology, 38,* 217–230.

Bushman, B. J. (1988). The effects of apparel on compliance: A field experiment with a female authority figure. *Personality and Social Psychology Bulletin, 14,* 459–467.

Bushman, B. J. (1996). Individual differences in the extent and development of aggressive cognitive-associative networks. *Personality and Social Psychology Bulletin, 22,* 811–819.

Bushman, B. J. (1998). Priming effects of violent media on the accessibility of aggressive constructs in memory. *Personality and Social Psychology Bulletin, 24,* 537–545.

Bushman, B. J. (2002). Does venting anger feed or extinguish the flame? Catharsis, rumination, distraction, anger, and aggressive responding. *Personality and Social Psychology Bulletin, 28,* 724–731.

Bushman, B. J., & Anderson, C. A. (2009). Comfortably numb: Desensitizing effects of violent media on helping others. *Psychological Science, 20,* 273–277.

Bushman, B. J., Anderson, C. A., Freedman, Jonathan L., & Nier, J. A. (2007). *Issue 18: Does media violence cause aggression?* New York: McGraw-Hill.

Bushman, B. J., & Cooper, H. M. (1990). Effects of alcohol on human aggression: An integrative research review. *Psychological Bulletin, 107,* 341–354.

Bushman, B. J., Giancola, P. R., Parrott, D. J., & Roth, R. M. (2012). Failure to consider future consequences increases the effects of alcohol on aggression. *Journal of Experimental Social Psychology, 48,* 591–595.

Bushman, B. J., & Huesmann, L. R. (2001). Effects of televised violence on aggression. In D. G. Singer & J. L. Singer (Eds.), *Handbook of children and the media* (pp. 223–254). Thousand Oaks, CA: Sage.

Bushman, B. J., Wang, M. C., & Anderson, C. A. (2005). Is the curve relating temperature to aggression linear or curvilinear? A response to Bell (2005) and to Cohn and Rotton (2005). *Journal of Personality and Social Psychology, 89,* 74–77.

Buss, A. H. (1980). *Self-consciousness and social anxiety.* San Francisco: Freeman.

Buss, D. M. (1989). Sex differences in human mate preferences: Evolutionary hypotheses tested in 37 cultures. *Behavioral and Brain Sciences, 12,* 1–14.

Buss, D. M. (2000). *The dangerous passion: Why jealousy is as necessary as love and sex.* New York: Free Press.

Buss, D. M. (2003). *The evolution of desire: Strategies of human mating* (rev. ed.). New York: Basic Books.

Buss, D. M. (2004). *Evolutionary psychology: The new science of the mind* (2nd ed.). Boston: Allyn & Bacon.

Buss, D. M. (2007). The evolution of human mating strategies: Consequences for conflict and cooperation. In S. W. Gangestad & J. A. Simpson (Eds.), *The evolution of mind: Fundamental questions and controversies.* New York: Guilford.

Buss, D. M., Larsen, R. J., Westen, D., & Semmelroth, J. (1992). Sex differences in jealousy: Evolution, physiology, and psychology. *Psychological Science, 3,* 251–255.

Buss, D. M., & Schmitt, D. P. (1993). Sexual strategies theory: An evolutionary perspective on human mating. *Psychological Review, 100,* 204–232.

Buss, D. M., & Shackelford, T. K. (1997). From vigilance to violence: Mate retention tactics in married couples. *Journal of Personality and Social Psychology, 72,* 346–361.

Buunk, A. P., Solano, A. C., Zurriaga, R., & González, P. (2011). Gender differences in the jealousy-evoking effect of rival characteristics: A study in Spain and Argentina. *Journal of Cross-Cultural Psychology, 42,* 323–339.

Byrne, D. (1971). *The attraction paradigm.* New York: Academic Press.

Byrne, D. (1997). An overview (and underview) of research and theory within the attraction paradigm. *Journal of Social and Personal Relationships, 14,* 417–431.

Byrne, D., & Clore, G. L. (1970). A reinforcement model of evaluative processes. *Personality: An International Journal, 1,* 103–128.

Byrne, D., Clore, G. L., & Smeaton, G. (1986). The attraction hypothesis: Do similar attitudes affect anything? *Journal of Personality and Social Psychology, 51,* 1167–1170.

Byrne, R. M. J., & McEleney, A. (2000). Counterfactual thinking about actions and failures to act. *Journal of Experimental Psychology: Learning Memory, and Cognition, 26,* 1318–1331.

Byrne, S. (2009). Media literacy interventions: What makes them boom or boomerang? *Communication Education, 58,* 1–14.

Cacioppo, J. T., Crites, S. L., Berntson, G. G., & Coles, M. G. H. (1993). If attitudes affect how stimuli are processed, should they not affect the event-related brain potential? *Psychological Science, 4,* 108–112.

Cacioppo, J. T., Gardner, W. L., & Bernston, G. G. (1997). Beyond bipolar conceptualizations and measures: The case of attitudes and evaluative space. *Personality and Social Psychology Review, 1,* 3–25.

Cacioppo, J. T., & Petty, R. E. (1981). Electromyograms as measures of extent and affectivity of information processing. *American Psychologist, 36,* 441–456.

Cacioppo, J. T., & Petty, R. E. (1982). The need for cognition. *Journal of Personality and Social Psychology, 42,* 116–131.

Cacioppo, J. T., Petty, R. E., Feinstein, J. A., & Jarvis, W. B. G. (1996). Dispositional differences in cognitive motivation: The life and times of individuals varying in need for cognition. *Psychological Bulletin, 119,* 197–253.

Cacioppo, J. T., Petty, R. E., Losch, M. E., & Kim, H. S. (1986). Electromyographic activity over facial muscle regions can differentiate the valence and intensity of affective reactions. *Journal of Personality and Social Psychology, 50,* 260–268.

Cacioppo, J. T., Petty, R. E., & Morris, K. (1983). Effects of need for cognition on message evaluation, recall, and persuasion. *Journal of Personality and Social Psychology, 45,* 805–818.

Cacioppo, J. T., Priester, J. R., & Bernston, G. G. (1993). Rudimentary determinants of attitudes. II. Arm flexion and extension have differential effects on attitudes. *Journal of Personality and Social Psychology, 65,* 5–17.

Cameron, J., & Pierce, W. D. (1994). Reinforcement, reward, and intrinsic motivation: A meta-analysis. *Review of Educational Research, 64,* 363–423.

Campbell, A. (1999). Staying alive: Evolution, culture, and women's intrasexual aggression. *Behavioral and Brain Sciences, 22,* 203–252.

Campbell, L., Simpson, J. A., Boldry, J., & Kashy, D. A. (2005). Perceptions of conflict and support in romantic relationships: The role of attachment anxiety. *Journal of Personality and Social Psychology, 88,* 510–531.

Canadian Automobile Association (CAA). *Bad driving habits on the rise, Canadians tell CAA,* July 19, 2011.

Canadian Community Health Survey (CCHS): Mental Health and Well-Being, 2002.

Canadian Community Health Survey – Annual Component (CCHS), 2009.

Canadian Federation of Students. (1999). *No means no: Violence against women fact sheet.* Retrieved April 29, 2012, from http://www.cfs-fcee.ca/nomeansno/Downloads/NMN_Facts-English.pdf

Canadian Institutes of Health Research, Natural Sciences and Engineering Research Council of Canada, and Social Sciences and Humanities Research Council of Canada. *Tri-Council Policy Statement: Ethical Conduct for Research Involving Humans,* December 2010.

Canadian Psychological Association. (2000). *Canadian Code of Ethics for Psychologists* (3rd ed.). Ottawa.

Caporael, L. R. (1997). The evolution of truly social cognition: The core configurations model. *Personality and Social Psychology Review, 1,* 276–298.

Capozza, D., & Brown, R. (2000). *Social identity processes: Trends in theory and research.* London: Sage.

Capozza, D., Voci, A., & Licciardello, O. (2000). Individualism, collectivism, and social identity theory. In D. Capozza & R. Brown (Eds)., *Social identity processes: Trends in theory and research.* London: Sage.

Caprariello, P. A., Cuddy, A. J. C., & Fiske, S. T. (2009). Social structure shapes cultural stereotypes and emotions: A causal test of the stereotype content model. *Group Processes & Intergroup Relations, 12,* 147–155.

Carbonneau, R., Kersten, G. E., & Vahidov, R. M. (2011). Pairwise issue modeling for negotiation counteroffer prediction using neural networks. *Decision Support Systems, 50,* 449–459.

Card, N. A., Stucky, B. D., Sawalani, G. M., & Little, T. D. (2008). Direct and indirect aggression during childhood and adolescence: A meta-analytic review of gender differences, intercorrelations, and relations to maladjustment. *Child Development, 79,* 1185–1229.

Carey, H. R., & Laughlin, P. R. (2012). Groups perform better than the best individuals on letters-to-numbers problems: Effects of induced strategies. *Group Processes & Intergroup Relations, 15,* 231–242.

Carlo, G., Mestre, M. V., Samper, P., Tur, A., & Armenta, B. E. (2011). The longitudinal relations among dimensions of parenting styles, sympathy, prosocial moral reasoning, and prosocial behaviors. *International Journal of Behavioral Development, 35,* 116–124.

Carlo, G., Okun, M. A., Knight, G. P., & de Guzman, M. R. T. (2005). The interplay of traits and motives on volunteering: Agreeableness, extraversion and prosocial value motivation. *Personality and Individual Differences, 38,* 1293–1305.

Carlsmith, K. M. (2006). The roles of retribution and utility in determining punishment. *Journal of Experimental Social Psychology, 42,* 437–451.

Carlsmith, K. M., Darley, J. M., & Robinson, P. H. (2002).Why do we punish?: Deterrence and just desserts as motives for punishment. *Journal of Personality and Social Psychology, 83,* 284–299.

Carlson, M., & Miller, N. (1987). Explanation of the relation between negative mood and helping. *Psychological Bulletin, 102,* 91–108.

Carnaghi, A., & Yzerbyt, V. Y. (2007). Subtyping and social consensus: The role of the audience in the maintenance of stereotypic beliefs. *European Journal of Social Psychology, 37,* 902–922.

Carnahan, T., & McFarland, S. (2007). Revisiting the Stanford Prison Experiment: Could participant self-selection have led to the cruelty? *Personality and Social Psychology Bulletin, 33,* 603–614.

Carnegie, D. (1936). *How to win friends and influence people.* New York: Pocket Books. (Reprinted in 1972)

Carnevale, P. J. (2002). Mediating from strength. In J. Bercovitch (Ed.), *Studies in international mediation: Essays in honor of Jeffrey Z. Rubin* (pp. 25–40). London: Palgrave-MacMillan.

Carpenter, C. J. (2012). Meta-analyses of sex differences in responses to sexual versus emotional infidelity: Men and women are more similar than different. *Psychology of Women Quarterly, 36,* 25–37.

Carr, A. (2011) *Positive psychology: The science of happiness and human strengths* (2nd ed.). New York: Routledge/Taylor & Francis Group.

Carrillo, M., Ricci, L. A., Coppersmith, G. A., & Melloni, R. H., Jr. (2009). The effect of increased serotonergic neurotransmission on aggression: A critical meta-analytic review of preclinical studies. *Psychopharmacology, 205,* 349–368.

Carron, A. V., Colman, M. M., Wheeler, J., & Stevens, D. (2002). Cohesion and performance in sport: A meta analysis. *Journal of Sport and Exercise Psychology, 24,* 168–188.

Cartwright, D. (1971). Risk taking by individuals and groups: An assessment of research employing choice dilemmas. *Journal of Personality and Social Psychology, 20,* 245–261.

Cartwright, D., & Zander, A. (1960). Group cohesiveness: Introduction. In D. Cartwright & A. Zander (Eds.), *Group dynamics: Research and theory* (2nd ed., pp. 69–94). Evanston, IL: Row, Peterson.

Carver, C. S., Harris, S. D., Lehman, J. M., Durel, L. A., Antoni, M. H., Spencer, S. M., & Pozo-Kaderman, C. (2000). How important is the perception of personal control? Studies of early stage breast cancer patients. *Personality and Social Psychology Bulletin, 26,* 139–149.

Carver, C. S., & Scheier, M. F. (1981). *Attention and self-regulation: A control-theory approach to human behavior.* New York: Springer-Verlag.

Carver, C. S., & Scheier, M. F. (1990). Origins and functions of positive and negative affect: A control-process view. *Psychological Review, 97,* 19–35.

Carver, C. S., & Scheier, M. F. (1998). *On the self-regulation of behavior.* New York: Cambridge University Press.

Carver, C. S., Scheier, M. F., & Segerstrom, S. C. (2010). Optimism. *Clinical Psychology Review, 30*(7), 879–889.

Case, R. B., Moss, A. J., Case, N., McDermott, M., & Eberly, S. (1992). Living alone after myocardial infarction: Impact on prognosis. *Journal of the American Medical Association, 267,* 515–519.

Cashdan, E. (2003). Hormones and competitive aggression in women. *Aggressive Behavior, 29,* 107–115.

Caspi, A. (2000). The child is the father of man: Personality continuities from childhood to adulthood. *Journal of Personality and Social Psychology, 78,* 158–172.

Cassidy, J., Kirsh, S. J., Scolton, K. L., & Parke, R. D. (1996). Attachment and representations of peer relationships. *Developmental Psychology, 32,* 892–904.

Cassidy, J., & Shaver, P. R. (Eds.) (1999). *Handbook of attachment: Theory, research, and clinical applications.* New York: Guilford Press.

Cassidy, T. (2009). Bullying and victimisation in school children: The role of social identity, problem-solving style, and family and school context. *Social Psychology of Education, 12,* 63–76.

Castano, E., Yzerbyt, V. Y., Bourguignon, D., & Seron, E. (2002). Who may enter? The impact of in-group identification on in-group/out-group categorization. *Journal of Experimental Social Psychology, 38,* 315–322.

Castelli, L., Arcuri, L., & Zogmaister, C. (2003). Perceiving ingroup members who use stereotypes: Implicit conformity and similarity. *European Journal of Social Psychology, 33,* 163–175.

Castelli, L., Macrae, N., Zogmaister, C., Arcuri, L. (2004). A tale of two primes: Contextual limits on stereotype activation. *Social Cognition, 22,* 233–247.

Castelli, L., Zogmaister, C., & Tomelleri, S. (2009). The transmission of racial attitudes within the family. *Developmental Psychology, 45,* 586–591.

Cate, R. M., & Lloyd, S. A. (1992). *Courtship.* Newbury Park, CA: Sage.

Ceci, S. J., Ross, D. F., & Toglia, M. P. (1987). Suggestibility of children's memory: Psycholegal implications. *Journal of Experimental Psychology, 116,* 38–49.

Ceci, S. J., & Williams, W. M. (2011). Understanding current causes of women's underrepresentation in science. *PNAS Proceedings of the National Academy of Sciences of the United States of America, 108,* 3157–3162.

Cesario, J., Plaks, J. E., & Higgins, E. T. (2006). Automatic social behavior as motivated preparation to interact. *Journal of Personality and Social Psychology, 90,* 893–910.

Chaiken, S. (1979). Communicator physical attractiveness and persuasion. *Journal of Personality and Social Psychology, 37,* 1387–1397.

Chaiken, S. (1980). Heuristic versus systematic information processing and the use of source versus message cues in persuasion. *Journal of Personality and Social Psychology, 39,* 752–766.

Chaiken, S. (1987). The heuristic model of persuasion. In M. P. Zanna, J. M. Olson, & C. P. Herman (Eds.), *Social influence: The Ontario symposium* (Vol. 5, pp. 3–39). Hillsdale, NJ: Erlbaum.

Chaiken, S., & Baldwin, M. W. (1981). Affective-cognitive consistency and the effect of salient behavioral information on the self-perception of attitudes. *Journal of Personality and Social Psychology, 41,* 1–12.

Chaiken, S., & Maheswaran, D. (1994). Heuristic processing can bias systematic processing: Effects of source credibility, argument ambiguity, and task importance on attitude judgment. *Journal of Personality and Social Psychology, 66,* 460–473.

Chanal, J. P., & Sarrazin, P. G. (2007). Big-fish-little-pond effect versus positive effect of upward comparisons in the classroom: How does one reconcile contradictory results? *Revue Internationale De Psychologie Sociale, 20,* 69–86.

Chang, A., Duck, J., & Bordia, P. (2006). Understanding the multidimensionality of group development. *Small Group Research, 37,* 327–350.

Chang, A., Sandhofer, C. M., & Brown, C. S. (2011). Gender biases in early number exposure to preschool-aged children. *Journal of Language and Social Psychology, 30,* 440–450.

Chang, H. (2007). Psychological distress and help-seeking among Taiwanese college students: Role of gender and student status. *British Journal of Guidance & Counselling, 35,* 347–355.

Chapdelaine, A., Kenny, D. A., & LaFontana, K. M. (1994). Matchmaker, matchmaker, can you make me a match? Predicting liking between two unacquainted persons. *Journal of Personality and Social Psychology, 67,* 83–91.

Chapleau, K., Oswald, D., & Russell, B. (2007). How ambivalent sexism toward women and men supports rape myth acceptance. *Sex Roles, 57,* 131–136.

Chaplin, W. F., Phillips, J. B., Brown, J. D., Clanton, N. R., & Stein, J. L. (2000). *Journal of Personality and Social Psychology, 79,* 110–117.

Chapman, L. J. (1967). Illusory correlation in observational report. *Journal of Verbal Learning and Verbal Behavior, 6,* 151–155.

Chartrand, T. L., & Bargh, J. A. (1999). The chameleon effect: The perception-behavior link and social interaction. *Journal of Personality and Social Psychology, 76,* 893–910.

Chasteen, A. L., Bhattacharyya, S., Horhota, M., Tam, R., & Hasher, L. (2005). How feelings of stereotype threat influence older adults' memory performance. *Experimental Aging Research, 31,* 235–260.

Cheah, C. S. L., & Nelson, L. J. (2004). The role of acculturation in the emerging adulthood of Aboriginal college students. *International Journal of Behavioral Development, 28,* 495–507.

Cheek, J. M., & Melchior, L. A. (1990). Shyness, self-esteem, and self-consciousness. In H. Leitenberg (Ed.), *Handbook of social and evaluation anxiety.* New York: Plenum.

Chen, F. F., & Kenrick, D. T. (2002). Repulsion or attraction: Group membership and assumed attitude similarity. *Journal of Personality and Social Psychology, 83,* 111–125.

Chen, P., Coccaro, E. F., Lee, R., & Jacobson, K. C. (2012). Moderating effects of childhood maltreatment on associations between social information processing and adult aggression. *Psychological Medicine: A Journal of Research in Psychiatry and the Allied Sciences, 42,* 1293–1304.

Chen, S., & Chaiken, S. (1999). The heuristic-systematic model in its broader context. In S. Chaiken & Y. Trope (Eds.), *Dual-process theories in social psychology* (pp. 73–96). New York: Guilford.

Chen, S., Langner, C. A., & Mendoza-Denton, R. (2009). When dispositional and role power fit: Implications for self-expression and self–other congruence. *Journal of Personality and Social Psychology, 96,* 710–727.

Chen, Y-R., Brockner, J., & Chen, X-P. (2002). Individual-collective primacy and ingroup favoritism: Enhancement and protection effects. *Journal of Experimental Social Psychology, 38,* 482–491.

Cheng, C. M., Chartrand, Tanya L. (2003). Self-monitoring without awareness: Using mimicry as a nonconscious affiliation strategy. *Journal of Personality and Social Psychology, 85,* 1170–1179.

Cheng, C.-Y., Chua, R. Y. J., Morris, M. W., & Lee, L. (2012). Finding the right mix: How the composition of self-managing multicultural teams cultural value orientation influences performance over time. *Journal of Organizational Behavior, 33,* 389–411.

Cheng, P. W., & Novick, L. R. (1990). A probabilistic contrast model of causal induction. *Journal of Personality and Social Psychology, 58,* 545–567.

Cheryan, S., & Bodenhausen, G. V. (2000). When positive stereotypes threaten intellectual performance: The psychological hazards of "model minority" status. *Psychological Science, 11,* 399–402.

Chiroro, P. M., Tredoux, C. G., Radaelli, S., & Meissner, C. A. (2008). Recognizing faces across continents: The effect of within-race variations on the own-race bias in face recognition. *Psychonomic Bulletin & Review, 15,* 1089–1092.

Choi, I., Nisbett, R. E., & Norenzayan, A. (1999). Causal attribution across cultures: Variation and universality. *Psychological Bulletin, 125,* 47–63.

Choi, J. N., & Kim, M. U. (1999). The organizational application of groupthink and its limitations in organizations. *Journal of Applied Psychology, 84,* 297–306.

Choi, S. M., Lee, W.-N., & Kim, H.-J. (2005). Lessons from the rich and famous: A cross-cultural comparison of celebrity endorsement in advertising. *Journal of Advertising, 34,* 85–98.

Chow, T.W., Pio F.J. & Rockwood K. (2011). An international needs assessment of caregivers for frontotemporal dementia. *The Canadian Journal of Neurological Sciences/Le Journal Canadien des Sciences Neurologiques, 38, 753–757.*

Christensen, A., & Heavey, C. L. (1993). Gender differences in marital conflict: The demand/withdraw interaction pattern. In S. Oskamp & M. Costanzo (Eds.), *Gender issues in contemporary society* (pp. 113–141). Newbury Park, CA: Sage.

Christensen, A. J., Turner, C. W., Smith, T. W., Holman, J. M., Jr., & Gregory, M. C. (1991). Health locus of control and depression in end-stage renal disease. *Journal of Counseling and Clinical Psychology, 59,* 419–424.

Christensen, L. (1988). Deception in psychological research: When is its use justified? *Personality and Social Psychology Bulletin, 14,* 664–675.

Christianson, S. (1992). Emotional stress and eyewitness memory: A critical review. *Psychological Bulletin, 112,* 284–309.

Cialdini, R. B. (2001). *Influence: Science and practice* (4th ed.). Needham Heights, MA: Allyn & Bacon.

Cialdini, R. B. (2007). *Influence: The psychology of persuasion.* New York: HarperCollins.

Cialdini, R. B., & Ascani, K. (1976). Test of a concession procedure for inducing verbal, behavioral, and further compliance with a request to give blood. *Journal of Applied Psychology, 61,* 295–300.

Cialdini, R. B., Baumann, D. J., & Kenrick, D. T. (1981). Insights from sadness: A three-step model of the development of altruism as hedonism. *Developmental Review, 1,* 207–223.

Cialdini, R. B., Borden, R. J., Thorne, A., Walker, M. R., Freeman, S., & Sloan, L. R. (1976). Basking in reflected glory: Three (football) field studies. *Journal of Personality and Social Psychology, 34,* 366–375.

Cialdini, R. B., Cacioppo, J. T., Bassett, R., & Miller, J. A. (1978). Low-ball procedure for producing compliance: Commitment then cost. *Journal of Personality and Social Psychology, 36,* 463–476.

Cialdini, R. B., & De Nicholas, M. E. (1989). Self-presentation by association. *Journal of Personality and Social Psychology, 57,* 626–631.

Cialdini, R. B., Kallgren, C. A., & Reno, R. R. (1991). A focus theory of normative conduct: A theoretical refinement and reevaluation of the role of norms in human behavior. *Advances in Experimental Social Psychology, 24,* 201–234.

Cialdini, R. B., Reno, R. R., & Kallgren, C. A. (1990). A focus theory of normative conduct: Recycling the concept of norms to reduce littering in public places. *Journal of Personality and Social Psychology, 58,* 1015–1026.

Cialdini, R. B., Schaller, M., Houlihan, D., Arps, K., Fultz, J., & Beaman, A. L. (1987). Empathy-based helping: Is it selflessly or selfishly motivated? *Journal of Personality and Social Psychology, 52,* 749–758.

Cialdini, R. B., Trost, M. R., & Newsom, J. T. (1995). Preference for consistency: The development of a valid measure and the discovery of surprising behavioral implications. *Journal of Personality and Social Psychology, 69,* 318–328.

Cialdini, R. B., Vincent, J. E., Lewis, S. K., Catalan, J., Wheeler, D., & Darby, B. L. (1975). Reciprocal concessions procedure for inducing compliance: The door-in-the-face technique. *Journal of Personality and Social Psychology, 31,* 206–215.

Cioffi, D., & Holloway, J. (1993). Delayed costs of suppressed pain. *Journal of Personality and Social Psychology, 64,* 274–282.

Cismaru, M., Jensen, G., & Lavack, A. M. (2010). If the noise coming from next door were loud music, you'd do something about it: Using mass media campaigns encouraging bystander intervention to stop partner violence. *Journal of Advertising, 39,* 69–82.

Clark, M. S. (1984). Record keeping in two types of relationships. *Journal of Personality and Social Psychology, 47,* 549–557.

Clark, M. S., & Mills, J. (1979). Interpersonal attraction in exchange and communal relationships. *Journal of Personality and Social Psychology, 37,* 12–24.

Clark, M. S., & Mills, J. (1993). The difference between communal and exchange relationships: What it is and is not. *Personality and Social Psychology Bulletin, 19,* 684–691.

Clark, R. D., III. (2001). Effects of majority defection and multiple minority sources on minority influence. *Group Dynamics, 5,* 57–62.

Clark, R. D., III, & Maass, A. (1990). The effects of majority size on minority influence: *European Journal of Psychology, 20,* 99–117.

Clark, R. D., III, & Word, L. E. (1972). Why don't bystanders help? Because of ambiguity? *Journal of Personality and Social Psychology, 24,* 392–400.

Clark, S. E. (2005). A re-examination of the effects of biased lineup instructions in eyewitness identification. *Law and Human Behavior, 29,* 575–604.

Clifford, M. M., & Walster, E. H. (1973). The effect of physical attractiveness on teacher expectations. *Sociology of Education, 46,* 248–258.

Coenders, M., Lubbers, M., Scheepers, P., & Verkuyten, M. (2008). More than two decades of changing ethnic attitudes in the Netherlands. *Journal of Social Issues, 64,* 269–285.

Cohen, S., Kessler, R. C., & Gordon, L. U. (1995). *Measuring stress: A guide for health and social scientists.* New York: Oxford University Press.

Cohen, D., & Nisbett, R. E. (1997). Field experiments examining the culture of honor: The role of institutions in perpetuating norms about violence. *Personality and Social Psychology Bulletin, 23,* 1188–1199.

Cohen, D., Nisbett, R. E., Bowdle, B. F., & Schwarz, N. (1996). Insult, aggression, and the southern culture of honor: An "experimental ethnography." *Journal of Personality and Social Psychology, 70,* 945–960.

Cohen, D., Vandello, J., & Rantilla, A. K. (1998). The sacred and the social: Cultures of honor and violence. In P. Gilbert & B. Andrews (Eds.), *Shame: Interpersonal behavior, psychopathology, and culture* (pp. 261–282). Cambridge: Oxford University Press.

Cohen, G. L., Steele, C. M., & Ross, L. D. (1999). The mentor's dilemma: Providing critical feedback across the racial divide. *Personality and Social Psychology Bulletin, 25,* 1302–1318.

Cohen, S. (2004). Social relationships and health. *American Psychologist, 59,* 676–684.

Cohen, S., Alper, C. M., Doyle, W. J., Adler, N. E., Treanor, J. J., & Turner, R. B. (2008). Objective and subjective socioeconomic status and susceptibility to the common cold. *Health Psychology, 27,* 268–274.

Cohen, S., Doyle, W. J., Turner, R., Alper, C. M., & Skoner, D. P. (2006). Sociability and susceptibility to the common cold. *Psychological Science, 14,* 389–395.

Cohen, S., Frank, E., Doyle, W. J., Skoner, D. P., Rabin, B. S., & Gwaltney, J. M. (1998). Types of stressors that increase susceptibility to the common cold in healthy adults. *Health Psychology, 17,* 214–223.

Cohen, S., & Herbert, T. (1996). Health psychology: Psychological factors and physical disease from the perspective of human psychoneuroimmunology. *Annual Review of Psychology, 47,* 113–142.

Cohen, S., & Janicki-Deverts, D. (2009). Can we improve our physical health by altering our social networks? *Perspectives on Psychological Science, 4,* 375–378.

Cohen, S., Kessler, R. C., & Gordon, L. U. (1995). *Measuring stress: A guide for health and social scientists.* New York: Oxford University Press.

Cohen, S., Underwood, L. G., & Gottlieb, B. H. (Eds.). (2000). *Social support measurement and intervention: A guide for health and social scientists.* New York: Oxford University Press.

Cohen-Ketteinis, P. T., & Van Goozen, S. H. M. (1997). Sex reassignment of adolescent transsexuals: A follow-up study. *Journal of the American Academy of Child and Adolescent Psychiatry, 36,* 263–271.

Collins, N. L., & Miller, L. C. (1994). Self-disclosure and liking: a meta-analytic review. *Psychological Bulletin, 116,* 457–475.

Colvin, C. R., Block, J., & Funder, D. C. (1995). Overly positive self-evaluations and personality: Negative implications for mental health. *Journal of Personality and Social Psychology, 68,* 1152–1162.

Conger, R. D., Reuter, M. A., & Elder, G. H., Jr. (1999). Couple resilience to economic pressure. *Journal of Personality and Social Psychology, 76,* 54–71.

Conklin, L. R., Strunk, D. R., & Fazio, R. H. (2009). Attitude formation in depression: Evidence for deficits in forming positive attitudes. *Journal of Behavior Therapy and Experimental Psychiatry, 40,* 120–126.

Conner, M., Norman, P., & Bell, R. (2002). The theory of planned behavior and healthy eating. *Health Psychology, 21,* 194–201.

Connolly, D. A., & Gordon, H. M. (2011). He-said–she-said: Contrast effects in credibility assessments and possible threats to fundamental principles of criminal law. *Legal and Criminological Psychology, 16,* 227–241.

Connolly, D. A., Price, H. L., & Read, J D. (2006) Predicting expert social science testimony in criminal prosecutions of historic child sexual abuse *Legal and Criminological Psychology, 11,* 55–74

Connolly, J., Nocentini, A., Menesini, E., Pepler, D., Craig, W., & Williams, T. S. (2010). Adolescent dating aggression in Canada and Italy: A cross-national comparison. *International Journal of Behavioral Development, 34,* 98–105.

Connors, E., Lundregan, T., Miller, N., & McEwen, T. (1996). *Convicted by juries, exonerated by science: Case studies in the use of DNA evidence to establish innocence after trial.* Washington, DC: U.S. Department of Justice.

Conway, L. G., Ryder, A. G., Tweed, R. G., & Sokol, B. W. (2001). Intranational cultural variation: Exploring further implications of collectivism within the United States. *Journal of Cross-Cultural Psychology, 32,* 681–697.

Conway, M. A. (1995). *Flashbulb memories.* Mahwah, NJ: Erlbaum.

Conway, M. A., & Pleydell-Pearce, C. W. (2000). The construction of autobiographical memories in the self-memory system. *Psychological Review, 107,* 261–288.

Conway, M. A., Wang, Q., Hanyu, K., & Haque, S. (2005). A cross-cultural investigation of autobiographical memory: On the universality and cultural variation of the reminiscence bump. *Journal of Cross-Cultural Psychology, 36,* 739–749.

Cook, T. D., & Campbell, D. T. (1979). *Quasi-experimentation: Design and analysis issues for field settings.* Chicago: Rand McNally.

Cooke, C. A. (2004). Young people's attitudes towards guns in America, Great Britain, and Western Australia. *Aggressive Behavior, 30,* 93–104.

Cooley, C. H. (1902). *Human nature and the social order.* New York: Schocken Books. (Reprinted in 1964)

Cooper, J. (2007). *Cognitive dissonance: Fifty years of classic theory.* London: Sage.

Cooper, J., & Fazio, R. H. (1984). A new look at dissonance theory. In L. Berkowitz (Ed.), *Advances in experimental social psychology* (Vol. 17, pp. 229–267). New York: Academic Press.

Cooper, J., & Hogg, M. (2007). Feeling the anguish of others: A theory of vicarious dissonance. *Advances in Experimental Social Psychology, 39,* 359–403.

Cooper, J., & Neuhaus, I. M. (2000). The "hired gun" effect: Assessing the effect of pay, frequency of testifying, and credentials on the perception of expert testimony. *Law and Human Behavior, 24,* 149–171.

Cooper, J., Zanna, M. P., & Goethals, G. R. (1974). Mistreatment of an esteemed other as a consequence affecting dissonance reduction. *Journal of Experimental Social Psychology, 10,* 224–233.

Cooper, M. L., Frone, M. R., Russell, M., & Mudar, P. (1995). Drinking to regulate positive and negative emotions: A motivational model of alcohol use. *Journal of Personality and Social Psychology, 69,* 990–1005.

Coopersmith, S. (1967). *The antecedents of self-esteem.* San Francisco: Freeman.

Copeland, J. T. (1994). Prophecies of power: Motivational implications of social power for behavioral confirmation. *Journal of Personality and Social Psychology, 67,* 264–277.

Cordery, J. L., & Soo, C. (2008). Overcoming impediments to virtual team effectiveness. *Human Factors and Ergonomics in Manufacturing, 18,* 487–500.

Correll, J., Spencer, S. J. & Zanna, M. P. (2004). An affirmed self and an open mind: Self-affirmation and sensitivity to argument strength. *Journal of Experimental Social Psychology, 40,* 350–356.

Cose, E. (1997). *Color-blind: Seeing beyond race in a race-obsessed world.* New York: HarperCollins.

Cottrell, N. B., Wack, D. L., Sekerak, G. J., & Rittle, R. H. (1968). Social facilitation of dominant responses by the presence of an audience and the mere presence of others. *Journal of Personality and Social Psychology, 9,* 245–250.

Covington, M. V. (2000). Intrinsic versus extrinsic motivation in schools: A reconciliation. *Current Directions in Psychological Science, 9,* 22–25.

Craig, W. M., Pepler, D., & Atlas, R. (2000). Observations of bullying in the playground and in the classroom. *School Psychology International, 21,* 22–36.

Cramer, R. E., McMaster, M. R., Bartell, P. A., & Dragna, M. (1988). Subject competence and the minimization of the bystander effect. *Journal of Applied Social Psychology, 18,* 1133–1148.

Crandall, C. S., Bahns, A. J., Warner, R., & Schaller, M. (2011). Stereotypes as justifications of prejudice. *Personality and Social Psychology Bulletin, 37,* 1488–1498.

Crandall, C. S., & Eshleman, A. (2003). A justification-suppression of the expression and experience of prejudice. *Psychological Bulletin, 129,* 414–446.

Crano, W. D. (2000). Milestones in the psychological analysis of social influence. *Group Dynamics: Theory, Research, and Practice, 4,* 68–80.

Crano, W. D., & Prislin, R. (Eds.). (2008). *Attitudes and attitude change.* New York: Psychology Press.

Crawford, M. T., & Salaman, L. (2012). Entitativity, identity, and the fulfilment of psychological needs. *Journal of Experimental Social Psychology,*

Crescioni, A. W., & Baumeister, R. F. (2009). In M. J. Harris (Ed.), *Alone and aggressive: Social exclusion impairs self-control and empathy and increases hostile cognition and aggression.* New York: Springer Publishing Co.

Crick, N. R., & Dodge, K. A. (1994). A review and reformulation of social information-processing mechanisms in children's social adjustment. *Psychological Bulletin, 115,* 74–101.

Crick, N. R., & Rose, A. J. (2000). Toward a gender-balanced approach to the study of social-emotional development: A look at relational aggression. In R. G. Geen & E. Donnerstein (Eds.), *Human aggression: Theories, research, and implications for social policy* (pp. 153–168). San Diego: Academic Press.

Crick, N. R., Werner, N. E., Casas, J. F., O'Brien, K. M., Nelson, D. A., Grotpeter, J. K., & Markon, K. (1999). Childhood aggression and gender: A new look at an old problem. In D. Bernstein (Ed.), *Nebraska symposium on motivation* (vol. 45, pp. 75–141). Lincoln: University of Nebraska Press.

Crocker, J., & Park, L. E. (2004). The costly pursuit of self-esteem. *Psychological Bulletin, 130,* 392–414.

Crocker, J., Voelkl, K., Testa, M., & Major, B. (1991). Social stigma: The affective consequences of attributional ambiguity. *Journal of Personality and Social Psychology, 60,* 218–228.

Crockett, M. J., Clark, L., Tabibnia, G., Lieberman, M. D., & Robbins, T. W. (2008). Serotonin modulates behavioral reactions to unfairness. *Science, 320,* 1739.

Croizet, J. C., & Claire, T. (1998). Extending the concept of stereotype and threat to social class: The intellectual underperformance of students from low socioeconomic backgrounds. *Personality and Social Psychology Bulletin, 24,* 588–594.

Croizet, J. C., Després, G., Gauzins, M. E., Huguet, P., Leyens, J.-P., & Meot, A. (2004). Stereotype threat undermines intellectual performance by triggering a disruptive mental load. *Personality and Social Psychology Bulletin, 30,* 721–731.

Cronbach, L. J. (1955). Processes affecting scores on "understanding of others" and "assumed similarity." *Psychological Bulletin, 52,* 177–193.

Cronin, P., & Reicher, S. (2009). Accountability processes and group dynamics: A SIDE perspective on the policing of an anti-capitalist riot. *European Journal of Social Psychology, 39,* 237–254.

Cronley, M. L., Mantel, S. P., & Kardes, F. R. (2010). Effects of accuracy motivation and need to evaluate on mode of attitude formation and attitude–behavior consistency. *Journal of Consumer Psychology, 20,* 274–281.

Crosby, J. R., Monin, B., & Richardson, D. (2008). Where do we look during potentially offensive behavior? *Psychological Science, 19,* 226–228.

Croyle, R., & Cooper, J. (1983). Dissonance arousal: Physiological evidence. *Journal of Personality and Social Psychology, 45,* 782–791.

Crozier, W. R. (Ed.) (2001). *Shyness: Development, consolidation, and change.* London: Routledge.

Crozier, W. R., & Alden, L. E. (2005). In W. R. Crozier, and L. E. Alden (Eds.), *Introduction: The development of social anxiety.* New York: John Wiley & Sons Ltd.

Crutchfield, R. S. (1955). Conformity and character. *American Psychologist, 10,* 195–198.

Csikszentmihalyi, M., & Figurski, T. J. (1982). Self-awareness and aversive experience in everyday life. *Journal of Personality, 50,* 15–28.

Cuddy, A. J. C., Fiske, S. T., & Glick, P. (2008). Warmth and competence as universal dimensions of social perception: The Stereotype Content Model and the BIAS Map. In M. P. Zanna (Ed.), *Advances in Experimental Social Psychology* (Vol. 40, pp. 61–149). New York: Academic Press.

Cuddy, A. J., Fiske, S. T., Kwan, V., S. Y. Glick, P., Demoulin, S., Leyens, J. P., et al. (2009). Stereotype content model across cultures: Towards universal similarities and some differences. *British Journal of Social Psychology, 48,* 1–33.

Cuddy, A. J. C., Norton, M. I., & Fiske, S. T. (2004). This old stereotype: The pervasiveness and persistence of the elderly stereotype. *Journal of Social Issues, 61,* 267–285.

Cunningham, M. R. (1979). Weather, mood, and helping behavior: Quasi experiments with the sunshine Samaritan. *Journal of Personality and Social Psychology, 37,* 1947–1956.

Cunningham, M. R., Roberts, A. R., Wu, C., Barbee, A. P., & Druen, P. B. (1995). "Their ideas of beauty are, on the whole, the same as ours": Consistency and variability in the cross-cultural perception of female physical attractiveness. *Journal of Personality and Social Psychology, 68,* 261–279.

Cunningham, M. R., Steinberg, J., & Grev, R. (1980). Wanting to and having to help: Separate motivations for positive mood and guilt-induced helping. *Journal of Personality and Social Psychology, 38,* 181–192.

Cunningham, W. A., Johnson, M. K., Gatenby, J. C., Gore, J. C., & Banaji, M. R. (2003). Neural components of social evaluation. *Journal of Personality and Social Psychology, 85,* 639–649.

Curtis, N. M., Ronan, K. R., Heiblum, N., & Crellin, K. (2009). Dissemination and effectiveness of multisystemic treatment in New Zealand: A benchmarking study. *Journal of Family Psychology, 23,* 119–129.

Cutler, B. L., & Penrod, S. D. (1995). *Mistaken identification: The eyewitness, psychology, and the law.* New York: Cambridge University Press.

Cutler, B. L., Penrod, S. D., & Stuve, T. E. (1988). Juror decision making in eyewitness identification cases. Law and *Human Behavior, 12,* 41–55.

Dabbs, J. M., & Dabbs, M. G. (2005). Why men and women fight: The role of testosterone in mate relations. In S. Fein, G. R. Goethals, & M. J. Sandstrom (Eds.), *Gender and aggression: Interdisciplinary perspectives.* Mahwah, NJ: Erlbaum.

Dabbs, J. M., Jr., Hargrove, M. F., & Heusel, C. (1996).Testosterone differences among college fraternities: Well-behaved vs. rambunctious. *Personality and Individual Differences, 20,* 157–161.

Daly, M., & Wilson, M. (1988). *Homicide.* New York: Aldine de Gruyter.

Daly, M., & Wilson, M. (1989). Homicide and cultural evolution. *Ethology and Sociobiology, 10,* 99–110.

Daly, M., & Wilson, M. (1996). Violence against stepchildren. *Current Directions in Psychological Science, 5,* 77–81.

Daly, M., & Wilson, M. (2005). The 'Cinderella effect' is no fairy tale: Comment. *Trends in Cognitive Sciences, 9,* 507–508.

Danziger, K. (2001). In R. W. Rieber, and D. K. Robinson (Eds.), *Wundt and the temptations of psychology.* New York: Kluwer Academic/Plenum Publishers.

Darke, P. R., & Chaiken, S. (2005). The pursuit of self-interest: Self-interest bias in attitude judgment and persuasion. *Journal of Personality and Social Psychology, 89,* 864–883.

Darley, J. M., & Batson, C. D. (1973). From Jerusalem to Jericho: A study of situational and dispositional variables in helping behavior. *Journal of Personality and Social Psychology, 27,* 100–108.

Darley, J. M., Carlsmith, K. M., & Robinson, P. H. (2000). Incapacitation and just desserts as motives for punishment. *Law and Human Behavior, 24,* 659–684.

Darley, J. M., & Fazio, R. (1980). Expectancy confirmation processes arising in the social interaction sequence. *American Psychologist, 35,* 867–881.

Darley, J. M., & Gross, P. H. (1983). A hypothesis-confirming bias in labeling effects. *Journal of Personality and Social Psychology, 44,* 20–33.

Darley, J. M., & Latané, B. (1970). Norms and normative behavior: Field studies of social interdependence. In J. Macauley & L. Berkowitz (Eds.), *Altruism and helping behavior* (pp. 83–101). New York: Academic Press.

Darwin, C. (1872). *The expression of the emotions in man and animals.* London: John Murray.

Das, E. H. H. J., de Wit, J. B. F., & Stroebe, W. (2003). Fear appeals motivate acceptance of action recommendations: Evidence for a positive bias in the processing of persuasive messages. *Personality and Social Psychology Bulletin, 29,* 650–664.

Dasgupta, N. (2009). Mechanisms underlying the malleability of implicit prejudice and stereotypes: The role of automaticity and cognitive control. In T. D. Nelson (Ed.), *Handbook of prejudice, stereotyping, and discrimination* (pp. 267–284). New York: Psychology Press.

David, N., Bewernick, B. H., Cohen, M. X., Newen, A., Lux, S., Fink, G. R., Shah, N. J., & Vogeley, K. (2006). Neural representations of self versus other: Visual-spatial perspective taking and agency in a virtual ball-tossing game. *Journal of Cognitive Neuroscience, 18,* 898–910.

Davidson, A. R., & Jaccard, J. J. (1979). Variables that moderate the attitude-behavior relation: Results of a longitudinal survey. *Journal of Personality and Social Psychology, 37,* 1364–1376.

Davies, P. G., Spencer, S. J., Quinn, D. M., & Gerhardstein, R. (2002). Consuming images: How television commercials that elicit stereotype threat can restrain women academically and professionally. *Personality and Social Psychology Bulletin, 28,* 1615–1628.

Davies, P. T., & Cummings, E. M. (1994). Marital conflict and child adjustment: An emotional security hypothesis. *Psychological Bulletin, 116,* 387–411.

Davis, B. P., & Knowles, E. S. (1999). A Disrupt-Then-Reframe technique of social influence. *Journal of Personality and Social Psychology, 76,* 192–199.

Davis, D., & Leo, R. A. (2012). INTERROGATION-RELATED REGULATORY DECLINE: Ego depletion, failures of self-regulation, and the decision to confess. *Psychology, Public Policy, and Law.*

Davis, J. H., Kameda, T., Parks, C., Stasson, M., & Zimmerman, S. (1989). Some social mechanics of group decision-making: The distribution of opinion, polling sequence, and implications for consensus. *Journal of Personality and Social Psychology, 57,* 1000–1012.

Davis, J. L., & Rusbult, C. E. (2001). Attitude alignment in close relationships. *Journal of Personality and Social Psychology, 81,* 65–84.

Davis, M. H., Soderlund, T., Cole, J., Gadol, E., Kute, M., Myers, M., & Wiehing, J. (2004). Cognitions associated with attempts to empathize: How do we imagine the perspective of another? *Personality and Social Psychology Bulletin, 30,* 1625–1635.

Davis, S. (1990). Men as success objects and women as sex objects: A study of personal advertisements. *Sex Roles, 23,* 43–50.

Dawes, R. M. (1980). Social dilemmas. *Annual Review of Psychology, 31,* 169–193.

Dawkins, R. (1989). *The selfish gene* (2nd ed.). Oxford: Oxford University Press.

Day, D. V., Shleicher, D. J., Unckless, A. L., & Hiller, N. J. (2002). Self-monitoring personality at work: A meta-analytic investigation of construct validity. *Journal of Applied Psychology, 87,* 390–401.

De Cremer, D., Van Knippenberg, D., Van Dijk, E., & Van Leeuwen, E. (2008). Cooperating if one's goals are collective-based: Social identification effects in social dilemmas as a function of goal transformation. *Journal of Applied Social Psychology, 38,* 1562–1579.

De Dreu, C. K. W., Beersma, B., Steinel, W., Van Kleef, G. A. (2007). The psychology of negotiation: Principles and basic processes (pp. 608–629). In A. W. Kruglanski & E. T. Higgins (Eds.), *Social psychology: Handbook of basic principles* (2nd ed.). New York: Guilford.

De Dreu, C. K. W., Beersma, B., Stroebe, K., & Euwema, M. C. (2006). Motivated information processing, strategic choice, and the quality of negotiated agreement. *Journal of Personality and Social Psychology, 90,* 927–943.

De Dreu, C., & De Vries, N. (Eds.) (2001). Group Consensus and Minority Influence: Implications for innovation. London: Blackwell.

de Hoog, N., Stroebe, W., & de Wit, J. B. F. (2005). The impact of fear appeals on processing and acceptance of action recommendations. *Personality and Social Psychology Bulletin, 31,* 24–33.

de Hoog, N., Stroebe, W., & de Wit, J. B. F. (2007). The impact of vulnerability to and severity of a health risk on processing and acceptance of fear-arousing communications: A meta-analysis. *Review of General Psychology, 11,* 258–285.

De Houwer, J., Thomas, S., & Baeyens, F. (2001) Associative learning of likes and dislikes: A review of 25 years of research on human evaluative conditioning. *Psychological Bulletin, 127,* 853–869.

DeNeve, K. M., & Cooper, H. (1998). The happy personality: A meta-analysis of 137 personality traits and subjective well-being. *Psychological Bulletin, 124,* 197–229.

De Pelsmacker, P., Cauberghe, V., & Dens, N. (2011). Fear appeal effectiveness for familiar and unfamiliar issues. *Journal of Social Marketing, 1,* 171–191.

De Raad, B. (2000). *The big five personality factors: Theory and applications.* Germany: Hogrefe & Huber.

de Veer, M. W., Gallup, G. G., Theall, L. A., van den Bos, R., & Povinelli, D. J. (2003). An 8-year longitudinal study of mirror self-recognition in chimpanzees *(Pan troglodytes). Neuropsychologia, 41,* 229–234.

de Waal, F. B. M. (1996). *Good natured: The origins of right and wrong in humans and other animals.* Cambridge, MA: Harvard University Press.

de Waal, F. B. M. (2006). *Primates and philosophers: How morality evolved.* Princeton, NJ: Princeton University Press.

de Waal, F. B. M. (2008). Putting the altruism back into altruism: The evolution of empathy. *Annual Review of Psychology, 59,* 279–300.

de Waal, F. B. M. (2009). *The age of empathy: Nature's lesson for a kinder society.* New York: Harmony.

de Waal, F. B., & Berger, M. L. (2000). Payment for labor in monkeys. *Nature, 404,* 563.

Dear Abby (2003, December 17). *The Berkshire Eagle,* p. C7.

Deater-Deckard, K., Dodge, K. A., Bates, J. E., & Pettit, G. S. (1998). Multiple-risk factors in the development of externalizing behavior problems: Group and individual differences. *Development and Psychopathology, 10,* 469–493.

Deaux, K., & Emswiller, T. (1974). Explanations for successful performance on sex-linked tasks: What is skill for the male is luck for the female. *Journal of Personality and Social Psychology, 29,* 80–85.

DeBono, K. G., Leavitt, A., & Backus, J. (2003). Product packaging and product evaluation: An individual difference approach. *Journal of Applied Social Psychology, 33,* 513–521.

Decety, J., Michalska, K. J., Akitsuki, Y., & Lahey, B. B. (2009). Atypical empathic responses in adolescents with aggressive conduct disorder: A functional MRI investigation. *Biological Psychology, 80,* 203–211.

Deci, E. L., & Ryan, R. M. (1985). *Intrinsic motivation and self-determination in human behavior.* New York: Plenum.

Deffenbacher, K. A., Bornstein, B. H., & Penrod, S. D. (2006). Mugshot exposure effects: Retroactive interference, mugshot commitment, source confusion, and unconscious transference. *Law and Human Behavior, 30,* 287–307.

DeKeseredy, W. S., Schwartz, M. D., & Tait, K. (1993) Sexual assault and stranger aggression on a Canadian university campus. *Sex Roles, 28,* 263–277.

Delfour, F., & Marten, K. (2001). Mirror image processing in three marine mammal species: Killer whales (orchinus orca), false killer whales (pseudorca crassidens) and California sea lions (zalophus californianus). *Behavioural Processes, 53,* 181–190.

Demaré, D., Lips, H. M., & Briere, J. (1993). Sexually violent pornography, anti-women attitudes, and sexual aggression: A structural equation model. *Journal of Research in Personality, 27,* 285–300.

DeMarree, Kenneth G., Wheeler, S. C., & Petty, R. E. (2005). Priming a new identity: Self-monitoring moderates the effects of nonself primes on self-judgments and behavior. *Journal of Personality and Social Psychology, 89,* 657–671.

Demoulin, S., Pozo, B. C., & Leyens, J.-P. (2009). Infrahumanization: The differential interpretation of primary and secondary emotions. In S. L. Demoulin, J.-P. Leyens, & J. F. Dovidio (Eds.), *Intergroup misunderstandings: Impact of divergent social realities* (pp. 153–171). New York: Psychology Press.

DeNeve, K. M., & Cooper, H. (1998). The happy personality: A meta-analysis of 137 personality traits and subjective well-being. *Psychological Bulletin, 124,* 197–229.

Denissen, J. A., Penke, L., & Schmitt, D. P. (2008). Self-esteem reactions to social interactions: Evidence for sociometer mechanisms across days, people, and nations. *Journal of Personality and Social Psychology, 95,* 181–196.

Denrell, J. (2005). Why most people disapprove of me: Experience sampling in impression formation. *Psychological Review, 112,* 951–978.

DePaulo, B. M., Lindsay, J. J., Malone, B. E., Muhlenbruck, L., Charlton, K., & Cooper, H. (2003). Cues to deception. *Psychological Bulletin, 129,* 74–112.

Deppe, R. K., & Harackiewicz, J. M. (1996). Self-handicapping and intrinsic motivation: Buffering intrinsic motivation from the threat of failure. *Journal of Personality and Social Psychology, 70,* 868–876.

Derlega, V. J., Metts, S., Petronio, S., & Margulis, S. T. (1993). *Self-disclosure.* Newbury Park, CA: Sage.

Derlega, V. J., Wilson, M., & Chaikin, A. L. (1976). Friendship and disclosure reciprocity. *Journal of Personality and Social Psychology, 34,* 578–587.

DeRosa, D. M., Smith, C. L., & Hantula, D. A. (2007). The medium matters: Mining the long-promised merit of group interaction in creative idea generation tasks in a meta-analysis of the electronic group brainstorming literature. *Computers in Human Behavior, 23,* 1549–1581.

DeSteno, D. A., & Salovey, P. (1996). Evolutionary origins of sex differences in jealousy? Questioning the "fitness" model. *Psychological Science, 7,* 367–372.

Deutsch, F. M. (1989). The false consensus effect: Is the self-justification hypothesis justified? *Basic and Applied Social Psychology, 10,* 83–99.

Deutsch, M., & Gerard, H. B. (1955). A study of normative and informational social influences upon individual judgment. *Journal of Abnormal and Social Psychology, 51,* 629–636.

Deutsch, M., & Krauss, R. M. (1960). The effect of threat upon interpersonal bargaining. *Journal of Abnormal and Social Psychology, 61,* 181–189.

Deutsch, R., & Fazio, R. H. (2008). How subtyping shapes perception: Predictable exceptions to the rule reduce attention to stereotype-associated dimensions. *Journal of Experimental Social Psychology, 44,* 1020–1034.

Devine, P. G. (1989). Stereotypes and prejudice: Their automatic and controlled components. *Journal of Personality and Social Psychology, 56,* 5–18.

Devine, P. G., Brodish, A. B., & Vance, S. L. (2005). Self-regulatory processes in interracial interactions: The role of internal and external motivation to respond without prejudice. In J. P. Forgas, K. D. Williams, & W. von Hippel (Eds.), *Social motivation: Conscious and unconscious processes* (pp. 249–273). New York: Psychology Press.

DeWall, C. N., & Bushman, B. J. (2009). Hot under the collar in a lukewarm environment: Words associated with hot temperature increase aggressive thoughts and hostile perceptions. *Journal of Experimental Social Psychology, 45,* 1045–1047.

DeWall, C. N., Maner, J. K., & Rouby, D. A. (2009). Social exclusion and early-stage interpersonal perception: Selective attention to signs of acceptance. *Journal of Personality and Social Psychology, 96,* 729–741.

DeWall, C. N., Twenge, J. M., Bushman, B., Im, C., & Williams, K. (2010). A little acceptance goes a long way: Applying social impact theory to the rejection-aggression link. *Social Psychological and Personality Science, 1,* 168–174.

Diamond, L. M. (2003). Was it a phase? Young women's relinquishment of lesbian/bisexual identities over a 5-year period. *Journal of Personality and Social Psychology, 84,* 352–364.

Diamond, L. M. (2008). Female bisexuality from adolescence to adulthood: Results from a 10-year longitudinal study. *Developmental Psychology, 44,* 5–14.

Diamond, M. (1993). Homosexuality and bisexuality in different populations. *Archives of Sexual Behavior, 22,* 291–310.

Dickson, R. A., Pillemer, D. B., & Bruehl, E. C. (2011). The reminiscence bump for salient personal memories: Is a cultural life script required? *Memory & Cognition, 39,* 977–991.

Diekmann, K. A., Tenbrunsel, A. E., & Galinsky, A. D. (2003). From self-prediction to self-defeat: Behavioral forecasting, self-fulfilling prophecies, and the effect of competitive expectations. *Journal of Personality and Social Psychology, 85,* 672–683.

Diener, E. (1979). Deindividuation, self-awareness, and disinhibition. *Journal of Personality and Social Psychology, 37,* 1160–1171.

Diener, E. (1980). Deindividuation: The absence of self-awareness and self-regulation in group members. In P. B. Paulus (Ed.), *Psychology of group influence* (pp. 209–242). Hillsdale, NJ: Erlbaum.

Diener, E., & Biswas-Diener, R. (2008). *Happiness: Unlocking the mysteries of psychological wealth.* Malden, MA: Blackwell.

Diener, E., Emmons, R. A., Larsen, R. J., & Griffin, S. (1984). The Satisfaction with Life Scale. *Journal of Personality Assessment, 49,* 71–75.

Diener, E., Fraser, S. C., Beaman, A. L., & Kelem, R. T. (1976). Effects of deindividuation variables on stealing among Halloween trick-or-treaters. *Journal of Personality and Social Psychology, 33,* 178–183.

Diener, E., & Suh, E. M. (Eds.). (2000). Culture and subjective well-being. Cambridge, MA: MIT Press.

Diener, E., Suh, E. M., Lucas, R. E., & Smith, H. L. (1999). Subjective well-being: Three decades of progress. *Psychological Bulletin, 125,* 276–302.

Diener, E., Wolsic, B., & Fujita, F. (1995). Physical attractiveness and subjective well-being. *Journal of Personality and Social Psychology, 69,* 120–129.

Dietz, T. L. (1998). An examination of violence and gender role portrayals in video games: Implications for gender socialization and aggressive behavior. *Sex Roles, 38,* 425–442.

Dietz-Uhler, B. (1996). The escalation of commitment in political decision-making groups: A social identity approach. *European Journal of Social Psychology, 26,* 611–629.

Dijksterhuis, A., & Aarts, H. (2003). Of wildebeests and humans: The preferential detection of negative stimuli. *Psychological Science, 14,* 14–18.

Dijksterhuis, A., & Bargh, J. A. (2001). The perception-behavior expressway: Automatic effects of social perception on social behavior. *Advances in Experimental Social Psychology, 33,* 1–40.

Dill, K. E., Anderson, C. A., Anderson, K. B., & Deuser, W. E. (1997). Effects of aggressive personality on social expectations and social perceptions. *Journal of Research in Personality, 31,* 272–292.

Dimberg, U., & Ohman, A. (1996). Behold the wrath: Psychophysiological responses to facial stimuli. *Motivation and Emotion, 20,* 149–181.

Dimberg, U., Thunberg, M., & Elmehed, K. (2000). Unconscious facial reactions to emotional facial expressions. *Psychological Science, 11,* 86–89.

Dindia, K., & Allen, M. (1992). Sex differences in self-disclosure: A meta-analysis. *Psychological Bulletin, 112,* 106–124.

Dion, K. K., Berscheid, E., & Walster, E. (1972). What is beautiful is good. *Journal of Personality and Social Psychology, 24,* 285–290.

Dion, K. K., & Dion, K. L. (1996). Cultural perspectives on romantic love. *Personal Relationships, 3,* 5–17.

Dion, K. L. (2000). Group cohesion: From "field of forces" to multidimensional construct. *Group Dynamics, 4,* 7–26.

Dion, K. L., & Dion, K. K. (1976). Love, liking and trust in heterosexual relationships. *Personality and Social Psychology Bulletin, 2,* 187–190.

Dionisio, D. P., Granholm, E., Hillix, W. A., & Perrine, W. F. (2001). Differentiation of deception using pupillary responses as an index of cognitive processing. *Psychophysiology, 38,* 205–211.

Doh, H., Shin, N., Kim, M., Hong, J. S., Choi, M., & Kim, S. (2012). Influence of marital conflict on young childrens aggressive behavior in South Korea: The mediating role of child maltreatment. *Children and Youth Services Review.*

Dolinski, D. (2000). On inferring one's beliefs from one's attempt and consequences for subsequent compliance. *Journal of Personality and Social Psychology, 78,* 260–272.

Dollard, J., Doob, L. W., Miller, N. E., Mowrer, O. H., & Sears, R. R. (1939). *Frustration and aggression.* New Haven, CT: Yale University Press.

Donnerstein, E., & Berkowitz, L. (1981). Victim reactions in aggressive erotic films as a factor in violence against women. *Journal of Personality and Social Psychology, 41,* 710–724.

Donnerstein, E., & Donnerstein, M. (1976). Research in the control of interracial aggression. In R. G. Geen and E. C. O'Neal (Eds.), *Perspectives on aggression* (pp. 133–168). New York: Academic Press.

Donnerstein, E., Linz, D., & Penrod, S. (1987). *The question of pornography.* New York: Free Press.

Donnerstein, E., & Malamuth, N. (1997). Pornography: Its consequences on the observer. In L. B. Schlesinger & E. Revitch (Eds.), *Sexual dynamics of anti-social behavior* (2nd ed., pp. 30–49). Springfield, IL: Charles C Thomas.

Dooley, P. A. (1995). Perceptions of the onset controllability of AIDS and helping judgments: An attributional analysis. *Journal of Applied Social Psychology, 25,* 858–869.

Dornbusch, S. M., Hastorf, A. H., Richardson, S. A., Muzzy, R. E., & Vreeland, R. S. (1965). The perceiver and the perceived: Their relative influence on categories of interpersonal perception. *Journal of Personality and Social Psychology, 1,* 434–440.

Douglas, E. M., & Straus, M. A. (2006). Assault and injury of dating partners by university students in 19 countries and its relation to corporal punishment experienced as a child. *European Journal of Criminology, 7,* 293–318.

Dovidio, J. F. (1984). Helping behavior and altruism: An empirical and conceptual overview. In L. Berkowitz (Ed.), *Advances in experimental social psychology* (Vol. 17, pp. 361–427). New York: Academic Press.

Dovidio, J. F., Brigham, J. C., Johnson, B. T., & Gaertner, S. L. (1996). Stereotyping, prejudice, and discrimination: Another look. In C. N. Macrae, C. Stangor, & M. Hewstone (Eds.), *Stereotypes and stereotyping* (pp. 276–319). New York: Guilford.

Dovidio, J. F., & Gaertner, S. L. (1998). On the nature of contemporary prejudice: The causes, consequences, and challenges of aversive racism. In J. L. Eberhardt, & S. T. Fiske (Eds.), *Confronting racism: The problem and the response* (pp. 3–32). Thousand Oaks, CA: Sage.

Dovidio, J. F., & Gaertner, S. L. (2010). Intergroup bias. In S. T. Fiske, D. T. Gilbert, & G. Lindzey (Eds.), *Handbook of social psychology* (5th ed.). New York: Wiley.

Dovidio, J. F., Gaertner, S. L., Kawakami, K., & Hodson, G. (2002). Why can't we just get along? Interpersonal biases and interracial distrust. *Cultural Diversity and Ethnic Minority Psychology, 8,* 88–102.

Dovidio, J. F., Gaertner, S. L., & Saguy, T. (2009). Commonality and the complexity of 'we': Social attitudes and social change. *Personality and Social Psychology Review, 13,* 3–20.

Dovidio, J. F., Kawakami, K., Johnson, C., Johnson, B., & Howard, A. (1997). On the nature of prejudice: Automatic and controlled processes. *Journal of Experimental Social Psychology, 33,* 510–540.

Dovidio, J. F., Pagotto, L., & Hebl, M. R. (2011). Impicit attitudes and discrimination against people with physical disabilities. In R. Wiener & S. L. Willborn (Eds.), *Disability and aging discrimination: Perspectives in law and psychology.* New York: Springer Science + Business Media, x, 270 pp.

Dovidio, J. F., Piliavin, J.A., Schroeder, D.A., & Penner, L. A. (2006). The social psychology of prosocial behavior. Mahwah, NJ: Lawrence Erlbaum Associates Publishers.

Downie, M., Mageau, G. A., & Koestner, R. (2008). What makes for a pleasant social interaction? Motivational dynamics of interpersonal relationships. *The Journal of Social Psychology, 148,* 523–534.

Downs, A. C., & Lyons, P. M. (1991). Natural observations of the links between attractiveness and initial legal judgments. *Personality and Social Psychology Bulletin, 17,* 541–547.

Drigotas, S. M., & Rusbult, C. E. (1992). Shall I stay or should I go? A dependence model of breakups. *Journal of Personality and Social Psychology, 62,* 62–87.

Duck, S., & Wright, P. H. (1993). Reexamining gender differences in same-gender friendships: A close look at two kinds of data. *Sex Roles, 28,* 709–727.

Duckitt, J., & Mphuthing, T. (1998). Group identification and intergroup attitudes: A longitudinal analysis in South Africa. *Journal of Personality and Social Psychology, 74,* 80–85.

Duckitt, J., & Sibley, C. G. (2009). A dual process motivational model of ideological attitudes and system justification. In J. T. Jost & A. C. Kay (Eds.), *Social and psychological bases of ideology and system justification* (pp. 292–313). New York: Oxford University Press.

Duclos, S. E., Laird, J. D., Schneider, E., Sexter, M., Stern, L., & Van Lighten, O. (1989). Emotion-specific effects of facial expressions and postures on emotional experience. *Journal of Personality and Social Psychology, 57,* 100–108.

Due, P., & Holstein, B. (2008). Bullying victimization among 13 to 15 year old school children: Results from two comparative studies in 66 countries and regions. *International Journal of Adolescent Medicine and Health, 20,* 209–221.

Dunbar, R. I. M. (2008). Cognitive constraints on the structure and dynamics of social networks. *Group Dynamics: Theory, Research, and Practice, 12,* 7–16.

Dunbar, R. I. M. (2012). The social brain meets neuroimaging. *Trends in Cognitive Sciences, 16,* 101–102.

Dunham, Y., Baron, A. S., & Banaji, M. R. (2008). The development of implicit intergroup cognition. *Trends in Cognitive Sciences, 12,* 248–253.

Dunning, D., Griffin, D. W., Milojkovic, J. D., & Ross, L. (1990). The overconfidence effect in social prediction. *Journal of Personality and Social Psychology, 58,* 568–581.

Dunning, D., & Hayes, A. F. (1996). Evidence for egocentric comparison in social judgment. *Journal of Personality and Social Psychology, 71,* 213–229.

Dunning, D., Johnson, K., Ehrlinger, J., & Kruger, J. (2003). Why people fail to recognize their own incompetence. *Current Directions in Psychological Science, 12,* 83–87.

Dunning, D., & Sherman, D. A. (1997). Stereotypes and tacit inference. *Journal of Personality and Social Psychology, 73,* 459–471.

Duntley, J., & Buss, D. (2008). The origins of homicide. In J. D. Duntley & T. K. Shackelford (Eds.), *Evolutionary forensic psychology: Darwinian foundations of crime and law* (pp. 41–63). New York: Oxford University Press.

Dunton, B. C., & Fazio, R. H. (1997). An individual difference measure of motivation to control prejudiced reactions. *Personality and Social Psychology Bulletin, 23,* 316–326.

Durán, M., Moya, M., & Megías, J. L. (2011). Its his right, its her duty: Benevolent sexism and the justification of traditional sexual roles. *Journal of Sex Research, 48,* 470–478.

Durik, Amanda M., & Harackiewicz, Judith M. (2007). Different strokes for different folks: How individual interest moderates the effects of situational factors on task interest. *Journal of Educational Psychology, 99,* 597–610.

Dutton, D. G., & Aron, A. P. (1974). Some evidence for heightened sexual attraction under conditions of high anxiety. *Journal of Personality and Social Psychology, 30,* 510–517.

Duval, S., & Wicklund, R. A. (1972). *A theory of objective self-awareness.* New York: Academic Press.

Duval, S., Duval, V. H., & Mulilis, J. P. (1992). Effects of self-focus, discrepancy between self and standard, and outcome expectancy favorability on the tendency to match self to standard or to withdraw. *Journal of Personality and Social Psychology, 62,* 340–348.

Dweck, C. S., Chiu, C., & Hong, Y. (1995). Implicit theories and their role in judgments and reactions: A world from two perspectives. *Psychological Inquiry, 6,* 267–285.

Dysart, J. E., Lindsay, R. C. L., MacDonald, T. K., & Wicke, C. (2002). The intoxicated witness: Effects of alcohol on identification accuracy from showups. *Journal of Applied Psychology, 87,* 170–175.

Eagly, A. H. (1987). *Sex differences in social behavior: A social-role interpretation.* Hillsdale, NJ: Erlbaum.

Eagly, A. H. (2004a). Few women at the top: How role incongruity produces prejudice and the glass ceiling. In D. van Knippenberg & M. A. Hogg (Eds.), *Identity, leadership, and power.* London: Sage.

Eagly, A. H. (2004b). Prejudice: Toward a more inclusive understanding. In A. Eagly, R. M. Baron, & V. L. Hamilton (Eds.), *The social psychology of group identity and social conflict: Theory, application, and practice.* Washington, DC: APA Books.

Eagly, A. H., Ashmore, R. D., Makhijani, M. G., & Longo, L. C. (1991). What is beautiful is good, but ...: A meta-analytic review of research on the physical attractiveness stereotype. *Psychology Bulletin, 110,* 107–128.

Eagly, A. H., & Carli, L. L. (1981). Sex of researchers and sex-typed communications as determinants of sex differences in influenceability: A meta-analysis of social influence studies. *Psychological Bulletin, 90,* 1–20.

Eagly, A. H., & Chravala, C. (1986). Sex differences in conformity: Status and gender-role interpretations. *Psychology of Women Quarterly, 10,* 203–220.

Eagly, A. H., & Crowley, M. (1986). Gender and helping behavior: A meta-analytic review of the social psychological literature. *Psychological Bulletin, 100,* 283–308.

Eagly, A. H., & Fischer, A. (2009). Gender inequalities in power in organizations. In B. van Knippenberg & D. Tjosvold (Eds.), *Power and interdependence in organizations.* New York: Cambridge University Press.

Eagly, A. H, Mladinic, A., & Otto, S. (1994). Are women evaluated more favorably than men? An analysis of attitudes, beliefs, and emotions. *Psychology of Women Quarterly, 15,* 203–216.

Eagly, A. H., Wood, W., & Chaiken, S. (1978). Causal inferences about communicators and their effect on opinion change. *Journal of Personality and Social Psychology, 36,* 424–435.

Eagly, A. H., Wood, W., & Johannesen-Schmidt, M. C. (2004). Social role theory of sex differences and similarities: Implications for the partner preferences of women and men. In A. H. Eagly, A. Beall, & R. J. Sternberg (Eds.), *The psychology of gender* (2nd ed.). New York: Guilford.

Easton, J. A., & Shackelford, T. K. (2009). Morbid jealousy and sex differences in partner-directed violence. *Human Nature, 20,* 342–350.

Eastwick, P. W., & Finkel, E. J. (2008). Sex differences in mate preferences revisited: Do people know what they initially desire in a romantic partner? *Journal of Personality and Social Psychology, 94,* 245–264.

Eastwick, Paul W., Finkel, E. J., & Eagly, A. H. (2011). When and why do ideal partner preferences affect the process of initiating and maintaining romantic relationships? *Journal of Personality and Social Psychology, 101,* 1012–1032.

Eberhardt, J. L., Davies, P. G., Purdie-Vaughns, V. J., & Johnson, S. L. (2006). Looking deathworthy: Perceived stereotypicality of black defendants predicts capital-sentencing outcomes. *Psychological Science, 17,* 383–386.

Eberhardt, J. L., & Goff, P. A. (2004). Seeing race. In C. S. Crandall & M. Schaller (Eds.), *The social psychology of prejudice: Historical perspectives.* Seattle, WA: Lewinian.

Eberle, M., & Kappeler, P. M. (2008). Mutualism, reciprocity, or kin selection? Cooperative rescue of a conspecific from a boa in a nocturnal solitary forager the gray mouse lemur. *American Journal of Primatology, 70,* 410–414.

Eden, D. (1990). Pygmalion without interpersonal contrast effects: Whole groups gain from raising manager expectations. *Journal of Applied Psychology, 75,* 394–398.

Edlund, J. E., & Sagarin, B. J. (2009). Sex differences in jealousy: Misinterpretation of nonsignificant results as refuting the theory. *Personal Relationships, 16,* 67–78.

Edwards, K. (1990). The interplay of affect and cognition in attitude formation and change. *Journal of Personality and Social Psychology, 59,* 202–216.

Edwards, K., & Smith, E. E. (1996). A disconfirmation bias in the evaluation of arguments. *Journal of Personality and Social Psychology, 71,* 5–24.

Eggum, N. D., Eisenberg, N., Kao, K., Spinrad, T. L., Bolnick, R., Hofer, C., Kupfer, A.S., & Fabricius, W. V. (2011). Emotion understanding, theory of mind, and prosocial orientation: Relations over time in early childhood. *The Journal of Positive Psychology, 6,* 4–16.

Ehrlichman, H., & Eichenstein, R. (1992). Private wishes: Gender similarities and differences. *Sex Roles, 26,* 399–422.

Ehrlinger, J., Gilovich, T., & Ross, L. (2005). Peering into the bias blind spot: People's assessments of bias in themselves and others. *Personality and Social Psychology Bulletin, 31,* 680–692.

Eibach, R. P., & Ehrlinger, J. (2006). "Keep your eyes on the prize": Reference points and racial differences in assessing progress toward equality. *Personality and Social Psychology Bulletin, 32,* 66–77.

Eichstaedt, J., & Silvia, Paul J. (2003). Noticing the self: Implicit assessment of self-focused attention using word recognition latencies. *Social Cognition, 21,* 349–361.

Eisenberg, N. (2010). In M. Mikulincer & P. R. Shaver (Eds.), *Empathy-related responding: Links with self-regulation, moral judgment, and moral behavior.* Washington, DC: American Psychological Association.

Eisenberg, N., & Eggum, N. D. (2008). Empathy-related and prosocial responding: Conceptions and correlates during development. In B. A. Sullivan, M. Snyder, & J. L. Sullivan (Eds.), *Cooperation: The political psychology of effective human interaction* (pp. 53–74). Oxford: Blackwell.

Eisenberg, N., Guthrie, I. K., Cumberland, A., Murphy, B. C., Shepard, S. A., Zhou, Q., & Carlo, G. (2002). Prosocial development in early adulthood: A longitudinal study. *Journal of Personality and Social Psychology, 82,* 993–1006.

Eisenberger, N. I. (2012). Broken hearts and broken bones: A neural perspective on the similarities between social and physical pain. *Current Directions in Psychological Science, 21,* 42–47.

Eisenberger, N. I., Gable, S. L., & Lieberman, M. D. (2007). fMRI responses relate to differences in real world social experiences. *Emotion, 7,* 745–754.

Eisenberger, N. I., Lieberman, M. I., & Williams, K. D. (2003).Does rejection hurt? An fMRI study of social exclusion. *Science, 302,* 290–292.

Eisenberger, R., & Cameron, J. (1996). Detrimental effects of reward: Reality or myth? *American Psychologist, 51,* 1153–1166.

Eisenberger, R., Cotterell, N., & Marvel, J. (1987). Reciprocation ideology. *Journal of Personality and Social Psychology, 53,* 743–750.

Ekman, P., & Friesen, W. V. (1974). Detecting deception from the body or face. *Journal of Personality and Social Psychology, 29,* 288–298.

Ekman, P., Friesen, W. V., O'Sullivan, M., Chan, A., Diacoyanni-Tarlatzis, I., Heider, K., Krause, R., LeCompte, W. A., Pitcairn, T., Ricci-Bitti, P., Scherer, K., Tomita, M., & Tzavaras, A. (1987). Universals and cultural differences in the judgments of facial expressions of emotion. *Journal of Personality and Social Psychology, 53,* 712–717.

Ekman, P., & O'Sullivan, M. (1991). Who can catch a liar? *American Psychologist, 46,* 913–920.

Elfenbein, H. A., & Ambady, N. (2002). On the universality and cultural specificity of emotion recognition: A meta-analysis. *Psychological Bulletin, 128,* 203–235.

Elkin, R. A., & Leippe, M. R. (1986). Physiological arousal, dissonance, and attitude change: Evidence for a dissonance-arousal link and a "don't remind me" effect. *Journal of Personality and Social Psychology, 51,* 55–65.

Elliot, A. J., & Devine, P. G. (1994). On the motivational nature of cognitive dissonance: Dissonance as psychological discomfort. *Journal of Personality and Social Psychology, 67,* 382–394.

Elliot, A. J., & Niesta, D. (2008). Romantic red: Red enhances men's attraction to women. *Journal of Personality and Social Psychology, 95,* 1150–1164.

Elliott, M. A., Armitage, C. J., & Baughan, C. J. (2003). Drivers' compliance with speed limits: An application of the theory of planned behavior. *Journal of Applied Psychology, 88,* 964–972.

Ellis, M. L., Weiss, B., & Lochman, J. E. (2009). Executive functions in children: Associations with aggressive behavior and appraisal processing. *Journal of Abnormal Child Psychology: An Official Publication of the International Society for Research in Child and Adolescent Psychopathology, 37,* 945–956.

Elms, A. C. (2009). Obedience lite. *American Psychologist, 64,* 32–36.

Elms, A., & Milgram, S. (1966). Personality characteristics associated with obedience and defiance toward authoritative command. *Journal of Experimental Research in Personality, 1,* 282–289.

Elwork, A., Sales, B. D., & Alfini, J. J. (1982). *Making jury instructions understandable.* Charlottesville, VA: Miche.

English, P. W., & Sales, B. D. (1997). A ceiling or consistency effect for the comprehension of jury instructions. *Psychology, Public Policy, and Law, 3,* 381–401.

Enzle, M. E., & Anderson, S. C. (1993). Surveillant intentions and intrinsic motivation. *Journal of Personality and Social Psychology, 64,* 257–266.

Epley, N., & Huff, C. (1998). Suspicion, affective response, and educational benefit as a result of deception in psychology research. *Personality and Social Psychology Bulletin, 24,* 759–768.

Erber, R., & Tesser, A. (1992). Task effort and the regulation of mood: The absorption hypothesis. *Journal of Experimental Social Psychology, 28,* 339–359.

Erber, R., & Tesser, A. (1994). Self-evaluation maintenance: A social psychological approach to interpersonal relationships. In R. Erber & R. Gilmour (Eds.), *Theoretical frameworks for personal relationships* (pp. 211–233). Hillsdale, NJ: Erlbaum.

Ericksen, J. A., & Steffen, S. A. (1999). *Kiss and tell: Surveying sex in the twentieth century.* Cambridge, MA: Harvard University Press.

Ernest-Jones, M., Nettle, D., & Bateson, M. (2011). Effects of eye images on everyday cooperative behavior: A field experiment. *Evolution and Human Behavior, 32,* 172–178.

Esquivel-Santoveña, E. E., & Dixon, L. (2012). Investigating the true rate of physical intimate partner violence: A review of nationally representative surveys. *Aggression and Violent Behavior, 17,* 208–219.

Esser, J. K. (1998). Alive and well after 25 years: A review of groupthink research. *Organizational Behavior and Human Decision Processes, 73,* 116–141.

Esses, V. M., Veenvliet, S., Hodson, G., & Mihic, L. (2008). Justice, morality, and the dehumanization of refugees. *Social Justice Research, 21,* 4–25.

Estrada-Hollenbeck, M., & Heatherton, T. F. (1998). Avoiding and alleviating guilt through prosocial behavior. In J. Bybee (Ed.), *Guilt and children* (pp. 215–231). San Diego: Academic Press.

Evans, G. W., & Lepore, S. J. (1993). Household crowding and social support: A quasiexperimental analysis. *Journal of Personality and Social Psychology, 65,* 308–316.

Evans, R. I., Smith, C. K., & Raines, B. E. (1984). Deterring cigarette smoking in adolescents: A psychosocial-behavioral analysis of an intervention strategy. In A. Baum, S. E. Taylor, & J. E. Singer (Eds.), *Handbook of psychology and health: Vol. 4. Social psychological aspects of health* (pp. 301–318). Hillsdale, NJ: Erlbaum.

Ewing, L., Rhodes, G., & Pellicano, E. (2010). Have you got the look? gaze direction affects judgements of facial attractiveness. *Visual Cognition, 18,* 321–330.

Exum, M. L. (2006). Alcohol and aggression: An integration of findings from experimental studies. *Journal of Criminal Justice, 34,* 131–145.

Fagan, A. A. (2005). The relationship between adolescent physical abuse and criminal offending: Support for an enduring and generalized cycle of violence. *Journal of Family Violence, 20,* 279–290.

Fagin-Jones, S., & Midlarsky, E. (2007). Courageous altruism: Personal and situational correlates of rescue during the Holocaust. *Journal of Positive Psychology, 2,* 136–147.

Falk, C. F., Heine, S. J., Yuki, M., & Takemura, K. (2009). Why do Westerners self-enhance more than East Asians? *European Journal of Personality, 23,* 183–203.

Fanti, K. A., Vanman, E., Henrich, C. C., & Avraamides, M. N. (2009). Desensitization to media violence over a short period of time. *Aggressive Behavior, 35,* 179–187.

Fard, S. A. (2010). Effect of gender and social status on conformity. *Psychological Research, 13,* 30–50.

Farrelly, D., Lazarus, J., & Roberts, G. (2007). Altruists attract. *Evolutionary Psychology, 5,* 313–329.

Farris, C., Treat, T. A., & Viken, R. J. (2010). Alcohol alters men's perceptual and decisional processing of women's sexual interest. *Journal of Abnormal Psychology, 119,* 427–432.

Farris, C., Treat, T. A., Viken, R. J., & McFall, R. M. (2008). Sexual coercion and the misperception of sexual intent. *Clinical Psychology Review, 28,* 48–66.

Fazio, R. H. (1990). Multiple processes by which attitudes guide behavior: The MODE model as an integrative framework. In M. P. Zanna (Ed.), *Advances in experimental social psychology* (Vol. 23, pp. 75–109). New York: Academic Press.

Fazio, R. H., Effrein, E. A., & Falender, V. J. (1981). Self-perceptions following social interactions. *Journal of Personality and Social Psychology, 41,* 232–242.

Fazio, R. H., Ledbetter, J. E., & Towles-Schwen, T. (2000). On the costs of accessible attitudes: Detecting that the attitude object has changed. *Journal of Personality and Social Psychology, 78,* 197–210.

Fazio, R. H., & Olson, M. A. (2003). Implicit measures in social cognition research: Their meaning and use. *Annual Review of Psychology, 54,* 297–327.

Fazio, R. H., & Towles-Schwen, T. (1999). The MODE model of attitude-behavior processes. In S. Chaiken & Y. Trope (Eds.), *Dual-process theories in social psychology* (pp. 97–116). New York: Guilford.

Fazio, R. H., & Zanna, M. P. (1981). Direct experience and attitude-behavior consistency. In L. Berkowitz (Ed.), *Advances in experimental social psychology* (Vol. 14, pp. 162–202). New York: Academic Press.

Fazio, R. H., Zanna, M. P., & Cooper, J. (1977). Dissonance and self perception: An integrative view of each theory's proper domain of application. *Journal of Experimental Social Psychology, 13,* 464–479.

Feeney, J. A., & Noller, P. (1990). Attachment style as a predictor of adult romantic relationships. *Journal of Personality and Social Psychology, 58,* 281–291.

Fehr, B., & Russell, J. A. (1991). The concept of love viewed from a prototype perspective. *Journal of Personality and Social Psychology, 60,* 425–438.

Fein, E., & Schneider, S. (1996). *The rules: Time-tested secrets for capturing the heart of Mr. Right.* New York: Warner Books.

Fein, S., & Eustis, E. F. (2001). *Effects of violent and sexist content in video games on men's sexist attitudes and judgments.* Paper presented at the second annual meeting of the Society of Personality and Social Psychology, San Antonio, TX.

Fein, S., Hoshino-Browne, E., Davies, P. G., & Spencer, S. J. (2003). Self-image maintenance goals and sociocultural norms in motivated social perception. In S. J. Spencer, S. Fein, M. P. Zanna, & J. M. Olson (Eds.), *Motivated social perception: The Ontario symposium* (Vol. 9, pp. 21–44). Mahwah, NJ: Erlbaum.

Fein, S., Morgan, S. J., Norton, M. I., & Sommers, S. R. (1997). Hype and suspicion: The effects of pretrial publicity, race, and suspicion on jurors' verdicts. *Journal of Social Issues, 53,* 487–502.

Fein, S., & Spencer, S. J. (1997). Prejudice as self-image maintenance: Affirming the self through derogating others. *Journal of Personality and Social Psychology, 73,* 31–44.

Fein, S., & Spencer, S. J. (2008). In R. H. Fazio & R. E. Petty (Eds.), *Prejudice as self-image maintenance: Affirming the self through derogating others.* New York: Psychology Press.

Feinberg, T. E., & Keenan, J. P. (Eds.). (2005). *The lost self: Pathologies of the brain and identity.* New York: Oxford University Press.

Feingold, A. (1988). Matching for attractiveness in romantic partners and same-sex friends: A meta-analysis and theoretical critique. *Psychological Bulletin, 104,* 226–235.

Feingold, A. (1992a). Gender differences in mate selection preferences: A test of the parental investment model. *Psychological Bulletin, 112,* 125–139.

Feingold, A. (1992b). Good-looking people are not what we think. *Psychological Bulletin, 111,* 304–341.

Fejfar, M. C., & Hoyle, R. H. (2000). Effect of private self-awareness on negative affect and self-referent attribution: A quantitative review. *Personality and Social Psychology Review, 4,* 132–142.

Fenigstein, A., & Abrams, D. (1993). Self-attention and the egocentric assumption of shared perspectives. *Journal of Experimental Social Psychology, 29,* 287–303.

Fenigstein, A., Scheier, M. F., & Buss, A. H. (1975). Public and private self-consciousness: Assessment and theory. *Journal of Consulting and Clinical Psychology, 43,* 522–527.

Ferguson, G. A. (1992) Psychology in Canada: 1939–1945. *Canadian Psychology. 33,* 697–705.

Ferguson, M. J., & Zayas, V. (2009). Automatic evaluation. *Current Directions in Psychological Science, 18,* 362–366.

Ferrari, J. R. (1998). Procrastination. In H. S. Friedman (Ed.), *Encyclopedia of Mental Health* (pp. 5.1–5.7). San Diego: Academic Press.

Ferrari, J. R., Johnson, J. A., & McCowan, W. G. (1995). *Procrastination and task avoidance: Theory, research, and treatment.* New York: Plenum.

Ferreira, A., Antunes, P., & Herskovic, V. (2011). Improving group attention: An experiment with synchronous brainstorming. *Group Decision and Negotiation, 20,* 643–666.

Ferreira, A., Picazo, O., Uriarte, N., Pereira, M., & Fernandez-Guasti, A. (2000). Inhibitory effect of buspirone and diazepam, but not of 8-OH-DPAT, on maternal behavior and aggression. *Pharmacology, Biochemistry and Behavior, 66,* 389–396.

Festinger, L. (1950). Informal social communication. *Psychological Review, 57,* 271–282.

Festinger, L. (1954). A theory of social comparison processes. *Human Relations, 7,* 117–140.

Festinger, L. (1957). *A theory of cognitive dissonance.* Stanford, CA: Stanford University Press.

Festinger, L., & Carlsmith, J. M. (1959). Cognitive consequences of forced compliance. *Journal of Abnormal and Social Psychology, 58,* 203–210.

Festinger, L., Pepitone, A., & Newcomb, T. (1952). Some consequences of de-individuation in a group. *Journal of Abnormal and Social Psychology, 47,* 382–389.

Festinger, L., Schachter, S., & Back, K. W. (1950). *Social pressures in informal groups: A study of human factors in housing.* New York: Harper.

Fincham, F., Beach, S., & Davila, J. (2007). Longitudinal relations between forgiveness and conflict resolution in marriage. *Journal of Family Psychology, 21,* 542–545.

Fincham, F. D. (2003). Marital conflict, correlates, structure, and context. *Current Directions in Psychological Science, 12,* 23–27.

Fincham, F. D., Harold, G. T., & Gano-Phillips, S. (2000). The longitudinal association between attributions and marital satisfaction: Direction of effects and role of efficacy expectations. *Journal of Family Psychology, 14,* 267–285.

Fine, M. A., & Harvey, J. H. (Eds.). (2006). *Handbook of divorce and relationship dissolution.* Hillsdale, NJ: Erlbaum.

Fine, M. A., & Sacher, J. A. (1997). Predictors of distress following relationship termination among dating couples. *Journal of Social and Clinical Psychology, 16,* 381–388.

Fingerhut, A. W., Riggle, E. D. B., & Rostosky, S. S. (2011). Same-sex marriage: The social and psychological implications of policy and debates. *Journal of Social Issues, 67,* 225–241.

Fink, B., Weege, B., Flügge, J., Röder, S., Neave, N., & McCarty, K. (2012). Men's personality and women's perception of their dance quality. *Personality and Individual Differences, 52,* 232–235.

Finkel, E. J., & Eastwick, P. W. (2008). Speed-dating. *Current Directions in Psychological Science, 17,* 193–197.

Finkel, E. J., Rusbult, C. E., Kumashiro, M., & Hannon, P. A. (2002). Dealing with betrayal in close relationships: Does commitment promote forgiveness? *Journal of Personality and Social Psychology, 82,* 956–974.

Finkel, N. J. (1995). *Commonsense justice: Jurors' notions of the law.* Cambridge, MA: Harvard University Press.

Finkelstein, M. A. (2009). Intrinsic vs. extrinsic motivational orientations and the volunteer process. *Personality and Individual Differences, 46,* 653–658.

Fischer, C. S. (1976). *The urban experience.* New York: Harcourt Brace Jovanovich.

Fischer, P., & Greitemeyer, T. (2006). Music and aggression: The impact of sexual-aggressive song lyrics on aggression-related thoughts, emotions, and behavior toward the same and the opposite sex. *Personality and Social Psychology Bulletin, 32,* 1165–1176.

Fischer, P., Krueger, J. I., Greitemeyer, T., Vogrincic, C., Kastenmüller, A., Frey, D., Heene, M., Wicher, M., & Kainbacher, M. (2011). The bystander-effect: A meta-analytic review on bystander intervention in dangerous and non-dangerous emergencies. *Psychological Bulletin, 137,* 517–537.

Fishbein, M. (1980). A theory of reasoned action: Some applications and implications. In H. E. Howe & M. M. Page (Eds.), *Nebraska symposium on motivation* (Vol. 27, pp. 65–116). Lincoln: University of Nebraska Press.

Fishbein, M., & Ajzen, I. (1972). Attitudes and opinions. In P. H. Mussen & M. R. Rosenzweig (Eds.), *Annual Review of Psychology, 23,* 487–544.

Fisher, H. E. (2004). *Why we love: The nature and chemistry of romantic love.* New York: Henry Holt.

Fisher, J. D., Nadler, A., & Whitcher-Alagna, S. (1982). Recipient reactions to aid. *Psychological Bulletin, 91,* 27–54.

Fisher, R. J., Vandenboosh, M., & Kersi, A. (2008). An empathy-helping perspective on consumers' responses to fund-raising appeals. *Journal of Consumer Research, 35,* 519–531.

Fiske, A. P. (1991). The cultural relativity of selfish individualism: Anthropological evidence that humans are inherently sociable. In M. S. Clark (Ed.), *Review of personality and social psychology: Vol. 12. Prosocial behavior* (pp. 176–214). Newbury Park, CA: Sage.

Fiske, A. P. (1992). The four elementary forms of sociality: Framework for a unified theory of social relations. *Psychological Review, 99,* 689–723.

Fiske, A. P. (2002). Using individualism and collectivism to compare cultures—A critique of the validity and measurement of the constructs: Comment on Oyserman et al. (2002). *Psychological Bulletin, 128,* 78–88.

Fiske, S. T. (2012). Warmth and competence: Stereotype content issues for clinicians and researchers. *Canadian Psychology/Psychologie canadienne, 53,* 14–20.

Fiske, S. T., Harris, L. T., Russell, A. M., & Shelton, J. N. (2009). Divergent social realities, depending on where you sit: Perspectives from the stereotype content model. In S. Demoulin, J. P. Leyens, & J. F. Dovidio (Eds.), *Intergroup misunderstandings: Impact of divergent social realities* (pp. 173–189). New York: Psychology Press.

Fiske, S. T., Lin, M., & Neuberg, S. L. (1999). The continuum model: Ten years later. In S. Chaiken & Y. Trope (Eds.), *Dual-process theories in social psychology* (pp. 231–254). New York: Guilford.

Fiske, S. T., & Neuberg, S. L. (1990). A continuum model of impression formation: From category-based to individuating processes: Influence of information and motivation on attention and interpretation. In M. P. Zanna (Ed.), *Advances in experimental social psychology* (Vol. 23, pp. 1–74). San Diego, CA: Academic Press.

Fiske, S. T., & Taylor, S. E. (2008). *Social cognition: From brains to culture.* New York: McGraw-Hill.

Fitzgerald, J. M. (1988). Vivid memories and the reminiscence phenomenon: The role of self-narrative. *Human Development, 31,* 261–273.

Fivush, R., Haden, C. A., & Dimmick, J. W. (Eds.) (2003). *Autobiographical memory and the construction of a narrative self: Developmental and cultural perspectives.* Mahwah, NJ: Erlbaum.

Fletcher, G. J. O., Danilovics, P., Fernandez, G., Peterson, D., & Reeder, G. D. (1986). Attributional complexity: An individual differences measure. *Journal of Personality and Social Psychology, 51,* 875–884.

Florian, V., Mikulincer, M., & Taubman, O. (1995). Does hardiness contribute to mental health during a stressful real-life situation? The roles of appraisal and coping. *Journal of Personality and Social Psychology, 68,* 687–695.

Flory, J. D., Raikkonen, K., Matthews, K. A., & Owens, J. F. (2000). Self-focused attention and mood during everyday social interactions. *Personality and Social Psychology Bulletin, 26,* 875–883.

Folger, R., & Greenberg, J. (1985). Procedural justice: An interpretive analysis of personnel systems. In K. Rowland & G. Ferris (Eds.), *Research in personnel and human resource management* (Vol. 3, pp. 141–183). Greenwich, CT: JAI Press.

Follett, M. P. (1942). Constructive conflict. In H. C. Metcalf & L. Urwick (Eds.), *Dynamic administration: The collected papers of Mary Parker Follett* (pp. 30–49). New York: Harper.

Forbes, G. B., Adams-Curtis, L. E., Pakalka, A. H., & White, K. B. (2006). Dating aggression, sexual coercion, and aggression-supporting attitudes among college men as a function of participation in aggressive high school sports. *Violence Against Women, 12,* 441–455.

Forbes, G., Zhang, X., Doroszewicz, K., & Haas, K. (2009). Relationships between individualism-collectivism, gender, and direct or indirect aggression: A study in China, Poland, and the U.S. *Aggressive Behavior, 35,* 24–30.

Ford, T. E., Ferguson, M. A., Brooks, J. L., & Hagadone, K. M. (2004). Coping sense of humor reduces effects of stereotype threat on women's math performance. *Personality and Social Psychology Bulletin, 30,* 643–653.

Ford, T. E., & Tonander, G. R. (1998). The role of differentiation between groups and social identity in stereotype formation. *Social Psychology Quarterly, 61,* 372–384.

Forest, A. L., & Wood, J. V. (2011). When partner caring leads to sharing: Partner responsiveness increases expressivity, but only for individuals with low self-esteem. *Journal of Experimental Social Psychology, 47,* 843–848.

Forgas, J. P. (Ed.) (2000). *Feeling and thinking: Affective influences on social cognition.* New York: Cambridge University Press.

Forgas, J. P., Baumeister, R. F., & Tice, D. M. (2009). *The psychology of self-regulation: An introductory review.* New York: Psychology Press.

Forgas, J. P., & Bower, G. H. (1987). Mood effects on person perception judgments. *Journal of Personality and Social Psychology, 53,* 53–60.

Forgas J. P., Cooper J. and Crano W. D. (Eds.),*The psychology of attitudes and attitude change* (2010). New York: Psychology Press.

Forgas, J. P., Dunn, E., & Granland, S. (2008). Are you being served...? an unobtrusive experiment of affective influences on helping in a department store. *European Journal of Social Psychology, 38,* 333–342.

Forgas, J. P., & East, R. (2008). How real is that smile? Mood effects on accepting or rejecting the veracity of emotional facial expressions. *Journal of Nonverbal Behavior, 32,* 157–170.

Forgas, J. P., & Fitness, J. (Eds.). (2008). *Social relationships: Cognitive, affective, and motivational processes.* New York: Psychology Press.

Forgas, J. P., & Locke, J. (2005). Affective influences on causal inferences: The effects of mood on attributions for positive and negative interpersonal episodes. *Cognition and Emotion, 19,* 1071–1081.

Foster, C. A., Foster, J. D., & Campbell, W. K. (2010). Are secret relationships hot, then not? Romantic secrecy as a function of relationship duration. *The Journal of Social Psychology, 150,* 668–688.

Foster, C. A., Witcher, B. S., Campbell, W. K., & Green, J. D. (1998). Arousal and attraction: Evidence for automatic and controlled processes. *Journal of Personality and Social Psychology, 74,* 86–101.

Fosterling, F. (1992). The Kelley model as an analysis of variance analogy: How far can it be taken? *Journal of Experimental Social Psychology, 28,* 475–490.

Fox, E., Russo, R., & Dutton, K. (2002). Attentional bias for threat: Evidence for delayed disengagement from emotional faces. *Cognition and Emotion, 16,* 355–379.

Franck, E., De Raedt, R., Barbez, C., & Rosseel, Y. (2008). Psychometric properties of the Dutch Rosenberg self-esteem scale. *Psychologica Belgica, 48,* 25–35.

Franck, K. A. (1980). Friends and strangers: The social experience of living in urban and non-urban settings. *Journal of Social Issues, 36*(3), 52–71.

Frank, J. (1949). *Courts on trial.* Princeton, NJ: Princeton University Press.

Franklin, S. S. (2010). *The psychology of happiness: A good human life.* New York: Cambridge University Press.

Frantz, C. M., Cuddy, A. J. C., Burnett, M., Ray, H., & Hart, A. (2004). A threat in the computer: The race Implicit Association Test as a stereotype threat experience. *Personality and Social Psychology Bulletin, 30,* 1611–1624.

Frattaroli, J. (2006). Experimental disclosure and its moderators: A meta-analysis. *Psychological Bulletin, 132,* 823–865.

Frazier, P. A. (2003). Perceived control and distress following sexual assault: A longitudinal test of a new model. *Journal of Personality and Social Psychology, 84,* 1257–1269.

Frazier, P., Steward, J., & Mortensen, H. (2004). Perceived control and adjustment to trauma: A comparison across events. *Journal of Social and Clinical Psychology, 23,* 303–324.

Fredrickson, B. L. (2009). *Positivity: Groundbreaking research reveals how to embrace the hidden strength of positive emotions, overcome negativity, and thrive.* New York: Crown Books.

Fredrickson, B. L., Roberts, T. A., Noll, S. M., Quinn, D. M., & Twenge, J. M. (1998). The swimsuit becomes you: Sex differences in self-objectification, restrained eating, and math performance. *Journal of Personality and Social Psychology, 75,* 269–284.

Freedman, J. L. (2002). *Media violence and its effects on aggression: Assessing the scientific evidence.* Toronto: University of Toronto Press.

Freedman, J. L. (2007) *Television Violence and Aggression: Setting the Record Straight.* The Media Institute. http://www.mediainstitute.org

Freedman, J. L., & Burke, T.M. (1996). The effect of pretrial publicity: The Bernardo case. *Canadian Journal of Criminology, 38, 253–270.*

Freedman, J. L., & Fraser, S. C. (1966). Compliance without pressure: The foot-in-the-door technique. *Journal of Personality and Social Psychology, 4,* 195–202.

Freedman, J. L., & Sears, D. O. (1965). Warning, distraction, and resistance to influence. *Journal of Personality and Social Psychology, 1,* 262–266.

French, D. C., Jansen, E. A., & Pidada, S. (2002). United States and Indonesian children's and adolescents' reports of relational aggression by disliked peers. *Child Development, 73,* 1143–1150.

Freud, S. (1905). Fragments of an analysis of a case of hysteria. *Collected papers* (Vol. 3). New York: Basic Books. (Reprinted in 1959)

Frey, K. S., Hirschstein, M. K., Edstrom, L. V., & Snell, J. L. (2009). Observed reductions in school bullying, nonbullying aggression, and destructive bystander behavior: A longitudinal evaluation. *Journal of Educational Psychology, 101,* 466–481.

Friedman, H. S. (1991). *The self-healing personality.* New York: Henry Holt.

Friedman, H. S. (2011). (Editor). The Oxford Handbook of Health Psychology. NY: Oxford University Press.

Friedrich, J., Fethersonhaugh, D., Casey, S., & Gallagher, D. (1996). Argument integration and attitude change: Suppression effects in the integration of one-sided arguments that vary in persuasiveness. *Personality and Social Psychology Bulletin, 22,* 179–191.

Friend, R., Rafferty, Y., & Bramel, D. (1990). A puzzling misinterpretation of the Asch "conformity" study. *European Journal of Social Psychology, 20,* 29–44.

Fritzsche, B. A., Finkelstein, M. A., & Penner, L. A. (2000). To help or not to help: Capturing individuals' decision policies. *Social Behavior and Personality, 28,* 561–578.

Frye, N. E., & Karney, B. R. (2004). Revision in memories of relationship development: Do biases persist over time? *Personal Relationships, 11,* 79–97.

Frye, N. E., & Karney, B. R. (2006). The context of aggressive behavior in marriage: A longitudinal study of newlyweds. *Journal of Family Psychology, 20,* 12–20.

Fujino, N., & Okamura, H. (2009). Factors affecting the sense of burden felt by family members caring for patients with mental illness. *Archives of Psychiatric Nursing, 23,* 128–137.

Funk, S. C. (1992). Hardiness: A review of theory and research. *Health Psychology, 11,* 335–345.

Furnham, A. (2003). Belief in a just world: Research progress over the past decade. *Personality and Individual Differences, 34,* 795–817.

Gabbert, F., Memon, A., & Allan, K. (2003). Memory conformity: Can eyewitnesses influence each other's memories for an event? *Applied Cognitive Psychology, 17,* 533–543.

Gaertner, S. L., & Dovidio, J. F. (2000). *Reducing intergroup bias: The common ingroup identity model.* Philadelphia, PA: Psychology Press.

Gaertner, S. L., & Dovidio, J. F. (2009). A common intergroup identity: A categorization-based approach for reducing intergroup bias. In T. D. Nelson (Ed.), *Handbook of prejudice, stereotyping, and discrimination* (pp. 489–505). New York: Psychology Press.

Gaertner, S. L., Dovidio, J. F., & Houlette, M. A. (2010). Social categorization. In J. F. Dovidio, M. Hewstone, P. Glick, & V. M. Esses (Eds.), *Hand-book of prejudice, stereotyping, and discrimination.* London: Sage.

Gagne, F. M., & Lydon, J. E. (2001). Mindset and relationship illusions: The moderating effects of domain specificity and relationship commitment. *Personality and Social Psychology Bulletin, 27,* 1144–1155.

Gagné, M., Tourigny, M., Joly, J., & Pouliot-Lapointe, J. (2007). Predictors of adult attitudes toward corporal punishment of children. *Journal of Interpersonal Violence, 22,* 1285–1304.

Gagnon, A., & Bourhis, R. Y. (1996). Discrimination in the minimal group paradigm: Social identity or self-interest? *Personality and Social Psychology Bulletin, 22,* 1289–1301.

Gailliot, M., Baumeister, R., DeWall, C., Maner, J., Plant, E., Tice, D., Brewer, L., & Schmeichel, B. (2007). Self-control relies on glucose as a limited energy source: Willpower is more than just a metaphor. *Journal of Personality and Social Psychology, 92,* 325–336.

Gailliot, M. T., Peruche, B. M., Plant, E. A., & Baumeister, R. F. (2009). Stereotypes and prejudice in the blood: Sucrose drinks reduce prejudice and stereotyping. *Journal of Experimental Social Psychology, 45,* 288–290.

Galanter, M. (1999). *Cults: Faith, healing, and coercion* (2nd ed.).New York: Oxford University Press.

Galen, B. R., & Underwood, M. K. (1997). *Developmental Psychology, 33,* 589–600.

Galinsky, A. D., & Kray, L. J. (2004). From thinking about what might have been to sharing what we know: The role of counterfactual mind-sets in information sharing in groups. *Journal of Experimental Social Psychology, 40,* 606–618.

Galinsky, A. D., & Ku, G. (2004). The effects of perspective-taking on prejudice: The moderating role of self-evaluation. *Personality and Social Psychology Bulletin, 30,* 594–604.

Galinsky, A. D., Stone, J., & Cooper, J. (2000). The reinstatement of dissonance and psychological discomfort following failed affirmations. *European Journal of Social Psychology, 30,* 123–147.

Galinsky, A. D., Wang, C. S., & Ku, G. (2008). Perspective-takers behave more stereotypically. *Journal of Personality and Social Psychology, 95,* 404–419.

Gallo, L. C., & Matthews, K. A. (2003). Understanding the association between socioeconomic status and physical health: Do negative emotions play a role? *Psychological Bulletin, 129,* 10–51.

Gallup, G. G., Jr. (1977). Self-recognition in primates: A comparative approach to the bidirectional properties of consciousness. *American Psychologist, 32,* 329–337.

Game, F., Carchon, I., & Vital-Durand, F. (2003). The effect of stimulus attractiveness on visual tracking in 2- to 6-month-old infants. *Infant Behavior & Development, 26,* 135–150.

Gámez-Guadix, M., Straus, Murray A., Carrobles, J. A., Muñoz-Rivas, M. J., & Almendros, C. (2010). Corporal punishment and long-term behavior problems: The moderating role of positive parenting and psychological aggression. *Psicothema, 22,* 529–536.

Gammie, S. C., Olaghere-da-Silva, U. B., & Nelson, R. J. (2000). 3-Bromo-7-nitroindazole, a neuronal nitric oxide synthase inhibitor, impairs maternal aggression and citrulline immunoreactivity in prairie voles. *Brain Research, 870,* 80–86.

Gamson, W. A., Fireman, B., & Rytina, S. (1982). *Encounters with unjust authority.* Homewood, IL: Dorsey.

Gangestad, S. W. (1993). Sexual selection and physical attractiveness: Implications for mating dynamics. *Human Nature, 4,* 205–235.

Gangestad, S. W., & Simpson, J. A. (2000). The evolution of human mating: Trade-offs and strategic pluralism. *Behavioral and Brain Sciences, 23,* 573–587.

Gangestad, S. W., & Snyder, M. (2000). Self-monitoring: Appraisal and reappraisal. *Psychological Bulletin, 126,* 530–555.

Gannon, T. A., Keown, K., & Polaschek, D. L. L. (2007). Increasing honest responding on cognitive distortions in child molesters: The bogus pipeline revisited. *Sexual Abuse: Journal of Research and Treatment, 19,* 5–22.

Garandeau, C. F., Ahn, H., & Rodkin, P. C. (2011). The social status of aggressive students across contexts: The role of classroom status hierarchy, academic achievement, and grade. *Developmental Psychology, 47,* 1699–1710.

Garcia, S. M., Weaver, K., Moskowitz, G. B., & Darley, J. M. (2002). Crowded minds: The implicit bystander effect. *Journal of Personality and Social Psychology, 83,* 843–853.

Garcia, S. M., Weaver, K., Darley, J. M., & Spence, B.T. (2009). Dual effects of implicit bystanders: Inhibiting vs. facilitating helping behavior. *Journal of Consumer Psychology, 19,* 215–224.

Gardner, W. L., Gabriel, S., & Hochschild, L. (2002). When you and I are "we," you are not threatening: The role of self-expansion in social comparison. *Journal of Personality and Social Psychology, 82,* 239–251.

Garrett, B. (2008). Judging innocence. *Columbia Law Review, 108,* 55–142.

Garry, M., French, L., Kinzett, T., & Mori, K. (2008). Eyewitness memory following a discussion: Using the MORI technique with a western sample. *Applied Cognitive Psychology, 22,* 431-431-439.

Gawronski, B., & Bodenhausen, G. V. (2006). Associative and propositional processes in evaluation: An integrative review of implicit and explicit attitude change. *Psychological Bulletin, 132,* 692–731.

Gawronski, B., Peters, K. R., Brochu, P. M., & Strack, F. (2008). Understanding the relations between different forms of racial prejudice: A cognitive consistency perspective. *Personality and Social Psychology Bulletin, 34,* 648–665.

Geary, D. C. (2000). Evolution and proximate expression of human paternal investment. *Psychological Bulletin, 126,* 55–77.

Geen, R. G. (1981). Behavioral and physiological reactions to observed violence: Effects of prior exposure to aggressive stimuli. *Journal of Personality and Social Psychology, 40,* 868–875.

Geen, R. G. (1991). Social motivation. *Annual Review of Psychology, 42,* 377–399.

Geen, R. G., & Quanty, M. B. (1977). The catharsis of aggression: An evaluation of a hypothesis. In L. Berkowitz (Ed.), *Advances in experimental social psychology* (Vol. 10, pp. 1–37). New York: Academic Press.

Geis, F. L., Brown, V., Jennings (Walstedt), J., & Porter, N. (1984). TV commercials as achievement scripts for women. *Sex Roles, 10,* 513–525.

Geiselman, R. E., Haight, N. A., & Kimata, L. G. (1984).Context effects in the perceived physical attractiveness of faces. *Journal of Experimental Social Psychology, 20,* 409–424.

George, D. M., Carroll, P., Kersnick, R., & Calderon, K. (1998). Gender-related patterns of helping among friends. *Psychology of Women Quarterly, 22,* 685–704.

Gerard, H. B., Whilhelmy, R. A., & Connolley, R. S. (1968).Conformity and group size. *Journal of Personality and Social Psychology, 8,* 79–82.

Gerber, J., & Wheeler, L. (2009). On being rejected: A meta-analysis of experimental research on rejection. *Perspectives on Psychological Science, 4,* 468–488.

Gerbner, G., Gross, L., Morgan, M., & Signorielli, N. (1986).Living with television: The dynamics of the cultivation process. In J. Bryant & D. Zillmann (Eds.), *Perspectives on media effects* (pp. 17–40). Hillsdale, NJ: Erlbaum.

Gergen, K. J. (1973). Social psychology as history. *Journal of Personality and Social Psychology, 26,* 309–320.

Gergen, K. J. (1994). Exploring the postmodern: Perils or potentials? *American Psychologist, 49,* 412–416.

Gershoff, E. T. (2002). Corporal punishment by parents and associated child behaviors and experiences: A meta-analytic and theoretical review. *Psychological Bulletin, 128,* 539–579.

Gersick, C. J. G. (1988). Time and transition in work teams: Toward a new model of group development. *Academy of Management Journal, 21,* 9–41.

Gersick, C. J. G. (1994). Pacing strategic change: The case of a new venture. *Academy of Management Journal, 37,* 9–45.

Gibbons, F. X. (1990). Self-attention and behavior: A review and theoretical update. In M. P. Zanna (Ed.), *Advances in experimental social psychology* (Vol. 23, pp. 249–303). New York: Academic Press.

Gibbons, F. X., Gerrard, M., Cleveland, M. J., Wills, T. A., & Brody, G. (2004). Perceived discrimination and substance use in African

American parents and their children: A panel study. *Journal of Personality and Social Psychology, 86,* 517–529.

Gibbons, F. X., Lane, D. J., Gerrard, M., Reis-Bergan, M., Lautrup, C., Pexa, N., & Blanton, H. (2002). Comparison level preferences after performance: Is downward comparison theory still useful? *Journal of Personality and Social Psychology, 83,* 865–880.

Gibbons, F. X., & McCoy, S. B. (1991). Self-esteem, similarity, and reactions to active versus passive downward comparison. *Journal of Personality and Social Psychology, 60,* 414–424.

Gibbons, F. X., O'Hara, R. E., Stock, M. L., Gerrard, M., Weng, C., & Wills, T. A. (2012). The erosive effects of racism: Reduced self-control mediates the relation between perceived racial discrimination and substance use in African American adolescents. *Journal of Personality and Social Psychology, 102,* 1089-1104.

Gibbons, S. L., & Ebbeck, V. (1997). The effect of different teaching strategies on the moral development of physical education students. *Journal of Teaching in Physical Education, 17,* 85–98.

Gibson, B., & Sachau, D. (2000). Sandbagging as a self-presentational strategy: Claiming to be less than you are. *Personality and Social Psychology Bulletin, 26,* 56–70.

Giesler, R. B., Josephs, R. A., & Swann, W. B., Jr. (1996). Self-verification in clinical depression: The desire for negative evaluation. *Journal of Abnormal Psychology, 105,* 358–368.

Gigerenzer, G., Todd, P. M., & the ABC Research Group (1999). *Simple heuristics that make us smart.* New York: Oxford University Press.

Gilbert, D. (2006). *Stumbling on happiness.* New York: Alfred A. Knopf.

Gilbert, D. T., Giesler, R. B., & Morris, K. A. (1995). When comparisons arise. *Journal of Personality and Social Psychology, 69,* 227–236.

Gilbert, D. T., & Hixon, J. G. (1991). The trouble of thinking: Activation and application of stereotypic beliefs. *Journal of Personality and Social Psychology, 60,* 509–517.

Gilbert, D. T., & Jones, E. E. (1986). Perceiver-induced constraint: Interpretations of self-generated reality. *Journal of Personality and Social Psychology, 50,* 269–280.

Gilbert, D. T., & Malone, P. S. (1995). The correspondence bias. *Psychological Bulletin, 117,* 21–38.

Gilbert, D. T., McNulty, S. E., Giuliano, T. A., & Benson, J. E. (1992). Blurry words and fuzzy deeds: The attribution of obscure behavior. *Journal of Personality and Social Psychology, 62,* 18–25.

Gilbert, D. T., Pelham, B. W., & Krull, D. S. (1988). On cognitive busyness: When person perceivers meet persons perceived. *Journal of Personality and Social Psychology, 54,* 733–740.

Gilbert, D. T., Pinel, E. C., Wilson, T. D., Blumberg, S. J., & Wheatley, T. (1998). Immune neglect: A source of durability bias in affective forecasting. *Journal of Personality and Social Psychology, 75,* 617–638.

Gilbert, S. J. (1981). Another look at the Milgram obedience studies: The role of the gradated series of shocks. *Personality and Social Psychology Bulletin, 7,* 690–695.

Gillig, P. M., & Greenwald, A. G. (1974). Is it time to lay the sleeper effect to rest? *Journal of Personality and Social Psychology, 29,* 132–139.

Gilovich, T. (1991). *How we know what isn't so: The fallibility of human reason in everyday life.* New York: Free Press.

Gilovich, T., Grifin, D., & Kahneman, D. (Eds.) (2002).*Heuristics and biases: The psychology of intuitive judgment.* New York: Cambridge University Press.

Gilovich, T., Medvec, V. H., & Savitsky, K. (2000). The spotlight effect in social judgment: An egocentric bias in estimates of the salience of one's own actions and appearance. *Journal of Personality and Social Psychology, 78,* 211–222.

Giner-Sorolla, R., & Chaiken, S. (1997). Selective use of heuristic and systematic processing under defensive motivation. *Personality and Social Psychology Bulletin, 23,* 84–97.

Gladue, B. A., Boechler, M., & McCaul, K. D. (1989). Hormonal response to competition in human males. *Aggressive Behavior, 15,* 409–422.

Gladstone, G. L., Parker, G. B., & Malhi, G. S. (2006). Do bullied children become anxious and depressed adults? A cross-sectional investigation of the correlates of bullying and anxious depression. *Journal of Nervous and Mental Disease, 19,* 201–208.

Gladwell, M. (2005). *Blink: The power of thinking without thinking.* New York: Little, Brown, and Company.

Glasman, L. R., & Albarracín, D. (2006). Forming attitudes that predict future behavior: A meta-analysis of the attitude-behavior relation. *Psychological Bulletin, 132,* 778–822.

Glass, D. C., & Singer, J. E. (1972). *Urban stress.* New York: Academic Press.

Glick, P., & Fiske, S. T. (2001). Ambivalent sexism. In M. P. Zanna (Ed.), *Advances in experimental social psychology* (Vol. 33, pp. 115–188). San Diego, CA: Academic Press.

Glick, P., & Fiske, S. T. (2011). Ambivalent sexism revisited. *Psychology of Women Quarterly, 35,* 530–535.

Glick, P., Fiske, S. T., et al. (2000). Beyond prejudice as simple antipathy: Hostile and benevolent sexism across cultures. *Journal of Personality and Social Psychology, 79,* 763–775.

Glomb, T. M., Bhave, D. P., Miner, A. G., & Wall, M. (2011). Doing good, feeling good: Examining the role of organizational citizenship behaviors in changing mood. *Personnel Psychology, 64,* 191–223.

Godfrey, D. K., Jones, E. E., & Lord, C. G. (1986). Self-promotion is not ingratiating. *Journal of Personality and Social Psychology, 50,* 106–115.

Goethals, G. R., Cooper, J., & Naficy, A. (1979). Role of foreseen, foreseeable, and unforeseeable behavioral consequences in the arousal of cognitive dissonance. *Journal of Personality and Social Psychology, 37,* 1179–1185.

Goethals, G. R., & Darley, J. (1977). Social comparison theory: An attributional approach. In J. M. Suls & R. L. Miller (Eds.), *Social comparison processes: Theoretical and empirical perspectives* (pp. 259–278). Washington, DC: Hemisphere.

Goff, P. A., Steele, C. M., & Davies, P. G. (2008). The space between us: Stereotype threat and distance in interracial contexts. *Journal of Personality and Social Psychology, 94,* 91–107.

Goffman, E. (1955). On face-work: An analysis of ritual elements in social interaction. *Psychiatry, 18,* 213–231.

Goffman, E. (1959). *The presentation of self in everyday life.* Garden City: Doubleday.

Goldberg, L. R. (1978). Differential attribution of trait-descriptive terms to oneself as compared to well-liked, neutral, and disliked others: A psychometric analysis. *Journal of Personality and Social Psychology, 36,* 1012–1028.

Goldberg, P. (1968). Are women prejudiced against women? *Transaction, 5,* 28–30.

Goldhagen, D. J. (1996). Hitler's willing executioners: Ordinary Germans and the Holocaust. New York: Knopf.

Goldstein, A. G., Chance, J. E., & Schneller, G. R. (1989). Frequency of eyewitness identification in criminal cases: A survey of prosecutors. *Bulletin of the Psychonomic Society, 27,* 71–74.

Goldstein, Noah J., & Cialdini, Robert B. (2007). The spyglass self: A model of vicarious self-perception. *Journal of Personality and Social Psychology, 92,* 402417.

Gollwitzer, P. M., & Schaal, B. (2001). How goals and plans affect action. In J. M. Collis & S. Messick (Eds.), *Intelligence and personality: Bridging the gap in theory and measurement* (pp. 139–161). Mahwah, NJ: Erlbaum.

Golombok, S., & Hines, M. (2002). Sex differences in social behavior. In P. K. Smith & C. H. Hart (Eds.), *Blackwell handbook of childhood social development* (pp. 117–136). Malden, MA: Blackwell.

Gonsalkorale, K., Sherman, J. W., Allen, T. J., Klauer, Karl Christoph, & Amodio, D. M. (2011). Accounting for successful control of implicit racial bias: The roles of association activation, response monitoring, and overcoming bias. *Personality and Social Psychology Bulletin, 37,* 1534–1545.

Gonzaga, G., Campos, B., & Bradbury, T. (2007). Similarity, convergence, and relationship satisfaction in dating and married couples. *Journal of Personality and Social Psychology, 93,* 34–48.

Gonzales, P. M., Blanton, H., & Williams, K. J. (2002). The effects of stereotype threat and double-minority status on the test performance of Latino women. *Personality and Social Psychology Bulletin, 28,* 659–670.

Goodwin, S. A., Fiske, S. T., Rosen, L. D., & Rosenthal, A. M. (2002). The eye of the beholder: Romantic goals and impression biases. *Journal of Experimental Social Psychology, 38,* 232–241.

Gopnik, A., Meltzoff, A. N., & Kuhl, P. K. (1999). *The scientist in the crib: Minds, brains, and how children learn.* New York: Morrow.

Gorchoff, S., John, O., & Helson, R. (2008). Contextualizing change in marital satisfaction during middle age: An 18-year longitudinal study. *Psychological Science, 19,* 1194–1200.

Gordijn, E. H., Hindriks, I., Koomen, W., Dijksterhuis, A., & van Knippenberg, A. (2004). Consequences of stereotype suppression and internal suppression motivation: A self-regulation approach. *Personality and Social Psychology Bulletin, 30,* 212–224.

Gorman, C. (1994, September 19). Let's not be too hasty. *Time,* p. 71.

Gorman, E. H., & Kmec, J. A. (2009). Hierarchical rank and women's organizational mobility: Glass ceilings in corporate law firms. *American Journal of Sociology, 114,* 1428–1474.

Gosling, P., Denizeau, M., & Oberlé, D. (2006). Denial of responsibility: A new mode of dissonance reduction. *Journal of Personality and Social Psychology, 90,* 722–733.

Gosling, S. (2008). *Snoop: What your stuff says about you.* New York: Basic Books.

Gosselin, P., Kirouac, G., & Dore, F. Y. (1995). Components and recognition of facial expression in the communication of emotion by actors. *Journal of Personality and Social Psychology, 68,* 83–96.

Gossett, J. L., & Byrne, S. (2002). "CLICK HERE": A content analysis of Internet rape sites. *Gender and Society, 16,* 689–709.

Gotlib, I. H., & Hammen, C. L. (Eds.). (2009). *Handbook of depression* (2nd ed.). New York: Guilford.

Gottman, J. M. (1994). *What predicts divorce?* Hillsdale, NJ: Erlbaum.

Gottman, J. M. (1998). Psychology and the study of marital processes. *Annual Review of Psychology, 49,* 169–197.

Gottman, J. M., & Levenson, R. W. (1992). Marital processes predictive of later dissolution: Behavior, physiology, and health. *Journal of Personality and Social Psychology, 63,* 221–233.

Gouin, J., Glaser, R., Malarkey, W. B., Beversdorf, D., & Kiecolt-Glaser, J. (2012). Chronic stress, daily stressors, and circulating inflammatory markers. *Health Psychology, 31,* 264–268.

Gouldner, A. W. (1960). The norm of reciprocity: A preliminary statement. *American Sociological Review, 25,* 161–178.

Grammer, K., & Thornhill, R. (1994). Human facial attractiveness and sexual selection: The role of averageness and symmetry. *Journal of Comparative Psychology, 108,* 233–242.

Granhag, P. A., & Strömwall. L. A. (Eds.). (2004). *Deception detection in forensic contexts.* Cambridge, England: Cambridge University Press.

Grant, D., ONeil, K., & Stephens, L. (2009). Pluralistic ignorance among assembled peers. *Sociological Perspectives, 52,* 59–79.

Grant, M. J., Button, C. M., Hannah, T. E., & Ross, A. S. (2002). Uncovering the multidimensional nature of stereotype inferences: A within-participants study of gender, age, and physical attractiveness. *Current Research in Social Psychology, 8,* 19–39.

Gray, H. M., Gray, K., & Wegner, D. M. (2007, February 2). Dimensions of mind perception. *Science, 315,* 619.

Gray, J. (1997). *Men are from Mars, women are from Venus.* New York: HarperCollins.

Gray, J. J., & Ginsberg, R. L. (2007). Muscle dissatisfaction: An overview of psychological and cultural research and theory. In J. K. Thompson & G. Cafri (Eds.), *The muscular ideal: Psychological, social, and medical perspectives* (pp. 15–39). Washington, DC: American Psychological Association.

Gray, K., Knobe, J., Sheskin, M., Bloom, P., & Barrett, L. F. (2011). More than a body: Mind perception and the nature of objectification. *Journal of Personality and Social Psychology, 101,* 1207–1220.

Gray-Little, B., & Hafdahl, A. R. (2000). Factors influencing racial comparisons of self-esteem: A quantitative review. *Psychological Bulletin, 126,* 26–54.

Green, D. P., Glaser, J., & Rich, A. (1998). From lynching to gay bashing: The elusive connection between economic conditions and hate crime. *Journal of Personality and Social Psychology, 75,* 82–92.

Green, J. D., Sedikides, C., & Gregg, A. P. (2008). Forgotten but not gone: The recall and recognition of self-threatening memories. *Journal of Experimental Social Psychology, 44,* 547–561.

Greenberg, D. L. (2004). President Bush's false "flashbulb" memory of 9/11/01. *Applied Cognitive Psychology, 18,* 363–370.

Greenberg, J., & Pyszczynski, T. (1985). The effects of an overheard ethnic slur on evaluations of the target: How to spread a social disease. *Journal of Experimental Social Psychology, 21,* 61–72.

Greenberg, J., Solomon, S., & Pyszczynski, T. (1997). Terror management theory of self-esteem and cultural worldviews: Empirical assessments and conceptual refinements. *Advances in Experimental Social Psychology, 29,* 61–139.

Greenberg, M. S., & Westcott, D. R. (1983). Indebtedness as a mediator of reactions to aid. In J. D. Fisher, A. Nadler, & B. M. DePaulo (Eds.), *New directions in helping: Vol. 1. Recipient reactions to aid* (pp. 85–112). New York: Academic Press.

Greene, E., & Heilbrun, K. (2011). *Wrightsman's psychology and the legal system* (7th ed.). Belmont, CA: Wadsworth.

Greenwald, A. G. (1968). Cognitive learning, cognitive responses to persuasion, and attitude change. In A. Greenwald, T. Brock, & T. Ostrom (Eds.), *Psychological foundations of attitudes* (pp. 147–170). New York: Academic Press.

Greenwald, A. G. (1980). The totalitarian ego: Fabrication and revision of personal history. *American Psychologist, 35,* 603–618.

Greenwald, A. G. (1992). New look 3: Unconscious cognition reclaimed. *American Psychologist, 47,* 766–779.

Greenwald, A. G., & Farnham, S. D. (2000). Using the Implicit Association Test to measure self-esteem and self-concept. *Journal of Personality and Social Psychology, 79,* 1022–1038.

Greenwald, A. G., McGhee, D. E., & Schwartz, J. L. K. (1998). Measuring individual differences in implicit cognition: The implicit association test. *Journal of Personality and Social Psychology, 74,* 1464–1480.

Greenwald, A. G., Nosek, B. A., & Banaji, M. R. (2003). Understanding and using the Implicit Association Test: I. An improved scoring algorithm. *Journal of Personality and Social Psychology, 85,* 197–216.

Greenwald, A. G., Poehlman, T. A., Uhlmann, E. L., & Banaji, M. R. (2009). Understanding and using the Implicit Association Test: III. Meta-analysis of predictive validity. *Journal of Personality and Social Psychology, 97,* 17–41.

Greenwald, A. G., Pratkanis, A. R., Leippe, M. R., & Baumgardner, M. H. (1986). Under what conditions does theory obstruct research progress? *Psychological Review, 93,* 216–229.

Greenwald, A. G., Spangenberg, E. R., Pratkanis, A. R., & Eskenazi, J. (1991). Double-blind tests of subliminal self-help audiotapes. *Psychological Science, 2,* 119–122.

Gregory, A. M., Light-Häusermann, J. H., Rijsdijk, F., & Eley, T. C. (2009). Behavioral genetic analyses of prosocial behavior in adolescents. *Developmental Science, 12,* 165–174.

Greitemeyer, T. (2011). Exposure to music with prosocial lyrics reduces aggression: First evidence and test of the underlying mechanism. *Journal of Experimental Social Psychology, 47,* 28–36.

Greitemeyer, T., Agthe, M., Turner, R., & Gschwendtner, C. (2012). Acting prosocially reduces retaliation: Effects of prosocial video games on aggressive behavior. *European Journal of Social Psychology, 42,* 235–242.

Greitemeyer, T., Schulz-Hardt, S., Brodbeck, F. C., & Frey, D. (2006). Information sampling and group decision making: The effects of an advocacy decision procedure and task experience. *Journal of Experimental Psychology: Applied, 12,* 31–42.

Grossman, M., & Wood, W. (1993). Sex differences in intensity of emotional experience: A social role interpretation. *Journal of Personality and Social Psychology, 65,* 1010–1020.

Grote, N. K., & Clark, M. S. (2001). Perceiving unfairness in the family: Cause or consequence of marital distress? *Journal of Personality and Social Psychology, 80,* 281–293.

Grover, K. W., & Miller, C. T. (2012). Does expressed acceptance reflect genuine attitudes? A bogus pipeline study of the effects of mortality salience on acceptance of a person with AIDS. *The Journal of Social Psychology, 152,* 131.

Gruder, C. L., Cook, T. D., Hennigan, K. M., Flay, B. R., Alessis, C., & Halamaj, J. (1978). Empirical tests of the absolute sleeper effect predicted from the discounting cue hypothesis. *Journal of Personality and Social Psychology, 36,* 1061–1074.

Grusec, J. E. (1991). The socialization of altruism. In M. S. Clark (Ed.), *Prosocial behavior. Review of personality and social psychology* (Vol. 12, pp. 9–33). Newbury Park, CA: Sage.

Gudjonsson, G. H. (2003). *The psychology of interrogations and confessions.* London: Wiley.

Gudykunst, W., & Bond, M. H. (1997). Intergroup relations across cultures. In J. W. Berry, M. H. Segall, & C. Kagitçibasi (Eds.), *Handbook of cross-cultural psychology: Social behavior and applications* (2nd ed., Vol. 3, pp. 119–161). Needham Heights, MA: Allyn & Bacon.

Guerin, B. (2003). Social behaviors as determined by different arrangements of social consequences: Diffusion of responsibility effects with competition. *Journal of Social Psychology, 143,* 313–329.

Guimond, S. (2000). Group socialization and prejudice: The social transmission of intergroup attitudes and beliefs. *European Journal of Social Psychology,* 30, 335–354.

Gully, S. M., Devine, D. J., & Whitney, D. J. (1995). A meta-analysis of cohesion and performance: Effects of level of analysis and task interdependence. *Small Group Research, 26,* 497–520.

Gump, B. B., & Kulik, J. A. (1997). Stress, affiliation, and emotional contagion. *Journal of Personality and Social Psychology, 72,* 305–319.

Günaydin, G., Zayas, V., Selcuk, E., & Hazan, C. (2012). I like you but I dont know why: Objective facial resemblance to significant others influences snap judgments. *Journal of Experimental Social Psychology, 48,* 350–353.

Gurtner, A.,Tschan, F., Semmer, N. K., & Nägele, C. (2007). Getting groups to develop good strategies: Effects of reflexivity interventions on team process, team performance, and shared mental models. *Organizational Behavior and Human Decision Processes, 102,* 127–142.

Gurung, A.R. (2010). Health psychology: A cultural approach (2nd ed.). Belmont, CA: Wadsworth/Cengage Learning.

Haas, S. A., Schaefer, D. R., & Kornienko, O. (2010). Health and the structure of adolescent social networks. *Journal of Health and Social Behavior, 51,* 424–439.

Haberstroh, S., Oyserman, D., Schwarz, N., Kuehnen, U., & Ji, L. J. (2002). Is the interdependent self more sensitive to question context than the independent self? Self-construal and the observation of conversational norms. *Journal of Experimental Social Psychology, 38,* 323–329.

Hackman, J. R., & Katz, N. (2010). Group behavior and performance. In S. T. Fiske, D. T. Gilbert, & G. Lindzey (Eds.), *Handbook of social psychology* (5th ed.). New York: McGraw-Hill.

Hafer, C. L. (2000). Do innocent victims threaten the belief in a just world? Evidence from a modified Stroop task. *Journal of Personality and Social Psychology, 79,* 165–173.

Hafer, C. L., Begue, L., Choma, B. L.& Dempsey, J. L. (2005). Belief in a just world and commitment to long-term deserved outcomes. *Social Justice Research, 18,* 429–444.

Hakmiller, K. L. (1966). Threat as a determinant of downward comparison. *Journal of Experimental Social Psychology* (Suppl. 1), 32–39.

Halberstadt, J., & Rhodes, G. (2000). The attractiveness of nonface averages: Implications for an evolutionary explanation of the attractiveness of average faces. *Psychological Science, 11,* 285–289.

Halberstadt, J., & Rhodes, G. (2003). It's not just average faces that are attractive: Computer-manipulated averageness makes birds, fish, and automobiles attractive. *Psychonomic Bulletin and Review, 10,* 149–156.

Halberstam, D. (1972). *The best and the brightest.* New York: Random House.

Halbesleben, J. R. B. (2009). The role of pluralistic ignorance in the reporting of sexual harassment. *Basic and Applied Social Psychology, 31,* 210–217.

Hald, G. M., Malamuth, N. M., & Yuen, C. (2010). Pornography and attitudes supporting violence against women: Revisiting the relationship in nonexperimental studies. *Aggressive Behavior, 36,* 14–20.

Hall, J. A., Coats, E. J., & LeBeau, L. S. (2005). Nonverbal behavior and the vertical dimension of social relations: A metaanalysis. *Psychological Bulletin, 131,* 898–924.

Hamer, D. H., Rice, G., Risch, N., & Ebers, G. (1999). Genetics and male sexual orientation. *Science, 285,* 803.

Hamermesh, D. S., & Biddle, J. E. (1994). Beauty and the labor market. *American Economic Review, 84,* 1174–1195.

Hamilton, D. L., & Rose, T. L. (1980). Illusory correlation and the maintenance of stereotypic beliefs. *Journal of Personality and Social Psychology, 39,* 832–845.

Hamilton, R., Vohs, Kathleen D., Sellier, A., & Meyvis, T. (2011). Being of two minds: Switching mindsets exhausts self-regulatory resources. *Organizational Behavior and Human Decision Processes, 115,* 13–24.

Hamilton, W. D. (1964). The genetical evolution of social behavior: I and II. *Journal of Theoretical Biology, 7,* 1–52.

Hammersla, J. F., & Frease-McMahan, L. (1990). University students' priorities: Life goals vs. relationships. *Sex Roles, 23,* 1–14.

Hampson, R. B. (1984). Adolescent prosocial behavior: Peer-group and situational factors associated with helping. *Journal of Personality and Social Psychology, 46,* 153–162.

Han, S., & Shavitt, S. (1994). Persuasion and culture: Advertising appeals in individualistic and collectivistic societies. *Journal of Experimental Social Psychology, 30,* 326–350.

Hanc, J. (2006, September 12). Muscle men: Today's culture has produced fitness buffs obsessed with becoming muscular. But how much is too much? *Newsday* (New York), p. B12.

Haney, C., Banks, C., & Zimbardo, P. (1973). Interpersonal dynamics in a simulated prison. *International Journal of Criminology and Penology, 1,* 69–97.

Haney, C., & Zimbardo, P. G. (1998). The past and future of U.S. prison policy: Twenty-five years after the Stanford Prison Experiment. *American Psychologist, 53,* 709–727.

Haney, C., & Zimbardo, P. G. (2009). Persistent dispositionalism in interactionist clothing: Fundamental attribution error in explaining prison abuse. *Personality and Social Psychology Bulletin, 35,* 807–814.

Hansen, C. H., & Hansen, R. D. (1988). Finding the face in the crowd: An anger superiority effect. *Journal of Personality and Social Psychology, 54,* 917–924.

Harackiewicz, J. M., & Elliot, A. J. (1993). Achievement goals and intrinsic motivation. *Journal of Personality and Social Psychology, 65,* 904–915.

Hardin, G. (1968). The tragedy of the commons. *Science, 162,* 1243–1248.

Haritos-Fatouros, M. (2002). *Psychological origins of institutionalized torture.* London: Routledge.

Hargreaves, D. A., & Tiggemann, M. (2009). Muscular ideal media images and men's body image: Social comparison processing and

individual vulnerability. *Psychology of Men and Masculinity, 10,* 109–119.
Harinck, F., & De Dreu, Carsten K. W. (2011). When does taking a break help in negotiations? the influence of breaks and social motivation on negotiation processes and outcomes. *Negotiation and Conflict Management Research, 4*(1), 33–46.
Harkins, S. G., & Petty, R. E. (1981). Effects of source magnification of cognitive effort on attitudes: An information processing view. *Journal of Personality and Social Psychology, 40,* 401–413.
Harkins, S. G., & Petty, R. E. (1987). Information utility and the multiple source effect. *Journal of Personality and Social Psychology, 52,* 260–268.
Harmon-Jones, E., Brehm, J. W., Greenberg, J., Simon, L., & Nelson, D. E. (1996). Evidence that the production of aversive consequences is not necessary to create cognitive dissonance. *Journal of Personality and Social Psychology, 70,* 5–16.
Harmon-Jones, E., & Mills, J. (Eds.) (1999). *Cognitive dissonance: Progress on a pivotal theory in social psychology.* Washington, DC: American Psychological Association.
Harris, C. R. (2002). Sexual and romantic jealousy in heterosexual and homosexual adults. *Psychological Science, 13,* 7–12.
Harris, C. R. (2003). A review of sex differences in sexual jealousy, including self-report data, psychophysiological responses, interpersonal violence, and morbid jealousy. *Personality and Social Psychology Review, 7,* 102–128.
Harris, C. R., & Christenfeld, N. (1996). Gender, jealousy, and reason. *Psychological Science, 7,* 364–366.
Harris, L. T., & Fiske, S. T. (2006). Dehumanizing the lowest of the low: Neuroimaging responses to extreme out-groups. *Psychological Science, 17,* 847–853.
Harris, L. T., & Fiske, S. T. (2011). Dehumanized perception: A psychological means to facilitate atrocities, torture, and genocide? *Zeitschrift Für Psychologie/Journal of Psychology, 219*(3), 175–181.
Harris, M. B. (1995). Ethnicity, gender, and evaluations of aggression. *Aggressive Behavior, 21,* 343–357.
Harris, M. J., & Perkins, R. (1995). Effects of distraction on interpersonal expectancy effects: A social interaction test of the cognitive busyness hypothesis. *Social Cognition, 13,* 163–182.
Harris, M. J., & Rosenthal, R. (1985). Mediation of interpersonal expectancy effects. *Psychological Bulletin, 97,* 363–386.
Hart, A. J. (1995). Naturally occurring expectation effects. *Journal of Personality and Social Psychology, 68,* 109–115.
Hart, A. J., Whalen, P. J., Shin, L. M., McInerney, S. C., Fischer, H., & Rauch, S. L. (2000). Differential response in the human amygdala to racial outgroup vs ingroup face stimuli. *NeuroReport, 11,* 2351–2355.
Hart, J. W., Karau, S. J., Stasson, M. F., & Kerr, N. A. (2004). Achievement motivation, expected coworker performance, and collective task motivation: Working hard or hardly working? *Journal of Applied Social Psychology, 34,* 984–1000.
Hartwig, M., Granhag, P. A., Strömwall, L. A., & Vrij, A. (2005). Detecting deception via strategic disclosure of evidence. *Law and Human Behavior, 29,* 469–484
Harvey, J. H., & Manusov, V. L. (Eds.) (2001). *Attribution, communication behavior, and close relationships.* New York: Cambridge University Press.
Harvey, J. H., & Omarzu, J. (2000). *Minding the close relationship: A theory of relationship enhancement.* New York: Cambridge University Press.
Hasan, Y., Bègue, L., & Bushman, B. J. (2012). Viewing the world through "blood-red tinted glasses": The hostile expectation bias mediates the link between violent video game exposure and aggression. *Journal of Experimental Social Psychology, 48,* 953–956.
Hasel, L. E., & Kassin, S. M. (2009). On the presumption of evidentiary independence: Can confessions corrupt eyewitness identifications? *Psychological Science, 20,* 122–126.
Haslam, N., Loughnan, S., Kashima, Y., & Bain, P. (2008). Attributing and denying humanness to others. *European Review of Social Psychology, 19,* 55–85.
Haslam, S. A., Jetten, J., Postmes, T., Haslam, C. (2009). Social identity, health and well-being: An emerging agenda for applied psychology. *Applied Psychology: An International Review, 58,* 1–23.
Haslam, S. A., Ryan, M. K., Postmes, T., Spears, R., Jetten, J., & Webley, P. (2006). Sticking to our guns: Social identity as a basis for the maintenance of commitment to faltering organizational projects. *Journal of Organizational Behavior, 27,* 607–628.
Hass, R. G. (1981). Effects of source characteristics on the cognitive processing of persuasive messages and attitude change. In R. Petty, T. Ostrom, & T. Brock (Eds.), *Cognitive responses in persuasion* (pp. 141–172). Hillsdale, NJ: Erlbaum.
Hass, R. G. (1984). Perspective taking and self-awareness: Drawing an E on your forehead. *Journal of Personality and Social Psychology, 46,* 788–798.
Hass, R. G., & Eisenstadt, D. (1990). The effects of self-focused attention on perspective-taking and anxiety. *Anxiety Research, 2,* 165–176.
Hass, R. G., & Grady, K. (1975). Temporal delay, type of forewarning, and resistance to influence. *Journal of Experimental Social Psychology, 11,* 459–469.
Hass, R. G., Katz, I., Rizzo, N., Bailey, J., & Moore, L. (1992). When racial ambivalence evokes negative affect, using a disguised measure of mood. *Personality and Social Psychology Bulletin, 18,* 786–797.
Hassin, R. R., Bargh, J. A., & Zimerman, S. (2009). Automatic and flexible: The case of nonconscious goal pursuit. *Social Cognition, 27,* 27–36.
Hassin, R., & Trope, Y. (2000). Facing faces: Studies on the cognitive aspects of physiognomy. *Journal of Personality and Social Psychology, 78,* 837–852.
Hastie, R. (1984). Causes and effects of causal attribution. *Journal of Personality and Social Psychology, 46,* 44–56.
Hastie, R., Penrod, S. D., & Pennington, N. (1983). *Inside the jury.* Cambridge, MA: Harvard University Press.
Hatfield, E. (1988). Passionate and companionate love. In R. J. Sternberg & M. L. Barnes (Ed.), *The psychology of love* (pp. 191–217). New Haven, CT: Yale University Press.
Hatfield, E., Bensman, L., & Rapson, R. L. (2012). A brief history of social scientists' attempts to measure passionate love. *Journal of Social and Personal Relationships, 29,* 143–164.
Hatfield, E., Rapson, R. L., & Martel, L. D. (2007). Passionate love. In S. Kitayama & D. Cohen (Eds.), *Handbook of cultural psychology.* New York: Guilford.
Haverkamp, B. E. (1993). Confirmatory bias in hypothesis testing for client-identified and counselor self-generated hypotheses. *Journal of Counseling Psychology, 40,* 303–315.
Hawkins, D. L., Pepler, D. J., & Craig, W. M. (2001). Naturalistic observations of peer interventions in bullying. *Social Development, 10,* 512–527.
Hawkley, L. C., & Cacioppo, J. T. (2010). Loneliness matters: A theoretical and empirical review of consequences and mechanisms. *Annals of Behavioral Medicine, 40*(2), 218–227.
Hay, D. F., & Cook, K. V. (2007). The transformation of prosocial behavior from infancy to childhood. In C. A. Brownell & C. B. Kopp (Eds.), *Socioemotional development in the toddler years: Transitions and transformations* (pp. 100–131). New York: Guilford.
Hays, R. B. (1985). A longitudinal study of friendship development. *Journal of Personality and Social Psychology, 48,* 909–924.
Hazan, C., & Diamond, L. M. (2000). The place of attachment in human mating. *Review of General Psychology, 4,* 186–204.
Hazan, C., & Shaver, P. (1987). Romantic love conceptualized as an attachment process. *Journal of Personality and Social Psychology, 52,* 511–524.

Hearold, S. (1986). A synthesis of 1043 effects of television on social behavior. In G. Comstock (Ed.), *Public communication and behavior* (Vol. 1, pp. 65–133). Orlando, FL: Academic Press.

Heatherton, T. F., & Polivy, J. (1991). Development and validation of a scale for measuring state self-esteem. *Journal of Personality and Social Psychology, 60,* 895–910.

Heatherton, T. F., & Vohs, K. D. (2000). Interpersonal evaluations following threats to self: Role of self-esteem. *Journal of Personality and Social Psychology, 78,* 725–736.

Heatherton, T. F., & Wyland, C. L. (2003). Assessing self-esteem. In S. J. Lopez & C. R. Snyder (Eds.), *Positive psychological assessment: A handbook of models and measures* (pp. 219–233). Washington, DC: American Psychological Association.

Hedge, A., & Yousif, Y. H. (1992). Effects of urban size, urgency, and cost on helpfulness: A cross-cultural comparison between the United Kingdom and the Sudan. *Journal of Cross Cultural Psychology, 23,* 107–115.

Heider, F. (1958). *The psychology of interpersonal relations.* New York: Wiley.

Heilman, M. E., Rivero, J. C., & Brett, J. F. (1991). Skirting the competence issue: Effects of sex-based preferential selection on task choices of women and men. *Journal of Applied Psychology, 76,* 99–105.

Heine, S. J. (2005). Where is the evidence for pancultural self-enhancement? A reply to Sedikides, Gaertner, & Toguchi (2003). *Journal of Personality and Social Psychology, 89,* 531–538.

Heine, S. J. (2007). Culture and motivation. In S. Kitayama & D. Cohen (Eds.), *Handbook of cultural psychology.* New York: Guilford.

Heine, S. J., & Hamamura, T. (2007). In search of East Asian self-enhancement. *Personality and Social Psychology Review, 11,* 1–24.

Heine, S. J., Kitayama, S., Lehman, D. R., Takata, T., Ide, E., Lueng, C., & Matsumoto, H. (2001). Divergent consequences of success and failure in Japan and North America: An investigation of self-improving motivations and malleable selves. *Journal of Personality and Social Psychology, 81,* 599–615.

Heine, S. J., & Lehman, D. R. (1997). Culture, dissonance, and self-affirmation. *Personality and Social Psychology Bulletin, 23,* 389–400.

Heine, S. J., Lehman, D. R., Markus, H. R., & Kitayama, S. (1999). Is there a universal need for positive self-regard? *Psychological Review, 106,* 756–794.

Heine, S. J., & Raineri, A. (2009). Self-improving motivations and collectivism: The case of Chileans. *Journal of Cross-Cultural Psychology, 40,* 158–163.

Heine, S. J., Takata, T., & Lehman, D. R. (2000). Beyond self-presentation: Evidence for self-criticism among Japanese. *Personality and Social Psychology Bulletin, 26,* 71–78.

Heine, S. J., Takemoto, T., Moskalenko, S., Lasaleta, J., & Henrich, J. (2008). Mirrors in the head: Cultural variation in objective self-awareness. *Personality and Social Psychology Bulletin, 34,* 879–887.

Helgeson, V. S., Cohen, S., Schulz, R., & Yasko, J. (2000). Group support interventions for women with breast cancer: Who benefits from what? *Health Psychology, 19,* 107–114.

Helgeson, V. S., Reynolds, K. A., & Tomich, P. L. (2006). A meta-analytic review of benefit finding and growth. *Journal of Consulting and Clinical Psychology, 74,* 797–816.

Heller, J. F., Pallak, M. S., & Picek, J. M. (1973). The interactive effects of intent and threat on boomerang attitude change. *Journal of Personality and Social Psychology, 26,* 273–279.

Henchy, T., & Glass, D. C. (1968). Evaluation apprehension and the social facilitation of dominant and subordinate responses. *Journal of Personality and Social Psychology, 10,* 446–454.

Henderlong, J., & Lepper, M. R. (2002). The effects of praise on children's intrinsic motivation: A review and synthesis. *Psychological Bulletin, 128,* 774–795.

Henderson, L., & Zimbardo, P. (1998). Shyness. In H. S. Friedman (Ed.), *Encyclopedia of Mental Health.* San Diego: Academic Press.

Henderson-King, D., Henderson-King, E., & Hoffman, L. (2001). Media images and women's self-evaluations: Social context and importance of attractiveness as moderators. *Personality and Social Psychology Bulletin, 27,* 1407–1416.

Henderson-King, E., & Henderson-King, D. (1997). Media effects on women's body esteem: Social and individual differences factors. *Journal of Applied Social Psychology, 27,* 399–417.

Hendrick, C., & Hendrick, S. S. (Eds.) (2000). *Close relationships: A sourcebook.* Thousand Oaks, CA: Sage.

Hendrick, S. S., & Hendrick, C. (1995). Gender differences and similarities in sex and love. *Personal Relationships, 2,* 55–65.

Henggeler, S. W., Letourneau, E. J., Chapman, J. E., Borduin, C. M., Schewe, P. A., & McCart, M. R. (2009). Mediators of change for multisystemic therapy with juvenile sexual offenders. *Journal of Consulting and Clinical Psychology, 77,* 451–462.

Henig, R. M. (2006, February 5). Looking for the lie. *The New York Times.*

Henle, C. A., Kohut, G., & Booth, R. (2009). Designing electronic use policies to enhance employee perceptions of fairness and to reduce cyberloafing: An empirical test of justice theory. *Computers in Human Behavior, 25,* 902–910.

Henley, N. M. (1977). *Body politics: Power, sex, and nonverbal communication.* Englewood Cliffs, NJ: Prentice-Hall.

Henningsen, D. D., Henningsen, M.,Lynn Miller, Eden, J., & Cruz, M. G. (2006). Examining the symptoms of groupthink and retrospective sensemaking. *Small Group Research, 37,* 36–64.

Henry, J. D., von Hippel, W., & Baynes, K. (2009). Social inappropriateness, executive control, and aging. *Psychology and Aging, 24,* 239–244.

Herdt, G. (1998). *Same sex, different cultures: Exploring gay and lesbian lives.* Boulder, CO: Westview Press.

Herman, C. P., Zanna, M. P., & Higgins, E. T. (1986). *Physical appearance, stigma, and social behavior: The Ontario symposium* (Vol. 3). Hillsdale, NJ: Erlbaum.

Herring, C. (2009). Does diversity pay? Race, gender, and the business case for diversity. *American Sociological Review, 74,* 208–224.

Hertwig, R., & Ortmann, A. (2008). Deception in social psychological experiments: Two misconceptions and a research agenda. *Social Psychology Quarterly, 71*(3), 222–227.

Herzberger, S. D. (1996). *Violence within the family: Social psychological perspectives.* Madison, WI: Brown & Benchmark.

Herzberger, S. D. (2005). Snips, snails, sugar, and spice: Decisions about family violence through the lens of gender. In S. Fein, G. R. Goethals, & M. J. Sandstrom (Eds.), *Gender and aggression: Interdisciplinary perspectives.* Mahwah, NJ: Erlbaum.

Hétu, S., Taschereau-Dumouchel, V., & Jackson, P. L. (2012). Stimulating the brain to study social interactions and empathy. *Brain Stimulation, 5,* 95-102.

Hewitt, P. L., Flett, G. L., Sherry, S. B., Habke, M., Parkin, M., Lam, R., McMurtry, B., Ediger, E., Fairlie, P., & Stein, M. B. (2003). The interpersonal expression of perfection: Perfectionistic self-presentation and psychological distress. *Journal of Personality and Social Psychology, 84,* 1303–1325.

Hewstone, M., & Lord, C. G. (1998). Changing intergroup cognitions and intergroup behavior: The role of typicality. In C. Sedikides, J. Schopler, & C. A. Insko (Eds.), *Intergroup cognition and intergroup behavior* (pp. 367–392). Mahwah, NJ: Erlbaum.

Higgins, E. T. (1989). Self-discrepancy theory: What patterns of self-beliefs cause people to suffer? In L. Berkowitz (Ed.), *Advances in experimental social psychology* (Vol. 22, pp. 93–136). New York: Academic Press.

Higgins, E. T. (1999). Self-discrepancy: A theory relating self and affect. In R. F. Baumeister (Ed.), *The self in social psychology* (pp. 150–181). Philadelphia, PA: Psychology Press/ Taylor & Francis.

Higgins, E. T., King, G. A., & Mavin, G. H. (1982). Individual construct accessibility and subjective impressions and recall. *Journal of Personality and Social Psychology, 43,* 35–47.

Higgins, E. T., Rholes, C. R., & Jones, C. R. (1977). Category accessibility and impression formation. *Journal of Experimental Social Psychology, 13,* 141–154.

Higgins, E. T., & Rholes, W. S. (1978). "Saying is believing": Effects of message modification on memory and liking for the person described. *Journal of Experimental Social Psychology, 14,* 363–378.

Higgins, L. T., Zheng, M., Liu, Y., & Sun, C. H. (2002). Attitudes to marriage and sexual behaviors: A survey of gender and culture differences in China and the United Kingdom. *Sex Roles, 46,* 75–89.

Higgins, R. L., & Harris, R. N. (1988). Strategic "alcohol" use: Drinking to self-handicap. *Journal of Social and Clinical Psychology, 6,* 191–202.

Hill, C. A. (1987). Affiliation motivation: People who need people . . . but in different ways. *Journal of Personality and Social Psychology, 52,* 1008–1018.

Hill, C., Memon, A., & McGeorge, P. (2008). The role of confirmation bias in suspect interviews: A systematic evaluation. *Legal and Criminological Psychology, 13,* 357–371.

Hilmert, C. J., Kulik, J. A., & Christenfeld, N. J. S. (2006). Positive and negative opinion modeling: The influence of another's similarity and dissimilarity. *Journal of Personality and Social Psychology, 90,* 440–452.

Hilton, J. L., & Darley, J. M. (1985). Constructing other persons: A limit on the effect. *Journal of Experimental Social Psychology, 21,* 1–18.

Hilton, J. L., & Darley, J. M. (1991). The effects of interaction goals on person perception. *Advances in Experimental Social Psychology, 24,* 235–267.

Hilton, J. L., & Fein, S. (1989). The role of typical diagnosticity in stereotype-based judgments. *Journal of Personality and Social Psychology, 57,* 201–211.

Hines, D. A., & Saudino, K. J. (2002). Intergenerational transmission of intimate partner violence: A behavioral genetic perspective. *Trauma Violence and Abuse, 3,* 210–225.

Hinsz, V. B., Tindale, R. S., & Vollrath, D. A. (1997). The emerging conceptualization of groups as information processors. *Psychological Bulletin, 121,* 43–64.

Hirt, E. R., Deppe, R. K., & Gordon, L. J. (1991). Self-reported versus behavioral self-handicapping: Empirical evidence for a theoretical distinction. *Journal of Personality and Social Psychology, 61,* 981–991.

Hirt, E. R., McCrea, S. M., & Boris, H. I. (2003). "I know you self-handicapped last exam": Gender differences in reactions to self-handicapping. *Journal of Personality and Social Psychology, 84,* 177–193.

Hirt, E. R., Zillman, D., Erickson, G. A., & Kennedy, C. (1992). Costs and benefits of allegiance: Changes in fans' self-ascribed competencies after team victory versus defeat. *Journal of Personality and Social Psychology, 63,* 724–738.

Hitler, A. (1933). *Mein Kampf* (E. T. S. Dugdale, Trans.).Cambridge, MA: Riverside.

Hittner, J. B., & Kennington, L. E. (2008). Normative perceptions, substance use, age of substance use initiation, and gender as predictors of HIV-risky sexual behavior in a college student sample. *Journal of Applied Biobehavioral Research, 13,* 86–101.

Hixon, J. G., & Swann, W. B., Jr. (1993). When does introspection bear fruit? Self-reflection, self-insight, and interpersonal choices. *Journal of Personality and Social Psychology, 64,* 35–43.

Hoaken, P. N. S., Allaby, D. B., & Earle, J. (2007). Executive cognitive functioning and the recognition of facial expressions of emotion in incarcerated violent offenders, non-violent offenders, and controls. *Aggressive Behavior, 33,* 412–421.

Hobza, C. L., & Rochlen, A. B. (2009). Gender role conflict, drive for muscularity, and the impact of ideal media portrayals on men. *Psychology of Men and Masculinity, 10,* 120–130.

Hodson, G., Hooper, H., Dovidio, J. F., & Gaertner, S. L. (2005). Aversive racism in Britain: The use of inadmissible evidence in legal decisions. *European Journal of Social Psychology, 35,* 437–448.

Hoertel, N., Le Strat, Y., Lavaud, P., & Limosin, F. (2012). Gender effects in bullying: Results from a national sample. *Psychiatry Research.*

Hoffman, M. L. (2000). Empathy and moral development: Implications for caring and justice. New York: Cambridge University Press.

Hofling, C. K., Brotzman, E., Dalrymple, S., Graves, N., & Pierce, C. (1966). An experimental study of nurse-physician relations. *Journal of Nervous and Mental Disease, 143,* 171–180.

Hofstede, G. (1980). *Culture's consequences.* Beverly Hills, CA: Sage.

Hofstede, G. (2001). *Culture's consequences: Comparing values, behaviors, institutions and organizations across nations,* 2nd ed. Thousand Oaks, CA: SAGE Publications.

Hogg, M. A., Turner, J. C., & Davidson, B. (1990). Polarized norms and social frames of reference: A test of the self-categorization theory of group polarization. *Basic and Applied Social Psychology, 11,* 77–100.

Hogh, A., Hansen, Å. M., Mikkelsen, E. G., & Persson, R. (2012). Exposure to negative acts at work, psychological stress reactions and physiological stress response. *Journal of Psychosomatic Research.*

Høigaard, R., & Ommundsen, Y. (2007). Perceived social loafing and anticipated effort reduction among young football (soccer) players: An achievement goal perspective. *Psychological Reports, 100,* 857–875.

Hollander, E. P. (1985). Leadership and power. In G. Lindzey & E. Aronson (Eds.), *Handbook of social psychology* (3rd ed., Vol. 2, pp. 485–537). New York: Random House.

Holloway, R., & Johnston, L. (2006). Evaluating the evaluators: Perceptions of interviewers by rejected job applicants as a function of interviewer and applicant sex. *Journal of Applied Social Psychology, 36,* 2635–2648.

Holmes, T. H., & Rahe, R. H. (1967). The Social Readjustment Rating Scale. *Journal of Psychosomatic Research, 11,* 213–218.

Holt, J. L., & Gillespie, W. (2008). Intergenerational transmission of violence, threatened egoism, and reciprocity: A test of multiple psychosocial factors affecting intimate partner violence. *American Journal of Criminal Justice, 33,* 252–266.

Holwerda, T. J., Beekman, A. T. F., Deeg, D. J. H., Stek, M. L., van Tilburg, T. G., Visser, P. J., Schmand, B., Jonker, C., & Schoevers, R. A. (2012). Increased risk of mortality associated with social isolation in older men: Only when feeling lonely? results from the amsterdam study of the elderly (AMSTEL). *Psychological Medicine: A Journal of Research in Psychiatry and the Allied Sciences, 42,* 843–853.

Homans, G. C. (1961). *Social behavior.* New York: Harcourt, Brace & World.

Honeycutt, J. M., Woods, B. L., & Fontenot, K. (1993). The endorsement of communication conflict rules as a function of engagement, marriage and marital ideology. *Journal of Social and Personal Relationships, 10,* 285–304.

Hong, J. S., & Espelage, D. L. (2012). A review of research on bullying and peer victimization in school: An ecological system analysis. *Aggression and Violent Behavior.*

Hong, L. (2000). Toward a transformed approach to prevention: Breaking the link between masculinity and violence. *Journal of American College Health, 48,* 269–279.

Hong, Y., Morris, M. W., Chiu, C., & Benet-Martinez, V. (2000). Multicultural minds: A dynamic constructivist approach to culture and cognition. *American Psychologist, 55,* 709–720.

Hong, Y., Wyer, R. S., & Fong, C. P. S. (2008). Chinese working in groups: Effort dispensability versus normative influence. *Asian Journal of Social Psychology, 11*(3), 187–195.

Honts, C. R., Raskin, D. C., & Kircher, J. C. (2002). The scientific status of research on polygraph techniques: The case for polygraph tests (pp. 446–483). In D. L. Faigman, D. Kaye, M. J. Saks, & J. Sanders (Eds.), *Modern scientific evidence: The law and science of expert testimony.* St. Paul, MN: West.

Hoorens, V., & Nuttin, J. M. (1993). Overvaluation of own attributes: Mere ownership or subjective frequency? *Social Cognition, 11,* 177–200.

Hope, L., Memon, A., & McGeorge, P. (2004). Understanding pretrial publicity: Predecisional distortion of evidence by mock jurors. *Journal of Experimental Psychology: Applied, 10,* 111–119.

Horowitz, I. A., & Willging, T. E. (1991). Changing views of jury power: The nullification debate, 1787–1988. *Law and Human Behavior, 15,* 165–182.

Horstmann, G., & Bauland, A. (2006). Search asymmetries with real faces: Testing the anger-superiority effect. *Emotion, 6,* 193–207.

Hortensius, R., Schutter, D. J. L. G., & Harmon-Jones, E. (2012). When anger leads to aggression: Induction of relative left frontal cortical activity with transcranial direct current stimulation increases the anger–aggression relationship. *Social Cognitive and Affective Neuroscience, 7*(3), 342–347.

Horvath, A. O., & Luborsky, L. (1993). The role of the therapeutic alliance in psychotherapy. *Journal of Consulting and Clinical Psychology, 61,* 561–573.

Hoshino-Browne, E., Zanna, A. S., Spencer, S. J.; Zanna, M. P., Kitayama, S., & Lackenbauer, S. (2005). On the cultural guises of cognitive dissonance: The case of Easterners and Westerners. *Journal of Personality and Social Psychology, 89,* 294–310.

Hosoda, M., Stone-Romero, E. F., & Coats, G. (2003). The effects of physical attractiveness on job-related outcomes: A meta-analysis of experimental studies. *Personnel Psychology, 56,* 431–462.

Houldsworth, C., & Mathews, B. P. (2000). Group composition, performance and educational attainment. *Education and Training, 42,* 40–53.

House, J. S., Landis, K. R., & Umberson, D. (1988). Social relationships and health. *Science, 241,* 540–545.

Hove, M. J., & Risen, J. L. (2009). It's all in the timing: Interpersonal synchrony increases affiliation. *Social Cognition, 27,* 949–961.

Hovland, C. I., & Sears, R. R. (1940). Minor studies in aggression: VI. Correlation of lynchings with economic indices. *Journal of Psychology, 9,* 301–310.

Hovland, C. I., & Weiss, W. (1951). The influence of source credibility on communication effectiveness. *Public Opinion Quarterly, 15,* 635–650.

Hovland, C. I., Janis, I. L., & Kelley, H. H. (1953). *Communication and persuasion: Psychological studies of opinion change.* New Haven, CT: Yale University Press.

Hovland, C. I., Lumsdaine, A. A., & Sheffield, F. D. (1949). *Experiments on mass communication.* Princeton, NJ: Princeton University Press.

Howard, D. E., Griffin, M. A., & Boekeloo, B. O. (2008). Prevalence and psychosocial correlates of alcohol-related sexual assault among university students. *Adolescence, 43,* 733–750.

Howard, D. J. (1990). The influence of verbal responses to common greetings on compliance behavior: The foot-in-the-mouth effect. *Journal of Applied Social Psychology, 20,* 1185–1196.

Howell, J. L., & Shepperd, J. A. (2011). Demonstrating the correspondence bias. *Teaching of Psychology, 38*(4), 243–246.

Huesmann, L. R., Dubow, E. F., & Boxer, P. (2009). Continuity of aggression from childhood to early adulthood as a predictor of life outcomes: Implications for the adolescent-limited and life-course-persistent models. *Aggressive Behavior, 35,* 136–149.

Huesmann, L. R., & Guerra, N. G. (1997). Children's normative beliefs about aggression and aggressive behavior. *Journal of Personality and Social Psychology, 72,* 408–419.

Huesmann, L. R., Moise-Titus, J., Podolski, C. P., & Eron, L. D. (2003). Longitudinal relations between children's exposure to TV violence and their aggressive and violent behavior in young adulthood: 1977–1992. *Developmental Psychology, 39,* 201–229.

Hugenberg, K., & Bodenhausen, G. V. (2003). Facing prejudice: Implicit prejudice and the perception of facial threat. *Psychological Science, 14,* 640–643.

Hugenberg, K., & Bodenhausen, G. V. (2004). Ambiguity in social categorization: The role of prejudice and facial affect in race categorization. *Psychological Science, 15,* 342–345.

Hugenberg, K., & Corneille, O. (2009). Holistic processing is tuned for in-group faces. *Cognitive Science, 33,* 1173–1181.

Hull, J. G., & Young, R. D. (1983). Self-consciousness, self-esteem, and success-failure as determinants of alcohol consumption in male social drinkers. *Journal of Personality and Social Psychology, 44,* 1097–1109.

Hur, M. H. (2006). Exploring the motivation factors of charitable giving and their value structure: A case study of Seoul, Korea. *Social Behavior and Personality, 34,* 661–680.

Huston, T. L., & Vangelisti, A. L. (1991). Socioemotional behavior and satisfaction in marital relationships: A longitudinal study. *Journal of Personality and Social Psychology, 61,* 721–733.

Hutchings, P. B., & Haddock, G. (2008). Look black in anger: The role of implicit prejudice in the categorization and perceived emotional intensity of racially ambiguous faces. *Journal of Experimental Social Psychology, 44,* 1418–1420.

Hütter, M., & Diehl, M. (2011). Motivation losses in teamwork: The effects of team diversity and equity sensitivity on reactions to free-riding. *Group Processes & Intergroup Relations, 14,* 845–856.

Iacono, W. G., & Lykken, D. T. (1997). The validity of the lie-detector test: Two surveys of scientific opinion. *Journal of Applied Psychology, 82,* 426–433.

Igou, Eric R. (2008). "How long will I suffer?" versus "how long will you suffer?" A self-other effect in affective forecasting. *Journal of Personality and Social Psychology, 95,* 899–917.

Imai, Y. (1991). Effects of influence strategies, perceived social power and cost on compliance with requests. *Japanese Psychological Research, 33,* 134–144.

Imhoff, R., & Banse, R. (2009). Ongoing victim suffering increases prejudice: The case of secondary anti-semitism. *Psychological Science, 20,* 1443–1447.

Inbau, F. E., Reid, J. E., Buckley, J. P., & Jayne, B. C. (2001). *Criminal interrogation and confessions* (4th ed.). Gaithersburg, MD: Aspen.

Ingham, A. G., Levinger, G., Graves, J., & Peckham, V. (1974). The Ringelmann effect: Studies of group size and group performance. *Journal of Experimental Social Psychology, 10,* 371–384.

Inglehart, R., Foa, R., Peterson, C., & Welzel, C. (2008). Development, freedom, and rising happiness: A global perspective (1981–2007). *Current Perspectives on Psychological Science, 3,* 264–285.

Ingoldsby, B. B. (1991). The Latin American family: Familism vs. machismo. *Journal of Comparative Family Studies, 23,* 47–62.

Ingram, R. E. (1990). Self-focused attention in clinical disorders: Review and a conceptual model. *Psychological Bulletin, 107,* 156–176.

Insko, C. A., Sedlak, A. J., & Lipsitz, A. (1982). A two-valued logic or two-valued balance resolution of the challenge of agreement and attraction effects in p-o-x triads, and a theoretical perspective on conformity and hedonism. *European Journal of Social Psychology, 12,* 143–167.

Internet World Stats. (2011). *Internet usage statistics: The big picture.* Retrieved July 17, 2011, from http://www.internetworldstats.com/stats.htm.

Inzlicht, M., Kaiser, C. R., & Major, B. (2008). The face of chauvinism: How prejudice expectations shape perceptions of facial affect. *Journal of Experimental Social Psychology, 44,* 758–766.

Ireland, T. O., & Smith, C. A. (2009). Living in partner-violent families: Developmental links to antisocial behavior and relationship violence. *Journal of Youth and Adolescence, 38*(3), 323–339.

Ipsos-Reid. (2012). Retrieved from http://www.ipsos.ca/pa/polls.cfm.

Isen, A. M. (1984). Toward understanding the role of affect in cognition. In R. S. Wyer & T. K. Srull (Eds.), *Handbook of social cognition* (Vol. 3, pp. 179–236). Hillsdale, NJ: Erlbaum.

Isen, A. M. (2008). Positive affect and decision processes: Some recent theoretical developments with practical implications. In C. P.

Haugtvedt, P. M. Herr, & F. R. Kardes (Eds), *Handbook of consumer psychology* (pp. 273–296). NY: Taylor & Francis.

Isen, A. M., & Levin, P. A. (1972). Effect of feeling good on helping: Cookies and kindness. *Journal of Personality and Social Psychology, 21,* 384–388.

Ishii, K., & Kurzban, R. (2008). Public goods games in Japan: Cultural and individual differences in reciprocity. *Human Nature, 19,* 138–156.

Ishii, K., Reyes, J., & Kitayama, S. (2003). Spontaneous attention to word content versus emotional tone: Differences among three cultures. *Psychological Science, 14,* 39–46.

Ito, T. A., Larsen, J. T., Smith, N. K., & Cacioppo, J. T. (1998). Negative information weighs more heavily on the brain: The negativity bias in evaluative categorizations. *Journal of Personality and Social Psychology, 75,* 887–900.

Ito, T. A., Miller, N., & Pollock, V. E. (1996). Alcohol and aggression: A meta-analysis on the moderating effects of inhibitory cues, triggering events, and self-focused attention. *Psychological Bulletin, 120,* 60–82.

Ito, T. A., & Urland, G. R. (2003). Race and gender on the brain: Electrocortical measures of attention to the race and gender of multiply categorizable individuals. *Journal of Personality and Social Psychology, 85,* 616–626.

Jacks, J. Z., & Cameron, K. A. (2003). Strategies for resisting persuasion. *Basic and Applied Social Psychology, 25,* 145–161.

Jackson, J. M. (1986). In defense of social impact theory: Comment on Mullin. *Journal of Personality and Social Psychology, 50,* 511–513.

Jackson, J. M., & Williams, K. D. (1985). Social loafing on difficult tasks: Working collectively can improve performance. *Journal of Personality and Social Psychology, 49,* 937–942.

Jackson, L. M. (2011). *The psychology of prejudice. From attitudes to social action.* Washington, DC: American Psychological Association.

Jackson, L. M., Esses, V. M., & Burris, C. T. (2001). Contemporary sexism and discrimination: The importance of respect for men and women. *Personality and Social Psychology Bulletin, 27,* 48–61.

Jackson, S. E., May, K. E., & Whiteney, K. (1995). Understanding the dynamics of diversity in decision making teams. In R. A. Guzzo & E. Salas (Eds.), *Team effectiveness and decision making in organizations* (pp. 204–261). San Francisco: Jossey-Bass.

Jackson, T., Chen, H., Guo, C., & Gao, X. (2006). Stories we love by: Conceptions of love among couples from People's Republic of China and the United States. *Journal of Cross-Cultural Psychology, 4,* 446–464.

Jackson, T., Fritch, A., Nagasaka, T., & Gunderson, J. (2002). Towards explaining the association between shyness and loneliness: A path analysis with American college students. *Social Behavior and Personality, 30,* 263–270.

Jacob, C., Guéguen, N., & Boulbry, G. (2010). Effects of songs with prosocial lyrics on tipping behavior in a restaurant. *International Journal of Hospitality Management, 29,* 761–763.

James, W. (1890). *Principles of psychology* (Vols. 1–2). New York: Holt.

James, W. H. (2005). Biological and psychosocial determinants of male and female human sexual orientation. *Journal of Biosocial Science, 37,* 555–567.

Jamison, J., Karlan, D., & Schechter, L. (2008). To deceive or not to deceive: The effect of deception on behavior in future laboratory experiments. *Journal of Economic Behavior & Organization, 68*(3–4), 477–488.

Janis, I. L. (1968). Attitude change via role playing. In R. Abelson, E. Aronson, W. McGuire, T. Newcomb, M. Rosenberg, & P. Tennenbaum (Eds.), *Theories of cognitive consistency: A sourcebook* (pp. 810–818). Chicago: Rand McNally.

Janis, I. L. (1982). *Groupthink* (2nd ed.). Boston: Houghton Mifflin.

Janis, I. L., & Feshbach, S. (1953). Effects of fear arousing communications. *Journal of Abnormal and Social Psychology, 48,* 78–92.

Janis, I. L., Kaye, D., & Kirschner, P. (1965). Facilitating effects of "eating while reading" on responsiveness to persuasive communications. *Journal of Personality and Social Psychology, 1,* 181–186.

Janis, I. L., & King, B. T. (1954). The influence of role playing on opinion change. *Journal of Abnormal and Social Psychology, 49,* 211–218.

Jankowiak, W. R., & Fischer, E. F. (1992). A cross-cultural perspective on romantic love. *Ethnology, 31,* 149–155.

Janoff-Bulman, R. (1979). Characterological versus behavioral self-blame: Inquiries into depression and rape. *Journal of Personality and Social Psychology, 37,* 1798–1809.

Jansari, A., & Parkin, A. J. (1996). Things that go bump in your life: Explaining the reminiscence bump in autobiographical memory. *Psychology and Aging, 11,* 85–91.

Jarvis, W. B. G., & Petty, R. E. (1996). The need to evaluate. *Journal of Personality and Social Psychology, 70,* 172–194.

Jeffery-Tosoni, S., Eys, M. A., Schinke, R. J., & Lewko, J. (2011). Youth sport status and perceptions of satisfaction and cohesion. *Journal of Sport Behavior, 34,* 150–159.

Jennings (Walstedt), J., Geis, F. L., & Brown, V. (1980). Influence of television commercials on women's self-confidence and independent judgment. *Journal of Personality and Social Psychology, 38,* 203–210.

Jepson, C., & Chaiken, S. (1990). Chronic issue-specific fear inhibits systematic processing of persuasive communications. *Journal of Social Behavior and Personality, 5,* 61–84.

Jetten, J., Hornsey, M. J., & Adarves-Yorno, I. (2006). When group members admit to being conformist: The role of relative intragroup status in conformity self-reports. *Personality and Social Psychology Bulletin, 32*(2), 162–173.

Johansson, G., von Hofsten, C., & Jansson, G. (1980). Event perception. *Annual Review of Psychology, 31,* 27–53.

Johnco, C., Wheeler, L., & Taylor, A. (2010). They do get prettier at closing time: A repeated measures study of the closing-time effect and alcohol. *Social Influence, 5,* 261–271.

Johns, M., Schmader, T., & Martens, A., (2005). Knowing is half the battle: Teaching stereotype threat as a means of improving women's math performance. *Psychological Science, 16,* 175–179.

Johnson, D. J., & Rusbult, C. E. (1989). Resisting temptation: Devaluation of alternative partners as a means of maintaining commitment in close relationships. *Journal of Personality and Social Psychology, 57,* 967–980.

Johnson, H. (1996). Dangerous Domains: Violence Against Women in Canada. Toronto: Nelson, Canada.

Johnson, H. M., & Seifert, C. M. (1998). Updating accounts following a correction of misinformation. *Journal of Experimental Psychology: Learning, Memory, and Cognition, 24,* 1483–1494.

Johnson, R. D., & Downing, L. L. (1979). Deindividuation and valance of cues: Effects on prosocial and antisocial behavior. *Journal of Personality and Social Psychology, 37,* 1532–1538.

Johnson, R. W., Kelly, R. J., & LeBlane, B. A. (1995). Motivational basis of dissonance: Aversive consequences or inconsistency. *Personality and Social Psychology Bulletin, 21,* 850–855.

Johnson, W., & Krueger, R. F. (2006). How money buys happiness: Genetic and environmental processes linking finances and life satisfaction. *Journal of Personality and Social Psychology, 90,* 680–691.

Johnston, K. E., & Jacobs, J. E. (2003). Children's illusory correlations: The role of attentional bias in group impression formation. *Journal of Cognition and Development, 4,* 129–160.

Jones, A. D. (2012). Intimate partner violence in military couples: A review of the literature. *Aggression and Violent Behavior, 17,* 147–157.

Jones, B. C., DeBruine, L. M., & Little, A. C. (2007). The role of symmetry in attraction to average faces. *Perception & Psychophysics, 69,* 1273–1277.

Jones, E. E. (1964). *Ingratiation: A social psychological analysis.* New York: Appleton-Century-Crofts.

Jones, E. E. (1990). *Interpersonal perception.* New York: Freeman.

Jones, E. E., Carter-Sowell, A., & Kelly, J. R. (2011). Participation matters: Psychological and behavioral consequences of information exclusion in groups. *Group Dynamics: Theory, Research, and Practice, 15*(4), 311–325.

Jones, E. E. & Davis, K. E. (1965). From acts to dispositions: The attribution process in person perception. *Advances in Experimental Psychology, 2,* 219–266.

Jones, E. E., Davis, K. E., & Gergen, K. (1961). Role playing variations and their informational value for person perception. *Journal of Abnormal and Social Psychology, 63,* 302–310.

Jones, E. E., & Harris, V. A. (1967). The attribution of attitudes. *Journal of Experimental Social Psychology, 3,* 1–24.

Jones, E. E., & Nisbett, R. E. (1972). The actor and the observer: Divergent perceptions of causality. In E. E. Jones, D. E. Kanouse, H. H. Kelley, R. E. Nisbett, S. Valins, & B. Weiner (Eds.), *Attribution: Perceiving the causes of behavior* (pp. 79–94). Morristown, NJ: General Learning Press.

Jones, E. E., & Pittman, T. S. (1982). Toward a general theory of strategic self presentation. In J. Suls (Ed.), *Psychological perspectives on the self.* Hillsdale, NJ: Erlbaum.

Jones, E. E., Rhodewalt, F., Berglas, S., & Skelton, J. A. (1981). Effects of strategic self-presentation on subsequent self-esteem. *Journal of Personality and Social Psychology, 41,* 407–421.

Jones, E. E., Rock, L., Shaver, K. G., Goethals, G. R., & Ward, L. M. (1968). Pattern of performance and ability attribution: An unexpected primary effect. *Journal of Personality and Social Psychology, 10,* 317–340.

Jones, E. E., & Sigall, H. (1971). The bogus pipeline: A new paradigm for measuring affect and attitude. *Psychological Bulletin, 76,* 349–364.

Jones, J. H. (1997). *Alfred C. Kinsey: A Public/Private Life.* New York: Norton.

Jones, J. M. (1997). *Prejudice and racism* (2nd ed.). New York: McGraw-Hill.

Jones, J. T., Pelham, B. W., Carvallo, M., & Mirenberg, M. C. (2004). How do I love thee? let me count the js: Implicit egotism and interpersonal attraction. *Journal of Personality and Social Psychology, 87,* 665–683.

Jones, T. F., Craig, A. S., Hoy, D., Gunter, E. W., Ashley, D. L., Barr, D. B., Brock, J. W., & Schaffner, W. (2000). Mass psychogenic illness attributed to toxic exposure at a high school. *New England Journal of Medicine, 342,* 96–100.

Jordan, C. H., Spencer, S. J., & Zanna, M. P. (2005). Types of high self-esteem and prejudice: How implicit self-esteem relates to racial discrimination among high explicit self-esteem individuals. *Personality and Social Psychology Bulletin, 31,* 693–702.

Jorgensen, S., Fichten, C. S., Havel, A., Lamb, D., James, C., & Barile, M. (2005). Academic performance of college students with and without disabilities: An archival study. *Canadian Journal of Counselling, 39,* 101–117

Josephs, R. A., Bosson, J. K., & Jacobs, C. G. (2003). Self-esteem maintenance processes: When low self-esteem may be resistant to change. *Personality and Social Psychology Bulletin, 29,* 920–933.

Jost, J. T., Kay, A. C., & Thorisdottir, H. (Eds.). (2009). *Social and psychological bases of ideology and system justification.* New York: Oxford University Press.

Judge, T. A., & Cable, D. M. (2011). When it comes to pay, do the thin win? the effect of weight on pay for men and women. *Journal of Applied Psychology, 96,* 95–112.

Judge, T. A., Hurst, C., & Simon, L. S. (2009). Does it pay to be smart, attractive, or confident (or all three)? Relationships among general mental ability, physical attractiveness, core self-evaluations, and income. *Journal of Applied Psychology, 94,* 742–755.

Jung, J., & Lee, S. H. (2006). Cross-cultural comparisons of appearance self-schema, body image, self-esteem, and dieting behavior between Korean and U.S. women. *Family and Consumer Sciences Research Journal, 34,* 350–365.

Jussim, L., Cain, T. R., Crawford, J. T., Harber, K., & Cohen, F. (2009). The unbearable accuracy of stereotypes. In T. D. Nelson (Ed.), *Handbook of prejudice, stereotyping, and discrimination* (pp. 199–227). New York: Psychology Press.

Jussim, L., Eccles, J., & Madon, S. (1996). Social perception, social stereotypes, and teacher expectations: Accuracy and the quest for the powerful self-fulfilling prophecy. In M. P. Zanna (Ed.), *Advances in experimental social psychology* (Vol. 28, pp. 281–388). San Diego, CA: Academic Press.

Jussim, L., & Harber, K. D. (2005). Teacher expectations and self-fulfilling prophecies: Knowns and unknowns, resolved and unresolved controversies. *Personality and Social Psychology Review, 9,* 131–155.

Juvonen, J., Nishina, A., & Graham, S. (2006). Ethnic diversity and perceptions of safety in urban middle schools. *Psychological Science, 17,* 393–400.

Kafer, R., Hodkin, B., Furrow, D. & Landry, T. (1993). What do the Montreal murders mean? Attitudinal and demographic predictors of attribution. *Canadian Journal of Behavioural Science, 25,* 541–558.

Kagan, J. (1994). Galen's prophecy: Temperament in human nature. New York: Basic Books.

Kahneman, D., & Miller, D. T. (1986). Norm theory: Comparing reality to its alternatives. *Psychological Review, 93,* 136–153.

Kahneman, D., Slovic, P., & Tversky, A. (Eds.) (1982). *Judgment under uncertainty: Heuristics and biases.* New York: Cambridge University Press.

Kaiser, C. R., Drury, B. J., Spalding, K. E., Cheryan, S., & O'Brien, L. T. (2009). The ironic consequences of Obama's election: Decreased support for social justice. *Journal of Experimental Social Psychology, 45,* 556–559.

Kalin, R., & Berry, J. W. (1995). Ethnic and civic self-identity in Canada: Analyses of 1974 and 1991 national surveys. *Canadian Ethnic Studies, 27,* 1–15.

Kallgren, C. A., & Wood, W. (1986). Access to attitude-relevant information in memory as a determinant of attitude-behavior consistency. *Journal of Experimental Social Psychology, 22,* 328–338.

Kalven, H., & Zeisel, H. (1966). *The American jury.* Boston: Little, Brown.

Kanetsuna, T., Smith, P. K., & Morita, Y. (2006). Coping with bullying at school: Children's recommended strategies and attitudes to school-based interventions in England and Japan. *Aggressive Behavior, 32,* 570–580.

Kaplan, M. F., & Schersching, C. (1981). Juror deliberation: An information integration analysis. In B. Sales (Ed.), *The trial process* (pp. 235–262). New York: Plenum.

Karasek, D., Ahern, J., & Galea, S. (2012). Social norms, collective efficacy, and smoking cessation in urban neighborhoods. *American Journal of Public Health, 102*(2), 343–351.

Karau, S. J., & Williams, K. D. (1993). Social loafing: A meta-analytic review and theoretical integration. *Journal of Personality and Social Psychology, 65,* 681–706.

Karau, S. J., & Williams, K. D. (2001). Understanding individual motivation in groups: The collective effort model. In M. E. Turner (Ed.), *Groups at work: Theory and research. Applied social research* (pp. 113–141). Mahwah, NJ: Erlbaum.

Karney, B. R., & Bradbury, T. N. (2000). Attributions in marriage: State or trait? A growth curve analysis. *Journal of Personality and Social Psychology, 78,* 295–309.

Karniol, R. (2003). Egocentrism versus protocentrism: The status of self in social prediction. *Psychological Review, 110,* 564–580.

Karpinski, A., & Hilton, J. L. (2001). Attitudes and the Implicit Association Test. *Journal of Personality and Social Psychology, 81,* 774–788.

Karpinski, A. T., & von Hippel, W. (1996). The role of the linguistic intergroup bias in expectancy maintenance. *Social Cognition, 14,* 141–163.

Karremans, J. C., Stroebe, W., & Claus, J. (2006). Beyond Vicary's fantasies: The impact of subliminal priming and brand choice. *Journal of Experimental Social Psychology, 42,* 792–798.

Kashima, Y., & Kerekes, A. R. Z. (1994). A distributed memory model of averaging phenomena in person impression formation. *Journal of Experimental Social Psychology, 30,* 407–455.

Kassin, S. M. (2002, November 1). False confessions and the jogger case. *New York Times,* p. A31.

Kassin, S. M., Drizin, S. A., Grisso, T., Gudjonsson, G. H., Leo, R. A., & Redlich, A. D. (2010). Police-induced confessions: Risk factors and recommendations. *Law and Human Behavior, 34,* 3–38.

Kassin, S. M., Goldstein, C. J., & Savitsky, K. (2003).Behavioral confirmation in the interrogation room: On the dangers of presuming guilt. *Law and Human Behavior, 27,* 187–203.

Kassin, S. M., & Kiechel, K. L. (1996). The social psychology of false confessions: Compliance, internalization, and confabulation. *Psychological Science, 7,* 125–128.

Kassin, S. M., & Sukel, H. (1997). Coerced confessions and the jury: An experimental test of the "harmless error" rule. *Law and Human Behavior, 21,* 27–46.

Katz, D., & Braly, K. W. (1933). Racial stereotypes of 100 college students. *Journal of Abnormal and Social Psychology, 28,* 280–290.

Kaufman, D. Q., Stasson, M. F., & Hart, J. W. (1999). Are the tabloids always wrong or is that just what we think? Need for cognition and perceptions of articles in print media. *Journal of Applied Social Psychology, 29,* 1984–1997.

Kawakami, K., Dion, K. L., & Dovidio, J. F. (1998). Racial prejudice and stereotype activation. *Personality and Social Psychology Bulletin, 24,* 407–416.

Kawakami, K., Dovidio, J. F., Moll, J., Hermsen, S., & Russin, A. (2000). Just say no (to stereotyping): Effects of training in the negation of stereotypic association on stereotype activation. *Journal of Personality and Social Psychology, 78,* 871–888.

Kawakami, K., Dovidio, J. F., & van Kamp, S. (2007). The impact of naïve theories related to strategies to reduce biases and correction processes on the application of stereotypes. *Group Processes and Intergroup Relations, 10,* 139–156.

Kay, A. C., & Jost, J. T. (2003). Complementary justice: Effects of "poor but happy" and "poor but honest" stereotype exemplars on system justification and implicit activation of the justice motive. *Journal of Personality and Social Psychology, 85,* 823–837.

Kay, A. C., Jost, J. T., & Young, S. (2005). Victim derogation and victim enhancement as alternate routes to system justification. *Personality and Social Psychology Bulletin, 16,* 240–246.

Keelan, J. P. R., Dion, K. L., & Dion, K. K. (1994). Attachment style and heterosexual relationships among young adults: A short-term panel study. *Journal of Social and Personal Relationships, 11,* 201–214.

Keenan, J. P., Gallup, G., & Falk, D. (2003). The face in the mirror: The search for the origins of consciousness. New York: New York: Harper Collins Publishers Inc.

Keil, M., Depledge, G., & Rai, A. (2007). Escalation: The role of problem recognition and cognitive bias. *Decision Sciences, 38,* 391–421.

Keillor, J. M., Barrett, A. M., Crucian, G. P., Kortenkamp, S., & Heilman, K. M. (2003). Emotional experience and perception in the absence of facial feedback. *Journal of the International Neurological Society, 8,* 130–135.

Keller, J., & Dauenheimer, D. (2003). Stereotype threat in the classroom: Dejection mediates the disrupting threat effect on women's math performance. *Personality and Social Psychology Bulletin, 29,* 371–381.

Keller, P. A. (1999). Converting the unconverted: The effect of inclination and opportunity to discount health-related fear appeals. *Journal of Applied Psychology, 84,* 403–415.

Kelley, H. H. (1950). The warm-cold variable in first impressions of persons. *Journal of Personality, 18,* 431–439.

Kelley, H. H. (1967). Attribution in social psychology. *Nebraska symposium on motivation, 15,* 192–238.

Kelly, A. E., & McKillop, K. J. (1996). Consequences of revealing personal secrets. *Psychological Bulletin, 120,* 450–465.

Kelly, A. E., & Rodriguez, Robert R. (2006). Publicly committing oneself to an identity. *Basic and Applied Social Psychology, 28,* 185–191.

Kelly, M. M., Tyrka, A. R., Anderson, G. M., Price, L. H., Carpenter, L. L. (2008). Sex differences in emotional and physiological responses to the Trier Social Stress Test. *Journal of Behavior Therapy and Experimental Psychiatry, 39,* 87–98.

Kelman, H. C. (1961). Processes of opinion change. *Public Opinion Quarterly, 25,* 57–78.

Kelman, H. C. (1967). Human use of human subjects: The problem of deception in social psychology experiments. *Psychological Bulletin, 67,* 1–11.

Kelman, H. C., & Hamilton, V. L. (1989). *Crimes of obedience: Toward a social psychology of authority and responsibility.* New Haven, CT: Yale University Press.

Kelman, H. C., & Hovland, C. I. (1953). "Reinstatement" of the communicator in delayed measurement of opinion change. *Journal of Abnormal and Social Psychology, 48,* 327–335.

Kemmelmeier, M., Jambor, E. E., & Letner, J. (2006). Individualism and good works: Cultural variation in giving and volunteering across the united states. *Journal of Cross-Cultural Psychology, 37,* 327–344.

Kennedy, H. (2003). He takes fatal OD as internet pals watch: Chatroom vultures egged him to pop more Rx pills. *New York Daily News,* February 2, p. 5.

Kenny, D. A. (1994). *Interpersonal perception: A social relations analysis.* New York: Guilford.

Kenny, D. A., & Acitelli, L. K. (2001). Accuracy and bias of perceptions of the partner in close relationships. *Journal of Personality and Social Psychology, 80,* 439–448.

Kenny, D. A., Albright, L., Malloy, T. E., & Kashy, D. A. (1994). Consensus in interpersonal perception: Acquaintance and the Big Five. *Psychological Bulletin, 116,* 245–258.

Kenny, D. A., & DePaulo, B. M. (1993). Do people know how others view them? An empirical and theoretical account. *Psychological Bulletin, 114,* 145–161.

Kenrick, D. T., Gabrielidis, C., Keefe, R. C., & Cornelius, J. S. (1996). Adolescents' age preferences for dating partners: Support for an evolutionary model of life-history strategies. *Child Development, 67,* 1499–1511.

Kenrick, D. T., & Keefe, R. C. (1992). Age preferences in mates reflect sex differences in human reproductive strategies. *Behavioral and Brain Sciences, 15,* 75–133.

Kenrick, D. T., & MacFarlane, S. W. (1986). Ambient temperature and horn honking: A field study of the heat/ aggression relationship. *Environment and Behavior, 18,* 179–191.

Kenrick, D. T., Neuberg, Steven L., Griskevicius, V., Becker, D. V., & Schaller, M. (2010). Goal-driven cognition and functional behavior: The fundamental-motives framework. *Current Directions in Psychological Science, 19,* 63–67.

Kernis, M. H., & Waschull, S. B. (1995). The interactive roles of stability and level of self-esteem: Research and theory. *Advances in Experimental Social Psychology, 27,* 93–141.

Kerr, N. L. (1981). Social transition schemes: Charting the group's road to agreement. *Journal of Personality and Social Psychology, 41,* 684–702.

Kerr, N. L. (1983). Motivation losses in small groups: A social dilemma analysis. *Journal of Personality and Social Psychology, 45,* 819–828.

Kerr, N. L., Harmon, D. L., & Graves, J. K. (1982). Independence of multiple verdicts by jurors and juries. *Journal of Applied Social Psychology, 12,* 12–29.

Kerr, N. L., Kramer, G. P., Carroll, J. S., & Alfini, J. J. (1991). On the effectiveness of voir dire in criminal cases with prejudicial pretrial publicity: An empirical study. *American University Law Review, 40,* 665–701.

Key, W. B. (1973). *Subliminal seduction.* Englewood Cliffs, NJ: Signet.
Key, W. B. (1989). *The age of manipulation.* New York: Holt.
Keysar, B., & Henly, A. S. (2002). Speakers' overestimation of their effectiveness. *Psychological Science, 13,* 207–212.
Khanfer, R., Lord, J. M., & Phillips, A. C. (2011). Neutrophil function and cortisol:DHEAS ratio in bereaved older adults. *Brain, Behavior, and Immunity, 25,* 1182–1186.
Kiecolt-Glaser, J. K. (2009). Psychoneuroimmunology: Psychology's gateway to the biomedical future. *Perspectives on Psychological Science, 4,* 367–369.
Kierein, N. M., & Gold, M. A. (2000). Pygmalion in work organizations: A meta-analysis. *Journal of Organizational Behavior, 21,* 913–928.
Kiesler, C. A. (1971). *The psychology of commitment.* New York: Academic Press.
Kiesler, C. A., & Kiesler, S. B. (1969). *Conformity.* Reading, MA: Addison-Wesley.
Kilham, W., & Mann, L. (1974). Level of destructive obedience as a function of transmitter and executant roles in the Milgram obedience paradigm. *Journal of Personality and Social Psychology, 29,* 696–702.
Kilianski, S. E., & Rudman, L. A. (1998). Wanting it both ways: Do women approve of benevolent sexism? *Sex Roles, 39,* 333–352.
Kim, H., & Markus, H. R. (1999). Deviance or uniqueness, harmony or conformity? A cultural analysis. *Journal of Personality and Social Psychology, 77,* 785–800.
Kim, H. S., Sherman, D. K., & Taylor, S. (2008). Culture and social support. *American Psychologist, 63,* 518–526.
Kim, H. S., Sherman, D. K., Taylor, S. E., Sasaki, J. Y., Chu, T. Q., Ryu, C., . . . Xu, J. (2010). Culture, serotonin receptor polymorphism and locus of attention. *Social Cognitive and Affective Neuroscience, 5*(2–3), 212–218.
Kim, J., & Park, H. S. (2011). The effect of uniform virtual appearance on conformity intention: Social identity model of deindividuation effects and optimal distinctiveness theory. *Computers in Human Behavior, 27,* 1223–1230.
Kim, Y., & Chiu, C. (2011). Emotional costs of inaccurate self-assessments: Both self-effacement and self-enhancement can lead to dejection. *Emotion, 11,* 1096–1104.
Kimmel, A. J., Smith, N. C., & Klein, J. G. (2011). Ethical decision making and research deception in the behavioral sciences: An application of social contract theory. *Ethics & Behavior, 21,* 222–251.
Kimmel, P. R. (1994). Cultural perspectives on international negotiations. *Journal of Social Issues, 50,* 179–196.
Kimmel, P. R. (2000). Culture and conflict. In M. Deutsch & P. T. Coleman (Eds.), *The handbook of conflict resolution: Theory and practice* (pp. 453–474). San Francisco, CA: Jossey-Bass.
Kingston, D. A., Malamuth, N. M., Fedoroff, P., & Marshall, W. L. (2009). The importance of individual differences in pornography use: Theoretical perspectives and implications for treating sexual offenders. *Journal of Sex Research, 46,* 216–232.
Kinsey, A. C., Pomeroy, W. B., & Martin, C. E. (1948). *Sexual behavior in the human male.* Philadelphia: Saunders.
Kinsey, A. C., Pomeroy, W. B., Martin, C. E., & Gebhard, P. H. (1953). *Sexual behavior in the human female.* Philadelphia: Saunders.
Kinzer, S. (1999, September 13). A sudden friendship blossoms between Greece and Turkey. *New York Times* (http:www.nytimes.com/library/world/europe/ 091399greece-turkey.html).
Kirkman, B. L., Rosen, B., Gibson, C. B., Tesluk, P., & McPherson, S. O. (2002). Five challenges to virtual team success: Lessons from Sabre, Inc. *Academy of Management Executive, 16,* 67–79.
Kirkpatrick, L. A., & Hazan, C. (1994). Attachment styles and close relationships: A four-year prospective study. *Personal Relationships, 1,* 123–142.
Kitayama, S., Duffy, S., Kawamura, T., & Larsen, J. T. (2003). Perceiving an object and its context in different cultures: A cultural look at New Look. *Psychological Science, 14,* 201–206.
Klapwijk, A., & Van Lange, P. A. M. (2009). Promoting cooperation and trust in "noisy" situations: The power of generosity. *Journal of Personality and Social Psychology, 96,* 83–103.
Klassen, R. M., & Krawchuk, L. L. (2009). Collective motivation beliefs of early adolescents working in small groups. *Journal of School Psychology, 47,* 101–120.
Klein, H., & Shiffman, K. (2009). Underrepresentation and symbolic annihilation of socially disenfranchised groups ('out groups') in animated cartoons. *Howard Journal of Communications, 20,* 55–72.
Klein, W. M. (1997). Objective standards are not enough: Affective, self-evaluative, and behavioral responses to social comparison information. *Journal of Personality and Social Psychology, 72,* 763–774.
Klein, W. M. P., Monin, M. M., Steers-Wentzell, K. L., & Buckingham, J. T. (2006). Effects of standards on self-enhancing interpretations of ambiguous social comparison information. *Basic and Applied Social Psychology, 28,* 65–79.
Kleinke, C. L. (1986). Gaze and eye contact: A research review. *Psychological Bulletin, 100,* 78–100.
Kleinke, C. L., Peterson, T. R., & Rutledge, T. R. (1998). Effects of self-generated facial expressions on mood. *Journal of Personality and Social Psychology, 74,* 272–279.
Klettke, B., Graesser, A. C., & Powell, M. B. (2010). Expert testimony in child sexual abuse cases: The effects of evidence, coherence and credentials on juror decision making. *Applied Cognitive Psychology, 24,* 481–494.
Klinesmith, J., Kasser, T., & McAndrew, F. T. (2006). Guns, testosterone, and aggression: An experimental test of a mediational hypothesis. *Psychological Science, 17,* 568–571.
Kluemper, D. H., Rosen, P. A. and Mossholder, K. W. (2012). Social Networking Websites, Personality Ratings, and the Organizational Context: More Than Meets the Eye? *Journal of Applied Social Psychology, 42,* 1143–1172.
Knafo, A., & Plomin, R. (2006). Prosocial behavior from early to middle childhood: Genetic and environmental influences on stability and change. *Developmental Psychology, 42,* 771–786.
Knafo, A., Zahn-Waxler, C., Van Hulle, C., Rhee, S., & Robinson, J. L. (2008). The developmental origins of a disposition toward empathy: Genetic and environmental contributions. *Emotion, 8,* 737–752.
Knauper, B., & Schwarz, N. (2004). Why your research may be out of order. *Psychologist, 17,* 28–31.
Kniffin, K., & Wilson, D. S. (2004). The effect of nonphysical traits on the perception of physical attractiveness: Three naturalistic studies. *Evolution and Human Behavior, 25,* 88–101.
Knobloch, S., Callison, C., Chen, L., Fritzsche, A., & Zillmann, D. (2005). Children's sex-stereotyped self-socialization through selective exposure to entertainment: Cross-cultural experiments in Germany, China, and the United States. *Journal of Communication, 55,* 122–138.
Knowles, E. S. (1983). Social physics and the effects of others: Tests of the effects of audience size and distance on social judgments and behavior. *Journal of Personality and Social Psychology, 45,* 1263–1279.
Knox, R. E., & Inskter, J. A. (1968). Postdecision dissonance at post time. *Journal of Personality and Social Psychology, 8,* 319–323.
Knox, R. E., & Safford, R. K. (1976). Group caution at the race track. *Journal of Experimental Social Psychology, 12,* 317–324.
Kobasa, S. C., Maddi, S. R., & Kahn, S. (1982). Hardiness and health: A prospective study. *Journal of Personality and Social Psychology, 42,* 168–177.
Kogut, T., & Ritov, I. (2007). 'One of us': Outstanding willingness to help save a single identified compatriot. *Organizational Behavior and Human Decision Processes, 104,* 150–157
Kohn, A. (1993). *Punished by rewards.* Boston: Houghton Mifflin.
Kohn, P. M., Lafreniere, K., & Gurevich, M. (1991). Hassles, health, and personality. *Journal of Personality and Social Psychology, 61,* 478–482

Kohut, A., & Wike, R. (2008, October 30). Xenophobia on the Continent. Retrieved June 16, 2009, from http://nationalinterest.org/Article.aspx?id=20124.

Kokko, K., Pulkkinen, L., Huesmann, L. R., Dubow, E. F, & Boxer, P. (2009). Intensity of aggression in childhood as a predictor of different forms of adult aggression: A two-country (Finland and the United States) analysis. *Journal of Research on Adolescence, 19,* 9–34.

Kokolakis, A., Smith, C. L., & Evans, C. S. (2010). Aerial alarm calling by male fowl (gallus gallus) reveals subtle new mechanisms of risk management. *Animal Behaviour, 79,* 1373–1380.

Kolditz, T. A., & Arkin, R. M. (1982). An impression management interpretation of the self-handicapping strategy. *Journal of Personality and Social Psychology, 43,* 492–502.

Konijn, E. A., Nije Bijvank, M., & Bushman, B. J. (2007). I wish I were a warrior: The role of wishful identification in the effects of violent video games on aggression in adolescent boys. *Developmental Psychology, 43,* 1038–1044.

Kopelman, S. (2009). The effect of culture and power on cooperation in commons dilemmas: Implications for global resource management. *Organizational Behavior and Human Decision Processes, 108,* 153–163.

Korte, C. (1980). Urban-nonurban differences in social behavior and social psychological models of urban impact. *Journal of Social Issues, 36* (3), 29–51.

Korte, C., Ypma, I., & Toppen, A. (1975). Helpfulness in Dutch society as a function of urbanization and environmental input level. *Journal of Personality and Social Psychology, 32,* 996–1003.

Kosonen, P., & Winne, P. (1995). Effects of teaching statistical laws of reasoning about everyday problems. *Journal of Educational Psychology, 87,* 33–46.

Kovacs, L. (1983). A conceptualization of marital development. *Family Therapy, 3,* 183–210.

Kovera, M. B. (2002). The effects of general pretrial publicity on juror decisions: An examination of moderators and mediating mechanisms. *Law and Human Behavior, 26,* 43–72.

Kowalski, R. M. (1993). Inferring sexual interest from behavioral cues: Effects of gender and sexually relevant attitudes. *Sex Roles, 29,* 13–36.

Kowalski, R. M. (1996). Complaints and complaining: Functions, antecedents, and consequences. *Psychological Bulletin, 119,* 179–196.

Kowalski, R. M., & Limber, S. P. (2007). Electronic bullying among middle school students. *Journal of Adolescent Health, 41*(6), S22–S30.

Kozak, M. N., Marsh, A. A., & Wegner, D. M. (2006). What do I think you're doing? Action identification and mind attribution. *Journal of Personality and Social Psychology, 90,* 543–555.

Kramer, G. P., Kerr, N. L., & Carroll, J. S. (1990). Pretrial publicity, judicial remedies, and jury bias. *Law and Human Behavior, 14,* 409–438.

Kramer, R. M. (1998). Revisiting the Bay of Pigs and Vietnam decisions 25 years later: How well has the groupthink hypothesis stood the test of time? *Organizational Behavior and Human Decision Processes, 73,* 236–271.

Kraus, S. J. (1995). Attitudes and the prediction of behavior: A meta-analysis of the empirical literature. *Personality and Social Psychology Bulletin, 21,* 58–75.

Krauss, R. M., Chen, Y., & Chawla, P. (1996). Nonverbal behavior and nonverbal communication: What do conversational hand gestures tell us? *Advances in Experimental Social Psychology, 28,* 389–450.

Kravitz, D. A., & Martin, B. (1986). Ringelmann rediscovered: The original article. *Journal of Personality and Social Psychology, 50,* 936–941.

Kray, L. J., Galinsky, A. D., & Thompson, L. (2002). Reversing the gender gap in negotiations: An exploration of stereotype regeneration. *Organizational Behavior and Human Decision Processes, 87,* 386–409.

Krebs, D. (1987). The challenge of altruism in biology and psychology. In C. Crawford, M. Smith, & D. Krebs (Eds.), *Sociobiology and psychology: Ideas, issues, and applications* (pp. 81–118). Hillsdale, NJ: Erlbaum.

Krebs, D., & Rosenwald, A. (1994). Moral reasoning and moral behavior in conventional adults. In B. Puka (Ed.), *Fundamental research in moral development* (pp. 111–121). New York: Garland.

Kringelbach, M. L., et al. (2008). A specific and rapid neural signature for parental instinct. *PLoS ONE, 3*(2): 1–7.

Kroger, R. O., & Scheibe, K. E. (1990). A reappraisal of wundts influence on social psychology. *Canadian Psychology/Psychologie Canadienne, 31,* 220–228.

Kroon, M. B. R., 't Hart, P., & van Kreveld, D. (1991). Managing group decision making processes: Individual versus collective accountability and groupthink. *International Journal of Conflict Management, 2,* 91–115.

Kross, E., Berman, M. G., Mischel, W., Smith, E. E., & Wager, T. D. (2011). Social rejection shares somatosensory representations with physical pain. *PNAS Proceedings of the National Academy of Sciences of the United States of America, 108,* 6270–6275.

Krueger, J. (1998). On the perception of social consensus. *Advances in Experimental Social Psychology, 30,* 163–240.

Krueger, J. (2000). The projective perception of the social world: A building block of social comparison processes. In J. Suls & L. Wheeler (Eds.), *Handbook of social comparison: Theory and research* (pp. 323–351). New York: Plenum/Kluwer.

Krueger, J., Rothbart, M., & Sriram, N. (1989). Category learning and change: Differences in sensitivity to information that enhances or reduces intercategory distinctions. *Journal of Personality and Social Psychology, 56,* 866–875.

Kruger, D. J. (2003). Evolution and altruism: Combining psychological mediators with naturally selected tendencies. *Evolution and Human Behavior, 24,* 118–125.

Kruger, J., & Dunning, D. (1999). Unskilled and unaware of it: How difficulties in recognizing one's own incompetence lead to inflated self-assessments. *Journal of Personality and Social Psychology, 77,* 1121–1134.

Kruger, J., Wirtz, D., & Miller, D. T. (2005). Counterfactual thinking and the first instinct fallacy. *Journal of Personality and Social Psychology, 88,* 725–735.

Kruglanski, A. W. (2001). That "vision thing": The state of theory in social and personality psychology at the edge of the new millennium. *Journal of Personality and Social Psychology, 80,* 871–875.

Kruglanski, A. W., & Freund, T. (1983). The freezing and unfreezing of lay-inferences: Effects of impressional primacy, ethnic stereotyping, and numerical anchoring. *Journal of Experimental Social Psychology, 19,* 448–468.

Kruglanski, A. W., & Mayseless, O. (1988). Contextual effects in hypothesis testing: The role of competing alternatives and epistemic motivations. *Social Cognition, 6,* 1–20.

Kruglanski, A. W., & Webster, D. M. (1996). Motivated closing of the mind: "Seizing" and "freezing." *Psychological Review, 103,* 263–283.

Kubany, E. S., Leisen, M. B., Kaplan, A. S., Watson, S. B., Haynes, S. N., Owens, J. A., & Burns, K. (2000). Development and preliminary validation of a brief broad-spectrum measure of trauma exposure: The Traumatic Life Events Questionnaire. *Psychological Assessment, 12,* 210–224.

Kuepper, Y., Alexander, N., Osinsky, R., Mueller, E., Schmitz, A., Netter, P., & Hennig, J. (2010). Aggression—Interactions of serotonin and testosterone in healthy men and women. *Behavioural Brain Research, 206,* 93–100.

Kugihara, N. (1999). Gender and social loafing in Japan. *Journal of Social Psychology, 139,* 516–526.

Kulik, J. A., & Mahler, H. I. M. (1989). Stress and affiliation in a hospital setting: Preoperative roommate preferences. *Personality and Social Psychology Bulletin, 15,* 183–193.

Kulik, J. A., Mahler, H. I. M., & Earnest, A. (1994). Social comparison and affiliation under threat: Going beyond the affiliate-choice paradigm. *Journal of Personality and Social Psychology, 66,* 301–309.

Kulik, J. A., Mahler, H. I. M., & Moore, P. J. (1996). Social comparison and affiliation under threat: Effects of recovery from major surgery. *Journal of Personality and Social Psychology, 71,* 967–979.

Kunda, Z. (1990). The case of motivated reasoning. *Psychological Bulletin, 108,* 480–498.

Kunda, Z., Adams, B., Davies, P. G., Hoshino-Browne, E., & Jordan, C. (2003). The impact of comprehension goals on the ebb and flow of stereotype activation during interaction. In S. J. Spencer, S. Fein, M. P. Zanna, & J. M. Olson (Eds.), *Motivated social perception: The Ontario symposium* (Vol. 9, pp. 1–20). Mahwah, NJ: Erlbaum.

Kunda, Z., Davies, P. G., Adams, B. D., & Spencer, S. J. (2002). The dynamic time course of stereotype activation: Activation, dissipation, and resurrection. *Journal of Personality and Social Psychology, 82,* 283–299.

Kunda, Z., Sinclair, L., & Griffin, D. (1997). Equal ratings but separate meanings: Stereotypes and the construal of traits. *Journal of Personality and Social Psychology, 72,* 720–734.

Kunda, Z., & Spencer, S. J. (2003). When do stereotypes come to mind and when do they color judgment? A goal-based theoretical framework for stereotype activation and application. *Psychological Bulletin, 129,* 522–544.

Kunstman, J. W., & Maner, Jon K. (2011). Sexual overperception: Power, mating motives, and biases in social judgment. *Journal of Personality and Social Psychology, 100,* 282–294.

Kuntz-Wilson, W., & Zajonc, R. B. (1980). Affective discrimination of stimuli that cannot be recognized. *Science, 207,* 557–558.

Kurdek, L. A. (1991a). Correlates of relationship satisfaction in cohabiting gay and lesbian couples: Interpretation of contextual, investment, and problem-solving models. *Journal of Personality and Social Psychology, 61,* 910–922.

Kurdek, L. A. (1991b). The dissolution of gay and lesbian couples. *Journal of Social and Personal Relationships, 8,* 265–278.

Kurdek, L. A. (1999). The nature and predictors of the trajectory of change in marital quality for husbands and wives over the first 10 years of marriage. *Developmental Psychology, 35,* 1283–1296.

Kurdek, L. A. (2005). What do we know about gay and lesbian couples? *Current Directions in Psychological Science, 14,* 251–254.

Kurdek, L. A. (2008). A general model of relationship commitment: Evidence from same-sex partners. *Personal Relationships, 15,* 391–405.

Kurebayashi, K., Hoffman, L., Ryan, C. S., & Murayama, A. (2012). Japanese and american perceptions of group entitativity and autonomy: A multilevel analysis. *Journal of Cross-Cultural Psychology, 43,* 349–364.

Kwan, V. S. Y., & Fiske, S. T. (2008). Missing links in social cognition: The continuum from nonhuman agents to dehumanized humans. *Social Cognition, 26,* 125–128.

Lacetera, N., & Macis, M. (2010). Do all material incentives for prosocial activities backfire? the response to cash and non-cash incentives for blood donations. *Journal of Economic Psychology, 31,* 738–748.

Laird, J. D. (1974). Self-attribution of emotion: The effects of expressive behavior on the quality of emotional experience. *Journal of Personality and Social Psychology, 29,* 475–486.

Lakey, B., & Cassady, P. B. (1990). Cognitive processes in perceived social support. *Journal of Personality and Social Psychology, 59,* 337–343.

Lakin, J. L., & Chartrand, T. L. (2003). Using nonconscious behavioral mimicry to create affiliation and rapport. *Psychological Science, 14,* 334–339.

Lalwani, A. K., Shavitt, S., & Johnson, T. (2006). What is the relation between cultural orientation and socially desirable responding? *Journal of Personality and Social Psychology, 90,* 165–178.

Lam, K. C. H., Buehler, R., McFarland, C., Ross, M., & Cheung, I. (2005). Culture and affective forecasting: The role of focalism. *Personality and Social Psychology Bulletin, 31,* 1296–1309.

Lambert, A. J., Payne, B. K., Jacoby, L. L., Shaffer, L. M., Chasteen, A. L., & Khan, S. R. (2003). Stereotypes as dominant responses: On the "social facilitation" of prejudice in anticipated public contexts. *Journal of Personality and Social Psychology, 84,* 277–295.

Lamm, H., & Myers, D. G. (1978). Group-induced polarization of attitudes and behavior. In L. Berkowitz (Ed.), *Advances in experimental social psychology* (Vol. 11, pp. 145–195). New York: Academic Press.

Landau, T. (1989). About faces: The evolution of the human face. New York: Anchor Books.

Lane, K. A., Kang, J., & Banaji, M. R. (2007). Implicit social cognition and law. *Annual Review of Law and Social Science, 3,* 427–451.

Langer, E. J. (1975). The illusion of control. *Journal of Personality and Social Psychology, 32,* 311–328.

Langer, E. J. (1989). *Mindfulness.* Reading, MA: Addison-Wesley.

Langer, E. J., Blank, A., & Chanowitz, B. (1978). The mindlessness of ostensibly thoughtful action. *Journal of Personality and Social Psychology, 36,* 635–642.

Langer, E. J., & Rodin, J. (1976). The effects of choice and enhanced personal responsibility for the aged: A field experiment in an institutional setting. *Journal of Personality and Social Psychology, 34,* 191–198.

Langfred, C. W. (1998). Is group cohesiveness a double-edged sword? An investigation of the effects of cohesiveness on performance. *Small Group Research, 29,* 124–143.

Langlois, J. H., Kalakanis, L., Rubenstein, A. J., Larson, A., Hallam, M., & Smoot, M. (2000). Maxims or myths of beauty? A meta-analytic and theoretical review. *Psychological Bulletin, 126,* 390–423.

Langlois, J. H., Ritter, J. M., Roggman, L. A., & Vaughn, L. S. (1991). Facial diversity and infant preferences for attractive faces. *Developmental Psychology, 27,* 79–84.

Langlois, J. H., & Roggman, L. A. (1990). Attractive faces are only average. *Psychological Science, 1,* 115–121.

Langlois, J. H., Roggman, L. A., & Musselman, L. (1994).What is average and what is not average about attractive faces? *Psychological Science, 5,* 214–220.

Langton, S. R. H., Watt, R. J., & Bruce, V. (2000). Do the eyes have it? Cues to the direction of social attention. *Trends in Cognitive Sciences, 4,* 50–59.

Lansford, J. E., Wager, L. B., Bates, J. E., Dodge, K. A., & Pettit, G. S. (2012). Parental reasoning, denying privileges, yelling, and spanking: Ethnic differences and associations with child externalizing behavior. *Parenting: Science and Practice, 12,* 42–56.

LaPiere, R. T. (1934). Attitudes vs. action. *Social Forces, 13,* 230–237.

La Rooy, D., Katz, C., Malloy, L. C., & Lamb, M. E. (2010). Do we need to rethink guidance on repeated interviews? *Psychology, Public Policy, and Law, 16,* 373–392.

Larsen, K. S. (1990). The Asch conformity experiment: Replication and transhistorical comparisons. *Journal of Social Behavior and Personality, 5,* 163–168.

Larsen, R. J., & Kasimatis, M. (1990). Individual differences in entrainment of mood to the weekly calendar. *Journal of Personality and Social Psychology, 58,* 164–171.

Larson, J. R., Jr., Foster-Fishman, P. G., & Franz, T. M. (1998). Leadership style and the discussion of shared and unshared information in decision-making groups. *Personality and Social Psychology Bulletin, 24,* 482–495.

Lassiter, G. D. (2010). Psychological science and sound public policy: Video recording of custodial interrogations. *American Psychologist, 65,* 768–779.

Lassiter, G. D., Diamond, S. S., Schmidt, H. C., & Elek, J. K. (2007). Evaluating videotaped confessions: Expertise provides no defense against the camera-perspective effect. *Psychological Science, 18,* 224–226.

Lassiter, G. D., Geers, A. L., Munhall, P. J., Handley, I. M., & Beers, M. J. (2001). Videotaped confessions: Is guilt in the eye of the camera? *Advances in Experimental Social Psychology, 33,* 189–254.

Lassiter, G. D., Stone, J. I., & Rogers, S. L. (1988). Memorial consequences of variation in behavior perception. *Journal of Experimental Social Psychology, 24,* 222–239.

Latané, B. (1981). The psychology of social impact. *American Psychologist, 36,* 343–356.

Latané, B., & Darley, J. M. (1968). Group inhibition of bystander intervention. *Journal of Personality and Social Psychology, 10,* 215–221.

Latané, B., & Darley, J. M. (1970). *The unresponsive bystander: Why doesn't he help?* New York: Appleton-Century-Crofts.

Latané, B., & L'Herrou, T. (1996). Spatial clustering in the conformity game: Dynamic social impact in electronic groups. *Journal of Personality and Social Psychology, 70,* 1218–1230.

Latané, B., Liu, J. H., Nowak, A., Bonevento, M., & Zheng, L. (1995). Distance matters: Physical space and social impact. *Personality and Social Psychology Bulletin, 21,* 795–805.

Latané, B., & Werner, C. (1978). Regulation of social contact in laboratory rats: Time, not distance. *Journal of Personality and Social Psychology, 36,* 1128–1137.

Latané, B., Williams, K., & Harkins, S. (1979). Many hands make light the work: The causes and consequences of social loafing. *Journal of Personality and Social Psychology, 37,* 822–832.

Latané, B., & Wolf, S. (1981). The social impact of majorities and minorities. *Psychological Review, 88,* 438–453.

Latham, G. P., & Locke, E. A. (2007). New developments in and directions for goal-setting research. *European Psychologist, 12,* 290–300.

Latkin, C., Donnell, D., Celentano, D. D., Aramrattna, A., Liu, T., Vongchak, T., Wiboonnatakul, K., Davis-Vogel, A., & Metzger, D. (2009). Relationships between social norms, social network characteristics, and HIV risk behaviors in Thailand and the United States. *Health Psychology, 28,* 323–329.

Laughlin, P. R., Carey, H. R., & Kerr, N. L. (2008). Group-to-individual problem-solving transfer. *Group Processes & Intergroup Relations, 11,* 319–330.

Law, D. M., Shapka, J. D., Hymel, S., Olson, B. F., & Waterhouse, T. (2012). The changing face of bullying: An empirical comparison between traditional and internet bullying and victimization. *Computers in Human Behavior, 28,* 226–232.

Lawrence, E., Rothman, A., Cobb, R., Bradbury, T., & Rothman, M. (2008). Marital satisfaction across the transition to parenthood. *Journal of Family Psychology, 22,* 41–50.

Lawson, T. J. (2010). The social spotlight increases blindness to change blindness. *Basic and Applied Social Psychology, 32,* 360–368.

Lawyer, S., Resnick, H., Bakanic, V., Burkett, T., & Kilpatrick, D. (2010). Forcible, drug-facilitated, and incapacitated rape and sexual assault among undergraduate women. *Journal of American College Health, 58,* 453–460.

Lazarus, R. S., & Folkman, S. (1984). *Stress, appraisal, and coping.* New York: Springer.

Le, B., & Agnew, C. R. (2003). Commitment and its theorized determinants: A meta-analysis of the investment model. *Personal Relationships, 10,* 37–57.

Le Bon, G. (1895). *Psychologie des foules.* Paris: Félix Alcan.

Leary, M. R. (Ed.) (2001). *Interpersonal rejection.* New York: Oxford University Press.

Leary, M. R. (2012). In P.A.M. Van Lange., A. W. Kruglanski, and E. T. Higgins (Eds.), *Sociometer theory.* Thousand Oaks, CA: Sage Publications Ltd.

Leary, M. R., & Baumeister, R. F. (2000). The nature and function of self-esteem: Sociometer theory. In M. P. Zanna (Ed.), *Advances in Experimental Social Psychology* (Vol. 32, pp.1–62). San Diego, CA: Academic Press.

Leary, M. R., & Kowalski, R. M. (1995). *Social anxiety.* New York: Guilford Press.

Leary, M. R., Kowalski, R. M., Smith, L., & Phillips, S. (2003). Teasing, rejection, and violence: Case studies of the school shootings. *Aggressive Behavior, 29,* 202–214.

Leary, M. R., & Tangney, J. P. (Eds.) (2003). *Handbook of self and identity.* New York: Guilford.

Leary, M. R., Tchividjian, L. R., & Kraxberger, B. E. (1994). Self-presentation can be hazardous to your health: Impression management and health risk. *Health Psychology, 13,* 461–470.

Leary, M. R., Twenge, J. M., & Quinlivan, E. (2006). Interpersonal rejection as a determinant of anger and aggression. *Personality and Social Psychology Review, 10,* 111–132.

LeDoux, J. (2002). *The synaptic self: How our brains become who we are.* New York: Penguin Books.

Lee, E. (2008). When are strong arguments stronger than weak arguments?: Deindividuation effects on message elaboration in computer-mediated communication. *Communication Research, 35,* 646–665.

Lee, J. A. (1988). Love-styles. In R. J. Sternberg & M. L. Barnes (Ed.), *The psychology of love* (pp. 38–67). New Haven, CT: Yale University Press.

Lee, K., & Ashton, M. C. (2012). Getting mad and getting even: Agreeableness and honesty-humility as predictors of revenge intentions. *Personality and Individual Differences, 52,* 596–600.

Lee, W. B., Fong, G. T., Zanna, M. P., Borland, R., Omar, M., & Sirirassamee, B. (2009). Regret and rationalization among smokers in Thailand and Malaysia: Findings from the international tobacco control Southeast Asia survey. *Health Psychology, 28,* 457-464.

Lehman, D. R., Chiu, C.-Y., & Schaller, M. (2004). Psychology and culture. *Annual Review of Psychology, 55,* 689–714.

Lehman, D. R., Lempert, R. O., & Nisbett, R. E. (1988). The effects of graduate training on reasoning: Formal discipline and thinking about everyday-life events. *American Psychologist, 43,* 431–442.

Leicht, K. T. (2008). Broken down by race and gender? Sociological explanations of new sources of earnings inequality. *Annual Review of Sociology, 34,* 237–255.

Leigh, B. C., & Stacy, A. W. (1993). Alcohol outcome expectancies: Scale construction and predictive utility in higher-order confirmatory models. *Psychological Assessment, 5,* 216–229.

Leippe, M. R., & Eisenstadt, D. (1994). Generalization of dissonance reduction: Decreasing prejudice through induced compliance. *Journal of Personality and Social Psychology, 67,* 395–413.

Leland, J. (1995, December 11). "Copycat" crimes in New York's subways reignite the debate: Do TV and movies cause actual mayhem? *Newsweek,* p. 46.

Lench, Heather C. (2009). Automatic optimism: The affective basis of judgments about the likelihood of future events. *Journal of Experimental Psychology: General, 138,* 187–200.

Leo, R. A., & Davis, D. (2010). From false confession to wrongful conviction: Seven psychological processes. *Journal of Psychiatry & Law, 38*(1–2), 9–56.

Leonard, K. E. (1989). The impact of explicit aggressive and implicit nonaggressive cues on aggression in intoxicated and sober roles. *Personality and Social Psychology Bulletin, 15,* 390–400.

Leonard, K. E., Collins, R. L., & Quigley, B. M. (2003). Alcohol consumption and the occurrence and severity of aggression: An event-based analysis of male-to-male barroom violence. *Aggressive Behavior, 29,* 346–365.

Lepore, L., & Brown, R. (1997). Category and stereotype activation: Is prejudice inevitable? *Journal of Personality and Social Psychology, 72,* 275–287.

Lepore, L., & Brown, R. (2002). The role of awareness: Divergent automatic stereotype activation and implicit judgment correction. *Social Cognition, 20,* 321–351.

Lepore, S. J., & Smyth, J. M. (2002). *The writing cure: How expressive writing promotes health and emotional well-being.* Washington, DC: American Psychological Association.

Lepper, M. R., Greene, D., & Nisbett, R. E. (1973).Undermining children's intrinsic interest with extrinsic reward: A test of the "overjustification" hypothesis. *Journal of Personality and Social Psychology, 28,* 129–137.

Lerner, M. J. (1980). *The belief in a just world: A fundamental delusion.* New York: Plenum.

Lerner, M. J. (1998). The two forms of belief in a just world: Some thoughts on why and how people care about justice. In L. Montada, & M. J. Lerner (Eds.), *Responses to victimization and belief in a just world: Critical issues in social justice* (pp. 247–269). NY: Plenum.

Lerner, M. J., & Simmons, C. H. (1966). Observers' reaction to the "innocent victim": Compassion or rejection? *Journal of Personality and Social Psychology, 4,* 203–210.

Leshowitz, B., Eignor DiCerbo, K., & Okun, M. A. (2002). Effects of instruction in methodological reasoning on information evaluation. *Teaching of Psychology, 29,* 5–10.

Letourneau, E. J., Henggeler, S. W., Borduin, C. M., Schewe, P. A., McCart, M. R., Chapman, J. E., & Saldana, L. (2009). Multisystemic therapy for juvenile sexual offenders: 1-year results from a randomized effectiveness trial. *Journal of Family Psychology, 23,* 89–102.

LeVay, S. (1991). A difference in hypothalamic structure between heterosexual and homosexual men. *Science, 253,* 1034–1037.

LeVay, S. (1993). *The sexual brain.* Cambridge, MA: MIT Press.

LeVay, S. (2011). From mice to men: Biological factors in the development of sexuality. *Frontiers in Neuroendocrinology, 32,* 110–113.

Leventhal, H. (1970). Findings and theory in the study of fear communications. In L. Berkowitz (Ed.), *Advances in experimental social psychology* (Vol. 5, pp. 119–186). New York: Academic Press.

Leventhal, H., Watts, J. C., & Pagano, F. (1967). Effects of fear and instructions on how to cope with danger. *Journal of Personality and Social Psychology, 6,* 313–321.

Leventhal, H., Weinman, J., Leventhal, E. A., & Phillips, L. A. (2008). Health psychology: The search for pathways between behavior and health. *Annual Review of Psychology, 59,* 477–505.

Levesque, M. J. (1997). Meta-accuracy among acquainted individuals: A social relations analysis of interpersonal perception and metaperception. *Journal of Personality and Social Psychology, 72,* 66–74.

Levesque, M. J., Nave, C. S., & Lowe, C. A. (2006). Toward an understanding of gender differences in inferring sexual interest. *Psychology of Women Quarterly, 30,* 150–158.

Levin, S., Henry, P. J., Pratto, F., & Sidanius, J. (2003). Social dominance and social identity in Lebanon: Implications for support of violence against the West. *Group Processes and Intergroup Relations, 6,* 353–368.

Levin, S., Henry, P. J., Pratto, F., & Sidanius, J. (2009). Social dominance and social identity in Lebanon: Implications for support of violence against the West. In J. Victoroff & A. W. Kruglanski (Eds.), *Psychology of terrorism: Classic and contemporary insights* (pp. 253–267). New York: Psychology Press.

Levin, S., Taylor, P. L., & Caudle, E. (2007). Interethnic and interracial dating in college: A longitudinal study of social psychological predictors and outcomes. *Journal of Social and Personal Relationships, 24,* 323–341.

Levine, J. M. (1989). Reaction to opinion deviance in small groups. In P. B. Paulus (Ed.), *Psychology of group influence* (2nd ed., pp. 187–231). Hillsdale, NJ: Erlbaum.

Levine, J. M., & Choi, H.-S. (2010). Newcomers as change agents: Minority influence in task groups. In R. Martin & M. Hewstone (Eds.), *Minority influence and innovation: Antecedents, processes, and consequences.* New York: Psychology Press.

Levine, J. M., & Moreland, R. L. (1998). Small groups. In D. T. Gilbert, S. T. Fiske, & G. Lindzey (Eds.), *The handbook of social psychology* (4th ed., Vol. 2, pp. 415–469). New York: McGraw-Hill.

Levine, M., & Cassidy, C. (2010). Groups, identities, and bystander behavior: How group processes can be used to promote helping. In S. Stürmer & M. Snyder (Eds.), *The psychology of prosocial behavior: Group processes, intergroup relations, and helping.* (pp. 209–222). Wiley-Blackwell.

Levine, M., & Crowther, S. (2008). The responsive bystander: How social group membership and group size can encourage as well as inhibit bystander intervention. *Journal of Personality and Social Psychology, 95,* 1429–1439.

Levine, M., Prosser, A., Evans, D., & Reicher, S. (2005, April). Identity and emergency intervention: How social group membership and inclusiveness of group boundaries shape helping behavior. *Personality and Social Psychology Bulletin, 31,* 443–453.

Levine, R., Sato, S., Hashimoto, T., & Verma, J. (1995). Love and marriage in eleven cultures. *Journal of Cross-Cultural Psychology, 26,* 554–571.

Levine, R. A., & Campbell, D. T. (1972). *Ethnocentrism: Theories of conflict, ethnic attitudes, and group behavior.* New York: Wiley.

Levine, R. V., Norenzayan, A., & Philbrick, K. (2001). Crosscultural differences in helping strangers. *Journal of Cross-Cultural Psychology, 32,* 543–560.

Levine, R. V., Reysen, S., & Ganz, E. (2008). The kindness of strangers revisited: A comparison of 24 US cities. *Social Indicators Research, 85,* 461–481.

Levy, D. A., & Nail, P. R. (1993). Contagion: A theoretical and empirical review and reconceptualization. *Genetic, Social, and General Psychology Monographs, 119,* 233–284.

Levy, S. R., Chiu, C.-Y., & Hong, Y.-Y. (2006). Lay theories and intergroup relations. *Group Processes and Intergroup Relations, 9,* 5–24.

Levy, S. R., & Hughes, J. M. (2009). Development of racial and ethnic prejudice among children. In T. D. Nelson (Ed.), *Handbook of prejudice, stereotyping, and discrimination* (pp. 23–42). New York: Psychology Press.

Lewin, K. (1935). *A dynamic theory of personality.* New York: McGraw-Hill.

Lewin, K. (1947). Group decision and social change. In T. M. Newcomb & E. L. Hartley (Eds.), *Readings in social psychology* (pp. 330–344). New York: Holt.

Lewin, K. (1951). Problems of research in social psychology. In D. Cartwright (Ed.), *Field theory in social science* (pp. 155–169). New York: Harper & Row.

Lewis, B. P., & Linder, D. E. (1997). Thinking about choking? Attentional processes and paradoxical performance. *Personality and Social Psychology Bulletin, 23,* 937–944.

Lewis, M., & Brooks-Gunn, J. (1979). *Social cognition and the acquisition of self.* New York: Plenum.

Leye, E., Powell, R. A., Nienhuis, G., Claeys, P., & Temmerman, M. (2006). Health care in Europe for women with genital mutilation. *Health Care for Women International, 27,* 362–378.

Li, L., Borland, R., Yong, H., Hitchman, S. C., Wakefield, M. A., Kasza, K. A., & Fong, Geoffrey T. (2012). The association between exposure to point-of-sale anti-smoking warnings and smokers interest in quitting and quit attempts: Findings from the international tobacco control four country survey. *Addiction, 107,* 425–433.

Li, N. P., & Kenrick, D. T. (2006). Sex similarities and differences in preferences for short-term mates: What, whether, and why. *Journal of Personality and Social Psychology, 90,* 468–489.

Li, N. P., Valentine, K. A., & Patel, L. (2011). Mate preferences in the US and Singapore: A cross-cultural test of the mate preference priority model. *Personality and Individual Differences, 50,* 291–294.

Liberman, B., Seidman, G., McKenna, K. Y. A., & Buffardi, L. E. (2011). Employee job attitudes and organizational characteristics as predictors of cyberloafing. *Computers in Human Behavior, 27,* 2192–2199.

Liden, R. C., Wayne, S. J., Jaworski, R. A., & Bennett, N. (2004). Social loafing: A field investigation. *Journal of Management, 30,* 285–304.

Lieberman, J. D., & Arndt, J. (2000). Understanding the limits of limiting instructions. *Psychology, Public Policy, and Law, 6,* 677–711.

Lieberman, M. D. (2010). Social cognitive neuroscience. In S. T. Fiske, D. T. Gilbert, & G. Lindzey (Eds.), *Handbook of social psychology* (5th ed.). NY: McGraw-Hill.

Lieberman, M. D., Gaunt, R., Gilbert, D. T., & Trope, Y. (2004). Reflection and reflexion: A social cognitive neuroscience approach to attributional inference. In M. P. Zanna (Ed.), *Advances in experimental social psychology* (Vol. 34, pp. 199–249). San Diego, CA: Academic Press.

Lieberman, M. D., Jarcho, J. M., & Obayashi, J. (2005). Attributional inference across cultures: Similar automatic attributions and different controlled corrections. *Personality and Social Psychology Bulletin, 31,* 889–901.

Lifton, R. J. (1986). *The Nazi doctors: Medical killing and the psychology of genocide.* New York: Basic Books.

Likert, R. (1932). A technique for the measurement of attitudes. *Archives of Psychology, 140,* 1–55.

Lim, J., & Guo, X. (2008). A study of group support systems and the intergroup setting. *Decision Support Systems, 45,* 452–460.

Linardatos, L., & Lydon, J. E. (2011). Relationship-specific identification and spontaneous relationship maintenance processes. *Journal of Personality and Social Psychology, 101,* 737–753.

Lind, E. A., Erickson, B. E., Friedland, N., & Dickenberger, M. (1978). Reactions to procedural models for adjudicative conflict resolution: A cross national study. *Journal of Conflict Resolution, 22,* 318–341.

Lind, E. A., Kanfer, R., & Farley, P. C. (1990). Voice, control, and procedural justice: Instrumental and noninstrumental concerns in fairness judgments. *Journal of Personality and Social Psychology, 59,* 952–959.

Linde, J. A., Rothman, A. J., Baldwin, A. S., & Jeffery, R. W. (2006). The impact of self-efficacy on behavior change and weight change among overweight participants in a weight loss trial. *Health Psychology, 25,* 282–291.

Linder, D. E., Cooper, J., & Jones, E. E. (1967). Decision freedom as a determinant of the role of incentive magnitude in attitude change. *Journal of Personality and Social Psychology, 6,* 245–254.

Lindsay, D. S., Hagen, L., Read, J. D., Wade, K. A., & Garry, M. (2004). True photographs and false memories. *Psychological Science, 15,* 149–154.

Lindsay, R. C. L., Ross, D. F., Read, J. D., & Toglia, M. P. (Eds.). (2007). *The handbook of eyewitness psychology: Vol. 2, Memory for people.* Mahwah, NJ: Erlbaum.

Lindsay, R. C. L., Wells, G. L., & Rumpel, C. M. (1981). Can people detect eyewitness-identification accuracy within and across situations? *Journal of Applied Psychology, 66,* 79–89.

Lindskold, S., & Han, G. (1988). GRIT as a foundation for integrative bargaining. *Personality and Social Psychology Bulletin, 14,* 335–345.

Linville, P. (1998). The heterogeneity of homogeneity. In J. Cooper & J. Darley (Eds.), *Attribution processes, person perception, and social interaction: The legacy of Ned Jones.* Washington, DC: American Psychological Association.

Linville, P. W., & Jones, E. E. (1980). Polarized appraisals of out-group members. *Journal of Personality and Social Psychology, 38,* 689–703.

Linville, P. W., Fischer, G. W., & Fischoff, B. (1992). Perceived risk and decision making involving AIDS. In J. B. Pryor & G. D. Reeder (Eds.), *The social psychology of HIV infection.* Hillsdale, NJ: Erlbaum.

Linville, P. W., Fischer, G. W., & Salovey, P. (1989). Perceived distributions of the characteristics of in-group and out-group members: Empirical evidence and a computer simulation. *Journal of Personality and Social Psychology, 57,* 165–188.

Linz, D., Donnerstein, E., & Penrod, S. (1987). The findings and recommendations of the Attorney General's Commission on Pornography: Do the psychological "facts" fit the political fury? *American Psychologist, 42,* 946–953.

Linz, D., Wilson, B. J., & Donnerstein, E. (1992). Sexual violence in the mass media: Legal solutions, warnings, and mitigation through education. *Journal of Social Issues, 48,* 145–171.

Lippa, R. A. (2006). Is high sex drive associated with increased sexual attraction to both sexes? *Psychological Science, 17,* 46–52.

Littlepage, G. E., Hollingshead, A. B., Drake, L. R., & Littlepage, A. M. (2008). Transactive memory and performance in work groups: Specificity, communication, ability differences, and work allocation. *Group Dynamics: Theory, Research, and Practice, 12,* 223–241.

Lo, C., Helwig, C. C., Chen, S. X., Ohashi, M. M., & Cheng, C. M. (2011). The psychology of strengths and weaknesses: Assessing self-enhancing and self-critical tendencies in eastern and western cultures. *Self and Identity, 10,* 203–212.

Lobchuk, M. M., McClement, S. E., McPherson, C., & Cheang, M. (2008). Does blaming the patient with lung cancer affect the helping behavior of primary caregivers? *Oncology Nursing Forum, 35,* 681–689.

Locke, E. A., & Latham, G. P. (2002). Building a practically useful theory of goal setting and task motivation: A 35-year odyssey. *American Psychologist, 57,* 705–717.

Lockwood, P., Jordan, C. H., & Kunda, Z. (2002). Motivation by positive or negative role models: Regulatory focus determines who will best inspire us. *Journal of Personality and Social Psychology, 83,* 854–864.

Lockwood, P., & Kunda, Z. (2000). Outstanding role models: Do they inspire or demoralize us? In A. Tesser, J. Suls, & R. Felson (Eds.), *Psychological perspectives on self and identity,* pp. 147–171. Washington, D. C. APA Press.

Loewenstein, G. F., Weber, E. U., Hsee, C. K., & Welch, N. (2001). Risk as feelings. *Psychological Bulletin, 127,* 267–286.

Loftus, E. F. (1996). *Eyewitness testimony* (reprint ed.). Cambridge, MA: Harvard University Press.

Loftus, E. F. (2003). Memory in Canadian courts of law. *Canadian Psychology, 44,* 207–212.

Loftus, E. F., & Palmer, J. C. (1974). Reconstruction of automobile destruction: An example of the interaction between language and memory. *Journal of Verbal Learning and Verbal Behavior, 13,* 585–589.

Logel, C., Iserman, E. C., Davies, P. G, Quinn, D. M, & Spencer, S. J. (2009). The perils of double consciousness: The role of thought suppression in stereotype threat. *Journal of Experimental Social Psychology, 45,* 299–312.

Logel, C. R., Walton, G. M., Spencer, S. J., Peach, J, & Mark, Z. P. (2012). Unleashing latent ability: Implications of stereotype threat for college admissions. *Educational Psychologist, 47,* 42–50.

Loke, I. C., Evans, A. D., & Lee, K. (2011). The neural correlates of reasoning about prosocial-helping decisions: An event-related brain potentials study. *Brain Research, 1369,* 140–148.

Long, E. C. J., & Andrews, D. W. (1990). Perspective taking as a predictor of marital adjustment. *Journal of Personality and Social Psychology, 59,* 126–131.

Lorenzo, G. L., Biesanz, J. C., & Human, L. J. (2010). What is beautiful is good and more accurately understood: Physical attractiveness and accuracy in first impressions of personality. *Psychological Science, 21,* 1777–1782.

Lortie-Lussier, M. (1987). Minority influence and idiosyncrasy credit: A new comparison of the Moscovici and Hollander theories of innovation. *European Journal of Social Psychology, 17,* 431–446.

Losch, M. E., & Cacioppo, J. T. (1990). Cognitive dissonance may enhance sympathetic tonus, but attitudes are changed to reduce negative affect rather than arousal. *Journal of Experimental Social Psychology, 26,* 289–304.

Lott, A. J., & Lott, B. E. (1974). The role of reward in the formation of positive interpersonal attitudes. In T. L. Huston (Ed.), *Foundations of interpersonal attraction* (pp. 171–189). New York: Academic Press.

Lott, B. (1985). The devaluation of women's competence. *Journal of Social Issues, 41,* 43–60.

Loula, F., Prasad, S., Harber, K., & Shiffrar, M. (2005). Recognizing people from their movement. *Journal of Experimental Psychology: Human Perception & Performance, 31,* 210–220.

Lu, H., While, A. E., & Barriball, K. L. (2008). Role perceptions and reported actual role content of hospital nurses in Mainland China. *Journal of Clinical Nursing, 17,* 1011–1022.

Lubek, I., & Apfelbaum, E. (2000). A critical gaze and wistful glance at handbook histories of social psychology: Did the successive accounts by Gordon Allport and successors historiographically succeed? *Journal of the History of the Behavioral Sciences, 36,* 405–428.

Lucier-Greer, M., & Adler-Baeder, F. (2011). An examination of gender role attitude change patterns among continuously married, divorced, and remarried individuals. *Journal of Divorce & Remarriage, 52,* 225–243.

Lun, J., Sinclair, S., Whitchurch, E. R., & Glenn, C. (2007). (Why) do I think what you think? epistemic social tuning and implicit prejudice. *Journal of Personality and Social Psychology, 93,* 957–972.

Lund, R., Nielsen, K. K., Hansen, D. H., Kriegbaum, M., Molbo, D., Due, P., et al. (2009). Exposure to bullying at school and depression in adulthood: A study of Danish men born in 1953. *European Journal of Public Health, 19,* 111–116.

Lüüs, C. A. E., & Wells, G. L. (1994). The malleability of eyewitness confidence: Co-witness and perseverance effects. *Journal of Applied Psychology, 79,* 714–723.

Lykken, D. T. (1998). *A tremor in the blood: Uses and abuses of the lie detector* (2nd ed.). Cambridge, MA: Perseus.

Lykken, D. T. (2000). *Happiness: The nature and nurture of joy and contentment.* New York: St. Martin's Press.

Lykken, D. T., & Tellegen, A. (1993). Is human mating adventitious or the result of lawful choice? A twin study of mate selection. *Journal of Personality and Social Psychology, 65,* 56–68.

Lyubomirsky, S., Sheldon, K. M., & Schkade, D. (2005). Pursuing happiness: The architecture of sustainable change. *Review of General Psychology, 9,* 111–131.

Maass, A., & Clark, R. D., III. (1984). Hidden impact of minorities: Fifteen years of minority influence research. *Psychological Bulletin, 95,* 428–450.

Maass, A., D'Ettole, C., & Cadinu, M. (2008). Checkmate? The role of gender stereotypes in the ultimate intellectual sport. *European Journal of Social Psychology, 38,* 231–245.

Maass, A., Volpato, C., & Mucchi-Faina, A. (1996). Social influence and the verifiability of the issue under discussion: Attitudinal versus objective items. *British Journal of Social Psychology, 35,* 15–26.

Macionis, J. J. (2003). *Sociology* (9th ed.). Upper Saddle River, NJ: Prentice Hall.

Mackenzie, C. S., Gekoski, W. L., & Knox, V. J. (2006). Age, gender, and the underutilization of mental health services: The influence of help-seeking attitudes. *Aging & Mental Health, 10,* 574–582.

Mackie, D. M., Asuncion, A. G., & Rosselli, F. (1992). Impact of positive affect on persuasion processes. *Review of Personality and Social Psychology, 14,* 247–270.

Mackie, D. M., & Worth, L. T. (1989). Processing deficits and the mediation of positive affect in persuasion. *Journal of Personality and Social Psychology, 57,* 27–40.

Mackinnon, Sean P., Jordan, C. H., & Wilson, A. E. (2011). Birds of a feather sit together: Physical similarity predicts seating choice. *Personality and Social Psychology Bulletin, 37,* 879–892.

MacLeod, C., & Campbell, L. (1992). Memory accessibility and probability judgments: An experimental evaluation of the availability heuristic. *Journal of Personality and Social Psychology, 63,* 890–902.

MacNeil, S., & Byers, E. S. (2009). Role of sexual self-disclosure in the sexual satisfaction of long-term heterosexual couples. *Journal of Sex Research, 46,* 3–14.

Macrae, C. N., Bodenhausen, G. V., Milne, A. B., & Jetten, J. (1994). Out of mind but back in sight: Stereotypes on the rebound. *Journal of Personality and Social Psychology, 67,* 808–817.

Madden, T. J., Ellen, P. S., & Ajzen, I. (1992). A comparison of the theory of planned behavior and the theory of reasoned action. *Personality and Social Psychology Bulletin, 18,* 3–9.

Maddux, J. E. (1995). *Self-efficacy, adaptation, and adjustment: Theory, research, and application.* New York: Perseus.

Maddux, J. E., & Rogers, R. W. (1980). Effects of source expertness, physical attractiveness, and supporting arguments on persuasion: A case of brains over beauty. *Journal of Personality and Social Psychology, 39,* 235–244.

Maddux, W. W., & Galinsky, A. D. (2009). Cultural borders and mental barriers: The relationship between living abroad and creativity. *Journal of Personality and Social Psychology, 96,* 1047–1061.

Madera, J. M., & Hebl, M. R. (2012). Discrimination against facially stigmatized applicants in interviews: An eye-tracing and face-to-face investigation. *Journal of Applied Psychology*, 97, 317–330.

Madey, S. F., Simo, M., Dillworth, D., Kemper, D., Toczynski, A., & Perella, A. (1996). They do get more attractive at closing time, but only when you are not in a relationship. *Basic and Applied Social Psychology, 18,* 387–393.

Madon, S, Guyll, M., Aboufadel, K., Montiel, E., Smith, A., Palumbo, P., & Jussim, L. (2001). Ethnic and national stereotypes: The princeton trilogy revisited and revised. *Personality and Social Psychology Bulletin, 27,* 996–1010.

Madon, S., Jussim, L., Keiper, S., Eccles, J., Smith, A., & Palumbo, P. (1998). The accuracy and power of sex, social class, and ethnic stereotypes: A naturalistic study in person perception. *Personality and Social Psychology Bulletin, 24,* 1304–1318.

Madsen, E. A., Tunney, R. J., Fieldman, G., Plotkin, H. C., Dunbar, R. I. M., Richardson, J. M., & McFarland, D. (2007). Kinship and altruism: A cross-cultural experimental study. *British Journal of Psychology, 98,* 339–359.

Maeder, E., Dempsey, J., & Pozzulo, J. (2012). Behind the veil of juror decision making: Testing the effects of muslim veils and defendant race in the courtroom. *Criminal Justice and Behavior, 39,* 666–678.

Magnussen, S., & Melinder, A. (2012). What psychologists know and believe about memory: A survey of practitioners. *Applied Cognitive Psychology, 26,* 54–60.

Magnussen, S., Wise, R. A., Raja, A. Q., Safer, M. A., Pawlenko, N., & Stridbeck, U. (2008). What judges know about eyewitness testimony: A comparison of Norwegian and US judges. *Psychology, Crime & Law, 14,* 177–188.

Maio, G., & Olson, J. M. (Eds.) (2000). *Why we evaluate: Functions of attitudes.* Mahwah, NJ: Erlbaum.

Major, B., Carrington, P. I., & Carnevale, P. J. D. (1984). Physical attractiveness and self-esteem: Attributions for praise from an other-sex evaluator. *Personality and Social Psychology Bulletin, 10,* 43–50.

Major, B., & Crocker, J. (1993). Social stigma: The affective consequences of attributional ambiguity. In D. M. Mackie & D. L. Hamilton (Eds.), *Affect, cognition, and stereotyping: Interactive processes in intergroup perception* (pp. 345–370). New York: Academic Press.

Major, B., Kaiser, C. R., O'Brien, L. T., & McCoy, S. K. (2007). Perceived discrimination as worldview threat or worldview confirmation: Implications for self-esteem. *Journal of Personality and Social Psychology, 92,* 1068–1086.

Major, B., Quinton, W. J., & Schmader, T. (2003). Attributions to discrimination and self-esteem: Impact of group identification and situational ambiguity. *Journal of Experimental Social Psychology, 39,* 220–231.

Malamuth, N. M. (1983). Factors associated with rape as predictors of laboratory aggression against women. *Journal of Personality and Social Psychology, 45,* 432–442.

Malamuth, N. M. (1986). Predictors of naturalistic sexual aggression. *Journal of Personality and Social Psychology, 50,* 953–962.

Malamuth, N. M. (1996). The confluence model of sexual aggression: Feminist and evolutionary perspectives. In D. M. Buss & N. M. Malamuth (Eds.), *Sex, power, conflict: Evolutionary and feminist perspectives* (pp. 269–295). New York: Oxford University Press.

Malamuth, N. M., & Donnerstein, E. I. (1982). The effects of aggressive-pornographic mass media stimuli. In L. Berkowitz (Ed.), *Advances in experimental social psychology* (Vol. 15, pp. 103–136). New York: Academic Press.

Malle, B. F., & Knobe, J. (1997). Which behaviors do people explain? A basic actor-observer asymmetry. *Journal of Personality and Social Psychology, 72,* 288–304.

Malle, B. F., Knobe, J., O'Laughlin, M. J., Pearce, G. E., & Nelson, S. E. (2000). Conceptual structure and social functions of behavior explanations: Beyond person-situation attributions. *Journal of Personality and Social Psychology, 79,* 309–326.

Malloy, T. E., & Albright, L. (1990). Interpersonal perception in a social context. *Journal of Personality and Social Psychology, 58,* 419–428.

Malpass, R. S., & Devine, P. G. (1981). Eyewitness identification: Lineup instructions and the absence of the offender. *Journal of Applied Psychology, 66,* 482–489.

Malpass, R. S., & Kravitz, J. (1969). Recognition for faces of own and other race. *Journal of Personality and Social Psychology, 13,* 330–334.

Malti, T., Gasser, L., & Buchmann, M. (2009). Aggressive and prosocial children's emotion attributions and moral reasoning. *Aggressive Behavior, 35,* 90–102.

Manago, A. M., Taylor, T., & Greenfield, P. M. (2012). Me and my 400 friends: The anatomy of college students facebook networks, their communication patterns, and well-being. *Developmental Psychology, 48,* 369–380.

Maner, J. K., Kenrick, D. T., Becker, D. V., Robertson, T. E., Hofer, B., Neuberg, S. L., et al. (2005). Functional projection: How fundamental social motives can bias interpersonal perception. *Journal of Personality and Social Psychology, 88,* 63–78.

Manning, R., Levine, M., & Collins, A. (2008). The legacy of the 38 witnesses and the importance of getting history right. *American Psychologist, 63,* 562–563.

Mannino, C. A., Snyder, M., & Omoto, A. M. (2011). In D. Dunning (Ed.), *Why do people get involved? motivations for volunteerism and other forms of social action.* New York: Psychology Press.

Mantonakis, A., & Galiffi, B. (2011, June). "Does the fluency of a winery name affect taste perception?" Academy of Wine Business Research International Conference, Bordeaux, France.

Maoz, I., & McCauley, C. (2008). Threat, dehumanization, and support for retaliatory aggressive policies in asymmetric conflict. *Journal of Conflict Resolution, 52,* 93–116.

Marcus-Newhall, A., Pedersen, W. C., Carlson, M., & Miller, N. (2000). Displaced aggression is alive and well: A meta-analytic review. *Journal of Personality and Social Psychology, 78,* 670–689.

Mares, M.-L., & Woodard, E. (2005). Positive effects of television on children's social interactions: A meta-analysis. *Media Psychology, 7,* 301–322.

Margolin, G., & Wampold, B. E. (1981). A sequential analysis of conflict and accord in distressed and nondistressed marital partners. *Journal of Consulting and Clinical Psychology, 49,* 554–567.

Markey, P. M. (2000). Bystander intervention in computer-mediated communication. *Computers in Human Behavior, 16,* 183–188.

Markman, K. D., & Weary, G. (1996). The influence of chronic control concerns on counterfactual thought. *Social Cognition, 14,* 292–316.

Marks, J. (1995). *Human biodiversity: Genes, race, and history.* New York: Aldine de Gruyter.

Markus, H. (1977). Self-schemata and processing information about the self. *Journal of Personality and Social Psychology, 35,* 63–78.

Markus, H., Hamill, R., & Sentis, K. P. (1987). Thinking fat: Self-schemas for body weight and the processing of weight-relevant information. *Journal of Applied Social Psychology, 17,* 50–71.

Markus, H. R. (2008). Pride, prejudice, and ambivalence: Toward a unified theory of race and ethnicity. *American Psychologist, 63,* 651–670.

Markus, H. R., & Kitayama, S. (1991). Culture and the self: Implications for cognition, emotion, and motivation. *Psychological Review, 98,* 224–253.

Markus, H. R., & Lin, L. R. (1999). Conflictways: Cultural diversity in the meanings and practices of conflict. In D. A. Prentice & D. T. Miller (Eds.), *Cultural divides: Understanding and overcoming group conflict* (pp. 302–333). New York: Russell Sage.

Martey, R. M., & Stromer-Galley, J. (2007). The digital dollhouse: Context and social norms in The Sims online. *Games and Culture: A Journal of Interactive Media, 2,* 314–334.

Martin, C. L., Eisenbud, L., & Rose, H. (1995). Children's gender-based reasoning about toys. *Child Development, 66,* 1453–1471.

Martinie, M., Olive, T., & Milland, L. (2010). Cognitive dissonance induced by writing a counterattitudinal essay facilitates performance on simple tasks but not on complex tasks that involve working memory. *Journal of Experimental Social Psychology, 46,* 587–594.

Marx, B. P., Gross, A. M., & Adams, H. E. (1999). The effect of alcohol on the responses of sexually coercive and noncoercive men to an experimental rape analogue. *Sexual Abuse: Journal of Research and Treatment, 11,* 131–145.

Maslach, C. (1979). Negative emotional biasing of unexplained arousal. *Journal of Personality and Social Psychology, 37,* 953–969.

Mason, M. F., Tatkow, E. P., & Macrae, C. N. (2005). The look of love: Gaze shifts and person perception. *Psychological Science, 16,* 236–239.

Massey, C., Simmons, J. P., & Armor, D. A. (2011). Hope over experience: Desirability and the persistence of optimism. *Psychological Science, 22,* 274–281.

Masten, A. S. (2001). Ordinary magic: Resilience processes in development. *American Psychologist, 56,* 227–238.

Masten, C. L., Morelli, S. A., & Eisenberger, N. I. (2011). An fMRI investigation of empathy for social pain and subsequent prosocial behavior. *NeuroImage, 55,* 381–388.

Masuda, T., & Kitayama, S. (2004). Perceiver-induced constraint and attitude attribution in Japan and the US: A case for the cultural dependence of the correspondence bias. *Journal of Experimental Social Psychology, 40,* 409–416.

Masuda, T., & Nisbett, R. E. (2001). Attending holistically vs. analytically: Comparing the context sensitivity of Japanese and Americans. *Journal of Personality and Social Psychology, 81,* 922–934.

Mathieu, J., Maynard, M. T., Rapp, T., & Gilson, L. (2008). Team effectiveness 1997–2007: A review of recent advancements and a glimpse into the future. *Journal of Management, 34,* 410–476.

Mathur, M., & Chattopadhyay, A. (1991). The impact of moods generated by TV programs on responses to advertising. *Psychology and Marketing, 8,* 59–77.

Matthews, K. A. (1988). Coronary heart disease and Type A behaviors: Update on and alternative to the Booth-Kewley and Friedman (1987) quantitative review. *Psychological Bulletin, 104,* 373–380.

Matthews, K. A. (2005). Psychological perspectives on the development of coronary heart disease. *American Psychologist, 60,* 783–796.

Matz, D. C., & Wood, W. (2005). Cognitive dissonance in groups: The consequences of disagreement. *Journal of Personality and Social Psychology, 88,* 22–37

Maznevski, M. L. (1994). Understanding our differences: Performance in decision-making groups with diverse members. *Human Relations, 47,* 531–552.

Mazur, A., Booth, A., & Dabbs, J. M. (1992). Testosterone and chess competition. *Social Psychology Quarterly, 55,* 70–77.

McAdams, D. P. (1989). *Intimacy: The need to be close.* New York: Doubleday.

McArthur, L. A. (1972). The how and what of why: Some determinants and consequences of causal attribution. *Journal of Personality and Social Psychology, 22,* 171–193.

McAuliffe, B. J., Jetten, J., Hornsey, M. J., & Hogg, M. A. (2003). Individualist and collectivist norms: When it's ok to go your own way. *European Journal of Social Psychology, 33,* 57–70.

McCabe, D. P., Castel, A. D., & Rhodes, M. G. (2011). The influence of fMRI lie detection evidence on juror decision-making. *Behavioral Sciences & the Law, 29,* 566–577.

McCall, C., Blascovich, J., Young, A., & Persky, S. (2009). Proxemic behaviors as predictors of aggression towards Black (but not White) males in an immersive virtual environment. *Social Influence, 4,* 1–17.

McConahay, J. B. (1986). Modern racism, ambivalence, and the modern racism scale. In J. F. Dovidio & S. L. Gaertner (Eds.), *Prejudice, discrimination, and racism: Theory and research* (pp. 91–125). Orlando, FL: Academic Press.

McCrae, R. R., & Costa, P. T., Jr. (2003). *Personality in adulthood: A five-factor theory perspective* (2nd ed.). New York: Guilford Press.

McDougall, W. (1908). *An introduction to social psychology.* London: Methuen.

McElwee, R. O., Dunning, D., Tan, P. L., & Hollmann, S. (2001). Evaluating others: The role of who we are versus what we think traits mean. *Basic and Applied Social Psychology, 23,* 123–136.

McGarty, C., Turner, J. C., Hogg, M. A., David, B., et al. (1992). Group polarization as conformity to the prototypical group member. *British Journal of Social Psychology, 31,* 1–19.

McGlynn, R. P., Harding, D. J., & Cottle, J. L. (2009). Individual-group discontinuity in group-individual interactions: Does size matter? *Group Processes & Intergroup Relations, 12,* 129–143.

McGuire, A. M. (1994). Helping behaviors in the natural environment: Dimensions and correlates of helping. *Personality and Social Psychology Bulletin, 20,* 45–56.

McGuire, W. J. (1964). Inducing resistance to persuasion. In L. Berkowitz (Ed.), *Advances in experimental social psychology* (Vol. 1, pp. 192–229). New York: Academic Press.

McGuire, W. J. (1967). Some impending reorientations in social psychology: Some thoughts provoked by Kenneth Ring. *Journal of Experimental Social Psychology, 3,* 124–139.

McGuire, W. J. (1968). Personality and susceptibility to social influence. In E. F. Borgatta & W.W. Lambert (Eds.), *Handbook of personality theory and research* (pp. 1130–1187). Chicago: Rand McNally.

McGuire, W. J. (1969). The nature of attitudes and attitude change. In G. Lindzey & E. Aronson (Eds.), *Handbook of social psychology* (2nd ed., Vol. 3, pp. 136–314). Reading, MA: Addison-Wesley.

McGuire, W. J., & McGuire, C. V. (1988). Content and process in the experience of self. In L. Berkowitz (Ed.), *Advances in experimental social psychology* (Vol. 20, pp. 97–144). New York: Academic Press.

McIntyre, R. B., Paulson, R. M., & Lord, C. G. (2003). Alleviating women's mathematics stereotype threat through salience of group achievements. *Journal of Experimental Social Psychology, 39,* 83–90.

McKenna, K. Y. A., & Bargh, J. A. (1998). Coming out in the age of the Internet: "Demarginalization" through virtual group participation. *Journal of Personality and Social Psychology, 75,* 681–694.

McKibbin, W. F., Starratt, V. G., Shackelford, T. K., & Goetz, A. T. (2011). Perceived risk of female infidelity moderates the relationship between objective risk of female infidelity and sexual coercion in humans (homo sapiens). *Journal of Comparative Psychology, 125,* 370–373.

McKimmie, B. M., Terry, D. J., Hogg, M. A., Manstead, A. S. R., Spears, R., & Doosje, B. (2003). I'm a hypocrite, but so is everyone else: Group support and the reduction of cognitive dissonance. *Group Dynamics: Theory, Research, and Practice, 7,* 214–224.

McNatt, D. B. (2000). Ancient Pygmalion joins contemporary management: A meta-analysis of the result. *Journal of Applied Psychology, 85,* 314–322.

McPherson, M., Smith-Lovin, L., & Cook, J. M. (2001). Birds of a feather: Homophily in social networks. *Annual Review of Sociology, 27,* 415–444.

Mead, G. H. (1934). *Mind, self, and society.* Chicago: University of Chicago Press.

Mealey, L., Bridgstock, R., & Townsend, G. C. (1999). Symmetry and perceived facial attractiveness: A monozygotic co-twin comparison. *Journal of Personality and Social Psychology, 76,* 151–158.

Medvec, V. H., Madey, S. F., & Gilovich, T. (1995). When less is more: Counterfactual thinking and satisfaction among olympic medalists. *Journal of Personality and Social Psychology, 69,* 603–610.

Medvec, V. H., & Savitsky, K. (1997). When doing better means feeling worse: The effects of categorical cutoff points on counterfactual thinking and satisfaction. *Journal of Personality and Social Psychology, 72,* 1284–1296.

Meeus, W. H. J., & Raaijmakers, Q. A. W. (1995). Obedience in modern society: The Utrecht studies. *Journal of Social Issues, 51,* 155–175.

Meijer, E. H., & Verschuere, B. (2010). The polygraph and the detection of deception. *Journal of Forensic Psychology Practice, 10,* 325–338.

Meiser, T., & Hewstone, M. (2006). Illusory and spurious correlations: Distinct phenomena or joint outcomes of exemplar-based category learning? *European Journal of Social Psychology, 36,* 315–336.

Meissner, C. A., & Brigham, J. C. (2001). 30 years of investigating the own-race bias in memory for faces: A meta-analytic review. *Psychology, Public Policy, and Law, 7,* 3–35.

Meissner, C. A., & Kassin, S. M. (2002). "He's guilty!" Investigator bias in judgments of truth and deception. *Law and Human Behavior, 26,* 469–480.

Meltzer, H., Vostanis, P., Ford, T., Bebbington, P., & Dennis, M. S. (2011). Victims of bullying in childhood and suicide attempts in adulthood. *European Psychiatry, 26,* 498–503.

Mendes, W. B., Blascovich, J., Lickel, B., & Hunter, S. (2002). Challenge and threat during social interaction with white and black men. *Personality and Social Psychology Bulletin, 28,* 939–952.

Mendonca, P. J., & Brehm, S. S. (1983). Effects of choice on behavioral treatment of overweight children. *Journal of Social and Clinical Psychology, 1,* 343–358.

Merikle, P., & Skanes, H. E. (1992). Subliminal self-help audiotapes: A search for placebo effects. *Journal of Applied Psychology, 77,* 772–776.

Merton, R. (1948). The self-fulfilling prophecy. *Antioch Review, 8,* 193–210.

Mesmer-Magnus, J., & DeChurch, L. (2009). Information sharing and team performance: A meta-analysis. *Journal of Applied Psychology, 94,* 535–546.

Messick, D. M., & Cook, K. S. (Eds.) (1983). *Equity theory: Psychological and sociological perspectives.* New York: Praeger.

Messineo, M. J. (2008). Does advertising on Black Entertainment Television portray more positive gender representations compared to broadcast networks? *Sex Roles, 59,* 752–764.

Messner, M., Reinhard, M., & Sporer, S. L. (2008). Compliance through direct persuasive appeals: The moderating role of communicators attractiveness in interpersonal persuasion. *Social Influence, 3,* 67–83.

Meston, C. M., & Frohlich, P. F. (2003). Love at first sight: Partner salience moderates roller-coaster-induced excitation transfer. *Archives of Sexual Behavior, 32,* 537–544.

Mezulis, A. H., Abramson, L. Y., Hyde, J. S., & Hankin, B. L. (2004). Is there a universal positivity bias in attributions? A meta-analytic review of individual, developmental, and cultural differences in the self-serving attributional bias. *Psychological Bulletin, 130,* 711–747.

Mickelson, K. D., Kessler, R. C., & Shaver, P. R. (1997). Adult attachment in a nationally representative sample. *Journal of Personality and Social Psychology, 73,* 1092–1106.

Midha, V., & Nandedkar, A. (2012). Impact of similarity between avatar and their users on their perceived identifiability: Evidence from virtual teams in second life platform. *Computers in Human Behavior, 28,* 929–932.

Midlarsky, E., Fagan Jones, S., & Corley, R. P. (2005). Personality correlates of heroic rescue during the Holocaust. *Journal of Personality, 73,* 907–934.

Midlarsky, E., Kahana, E., Corley, R., Nemeroff, R., & Schonbar, R. A. (1999). Altruistic moral judgment among older adults. *International Journal of Aging and Human Development, 49,* 27–41.

Mikulincer, M., Shaver, P. R., & Avihou-Kanza, N. (2011). Individual differences in adult attachment are systematically related to dream narratives. *Attachment & Human Development, 13,* 105–123.

Miles, D. R., & Carey, G. (1997). Genetic and environmental architecture on human aggression. *Journal of Personality and Social Psychology, 72,* 207–217.

Miles, J. A., & Greenberg, J. (1993). Using punishment threats to attenuate social loafing effects among swimmers. *Organizational Behavior and Human Decision Processes, 56,* 246–265.

Milgram, S. (1963). Behavioral study of obedience. *Journal of Abnormal and Social Psychology, 67,* 371–378.

Milgram, S. (1970). The experience of living in cities. *Science, 167,* 1461–1468.

Milgram, S. (1974). Obedience to authority: An experimental view. New York: Harper & Row.

Milgram, S., Bickman, L., & Berkowitz, L. (1969). Note on the drawing power of crowds of different size. *Journal of Personality and Social Psychology, 13,* 79–82.

Milgram, S., & Sabini, J. (1978). On maintaining urban norms: A field experiment in the subway. In A. Baum, J. E. Singer, & S. Valins (Eds.), *Advances in environmental psychology* (Vol. 1). Hillsdale, NJ: Erlbaum.

Milgram, S., & Toch, H. (1969). Collective behavior: Crowds and social movements. In G. Lindzey & E. Aronson (Eds.), *The handbook of social psychology* (2nd ed., Vol. 4, pp. 507–610). Reading, MA: Addison-Wesley.

Millar, M. (2002). Effects of guilt induction and guilt reduction on door in the face. *Communication Research, 29,* 666–680.

Millar, M. G., & Millar, K. U. (1990). Attitude change as a function of attitude type and argument type. *Journal of Personality and Social Psychology, 59,* 217–228.

Miller, A. G. (1986). *The obedience experiments: A case study of controversy in social science.* New York: Praeger.

Miller, A. G. (2009). Reflections on "Replicating Milgram" (Burger, 2009). *American Psychologist, 64,* 20–27.

Miller, A. G., Gordon, A. K., & Buddie, A. M. (1999). Accounting for evil and cruelty: Is to explain to condone? *Personality and Social Psychology Review, 3,* 254–268.

Miller, A. G., Jones, E. E., & Hinkle, S. (1981). A robust attribution error in the personality domain. *Journal of Experimental Social Psychology, 17,* 587–600.

Miller, C. T. (1984). Self-schemas, gender, and social comparison: A clarification of the related attributes hypothesis. *Journal of Personality and Social Psychology, 46,* 1222–1229.

Miller, G., Chen, E., & Cole, S. W. (2009). Health psychology: Developing biologically plausible models linking the social world and physical health. *Annual Review of Psychology, 60,* 501–524.

Miller, J. G. (1984). Culture and the development of everyday social explanation. *Journal of Personality and Social Psychology, 46,* 961–978.

Miller, N., & Campbell, D. T. (1959). Recency and primacy in persuasion as a function of the timing of speeches and measurements. *Journal of Abnormal and Social Psychology, 59,* 1–9.

Miller, N. E. (1941). The frustration-aggression hypothesis. *Psychological Review, 48,* 337–342.

Miller, P. A., Eisenberg, N., Fabes, R. A., & Shell, R. (1996). Relations of moral reasoning and vicarious emotion to young children's prosocial behavior toward peers and adults. *Developmental Psychology, 32,* 210–219.

Miller, R., & Perlman, D. (2009). *Intimate relationships* (5th ed.). New York: McGraw-Hill.

Miller, T. Q., Smith, T. W., Turner, C. W., Guijarro, M. L., & Hallet, A. J. (1996). A meta-analytic review of research on hostility and physical health. *Psychological Bulletin, 119,* 322–348.

Miller, T. Q., Turner, C. W., Tindale, R. S., Posavac, E. J., & Dugon, B. L. (1991). Reasons for the trend toward null findings in research on Type A behavior. *Psychological Bulletin, 110,* 469–485.

Miller, W. R. (1985). Motivation for treatment: A review with special emphasis on alcoholism. *Psychological Bulletin, 98,* 84–107.

Miranda, S. M. (1994). Avoidance of groupthink: Meeting management using group support systems. *Small Group Research, 25,* 105–136.

Mita, T. H., Dermer, M., & Knight, J. (1977). Reversed facial images and the mere exposure hypothesis. *Journal of Personality and Social Psychology, 35,* 597–601.

Mitchell, J. P., Ames, D. L., Jenkins, A. C., Banaji, M. R. (2009). Neural correlates of stereotype application. *Journal of Cognitive Neuroscience, 21,* 594–604.

Miura, H. (2009). Differences in frontal lobe function between violent and nonviolent conduct disorder in male adolescents. *Psychiatry and Clinical Neurosciences, 63,* 161–166.

Miyamoto, Y., & Kitayama, S. (2002). Cultural variation in correspondence bias: The critical role of attitude diagnosticity of socially constrained behavior. *Journal of Personality and Social Psychology, 83,* 1239–1248.

Moghaddam, F. M., Taylor, D. M., & Wright, S. C. (1993). *Social psychology in cross-cultural perspective.* New York: W. H. Freeman.

Mondschein, E. R., Adolph, K. E., & Tamis-LeMonda, C. S. (2000). Gender bias in mothers' expectations about infant crawling. *Journal of Experimental Child Psychology, 77,* 304–316.

Monin, B., Sawyer, P. J., & Marquez, M. J. (2008). The rejection of moral rebels: Resenting those who do the right thing. *Journal of Personality and Social Psychology, 95,* 76–93.

Monteith, M. J., Ashburn-Nardo, L., Voils, C. I., & Czopp, A. M. (2002). Putting the brakes on prejudice: On the development and operation of cues for control. *Journal of Personality and Social Psychology, 83,* 1029–1050.

Monteith, M. J., & Mark, A.Y. (2005). Changing one's prejudice ways: Awareness, affect, and self-regulation. *European Review of Social Psychology, 16,* 113–154.

Monteith, M. J., & Mark, A. Y. (2009). The self-regulation of prejudice. In T. D. Nelson (Ed.), *Handbook of prejudice, stereotyping, and discrimination* (pp. 507–523). New York: Psychology Press.

Monteith. M. J., Sherman, J. W., & Devine, P. G. (1998). Suppression as a stereotype control strategy. *Personality and Social Psychology Review, 2,* 63–82.

Montepare, J. M., & McArthur, L. Z. (1988). Impressions of people created by age-related qualities of their gaits. *Journal of Personality and Social Psychology, 55,* 547–556.

Montoya, E. R., Terburg, D., Bos, P. A., & van Honk, J. (2012). Testosterone, cortisol, and serotonin as key regulators of social aggression: A review and theoretical perspective. *Motivation and Emotion, 36,* 65–73.

Montoya, R. M., Horton, R. S., & Kirchner, J. (2008). Is actual similarity necessary for attraction? A meta-analysis of actual and perceived similarity. *Journal of Social and Personal Relationships, 25,* 889–922.

Montoya, R. M., & Insko, C. A. (2008). Toward a more complete understanding of the reciprocity of liking effect. *European Journal of Social Psychology, 38,* 477–498.

Moons, W. G., Mackie, D. M., Garcia-Marques, T. (2009). The impact of repetition-induced familiarity on agreement with weak and strong arguments. *Journal of Personality and Social Psychology, 96,* 32–44.

Moore, B. S., Underwood, B., & Rosenhan, D. L. (1973). Affect and altruism. *Developmental Psychology, 8,* 99–104.

Moore, M. J., Nakano, T., Enomoto, A., & Suda, T. (2012). Anonymity and roles associated with aggressive posts in an online forum. *Computers in Human Behavior, 28,* 861–867.

Moore, T. E. (1982). Subliminal advertising: What you see is what you get. *Journal of Marketing, 46,* 38–47.

Mor, N., & Winquist, J. (2002). Self-focused attention and negative affect: A meta-analysis. *Psychological Bulletin, 128,* 638–662.

Moradi, B., Dirks, D., & Matteson, A. V. (2005). Roles of sexual objectification experiences and internalization of standards of beauty in eating disorder symptomatology: A test and extension of objectification theory. *Journal of Counseling Psychology, 52,* 420–428.

Morales, J. R., Cullerton-Sen, C., & Crick, N. R. (2005). Relational aggression and victimization in dyadic peer relationships: Once I ran to you, now I run from you. In S. Fein, G. R. Goethals, & M. J. Sandstrom (Eds.), *Gender and aggression: Interdisciplinary perspectives.* Mahwah, NJ: Erlbaum.

Moran, G., & Comfort, C. (1986). Neither "tentative" nor "fragmentary": Verdict preference of impaneled felony jurors as a function of attitude toward capital punishment. *Journal of Applied Psychology, 71,* 146–155.

Moran, G., & Cutler, B. L. (1991). The prejudicial impact of pretrial publicity. *Journal of Applied Social Psychology, 21,* 345–367.

Moray, N. (1959). Attention in dichotic listening: Affective cues and the influence of instructions. *Quarterly Journal of Experimental Psychology, 11,* 56–60.

Moreland, R. L., & Beach, S. R. (1992). Exposure effects in the classroom: The development of affinity among students. *Journal of Experimental Social Psychology, 28,* 255–276.

Moreland, R. L., & Levine, J. M. (2002). Socialization and trust in work groups. *Group Processes and Intergroup Relations, 5,* 185–201.

Morewedge, C. K., Preston, J., & Wegner, D. M. (2007). Timescale bias in the attribution of mind. *Journal of Personality and Social Psychology, 93,* 1–11.

Moriarty, D., & McCabe, A. E. (1977). Studies of television and youth sport. In *Ontario Royal Commission on Violence in the Communications Industry report* (Vol. 5). Toronto: Queen's Printer for Ontario.

Moriarty, T. (1975). Crime, commitment, and the responsive bystander: Two field experiments. *Journal of Personality and Social Psychology, 31,* 370–376.

Morrongiello, B. A., & Dawber, T. (2000). Mothers' responses to sons and daughters engaging in injury-risk behaviors on a playground: Implications for sex differences in injury rates. *Journal of Experimental Child Psychology, 76,* 89–103.

Morrongiello, B. A., Midgett, C., & Stanton, K. L. (2000). Gender biases in children's appraisals of injury risk and other children's risk-taking behaviors. *Journal of Experimental Child Psychology, 77,* 317–336.

Morr Serewicz, M. C., & Gale, E. (2008). First-date scripts: Gender roles, context, and relationship. *Sex Roles, 58*(3–4), 149–164.

Morse, B. J. (1995). Beyond the Conflict Tactics Scale: Assessing gender differences in partner violence. *Violence and Victims, 10,* 251–272.

Moscovici, S. (1980). Toward a theory of conversion behavior. In L. Berkowitz (Ed.), *Advances in Experimental Social Psychology, 6,* 149–202.

Moscovici, S., Lage, E., & Naffrechoux, M. (1969). Influence of a consistent minority on the responses of a majority in a color perception task. *Sociometry, 32,* 365–380.

Moscovici, S., Mugny, G., & Van Avermaet, E. (Eds.) (1985). *Perspectives on minority influence.* New York: Cambridge University Press.

Moscovici, S., & Personnaz, B. (1991). Studies in social influence VI: Is Lenin orange or red? Imagery and social influence. *European Journal of Social Psychology, 21,* 101–118.

Moscovici, S., & Zavalloni, M. (1969). The group as a polarizer of attitudes. *Journal of Personality and Social Psychology, 12,* 125–135.

Moskalenko, S., & Heine, S. J. (2003). Watching your troubles away: Television viewing as a stimulus for subjective self-awareness. *Personality and Social Psychology Bulletin, 29,* 76–85.

Moskowitz, G. B. (1996). The mediational effects of attributions and information processing in minority social influence. *British Journal of Social Psychology, 35,* 47–66.

Moskowitz, G. B., & Grant, H. (Eds.). (2009). *The psychology of goals.* New York: Guilford Press.

Moskowitz, G. B., Li, P., & Kirk, E. R. (2004). The implicit volition model: On the preconscious regulation of temporarily adopted goals. In M. P. Zanna (Ed.), *Advances in experimental social psychology.* San Diego, CA: Academic Press.

Mouilso, E. R., Fischer, S., & Calhoun, K. S. (2012). A prospective study of sexual assault and alcohol use among first-year college women. *Violence and Victims, 27,* 78–94.

Mouton, J., Blake, R., & Olmstead, J. (1956). The relationship between frequency of yielding and the disclosure of personal identity. *Journal of Personality, 24,* 339–347.

Moya, M., Glick, P., Expósito, F., de Lemus, S., & Hart, J. (2007). It's for your own good: Benevolent sexism and womens reactions to protectively justified restrictions. *Personality and Social Psychology Bulletin, 33,* 1421–1434.

Mueller, J. H. (1982). Self-awareness and access to material rated as self-descriptive and nondescriptive. *Bulletin of the Psychonomic Society, 19,* 323–326.

Mueller, J. S. (2012). Why individuals in larger teams perform worse. *Organizational Behavior and Human Decision Processes, 117,* 111–124.

Mugny, G., & Perez, J. A. (1991). *Social psychology of minority influence.* Cambridge: Cambridge University Press.

Mulder, L. B. (2008). Undermining trust and cooperation: The paradox of sanctioning systems in social dilemmas. *Journal of Experimental Social Psychology, 42,* 147–162.

Mullen, B. (1983). Operationalizing the effect of the group on the individual: A self-attention perspective. *Journal of Experimental Social Psychology, 19,* 295–322.

Mullen, B. (1985). Strength and immediacy of sources: A meta-analytic evaluation of the forgotten elements of social impact theory. *Journal of Personality and Social Psychology, 48,* 1458–1466.

Mullen, B. (1986). Atrocity as a function of lynch mob composition: A self-attention perspective. *Personality and Social Psychology Bulletin, 12,* 187–197.

Mullen, B., Anthony, T., Salas, E., & Driskell, J. E. (1994). Group cohesiveness and quality of decision making: An integration of tests of the groupthink hypothesis. *Small Group Research, 25,* 189–204.

Mullen, B., & Copper, C. (1994). The relation between group cohesiveness and performance: An integration. *Psychological Bulletin, 115,* 210–227.

Mullen, B., Dovidio, J. F., Johnson, C., & Copper, C. (1992). In-group and out-group differences in social projection. *Journal of Experimental Social Psychology, 28,* 422–440.

Mullen, B., Johnson, C., & Salas, E. (1991). Productivity loss in brainstorming groups: A meta-analytic integration. *Basic and Applied Social Psychology, 12,* 3–23.

Mullen, E., & Skitka, L. J. (2009). Comparing Americans' and Ukrainians' allocations of public assistance: The role of affective reactions in helping behavior. *Journal of Cross-Cultural Psychology, 40,* 301–318.

Muraven, M., & Baumeister, R. F. (1998). Self-control as a limited resource: Regulatory depletion patterns. *Journal of Personality and Social Psychology, 74,* 774–789.

Muraven, M., & Baumeister, R. F. (2000). Self-regulation and depletion of limited resources: Does self-control resemble a muscle? *Psychological Bulletin, 126,* 247–259.

Murray, G., Judd, F., Jackson, H., Komiti, A., Wearing, A., Robins, G., et al. (2008). Big boys don't cry: An investigation of stoicism and its mental health outcomes. *Personality and Individual Differences, 44,* 1369–1381.

Murray, K. B., & Häubl, G. (2012). Why dominant companies are vulnerable. *MIT Sloan Management Review, 53*(2), 12–14.

Murray, S. L., Aloni, M., Holmes, J. G., Derrick, J. L., Stinson, D. A., & Leder, S. (2009). Fostering partner dependence as trust insurance: The implicit contingencies of the exchange script in close relationships. *Journal of Personality and Social Psychology, 96,* 324–348.

Murray, S. L., & Holmes, J. G. (1999). The (mental) ties that bind: Cognitive structures that predict relationship resilience. *Journal of Personality and Social Psychology, 77,* 1228–1244.

Murray, S. L., & Holmes, J. G. (2008). The commitment insurance system: Self-esteem and the regulation of connection in close relationships. *Advances in Experimental Social Psychology, 40,* 1–60.

Murray, S. L., Holmes, J. G., & Collins, N. L. (2006). Optimizing assurance: The risk regulation system in relationships. *Psychological Bulletin, 132,* 641–666.

Murray, S. L., Holmes, J. G., & Griffin, D. W. (1996). The benefits of positive illusions: Idealization and the construction of satisfaction in close relationships. *Journal of Personality and Social Psychology, 70,* 79–98.

Murstein, B. I. (1986). *Paths to marriage.* Beverly Hills, CA: Sage.

Mussweiler, T., & Rüter, K. (2003). What friends are for! The use of routine standards in social comparison. *Journal of Personality and Social Psychology, 85,* 467–481.

Mussweiler, T., & Strack, F. (2000). The "relative self": Informational and judgmental consequences of comparative self-evaluation. *Journal of Personality and Social Psychology, 79,* 23–38.

Myers, D. G., & Bishop, G. D. (1970). Discussion effects on racial attitudes. *Science, 169,* 778–779.

Myers, D. G., & Diener, E. (1995). Who is happy? *Psychological Science, 6,* 10–19.

Myers, D. G., & Lamm, H. (1976). The group polarization phenomenon. *Psychological Bulletin, 83,* 602–627.

Myrtek, M. (2007). In Jordan J., Bardé B. and Zeiher A. M. (Eds.), *Type A behavior and hostility as independent risk factors for coronary heart disease.* Washington, DC: American Psychological Association.

Nabi, R. L., & Sullivan, J. L. (2001). Does television viewing relate to engagement in protective action against crime? A cultivation analysis from a theory of reasoned action perspective. *Communication Research, 28,* 802–825.

Nadler, A., & Fisher, J. D. (1986). The role of threat to self-esteem and perceived control in recipient reactions to help: Theory development and empirical validation. In L. Berkowitz (Ed.), *Advances in experimental social psychology* (Vol. 19, pp. 81–122). New York: Academic Press.

Nadler, A., Halabi, S., & Harpaz-Gorodeisky, G. (2009). Intergroup helping as status-organizing processes: Implications for intergroup misunderstandings. In S. Demoulin, J. P. Leyens, & J. F. Dovidio (Eds.), *Intergroup misunderstandings: Impact of divergent social realities* (pp. 311–330). New York: Psychology Press.

Nakao, H., & Itakura, S. (2009). An integrated view of empathy: Psychology, philosophy, and neuroscience. *Integrative Psychological & Behavioral Science, 43,* 42–52.

Nakashima, K., Isobe, C., & Ura, M. (2008). Effect of self-construal and threat to self-esteem on ingroup favouritism: Moderating effect of independent/interdependent self-construal on use of ingroup favouritism for maintaining and enhancing self-evaluation. *Asian Journal of Social Psychology, 11,* 286–292.

Naquin, C. E., & Kurtzberg, T. R. (2009). Team negotiation and perceptions of trustworthiness: The whole versus the sum of the parts. *Group Dynamics: Theory, Research, and Practice, 13,* 133–150.

Nassif, A., & Gunter, B. (2008). Gender representation in television advertisements in Britain and Saudi Arabia. *Sex Roles, 58,* 752–760.

National Forum on Health. (2000). *What makes a woman healthy or unhealthy?*

National Law Journal (1990). Rock group not liable for deaths (September 10), p. 33.

National Parole Board of Canada (2010/2011). *Performance Monitoring Report for 2010/2011.*

National Research Council, Committee to Review the Scientific Evidence on the Polygraph, Division of Behavioral and Social Sciences and Education. (2003). *The polygraph and lie detection.* Washington, DC: National Academies Press.

National Television Violence Study, Vol. 2 (1998). Thousand Oaks, CA: Sage.

Nattinger, A. B., et al. (1998). Celebrity medical care decisions can influence others. *Journal of the American Medical Association, 279,* 788–789.

Nedelec, J. L., & Beaver, K. M. (2011). Beauty is in the sex of the beholder: An examination of the effects of interviewer characteristics on assessments of respondent attractiveness. *Personality and Individual Differences, 51,* 930–934.

Neighbors, C., Dillard, A. J., Lewis, M. A., Bergstrom, R. L., & Neil, T. A. (2006). Normative misperceptions and temporal precedence of perceived norms and drinking. *Journal of Studies on Alcohol, 67,* 290–299.

Nelissen, R. M. A. (2008). The price you pay: Cost-dependent reputation effects of altruistic punishment. *Evolution and Human Behavior, 29,* 242–248.

Nemeth, C. (1986). Differential contributions of majority and minority influence. *Psychological Review, 93,* 23–32.

Nemeth, C., & Kwan, J. (1987). Minority influence, divergent thinking, and detection of correct solutions. *Journal of Applied Social Psychology, 17,* 788–799.

Nemeth, C., Mayseless, O., Sherman, J., & Brown, Y. (1990). Exposure to dissent and recall of information. *Journal of Personality and Social Psychology, 58,* 429–437.

Nes, L. S., & Segerstrom, S. C. (2006). Dispositional optimism and coping: A meta-analytic review. *Personality and Social Psychology Review, 10,* 235–251.

Nesdale, D., & Naito, M. (2005). Individualism-collectivism and the attitudes to school bullying of Japanese and Australian students. *Journal of Cross-Cultural Psychology, 36,* 537–556.

Neuberg, S. L. (1989). The goal of forming accurate impressions during social interactions: Attenuating the impact of negative expectancies. *Journal of Personality and Social Psychology, 56,* 374–386.

Neuberg, S. L., Kenrick, D. T., & Schaller, M. (2010). Evolutionary social psychology. In S. T. Fiske, D. T. Gilbert, & G. Lindzey (Eds.), *The handbook of social psychology* (5th ed.). New York: McGraw-Hill.

Neuman, W. R., Marcus, G. E., Crigler, A. N., & MacKuen, M. (Eds.). (2007). *The affect effect: Dynamics of emotion in political thinking and behavior.* Chicago: University of Chicago Press.

Newby-Clark, I. R., & Ross, M. (2003). Conceiving the past and future. *Personality and Social Psychology Bulletin, 29,* 807–818.

Newcomb, T. M. (1943). *Personality and social change: Attitude formation in a student community.* Ft. Worth, TX: Dryden Press.

Newcomb, T. M. (1961). *The acquaintance process.* New York: Holt, Rinehart and Winston.

Newheiser, A., & Olson, K. R. (2012). White and black american childrens implicit intergroup bias. *Journal of Experimental Social Psychology, 48,* 264–270.

Newman, C. (2000, January). The enigma of beauty. *National Geographic,* pp. 94–121.

Newman, L. S., & Uleman, J. S. (1989). Spontaneous trait inference. In J. S. Uleman & J. A. Bargh (Eds.), *Unintended thought* (pp. 155–188). New York: Guilford.

Newtson, D. (1974). Dispositional inference from effects of actions: Effects chosen and effects foregone. *Journal of Experimental Social Psychology, 10,* 487–496.

Newtson, D., Hairfield, J., Bloomingdale, J., & Cutino, S. (1987). The structure of action and interaction. *Social Cognition, 5,* 191–237.

Nezlek, John B., Schütz, A., Schröder-Abé, M., & Smith, C. V. (2011). A cross-cultural study of relationships between daily social interaction and the Five-Factor model of personality. *Journal of Personality, 79*(4), 811–840.

Nguyen, H. H. D., & Ryan, A. M. (2008). Does stereotype threat affect test performance of minorities and women? A meta-analysis of experimental evidence. *Journal of Applied Psychology, 93,* 1314–1334.

Nibler, R., & Harris, K. L. (2003). The effects of culture and cohesiveness on intragroup conflict and effectiveness. *The Journal of Social Psychology, 143,* 613–631.

Niedermeier, K. E., Horowitz, I. A., & Kerr, N. L. (1999). Informing jurors of their nullification power: A route to a just verdict or judicial chaos? *Law and Human Behavior, 23,* 331–351.

Nieva, V. F., & Gutek, B. A. (1981). *Women and work: A psychological perspective.* New York: Praeger.

Nijstad, B. A., & Stroebe, W. (2006). How the group affects the mind: A cognitive model of idea generation in groups. *Personality and Social Psychology Review, 10,* 186–213.

Nisbett, R. E. (2003). *The geography of thought: How Asians and Westerners think differently . . . and why.* New York: Free Press.

Nisbett, R. E., & Cohen, D. (1996). *Culture of honor: The psychology of violence in the South.* Boulder, CO: Westview.

Nisbett, R. E., Fong, G. T., Lehman, D. R., & Cheng, P.W. (1987). Teaching reasoning. *Science, 238,* 625–631.

Nisbett, R. E., & Ross, L. (1980). *Human inference: Strategies and shortcomings of social judgment.* Englewood Cliffs, NJ: Prentice-Hall.

Nisbett, R. E., & Wilson, T. D. (1977). Telling more than we can know: Verbal reports on mental processes. *Psychological Review, 84,* 231–259.

Nolan, J. M., Schultz, P. W., Cialdini, R. B., Goldstein, N. J., & Griskevicius, V. (2008). Normative social influence is underdetected. *Personality and Social Psychology Bulletin, 34,* 913–923.

Norenzayan, A., & Nisbett, R.E. (2000). Culture and causal cognition. *Current Directions in Psychological Science, 9,* 132–135.

Norman, R. M. G., Sorrentino, R. M., Gawronski, B., Szeto, A. C. H., Ye, Y., & Windell, D. (2010). Attitudes and physical distance to an individual with schizophrenia: The moderating effect of self-transcendent values. *Social Psychiatry and Psychiatric Epidemiology, 45,* 751–758.

North, A. C., Hargreaves, D. J., & McKendrick, J. (1999). The influence of in-store music on wine selections. *Journal of Applied Psychology, 84,* 271–276.

North, A. C., Tarrant, M., & Hargreaves, D. J. (2004). The effects of music on helping behavior: A field study. *Environment and Behavior, 36,* 266–275.

Northoff, G., Qin, P., & Feinberg, T. E. (2011). Brain imaging of the self—Conceptual, anatomical and methodological issues. *Consciousness and Cognition: An International Journal, 20,* 52–63.

Norton, K. I., Olds, T. S., Olive, S., & Dank, S. (1996). Ken and Barbie at life size. *Sex Roles, 34,* 287–294.

Norton, Michael I., Sommers, S. R., Vandello, J. A., & Darley, J. M. (2006). Mixed motives and racial bias: The impact of legitimate and illegitimate criteria on decision making. *Psychology, Public Policy, and Law, 12,* 36–55.

Nosek, B. A., Banaji, M. R., & Greenwald, A. G. (2002). Harvesting implicit attitudes and stereotype data from the Implicit Association Test website. *Group Dynamics, 6,* 101–115.

Nosek, B.,A., Greenwald, A. G., & Banaji, M. R. (2005). Understanding and using the implicit association test: II. method variables and construct validity. *Personality and Social Psychology Bulletin, 31,* 166–180.

O'Brien, L. T., & Crandall, C. S. (2003). Stereotype threat and arousal: Effects on women's math performance. *Personality and Social Psychology Bulletin, 29,* 782–789.

O'Connor, S. C., & Rosenblood, L. K. (1996). Affiliation motivation in everyday experience: A theoretical comparison. *Journal of Personality and Social Psychology, 70,* 513–522.

O'Gorman, R., Sheldon, K. M., & Wilson, D. S. (2008). For the good of the group? MaaExploring group-level evolutionary adaptations using multilevel selection theory. *Group Dynamics: Theory, Research, and Practice, 12,* 17–26.

O'Keefe, D. J., & Figge, M. (1997). A guilt-based explanation of the door-in-the-face influence strategy. *Human Communication Research, 42,* 64–81.

O'Leary, K. D., Acevedo, B. P., Aron, A., Huddy, L., & Mashek, D. (2012). Is long-term love more than a rare phenomenon? if so, what are its correlates? *Social Psychological and Personality Science, 3,* 241–249.

O'Leary, K. D., Barling, J., Arias, I., Rosenbaum, A., Malone, J., & Tyree, A. (1989). Prevalence and stability of physical aggression between spouses: A longitudinal analysis. *Journal of Consulting and Clinical Psychology, 57,* 263–268.

O'Leary, K. D., & Smith, D. A. (1991). Marital interaction. *Annual Review of Psychology, 42,* 191–212.

O'Neill, A. M., Green, M., & Cuadros, P. (1996, September 2). *People,* p. 72.

O'Neill, M. C., & Pozzulo, J. D. (2012). Jurors judgments across multiple identifications and descriptions and descriptor inconsistencies. *American Journal of Forensic Psychology, 30,* 39-66.

O'Sullivan, Maureen, Frank, M. G., Hurley, C. M., & Tiwana, J. (2009). Police lie detection accuracy: The effect of lie scenario. *Law and Human Behavior, 33,* 530–538.

Oddone-Paolucci, E., Genuis, M., & Violato, C. (2000). A meta-analysis of the published research on the effects of pornography. In C. Violato & E. Oddone-Paolucci (Eds.), *The changing family and child development* (pp. 48–59). Aldershot, England: Ashgate.

Ogilvy, D. (1985). *Ogilvy on advertising.* New York: Vintage Books.

Ogloff, J. R. P., & Vidmar, N. (1994). The impact of pretrial publicity on jurors: A study to compare the relative effects of television and print media in a child sex abuse case. *Law and Human Behavior, 18,* 507–525.

Olczak, P. V., Kaplan, M. F., & Penrod, S. (1991). Attorneys' lay psychology and its effectiveness in selecting jurors: Three empirical studies. *Journal of Social Behavior and Personality, 6,* 431–452.

Oliver, M. G., & Hyde, J. S. (1993). Gender differences in sexuality: A meta-analysis. *Psychological Bulletin, 114,* 29–51.

Olivola, C. Y., & Todorov, A. (2010). Fooled by first impressions? Reexamining the diagnostic value of appearance-based inferences. *Journal of Experimental Social Psychology, 46,* 315–324.

Olson, J. M., Vernon, P. A., Harris, J. A., & Jang, K. L. (2001). The heritability of attitudes: A study of twins. *Journal of Personality and Social Psychology, 80,* 845–860.

Olson, M. A., & Fazio, R. H. (2001). Implicit attitude formation through classical conditioning. *Psychological Science, 12,* 413–417.

Olson, M. A., & Fazio, R. H. (2004). Reducing the influence of extrapersonal associations on the Implicit Association Test: Personalizing the IAT. *Journal of Personality and Social Psychology, 86,* 653–667.

Olson, M. A., & Fazio, R. H. (2006). Reducing automatically activated racial prejudice through implicit evaluative conditioning. *Personality and Social Psychology Bulletin, 32,* 421–433.

Olson, M. A., & Kendrick, R. V. (2008). In Crano W. D., Prislin R. (Eds.), *Origins of attitudes.* New York: Psychology Press.

Olweus, D. (2004). The Olweus Bullying Prevention Programme: Design and implementation issues and a new national initiative in Norway. In P. K. Smith, D. Pepler, & K. Rigby (Eds.), *Bullying in schools: How successful can interventions be?* (pp. 13–36). New York: Cambridge University Press.

Omarzu, J. (2000). A disclosure decision model: Determining how and when individuals will self-disclose. *Personality and Social Psychology Review, 4,* 174–185.

Omoto, A. M., Malsch, A. M., & Barraza, J. A. (2009). Compassionate acts: Motivations for and correlates of volunteerism among older adults. In B. Fehr, S. Sprecher, & L. G. Underwood (Eds.), *The science of compassionate love: Theory, research, and applications.* Malden, MA: Wiley-Blackwell.

Omoto, A. M., & Snyder, M. (1995). Sustained helping without obligation: Motivation, longevity of service, and perceived attitude change among AIDS volunteers. *Journal of Personality and Social Psychology, 68,* 671–686.

Omoto, A. M., Snyder, M., & Hackett, J. D. (2010). Personality and motivational antecedents of activism and civic engagement. *Journal of Personality, 78,* 1703–1734.

Ore, T. E. (2000). *The social construction of difference and inequality: Race, gender, and sexuality.* Mountain View, CA: Mayfield.

Orenstein, P. (1994). *Schoolgirls: Young women, self-esteem, and the confidence gap.* New York: Anchor Books.

Orobio de Castro, B., Veerman, J. W., Koops, W., Bosch, J. D., & Monshouwer, H. J. (2002). Hostile attribution of intent and aggressive behavior: A meta-analysis. *Child Development, 73,* 916–934.

Orth, U., Robins, R. W., & Widaman, K. F. (2012). Life-span development of self-esteem and its effects on important life outcomes. *Journal of Personality and Social Psychology, 102,* 1271–1288.

Orwell, G. (1942). Looking back on the Spanish War. In S. Orwell & I. Angus (Eds.), *The collected essays, journalism and letters of George Orwell: Vol. 2. My country right or left, 1940–1943* (pp. 249–267). New York: Harcourt, Brace & World. (Reprinted in 1968)

Osborn, A. F. (1953). *Applied imagination.* New York: Scribner.

Osgood, C. E. (1962). *An alternative to war or surrender.* Urbana: University of Illinois Press.

Oshri, I., van Fenema, P., & Kotlarsky, J. (2008). Knowledge transfer in globally distributed teams: The role of transactive memory. *Information Systems Journal, 18,* 593–616.

Osterman, L. L., & Brown, R. P. (2011). Culture of honor and violence against the self. *Personality and Social Psychology Bulletin, 37,* 1611–1623.

Owens, L., Shute, R., & Slee, P. (2000). "Guess what I just heard!": Indirect aggression among teenage girls in Australia. *Aggressive Behavior, 26,* 67–83.

Oyserman, D., Coon, H. M., & Kemmelmeier, M. (2002). Rethinking individualism and collectivism: Evaluation of theoretical assumptions and meta-analyses. *Psychological Bulletin, 128,* 3–72.

Oyserman, D., & Lee, S. W. (2008). Does culture influence what and how we think? Effects of priming individualism and collectivism. *Psychological Bulletin, 134,* 311–342.

Packard, V. (1957). *The hidden persuaders.* New York: Pocket Books.

Packer, D. J. (2008). Identifying systematic disobedience in Milgram's obedience experiments. *Perspectives on Psychological Science, 3,* 301–304.

Pagani, L., Tremblay, R. E., Nagin, D., Zoccolillo, M., Vitaro, F., & McDuff, P. (2009). Risk factor models for adolescent verbal and physical aggression toward fathers. *Journal of Family Violence, 24,* 173–182.

Page-Gould, Elizabeth, Mendoza-Denton, R., & Tropp, L. R. (2008). With a little help from my cross-group friend: Reducing anxiety in intergroup contexts through cross-group friendship. *Journal of Personality and Social Psychology, 95,* 1080–1094.

Pager, D., & Shepherd, H. (2008). The sociology of discrimination: Racial discrimination in employment, housing, credit, and consumer markets. *Annual Review of Sociology, 34,* 181–209.

Paik, H., & Comstock, G. (1994). The effects of television violence on antisocial behavior: A meta-analysis. *Communication Research, 21,* 516–546.

Palazzolo, E. T., Serb, D. A., & She, Y. (2006). Coevolution of communication and knowledge networks in transactive memory systems: Using computational models for theoretical development. *Communication Theory, 16,* 223–250.

Paluck, E. L. (2009). Reducing intergroup prejudice and conflict using the media: A field experiment in Rwanda. *Journal of Personality and Social Psychology, 96,* 574–587.

Panee, C. D., & Ballard, M. E. (2002). High versus low aggressive priming during video-game training: Effects on violent action during game play, hostility, heart rate, and blood pressure. *Journal of Applied Social Psychology, 32,* 2458–2474.

Paquette, G. (2004). Violence on Canadian television networks. *Canadian Child and Adolescent Psychiatry Review, 13,* 13–15.

Parducci, A. (1995). *Happiness, pleasure, and judgment: The contextual theory and its applications.* Mahwah, NJ: Erlbaum.

Parent, M. C., & Moradi, B. (2011). His biceps become him: A test of objectification theorys application to drive for muscularity and propensity for steroid use in college men. *Journal of Counseling Psychology, 58,* 246–256.

Park, B. (1986). A method for studying the development of impressions of real people. *Journal of Personality and Social Psychology, 51,* 907–917.

Park, L. E., & Maner, J. K. (2009). Does self-threat promote social connection? The role of self-esteem and contingencies of self-worth. *Journal of Personality and Social Psychology, 96,* 203–217.

Park, S., & Catrambone, R. (2007). Social facilitation effects of virtual humans. *Human Factors, 49,* 1054–1060.

Parkinson, S. (1994). Scientific or ethical quality? *Psychological Science, 5,* 137–138.

Partridge, A., & Eldridge, W. B. (1974). *The second circuit sentencing study: A report to the judges of the second circuit.* Washington, DC: Federal Judicial Center.

Pascoe, E. A., & Smart Richman, L. (2009). Perceived discrimination and health: A meta-analytic review. *Psychological Bulletin, 135,* 531–554.

Patterson, M. L. (1983). *Nonverbal behavior: A functional perspective.* New York: Springer-Verlag.

Pauker, K., Weisbuch, M., Ambady, N., Sommers, S. R., Adams, R. B., Jr., & Ivcevic, Z. (2009). Not so black and white: Memory for ambiguous group members. *Journal of Personality and Social Psychology, 96,* 795–810.

Paulhus, D. L. (1998). Interpersonal and intrapsychic adaptiveness of trait self-enhancement: A mixed blessing? *Journal of Personality and Social Psychology, 74,* 1197–1208.

Paulhus, D., Graf, P., & Van Selst, M. (1989). Attentional load increases the positivity of self-presentation. *Social Cognition, 7,* 389–400.

Paulus, P. B. (1988). *Prison crowding: A psychological perspective.* New York: Springer-Verlag.

Paulus, P. B., & Brown, V. R. (2007). Toward more creative and innovative group idea generation: A cognitive-social-motivational perspective of brainstorming. *Social and Personality Psychology Compass, 1,* 248–265.

Paulus, P. B., Nakui, T., Putman, V. L., & Brown, V. (2006). Effects of task instructions and brief breaks on brainstorming. *Group Dynamics: Theory, Research, and Practice, 10,* 206–219.

Pavitt, C. (1994). Another view of group polarizing: The "reasons for" one-sided oral argumentation. *Communication Research, 21,* 625–642.

Pavot, W., & Diener, E. (1993). Review of the Satisfaction with Life Scale. *Psychological Assessment, 5,* 164–172.

Pawlowski, B., Dunbar, R. I. M., & Lipowicz, A. (2000). Evolutionary fitness: Tall men have more reproductive success. *Nature, 403,* 156.

Payne, B. K., Cheng, C. M., Govorun, O., & Stewart, B. D. (2005). An inkblot for attitudes: Affect misattribution as implicit measurement. *Journal of Personality and Social Psychology, 89,* 277–293.

Pedersen, W. C., Miller, L. C., Putch-Bhagavatula, A. D., & Yang, Y. (2002). Evolved sex differences in the number of partners desired? The long and the short of it. *Psychological Science, 13,* 157–161.

Pelham, B. W. (1995). Self-investment and self-esteem: Evidence for a Jamesian model of self-worth. *Journal of Personality and Social Psychology, 69,* 1141–1150.

Pelham, B.W., Mirenberg, M.C., & Jones, J.T. (2002). Why Susie sells seashells by the seashore: Implicit egotism and major life decisions. *Journal of Personality and Social Psychology, 82,* 469–487.

Pelham, B. W., & Swann, W. B., Jr. (1989). From self-conceptions to self-worth: The sources and structure of self-esteem. *Journal of Personality and Social Psychology, 57,* 672–680.

Peltokorpi, V. (2012). Organizational transactive memory systems: Review and extension. *European Psychologist, 17,* 11–20.

Peng, K., & Nisbett, R. E. (1999). Culture, dialectics, and reasoning about contradiction. *American Psychologist, 54,* 741–754.

Pennebaker, J. W. (1997). Writing about emotional experiences as a therapeutic process. *Psychological Science, 8,* 162–166.

Pennebaker, J. W., Dyer, M. A., Caulkins, R. J., Litowitz, D. L., Ackreman, P. L., Anderson, D. B., & McGraw, K. M. (1979). Don't the girls get prettier at closing time: A country and western application to psychology. *Personality and Social Psychology Bulletin, 5,* 122–125.

Penner, L. A. (2004). Volunteerism and social problems: Making things better or worse? *Journal of Social Issues, 60,* 645–666.

Penner, L. A., Dovidio, J. F., Piliavin, J. A., & Schroeder, D. A. (2005). Prosocial behavior: Multiple perspectives. *Annual Review of Psychology, 56,* 365–392.

Pennington, N., & Hastie, R. (1992). Explaining the evidence: Tests of the story model for juror decision making. *Journal of Personality and Social Psychology, 62,* 189–206.

Penrod, S. D., & Cutler, B. (1995). Witness confidence and witness accuracy: Assessing their forensic relation. *Psychology, Public Policy, and Law, 1,* 817–845.

People (1996, December 30). She gave a helping hand to a distant—very distant—relation. p. 66.

Peplau, L. A. (2003). Human sexuality: How do men and women differ? *Current Directions in Psychological Science, 12,* 37–40.

Peplau, L. A., & Fingerhut, A. W. (2007). The close relationships of lesbians and gay men. *Annual Review of Psychology, 58,* 405–424.

Peplau, L. A., Garnets, L. D., Spalding, L. R., Conley, T. D., & Veniegas, R. C. (1998). A critique of Bem's "Exotic becomes erotic" theory of sexual orientation. *Psychogical Review, 105,* 387–394.

Peplau, L. A., & Perlman, D. (Eds.) (1982). *Loneliness: A sourcebook of current theory, research, and therapy.* New York: Wiley.

Pepler, D. J., & Craig, W. M. (1995). A peek behind the fence: Naturalistic observations of aggressive children with remote audiovisual recording. *Developmental Psychology, 31,* 548–553.

Pepler, D. J., Craig, W. M., Connolly, J. A., Yuile, A., McMaster, L., & Jiang, D. (2006). A developmental perspective on bullying. *Aggressive Behavior, 32,* 376–384.

Perdue, C. W., Dovidio, J. F., Gurtman, M. B., & Tyler, R. B. (1990). Us and them: Social categorization and the process of intergroup bias. *Journal of Personality and Social Psychology, 59,* 475–486.

Peters, R. M., Butler, K., Gjini, K., Yeragani, V., & Boutros, N. N. (2011). The role of sensory gating in the racism/blood pressure relationship: A pilot study. *Journal of Psychophysiology, 25,* 40-49.

Petersen, L. E., & Blank, H. (2003). Ingroup bias in the minimal group paradigm shown by three-person groups with high or low state self-esteem. *European Journal of Social Psychology, 33,* 149–162.

Peterson, K. S. (1997, November 3). For today's teens, race "not an issue anymore." *USA Today,* p. 1A.

Pettigrew, T. F. (1958). Personality and sociocultural factors in intergroup attitudes: A cross-national comparison. *Journal of Conflict Resolution, 2,* 29–42.

Pettigrew, T. F., Christ, O., Wagner, U., van Dick, R., Zick, A., & Meertens, R. W. (2008). Relative deprivation and intergroup prejudice. *Journal of Social Issues, 64,* 385–401.

Pettigrew, T. F., & Meertens, R. W. (1995). Subtle and blatant prejudice in western Europe. *European Journal of Social Psychology, 25,* 57–75.

Pettigrew, T. F., & Tropp, L. R. (2000). Does intergroup contact reduce prejudice: Recent meta-analytic findings. In S. Oskamp (Ed.), *Reducing prejudice and discrimination: The Claremont symposium on applied social psychology* (pp. 93–114). Mahwah, NJ: Erlbaum.

Pettigrew, T. F., & Tropp, L. R. (2006). A meta-analytic test of intergroup contact theory. *Journal of Personality and Social Psychology, 90,* 751–783.

Pettigrew, T. F., & Tropp, L. R. (2008). How does intergroup contact reduce prejudice? Meta-analytic tests of three mediators. *European Journal of Social Psychology, 38,* 922–934.

Petty, R. E., & Cacioppo, J. T. (1983). The role of bodily responses in attitude measurement and change. In J. Cacioppo & R. Petty (Eds.), *Social psychophysiology: A sourcebook* (pp. 51–101). New York: Guilford.

Petty, R. E., & Cacioppo, J. T. (1984). The effects of involvement on response to argument quantity and quality: Central and peripheral routes to persuasion. *Journal of Personality and Social Psychology, 46,* 69–81.

Petty, R. E., & Cacioppo, J. T. (1986). *Communication and persuasion: Central and peripheral routes to attitude change.* New York: Springer-Verlag.

Petty, R. E., Cacioppo, J. T., & Goldman, R. (1981). Personal involvement as a determinant of argument-based persuasion. *Journal of Personality and Social Psychology, 41,* 847–855.

Petty, R. E., & Chaiken, S. (Eds.) (2004). *Key readings in attitudes and persuasion.* London: Taylor & Francis.

Petty, R. E., & Fazio, R. H., & Brinol, P. (Eds.). (2009). *Attitudes: Insights from the new implicit measures.* New York: Psychology Press.

Petty, R. E., & Krosnick, J. A. (Eds.) (1995). *Attitude strength: Antecedents and consequences.* Mahwah, NJ: Erlbaum.

Petty, R. E., Schumann, D. W., Richman, S. A., & Strathman, A. J. (1993). Positive mood and persuasion: Different roles for affect under high-and low-elaboration conditions. *Journal of Personality and Social Psychology, 64,* 5–20.

Petty, R. E., & Wegener, D. T. (1999). The Elaboration Likelihood Model: Current status and controversies. In S. Chaiken & Y. Trope (Eds.), *Dual-process theories in social psychology* (pp. 41–72). New York: Guilford.

Petty, R. E., Wegener, D. T., & Fabrigar, L. R. (1997). Attitudes and attitude change. *Annual Review of Psychology, 48,* 609–647.

Petty, R. E., Wegener, D. T., & White, P. (1998). Flexible correction processes in persuasion. *Social Cognition, 16,* 93–113.

Pfau, M., Kenski, H. C., Nitz, M., & Sorenson, J. (1990). Efficacy of inoculation strategies in promoting resistance to political attack messages: Application to direct mail. *Communication Monographs, 57,* 25–43.

Phelan, J. E., Moss-Racusin, C. A., & Rudman, L. A. (2008). Competent yet out in the cold: Shifting criteria for hiring reflect backlash toward agentic women. *Psychology of Women Quarterly, 32,* 406–413.

Phelps, E. A., O'Connor, K. J., Cunningham, W. A., Funayama, E. S., Gatenby, J. C., Gore, J. C., & Banaji, M. R. (2000). Performance on indirect measures of race evaluation predicts amygdala activation. *Journal of Cognitive Neuroscience, 12,* 729–738

Phillips, Ann G., & Silvia, Paul J. (2005). Self-awareness and the emotional consequences of self-discrepancies. *Personality and Social Psychology Bulletin, 31,* 703–713.

Picho, K., & Stephens, J. M. (2012). Culture, context and stereotype threat: A comparative analysis of young ugandan women in coed and single-sex schools. *The Journal of Educational Research, 105,* 52–63.

Pieters, R., Wedel, M., & Batra, R. (2010). The stopping power of advertising: Measures and effects of visual complexity. *Journal of Marketing, 74*(5), 48–60.

Piferi, R. L., Jobe, R. L., Jones, W. H., & Gaines, S. O., Jr. (2006). Giving to others during national tragedy: The effects of altruistic and egoistic motivations on long-term giving. *Journal of Social and Personal Relationships, 23,* 171–184.

Piff, P. K., Kraus, M. W., Côté, S., Cheng, B. H., & Keltner, D. (2010). Having less, giving more: The influence of social class on prosocial behavior. *Journal of Personality and Social Psychology, 99,* 771–784.

Pihl, R. O., Lau, M. L., & Assaad, J. M. (1997). Aggressive disposition, alcohol, and aggression. *Aggressive Behavior, 23,* 11–18.

Piliavin, I. M., Piliavin, J. A., & Rodin, J. (1975). Costs, diffusion, and the stigmatized victim. *Journal of Personality and Social Psychology, 32,* 429–438.

Piliavin, J. A. (2003). Doing well by doing good: Benefits for the benefactor. In C. L. M. Keyes & J. Haidt (Eds.), *Flourishing: Positive psychology and the life well-lived* (pp. 227–247). Washington, DC: American Psychological Association.

Piliavin, J. A., & Callero, P. L. (1991). *Giving blood: The development of an altruistic identity.* Baltimore: Johns Hopkins.

Piliavin, J. A., Dovidio, J. F., Gaertner, S. L., & Clark, R. D., III. (1981). *Emergency intervention.* New York: Academic Press.

Piliavin, J. A., Grube, J. A., & Callero, P. L. (2002). Role as a resource for action in public service. *Journal of Social Issues, 58,* 469–485.

Piliavin, J. A., & Siegl, E. (2008). Health benefits of volunteering in the Wisconsin Longitudinal Study. *Journal of Health and Social Behavior, 48,* 450–464.

Pillemer, D. B., Picariello, M. L., Law, A. B., & Reichman, J. S. (1996). Memories of college: The importance of educational episodes. In D. C. Rubin (Ed.), *Remembering our past: Studies in autobiographical memory* (pp. 318–337). New York: Cambridge University Press.

Pinderhughes, E. E., Dodge, K. A., Bates, J. E.. Pettit, G. S., & Zelli, A. (2000). Discipline responses: Influences of parents' socioeconomic status, ethnicity, beliefs about parenting, stress, and cognitive-emotional processes. *Journal of Family Psychology, 14,* 380–400.

Pinel, Elizabeth C., & Long, A. E. (2012). When I's meet: Sharing subjective experience with someone from the outgroup. *Personality and Social Psychology Bulletin, 38,* 296–307.

Pinto, I. R., Marques, J. M., Levine, J. M., & Abrams, D. (2010). Membership status and subjective group dynamics: Who triggers the black sheep effect? *Journal of Personality and Social Psychology, 99,* 107–119.

Pittman, T. S. (1975). Attribution of arousal as a mediator of dissonance reduction. *Journal of Experimental Social Psychology, 11,* 53–63.

Pittman, T. S., & Heller, J. F. (1987). Social motivation. *Annual Review of Psychology, 38,* 461–489.

Plaks, J. E., & Higgins, E. T. (2000). Pragmatic use of stereotyping in teamwork: Social loafing and compensation as a function of inferred partner-situation fit. *Journal of Personality and Social Psychology, 79,* 962–974.

Plant, E. A., & Devine, P. G. (1998). Internal and external motivation to respond without prejudice. *Journal of Personality and Social Psychology, 75,* 811–832.

Plant, E. A., & Devine, P. G. (2009). The active control of prejudice: Unpacking the intentions guiding control efforts. *Journal of Personality and Social Psychology, 96,* 640–652.

Platek, S. M., Wathne, K., Tierney, N. G., & Thomson, J. W. (2008). Neural correlates of self-face recognition: An effect-location meta-analysis. *Brain Research, 1232,* 173–184.

Platow, M. J., Byrne, L., & Ryan, M. K. (2005). Experimentally manipulated high in-group status can buffer personal self-esteem against discrimination. *European Journal of Social Psychology, 35,* 599–608.

Plotnik, J. M., de Waal, Frans B. M., & Reiss, D. (2006). Self-recognition in an asian elephant. *PNAS Proceedings of the National Academy of Sciences of the United States of America, 103,* 17053–17057.

Polivy, J., Garner, D. M., & Garfinkel, P. E. (1986). Causes and consequences of the current preference for thin female physiques. In C. P. Herman, M. P. Zanna, & E. T. Higgins (Eds.), *The Ontario symposium: Vol. 3. Physical appearance, stigma, and social behavior* (pp. 89–112). Hillsdale, NJ: Erlbaum.

Pontari, B. A., & Schlenker, B. R. (2000). The influence of cognitive load on self-presentation: Can cognitive busyness help as well as harm social performance? *Journal of Personality and Social Psychology, 78,* 1092–1108.

Poole, C., & Rietschlin, J. (2012). Intimate partner victimization among adults aged 60 and older: An analysis of the 1999 and 2004 general social survey. *Journal of Elder Abuse & Neglect, 24,* 120–137.

Poole, D. A., & White, L. T. (1991). Effects of question repetition on the eyewitness testimony of children and adults. *Developmental Psychology, 27,* 975–986.

Poon, M. K., Wong, J. P., Sutdhibhasilp, N., Ho, P. T., & Wong, B. (2011). Condom use among east and southeast asian men attending a gay bathhouse in Toronto. *The Canadian Journal of Human Sexuality, 20,* 67–74.

Poppen, P. J., & Segal, N. J. (1988). The influence of sex and sex role orientation on sexual coercion. *Sex Roles, 19,* 689–701.

Pornpitakpan, C. (2004). The persuasiveness of source credibility: A critical review of five decades' evidence. *Journal of Applied Social Psychology, 34,* 243–281.

Porter, S., Bellhouse, S., McDougall, A., ten Brinke, L., & Wilson, K. (2010). A prospective investigation of the vulnerability of memory for positive and negative emotional scenes to the misinformation effect. *Canadian Journal of Behavioural Science/Revue Canadienne Des Sciences Du Comportement, 42,* 55–61.

Posavac, H. D., Posavac, S. S., & Posavac, E. J. (1998). Exposure to media images of female attractiveness and concern with body weight among young women. *Sex Roles, 38,* 187–201.

Post, S. G. (2005). Altruism, happiness, and health: It's good to be good. *International Journal of Behavioral Medicine, 12,* 66–77.

Postmes, T., Spears, R., & Cihangir, S. (2001). Quality of decision making and group norms. *Journal of Personality and Social Psychology, 80,* 918–930.

Povinelli, D. J., Gallup, G. G. Jr., Eddy, T. J., Bierschwale, D. T., Engstrom, M. C., Perilloux, H. K., & Toxopeus, I. B. (1997). Chimpanzees recognize themselves in mirrors. *Animal Behaviour, 53,* 1083–1088.

Potegal, M. (2011). Temporal and frontal lobe initiation and regulation of the top-down escalation of anger and aggression. *Behavioural Brain Research, 231,* 386-395.

Powers, S. I., Pietromonaco, P. R., Gunlicks, M., & Sayer, A. (2006). Dating couples' attachment styles and patterns of cortisol reactivity and recovery in response to a relationship conflict. *Journal of Personality and Social Psychology, 90,* 613–628.

Pozzulo, J.D., Bennell, C., & Forth, A. (2011). *Forensic psychology* (3rd *Edition*). Toronto: Pearson Education Canada.

Pratkanis, A. R. (1992). The cargo-cult science of subliminal persuasion. *Skeptical Inquirer, 16,* 260–272.

Pratkanis, A. R., Greenwald, A. G., Leippe, M. R., & Baumgardner, M. H. (1988). In search of reliable persuasion effects: III. The sleeper effect is dead. Long live the sleeper effect. *Journal of Personality and Social Psychology, 54,* 203–218.

Pratkanis, A. R., & Turner, M. E. (1994). Nine principles of successful affirmative action: Mr. Branch Rickey, Mr. Jackie Robinson, and the integration of baseball. *Nine: A Journal of Baseball History and Social Policy Perspectives, 3,* 36–65.

Pratto, F., & John, O. P. (1991). Automatic vigilance: The attention-grabbing power of negative social information. *Journal of Personality and Social Psychology, 61,* 380–391.

Prentice, D. A., & Carranza, E. (2002). What women should be, shouldn't be, are allowed to be, and don't have to be: The contents of prescriptive gender stereotypes. *Psychology of Women Quarterly, 26,* 269–281.

Prentice, D. A., & Miller, D. T. (1996). Pluralistic ignorance and the perpetuation of social norms by unwitting actors. *Advances in Experimental Social Psychology, 28,* 161–209.

Prentice-Dunn, S., & Rogers, R. W. (1982). Effects of public and private self-awareness on deindividuation and aggression. *Journal of Personality and Social Psychology, 43,* 503–513.

Prentice-Dunn, S., & Rogers, R. W. (1983). Deindividuation in aggression. In R. G. Geen & E. I. Donnerstein (Eds.), *Aggression:*

Theoretical and empirical reviews: Vol. 2. Issues in research (pp. 155–171). New York: Academic Press.

Price, M. E. (2008). The resurrection of group selection as a theory of human cooperation. *Social Justice Research, 21,* 228–240.

Priester, J. R., Cacioppo, J. T., & Petty, R. E. (1996). The influence of motor processes on attitudes toward novel versus familiar semantic stimuli. *Personality and Social Psychology Bulletin, 22,* 442–447.

Priester, J. R., & Petty, R. E. (1995). Source attributions and persuasion: Perceived honesty as a determinant of message scrutiny. *Personality and Social Psychology Bulletin, 21,* 637–654.

Prioleau, L., Murdock, M., & Brody, N. (1983). An analysis of psychotherapy versus placebo studies. *Behavioral and Brain Sciences, 6,* 275–310.

Prokosch, M., Coss, R., Scheib, J., & Blozis, S. (2009). Intelligence and mate choice: Intelligent men are always appealing. *Evolution and Human Behavior, 30,* 11–20.

Pronin, E. (2007). Perception and misperception of bias in human judgment. *Trends in Cognitive Sciences, 11,* 37–43.

Pronin, E., Berger, J., & Molouki, S. (2007). Alone in a crowd of sheep: Asymmetric perceptions of conformity and their roots in an introspection illusion. *Journal of Personality and Social Psychology, 92,* 585–595.

Proto-Campise, L., Belknap, J., & Wooldredge, J. (1998). High school students' adherence to rape myths and the effectiveness of high school rape-awareness programs. *Violence Against Women, 4,* 308–328.

Pruitt, D. G. (1998). Social conflict. In D. T. Gilbert, S. T. Fiske, & G. Lindzey (Eds.), *The handbook of social psychology* (4th ed., Vol. 2, pp. 410–503). New York: McGraw-Hill.

Pryor, J. B., & Merluzzi, T. V. (1985). The role of expertise in processing social interaction scripts. *Journal of Experimental Social Psychology, 21,* 362–379.

Pumphrey-Gordon, Jennifer E., & Gross, A. M. (2007). Alcohol consumption and females recognition in response to date rape risk: The role of sex-related alcohol expectancies. *Journal of Family Violence, 22,* 475–485.

Pyszczynski, T., & Greenberg, J. (1987). Self-regulatory preservation and the depressive self-focusing style: A self-awareness theory of reactive depression. *Psychological Bulletin, 201,* 122–138.

Pyszczynski, T., & Greenberg, J. (1992). *Hanging on and letting go.* New York: Springer-Verlag.

Qin, P., & Northoff, G. (2011). How is our self related to midline regions and the default-mode network? *NeuroImage, 57,* 1221–1233.

Qualter, T. H. (1962). *Propaganda and psychological warfare.* New York: Random House.

Quattrone, G. A. (1986). On the perception of a group's variability. In S. Worchel & W. G. Austin (Eds.), *Psychology of intergroup relations* (2nd ed., pp. 25–48). Chicago: Nelson Hall.

Quigley, B. M., & Leonard, K. E. (2006). Alcohol expectancies and intoxicated aggression. *Aggression and Violent Behavior, 11,* 484–496.

Quinn, D. M., Kahng, S. K., & Crocker, J. (2004). Discreditable: Stigma effects of revealing a mental illness history on test performance. *Personality and Social Psychology Bulletin, 30,* 803–815.

Raaijmakers, M. A. J., Smidts, D. P., Sergeant, J. A., Maassen, G. H., Posthumus, J. A., van Engeland, H., et al. (2008). Executive functions in preschool children with aggressive behavior: Impairments in inhibitory control. *Journal of Abnormal Child Psychology, 36,* 1097–1107.

Rachlinski, J. J., Johnson, S. L., Wistrich, A. J., & Guthrie, C. (2009). Does unconscious racial bias affect trial judges? Notre Dame Law Review, 84, 1195–1246.

Rains, S. A. (2005). Leveling the organizational playing field—virtually: A meta-analysis of experimental research assessing the impact of group support system use on member influence behaviors. *Communication Research, 32,* 193–234.

Rajecki, D. W., Bledsoe, S. B., & Rasmussen, J. L. (1991). Successful personal ads: Gender differences and similarities in offers, stipulations, and outcomes. *Basic and Applied Social Psychology, 12,* 457–469.

Ramírez-Esparza, N., Gosling, S. D., & Pennebaker, J. W. (2008). Paradox lost: Unraveling the puzzle of Simpatía. *Journal of Cross-Cultural Psychology, 39,* 703–715.

Ramírez-Esparza, Nairán, Mehl, M. R., Álvarez-Bermúdez, J., & Pennebaker, J. W. (2009). Are Mexicans more or less sociable than Americans? Insights from a naturalistic observation study. *Journal of Research in Personality, 43,* 1-7.

Raskin, D. C. (1986). The polygraph in 1986: Scientific, professional, and legal issues surrounding application and acceptance of polygraph evidence. *Utah Law Review,* 29–74.

Rasmussen, A. S., & Bernsten,D. (2009). The possible functions of involuntary autobiographical memories. *Applied Cognitive Psychology, 23,* 1137-1152.

Ray, D. G., Mackie, D. M., Rydell, R. J., & Smith, E. R. (2008). Changing categorization of self can change emotions about outgroups. *Journal of Experimental Social Psychology, 44,* 1210–1213.

Ray, O. (2004). How the mind hurts and heals the body. *American Psychologist, 59,* 29–40.

Read, S. J. (1987). Constructing causal scenarios: A knowledge structure approach to causal reasoning. *Journal of Personality and Social Psychology, 52,* 288–302.

Read, S. J., & Urada, D. I. (2003). A neural network simulation of the outgroup homogeneity effect. *Personality and Social Psychology Review, 7,* 146–159.

Reader's Digest. *How polite are we?* July, 2006

Reeder, G. D. (1993). Trait-behavior relations and dispositional inference. *Personality and Social Psychology Bulletin, 19,* 586–593.

Reeder, G. D., & Brewer, M. B. (1979). A schematic model of dispositional attribution in interpersonal perception. *Psychological Review, 86,* 61–79.

Regan, D. T. (1971). Effects of a favor and liking on compliance. *Journal of Experimental Social Psychology, 7,* 627–639.

Regan, D. T., Williams, M., & Sparling, S. (1972). Voluntary expiation of guilt: A field experiment. *Journal of Personality and Social Psychology, 24,* 42–45.

Regan, P. C., & Berscheid, E. (1997). Gender differences in characteristics desired in a potential sexual and marriage partner. *Journal of Psychology and Human Sexuality, 9,* 25–37.

Regan, P. C., & Berscheid, E. (1999). *Lust: What we know about human sexual desire.* Thousand Oaks, CA: Sage.

Regan, P. C., & Gutierrez, D. M. (2005). Effects of participants' sex and targets' perceived need on supermarket helping behavior. *Perceptual and Motor Skills, 101,* 617–620.

Regan, P. C., Kocan, E. R., & Whitlock, T. (1998). Ain't love grand! A prototype analysis of the concept of romantic love. *Journal of Social and Personal Relationships, 15,* 411–420.

Reiber, C., & Garcia, J. R. (2010). Hooking up: Gender differences, evolution, and pluralistic ignorance. *Evolutionary Psychology, 8,* 390-404.

Reicher, S. D., & Haslam, S. A. (2006). Rethinking the psychology of tyranny: The BBC prison study. *British Journal of Social Psychology, 45,* 1–40.

Reifman, A. S., Larrick, R. P., & Fein, S. (1991). Temper and temperature on the diamond: The heat-aggression relationship in major-league baseball. *Personality and Social Psychology Bulletin, 17,* 580–585.

Reifman, A., Klein, J. G., & Murphy, S. T. (1989). Self-monitoring and age. *Psychology and Aging, 4,* 245–246.

Reisenzein, R. (1983). The Schachter theory of emotion: Two decades later. *Psychological Bulletin, 94,* 239–264.

Reiss, D., & Marino, L. (2001). Mirror self-recognition in the bottlenose dolphin: A case of cognitive convergence. *Proceedings of the National Academy of the Sciences, 98,* 5937–5942.

Remedios, R., Ritchie, K., & Lieberman, D.A. (2005). I used to like it but now I don't: The effect of the transfer test in Northern Ireland on pupils' intrinsic motivation. *British Journal of Educational Psychology, 75,* 435–452.

Remley, A. (1988, October). The great parental value shift: From obedience to independence. *Psychology Today,* 56–59.

Renfrew, J. W. (1997). *Aggression and its causes: A biopsychosocial approach.* New York: Oxford University Press. Responsible citizenship. (2002, December 31). *Ottawa Citizen,* p. A14.

Renouf, A., Brendgen, M., Parent, S., Vitaro, F., Zelazo, P. D., Boivin, M., Dionne, G., Trembley, R.E., Pérusse, D., & Séguin, J. R. (2010). Relations between theory of mind and indirect and physical aggression in kindergarten: Evidence of the moderating role of prosocial behaviors. *Social Development, 19,* 535-555.

Reysen, S., & Ganz, E. (2006). Gender differences in helping in six U.S. cities. *North American Journal of Psychology, 8,* 63–67.

Rhee, E., Uleman, J. S., Lee, H. K., & Roman, R. J. (1995). Spontaneous self-descriptions and ethnic identities in Individualistic and collectivistic cultures. *Journal of Personality and Social Psychology, 69,* 142–152.

Rhodes, G. (2006). The evolutionary psychology of facial beauty. *Annual Review of Psychology, 57,* 199–226.

Rhodes, G., Sumich, A., & Byatt, G. (1999). Are average facial configurations attractive only because of their symmetry? *Psychological Science, 10,* 52–58.

Rhodes, G., & Zebrowitz, L. A. (Eds.) (2002). *Facial attractiveness: Evolutionary, cognitive, and social perspectives.* Norwood, NJ: Ablex.

Rhodes, G., Zebrowitz, L. A., Clark, A., Kalick, S. M., Hightower, A., & McKay, R. (2001). Do facial averageness and symmetry signal health? *Evolution and Human Behavior, 22,* 31–46.

Rhodes, N., & Wood, W. (1992). Self-esteem and intelligence affect influenceability: The mediating role of message reception. *Psychological Bulletin, 111,* 156–171.

Rhodewalt, F. (1990). Self-handicappers: Individual differences in the preference for anticipatory, self-protective acts. In R. L. Higgins, C. R. Synder, & S. Berglas (Eds.), *Self-handicapping: The paradox that isn't* (pp. 69–106). New York: Plenum.

Rhodewalt, F., & Agustsdottir, S. (1986). Effects of self-presentation on the phenomenal self. *Journal of Personality and Social Psychology, 50,* 47–55.

Rhodewalt, F., Sandonmatsu, D. M., Tschanz, B., Feick, D. L., & Waller, A. (1995). Self-handicapping and interpersonal trade-offs: The effects of claimed self-handicaps on observers' performance evaluations and feedback. *Personality and Social Psychology Bulletin, 21,* 1042–1050.

Richardson, M. J., Marsh, K. L., & Schmidt, R. C. (2005). Effects of visual and verbal interaction on unintentional interpersonal coordination. *Journal of Experimental Psychology: Human Perception and Performance, 31,* 62-79.

Richeson, J. A., & Shelton, J. N. (2010). Prejudice and bias in intergroup interactions. In J. F. Dovidio, M. Hewstone, P. Glick, & V. M. Esses (Eds.), *Handbook of prejudice, stereotyping, and discrimination.* London: Sage.

Richeson, J. A., Todd, A. R., Trawalter, S., & Baird, A. A. (2008). Eye-gaze direction modulates race-related amygdala activity. *Group Processes & Intergroup Relations, 11,* 233–246.

Richeson, J. A., & Trawalter, S. (2005). Why do interracial interactions impair executive function? A resource depletion account. *Journal of Personality and Social Psychology, 88,* 934–947.

Richeson, J. A., & Trawalter, S. (2008). The threat of appearing prejudiced and race-based attentional biases. *Psychological Science, 19,* 98–102.

Rico, R., Sánchez-Manzanares, M., Antino, M., & Lau, D. (2012). Bridging team faultlines by combining task role assignment and goal structure strategies. *Journal of Applied Psychology, 97,* 407–420.

Rilling, J. K., Goldsmith, D. R., Glenn, A. L., Jairam, M. R., Elfenbein, H. A., Dagenais, J. E., Murdock, C. D., & Pagnoni, G. (2008). The neural correlates of the affective response to unreciprocated cooperation. *Neuropsychologia, 46,* 1256–1266.

Rilling, J. K., Gutman, D. A., Zeh, T. R., Pagnoni, G., Berns, G. S., & Kilts, C. D. (2002). A neural basis for social cooperation. *Neuron, 35,* 395–405.

Rilling, J. K., DeMarco, A. C., Hackett, P. D., Thompson, R., Ditzen, B., Patel, R., & Pagnoni, G. (2012). Effects of intranasal oxytocin and vasopressin on cooperative behavior and associated brain activity in men. *Psychoneuroendocrinology, 37,* 447–461.

Rind, B., & Strohmetz, D. B. (2001). Effect on restaurant tipping of a helpful message written on the back of customers' checks. *Journal of Applied Social Psychology, 31,* 1379–1384.

Rimal, Rajiv N., & Real, K. (2005). Assessing the perceived importance of skin cancer: How question-order effects are influenced by issue involvement. *Health Education & Behavior, 32,* 398–412.

Ringelmann, M. (1913). Recherches sur les moteurs animés: Travail de l'homme. *Annales de l'Institut National Agronomique, 2e série, tom XII,* 1–40.

Risen, J. L., Gilovich, T., & Dunning, D. (2007). One-shot illusory correlations and stereotype formation. *Personality and Social Psychology Bulletin, 33,* 1492–1502.

Roach, M. (2008). *Bonk: The curious coupling of science and sex.* New York: Norton.

Robert, L., Jr., Denis, A., & Hung, Y.-T. (2009). Individual swift trust and knowledge based trust in face-to-face and virtual team members. *Journal of Management Information Systems, 26,* 251–279.

Robins, R. W., Mendelsohn, G. A., Connell, J. B., & Kwan, V. S. Y. (2004). Do people agree about the causes of behavior? A social relations analysis of behavior ratings and causal attributions. *Journal of Personality and Social Psychology, 86,* 334–344.

Robinson, J. P., Shaver, P. R., & Wrightsman, L. S. (Eds.) (1991). *Measures of personality and social psychological attitudes.* New York: Academic Press.

Robinson, J. P., Shaver, P. R., & Wrightsman, L. S. (Eds.) (1998). *Measures of political attitudes.* New York: Academic Press.

Rockloff, M. J., & Greer, N. (2011). Audience influence on EGM gambling: The protective effects of having others watch you play. *Journal of Gambling Studies, 27,* 443–451.

Roddy, S., Stewart, I., & Barnes-Holmes, D. (2011). Facial reactions reveal that slim is good but fat is not bad: Implicit and explicit measures of body-size bias. *European Journal of Social Psychology, 41,* 688.

Rodkin, P. C., & Roisman, G. I. (2010). Antecedents and correlates of the popular-aggressive phenomenon in elementary school. *Child Development, 81,* 837–850.

Rodriguez, D. N., & Berry, M. A. (2010). System and estimator variables, eyewitness confidence, and the postidentification feedback effect. *American Journal of Forensic Psychology, 28,* 17–37.

Roese, N. J. (1997). Counterfactual thinking. *Psychological Bulletin, 121,* 133–148.

Roese, N. J., & Jamieson, D. W. (1993). Twenty years of bogus pipeline research: A critical review and meta-analysis. *Psychological Bulletin, 114,* 363–375.

Roese, N. J., & Olson, J. M. (Eds.) (1995). *What might have been: The social psychology of counterfactual thinking.* Hillsdale, NJ: Erlbaum.

Roese, N. J., & Summerville, A. (2005). What we regret most... and why. *Personality and Social Psychology Bulletin, 31,* 1273–1285.

Rofé, Y. (1984). Stress and affiliation: A utility theory. *Psychological Review, 91,* 235–250.

Rogers, M., Miller, N., Mayer, F. S., & Duval, S. (1982). Personal responsibility and salience of the request for help: Determinants of the relation between negative affect and helping behavior. *Journal of Personality and Social Psychology, 43,* 956–970.

Rogers, R. W. (1983). Cognitive and psychological processes in fear appeals and attitude change: A revised theory of protection motivation. In J. Cacioppo & R. Petty (Eds.), *Social psychophysiology: A sourcebook* (pp. 153–176). New York: Guilford.

Rogers, R. W., & Mewborn, R. C. (1976). Fear appeals and attitude change: Effects of a threat's noxiousness, probability of occurrence, and the efficacy of coping responses. *Journal of Personality and Social Psychology, 34,* 54–61.

Rohrer, J. H., Baron, S. H., Hoffman, E. L., & Swander, D. V. (1954). The stability of autokinetic judgments. *Journal of Abnormal and Social Psychology, 49,* 595–597.

Ronquillo, J., Denson, T., Lickel, B., Nandy, A., Maddox, K., & Lu, Z. (2007). The effects of skin tone on race-related amygdala activity: An fMRI investigation. *Social Cognitive and Affective Neuroscience, 2,* 39–44.

Ronzone, R. (2009, April 2). Video games not just children's play. *The Villanovan.*

Rook, K. S. (1984). The negative side of social interaction: Impact on psychological well-being. *Journal of Personality and Social Psychology, 46,* 1097–1108.

Rook, K. S. (1987). Reciprocity of social exchange and social satisfaction among older women. *Journal of Personality and Social Psychology, 52,* 145–154.

Rook, K. S., & Peplau, L. A. (1982). Perspectives on helping the lonely. In L. A. Peplau & D. Perlman (Eds.), *Loneliness: A sourcebook of current theory, research and therapy* (pp. 351–378). New York: Wiley.

Rose, H. A. (2012). Canada's same-sex marriage law: Exception to or exemplar of Canada's family policy? *Journal of Child and Family Studies, 21,* 88–94.

Rose, V. G., & Ogloff, J. R. P. (2001). Evaluating the comprehensibility of jury instructions: A method and an example. *Law and Human Behavior, 25,* 409–431.

Rosenbaum, M. E. (1986). The repulsion hypothesis: On the nondevelopment of relationships. *Journal of Personality and Social Psychology, 51,* 1156–1166.

Rosenbloom, T., Shahar, A., Perlman, A., Estreich, D., & Kirzner, E. (2007). Success on a practical drivers license test with and without the presence of another testee. *Accident Analysis and Prevention, 39,* 1296–1301.

Rosenman, R. H., Brand, R. J., Jenkins, C. D., Friedman, M., Strau, R., & Wurm, M. (1975). Coronary heart disease in the Western Collaborative Group Study: Final follow-up experience of 8 1/2 years. *Journal of the American Medical Association, 233,* 872–877.

Rosenthal, E. (2006, June 2). Genital cutting raises by 50% likelihood mothers or their newborns will die, study finds. *New York Times.* p. A10.

Rosenthal, H. E. S., & Crisp, R. J. (2006). Reducing stereotype threat by blurring intergroup boundaries. *Personality and Social Psychology Bulletin, 32,* 501–511.

Rosenthal, R. (1976). *Experimenter effects in behavioral research.* New York: Irvington.

Rosenthal, R. (1985). From unconscious experimenter bias to teacher expectancy effects. In J. B. Dusek, V. C. Hall, & W. J. Meyer (Eds.), *Teacher expectancies* (pp. 37–65). Hillsdale, NJ: Erlbaum.

Rosenthal, R. (2002). Covert communication in classrooms, clinics, courtrooms, and cubicles. *American Psychologist, 57,* 839–849.

Rosenthal, R., & Jacobson, L. (1968). *Pygmalion in the classroom: Teacher expectation and pupils' intellectual development.* New York: Holt, Rinehart and Winston.

Ross, E. A. (1908). Social psychology: An outline and source book. New York: Macmillan.

Ross, J., & Staw, B. M. (1986). Expo 86: An escalation prototype. *Administrative Science Quarterly, 31,* 274–297.

Ross, L. (1977). The intuitive psychologist and his shortcomings: Distortions in the attribution process. In L. Berkowitz (Ed.), *Advances in experimental social psychology* (Vol. 10, pp. 174–221). New York: Academic Press.

Ross, L., Amabile, T. M., & Steinmetz, J. L. (1977). Social roles, social control, and biases in social-perception processes. *Journal of Personality and Social Psychology, 35,* 485–494.

Ross, L., Bierbrauer, G., & Hoffman, S. (1976). The role of attribution processes in conformity and dissent. *American Psychologist, 31,* 148–157.

Ross, L., Greene, D., & House, P. (1977). The false consensus phenomenon: An attributional bias in self-perception and social-perception processes. *Journal of Experimental Social Psychology, 13,* 279–301.

Ross, M. (1989). The relation of implicit theories to the construction of personal histories. *Psychological Review, 96,* 341–357.

Ross, M., Xun, W. Q., & Wilson, A. E. (2002). Language and the bicultural self. *Personality and Social Psychology Bulletin, 28,* 1040–1050.

Rowatt, W. C., Cunningham, M. R., & Druen, P. B. (1999). Lying to get a date: The effect of facial physical attractiveness on the willingness to deceive prospective dating partners. *Journal of Social and Personal Relationships, 16,* 209–223.

Rowe, R., Rijsdijk, F. V., Maughan, B., Hosang, G. M., & Eley, T. C. (2008). Heterogeneity in antisocial behaviours and comorbidity with depressed mood: A behavioural genetic approach. *Journal of Child Psychology and Psychiatry, 49,* 526–534.

Rozin, P., & Fallon, A. E. (1987). A perspective on disgust. *Psychological Review, 94,* 23–41.

Rozin, P., Haidt, J., & McCauley, C. R. (2000). Disgust. In M. Lewis & J. Haviland-Jones (Eds.), *Handbook of emotions* (2nd ed., pp. 637–653). New York: Guilford.

Rozin, P., & Royzman, E. B. (2001). Negativity bias, negativity dominance, and contagion. *Personality and Social Psychology Review, 5,* 296–320.

Rubin, D. C. (Ed.) (1996). *Remembering our past: Studies in autobiographical memory.* New York: Cambridge University Press.

Rubin, J. Z., Provenzano, F. J., & Luria, Z. (1974). The eye of the beholder: Parents' views on sex of newborns. *American Journal of Orthopsychiatry, 44,* 512–519.

Rubin, J. Z., Pruitt, D. G., & Kim, S. H. (1994). *Social conflict: Escalation, stalemate, and settlement.* New York: McGraw-Hill.

Rubin, Z. (1973). *Liking and loving.* New York: Holt, Rinehart and Winston.

Rubonis, A. V., & Bickman, L. (1991). Psychological impairment in the wake of disaster: The disaster-psychopathology relationship. *Psychological Bulletin, 109,* 384–399.

Rudman, L. A., & Borgida, E. (1995). The afterglow of construct accessibility: The behavioral consequences of priming men to view women as sexual objects. *Journal of Experimental Social Psychology, 31,* 493–517.

Rudman, L. A., & Glick, P. (2001). Prescriptive gender stereotypes and backlash toward agentic women. *Journal of Social Issues, 57,* 743–762.

Rule, B. G., Taylor, B. R., & Dobbs, A. R. (1987). Priming effects of heat on aggressive thoughts. *Social Cognition, 5,* 131–143.

Rule, N. O., & Ambady, N. (2011). Face and fortune: Inferences of personality from managing partners' faces predict their law firms' financial success. *The Leadership Quarterly, 22,* 690–696.

Rule, N. O., Freeman, J. B., Moran, J. M., Gabrieli, J. D. E., Adams, R. B., & Ambady, N. (2010). Voting behavior is reflected in amygdala response across cultures. *Social Cognitive and Affective Neuroscience, 5,* 349–355.

Rusbult, C. E., & Buunk, B. P. (1993). Commitment processes in close relationships: An interdependence analysis. *Journal of Social and Personal Relationships, 10,* 175–204.

Rusbult, C. E., Martz, J. M., & Agnew, C. R. (1998). The investment model scale: Measuring commitment level, satisfaction level, quality of alternatives, and investment size. *Personal Relationships, 5,* 357–391.

Rushton, J. P. (1981a). Television as a socializer. In J. P. Rushton & R. M. Sorrentino (Eds.), *Altruism and helping behavior: Social, personality, and developmental perspectives* (pp. 91–108). Hillsdale, NJ: Erlbaum.

Rushton, J. P. (1981b). The altruistic personality. In J. P. Rushton & R. M. Sorrentino (Eds.), *Altruism and helping behavior: Social, personality, and developmental perspectives* (pp. 251–266). Hillsdale, NJ: Erlbaum.

Russell, G. W., Arms, R. L., & Bibby, R. W. (1995). Canadians' belief in catharsis. *Social Behavior and Personality, 23,* 223–228.

Russell, J. A. (1994). Is there universal recognition of emotion from facial expression? A review of cross-cultural studies. *Psychological Bulletin, 115,* 102–141.

Rutchick, A. M., Hamilton, D. L., & Sack, J. D. (2008). Antecedents of entitativity in categorically and dynamically construed groups. *European Journal of Social Psychology, 38,* 905–921.

Rutherford, A., Unger, R., & Cherry, F. (2011). Reclaiming SPSSIs sociological past: Marie jahoda and the immersion tradition in social psychology. *Journal of Social Issues, 67,* 42–58.

Rutkowski, G. K., Gruder, C. L., & Romer, D. (1983). Group cohesiveness, social norms, and bystander intervention. *Journal of Personality and Social Psychology, 44,* 545–552.

Ruva, C. L., Guenther, C. C., & Yarbrough, A. (2011). Positive and negative pretrial publicity: The roles of impression formation, emotion, and predecisional distortion. *Criminal Justice and Behavior, 38,* 511–534.

Ryan, C. S., & Bogart, L. M. (1997). Development of new group members' ingroup and outgroup stereotypes: Changes in perceived group variability and ethnocentrism. *Journal of Personality and Social Psychology, 73,* 719–732.

Rydell, R. J., McConnell, A. R., & Beilock, S. L. (2009). Multiple social identities and stereotype threat: Imbalance, accessibility, and working memory. *Journal of Personality and Social Psychology, 96,* 949–966.

Sacks, O. (1985). *The man who mistook his wife for a hat.* New York: Summit.

Sagar, H. A., & Schofield, J. W. (1980). Racial and behavioral cues in black and white children's perceptions of ambiguously aggressive acts. *Journal of Personality and Social Psychology, 39,* 590–598.

Saks, M. J. (1974). Ignorance of science is no excuse. *Trial, 10,* 18–20.

Saks, M. J., & Marti, M. W. (1997). A meta-analysis of the effects of jury size. *Law and Human Behavior, 21,* 451–468.

Saleton, W. (2009, April 15). Sex reversal. *Slate Magazine.*

Salomon, K. & Jagusztyn, N. E. (2008). Cardiovascular reactivity to an interpersonal conflict is moderated by reports of ethnic discrimination. *Health Psychology, 27,* 473–481.

Sallet, J., Mars, R. B., Noonan, M. P., Andersson, J. L., OReilly, ,J.X., Jbabdi, S., Croxson, P.L., Jenkinson, M., Miller, K.L., & Rushworth, M. F. S. (2011). Social network size affects neural circuits in macaques. *Science, 334,* 697–700.

Salovey, P. (1992). Mood-induced focus of attention. *Journal of Personality and Social Psychology, 62,* 699–707.

Salovey, P., Mayer, J. D., & Rosenhan, D. L. (1991). Mood and helping: Mood as a motivator of helping and helping as a regulator of mood. In M. S. Clark (Ed.), *Prosocial behavior* (Vol. 12, pp. 215–237). Newbury Park, CA: Sage.

Sanchez-Burks, J., Nisbett, R. E., & Ybarra, O. (2000). Relational schemas, cultural styles, and prejudice against outgroups. *Journal of Personality and Social Psychology, 79,* 174–189.

Sanders, G. S. (1981). Driven by distraction: An integrative review of social facilitation theory and research. *Journal of Experimental Social Psychology, 17,* 227–251.

Sanders, S. A., Hill, B. J., Yarber, W. L., Graham, C. A., Crosby, R. A., Milhausen, R. R. (2010) Misclassification bias: Diversity in conceptualisations about having 'had sex'. *Sexual Health, 7,* 31–34.

Sanderson, C. A., & Evans, S. M. (2001). Seeing one's partner through intimacy-colored glasses: An examination of the processes underlying the intimacy goals-relationship satisfaction link. *Personality and Social Psychology Bulletin, 27,* 463–473.

Sanderson, D. W. (1993). *Smileys.* Sebastopol, CA: O'Reilly.

Sanna, L. J. (1992). Self-efficacy theory: Implications for social facilitation and social loafing. *Journal of Personality and Social Psychology, 62,* 774–786.

Santalahti, P., Sourander, A., Aromaa, M., Helenius, H., Ikäheimo, K., & Piha, J. (2008). Victimization and bullying among 8-year-old Finnish children: A 10-year comparison of rates. *European Child and Adolescent Psychiatry, 17,* 463–472.

Santos, M. D., Leve, C., & Pratkanis, A. R. (1994). Hey buddy, can you spare seventeen cents? Mindful persuasion and the pique technique. *Journal of Applied Social Psychology, 24,* 755–764.

Sarason, I. G., Levine, H. M., Basham, R. B., & Sarason, B. R. (1983). Assessing social support: The social support questionnaire. *Journal of Personality and Social Psychology,* 49, 469–480.

Sarason, I. G., Sarason, B. R., Pierce, G. R., Shearin, E. N., & Sayers, M. H. (1991). A social learning approach to increasing blood donations. *Journal of Applied Social Psychology, 21,* 896–918.

Sarnoff, I., & Zimbardo, P. (1961). Anxiety, fear, and social affiliation. *Journal of Abnormal and Social Psychology, 62,* 356–363.

Saucier, D. A., Miller, C. T., & Doucet, N. (2005). Differences in helping whites and blacks: A meta-analysis. *Personality and Social Psychology Review, 9,* 2–16.

Sauer, S. J. (2011). Taking the reins: The effects of new leader status and leadership style on team performance. *Journal of Applied Psychology, 96,* 574–587.

Saulnier, K., & Perlman, D. (1981). The actor-observer bias is alive and well in prison: A sequel to Wells. *Personality and Social Psychology Bulletin, 7,* 559–564.

Saulny, S. (2002). Why confess to what you didn't do? *The New York Times,* December 8, Section 4.

Savin, H. B. (1973). Professors and psychological researchers: Conflicting values in conflicting roles. *Cognition, 2,* 147–149.

Savitsky, K., Epley, N., & Gilovich, T. (2001). Do others judge us as harshly as we think? Overestimating the impact of our failures, shortcomings, and mishaps. *Journal of Personality and Social Psychology, 81,* 44–56.

Savitsky, K., Gilovich, T., Berger, G., & Medvec, V. H. (2003). Is our absence as conspicuous as we think? Overestimating the salience and impact of one's absence from a group. *Journal of Experimental Social Psychology, 39,* 386–392.

Sawyer, J., Mishna, F., Pepler, D., & Wiener, J. (2011). The missing voice: Parents' perspectives of bullying. *Children and Youth Services Review, 33,* 1795–1803.

Sbarra, D. A., & Nietert, P. J. (2009). Divorce and death: Forty years of the Charleston Heart Study. *Psychological Science, 20,* 107–113.

Schachter, S. (1951). Deviation, rejection, and communication. *Journal of Abnormal and Social Psychology, 46,* 190–207.

Schachter, S. (1959). *The psychology of affiliation: Experimental studies of the sources of gregariousness.* Stanford, CA: Stanford University Press.

Schachter, S. (1964). The interaction of cognitive and physiological determinants of emotional state. In L. Berkowitz (Ed.), *Advances in experimental social psychology* (Vol. 1, pp. 49–80). New York: Academic Press.

Schachter, S., & Singer, J. (1962). Cognitive, social, and physiological determinants of the emotional state. *Psychological Review, 69,* 379–399.

Schachter, S., & Singer, J. (1979). Comments on the Maslach and Marshall-Zimbardo experiments. *Journal of Personality and Social Psychology, 37,* 989–995.

Schafer, R. B., & Keith, P. M. (1980). Equity and depression among married couples. *Social Psychology Quarterly, 43,* 430–435.

Schaller, M., Park, J. H., & Faulkner, J. (2003). Prehistoric dangers and contemporary prejudices. *European Review of Social Psychology, 14,* 105–137.

Schaller, C., Park, J. H., & Mueller, A. (2003). Fear of the dark: Interactive effects of beliefs about danger and ambient darkness on ethnic stereotypes. *Personality and Social Psychology Bulletin, 29,* 637–649.

Scharfe, E., & Bartholomew, K. (1994). Reliability and stability of adult attachment patterns. *Personal Relationships, 1,* 23–43.

Scheck, B., Neufeld, P., & Dwyer, J. (2000). *Actual innocence: Five days to execution and other dispatches from the wrongly convicted.* New York: Doubleday.

Scheepers, D., & Ellemers, N. (2005). When the pressure is up: The assessment of social identity threat in low and high status groups. *Journal of Experimental Social Psychology, 41,* 192–200.

Scheepers, D., Ellemers, N., & Sintemaartensdijk, N. (2009). Suffering from the possibility of status loss: Physiological responses to social identity threat in high status groups. *European Journal of Social Psychology, 39,* 1075–1092.

Scheepers, D., Spears, R., Doosje, B., & Manstead, A. S. R. (2006). The social functions of ingroup bias: Creating, confirming, or changing social reality. *European Review of Social Psychology, 17,* 359–396.

Scheier, M. F., & Carver, C. S. (1983). Two sides of the self: One for you and one for me. In J. Suls and A. G. Greenwald (Eds.), *Psychological perspectives on the self* (Vol. 2, pp. 123–157). Hillsdale, NJ: Erlbaum.

Scheier, M. F., & Carver, C. S. (1985). Optimism, coping, and health: Assessment and implications of generalized outcome expectancies. *Health Psychology, 4,* 219–247.

Scheier, M. F., & Carver, C. S. (1992). Effects of optimism on psychological and physical well-being: Theoretical overview and empirical update. *Cognitive Therapy and Research, 16,* 201–228.

Schel, A. M., Tranquilli, S., & Zuberbühler, K. (2009). The alarm call system of two species of black-and-white colobus monkeys (Colobus polykomos and Colobus guereza). *Journal of Comparative Psychology, 123,* 136–150.

Scher, S. J., & Cooper, J. (1989). Motivational basis of dissonance: The singular role of behavioral consequences. *Journal of Personality and Social Psychology, 56,* 899–906.

Schimel, J., Arndt, J., Pyszczynski, T., & Greenberg, J. (2001). Being accepted for who we are: Evidence that social validation of the intrinsic self reduces general defensiveness. *Journal of Personality and Social Psychology, 80,* 35–52.

Schimmack, U., Oishi, S., & Diener, E. (2005). Individualism: A valid and important dimension of cultural differences between nations. *Personality and Social Psychology Review, 9,* 17–31.

Schittekatte, M., & van Hiel, A. (1996). Effects of partially shared information and awareness of unshared information on information sampling. *Small Group Research, 27,* 431–448.

Schlauch, R. C., Lang, A. R., Plant, E. A., Christensen, R., & Donohue, K. F. (2009). Effect of alcohol on race-biased responding: The moderating role of internal and external motivations to respond without prejudice. *Journal of Studies on Alcohol and Drugs, 70,* 328–336.

Schlenker, B. R. (1982). Translating actions into attitudes: An identity-analytic approach to the explanation of social conduct. In L. Berkowitz (Ed.), *Advances in experimental social psychology* (Vol. 15, pp. 193–247). New York: Academic Press.

Schlenker, B. R. (2003). Self-presentation. In M. R. Leary & J. P. Tangney (Eds.), *Handbook of self and identity* (pp. 492–518). New York: Guilford.

Schlenker, B. R., & Trudeau, J. V. (1990). The impact of self-presentations on private self-beliefs: Effects of prior self-beliefs and misattribution. *Journal of Personality and Social Psychology, 58,* 22–32.

Schlenker, B. R., Weigold, M. F., & Hallam, J. R. (1990). Self-serving attributions in social context: Effects of self-esteem and social pressure. *Journal of Personality and Social Psychology, 58,* 855–863.

Schmader, T., & Johns, M. (2003). Converging evidence that stereotype threat reduces working memory capacity. *Journal of Personality and Social Psychology, 85,* 440–452.

Schmader, T., Johns, M., & Forbes, C. (2008). An integrated process model of stereotype threat effects on performance. *Psychological Review, 115,* 336–356.

Schmeichel, B. J., & Vohs, K. (2009). Self-affirmation and self-control: Affirming core values counteracts ego depletion. *Journal of Personality and Social Psychology, 96,* 770–782.

Schmitt, D. P. (2003). Universal sex differences in the desire for sexual variety: Tests from 52 nations, 6 continents, and 13 islands. *Journal of Personality and Social Psychology, 85,* 85–104.

Schmitt, M. T., Branscrombe, N. R., Kobrynowicz, D., & Owen, S. (2002). Perceiving discrimination against one's gender group has different implications for well-being in women and men. *Personality and Social Psychology Bulletin, 28,* 197–210.

Schmitt, M. T., Branscombe, N. R., Silvia, P. J., Garcia, D. M., & Spears, R. (2006). Categorizing at the group-level in response to intragroup social comparisons: A self-categorization theory integration of self-evaluation and social identity motives. *European Journal of Social Psychology, 36,* 297–314.

Schmitt, M. T., & Maes, J. (2002). Stereotypic ingroup bias as self-defense against relative deprivation: Evidence from a longitudinal study of the German unification process. *European Journal of Social Psychology, 32,* 309–326.

Schnake, S. B., & Ruscher, J. B. (1998). Modern racism as a predictor of the linguistic intergroup bias. *Journal of Language and Social Psychology, 17,* 484–491.

Schneider, D. J. (1973). Implicit personality theory: A review. *Psychological Bulletin, 79,* 294–309.

Schneider, D. M., & Watkins, M. J. (1996). Response conformity in recognition testing. *Psychonomic Bulletin & Review, 3,* 481–485.

Schneider, S. G., Taylor, S. E., Hammen, C., Kemeny, M. E., & Dudley, J. (1991). Factors influencing suicide intent in gay and bisexual suicide ideators: Differing models for men with and without human immunodeficiency virus. *Journal of Personality and Social Psychology, 61,* 776–778.

Schneider, M. E., Major, B., Luhtanen, R., & Crocker, J. (1996). Social stigma and the potential costs of assumptive help. *Personality and Social Psychology Bulletin, 22,* 201–209.

Schonert-Reichl, K. A. (1999). Relations of peer acceptance, friendship adjustment, and social behavior to moral reasoning during early adolescence. *Journal of Early Adolescence, 19,* 249–279.

Schooler, D. (2008). Real women have curves: A longitudinal investigation of TV and the body image development of Latina adolescents. *Journal of Adolescent Research, 23,* 132–153.

Schuldt, J. P., Konrath, S. H., & Schwarz, N. (2011). "Global warming" or "climate change"? whether the planet is warming depends on question wording. *Public Opinion Quarterly, 75,* 115–124.

Schultheiss, O. C., & Brunstein, J. C. (2000). Choice of difficult tasks as a strategy of compensating for identity-relevant failure. *Journal of Research in Personality, 34,* 269–277.

Schultz, B., Ketrow, S. M., & Urban, D. M. (1995). Improving decision quality in the small group: The role of the reminder. *Small Group Research, 26,* 521–541.

Schulz, R. (1976). Effects of control and predictability on the physical and psychological well-being of the institutionalized aged. *Journal of Personality and Social Psychology, 33,* 563–573.

Schuster, M. A., Stein, B. D., Jaycox, L. H., Collins, R. L., Marshall, G. N., Elliott, M. N., Zhou, A. J., Kanouse, D. E., Morrison, J. L., & Berry, S. H. (2001). A national survey of stress reactions after the September 11, 2001, terrorist attacks. *New England Journal of Medicine, 345,* 1507–1512.

Schwartz, C. E., Keyl, P. M., Marcum, J. P., & Bode, R. (2009). Helping others shows differential benefits on health and well-being for male and female teens. *Journal of Happiness Studies, 10,* 431–448.

Schwartz, S. H. (1990). Individualism-collectivism: Critique and proposed refinements. *Journal of Cross-Cultural Psychology, 21,* 139–157.

Schwartz, S. H., & Gottlieb, A. (1980). Bystander anonymity and reaction to emergencies. *Journal of Personality and Social Psychology, 39,* 418–430.

Schwarz, N. (1990). Feelings as information: Information and motivational functions as affective states. In E. T. Higgins et al. (Eds.), *Handbook of motivation and cognition: Foundations of social behavior* (Vol. 2, pp. 527–561). New York: Guilford.

Schwarz, N. (1999). Self-reports: How the questions shape the answers. *American Psychologist, 54,* 93–105.

Schwarz, N., Bless, H., & Bohner, G. (1991). Mood and persuasion: Affective states influence the processing of persuasive communications. In M. P. Zanna (Ed.), *Advances in experimental social psychology* (Vol. 24, pp. 161–199). New York: Academic Press.

Schwarz, N., Hippler, H. J., Deutsch, B., & Strack, F. (1985). Response scales: Effects of category range on reported behavior and comparative judgments. *Public Opinion Quarterly, 49,* 388–395.

Schwarz, N., Oyserman, D., & Peytcheva, E. (2010). Cognition, communication, and culture: Implications for the survey response process. In J. Harkness et al. (Eds.), *Survey methods in multinational, multiregional and multicultural contexts.* New York: Wiley.

Schwarzwald, J., Raz, M., & Zvibel, M. (1979). The applicability of the door-in-the-face technique when established behavioral customs exist. *Journal of Applied Social Psychology, 9,* 576–586.

Scott, L., & O'Hara, M. W. (1993). Self-discrepancies in clinically anxious and depressed university students. *Journal of Abnormal Psychology, 102,* 282–287.

Seacat, J. D., & Mickelson, K. D. (2009). Stereotype threat and the exercise/dietary health intentions of overweight women. *Journal of Health Psychology, 14,* 556–567.

Sears, D. O., & Henry, P. J. (2005). Over thirty years later: A contemporary look at symbolic racism. In M. P. Zanna (Ed.), *Advances in experimental social psychology* (Vol. 37, pp. 95–150). San Diego: Elsevier.

Sedikides, C. (1992). Attentional effects on mood are moderated by chronic self-conception valence. *Personality and Social Psychology Bulletin, 18,* 580–584.

Sedikides, C. (1993). Assessment, enhancement, and verification determinants of the self-evaluation process. *Journal of Personality and Social Psychology, 65,* 317–338.

Sedikides, C., & Anderson, C. A. (1994). Causal perceptions of intertrait relations: The glue that holds person types together. *Personality and Social Psychology Bulletin, 20,* 294–302.

Sedikides, C., Gaertner, L., & Toguchi, Y. (2003). Pancultural self-enhancement. *Journal of Personality and Social Psychology, 84,* 60–79.

Sedikides, C., Gaertner, L., & Vevea, J. L. (2005). Pancultural self-enhancement reloaded: A meta-analytic reply to Heine (2005). *Journal of Personality and Social Psychology, 89,* 539–551.

Sedikides, C., & Gregg, A. P. (2008). Self-enhancement: Food for thought. *Perspectives on Psychological Science, 3,* 102–116.

Sedikides, C., & Jackson, J. M. (1990). Social impact theory: A field test of source strength, source immediacy and number of targets. *Basic and Applied Social Psychology, 11,* 273–281.

Sedikides, C., & Spencer, S. J. (Eds.). (2007). *The self.* New York: Psychology Press.

Seeds, P. M., Harkness, K. L., & Quilty, L. C. (2010). Parental maltreatment, bullying, and adolescent depression: Evidence for the mediating role of perceived social support. *Journal of Clinical Child and Adolescent Psychology, 39,* 681–692.

Segerstrom, S. C. (2006a). *Breaking Murphy's law: How optimists get what they want from life and pessimists can too.* New York: Guilford Press.

Segerstrom, S. C. (2006b). How does optimism suppress immunity? Evaluation of three affective pathways. *Health Psychology, 25,* 653–657.

Segerstrom, S. C., & Miller, G. E. (2004). Psychological stress and the human immune system: A meta-analytic study of 30 years of inquiry. *Psychological Bulletin, 130,* 601–630.

Seguin, J. R., & Zelazo, P. D. (2005). Executive function in early physical aggression. In R. E. Tremblay, W. W. Hartup, & J. Archer (Eds.), *Developmental origins of aggression* (pp. 307–329). New York: Guilford.

Seih, Y., Chung, Cindy K., & Pennebaker, James W. (2011). Experimental manipulations of perspective taking and perspective switching in expressive writing. *Cognition and Emotion, 25,* 926–938.

Seijts, G. H., & Latham, G. P. (2000). The effects of goal setting and group size on performance in a social dilemma. *Canadian Journal of Behavioural Science, 32,* 104–116.

Sekaquaptewa, D., Espinoza, P., Thompson, M., Vargas, P., & von Hippel, W. (2003). Stereotypic explanatory bias: Implicit stereotyping as a predictor of discrimination. *Journal of Experimental Social Psychology, 39,* 75–82.

Sekaquaptewa, D., & Thompson, M. (2003). Solo status, stereotype threat, and performance expectancies: Their effects on women's performance. *Journal of Experimental Social Psychology, 39,* 68–74.

Seligman, M. E. P. (1975). *On depression, development, and death.* San Francisco: Freeman.

Seligman, M. E. P. (1991). *Learned optimism.* New York: Knopf.

Sellers, R. M., & Shelton, J. N. (2003). The role of racial identity in perceived racial discrimination. *Journal of Personality and Social Psychology, 84,* 1079–1092.

Selye, H. (1936). A syndrome produced by diverse nocuous agents. *Nature, 138,* 32.

Senju, A., & Johnson, M. (2009). The eye contact effect: Mechanisms and development. *Trends in Cognitive Sciences, 13,* 127–134.

Serbin, L. A., Poulin-Dubois, D., & Eichstedt, J. A. (2002). Infants' response to gender-inconsistent events. *Infancy, 3,* 531–542.

Seto, M. C., Marc, A., & Barbaree, H. E. (2001). The role of pornography in the etiology of sexual aggression. *Aggression and Violent Behavior, 6,* 35–53.

Seyfarth, R. M., & Cheney, D. L. (1984). Grooming, alliances and reciprocal altruism in vervet monkeys. *Nature, 308,* 541–543.

Shackelford, T. K. (2001). Cohabitation, marriage, and murder: Woman-killing by male romantic partners. *Aggressive Behavior, 27,* 284–291.

Shackelford, T. K., & Goetz, A. T. (2005). When we hurt the ones we love: Predicting violence against women from men's mate retention tactics. In S. M. Platek & T. K. Shackelford (Eds.), *Human paternal uncertainty and anti-cuckoldry tactics: How males deal with female infidelity.* Cambridge: Cambridge University Press.

Shackelford, T. K., & Larsen, R. J. (1999). Facial attractiveness and physical health. *Evolution and Human Behavior, 20,* 71–76.

Shanab, M. E., & Yahya, K. A. (1977). A behavioral study of obedience in children. *Journal of Personality and Social Psychology, 35,* 530–536.

Shanab, M. E., & Yahya, K. A. (1978). A cross cultural study of obedience. *Bulletin of the Psychonomic Society, 11,* 267–269.

Shapiro, P. N., & Penrod, S. (1986). Meta-analysis of facial identification studies. *Psychological Bulletin, 100,* 139–156.

Shaver, K. G. (1970). Defensive attribution: Effects of severity and relevance on the responsibility assigned for an accident. *Journal of Personality and Social Psychology, 14,* 101–113.

Shaver, P. R., & Mikulincer, M. (2012). In Van Lange P. A. M., Kruglanski A. W. and Higgins E. T. (Eds.), *Attachment theory.* Thousand Oaks, CA: Sage Publications Ltd.

Shaw, J. S., III (1996). Increases in eyewitness confidence resulting from postevent questioning. *Journal of Experimental Psychology: Applied, 2,* 126–146.

Shelton, J. N., & Richeson, J. A. (2007). Interracial interactions: A relational approach. In M. P. Zanna (Ed.), *Advances in experimental social psychology.* San Diego, CA: Elsevier.

Shelton, J. N., Richeson, J. A., & Bergsieker, H. B. (2009). Interracial friendship development and attributional biases. *Journal of Social and Personal Relationships, 26,* 179-193.

Shepela, S. T., Cook, J., Horlitz, E., Leal, R., Luciano, S., Lutfy, E., Miller, C., Mitchell, G., & Worden, E. (1999). Courageous resistance: A special case of altruism. *Theory and Psychology, 9,* 787–805.

Sheppard, B. H. (1985). Justice is no simple matter: Case for elaborating our model of procedural fairness. *Journal of Personality and Social Psychology, 49,* 953–962.

Shepperd, J. A. (1993). Productivity loss in performance groups: A motivation analysis. *Psychological Bulletin, 113,* 67–81.

Shepperd, J. A., & Taylor, K. M. (1999). Social loafing and expectancy-value theory. *Personality and Social Psychology Bulletin, 25,* 1147–1158.

Sherer, M. (2007). Advice and help-seeking intentions among youth in Israel: Ethnic and gender differences. *Journal of Sociology & Social Welfare, 34,* 53–76.

Sherif, M. (1936). *The psychology of social norms.* New York: Harper.

Sherif, M. (1966). *In common predicament: Social psychology of intergroup conflict and cooperation.* Boston: Houghton Mifflin.

Sherif, M., Harvey, L. J., White, B. J., Hood, W. R., & Sherif, C.W. (1961). *The Robbers Cave experiment: Intergroup conflict and cooperation.* Middletown, CT: Wesleyan University Press. (Reprinted in 1988)

Sherman, D. K., Bunyan, D. P., Creswell, J. D., & Jaremka, L. M. (2009). Psychological vulnerability and stress: The effects of self-affirmation on sympathetic nervous system responses to naturalistic stressors. *Health Psychology, 28,* 554–562.

Sherman, J. W., Kruschke, J. K., Sherman, S. J., Percy, E. J., Petrocelli, J. V., & Conrey, F. R. (2009). Attentional processes in stereotype formation: A common model for category accentuation and illusory correlation. *Journal of Personality and Social Psychology, 96,* 305–323.

Sherman, J. W., Stroessner, S. J., Conrey, F. R., & Azam, O. (2005). Prejudice and stereotype maintenance processes: Attention, attribution, and individuation. *Journal of Personality and Social Psychology, 89,* 607–622.

Shih, M., Pittinsky, T. L., & Ambady, N. (1999). Stereotype susceptibility: Identity salience and shifts in quantitative performance. *Psychological Science, 10,* 80–83.

Shotland, R. L., & Heinold, W. D. (1985). Bystander response to arterial bleeding: Helping skills, the decision-making process, and differentiating the helping response. *Journal of Personality and Social Psychology, 49,* 347–356.

Shotland, R. L., & Stebbins, C. A. (1980). Bystander response to rape: Can a victim attract help? *Journal of Applied Social Psychology, 10,* 510–527.

Shotland, R. L., & Stebbins, C. A. (1983). Emergency and cost as determinants of helping behavior and the slow accumulation of social psychological knowledge. *Social Psychology Quarterly, 46,* 36–46.

Shotland, R. L., & Straw, M. K. (1976). Bystander response to an assault: When a man attacks a woman. *Journal of Personality and Social Psychology, 34,* 990–999.

Shrauger, J. S., & Schoeneman, T. (1979). Symbolic interactionist view of the self-concept: Through the looking-glass darkly. *Psychological Bulletin, 86,* 549–573.

Shultz, S., & Dunbar, R. (2010). Encephalization is not a universal macroevolutionary phenomenon in mammals but is associated with sociality. *Proceedings of the National Academy of Sciences of the United States of America, 107,* 21582–21586

Sidanius, J., Haley, H., Molina, L., & Pratto, F. (2007). Vladimir's choice and the distribution of social resources: A group dominance perspective. *Group Processes and Intergroup Relations, 10,* 259–268.

Sidebotham, P., & Heron, J. (2006). Child maltreatment in the 'children of the nineties': A cohort study of risk factors. *Child Abuse & Neglect, 30,* 497–522.

Siegman, A. W., & Smith, T. W. (1994). *Anger, hostility, and the heart.* Hillsdale, NJ: Erlbaum.

Siever, L. (2008). Neurobiology of aggression and violence. *American Journal of Psychiatry, 165,* 429–442.

Silk, J. B., & House, B. R. (2011). Evolutionary foundations of human prosocial sentiments. *PNAS Proceedings of the National Academy of Sciences of the United States of America, 108,* 10910–10917.

Silke, A. (2003). Deindividuation, anonymity, and violence: Findings from Northern Ireland. *Journal of Social Psychology, 143,* 493–499.

Silverstein, B., Perdue, L., Peterson, B., & Kelly, E. (1986). The role of the mass media in promoting a thin standard of bodily attractiveness for women. *Sex Roles, 14,* 519–532.

Silvia, P. (2006). Reactance and the dynamics of disagreement: Multiple paths from threatened freedom to resistance to persuasion. *European Journal of Social Psychology, 36,* 673–685.

Silvia, Paul J., & Duval, T. S. (2001). Predicting the interpersonal targets of self-serving attributions. *Journal of Experimental Social Psychology, 37,* 333–340.

Simmons, R. G. (1978). Blacks and high self-esteem: A puzzle. *Social Psychology, 41,* 54–57.

Simon, H. A. (1956). Rational choice and the structure of the environment. *Psychological Review, 63,* 129–138.

Simpson, B., & Willer, R. (2008). Altruism and indirect reciprocity: The interaction of person and situation in prosocial behavior. *Social Psychology Quarterly, 71,* 37–52.

Simpson, J. A. (1987). The dissolution of romantic relationships: Factors involved in relationship stability and emotional distress. *Journal of Personality and Social Psychology, 53,* 683–692.

Simpson, J. A., Gangestad, S. W., & Lerma, M. (1990). Perception of physical attractiveness: Mechanisms involved in the maintenance of romantic relationships. *Journal of Personality and Social Psychology, 59,* 1192–1201.

Simpson, J. A., & Kenrick, D. T. (Eds.) (1997). *Evolutionary social psychology.* Mahwah, NJ: Erlbaum.

Sinatra, G. M., Kardash, C. M., Taasoobshirazi, G., & Lombardi, D. (2012). Promoting attitude change and expressed willingness to take action toward climate change in college students. *Instructional Science, 40,* 1–17.

Sinclair, L., & Kunda, Z. (1999). Reactions to a black professional: Motivated inhibition and activation of conflicting stereotypes. *Journal of Personality and Social Psychology, 77,* 885–904.

Sinclair, L., & Kunda, Z. (2000). Motivated stereotyping of women: She's fine if she praised me but incompetent if she criticized me. *Personality and Social Psychology Bulletin, 26,* 1329–1342.

Sinclair, R. C., Hoffman, C., Mark, M. M., Martin, L. M., & Pickering, T. L. (1994). Construct accessibility and the misattribution of arousal: Schachter and Singer revisited. *Psychological Science, 5,* 15–19.

Singelis, T. M. (1994). The measurement of independent and interdependent self-construals. *Personality and Social Psychology Bulletin, 20,* 580–591.

Singer, T., Seymour, B., O'Doherty, J. P., Stephan, K. E., Dolan, R. J., & Frith, C. D. (2006). Empathic neural responses are modulated by the perceived fairness of others. *Nature, 439,* 466–469.

Singh, D. (1993). Adaptive significance of female physical attractiveness: Role of waist-to-hip ratio. *Journal of Personality and Social Psychology, 65,* 293–307.

Singh, D. (1995). Female judgment of male attractiveness and desirability for relationships: Role of waist-to-hip ratio and financial status. *Journal of Personality and Social Psychology, 69,* 1089–1101.

Singh, D., & Randall, P. K. (2007). Beauty is in the eye of the plastic surgeon: Waist-hip ratio (WHR) and women's attractiveness. *Personality and Individual Differences, 43,* 329–340.

Sistrunk, F., & McDavid, J. W. (1971). Sex variable in conforming behavior. *Journal of Personality and Social Psychology, 17,* 200–207.

Siu, A. M. H., Cheng, H. C. H., & Leung, M. C. M. (2006). Pro-social norms as a positive youth development construct: Conceptual bases and implications for curriculum development. *International Journal of Adolescent Medicine and Health, 18,* 451–457.

Skinner, E. A. (1996). A guide to constructs of control. *Journal of Personality and Social Psychology, 71,* 549–570.

Skinner, E. A., Edge, K., Altman, J., & Sherwood, H. (2003). Searching for the structure of coping: A review and critique of category systems for classifying ways of coping. *Psychological Bulletin, 129,* 216–269.

Sklar, L. S., & Anisman, H. (1981). Stress and cancer. *Psychological Bulletin, 89,* 369–406.

Skov, R. B., & Sherman, S. J. (1986). Information-gathering processes: Diagnosticity, hypothesis confirmatory strategies, and perceived hypothesis confirmation. *Journal of Experimental Social Psychology, 22,* 93–121.

Skowronski, J. J., & Carlston, D. E. (1989). Negativity and extremity biases in impression formation: A review of explanations. *Psychology Bulletin, 105,* 131–142.

Slamecka, N. J., & Graff, P. (1978). The generation effect: Delineation of a phenomenon. *Journal of Experimental Psychology: Human Learning and Memory, 4,* 592–604.

Slovic, P. (2000). *The perception of risk.* London: Earthscan.

Slovic, P., Fischhoff, B., & Lichtenstein, S. (1982). Facts versus fears: Understanding perceived risk. In D. Kahneman, P. Slovic, & A. Tversky (Eds.), *Judgment under uncertainty: Heuristics and biases* (pp. 463–489). New York: Cambridge University Press.

Smart Richman, L., & Leary, M. R. (2009). Reactions to discrimination, stigmatization, ostracism, and other forms of interpersonal rejection: A multimotive model. *Psychological Review, 116,* 365–383.

Smeaton, G., Byrne, D., & Murnen, S. K. (1989). The repulsion hypothesis revisited: Similarity irrelevance or dissimilarity bias? *Journal of Personality and Social Psychology, 56,* 54–59.

Smith, A., Jussim, L., & Eccles, J. (1999). Do self-fulfilling prophecies accumulate, dissipate, or remain stable over time? *Journal of Personality and Social Psychology, 77,* 548–565.

Smith, C. T., & Nosek, B. A. (2010). Implicit Association Test. In I. B. Weiner & W. E. Craighead (Eds.), *Corsini Encyclopedia of Psychology.* Hoboken, NJ: Wiley.

Smith, D. L. (2007). *The most dangerous animal: Human nature and the origins of war.* New York: St. Martin's.

Smith, E. R., & Collins, E. C. (2009). Contextualizing person perception: Distributed social cognition. *Psychological Review, 116,* 343–364.

Smith, H. J., Spears, R., & Hamstra, I. J. (1999). Social identity and the context of relative deprivation. In N. Ellemers, R. Spears, & I. J. Hamstra (Eds.), *Social identity: Context, commitment, content* (pp. 205–229). Oxford, England: Blackwell.

Smith, M. L., Glass, G. V., & Miller, T. I. (1980). *The benefits of psychotherapy.* Baltimore: Johns Hopkins University Press.

Smith, N. K., Cacioppo, J. T., Larsen, J. T., & Chartrand, T. L. (2003). May I have your attention, please: Electrocortical responses to positive and negative stimuli. *Neuropsychologia, 41,* 171–183.

Smith, P. B., & Bond, M. H. (1993). *Social psychology across cultures: Analysis and perspective.* New York: Harvester/ Wheatsheaf.

Smith, S. M., McIntosh, W. D., & Bazzani, D. G. (1999). Are the beautiful good in Hollywood? An investigation of the beauty-and-goodness stereotype on film. *Basic and Applied Social Psychology, 21,* 69–80.

Smith, S. S., & Richardson, D. (1983). Amelioration of deception and harm in psychological research: The important role of debriefing. *Journal of Personality and Social Psychology, 44,* 1075–1082.

Smith, T.W., Snyder, C. R., & Perkins, S. C. (1983). The self-serving function of hypochondriacal complaints: Physical symptoms as self-handicapping strategies. *Journal of Personality and Social Psychology, 44,* 787–797.

Smith, V. L., & Kassin, S. M. (1993). Effects of the dynamite charge on the deliberations of deadlocked mock juries. *Law and Human Behavior, 17,* 625–643.

Smitherman, H. O. (1992). Helping: The importance of cost/ reward considerations on likelihood to help. *Psychological Reports, 71,* 305–306.

Smolak, L., & Thompson, J. K. (Eds.). (2009). *Body image, eating disorders, and obesity in youth: Assessment, prevention, and treatment* (2nd ed.). Washington, DC: American Psychological Association.

Snibbe, A. C., Kitayama, S., Markus, H. R., & Suzuki, T. (2003). They saw a game: A Japanese and American (football) field study. *Journal of Cross-Cultural Psychology, 34,* 581–595.

Snyder, C. R., & Higgins, R. L. (1988). Excuses: Their effective role in the negotiation of reality. *Psychological Bulletin, 104,* 23–35.

Snyder, C. R., Higgins, R. L., & Stucky, R. J. (1983). *Excuses: Masquerades in search of grace.* New York: Wiley.

Snyder, C. R., Lassegard, M. A., & Ford, C. E. (1986). Distancing after group success and failure: Basking in reflected glory and cutting off reflected failure. *Journal of Personality and Social Psychology, 51,* 382–388.

Snyder, M. (1974). The self-monitoring of expressive behavior. *Journal of Personality and Social Psychology, 30,* 526–537.

Snyder, M. (1987). *Public appearances private/realities: The psychology of self-monitoring.* New York: Freeman.

Snyder, M. (1993). Basic research and practical problems: The promise of a "functional" personality and social psychology. *Personality and Social Psychology Bulletin, 19,* 251–264.

Snyder, M., & DeBono, K. (1985). Appeals to image and claims about quality: Understanding the psychology of advertising. *Journal of Personality and Social Psychology, 49,* 586–597.

Snyder, M., & Gangestad, S. (1986). On the nature of self-monitoring: Matters of assessment, matters of validity. *Journal of Personality and Social Psychology, 51,* 125–139.

Snyder, M., & Monson, T. C. (1975). Persons, situations, and the control of social behavior. *Journal of Personality and Social Psychology, 32,* 637–644.

Snyder, M., & Omoto, A. (2008). Volunteerism: Social issues perspectives and social policy implications. *Social Issues and Policy Review, 2,* 1–36.

Snyder, M., & Stukas, A. A. (1999). Interpersonal processes: The interplay of cognitive, motivational, and behavioral activities in social interaction. *Annual Review of Psychology, 50,* 273–303.

Snyder, M., & Swann, W. B., Jr. (1978). Behavioral confirmation in social interaction: From social perception to social reality. *Journal of Personality and Social Psychology, 36,* 1202–1212.

Snyder, M., Tanke, E. D., & Berscheid, E. (1977). Social perception and interpersonal behavior: On the self-fulfilling nature of social stereotypes. *Journal of Personality and Social Psychology, 35,* 656–666.

Sober, E., & Wilson, D. S. (1998). *Unto others: The evolution and psychology of unselfish behavior.* Cambridge, MA: Harvard University Press.

Soll, J. B., & Larrick, R. P. (2009). Strategies for revising judgment: How (and how well) people use others' opinions. *Journal of Experimental Psychology: Learning, Memory, and Cognition, 35,* 780–805.

Sommers, S. R., & Norton, M. I. (2008). Race and jury selection: Psychological perspectives on the peremptory challenge debate. *American Psychologist, 63,* 527–539.

Song, H., & Schwarz, N. (2009). If it's difficult to pronounce, it must be risky: Fluency, familiarity, and risk perception. *Psychological Science, 20,* 135–138.

Son Hing, L. S., Chung-Yan, G. A., Hamilton, L. K., & Zanna, M. P. (2008). A two-dimensional model that employs explicit and implicit attitudes to characterize prejudice. *Journal of Personality and Social Psychology, 94,* 971–987.

Sparks, J. R., & Rapp, D. N. (2011). Readers reliance on source credibility in the service of comprehension. *Journal of Experimental Psychology: Learning, Memory, and Cognition, 37,* 230–247.

Spears, R. (2002). Four degrees of stereotype formation: Differentiation by any means necessary. In C. McGarty, V. Y. Yzerbyt, & R. Spears (Eds.), *Stereotypes as explanations: The formation of meaningful beliefs about social groups* (pp. 127–156). Cambridge, UK: Cambridge University Press.

Spencer, B., & Castano, E. (2007). Social class is dead. Long live social class! Stereotype threat among low socioeconomic status individuals. *Social Justice Research, 20,* 418–432.

Spencer, S. J., Fein, S., Wolfe, C. T., Fong, C., & Dunn, M. A. (1998). Automatic activation of stereotypes: The role of self-image threat. *Personality and Social Psychology Bulletin, 24,* 1139–1152.

Spencer, S. J., Fein, S., Zanna, M., & Olson, J.M. (Eds.) (2003). *Motivated social perception: The Ontario symposium* (Vol. 9). Mahwah, NJ: Erlbaum.

Spencer, S. J., Steele, C. M., & Quinn, D. M. (1999). Stereotype threat and women's math performance. *Journal of Experimental Social Psychology, 35,* 4–28.

Spencer-Rodgers, J., Boucher, H. C., Mori, S. C., Wang, L., & Peng, K. (2009). The dialectical self-concept: Contradiction, change, and holism in East Asian cultures. *Personality and Social Psychology Bulletin, 35,* 29–44.

Spiegel, D. (1993). Social support: How friends, family, and groups can help. In D. Goleman & J. Gurin (Eds.), *Mind body medicine: How to use your mind for better health* (pp. 331–350). Yonkers, NY: Consumer Reports Books.

Spivey, C. B., & Prentice-Dunn, S. (1990). Assessing the directionality of deindividuated behavior: Effects of deindividuation, modeling, and private self-consciousness on aggressive and prosocial responses. *Basic and Applied Social Psychology, 11,* 387–403.

Sporer, S. L., Penrod, S. D., Read, J. D., & Cutler, B. L. (1995). Choosing, confidence, and accuracy: A meta-analysis of the confidence-accuracy relation in eyewitness identification studies. *Psychological Bulletin, 118,* 315–327.

Sprafkin, J. N., Liebert, R. M., & Poulos, R. W. (1975). Effects of a prosocial televised example on children's helping. *Journal of Experimental Child Psychology, 20,* 119–126.

Sprecher, S. (1994). Two sides to the breakup of dating relationships. *Personal Relationships, 1,* 199–222.

Sprecher, S. (2001). Equity and social exchange in dating couples: Associations with satisfaction, commitment, and stability. *Journal of Marriage and the Family, 63,* 599–613.

Sprecher, S., & Fehr, B. (2011). Dispositional attachment and relationship-specific attachment as predictors of compassionate love for a partner. *Journal of Social and Personal Relationships, 28,* 558–574.

Sprecher, S., & Regan, P. C. (1998). Passionate and companionate love in courting and young married couples. *Sociological Inquiry, 68,* 163–185.

Sprecher, S., Sullivan, Q., & Hatfield, E. (1994). Mate selection preferences: Gender differences examined in a national sample. *Journal of Personality and Social Psychology, 66,* 1074–1080.

Sprecher, S., Sullivan, Q., & Hatfield, E. (1994). Mate selection preferences: Gender differences examined in a national sample. *Journal of Personality and Social Psychology, 66,* 1074–1080.

Sprott, J. B., & Doob, A. N. (2010). Gendered treatment: Girls and treatment orders in bail court. *Canadian Journal of Criminology and Criminal Justice, 52,* 427–441.

Sriram, N., & Greenwald, A. G. (2009). The Brief Implicit Association Test. *Experimental Psychology, 56,* 283–294.

Staats, A. W., & Staats, C. K. (1958). Attitudes established by classical conditioning. *Journal of Abnormal and Social Psychology, 57,* 37–40.

Stahl, J., Wiese, H., & Schweinberger, S. R. (2008). Expertise and own-race bias in face processing: An event-related potential study. *Neuroreport: For Rapid Communication of Neuroscience Research, 19,* 583–587.

Stalans, L. J., & Diamond, S. S. (1990). Formation and change in lay evaluations of criminal sentencing: Misperception and discontent. *Law and Human Behavior, 14,* 199–214.

Stalder, D. R. (2008). Revisiting the issue of safety in numbers: The likelihood of receiving help from a group. *Social Influence, 3*(1), 24–33.

Stangor, C. (2009). The study of stereotyping, prejudice, and discrimination within social psychology: A quick history of theory and research. In T. D. Nelson (Ed.), *Handbook of prejudice, stereotyping, and discrimination* (pp. 1–22). New York: Psychology Press.

Stangor, C., & Lange, J. E. (1994). Mental representations of social groups: Advances in understanding stereotypes and stereotyping. In M. P. Zanna (Ed.), *Advances in experimental social psychology* (Vol. 26, pp. 357–416). San Diego, CA: Academic Press.

Stangor, C., Sechrist, G. B., & Jost, J. T. (2001). Changing racial beliefs by providing consensus information. *Personality and Social Psychology Bulletin, 27,* 486–496.

Stanton, A. L., Kirk, S. B., Cameron, C. L., & Danoff-Berg, S. (2000). Coping through emotional approach: Scale construction and validation. *Journal of Personality and Social Psychology, 78,* 1150–1169.

Stapel, D. A., & Koomen, W. (2000). How far do we go beyond the information given? The impact of knowledge activation on interpretation and inference. *Journal of Personality and Social Psychology, 78,* 19–37.

Stark, E. M., Shaw, J. D., & Duffy, M. K. (2007). Preference for group work, winning orientation, and social loafing behavior in groups. *Group & Organization Management, 32,* 699–723.

Starzyk, K., Fabrigar, L., Soryal, A., & Fanning, J. (2009). A painful reminder: The role of level and salience of attitude importance in cognitive dissonance. *Personality and Social Psychology Bulletin, 35,* 126–137.

Stasser, G. (1992). Pooling of unshared information during group discussions. In S. Worchel, W. Wood, & J. A. Simpson (Eds.), *Group process and productivity* (pp. 48–67). Newbury Park, CA: Sage.

Stasser, G., & Birchmeier, Z. (2003). Group creativity and collective choice. In P. B. Paulus & B. A. Nijstad (Eds.), *Group creativity: Innovation through collaboration* (pp. 85–109). New York: Oxford University.

Stasser, G., & Davis, J. H. (1981). Group decision making and social influence: A social interaction sequence model. *Psychological Review, 88,* 523–551.

Stasser, G., Kerr, N. L., & Bray, R. M. (1982). The social psychology of jury deliberations: Structure, process, and product. In N. Kerr & R. Bray (Eds.), *The psychology of the courtroom* (pp. 221–256). New York: Academic Press.

Stasser, G., & Titus, W. (2003). Hidden profiles: A brief history. *Psychological Inquiry, 14,* 304–313.

Statistics Canada (2006). *Converging gender roles: Perspectives on labour and income.* Catalogue no. 75-001-X.

Statistics Canada (2008). *Family violence in Canada. A statistical profile 2008.* Canadian Centre for Justice Statistics. Retrieved June 4, 2012, from http://www.statcan.gc.ca/pub/85-224-x/85-224-x2008000-eng.pdf

Statistics Canada (2009). *General Social Survey on Victimization.*

Statistics Canada (2010). *Canada Survey of Giving, Volunteering and Participating.*

Statistics Canada (2010). *General Social Survey: Overview of the Time Use of Canadians.*

Staub, E. (1996). Cultural-societal roots of violence: The examples of genocidal violence and of contemporary youth violence in the United States. *American Psychologist, 51,* 117–132.

Staub, E. (2004). Understanding and responding to group violence: Genocide, mass killing, and terrorism. In F. M. Moghaddam, & A. J. Marsella (Eds.), *Understanding terrorism: Psychosocial roots, consequences, and interventions* (pp. 151–168). Washington, DC: American Psychological Association.

Staub, E., & Vollhardt, J. (2008). Altruism born of suffering: The roots of caring and helping after victimization and other trauma. *American Journal of Orthopsychiatry, 78,* 267–280.

Staw, B. M. (1997). The escalation of commitment: An update and appraisal. In Z. Shapira (Ed.), *Organizational decision making. Cambridge series on judgement and decision making* (pp. 191–215). New York: Cambridge University Press.

Steblay, N., Besirevic, J., Fulero, S., & Jiminez-Lorente, B. (1999). The effects of pretrial publicity on juror verdicts: A meta-analytic review. *Law and Human Behavior, 23,* 219–235.

Steblay, N., Hosch, H. M., Culhane, S. E., & McWethy, A. (2006). The impact on juror verdicts of judicial instruction to disregard inadmissible evidence: A meta-analysis. *Law and Human Behavior, 30,* 469–492.

Steblay, N. K., Dysart, J. E., & Wells, G. L. (2011). Seventy-two tests of the sequential lineup superiority effect: A meta-analysis and policy discussion. *Psychology, Public Policy, and Law, 17,* 99–139.

Steblay, N. M. (1987). Helping behavior in rural and urban environments: A meta-analysis. *Psychological Bulletin, 102,* 346–356.

Steblay, N. M. (1997). Social influence in eyewitness recall: A meta-analytic review of lineup instruction effects. *Law and Human Behavior, 21,* 283–297.

Steele, C. M. (1988). The psychology of self-affirmation: Sustaining the integrity of the self. In L. Berkowitz (Ed.), *Advances in experimental social psychology* (Vol. 21, pp. 261–302). New York: Academic Press.

Steele, C. M. (1997). A threat in the air: How stereotypes shape intellectual identity and performance. *American Psychologist, 52,* 613–629.

Steele, C. M. (1999). Thin ice: "Stereotype threat" and black college students. *Atlantic Monthly, 284,* 44–47, 50–54.

Steele, C. M., & Aronson, J. (1995). Stereotype vulnerability and the intellectual test performance of African Americans. *Journal of Personality and Social Psychology, 69,* 797–811.

Steele, C. M., & Josephs, R. A. (1990). Alcohol myopia: Its prized and dangerous effects. *American Psychologist, 45,* 921–933.

Steele, C. M., Spencer, S. J., & Aronson, J. (2002). Contending with group image: The psychology of stereotype and social identity threat. In M. P. Zanna (Ed.), *Advances in experimental social psychology* (Vol. 34, pp. 379–440). San Diego, CA: Academic Press.

Steele, C. M., Spencer, S. J., & Lynch, M. (1993). Self-image resilience and dissonance: The role of affirmational resources. *Journal of Personality and Social Psychology, 64,* 885–896.

Stein, M. B., Walker, J. R., & Forde, D. R. (1996). Public-speaking fears in a community sample. *Archives of General Psychiatry, 53,* 169–174.

Steiner, I. D. (1972). *Group process and productivity.* New York: Academic Press.

Stel, M., van Baaren, Rick B., Blascovich, J., van Dijk, E., McCall, C., Pollmann, M. M. H., van Leeuwen, M. L. , Mastop, J., & Vonk, R. (2010). Effects of a priori liking on the elicitation of mimicry. *Experimental Psychology, 57,* 412–418.

Stepanikova, I., Triplett, J., & Simpson, B. (2011). Implicit racial bias and prosocial behavior. *Social Science Research, 40,* 1186–1195.

Stephan, W. G. (1986). The effects of school desegregation: An evaluation 30 years after Brown. In M. J. Saks & L. Saxe (Eds.), *Advances in applied social psychology* (Vol. 3, pp. 181–206). Hillsdale, NJ: Erlbaum.

Stephan, W. G., Renfro, C. L., Esses, V. M., Stephan, C. W., & Martin, T. (2005). The effects of feeling threatened on attitudes toward immigrants. *International Journal of Intercultural Relations, 29,* 1–19.

Stepper, S., & Strack, F. (1993). Proprioceptive determinants of emotional and nonemotional feelings. *Journal of Personality and Social Psychology, 64,* 211–220.

Sternberg, R. J. (1986). A triangular theory of love. *Psychological Review, 93,* 119–135.

Sternberg, R. J. (1999). *Cupid's arrow: The course of love through time.* New York: Cambridge University Press.

Sternberg, R. J., & Barnes, M. L. (Eds.) (1998). *The psychology of love.* New Haven, CT: Yale University Press.

Stewart, A. J., Sokol, M., Healy, J. M., Jr., & Chester, N. L. (1986). Longitudinal studies of psychological consequences of life changes in children and adults. *Journal of Personality and Social Psychology, 50,* 143–151.

Stewart, B. D., & Payne, B. K. (2008). Bringing automatic stereotyping under control: Implementation intentions as efficient means of thought control. *Personality and Social Psychology Bulletin, 34,* 1332–1345.

Stewart, T. L., Latu, I. M., Kawakami, K., & Myers, A. C. (2010). Consider the situation: Reducing automatic stereotyping through situational attribution training. *Journal of Experimental Social Psychology, 46,* 221–225.

Stewart-Williams, S. (2007). Altruism among kin vs. nonkin: Effects of cost of help and reciprocal exchange. *Evolution and Human Behavior, 28,* 193–198.

Stewart-Williams, S. (2008). Human beings as evolved nepotists: Exceptions to the rule and effects of cost of help. *Human Nature, 19,* 414–425.

Stirrat, M., Stulp, G., & Pollet, T. V. (2012). Male facial width is associated with death by contact violence: Narrow-faced males are more likely to die from contact violence. *Evolution and Human Behavior.*

Stoltzfus, N. (1996). *Resistance of the heart: Intermarriage and the Rosenstrasse protest in Nazi Germany.* New York: Norton.

Stone, J. (2003). Self-consistency for low self-esteem in dissonance processes: The role of self-standards. *Personality and Social Psychology Bulletin, 29,* 846–858.

Stone, J., Lynch, C. I., Sjomeling, M., & Darley, J. M. (1999). Stereotype threat effects on black and white athletic performance. *Journal of Personality and Social Psychology, 77,* 1213–1227.

Stone J., Perry, Z. W., & Darley, J. M. (1997). "White men can't jump": Evidence for the perceptual confirmation of racial stereotypes following a basketball game. *Basic and Applied Social Psychology, 19,* 291–306.

Stone, J., Wiegand, A. W., Cooper, J., & Aronson, E. (1997). When exemplification fails: Hypocrisy and the motive for self-integrity. *Journal of Personality and Social Psychology, 72,* 54–65.

Stone, W. F., Lederer, G., & Christie, R. (Eds.) (1993). *Strength and weakness: The authoritarian personality today.* New York: Springer-Verlag.

Stoner, J. A. F. (1961). *A comparison of individual and group decisions involving risk.* Unpublished manuscript, Massachusetts Institute of Technology, Cambridge, MA.

Strahan, E. J., Lafrance, A., Wilson, A. E., Ethier, N., Spencer, S. J., & Zanna, M. P. (2008). Victoria's dirty secret: How sociocultural norms influence adolescent girls and women. *Personality and Social Psychology Bulletin, 34,* 288–301.

Strahan, E. J., Spencer, S. J., & Zanna, M. P. (2002). Subliminal priming and persuasion: Striking while the iron is hot. *Journal of Experimental Social Psychology, 38,* 556–568.

Strauman, T. J. (1992). Self-guides, autobiographical memory, and anxiety and dysphoria: Toward a cognitive model of vulnerability to emotional distress. *Journal of Abnormal Psychology, 101,* 87–95.

Strauman, T. J., Lemieux, A. M., & Coe, C. L. (1993). Self-discrepancy and natural killer cell activity: Immunological consequences of negative self-evaluation. *Journal of Personality and Social Psychology, 64,* 1042–1052.

Strauman, T. J., Woods, T. E., Schneider, K. L., Kwapil, L., & Coe, C. L. (2004). Self-regulatory cognition and immune reactivity: Idiographic success and failure feedback effects on the natural killer cell. *Brain, Behavior, and Immunity, 18,* 544–554.

Straus, M. A. (1999). The controversy over domestic violence by women: A methodical, theoretical, and sociology of science analysis. In X. B. Arriaga & S. Oskamp (Eds.), *Violence in intimate relationships* (pp. 17–44). Thousand Oaks, CA: Sage.

Straus, M. A. (2000). *Beating the devil out of them: Corporal punishment in American families and its effects on children* (2nd ed.). New Brunswick, NJ: Transaction Publishers.

Straus, M. A., & Douglas, E. M. (2008). Research on spanking by parents: Implications for public policy. *The Family Psychologist: Bulletin of the Division of Family Psychology, 43,* 18–20.

Straus, M. A., & Ramirez, I. L. (2005). Gender symmetry in prevalence, severity, and chronicity of physical aggression against dating partners by University students in Mexico and the USA. In S. Fein, G. R. Goethals, & M. J. Sandstrom (Eds.), *Gender and aggression: Interdisciplinary perspectives.* Mahwah, NJ: Erlbaum.

Strentz, T., & Auerbach, S. M. (1988). Adjustment to the stress of simulated captivity: Effects of emotion-focused versus problem-focused preparation on hostages differing in locus of control. *Journal of Personality and Social Psychology, 55,* 652–660.

Striegel-Moore, R., & Smolak, L. (Eds.) (2001). *Eating disorders: Innovative directions in research and practice.* Washington, DC: American Psychological Association.

Strodtbeck, F. L., & Hook, L. (1961). The social dimensions of a twelve-man jury table. *Sociometry, 24,* 397–415.

Strodtbeck, F. L., James, R., & Hawkins, C. (1957). Social status in jury deliberations. *American Sociological Review, 22,* 713–719.

Stroebe, W. (2012). The truth about triplett (1898), but nobody seems to care. *Perspectives on Psychological Science, 7,* 54–57.

Stroessner, S. J., & Plaks, J. E. (2001). Illusory correlation and stereotype formation: Tracing the arc of research over a quarter century. In G. B. Moskowitz (Ed.), *Cognitive social psychology: The Princeton symposium on the legacy and future of social cognition* (pp. 247–259). Mahwah, NJ: Erlbaum.

Strohmetz, D. B., Rind, B., Fisher, R., & Lynn, M. (2002). Sweetening the till: The use of candy to increase restaurant tipping. *Journal of Applied Social Psychology, 32,* 300–309.

Strube, M. J. (2005). What did triplett really find? A contemporary analysis of the first experiment in social psychology. *The American Journal of Psychology, 118,* 271–286.

Struck, D. (2006, September 15). Gunman's writings presaged rampage; blog described fascination with death, laid out events that would unfold in Montreal. *Washington Post,* p. A12.

Struckman-Johnson, C., & Struckman-Johnson, D. (1994). Men pressured and forced into sexual experience. *Archives of Sexual Behavior, 23,* 93–114.

Studebaker, C. A., & Penrod, S. D. (1997). Pretrial publicity: The media, the law, and common sense. *Psychology, Public Policy, and Law, 3,* 428–460.

Stürmer, S., Snyder, M., Kropp, A., & Siem, B. (2006). Empathy-motivated helping: The moderating role of group membership. *Personality and Social Psychology Bulletin, 32,* 943–956.

Sue, S., Smith, R. E., & Caldwell, C. (1973). Effects of inadmissible evidence on the decisions of simulated jurors: A moral dilemma. *Journal of Applied Social Psychology, 3,* 345–353.

Suls, J. M., & Wheeler, L. (Eds.) (2000). *Handbook of social comparison: Theory and research.* New York: Plenum.

Supple, A. J., & Plunkett, S. W. (2011). Dimensionality and validity of the Rosenberg self-esteem scale for use with latino adolescents. *Hispanic Journal of Behavioral Sciences, 33,* 39–53.

Swaab, R. I., & Swaab. D. F. (2009). Sex differences in the effects of visual contact and eye contact in negotiations. *Journal of Experimental Social Psychology, 45,* 129–136.

Swami, V., & Allum, L. (2012). Perceptions of the physical attractiveness of the self, current romantic partners, and former partners. *Scandinavian Journal of Psychology, 53,* 89–95.

Swami, V., Campana, A. N., & Coles, R. (2012). Acceptance of cosmetic surgery among British female university students: Are there ethnic differences? *European Psychologist, 17,* 55–62.

Swami, V., & Furnham, A. (2008). *The psychology of physical attraction.* New York: Routledge/Taylor & Francis.

Swami, V., Jones, J., Einon, D., & Furnham, A. (2009). Mens preferences for womens profile waist-to-hip ratio, breast size, and ethnic group in britain and south africa. *British Journal of Psychology, 100,* 313–325.

Swann, W. B., Jr. (1984). Quest for accuracy in person perception: A matter of pragmatics. *Psychological Review, 91,* 457–477.

Swann, W. B., Jr. (1987). Identity negotiation: Where two roads meet. *Journal of Personality and Social Psychology, 53,* 1038–1051.

Swann, W. B., Jr. (1999). *Resilient identities: Self, relationships, and the construction of social reality.* New York: Basic Books.

Swann, W. B., Jr., & Bosson, J. K. (2010). Self and identity. In S. T. Fiske, D. T. Gilbert, & G. Lindzey (Eds.), *Handbook of social psychology* (5th ed.). New York: McGraw-Hill.

Swann, W. B., Jr., Chang-Schneider, C., & Larsen McClarty, K. (2007). Do people's self-views matter? Self-concept and self-esteem in everyday life. *American Psychologist, 62,* 84–94.

Swann, W. B., Jr., & Ely, R. J. (1984). A battle of wills: Self-verification versus behavioral confirmation. *Journal of Personality and Social Psychology, 46,* 1287–1302.

Swann, W. B., Jr., & Hill, C. A. (1982). When our identities are mistaken: Reaffirming self-conceptions through social interaction. *Journal of Personality and Social Psychology, 43,* 59–66.

Swann, W. B., Jr., Hixon, J. G., & De La Ronde, C. (1992). Embracing the bitter "truth": Negative self-concepts and marital commitment. *Psychological Science, 3,* 118–121.

Swann, W. B., Jr., Stein-Seroussi, A., & Giesler, B. J. (1992). Why people self-verify. *Journal of Personality and Social Psychology, 62,* 392–401.

Sweet, P. R. (October 1, 2001). "Surely, Canada Is Our Best Friend, Closest Ally." *The Cleveland Plain Dealer.* p. B6.

Swim, J. K., & Sanna, L. J. (1996). He's skilled, she's lucky: A meta-analysis of observers' attributions for women's and men's successes and failures. *Personality and Social Psychology Bulletin, 22,* 507–519.

Swim, J. K., & Hyers, L. L. (2009). Sexism. In T. D. Nelson (Ed.), *Handbook of prejudice, stereotyping, and discrimination* (pp. 407–430). New York: Psychology Press.

't Hart, P. (1998). Preventing groupthink revisited: Evaluating and reforming groups in government. *Organizational Behavior and Human Decision Processes, 73,* 306–326.

't Hart, P., Stern, E., & Sundelius, B. (1995). *Beyond groupthink.* Stockholm: Stockholm Center for Organizational Research.

Tafarodi, R. W., Shaughnessy, S. C., Yamaguchi, S., & Murakoshi, A. (2011). The reporting of self-esteem in japan and canada. *Journal of Cross-Cultural Psychology, 42,* 155–164.

Tajfel, H. (1982). Social psychology of intergroup relations. *Annual Review of Psychology, 33,* 1–39.

Tajfel, H., Billig, M. G., Bundy, R. P., & Flament, C. (1971). Social categorization and intergroup behavior. *European Journal of Social Psychology, 1,* 149–178.

Takemura, K., & Yuki, M. (2007). Are Japanese groups more competitive than Japanese individuals? A cross-cultural validation of the interindividual-intergroup discontinuity effect. *International Journal of Psychology, 42,* 27–35.

Talarico, J. M., & Rubin, D. C. (2007). Flashbulb memories are special after all; in phenomenology, not accuracy. *Applied Cognitive Psychology, 21,* 557–578.

Tan, H. H., & Tan, M.-L. (2008). Organizational citizenship behavior and social loafing: The role of personality, motives, and contextual factors. *Journal of Psychology: Interdisciplinary and Applied, 142,* 89–108.

Tanford, S., & Penrod, S. (1984). Social influence model: A formal integration of research on majority and minority influence processes. *Psychological Bulletin, 95,* 189–225.

Tang, S., & Hall, V. C. (1995). The overjustification effect: A meta-analysis. *Applied Cognitive Psychology, 9,* 365–404.

Tangney, J. P., Wagner, P. E., Hill-Barlow, D., Marschall, D. E., & Gramzow, R. (1996). Relation of shame and guilt to constructive versus destructive responses to anger across the lifespan. *Journal of Personality and Social Psychology, 70,* 797–809.

Tannen, D. (1990). *You just don't understand: Women and men in conversation.* New York: Morrow.

Tarde, G. (1890). *Les lois de l'imitation. Étude sociologique.* Paris: Félix Alcan.

Tassinary, L. G., & Cacioppo, J. T. (1992). Unobservable facial actions and emotion. *Psychological Science, 3,* 28–33.

Taylor, K. A., Mesmer-Magnus, J., & Burns, T. M. (2008). Teaching the art of negotiation: Improving students negotiating confidence and perceptions of effectiveness. *Journal of Education for Business, 83,* 135–140.

Taylor, R. B. (2000). *Breaking away from broken windows: Baltimore neighborhoods and the nationwide fight against crime, grime, fear, and decline.* Boulder, CO: Westview Press.

Taylor, S. E. (1989). *Positive illusions: Creative self-deceptions and the healthy mind.* New York: Basic Books.

Taylor, S. E. (1990). Health psychology: The science and the field. *American Psychologist, 45,* 40–50.

Taylor, S. E. (1991). Asymmetrical effects of positive and negative events: The mobilization-minimization hypothesis. *Psychological Bulletin, 110,* 67–85.

Taylor, S. E. (2006). Tend and befriend: Biobehavioral bases of affiliation under stress. *Current Directions in Psychological Science, 15,* 273–277.

Taylor, S. E. (2009). *Health psychology* (7th ed.). New York: McGraw-Hill.

Taylor, S. E., & Brown, J. D. (1988). Illusion and well-being: A social psychological perspective on mental health. *Psychological Bulletin, 103,* 193–210.

Taylor, S. E., & Fiske, S. T. (1975). Point of view and perceptions of causality. *Journal of Personality and Social Psychology, 32,* 439–445.

Taylor, S. E., Kemeny, M. E., Reed, G. M., Bower, J. E., & Gruenewald, T. L. (2000). Psychological resources, positive illusions, and health. *American Psychologist, 55,* 99–109.

Taylor, S. E., Lerner, J. S., Sherman, D. K., Sage, R. M., & McDowell, N. K. (2003). Portrait of the self-enhancer: Well adjusted and well liked or maladjusted and friendless? *Journal of Personality and Social Psychology, 84,* 165–176.

Taylor, S. E., & Lobel, M. (1989). Social comparison activity under threat: Downward evaluation and upward contacts. *Psychological Review, 96,* 569–575.

Taylor, S. E., Sherman, D. K., Kim, H. S., Jarcho, J., Takgi, K., & Dunagan, M. S. (2004). Culture and social support: Who seeks it and why? *Journal of Personality and Social Psychology, 87,* 354–362.

Taylor, S. E., Welch, W. T., Kim, H. S., & Sherman, D. K. (2007). Cultural differences in the impact of social support on psychological and biological stress responses. *Psychological Science, 18,* 831–837.

Tedeschi, J. T., & Bond, M. H. (2001). Aversive behavior and aggression in cultural perspective. In R. M. Kowalski (Ed.), *Behaving badly: Aversive behaviors in interpersonal relationships* (pp. 257–293). Washington, DC: American Psychological Association.

Tedeschi, J. T., Schlenker, B. R., & Bonoma, T. V. (1971). Cognitive dissonance: Private ratiocination or public spectacle? *American Psychologist, 26,* 685–695.

Tenenbaum, H. R., & Leaper, C. (2002). Are parents' gender schemas related to their children's gender-related cognitions? A meta-analysis. *Developmental Psychology, 38,* 615–630.

Tekleab, A. G., Quigley, N. R., & Tesluk, P. E. (2009). A longitudinal study of team conflict, conflict management, cohesion, and team effectiveness. *Group & Organization Management, 34,* 170–205.

Tesser, A. (1978). Self-generated attitude change. In L. Berkowitz (Ed.), *Advances in experimental social psychology* (Vol. 11, pp. 288–338). New York: Academic Press.

Tesser, A. (1988). Toward a self-evaluation maintenance model of social behavior. In L. Berkowitz (Ed.), *Advances in experimental social psychology* (Vol. 21, pp. 181–227). New York: Academic Press.

Tesser, A. (1993). The importance of heritability in psychological research: The case of attitudes. *Psychological Review, 100,* 129–142.

Tesser, A., & Collins, J. E. (1988). Emotion in social reflection and comparison situations: Intuitive, systematic, and exploratory approaches. *Journal of Personality and Social Psychology, 55,* 695–709.

Tesser, A., Pilkington, C. J., & McIntosh, W. D. (1989). Self-evaluation maintenance and the mediational role of emotion: The perception of friends and strangers. *Journal of Personality and Social Psychology, 57,* 442–456.

Testa, M., & Hoffman., J. (2012). Naturally occurring changes in womens drinking from high school to college and implications for sexual victimization. *Journal of Studies on Alcohol and Drugs, 73,* 26–33.

Tetlock, P. E. (1998). Social psychology and world politics. In D. T. Gilbert, S. T. Fiske, & G. Lindzey (Eds.), *The handbook of social psychology* (4th ed., Vol. 2, pp. 868–912). New York: McGraw-Hill.

Thibaut, J. W., & Kelley, H. H. (1959). *The social psychology of groups.* New York: Wiley.

Thibaut, J., & Walker, L. (1975). *Procedural justice: A psychological analysis.* Hillsdale, NJ: Erlbaum.

Thomas, A. K., & Loftus, E. F. (2002). Creating bizarre false memories through imagination. *Memory and Cognition, 30,* 423–431.

Thompson, C. P., Herrmann, D. J., Read, J. D., Bruce, D., Payne, D. G., & Toglia, M. P. (Eds.) (1998). *Autobiographical memory: Theoretical and applied perspectives.* Mahwah, NJ: Erlbaum.

Thompson, L. (1990). Negotiation behavior and outcomes: Empirical evidence and theoretical issues. *Psychological Bulletin, 108,* 515–532.

Thompson, L. (1991). Information exchange in negotiation. *Journal of Experimental Social Psychology, 27,* 161–179.

Thompson, L., & Hrebec, D. (1996). Lose-lose agreements in interdependent decision making. *Psychological Bulletin, 120,* 396–409.

Thompson, S. C. (1999). Illusions of control: How we overestimate our personal influence. *Current Directions in Psychological Science, 8,* 187–190.

Thompson, W. M., Dabbs, J. M., Jr., & Frady, R. L. (1990). Changes in saliva testosterone levels during a 90-day shock incarceration program. *Criminal Justice and Behavior, 17,* 246–252.

Thornberg, R., & Knutsen, S. (2011). Teenagers' explanations of bullying. *Child & Youth Care Forum, 40,* 177–192.

Thornhill, R., & Gangestad, S. W. (1993). Human facial beauty: Averageness, symmetry, and parasite resistance. *Human Nature, 4,* 237–269.

Thornton, B. (1992). Repression and its mediating influence on the defensive attribution of responsibility. *Journal of Research in Personality, 26,* 44–57.

Thurstone, L. L. (1928). Attitudes can be measured. *American Journal of Sociology, 33,* 529–544.

Tice, D. M. (1991). Esteem protection or enhancement? Self-handicapping motives and attributions differ by trait self-esteem. *Journal of Personality and Social Psychology, 60,* 711–725.

Tice, D. M., & Baumeister, R. F. (1997). Longitudinal study of procrastination, performance, stress, and health: The costs and benefits of dawdling. *Psychological Science, 8,* 454–458.

Tice, D. M., & Wallace, H. M. (2003). The reflected self: Creating yourself as (you think) others see you. In M. R. Leary & J. P. Tangney (Eds.), *Handbook of self and identity* (pp. 91–105). New York: Guilford.

Tilker, H. A. (1970). Socially responsible behavior as a function of observer responsibility and victim feedback. *Journal of Personality and Social Psychology, 14,* 95–100.

Tiwari, G. K. (2012). The misinformation effect and fate of witnessed minutiae. *Indian Journal of Community Psychology, 8,* 134–142.

Tjaden, P., & Thoennes, N. (2000). *Extent, nature, and consequences of intimate partner violence.* Washington, DC: U.S. Department of Justice.

Tobin, A. M. (2006, October 3). "Copycat effect" may explain cluster. *Toronto Star,* p. A7.

Todorov, A., Said, C. P., Engell, A. D., & Oosterhof, N. A. (2008). Understanding evaluation of faces on social dimensions. *Trends in Cognitive Sciences, 12,* 455–460.

Todorov, A., & Uleman, J. S. (2004). The person reference process in spontaneous trait inferences. *Journal of Personality and Social Psychology, 87,* 482–493.

Tolstedt, B. E., & Stokes, J. P. (1984). Self-disclosure, intimacy, and the depenetration process. *Journal of Personality and Social Psychology, 46,* 84–90.

Toma, C. L., Hancock, J. T., Ellison, N. B. (2008). Separating fact from fiction: An examination of deceptive self-presentation in online dating profiles. *Personality and Social Psychology Bulletin, 34,* 1023–1036.

Tomada, G., & Schneider, B. H. (1997). Relational aggression, gender, and peer acceptance: Invariance across culture, stability over time, and concordance among informants. *Developmental Psychology, 33,* 601–609.

Top, T. J. (1991). Sex bias in the evaluation of performance in the scientific, artistic, and literary professions: A review. *Sex Roles, 24,* 73–106.

Tormala, Z. L., Brinol, P., & Petty, R. E. (2006). When credibility attacks: The reverse impact of source credibility on persuasion. *Journal of Experimental Social Psychology, 42,* 684–691.

Tormala, Z. L., & Petty, R. E. (2002). What doesn't kill me makes me stronger: The effects of resisting persuasion on attitude certainty. *Journal of Personality and Social Psychology, 83,* 1298–1313.

Tougas, F., Brown, R., Beaton, A. M., & Joly, S. (1995). Neosexism: Plus ça change, plus c'est pareil. *Personality and Social Psychology Bulletin, 21,* 842–849.

Tourangeau, R., Rips, L. J., & Rasinksi, K. (2000). *The psychology of survey response.* New York: Cambridge University Press.

Tourangeau, R., Smith, T. W., & Rasinski, K. A. (1997). Motivation to report sensitive behaviors on surveys: Evidence from a bogus pipeline experiment. *Journal of Applied Social Psychology, 27,* 209–222.

Trafimow, D., Triandis, H. C., & Goto, S. G. (1991). Some tests of the distinction between the private and collective self. *Journal of Personality and Social Psychology, 60,* 649–655.

Trawalter, S., Todd, A. R., Baird, A. A., & Richeson, J. A. (2008). Attending to threat: Race-based patterns of selective attention. *Journal of Experimental Social Psychology, 44,* 1322–1327.

Trawalter, S., Adam, E. K., Chase-Lansdale, P. L., & Richeson, J. A. (2012). Concerns about appearing prejudiced get under the skin: Stress system responses to interracial contact in the moment and across time. *Journal of Experimental Social Psychology, 48,* 682–693.

Triandis, H. C. (1994). *Culture and social behavior.* New York: McGraw-Hill.

Triandis, H., Chen, X. P., & Chan, D. K. (1998). Scenarios for the measurement of collectivism and individualism. *Journal of Cross-Cultural Psychology, 29,* 275–289.

Triplett, N. (1897–1898). The dynamogenic factors in pacemaking and competition. *American Journal of Psychology, 9,* 507–533.

Tripp, C., Jensen, T. D., & Carlson, L. (1994). The effects of multiple product endorsements by celebrities on consumers' attitudes and intentions. *Journal of Consumer Research, 20,* 535–547.

Trivers, R. L. (1971). The evolution of reciprocal altruism. *Quarterly Review of Biology, 46,* 35–57.

Trivers, R. L. (1972). Parental investment and sexual selection. In B. Campbell (Ed.), *Sexual selection and the descent of man* (pp. 136–179). Chicago: Aldine-Atherton.

Trivers, R. L. (1985). *Social evolution.* Menlo Park, CA: Benjamin/Cummings.

Troll, L. E., & Skaff, M. M. (1997). Perceived continuity of self in very old age. *Psychology and Aging, 12,* 162–169.

Trope, Y. (1986). Identification and inferential processes in dispositional attribution. *Psychological Review, 93,* 239–257.

Trope, Y., & Alfieri, T. (1997). Effortfulness and flexibility of dispositional judgment processes. *Journal of Personality and Social Psychology, 73,* 662–674.

Trope, Y., Bassock, M., & Alon, E. (1984). The questions lay interviewers ask. *Journal of Personality, 52,* 90–106.

Trzesniewski, K. H., Donnellan, M. B., & Robins, R. W. (2003). Stability of self-esteem across the life span. *Journal of Personality and Social Psychology, 84,* 205–220.

Tsai, W., Chen, C., & Liu, H. (2007). Test of a model linking employee positive moods and task performance. *Journal of Applied Psychology, 92,* 1570–1583.

Tsapelas, I., Aron, A., & Orbuch, T. (2009). Marital boredom now predicts less satisfaction 9 years later. *Psychological Science, 20,* 543–545.

Tubre, T. C., & Collins, J. M. (2000). Jackson and Schuler (1985) revisited: A meta-analysis of the relationships between role ambiguity, role conflict, and job performance. *Journal of Management, 26,* 155–169.

Tuckman, B. W. (1965). Developmental sequence in small groups. *Psychological Bulletin, 63,* 384–399.

Tuckman, B. W., & Jensen, M. A. (1977). Stages of small-group development revisited. *Group and Organization Studies, 2,* 419–427.

Turner, J. C. (1987). *Rediscovering the social group: A self-categorization theory.* Oxford, England: Basil Blackwell.

Turner, J. C. (1991). *Social influence.* Pacific Grove, CA: Brooks/Cole.

Tversky, A., & Kahneman, D. (1973). Availability: A heuristic for judging frequency and probability. *Cognitive Psychology, 5,* 207–232.

Twenge, J. M. (2009). Change over time in obedience: The jury's still out, but it might be decreasing. *American Psychologist, 64,* 28–31.

Twenge, J., & Crocker, J. (2002). Race and Self-Esteem. *Psychological Bulletin, 128,* 371–408.

Uchino, B. N. (2009). Understanding the links between social support and physical health: A life-span perspective with emphasis on the separability of perceived and received support. *Perspectives on Psychological Science, 4,* 236–255.

Uchino, B. N., Cacioppo, J. T., & Kiecolt-Glaser, J. K. (1996). The relationship between social support and physiological processes: A review with emphasis on underlying mechanisms and implications for health. *Psychological Bulletin, 119,* 488–531.

Underwood, J., & Pezdek, K. (1998). Memory suggestibility as an example of the sleeper effect. *Psychonomic Bulletin and Review, 5,* 449–453.

Underwood, M. K., Beron, K. J., Gentsch, J. K., Galperin, M. B., & Risser, S. D. (2008). Family correlates of children's social and physical aggression with peers: Negative interparental conflict strategies and parenting styles. *International Journal of Behavioral Development, 32,* 549–562.

Unger, Rhoda K., Sheese, K., & Main, A. S. (2010). Feminism and women leaders in SPSSI: Social networks, ideology, and generational change. *Psychology of Women Quarterly, 34,* 474–485.

U.S. Bureau of the Census (1994). *Statistical Abstract of the United States: 1994.* Washington, DC: The Reference Press.

U.S. Department of Health, Education, and Welfare. (1974, May 30). *Protection of human subjects.* Federal Register, 39(105): 18914–20 (45CFR, part 46).

U.S. Department of Justice (1999). *Eyewitness evidence: A guide for law enforcement.* Washington, DC: U.S. Department of Justice.

U.S. Department of Justice. (2007). *Black victims of violent crime.* Office of Justice Programs, Bureau of Justice Statistics. August 2007, NCJ 214258.

Uziel, L. (2007). Individual differences in the social facilitation effect: A review and meta-analysis. *Journal of Research in Personality, 41,* 579–601.

Uziel, L. (2010). Look at me, I'm happy and creative: The effect of impression management on behavior in social presence. *Personality and Social Psychology Bulletin, 36,* 1591–1602.

Vaish, A., Carpenter, M., & Tomasello, M. (2009). Sympathy through affective perspective taking and its relation to prosocial behavior in toddlers. *Developmental Psychology, 45,* 534–543.

Vaish, A., Grossmann, T., & Woodward, A. (2008). Not all emotions are created equal: The negativity bias in social-emotional development. *Psychological Bulletin, 134,* 383–403.

Vallacher, R. R., Read, S. J., & Nowak, A. (2002). The dynamical perspective in personality and social psychology. *Personality and Social Psychology Review, 6,* 264–273.

Van Bavel, J. J., & Cunningham, W. A. (2009). Self-categorization with a novel mixed-race group moderates automatic social and racial biases. *Personality and Social Psychology Bulletin, 35,* 321–335.

Van Bavel, J. J., Packer, D. J., & Cunningham, W. A. (2008). The neural substrates of in-group bias: A functional magnetic resonance imaging investigation. *Psychological Science, 19,* 1131–1139.

van Bokhoven, I., van Goozen, Stephanie H. M., van Engeland, H., Schaal, B., Arseneault, L., Séguin, J. R., Assaad, J-M., Nagin, D.S., Vitaro, F., & Tremblay, R. E. (2006). Salivary testosterone and aggression, delinquency, and social dominance in a population-based longitudinal study of adolescent males. *Hormones and Behavior, 50,* 118–125.

Van Cappellen, P., Corneille, O., Cols, S., & Saroglou, V. (2011). Beyond mere compliance to authoritative figures: Religious priming increases conformity to informational influence among submissive people. *International Journal for the Psychology of Religion, 21,* 97–105.

van der Toorn, J., Tyler, T. R., & Jost, J. T. (2011). More than fair: Outcome dependence, system justification, and the perceived legitimacy of authority figures. *Journal of Experimental Social Psychology, 47,* 127–138.

van Dijk, E., De Kwaadsteniet, E. W., & De Cremer, D. (2009). Tacit coordination in social dilemmas: The importance of having a common understanding. *Journal of Personality and Social Psychology, 96,* 665–678.

Van Dyne, L., & Saavedra, R. (1996). A naturalistic minority influence experiment: Effects on divergent thinking, conflict, and originality in work-groups. *British Journal of Social Psychology, 35,* 151–167.

Van Goozen, S. H. M., Cohen-Kettenis, P. T., Gooren, L. J. G., & Frijda, N. H., et al. (1995). Gender differences in behaviour: Activating effects of cross-sex hormones. *Psychoneuroendocrinology, 20,* 343–363.

van Knippenberg, D., & Schippers, M. C. (2007). Work group diversity. *Annual Review of Psychology, 58,* 515–541.

Van Lange, P. A. M., Klapwijk, A., & Van Munster, L. M. (2011). How the shadow of the future might promote cooperation. *Group Processes & Intergroup Relations, 14,* 857–870.

Van Vugt, M., & Schaller, M. (2008). Evolutionary approaches to group dynamics: An introduction. *Group Dynamics: Theory, Research, and Practice, 12,* 1–6.

Vandello, J. A., Cohen, D., Grandon, R., & Franiuk, R. (2009). Stand by your man: Indirect prescriptions for honorable violence and feminine loyalty in canada, chile, and the united states. *Journal of Cross-Cultural Psychology, 40,* 81–104.

Vandello, Joseph A., Cohen, D., & Ransom, S. (2008). U.S. southern and northern differences in perceptions of norms about aggression: Mechanisms for the perpetuation of a culture of honor. *Journal of Cross-Cultural Psychology, 39,* 162–177.

Vandello, J. A., & Cohen, D. (2005). Tenuous manhood and domestic violence against women. In S. Fein, G. R. Goethals, & M. J. Sandstrom (Eds.), *Gender and aggression: Interdisciplinary approaches.* Mahwah, NJ: Erlbaum.

VanderStoep, S. W., & Shaughnessy, J. J. (1997). Taking a course in research methods improves reasoning about real-life events. *Teaching of Psychology, 24,* 122–124.

VanderZee, K. I., Buunk, B. P., DeRuiter, J. H., Tempelaar, R., VanSonderen, E., & Sanderman, R. (1996). Social comparison and the subjective well-being of cancer patients. *Basic and Applied Social Psychology, 18,* 453–468.

Vathanophas, V., & Liang, S. Y. (2007). Enhancing information sharing in group support systems (GSS). *Computers in Human Behavior, 23,* 1675–1691.

Vazire, S., & Carlson, E. N. (2010). Self-knowledge of personality: Do people know themselves? *Social and Personality Psychology Compass, 4,* 605–620.

Veenhoven, R. (1993). *Happiness in nations.* Rotterdam, The Netherlands: Risbo.

Vega, V., & Malamuth, N. M. (2007). Predicting sexual aggression: The role of pornography in the context of general and specific risk factors. *Aggressive Behavior, 33,* 104–117.

Verkuyten, M. (2005). The puzzle of high self-esteem among ethnic minorities: Comparing explicit and implicit self-esteem. *Self and Identity, 4,* 171–192.

Verona, E., Patrick, C. J., & Lang, A. R. (2002). A direct assessment of the role of state and trait negative emotion in aggressive behavior. *Journal of Abnormal Psychology, 111,* 249–258.

Vidmar, N., & Hans, V. P. (2007). *American juries: The verdict.* Amherst, NY: Prometheus.

Vierikko, E., Pulkkinen, L., Kaprio, J., & Rose, R. J. (2006). Genetic and environmental sources of continuity and change in teacher-rated aggression during early adolescence. *Aggressive Behavior, 32,* 308–320.

Viki, G. T., Abrams, D., & Masser, B. (2004). Evaluating stranger and acquaintance rape: The role of benevolent sexism in perpetrator blame and recommended sentence length. *Law and Human Behavior, 28,* 295–303.

Vinokur, A., & Burnstein, E. (1974). Effects of partially shared persuasive arguments on group-induced shifts: A group-problem-solving approach. *Journal of Personality and Social Psychology, 29,* 305–315.

Visintainer, M., Volpicelli, J., & Seligman, M. (1982). Tumor rejection in rats after inescapable or escapable shock. *Science, 216,* 437–439.

Visser, P. S., & Mirabile, R. R. (2004). Attitudes in the social context: The impact of social network composition on individual-level attitude strength. *Journal of Personality and Social Psychology, 87,* 779–795.

Vittengl, J. R., & Holt, C. S. (2000). Getting acquainted: The relationship of self-disclosure and social attraction to positive affect. *Journal of Social and Personal Relationships, 17,* 53–66.

Vogel, D. L., Wester, S. R., & Heesacker, M. (1999). Dating relationships and the demand/withdraw pattern of communication. *Sex Roles, 41,* 297–306.

Vohs, K. D., Baumeister, R. F., & Ciarocco, N. J. (2005). Self-regulation and self-presentation: Regulatory resource depletion impairs impression management and effortful self-presentation depletes regulatory resources. *Journal of Personality and Social Psychology, 88,* 632–657.

Vohs, K. D., & Heatherton, T. F. (2000). Self-regulatory failure: A resource-depletion approach. *Psychological Science, 11,* 249–252.

Vokey, J. R., & Read, J. D. (1985). Subliminal messages: Between the devil and the media. *American Psychologist, 40,* 1231–1239.

Vollhardt, J. R. (2009). Altruism born of suffering and prosocial behavior following adverse life events: A review and conceptualization. *Social Justice Research, 22,* 53–97.

von der Pahlen, B., Lindman, R., Sarkola, T., Maekisalo, H., & Eriksson, C. J. P. (2002). An exploratory study on self-evaluated aggression and androgens in women. *Aggressive Behavior, 28,* 273–280.

von Hippel, W., & Henry, J. D. (2011). In Vohs K. D., Baumeister R. F. (Eds.), *Aging and self-regulation.* New York: Guilford Press.

von Hippel, William, Lakin, J. L., & Shakarchi, R. J. (2005). Individual differences in motivated social cognition: The case of self-serving information processing. *Personality and Social Psychology Bulletin, 31,* 1347–1357.

von Hippel, W., Sekaquaptewa, D., & Vargas, P. T. (2009). Linguistic markers of implicit attitudes. In R. E. Petty, R. H. Fazio, & P. Brinol (Eds.), *Attitudes: Insights from the new wave of implicit measures.* New York: Psychology Press.

Von Lang, J., & Sibyll, C. (Eds.) (1983). *Eichmann interrogated* (R. Manheim, Trans.). New York: Farrar, Straus & Giroux.

Vonk, R. (1998). The slime effect: Suspicion and dislike of likeable behavior toward superiors. *Journal of Personality and Social Psychology, 74,* 849–864.

Voracek, M., & Fisher, M. L. (2002). Shapely centrefolds? Temporal change in body measures: Trend analysis. *British Medical Journal, 325,* 1447–1448.

Vorauer, J. D. (2003). Dominant group members in intergroup interaction: Safety or vulnerability in numbers? *Personality and Social Psychology Bulletin, 29,* 498–511.

Vorauer, J. D., Cameron, J. J., Holmes, J. G., & Pearce, D. G. (2003). Invisible overtures: Fears of rejection and the signal amplification bias. *Journal of Personality and Social Psychology, 84,* 793–812.

Vorauer, J. D., & Claude, S. D. (1998). Perceived versus actual transparency of goals in negotiation. *Personality and Social Psychology Bulletin, 24,* 371–385.

Vorauer, J. D., & Sasaki, S. J. (2009). Helpful only in the abstract? Ironic effects of empathy in intergroup interaction. *Psychological Science, 20,* 191–197.

Vorauer, J. D., & Sasaki, S. J. (2011). The pitfalls of empathy as a default intergroup interaction strategy: Distinct effects of trying to empathize with a lower status outgroup member who does versus does not express distress. *Journal of Experimental Social Psychology, 48,* 519–524.

Vorauer, J. D., & Turpie, C. A. (2004). Disruptive effects of vigilance on dominant group members treatment of outgroup members: Choking versus shining under pressure. *Journal of Personality and Social Psychology, 87,* 384–399.

Vrij, A. (2008). *Detecting lies and deceit: Pitfalls and opportunities.* Chichester, UK: Wiley.

Vrij, A., Granhag, P., Mann, S., & Leal, S. (2011). Outsmarting the liars: Toward a cognitive lie detection approach. *Current Directions in Psychological Science, 20,* 28–32.

Vrij, A., Mann, S., Fisher, R., Leal, S., Milne, R., & Bull, R. (2008). Increasing cognitive load to facilitate lie detection: The benefit of recalling an event in reverse order. *Law and Human Behavior, 32,* 253–265.

Wageman, R., Fisher, C. M., & Hackman, J. R. (2009). Leading teams when the time is right: Finding the best moments to act. *Organizational Dynamics, 38,* 192–203.

Wageman, R., Gardner, H., & Mortensen, M. (2012). The changing ecology of teams: New directions for teams research. *Journal of Organizational Behavior, 33,* 301–315.

Wagner, L., & Druckman, D. (2012). The role of justice in historical negotiations. *Negotiation and Conflict Management Research, 5,* 49–71.

Wagstaff, G. F., Wheatcroft, J., Cole, J. C., Brunas-Wagstaff, J., Blackmore, V., & Pilkington, A. (2008). Some cognitive and neuropsychological aspects of social inhibition and facilitation. *European Journal of Cognitive Psychology, 20,* 828–846.

Walker, I., & Smith, H. J. (2002). *Relative deprivation: Specification, development, and integration.* Cambridge, UK: Cambridge University Press.

Walker, L., LaTour, S., Lind, E. A., & Thibaut, J. (1974). Reactions of participants and observers to modes of adjudication. *Journal of Applied Social Psychology, 4,* 295–310.

Walster, E. (1966). Assignment of responsibility for important events. *Journal of Personality and Social Psychology, 3,* 73–79.

Walster, E., Aronson, V., Abrahams, D., & Rottman, L. (1966). The importance of physical attractiveness in dating behavior. *Journal of Personality and Social Psychology, 4,* 508–516.

Walster, E., & Festinger, L. (1962). The effectiveness of "overheard" persuasive communications. *Journal of Abnormal and Social Psychology, 65,* 395–402.

Walster, E., Walster, G. W., & Berscheid, E. (1978). *Equity: Theory and research.* Boston: Allyn & Bacon.

Walster, E., Walster, G. W., Piliavin, J., & Schmidt, L. (1973). "Playing hard-to-get": Understanding an elusive phenomenon. *Journal of Personality and Social Psychology, 26,* 113–121.

Walther, E., Nagengast, B., & Trasselli, C. (2005). Evaluative conditioning in social psychology: Facts and speculations. *Cognition and Emotion, 19,* 175–196.

Walton, G., & Cohen, G. (2004). Stereotype lift. *Journal of Experimental Social Psychology, 39,* 456–467.

Wampold, B. E., Mondin, G. W., Moody, M., Stich, F., Benson, K., & Ahn, H. (1997). A meta-analysis of outcome studies comparing bona fide psychotherapies: Empirically, "all must have prizes." *Psychological Bulletin, 122,* 203–215.

Wang, J., Iannotti, R. J., & Luk, J. W. (2012). Patterns of adolescent bullying behaviors: Physical, verbal, exclusion, rumor, and cyber. *Journal of School Psychology,*

Wann, D. L., & Grieve, F. G. (2005). Biased evaluation of in-group and out-group spectator behavior at sporting events: The importance of team identification and threats to social identity. *Journal of Social Psychology, 145,* 531–545.

Want, S.C. (2009). Meta-analytic moderators of experimental exposure to media portrayals of women on female appearance satisfaction: Social comparisons as automatic processes. *Body Image, 6,* 257–269.

Warburton, W. A., Williams, K. D., & Cairns, D. R. (2006). When ostracism leads to aggression: The moderating effects of control deprivation. *Journal of Experimental Social Psychology, 42,* 213–220.

Ward, L. M., & Friedman, K. (2006). Using TV as a guide: Associations between television viewing and adolescents' sexual attitudes and behavior. *Journal of Research on Adolescence, 16,* 133–156.

Ward, M. L., Hansbrough, E., & Walker, E. (2005). Contributions of music video exposure to black adolescents' gender and sexual schemas. *Journal of Adolescent Research, 20,* 143–166.

Warneken, F., & Tomasello, M. (2006). Altruistic helping in human infants and young chimpanzees. *Science, 311,* 1301–1303.

Warren, B. L. (1966). A multiple variable approach to the assortive mating phenomenon. *Eugenics Quarterly, 13,* 285–298.

Watkins, Christopher D., Jones, B. C., Little, A. C., DeBruine, L. M., & Feinberg, D. R. (2012). Cues to the sex ratio of the local population influence women's preferences for facial symmetry. *Animal Behaviour, 83,* 545–553.

Watson, D. (1982). The actor and the observer: How are their perceptions of causality divergent? *Psychological Bulletin, 92,* 682–700.

Weary, G., & Edwards, J. A. (1994). Individual differences in causal uncertainty. *Journal of Personality and Social Psychology, 67,* 308–318.

Webster, D. M., Richter, L., & Kruglanski, A. W. (1996). On leaping to conclusions when feeling tired: Mental fatigue effects on impressional primacy. *Journal of Experimental Social Psychology, 32,* 181–195.

Weeden, J., & Sabini, J. (2005). Physical attractiveness and health in Western societies: A review. *Psychological Bulletin, 131,* 635–653.

Wegener, D. T., & Petty, R. E. (1994). Mood management across affective states: The hedonic contingency hypothesis. *Journal of Personality and Social Psychology, 66,* 1034–1048.

Wegener, D. T., Petty, R. E., & Smith, S. M. (1995). Positive mood can increase or decrease message scrutiny: The hedonic contingency view of mood and message processing. *Journal of Personality and Social Psychology, 69,* 5–15.

Wegge, J., Bipp, T., & Kleinbeck, U. (2007). Goal setting via videoconferencing. *European Journal of Work and Organizational Psychology, 16,* 169–194.

Wegner, D. M. (1994). Ironic processes of mental control. *Psychological Review, 101,* 34–52.

Wegner, D. M. (1997). When the antidote is the poison: Ironic mental control processes. *Psychological Science, 8,* 148–153.

Wegner, D. M., Ansfield, M., & Pilloff, D. (1998). The putt and the pendulum: Ironic effects of the mental control of action. *Psychological Science, 9,* 196–199.

Wegner, D. M., Erber, R., & Raymond, P. (1991). Transactive memory in close relationships. *Journal of Personality and Social Psychology, 61,* 923–929.

Wegner, D. M., Lane, J. D., & Dimitri, S. (1994). The allure of secret relationships. *Journal of Personality and Social Psychology, 66,* 287–300.

Weiner, B. (1985). "Spontaneous" causal thinking. *Psychological Bulletin, 97,* 74–84.

Weinstein, N. D. (1980). Unrealistic optimism about future life events. *Journal of Personality and Social Psychology, 39,* 806–820.

Weinstein, N. D. (1989). Effects of personal experience on self-protective behavior. *Psychological Bulletin, 105,* 31–50.

Weiner, B. (2008). Reflections on the history of attribution theory and research. *Social Psychology, 39,* 151–156.

Weisbuch, M., Ivcevic, Z., & Ambady, N. (2009). On being liked on the web and in the "real world": Consistency in first impressions across personal webpages and spontaneous behavior. *Journal of Experimental Social Psychology, 45,* 573–576.

Weldon, M. S., Blair, C., & Huebsch, D. (2000). Group remembering: Does social loafing underlie collaborative inhibition? *Journal of Experimental Psychology: Learning, Memory, and Cognition, 26,* 1568–1577.

Wells, G. L., & Bradfield, A. L. (1998). "Good, you identified the suspect": Feedback to eyewitnesses distorts their reports of the witnessing experience. *Journal of Applied Psychology, 83,* 360–376.

Wells, G. L., Lindsay, R. C. L., & Ferguson, T. J. (1979). Accuracy, confidence, and juror perceptions in eyewitness identification. *Journal of Applied Psychology, 64,* 440–448.

Wells, G. L., Malpass, R. S., Lindsay, R. C. L., Fisher, R. P., Turtle, J. W., & Fulero, S. M. (2000). From the lab to the police station: A successful application of eyewitness research. *American Psychologist, 55,* 581–598.

Wells, G. L., Memon, A., & Penrod, S. (2007). Eyewitness evidence: Improving its probative value. *Psychological Science in the Public Interest, 7,* 45–75.

Wells, G. L., & Murray, D. M. (1984). Eyewitness confidence. In G. Wells & E. Loftus (Eds.), *Eyewitness testimony: Psychological perspectives* (pp. 155–170). New York: Cambridge University Press.

Wells, G. L., & Petty, R. E. (1980). The effects of overt head-movements on persuasion: Compatibility and incompatibility of responses. *Basic and Applied Social Psychology, 1,* 219–230.

Wells, G. L., & Quinlivan, D. S. (2009). Suggestive eyewitness identification procedures and the Supreme Court's reliability test in light of eyewitness science: 30 years later. *Law and Human Behavior, 33,* 1–24.

Wells, G. L., Small, M., Penrod, S., Malpass, R. S., Fulero, S. M., & Brimacombe, C. A. E. (1998). Eyewitness identification procedures: Recommendations for lineups and photospreads, *Law and Human Behavior, 22,* 603–648.

Wenzlaff, R. M., & Wegner, D. M. (2000). Thought suppression. *Annual Review of Psychology, 51,* 59–91.

West, S. G., & Brown, T. J. (1975). Physical attractiveness, the severity of the emergency and helping: A field experiment and interpersonal simulation. *Journal of Experimental Social Psychology, 11,* 531–538.

Westen, D. (2007). *The political brain: The role of emotion in deciding the fate of the nation.* New York: Public Affairs.

Wheeler, B. C. (2008). Selfish or altruistic? An analysis of alarm call function in wild capuchin monkeys, Cebus apella nigritus. *Animal Behaviour, 76,*1465–1475.

Wheeler, L., & Kim, Y. (1997). What is beautiful is culturally good: The physical attractiveness stereotype has different content in collectivist cultures. *Personality and Social Psychology Bulletin, 23,* 795–800.

Wheeler, L., Koestner, R., & Driver, R. E. (1982). Related attributes in the choice of comparison others. *Journal of Experimental Social Psychology, 18,* 489–500.

Wheeler, M. E., & Fiske, S. T. (2005). Controlling racial prejudice: Social-cognitive goals affect amygdala and stereotype activation. *Psychological Science, 16,* 56–63.

Whitbeck, L. B., & Hoyt, D. R. (1994). Social prestige and assortive mating: A comparison of students from 1956 and 1988. *Journal of Social and Personal Relationships, 11,* 137–145.

White, G. L., Fishbein, S., & Rutstein, J. (1981). Passionate love: The misattribution of arousal. *Journal of Personality and Social Psychology, 41,* 56–62.

Whyte, G. (1993). Escalating commitment in individual and group decision making: A prospect theory approach. *Organizational Behavior and Human Decision Processes, 54,* 430–455.

Whyte, G. (1998). Recasting Janis's groupthink model: The key role of collective efficacy in decision fiascoes. *Organizational Behavior and Human Decision Processes, 73,* 185–209.

Wickens, C. M., Wiesenthal, D. L., Flora, D. B., & Flett, G. L. (2011). Understanding driver anger and aggression: Attributional theory in the driving environment. *Journal of Experimental Psychology: Applied, 17,* 354–370.

Wicker, A. W. (1969). Attitudes versus actions: The relationship between verbal and overt behavioral responses to attitude objects. *Journal of Social Issues, 25(4),* 41–78.

Wicker, B., Keysers, C., Plailly, J., Royet, J. P., Gallese, V., & Rizzolatti, G. (2003). Both of us disgusted in *my* insula: The common neural basis of seeing and feeling disgust. *Neuron, 40,* 655–664.

Wicklund, R. A. (1975). Objective self-awareness. In L. Berkowitz (Ed.), *Advances in experimental social psychology* (Vol. 8, pp. 233–275). New York: Academic Press.

Widen, S. C., Christy, A. M., Hewett, K., & Russell, J. A. (2011). Do proposed facial expressions of contempt, shame, embarrassment, and compassion communicate the predicted emotion? *Cognition and Emotion, 25,* 898–906.

Widen, S. C., & Russell, J. A. (2010). The "disgust face" conveys anger to children. *Emotion, 10,* 455–466.

Widmeyer, W. N., & Loy, J. W. (1988). When you're hot, you're hot! Warm-cold effects in first impressions of persons and teaching effectiveness. *Journal of Educational Psychology, 80,* 118–121.

Wigboldus, D. H. J., Sherman, J. W., Franzese, H. L., & van Knippenberg, A. (2004). Capacity and comprehension: Spontaneous stereotyping under cognitive load. *Social Cognition,* in press.

Wiggins, J. S. (Ed.) (1996). *The five-factor model of personality: Theoretical perspectives.* New York: Guilford.

Wilder, D. A. (1977). Perception of groups, size of opposition, and social influence. *Journal of Experimental Social Psychology, 13,* 253–268.

Wilder, D. A., Simon, A. F., & Myles, F. (1996). Enhancing the impact of counterstereotypic information: Dispositional attributions for deviance. *Journal of Personality and Social Psychology, 71,* 276–287.

Wildschut, T., Pinter, B., Vevea, J. L., Insko, C. A., & Schopler, J. (2003). Beyond the group mind: A quantitative review of the interindividual intergroup discontinuity effect. *Psychological Bulletin, 129,* 698–722.

Williams, D. R., Neighbors, H. W., & Jackson, J. S. (2003). Racial/ethnic discrimination and health: Findings from community studies. *American Journal of Public Health, 93,* 200–208.

Williams, J. E., & Best, D. L. (1982). *Measuring sex stereotypes: A thirty nation study.* Beverly Hills, CA: Sage.

Williams, K. D. (2001). *Ostracism: The power of silence.* New York: Guilford.

Williams, K. D. (2007). Ostracism: The kiss of social death. *Social and Personality Psychology Compass, 1,* 236–247.

Williams, K. D. (2009). Ostracism: A temporal need-threat model. In M. P. Zanna (Ed.), *Advances in experimental social psychology* (Vol. 41), pp. 275–314. Burlington: Academic Press.

Williams, K. D., Cheung, C., & Choi, W. (2000). Cyberostracism: Effects of being ignored over the internet. *Journal of Personality and Social Psychology, 79,* 748–762.

Williams, K. D., Govan, C. L., Croker, V., Tynan, D., Cruickshank, M., & Lam, A. (2002). Investigations into differences between social-and cyberostracism. *Group Dynamics: Theory, Research, and Practice, 6,* 65–77.

Williams, M. J., & Eberhardt, J. L. (2008). Biological conceptions of race and the motivation to cross racial boundaries. *Journal of Personality and Social Psychology, 94,* 1033–1047.

Williams, M. J., & Mendelsohn, G. A. (2008). Gender clues and cues: Online interactions as windows into lay theories about men and women. *Basic and Applied Social Psychology, 30,* 278–294.

Williams, R. (1993). *Anger kills.* New York: Times Books.

Williamson, G. M., Clark, M. S., Pegalis, L. J., & Behan, A. (1996). Affective consequences of refusing to help in communal and exchange relationships. *Personality and Social Psychology Bulletin, 22,* 34–47.

Willis, J., & Todorov, A. (2006). First impressions: Making up your mind after a 100-ms exposure to a face. *Psychological Science, 17,* 592–598.

Wills, T. A. (1981). Downward comparison principles in social psychology. *Psychological Bulletin, 90,* 245–271.

Wills, T. A., & DePaulo, B. M. (1991). Interpersonal analysis of the help-seeking process. In C. R. Snyder & D. R. Forsyth (Eds.), *Handbook of social and clinical psychology: The health perspective* (pp. 350–375). New York: Pergamon Press.

Wilson, A. E., & Ross, M. (2000). The frequency of temporal and social comparisons in people's personal appraisals. *Journal of Personality and Social Psychology, 78,* 928–942.

Wilson, A. E., & Ross, M. (2003). The identity function of autobiographical memory: Time is on our side. *Invited paper in Memory: Special Issue Exploring the Functions of Autobiographical Memory, 11,* 137–149.

Wilson, D. S., & Sober, E. (1994). Reintroducing group selection to the human behavioral sciences. *Behavioral and Brain Sciences, 17,* 585–654.

Wilson, D. S., Van Vugt, M., & O'Gorman, R. (2008). Multilevel selection theory and major evolutionary transitions: Implications for psychological science. *Current Directions in Psychological Science, 17,* 6–9.

Wilson, D.S., & Wilson, E.O. (2010). *Evolution "for the good of the group."* Sunderland, MA: Sinauer Associates.

Wilson, D. W. (1978). Helping behavior and physical attractiveness. *Journal of Social Psychology, 104,* 313–314.

Wilson, M. I., & Daly, M. (1996). Male sexual proprietariness and violence against wives. *Current Directions in Psychological Science, 5,* 2–7.

Wilson, T. D. (2002). *Strangers to ourselves: Discovering the adaptive unconscious.* Cambridge, MA: Belknap Press.

Wilson, T. D., & Gilbert, D. T. (2003). Affective forecasting. *Advances in Experimental Social Psychology, 35,* 345–411.

Wilson, T. D., & Gilbert, D. T. (2005). Affective forecasting: Knowing what to want. *Current Directions in Psychological Science, 14,* 131–134.

Wilson, T. D., Wheatley, T., Meyers, J. M., Gilbert, D. T., & Axsom, D. (2000). Focalism: A source of durability bias in affective forecasting. *Journal of Personality and Social Psychology, 78,* 821–836.

Winch, R. F., Ktsanes, I., & Ktsanes, V. (1954). The theory of complementary needs in mate selection: An analytic and descriptive study. *American Sociological Review, 19,* 241–249.

Winstok, Z., & Straus, Murray A. (2011). Perceived neighborhood violence and use of verbal aggression, corporal punishment, and physical abuse by a national sample of parents in Israel. *Journal of Community Psychology, 39,* 678–697.

Wise, R. A., Safer, M. A., & Maro, C. (2011). What U.S. law enforcement officers know and believe about eyewitness factors, eyewitness interviews, and identification procedures. Applied Cognitive Psychology, 25, 488–500.

Wishman, S. (1986). *Anatomy of a jury: The system on trial.* New York: Times Books.

Wissler, R. L., & Saks, M. J. (1985). On the inefficacy of limiting instructions: When jurors use prior conviction evidence to decide on guilt. *Law and Human Behavior, 9,* 37–48.

Wittenbrink, B., Judd. C. M., & Park, B. (1997). Evidence for racial prejudice at the implicit level and its relationship with questionnaire measures. *Journal of Personality and Social Psychology, 72,* 262–274.

Wittenbrink, B., & Schwarz, N. (Eds.). (2007). *Implicit measures of attitudes.* New York: Guilford.

Wolf, S., & Montgomery, D. A. (1977). Effects of inadmissible evidence and level of judicial admonishment to disregard on the judgments of mock jurors. *Journal of Applied Social Psychology, 7,* 205–219.

Wood, J. V. (1989). Theory and research concerning social comparisons of personal attributes. *Psychological Bulletin, 106,* 231–248.

Wood, N., & Cowan, N. (1995). The cocktail party phenomenon revisited: How frequent are attention shifts to one's name in an irrelevant auditory channel? *Journal of Experimental Psychology: Learning, Memory, and Cognition, 21,* 255–260.

Wood, W., Kallgren, C. A., & Preisler, R. M. (1985). Access to attitude-relevant information in memory as a determinant of persuasion: The role of message attributes. *Journal of Experimental Social Psychology, 21,* 73–85.

Wood, W., Lundgren, S., Ouellette, J. A., Busceme, S., & Blackstone, T. (1994). Minority influence: A meta-analytic review of social influence processes. *Psychological Bulletin, 115,* 323–345.

Wood, W., Pool, G. J., Leck, K., & Purvis, D. (1996). Self-definition, defensive processing, and influence: The normative impact of majority and minority groups. *Journal of Personality and Social Psychology, 71,* 1181–1193.

Wood, W., & Quinn, J. M. (2003). Forewarned and forearmed? Two meta-analysis syntheses of forewarnings of influence appeals. *Psychological Bulletin, 129,* 119–138.

Woolley, Anita Williams, Gerbasi, M. E., Chabris, C. F., Kosslyn, S. M., & Hackman, J. R. (2008). Bringing in the experts: How team composition and collaborative planning jointly shape analytic effectiveness. *Small Group Research, 39,* 352–371.

Word, C. O., Zanna, M. P., & Cooper, J. (1974). The nonverbal mediation of self-fulfilling prophecies in interracial interaction. *Journal of Experimental Social Psychology, 10,* 109–120.

World Health Organization. *World Report on Violence and Health,* October 3, 2002.

Worth, L. T., & Mackie, D. M. (1987). Cognitive mediation of positive affect in persuasion. *Social Cognition, 5,* 76–94.

Worthy, D. A., Markman, A. B., & Maddox, W. T. (2009). Choking and excelling at the free throw line. *The International Journal of Creativity and Problem Solving, 19,* 53–58.

Wright, N. S., & Drewery, G. P. (2006). Forming cohesion in culturally heterogeneous teams differences in japanese, pacific islander and anglo experiences. *Cross Cultural Management, 13,* 43–53.

Wright, P. H. (1982). Men's friendships, women's friendships and the alleged inferiority of the latter. *Sex Roles, 8,* 1–20.

Wright, R. A., & Contrada, R. J. (1986). Dating selectivity and interpersonal attraction: Toward a better understanding of the "elusive phenomenon." *Journal of Social and Personal Relationships, 3,* 131–148.

Wright, R. A., Wadley, V. G., Danner, M., & Phillips, P. N. (1992). Persuasion, reactance, and judgments of interpersonal appeal. *European Journal of Social Psychology, 22,* 85–91.

Wuthnow, R. (1991). *Acts of compassion.* Princeton, NJ: Princeton University Press.

Wyer, N. A. (2004). Not all stereotypic biases are created equal: Evidence for a stereotype *dis*confirmation bias. *Personality and Social Psychology Bulletin, 30,* 706–720.

Wyer, N. A. (2007). Motivational influences on compliance with and consequences of instructions to suppress stereotypes. *Journal of Experimental Social Psychology, 43,* 417–424.

Wyer, N. A., Sadler, M. S., & Judd, C. M. (2002). Contrast effects in stereotype formation and change: The role of comparative context. *Journal of Experimental Social Psychology, 38,* 443–458.

Xu, X., Zuo, X., Wang, X., & Han, S. (2009). Do you feel my pain? Racial group membership modulates empathic neural responses. *Journal of Neuroscience, 29,* 8525–8529.

Yamagishi, T., Makimura, Y., Foddy, M., Matsuda, M., Kiyonari, T., & Platow, M. J. (2005). Comparisons of Australians and Japanese on group-based cooperation. *Asian Journal of Social Psychology, 8,* 173–190.

Yamawaki, N. (2007). Rape perception and the function of ambivalent sexism and gender-role traditionality. *Journal of Interpersonal Violence, 22,* 406–423.

Yeargain, J. W., & Kessler, L. L. (2010). Organizational hostility toward whistleblowers. *Journal of Legal, Ethical and Regulatory Issues, 13,* 87–92.

Yeung, N. C. J., & von Hippel, C. (2008). Stereotype threat increases the likelihood that female drivers in a simulator run over jaywalkers. *Accident Analysis and Prevention, 40,* 667–674.

Yopyk, D. J. A., & Prentice, D. A. (2005). Am I an athlete or a student? Identity salience and stereotype threat in student-athletes. *Basic and Applied Social Psychology, 27,* 329–336.

Young, R. K., Kennedy, A. H., Newhouse, A., Browne, P., & Thiessen, D. (1993). The effects of names on perceptions of intelligence, popularity, and competence. *Journal of Applied Social Psychology, 23,* 1770–1788.

Young, S. G., & Hugenberg, K. (2012). Individuation motivation and face experience can operate jointly to produce the own-race bias. *Social Psychological and Personality Science, 3,* 80–87.

Young, S. G., Sacco, D. F., & Hugenberg, K. (2011). Vulnerability to disease is associated with a domain-specific preference for symmetrical faces relative to symmetrical non-face stimuli. *European Journal of Social Psychology, 41,* 558–563.

Yu, D. W., & Shepard, G. H. (1998). Is beauty in the eye of the beholder? *Nature, 296,* 321–322.

Yuille, J. C., & Tollestrup, P. A. (1990). Some effects of alcohol on eyewitness memory. *Journal of Applied Psychology, 75,* 268–273.

Yuki, M. (2003). Intergroup comparison versus intragroup relationships: A cross-cultural examination of social identity theory in North American and East Asian cultural contexts. *Social Psychology Quarterly, 66,* 166–183.

Yzerbyt, V. Y., Dardenne, B., & Leyens, J.-Ph. (1998). Social judgeability concerns in impression formation. In V. Y. Yzerbyt, G. Lories, & B. Dardenne (Eds.), *Metacognition: Cognitive and social dimensions* (pp. 126–156). London: Sage.

Yzerbyt, V., & Demoulin, S. (2010). Intergroup relations. In S. T. Fiske, D. T. Gilbert, & G. Lindzey (Eds.), *The handbook of social psychology* (5th ed.). New York: McGraw-Hill.

Zajonc, R. B. (1965). Social facilitation. *Science, 149,* 269–274.

Zajonc, R. B. (1968). Attitudinal effects of mere exposure. *Journal of Personality and Social Psychology Monograph Supplement, 9(2),* 1–27.

Zajonc, R. B. (1980). Compresence. In P. B. Paulus (Ed.), *Psychology of group influence* (pp. 35–60). Hillsdale, NJ: Erlbaum.

Zajonc, R. B. (2001). Mere exposure: A gateway to the subliminal. *Current Directions in Psychological Science, 10,* 224–228.

Zajonc, R. B., Heingartner, A., & Herman, E. M. (1969). Social enhancement and impairment of performance in the cockroach. *Journal of Personality and Social Psychology, 13,* 82–92.

Zanna, M. P., & Cooper, J. (1974). Dissonance and the pill: An attribution approach to studying the arousal properties of dissonance. *Journal of Personality and Social Psychology, 29,* 703–709.

Zárate, M. A., Garcia, B., Garza, A. A., & Hitlan, R. T. (2004). Cultural threat and perceived realistic group conflict as dual predictors of prejudice. *Journal of Experimental Social Psychology, 40,* 99–105.

Zebrowitz, L. A., Luevano, V. X., Bronstad, P. M., & Aharon, I. (2009). Neural activation to babyfaced men matches activation to babies. *Social Neuroscience, 4,* 1–10.

Zebrowitz, L. A., & McDonald, S. M. (1991). The impact of litigants' babyfacedness and attractiveness on adjudications in small claims courts. *Law and Human Behavior, 15,* 603–624.

Zeisel, H., & Diamond, S. (1978). The effect of peremptory challenges on jury and verdict: An experiment in a federal district court. *Stanford Law Review, 30,* 491–531.

Zell, E., & Alicke, Mark D. (2010). Comparisons over time: Temporal trajectories, social comparison, and self-evaluation. *European Journal of Social Psychology, 40,* 375–382.

Zhang, S., & Kline, S. L. (2009). Can I make my own decision? A cross-cultural study of perceived social network influence in mate selection. *Journal of Cross-Cultural Psychology, 40,* 3–23.

Zhu, D. H., & Westphal, J. D. (2011). Misperceiving the beliefs of others: How pluralistic ignorance contributes to the persistence of positive security analyst reactions to the adoption of stock repurchase plans. *Organization Science, 22,* 869–886.

Zick, A., Pettigrew, T. E., & Wagner, U. (2008). Ethnic prejudice and discrimination in Europe. *Journal of Social Issues, 64,* 233–251.

Zillmann, D. (1979). *Hostility and aggression.* Hillsdale, NJ: Erlbaum.

Zillmann, D. (1983). Arousal and aggression. In R. G. Geen & E. I. Donnerstein (Eds.), *Aggression: Theoretical and empirical reviews: Vol. I. Theoretical and methodological issues* (pp. 75–101). New York: Academic Press.

Zillmann, D. (1984). *Connections between sex and aggression.* Hillsdale, NJ: Erlbaum.

Zillmann, D. (2003). Theory of affective dynamics: Emotions and moods. In J. Bryant, D. Roskos-Ewoldsen, & J. Cantor (Eds.), *Communication and emotion: Essays in honor of Dolf Zillmann* (pp. 533–567). Mahwah, NJ: Erlbaum.

Zillmann, D., Bryant, J., Cantor, J. R., & Day, K. D. (1975). Irrelevance of mitigating circumstances in retaliatory behavior at high levels of excitation. *Journal of Research in Personality, 9,* 282–293.

Zimbardo, P. G. (1969). The human choice: Individuation, reason, and order versus deindividuation, impulse, and chaos. *Nebraska symposium on motivation, 17,* 237–307.

Zimbardo, P. G. (2007). *The Lucifer effect: How good people turn evil.* New York: Random House.

Zimbardo, P. G., Banks, W. C., Haney, C., & Jaffe, D. (1973, April 8). The mind is a formidable jailer: A Pirandellian prison. *New York Times Magazine,* pp. 38–60.

Zimbardo, P. G., LaBerge, S., & Butler, L. D. (1993). Psychophysiological consequences of unexplained arousal: A posthypnotic suggestion paradigm. *Journal of Abnormal Psychology, 102,* 466–473.

Zitek, E. M., & Hebl, M. R. (2007). The role of social norm clarity in the influenced expression of prejudice over time. *Journal of Experimental Social Psychology, 43,* 867–876.

Zuckerman, M., DePaulo, B. M., & Rosenthal, R. (1981). Verbal and nonverbal communication of deception. In L. Berkowitz (Ed.), *Advances in experimental social psychology* (Vol. 14, pp. 1–59). New York: Academic Press.

Zuckerman, M., Knee, C. R., Hodgins, H. S., & Miyake, K. (1995). Hypothesis confirmation: The joint effect of positive test strategy and acquiescence response set. *Journal of Personality and Social Psychology, 68,* 52–60.

Zuwerink, J. R., & Devine, P. G. (1996). Attitude importance and resistance to persuasion: It's not just the thought that counts. *Journal of Personality and Social Psychology, 70,* 931–944.

Name Index

Subject Index

Italicized *fs* and *ts* refer to figures and tables.